RXPREP COURSE BOOK
2014 EDITION

KAREN SHAPIRO, PHARMD, BCPS

SHERRY A. BROWN, PHARMD, MBA, BCPS

DANNY MCNATTY, PHARMD, MHA, BCPS

CONTRIBUTORS

JOHN AN
PHARMD, PHD, PPD

MAHFOUD ASSEM
PHARMD, PHD

PAUL BERINGER
PHARMD

HEATHER R. BREAM-ROUWENHORST
PHARMD, BCPS

GEORGE DEMAAGD
PHARMD, BCPS

JEFFREY FUDIN
BS, PHARMD, FCCP

MUOI GI
PHARMD, BCPS, BCOP

JENANA HALILOVIC
PHARMD, BCPS

BRETT HEINTZ
PHARMD, BCPS-ID, AAHIVE

ERIC IP
PHARMD, BCPS, CSCS, CDE

CYNTHIA JACKEVICIUS
BSCPHM, PHARMD, MSC, FCSHP, BCPS

JESS MARTINEZ
PHARMD

TIEN NG
PHARMD, FCCP, BCPS (AQ-C)

IFEANYI ONOR
BS, PHARMD, BCPS

LORI REISNER
PHARMD

RENU F. SINGH
PHARMD, BCACP, CDE

KIMBERLY B. TALLIAN
PHARMD, BCPP, FASHP, FCCP, FCSHP

NATHAN S. TEUSCHER
BS, MS, PHD

ROBIN WACKERNAH
PHARMD, BCPP

D. RAYMOND WEBER
PHARMD, BSPHARM, BCOP, BCPS, RPH

JEANETTE Y. WICK
RPH

TABLE OF CONTENTS

EXAM OVERVIEW

INTRODUCTION
This section includes four topics:

- NAPLEX® Overview
- Test Taking Tips
- How to Use this Book
- CPJE Pointers – for CA exam takers

NAPLEX® OVERVIEW

The NAPLEX® exam blueprint (outline) is effective for anyone taking the exam after March, 2010. This is available on the board's website at www.nabp.net. Please review the complete blueprint on the website. Below is a summary of the blueprint:

The first section is "Safe and Effective" use and is the majority of the exam (56%).

- These are largely asked in a patient-case format. You will need to identify aberrant labs, medical histories, medication use history – and recognize appropriate or inappropriate therapy options.

- This section includes expected dosing options, regimens, and formulations. Pharmaco-economic factors may be important: if a patient cannot afford a drug and a less-expensive, but valid option is available, you'll need to recognize it. Is the physician choosing a drug based on poor study data? This is an important area for pharmacists; manufacturers can entice clinicians to use their new, expensive drugs – but our job is to review study data and protect the patient. Occasionally, new drugs are lifesavers, but many times new agents are copy-cat drugs (similar to older agents) or are not superior to less-expensive, existing options. Review our pharmacoeconomics section for more information.

- Also included is the ability to monitor patient outcomes (is the dose level correct, is the patient responding well?). Be able to choose correct monitoring tests. Improving medication adherence and recommending better treatment options are tested on as well.

The second section is safe and accurate preparation and dispensing of medications (33%).

- This includes calculations, including nutritional requirements and basic <u>PN calculations</u>. Flow rates for drugs administered by IV infusion <u>are essential</u>, along with drug concentrations, and the other general calculations in the section. <u>If you do not know the calculations well in this text</u> (which are standard pharmacy calculations) <u>you are not likely to do well</u>.

- Trade/generics are tested, along with common dosage forms. See our tips on which drugs to review below. Be able to use PK parameters and quality assurance information to identify appropriate interchange, identify information regarding storage, packaging, handling, administration, and medication disposal. Some equipment questions may be asked (pumps, etc.).

The third section requires assessment, recommendations, and providing health care information to promote public health (11%).

- Know your drug reference sources.

- Be able to read simple study summaries and interpret the data.

- Review emergency care and vaccinations.

- Review basic information regarding dietary supplements.

- Review self-care products and durable medical equipment, and self-monitoring of health status by the patient.

NAPLEX® is a computer-adaptive exam that consists of 185 multiple-choice questions. Of these, 150 questions are used to calculate your test score.

- The majority of the questions are asked in a scenario-based format (such as patient profiles with accompanying questions). There are also stand alone questions. The exam is moving towards more stand-alone questions.

- The exam time is 4 hours and 15 minutes with an optional 10-minute break after approximately 2 hours. Any other breaks that are needed will be subtracted from the total testing time.

- On the day of the exam, arrive 30 minutes prior to your appointment to get signed in (fingerprints will be taken, you will need 2 forms of ID, etc.).

- If you arrive 30 minutes or later than your scheduled appointment, and are refused admission to sit for the exam, you will be required to forfeit your appointment.

- A computer-adaptive exam assesses the answer to a given question in order to determine the level of difficulty to be selected for the following question. If you answer a question correctly, the computer will select a more difficult question from the test pool in an appropriate content area. If you answer a question incorrectly, an easier question will be selected by the computer. <u>If you miss a calculation you are likely to get another similar item worth less and you may not accumulate enough points to pass</u>. Increasingly the math questions look more complex but are not; you will not have time to think about how to set up a math problem. These need to be done <u>repeatedly so that you can do them quickly and accurately</u>. The online video lecture in calculations <u>explains each type of problem and the simplest method to solve them</u>.

- The computer-adaptive format requires that ALL test questions be answered in the order in which they are presented. Therefore, you can NOT skip questions or go back to questions.

- Be sure to look at the website: www.nabp.net and take the pre-test prior to sitting for the exam. It is $50 and you can take it up to two times. Many students score poorly on the pre-test, and better on the actual exam. However, it gives a feel for how the cases look and for this reason is useful. The cases in our book (at the end of most of the therapeutics chapters) are also designed to be similar to exam-style cases.

TEST TAKING TIPS

<u>Study the top selling drugs</u> (group them together; you'll see all the statins are there, many ACE Is, etc) – and focus on the doses for the common agents. We have bolded most of them in this text. The RxPrep test bank can be used to check your retention of all the top sellers (and the essential others).

- For example, with beta blockers, focus on the dosing for atenolol, metoprolol, carvedilol (IR and CR) and propranolol (special uses). For loops, furosemide (1st); for thiazides, HCTZ, chlorthalidone. For NSAIDs, know dosing for ibuprofen, naproxen, and celecoxib.

Many times, the counseling and safety considerations will be similar for all agents in a particular class; therefore, if you know trade/generics, you can identify the SEs, ADRs, etc. for the group.

There are exceptions where individual agents have differences.

- For example, propranolol (lipophilic, non-selective), carvedilol (not beta-1 selective), SSRI's (fluoxetine is most activating and is taken in the AM), some have more DI's (fluvoxamine, then fluoxetine, then paroxetine) otherwise SEs are mostly similar (with some notable exceptions, such as teratogenicity). Study for the group, along with the individual exceptions.

When reading the case, take a quick moment to jot down allergies, abnormal labs and major enzyme inducers/inhibitors. They are there for a reason.

- You will have a dry erase board – take time to write these things down – so they are in your mind when looking at the questions.

Focus on the common, chronic conditions first (diabetes, hypertension, lipids, pain, geriatric conditions, asthma/COPD, psych, common ID, common OTC), basic calculations and contraception. Again, miss math and you'll likely miss the exam. Math cannot be "winged" as a pharmacist; a mistake is a dosing error.

- Conditions for which "lifestyle" is essential (heart failure, diabetes) will require that you know how to counsel on healthy-living and disease-monitoring.

- These usually make up a good bulk of the questions. If you miss the math you will likely not pass! Do the math problems repeatedly until they are second-nature. The math is not difficult; it only seems that way because most do not use these calculations in everyday life. Do them enough until they are easy. Make sure that you follow the instructions for the math, such as rounding to the nearest whole number, if instructed to do-so. Re-read the question before answering to make sure you are answering what is asked. You will need to type in most of the math answers; there is no guessing on math.

Study the drugs that pharmacists manage such as anticoagulation (warfarin, heparin, enoxaparin), infectious disease, coronary conditions, seizures, etc.

Pharmacoeconomics (with the necessary biostat equations) is a required competency; this area, similar to calculations, must be known well prior to sitting for licensure. The calculations in this area are not complex; you must do them repeatedly until they are mastered. If you have difficulty the RxPrep online course explains each calculation in a step-by-step format with an instructor, if the text is not sufficient for your needs. The course also includes assistance as needed.

- Pharmacists write the questions for the exam. You should be studying material developed by practicing pharmacists – they'll know what is important. It is not a wise idea to use outdated, or irrelevant material. It is not advisable to "memorize" old board questions, and is not ethical. If you use the RxPrep test bank you must understand why the answer is correct; the board's question bank is large and you should focus on the material content to do well.

When studying specialty topics (HIV, oncology, others), focus on the areas that each pharmacist should know (not what the specialists know).

- Know trade/generics of common oncology agents that are dispensed in the community setting.

- Know major toxicities of chemo drugs and how to prevent or mitigate them.

- Know how to manage the side effects of chemo agents (for example, N/V, ESA use).

- For HIV, know commonly used agents, major toxicities and side effects, current guidelines, prophylaxis of opportunistic infections. There have been many HIV drugs approved, yet only a handful are used commonly. The others are used for salvage therapy, but that is a specialty area, while the exam is focused on basic competency for all of us. It is not sufficient to focus in detail on the salvage drugs, just as it is not necessary to become an oncology pharmacist for this exam. Yet, there are areas of oncology that we all should know.

Make educated choices and have confidence

If you don't know the answer, narrow it down to 2 options, and then choose what seems most likely, focusing on <u>safety</u> issues first.

Example of a question where one might be tempted to answer incorrectly when the correct answer seems to be (too) obvious:

1.   Ibuprofen can cause

     a. Headache
     b. GI irritation
     c. Gastrectasis
     d. Peripheral neuropathy
     e. Phlebitis

- Almost all analgesics (not DHE) can cause rebound headaches – technically, this answer is correct. But don't choose it – choose the more obvious choice of GI irritation. Some people will choose gastrectasis – because it sounds scary and they may not be sure what it is!

If the answer seems too simple or obvious – that's likely because you know it.

Review the foundation topics at the beginning of this book, and study them first before the therapeutics, which begin with ID. These include:

- Key Drug References

- Immunizations (current graduates are trained immunizers; this area must be mastered)

- Biostatistics and Pharmacoeconomics

- Medication Safety (this is a responsibility of all pharmacists; drugs that are high-risk must be known, along with what to do to mitigate the risk, and other areas in the Medication Safety chapter, such as infection control, safe drug preparation, and others.)

<u>Review the Drug Interaction pages in this book.</u> You will see there are several key drugs that have significant interactions. Several key inducers and inhibitors. If you see a problem "substrate" drug or inducer or inhibitor, look for an interaction. Review carefully the additive drug interactions, including additive CNS effects, bleeding risk, QT prolongation, and the others – often, one drug alone may not be a problem, but when others with similar toxicities are taken together, and/or the doses are high, the pharmacist should notice the risk.

<u>You don't need to answer every question correctly.</u> You will realize that you answered a question wrong – after you have passed it. Some will freeze.

- Don't – forget about it and move on.

<u>When you are studying, use time efficiently.</u> Do not study for more than 45-50 minutes. Do some type of physical activity in short breaks. Do not study passively – use colleagues, write, talk. Most importantly <u>assess</u> your drug information retention. There is <u>a lot</u> of information. It will not work to "read" several sources alone – if this does not let you know that the material has been <u>retained. You need to ensure drug information retention.</u>

Be sure you know how to provide patient counseling

- Talk to patients about how to monitor for signs and symptoms of side effects/ADRs at home (e.g., liver impairment, hyperkalemia, etc.). Counseling in this text appears after the drug tables.

- Be sure to know device techniques and administration techniques (MDIs, eye drops, insulin pen, etanercept injection (SC), epinephrine pen, nasal inhalers, etc.). We demonstrate most of these in the online video lectures. If you have not dispensed an essential drug that is <u>not</u> oral (such as inhalers, self-injectables) and do not have the online course, go to the drug website at www.drugname.com (for example www.avonex.com) and watch the patient instruction short video-most big brands have them, or at least, will have nice demo pictures.

<u>Safety is key</u>. Of all things, pharmacy licensure exams want to make sure we "do no harm."

<u>Do not panic or worry excessively</u>. This will not benefit you in your studies nor on the exam. Be confident. Stay positive. This is not a rocket science exam. But, there is a lot to know. Take time to learn well. If you get to feeling low think of some kooky person you know who has passed and realize you can do it too! If you are not sure if you have mastered key material, <u>check your retention of key points with the matching test bank section</u> at www.rxprep.com. If you are missing these questions (which are basic, must-know knowledge) you may wish to consider using the online video course which will help your understanding and, consequently, your retention.

HOW TO USE THIS BOOK

This book is designed as a companion to our live or online courses. You can register for a review program at www.rxprep.com.

If you are using the book as a stand-alone, here are some pointers:

- If an item is bolded it is a key drug and if it is underlined it is essential information.

- Not all essential information is designated. Use the top seller list in the appendix as a guide to must-know drugs. You will also be tested on drugs that are not top sellers, but have safety considerations. Hospital drugs that are essential are noted in the text.

- This book is complete; you do not need to have a myriad of additional resources. If you are testing through most of 2014, this book is sufficient. However, if it is towards the latter part of the year, you should check for key updates. We often post these as they come along on our Facebook page. Only reputable resources should be used.

- This text has "foundation" type material in the beginning of the text that is increasingly important in pharmacy, such as pharmacoeconomics and medication errors. Do not skip these chapters. <u>It is best to review everything up to ID first</u>.

- Many key drugs have counseling points after the "box" that outlines the drug. Review the counseling points; for example, if a drug causes "hepatotoxicity" the counseling points will include symptoms that the patient should notice if the liver is failing. The counseling provides a review of key concerns with the drug and is an important part of a pharmacist's job.

- At the end of many of the core chapters are patient cases with practice questions. These are designed to be somewhat similar to NAPLEX® style cases – either in a written format, or the profile you might see on a pharmacy computer. The cases are designed to review key drugs points and should not be missed.

- You may wish to take the self-assessment <u>test bank</u> that is available on our website at www.rxprep.com. If you get 80%, <u>it is not enough, as these questions are designed to test the most basic drug competency knowledge</u>. The knowledge in these questions, including calculations, should be at 100%. If you get something wrong right it down and learn it. If you are not scoring well on a section it means that you need to go back and review that material. The test bank for 2014 has over 2,600 basic knowledge questions. When you do the questions take the time to think about why the answer is correct. It may be advisable to delay the exam date if these are not mastered. Taking time to carefully <u>write out 3" x 5" flash cards is helpful</u>; if you <u>think about why the answer is correct</u> you will find that you know about half of them when you go back to review the ones missed. The test bank will save the ones you missed, but it is <u>more of an active learning process (and more useful) to write out the missed material</u>.

- "Select ALL that apply" questions have become more common on the exam. These do not provide partial credit if one or more of the five choices are missed. Point-and-click questions are used, and some ranking questions. The board provides examples of each type in the exam blueprint. The format types are in the RxPrep test bank for practice.

- <u>Foreign graduates</u>: You have not had a year of clinical rotations; U.S. grads have and should not find it very difficult to read through cases on the exam. Please complete the practice cases at the end of the chapters in the book. These are in the common formats used on the exam. The cases do not take the place of the extensive test assessment, but should help you learn to manage time. The questions in the book do not overlap with the test bank questions.

- <u>A note to parents</u>: if there are children in the house, any loving parent will be listening for them. This is good – but makes it difficult to focus on studying! Studying for a board exam requires a dedicated mind. You may need to make arrangements with your family to get out of the house and prepare with study partners, or go to an environment with fewer distractions than will be present in the home. Studying in a coffee shop or a library can be helpful. During the spring exam season students can "connect" with study partners using the RxPrep Facebook page.

- Again, if the drug is bolded or underlined and is not given orally make sure you can explain to a patient (in patient-friendly language) how to safely store/use/dispose of the drug, and the side effect profile.

CPJE POINTERS – FOR CA EXAM TAKERS

Clinical Section of the Exam

Our text book, corresponding video lectures and test assessment cover the clinical topics on the blueprint, including topics specific to the CPJE blueprint (such as NPSGs, ADC safety, therapeutic interchange, P&T). We have covered these topics completely, along with the more advanced clinical concepts required for this exam.

If you are unsure what is on the exam you can find the list of exam topics (the blueprint) on the board website (under the Applicants tab, and then click for Exam Information). This is included in the exam handbook that is on the website, or is sent once you register.

Note that in the RxPrep test bank we have included the topics for CPJE – and we have attempted to "reword" the practice questions in the handbook. Hopefully, you will also do the practice questions in the exam handbook. If you do not know the topics listed on the blueprint thoroughly (such as how to choose therapeutic interchange drugs, how to safely use ADCs in remote facilities, the Joint Commission's medication safety goals, and others) you are not ready to test.

Law Section of the Exam

Fred Weissman's law book is a must-have resource (we believe) for those of us practicing in California. It is not only relevant – it is pleasant to read. You can purchase it by clicking on the store at www.rxprep.com or from the USC or Western bookstores.

The law questions should be points that are not missed. Although "law" or "administrative" type questions typically represent up to 20% on the exam, in a sense <u>they represent the more straight-forward material since there is certain information that is required knowledge for a pharmacist practicing legally in the state</u>, while the clinical questions can come from a much broader range of options. The board wants to make sure you are practicing legally.

There are "legal" items that are known to pharmacists practicing in California: such as when to do controlled drug inventory, requirements for an off-site waiver, requirements for the security form, for bottle labeling, and so on. <u>If you have NOT practiced in a community setting in California it may be a wise investment to use our 4-part video series (that comes with a corresponding quiz bank so that you can know if you have retained key law information.)</u> This is available by clicking on the CPJE link at www.rxprep.com.

Best wishes for your CPJE preparation.

CALCULATIONS

ABBREVIATIONS USED IN PRESCRIPTIONS

ABBREVIATION	MEANING	ABBREVIATION	MEANING
ss	one-half	mL	milliliter
ac	before meals	NTE	not to exceed
pc	after meals	MDI	metered-dose inhaler
gtt, gtts	drop, drops	q	every
au	each ear	qd	every day
as	left ear	qod	every other day
ad	right ear	PO	by mouth or orally
ATC	around the clock	NPO	nothing by mouth
hs	at bedtime	IV	intravenous
bid	twice a day	IVP	intravenous push
tid	three times a day	IVPB	intravenous piggy back
qid	four times a day	ID	intradermal
biw	two times a week	IM	intramuscular
tiw	three times a week	subc, subq, SC, SQ	subcutaneous
os	left eye	ung	ointment
od	right eye	top	topically
ou	each eye	WA	while awake
qs	sufficient quantity	prn	as needed
qs ad	a sufficient quantity to make	stat	immediately
NR	no refills	SL	sublingual
c or w/	with	sup or supp	suppository
s or w/o	without	PR	per rectum
inj	injection	BM	bowel movement
X	times	N/V or N & V	nausea and vomiting

Not all of the above are considered safe abbreviations; all are used outpatient. In hospital settings use abbreviations included on the approved abbreviation list.

EQUIVALENT MEASUREMENTS

MEASUREMENT	EQUIVALENT
tsp (t)	5 mL
tbsp (T)	15 mL
1 fl oz	30 mL (approx.); 29.6 mL (actual)
1 cup	8 oz
1 pint (16 oz)	473 mL
1 quart	2 pints; 946 mL
1 gallon	4 quarts; 3,785 mL

MEASUREMENT	EQUIVALENT
1 kg	2.2 pounds
1 oz	28.4 g
1 pound	454 g
1 in	2.54 cm
1 grain (gr)	65 mg (approx); 64.8 mg (actual)
% (w/v)	g/100 mL
% (v/v)	mL/100 mL
% (w/w)	g/100 g

METRIC CONVERSIONS

PREFIX	DEFINITION
kilo	1,000 (one thousand), as in kg
deci	1/10 (one-tenth), as in dL
milli	1/1,000 (one-thousandth), as in mL
micro	1/1,000,000 (one-millionth), as in mcg
nano	1/1,000,000,000 (one-billionth), as in ng

LABELING INSTRUCTIONS

- Begin with an instructive word (such as: Take, Place, Unwrap, Insert, Inhale).
- Follow with the quantity and dosage form (such as: 1 capsule).
- Follow by the location (such as: by mouth, rectally, vaginally, under tongue).
- Follow with the frequency (such as: daily, twice daily, at meals and bedtime).
- Finish with any noted instructions (such as: for pain, for cholesterol, on an empty stomach).

CPJE Students Only

Note in California, the 2011 new prescription label requirements include changes to the label layout such as 16 phrases of directions for use. In most cases, these phrases should be used on the prescription label. Please refer to *A Guide To California Community Pharmacy Law*, by Fred G. Weissman, PharmD, J.D. or, the law statement on the board's website or RxPrep's CPJE Course, which covers legal requirements and several items not covered in this book (including NPSG's, ADC requirements, P&T and Formulary, and Therapeutic Interchange).

Labeling Prescriptions

State of California
PRESCRIPTION BLANK

Joe Jackson, MD
927 Deep Valley Drive
Los Angeles, California
Phone (310) 555-3333

DEA#FJ 3829150
BATCH# HTS5058903765

CA LIC#568596

0200

Name _Edward Richards_   D.O.B. _May 15, 1949_

Address _177 Green Street_   Date _November 29, 2013_

Touch Rx symbol, color will disappear then reappear.

Rx   **Vicodin 5/325 mg #12**

Sig: i-ii tabs PO q 4-6 hrs prn pain X 2 days. NTE 6/d.

Qty/Units
☒ 1-24 / _12_
☐ 25-49 / _____
☐ 50-74 / _____
☐ 75-100 / _____
☐ 101-150 / _____
☐ 151 and over / _____

SUBSTITUTION PERMISSABLE _____   DO NOT SUBSTITUTE _____

DO NOT REFILL _____ REFILL _____ TIMES

SIGNATURE OF PRESCRIBER

Prescription is void if more than one controlled substance is written per blank.

Security Features. Details on Back

---

1. **Choose the correct wording for the prescription label:**

   a. Take 1-2 tablets by mouth every 4-6 hours as-needed for pain for 2 days. Do not exceed 6 tablets per day.

   b. Take up to 2 tablets by mouth every 4-6 hours as-needed for pain. Do not exceed 6 tablets per day.

   c. Take 1-2 tablets by mouth every 4-6 hours as-needed for pain. NTE 6 tablets per day.

   d. Take 1-2 tablets by mouth every 4-6 hours for pain. Do not exceed 6 tablets per day.

   e. Take 1-2 tablets by mouth up to 6 times daily as-needed for pain for 2 days. Do not exceed 6 tablets per day.

The correct answer is (A). Generally, the acetaminophen component has the higher risk of toxicity (liver toxicity).

2. Choose the correct wording for the prescription label:

JOE JACKSON, MD
927 DEEP VALLEY DRIVE
LOS ANGELES, CALIFORNIA

PHONE (310) 555-3333   DEA NO. FJ3829150

NAME _Melissa Atkins_   DATE _October 29, 2013_

ADDRESS _18469 Lotus Circle_   AGE _57_

℞

Keflex 500 mg PO QID: ac and hs. #28

☐ LABEL

REFILL ___0___ TIMES

_____, M.D.   _____, M.D.

DO NOT SUBSTITUTE   SUBSTITUTION PERMISSIBLE

- *a.* Take 1 capsule by mouth every six hours.
- *b.* Take 1 capsule by mouth four times daily: take 1 on an empty stomach and take 1 at bedtime.
- *c.* Take 1 capsule by mouth four times daily: take 1 after meals and take 1 at bedtime.
- *d.* Take 1 capsule by mouth four times daily: take 1 with meals and take 1 at bedtime.
- *e.* Take 1 capsule by mouth four times daily: take 1 before meals and take 1 at bedtime.

The correct answer is (E). The patient should be counseled to finish all of the medication even if they start to feel better. Cephalexin *(Keflex)* comes as tablets, capsules and powder for suspension.

---

3. A pharmacist receives a prescription for "APAP 5 gr supp #6 1 PR prn temperature > 102 degrees". Choose the correct wording for the prescription label:

- *a.* Insert 1 suppository as needed when temperature is greater than 102 degrees.
- *b.* Unwrap and insert 1 suppository rectally as needed for a temperature greater than 102°.
- *c.* Take 500 mg of APAP suspension as needed 6 times per day for a temperature greater than 102°.
- *d.* Take 6 suppositories vaginally as needed for a temperature greater than 102°.
- *e.* Insert 500 mg of APAP into the rectum as needed for a fever greater than 102°.

The correct answer is (B). It is important to tell patients exactly how to take a medication. Five grains is 325 milligrams (65 mg/gr x 5 gr).

4. A pharmacist receives a prescription for *"Vigamox* 0.5% #3 1 gtt tid ou x 5d". Choose the correct wording for the prescription label:

    a. Insert 3 mL into the right eye three times daily for 5 days.

    b. Insert 1 drop into the right eye three times daily for 3 days.

    c. Instill 1 drop into both eyes three times a day for 5 days.

    d. Instill 3 drops into the right eye three times a day for 5 days.

    e. Instill 3 drops into both eyes three times a day for 5 days.

The correct answer is (C). It is important to properly counsel patients on the correct technique for instilling eye drops. Refer to the Opthalmics chapter.

Calculating the Correct Dose and/or Amount for a Prescription

Instructions to perform with each calculation problem in order to increase accuracy:

- Check your math. Time permitting, double-check the calculations. It is very easy to make mistakes that you will catch when repeating the calculations.

- If you are using proportions to solve the problem, place your answer directly back into the equation as another accuracy check. For example:

$$\frac{5\,g}{100\,g} = \frac{X\,g}{1{,}000\,g} \qquad X = 50\,g$$

    Check: 5/100 = 0.05; 50/1,000 = 0.05

- When setting up proportions, make sure the units (including route and drug if applicable) in the numerators match, and the units (route and drug) in the denominators match as well.

- <u>Read the question again after solving the problem</u> to be certain you have answered with the correct units (g or mg, mEq, mL or L, etc.) and have rounded your answer as specified in the question. If rounding is required, look at the number to the right of the one you are rounding to; for example, if rounding to the nearest whole number look at the tenths column. If the number to the right is 0 to 4, round down. If it is 5 to 9, round up. For example, 31.<u>2</u>7 rounded to the nearest whole number is 31, and 31.<u>6</u>35 rounded to the nearest whole number is 32. <u>Round only at the end of the equation, not at each step.</u>

- <u>Make sure you are answering the question.</u> The next problem illustrates that the problem may have more than one step, and you want to be careful to get to the right step to get to the requested response.

- The math in this section, and on the exam, is not complex. Most formulas are not provided. How do you get to the point where you can do the math easily and accurately, in a timely fashion: by repetition. Do the math over and over until you are doing the problems easily. The problems shown here are repeated, with different numbers, in the RxPrep test bank which can be used for knowledge assessment. Your math ability should be at 100% prior to testing; math mistakes are not acceptable in this profession; a math mistake is a dosing mistake.

5. In the prescription to the right, the pharmacist dispensed 3 oz to Ms. Brooks. How many days of therapy will Ms. Brooks be short? Round to the nearest whole number. Use 30 mL for 1 fluid ounce.

　　　a. 10 mL
　　　b. 90 mL
　　　c. 1 day
　　　d. 3 days
　　　e. 9 days

The correct answer is (C). Use caution with calculations where a step of the answer (but not the final step) will be a selection. Always go back and read the question prior to selecting your response.

- 5 mL (per dose) x 2 times/day x 10 days = 100 mL needed

- Quantity dispensed: 3 oz x 30 mL/oz = 90 mL dispensed

- Difference: Quantity needed – Quantity dispensed = 100 mL – 90 mL = 10 mL

- Each tsp (t) is 5 mL. She needs 2 tsp (t) daily, which is 10 mL. She is 1 day short for her course of therapy.

Gene Tran, MD	005-1015
5445 Grand Ave. Fallbrook, California Phone (760) 555-2112	CA LIC. #A19666 D.E.A. #SK456789

Name _Angelina Brooks_　　Date _January 22, 2014_

Address _33 Walden Rd. N Falls_　D.O.B. _May 5, 1951_

Rx

TMP/SMX 40-200 mg/5 mL
Sig: 1 tsp PO BID x 10 days, until all taken.

❑ Do Not Substitute　　　　Refill _____ Times

Quantity　　**Units**
❑ 1-24　　　_____
❑ 25-49　　_____
❑ 50-74　　_____
❑ 75-100　_____
❑ 101-150　_____
❑ 151 and over　_____　　**Physician Signature**

Prescription is void if more than one controlled substance is written per blank.

---

6. How many milliliters (mL) of *Mylanta* suspension are contained in each dose of the prescription below? Round to the nearest whole number.

PRESCRIPTION	QUANTITY
Belladonna Tincture	10 mL
Phenobarbital	60 mL
Mylanta susp. qs. ad	120 mL
Sig. 5 mL BID	

The total prescription is 120 mL; 10 mL belladonna, 60 mL of phenobarbital, and that leaves 50 mL left for the *Mylanta*.

$$\frac{50 \text{ mL } \textit{Mylanta}}{120 \text{ mL total Rx}} = \frac{X \text{ mL } \textit{Mylanta}}{5 \text{ mL total Rx dose}} \quad X = 2.08, \text{ or 2 mL } \textit{Mylanta}/\text{dose}$$

After solving the problem, read the question again to be certain you have answered the question with the correct units (mL of *Mylanta* per dose).

7. You have tablets that contain 0.25 mg of levothyroxine per tablet. You are crushing the tablets and mixing with glycerol and water for a 36 pound child. How many levothyroxine tablets will be needed to compound the following prescription?

PRESCRIPTION	QUANTITY
Levothyroxine Liq.	0.1 mg/mL
Disp.	60 mL
Sig. 0.01 mg per kg PO BID	

$$60 \text{ mL total Rx} \times \frac{0.1 \text{ mg levo}}{\text{mL}} = 6 \text{ mg of levothyroxine needed}$$

$$6 \text{ mg levo} \times \frac{1 \text{ tab}}{0.25 \text{ mg levo}} = 24 \text{ tabs of levothyroxine needed}$$

Or, solving by dimensional analysis:

$$\frac{1 \text{ tab levo}}{0.25 \text{ mg levo}} \times \frac{0.1 \text{ mg levo}}{\text{mL}} \times 60 \text{ mL total Rx} = 24 \text{ tabs of levothyroxine needed}$$

After solving the problem, read the question again to be certain you have answered the question with the correct units (tablets).

---

8. How many milligrams of codeine will be contained in each capsule?

PRESCRIPTION	QUANTITY
Codeine Sulfate	0.6 g
Guaifenesin	1.2 g
Caffeine	0.15 g
M. ft. caps. no. 24	
Sig. One capsule TID prn cough	

Begin by converting to the unit requested in the answer (mg).

$$0.6 \text{ g Codeine} \times \frac{1{,}000 \text{ mg}}{1 \text{ g}} = 600 \text{ mg of codeine for the total prescription}$$

The prescription order is for 24 capsules.

$$\frac{600 \text{ mg codeine total}}{24 \text{ caps}} = 25 \text{ mg of codeine/capsule}$$

After solving the problem, read the question again to be certain you have answered the question with the correct units (mg of codeine per capsule).

9. A physician writes an order for aminophylline 500 mg IV, dosed at 0.5 mg per kg per hour for a patient weighing 165 pounds. There is only theophylline in stock. How many milligrams (mg) of theophylline will the patient receive per hour? Round to the nearest whole number.

$$\frac{0.5 \text{ mg Amino}}{\text{kg/hr}} \times \frac{1 \text{ kg}}{2.2 \text{ pounds}} \times 165 \text{ pounds} = 37.5 \text{ mg/hr aminophylline}$$

To get the theophylline dose, multiply by 0.8. Therefore, 37.5 mg/hr aminophylline x 0.8 = 30 mg/hr of theophylline. <u>You must know how to convert between aminophylline and theophylline.</u>

- Aminophylline to theophylline; multiply by 0.8

- Theophylline to aminophylline; divide by 0.8

After solving the problem, read the question again to be certain you have answered the question with the correct units (mg per hour of theophylline).

---

10. How many grains of aspirin will be contained in each capsule? Round to the nearest tenth.

PRESCRIPTION	QUANTITY
Aspirin	6 g
Phenacetin	3.2 g
Caffeine	0.48 g
M. ft. no. 20 caps	
Sig. One capsule Q6H prn pain	

$$6 \text{ g ASA} \times \frac{1{,}000 \text{ mg}}{1 \text{ g}} \times \frac{1 \text{ gr}}{65 \text{ mg}} = 92.3 \text{ grains}$$

We have 92.3 grains per 20 capsules.

$$\frac{92.3 \text{ gr}}{20 \text{ capsules}} = 4.6 \text{ grains/capsule}$$

After solving the problem, read the question again to be certain you have answered the question with the correct units (grains per capsule).

---

11. A 45 milliliter nasal spray delivers 20 sprays per milliliter of solution. Each spray contains 1.5 mg of active drug. How many milligrams of drug are contained in the 45 mL package?

First, add up the amount of drug per mL.

$$\frac{1.5 \text{ mg drug}}{\text{spray}} \times \frac{20 \text{ sprays}}{\text{mL}} = 30 \text{ mg/mL}$$

Then solve for milligrams of drug in 45 mL.

$$\frac{30 \text{ mg}}{\text{mL}} = \frac{X \text{ mg}}{45 \text{ mL}} \quad X = 1{,}350 \text{ mg}$$

12. A metered dose inhaler provides 90 micrograms of albuterol sulfate with each inhalation. The canister provides 200 inhalations. If the patient uses the entire canister, how many total milligrams will the patient have received?

$$200 \text{ inhalations} \quad \times \quad \frac{90 \text{ mcg}}{\text{inhalation}} = 18{,}000 \text{ mcg}$$

$$18{,}000 \text{ mcg} \quad \times \quad \frac{1 \text{ mg}}{1{,}000 \text{ mcg}} = 18 \text{ mg}$$

Proportions

A proportion represents the equality of two ratios. Given any three values of a proportion, it is easy to calculate the fourth. Remember to keep the same units (route, drug, etc.) in the numerator and the same units (route, drug, etc.) in the denominator.

$$\frac{a}{b} = \frac{c}{d}$$

13. If one 10 mL vial contains 0.05 g of diltiazem, how many milliliters should be administered to provide a 25 mg dose of diltiazem?

First, convert grams to milligrams. Usually, it is best practice to convert to the units required in the answer when you begin the problem.

$$0.05 \text{ gram of diltiazem} \quad \times \quad \frac{1{,}000 \text{ mg}}{1 \text{ g}} = 50 \text{ mg}$$

Use proportions to calculate the number of mL for a 25 mg dose.

$$\frac{50 \text{ mg}}{10 \text{ mL}} = \frac{25 \text{ mg}}{X \text{ mL}} \quad X = 5 \text{ mL dose}$$

14. If phenobarbital elixir contains 18.2 mg of phenobarbital per 5 mL, how many grams of phenobarbital would be used in preparing a pint of the elixir? Round to the nearest hundredth.

First, convert milligrams to grams.

$$18.2 \text{ mg} \quad \times \quad \frac{1 \text{ g}}{1{,}000 \text{ mg}} = 0.0182 \text{ g}$$

Use proportions to calculate the amount of grams needed for 1 pint.

$$\frac{0.0182 \text{ g}}{5 \text{ mL}} = \frac{X \text{ g}}{473 \text{ mL}} \quad X = 1.72 \text{ g}$$

15. Digoxin injection is supplied in ampules of 500 mcg per 2 mL. How many milliliters must a nurse administer to provide a dose of 0.2 mg? Round to the nearest tenth.

First, convert 500 mcg to mg.

$$500 \text{ mcg} \quad \times \quad \frac{1 \text{ mg}}{1,000 \text{ mcg}} \quad = \quad 0.5 \text{ mg}$$

$$\frac{0.5 \text{ mg}}{2 \text{ mL}} \quad = \quad \frac{0.2 \text{ mg}}{X \text{ mL}} \qquad X = 0.8 \text{ mL}$$

---

16. If 200 capsules contain 500 mg of an active ingredient, how many milligrams of the active ingredient will 76 capsules contain?

$$\frac{200 \text{ caps}}{500 \text{ mg}} \quad = \quad \frac{76 \text{ caps}}{X \text{ mg}} \qquad X = 190 \text{ mg}$$

---

17. A penicillin V 250 mg tablet equals 400,000 units of penicillin activity. A patient is taking penicillin V 500 mg tablets QID for 7 days. How much penicillin activity, in units, will this patient receive in the total prescription?

If 250 mg contains 400,000 units, then 500 mg contains 800,000 units. The patient is taking 4 tablets daily, for 7 days (or 28 total tablets), at 800,000 units each.

$$\frac{800,000 \text{ units}}{1 \text{ tab}} \quad = \quad \frac{X \text{ units}}{28 \text{ tabs}} \qquad X = 22,400,000 \text{ units}$$

---

18. A cough syrup contains 4 g of brompheniramine maleate per liter. How many milligrams are contained in a teaspoonful dose of the elixir?

First, convert grams to milligrams.

$$4 \text{ g} \quad \times \quad \frac{X \text{ mg}}{1 \text{ g}} \quad = \quad 4,000 \text{ mg per 1 liter}$$

- 1 L = 1,000 mL

- 1 teaspoonful = 5 mL

Next, solve using proportions.

$$\frac{4,000 \text{ mg}}{1,000 \text{ mL}} \quad = \quad \frac{X \text{ mg}}{5 \text{ mL}} \qquad X = 20 \text{ mg}$$

---

19. A patient is to receive acyclovir 5 mg/kg every 8 hours for an acute outbreak of herpes zoster. What daily dose, in milligrams, should a 110 pound female receive?

Begin by converting the patient's weight in pounds (lbs) to kilograms (kg).

- 2.2 pounds = 1 kg

$$110 \text{ pounds} \quad \times \quad \frac{1 \text{ kg}}{2.2 \text{ pounds}} \quad = \quad 50 \text{ kg}$$

$$\frac{5 \text{ mg}}{1 \text{ kg}} = \frac{X \text{ mg}}{50 \text{ kg}}$$ X = 250 mg/dose x 3 doses/day = 750 mg/day

---

20. MH is a 72 year old male patient hospitalized with decompensated heart failure and fever. Cultures are positive for aspergillosis. MH weighs 110 kg and will receive 0.25 mg/kg per day amphotericin B (reconstituted and diluted to 0.1 mg/mL) by IV infusion. What volume of solution, in milliliters, is required to deliver the daily dose?

Begin by calculating the total daily dose (mg) for this patient.

$$\frac{0.25 \text{ mg}}{1 \text{ kg}} = \frac{X \text{ mg}}{110 \text{ kg}}$$ X = 27.5 mg daily

Calculate the volume of reconstituted amphotericin B solution needed per day.

$$\frac{27.5 \text{ mg}}{X \text{ mL}} = \frac{0.1 \text{ mg}}{1 \text{ mL}}$$ X = 275 mL

---

21. An elixir of ferrous sulfate contains 220 milligrams of ferrous sulfate in each 5 milliliters. If each milligram of ferrous sulfate contains the equivalent of 0.2 milligrams of elemental iron, how many milligrams of elemental iron would be in each 5 milliliters of elixir?

Ferrous sulfate ($FeSO_4$) contains 20% elemental iron (Fe); this is given in the problem which states that 1 milligram has 0.2 milligrams of elemental iron, which is 20%.

$$\frac{0.2 \text{ mg Fe}}{1 \text{ mg FeSO}_4} = \frac{X \text{ mg Fe}}{220 \text{ mg FeSO}_4}$$ X = 44 mg Fe

---

22. A 10 gram packet of potassium chloride provides 20 mEq of potassium and 4 mEq of chloride. How many grams of powder would provide 8 mEq of potassium?

$$\frac{10 \text{ g}}{20 \text{ mEq K}^+} = \frac{X \text{ g}}{8 \text{ mEq K}^+}$$ X = 4 g

---

23. Oral potassium chloride 20% solution contains 40 mEq of potassium per 15 milliliters of solution. A patient needs 25 mEq of potassium daily. What is the amount, in milliliters, of 20% potassium chloride that the patient should take? Round to the nearest tenth.

$$\frac{40 \text{ mEq K}^+}{15 \text{ mL}} = \frac{25 \text{ mEq K}^+}{X \text{ mL}}$$ X = 9.375, or 9.4 mL

Percentage Strength

A percentage is a number or ratio as a fraction of 100. Expressions of concentration describe the amount of solute that will be contained in the total preparation. The percentage concentrations are defined as follows:

■ Percent weight-in-volume (% w/v) is expressed as g/100 mL (a solid mixed into a liquid)

■ Percent volume-in-volume (% v/v) is expressed as mL/100 mL (a liquid mixed into a liquid)

■ Percent weight-in-weight (% w/w) is expressed as g/100 g (a solid mixed into a solid)

24. How many grams of NaCl are in 1 liter of normal saline (NS)?

Normal saline (NS) is 0.9% (w/v) NaCl solution

Remember (w/v) is always expressed as grams per 100 mL, therefore, NS contains 0.9 g NaCl per 100 mL of solution.

$$\frac{0.9\ g}{100\ mL} = \frac{X\ g}{1{,}000\ mL} \quad X = 9\ g$$

---

25. How many grams of NaCl are in 500 mL of ½ NS? Round to the nearest hundredth.

NS is 0.9 g/100 mL; ½ NS is 0.45 g/100 mL.

$$\frac{0.45\ g}{100\ mL} = \frac{X\ g}{500\ mL} \quad X = 2.25\ g$$

---

26. How many grams of dextrose 5% are in 250 mL of D5W? Round to the nearest tenth.

$$\frac{5\ g}{100\ mL} = \frac{X\ g}{250\ mL} \quad X = 12.5\ g$$

---

27. How many milligrams of triamcinolone should be used in preparing the following prescription? Round to the nearest whole number.

PRESCRIPTION	QUANTITY
Triamcinolone (w/v)	5%
Glycerin qs	60 mL
Sig. Two drops in right ear	

$$\frac{5\ g}{100\ mL} = \frac{X\ g}{60\ mL} \quad X = 3\ g,\ or\ 3{,}000\ mg$$

---

28. A prescription reads as follows: Prepare a 3% w/w coal tar preparation qs with petrolatum to 150 g. How much petrolatum, in grams, will be needed to make the prescription? Round to the nearest tenth.

$$\frac{3\ g}{100\ g} = \frac{X\ g}{150\ g} \quad X = 4.5\ g$$

150 g (total weight) – 4.5 g (active ingredient) = 145.5 g petrolatum

---

29. JL has mucositis secondary to methotrexate chemotherapy. The physician has ordered lidocaine HCl 2% w/v solution; qs with pure water to 120 mL. How much lidocaine, in grams, is required to make the prescription? Round to the nearest tenth.

$$\frac{2\ g}{100\ mL} = \frac{X\ g}{120\ mL} = X = 2.4\ g$$

Compounding steps for this problem:

Weigh the drug (2.4 g), place in a beaker, add water to the 120 mL line, stir, and place into a container labeled: Lidocaine 2% solution, 120 mL, with additional labeling as required.

Common steps for compounding an ointment or cream:

- Weigh or measure the active ingredient/s.

- If you are using a dry powder or granules, you will need to triturate with the pestle to reduce the particle size.

- Levigate on an ointment slab <u>with a metal spatula (unless you are mixing metal ions, then use a plastic spatula)</u>.

- Package into a tube or jar. See further discussion in the Compounding chapter.

---

30. SS is a 79 year old female with dry mouth and dry eyes from Sjögren's syndrome. She is picking up the prescription below. What is the maximum milligrams of pilocarpine she will receive per day?

PRESCRIPTION	QUANTITY
Pilocarpine	1% (w/v)
Sodium Chloride qs ad	15 mL
Sig: 2 gtts (0.1 mL) po TID prn up to 5 days	

First, calculate the amount of pilocarpine in the prescription.

$$\frac{1\ g}{100\ mL} = \frac{X\ g}{15\ mL} \qquad X = 0.15\ g$$

Then, convert to mg since the problem wants the answer in mg.

$$0.15\ g \times \frac{1,000\ mg}{1\ g} = 150\ mg\ of\ pilocarpine$$

The patient will receive up to 3 doses per day (0.1 mL x 3 = 0.3 mL). Calculate the amount of pilocarpine in 0.3 mL.

$$\frac{150\ mg\ pilocarpine}{15\ mL} = \frac{X\ mg}{0.3\ mL} \qquad X = 3\ mg\ pilocarpine$$

31. If 1,250 g of a mixture contains 80 g of drug, what is the percentage strength (w/w) of the mixture? Round to the nearest tenth.

$$\frac{80\ g}{1,250\ g} = \frac{X\ g}{100\ g} \qquad X = 6.4\ g,\ which\ is\ 6.4\%$$

32. A mouth rinse contains 1/12% (w/v) of chlorhexidine gluconate. How many grams of chlorhexidine gluconate should be used to prepare 18 liters of mouth rinse? Round to the nearest whole number.

- 1/12% = 0.083 g per 100 mL (w/v)

- 18 L x 1,000 mL/L = 18,000 mL

$$\frac{0.083 \text{ g}}{100 \text{ mL}} = \frac{X \text{ g}}{18,000 \text{ mL}} \quad X = 14.94, \text{ or } 15 \text{ g}$$

33. If 12 grams of lanolin are combined with 2 grams of white wax and 36 grams of petrolatum to make an ointment, what is the percentage strength (w/w) of lanolin in the ointment?

$$\frac{12 \text{ g lanolin}}{50 \text{ grams ointment}} = \frac{X \text{ g}}{100 \text{ grams}} \quad X = 24\% \text{ w/w}$$

34. A pharmacist dissolves 6 tablets. Each tablet contains 250 mg of metronidazole. The pharmacist will put the drug into a liquid base to prepare 60 mL of a topical solution. What is the percentage strength (w/v) of metronidazole in the prescription? Round to the nearest tenth.

$$6 \text{ tablets} \quad x \quad \frac{250 \text{ mg}}{1 \text{ tab}} = 1,500 \text{ mg, or } 1.5 \text{ g}$$

$$\frac{1.5 \text{ g}}{60 \text{ mL}} = \frac{X \text{ g}}{100 \text{ mL}} \quad X = 2.5 \text{ g, which is } 2.5\% \text{ w/v}$$

35. A pharmacist adds 5.3 grams of hydrocortisone to 150 grams of a 2.5% hydrocortisone ointment. What is the percentage (w/w) of hydrocortisone in the finished product? Round to the nearest whole number.

First, determine the amount of hydrocortisone (HC) in the current product.

$$\frac{2.5 \text{ g HC}}{100 \text{ g}} = \frac{X \text{ g HC}}{150 \text{ g}} \quad X = 3.75 \text{ g HC}$$

Next, add this amount (3.75 g) to the amount of hydrocortisone being added (5.3 g): 3.75 g + 5.3 g = 9.05 g.

Then, find the percent concentration of the total product (5.3 g + 150 g = 155.3 g).

$$\frac{9.05 \text{ g}}{155.3 \text{ g}} = \frac{X}{100 \text{ g}} \quad X = 5.82743, \text{ or } 6\%$$

36. How many milliliters of hydrocortisone liquid (40 mg/mL) will be needed to prepare 30 grams of a 0.25% cream (w/w)? Round to the nearest hundredth.

First, calculate the amount of hydrocortisone in the current product.

$$\frac{0.25 \text{ g}}{100 \text{ g}} = \frac{X \text{ g}}{30 \text{ g}} \quad X = 0.075 \text{ g or } 75 \text{ mg}$$

Then, solve for mL of hydrocortisone liquid needed.

$$\frac{40 \text{ mg}}{\text{mL}} = \frac{75 \text{ mg}}{X \text{ mL}} \quad X = 1.875 \text{ mL, rounded to } 1.88 \text{ mL}$$

After solving the problem, read the question again to be certain you have answered the question with the correct units (mL).

---

37. What is the percentage strength of imiquimod in the following prescription? Round to the nearest hundredth.

PRESCRIPTION	QUANTITY
Imiquimod 5% cream	15 g
Xylocaine	20 g
Hydrophilic ointment	25 g

First, calculate the amount of imiquimod (5%) in the prescription.

$$\frac{5 \text{ g}}{100 \text{ g}} \times 15 \text{ g} = 0.75 \text{ grams of imiquimod}$$

The total weight of the prescription is 60 g (15 g + 20 g + 25 g).

$$\frac{0.75 \text{ g}}{60 \text{ g}} = \frac{X \text{ g}}{100 \text{ g}} \quad X = 1.25 \text{ g, which is } 1.25\%$$

Ratio Strength

The concentration of weak solutions can be expressed in terms of ratio strength. Ratio strength describes the drug concentration in terms of a ratio (as the name suggests). It is denoted as one unit of solute contained in the total amount of the solution or mixture (e.g., 1:500).

---

38. Express 0.04% as a ratio strength.

$$\frac{0.04}{100} = \frac{1 \text{ part}}{X \text{ parts}} \quad X = 2,500. \text{ Ratio strength is } 1:2,500$$

You can go back to 0.04% by taking 1/2500 x 100; try it.

Express 1:4,000 as a percentage strength.

$$\frac{1 \text{ part}}{4,000 \text{ part}} = \frac{X}{100} \quad X = 0.025, \text{ which is } 0.025\%$$

39. There are 50 mg of drug in 50 mL of solution. Express the concentration as a ratio strength (% w/v).

First, convert 50 mg to grams. 50 mg x 1 g/1,000 mg = 0.05 g

Then, find out how many grams per 100 mL.

$$\frac{0.05\ g}{50\ mL} = \frac{X\ g}{100\ mL} \quad X = 0.1\ g$$

Now solve for ratio strength.

$$\frac{0.1\ g}{100\ mL} = \frac{1\ part}{X\ parts} \quad X = 1{,}000,\ or\ 1{:}1{,}000$$

---

40. How many milligrams of iodine should be used in compounding the following prescription?

ITEM	QUANTITY
Iodine	1:400
Hydrophilic ointment ad	10 g
Sig. Apply as directed.	

First, convert the ratio strength to a percentage strength.

1:400 = 0.0025, or 0.25%

Then, multiply by the total amount in the prescription.

10 g x 0.0025 = 0.025 g, or 25 mg

Or, solve another way:

1:400 means 1 g in 400 g of ointment.

$$\frac{1\ g}{400\ g} = \frac{X\ g}{10\ g} \quad X = 0.025\ g,\ or\ 25\ mg$$

---

41. A 10 mL mixture contains 0.25 mL of active drug. Express the concentration as a ratio strength (% v/v).

First, find out how much drug is in 100 mL.

$$\frac{0.25\ mL\ drug}{10\ mL} = \frac{X\ mL\ drug}{100\ mL} \quad X = 2.5\ mL$$

Now solve for ratio strength.

$$\frac{2.5\ mL\ drug}{100\ mL} = \frac{1\ part}{X\ parts} \quad X = 40;\ or\ 1{:}40$$

42. What is the concentration, in ratio strength, of a trituration made by combining 150 mg of albuterol sulfate and 4.05 grams of lactose?

First, add up the total weight of the prescription.

0.150 g + 4.05 g = 4.2 g

Now solve for ratio strength.

$$\frac{0.150 \text{ g}}{4.2} = \frac{1}{X} \qquad X = 28, \text{ or } 1:28$$

Parts Per Million (PPM)

Parts indicate amount proportions. Parts per million (PPM) and parts per billion (PPB) are used to quantify strengths of very dilute solutions. It is defined as the number of parts of the drug per 1 million (or 1 billion) parts of the whole. The same default units are followed as for percentage systems (% w/w, % w/v and % v/v).

---

43. Express 0.00022% w/v as PPM. Round to the nearest tenth.

$$\frac{0.00022 \text{ g}}{100 \text{ mL}} = \frac{X \text{ g}}{1,000,000} \qquad X = 2.2 \text{ PPM}$$

---

44. Express 30 PPM of copper in solution as a percentage.

$$\frac{30}{1,000,000} = \frac{X \text{ g}}{100 \text{ mL}} \qquad X = 0.003\%$$

---

45. Express 5 PPM of iron in water as a percentage.

$$\frac{5}{1,000,000} = \frac{X \text{ g}}{100 \text{ mL}} \qquad X = 0.0005\%$$

---

46. A patient's blood contains 0.085 PPM of selenium. How many micrograms of selenium does the patient's blood contain if the blood volume is 6 liters?

$$\frac{0.085 \text{ g}}{1,000,000 \text{ mL}} = \frac{X \text{ g}}{6,000 \text{ mL}} \qquad X = 0.00051 \text{ g, or } 510 \text{ mcg}$$

---

47. A sample of an intravenous solution is found to contain 0.4 PPM of DEHP. How much of the solution, in milliliters, will contain 50 micrograms of DEHP?

$$\frac{0.4 \text{ g}}{1,000,000 \text{ mL}} = \frac{0.00005 \text{ g}}{X} \qquad X = 125 \text{ mL}$$

If asked to express something in PPB (parts per billion), you divide by 1,000,000,000 (9 zeros).

Body Mass Index (BMI)

BMI is a measure of body fat based on height and weight that applies to adult men and women. A primary health problem is overweight and obesity which increases the risk of morbidity from hypertension, dyslipidemia, diabetes, coronary heart disease, stroke, gallbladder disease, osteoarthritis and some other conditions. Higher body weights are also associated with increases in all-cause mortality. BMI is a useful measure of body fat, but the BMI can over-estimate body fat in persons who are muscular, and can under-estimate body fat in frail elderly and others who have lost muscle mass. Waist circumference is used concurrently. If most of the fat is around the waist, there is higher disease risk. High risk is defined as a waist size > 35 inches for women or > 40 inches for men. Underweight can be a problem if a person is fighting a disease such as a frail, hospitalized patient with an infection.

BMI is calculated as follows:

$$BMI = \frac{weight\ (kg)}{height\ (m^2)}$$

Alternatively, BMI can be calculated using the following formula:

$$BMI = \frac{weight\ (pounds)}{height\ (in)^2} \times 704.5$$

BMI Classifications

SCORE	CLASSIFICATION
< 18.5	Underweight
18.5-24.9	Normal weight
25-29.9	Overweight
≥ 30	Obese

48. A male comes to the pharmacy and tells you he is 6'7" tall and 250 pounds. His waist circumference is 43 inches. Calculate his BMI. Round to the nearest whole number. Is the patient underweight, normal weight, overweight, or obese?

- Convert weight to kg: 250 pounds x 1 kg/2.2 lbs. = 113.6 kg

- Convert height to cm: 6'7" = 79" x 2.54 cm/inch = 200.66 cm.

- 200.66 cm = 2 m (divide cm by 100 to get the height in meters)

$$BMI\ (kg/m^2) = \frac{113.6}{2^2} = 28.4,\ or\ 28\ which\ is\ overweight.$$

49. Calculate the BMI for a male who is 6' tall and weighs 198 lbs. Round to the nearest tenth. Is the patient underweight, normal weight, overweight, or obese?

$$BMI\ (pounds/in^2) = \frac{198\ pounds}{(72\ in)^2} \times 704.5 = 26.9,\ or\ 27\ which\ is\ overweight.$$

Ideal Body Weight (IBW)

IBW is the healthy (ideal) weight for a person. Some medications which are hydrophilic do not distribute much into fat and should be dosed on IBW to prevent giving the patient too much drug. <u>Know these formulas and the creatinine clearance formula below:</u>

- IBW (males) = 50 kg + (2.3 kg)(each inch over 5 feet)

- IBW (females) = 45.5 kg + (2.3 kg)(each inch over 5 feet)

Renal Function and Creatinine Clearance (CrCl) Estimation

A normal range of serum creatinine is approximately 0.6 to 1.2 mg/dL. A serum creatinine above this range usually indicates that the kidneys are not functioning properly. However, the values can appear normal even when renal function is compromised.

Creatinine is a break-down product produced when muscle tissue makes energy. If the kidneys are declining and cannot clear (excrete) the creatinine, the creatinine level will increase in the blood and the creatinine clearance (CrCl) will decrease. This tells us that the concentration of drugs that are renally cleared will also increase and a dose reduction may be required.

Patients should be assessed for dehydration when the serum creatinine value is elevated. Dehydration can cause both the serum creatinine (SCr) and the blood urea nitrogen (BUN) values to increase. <u>Generally, a BUN:SCr ratio > 20 indicates dehydration</u>. Correcting the dehydration will reduce both BUN and SCr, and can prevent or treat acute renal failure. Signs of dehydration should also be assessed and these can include decreased urine output, tachycardia, tachypnea, dry skin/mouth/mucous membranes, skin tenting (skin does not bounce back when pinched into a fold) and possibly fever. Dehydration is usually caused by diarrhea, vomiting, and/or a lack of adequate fluid intake.

---

50. Looking at the laboratory values below, make an assessment of the patient's hydration status.

	NORMAL RANGE	PATIENT'S RANGE
BUN	7-25 mg/dL	54
Creatinine	0.6-1.2 mg/dL	1.8

- *a.* The patient appears to be well hydrated given the laboratory results.
- *b.* The patient appears to be too hydrated given the laboratory results.
- *c.* The patient is not experiencing dehydration given the laboratory results.
- *d.* The patient is experiencing dehydration and the patient may need to be started on fluids.
- *e.* The patient has subjective information indicating dehydration but the patient needs to be assessed objectively as well.

The correct answer is [D]. The patient's BUN:SCr ratio is 54/1.8 = 30. Since 30 > 20, the BUN is disproportionately elevated relative to the creatinine, indicating that the patient is dehydrated.

51. Nancy is receiving a furosemide infusion at 5 mg/hr. The nurse notices her urine output has decreased in the last hour. Laboratory values are drawn and the patient has a SCr 1.5 mg/dL and a BUN 26 mg/dL. The nurse wants to know if she should stop the furosemide infusion due to the patient becoming dehydrated. What is the correct assessment of the patient's hydration status?

    a. The patient appears to be too hydrated given the laboratory results.

    b. The patient is not experiencing dehydration given the laboratory results.

    c. The patient is experiencing dehydration and the patient may need to be started on fluids.

    d. The patient has objective information indicating dehydration but the patient needs to be assessed subjectively as well.

    e. None of the above are correct.

The correct answer is [B]. The BUN:SCr ratio is 26/1.5 = 17.3, which is < 20. Continue to monitor the patient.

The Cockcroft-Gault Equation

This formula is used commonly by pharmacists to estimate renal function. However, it is not commonly used in very young children, ESRD patients or when renal function is fluctuating rapidly. There are different methods used to estimate renal function in these circumstances. The Cockcroft-Gault formula should be known, as it is commonly used in practice.

$$CrCl = \frac{140-(\text{age of patient})}{72 \times SCr} \times \text{wt in kg } (\times 0.85 \text{ if female})$$

A problem may specify which weight to use in the equation. If not, it is advisable to use the following weights:

- Underweight (BMI < 18.5 kg/m^2), use the patient's actual weight

- Normal weight (BMI 18.5-24.9 kg/m^2), use the Ideal Body Weight (IBW)

- Overweight (BMI ≥ 25 kg/m^2), use the Adjusted Body Weight$_{0.4}$

The adjusted body weight formula should be known:

$$AdjBW_{0.4} = IBW + 0.4(TBW-IBW)$$

As mentioned above, the IBW is commonly used for drugs that are hydrophilic, such as aminoglycosides, theophylline and others (except if thin). If the actual weight is used, a drug that primarily stays in the blood compartment and does not distribute into fat may be overdosed. The abbreviation ABW can indicate either actual or adjusted body weight and is best avoided.

GFR LEVEL (mL/min/1.73m^2)	INTERPRETATION
60-89	mild renal insufficiency (Stage 2 CKD)
30-59	moderate renal insufficiency (Stage 3 CKD)
15-29	severe renal insufficiency (Stage 4 CKD)
< 15 or on dialysis	renal failure (Stage 5 CKD)

52. An 87 year old female patient (height 5′4″, weight 103 pounds) is placed on levofloxacin, dosing per pharmacy. Her labs include BUN 22 mg/dL and SCr 1 mg/dL. Choose the correct dosing regimen based on the chart below.

CRCL	≥ 50 ML/MIN	20-49 ML/MIN	< 20ML/MIN
Levofloxacin Dose	500 mg Q 24 hours	250 mg Q 24 hours	250 mg Q 48 hours

First, convert weight to kg: 103 pounds x 1 kg/2.2 pounds = 46.8 kg. Use her actual body weight for calculating CrCl since her actual body weight is lower than her IBW.

$$CrCL = \frac{140-87}{72 \times 1} \times 46.8 \; (\times 0.85) = 29 \; mL/min.$$ The correct dose of levofloxacin is 250 mg Q 24H.

---

53. A 34 year old male (height 6′7″, weight 227 pounds) is hospitalized after a motor vehicle accident. He develops a *P. aeruginosa* infection. The physician orders tobramycin 2 mg/kg IV Q8H. Calculate the tobramycin dose. Round to the nearest 10 milligrams.

IBW (males) = 50 kg + (2.3 kg x height in inches over 5 feet):

$$IBW = 50 \; kg + (2.3 \times 19 \; in) = 93.7 \; kg$$

Tobramycin 2 mg/kg x 93.7 kg = 187.4 mg, round to 190 mg IV Q8H.

---

54. A 50 year old male (height 6′1″, weight 177 pounds) has HIV and is being started on tenofovir, emtricitabine and efavirenz therapy. His laboratory values include K⁺ 4.4 mEq/L, BUN 40 mg/dL, SCr 1.8 mg/dL, and CD4 count of 455 cells/mm³. Using the information below, what is the correct dose of tenofovir for this patient. If the IBW is less than the actual weight, use the actual weight.

CRCL	≥ 50 ML/MIN	30-49 ML/MIN	10-29 ML/MIN	< 10 ML/MIN
Tenofovir Dose	300 mg daily	300 mg Q 48 hours	300 mg Q 72-96 hours	300 mg weekly

First, calculate the patient's IBW.

$$IBW = 50 \; kg + (2.3 \times 13 \; in) = 79.9, \text{ or } 80 \; kg$$

The IBW is the same as the actual weight. If the IBW is less than the actual weight, use the actual weight.

Next, calculate the CrCl.

$$CrCL = \frac{140-50}{72 \times 1.8} \times 80 \; kg = 55.5 \; mL/min$$

The dose of tenofovir should be 300 mg daily.

55. A 64 year old female patient (height 5'5", weight 205 pounds) is hospitalized with a nosocomial pneumonia which is responding to treatment. Her current antibiotic medications include ceftazidime, imipenem and vancomycin. Her morning laboratory values include K⁺ 4.0 mEq/L, BUN 60 mg/dL, SCr 2.7 mg/dL, and glucose 222 mg/dL. Based on the chart below, what is the correct dose of imipenem for this patient?

CRCL	≥ 71 ML/MIN	41-70 ML/MIN	21-40 ML/MIN	≤ 20 ML/MIN
Imipenem Dose	500 mg IV Q6H	500 mg IV Q8H	250 mg IV Q6H	250 mg IV Q12H

Since her BMI ≥ 25, we would use the adjusted body weight unless otherwise instructed. Calculate her IBW.

$$IBW = 45.5 \text{ kg} + (2.3 \times 5 \text{ in}) = 57 \text{ kg}$$

Now we can calculate her adjusted body weight.

$$AdjBW_{0.4} = 57 + 0.4(93-57) = 71.4 \text{ kg}$$

Then, solve using the Cockcroft-Gault equation.

$$CrCL = \frac{140-64}{72 \times 2.7} \times 71.4(0.85) = 23.7 \text{ mL/min. Therefore, the correct dose of imipenem is 250 mg IV Q6H.}$$

---

56. A female patient is to receive 5 mg/kg/d of theophylline. The patient is 5'7" and weighs 243 pounds. Calculate the theophylline dose the patient should receive.

$$IBW \text{ (females)} = 45.5 \text{ kg} + (2.3 \times 7 \text{ in}) = 61.6 \text{ kg}$$

$$\text{Theophylline 5 mg/kg} \times 61.6 \text{ kg} = 308 \text{ mg}$$

Theophylline and aminophylline which are generally dosed on IBW. Check if there were any instructions in the problem regarding rounding, or which weight to use.

Specific Gravity (SG)

Specific gravity is the ratio of the density of a substance to the density of water. SG can be important for calculating IV medications, in compounding, and in urinalysis for use in diagnosis. Water has a specific gravity of 1 where 1 g water = 1 mL water. Substances that have a SG < 1 are lighter than water. Substances that have a SG > 1 are heavier than water. SG does not have units.

$$SG = \frac{\text{weight (g)}}{\text{volume (mL)}}$$

---

57. What is the specific gravity of 150 mL of glycerin weighing 165 grams? Round to the nearest tenth.

$$SG = \frac{165 \text{ g}}{150 \text{ mL}} \quad SG = 1.1$$

Check the answer: 150 mL x 1.1 = 165 g

58. What is the weight of 750 mL of concentrated acetic acid (SG=1.2)?

$$1.2 \ = \ \frac{X \text{ g}}{750 \text{ mL}} \qquad X = 900 \text{ g}$$

Check the answer: 900 g/750 mL = 1.2

---

59. How many mL of polysorbate 80 (SG = 1.08) are needed to prepare a prescription that includes 48 g of the surfactant/emulsifier (polysorbate)? Round to the nearest hundredth.

$$1.08 \ = \ \frac{48 \text{ g}}{X \text{ mL}} \qquad X = 44.44 \text{ mL}$$

Check the answer: 48 g/44.44 mL = 1.08

---

60. What is the specific gravity of 30 mL of a liquid weighing 23,400 milligrams? Round to the nearest hundredth.

$$SG \ = \ \frac{23.4 \text{ g}}{30 \text{ mL}} \qquad SG = 0.78$$

---

61. What is the weight of 0.5 L of polyethylene glycol 400 (SG = 1.13).

$$1.13 \ = \ \frac{X \text{ g}}{500 \text{ mL}} \qquad X = 565 \text{ grams}$$

---

62. Nitroglycerin has a specific gravity of 1.59. How much would 1 quart weigh in grams? Round to the nearest whole number.

- One quart = 946 mL

$$1.59 \ = \ \frac{X \text{ g}}{946 \text{ mL}} \qquad X = 1,504 \text{ g}$$

Check the answer: 1,504 g/946 mL = 1.59

Note that the SG is <u>equivalent</u> to the <u>density in g/mL (with units)</u>. If asked for the density in the above problem, the answer would be 1.59 g/mL.

Flow Rates

Intravenous infusions are commonly used to deliver medications in different settings, including hospitals. Flow rates are used to calculate the volume or amount of drug a patient will receive over a given period of time. An order can specify the rate of flow of continuous intravenous fluids in milliliters per minute, drops per minute, milligrams per hour, or as the total time to administer the entire volume of the infusion (e.g., give over 8 hours). Intravenous (IV) tubing is set to deliver a certain number of drops per minute (gtts/min). There are various types of IV tubing and each has a hollow plastic chamber called a drip chamber. One can count the number of drops per minute by looking at the drip chamber. Also, it is important to know how big the drops are to calibrate the tubing in terms of drops/mL. This is called the drop factor.

63. **The pharmacist has an order for heparin 25,000 units in 250 mL D5W to infuse at 1,000 units/ hour. The pharmacy has the following premixed heparin bags in stock: 25,000 units in 500 mL 1/2 NS, 10,000 units in 250 mL D5W, and 25,000 units in 250 mL D5W. What should the infusion rate be set at in mL/hour?**

The pharmacy has the heparin concentration needed in stock. First, calculate units per mL.

$$\frac{25{,}000 \text{ units}}{250 \text{ mL}} = 100 \text{ units/mL}$$

Since there are 100 units in each mL and 1,000 units/hour must be delivered to the patient, the pump should be programmed for an infusion rate of 10 mL/hr.

$$\frac{1 \text{ mL}}{100 \text{ units}} \times \frac{1{,}000 \text{ units}}{\text{hour}} = 10 \text{ mL/hour}$$

Another way to solve the problem simply is to use the following ratio:

$$\frac{25{,}000 \text{ units}}{250 \text{ mL}} = \frac{1{,}000 \text{ units}}{X \text{ mL}} \qquad X = 10 \text{ mL (per hour since we had 1,000 units given in 1 hour)}$$

---

64. **If 50 mg of drug are added to a 500 mL bag, what will be the rate of flow, in milliliters per hour, to deliver 5 mg of drug per hour?**

$$\frac{50 \text{ mg}}{500 \text{ mL}} = \frac{5 \text{ mg}}{X} \qquad X = 50 \text{ mL/hour}$$

---

65. **If 200 mg of drug are added to a 500 mL bag, what will be the rate of flow, in milliliters per hour, to deliver 500 mcg of drug per hour? Round to the nearest hundredth.**

$$200 \text{ mg} \times \frac{1{,}000 \text{ mcg}}{1 \text{ mg}} = 200{,}000 \text{ mcg}$$

$$\frac{200{,}000 \text{ mcg}}{500 \text{ mL}} = \frac{500 \text{ mcg}}{X} \qquad X = 1.25 \text{ mL/hour}$$

---

66. **A 68 kg patient is receiving a drug in standard concentration of 400 mg/250 mL of 1/2 NS running at 15 mL/hr. Calculate the dose in mcg/kg/min. Round to the nearest hundredth.**

$$\frac{15 \text{ mL}}{\text{hr}} \times \frac{400 \text{ mg drug}}{250 \text{ mL}} = 24 \text{ mg drug/hr}$$

$$\frac{24 \text{ mg drug}}{\text{hr}} \times \frac{1{,}000 \text{ mcg}}{1 \text{ mg}} = 24{,}000 \text{ mcg/hr}$$

$$\frac{24{,}000 \text{ mcg}}{\text{hr}} \times \frac{1 \text{ hr}}{60 \text{ min}} = 400 \text{ mcg/min}$$

$$\frac{400 \text{ mcg/min}}{68 \text{ kg}} = 5.88 \text{ mcg/kg/min}$$

67. The pharmacist has an order for heparin 25,000 units in 250 mL D5W to infuse at 1,000 units/ hour. How much time, in hours, will be needed to infuse the entire bag?

$$25,000 \text{ units} \quad \times \quad \frac{1 \text{ hr}}{1,000 \text{ units}} \quad = \quad 25 \text{ hours}$$

You may need to calculate how many drops will be administered per minute (or per hour). The problem would state the number of drops/mL, which depends on the infusion set.

68. A physician orders an IV infusion of D5W 1 Liter to be delivered over 8 hours. The IV infusion set delivers 15 drops/mL. How many drops/min will the patient receive? Round to the nearest whole number.

$$\frac{15 \text{ drops}}{1 \text{ mL}} \quad \times \quad \frac{1,000 \text{ mL}}{8 \text{ hr}} \quad \times \quad \frac{1 \text{ hr}}{60 \text{ min}} \quad = \quad 31.25 \text{ drops/min; or 31 drops/min}$$

69. A nurse is hanging a 4% lidocaine solution for a patient. If the dose is 6 mg/min, how many hours will a 250 mL bag last? Round to the nearest tenth.

$$\frac{4 \text{ g}}{100 \text{ mL}} \quad = \quad \frac{X}{250 \text{ mL}} \quad X = 10 \text{ g or 10,000 mg}$$

$$\frac{6 \text{ mg}}{\text{min}} \quad = \quad \frac{10,000 \text{ mg}}{X \text{ min}} \quad X = 1,666.67 \text{ minutes or 27.8 hours}$$

Or, solve another way:

$$\frac{1 \text{ hr}}{60 \text{ min}} \quad \times \quad \frac{1 \text{ min}}{6 \text{ mg}} \quad \times \quad \frac{1,000 \text{ mg}}{1 \text{ g}} \quad \times \quad \frac{4 \text{ g}}{100 \text{ mL}} \quad \times \quad 250 \text{ mL} \quad = \quad 27.8 \text{ hours}$$

70. A patient is to receive *Keppra* at a rate of 5 mg/min. The pharmacy has a 5 mL (100 mg/mL) *Keppra* injection vial to be diluted in 100 mL of NS. What is the rate of infusion, in mL/min, of *Keppra?* Do not include the volume of the 5 mL additive.

First, calculate the amount of *Keppra* in the vial.

$$\frac{100 \text{ mg}}{\text{mL}} \quad = \quad \frac{X \text{ mg}}{5 \text{ mL}} \quad X = 500 \text{ mg}$$

Then, solve for the answer in mL/min.

$$\frac{100 \text{ mL}}{500 \text{ mg}} \quad \times \quad \frac{5 \text{ mg}}{\text{min}} \quad = \quad 1 \text{ mL/min}$$

71. A physician orders 15 units of insulin to be added to a liter of D5W to be given over 10 hours. What is the infusion rate, in drops/minute, if the IV set delivers 15 drops/mL? Do not round your answer.

$$\frac{15 \text{ drops}}{\text{mL}} \times \frac{1,000 \text{ mL}}{10 \text{ hours}} \times \frac{1 \text{ hour}}{60 \text{ min}} = 25 \text{ drops/min}$$

---

72. The pharmacy has insulin vials containing 100 units of insulin/mL. A physician orders 15 units of insulin to be added to a liter of D5W to be given over 10 hours. How many units of insulin will the patient receive each hour if the IV set delivers 15 drops/mL? Do not round the answer.

$$\frac{15 \text{ units}}{10 \text{ hours}} = \frac{X \text{ units}}{1 \text{ hour}} \qquad X = 1.5 \text{ units/hour}$$

---

73. An order is written for 10 mL of a 10% calcium chloride injection and 10 mL of multivitamin injection (MVI) to be added to 500 mL of D5W. The infusion is to be administered over 6 hours. The IV set delivers 15 drops/mL. What should be the rate of flow in drops/minute to deliver this infusion? Round to the nearest whole number.

Total volume of the infusion = 500 mL (D5W) + 10 mL (CaCl$_2$) + 10 mL (MVI) = 520 mL

$$\frac{15 \text{ drops}}{\text{mL}} \times \frac{520 \text{ mL}}{6 \text{ hr}} \times \frac{1 \text{ hr}}{60 \text{ min}} = 22 \text{ drops/min}$$

---

74. RS is a 45 year old male, 5'5", 168 pounds, hospitalized with a diabetic foot infection. The pharmacist prepared a 500 mL bag of D5W contains 1 gram of vancomycin to be infused over 4 hours using a 20 gtts/mL IV tubing set. How many mg of vancomycin will the patient receive each minute? Round to the nearest tenth.

$$\frac{1,000 \text{ mg vanco}}{4 \text{ hrs}} \times \frac{1 \text{ hr}}{60 \text{ min}} = 4.16 \text{ mg/min or } 4.2 \text{ mg/min}$$

---

75. A patient is to receive 600,000 units of penicillin G potassium in 100 mL D5W. A vial of penicillin G potassium 1,000,000 units is available. The manufacture states that when 4.6 mL of diluent is added, a 200,000 units/mL solution will result. How many milliliters of reconstituted solution should be withdrawn and added to the bag of D5W?

$$\frac{200,000 \text{ units}}{\text{mL}} = \frac{600,000 \text{ units}}{X \text{ mL}} \qquad X = 3 \text{ mL}$$

---

76. A patient is to receive 1.5 liters of NS running at 45 gtts/min using a 15 gtts/mL IV tubing set. Calculate the total infusion time in hours. Round to the nearest tenth.

$$\frac{45 \text{ gtts}}{X \text{ mL}} = \frac{15 \text{ gtts}}{1 \text{ mL}} \qquad X = 3 \text{ mL}$$

$$\frac{3 \text{ mL}}{\text{min}} = \frac{1,500 \text{ mL}}{X \text{ min}} \qquad X = 500 \text{ min}$$

$$500 \text{ min} \quad x \quad \frac{1 \text{ hour}}{60 \text{ min}} \quad = \quad 8.3 \text{ hours}$$

---

77. An intravenous infusion contains 2 mL of a 1:1,000 (w/v) solution of epinephrine and 250 mL of D5W. At what flow rate, in mL/min, should the infusion be administered to provide 0.3 mcg/kg/min of epinephrine to an 80 kg patient? Round to the nearest whole number.

- 1:1,000 = 0.1% (w/v)

$$\frac{0.1 \text{ g}}{100 \text{ mL}} = \frac{X \text{ g}}{2 \text{ mL}} \qquad X = 0.002 \text{ g, or 2 mg}$$

The patient is 80 kg x 0.3 mcg/kg/min = 24 mcg/min

$$\frac{252 \text{ mL}}{2 \text{ mg}} \quad x \quad \frac{1 \text{ mg}}{1,000 \text{ mcg}} \quad x \quad \frac{24 \text{ mcg}}{\text{min}} \quad = \quad 3 \text{ mL/min}$$

---

78. A patient is to receive *Flagyl* at a rate of 12.5 mg/min. The pharmacy has a 5 mL (100 mg/mL) *Flagyl* injection vial to be diluted in 100 mL of NS. How much drug in milligrams will the patient receive over 20 minutes?

$$\frac{12.5 \text{ mg}}{\text{min}} \quad x \quad 20 \text{ minutes} \quad = \quad 250 \text{ mg}$$

---

79. A physician has ordered 2 grams of cefotetan to be added to 100 mL NS for a 56 year old female with an anaerobic infection. Using a reconstituted injection containing 154 mg/mL, how many milliliters should be added to prepare the order? Round to the nearest whole number.

$$2,000 \text{ mg} \quad x \quad \frac{1 \text{ mL}}{154 \text{ mg}} \quad = \quad 13 \text{ mL}$$

---

80. JY is a 58 year old male who was hospitalized for a total knee replacement. He was given unfractionated heparin and developed heparin-induced thrombocytopenia (HIT). Argatroban was ordered at a dose of 2 mcg/kg/min. The pharmacy mixes a concentration of 100 mg argatroban in 250 mL of D5W. JY weighs 85 kg. How many mL/hour should the nurse infuse to provide the desired dose? Round to the nearest whole number.

First, determine the amount of drug needed based on body weight.

2 mcg/kg/min x 85 kg = 170 mcg/min

Then, calculate mL/hr.

$$\frac{250 \text{ mL}}{100 \text{ mg}} \quad x \quad \frac{1 \text{ mg}}{1,000 \text{ mcg}} \quad x \quad \frac{170 \text{ mcg}}{\text{min}} \quad x \quad \frac{60 \text{ min}}{\text{hr}} \quad = \quad 25.5 \text{ mL/hr, rounded up to 26 mL/hr}$$

81. The 8 a.m. medications scheduled for your patient include *Tygacil* dosed at 6 mg/kg. The patient weighs 142 pounds. *Tygacil* comes as 500 mg vials to be reconstituted and diluted in 50 mL NS. According to the pharmacy, this preparation should be administered over thirty minutes. The IV tubing in the unit delivers 15 drops per milliliter. What is the correct rate of flow in drops per minute? Round to the nearest drop.

$$\frac{142 \text{ pounds}}{2.2 \text{ pounds/kg}} \quad \times \quad \frac{6 \text{ mg}}{\text{kg}} \quad = \quad 387.27 \text{ mg required dose}$$

The drug comes as 500 mg in a 50 mL bag: 500 mg/50 mL = 10 mg/mL

$$\frac{500 \text{ mg}}{50 \text{ mL}} \quad = \quad 10 \text{ mg/mL}$$

The patient requires 387.27 mg x 10 mg/mL = 38.727 mL

$$\frac{38.727 \text{ mL}}{30 \text{ min}} \quad = \quad \frac{1.29 \text{ mL}}{\text{min}} \quad \times \quad \frac{15 \text{ drops}}{\text{mL}} \quad = \quad 19.36 \text{ drops per minute, rounded to 19 drops/minute}$$

---

82. A 165 pound patient is to receive 250 mL of a dopamine drip at a rate of 17 mcg/kg/min. The pharmacy has dopamine premixed in concentration of 3.2 mg/mL in D5W. Calculate the infusion rate in mL/minute. Round to the nearest tenth.

Step 1 – Calculate amount of drug in the 250 mL bag.

$$\frac{3.2 \text{ mg}}{\text{mL}} \quad \times \quad 250 \text{ mL} \quad = \quad 800 \text{ mg}$$

Step 2 – Calculate amount of drug the patient needs.

$$\frac{17 \text{ mcg}}{\text{kg/min}} \quad \times \quad \frac{1 \text{ kg}}{2.2 \text{ lbs}} \quad \times \quad 165 \text{ lbs.} \quad = \quad 1,275 \text{ mcg/min or } 1.275 \text{ mg/min}$$

Step 3–Solve for milliliters per minute.

$$\frac{250 \text{ mL}}{800 \text{ mg}} \quad \times \quad \frac{1.275 \text{ mg}}{\text{min}} \quad = \quad 0.4 \text{ mL/min}$$

---

83. An order is written for phenytoin to be given by intravenous infusion at a loading dose of 15 mg/kg to be infused at 0.5 mg/kg/min for a 33 pound child. The pharmacy has phenytoin injection solution 50 mg/mL in a 5 mL vial in stock. The pharmacist will put the dose into 50 mL NS. Over how many minutes should the dose be administered? Round to the nearest whole number.

First, calculate the child's body weight in kg.

$$33 \text{ lbs} \quad \times \quad \frac{1 \text{ kg}}{2.2 \text{ lbs}} \quad = \quad 15 \text{ kg}$$

Next, find the dose the child will receive.

$$\frac{15 \text{ mg}}{\text{kg}} \quad \times \quad 15 \text{ kg} \quad = \quad 225 \text{ mg}$$

Then, calculate the time it will take to infuse this amount of drug at the given rate.

0.5 mg/kg/min x 15 kg = 7.5 mg/min

$$\frac{1 \text{ min}}{7.5 \text{ mg}} \quad x \quad 225 \text{ mg} \quad = \quad 30 \text{ minutes}$$

Dilution and Concentration

Often the strength of a concentration must be increased or decreased. Or, a new quantity is required. This formula can be used to change the strength or quantity. Be careful: <u>the units on each side must match</u> and one or more may need to be changed, such as mg to gram, or vice-versa.

$Q_1 \times C_1 = Q_2 \times C_2$

Q_1 = old quantity

C_1 = old concentration

Q_2 = new quantity

C_2 = new concentration

---

84. How many mL of a 1:2,500 (w/v) solution of aluminum acetate can be made from 100 mL of a 0.2% solution?

1:2,500 is converted to a percentage by making it into a fraction and multiplying by 100.

$$1{:}2{,}500 \quad = \quad \frac{1}{2{,}500} \quad x \quad 100 \quad = \quad 0.04\%$$

Now we can use the formula.

$Q_1 \quad x \quad C_1 \quad = \quad Q_2 \quad x \quad C_2$

100 mL x 0.2% = Q_2 x 0.04%

Q_2 = 500 mL

---

85. Using 20 g of a 9% boric acid ointment base, the pharmacist will manufacture a 5% ointment. How much diluent is required?

Note the difference from the previous problem where the calculation provided the total volume. Here, you will get the final quantity (weight) but are asked how much diluent should be added to make the final weight.

20 g x 9% = Q_2 x 5%

Q_2 = 36 g total

Then take 36 g – 20 g (already present) = 16 g diluent required

86. How many grams of petrolatum (diluent) should be added to 250 g of a 20% ichthammol ointment to make a 7% ichthammol ointment? Round to the nearest tenth.

250 g x 20% = Q_2 x 7%

Q_2 = 714.3 g total

714.3 g – 250 g present = 464.3 g petrolatum required

---

87. What is the ratio strength (w/v) of 50 mL containing a 1:20 (w/v) ammonia solution diluted to 1 liter?

1:20 is converted to a percentage by making it into a fraction and multiplying by 100:

1:20 = $\dfrac{1}{20}$ x 100 = 5%

50 mL x   5%   = 1,000 mL x C_2

C_2 = 0.25% = 1:400

---

88. If 1 gallon of a 20% (w/v) solution is evaporated to a solution with a 50% (w/v) strength, what will be the new volume (in mL)?

3,785 mL x 20% = Q_2 x 50%

Q_2 = 1,514 mL

Alligation

Alligation is used to obtain a new strength (percentage) that is between two strengths the pharmacist has in stock. Occasionally, no math is required to solve this type of problem if the new strength needed is exactly in the middle of the 2 strengths that are given. If the prescription calls for an ingredient that is <u>pure, the concentration is 100%</u>. If you are given a diluent, such as petrolatum, lanolin, alcohol, "ointment base", etc., the concentration of the <u>diluent is 0%</u>.

---

89. Measure out 100 g of a 50% hydrocortisone powder using the 25% and 75% in stock.

- Use 50g of the 75%, and 50g of the 25% (total is 100 grams).

---

90. You are asked to prepare 80 g of a 12.5% ichthammol ointment. You have 16% and 12% ichthammol ointments in stock.

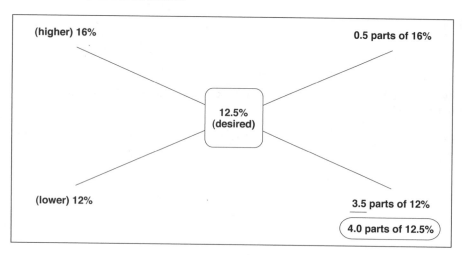

- To set up the X method:

  - Put the more concentrated product at the top left (high goes high)

  - Put the less concentrated product at the bottom left (low goes low)

  - Place the desired concentration in the middle of the X

- Subtract down the "X" lines to obtain the # of parts on the right (16%–12.5% = 3.5 parts; 12%–12.5% = 0.5 parts).

- Add the # of parts on the right to find the total # of parts (4 parts).

- Divide by the total weight (80 g) by the number of parts to obtain the weight per part.

$$\frac{80\ g}{4\ parts} = \frac{20\ g}{part}$$

- Take the amount per part (20 g) and multiply it by the parts from each of the concentrations (from the high, and from the low).

$$0.5\ parts \quad x \quad \frac{20\ g}{part} \quad = \quad 10\ g\ of\ the\ 16\%\ ichthammol\ ointment$$

$$3.5 \text{ parts} \quad x \quad \frac{20 \text{ g}}{\text{part}} \quad = \quad 70 \text{ g of the 12\% ichthammol ointment}$$

Mix together; the end product provides 80 g of a 12.5% ichthammol ointment.

---

91. You are asked to prepare 1 gallon of tincture containing 5.5% iodine. The pharmacy has 3% iodine tincture and 8.5% iodine tincture in stock. How many mL of each 3% and 8.5% iodine tincture should be used? (Use 1 gallon = 3,785 mL)

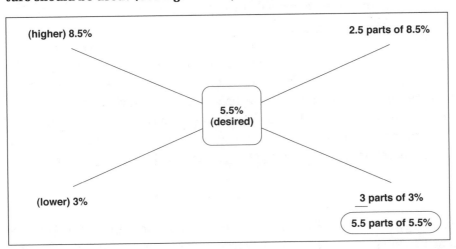

- To set up the X method:

  - Put the more concentrated product at the top left (high goes high)

  - Put the less concentrated product at the bottom left (low goes low)

  - Place the desired concentration in the middle of the X

- Subtract down the "X" lines to obtain the # of parts on the right (e.g., 8.5%–5.5% = 3 parts; 3%–5.5% = 2.5 parts for this problem).

- Add the # of parts on the right to find the total # of parts (5.5 parts in this problem).

- Divide the total volume (3,785 mL) by the number of parts to obtain the volume per part.

$$\frac{3,785 \text{ mL}}{5.5 \text{ parts}} \quad = \quad 688.2 \text{ mL per part}$$

$$2.5 \text{ parts} \quad x \quad \frac{688.2 \text{ mL}}{\text{part}} \quad = \quad 1,720 \text{ mL of the 8.5\% iodine tincture}$$

$$3 \text{ parts} \quad x \quad \frac{688.2 \text{ mL}}{\text{part}} \quad = \quad 2,065 \text{ mL of the 3\% iodine tincture}$$

The end product provides 3,785 mL of a 5.5% iodine tincture.

Calorie Sources and Nutrition Calculations

Kilocalories (kcals), "Calories" and "calories"

A calorie is a measurement of the energy, or heat, it takes to raise the temperature of 1 gram of water by 1° C. Calories are associated with nutrition because humans obtain energy from the food they consume, or from enteral nutrition (EN) formulas delivered by "feeding" tubes into the stomach or intestine, or from parenteral nutrition (PN), which is delivered peripherally through a vein, or centrally through an artery. Calories from any of these nutrition sources are provided by these 3 components: carbohydrates, fat and protein.

A calorie is a very small unit, and these are therefore measured in kilocalories, or kcals, where 1,000 calories = 1 kcal. It is common to find the term "calories" used interchangeably for kcals. For example, the "Nutrition Facts" box on the side of a container of Honey Nut Cheerios® states that a serving of ¾ cup of the cereal provides 110 Calories. Precisely, this is 110 kcals. If you were to look at the box, the word "Calories" is written with a capital "C" which is sometimes used to indicate kcals, versus a lower case "c". It is not consistent; for pharmacy calculations, "calories" or "Calories" are meant to refer to kilocalories, or kcals.

Carbohydrates

Glucose is the primary energy source. Unless a patient purchases glucose tablets or gel, carbohydrates are consumed as simple sugars, such as fruit juice, or complex "starchy" sugars, such as legumes and grains. These are hydrolyzed by the gut into the monosaccharides fructose, galactose and glucose, which are absorbed. The liver converts the first two into glucose, and excess glucose is stored as glycogen.

Carbohydrates from food or in EN formulas provide 4 kcal/gram, although the formula calories are measured together (that's the carbs, fat and protein) in total kcal provided by each mL (kcal/mL). In PN, dextrose monohydrate provides the carbohydrate source. This is the isomer of glucose (D-glucose) which can be metabolized for energy. The dextrose in PN provides 3.4 kcal/gram. Occasionally, glycerol is used as an alternative to dextrose in patients with impaired insulin secretion. Glycerol provides 4.3 kcal/gram and comes premixed with amino acids.

Fat

Fats, or lipids, are used by the body for energy or for various critical functions, including being an essential component of cell membranes, a solvent for fat soluble vitamins, in hormone production and activity, in cell signaling, and other functions. In food or from EN formulas, fat is provided as four types: saturated, *trans*, monounsaturated and polyunsaturated. Each of these provides 9 kcal/gram. In PN, lipids are not measured in grams but in kcal/mL due to the caloric contribution provided by the egg phospholipid and glycerol components in the Intravenous Fat Emulsion (IVFE). 10% IVFE provides 1.1 kcal/mL, 20% provides 2 kcal/mL and 30% provides 3 kcal/mL.

Protein

Protein is used either to <u>repair or build muscle cells</u>, or as a source of <u>energy</u>. Protein in enteral intake is present in various forms, and in PN as the constituent amino acids. If adequate energy is provided by carbohydrates and fat, the protein may be "<u>spared</u>" and can be used by muscle, (although the protein calories may not end up in the intended location.) If "protein sparing" is used, the energy required by the patient will come from only the dextrose and lipids, which are the "Non-Protein Calories" (NPC).

Protein calories from food, enteral nutrition formulas or as parenteral amino acid solutions each provide <u>4 kcal/gram. The kcal amounts in the chart below should be known:</u>

USUAL DIET*			EN FORMULAS*		PN FORMULAS	
Carbs	Bread, Rice….	4 kcal/g	Corn syrup solids, cornstarch, sucrose….	The components contribute the same as from the diet, but are measured (together) as kcal/mL	Dextrose Monohydrate	3.4 kcal/gram
					Glycerol/ Glycerin**	4.3 kcal/gram
Fat	Butter, Oil….	9 kcal/g	Borage oil, canola oil, corn oil….		IV Fat Emulsion (IVFE) 10%	1.1 kcal/mL
					IVFE 20%	2 kcal/mL
					IVFE 30%	3 kcal/mL
Protein	Fish, Meat….	4 kcal/g	Casein, soy, whey….		Amino Acid Solutions (Aminosyn, Freamine….)	4 kcal/gram

* The diet and enteral formula components are common examples; there are others.

** Glycerol may be used to decrease hyperglycemia; more commonly, the dextrose load is decreased or the insulin dose is increased.

PARENTERAL NUTRITION (PN)

It is preferable to use the <u>least invasive</u> and <u>most physiologic</u> method of feeding. PN is neither and has a higher risk of complications, including infection and thrombosis. It may be indicated when the patient is not able to absorb adequate nutrition via the GI tract for greater than 5 days. Usual conditions that may require PN include bowel obstruction, ileus, severe diarrhea, radiation enteritis and untreatable malabsorption.

There are 2 types of PN admixtures. Mixtures that contain dextrose, amino acids, sterile water for injection, electrolytes, vitamins and minerals are referred to as 2-in-1 formulations, while the intravenous fat emulsion (IVFE) is infused separately. When the IVFE in contained in the same bag, it is referred to as total nutrient admixtures (TNAs), or 3-in-1, or all-in-one formulations.

If the PN is expected to be short-term (<1 week), peripheral access may be possible, but has a high risk of phlebitis and vein damage. Central line placement allows a higher osmolarity and a wider variation in pH. Common types of central lines include peripherally-inserted central catheters ("PICC" lines), Hickman, Broviac, Groshong and others.

The fluid, kcal, protein and lipid requirements, plus the initial electrolyte, vitamin and trace element requirements will be determined. Additional additives may be needed, such as insulin and H2-blockers. PN requires monitoring, including assessing the need, the degree of glucose intolerance and the risk of refeeding syndrome, which is an intracellular loss of electrolytes, particularly phosphate, which causes serious complications. The calculations for PN that follow are basic and should be known by pharmacists who work in the hospital setting. Nutrition pharmacy itself is more complex and is a specialty area.

Determining Fluid Needs

Fluid requirements are often calculated 1st in the PN. Enough (but not too much) fluid needs to be given to maintain adequate hydration. Daily fluid needs can be calculated using this formula:

When weight > 20 kg: 1,500 mL + (20 mL)(Wt in kg – 20)

Alternatively, some institutions estimate adult fluid requirements using a general guideline of 30-40 mL/kg/day. The PN and fluid volume should be tailored to the patient. If the patient has problems with fluid accumulation (such as heart failure, renal dysfunction, etc.), the amount of fluid they can handle will be reduced. Fluid volume from medications (including IVPBs) should be included in the overall volume the patient is receiving.

---

92. GG is a 57 year old female admitted to the hospital with bowel obstruction. She is made NPO for the next 5-7 days. The decision was made to start PN therapy. She weighs 65 kg and is 5'6". The SCr is 1.3 mg/dL. Calculate GG's daily fluid requirements.

1,500 mL + (20 mL)(65 – 20) = 2,400 mL/day

---

93. A 76 year old, 154 lbs (IBW) patient is made NPO and needs hydration. She is afebrile and does not have CHF, renal disease, or ascites. What volume of fluid should the patient receive per day?

1,500 mL + (20 mL)(70 – 20) = 2,500 mL/day

Calculating Protein Calories

Typical protein requirements for a non-stressed, ambulatory patient are 0.8-1 g/kg/day. Protein requirements increase as the patient is placed under stress, which is defined as illness severity. The more severely ill, the greater the protein requirements will be per day. In patients with a high degree of metabolic stress the protein requirements can be as high as 1.8-2 g/kg/day.

CONDITION	PROTEIN REQUIREMENTS
Ambulatory, non-hospitalized (non-stressed)	0.8-1 g/kg/day
Hospitalized, or malnourished	1.2-2 g/kg/day

94. MK is a 62 year old female who has been admitted with enteritis and pneumonia. She has a history of Crohn's disease and COPD. The staff gastroenterologist has ordered PN therapy, to be prepared by pharmacy. She is 158 pounds, 5'4". Calculate her protein requirements using her actual weight. She is hospitalized and should receive 1.5 g/kg/day of protein. Round to the nearest whole number.

First, convert pounds to kg. 158 pounds x 1 kg/2.2 lbs = 71.8 kg

Then, calculate the protein requirements. 71.8 kg x 1.5 g/kg/day = 108 g protein/day

---

95. PP is a 46 year old male (207 pounds, 5'11") who has been admitted for bowel resection surgery. Post surgery, he is to be started on PN therapy. The physician wants the patient to receive 1.3 g/kg/day of protein. Calculate his protein requirements using his actual weight. Round to the nearest whole number.

First, convert pounds to kg. 207 pounds x 1 kg/2.2 pounds = 94.1 kg

Then, calculate the protein requirements. 94.1 kg x 1.3 g/kg/day = 122 g protein/day

Calculating Non-Protein Calories

Basal Energy Expenditure (BEE) and Total Energy Expenditure (TEE)

The basal energy expenditure (BEE), otherwise referred to as the basal metabolic rate (BMR), is the energy expenditure in the resting state, exclusive of eating and activity. It is estimated differently in male and female patients using the Harris-Benedict equations (it can also be estimated in adults at 15-25 kcal/kg/day). The Harris-Benedict equations are:

- BEE (males): 66.47 + 13.75(weight in kg) + 5(height in cm)–6.76(age in years)

- BEE (females): 655.1 + 9.6(weight in kg) + 1.85(height in cm)–4.68(age in years)

Total energy expenditure (or total daily expenditure or TDE) is a measure of basal energy expenditure plus excess metabolic demands as a result of stress, the thermal effects of feeding, and energy expenditure for activity.

TEE = BEE x activity factor x stress factor

- Once the BEE is calculated, calculate the TEE by taking the BEE calories and multiplying by the appropriate activity factor and stress factor. This will increase the calories required. Energy requirements are increased 12% with each degree of fever over 37° C.

The activity factor is either 1.2 if confined to bed (non-ambulatory), or 1.3 if out of bed (ambulatory). Commonly used stress factors are listed in the table:

STATE OF STRESS	STRESS FACTOR
Minor surgery	1.2
Infection	1.4
Major trauma, sepsis, burns up to 30% BSA	1.5
Burns over 30% BSA	1.5-2

96. Using the Harris-Benedict equation, calculate the resting non-protein caloric requirement for a major trauma patient (stress factor 1.5) who is a 66 year old male, 174 pounds and 5'10" in height. Activity factor is 1.2. Round to the nearest whole number.

- Height = 70" x 2.54 cm/inch = 177.8 cm. Weight 174 pounds x 1 kg/2.2 pounds = 79.1 kg.

BEE (males): 66.47 + 13.75(weight in kg) + 5(height in cm)–6.76(age in years)

BEE = 66.47 + (13.75 x 79.1) + (5 x 177.8) - (6.76 x 66)

BEE = 66.47 + 1,087.6 + 889 - 446.16 = 1,597 kcal/day

The BEE can be estimated using 15-25 kcal/kg (adults). You may want to check your calculations by using the estimates and seeing if the numbers are close. In this case, an estimation using 20 kcal/kg/day would provide 1,582 kcal/day (close to 1,597 kcal/day as above).

---

97. Using the total energy expenditure equation, calculate the total non-protein caloric requirement for a major trauma patient (stress factor is 1.5, activity factor is 1.2) who is a 66 year old male, weighing 174 pounds and measures 5'10" in height. (Use the kcal from the patient in the previous problem.) Round to the nearest whole number.

TEE = BEE x activity factor x stress factor. BEE was calculated above.

TEE = 1,597 x 1.2 x 1.5 = 2,875 kcal/day

---

98. A 25 year old female major trauma patient survives surgery and is recovering in the surgical intensive care unit. The medical team wants to start PN therapy. She is 122 pounds, 5' 7" with some mild renal impairment. Calculate her BEE using the Harris-Benedict equation and her TEE non-protein caloric requirements (stress factor = 1.7 and activity factor =1.2). Round to the nearest whole number.

- Height = 67" x 2.54 cm/inch = 170 cm. Weight 122 pounds x 1 kg/2.2 pounds = 55.5 kg.

BEE (females): 655.1 + 9.6(weight in kg) + 1.85(height in cm)–4.68(age in years)

BEE = 655.1 + (9.6 x 55.5) + (1.85 x 170) - (4.68 x 25)

BEE = 655.1 + 532.8 + 314.5 - 117 = 1,385 kcal/day

TEE = BEE x activity factor x stress factor

TEE = 1,385 x 1.2 x 1.7 = 2,825 kcal/day

Calculating Amino Acids

Amino acids are the source of proteins in PN. Amino acids are used to build muscle mass and may not be counted as an energy source in critically ill patients because they are catabolic. Amino acids come in stock preparations of 5%, 8.5%, 10%, 15%, and others. Amino acids provide 4 kcal/gram.

---

99. If the pharmacy stocks *Aminosyn* 8.5%, how many mL will be needed to provide 108 g of protein? Round to the nearest whole number.

$$\frac{8.5\ g}{100\ mL} = \frac{108\ g}{X\ mL} \quad X = 1{,}271\ mL$$

---

100. How many calories are provided by 108 grams of protein?

$$\frac{4\ kcal}{g} \times 108\ g = 432\ kcal\ of\ protein$$

---

101. The pharmacy stocks *FreAmine* 10%. A patient requires 122 grams of protein per day. How many mL of *FreAmine* will the patient need?

$$\frac{10\ g}{100\ mL} = \frac{122\ g}{X\ mL} \quad X = 1{,}220\ mL$$

---

102. JR is requiring 1.4 g/kg/day of protein and the pharmacy stocks *Aminosyn* 8.5%. JR is a 55 year old male (weight 189 pounds) who is confined to bed (activity factor 1.2) due to his current infection (stress factor 1.5). Calculate the amount of *Aminosyn*, in milliliters, JR should receive. Round to the nearest whole number. (The answer will be accurate if rounding is done at the last step; the final number should be 1,415 mL.)

First, convert weight to kg. 189 pounds x 1 kg/2.2 pounds = 85.9 kg

Next, calculate protein requirements. 1.4 g/kg/day x 85.9 kg = 120.27 g/day

Then, calculate the amount of *Aminosyn* (mL) needed. Note the activity factor and stress factor are not required to calculate the protein requirements.

$$\frac{8.5\ g}{100\ mL} = \frac{120.27\ g}{X\ mL} \quad X = 1{,}415\ mL$$

---

103. JR is receiving 97 grams of protein in an *Aminosyn* 8.5% solution on day 8 of his hospitalization. How many calories are provided by this amount of protein?

$$\frac{4\ kcal}{g} \times 97\ g = 388\ kcal\ of\ protein$$

104. A PN order is written to add 800 mL of 10% amino acid solution. The pharmacy only has 15% amino acid solution in stock. Using the 15% amino acid solution instead, how many mL should be added to the PN bag? Round to the nearest whole number.

First, calculate the the grams that would be provided with the 10% solution.

$$\frac{10 \text{ g}}{100 \text{ mL}} = \frac{X \text{ g}}{800 \text{ mL}} \quad X = 80 \text{ g}$$

Next, supply the 80 grams of protein with the 15% amino acid solution.

$$\frac{15 \text{ g}}{100 \text{ mL}} = \frac{80 \text{ g}}{X \text{ mL}} \quad X = 533 \text{ mL}$$

Nitrogen Balance

Determining The Grams Of Nitrogen From Protein

Nitrogen is released during protein catabolism and is mainly excreted as urea in the urine. Nitrogen balance is the difference between the body's nitrogen gains and losses. While grams of protein are calculated in a nutritional plan, grams of nitrogen are used as an expression of the amount of protein received by the patient. There is 1 g of nitrogen (N) for each 6.25 g of protein. To calculate the grams of nitrogen in a certain weight of protein, divide the protein grams by 6.25.

$$\text{Nitrogen intake} = \frac{\text{grams of protein intake}}{6.25}$$

---

105. A patient is receiving PN containing 540 mL of 12.5% amino acids per day. How many grams of nitrogen will the patient be receiving? Round to the nearest tenth.

$$\frac{12.5 \text{ g}}{100 \text{ mL}} = \frac{X \text{ g}}{540 \text{ mL}} \quad X = 67.5 \text{ g of protein}$$

$$\frac{67.5 \text{ g of protein}}{6.25} = 10.8 \text{ g of nitrogen}$$

Calculating the Non-Protein Calories to Nitrogen (NPC:N) Ratio

The non-protein calorie to nitrogen ratio (NPC:N) is calculated as:

- First, calculate the grams of nitrogen supplied per day (1 g N = 6.25 g of protein).

- Then, divide the total non-protein calories (dextrose + lipids) by the grams of nitrogen.

Desirable NPC:N ratios are:

- 80:1 the most severely stressed patients

- 100:1 severely stressed patients

- 150:1 unstressed patient

106. A patient is receiving PN containing 480 mL of dextrose 50% and 50 grams of amino acids plus electrolytes. Calculate the non-protein calories to nitrogen ratio for this patient.

First, calculate the nitrogen intake.

$$\text{Nitrogen} = \frac{50 \text{ g of protein}}{6.25} = 8 \text{ g}$$

Next, calculate the non-protein calories.

$$\frac{50 \text{ g dextrose}}{100 \text{ mL}} = \frac{X \text{ g}}{480 \text{ mL}} \qquad X = 240 \text{ g dextrose}$$

$$240 \text{ g dextrose} \quad x \quad \frac{3.4 \text{ kcal dextrose}}{1 \text{ g}} = 816 \text{ kcal of dextrose}$$

Then, set up the NPC:N ratio.

NPC:N ratio is 816:8, or 102:1

Calculating Dextrose

Dextrose is the source of carbohydrates in PN. The usual distribution of non-protein calories is 70-85% as carbohydrate (dextrose) and 15-30% as fat (lipids). Dextrose comes in concentrations of 5%, 10%, 20%, 30%, 50%, 70% and others. The higher concentrations are used for PN. When calculating the dextrose, do not exceed 4 mg/kg/min (some use 7 g/kg/day). These are conservative estimates of the maximum amount of dextrose that the liver can handle.

---

107. Using 50% dextrose in water, how many mL are required to fulfill a PN order for 405 g of dextrose?

$$\frac{50 \text{ g}}{100 \text{ mL}} = \frac{405 \text{ g}}{X \text{ mL}} = 810 \text{ mL}$$

---

108. DF, a 44 year old male, is receiving 1,235 mL of D30W, 1,010 mL of *FreAmine* 8.5%, 200 mL of *Intralipid* 20% and 50 mL of electrolytes/minerals in his PN. How many calories from dextrose is DF receiving from the PN? Round to the nearest whole number.

$$\frac{30 \text{ g}}{100 \text{ mL}} \quad x \quad \frac{1,235 \text{ mL}}{\text{day}} \quad x \quad \frac{3.4 \text{ kcal}}{\text{g}} = 1,260 \text{ kcal/day}$$

---

109. A pharmacy is preparing a PN order for 280 g of dextrose. How many mL of dextrose are required if the concentration of dextrose is 20%?

$$\frac{20 \text{ g}}{100 \text{ mL}} = \frac{280 \text{ g}}{X \text{ mL}} \qquad X = 1,400 \text{ mL}$$

110. If a 50% dextrose injection provides 170 kcal in each 100 mL, how many milliliters of a 70% dextrose injection would provide the same caloric value? Round to the nearest tenth. Or, to solve more simply: since the calories are from 50 g of dextrose, and the pharmacist is using D70, solve by:

$$\frac{70 \text{ g}}{100 \text{ mL}} = \frac{50 \text{ g}}{\text{X mL}}$$

$$\frac{100 \text{ mL}}{70 \text{ g}} \times \frac{1 \text{ g}}{3.4 \text{ kcal}} \times 170 \text{ kcal} = 71.4 \text{ mL}$$

---

111. AH is receiving 640 mL of D50W in her PN. How many calories does this provide?

$$\frac{50 \text{ g}}{100 \text{ mL}} \times \frac{640 \text{ mL}}{\text{day}} \times \frac{3.4 \text{ kcal}}{\text{g}} = 1{,}088 \text{ kcal}$$

---

112. A PN order is written for 500 mL of 50% dextrose. The pharmacy only has D70W in stock. How many mL of D70W would you add to the PN bag? Round to the nearest whole number.

First, calculate the grams of dextrose needed for the PN as written.

$$\frac{50 \text{ g}}{100 \text{ mL}} = \frac{\text{X g}}{500 \text{ mL}} \qquad \text{X} = 250 \text{ g}$$

Next, supply the 250 grams of dextrose with the 70% dextrose solution.

$$\frac{70 \text{ g}}{100 \text{ mL}} = \frac{250 \text{ g}}{\text{X mL}} \qquad \text{X} = 357 \text{ mL of D70W}$$

Calculating Lipids

Lipids are the source of fat in PN. The standard distribution of non-protein calories is 70-85% as carbohydrate (dextrose) and 15-30% as fat (lipids). Lipids are available as 10%, 20% or 30% emulsions. Do not exceed 2.5 g/kg/day of lipids. Lipids do not need to be given daily, especially if the triglycerides are high. The recommended hang time limit for IV fat emulsions (IVFE) is 12 hours if infused separately by itself due to the risk of infection. However, an admixture containing IVFE, such as a TNA, may be administered over 24 hours. Patients receiving lipids should have their triglycerides monitored. If lipids are given once weekly, then divide the total calories by 7 to determine the daily amount of fat the patient receives. Lipid emulsions cannot be filtered through 0.22 micron filters; 1.2 micron filters are used in most formulations. PN requires a filter itself due to the risk of a precipitate.

---

113. A patient is receiving 500 mL of 10% lipids. How many calories is the patient receiving from the lipids? Round to the nearest whole number.

$$\frac{1.1 \text{ kcal}}{\text{mL}} = \frac{\text{X kcal}}{500 \text{ mL}} \qquad \text{X} = 550 \text{ kcal}$$

114. The total energy expenditure (TEE) for a patient is 2,435 kcal/day. The patient is receiving 1,446 kcal from dextrose and 810 kcal from protein. How many kcal should be provided by the lipids?

TEE refers to the non-protein calories. Therefore, 2,435 kcal (total)–1,446 kcal (dextrose) = 989 kcal remaining. 989 kcal should be provided by the lipids.

---

115. Using a 20% lipid emulsion, how many mL are required to meet 989 calories? Round to the nearest whole number.

$$\frac{2 \text{ kcal}}{\text{mL}} = \frac{989 \text{ kcal}}{X \text{ mL}} \qquad X = 495 \text{ mL}$$

---

116. A patient is receiving 660 mL of 10% *Intralipid* on Saturdays along with his normal daily PN therapy of 1,420 mL of D20W, 450 mL *Aminosyn* 15%, and 30 mL of electrolytes. What is the daily amount of calories provided by the lipids? Round to the nearest whole number.

$$\frac{1.1 \text{ kcal}}{\text{mL}} = \frac{X \text{ kcal}}{660 \text{ mL}} \qquad X = 726 \text{ kcal/week. Need to divide by 7 to get daily amount} = 104 \text{ kcal/day}$$

---

117. A patient is receiving 180 mL of 30% lipids. How many calories is the patient receiving from the lipids?

$$\frac{3 \text{ kcal}}{\text{mL}} = \frac{X \text{ kcal}}{180 \text{ mL}} \qquad X = 540 \text{ kcal}$$

---

118. A PN order calls for 475 calories to be provided by lipids. The pharmacy has 10% lipid emulsion in stock. How many mL should be administered to the patient? Round to the nearest whole number.

$$\frac{1.1 \text{ kcal}}{\text{mL}} = \frac{475 \text{ kcal}}{X \text{ mL}} \qquad X = 432 \text{ mL}$$

---

119. TE is a 35 year old female who is receiving 325 grams of dextrose, 85 grams of amino acids, and 300 mL of 10% lipids via her PN therapy. What percentage of calories is provided by the protein content? Round to the nearest whole number.

First, calculate the calories from all sources; dextrose, amino acids, and lipids.

DEXTROSE

$$\frac{3.4 \text{ kcal}}{\text{g}} \times 325 \text{ g} = 1,105 \text{ kcal of dextrose}$$

PROTEIN

$$\frac{4 \text{ kcal}}{\text{g}} \times 85 \text{ g} = 340 \text{ kcal of protein}$$

LIPIDS

$$\frac{1.1 \text{ kcal}}{\text{mL}} \times 300 \text{ mL} = 330 \text{ kcal of fat}$$

Then, add up the total calories from all the sources. 1,105 + 340 + 330 = 1,775 kcal

Finally, calculate the percent of protein.

$$\frac{340 \text{ kcal}}{1{,}775 \text{ kcal}} \times 100 = 19\%$$

---

120. WC, a 57 year old male, is receiving 1,145 mL of D30W, 850 mL of *FreAmine* 8.5%, and 350 mL of *Intralipid* 10% in his PN therapy. What percentage of the non-protein calories are represented by dextrose? Round to the nearest whole number.

First, calculate the non-protein calories (dextrose and lipids).

DEXTROSE

$$\frac{3.4 \text{ kcal}}{g} \times \frac{30 \text{ g}}{100 \text{ mL}} \times 1{,}145 \text{ mL} = 1{,}168 \text{ kcal}$$

LIPIDS

$$\frac{1.1 \text{ kcal}}{mL} \times 350 \text{ mL} = 385 \text{ kcal}$$

Then, add up the calories from these non-protein sources. 1,168 + 385 = 1,553 kcal

Finally, calculate the percent from dextrose.

$$\frac{1{,}168 \text{ kcal}}{1{,}553 \text{ kcal}} \times 100 = 75\%$$

---

121. A 46 year old female with radiation enteritis is receiving 1,800 kcal from her parental nutrition. The solution contains amino acids, dextrose and electrolytes. There are 84.5 grams of protein in the PN and it is running at 85 mL/hour over 24 hours. What is the final concentration of dextrose in the PN solution? Round to the nearest whole number.

First, calculate the amount of dextrose the patient is receiving by subtracting out the protein component.

$$84.5 \text{ g} \times \frac{4 \text{ kcal}}{g} = 338 \text{ kcal}$$

1,800 kcal - 338 kcal of protein = 1,462 kcal from dextrose

Next, calculate the grams of dextrose in this PN.

$$1{,}462 \text{ kcal} \times \frac{1 \text{ g}}{3.4 \text{ kcal}} = 430 \text{ grams of dextrose}$$

Then, calculate the final concentration. This requires calculating the total volume the patient is receiving.

$$\frac{85 \text{ mL}}{\text{hr}} \times 24 \text{ hours} = 2,040 \text{ mL or } 2.04 \text{ L}$$

$$\frac{430 \text{ g dextrose}}{2,040 \text{ mL}} = \frac{X \text{ g}}{100 \text{ mL}} \quad X = 21\%$$

Determining the Amount of Electrolytes

Sodium Considerations

Sodium is the principal <u>extra</u>cellular cation. Sodium may need to be reduced in renal dysfunction or cardiovascular disease, including hypertension. Sodium chloride comes in many concentrations, such as 0.9% (NS), 0.45% (1/2 NS) and others. Sodium chloride 23.4% is used for PN preparation and contains 4 mEq/mL.

Sodium can be added to PN as either sodium chloride or sodium acetate. If a patient is acidotic, sodium acetate should be added. Sodium acetate is converted to sodium bicarbonate and may help correct the acidosis. A patient may require a certain quantity from each formulation. Or, they may get sodium chloride alone. Hypertonic saline (> 0.9%) is dangerous if used incorrectly and is discussed in the Medication Safety chapter.

---

122. The pharmacist is going to add 80 mEq of sodium to the PN; half will be given as sodium acetate (2 mEq/mL) and half as sodium chloride (4 mEq/mL). How many mL of sodium chloride will be needed?

40 mEq will be provided by the NaCl.

$$\frac{4 \text{ mEq}}{\text{mL}} = \frac{40 \text{ mEq}}{X \text{ mL}} \quad X = 10 \text{ mL}$$

---

123. The pharmacist is making PN that needs to contain 80 mEq of sodium and 45 mEq of acetate. The available pharmacy stock solutions contain 4 mEq/mL sodium as sodium chloride and 2 mEq/mL sodium as sodium acetate. The final volume of the PN will be 2.5 liters to be given at 100 mL/hr. What quantity, in milliliters, of each stock solution should be added to the PN to meet the requirements? Round to the nearest hundredth.

First, calculate the acetate component as this contributes sodium as well.

$$\frac{2 \text{ mEq}}{\text{mL}} = \frac{45 \text{ mEq}}{X \text{ mL}} \quad X = 22.5 \text{ mL of sodium acetate}$$

This amount (22.5 mL of sodium acetate) also supplies 45 mEq of sodium. So, now we only need 35 mEq of sodium (80 mEq–45 mEq = 35 mEq).

$$\frac{2 \text{ mEq}}{\text{mL}} \times 22.5 \text{ mL sodium acetate} = 45 \text{ mEq of sodium}$$

80 mEq - 45 mEq = 35 mEq of sodium still needed

Supply the remaining needed sodium (35 mEq) with sodium chloride.

$$\frac{4\ mEq}{mL} = \frac{35\ mEq}{X\ mL} \qquad X = 8.75\ mL\ of\ sodium\ chloride$$

---

124. A 2 liter PN solution is to contain 60 mEq of sodium and 30 mEq of acetate. The pharmacy has in stock sodium chloride (4 mEq/mL) and sodium acetate (2 mEq/mL). What quantity, in milliliters, of each solution should be added to the PN? Round to the nearest tenth.

First, calculate the amount of sodium acetate needed.

$$\frac{2\ mEq}{mL} = \frac{30\ mEq}{X\ mL} \qquad X = 15\ mL\ of\ sodium\ acetate$$

This amount (15 mL of sodium acetate) also supplies 30 mEq of sodium. The additional amount required is 30 mEq of sodium (60 mEq–30 mEq).

Calculate the amount of sodium chloride needed.

$$\frac{4\ mEq}{mL} = \frac{30\ mEq}{X\ mL} \qquad X = 7.5\ mL\ of\ NaCl$$

Potassium, Calcium and Phosphate Considerations

Potassium

Potassium is the principal <u>intra</u>cellular cation. Potassium may need to be reduced in renal or cardiovascular disease. Potassium can be provided by potassium chloride (KCl) or potassium phosphate (K Phos) or potassium acetate. <u>The normal range for serum potassium is 3.5-5.0 mEq/L.</u>

Calcium

Calcium is important for many functions including cardiac conduction, muscle contraction, and bone homeostasis. The normal serum calcium level is 8.5-10.5 mg/dL. Almost half of serum calcium is bound to albumin. Low albumin will lead to an incorrect calcium concentration. If albumin is low (< 3.5 g/dL), calcium levels will need to be corrected with this equation prior to the addition of calcium into the PN:

$$Ca_{corrected} = (calcium_{reported(serum)}) + [(4.0 - albumin) \times (0.8)]$$

125. Calculate the corrected calcium value for a patient with the following lab values:

LAB	VALUE
Calcium	7.6 mg/dL (normal range 8.5 – 10.5 mg/dL)
Albumin	1.5 g/dL (normal range 3.5 – 5 g/dL)

- $Ca_{corrected} = (calcium_{reported(serum)}) + [(4.0 - albumin) \times (0.8)]$

- $Ca_{corrected} = (7.6) + [(4.0 - 1.5) \times (0.8)] = 9.6$ mg/dL

Calcium and Phosphate Solubility

Phosphorus (or phosphate, PO_4) is present in DNA, cell membranes, ATP, acts as an acid-base buffer, and is vital in bone metabolism. Phosphate and calcium need to be added carefully, or they can bind together and precipitate which can cause a pulmonary embolus. This can be fatal. The following considerations can help reduce the risk of a calcium-phosphate precipitate:

- Choose <u>calcium gluconate</u> over calcium chloride ($CaCl_2$) due to being less reactive and lower risk of precipitation with phosphates. Calcium gluconate has a lower dissociation constant compared to calcium chloride, leaving less free calcium available in solution to bind phosphates.

- <u>Add phosphate first</u> (after the dextrose and amino acids), followed by other PN components, agitate the solution, then calcium should be added near the end to take advantage of the maximum volume of the PN formulation.

- The calcium and phosphate added together (units must be the same to do this) should not exceed 45 mEq/L.

- Maintain a proper pH (lower pH; less risk of precipitation) to eliminate binding and refrigerate the bag once prepared (PNs are kept in the refrigerator until they are needed). When temperature increases, more calcium and phosphate dissociate in solution and precipitation risk increases.

An additional safety consideration involves ordering the correct dose of phosphate. Phosphate can be ordered as potassium or sodium salts. The two forms do not provide equivalent amounts of phosphate. The order should be written in mmol (of phosphate), followed by the type of salt form (potassium or sodium).

---

126. The pharmacist has calculated that a patient requires 30 mmol of phosphate and 80 mEq of potassium. The pharmacy has stock solutions of potassium phosphate (3 mmol of phosphate with 4.4 mEq of potassium/mL) and potassium chloride (2 mEq K^+/mL). How much potassium phosphate and how much potassium chloride will be required to meet the patient's needs?

First, calculate the phosphate required (since potassium comes along with the phosphate in the potassium-phosphate solution).

$$\frac{3 \text{ mmol Phosphate}}{mL} = \frac{30 \text{ mmol Phosphate}}{X \text{ mL}} \quad X = 10 \text{ mL K-Phos}$$

Each mL of the potassium phosphate (K-Phos) supplies 4.4 mEq of potassium. Calculate the amount of potassium the patient received from the 10 mL of K-Phos.

- 10 mL x 4.4 mEq/mL = 44 mEq potassium

- The remaining potassium will be provided by KCl.

- 80 mEq K required – 44 mEq potassium (from K-Phos) = 36 mEq to be obtained from the KCl.

$$\frac{2 \text{ mEq K}^+}{\text{mL}} = \frac{36 \text{ mEq K}^+}{X \text{ mL}} \quad X = 18 \text{ mL KCl}$$

The patient requires 10 mL of potassium phosphate and 18 mL of potassium chloride.

---

127. A patient is to receive 8 mEq of calcium. The pharmacy has calcium gluconate 10% in stock which provides 0.465 mEq/mL. How many mL of calcium gluconate should be added to the PN? Round to the nearest whole number.

$$\frac{1 \text{ mL}}{0.465 \text{ mEq Ca}^{2+}} \times 8 \text{ mEq Ca}^{2+} = 17.2, \text{ or } 17 \text{ mL calcium gluconate}$$

---

128. A patient is receiving 30 mmol of phosphate and 8 mEq of calcium. The volume of the PN is 2,000 mL. There are 2 mEq PO$_4$/mmol. Confirm that the calcium and phosphorus added together does not exceed 45 mEq/L.

First, calculate mEq from the phosphate.

$$\frac{2 \text{ mEq PO}_4}{\text{mmol}} \times 30 \text{ mmol PO}_4 = 60 \text{ mEq phosphate}$$

Then, add the phosphate to the calcium. 60 mEq phosphate + 8 mEq calcium = 68 mEq.

The volume of the PN is 2,000 mL, or 2 L. Find the mEq per liter. 68 mEq/2 L = 34 mEq/L, which is less than 45 mEq/L.

QUESTIONS 130-139 RELATE TO PN ORDER BELOW.

129. A pharmacy receives the following PN order. Calculate the amount, in mL, of dextrose 70% that should be added to the PN. Round to the nearest whole number.

ITEM	QUANTITY
Dextrose 70%	250 g
Amino acids	50 g
Sodium chloride	44 mEq
Sodium acetate	20 mEq
Potassium	40 mEq
Magnesium sulfate	12 mEq
Phosphate	18 mmol
Calcium	4.65 mEq
MVI-12	5 mL
Trace elements-5	1 mL
Vitamin K-1	0.5 mg
Famotidine	10 mg
Regular insulin	20 units
Sterile water qs ad	960 mL

$$\frac{70\ g}{100\ mL} = \frac{250\ g}{X\ mL} \qquad X = 357\ mL\ of\ dextrose\ 70\%$$

---

130. Using amino acids 10%, calculate the amount of amino acids that should be added to the PN.

$$\frac{10\ g}{100\ mL} = \frac{50\ g}{X\ mL} \qquad X = 500\ mL$$

---

131. Calculate the amount of sodium chloride 23.4% (4 mEq/mL) that should be added to the PN.

$$\frac{4\ mEq}{mL} = \frac{44\ mEq}{X\ mL} \qquad X = 11\ mL$$

**This concentration of NaCl is hypertonic and is a high-alert drug due to heightened risk of patient harm when dosed incorrectly.

---

132. Calculate the amount of sodium acetate 16.4% (2 mEq/mL) that should be added to the PN.

$$\frac{2\ mEq}{mL} = \frac{20\ mEq}{X\ mL} \qquad X = 10\ mL$$

133. Using the potassium phosphate (3 mmol of phosphate and 4.4 mEq of potassium/mL) vials in stock, calculate the amount of potassium phosphate that should be added to the PN to meet the needs of the phosphate requirements.

$$\frac{3 \text{ mmol Phosphate}}{\text{mL}} = \frac{18 \text{ mmol Phosphate}}{X \text{ mL}} \qquad X = 6 \text{ mL K-Phos}$$

---

134. The PN contains 6 mL of potassium phosphate (3 mmol of phosphate and 4.4 mEq of potassium/mL). The daily potassium requirement is 40 mEq. How much potassium chloride (2 mEq/mL), in milliliters, should be added to the PN? Round to the nearest tenth.

First, calculate the amount of K^+ already in the PN.

$$\frac{4.4 \text{ mEq K}^+}{\text{mL}} \times 6 \text{ mL} = 26.4 \text{ mEq K}^+$$

Total K^+ needed is 40 mEq. 40 mEq–26.4 mEq = 13.6 mEq still needed.

$$\frac{2 \text{ mEq K}^+}{\text{mL}} = \frac{13.6 \text{ mEq K}^+}{X \text{ mL}} \qquad X = 6.8 \text{ mL KCL}$$

---

135. The PN order calls for 4.65 mEq of calcium. The pharmacy has calcium gluconate 10% (0.465 mEq/mL) in stock. How many mL of calcium gluconate 10% should be added to the PN?

$$\frac{0.465 \text{ mEq Ca}^{2+}}{\text{mL}} = \frac{4.65 \text{ mEq Ca}^{2+}}{X \text{ mL}} \qquad X = 10 \text{ mL calcium gluconate 10\%}$$

---

136. The PN calls for 18 mmol of phosphate and 4.65 mEq of calcium (provided by 10 mL of calcium gluconate 10%, as calculated in the previous problem) in a volume of 960 mL. There are 2 mEq PO_4/mmol. Confirm that the calcium and phosphorus added together do not exceed 45 mEq/L.

First, calculate mEq from the phosphate.

$$\frac{2 \text{ mEq PO}_4}{\text{mmol}} \times 18 \text{ mmol PO}_4 = 36 \text{ mEq phosphate}$$

Then, add the phosphate to the calcium. 36 mEq phosphate + 4.65 mEq calcium = 40.65 mEq. The volume of the PN is 960 mL, or 0.96 L. 40.65 mEq/0.96 L = 42.3 mEq/L, which is less than 45 mEq/L.

---

137. Calculate the amount of magnesium sulfate (4 mEq/mL) that should be added to the PN.

$$\frac{4 \text{ mEq}}{\text{mL}} = \frac{12 \text{ mEq}}{X \text{ mL}} \qquad X = 3 \text{ mL magnesium sulfate}$$

---

138. What percentage of the total calories from the above PN are represented by the protein component? Round to the nearest whole number.

First, calculate the total calories.

DEXTROSE

$$\frac{3.4 \text{ kcal dextrose}}{g} \times 250 \text{ g dextrose} = 850 \text{ kcal of dextrose}$$

PROTEIN

$$\frac{4 \text{ kcal protein}}{g} \times 50 \text{ g protein} = 200 \text{ kcal of protein}$$

Total calories = 850 + 200 = 1,050 kcal. Now, calculate the amount of calories from protein.

$$\frac{200 \text{ kcal}}{1,050 \text{ kcal}} \times 100 = 19\%$$

Add-in Multivitamins, Trace Elements, and Insulin

Multivitamins: There are 4 fat-soluble vitamins (A, D, E and K) and 9 water-soluble vitamins (thiamine, riboflavin, niacin, pantothenic acid, pyridoxine, ascorbic acid, folic acid, cyanocobalamin, biotin) in the standard MVI-13 mixture. The MVI-12 mixture does not contain vitamin K since certain patients may need less or more of this vitamin. If patients on PN therapy are using warfarin, the INR will need to be monitored.

Trace Elements

The standard mix includes zinc, copper, chromium and manganese (and may include selenium). Manganese and copper should be withheld in severe liver disease. Chromium, molybdenum and selenium should be withheld in severe renal disease. Iron is not routinely given in a PN.

Insulin

PNs may contain insulin, usually 50% or less than what the person is expected to require per day, supplemented by a sliding scale. A minimum dose to add is 10 units, and is usually increased by 10 unit increments. It is important to avoid adding too much insulin. Half the previous day's sliding scale or less can be used as a safe amount.

Enteral Nutrition

Enteral nutrition (EN) is the provision of nutrients via the gastrointestinal (GI) tract through a feeding tube. Nasogastric (NG) tubes are often used, primarily for short-term administration. For longer-term, or if the stomach cannot be used, tubes are placed further down the GI tract. EN is the preferred route for patients who cannot meet their nutrition needs through voluntary oral intake. Tube feedings can range from providing adjunctive support to providing complete nutrition support. Several advantages of EN over PN include lower cost, using the gut which prevents atrophy and other problems, and a lower risk of complications (less infections, less hyperglycemia, reduced risk of cholelithiasis and cholestasis). The most common risk associated with enteral feeding is aspiration which can lead to pneumonia. Enteral feedings can cause drug interactions. The general rule for preventing drug/enteral feeding interactions is to hold the feedings one hour before or two hours after the drug is administered. Some drugs may require further separation.

Tube feeds do not, by themselves, provide enough water. Water is given in addition to the tube feeds. If fluid intake is inadequate, it will be uncomfortable for the patient and put them at risk for complications, including hypernatremia.

Drug-Nutrient interactions with enteral feedings (most common problems):

- Warfarin: many enteral products bind warfarin, resulting in low INRs and the need for dose adjustments. Hold tube feeds one hour before and one hour after warfarin administration.

- Tetracycline: will chelate with metals, including calcium, magnesium, and iron, which reduces drug availability, and is separated from tube feeds.

- Ciprofloxacin: the oral suspension is not used with tube feeds because the oil-based suspension adheres to the tube. The immediate-release tablets are used instead; crush and mix with water, flush line with water before and after administration.

- Phenytoin *(Dilantin suspension)*: is reduced when the drug binds to the feeding solution, leading to less free drug availability and sub-therapeutic levels. Separate tube feeds by 2 hours.

Tube Names

- A tube in the nose to the stomach is called a nasogastric (NG), or nasoenteral, tube.

- A tube that goes through the skin into the stomach is called a gastrostomy, or percutaneous endoscopic gastrostomy (PEG, or G) tube.

- A tube into the small intestine is called a jejunostomy, or percutaneous endoscopic jejunostomy (PEJ, or J) tube.

Patient Case (For Questions 140-142)

Wilma is a patient starting enteral nutrition therapy. Wilma has a past medical history significant for diabetes. She will be started on *Glucerna* Ready-to-Drink Vanilla shakes. See the nutrient label below.

Serving Size: 8 fl oz (237 mL)

NUTRIENT DATA PER SERVING OF GLUCERNA

ITEM	QUANTITY
Protein	19.6 g
Fat	17.8 g
Carbohydrate	31.5 g
Dietary Fiber	3.8 g
L-Carnitine	51 mg
Taurine	40 mg
m-Inositol	205 mg
Calories	356 kcal

139. According to the case above, what percent of calories will Wilma receive from the protein component? Round to the nearest whole number.

First, calculate the amount of calories coming from the protein component.

$$19.6 \text{ g protein} \times \frac{4 \text{ kcal}}{g} = 78.4 \text{ kcal}$$

Next, find the percentage of protein calories.

$$\frac{78.4 \text{ kcal}}{356 \text{ kcal}} \times 100 = 22\%$$

140. How many calories will Wilma receive from the fat component of 1 (8 fl oz.) shake? Round to the nearest whole number.

$$17.8 \text{ g} \times \frac{9 \text{ kcal}}{g} = 160.2, \text{ or } 160 \text{ kcal}$$

141. What percent of calories are derived from the fat component? Round to the nearest whole number.

$$\frac{160.2 \text{ kcal}}{356 \text{ kcal}} \times 100 = 45\%$$

Patient Case (For Questions 143-145)

Jonathan is a patient receiving *Osmolite* (a high-protein, low-residue formula) enteral nutrition through his PEG tube. See the nutrient label below.

Serving Size: 8 fl oz (237 mL)

NUTRIENT DATA PER SERVING OF OSMOLITE

ITEM	QUANTITY
Protein	13.2 g
Fat	9.2 g
Carbohydrate	37.4 g
L-Carnitine	36 mg
Taurine	36 mg
Calories	285 kcal

142. According to the case above, how many calories will Jonathan receive from the carbohydrate component in 4 fl oz? Round to the nearest whole number.

First, calculate the total calories from carbohydrates per 1 can (8 fl oz).

$$37.4 \text{ g carbohydrate} \quad \times \quad \frac{4 \text{ kcal}}{\text{g}} \quad = \quad 149.6 \text{ kcal from 8 fl oz.}$$

Then, take half of the amount of calories (4 fl oz).

$$\frac{149.6}{2} \quad = \quad 74.8, \text{ or 75 kcal from 4 fl oz.}$$

---

143. What percent of calories will Jonathan receive from the carbohydrate component? Round to the nearest whole number.

First, calculate the amount of calories coming from the carbohydrate component.

$$37.4 \text{ g carbohydrate} \quad \times \quad \frac{4 \text{ kcal}}{\text{g}} \quad = \quad 149.6 \text{ kcal}$$

Next, find the percentage of carbohydrate calories.

$$\frac{149.6 \text{ kcal}}{285 \text{ kcal}} \quad \times \quad 100 \quad = \quad 52.5, \text{ or 53\%}$$

---

144. The nurse was administering 1 can (8 fl oz.) of *Osmolite* to Jonathan when she accidentally spilled 2 fl oz. onto the floor. The remaining amount in the can was accurately delivered to Jonathan. How many calories did he actually receive from this can? Do not round the answer.

1 can = 8 fl oz

$$\frac{8 \text{ fl oz}}{285 \text{ kcal}} \quad = \quad \frac{6 \text{ fl oz}}{X \text{ kcal}} \qquad X = 213.75 \text{ kcal}$$

Osmolarity

The total number of particles in a given solution is directly proportional to its osmotic pressure. The particles are usually measured in milliosmoles. Osmolarity is the measure of total number of particles (or solutes) per liter (L) of solution, defined as osmoles/Liter (Osmol/L) or, more commonly as milliosmoles/Liter (mOsmol/L). Solutes can be either ionic (such as NaCl, which dissociates into 2 solutes in solution, Na^+ and Cl^-) or non-ionic, which do not dissociate (such as glucose and urea). The term for osmolarity when used to refer to the solute concentration of body fluids is tonicity, and solutions are thus isotonic (osmolarity is the same as blood, which is ~ 300 mOsmol/L), or is lower (hypotonic) or is higher (hypertonic).

If the osmolarity is higher in one cellular compartment, it will cause water to move from the lower to the higher concentration of solutes. If a PN solution is injected with a higher osmolarity than blood, fluid will flow into the vein, resulting in edema, inflammation, phlebitis and possible thrombosis.

Milliosmole calculation problems differ from osmolarity calculation problems in that osmolarity will always need to be normalized to a volume of 1 liter. Some compounds for which it may be useful to know dissociations are listed to the right:

COMPOUND	# OF DISSOCIATION PARTICLES
Dextrose	1
Mannitol	1
Potassium chloride (KCl)	2
Sodium chloride (NaCl)	2
Sodium acetate ($NaC_2H_3O_2$)	2
Calcium chloride ($CaCl_2$)	3
Sodium citrate ($Na_3C_6H_5O_7$)	4

Osmolarity Calculations

Use this formula to find the mOsmol/L.

$$mOsmol/L = \frac{\text{Wt of substance (g/L)}}{\text{MW (g/mole)}} \times (\text{\# of particles}) \times 1{,}000$$

- Add up the number of particles into which the compound dissociates.

- Calculate the number of grams of the compound present in 1 L.

- Use the Molecular Weight (M.W.) to solve the problem.

Milliosmole calculations do not normalize to 1 liter.

---

145. What is the osmolarity, in mOsmol/L, of normal saline (0.9% NaCl)? M.W. = 58.5. Round to the nearest whole number.

NaCl dissociates into 2 particles; Na^+ and Cl^-.

Calculate the number of grams of the compound (NaCl) present in 1 L.

$$\frac{0.9\text{ g}}{100\text{ mL}} = \frac{X\text{ g}}{1{,}000\text{ mL}} \qquad X = 9\text{ g}$$

Use the molecular weight to solve the problem.

$$mOsmol/L = \frac{9\text{ g/L}}{58.5\text{ g/mole}} \times 2 \times 1{,}000 = 308\text{ mOsmol/L}$$

146. What is the osmolarity, in mOsmol/L, of D5W? M.W. = 198. Round to the nearest tenth.

Dextrose does not dissociate and is counted as 1 particle.

$$\frac{5 \text{ g}}{100 \text{ mL}} = \frac{X \text{ g}}{1,000 \text{ mL}} \qquad X = 50 \text{ g}$$

Use the molecular weight to solve the problem.

$$\text{mOsmol/L} = \frac{50 \text{ g/L}}{198 \text{ g/mole}} \times 1 \times 1,000 = 252.5 \text{ mOsmol/L}$$

---

147. A solution contains 373 mg Na⁺ ions per liter. How many milliosmoles are represented in the solution? M.W. = 23. Round to the nearest tenth.

First, convert the units to match the formula.

$$\frac{373 \text{ mg Na}^+}{L} \times \frac{1 \text{ g}}{1,000 \text{ mg}} = 0.373 \text{ g/L}$$

$$\text{mOsmol} = \frac{0.373 \text{ g/L}}{23 \text{ g/mole}} \times 1 \times 1,000 = 16.2 \text{ mOsmol}$$

Note that the problem is asking for milliosmoles and not osmolarity. Therefore, the answer is in milliosmoles and not mOsmol/L although the problem is in 1 liter so you would get the same numeric answer.

---

148. Calculate the osmolar concentration, in milliosmoles, represented by 1 liter of a 10% (w/v) solution of anhydrous dextrose (M.W. = 180) in water. Round to the nearest tenth.

$$\frac{10 \text{ g}}{100 \text{ mL}} = \frac{X \text{ g}}{1,000 \text{ mL}} \qquad X = 100 \text{ g}$$

$$\text{mOsmol} = \frac{100 \text{ g/L}}{180 \text{ g/mole}} \times 1 \times 1,000 = 555.6 \text{ mOsmol}$$

Note that the problem is asking for milliosmoles and not osmolarity. Therefore, the answer is in milliosmoles and not mOsmol/L although the problem is in 1 liter so you would get the same numeric answer.

---

149. How many milliosmoles of CaCl₂ (M.W.= 147) are represented in 150 mL of a 10% (w/v) calcium chloride solution? Round to the nearest whole number.

$$\frac{10 \text{ g}}{100 \text{ mL}} = \frac{X \text{ g}}{150 \text{ mL}} \qquad X = 15 \text{ g}$$

$$\text{mOsmol} = \frac{15 \text{ g}}{147 \text{ g/mole}} \times 3 \times 1,000 = 306 \text{ mOsmol}$$

Note that the problem is asking for milliosmoles and not osmolarity. Therefore, the answer is in milliosmoles and not mOsmol/L. It is not normalized to 1 liter.

150. A solution contains 200 mg Ca⁺ ions per liter. How many milliosmoles are represented in the solution? M.W = 40

$$\text{mOsmol} \quad = \quad \frac{0.2 \text{ g/L}}{40 \text{ g}} \quad \times \quad 1 \quad \times \quad 1,000 \quad = \quad 5 \text{ mOsmol}$$

Please note that the problem is asking for milliosmoles and not osmolarity. Therefore, the answer is in milliosmoles and not mOsmol/L.

---

151. Calculate the amount of grams of potassium chloride needed to make 200 mL of a solution contain 250 mOsmol/L. M.W. = 74.5. Round to the nearest hundredth.

$$250 \text{ mOsmol/L} \quad = \quad \frac{X}{74.5 \text{ g/mole}} \quad \times \quad 2 \quad \times \quad 1,000 \qquad X = 9.31 \text{ g/L}$$

$$\frac{9.31 \text{ g}}{1,000 \text{ mL}} \quad = \quad \frac{X \text{ g}}{200 \text{ mL}} \qquad X = 1.86 \text{ g}$$

Isotonicity

Osmolarity is the measure of total number of particles (or solutes) per liter (L) of solution. Tonicity is the term used to describe osmolarity used in the context of body fluids. When solutions are prepared, they need to match the tonicity of the body fluid as closely as possible. Solutions that are not isotonic with the body fluid produce pain upon administration, and cause fluid transfer. In pharmacy, the terms hypotonic rather than hypo-osmotic, hyper-

NUMBER OF DISSOCIATED IONS	DISSOCIATION FACTOR (OR IONIZATION) *i*
1	1
2	1.8
3	2.6
4	3.4
5	4.2

tonic rather than hyperosmotic, and isotonic rather than iso-osmotic, are used. Isotonicity is commonly used when preparing eye drops and nasal solutions.

Since isotonicity is related to the number of particles in solution, the dissociation factor (or ionization), symbolized by the letter *i*, is determined for the compound (drug). Non-ionic compounds do not dissociate and will have a dissociation factor, *i*, of 1. The chart above shows the dissociation factors (*i*) based on the percentage that dissociates into ions; for example, a dissociation factor of 1.8 means that 80% of the compound will dissociate in a weak solution.

As mentioned above, body fluids are isotonic, having an osmotic pressure equivalent to 0.9% sodium chloride. When making a medication to place into a body fluid, the drug provides solutes to the solvent and needs to be accounted for in the prescription in order to avoid making the prescription hypertonic. The relationship between the amount of drug that produces a particular osmolarity and the amount of sodium chloride that produces the same osmolarity is called the <u>sodium chloride equivalent, or "E value"</u> for short. This is the formula for calculating the E value of a compound:

$$E = \frac{(58.5)(i)}{(MW\ of\ drug)(1.8)}$$

The "E value" formula takes into account the molecular weight of NaCl (58.5) and the dissociation factor of 1.8 since normal saline is around 80% ionized- adding 0.8 for each additional ion beyond 1 into which the drug dissociates. The reason the compound is compared to NaCl is because NaCl is the major determinate of the isotonicity of body fluid.

Once the "E value" is determined, isotonicity problems can be calculated. The following steps outline the process of doing isotonicity problems:

1. Calculate the total amount of NaCl needed to make the final product/prescription isotonic. This is done by multiplying 0.9% NS by the desired volume of the prescription.

2. Multiply the total drug amount, in grams, by the "E value".

3. Subtract step 2 from step 1 to determine the total amount of NaCl needed to prepare an isotonic prescription.

Isotonicity Calculations

152. Calculate the E value for mannitol (M.W. = 182). Round to the nearest hundredth.

$$\frac{(58.5)(i)}{(MW\ of\ drug)(1.8)} = \frac{58.5\ (1)}{182\ (1.8)} = 0.18$$

---

153. Calculate the E value for potassium iodide, which dissociates into 2 particles (M.W. = 166). Round to two decimal places.

$$\frac{(58.5)(i)}{(MW\ of\ drug)(1.8)} = \frac{58.5\ (1.8)}{166\ (1.8)} = 0.35$$

---

154. Physostigmine salicylate (M.W. = 413) is a 2- ion electrolyte, dissociating 80% in a given concentration (therefore, use a dissociation factor of 1.8). Calculate its sodium chloride equivalent. Round to two decimal places.

$$\frac{(58.5)(i)}{(MW\ of\ drug)(1.8)} = \frac{58.5\ (1.8)}{413\ (1.8)} = 0.14$$

155. The E-value for ephedrine sulfate is 0.23. How many grams of sodium chloride are needed to make the following prescription? Round to 3 decimal places.

PRESCRIPTION	QUANTITY
Ephedrine sulfate	0.4 g
Sodium chloride	q.s.
Purified water qs	30 mL
Make isotonic soln.	
Sig. For the nose.	

Step 1. Determine how much NaCl would make the product isotonic.

$$\frac{0.9 \text{ g}}{100 \text{ mL}} = \frac{X}{30 \text{ mL}} \quad X = 0.27 \text{ g}$$

Step 2. Determine amount of sodium chloride represented from ephedrine sulfate.

- 0.4 g x 0.23 ("E value") = 0.092 g of sodium chloride

Step 3. Subtract step 2 from step 1.

- 0.27 g–0.092 g = 0.178 g of NaCl are needed to make an isotonic solution

---

156. The pharmacist receives an order for 10 mL of tobramycin 1% ophthalmic solution. You have tobramycin 40 mg/mL solution. Tobramycin does not dissociate and has a M.W. of 468. Find the E value for tobramycin and determine the amount of NaCl needed to make the solution isotonic. Round to two decimal places.

$$\frac{(58.5)(i)}{(\text{MW of drug})(1.8)} = \frac{58.5 \, (1)}{468 \, (1.8)} = 0.07, \text{ which is the "E value" for tobramycin.}$$

The "E value" for tobramycin is 0.07. The prescription asks for 10 mL of 1% solution.

Step 1. Determine how much NaCl would make the product isotonic (if that is all you were using).

$$\frac{0.9 \text{ g}}{100 \text{ mL}} = \frac{X}{10 \text{ mL}} \quad X = 0.09 \text{ g, or } 90 \text{ mg}$$

Step 2. Determine amount of sodium chloride represented from tobramycin.

$$\frac{1 \text{ g}}{100 \text{ mL}} = \frac{X}{10 \text{ mL}} \quad X = 0.1 \text{ g, or } 100 \text{ mg}$$

- 100 mg x 0.07 ("E value") = 7 mg

Step 3. Subtract step 2 from step 1.

You are using tobramycin, so you do not need all the NaCl – subtract out the equivalent amount of tonicity provided by the tobramycin, which is 7 mg.

90 mg-7 mg = 83 mg (83 mg additional sodium chloride is needed to make an isotonic solution)

To calculate how much of the original stock solution is required, use the stock solution that is 40 mg/mL. The prescription is written for 10 mL of a 1% solution. In the previous steps it was found that 100 mg of tobramycin is needed to provide 10 mL of a 1% solution.

$$\frac{40 \text{ mg}}{1 \text{ mL}} = \frac{100 \text{ mg}}{X \text{ mL}} \quad X = 2.5 \text{ mL of the original stock solution.}$$

Moles (mols)/Millimoles (mmols)

A mole is the molecular weight of a substance in grams, or g/mole. A millimole is 1/1,000 of the molecular weight in grams, or 1/1,000 of a mole. For monovalent species, the numeric value of the milliequivalent and millimole are identical.

Useful equations

$$\text{mols} = \frac{\text{g}}{\text{MW}} \quad \text{or} \quad \text{mmols} = \frac{\text{mg}}{\text{MW}}$$

---

157. How many moles of anhydrous magnesium sulfate (M.W. = 120.4) are present in 250 grams of the substance? Round to the nearest hundredth.

$$\text{mols} = \frac{\text{g}}{\text{MW}}$$

$$\text{mols} = \frac{250 \text{ g}}{120.4} = 2.08 \text{ mols}$$

158. How many moles are equivalent to 875 milligrams of aluminum acetate (M.W. = 204)? Round to 3 decimal places.

First, convert 875 mg to grams.

$$875 \text{ mg} \times \frac{1 \text{ g}}{1,000 \text{ mg}} = 0.875 \text{ g}$$

Next, solve for mols.

$$\text{mols} = \frac{\text{g}}{\text{MW}} = \frac{0.875 \text{ g}}{204} = 0.004 \text{ mols}$$

---

159. How many millimoles of sodium phosphate (M.W. = 138) are present in 90 g of the substance? Round to the nearest whole number.

$$\frac{90,000 \text{ mg}}{138} = 652 \text{ mmols}$$

Or, solve another way:

$$\frac{90\ g}{138} = 0.652 \text{ mols, which is } 652 \text{ mmols}$$

160. How many moles are equivalent to 45 grams of potassium carbonate (M.W. = 138)? Round to the nearest thousandth.

$$\text{mols} = \frac{g}{MW}$$

$$\text{mols} = \frac{45\ g}{138} = 0.326 \text{ mols}$$

161. How many millimoles of calcium chloride (M.W. = 147) are represented in 147 mL of a 10% (w/v) calcium chloride solution?

Step 1: Calculate the amount (g) of $CaCl_2$ in 147 mL of 10% $CaCl_2$ solution.

$$\frac{10\ g}{100\ mL} = \frac{X\ g}{147\ mL} \qquad X = 14.7\ g$$

Step 2: Calculate the mols of $CaCl_2$ in 147 mL of 10% $CaCl_2$ solution.

$$\frac{14.7\ g}{147} \qquad X = 0.1\ mol$$

Step 3: Solve the problem by converting moles to millimoles; 0.1 mol x 1,000 = 100 mmols

162. How many milligrams of sodium chloride (MW = 58.5) represent 0.25 mmol? Do not round the answer.

$$0.25 \text{ mmols} = \frac{X\ mg}{58.5} \qquad X = 14.625\ mg$$

163. How many grams of sodium chloride (MW = 58.5) should be used to prepare this solution? Do not round the answer.

PRESCRIPTION	QUANTITY
Methylprednisolone	0.5 g
NaCl solution	60 mL
Each 5 mL should contain 0.6 mmols of NaCl	

$$\frac{0.6 \text{ mmols}}{5\ mL} = \frac{X \text{ mmols}}{60\ mL} \qquad X = 7.2 \text{ mmols}$$

$$7.2 \text{ mmols} = \frac{X\ mg}{58.5} \qquad X = 421.2\ mg \text{ or } 0.4212\ g$$

Milliequivalents (mEq)

Drugs can be expressed in solution in different ways:

- Milliosmoles refers to the number of particles in solution.

- Millimoles refers to the molecular weight (MW).

- Milliequivalents represent the amount, in milligrams (mg), of a solute equal to 1/1,000 of its gram equivalent weight, taking into account the valence of the ions. Like osmolarity, the quantity of particles is important – but so is the electrical charge. Milliequivalents refers to the chemical activity of an electrolyte and is related to the total number of ionic charges in solution and considers the valence (charge) of each ion.

To count the valence, divide the compound into its positive and negative components, and then count the number of either the positive or the negative charges. For a given compound, the milliequivalents of cations equals that of anions. Some common compounds and their valence are listed in the chart to the right.

COMPOUND	VALENCE
ammonium chloride (NH_4Cl)	1
potassium chloride (KCl^-)	1
potassium gluconate ($KC_6H_{11}O_7$)	1
sodium acetate ($NaC_2H_3O_2$)	1
sodium bicarbonate ($NaHCO_3$)	1
calcium carbonate ($CaCO_3$)	2
calcium chloride ($CaCl_2$)	2
disodium phosphate	2
ferrous sulfate ($FeSO_4^{2-}$)	2
magnesium sulfate ($MgSO_4^{2-}$)	2

mEq formula

$$mEq = \frac{mg \times valence}{MW} \qquad or \qquad mEq = mmols \times valence$$

164. A 20 mL vial is labeled potassium chloride (2 mEq/mL). How many grams of potassium chloride (M.W. = 74.5) are present? Round to the nearest hundredth.

$$20 \text{ mL} \times \frac{2 \text{ mEq}}{mL} = 40 \text{ mEq KCl total}$$

$$mEq = \frac{mg \times valence}{MW}$$

$$40 \text{ mEq} = \frac{mg \times 1}{74.5} = 2,980 \text{ mg, which is 2.98 g}$$

* Note: if asked to convert KCl liquid to tablets, you can use simple proportion since KCl 10% = 20 mEq/15 mL. For example, if someone is using Klor-Con 20 mEq BID, the total daily dose is 40 mEq, and convert to KCl 10%, solve the following equation to get the 30 mL required dose:

$$\frac{40 \text{ mEq}}{X \text{ mL}} = \frac{20 \text{ mEq}}{15 \text{ mL}}$$

165. How many milliequivalents of potassium chloride are present in a 12 mL dose of a 10% (w/v) potassium chloride (M.W. = 74.5) elixir? Round to 1 decimal place.

$$\frac{10\ g}{100\ mL} = \frac{X\ g}{12\ mL} \qquad X = 1.2\ g,\ or\ 1{,}200\ mg$$

$$mEq = \frac{1{,}200\ mg \times 1}{74.5} = 16.1\ mEq$$

---

166. Calculate the milliequivalents of a standard ammonium chloride (M.W. = 53.5) 21.4 mg/mL sterile solution in a 500 mL container.

$$\frac{21.4\ mg}{mL} \times 500\ mL = 10{,}700\ mg$$

$$mEq = \frac{10{,}700\ mg \times 1}{53.5} = 200\ mEq$$

---

167. How many milliequivalents of $MgSO_4$ (M.W. = 120.4) are represented in 1 gram of anhydrous magnesium sulfate? Round to the nearest tenth.

$$mEq = \frac{mg \times valence}{MW}$$

$$mEq = \frac{1{,}000\ mg \times 2}{120.4} = 16.6\ mEq$$

---

168. How many milliequivalents of sodium are in a 50 mL vial of sodium bicarbonate (M.W. = 84) 8.4%?

$$\frac{8.4\ g}{100\ mL} = \frac{X\ g}{50\ mL} \qquad X = 4.2\ g,\ or\ 4{,}200\ mg$$

$$mEq = \frac{4{,}200\ mg \times 1}{84} = 50\ mEq$$

Temperature Conversions

Converting Fahrenheit to Celsius and Celsius to Fahrenheit

FORMULAS

$°C = (°F - 32)/1.8$

$°F = (°C \times 1.8) + 32$

---

169. Convert 88°F to Celsius. Round to the nearest tenth.

Answer: $(88-32)/1.8 = 31.1°C$

170. Convert 134°F to Celsius. Round to the nearest tenth.

Answer: (134-32)/1.8 = 56.7°C

---

171. Convert 26°C to Fahrenheit. Round to the nearest tenth.

Answer: (26 x 1.8) + 32 = 78.8°F

---

172. Convert -15°C to Fahrenheit.

Answer: (-15 x 1.8) + 32 = 5°F

Calcium Carbonate and Calcium Citrate Tablet Conversion

Calcium carbonate (*Oscal*, *Tums*, etc) has acid-dependent absorption and should be taken with meals. Calcium carbonate is a dense form of calcium and contains 40% elemental calcium. A tablet that advertises 500 mg of elemental calcium weighs 1,250 mg. If 1,250 mg is multiplied by 0.40 (which is 40%), it will yield 500 mg elemental calcium.

Calcium citrate (*Citracal*, etc) has acid-independent absorption and can be taken with or without food. Calcium citrate is less dense and contains 21% elemental calcium. A tablet that advertises 315 mg calcium weighs 1,500 mg. If 1,500 mg is multiplied by 0.21 (or 21%), it will yield 315 mg elemental calcium. This is why the larger calcium citrate tablets provide less elemental calcium per tablet. They may be preferred if the gut fluid is basic, rather than acidic.

---

173. A patient is taking 3 calcium citrate tablets daily (one tablet, TID). Each weighs 1,500 mg total (non-elemental) weight. She wishes to trade her calcium tablets for the carbonate form. If she is going to use 1,250 mg carbonate tablets (by weight), how many tablets will she need to take to provide the same total daily dose?

1,500 x 0.21 x 3 = 945 mg elemental calcium, daily.

Each of the carbonate tablets (1,250 mg x 0.4) = 500 mg per tablet. She would need 2 tablets to provide a similar dose. Calcium absorption increases with lower doses. The tablets should be taken apart with two different meals.

CBC and CBC with Differential

When a CBC is ordered, it usually contains these components (for ranges refer to the Appendix).

- RBCs (red blood cells or erythrocytes), which have an average life span of 120 days.

- WBCs (white blood cells or leukocytes) are important for fighting infections. When the WBC count is low, it is called leukopenia. When the WBC count is high, it is called a leukocytosis (and may indicate an infection).

- Hgb (hemoglobin)

- Hct (hematocrit)

- Platelets (Plt) have an average life span of 7-10 days. A low platelet count is called thrombocytopenia.

- MCV (mean corpuscular volume)

- MCH (mean corpuscular hemoglobin)

- MCHC (mean corpuscular hemoglobin concentration)

- RDW (red cell distribution width)

When a CBC with differential is ordered, the types of WBCs are analyzed, and would include the percentage of polymorphonuclear neutrophils ("segs" or "polys"), band neutrophils ("bands"), lymphocytes, monocytes, eosinophils (an increase may indicate inflammation or a parasite infection), and basophils.

CBC may be reflected in the stick diagram as below:

Absolute Neutrophil Count (ANC)

Neutrophils make up most of the WBCs and represent the primary cells that fight infection. A low absolute neutrophil count (ANC) indicates higher infection risk. This can be caused by drugs (most commonly chemotherapy agents), clozapine, carbamazepine and others.

The normal range for the ANC is 2,200-8,000/microliter. The microliter may be written as mm^3, or µL, but it is preferable to avoid this designation for safety reasons. A level < 2,000 is high-risk; for example, clozapine cannot be refilled if the ANC is < 2,000. A level < 500 is very high-risk for developing an infection.

A neutropenic patient should be watched for signs of infection, including fever, shaking, general weakness or flu-like symptoms. Precautions to reduce infection risk, such as proper hand-washing and avoiding others with infection, should be followed.

Calculating the ANC

Multiply the WBC by the percentage of neutrophils (the segs plus the bands) and divide by 100.

ANC (cells/mm^3) = WBC x (% segs + % bands)/100

---

174. A patient is being followed up at the oncology clinic today after her first round of chemotherapy one week ago. A CBC with differential is ordered and reported back as WBC = 14.8 x 10³ cells/mm³, segs are 10%, bands are 11%. Calculate this patient's ANC.

Segs = 10% Bands = 11%

14,800 x (10% + 11%)/100 = 14,800 x 0.21 = ANC of 3,108

175. A patient is taking clozapine and is at the clinic for a routine visit. Today's labs include WBC = 4,300 with 48% segs and 2% bands. Calculate this patient's ANC.

Segs = 48% Bands = 2%

4,300 x (48% + 2%)/100 = 4,300 x 0.5 = ANC of 2,150

Basic Metabolic Panel (BMP)/Comprehensive Metabolic Panel (CMP)

The BMP is 8 tests (see Appendix for values) and includes sodium, potassium, CO_2 (bicarbonate), chloride, calcium, BUN, creatinine and glucose. A stick diagram is commonly used in practice to denote 7 of these laboratory parameters:

A CMP is 14 tests. All the tests in the BMP are included, plus albumin and the liver tests ALT, AST, Alk Phos (alkaline phosphatase), bilirubin and total bilirubin. The CMP used to be called the Chem 12.

pH, Anion Gap, Buffer Systems and Ionization

pH

The pH refers to the acidity or basicity of the solution. As a solution becomes more acidic (the concentration of protons increases), the pH decreases. Conversely, when the pH increases, protons decrease, and the solution is more basic, or alkaline. Pure water is neutral at a pH of

> **pH NOTES**
>
> A lower pH means more hydronium ions (H_3O^+, or H^+) in solution and is therefore more acidic. A higher pH is more basic and has less hydronium ions and more hydroxide (OH^-) ions in solution. The pH of 7 is said to be neutral. Blood is just slightly alkaline with a pH that should stay between 7.35-7.45.

7, and blood, with a pH of 7.4, is slightly alkaline. Stomach acid has a pH of ~2, is therefore acidic, with many protons in solution.

Calculating Anion Gap

When a patient is experiencing metabolic acidosis, it is common to calculate an anion gap. The anion gap is the difference in the measured cations and the measured anions in the blood. An anion gap assists in determining the cause of the acidosis. A mnemonic to remember the causes of a gap acidosis is CUTE DIMPLES [cyanide, uremia, toluene, ethanol (alcoholic ketoacidosis), diabetic ketoacidosis, isoniazid, methanol, propylene glycol, lactic acidosis, ethylene glycol, salicylates]. A gap is considered high if it is > 12 mEq/L (meaning the patient has a gap acidosis). The anion gap can also be low, which is less common. A non-gap acidosis is caused by other factors, mainly hyperchloremic acidosis. Here is the formula to calculate the anion gap:

Anion gap (AG) = $Na^+ - Cl^- - HCO_3^-$

176. A patient in the ICU has recently developed an acidosis. Using the laboratory parameters below, calculate the patient's anion gap.

Na^+	139
Cl^-	101
K^+	4.6
HCO_3	19
SCr	1.6
BUN	38

Anion Gap = 139–101–19

Anion Gap = 19; therefore, the patient has a gap acidosis.

---

177. SJ was recently admitted to the ICU with a pH=7.27. Below is her laboratory data. Calculate SJ's anion gap.

144	95	68	
3.2	21	2.1	414

Anion Gap = 144–95–21 = 28; therefore, SJ has a gap acidosis.

Buffer Systems/Ionization

Buffer systems help to reduce the impact of too few or too many hydrogen ions in body fluids. These hydrogen ions could cause harm including degrading some drugs, destabilizing proteins, inhibiting cellular functions, and with too much of a change outside of the narrow range, cells die and death can occur. Therefore, buffers minimize fluctuations in pH so that harm is avoided. Buffer systems are common in the body and are composed of either a weak acid and salt of the acid (e.g., acetic acid and sodium acetate), or weak base and salt of the base (e.g., ammonium hydroxide and ammonium chloride). An <u>acid</u> is a compound that dissociates, <u>releasing (donating) protons into solution</u>. Once the proton is released, the compound is now a conjugate base, or its salt form. For example, HCl in solution is an acid and dissociates (giving up the proton) into H^+ and Cl^-. <u>A base picks up, or binds, the proton</u>. For example, NH_3 is a base that can pick up a proton and become NH_4^+.

Acid-base reactions are equilibrium reactions; there is drug moving back and forth between the acid and base state. The pH and the pKa are used to determine if the drug is acting as an acid or a base. When the pH = pKa, the molar concentration of the salt form and the molar concentration of the acid form of the buffer acid-base pair will be equal: 50% of the buffer will be in salt form and 50% in acid form. Notice that the percentage of buffer in the acid form when added to the percentage of buffer in the salt form will equal 100%. <u>When the pH = pKa, this is the point at which half the compound is protonated (ionized), and half is not protonated (un-ionized).</u>

A 'strong' acid or base means that you get 100% dissociation and a 'weak' acid or base means you get very limited dissociation. Any time you are given a pKa, it refers to the acid form losing protons to give to the base, or salt, form.

If you were given the 'pKb' then you would say, 'base' simply because of the definitions of the two terms.

If the pH > pKa, more of the acid is ionized, and more of the conjugate base is un-ionized.

If the pH = pKa, the ionized and un-ionized forms are equal.

If the pH < pKa, more of the acid is un-ionized, and more of the conjugate base is ionized.

The percentage of drug in the ionized versus un-ionized state is important because an ionized drug is soluble but cannot easily cross lipid membranes. An un-ionized drug is not soluble but can cross the membranes and reach the proper receptor site. Most drugs are weak acids. They are soluble, and can pick up a proton to cross the lipid layer.

Most drugs molecules are weak acids (or weak bases). These molecules can exist in either the un-ionized or the ionized state, and the degree of ionization depends on the dissociation constant (Ka) of the drug and the pH of the environment. This leads to the Henderson-Hasselbalch equation, also known as the buffer equation, which is used to solve for the pH.

WEAK ACID FORMULA

$$pH = pK_a + \log\left[\frac{salt}{acid}\right]$$

WEAK BASE FORMULAS

$$pH = pK_w - pK_b + \log\left[\frac{base}{salt}\right] \text{, where pKw = 14} \quad \text{or} \quad pH = pK_a + \log\left[\frac{base}{salt}\right]$$

---

178. What is the pH of a solution prepared to be 0.5 M sodium citrate and 0.05 M citric acid (pKa for citric acid = 3.13)? Round to the nearest hundredth.

$$pH = pK_a + \log\left[\frac{salt}{acid}\right]$$

$$pH = 3.13 + \log\left[\frac{0.5M}{0.05M}\right]$$

$$pH = 3.13 + \log[10]$$

$$pH = 3.13 + 1$$

$$pH = 4.13$$

---

179. What is the pH of a solution prepared to be 0.4 M ammonia and 0.04 M ammonium chloride (pKb for ammonia = 4.76)? Round to the nearest hundredth.

$$pH = pK_w - pK_b + \log\left[\frac{base}{salt}\right]$$

$$pH = 14 - 4.76 + \log\left[\frac{0.4}{0.04}\right]$$

pH = 9.24 + log(10)

pH = 9.24 + 1

pH = 10.24

---

180. What is the pH of a buffer solution containing 0.5 M acetic acid and 1 M sodium acetate in 1 liter of solution (pKa for acetic acid = 4.76)? Round to the nearest hundredth.

$$pH \ = \ pK_a \ + \ \log\left[\frac{salt}{acid}\right]$$

$$pH \ = \ 4.76 \ + \ \log\left[\frac{1}{0.5}\right]$$

pH = 4.76 + log(2)

pH = 4.76 + 0.3

pH = 5.06

---

181. What is the pH of a solution containing 0.2 mole of a weakly basic drug and 0.02 mole of its salt per liter of solution (pKa of the drug = 9.36)? Round to the nearest hundredth.

$$pH \ = \ pK_a \ + \ \log\left[\frac{base}{salt}\right]$$

$$pH \ = \ 9.36 \ + \ \log\left[\frac{0.2}{0.02}\right]$$

pH = 9.36 + 1

pH = 10.36

Percent of Ionization

The Henderson-Hasselbalch equation can be modified to calculate the percent of ionization of a drug.

To calculate the % ionization of a weak acid:

$$\% \ ionization \ = \ \frac{100}{1+10^{(pKa-pH)}}$$

To calculate % ionization of a weak base:

$$\% \ ionization \ = \ \frac{100}{1+10^{(pH-pKa)}}$$

---

182. What is the % ionization of amitriptyline, a weak base with a pKa = 9.4, at a physiologic pH of 7.4?

Use the weak base formula:

$$\% \ ionization \ = \ \frac{100}{1+10^{(pH-pKa)}}$$

$$\% \text{ ionization} = \frac{100}{1+10^{(7.4-9.4)}}$$

$$\% \text{ ionization} = \frac{100}{1+10^{(7.4-9.4)}}$$

$$\% \text{ ionization} = \frac{100}{1.01}$$

$$\% \text{ ionization} = 99\%$$

---

183. What is the % ionization of naproxen, a weak acid with a pKa of 4.2, in the stomach at a pH of 3?

Use the weak acid formula:

$$\% \text{ ionization} = \frac{100}{1+10^{(pKa-pH)}}$$

$$\% \text{ ionization} = \frac{100}{15.85}$$

$$\% \text{ ionization} = 6\%$$

Aliquot Measurement

An aliquot is a portion or part that is contained in the exact number of times in another (2 is an aliquot of 6). Aliquots are used when you need to make a prescription but cannot weigh out the small amount needed directly since the scale is not accurate to such a small degree. In the aliquot method, a larger-than-needed portion of active drug is measured out, diluted and mixed with an inert substance, and then a portion (or aliquot) is obtained to provide the desired amount of active drug needed.

Note on balances: Most pharmacists now commonly use electronic balances, which have a capacity to measure small amounts. These problems are using a Class A balance (or torsion balance) which is a standard piece of equipment. Balances of this type have a sensitivity requirement (SR) of 6 mg. The sensitivity requirement means that as much as 6 mg could be added to or removed from the pan before the balance marker will move 1 division.

To calculate the minimum weighable quantity (MWQ) that can be weighed accurately, take the SR of the scale, which is generally 6, and divide by the percentage of error. The maximum acceptable percentage of error is 5% (or 0.05), but some problems may suggest to use other percentages of error.

$$MWQ = \frac{SR}{\% \text{ of error}}$$

If the balance has an SR of 6 mg with a 5% error, the MWQ = 6 mg/0.05 = 120 mg, which is the least weighable amount (you can weigh at or above the MWQ). Most Class A balances have a maximum capacity of 120 grams.

ALIQUOT STEPS

1. Calculate the MWQ (as mentioned above).

2. Select a multiple (or factor) of the desired quantity needed in the prescription that can be weighed with the required precision (must be ≥ MWQ and must be a whole number). A simple way to determine this is to divide the MWQ by the total amount of drug needed. This will provide the multiple quantity.

3. Dilute the multiple quantity from step #2 with an inert substance (lactose is commonly used; check to make sure the patient is not lactose intolerant) by using the same multiple from step #2. This will give the quantity of the total dilution (drug + diluent).

4. Weigh out the aliquot portion (1 divided by the multiple used) of the dilution as this contains the desired quantity of drug.

184. What is the minimum weighable quantity with a maximum error of 5% on a balance whose sensitivity requirement is 20 mg?

$$MWQ = \frac{SR}{\% \text{ of error}}$$

$$MWQ = \frac{20 \text{ mg}}{0.05} = 400 \text{ mg}$$

185. What is the smallest quantity that can be weighed with a 1% maximal error on a balance whose sensitivity requirement is 1 mg?

$$MWQ = \frac{SR}{\% \text{ of error}}$$

$$MWQ = \frac{1}{0.01} = 100 \text{ mg}$$

186. A prescription calls for 10 capsules, each containing 0.5 mg of lorazepam. A torsion balance has a sensitivity requirement of 6 mg. Explain how you would weigh 5 mg of lorazepam with an accuracy of ± 5%, using lactose as the diluent.

1. Calculate the MWQ.

$$MWQ = \frac{SR}{\% \text{ of error}} = \frac{6 \text{ mg}}{0.05} = 120 \text{ mg}$$

2. Select a multiple of the desired quantity that can be weighed with the required precision (≥ MWQ and must be a whole number).

Select a multiple of 5 mg (the desired quantity from the problem above–0.5 x 10 caps = 5 mg) that can be weighed with the desired accuracy. For this scale, we cannot weigh less than 120 mg. We need to find a multiple of 5 that will give us 120 mg (or more). In this case, we can use the multiple 24: 5 mg x 24 = 120 mg of lorazepam. A simple way to get the multiple is to divide the MWQ by the amount of drug needed (120/5 = 24).

3. Dilute the multiple quantity above (120 mg) with an inert substance using the same multiple (24). This will give us the quantity of the total dilution.

- 120 mg (the multiple quantity from above) x 24 = 2,880 mg (this is the total dilution which contains drug + lactose)

4. Weigh the aliquot portion of the dilution (1 divided by the multiple–1/24) that contains the desired quantity.

Since 24 times the needed amount of active drug was weighed in Step 2, an aliquot part equal to 1/24th of the 2,880 mixture (or 120 mg) will give us the required quantity of drug substance. Therefore, 1/24 x 2,880 mg = 120 mg. Weigh 1/24 of the dilution (2,880 mg), or 120 mg of dilution (the aliquot), which will contain 5 mg of drug (answer).

You have calculated the total amount of the dilution. We do not need this much, but the purpose of doing this was to get the exact amount of drug (5 mg) in each 120 mg aliquot portion.

---

187. A prescription requires 30 mg diphenhydramine. A torsion balance has a sensitivity requirement of 6 mg with a maximum of 4% error. Explain how would you prepare this prescription.

1. Calculate the MWQ.

$$MWQ = \frac{SR}{\% \text{ of error}}$$

$$MWQ = \frac{6 \text{ mg}}{0.04} = 150 \text{ mg}$$

2. Select a multiple of the desired quantity that can be weighed with the required precision.

Select a multiple of 30 mg (the desired quantity stated in the problem above) that can be weighed with the desired accuracy. For this scale, we cannot weigh less than 150 mg. We need to find a multiple that will give us 150 mg (or more). In this case, we can use the multiple 5.

30 mg x 5 = 150 mg of diphenhydramine.

3. Dilute the multiple quantity with an inert substance. This will give us the quantity of the total dilution.

150 mg (the multiple quantity from above) x 5 = 750 mg of dilution

4. Weigh the aliquot portion of the dilution that contains the desired quantity.

Since 5 times the needed amount of active drug was weighed in Step 2, an aliquot part equal to 1/5th of the 750 mg dilution (or 150 mg) will give us the required quantity of drug (30 mg). 1/5 x 750 mg = 150 mg (aliquot that contains 30 mg of diphenhydramine)

188. A prescription calls for 15 capsules, each containing 1 mg doxazosin. A torsion balance has a sensitivity requirement of 6.5 mg. Explain how you would weigh 15 mg of doxazosin with an accuracy of ± 5%, using lactose as the diluent.

1. Calculate the MWQ.

$$MWQ = \frac{SR}{\% \text{ of error}} = \frac{6.5 \text{ mg}}{0.05} = 130 \text{ mg}$$

2. Select a multiple of the desired quantity that can be weighed with the required precision.

Select a multiple of 15 mg that can be weighed with the desired accuracy. For this scale, we cannot weigh less than 130 mg. We need to find a multiple of 15 that will give us 130 mg (or more). In this case, we are going to use the multiple 9; 15 mg x 9 = 135 mg of doxazosin.

3. Dilute the multiple quantity with an inert substance.

■ 135 mg (the multiple quantity) x 9 = 1,215 mg (dilution).

4. Weigh the aliquot portion of the dilution that contains the desired quantity.

Weigh 1/9 of dilution (1,215 mg), or 135 mg of dilution (the aliquot), which will contain 15 mg of doxazosin (answer).

Aliquots Using Liquids

189. A prescription calls for 0.5 mL of cherry oil. Using a 10 mL graduate cylinder calibrated from 2-10 mL, in 1 mL divisions and 95% ethyl alcohol as a diluent, calculate how the desired quantity could be measured?

1. Find the MWQ.

2. The minimum measurable amount is 2 mL and the maximum amount is 10 mL as stated in the problem. Therefore, the MWQ was given to you (2 mL). Additionally, the volume can be measured in 1 mL increments from 2-10 mLs.

3. Select a multiple of the desired quantity that can be weighed with the required precision. Select a multiple of 0.5 mL that will be equal to or greater than 2 mL. In this case, we will choose the multiple 4; 0.5 mL (cherry oil) x 4 = 2 mL. Remember, a simple way to determine this is to take the MWQ and divide by the amount of drug needed (2 mL/0.5 mL = 4).

4. Dilute the multiple quantity with an inert substance using the same multiple.

2 mL x 4 = 8 mL total dilution

5. Weigh the aliquot portion of the dilution that contains the desired quantity.

1/4 x 8 mL = 2 mL aliquot which will contain 0.5 mL of cherry oil

Please note the graduated cylinder can measure this quantity and each step in the calculation.

3

COMPOUNDING REQUIREMENTS & TERMINOLOGY

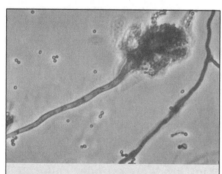

Fungal Meningitis Outbreak Linked to Compounded Medication

In 2012 a compounding pharmacy prepared methylprednisolone injections that were contaminated and caused fungal meningitis (*aspergillis*), with resultant illness and fatalities. In addition to improper aseptic technique (sterile compounding is required for injectables) and a lack of improper policies and procedures – a primary concern is that the pharmacy prepared multiple batches for mass distribution. Compounding is limited to patient-specific doses (or, in some cases, production of limited quantities of the same product prepared in advance of expected patient prescriptions.) The primary purpose of compounding is to provide medications that are not commercially available to meet the unique needs of individual patients, as designated on the prescription. Compounding is the preparation of *patient-specific* medications.

GUIDELINE

Non-Sterile Preparations: US Pharmacopeia (USP) Chapter 795.

We gratefully acknowledge the assistance of Jess Martinez, PharmD, Clinical Associate Professor & Vice Dean, Western University College of Pharmacy, in preparing this chapter.

NONSTERILE COMPOUNDING VERSUS FDA-APPROVED DRUGS

Compounding is different from manufacturing since it is patient-specific (ordered by a prescriber for the patient) and regulated by the state boards of pharmacy. For example, a prescriber designates specific percentages of hormone cream for an individual female patient. Or, a hospitalized patient is getting powders prepared since she cannot swallow pills.

- <u>Beyond use dates</u> must be applied to each compounded product, using either the USP <795> guidelines for Nonaqueous Liquids and Solid Formulations and for Water-Containing Formulations. For all other formulations the beyond use date is not later than the intended duration of therapy or 30 days, whichever is earlier.

- The recipe must be kept in a log book (see next section).

- Advertisement of compounded products is not permitted.

- Compounded products do not have NDC numbers.

- In contrast, <u>FDA-approved and regulated drugs must have an approved NDA, must be produced under Good Manufacturing Practices (GMP), have NDC numbers, and carry a set expiration date</u> (provided to the pharmacy).

GENERAL NON-STERILE COMPOUNDING RULES

- Compounding space should be separate and away from the dispensing section.

- Ideally, use only USP or NF chemicals from FDA-inspected manufacturers.

- Required logs that must be in pharmacy: compounding formulas and procedures, compounded item log, equipment maintenance records (includes refrigerator and freezer temp logs), record of chemicals, bulk drug substances, drug products, and components used to compound products (which must be obtained from reliable sources).

- For each compounded product, pharmacy records must include: master formula, date the product was compounded, pharmacy personnel who compounded the product, pharmacist with final review, quantity of each product used in compounding the product, manufacturer and lot number of each component, equipment used, pharmacy assigned reference number or lot number, expiration date, quantity or amount of product compounded.

Labels on Pharmacy-Compounded Products

- Expiration Dates (Beyond Use Dates)

  - Solids (non-aqueous) preparations: Label up to 6-months duration if the ingredients are all USP or NF products OR use a date that is no later than 25% of the time left on the manufacturer's date, whichever is sooner.

  - Aqueous (a water-containing, liquid preparation) no more than 14 days IF the preparation is stored in the refrigerator (2-8°C, 36-46°F).

  - Anything else should expire no more than the intended length of treatment OR 30 days, whichever is sooner.

- Auxiliary Labels for Compounded Creams and Lotions

  - Refrigerate

  - Shake Well Before Using (emulsions and suspensions)

  - External Use Only

- The product label must include generic or chemical name of active ingredients, strength or quantity, pharmacy lot number, beyond-use date, and any special storage requirements.

- A statement that the product has been compounded by the pharmacy must be placed on the label of the container.

- For capsules, the label must include mcg or mg/capsule.

- For liquids, the strength should be in concentration (e.g., 125 mg/5 mL), or provided as a percentage.

- The coining of short names for marketing or convenience (e.g., *Johnson's Solution*) is strongly discouraged.

- Purified water (not tap water) is used. Purified water is also used for rinsing equipment.

- If compounding a prescription that calls for alcohol and the type is not specified, use USP 95% ethyl alcohol.

Selected Notes on Sterile Compounding
(see Medication Safety Chapter for further requirements)

- The following products must be compounded in a sterile environment: injections, inhalations, wound and cavity irrigation baths, eye drops and eye ointments. Water used in preparation must be sterile water for injection, or bacteriostatic water for injection.

- Sterile compounding requires personnel trained and evaluated annually for competency in aseptic techniques, environmental control, quality assurance testing and end-product evaluation and sterility testing.

- If the product is an injectable, the certified sterile compounding environment must be either an ISO class 5 (class 100) laminar air flow hood within a ISO class 7 (class 10,000) clean room (with positive air pressure differential relative to adjacent areas) or an ISO class 5 (class 100) clean room with positive air pressure differential relative to adjacent areas or a barrier isolator that provides a ISO class 5 (class 100) environment for compounding.

- Clean room garb (low-shedding coverall, head cover, face mask and shoe covers) is required and should be put on and taken off outside the designated area. Hand, finger and wrist jewelry is not allowed. Head and facial hair have to be out of the way (tied up) and covered.

- When preparing cytotoxic agents, gowns and gloves are worn. All cytotoxic agents must be labeled "cytotoxic agents – dispose of properly" and disposal and spill policies and spill kits must be kept in the pharmacy.

- Sterile and non-sterile areas must be separate.

NONSTERILE COMPOUNDING EQUIPMENT USED IN A COMMUNITY PHARMACY
Required balances: a torsion balance (a "class A balance" is a torsion type balance that utilizes both internal and external weights and requires the use of external weights for measurements exceeding 1 g), and if compounding routinely, a top-loading electronic balance. Most pharmacists will make their weight measurements on an electronic balance.

Torsion balance

Electronic balance

Measuring Devices

Caution! All equipment, including scales, measuring devices, slabs, spatulas and anything else used must be selected to avoid selecting surfaces that may make contact with pharmaceutical components, in process materials, or finished preparations that may be reactive, additive, or absorptive to avoid altering the safety, identity, strength, quality, or purity of the preparation.

When measuring, select a device equal to or slightly larger than the amount to be measured.

- If the volume to be measured is viscous use a syringe, rather than a cylinder. Pipettes are used for measuring 1.5 mL or less of liquids; they are long thin tubes made of glass.

- Liquids in a container curve up, therefore measure at the bottom of the meniscus.

Pipette

Volumetric Flask

Graduated Cylinder
(measure from the bottom of the meniscus)

Mortar & Pestle

Compounding requires a minimum of two types of mortar and pestles: 1 glass and 1 Wedgewood or porcelain (ceramic). Wedgewood or porcelain is used most commonly and is best for reducing particle size of dry powders and crystals. Porcelain has a smoother surface than Wedgewood and is preferred for blending powders or pulverizing soft materials. If Wedgewood is used for powders or crystals, first coat the inside with lactose to fill in the crevices.

Glass is used for liquids and chemicals that are oily or that will stain the porcelain, including many chemotherapeutics. Glass is preferred for mixing liquids and semi-soft dosage forms.

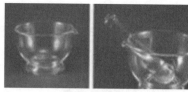

Glass mortar & pestle

Ceramic mortar and pestle

Surfaces & Spatulas

Glassine weighing paper (as opposed to bond paper) should be used for weighing ointments and some dry chemicals. It is safest not to use ointment paper to prepare creams and lotions (use a slab and spatula instead) because the water content will cause the paper to moisten, and possibly tear.

Parchment ointment paper is convenient and easy to clean, but cannot be used for creams or other aqueous mixtures because the paper will absorb water – use a slab instead.

Generally, large metal (stainless steel) spatula blades are used, but small spatula blades (< 6 inches) can be used for removing product from the large spatula and putting it into the jar.

Plastic spatulas should be used for chemicals (e.g., potassium, iodine) that can react with stainless steel blades. The third type is the rubber spatula. Compounding slabs are also called ointment slabs, they are generally glass, and have nonabsorbent surfaces.

COMPOUNDING TERMINOLOGY AND INGREDIENTS

Levigation

Levigation is the process of reducing the size of a particle of a solid by triturating it (grinding it down to smaller particles) in a mortar or spatulating it on an ointment slab with a small amount of liquid (the wetting agent) in which the solid is not soluble. The goal is to transfer it from a solid to a paste-like substance utilizing a levigating agent. This incorporates the solid into a cream or ointment base. It also makes the solid more uniform throughout the base and gets rid of the gritty feeling.

- The levigation agent must be miscible (compatible) with the ointment base.

- Levigating Agents used in preparing ointments are:

  - For aqueous systems (O/W dispersions) – Glycerin, propylene glycol, polyethylene glycol 80.

  - For oleaginous systems (W/O dispersions)- Mineral oil (light & heavy), castor oil, cottonseed oil, *Tween 80.*

- Mineral oil is good to use for levigating a hydrophobic ointment such as white petrolatum.

- If heat is used (to mix things easier), the use should be limited and the ingredient with the higher melting point should be heated. Otherwise, undesired chemical reactions could occur.

- A water bath will help prevent over-heating.

Trituration

Trituration is the process of reducing fracturable powder substances into fine particles by rubbing (or grinding) them with a mortar and pestle, or on an ointment slab.

Extemporaneous

Extemporaneous compounding refers to a compound prepared without a specific formula from an official compendium and made especially to fill the needs of a specific patient.

Emollients

An emollient is a single agent that is used to soften and smooth the skin. A moisturizer is sometimes referred to as an emollient, but the term emollient is used for single agents, and moisturizers often have coloring, scents, and other ingredients added. Astringents tighten the skin.

Emulsions & Emulsifiers

Emulsions are a two-phase system of two immiscible liquids, one of which is dispersed through the other as small droplets. They can be oil in water, or water in oil. Emulsifiers (or emulgent) is used to stabilize the emulsion. Emulsifiers are usually surfactants (or wetting agents) that reduce surface tension so that the 2 substances can move closer to each other. Emulsions are immiscible (they do not form a suspension – which means the two liquids stay separate when you combine them). Emulsions are used as a dosage form whenever two immiscible liquids must be dispensed in the same preparation.

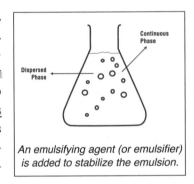

An emulsifying agent (or emulsifier) is added to stabilize the emulsion.

- Emulsifiers include acacia, agar, pectin, lipophilic esters of sorbitan (*Arlacel* and *Span*) and the hydrophilic esters (*Myrj* and *Tween*). Other emulsifier names that may be good to recognize are polyethylene glycol (PEG, which is also commonly used as a laxative), acacia, glyceryl monostearate and sodium laurel sulfate.

- The Continental or dry gum method of preparing an emulsion uses oil, purified water and gum (such as acacia) in the ratio of 4:2:1. The English, or wet gum method uses the same ingredients (oil, water, gum) but the order of mixing is different. In the dry gum method, the gum is mixed rapidly with oil, and then the water is added all at once, while the wet gum method is a slower process in which the gum is dissolved in water first, and then the oil is slowly added.

- The hydrophilic-lipophilic balance (HLB) number determines how much surfactant will be required to form the mixture together. Agents with a low HLB number are more oil-soluble. Agents with a high HLB number are more water-soluble. The HLB scale range is 0-20 and a value of 10, the midpoint, is the break-point between water and oil solubility. A value less than 10, therefore, is lipid-soluble and a value greater than 10 is water-soluble.

Lotions, Creams, Ointments, Pastes

Lotions, creams, ointments and pastes are all water and oil emulsions (either oil in water, or water in oil), but in different amounts and for different uses. Be CAREFUL when choosing a product because many come in various formulations. For example, terbinafine *(Lamisil AT)* comes as a cream, gel and solution and mupirocin *(Bactroban)* comes as an ointment and a cream.

Note on medication potency and choice of the delivery vehicle: The Common Skin Conditions chapter reviews how different formulations are used on different types of skin. For example, you cannot apply an antifungal ointment well to hairy skin; it will be difficult to spread. Yet, ointments promote medication absorption better than creams and lotions. BOTH site and potency must be considered. A medication packaged in an ointment will have a higher potency than the same medication packaged in a cream or lotion. Examples: Mometasone *(Elocon)* ointment is high-potency and mometasone *(Elocon)* cream is low-medium potency.

- Lotions have the MOST water, and are most often oil-in-water (a small amount of oil). They absorb quickly and are easy to spread on the skin. Since lotions contain a lot of water, they often come in pumps. Some of the lotions contain alcohol, but this can be drying. Example: Most of the OTC moisturizers are lotions, such as *Keri* and *Cetaphil.*

- Creams are emulsions of about half oil and half water. They spread easily and are reasonably hydrating. Creams are packaged in tubes, and sometimes in tubs; they are too thick to be dispensed in a pump. Examples: terbinafine *(Lamisil AT)* antifungal cream, docosanol *(Abreva)* antiviral cream.

- Ointments are ~80% oil and 20% water. They do not absorb well and are not easy to use on large areas. They are used for the occlusive benefit—they block (trap in) moisture, and are preferred for dry or dry/cracked skin. They are useful to help injured skin from burns or lasers, since the moisture is needed for these types of injuries. They are often used for medication delivery and are usually packaged in tubes, and sometimes in tubs. Examples: Mupirocin *(Bactroban)* ointment, nitroglycerin ointment, *Aquaphor, Aquabase.*

- Pastes are the thickest ointments and are also used as protective barriers. Example: *Triple Paste* medicated diaper rash ointment.

Gels

Gels are oil in water emulsions, usually with an alcohol base. They are easy to spread and dry into a thin film. Example: Benzoyl peroxide and erythromycin topical acne gel *(Benzamycin).*

Gels are also used as thickeners. They have a solid and a liquid that are dispersed evenly throughout a material (the suspension is inter-penetrated by the liquid). Example – *BenzaClin* acne gel.

- Common gels used as thickeners are the alginates (including Na$^+$, K$^+$, Ca^{2+} alginate), agar, carrageenan, gelatin, carbomer, tragacanth, bentonite). A commercial product that is used commonly is called *Liqua-Gel.*

Powders

Powders are finely divided drugs, or other chemicals. Powders range in size from very coarse (No. 8) to very fine (No. 80).

Solutions

Solutions are liquid preparations of soluble chemicals dissolved in solvents such as water, alcohol, or propylene glycol. When alcohol is used as a solvent in a systemic formulation, the pharmacist should consider effects on the patient, and if the alcohol may interact with medications.

Suspensions

Suspensions are two phased-system of a finely divided solid in a liquid medium. The drug must be uniformly dispersed in the medium. The suspension should be deflocculated: this means that the repulsive forces between particles predominate so that the particles in the suspension repel each other and remain as discrete, single particles. Suspensions should settle slowly, be easy to re-disperse by gently shaking and have uniform particles that are of small size. Suspending agents used in suspensions:

- Natural hydrocolloids, including acacia, alginic acid, gelatin, guar gum, alginate, xanthan gum

- Semi-synthetic hydrocolloids, including methylcellulose

- Synthetic hydrocolloids, including carbomers and polyvinyl alcohol

- Clays, including bentonite and veegum

Suppositories

Suppositories are solid dosage forms used to deliver medicine into the rectum, vagina or urethra. They are formed in a mold. They melt, soften or dissolve in the body cavity. Suppositories bypass the oral route and avoid first-pass metabolism.

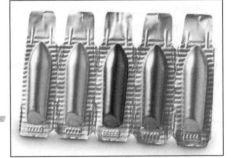

- The base must be compatible with the medication, it must not melt too quickly (in your hands while inserting), must be stable and must not have a disagreeable look or scent.

- Examples include the following rectal suppositories: acetaminophen suppository (good for feverish infant who is not eating or is vomiting), hemorrhoid suppository, mesalamine suppository (used to treat distal disease – the suppository provides medication where the disease is located, and avoids systemic toxicity – mesalamine also comes as an enema), and vaginal suppositories of antifungal medication for vaginal candida infections.

- Commonly used bases utilized in suppositories include cocoa butter (theobroma oil), glycerin, hydrogenated vegetable oils, and polyethylene glycol (Carbowax).

Syrups

Syrups are concentrated, aqueous preparations of sugar or sugar-substitute, medicinal agents, or flavoring in water, such as cough syrups.

Elixirs

Elixirs are clear, sweetened, hydroalcoholic solutions suitable for water-insoluble drugs, such as mouthwashes.

Lozenges/Troches

Lozenges are called troches and deliver drug to the oral mucosa. They can also be used for patients who have trouble swallowing since the lozenge dissolves in the mouth. Clotrimazole troche *(Mycelex)* is an antifungal troche that dissolves in the mouth and is used to treat oral thrush. Troches are made in molds, with any required flavorings or colorings.

Clotrimazole (Mycelex) Troche

Flavorings/Sweeteners

Products or preparations that have an unpleasant taste are not usually used, or they will result in decreased adherence. Flavor is one of the key attributes in determining the palatability of drugs given in oral liquid and oral semisolid dosage forms. Salty, sweet or bitter tastes can be used to mask a bitter flavor. Mint and spices can be used to mask poor flavor. Acids (such as citric acid) are used to enhance fruit flavors. Adding saltiness can be useful. Another option is to put the drug into an emulsion (in the internal phase) where it is less likely to interact with the patient's taste buds. A few concerns with sweeteners used in chewables is described under tablets.

Capsules

Capsules are unit doses made in soluble shells of gelatin, or can be made of hypromellose (a non-animal product) to accommodate cultural and dietary requirements. Unpleasant drug tastes and odors can be masked by the capsule shell. Capsules are made by triturating the powders to a small particle size, mixing by geometric dilution, and calculating the weight needed to fill a capsule. Sorbitol is used as a plasticizer for gelatin capsules.

Capsule size: the largest is 000, where the smaller the size, the higher the number. The smallest capsule size is 5.

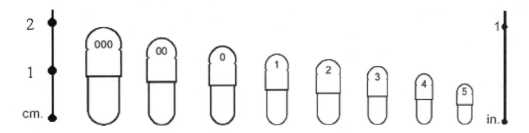

Tablets

In large-scale manufacturing, the formulation that is often the least expensive to make (and the most common dispensed in everyday practice) are compressed tablets. Tablets may contain excipients (also called binders) that hold the tablet together. Capsules may also use similar ingredients as fillers. Sorbitol is used (particularly in chewables as it is sweet). Sorbitol is also used as a thickening agent in liquids. Sorbitol can cause considerable GI distress in some patients with IBS; it has laxative properties. If lactose is used, this may present a problem for patients with lactose-intolerance.

Calculations for compounding require the math skills discussed in the Calculations chapter, which includes compounding problems.

4

PHARMACOKINETICS, PHARMACODYNAMICS AND DRUG FORMULATIONS

We gratefully acknowledge the assistance of Nathan S. Teuscher, BS, MS, PhD, Founder & President, PK/PD Associates, and Ifeanyi Onor, BS, PharmD, BCPS, Clinical Assistant Professor & Adult Medicine Clinical Pharmacist, Xavier University College of Pharmacy, in preparing this chapter.

Pharmacokinetics is the study of the time course of drug absorption, distribution, metabolism and excretion. Pharmacokinetics attempts to use mathematical relationships to describe how drug molecules enter the body, circulate to different tissues and organs, and are then eliminated by metabolic and excretory processes. Pharmacokinetic analysis provides insights into the time course of drug pharmacology by correlating therapeutic and toxic effects with circulating drug levels. Pharmacodynamics refers to the effects of drugs on the patient's body (the mechanism of action, or how they work), the drug's therapeutic benefit and the toxicity profile. Pharmacodynamics is also used to explain the effect of the drug on an organism (such as a bacteriostatic or bactericidal effect).

PHARMACOKINETICS: ABSORPTION, DISTRIBUTION, METABOLISM AND EXCRETION

Absorption

Absorption is the process by which a drug moves from the site of administration to the circulatory system. Sites of drug administration are divided into two main areas, intravascular administration, where the drug is placed directly into the blood either intravenously or intra-arterially, or extravascular administration. Examples of extravascular administration include oral, sublingual, buccal, intramuscular, subcutaneous, dermal, pulmonary, topical ocular, intraocular and rectal. If a drug is administered via intravascular administration, (into the vein directly, with an IV infusion) there is no drug absorption as the drug is placed directly in the systemic circulation. However, if a drug is administered by extravascular administration, drug absorption occurs as the drug moves from the site of administration to the circulatory system.

Site of Administration

Extravascular administration can be divided into two groups: drugs intended for local effects and drugs intended for systemic effects. Drugs intended for local effects are often applied topically to the site of action. Examples of drugs intended for local effects include eyedrops for glaucoma (e.g., latanoprost), dermal preparations for psoriasis (e.g., coal tar preparations), and nasal sprays for allergies (e.g., fluticasone nasal spray). In general, drug absorption is low with most, but not all, topical products. The extent of topical absorption is affected by other factors, including open wounds on the skin (increases absorption) and the amount that is applied. Therapeutic effects can be observed with local administration, and systemic toxicity can often be avoided due to low systemic exposure. Drugs intended for systemic effects are generally applied in such a way to encourage absorption to the circulatory system. Examples of drugs intended for systemic effects are oral tablets for seasonal allergies (e.g., loratidine), injectables for osteoporosis (e.g., teriparatide), and sublingual tablets for angina chest pain (nitroglycerin SL). With systemic absorption, some percentage of the drug will move from the site of administration into the systemic circulation.

Dosage Form Dissolution and Drug Solubility

When an oral dosage form is ingested, it begins to dissolve in the gastrointestinal (GI) tract and drug is released from the dosage form which is typically a compressed tablet or a capsule. This is called dissolution. Dissolution is a function of the inactive matrix that is used to formulate the drug dosage form. Many pharmaceutical companies utilize biocompatible polymers to develop controlled release drug products that have a pre-defined dissolution process. This can provide a more even drug concentration and reduce the dosing frequency. Or, the drug may be given in an immediate release formulation that dissolves fast and is absorbed rapidly. The formulation can be chosen to limit drug degradation in the gut; the drug can be destroyed in the gut (primarily by hydrolysis, or lysis with water) and less would be available for absorption. Examples of drugs with "protective" coatings include enteric-coated formulations such as bisacodyl and *Entocort*. Typically, the coating prevents drug dissolution in the acidic gut medium but permits dissolution in the basic medium of the intestine. If the drug has poor absorption, one of the methods used to increase the dissolution rate is to reduce the particle diameter, which increases the surface area. Drugs with very small particle diameters are referred to as micronized, which used to mean the diameter was measured in micrometers, but now may refer to even smaller particle sizes measured in nanometers. Drugs with poor absorption that are "micronized" include progesterone and fenofibrate formulations. Without micronization, these drugs would be poorly absorbed. The rate of dissolution is described by the Noyes-Whitney equation.

Following dissolution, the drug that is released from the dosage form can be dissolved in GI fluids. The rate and extent to which the drug dissolves in the GI fluid depends on the solubility. Poorly soluble drugs are generally lipophilic, or lipid-loving. Freely soluble drugs are generally hydrophilic, or water-loving. As a drug moves through the GI tract, only dissolved drug is absorbed into the body. Thus poorly soluble drugs generally have poor systemic absorption and highly soluble drugs often have good systemic absorption.

Systemic Absorption

Absorption into the systemic circulation occurs via two primary processes, passive diffusion across the gut wall, or active transport via transporter proteins. Passive diffusion occurs when a high concentration of drug in the gut lumen moves to equalize drug concentration (reach an equilibrium) across the gut wall. Drug particles move through the gut wall into the portal vein, unassisted by cellular machinery. Active transport occurs when drugs are moved across the gut wall via transporter proteins that are normally used to absorb nutrients from food.

Bioavailability

The extent to which a drug is absorbed into the systemic circulation is called bioavailability. Bioavailability is the percentage of drug absorbed from extravascular administration relative to intravascular administration (e.g., IV bolus). Bioavailability is reported as a percentage from 0 to 100%. If the oral dose of a drug is the same as the IV dose (such as with levofloxacin or linezolid) then the bioavailability is 1, or 100%. With these two drugs, nearly 100% is absorbed and it makes it simple to convert from IV to PO. In many hospitals, these drugs are automatically converted to the same dose orally if the prescriber has written for the IV form and the patient can use the oral dose instead. This is part of the hospital's "therapeutic interchange" protocol. With most drugs not all of the dose is absorbed, and the bioavailability is less than 100%; this means that the oral dose will need to be higher than the corresponding IV dose. A drug with good absorption characteristics will generally have high bioavailability (> 70%), while a drug with poor absorption characteristics will have low bioavailability (< 10%). Levofloxacin has high bioavailability; the oral and IV drug doses are the same. Bisphosphonates have low bioavailability and the annual IV dose will be less than the weekly dose of the oral formation.

Bioavailability can be calculated using the area under the plasma concentration time curve, or AUC. The AUC represents the total exposure of drug following administration. The figure below illustrates the plasma concentration time curve (outside line) and the AUC (the shaded area).

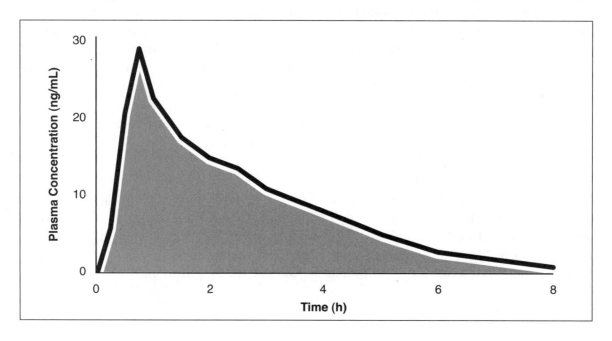

Area under the plasma concentration-time curve

Absolute bioavailability, represented by F, is calculated using the following equation:

$$F\ (\%)\ =\ 100\ \times\ \frac{AUC_{extravascular}}{AUC_{intravenous}}\ \times\ \frac{Dose_{intravenous}}{Dose_{extravascular}}$$

Bioavailability Example

Data was obtained after oral and intravenous administration of Drug X. Following a 250 mg intravenous dose, administered as a bolus injection, the AUC was 3.8 mg x hr/mL. Following a 500 mg oral dose, administered as a solution, the AUC was 3.5 mg x hr/mL. Calculate the absolute bioavailability of Drug X.

ITEM	VALUE
$Dose_{extravascular}$	500 mg
$AUC_{extravascular}$	3.5 mg x hr/mL
$Dose_{intravenous}$	250 mg
$AUC_{intravenous}$	3.8 mg x hr/mL

Using the equation for absolute bioavailability, we can calculate the following:

$$F\ (\%)\ =\ 100\ \times\ \frac{3.5\ mg\ x\ hr/mL}{3.8\ mg\ x\ hr/mL}\ \times\ \frac{250\ mg}{500\ mg}\ =\ 46\%$$

Distribution

Distribution is the process by which drug molecules move from the systemic circulation to the various tissues and organs of the body. Distribution occurs for intravascular and extra-vascular routes of administration. Distribution to tissues and organs in the body depends on the physiochemical properties of the drug molecule and its interactions with membranes and tissues throughout the body. In general, drugs distribute evenly throughout the body based on properties such as lipophilicity, molecular weight, solubility, ionization status and the extent of protein binding. Human plasma contains many proteins, and albumin is the primary protein which accounts for most drug binding. If a drug is highly protein-bound (> 90%) and the albumin is low (< 3.5 g/dL) then a higher percentage of the drug will be in the unbound form, which is able to interact with receptors and cause therapeutic or toxic effects. For two drugs in particular (phenytoin and valproate), and for calcium, if the albumin is low the level will be higher than given on the lab report, unless the "free" level of phenytoing or the ionized calcium is reported. If the free phenytoin or ionized calcium is reported, there is no adjustment required. Otherwise, there is and the formulas to adjust the levels for low albumin are in the calculation chapter (calcium) and epilepsy chapter (phenytoin and valproate). The advent of therapeutic antibodies has permitted target-mediated drug distri-bution, where targeting antibodies are attached to drug molecules to specifically direct distribution to a target tissue (e.g., tumor cells). The drug does not "know" where it is supposed to go; it will interact with various receptors as it travels through the body. In general, "side effects" are caused by the drug hitting the "wrong" receptor (where it happened to fit) and therapeutic benefit occurs when the drug hits the "right" receptor. This makes drug targeting an important area of research. If the drug goes only where it is intended, the side effect profile (and toxicity) can be reduced and the therapeutic benefit can be increased.

Volume of Distribution

The volume of distribution (V or Vd) is how large an area in the patient's body the drug has distributed into, and is based on the properties of that drug. The volume of distribution relates the amount of drug in the body to the concentration of drug measured in plasma (or serum). A dose of drug is administered using amounts of drug (e.g., 10 mg), however, drug is measured as a concentration (amount per volume) from a sample of biological fluid. To convert between amounts and concentrations, a volume is needed. The equation for volume of distribution is:

$$Vd = \frac{\text{Amount of drug in body}}{\text{Concentration of drug in plasma}}$$

For example, 500 mg of acetaminophen is administered to a patient, and a blood sample is drawn one hour after dose administration. The concentration of acetaminophen is measured as 8 mcg/mL (which is 8 mg/L). To determine the total amount of drug remaining in the body, we need to multiply the concentration (8 mg/L) by a volume parameter. Acetaminophen has a volume of distribution of 51 L. Therefore, the amount of acetaminophen in the body 1 hour after dose administration is:

$$\text{Amount} = 8 \text{ mg/L} \times 51 \text{ L} = 408 \text{ mg}$$

Volume of distribution and physical volumes

Volume of distribution is not a physical volume and can be very small, such as erythropoietin (Vd = 0.076 L/kg), or very large, such as chloroquine (Vd = 200 L/kg). While volume of distribution is not a physical volume, it can be useful to compare Vd to physical volumes in the body to make inferences regarding the distribution of drug in the body. Total body water is 42 L (0.6 L/kg), extracellular water is 16 L (0.23 L/kg), and plasma volume is 3 L (0.04 L/kg). Drugs with small volumes of distribution (e.g., erythropoietin) are generally confined to plasma circulation or extracellular spaces. These drugs rarely distribute to other tissues (e.g., fat, muscle, etc.). Drugs with large volumes of distribution are widely distributed in the tissues of the body, and are often sequestered in fat cells or membranes.

Calculation of volume of distribution

Volume of distribution can be calculated using the following equation:

$$Vd = \frac{F \times Dose}{k_{el} \times AUC}$$

where F is bioavailability, k_{el} is the terminal elimination rate constant, and AUC is the area under the plasma concentration-time curve. With intravenous administration, the bioavailability is assumed to be 1. With extravascular administration, the bioavailability is generally unknown, therefore V/F, or the <u>apparent volume of distribution</u> is calculated using the following equation:

$$\frac{Vd}{F} = \frac{Dose}{k_{el} \times AUC}$$

In the specific case of a bolus intravenous injection, volume of distribution can be calculated using the following equation:

$$Vd = \frac{Dose}{C_0}$$

where C_0 is the extrapolated concentration at time = 0 from the plasma concentration-time curve.

Volume of distribution following IV bolus example

Following a 0.1 mg intravenous bolus dose of fentanyl, plasma levels of fentanyl were measured. The extrapolated concentration at time = 0 was 0.357 mcg/L. Calculate the volume of distribution for fentanyl.

Dose = 0.1 mg = 100 mcg

C_0 = 0.357 mcg/L

Using the equation for a bolus intravenous injection, we can calculate the following:

$$Vd = \frac{100 \text{ mcg}}{0.357 \text{ mcg/L}} = 280 \text{ L}$$

Volume of distribution following oral dose example

Following an oral dose of 250 mg of cefuroxime *(Ceftin)*, the terminal elimination rate constant was determined to be 0.41 hr^{-1}, and the AUC was determined to be 29.62 mg x hr/L. Calculate the apparent volume of distribution of cefuroxime.

ITEM	VALUE
Dose	250 mg
AUC	29.62 mg x hr/L
K_{el}	50 mg

Because cefuroxime was administered as an oral dose, and the bioavailability was not provided, we will use the equation for apparent volume of distribution and calculate the apparent volume of distribution:

$$\frac{Vd}{F} = \frac{250 \text{ mg}}{0.41 \text{hr}^{-1} \times 29.62 \text{ mg x hr/L}} = 20.6 \text{ L}$$

Metabolism

Metabolism is the process by which a drug is converted from its original chemical structure into other forms to facilitate elimination from the body. The original chemical form is called the "parent drug" and the additional forms are called "metabolites". Metabolism can occur throughout the body; however, the gut and liver are primary sites for drug metabolism due to high levels of metabolic enzymes in those tissues.

Metabolism is described in detail in the <u>Drug Interactions</u> chapter.

Excretion

Excretion is the process of irreversible removal of drugs from the body. Excretion can occur via the kidney (urine), liver (bile), gut (feces), lungs (exhaled air) and skin (sweat). The primary routes of excretion for most drugs include the kidney (renal excretion) and the gut/liver (via metabolism). It should be noted that drug that is never absorbed cannot be excreted. Thus only drug that has been absorbed into the systemic circulation can be excreted from the body. Renal excretion is described in detail in the <u>Renal Disease and Dosing Considerations</u> chapter, and in the <u>Calculations</u> chapter.

Clearance

The rate of drug elimination from the body is proportional to the concentration of drug present in the body. The proportionality constant used to relate the rate of elimination and drug concentration is <u>clearance</u> (Cl). Clearance is a pharmacokinetic parameter that converts a concentration of drug in the body to an amount of drug eliminated per unit time, and is generally described by the following equation:

$$\text{Rate of elimination} = Cl \times \text{Concentration}$$

The rate of elimination has units of mass per time (e.g., mg/hr), and drug concentration has units of concentration (e.g., mg/L), therefore clearance has units of volume per time (e.g., L/hr). Because the rate of elimination is difficult to assess clinically, another method is used to calculate the clearance of a drug from the body:

$$F \times \text{Dose} = Cl \times AUC$$

The area under the curve (AUC) represents the total exposure to the drug in the systemic circulation, or an average concentration over the time measured. The bioavailable dose (F x Dose) represents the total amount of drug administered and eliminated. By rearranging this equation, the <u>apparent clearance</u> (Cl/F) for extravascular administration can be calculated:

$$\frac{Cl}{F} = \frac{\text{Dose}}{AUC}$$

Following intravenous administration, F = 1, which can be inserted into the previous equation to determine clearance.

Half-life

The time required for the drug concentration (and drug amount) <u>to decrease by 50%</u> is called the elimination half-life. For example, it takes 5 hours for theophylline concentrations to fall from 16 to 8 mg/L. Thus the half-life of theophylline is 5 hours. It would take 5 more hours for the drug concentration to fall from 8 mg/L to 4 mg/L. It is important to note that the half-life is independent of the drug concentration.

The half-life of a drug can be calculated from the terminal elimination rate constant (k_{el}) as shown below

$$t_{\frac{1}{2}} = \frac{0.693}{k_{el}}$$

The terminal elimination rate constant can be calculated using linear regression of concentration-time data, or it can be calculated from the volume of distribution (Vd) and clearance (Cl) of a drug:

$$k_{el} = \frac{Cl}{Vd}$$

The half-life of a drug can be used to calculate the time required for drug washout or the time required to achieve steady-state as shown in the following table. <u>Steady state</u> is an important concept in pharmacy, because drug levels are generally (but not always) collected at <u>steady state</u> to obtain clinically useful serum drug concentrations. When a fixed dose is administered at regular intervals, the drug accumulates until it reaches steady state where <u>the rate of drug intake equals the rate of drug elimination</u>. The time required to reach steady state depends on the elimination half-life of the drug. If the drug follows first-order kinetics (described later in this chapter) in a one-compartment distribution model (the drug is rapidly and evenly distributed throughout the body) and if a loading dose has not been given, it takes <u>~5-6 half-lives to reach steady state</u>.

Relationship between half-life, percent of drug remaining and percent of steady-state achieved.

# OF HALF-LIVES	% OF DRUG REMAINING	% OF STEADY-STATE ACHIEVED
1	50	50
2	25	75
3	12.5	87.5
4	6.25	93.8
5	3.13	96.9
6	1.56	98.4
7	0.78	99.2

Clearance example

Following a 200 mg dose of ketoconazole the area under the curve is measured at 5.67 mcg x hr/mL. Calculate the apparent clearance. Round to the nearest liter. Refer to the preceding table.

ITEM	VALUE
Dose	200 mg
AUC	5.67 mcg x hr/mL

Using the equation for apparent clearance, we can calculate the following

$$\frac{CL}{F} = \frac{200,000 \text{ mcg}}{5.67 \text{ mcg x hr/mL}} = 35,273 \text{ mL/hr} = 35 \text{ L/hr}$$

Half-life example

Tetracycline has a clearance of 7.014 L/hr and a volume of distribution of 105 L. Calculate the half-life of tetracycline and the time required for elimination of greater than 95% of the drug from the body.

ITEM	VALUE
Cl	7.014 L/hr
V	105 L

Using the equation for the terminal elimination rate constant and the equation for half-life, we can calculate the following:

> 95% of the drug, we use the values in the table on the preceding page and note that <u>5 half-lives are required to eliminate more than 95% of the drug</u>. Thus, the time required is 5 x 10.4 hr = 52 hr.

Examples of Various Half-Life Calculations Solved Without the Half-Life Formulas

A patient receives 200 mg of a drug with a half-life of 5 hrs. How much of the drug still remains in the patient after 10 hours?

- 10 hrs = 2 half-lives:

- 200 mg/2 (or reduced by 50%) = 100 mg (amount of drug left after one half-life)

- 100 mg/2 = 50 mg is left after 10 hours (2 half-lives)

The serum concentration of Drug A over time is plotted below. What is the half-life of Drug A?

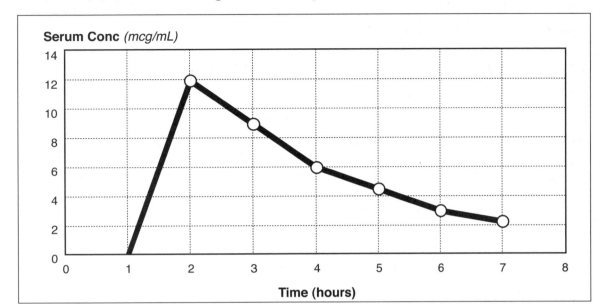

- Choose two times (in hours) where the drug concentration has decreased by half to find the half-life

- For example, at 2 hours the concentration is 12 mcg/ml and at 4 hours the concentration is 6 mcg/mL.

- It takes 2 hours for the concentration to decrease by 50%; the half-life is 2 hours.

FIRST-ORDER KINETICS

The lower left corner of the chart (up to the arrow) indicates first-order kinetics. The absorption of <u>most drugs follows first-order kinetics</u>. The <u>amount of drug given is proportional to the increase seen in plasma concentration</u>.

In first-order kinetics, the more drug given, the higher the drug concentration, in a linear manner.

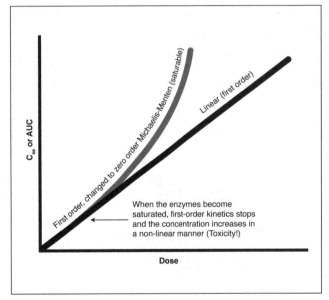

When the enzymes become saturated, first-order kinetics stops and the concentration increases in a non-linear manner (Toxicity!)

MICHAELIS-MENTEN KINETICS

Michaelis-Menten, or saturable kinetics, begins as first-order, but when the metabolism <u>becomes saturated, the concentration increases rapidly. Drugs with this type of kinetics begin as first-order kinetics, but can change to zero order once a certain dose is reached</u>

and metabolizing enzymes are saturated. In zero order elimination, the elimination rate is independent of the drug's concentration. At this point, toxicity is likely to result. Phenytoin, theophylline and voriconazole have this type of saturable kinetics.

With saturable kinetics, a small increase in dose may result in a large increase in drug concentration.

Michaelis-Menten Kinetics – Example

A patient has been using phenytoin 100 mg three times daily. The phenytoin level was taken and found to be 9.8 mcg/mL. The physician increased the dose to 100 mg with breakfast and lunch, and 200 mg with dinner. The patient started to slur her words, felt fatigued and returned to the physician's office. The level was retaken and found to be 22.7 mcg/mL.

The most likely explanation for the increase in phenytoin level is that although first-order kinetics took place initially, when the dose was increased, the metabolism became saturated, and the level increased dramatically, as shown in the above figure.

Drug Formulation Considerations

It may be necessary to choose whether or not a drug comes in a specific formulation. It is difficult to memorize all the various formulations, but consider that it takes money to develop unique dosing forms. If a drug is available in something unusual – there has to be a market for the formulation or the manufacturer would not have spent money to develop a novel method of delivery. Think about who would need the drug in that form to help remember the various formulations.

Dysphagia, Trouble Swallowing Large Capsules or Tablets

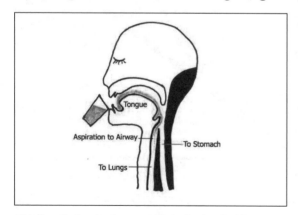

Elderly with dysphagia can aspirate food or liquids into the lungs, resulting in a pneumonia

Children can have difficulty swallowing large tablets or capsules

Patients with swallowing difficulty (elderly, frail, dementia, stroke, young children, etc.) may need a formulation other than a traditional tablet or capsule. Tablets that dissolve in the mouth (orally disintegrating (or dissolving, or dispersable) tablets, or ODT) are available for many drugs that are used in elderly patients: dementia drugs such as donepezil *(Aricept ODT)*, memantine comes as solution *(Namenda* solution), the Parkinson drug ODT form of carbidopa-levodopa *(Parcopa)*, the antidepressant mirtazapine *(Remeron SolTab* – an ODT) – this medication is often given to frail elderly due to the side effect profile (sedation and increased appetite), among others.

Remeron SolTab

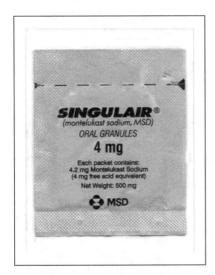

Singulair granules

Rivastigmine, a dementia drug, comes in a patch formulation that makes it easy to give to a person with dementia – it is applied once daily. Some patients with dysphagia need to grind up tablets – be careful patients do not grind up long-acting formulations. Medications that come as beads in capsules can sometimes be sprinkled on a small amount of soft food or mixed with beverages. Typically these are long-acting beads – if they sit in applesauce or pudding the liquid will ruin the slow release. Instruct patients to consume right after they sprinkle; do not chew if long-acting or an irritant. To swallow without chewing requires that the drug be placed in a small amount of soft food. Children can have trouble swallowing some tablets or capsules and montelukast *(Singulair* – used for asthma or allergies) comes in packets that can be sprinkled on food. Valproate, used for seizures in children, also comes as a sprinkle-filled capsule. Many of the ADHD medications can be sprinkled on applesauce or pudding – since young children may have difficulty swallowing tablets or capsules. Lisdexamfetamine *(Vyvanse)*, a popular ADHD drug, comes in a small capsule that can be opened so the parent can mix the contents in a small amount of water. Like *Concerta*, it is designed to be small to make it easier for younger people to swallow. Both are designed to be more difficult to abuse; see the ADHD chapter for more details on the design.

Nausea

If a medication causes nausea it is easier to tolerate if it comes as a dissolving form. The medical condition itself may be causing nausea – and it would be worsened by administering medications that cause additional nausea.

Migraine medications come in various formulations because nausea is common with these types of headaches. Rizatriptan *(Maxalt MLT)* and Zolmitriptan *(Zomig ZMT)* are both ODTs. The primary side effect of the acetylcholinesterase inhibitors used for dementia is nausea – and the *Aricept ODT* or the *Exelon* patch could be helpful. Patches bypass the oral route. [As an interesting aside, most medications that are dosed at night are dosed QHS due to sedation – but donepezil is dosed at night so the nausea is lessened during the day.] Suppositories may be useful to avoid the GI route and reduce any GI complaint. IV is another option. If a hospitalized patient is vomiting or NPO (no oral intake, or not-by-mouth), they will primarily receive the IV route.

Many drugs that cause stomach upset come in long-acting formulations – if less of the drug is released initially (versus disintegrating in the stomach all at once), stomach upset (nausea, abdominal pain, sometimes diarrhea) can be lessened. Metformin XR is a key example – this can be dosed with dinner and is once daily – both are helpful to reduce daytime stomach upset.

STAT Onset Needed!

If the condition causes pain onset FAST then it may be required to bypass the oral route – oral absorption requires at least ½ an hour, and usually an hour, for onset. Sumatriptan (*Imitrex STAT dose, Sumavel DosePro*) is used by many patients who require fast onset for acute migraine pain. Fentanyl sublingual forms are used for acute breakthrough pain in patients being treated for cancer. Injections provide fast relief and are frequently used in acute care settings for treating severe pain, such as with the use of patient controlled analgesia (PCA) devices. Sublingual (SL) formulations work faster than oral absorption and drugs that are designed to work faster by SL absorption include fentanyl (for breakthrough cancer pain), buprenorphine, some of the hypnotics, and others.

Nonadherence

If a patient is likely to forget their medicine, or refuses to take it, it is useful to choose a formulation that can be dosed less frequently. Not all long-acting tablets are once daily, however – some are BID. Some of the psychosis medications have been formulated in long-acting formulations to enable caregivers to administer the drug less frequently. Haloperidol comes as the *Haldol decanoate*, which is given every 4 weeks. Paliperidone comes in a monthly injection. Risperidone in the *Risperdal Consta* injection is a 2-week formulation. Another 2-week formulation is the older antipsychotic fluphenazine (*Prolixin decanoate*). Divalproex comes in a sprinkle formulation that can be used on food for patients with bipolar who require a mood stabilizer – this way, they may not be aware they have received the drug. This formulation is also used for seizure control in children who cannot swallow capsules or tablets.

Risperdal Consta

School-Time Dosing

Many of the stimulant medications that are used for ADHD are designed to avoid noon-time dosing (and to provide a more steady drug response). If a child has to go to the nurse's office to get the dose, they are stigmatized, and may have to wait in line (with the children getting inhalers, or insulin) and miss playtime. In addition they may need a little bit of medication to get them going in the morning (IR) so they are alert in homeroom, and more later (via a long-acting formulation) to carry them throughout the day. *Concerta* comes in the *OROS* deliver system that provides both IR/ER release – and there are others that provide a similar delivery. Methylphenidate comes in a patch (*Daytrana*) that <u>is applied each morning</u> (to the hip) to provide a steady release of medication throughout the day.

Long-Acting Formulations

These are useful to primarily permit once-daily dosing but are not always once-daily, and may help with side effects such as reduced GI upset or reduced dry mouth (for example, from long-acting anticholinergics used for OAB). When a drug delivery is spread-out (in a more even, smooth delivery), side effects are generally lessened since the "peak" is lower. <u>Side effects occur more readily when more of the drug is available to interact with the wrong receptors</u>. Patches generally cause decreased side effects due to slow, even delivery.

<u>Certain drugs are designed as slow release to avoid irritation to the GI lining. Or, they may be enteric-coated. Do not crush or chew</u> any drug that has the following suffix that indicates it is a long-acting formulation: XR, ER, LA, SR, CR, CRT, SA, TR, TD, or have 24 in the name, or the ending –cont (for controlled release, such as *MS Contin* or *OxyContin*), or timecaps or sprinkles.

Note the danger: <u>There are certain drugs that, if crushed, could KILL the patient!</u> These include opioids – where a 24H dose could be released in less than an hour. Be sure to look for the suffix and counsel. There are a few long-acting formulations that can be cut at the score line – but still NOT crushed, such as *Toprol XL.*

Suppositories

<u>Mesalamine comes in a suppository because the disease is often present in the distal portion of the intestine. There is no reason to expose the patient to the drug systemically if the disease is local.</u> With a mesalamine suppository (or enema) the diseased area is treated and the

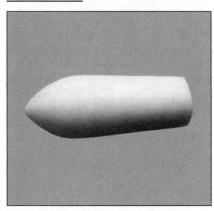

patient suffers less side effects. <u>Suppositories are useful if nausea is present</u>. They can also <u>provide stat relief – including for constipation</u>. Glycerin suppositories are useful to treat (not prevent) constipation in small children and elderly. The bisacodyl suppository is another fast-relief option for constipation. The bisacodyl suppository is to treat constipation (when a bowel movement is needed now) versus the tablet, which is generally dosed QHS in order for the patient to have a bowel movement the following morning. Suppositories are used for either local or systemic drug delivery.

Mesalamine Canasa Suppository

Marketing Formulations that may not Provide Benefit

Sometimes long-acting formulations, or other formulations, <u>are released only because the drug went generic and the manufacturer is looking to retain market share.</u> *Paxil CR* was promoted to help with GI side effects when paroxetine generic became available – but the IR formulation does not usually cause much stomach problems. Most patients using *Ambien*

CR would find the same benefit with zolpidem generic. The new higher dose *Aricept* was promoted when donepezil went generic, but the higher dose does not provide noticeable benefit for the majority of patients.

Patches

Patches applied to the skin (transdermal) have several advantages: the drug delivery is painless (although skin irritation may occur), there are no needles or devices to manage or dispose of, GI side effects are largely absent, peaks are more level (and thus, decreased side effects associated with peaks), and troughs are not as "low"—the drug delivery is smooth. Patches bypass the liver (the drug enters the systemic circulation directly) and can provide better drug delivery for agents with high first-pass metabolism. Bypassing the GI tract can be useful for drugs that degrade in stomach acid. Patches require patient counseling, in primarily these areas:

QUESTION	RESPONSE
Can I cut the patch into pieces?	■ Usually NO, except *Lidoderm*, which is designed to be cut and applied over the painful area. ■ Some patients cut matrix patches because they were instructed to cut them, such as with some of the fentanyl patches; this is NOT advisable as the dose is changed. Fentanyl patches are available in enough doses (5) to make this avoidable, and in generics, to help with cost.
Can the patch be exposed to heat, such as from a fever, or from an electric blanket or heating pad?	In almost all cases NO heat exposure; this causes the drug to pour out of the patch, resulting in toxicity. With fentanyl and buprenorphine this can be quickly toxic (fatal).
The patch is bothering my skin. What can I do?	■ Check if patient is alternating the application site. An alternative site (if permitted) may be beneficial. ■ The skin should not be shaved beforehand; shaving is irritating. ■ In some cases a topical steroid, such as hydrocortisone (OTC) can be applied (only afterwards; the vehicle is an emollient and will prevent the patch from sticking well.)
Which patches need to be removed prior to an MRI? If the patch contains metal (usually aluminum) it will burn the skin during an MRI procedure.	Testosterone *(Androderm)* Clonidine *(Catapres-TTS)* Fentanyl *(Duragesic,* generics) Rotigotine *(Neupro)* Scopolamine *(Transderm Scop)* *Salon Pas Power Plus* (OTC) Nicotine *(NicoDerm CQ)* These change; check the instructions.

Patch Questions Continued

QUESTION	RESPONSE
The patch does not stick (it falls or peels off). Can the patch be covered with tape if it will not stick? With most patches, if it comes off, a new patch is reapplied, to the same or a different site.	■ NO; most CANNOT be covered with tape. A few permit tape around the edges. ■ If patches are placed on lubricated skin they will not stick! Place on dry, non-lubricated skin. No moisturizer or bath oils beforehand. ■ Press down for the right amount of time, with palm over the patch; some require a rather long time (check), such as the fentanyl patch which takes 30 seconds to adhere to the skin. ■ If the skin is hairy the patch will not stick. Although patches are NOT placed on hairy skin, do NOT shave right before the patch application. This can cause little bumps on delicate skin, and patches cannot be placed on irritated or broken skin. Cut hair close to the skin or shave days in advance. Or, use a permitted site that is not as hairy. ■ Try NOT to touch the sticky-side of the patch. ■ DANGER: Do NOT cover fentanyl patches except for the *Duragesic* or buprenorphine (*Butrans*) patches but only with permitted coverings; these two products state: "Can be covered with *Bioclusive* or *Tegaderm* see-through dressings." (NEVER with any other bandage or tape.) ■ *Catapres-TTS* has a cover that goes over the patch to hold it in place.
Patch Application Frequency	Testosterone *(Androderm):* Nightly, not to scrotum, use steroid cream if irritation (after patch has been removed). Clonidine *(Catapres-TTS)*: Weekly Estradiol (*Climara, Menostar*): Weekly, not on breasts. Estradiol (*Alora, Vivelle*): Twice weekly, not on breasts. Estradiol/norethindrone (*Climara Pro*): Weekly, not on breasts. Fentanyl (*Duragesic*): Q72H, if runs out after two days, change to Q48H. Diclofenac (*Flector*): Twice daily *Lidoderm*: 1-3 patches/12 hours, then leave off 12 hours. Methylphenidate (*Daytrana*): Daily, early morning, 2 hours prior to school, alternate hips daily. Nicotine (*NicoDerm CQ*): Daily Nitroglycerin patches: On 12-14 hours a day, off 10-12 hours. *Ortho-Evra* contraception patch: Apply once weekly for 3 weeks, off for the 4th week. Oxybutinin (*Oxytrol*): Twice weekly Rivastigmine (*Exelon*): Daily; remove/reduce strength if nausea. Rotigotine (*Neupro*): Daily Scopolamine (*Transderm Scop*): 4 hours before expected motion sickness, remove after 3 days, or sooner. Selegiline (*Emsam)*: Daily

Patch Questions Continued

QUESTION	RESPONSE
Where is the patch applied? Most require alternating sites to reduce skin irritation.	Check individual agent. Common application sites include upper chest or upper/sides of back (below the neck), upper thigh, upper outer arm. ■ *Daytrana* is on hip, alternating R/L hips daily. ■ *Transderm Scop* is behind an ear, alternating ears. ■ Estrogen patches are mostly lower abdomen; some can be applied to upper buttock. Never to breasts. ■ Testosterone patch is never to scrotum (testicles and surrounding sac). ■ Topical pain patches are over the painful area/s –this is NOT the opioid patches, which work systemically, but for patches such as *Flector, Lidoderm* and *SalonPas,* other OTCs.
How do I dispose of used patches?	■ For most: Remove, fold patch to press adhesive surfaces together, then discard but NOT in the toilet—no flushing! ■ Flushing exception: The DEA permits flushing of highly potent narcotic patches (fentanyl, methylphenidate patch *(Daytrana)*, since these are dangerous (a child or animal could ingest fatal amount.) ■ Alternatively, the fentanyl patch can be cut up and mixed with noxious substance, then disposed in the trash—more information in drug disposal chapter. ■ The *Butrans* patch can be placed and sealed into the Patch-Disposal Unit that comes with the drug, then disposed in the trash (the package labeling states it can be flushed as an alternative; however, this is not on the FDA's list of drugs that can be flushed. The buprenorphine patch would be dangerous if placed in the mouth; it has good SL absorption.)

BIOSTATISTICS & PHARMACOECONOMICS

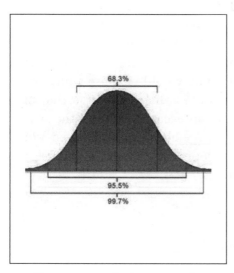

BIOSTATISTICS

Background

Health care is evolving at an exponential rate. As pharmacists, the "drug experts," it is our responsibility to review and evaluate biomedical literature assessing safety, efficacy and economic issues related to new drugs and innovative uses of current medications. Biomedical literature presents clinical data, using statistical methods and tools to answer research questions and aid in clinical guideline development and consensus statements on the optimal treatment of various medical conditions. While there are few types of studies that do not require statistical analysis (e.g., case studies, case series), most robust studies are based on statistical analysis and pharmacists should acquire the basic knowledge of statistical methods to best interpret available data.

Descriptive Statistics

Descriptive statistics are designed to describe the basic features of the data and provide simple summaries in a meaningful way. They are utilized to present quantitative descriptions in a manageable form. One of the most common ways to evaluate data is to analyze its distribution. Measures of central tendency estimate the "center" of a distribution of values, or the point around where the numbers cluster. There are three primary ways of estimating central tendency: the mean, the median and the mode. Although they all estimate the "center," the values obtained can be quite different.

Mean

The mean is the average value of a sample distribution. It is calculated by adding up the values in a list, and dividing by the number of values present. The mean will reflect (or be sensitive to) the outlying values – which may not be representative of the norm. For example, in the list 1,3,4,3,4,2,11, the outlier is 11, and the mean would be affected by this value. Means can be used when the data are not skewed. The mean is used for continuous data.

$$\text{Mean} = \frac{\text{Sum of all values}}{\text{Number of values}}$$

In this example, the mean would be 4 (1+3+4+3+4+2+11/7).

Median

The median is the value in the middle of a ranked list – to calculate it, arrange all the observations in numerical order (lowest to highest) and pick the middle value. Half of the values will be above the median, and half will be below. If the list contains an even number of values, then select the 2 values in the middle of the ranked list, add them together and divide by 2 to get the median. Unlike the mean, the median is not influenced by outliers. Another term for the median is the 50th percentile, which means that 50% of the values are below and the other 50% are above the median. For example, if students are ranking a professor from 1-10 (10 being the best) and the class size is small, the median would be more appropriate to represent the data than the mean. If only 1 or 2 students did not like the course, they may rank the professor low (1 or 2). By using the median value to represent the middle, the outlier effect on the data is minimized. Median values should be used when data are skewed. When the mean and the median values are very different, the data set is skewed. Median values can be used with both continuous and ordinal, or ranked, data.

Mode

The mode is the value that occurs most frequently in a set of data.

Range

The range is the difference between the highest and the lowest values.

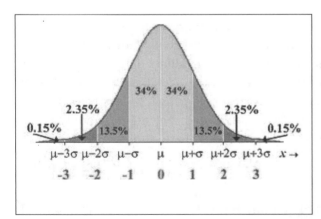

Normal Distribution

A "normal" distribution is also known as a bell shaped, or Gaussian, curve. Generally, clinical studies rely on "sample" populations that appear to be representative of the population of interest. When we look at a sample, we do not have the entire population and thus are forced to estimate. When the population group is large, the distribution approximates a normal, bell shaped curve (see picture) where μ is the mean, and σ is the standard deviation (SD). In a Gaussian or normal distribution, the mean, mode and median would all have the same (or similar) value and would look like the figure above. Notice the curve is symmetric around the mean and the skew is zero.

Standard Deviation (SD)

The standard deviation shows how much variation, or dispersion, there is from the mean. The closer the numbers cluster around the mean, the smaller the standard deviation. If the SD is small, one would conclude that the drug being studied had a similar effect on most subjects. SD is expressed in the same units as the data, is used for data that is normally distributed, is always a positive number, and can be used for continuous data only. In a normal distribution, roughly 68% of the values are within 1 standard deviation from the mean and 95% are within 2 standard deviations. Standard deviation is calculated by taking the square root of the variance.

Skewness

Data that do not have a normal distribution are said to be skewed data. The asymmetric data can be skewed to the right or skewed to the left. Data that are skewed to the right have a positive skew (curve C in figure below) and data that are skewed to the left have a negative skew (curve A in figure below). The direction of the skew refers to the direction of the longer tail, not to the bulk of the data or curve hump. Notice that in curve B, the right and left are perfect mirrors of one another indicating symmetrical data.

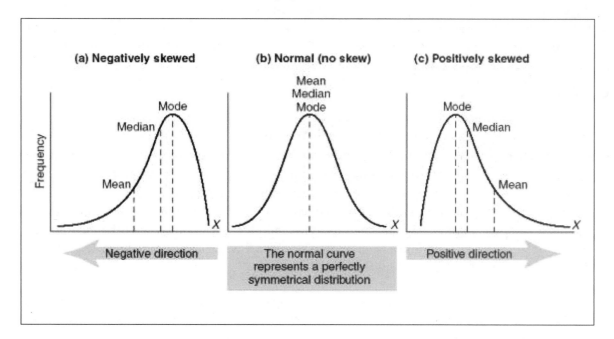

Null Hypothesis (H$_o$)

The null hypothesis states that there is no difference (or relationship) between groups (e.g., Drug A = Drug B). A study is designed to disprove this assertion by testing for a statistically significant difference between Drug A and Drug B (this is called the alternate hypothesis or H$_A$). If the study data concluded that there was a statistically significant difference between Drug A and Drug B, then the null hypothesis would fail to be accepted (therefore, it would be rejected).

Alternative Hypothesis (H_A)

The alternative hypothesis states that there is a treatment difference (or a relationship among variables) between groups in the trial (e.g., Drug A ≠ Drug B). If you fail to accept (or reject) the null hypothesis (H_0), you are accepting the alternative hypothesis.

p-value

The p-value is the likelihood (or probability) that chance would produce a difference as large or larger than the one found in the study, if the null hypothesis is true. In simple terms, it is the probability that the result obtained was due to chance. Generally, a p-value of < 0.05 (and sometimes < 0.01 or others, depending on the trial design) indicates statistical significance. If the p-value is less than 0.05, then there is less than a 5% probability that the result was obtained by chance. In other words, the p-value is the probability of a random difference, given that the null hypothesis is true.

Conversely, there is a high probability the result was not obtained by chance and we can state that the conclusion is "statistically significant." When the p-value is smaller than the significance level (or alpha level), we say that the difference found between groups is statistically significant and we fail to accept (or reject) the null hypothesis. Again, we fail to accept (or reject) the null hypothesis when the p-value is less than the predetermined significance level (say <0.05), indicating that the observed result is highly unlikely under the null hypothesis.

Confidence Interval (CI)

The confidence interval (CI) is a range of values derived from the sample that has a given probability of encompassing the "true" value. It reflects the margin of error that inherently goes along when we use a sample statistic to estimate the true value of the population parameter. Therefore, CIs are used to help determine the validity of the sample statistic by attempting to capture the true population parameter. The confidence interval tells us that there is a given probability that the population's true value is contained within this interval. The most common confidence coefficient used in medicine is 95%; however, other coefficients may be used. A higher confidence interval will produce a wider range of values. A 95% CI can also be stated as a 5% degree of uncertainty.

CIs can be used descriptively or inferentially. An example of descriptive use: a study reports that the mean weight of newborns at one hospital in the past 12 months was 7.7 lbs, with a 95% confidence interval (6.6 - 8.8 lbs) – meaning we are 95% confident that the confidence interval contains the sample statistic. Inferential use looks at the values as a way of comparing groups and determining level of significance. Few rules apply when looking at CIs for inferential use:

- When the 95% CI for the estimated difference between groups (or within the same group over time) does not include zero, the results are significant at the 0.05 level.

- When the 95% CI for an odds ratio, risk ratio or hazard ratio that compares 2 groups does not include 1, the results are significant at the 0.05 level.

See examples of inferential use of CIs below using the difference in table 1 and RR in table 2.

LUNG FUNCTION	ROFLUMILAST (N = 745)	PLACEBO (N = 745)	DIFFERENCE (95% CI)	P-VALUE
Change in pre-bronchodilator FEV$_1$ (mL)	46	8	38 (18 – 58)	p = 0.0003
Change in pre-bronchodilator FEV$_1$/FVC (%)	0.314	0.001	0.313 (-0.26 – 0.89)	p = 0.2858

EXACERBATIONS	ROFLUMILAST	PLACEBO	RR (95% CI)	P-VALUE
Severe (mean rate, per patient per year)	0.11 (n = 69)	0.12 (n = 81)	RR 0.89 (0.61 – 1.29)	p = 0.5275
Moderate (mean rate, per patient per year)	0.94 (n = 299)	1.11 (n = 343)	RR 0.84 (0.72 – 0.99)	p = 0.0325

Clinical Significance

Note that a measure of statistical significance is not the same as "clinical significance". Statistical significance reflects the influence of chance on the outcome; clinical significance reflects the biological value of the outcome. For example, if a blood pressure drug lowers SBP by 3 mmHg, it may be statistically significant (with a p-value < 0.05) versus placebo, but clinically the drug will not be used since other drugs lower BP to a greater degree. It would not be "clinically significant" because it does not measure up to other available drugs and would not have a useful clinical benefit.

Type I error

The alpha level (α) is the probability chosen by the researcher to be the threshold of statistical significance. A type I error occurs when the null hypothesis is true, yet it is rejected in error. Said another way, it was concluded that there was a difference between two groups when, in fact, there was not. The probability of a type I error is represented by the Greek letter, alpha (α). Commonly, α is set to 0.05, which means that 5% of the time the null hypothesis will be rejected in error. When we choose the p-value of < 0.05 for statistical significance, we accept the fact that this error will occur < 5% of the time. A type I error is also known as a false positive (e.g., a drug is concluded to be better than placebo when it is not).

Type II error

A type II error occurs when the null hypothesis is false, yet it is accepted in error. Said another way, it was concluded that there was no difference between two groups when, in fact, there was. The probability of a type II error is represented by the Greek letter, beta (β). Beta is generally set at 0.1 or 0.2, indicating a willingness to accept a type II error 10 or 20 times in 100 comparisons. A type II error is also known as a false negative (e.g., a drug is concluded not to have benefit over placebo when it truly has). Beta is usually expressed in terms of statistical power, which is calculated as 1-beta.

DECISION BASED ON DATA	UNDERLYING "TRUTH"	
	Ho TRUE	Ho FALSE
Accept Ho	No error	Type II error
Reject Ho	Type I error	No error

Statistical Power

Power of a statistical test is the probability that the test will reject the null hypothesis when the null hypothesis is false (avoiding a type II error). As the power increases, the chance of a type II error occurring decreases. Therefore, power is equal to $1-\beta$. A higher statistical power means that we can be more certain that the null hypothesis was correctly rejected. The power of a study is determined by several factors including the sample size, the number of events (MIs, strokes, deaths, etc.), the effect size and the statistical significance criterion used.

Relative Risk (RR)

The relative risk (or risk ratio) is the probability of an unfavorable event occurring in the treatment group versus the control group. First, the risk must be calculated in each of the groups and then the relative risk compares the risk of developing the event in the treatment group (numerator) over the risk of developing the event in the control group (denominator). The RR is generally expressed as a decimal or can be converted to a percentage. RR is simply a ratio of risks in the 2 groups.

$$Risk = \frac{\text{Number of subjects with unfavorable event}}{\text{Number of subjects in that arm}}$$

$$RR = \frac{\text{Risk in treatment group}}{\text{Risk in control group}}$$

INTERPRETING RR

- RR = 1: no difference in risk between the 2 groups

- RR < 1: the event is less likely to occur in the treatment group than in the control group

- RR > 1: the event is more likely to occur in the treatment group than in the control group

Example #1: A study compared metoprolol vs. placebo in heart failure patients over 12 months. If heart failure progression occurred in 28% of placebo-treated patients and in 16% of metoprolol-treated patients, then the risk ratio is 0.16/0.28 = 0.57, or 57%. Therefore, subjects treated with metoprolol were only 57% as likely as placebo-treated patients to have heart failure progression.

Example #2: Drug A was studied for the prevention of chemotherapy-induced nausea and vomiting (CINV). The trial included 245 patients; 120 patients randomized to Drug A and 125 patients randomized to placebo. There were 20 patients in the placebo group versus 6 patients in the Drug A group who developed CINV. The risk in the Drug A arm is 6 patients divided by 120 patients in this arm, or 5% (6/120 = 0.05 x 100 = 5%). The risk in the placebo arm is 20 patients divided by 125 patients in this arm, or 16% (20/125 = 0.16 x 100 = 16%). The relative risk can be calculated as 0.05/0.16 = 0.3125, or 31%. Therefore, subjects treated with Drug A were only 31% as likely as placebo-treated patients to have CINV. By reporting only the relative risk (as opposed to absolute risk), the value of the treatment may be overstated (as is often done in the lay press).

Another formula that can be used for calculating RR is below:

$$RR = \frac{a/(a+b)}{c/(c+d)}$$

EXPOSURE OR TREATMENT	DISEASE	
	PRESENT	ABSENT
Present (Drug group)	a	b
Absent (Placebo group)	c	d

Example #3: In a group of 100 smokers, 40 people developed lung cancer (CA) while 60 people did not. In a similar group of 100 non-smokers, lung CA developed in 10 people. Calculate the relative risk of developing lung CA from smoking.

$$RR = \frac{40/(40 + 60)}{10/(10+90)} = 4$$

The RR of 4 means that smokers are 4 times as likely to develop lung CA than non-smokers.

Relative Risk Reduction (RRR)

Relative risk reduction measures how much the risk is reduced in the treatment group compared to the control group. It can be calculated by dividing the absolute risk reduction by the control group event rate or by subtracting the relative risk (expressed as a decimal) from 1.

$$RRR = \frac{(\% \text{ risk in control group} - \% \text{ risk in treatment group})}{\% \text{ risk in the control group}} \quad OR \quad 1 - RR$$

Using Example #1 from above: (28% - 16%)/28% = 0.43 or 1-0.57 = 0.43, or 43%; meaning there is a 43% relative risk reduction in heart failure progression in patients being treated with metoprolol.

Using Example #2 from above: (16% - 5%)/16% = 0.69 or 1-0.31 = 0.69, or 69%; meaning there is a 69% relative risk reduction in CINV in patients being treated with Drug A. Expressing the result as a relative risk reduction is more intuitively understandable. RR and RRR are limited in that these data do not reflect how important, or large, the treatment effect is in the population at-large. They only provide a measure of what the risk of an event is in one group (treatment or exposed) compared to the risk of that event in a comparison (or control) group.

Absolute Risk Reduction (ARR)

Absolute risk reduction, or attributable risk, is the difference between the control group's event rate and the treatment group's event rate.

$$ARR = (\% \text{ risk in control group}) - (\% \text{ risk in treatment group})$$

Using Example #1 from above: 28% - 16% = 12%. The ARR is 12%. This is the difference in risk that can be attributed to the intervention (drug).

Using Example #2 from above: 16% - 5% = 11%. The ARR is 11%, therefore, the risk of developing CINV was 11% less with Drug A than with placebo.

Number Needed to Treat (NNT)

The number needed to treat represents the number of people who would need to be treated with the intervention (drug) for a certain period of time in order to prevent 1 adverse outcome.

$$NNT = \frac{1}{(\% \text{ risk in control group}) - (\% \text{ risk in treatment group})} \quad OR \quad \frac{1}{ARR \text{ (expressed as a decimal)}}$$

Example #1 from above: 1/0.12 = 8.3, or 9 (must always round up since you cannot divide a person into fractions). Therefore, for every 9 patients who received metoprolol for 1 year, you would expect heart failure progression to be prevented in one patient.

Using Example #2 from above: 1/0.11 = 9.09 or 10 (must always round up). You would need to treat 10 patients to prevent CINV in 1 patient. The NNT puts the results of a trial in a clinically relevant context. When the treatment or exposure causes harm (e.g., cigarette smoking, *Vioxx*, etc), the term NNT does not work and it is more accurate to report the results as the number needed to harm (NNH) which is calculated the same way as NNT. However, with NNH, we always round down.

Odds

Odds are not the same as risks. Risk is the probability of an event occurring with all possibilities for it to occur whereas odds represent the probability of the event occurring compared with the probability that it will not occur. Using the example of 100 smokers, if 40 smokers developed lung cancer and 60 smokers did not develop lung cancer, the risk would be 40/100, or 40% vs. the odds which would be 40/60, or 67%.

Odds Ratio (OR)

The odds ratio is the ratio of two odds, or the ratio of the odds of an event occurring in the treatment group to the odds of an event occurring in the control group. It is a measure of association between an exposure and an outcome. Odds ratios are used mostly in case-control studies, but they are the unit of outcome provided by logistic regression analyses which is a valuable statistical tool.

EXPOSURE OR TREATMENT	DISEASE	
	PRESENT	ABSENT
Present (Drug group)	a	b
Absent (Placebo group)	c	d

$$\text{Odds Ratio (OR)} = \frac{ad}{bc}$$

Using Example #3 from above: In a group of 100 smokers, 40 people developed lung CA while 60 people did not. In a similar group of 100 non-smokers, lung CA developed in 10 people. The odds of a smoker developing lung CA would be 40/60 = 0.67, whereas the odds of a non-smoker developing lung CA would be 10/90 = 0.11. The odds ratio is then 0.67/0.11, or 6, meaning that smokers are 6 times as likely to develop lung cancer compared to non-smokers. An odds ratio of 1 indicates no difference between groups. When the event rate is small, odds ratios are very similar to the relative risk.

Hazard Ratio (HR)

A hazard rate is the estimated risk of an unfavorable event occurring by a given point in time. A hazard ratio is the effect of the hazard rate between the different groups (e.g., treatment group vs. control group, men vs. women) or a ratio of the 2 hazards. Hazard ratios are used in clinical trials with time-to-event (or survival) analysis. Hazard ratios assume that the ratio is constant over time.

$$\text{HR} = \frac{\text{Hazard in the treatment arm}}{\text{Hazard in the control arm}}$$

- HR = 1: no difference between the 2 groups

- HR < 1: unfavorable event (hazard) is happening slower for the treatment group than the control group

- HR > 1: unfavorable event is happening faster for the treatment group than the control group

For example, a clinical trial reports that the drug treated group died at 4 times the rate per unit of time as the control group. The hazard ratio would be 4, indicating patients in the treatment group are 4 times as likely to die compared to the control group.

Correlation

Correlation is a measure of the relation between two variables. The direction and magnitude of the linear correlation can be quantified with a correlation coefficient. The most widely-used type of correlation coefficient is the Pearson Correlation Coefficient, abbreviated r. Values of the correlation coefficient vary from -1 to 1. If the coefficient is 0, then the two variables do not vary together at all (no correlation). If the coefficient is positive, the 2 variables tend to increase or decrease together. If the coefficient is negative, the 2 variables are inversely related, that is, as one variable decreases, the other variable increases. If the coefficient is 1 or -1, the two variables vary together completely, that is, a graph of the data points forms a straight line.

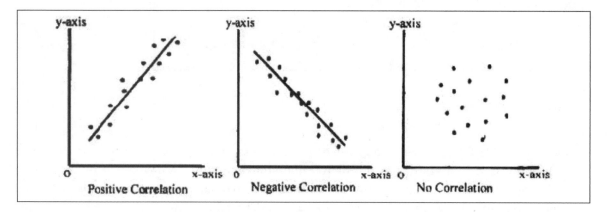

Variables

A dependent variable is the outcome of interest, which should change in response to some intervention. An independent variable is the intervention, or what is being manipulated. For example, aspirin is compared against placebo to see if it leads to a reduction in coronary events. The dependent variable (or outcome of interest) is the number of coronary events while the independent variable (the intervention) is aspirin.

Types of Data

Discrete Data

Discrete data can have only a limited, or finite, set of values (i.e., not continuous) and can assume only whole numbers. There are 2 types of discrete data:

1. NOMINAL DATA

Consists of categories, where the order of the categories is arbitrary (e.g., marital status, gender, ethnicity). The numbers do not have a true numerical, or quantitative, value (e.g., 0 = male, 1 = female).

2. ORDINAL DATA

Consists of ranked categories, where the order of the ranking is important. However, the difference between categories cannot be considered to be equal. These are usually scoring systems that are ranked by severity (e.g., Apgar score, Likert scales, NYHA functional class) but cannot be measured/quantified. There is no consistent correlation between the rank and the degree of severity. For example, a trauma score of 4 does not necessarily mean you are twice as ill as a trauma score of 2.

Continuous Data

Continuous data can take an infinite number of possible values (such as height, weight, A1C, blood pressure) within a defined range. Continuous data can include fractional data (e.g., A1C of 7.3%). Types of continuous data include:

1. INTERVAL DATA

Interval data is used to measure continuous data that have legitimate mathematical values. The difference between 2 consecutive values is consistent along any point of the scale, but the zero point is arbitrary. (e.g., Celsius temperature scale).

2. RATIO DATA

Ratio data has equal intervals between values and a meaningful zero point (e.g., height, weight, time, length).

Determining the appropriate statistical test depends on many factors including the type of data, number of groups being compared, whether the samples are independent or paired and the assumptions within a specific test. Below is a chart outlining some of the statistical tests commonly used in clinical trials.

COMPARISON OF STATISTICAL TESTS*

NUMBER OF GROUPS COMPARED	INDEPENDENT SAMPLES	PAIRED SAMPLES	CORRELATION
Nominal Data			
2	Chi-squared test or Fisher's Exact test	McNemar test	Phi
3 or more	Chi-squared test	Cochran Q	
Ordinal Data			
2	Wilcoxon rank sum test or Mann-Whitney U test ‡	Wilcoxon signed-rank test ‡	Spearman's
3 or more	Kruskal-Wallis test ‡	Friedman test ‡	
Continuous Data			
2	Student's t-test**	Paired Student's t-test** or Wilcoxon signed-rank test ‡	Pearson's
3 or more	Analysis of variance (ANOVA)** or Kruskal-Wallis test ‡	ANOVA	

* Other tests may also apply   *** Parametric test*   *‡ Nonparametric test*

ADDITIONAL DESCRIPTIVE TERMINOLOGY WITH CLINICAL TRIALS

Placebo

A placebo is made to look exactly like a real drug but consists of an inactive substance, such as a starch or sugar. Placebos are now used only in research. A placebo administered to study participants serves as a reference to distinguish the true effects of an active drug from anticipatory or coincidental effects. Placebos are used in clinical trials to "blind" people to their treatment allocation and to minimize bias. Placebos should be indistinguishable from the active intervention (the actual drug) to ensure adequate blinding.

Study Design Types

Observational Study

An observational study is a type of study in which individuals are observed or certain outcomes are measured under precisely defined conditions in a systematic and objective manner. No attempt is made to affect the outcome (no intervention). Observational studies follow subjects with a certain condition or those who receive a particular treatment over time. They may be compared to another group who are not affected by the condition or taking the particular treatment. Large observational studies can clarify the tolerability profile of marketed medicines. A example of an observational study is the Women's Health Initiative trial.

Case-Control Study

Case-control studies compare patients who have a disease or outcome of interest (the cases) with patients who do not have the disease or outcome (the controls), and look back retrospectively to compare how frequently the exposure to a risk factor is present in each group to determine the relationship between the risk factor and the disease. Case control studies are observational because no intervention is implemented and no attempt is made to alter the course of the disease. For example, did subjects exposed to statins have a higher incidence of liver damage? Case control studies are good for studying rare diseases or outcomes, can be conducted in less time since the condition has already occurred, and are useful to establish an association. They are often used to generate hypotheses that can then be studied via a prospective cohort or other studies.

Cohort Study

A cohort is a group of people who share a common characteristic or experience within a defined period (e.g., year born, exposure to pollutant/drug/vaccine, having undergone a certain procedure, etc.). This study type follows the cohort over time (longitudinal) and the outcomes are compared to a subset of the group who were not exposed to the intervention, such as a drug (e.g., the Framingham studies). They are also good studies for outcomes when a randomized study is unethical. Cohort studies may be prospective in design (they are carried out into the future) but can be done retrospectively as well (e.g., patient medical charts).

Cross-Sectional Study

Cross-sectional studies are descriptive and are used to estimate the relationship between an outcome of interest and population variables as they exist at one particular time. Cross-sectional studies are used to determine prevalence of disease. By identifying associations between exposures and outcomes, they can be used to generate hypotheses about causation that can be tested with other study designs.

Randomized Controlled Trial (RCT)

A study design that randomly assigns participants into an experimental (or treatment) group or a control group, thus reducing allocation bias. The clinical trial setting can be controlled in many ways. "Blinding" on the part of the subjects and researchers reduces bias. Single blinding means that the subjects do not know if they received the active drug or placebo. Double-blinding means that neither the subjects nor the researchers know which subjects received the active drug and which subjects received the placebo. RCTs are commonly used to test a medication for efficacy and safety within a given patient population. A randomized, placebo-controlled, double-blinded, multicenter trial with adequate statistical power is the gold standard for drug trials. These types of trials are scientifically robust (having high degree of internal validity) but they are expensive in terms of time and money.

Crossover Study

A longitudinal trial in which the study participants receive each treatment in a random order. With this type of study, every patient serves as his or her own control. For example, comparing drugs A and B, half of the participants are randomly allocated to receive them in the order A then B and half of the participants are to receive them in the order B then A. A washout period is required in crossover studies. This is the time between discontinuing the first treatment and before the initiation of the second treatment and is designed in an attempt to reduce the influence of the 1st phase of the trial on the 2nd phase.

Non-Inferiority Trial

A non-inferiority trial is a comparison with an active control to determine whether the difference in response between the new drug and the active control is small enough (less than a pre-specified margin) to demonstrate that the new treatment is not less effective (or is only slightly less effective) than the control in achieving the primary outcome. Non-inferiority trials are appropriate when a proven effective treatment already exists and assigning some patients to a placebo would be unethical because the treatment is life-saving or prevents irreversible damage.

Clinical trials may not provide "real life" comparisons

Patients in clinical trials may not be reflective of those treated in everyday clinical practice. Patients in clinical trials tend to be younger, more compliant with therapy, more likely to reach target doses of the drug and do so more quickly than in everyday practice. They are not as likely to have a complex presentation as real-life patients. For example, practitioners may be using a drug that is cleared renally in patients with moderate to severe renal impairment, where this subgroup of patients may have been excluded from clinical trials related to the drug in question. Therefore, we will not know how to use the drug safely in this patient population.

Meta-Analysis

A method for systematically combining pertinent qualitative and quantitative study data from several selected studies (primary research) to develop a single conclusion that has greater statistical power. Meta-analysis can be used for the following purposes:

- To establish statistical significance with studies that have conflicting results

- To develop a more correct estimate of effect magnitude

- To provide a more complex analysis of harms, safety data, and/or benefits

- To examine subgroups with individual numbers that are not statistically significant

However, there are many potential flaws in this type of pooled data. For example, the populations studied can differ, there can be different lengths of treatment and the inclusion and exclusion criteria may not be identical. The differences in the trials will confound the results of the meta-analysis. For example, a meta-analysis that looked at the effects of different studies of *Echinacea* for common cold prevention compared studies that used different parts of the *Echinacea* plant, harvested at different seasons, and used in patients with different criteria for defining common cold. This will question the validity of the results, and if any firm conclusion can be drawn.

PHARMACOECONOMICS

Background

Health care costs in the United States rank among the highest of all industrialized countries. In 2011 (the most recent data available), total health care expenditures reached 2.7 trillion dollars, which translates to an average of $8,680 per person, or about 17.9% of the nation's gross domestic product. This increase continues to outpace inflation and the growth in national income and is not sustainable. The increasing costs have resulted in a need to understand how our limited resources can be used most effectively and efficiently in the care of our patients and society as a whole. Therefore, it is necessary to scientifically evaluate the costs and outcomes of interventions such as drug therapy.

Definitions

Pharmacoeconomics is a collection of descriptive and analytic techniques for evaluating pharmaceutical interventions (drugs, devices, procedures, etc.) in the health care system. Pharmacoeconomic research identifies, measures, and compares the costs (direct, indirect and intangible) and consequences (clinical, economic and humanistic) of pharmaceutical products and services. Various research methods can be used to determine the impact of the pharmaceutical product or service. These methods include, but not limited to: cost-effectiveness analysis, cost-minimization analysis, cost-utility analysis, and cost-benefit analysis. Pharmacoeconomics is often termed health outcomes research particularly when a process or clinical/care pathway is evaluated (not a medication).

Clinicians and other decision makers can use these methods to evaluate and compare the total costs and consequences of pharmaceutical products and services. When looking at certain analyses, it is important to consider whose interests are being taken into account. What may be viewed as cost-beneficial for society or for the patient may not be cost-beneficial for hospital administrators and/or hospital employees (e.g., a shorter length of stay when a longer length of stay is fully reimbursed).

Pharmacoeconomic analyses are done as a supplement to the randomized clinical trials. From clinical trials, a drug may demonstrate safety and efficacy. With pharmacoeconomic studies, health care providers can decide where, if at all, this drug fits into the decision tree for a specific condition. They may decide, in some cases, not to use the drug at all (even if a mortality benefit is present) due to high cost and a limited budget. Pharmacoeconomic studies serve to guide optimal healthcare resource allocation, in a standardized and scientifically based manner.

The ECHO model (Economic, Clinical and Humanistic Outcomes) can be used to determine pharmacoeconomic benefit and incorporates these elements:

- Economic outcomes: Include direct, indirect and intangible costs of the drug compared to a medical intervention.

- Clinical outcomes: Include medical events that occur as a result of the treatment or intervention.

- Humanistic Outcomes: Include consequences of the disease or treatment as reported by the patient or caregiver (patient satisfaction, quality of life).

Costs

The majority of pharmacoeconomic methods require proper identification of the costs involved with an intervention. Costs can be categorized into 4 types:

Direct medical costs: Include medications, medication administration, hospitalizations, clinic visits, emergency room visits, nursing services

Direct non-medical costs: Include travel costs (gas, bus, hotel stays for family), child care services (for children of patients)

Indirect costs: Include loss of productivity of the patient (and possibly of caregiver)

Intangible costs: Include pain and suffering, anxiety, weakness

Pharmacoeconomic Methodologies

Cost-Effectiveness Analysis

Cost-effectiveness analysis (CEA) is defined as a series of analytical and mathematical procedures that aid in the selection of a course of action from various alternative approaches. Inputs are usually measured in dollars and outputs are usually measured in natural units (e.g., LDL values in mg/dL, clinical cures, length of stay). The main advantage of this method is that the outcomes are easier to quantify when compared to other analyses, and clinicians and decision makers are familiar with these types of outcomes since they are similar to outcomes seen in clinical trials. Therefore, CEA is the most common methodology seen in the literature today. A disadvantage of CEA is the inability to directly compare different types of outcomes. For example, one cannot compare the cost effectiveness of implementing a diabetes program with implementing an asthma program where the outcome units are different (e.g., blood glucose values versus asthma exacerbations). It is also difficult to combine two or more outcomes into one value of measurement (e.g., comparing one chemotherapeutic agent that prolongs survival but has significant side effects to another chemotherapeutic agent that has less effect on prolonging survival and has fewer side effects).

Cost-Minimization Analysis

Cost-minimization analysis (CMA) is used when two or more interventions have already demonstrated equivalency in outcomes and the costs of each intervention are being compared. CMA measures and compares the input costs and assumes outcomes are equivalent. For example, two ACE-inhibitors, captopril and lisinopril, are considered therapeutically equivalent in the literature but the acquisition cost (the price paid for the drug) and administrative costs may be different (captopril is administered TID and lisinopril is administered once daily). A CMA would look at "minimizing costs" when multiple drugs have equal efficacy and tolerability. Another example of CMA is looking at the same drug regimen given in two different settings (e.g., hospital versus home health care). CMA is considered the easiest analysis to perform. However, the use of this method is limited given its ability to compare only alternatives with the same outcome.

Cost-Benefit Analysis

Cost-benefit analysis (CBA) is a systematic process for calculating and comparing benefits and costs of an intervention in terms of monetary units. CBA consists of identifying all the benefits from an intervention and converting them into dollars in the year that they will occur. Also, the costs associated with the intervention are identified and are allocated to the year when they occur. Then, all costs are discounted back to their present day value. Given that all other factors remain constant, the program with the largest present day value of benefits minus costs is the best economic value. In CBA, both benefits and costs are expressed in terms of dollars and are adjusted to their present value. This can be difficult when required to measure the benefits and then assign a dollar amount to that benefit (e.g., when measuring the benefit of patient quality of life, an outcome difficult to measure and assign a dollar value to it. One advantage to using CBA is the ability to determine if the benefits of the intervention exceed the costs of implementation. CBA can also be used to compare multiple programs for similar or unrelated outcomes, as long as the outcome measures can be converted to dollars.

Cost-Utility Analysis

Cost-utility analysis (CUA) is a specialized form of CEA that includes a quality-of-life component associated with morbidity using common health indices such as quality-adjusted life years (QALYs) and disability-adjusted life years (DALYs). With CEA, you can measure the quantity of life (years gained) but not the "quality" or "utility" of those years. In a CUA, the intervention outcome is measured in terms of quality-adjusted life-years (QALY) gained. QALY takes into account both the quality (morbidity) and the quantity (mortality) of life gained. CUA measures outcomes based on years of life that are adjusted by utility weights, which range from 1 for "perfect health" to 0 for "dead". These weights take into account patient and society preferences for specific health states; however, there is no consensus on the measurement, since both patient and society preferences may vary based on culture. An advantage of CUA is that different types of outcomes and diseases with multiple outcomes of interest can be compared (unlike CEA) using one common unit, like QALY. In addition, CUA combines morbidity and mortality into one unit without having to assign a dollar value to it (unlike CBA). Outcome units may also be expressed as quality-adjusted life months (QALMs) and healthy-year equivalents (HYEs).

Four Basic Pharmacoeconomic Methodologies

METHODOLOGY	COST MEASUREMENT UNIT	OUTCOME UNIT
Cost-effectiveness analysis	Dollars	Natural units (life-years gained, mmHg blood pressure, mg/dL LDL, etc.)
Cost-minimization analysis	Dollars	Assumed to be equivalent in comparative groups
Cost-benefit analysis	Dollars	Dollars
Cost-utility analysis	Dollars	Quality-adjusted-life-year (QALY) or other utilities

PRACTICE CASE

A major clinical trial published in *NEJM* is evaluating a new drug (Drug X) to the current standard of care drug (Drug Y) in patients presenting with MIs to the emergency department. The study was a prospective, open-label, randomized, multicenter trial including 3,600 patients (1,800 patients in each arm). Partial results of the trial are depicted below.

Outcomes at 30 days

ENDPOINTS	DRUG X	DRUG Y	P-VALUE
Primary Endpoints			
Death, MI, and urgent revascularization	166 (9.2%)	218 (12.1%)	0.045
Major Bleeding	89 (4.9%)	99 (5.5%)	0.1
Secondary endpoints			
Strokes	13 (0.7%)	11 (0.6%)	0.48
Blood Transfusions	49 (2.7%)	72 (4.0%)	0.02
Revascularization	47 (2.6%)	35 (1.9%)	0.18

Questions

1. Looking at the results of the trial above, which of the following statements is correct?

   a. Drug Y has demonstrated a statistically significant benefit over Drug X in reducing death, MI, urgent revascularization and major bleeding.

   b. Drug X has demonstrated a statistically significant benefit over Drug Y in reducing death, MI, urgent revascularization and major bleeding.

   c. Drug Y has demonstrated a statistically significant benefit over Drug X in reducing death, MI, and urgent revascularization but not in reducing major bleeds.

   d. Drug X has demonstrated a statistically significant benefit over Drug Y in reducing death, MI, and urgent revascularization but not in reducing major bleeds.

   e. There is no statistical difference between Drug X and Drug Y in the primary endpoints.

2. Which of the following statements below are true regarding the clinical trial results above?

   a. Strokes, transfusions and revascularization all met statistical significance.

   b. Drug Y resulted in statistically significantly fewer strokes than Drug X.

   c. Drug X resulted in more clinically significant major bleeding than Drug Y.

   d. Drug Y resulted in statistically significantly fewer revascularizations than Drug X.

   e. None of the above statements are true.

3. In the trial above, which of the following parameter changes would make this data subject to less bias?

    a. Single center
    b. Allowing only one gender type
    c. Cohort study
    d. Non-randomized
    e. Double blind

4. In the trial above, what is the absolute risk reduction in death, MI, and urgent revascularization?

    a. 0.4%
    b. 1.5%
    c. 2.9%
    d. 9.2%
    e. 12.1%

5. In the trial above, what is the relative risk of major bleeding between the two groups?

    a. 0.24
    b. 0.52
    c. 0.67
    d. 0.89
    e. 0.94

Questions 6-15 do not relate to the case.

6. Students took a statistics course in pharmacy school. When the class was completed, the students ranked the course on a scale of 1 to 5, with 1 corresponding to the worst topic possible, and 5 to the most desirable. What type of variable is described above?

    a. Normal distribution
    b. Ordinal
    c. Nominal
    d. Ratio
    e. Correlation

7. A trial is conducted between 2 different beta blockers, referred to as Drug A and Drug B. The null hypothesis is that both drugs will be equal in their effects on lowering BP. The study concluded that the effects of Drug A were better than Drug B in lowering BP (p-value < 0.01). Which of the following statements is correct?

    a. We can accept the null hypothesis.
    b. We can fail to accept the null hypothesis.
    c. There is a 10% chance that Drug A is superior.
    d. There is a 0.1% chance that Drug B is superior.
    e. This trial did not reach statistical significance.

8. Correlation in a clinical trial describes:

    a. The ability of 1 or more variables to predict another
    b. The relationship between 2 variables
    c. Nominal data
    d. Confounding variables
    e. A cause and effect relationship

9. Which of the following statements concerning a Type I error is correct?

    a. A type I error means that the null hypothesis is accepted in error.
    b. A type I error means that the null hypothesis is rejected in error.
    c. A type I error means failing to reject the null hypothesis in error.
    d. A type I error means that the null hypothesis is accepted.
    e. A type I error is a beta error.

10. Which of the following statements concerning case-control studies is correct? (Select **ALL** that apply)

    a. They are retrospective.
    b. The patient serves as their own control.
    c. The researcher analyzes individual patient cases.
    d. They include cases without the intervention.
    e. They provide conclusive evidence of cause and effect.

11. Which of the following statements regarding the median is correct? (Select **ALL** that apply)

    a. It is the value in the middle of a ranked list.

    b. It is not appropriate to use with skewed data.

    c. It is not sensitive to outliers.

    d. It is a measure of dispersion.

    e. In a Gaussian distribution, it is the same as the mean.

12. Choose the best description of the purpose of a pharmacoeconomic analysis:

    a. To measure and compare the costs and outcomes of drug therapy and other medical interventions.

    b. To reduce health care expenditures by limiting medication use to only those who need it most.

    c. To get the best treatments available to as many people as possible.

    d. To examine the indirect costs of medical care in each medical specialty within hospitals, clinics, and outpatient surgery centers.

    e. To reduce the pharmacy drug budget within a hospital setting as a way to control health care costs.

13. Choose the example that represents a direct medical cost: (Select **ALL** that apply)

    a. Lost productivity

    b. Quality of life

    c. Clinic visit

    d. Nursing services

    e. Cost of taking the bus to the hospital

14. A pharmacist is conducting an analysis to determine the best way to manage patients with diabetes based on A1C values. Three treatment regimens will be evaluated based on cost and effects on A1C reduction. Choose the type of analysis the pharmacist should perform:

    a. A cost-utility analysis

    b. A cost-minimization analysis

    c. A cost-optimization analysis

    d. A cost-benefit analysis

    e. A cost-effectiveness analysis

15. A pharmacist is considering which intravenous vasodilator should be preferred at his institution. He has narrowed his search down to two agents. Each drug provides similar health benefits and similar tolerability. The pharmacist will base his decision on drug acquisition, administration, and monitoring costs. The pharmacist should use the following analysis to decide which intravenous vasodilator should be added to his institution's formulary:

    a. A cost-utility analysis

    b. A cost-minimization analysis

    c. A cost-effectiveness analysis

    d. A cost-benefit analysis

    e. A cost-optimization analysis

Answers

1-d, 2-e, 3-e, 4-c, 5-d, 6-b, 7-b, 8-b, 9-b, 10-a,c,d, 11-a,c,e, 12-a, 13-c,d, 14-e, 15-b

PHARMACOGENOMICS

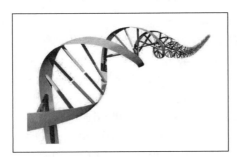

We gratefully acknowledge the assistance of Mahfoud Assem, PharmD, PhD, The University of Iowa College of Pharmacy, in preparing this chapter.

BACKGROUND

Pharmacogenomics is the science which examines <u>inherited variations in genes</u> that dictate drug response and explores ways that the variations can be used <u>to predict whether a patient will have a good response to a drug, a bad response, or no response at all</u>. It is estimated that <u>genetic factors contribute between 20-40%</u> of the <u>differences in drug metabolism and response</u> between patients. The goal of pharmacogenomics is to identify these factors and develop treatment strategies that are tailored to maximize the benefits of a drug (increase efficacy and/or reduce toxicity). Pharmacogenomics is called "personalized medicine" where the drugs are optimized for a persons unique genotype.

DEFINITIONS

<u>Deoxyribonucleic acid (DNA)</u>: Self-replicating genetic material that is the main component of chromosomes. DNA carries genetic information.

<u>Gene</u>: A stretch of DNA that codes for a single protein. One or many genes can be responsible for an observable trait, or phenotype (e.g., hair/eye color, height, drug metabolism efficiency).

<u>Chromosome</u>: A threadlike structure, made up of many genes, that carries genetic information. In most cells, humans have 23 pairs of chromosomes.

<u>Allele</u>: One form of a gene or gene locus (the location on a chromosome, typically forming a group of genes). Each person has two alleles (one from the mother and one from the father) for each gene. If both alleles are the <u>same</u>, the person is <u>homozygous</u> for that gene or trait. If the alleles are different, the <u>person</u> is <u>heterozygous</u> for that gene or trait.

Nucleotide: The basic structural unit of DNA. Nucleotides are named based on their nitrogenous bases – G (guanine), C (cytosine), A (Adenine) and T (thymine). G-C and A-T are the base pairs that link together to form the DNA into the double-stranded, helical structure. RNA is a single strand with the same bases except for Uracil (U), which replaces thymine.

Polymorphism: An inherited variation in the DNA sequence. Polymorphisms occur with fairly high frequency; however, most do not result in a change in phenotype. Polymorphisms most commonly involve variation at a single base pair with the DNA. This is called a single nucleotide polymorphism (SNP, pronounced "snip"). Polymorphisms can also involve larger stretches of DNA; these are called structural variations (SV), which produce structural variants. Human leukocyte antigens (HLAs) are an important part of the immune response; HLAs alert the immune system to target a pathogen for destruction. Certain HLA variants put the patient at high risk for hypersensitivity reactions.

SINGLE NUCLEOTIDE POLYMORPHISMS AND STRUCTURAL VARIANTS

SNPs are the most common genetic polymorphisms in DNA. They occur every 100-300 base pairs and account for about 90% of all differences in human DNA. SVs are more rare than SNPs; however, they affect a large chunk of DNA and have a greater impact on genes than SNPs. Whether the SNP or SV has an effect on gene function (and the action of a drug) depends on the location of the polymorphism and whether it is present on one or both alleles. Pharmacogenomic testing can identify whether a SNP or SV is homozygous or heterozygous and therefore help predict what type of response a patient is likely to have to a drug.

THE EFFECT OF POLYMORPHISMS ON PHARMACOKINETICS AND PHARMACO-DYNAMICS

Genetic polymorphisms can significantly alter the pharmacokinetics of a drug and/or the pharmacodynamic response in a particular patient or population. An example of a pharmacokinetic change is metabolism of drugs by CYP450 2D6. Based on the presence or absence of polymorphisms, patients can be ultra-rapid metabolizers (UMs), extensive metabolizers (EMs), intermediate metabolizers (IMs) or poor metabolizers (PMs). Codeine is converted to morphine by 2D6; therefore, UMs and EMs have an increased risk of toxicity, while PMs are unlikely to benefit from the administration of codeine. An example of a pharmacodynamic change is the presence of a polymorphism in the DNA coding for the solute carrier organic anion transporter family member 1B1 (SLCO1B1) gene. Patients with a variant allele have an increased risk of myalgia when taking statins. Another example is the expression of the HLA-B*1502 allele, which, if present, gives the recipient a 5-10% chance of having a severe skin reaction (e.g., Stevens Johnson syndrome) if they use carbamazepine. The risk in patients without this allele is < 1%. This variant allele is more common in patients of Asian descent; therefore, Asian patients should be tested prior to starting carbamazepine therapy. A fourth example is the necessary expression of the HER2/neu oncogene for the patient to benefit from using trastuzumab (Herceptin) and ado-trastuzumab emtansine (Kadcyla) for the treatment of breast cancer. Patients must be tested prior to starting treatment to ensure the tumor expresses HER2/neu.

The Drugs With Pharmacogenomic Testing table includes drugs where genetic testing is routinely done and/or required according to the product labeling. Following this list are the drugs known to have genetic risk, but where standardized testing is not yet routine. The FDA has recently published guidelines for drug companies that require diagnostic tests to be approved at the same time as the drug if genetic testing is necessary for the safe and effective use of the drug. This, along with a growing body of evidence supporting the benefits of "personalized medicine", will lead to further increases in genetic testing.

Genetic Variation in Warfarin Response

Warfarin consists of two racemic isomers – an S-isomer and an R-isomer. The S-isomer is 3-4 times more potent than the R-isomer. The S-isomer is metabolized by CYP450 2C9, and a reduction in the ability of this enzyme to metabolize warfarin will result in slow metabolism. If lower doses are not used, bleeding risk is increased. The 2C9*2 and the 2C9*3 alleles are loss-of-function alleles; therefore, they are associated with more bleeding. The 2C9*2 allele can lead to a large reduction in metabolism of warfarin whereas the 2C9*3 allele causes an even larger reduction in metabolism. Patients who are homozygous for the 2C9*3 allele have the greatest risk of bleeding.

The 2nd variation resulting in an increased bleeding risk is a variation in the VKORC1 gene. In the VKORC1 SNPs, several SNPs are associated with alteration of VKORC1 activity. These SNPs are grouped together as haplotype A or G. A haplotype is a group of genetic polymorphisms that are inherited together because they are physically present in the same genetic region. Patients with the 'A haplotype' produce less VKORC1 and will require a lower dose of warfarin.

With the patient's genetic information, the warfarin starting dose can be more accurately determined. Genetic testing has been simplified by the availability of several outside companies that test for these variations; however, testing is not yet routinely performed nor has testing been adequately validated. In warfarin initiation, always proceed cautiously and monitor the INR frequently. The chart below shows the ranges of expected maintenance doses of warfarin based on the presence of the 2C9 and VKORC1 alleles.

Expected Maintenance Dose Ranges Based on Warfarin Genotypes

VKORC1	CYP2C9					
	*1/*1	*1/*2	*1/*3	*2/*2	*2/*3	*3/*3
GG	5-7 mg	5-7 mg	3-4 mg	3-4 mg	3-4 mg	0.5-2 mg
AG	5-7 mg	3-4 mg	3-4 mg	3-4 mg	0.5-2 mg	0.5-2 mg
AA	3-4 mg	3-4 mg	0.5-2 mg	0.5-2 mg	0.5-2 mg	0.5-2 mg

Drugs With Required/Strongly Recommended Genetic Testing

DRUG	USED TO TREAT	TESTING	REACTION/PACKAGE WARNINGS
Abacavir *(Ziagen)* abacavir + lamivudine *(Epzicom)* abacavir + zidovudine + lamivudine *(Trizivir)*	HIV	Test for HLA-B*5701 If positive, do not give drug.	Hypersensitivity to abacavir is a multi-organ clinical syndrome; see HIV chapter Discontinue as soon as a hypersensitivity reaction is suspected.
Clopidogrel *(Plavix)*	Acute coronary syndromes, PAD, stroke	Testing of CYP2C19 genotype	Effectiveness of the drug depends on activation to an active metabolite, mainly by 2C19. Poor metabolizers exhibit higher cardiovascular event rates than patients with normal 2C19 function. Tests are available to identify a patient's 2C19 genotype. Consider alternative treatment in patients identified as CYP2C19 poor metabolizers.
Carbamazepine *(Tegretol,* others)	Seizures, other occasional uses	Test for HLA-B*1502 if of Asian ancestry. If positive, do not use unless benefit clearly outweighs risk.	Serious dermatologic reactions with positive HLA-B*1502 alelle, including Toxic Epidermal Necrolysis (TEN) and Stevens-Johnson Syndrome (SJS), have occurred.
Trastuzumab *(Herceptin)*/ **Ado-trastuzumab emtansine** *(Kadcyla)*/ lapatinib *(Tykerb)*/ pertuzumab *(Perjeta)*	Breast and gastric cancer	HER2/neu oncogene If positive, can give drug	HER2/neu over-expression required for use. The test must be 2+ or 3+ positive on immunohistochemical (IHC) testing as weakly positive (1+) tumors do not respond well to therapy
Cetuximab *(Erbitux)*/ **panitumumab** *(Vectibix)*	Colorectal cancer	K-Ras mutations If positive, do not give drug	K-Ras mutations indicate a poor response to therapy. These agents will not work in patients with colorectal cancer who have a K-Ras mutation (~40% of patients). Package inserts state that there is no benefit in patients with K-Ras mutations in codon 12 or 13. Therefore, only patients who are K-Ras mutation-negative (wild type) should receive these medications.
Cetuximab *(Erbitux)*/erlotinib *(Tarceva)*	Non-small cell lung cancer	EGFR If positive, can give drug	These medications have enhanced effectiveness in tumors expressing EGFR or who are EGFR-TK mutation positive
Imatinib *(Gleevec)*	Gastrointestinal stromal tumors (GIST)	cKIT If positive, can give drug	Patients will respond to therapy if GIST is KIT (CD117)+
Maraviroc *(Selzentry)*	HIV	Tropism testing, using the Trofile test If CCR5-positive, can give drug	Adult patients infected with only CCR5-tropic HIV-1 should use maraviroc. Do not use in patients with dual/mixed or CXCR-4-tropic HIV-1 disease as efficacy was not demonstrated in a Phase 2 trial of this patient population.
Imatinib *(Gleevec)*/dasatinib *(Sprycel)*/nilotinib *(Tasigna)*/nosutinib *(Bosulif)*	CML	BCR-ABL If positive, can give drug	In chronic myelogenous leukemia, the Philadelphia chromosome leads to a fusion protein of abl with bcr (breakpoint cluster region), termed bcr-abl. These drugs target and inhibit this kinase.

Drugs With Required/Strongly Recommended Genetic Testing Continued

DRUG	USED TO TREAT	TESTING	REACTION/PACKAGE WARNINGS
Rituximab (Rituxan)/ ofatumumab (Arzerra)	Non-Hodgkin Lymphomas, Hodgkin Lymphoma, Chronic Lymphocytic Leukemia, etc.	CD-20 receptor status on cell surface If positive, can give drug	Directed against CD-20 receptor site on malignant cells but also normal lymphocytes resulting in efficacy and toxicity with antibody dependent cellular cytoxicity (ADCC), complement fixation, natural killer cell activation and apoptosis.
Simeprevir (Olysio)	Hepatitis C	NS3 Q80K polymorphism If positive, do not give drug	Screening patients with HCV gentotype 1a infection for the presence of virus with the NS3 Q80K polymorphism at baseline is strongly recommended. Patients with this polymorphism will not respond and alternative therapy should be given.
Crizotinib (Xalkori)	Metastatic non-small cell lung cancer (NSCLC)	Anaplastic lymphoma kinase (ALK) If positive, can give drug	Crizotinib is a kinase inhibitor indicated for the treatment of patients with locally advanced or metastatic non-small cell lung cancer (NSCLC) that is anaplastic lymphoma kinase (ALK) positive as detected by an FDA-approved test
Vemurafenib (Zelboraf)	Metastatic melanoma	BRAF V600E mutation If positive, can give drug	Vemurafenib is a kinase inhibitor for patients with unresectable or metastatic melanoma with BRAF V600E mutation as detected by an-FDA approved test. This agent is contraindicated in patients with wild-type BRAF melanoma.
Azathioprine and mercaptopurine	Solid organ cancers; leukemia; Crohn's disease, ulcerative colitis	Monitor for TPMT (thiopurine methyltransferase)	Patients with a genetic deficiency of TPMT may have ↑ risk of myelosuppressive effects; those patients with low or absent TPMT activity are at risk for severe myelotoxicity; occurs in ~10% of patients
Lenalidomide (Revlimid)	Myelodysplastic syndrome, others	5q deletion	Patients with 5q deletion myelodysplanstic syndrome have increased risk of hematologic toxicity (neutropenia and thrombocytopenia) from their MDS but also a better response to lenalidomide therapy
Tositumomab (Bexxar)	Non-Hodgkin lymphoma after relapse or failure of standard chemotherapies	MS4A1 testing (CD-20 antigen) If positive, can give drug	Directed against CD-20 receptor site on malignant cells but also normal B- and pre-B-lymphocytes resulting in efficacy and toxicity.
Brentuximab Vedotin (Adcetris)	Hodgkin Lymphoma after failure of autologous stem cell transplant. Systemic anaplastic large cell lymphoma after failure of previous chemotherapies.	TNFRSF8 testing (CD-30 antigen) If positive, can give drug	Directed against CD-30 receptor site on malignant cells but also normal resulting in efficacy and toxicity.
Denileukin Diftitox (Ontak)	Cutaneous T-cell lymphoma	IL2RA testing (CD-25 antigen) If positive, can give drug	Directed against CD-25 receptor site on positive malignant cells.
Ivacaftor (Kalydeco)	CFTR	Should test for CFTR G551D carriers If positive, can give drug	Patients age six years and older who have the specific G551D mutation in the CFTR gene.

Select Drugs Where Pharmacogenomic Testing Should Be Considered

DRUG	USED TO TREAT	TESTING	REACTION/PACKAGE WARNINGS
Allopurinol *(Zyloprim)*	Gout	Increased risk of severe cutaneous reactions with HLA-B*5801 No recommendations for testing.	Discontinue at 1st appearance of skin rash or other signs which may indicate an allergic reaction. In some instances, a skin rash may be followed by more severe hypersensitivity reactions such as exfoliative, urticarial, and purpuric lesions, as well as SJS, (and/or generalized vasculitis, irreversible hepatotoxicity, and, on rare occasions, death).
Codeine	Pain, cough	Extensive metabolizers of CYP2D6 may have exaggerated response to drug due to extensive conversion to morphine metabolite. No recommendation, but use caution – CYP2D6 extensive metabolizers are common.	Over-production of morphine can result in CNS effects, including an ↑ risk of respiratory depression. Use extreme caution in lactating women as most opioids are excreted in breast milk. While use may be acceptable in small amounts, the risk to the infant must be considered. Do not use codeine (in *Tylenol #3*, others), since rapid metabolizers of the CYP2D6 enzyme will produce excessive amounts of morphine, which could be fatal to the infant. See contraindications and warnings in Pain chapter.
Warfarin *(Coumadin, Jantoven)*	Clot Prevention	From package insert: Identification of risk factors for bleeding and certain genetic variations in CYP2C9 and VKORC1 in a patient may increase the need for more frequent INR monitoring and the use of lower warfarin doses.	Increased bleeding risk. Loss-of-function alleles (CYP2C9*2 and CYP2C9*3) and VKORC1 G > A variant, can lead to an increased risk of bleeding. If not testing, use caution by selecting a low starting dose, increasing slowly, and frequent INR monitoring – especially at initiation. If the test indicates variations, a safer starting dose can be calculated.
Capecitabine *(Xeloda)*/fluorouracil (5-FU)	Breast, colon, pancreatic cancers	Dihydropyrimidine dehydrogenase (DPD)	A deficiency in dihydropyrimidine dehydrogenase (DPD) can increase toxicity associated with these agents. The incidence is low but potentially fatal. Most of the testing is performed after unexpected toxicity occurs.
Phenytoin and fosphenytoin *(Dilantin)*	Seizures	Test for HLA-B*1502 if of Asian ancestry. <u>If positive, do not use unless benefit clearly outweighs risk.</u>	Strong association between the risk of developing Stevens-Johnson Syndrome (SJS) and Toxic Epidermal Necrolysis (TEN) and the presence of the HLA-B*1502 allele.
Atomoxetine *(Strattera)*	ADHD	Poor metabolizers of CYP2D6 may have exaggerated response (5 fold increase) to drug due to reduced rate of metabolism. No recommendation, but use caution.	Atomoxetine concentrations have been measured at 5-fold higher concentrations in poor metabolizers versus extensive metabolizers. This can lead to an increase in adverse effects. See ADHD chapter.

Drugs Where Pharmacogenomic Testing Should Be Considered Continued

DRUG	USED TO TREAT	TESTING	REACTION/PACKAGE WARNINGS
Fluorouracil, methotrexate	Lymphomas, leukemias, psoriasis, RA, other	Methylenetetrahy-drofolate Reductase (MTHFR)	Methylenetetrahydrofolate Reductase (MTHFR) polymorphisms influence the metabolism of folates and could modify the pharmacodynamics of antifolates and many other drugs whose metabolism, biochemical effects, or target structures require methylation reactions.
Irinotecan (*Camptosar*)	Colon cancer and other cancers	May test for the UGT1A1*28 allele (homozygous vs. heterozygous carriers)	Patients homozygous for the UGT1A1*28 allele are at risk of neutropenia; initial one-level dose reduction should be considered. Heterozygous carriers of the UGT1A1*28 allele may also be at risk, however, most patients tolerate normal starting doses
Many pain and psych drugs – see Drug Interactions chapter	Various psychiatric disorders	May test for the CYP2D6*2 and CYP2D6*10 alleles.	CYP2D6 poor metabolizers are at risk of variable response to therapies, inappropriate dosage (reduce dosage by 25% for some anti-psychotics) and drug interactions (reduce doses when co-administered with CYP2D6 inhibitors).
Cisplatin (*Platinol*)	Several cancers	Monitor for TPMT	TPMT intermediate or poor metabolizers are at risk of severe toxicity. The drug label states that all children undergoing Platinol treatment have a risk of ototoxicity, and all children should undergo audiometric testing.
Gefitinib (*Iressa*)	Non-small cell lung cancer	EGFR	Better response in Asian population. Limit use to patients that currently benefit, have previously benefited or are enrolled in non-Investigational New Drug (IND) clinical trials.
Tamoxifen (*Nolvadex*)	Breast cancer	Hormone receptors ESR1, PGR status	Available evidence indicates that patients whose tumors are estrogen receptor positive are more likely to benefit from tamoxifen therapy.
Chloroquine (*Aralen*), dapsone (*Aczone*)	Infectious diseases	G6PDH deficiency test not required but follow up with blood count	Hemolytic anemia is more common in G6PDH deficient patients.
Rifampin, isoniazid, and pyrazinamide (*Rifater*)	Tuberculosis	NAT1-2 slow acetylators test not required but monitor liver function monthly	Neuropathy and liver toxicity more common in slow acetylators.

PRACTICE QUESTIONS

1. A 15 year-old girl of Asian ancestry presents with a seizure disorder. The physician plans to initiate carbamazepine therapy, but first orders genetic testing in order to determine if she is at an increased risk for the following adverse drug reaction:

    a. Gastrointestinal bleeding
    b. Hemorrhage
    c. Serious skin reactions
    d. Neuropathy
    e. Tendon rupture

2. When initiating carbamazepine in a patient of Asian descent, test for the following allele:

    a. HLA-B *5701
    b. HLA-B *1502
    c. HLA-B *5801
    d. HLA-B *1501
    e. TPMT activity

3. Trastuzumab is indicated in cancers with an overexpression of this gene:

    a. ALK
    b. BCR ABL+
    c. cKIT
    d. HER2/neu
    e. BRCA2

4. A patient was started on warfarin 5 mg once daily. She presents to the clinic 2 weeks later and is found to have an INR of 4.7 with excessive oral bleeding when she brushes her teeth. Which of the following most likely describes the patient's genotype?

    a. Slow metabolizer of CYP 2C9
    b. Rapid metabolizer of CYP 2C9
    c. Slow metabolizer of CYP 3A4
    d. Rapid metabolizer of CYP 3A4
    e. Rapid metabolizer of CYP 2D6

5. Which of the following statements regarding abacavir is correct? (Select **ALL** that apply.)

    a. Testing for HLA-B*5701 is recommended on initiation or re-initiation of therapy.
    b. If the testing is positive for HLA-B*5701, abacavir cannot be used.
    c. Abacavir is a protease inhibitor that should be boosted with ritonavir.
    d. Abacavir can be taken with or without food.
    e. Abacavir is recommended as a preferred first line agent for newly diagnosed HIV+ patients.

Answers

1-c, 2-b, 3-d, 4-a, 5-a,b,d

DRUG ALLERGIES, ADRs & ADR REPORTING

REFERENCE

FDA MedWatch program, available at: http://www.fda.gov/Safety/MedWatch/default.htm (accessed 2013 Nov 20)

WHAT IS IT? A SIDE EFFECT? AN ADVERSE EFFECT? AN ALLERGY? ANAPHYLAXIS?

Adverse Drug Reactions: Side Effects, Adverse Events and MedWatch Reporting

Side effects or adverse events are <u>not generally avoidable</u> and can <u>occur in anyone with normal doses</u> (although higher doses can increase the side effect severity). <u>Side effects are more common and generally less severe</u> (such as orthostatic hypotension from doxazosin) while <u>adverse events are known complications of a drug but are generally rarer and more severe</u> (such as rash from lamotrigine).

[Note: do not mix these up with medication errors, which are due to someone doing something incorrectly, such as giving the wrong drug to a patient. Medication errors are an important area and are discussed in the Medication Safety chapter.]

True drug allergies, or hypersensitivity reactions, are classified into four types. Type I reactions are immediate (within 15-30 minutes of exposure). The severity can range from minor inconvenience to death. Type II reactions occur minutes to hours after exposure. Examples include hemolytic anemia and thrombocytopenia. Type III reactions are immune-complex reactions. They occur 3-10 hours after exposure. Examples include drug-induced lupus and serum sickness. Type IV reactions are delayed hypersensitivity reactions. They can occur anywhere from 48 hours to several weeks after exposure. The classic example of a type IV reaction is the PPD skin test for tuberculosis, which peaks at 48 hours.

Most drug reactions are characterized as "type A" which means that they are dose-dependent and predictable from the drug's pharmacology. For example, if a patient starts doxazosin at 1 mg QHS they will have much less orthostatic hypotension and dizziness than if they began the medication at a 4 mg dose; <u>thus</u>, this drug is slowly titrated upward to reduce the severity of the side effects. Type B reactions [which are idiosyncratic – this means a particular patient has an independent peculiar reaction (or hypersensitivity) to the drug] are not predictable from the known pharmacology of the drug and the reaction is determined by patient-specific susceptibility factors.

Although side effects or adverse effects can occur in anyone, we need to consider that they may be more likely if a drug is given to a patient at high risk for a certain condition. For example, anyone taking an aminoglycoside for longer than a few days would expect to suffer some degree of renal damage. However, if a patient with impaired renal function receives an aminoglycoside they would be more susceptible to further damage sooner.

- Side effects, adverse events and allergies (which are discussed below) should be reported to the <u>FDA's MedWatch program</u>. This is called an adverse event reporting system (AERS) that provides a central collection for problems caused by drugs. [Note that vaccines are an exception that are not reported under AERS; vaccine adverse drug reactions are reported under a different program called VAERS; this is described in the Immunization chapter.]

- <u>The FDA conducts Phase IV (post-marketing safety surveillance programs)</u> for approved drug and therapeutic biologic products and collates the reports to better understand the drug safety profile in a real world setting. When drugs are tested in trials, high-risk patients are typically excluded. Yet, in real life settings high risk patients are often included. If a drug causes a reaction in 1 out of every 3,000 people, you might not even see the reaction appear in a smaller clinical trial. This is why <u>community-based adverse event reporting is critical</u>.

> **EXAMPLE OF "REAL LIFE" ADVERSE EVENT INCIDENCE VERSUS THAT IN A CLINICAL TRIAL SETTING**
>
> When spironolactone was studied in heart failure patients during the RALES trial, patients with renal insufficiency or elevated potassium levels were excluded due to the known risk of additional hyperkalemia from the use of spironolactone. The drug was found to have benefit in advanced heart failure patients and doctors in the community began to use it in their heart failure patients. In this real life setting, patients with renal insufficiency or elevated potassium were occasionally prescribed spironolactone, and arrhythmias and sudden death due to hyperkalemia were reported.

- Reporting is voluntary. Healthcare professionals and patients may also report adverse events to the drug manufacturer, who is required by law to send the report to the FDA's MedWatch program. The MedWatch form that is used for reporting can be found online via the link provided in the references at the beginning of this chapter. We can also report by calling the FDA directly. We can also call in or report online via the link provided in the references at the beginning of this section. MedWatch is not only used to report problems with drugs; it is also used for reporting problems with biologics, medical devices and some nutritional products and cosmetics.

- If the FDA receives enough reports that a drug is linked to a particular problem they may require that the product's drug information, such as the package insert or labeling, be changed. In especially risky cases they will issue safety alerts to prescribers, usually before the labeling is changed.

EXAMPLE OF A SIDE EFFECT THAT WAS ADDED TO THE PACKAGE INSERT MANY YEARS AFTER THE DRUG HAD BEEN RELEASED DUE TO THE ADR REPORTS RECEIVED BY THE FDA

Oseltamivir *(Tamiflu)* was initially released without any warning of unusual behavior in children. The FDA received enough reports that they issued a warning to prescribers in 2006. After many more reports, in 2008, the FDA required the drug company to update the prescribing information to include a precaution about hallucinations, confusion and other strange behavior in children.

Example of a Posting on the FDA Website of a Drug that is Being Monitored Under Phase IV

DRUG	USAGE	ADVERSE EVENTS	NOTES
Ticagrelor *(Brilinta)*	To reduce the rate of thrombotic cardiovascular events in patients with acute coronary syndrome (ACS) (unstable angina, non-ST elevation myocardial infarction, or ST elevation myocardial infarction).	Adverse event reports of neutropenia, thrombocytopenia, pancytopenia, and clinical gout were identified.	FDA is continuing to evaluate neutropenia, thrombocytopenia, pancytopenia, and clinical gout to determine if regulatory action is required.

Assessing Causality of an Adverse Drug Reaction

When an adverse reaction occurs, it can sometimes be difficult to determine whether a particular drug is the cause. The Naranjo Scale is a validated causality assessment scale that can help pharmacists determine the likelihood that a drug caused an ADR. The pharmacist simply answers the questions on the scale and a probability score is calculated:

QUESTIONNAIRE	YES	NO	DO NOT KNOW
Are there previous conclusive reports on this reaction?	+1	0	
Did the adverse event appear after the suspected drug was given?	+2	-1	
Did the adverse reaction improve when the drug was discontinued or a specific antagonist was given?	+1	0	
Did the adverse reaction appear when the drug was readministered?	+2	-1	
Are there alternative causes that could on their own have caused the reaction?	-1	+2	
Did the reaction reappear when a placebo was given?	-1	+1	
Was the drug detected in any body fluid in toxic concentrations?	+1	0	
Was the reaction more severe when the dose was increased or less severe when the dose was decreased?	+1	0	
Did the patient have a similar reaction to the same or similar drugs in any previous exposure?	+1	0	
Was the adverse event confirmed by any objective evidence?	+1	0	

Scoring > 9 = definite ADR; 5-8 = probable ADR; 1-4 = possible ADR; 0 = doubtful ADR

Characterizing an Adverse Drug Reaction

In order to properly characterize an adverse reaction, sensitivity to a drug or a true drug allergy, pharmacists need to ask the right questions. When patients report an "allergy" to a drug these questions can help place the reaction into the proper context:

- What reaction occurred (was it a mild rash, a severe rash with blisters, trouble breathing?)

- When did it occur? (about how old were you?)

- Can you use similar drugs in the same class (for example, if they report an allergy to penicillin, have they ever used *Keflex*?)

- Ask and include any food allergies and latex allergies in the patient record. Latex allergies should be recorded since some drugs require tubing, have latex vial stoppers, or require gloves for administration.

DRUG SIDE EFFECTS (SENSITIVITIES OR INTOLERANCES)

EXAMPLE OF STOMACH UPSET DUE TO CODEINE BEING REPORTED INCORRECTLY AS A DRUG ALLERGY

Carmen received acetaminophen 300 mg-codeine 30 mg *(Tylenol #3)* for pain relief after a dental extraction several years ago. Carmen got very nauseated from the medicine. When Carmen was admitted to the hospital for a left hip replacement, she reported to the intake coordinator that she was "allergic" to codeine. The intake coordinator did not attempt to clarify the reaction. The hospital's pain management protocol calls for hydromorphone in a patient-controlled analgesic device for post-op pain control. The physician used a less desirable option for pain control due to the reported allergy.

Stomach Upset/Nausea

Stomach upset or nausea is often incorrectly reported as an allergy. The reaction should be listed on the patient profile because the drug bothered the patient and, if possible, the drug should be avoided in the future, but this is not an allergy and should not prevent drugs in the same class from being used. This is more accurately categorized as an intolerance. Modern electronic medical records often allow for documentation of intolerances separate from allergies. An example of an intolerance is the patient who gets stomach upset from codeine (but not hydrocodone or other drugs in the morphine class) or from erythromycin (but not azithromycin or other macrolides).

Mild Rash

Opioids can commonly cause histamine-induced skin rash or itching, particularly in the inpatient setting post-op when opioid-naïve patients are receiving the medication or non-naïve patients are receiving higher-than-normal dosing. This reaction can be reduced or avoided if the patient is pre-medicated with an antihistamine before use, such as diphenhydramine.

Photosensitivity

Many drugs can cause photosensitivity, which requires limiting sun exposure and using sunscreens that block both UVA (causes aging, skin cancer) and UVB (causes sunburn). Sunscreens that cover both UVA and UVB are labeled broad-spectrum.

[Note that there is a different type of skin reaction that occurs when sunlight causes the drug to become toxic; this is an allergic reaction and is rare. The reaction looks like a bad sunburn on only sun-exposed skin.]

Another sensitivity that some people have is to the iodine in contrast dyes. This reaction can cause itching, flushing and a drop in blood pressure, but is not technically a true allergy.

NSAIDs can cause issues with either sensitivity or true allergy; these are discussed in the next section.

Severe Skin Rashes

There are several severe skin rashes that can be caused by drugs, including Stevens-Johnson syndrome (SJS), toxic epidermal necrolysis (TEN), drug reaction with eosinophilia and systemic symptoms (DRESS) and thrombotic thrombocytopenic purpura (TTP). All of these can be life-threatening and require prompt treatment. SJS and TEN result in severe, explosive mucosal erosions, a high temperature and damage to organs (eyes, liver, kidney, lungs). SJS and TEN are not easily distinguished and the key to treating both is stopping the offending agent as soon as possible. In addition, patients will receive fluid/electrolyte replacement, wound care and pain medications. Corticosteriods may be used in SJS (benefit is controversial) but are contraindicated in TEN. Due to the severity of the mucosal involvement, antibiotics are usually necessary to prevent infection. DRESS can include a variety of skin eruptions as well as systemic symptoms (fever, hepatic dysfunction, renal dysfunction, lymphadenopathy). Treatment is stopping the offending agent, although symptoms may actually worsen for a period of time after the agent has been discontinued. TTP can cause purpura (bruises) and petechiae (dots) on the skin. These are caused by bleeding under the skin. TTP should be treated emergently with plasma exchange. The table contains the drugs most commonly associated with severe skin rashes. Note that it is not complete; recently, cases of severe rash were associated with the use of the (generally-safe) OTC analgesics acetaminophen and ibuprofen.

DRUGS MOST COMMONLY ASSOCIATED WITH PHOTOSENSITIVITY

Sulfa antibiotics	Diuretics, thiazides and loops
Tetracyclines	Topical fluorouracil
NSAIDs	Metronidazole
Amiodarone	St John's Wort
Chloroquine	PDE-5 inhibitors
Coal Tar	Cyclosporine
Oral and topical retinoids	
Phenothiazines	
Psoralens	
Quinidine	
Fluoroquinolones	
Tacrolimus	

DRUGS ASSOCIATED WITH SEVERE SKIN RASHES

Not complete; these are well known.

SJS/TEN	
Sulfamethoxazole	Letrozole
Allopurinol	Hydroxychloroquine
Carbamazepine	Piroxicam
Oxcarbazepine	Tetracyclines
Phenobarbital	**DRESS**
Ethosuximide	Ethosuximide
Lamotrigine	Phenytoin
Phenytoin	Tetracyclines
Clopidogrel	
Ticlopidine	**TTP**
Quinine	Clopidogrel
Abacavir	Ticlopidine
Nevirapine	Sulfamethoxazole
	Quinine

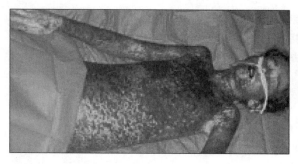
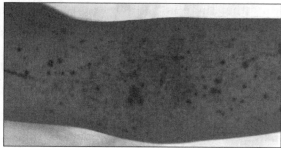

Patient with Stevens-Johnson Syndrome   *Patient with Thrombotic Thrombocytopenic Purpura*

TRUE DRUG ALLERGIES AND ANAPHYLAXIS

Penicillins and sulfonamides cause the most drug allergies. For a true drug allergy to occur the person must have taken the drug previously. Initial exposure will cause a Type I hypersensitivity reaction, resulting in IgE production, which primes the body to release excessive histamine at the next drug exposure.

A reaction without breathing difficulty may sometimes be treated by simply stopping the offending drug. Antihistamines can be used to counteract the histamine release that causes itching, swelling and rash. Steroids, and sometimes NSAIDs, can be used to decrease swelling. Severe swelling may necessitate a steroid injection. Epinephrine is used if needed to reverse bronchoconstriction if the patient is wheezing or has other signs of trouble breathing.

Anaphylaxis is a severe, life-threatening allergic reaction that occurs seconds to minutes after taking the drug. Anaphylaxis can occur after an initial exposure and subsequent immune response, but some drugs can cause anaphylaxis with the first exposure.

Signs/Symptoms of Anaphylaxis

- Swelling, with or without urticaria

- Bronchoconstriction, difficulty breathing, pulmonary edema

- Light headedness or dizziness, confusion

- Nausea, vomiting

- Sudden drop in blood pressure, with or without loss of consciousness

- Shock, with possible organ damage

How to Treat Anaphylaxis

If a patient has an anaphylactic reaction, they will need to go to the ED right away (or call 911) and receive an epinephrine injection ± diphenhydramine and ± IV fluids. Do not put a pillow under a patient's head because this makes it more difficult to get air into the lungs. Do not attempt to put anything into their mouth.

Swollen airways can be quickly fatal and patients who have had such a reaction should carry injectable single-use epinephrine *(EpiPen, EpiPen Jr, Adrenaclick, Auvi-Q)*, if they may be at future risk. These contain 0.3 mg of epinephrine (*EpiPen Jr* is 0.15 mg). Their emergency kit should include diphenhydramine tablets (25 mg x 2) and emergency contact information.

EpiPen Injection Instructions (For patients; detailed information on epinephrine use for health care professionals is in the Immunization chapter.)

- If using *Auvi-Q*, pull off outer case, then follow the audio instructions to administer.

- Grasp the epinephrine shot injector in one fist with the black tip pointing down. Do not touch the black tip. (Color may be different.)

- With the other hand, pull off the cap.

- Hold the tip close to your outer thigh. Swing and jab the tip into your outer thigh (through clothing if necessary). The injector should be at a 90-degree angle to your thigh.

- Keep the injector in your outer thigh while you slowly count to 5.

- Remove the injector and <u>rub the area</u> where the medicine entered your skin.

- Look at the black tip: If the needle is showing, you received the dose. If not, you need to inject again. It is normal for some of the liquid to be left in the injector. Do not try to inject the remaining liquid.

- Patients may have two pens, and may need to use the second (in the opposite thigh) to maintain breathing prior to the arrival of medical help.

- Take the antihistamine tablet s (2 x 25 mg) in your allergy kit.

- Anyone with serious allergies to food or drugs should wear a *Medic Alert* bracelet. These are available in the pharmacy, and link the patient and reactions to a 24-hour information line. Patients with serious allergies and medical conditions (including hypoglycemia that may require glucagon) should wear this type of identification.

DRUG CLASSES THAT CAN CAUSE ALLERGIC REACTIONS

While any drug can lead to an allergic reaction, some are more common. These are discussed below. Often the drug that caused the reaction can be replaced with another drug. Rarely this is not possible and desensitization may be recommended. This requires administering the drug in a medical setting in increasing amounts until the patient can tolerate the needed dose. "Patch testing" is occasionally used to try and determine possible rash reactions, including severe skin reactions such as toxic epidermal necrolysis (TEN), but the tests do not always work and the research on patch testing is inconsistent.

Beta Lactam Allergy

Penicillin is a beta lactam antibiotic and there are many related compounds in this family, including nafcillin, oxacillin, ampicillin, amoxicillin, ticarcillin, piperacillin and others. <u>Anyone who is allergic to one of the penicillins should be presumed to be allergic to all penicillins and should avoid the entire group, unless they have been specifically evaluated for this problem.</u>

Cephalosporins are closely related to penicillin. <u>People with a history of penicillin allergy have a small risk of having an allergic reaction to a cephalosporin or carbapenem</u>. It is prudent on the exam to avoid any beta lactam with a stated allergy to another, unless there is no alternative agent.

Sulfa Allergies

<u>These are most commonly reported with sulfamethoxazole</u> (in *Bactrim, Septra)*, and the patient should avoid using sulfapyridine, sulfadiazine and sulfisoxazole. "Non-arylamine" sulfonamides (thiazide diuretics, loop diuretics, sulfonylureas, acetazolamide, zonisamide and celecoxib) usually do not cross react with a sulfamethoxazole allergy, but on the exam you will likely have to recognize the reaction. Since the cross-reactivity between sulfamethoxazole and thiazides and loops is very small, the reaction is usually not considered when the need for these drugs is present – but the patient should be aware to watch for a possible reaction. There are other sulfa-type groups that also have low cross-reactivity. <u>Sulfites or sulfate allergies do not cross react with a sulfonamide</u>. The rotigotine patch, orphenadrine injection, some dobutamine formulations and some eye drops contain sulfites.

Opioid Allergy

Opioid allergies and cross-reactivity is described in detail in the pain section. Fentanyl (*Duragesic)*, meperidine (*Demerol)* and methadone (*Dolophine)* do not cross-react with opioids of the morphine-type. However, they each have safety considerations and can <u>only</u> be used in select groups of patients (see pain chapter). Meperidine is in the same chemical class as fentanyl (and alfentanil, remifentanil and sufentanil) and could cross-react. The tramadol package insert states that if the patient has an allergic reaction to codeine or other opioids they should not use tramadol. Tramadol is not in the morphine class, which includes codeine, oxycodone, morphine, oxymorphone, hydrocodone, hydromorphone, levorphanol, pentazocine and butorphanol. However, technically it is contraindicated according to the package insert. In the case of a true morphine allergy, it should not be used. Tapentadol does not have the same warning, however (interestingly) tapentadol is structurally similar to tramadol. Per the package insert, it could be recommended. Bottom line is safety, it's best to avoid use, but if you use it, monitor the patient.

Breathing Difficulties and NSAIDs

Reactions to NSAIDs, including aspirin, can be either a drug sensitivity (which can cause rhinitis, mild asthmatic type reactions or skin reactions) or a true allergic reaction. If a true allergy is present the patient will experience urticaria and angioedema, and occasionally anaphylaxis. COX-2 selective NSAIDs are used clinically, but on licensing exams it may be prudent to avoid all NSAIDs.

Peanut/Soy Allergy

A food allergy that is important for pharmacists to know is a peanut allergy, since soy is used in some medications. <u>Peanuts and soy are in the same family and can have cross-re-</u>

activity. Parents of children with peanut allergies should be trained in CPR. An *EpiPen* may need to be kept within close reach. Most likely, a reaction will be due to consuming peanuts or soy unknowingly in food products. Drugs to avoid with peanut allergy:

- Clevidipine *(Cleviprex)*

- Propofol *(Diprivan)*

- Progesterone in *Prometrium*

Egg Allergy

If a patient has a true allergy to eggs (which means they cannot enjoy birthday cake), they cannot use:

- Clevidipine *(Cleviprex)*

- Propofol *(Diprivan)*

- Influenza vaccine: Per ACIP, people who have experienced only hives from consuming eggs can receive TIV (the shot, given IM), as long as they are treated by a health care provider who is familiar with the potential manifestations of egg allergies and can be observed by a health care professional for at least 30 minutes after receiving each dose. If the person has more severe symptoms (such as wheezing, requiring epinephrine, hypotension, cardiovascular changes) they may not be able to receive the vaccine, but should be evaluated further by an allergist physician. *Flublok* is the first seasonal influenza vaccine made using recombinant techniques and does not use eggs at all in its production.

8

MEDICATION ERRORS, PATIENT SAFETY & THE JOINT COMMISSION

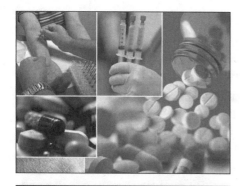

GUIDELINES/REFERENCES

Institute for Safe Medication Practices, www.ismp.org (accessed 2013 Nov 20)

Cohen, Michael R (2007). *Medication Errors*. Washington DC: American Pharmacists Association.

Joint Commission, www.jointcommission.org (accessed 2013 Nov 20)

MMWR Guideline for Hand Hygiene in Health-Care Settings October 25, 2002, 51(RR16);1-44.

CDC Guideline for Isolation Precautions: Preventing Transmission of Infectious Agents in Healthcare Settings, http://www.cdc.gov/hicpac/2007ip/2007isolationprecautions.html (accessed 2013 Dec 1)

US Pharmacopeia (USP) Chapter <797>, www.usp.org (accessed 2013 Dec 1)

BACKGROUND

Awareness of the prevalence of medical errors increased after the release of a study from the Institute of Medicine (IOM), *To Err is Human* (1999), which found that up to 98,000 Americans die each year in U.S. hospitals due to preventable medical errors, 7,000 from medication errors alone. These numbers understated the problem because they did not include preventable deaths due to medical treatments outside of hospitals. Since the release of the IOM study, there has been a greater focus on the quality of healthcare provided in the U.S. and the need to reduce medical errors, which are preventable. As pharmacists we are most concerned with errors involving medications.

This chapter begins with an overview of medication errors, followed by specific measures to limit medication errors in the community and institution settings. Included is a discussion of two types of medication devices that have important benefits but known safety risks – patient controlled analgesia (PCA) devices and automated dispensing cabinets (ADCs).

Patient safety includes reducing infection risk. Essential methods to reduce infections, such as proper handwashing technique, enforcing universal precautions and using safe injection technique are included. The chapter concludes with a discussion of The Joint Commission (TJC), which provides accreditation for healthcare facilities. A primary focus of TJC is patient safety.

Definition of a Medication Error

The formal definition of a medication error developed by the National Coordinating Council on Medication Error Reporting and Prevention (NCC MERP) is "any preventable event that may cause or lead to inappropriate medication use or patient harm while the medication is in the control of the health care professional, patient, or consumer. Such events may be related to professional practice, health care products, procedures, and systems, including prescribing; order communication; product labeling, packaging, and nomenclature; compounding; dispensing; distribution; administration; education; monitoring; and use."

Do not confuse medication errors with adverse drug reactions (ADRs) – these are generally not avoidable although they may be more likely to occur if the drug is given to a patient at high risk for certain complications.

EXAMPLE OF AN ADR (NOT A MEDICATION ERROR)

A 55-year old female had a history of herpes zoster. She has no other known medical conditions. The patient reported considerable "shingles pain" that "run from my back through my left breast." The physician prescribed pregabalin. The patient returned to the physician with complaints of ankle swelling, which required drug discontinuation.

This problem would not be attributable to a medication error made by the physician who prescribed pregabalin or by the pharmacist who dispensed it. Although this drug can cause fluid retention, it does not occur with everyone and there is no way to know in advance if the patient would suffer this problem.

SYSTEM-BASED CAUSES OF MEDICATION ERRORS

Experts in medication safety concur that the most common cause of medication errors is not individual error but problems with the design of the medical system itself. Currently, instead of blaming the "lousy pharmacist" or the "lousy technician" (or the prescriber), health care professionals should find ways to improve the system in order to reduce the chance that the error will occur again. The idea is to design systems in order to prevent medication errors from reaching the patient.

Root Cause Analysis to Prevent Future Errors

One reason the error described in the sidebar to the left occurred is because the pharmacy stored two strengths of phenobarbital tablets next to each other on the shelf. The technician who pulled the medication grabbed the

EXAMPLE OF BLAMING A HEALTH CARE PROFESSIONAL RATHER THAN FOCUSING EFFORTS TO IMPROVE THE SYSTEM

A young man graduated from pharmacy school shortly after the release of the IOM report. He was a top student, a class leader and was well-liked by co-workers. During his first year of practice as a licensed pharmacist he dispensed the wrong strength of phenobarbital tablets for a 10 year-old child. The child was overdosed and hospitalized for several days. Fortunately, the child recovered. The pharmacist was fired by his employer and subsequently suffered from a lack of self-confidence and depression. Eventually, he returned to pharmacy in a different practice setting.

wrong bottle and the pharmacist missed the error during the check. Errors like this can be prevented from occurring again when the contributing factors are made known and appropriate prevention strategies are employed. A root cause analysis (RCA) is a retrospective investigation of an event that has already occurred which includes reviewing the sequence of events that led to the error. The information obtained in the analysis is used to design changes that will hopefully prevent future errors.

Findings from the RCA (the identification of the factors that contributed to the event and led to a "sentinel event" – the unexpected occurrence involving death or serious physical or psychological injury, or risk thereof) can be applied proactively to analyze and improve processes and systems before they breakdown again.

The RCA can be of enormous value in capturing both the big-picture perspective and the details of the error. This type of analysis facilitates system evaluation and the need for corrective action. Targeting corrective measures at the identified root causes is the best way to prevent similar problems from occurring in the future. However, it is recognized that complete prevention of recurrence by a single intervention is not always possible. Thus, RCA is often considered to be a repetitive process, and is frequently viewed as a continuous quality improvement (CQI) tool.

After an analysis of the various factors contributing to the error described above, changes were implemented to make it much more difficult for anyone to make the same mistake. These included the following:

- Alerts regarding safety concerns with this medication (and others labeled as "high-alert") were built into the computer system. Pharmacists are now required to acknowledge and accept or reject high doses in the system.

- The pharmacy now requires that the bottles of phenobarbital tablets and the suspension be placed in separate high-alert medication bins that are labeled with a warning to double check the dosage.

- Pharmacists now flag these medications for mandatory patient education/counseling at the point of sale.

An analysis can also be done prospectively to identify pathways that could lead to errors and to identify ways to reduce the error risk. Failure Mode and Effects Analysis (FMEA) is a proactive method used to reduce the frequency and consequences of errors. FMEA is used to analyze the design of the system in order to evaluate the potential for failures, and to determine what potential effects could occur when the medication delivery system changes in any substantial way or if a potentially dangerous new drug will be added to the formulary.

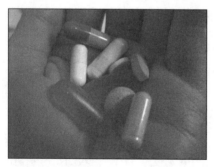

MEDICAL ERROR CLASSIFICATION: ERRORS OF OMISSION AND ERRORS OF COMMISSION

Errors of Omission

An error of omission means leaving something out that is needed for safety, such as missed instructions, or failure to provide a dose at the required time. For example, consider the drug chloral hydrate, which is occasionally used in children as a pre-operative sedative. There have been instances of overdose (some with fatalities) due to incorrect dosing and incorrect administration. It is critical that the pharmacist check that the mg/kg dose is reasonable and help to ensure that the correct dose

EXAMPLE OF AN ERROR OF OMISSION

A physician prescribed warfarin 5 mg to a 70 year-old frail female with atrial fibrillation, heart failure and renal insufficiency. The bottle label was incorrectly prepared as "warfarin 5 mg daily." Neither the technician who typed the label nor the pharmacist who checked the label noticed that the dosing schedule had not been provided on the prescription. The physician had intended to instruct the patient to begin the medication at 1/2 tablet daily, but had left this off the instructions and did not inform the patient or her caregiver. The patient took one tablet daily for ten days and reported to the medical office. The INR was measured at 4.8. Fortunately, the patient did not have any noticeable bleeding and the dosage was decreased.

EXAMPLE OF AN ERROR OF COMMISSION

Manuel is a 38 year-old male patient with a creatinine clearance of 24 mL/min. He is an inpatient in the amputation unit. Manuel's tissue sample is positive for gram positive cocci. The physician ordered vancomycin 1 gram IV Q 8 hours. The pharmacist approved the order and the patient received the medication, at this dose, for the next two days. He suffered further renal damage. This is considered an error of commission because the vancomycin was dosed too high for a patient with reduced clearance.

is given by providing an oral dosing syringe or measuring cup, with instructions, to the parent. If the pharmacist does not provide the measuring device with clear instructions (an error of omission) the parent may be receiving doses for several procedures in one bottle and could mistakenly provide the entire bottle of syrup prior to one procedure. Another example of omission: if hydrochlorothiazide is dispensed when the combination of hydrochlorothiazide/lisinopril was prescribed, the omission of hydrochlorothiazide is an error of omission even though lisinopril was dispensed correctly.

Errors of Commission

An error of commission means that something was done incorrectly, such as prescribing bupropion to a patient with a history of epilepsy or dispensing sulfamethoxazole to a patient with a sulfa allergy.

Reporting Medication Errors

Medication errors, preventable adverse drug reactions, close calls, or hazardous conditions should be reported. We report medication errors so that changes can be made to the system to prevent similar errors in the future. Without reporting, such events may go unrecognized and thus important epidemiological and preventive information would be unavailable.

In a community pharmacy, the staff member who discovers the error should immediately report it to the corporate office or in the case of an independently owned pharmacy, the owner, who is involved with the quality assurance program. These are mandated by many state boards of pharmacy and have the purpose (in the words of the California state board) "to develop pharmacy systems and workflow processes designed to prevent medication errors." Error investigations need to take place quickly – often as soon as within 48 hours of the incident so that the sequence of events remains clear to those involved. Many states mandate the ethical requirement that errors be reported to the patient and their prescriber as soon as possible.

In a hospital setting, the staff member should report a medication error through the hospital's specific medication event reporting system. Many medication error reporting systems within hospitals are electronic, however some hospitals may still maintain a paper reporting system. The hospital's Pharmacy and Therapeutics (P&T) committee should be informed of the error as well as the Medication Safety Committee.

Reporting to Organizations that Specialize in Error Prevention

The Patient Safety and Quality Improvement Act of 2005 (Patient Safety Act) authorized the creation of Patient Safety Organizations (PSOs) to improve the quality and safety of health care delivery in the United States. The Patient Safety Act encourages clinicians and health care organizations to voluntarily report and share quality and patient safety information without fear of this information being used in legal proceedings.

> **Those who cannot remember the past are condemned to repeat it.**
>
> *Poet and Philosopher George Santayana 1863-1952*

EXAMPLE OF A CLOSE CALL THAT SHOULD BE REPORTED

A pain specialist pharmacist worked at a large county hospital. She was asked to provide a pain consult for a patient hospitalized due to pneumonia. The patient had been taking oxycodone immediate release 20 mg on an as-needed basis for chronic pain. She used 6-7 tablets daily and remained in significant pain. At 10:00 the pharmacist went to the bedside, conducted a pain assessment and wrote an order to discontinue the current pain medication. She replaced the oxycodone with morphine controlled-release 60 mg Q 12 hours, with a lower dose of morphine immediate-release as-needed. At 16:00 the pharmacist went to check on the patient and saw that a feeding tube had been inserted. She panicked and ran to find the nurse and the patient's medication administration record. Fortunately, the nurse was an experienced practitioner who knew not to crush a long-acting opioid. The nurse had contacted the physician for a replacement order.

If this close call was reported, the hospital would have the opportunity to implement procedures to avoid this situation in the future. At this hospital nursing students often administer medications with little supervision. By reporting this "close call" the hospital was provided an opportunity to intervene and avoid a potentially fatal mistake in the future.

Other organizations involved in helping to reduce medication errors and promote patient safety are the American Society of Health-System Pharmacists (ASHP), the National Coordinating Council for Medication Error Reporting and Prevention (NCC MERP), and the Agency for Healthcare Research and Quality (AHRQ).

The Agency for Healthcare Research and Quality (AHRQ) administers the provisions of the Patient Safety Act and the Patient Safety Rule dealing with PSO operations. More information regarding PSOs can be found at the Agency for Healthcare Research and Quality website (http://www.pso.ahrq.gov/).

Organizations that specialize in error prevention can analyze the system-based causes of the errors and make recommendations to others who can learn from the mistakes. Every pharmacist should make it a practice to read medication error reports in order to use this history to improve their own practice settings. Information sources include the Institute for Safe Medication Practices (ISMP) newsletters which have information about medication-related errors, adverse drug reactions, as well as recommendations that will help reduce the risk of medication errors and other adverse drug events at the practice site. ISMP publishes monthly medication error report analysis and adverse drug reaction articles in the journal, *Hospital Pharmacy*. This journal is available free of charge for hospital pharmacists.

The ISMP National Medication Errors Reporting Program (MERP) is a confidential national voluntary reporting program that provides expert analysis of the system causes of medication errors and disseminates recommendations for prevention.

On the ISMP website (www.ismp.org), medication errors <u>and</u> close calls can be reported. Click on "Report Errors." Professionals and consumers should be encouraged to report medication errors using this site even if the error was reported internally.

COMMON METHODS USED TO REDUCE MEDICATION ERRORS

Patient Profiles

Pharmacies should maintain current patient profiles that include all prescription drugs, over the counter (OTC) medications, and anything else the patient is taking such as natural products and other supplements. Allergies and the type of allergic reaction (e.g., rash, lip swelling) should be recorded. Intolerances should be noted and the drug avoided, if possible, or the intolerance can be proactively managed (such as using an anti-emetic agent if the intolerance is nausea from an opioid). See the Drug Allergy chapter for pointers on proper documentation. The most common use of the profile is to check for allergies and drug interactions, but it can also be used for monitoring appropriateness of therapy, checking for polypharmacy (polypharmacy means "many drugs" and refers to problems that can occur when a patient is taking more medications than are necessary) and assessing patient adherence with their medication regimen. Patient disease-state information and diagnosis is also important information in order to check the appropriateness of medication selection and dosage.

> **EXAMPLE OF POLYPHARMACY DISCOVERED BY A REVIEW OF A PATIENT'S PROFILE**
>
> Jessica is a 52 year-old female with a history of bipolar II disorder, anxiety, insomnia and restless leg syndrome. She is taking olanzapine 10 mg QAM, fluoxetine 20 mg QHS, zolpidem 10 mg QHS and ropinirole 1 mg QHS. The pharmacist recording the patient's profile asked about the patient's general health and was told that since the initiation of olanzapine therapy eighteen months ago the patient's weight has increased by 8 pounds and she was told recently that her blood glucose and LDL cholesterol are high. The pharmacist considers the possibility that the olanzapine is typically sedating (and might be moved to QHS dosing) and the fluoxetine is typically activating (and might be moved to QAM dosing). Perhaps if this was done the patient might not require a hypnotic. The pharmacist also asked about the patient's sleep schedule and whether the restless leg began after the initiation of fluoxetine therapy. The physician is considering the addition of diabetes and hypertension medications. The pharmacist informs the physician that the metabolic changes may be due to the olanzapine therapy and has suggested an alternative. (Hopefully, these suggestions are not all implemented concurrently.)

Medication Therapy Management

The example above may have been discovered during a more comprehensive medication review (CMR), through the process of medication therapy management (MTM). A personal medication record (PMR) is prepared, and a medication-related action plan (MAP) is developed, preferably by a pharmacist-led team. The next steps involve interventions, referrals, documentation and plans for follow-up. This is a program mandated under the Medicare drug benefit (Medicare Part D) to promote safe and effective medication use. Medicare's drug benefit provides outpatient prescription drug coverage. It is available only through private companies. At a minimum, beneficiaries targeted for MTM include members with multiple chronic conditions who are taking multiple drugs and are likely to incur annual costs for covered drugs that exceed a predetermined level. Computer databases are used to identify patients with certain high-risk conditions (such as heart failure or uncontrolled diabetes) who are generally using many medications (some systems tag patients taking many chronic medications daily) and assign a pharmacist (preferably) to review profiles for proper use. This program is a Medicare requirement and therefore the majority of MTM programs exist within Medicare-funded health care plans. MTM may also apply to populations outside of Medicare.

The pharmacist can form a partnership with the patient and prescriber to remedy any issues or lapses. Often, these reviews identify missed therapy such as lack of an ACE inhibitor or ARB in patients with diabetes, missing beta blocker therapy post-MI, missing bisphospho-nate therapy with high-dose chronic steroids, and others, since these are easily searchable in databases. A popular MTM initiative is to improve non-adherence in heart failure patients due to the high-rate of ED visits due to decompensated heart failure. MTM is also used to identify cost-savings, by promoting switches to generics or more affordable brands, or by suggesting patient assistance programs or low income subsidies for eligible members.

Drug Utilization Reviews (DURs) and Retrospective Analysis

The DUR is designed to address some combination of inappropriate medication use, including therapeutic duplications, drug-drug and drug-disease contraindications, incorrect dosage or treatment durations, abuse (of either patients, or poor prescribing) and clinical misuse, such as prescribing out of formulary for unnecessary indications.

EXAMPLE OF A DRUG UTILIZATION REVIEW BY THE STATE OF WYOMING

In 2010 many regions in the U.S. experienced fiscal restraints, including the state of Wyoming, which has high costs due to ED visits. The state wished to reduce the prevalence of ED admits due to asthma exacerbations. The state conducted a DUR of asthma medication adherence and found that adher-ence rates of asthma medications declined during pregnancy, although the medication was covered under the state's low income medication plan. Through further follow-up the researchers discovered that the primary reason many women decreased asthma medication adherence during pregnancy was due to safety concerns. Based on the data provided by the DUE the state initiated a campaign to increase awareness of the health risks associated with discontinuation of asthma medications during pregnancy.

Retrospective DURs can be done indi-vidually (such as with an MTM review) or, more commonly, with a system-wide review using aggregate data. The retro-spective DUR program involves reviews of patient drug history profiles generat-ed from medical assistance paid claims data by a panel of active practicing phy-sicians and pharmacists. DURs used to be performed more commonly but they are still done and can serve a useful purpose, such as a DUR conducted in a healthcare group to determine which physician's handwriting contributes to the most prescribing errors, or which prescribers use the highest percentage of branded drugs, when less-expensive alternatives are available.

Medication Reconciliation

According to TJC, "Medication reconciliation is the process of comparing a patient's medication orders to all of the medications that the patient has been taking." This reconciliation is done to avoid medication errors such as omissions, duplications, dosing errors, or drug interactions. It should be done at every transition of care in which new medications are ordered or existing orders are rewritten.

Transitions in care include changes in setting, service, practitioner or level of care. This process comprises five steps:

1. Develop a list of current medications;

2. Develop a list of medications to be prescribed;

3. Compare the medications on the two lists;

BAYSHORE COMMUNITY HOSPITAL
727 North Beers Street • Holmdel, New Jersey 07733-1598

MEDICATION RECONCILIATION ORDER FORM

List all patient medications prior to assessment. Include OTCs & alternative meds (herbals). (Alternative meds will not be continued on admission).

Before an outpatient receives any medication as part of their test or procedure, list all of their current home medications looking for allergies, interactions, duplications, or other concerns. A complete reconciliation is required only if the patient is to be admitted to the hospital.

Allergies: _____

DO NOT USE ABBREVIATIONS: .#, #.0, IU, MS, MgSO4, MSO4, QD, QOD, U

Information Source: ____ Patient ____ Family ____ Primary Care Physician
____ Patient's Pharmacy(s) _____ (See Back)
____ MAR from _____ Other, specify _____

☐ Check here if patient is not currently on any medication.

Medication Name	Dose	Route	Frequency	Last Dose Date	Time	Physician Decision: Continue? Circle one
1						Y N
2						Y N
3						Y N
4						Y N
5						Y N
6						Y N
7						Y N
8						Y N
9						Y N
10						Y N
11						Y N
12						Y N
13						Y N
14						Y N
15						Y N

On the lines below, enter orders for new medications that the patient isn't currently taking or changes to their current regimen.

Completed by _____ Nurse Signature _____ Date/Time _____
(print name)

I have reviewed this list of patient medications and to the best of my knowledge, the additional medications I have ordered will not result in any adverse reaction(s).

Completed by _____ MD Signature _____ Date/Time _____
(print name)

Faxed/Given to _____ By _____ Date/Time _____
(sign & print name)

70811 (REV 6/06)   Sheet ____ of ____

4. Make clinical decisions based on the comparison; and

5. Communicate the new list to appropriate caregivers and to the patient.

EXAMPLE OF THE BENEFIT OF MEDICATION RECONCILIATION

Ann is an 82 year-old female. Her only medication for the previous ten years has been amlodipine 10 mg daily. Ann recently developed influenza. She began to have trouble breathing and was taken to the hospital. It was discovered that Ann had pneumonia and new-onset atrial fibrillation. She was prescribed diltiazem, dabigatran and digoxin. Ann was discharged to transitional care and received the new medications plus the previous medication amlodipine. The consultant pharmacist conducted a medication review to reconcile the medications and, after discussion with the physician on the patient's rate control, the pharmacist wrote an order to discontinue the diltiazem.

This is accomplished by reviewing the patient's complete medication regimen at the time of admission, transfer, and discharge and comparing it with the regimen being considered for the new setting of care. At discharge, give the patient a list of medications and educate about those to be continued at home. Address any discrepancies. Though most often discussed in the hospital context, medication reconciliation can be equally important in ambulatory care, as many patients receive prescriptions from more than one outpatient provider and may go to several pharmacies.

Medication reconciliation is a part of the National Patient Safety Goals (NPSGs) issued by TJC. An effective medication reconciliation process must be in place for healthcare facilities to be in compliance with many of the NPSGs.

Medication Guides

Medication Guides (or MedGuides) present <u>important adverse events</u> that can occur with over 300 medications. MedGuides are <u>FDA-approved patient handouts</u> and are considered part of the drug's labeling. If a medication has a MedGuide, it should be dispensed with the <u>original prescription</u> and with <u>each refill</u>. Some medications dispensed while inpatient require MedGuides and these should be available to the patient or family upon request. It is not necessary to dispense them to inpatients routinely as the patient is being monitored. <u>MedGuides are required for many individual agents and some entire classes of medications</u> (including anticonvulsants, antidepressants, long-acting opioids, NSAIDs and the ADHD stimulants and atomoxetine).

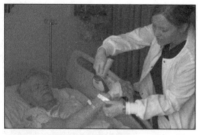

Barcoding

Barcoding may be the <u>most important medication error reduction tool</u> in the arsenal right now. The barcode <u>follows the drug through the medication use process</u> to make sure it is being properly stocked (such as in the right space in the pharmacy or in the right pocket in the dispensing cabinet), through compounding (if required), and to the patient. The barcode is used at the bedside to identify that the correct drug (by scanning the code on the drug's packaging) is going to the right patient (via scanning the patient's wristband) and confirms that the dose is being given at the right time. The nurse may have a badge barcode that can track who administered the dose. Barcodes are now on many pumps and can prevent errors involving medications being given IV that are not meant to be administered in this manner. The FDA requires bar coding on medications with (minimally) the drug's national drug code (NDC) number. It may also include other items, such as the lot number and expiration date. <u>Nurses using bedside barcode medication administration records (MARs) spend more time providing direct patient care, versus nurses who use paper-based MARs.</u>

Look-Alike, Sound-Alike Medications

Confusing drug names is a common cause of medication errors. Poor handwriting and similar product labeling aggravate the problem of pulling a look-alike or sound-alike agent instead of the intended medication. Drug dictionaries within computer systems are being built with alerts to attempt to double-check that the correct medication is being ordered or withdrawn. For example a warning may appear on the screen of the ADCs which will state: "This is DILAUDID. Did you want hydroMORPHONE? (to avoid confusions with morphine)."

Drugs that are easily mixed up should be labeled with tall man letters (e.g., CeleXA, Cele-BREX). Using tall man letters, which mix upper and lower case letters, draws attention to the <u>dissimilarities</u> in the drug names. The letters that are upper cases are the ones that are <u>different between the two sound-alike drugs</u>. Tall man lettering makes the drugs with names that look or sound like others less prone to mix-ups. <u>ISMP, FDA, The Joint Commission, and other safety-conscious organizations have promoted the use of tall man letters as one means of reducing confusion between similar drug names</u>. If receiving a verbal order for a drug that is easily confused with another be sure to repeat the drug name back, with spelling as necessary if useful, to the prescriber. It may be possible to remove a drug that is easily confused with another from the institution's formulary.

The FDA's and ISMP's approved tall man lettering information is available at: http://www.ismp.org/tools/tallmanletters.pdf

Do Not Use Error-Prone Abbreviations, Symbols, and Dosage Designations

<u>Abbreviations are unsafe and contribute to many medical errors.</u> TJC standards include recommendations against the use of unsafe abbreviations. The ISMP's list of error-prone abbreviations, symbols, and dosage designations includes those on TJC's do-not-use list (designated by **). Try writing the number 5.0 on a lined paper and you can see how easily the number could be mistaken for 50; this is why trailing zeros (after a whole number) are not permitted. Leading zeros are required because it would be easy to miss a decimal point placed before a number (such as .5) if the leading zero was not present (the correct way to write this is 0.5). The other items on the list are important enough that it is almost misleading to give one example – such as the long history of mix-ups between morphine and magnesium and resultant fatalities. Review the TJC list carefully. If abbreviations are used within an institution (such as a hospital) they must not be on <u>that institution's</u> unapproved abbreviation list (and not include any on the Joint Commission's do-not use list). The unapproved abbreviations list is supposed to be kept readily accessible in the unit and may be placed at the back of the patient chart. It is best to attempt to avoid abbreviations entirely.

Official "Do Not Use" List[1]

Do Not Use	Potential Problem	Use Instead
U, u (unit)	Mistaken for "0" (zero), the number "4" (four) or "cc"	Write "unit"
IU (International Unit)	Mistaken for IV (intravenous) or the number 10 (ten)	Write "International Unit"
Q.D., QD, q.d., qd (daily)	Mistaken for each other	Write "daily"
Q.O.D., QOD, q.o.d, qod (every other day)	Period after the Q mistaken for "I" and the "O" mistaken for "I"	Write "every other day"
Trailing zero (X.0 mg)* Lack of leading zero (.X mg)	Decimal point is missed	Write X mg Write 0.X mg
MS	Can mean morphine sulfate or magnesium sulfate	Write "morphine sulfate" Write "magnesium sulfate"
MSO₄ and MgSO₄	Confused for one another	

[1] Applies to all orders and all medication-related documentation that is handwritten (including free-text computer entry) or on pre-printed forms.

*Exception: A "trailing zero" may be used only where required to demonstrate the level of precision of the value being reported, such as for laboratory results, imaging studies that report size of lesions, or catheter/tube sizes. It may not be used in medication orders or other medication-related documentation.

The ISMP's list of error-prone abbreviations is available at: http://www.ismp.org/tools/errorproneabbreviations.pdf

Indications for Use on Prescriptions

An <u>indication for use</u> that is written on the prescription (such as lisinopril 10 mg once daily for hypertension) <u>helps pharmacists ensure appropriate prescribing and drug selection</u>. If the pharmacist does not know the indication for the prescribed medication, the prescriber should be contacted. Indications provide information in order to appropriately provide counseling to a patient. In this example, the pharmacist can inform the patient this medication is to help keep their blood pressure at the right level and they can make sure the patient is aware of the blood pressure goal. The retail pharmacist should open the bag, open the vial and show the patient the medication (this can be tricky; lisinopril comes in various tablet sizes and colors – hopefully the same generic manufacturer can be chosen). Many pharmacies now provide the tablet description on the patient label. The patient should be instructed always to read this description so they are sure that what is in the vial looks like the description provided on the label. The patient is now equipped to monitor their condition <u>and</u> to help catch a dispensing error if one occurs. The pharmacist who has educated the patient on their blood pressure goal (or any other therapeutic goal) has helped improve the patient's health.

Measurements Should be in the Metric System

<u>Measurements should be kept in the metric system only</u>. Prescribers should use the metric system to express all weights, volumes and units.

Provide Instructions on Prescriptions; Avoid Using "As Directed"

Using <u>the term "as directed" is not acceptable</u> on prescriptions because the patient often has no idea what this means and the pharmacist cannot verify a proper dosing regimen. Occasionally, this term is used on the bottle along with a separate dosing calendar, such as with warfarin. It would be preferable to write "use per instructions on the dosing calendar" since the patient may not understand how to take the medication and may not be aware that a separate dosing calendar exists.

Special Bins and Labeling for High-Alert Drugs

<u>Drugs that bear a heightened risk of causing significant patient harm when used in error should be designated as "High-alert"</u>. Any drug that is high risk for significant harm if dispensed incorrectly can be placed in a medication bin that provides a visual alert to the person pulling the medication. The bin can be labeled with warnings and include materials (placed inside the bin) that should be dispensed with the drug (such as oral syringes or MedGuides). In the hospital setting certain drugs are classified as "high-alert" and these can be placed in bins labeled with dispensing requirements.

There are many drugs considered high-alert, including insulin and oral hypoglycemics, opioids, anticoagulants, antiarrhythmics, anesthetics, chemotherapeutics, injectable KCl, phosphate, magnesium and hypertonic saline.

Use the ISMP "high-alert" list to determine which medications require special safeguards to reduce the risk of errors. It is available at: www.ismp.org/tools/highalertmedications. Keep in mind that the ISMP's list represents the most common agents that are high risk, and need special precautions. An institution's list should be based on the experience in that setting. Many of these drugs will be the same, and others may be unique to your practice. Here are examples of high-risk drugs and precautions used in a hospital setting to reduce risk:

High-Alert Drugs and Safe-Use Precautions

DRUG	PRECAUTIONS
Hypertonic Saline	Allow only commercially available, standard (e.g., isotonic) concentrations of sodium chloride outside the pharmacy
	Limit options – do not stock the 3% sodium chloride injection
	Develop a protocol for administering sodium chloride for use in treating hyponatremia – covering the rate and volume of administration and the frequency of serum sodium monitoring
	Limit addition of sodium to enteral feedings to the pharmacy
	In dialysis units, stock a single hypertonic concentration and store in a locked area with limited access and affix special hazard labeling
Insulin	Eliminate insulin pens from the inpatient setting
	If U-500 is stocked, specify conditions under which it is to be used
	Standardize all insulin infusions to one concentration
	Develop protocols for insulin infusions, transition from infusion to SC and sliding scale orders
	Have standard orders in place for management of hypoglycemia
	Do not use "U" for units
	Always label with "units" or "units = mL", but never just "mL"
	Do not place in ADCs; all insulin orders should be reviewed by a pharamcist prior to dispensing
Heparin	Standardize heparin solutions – use premixed and reduce the number of concentrations available
	Standardize administration procedures – place dose stickers on heparin bags and double check all rate changes. If a bolus is ordered, give it from a syringe, rather than modifying the rate of the infusion
	Differentiate all look-alike products
	Separate the storage of all drugs ordered in units
	Standardize the dosing using weight-based protocols
	Have infusion pump rate settings and line placement on dual-channel pumps checked by two persons
	Develop and follow standard treatment protocols
	Do not use "U" for units
	Use only 'free flow' protected pumps

High-Alert Drugs and Safe-Use Precautions Continued

DRUG	PRECAUTIONS
Potassium Chloride	Remove all KCl vials from floor stock
	Centralize KCl infusion preparation in the pharmacy
	Use premixed containers
	Use protocols for KCl delivery, including indications for:
	■ KCl infusion
	■ Maximum rate of infusion
	■ Maximum allowable concentration
	■ Guidelines for when cardiac monitoring is required
	■ Stipulation that all KCl infusions must be given via a pump
	■ Prohibition of multiple simultaneous KCl solutions (e.g., no IV KCl while KCl is being infused in another IV)
	Allow for automatic substitution of oral KCl for IV KCl, when appropriate
	Label all fluids containing potassium with a "Potassium Added" sticker
Opioids	Use of tools to screen patients for risk factors for oversedation and respiratory depression
	Monitor vitals, use of telemetry when indicated, and sedation scales per protocol
	Build red flag alerts into e-prescribing systems for dosing limits
	Use of tall man lettering
	Separation of sound-alike and look-alike agents
	Use of conversion support systems to calculate correct doses
	Use of infusion pump technology when administering IV

EXAMPLE OF AN ERROR DUE TO MISIDENTIFICATION OF A CONCENTRATION BASED ON THE PACKAGING

The intravenous catheters of three neonates in a NICU unit in Los Angeles were flushed with the adult therapeutic dose of heparin (10,000 units/mL) rather than the heparin flush dose of 10 units/mL. This accident did not result in fatalities although two of the babies required the reversal agent protamine. Three babies died from a similar incident the previous year at a different hospital. The overdose was administered because the nurse thought she was using a lower concentration of heparin.

Due to the high risk associated with heparin overdose, high concentration heparin vials should not be present in patient care areas. Instead, therapeutic doses should be sent by the pharmacy department.

Do Not Rely on Medication Packaging for Identification Purposes

Look-alike packaging can contribute to errors. If unavoidable, separate look-alike drugs in the pharmacy and patient care units units, or repackage.

Avoid Multiple-Dose Vials, if Possible

These pose risk for cross-contamination (infection) and over-dosing. If used, they should be (ideally) designated for a single patient and labelled appropriately. Discard the remainder when the patient is done with the medication, or is discharged.

CODE BLUE
Code Blue refers to a patient requiring emergency medical care, typically for cardiac or respiratory arrest. The overhead announcement will provide the patient's location. The code team will rush to the room and begin immediate resuscitative efforts.

Use Safe Practices for Emergency Medications/ Crash Carts

Staff must be properly trained to handle emergencies and use crash cart medications. The medications should be <u>unit dose</u> and <u>age-specific</u>, including pediatric-specific doses. A weight-based dosing chart can be placed in the trays used in the pediatric units. If a unit dose medication is not available it is best to have prefilled syringes and drips in the cart as much as possible because it is easy to make a mistake under the stress of a code. The emergency medications should be stored in sealed or locked containers in a locked room and replaced as soon as possible after use (through a cart exchange so that the area is not left without required medications). Monitor the drug expiration dates. Trained pharmacists should be present at codes when possible.

Dedicate Pharmacists to the ICU, Pediatric Units and Emergency Departments

<u>These are units with a high incidence of preventable medication errors,</u> and pharmacist working in these units can assist in identifying and preventing medication errors by developing process improvements designed to reduce drug errors.

Organize Educational Programs

<u>Staff education programs such as "in-services"</u> should be provided whenever new high-alert drugs are being used in the facility, to introduce new procedural changes aimed at preventing medication errors and to introduce any new guidelines. The information provided in these "in-services" should be unbiased and should not be provided in a skewed manner by drug company representatives. Many hospitals now <u>limit the use of pharmaceutical companies to provide drug education</u> due to the inherent bias.

Develop and Use Standard Protocols

<u>Standard protocols</u> for high-risk drugs increase the rate of appropriate prescribing based on published recommended guidelines and reduce the chance of errors due to inappropriate prescribing. <u>The Joint Commission requires that standard order sets be used for all antithrombotics.</u> The standard order sheet should include instructions for initial doses of heparin and other high-risk antithrombotics, monitoring for bleeding, using appropriate antidotes, monitoring for HIT and discontinuing heparin if HIT is suspected. The prescriber should be <u>required to justify any order outside the protocol and a pharmacist should approve the request.</u>

Implement Computerized Prescriber Order Entry (CPOE)

Computerized physician/provider order entry is a computer system that <u>allows direct entry of medical orders</u> by prescribers. Directly entering orders into a computer has the benefit of reducing errors by <u>minimizing the ambiguity</u> resulting from hand-written orders. A

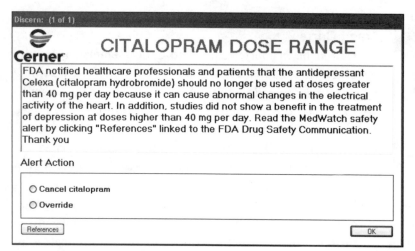

much greater benefit is seen with the <u>combination of CPOE and clinical decision support tools</u>. Clinical guidelines and patient labs can be built into the CPOE system and alerts can notify a prescriber if the drug is inappropriate, or if labs indicate the drug could be unsafe (such as a high potassium level and a new order for a potassium-sparing agent). CPOE can include standard order sets. In addition to medication orders, CPOE is used for laboratory orders and procedures. An example of an on-screen alert from a clinical decision support system is below. The alert in this example pops-up when a prescriber attempts to order citalopram with a dose greater than 40 mg/day.

Educate Patients and their Families

Patients can play a <u>vital role in preventing medication errors</u> when they have been encouraged to ask questions and seek satisfactory answers about their medications before drugs are dispensed at a pharmacy. If a patient questions any part of the medication dispensing process, whether it is about the drug's appearance, or dose, or something else, the pharmacist must be receptive and responsive (<u>not</u> defensive). All patient inquiries should be thoroughly investigated before the medication is dispensed. The written information about the medications should be at a reading level that is comprehensible for the patient.

It may be necessary to provide pictograms or other means of instruction to patients who do not speak English or are unable to read English. In certain communities there is a high percentage of patients who are functionally illiterate, which may include many native English speakers. An inability to understand written English has no correlation with intelligence and does not imply an inability to understand simple instructions; it is still necessary for pharmacists to ensure that these patients understand how to use their medications safely.

Monitor for Drug-Food Interactions

<u>Check for drug-food interactions routinely</u> and have nutrition involved with this effort when drugs with a high rate of food interactions (such as warfarin) are ordered.

Follow Requirements for Risk Evaluation and Mitigation Strategies (REMS) Drugs

REMS is an FDA program that requires <u>specified training and various restrictions</u> (patient requirements, user registries, etc.) on certain drugs. Examples include the clozapine patient registry, the APPRISE program for erythropoietin use in oncology, the iPLEDGE program for isotretinoin, and others. In 2011 the FDA began new REMS to reduce the misuse of long-acting opioids, which covers many drugs (morphine extended-release, fentanyl patches, hydromorphone, oxycodone and oxymorphone, methadone and buprenorphine). The list of REMS drugs keeps growing. When working your way through this book note the many drugs that have prescribing qualifications. As pharmacists, we are hopeful the REMS information on the FDA website becomes more standardized, and there is improvement on the reimbursement end for pharmacists involved with implementing REMS requirements.

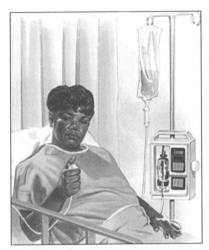

PATIENT CONTROLLED ANALGESIC (PCA) DEVICE OVERVIEW AND SAFETY CONCERNS

Opioids are effective agents used for moderate to severe post-surgical pain and are the mainstay of treatment. These may be administered through PCA devices. PCAs allow the patient <u>to treat pain quickly</u> (there is no need to call the nurse and wait for the dose to arrive) They allow the administration of small doses, which helps reduce side effects (particularly over-sedation). However, as some patients will be opioid-naïve or receiving higher-than-normal doses post-surgically, antiemetics or antihistamines may be required. <u>PCA drug delivery can mimic the pain pattern more closely and provide good pain control</u>. Increasingly, the PCA is administered with anesthetics for a synergistic benefit in pain relief.

PCAs have important safety considerations

- The devices can be complex and require set-up and programming. This is a <u>significant cause of preventable medication errors</u>. PCAs should be used only with well-coordinated health care teams.

- Patients may not be appropriate candidates for PCA treatment. They should be cooperative and should have a cognitive assessment prior to using the PCA to ensure they can follow instructions.

- <u>Friends and family members should not administer PCA doses. This is a Joint Commission requirement.</u>

- PCAs do not frequently cause respiratory depression, but the risk is present. Advanced age, obesity and concurrent use of CNS depressants (in addition to higher opioid doses) increases risk.

With PCAs it is important to follow these safety steps

- <u>Limit the opioids</u> available in floor stock. Use standard orders (set drug dosages, especially for opioid-naïve patients) so that drugs are not over-dosed.

- <u>Educate staff</u> about HYDROmorphone and morphine mix-ups.

- Implement PCA <u>protocols</u> that include independent double-checking of the drug, pump setting, and dosage. The concentration on the <u>Medication Administration Record (MAR)</u> should match the PCA label.

- Use <u>bar-coding</u> technology. Some infusion pumps incorporate bar-coding technology. Scanning the barcode on the PCA bag would help ensure the correct concentration is entered during PCA programming. It will also ensure that the right patient is getting the medication.

- Assess the patient's <u>pain, sedation and respiratory rate</u> on a scheduled basis.

AUTOMATED DISPENSING CABINET OVERVIEW AND SAFETY CONCERNS

Most pharmacy interns will have seen automated dispensing cabinets (ADCs) while on clinical rotations. Common names are *Pyxis, Omnicell, ScriptPro* and *AccuDose*. Over half of the hospitals in the U.S. now use ADCs. In about half of these, the ADCs have replaced patient cassettes that had to be filled at least once daily and exchanged.

ADCs provide practical benefits

The drug inventory and medication can be automated when drugs are placed into the cabinet and removed. Controlled drug security can be improved (versus the previous method of keeping the controlled drugs locked in a metal cabinet or in a drawer in the nurses' station). The drugs are easily available at the unit and do not require individual delivery from the pharmacy. ADCs provide alerts, usage reports and work well with bar-coding.

ADCs have important safety considerations

- Stocking errors, such as a drug being placed in an incorrect drawer or bin, can lead to the wrong drug being dispensed (barcode scanning can be used to make sure that the correct drug is being placed into the ADC or dispensed).

- The wrong drug can be selected from the screen or ADC.

- The wrong dose can be selected from the screen.

- Errors can occur due to overrides that are not subject to a pharmacist's prospective order review.

Methods to improve ADC safety

- <u>The Joint Commission requires that the pharmacist review the order before the medication can be removed from the ADC for a patient, except in special circumstances.</u> The override function should be limited to true emergencies and all overrides should be investigated.

- The most common error associated with ADC use is giving the wrong drug or dose to a patient. The patient medication administration records (MARs) should be accessible to practitioners while they are removing medications from the ADC. <u>Barcode scanning improves ADC safety.</u> The drug can be scanned to make sure it is going into the right place into the cabinet and can ensure that the right drug is being pulled. Prior to administration the patient's wrist band can be scanned to make sure the drug is going to the right patient.

- <u>Look-alike and sound-alike medications should be stored in different locations within the ADC.</u> Using computerized alerts, ideally pop-ups that require a confirmation, when medications with high potential for mix-up in a given setting are selected, can help reduce error risk.

- Certain medications should not be put into the ADCs, including insulin, warfarin and high-dose narcotics (such as hydromorphone 10 mg/mL and morphine 20 mg/mL).

- Do not let nurses put medications back into the medication compartment because it might be placed in the wrong area; it is best to have a separate drawer for all "returned" medications.

- If the machine is in a busy, noisy environment, or in one with poor lighting, errors increase.

The California board specifically states that all drugs that are stocked in the ADC in a nursing facility are restocked by a pharmacist or by an intern or technician working under the supervision of a pharmacist. Removable pockets or drawers transported between the pharmacy and a stocking facility must be transported in a secure tamper-evident container.

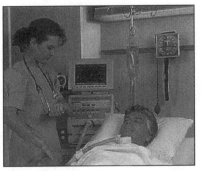

INFECTION CONTROL IN HOSPITALS

Nearly two million infections occur in hospitals annually – about one infection for every twenty patients. It is somewhat incredulous that so many patients enter hospitals for treatment of a condition and contract a different condition at the same facility.

The organisms in healthcare settings are highly pathogenic – this means that resistant bacteria are in the hospitals because that is where the sickest patients are and certain organisms grow in hospital settings, such as *Pseudomonas* in the moist environment of the ventilator.

Hospital infections cause avoidable illness and death and add enormous financial costs. The worst part of this sad state of affairs is that many of these infections are preventable if proper techniques (which are often simple measures) are followed. Many states now require hospitals to report infection rates and Medicare has begun to refuse reimbursement for hospital-acquired infections that are largely avoidable.

Common Types of Hospital (Nosocomial) Acquired Infections

■ Urinary tract infections, from indwelling catheters (very common), <u>remove the catheter as soon as possible)</u> – preventing catheter associated infections is a Joint Commission National Patient Safety Goal (NPSG).

■ Blood stream infections <u>from IV lines (central lines have the highest risk) and catheters</u>

■ Surgical site infections (<u>see the section on antibiotic prophylaxis in the ID chapter</u>)

■ Decubitis ulcers

■ Hepatitis

■ *Clostridium difficile,* <u>other GI infections</u>

■ <u>Pneumonia (mostly due to ventilator use)</u>, bronchitis

Universal Precautions for the Spread of Infectious Agents in the Healthcare Setting

Universal precautions is an approach to infection control that treats human blood and body fluids as if they are known to be infectious for HIV, HBV and other bloodborne pathogens. Contact with bodily fluids should be avoided through the use of good hand hygiene and, in select cases, the use of gowns, masks, or patient isolation.

There are 3 categories of transmission-based precautions defined by the CDC:

Contact precautions

■ Intended to prevent transmission of infectious agents which are spread by direct and indirect contact with the patient and patient's environment.

■ Single patient rooms are preferred. If not available, keep ≥ 3 feet spatial separation between beds to prevent inadvertent sharing of items between patients.

■ Healthcare personnel caring for these patients wear a gown and gloves for all interactions that may involve contact with the patient or contaminated areas in the patient's room.

■ <u>Contact precautions are recommended for patients colonized with MRSA and VRE.</u>

Droplet precautions

■ Intended to prevent transmission of pathogens spread through close respiratory contact with respiratory secretions.

■ Single patient rooms are preferred. If not available, keep ≥ 3 feet spatial separation and drawing a curtain between beds is especially important for diseases transmitted via droplet.

■ Healthcare personnel wear a mask (a respirator is not necessary) for close contact with the patient. The mask is donned upon room entry.

■ Droplet precautions are recommended for patients with active *B. pertussis*, influenza virus, adenovirus, rhinovirus, *N. meningitides*, and group A streptococcus (for the first 24 hours of antimicrobial therapy).

Airborne Precautions

■ Intended to prevent transmission of infectious agents that remain infectious over long distances when suspended in the air.

■ Patient should be placed in an airborne infection isolation room (AIIR). An AIIR is a single-patient room that is equipped with special air and ventilation handling negative pressure rooms, air exhausted directly to the outside or re-circulated through HEPA filtration before return.

■ Healthcare personnel wear a mask or respirator (N95 level or higher), depending on the disease, which is donned prior to room entry.

■ Airborne precautions are recommended for patients with rubella virus (measles), varicella virus (chickenpox), or *M. tuberculosis*.

Prevention Of Catheter Associated Bloodstream Infections (CRBSI)

■ The most important and most cost-effective strategy to minimize catheter-associated bloodstreatm infections is through aseptic technique during catheter insertion, including proper handwashing and utilization of standard protocols/catheter insertion checklist.

■ It is also important to minimize use of intravascular catheters, if possible, through intravenous to oral route protocols and setting appropriate time limits for catheter use. For example, peripheral catheters should be removed/replaced every 2-3 days to minimize risk for infection.

■ Other strategies shown to reduce the risk of CRBSI, include use of skin antiseptics (2% chlorhexidine), antibiotic impregnated central venous catheters, and antibiotic/ethanol lock therapy, but must be weighed against to potential risk for increased rates of resistance.

Hand Hygiene

Many hospital infections are spread by hospital worker's hands and numerous studies show that proper hand hygiene reduces the spread of nosocomial infection. Patients are often carriers of resistant bacteria, including MRSA and VRE. Alcohol-based hand rubs (gel, rinse or foam) are considered more effective in the healthcare setting than plain soap or antimicrobial soap and water. Review the conditions below in which soap and water are preferable. Do not wear jewelry under gloves – these harbor bacteria and can tear the gloves. Keep fingernails clipped short and clean.

Antimicrobial hand soaps that contain chlorhexidine (*Hibiclens*, others) may be preferable to soap and water to reduce infections in healthcare facilities. Triclosan may also be better but this compound gets into the water supply and has environmental concerns.

When to Wash Hands

- Before entering and after leaving patient rooms.

- Between patient contacts if there is more than one patient per room.

- Before and after removing gloves (new gloves with each patient).

- Before handling invasive devices, including injections.

- After coughing or sneezing.

- Before handling food and oral medications.

Use Soap and Water (not alcohol-based rubs) in these situations

- Before eating.

- After using the restroom.

- Anytime there is visible soil (anything noticeable on the hands).

- After caring for a patient with diarrhea or known *C. difficile* or spore forming organisms – alcohol-based hand rubs have poor activity against spores.

- Before caring for patients with food allergies.

Soap and Water Technique

- Wet both sides of hands, apply soap, rub together for at least 15 (slow) seconds.

- Rinse thoroughly.

- Dry with paper towel and use the towel to turn off the water.

Alcohol-Based Hand Rubs Technique

- Use enough gel (2-5 mL or about the size of a quarter).

- Rub hands together until the rub dries (15-25 seconds).

- Hands should be completely dry before putting on gloves.

Hand-Hygiene for Sterile Compounding

- Wash with soap and water up to the elbows using an alcohol-based surgical hand scrub.

It is important to properly clean surfaces, including bed rails, eating trays, and other room surfaces. Health care professionals should be careful not to be sources of infection from contaminated clothing (including white coats and ties). Organisms that spread via surface contact include VRE, *C. difficile*, noroviruses and other intestinal tract pathogens.

Safe Injection Practices

Outbreaks involving the transmission of blood borne pathogens or other microbial pathogens to patients (and occasionally to healthcare workers) continue to occur due to unsafe injection technique. The majority of safety breaches involve the reuse of syringes in multiple patients, contamination of IV bags with used syringes, failure to follow basic injection safety when administering IV medications and inappropriate care or maintenance of glucometer equipment that is used on multiple patients.

The following practices ensure safe injection of medications. These recommendations are meant for healthcare facilities; see the Drug Disposal chapter for more information on syringe disposal for patients.

- Never administer an oral solution/suspension IV. Many medication errors (sometimes fatal) have occurred this way. Always label oral syringes "for oral use only."

- Never reinsert used needles into a multiple-dose vial or solution container (whenever possible, use of single-dose vials is preferred over multiple-dose vials, especially when medications will be administered to multiple patients).

- Needles used for withdrawing blood or any other body fluid, or used for administering medications or other fluids should preferably have "engineered sharps protection" which reduces the risk of an exposure incident by a mechanism such as drawing the needle into the syringe barrel after use.

- To avoid contamination to the patient, never touch the tip or plunger of a syringe.

- Disposable needles contaminated with drugs, chemicals or blood products should never be removed from their original syringes unless no other option is available. Throw the entire needle/syringe assembly (needle attached to the syringe) into the red plastic sharps container.

- Never remove a needle by unscrewing it.

- Used disposable needles/sharps should be discarded immediately after use without recapping into a sharps container (a non-reusable plastic container that is puncture resistant, leak proof on the sides and bottom, properly labeled and closable).

- Sharps containers should be easily accessible, replaced routinely, and not allowed to overfill. Never compress or "push down" on the contents of any sharps container.

- If someone is stuck with a needle the proper department at the facility should be contacted immediately.

STERILE MEDICATION PREPARATION AND LAMINAR FLOW HOODS

Medications given intravenously bypass the protective mechanisms of the skin barrier and gastrointestinal tract. About half of medications given in the hospital setting are given IV. If the medication is contaminated the patient will suffer severe adverse effects and possible death. In addition to IV preparations, items that must be prepared in a sterile manner are opthalmics, inhalations, tissue soaks (for organ transplants), other implants, and irrigations.

Hoods are ventilation devices used to keep sterile compounded or parenteral drugs free of contaminants, and are used to keep the pharmacy area free of noxious fumes. The picture shows a horizontal hood. Vertical flow hoods (also called biological safety cabinets or chemotherapy hoods) blow air <u>from the top down</u> to maintain sterility and to protect the pharmacist or technician preparing the medication from breathing in dangerous fumes. Vertical hoods are used for <u>chemotherapy</u> and other hazardous medications. <u>Laminar flow means that the air is moving in an uninterrupted, constant stream. The air is drawn through a High Efficiency Particulate Air (HEPA) filter that catches particulates.</u> The air is may be directed horizontally toward the user, as shown in the picture of the horizontal hood. Some laminar flow hoods move the air vertically. HEPA filters remove 99.97% of all air particles <u>0.3 mm or larger</u>. This keeps the workspace area free of contaminants, including bacterial and viral organisms. The cabinet is stainless steel with a smooth design to keep out contaminants and is designed to reduce the risk of joints and other spaces where spores might accumulate.

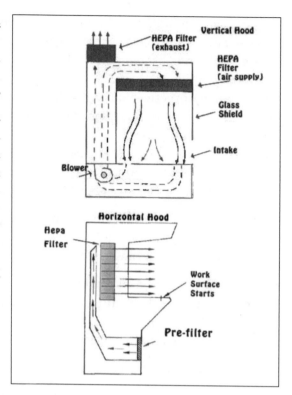

Sterile Compounding Technique and Safety

IV solutions should be isotonic (osmotic pressure matches to human blood by having the same number of particles in solution), measured via milliosmoles (mOsm) or mOsm/Liter. Human blood has 285 mOsm/L. This prevents fluid transfer across the (biological) semipermeable membranes. The pH should be close to neutral (pH of 7); blood is slightly alkaline at a pH of 7.35-7.45. No eating, drinking coughing or talking is permitted. No distractions or interruptions. Non-PVC bags should be used for medications that have leaching or sorption issues. The IV set must be sterile and nonpyrogenic.

Proper Procedure for IV Preparation Includes:

- Hand, finger and wrist jewelry is removed prior to scrubbing. Do not wear make-up if working in the hood. Wash hands using a germicidal agent (such as chlorhexidine gluconate or povidone-iodine) for at least thirty seconds being careful to clean under the fingernails, which should be kept short enough to avoid tearing the gloves. Clean up to the elbows. Dry hands completely.

- Garb up in the following order: shoe covers, a hair/head cover, facial mask. Wash hands again, dry, put on sterile powder-free gloves. If the gloves rip at any time, replace immediately.

- Laminar flow hoods are kept running and cleaned as directed. Prior to use (at least at beginning of each work shift and as-scheduled) all surfaces should be thoroughly cleaned with 70% sterile isopropyl alcohol in a side-to-side motion, starting from the back of the hood. In addition, clean whenever there is a spill or if the hood looks like it requires cleaning.

- Gather all components and check expiration dates, discoloration, particulates (discard) and leaks.

- Only required items can be placed in the hood, side by side (not behind each other except possibly for items such as consecutive bags that additives are being placed into, for example – if this is done, place the larger items behind the smaller ones and do not put more than a few in this manner) and do not block three inches from the back of the hood.

- Leave <u>six inches from the front edge of the hood clear (this is where the air starts to mingle)</u>, with no blockage to the HEPA filter. Only essential objects and materials necessary for product preparation should be placed in the airflow hood (no pens or calculators.) Leave three inches in front of the back of the hood clear.

- Do not tear open components. Open along seal within the hood. Do not touch the syringe tip or plunger, even with gloved hands.

- Work in the center and place critical items reasonably close to the air source.

- Nothing should pass behind a sterile object and the HEPA filter in a horizontal airflow hood or above a sterile object in a vertical airflow hood. Chemotherapy must be done in a vertical hood.

- For greatest accuracy, use the smallest syringe that can hold the desired amount of solution. The syringe should not be larger than twice the volume to be measured.

- The volume of solution drawn into a syringe is measured at the point of contact between the rubber piston and the side of the syringe barrel.

- Powders are reconstituted by introducing a diluent such as sterile water for injection.

- Prior to withdrawing any liquid from a vial, first inject an equal volume of air to the fluid removed (Exception: do not inject air prior to removing cytotoxic drugs from vials).

- Swab the rubber top (or ampule neck) with sterile isopropyl alcohol, and wait for it to air-dry; do not blow on or wave over it to dry faster.

- Puncture the rubber top of the vial with the needle bevel up. Then bring the syringe and needle straight up, penetrate the stopper, and depress the plunger of the syringe, emptying the air into the vial. Invert the vial with the attached syringe. Draw up from the vial the amount of liquid required. Withdraw the needle from the vial. In the case of a multi-dose vial, the rubber cap will close, sealing the contents of the vial.

- If the medication is in a glass ampule, open the ampule by forcefully snapping the neck away from you, then tilt the ampule, place the needle bevel of a filter needle or tip of a filter straw in the corner near the opening, and withdraw the medication. Use a needle equipped with a filter for filtering out any tiny glass particles, fibers, or paint chips that may have fallen into the ampule. Before injecting the contents of a syringe into an IV, the needle must be changed to avoid introducing glass or particles into the admixture. A standard needle could be used to withdraw the drug from the ampule; it is then replaced with a filter device before the drug is pushed out of the syringe.

- Instruct the technicians to keep all the additives with the bag and the syringes used (pulled up to the precise volume that was injected into the bag) for the pharmacist to check.

IV Bag Preparation, Label Includes:

- Patient name, location, other identification such as medical record number, DOB

- Active ingredient(s) and quantity of each

- IV solution (diluent)

- Run rate or frequency

- Scheduled hang time, using a 24 hour scale (where midnight is 0000, noon is 1200, 11:59PM is 2359)

- Any special storage conditions, auxiliary labels, precautions, date prepared

- Expiration date and time and device specific instructions, if needed

- Initials of pharmacist (and tech)

THE JOINT COMMISSION ON ACCREDITATION OF HEALTHCARE ORGANIZATIONS (JOINT COMMISSION, OR TJC)

The Joint Commission is an independent, not-for-profit organization that accredits and certifies more than 17,000 health care organizations and programs in the U.S. including hospitals, health care networks, long term care facilities, home care organizations, office-based surgery centers and independent laboratories. The Joint Commission focuses on the highest quality and safety of care and sets standards that institutions must meet to be accredited. An accredited organization must undergo an on-site survey at least every three years and surveys can be unannounced.

National patient safety goals (NPSGs) are set annually by the Joint Commission for different types of health care settings in order to improve patient safety. Each goal includes defined measures called "Elements of Performance" that must be met. These will be included in the institution's protocol. There are other NPSGs not discussed here, such as a goal for conducting a preprocedure verification process and another for identifying patients at risk of suicide. Pharmacists focus on medication-related NPSGs. Current hospital NPSGs related to medication safety include the following:

NPSG 03.04.01: Label all medications, medication containers and other solutions on and off the sterile field in perioperative and other procedural settings.

Numerous errors, sometimes fatal, have occurred due to medications and other solutions that were removed from their original containers and placed into unlabeled containers. This is of particular concern in perioperative and other procedural areas. Pharmacists should ensure that all medications and medication containers are labeled. The exception is when an agent is to be immediately administered without a break in the medication use process. Medication and solution labels should contain medication name, strength, quantity, diluent and volume and expiration date/time.

NPSG 03.05.01: Reduce the likelihood of harm associated with anticoagulant therapy.

There are many elements to this goal, including the requirement to use standardized dosing protocols, monitoring INRs, using programmable pumps for heparin, and providing education to patients and families. In the protocol, starting dose ranges are included; if the prescriber requests a dose out of the range the pharmacist will need to confirm agreement. The protocol will note alternative dosing ranges for a drug that increases or decreases the therapeutic effect of the anticoagulant. For example, if a drug that inhibits warfarin metabolism is being used concurrently, a lower starting dose will be required. INR monitoring frequency (plus baseline INR) will be in the protocol, along with the requirement to notify dietary.

NPSG 03.06.01: Maintain and communicate accurate patient medication information

This includes medication reconciliation, providing written information to the patient and conducting discharge counseling. In conducting the reconciliation the medication name, dose, frequency, route, and purpose (at the minimum) should be confirmed. Refer to Medication Reconciliation earlier in this chapter.

NSPG 02.03.01: Report critical results of tests and diagnostic procedures on a timely basis

This includes identifying and acting upon critical lab values, blood culture results, and other critical results as defined in the protocol. It should state the acceptable length of time between the availability and the reporting. The process should be evaluated to make sure the time is being met. Pharmacists should play an active role in this communication process.

NPSG 07.01.01: Comply with the Centers for Disease Control (CDC) hand hygiene guidelines

Proper hand hygiene technique as described previously in this chapter. The goals for improving compliance should be stated, and the frequency of monitoring to ensure the goals are being met must be included.

NPSG 07.03.01; 07.04.01; 07.05.01; 07.06.01: Implement evidence-based practices to reduce healthcare associated infections

These include recommendations to reduce the likely sources of infection, such as from urinary catheters [only use if warranted, proper hand hygiene prior to insertion by qualified personnel only, properly secure the indwelling catheter, use the smallest bore catheter possible, with good drainage (to minimize tissue damage – all insertion and removal should be done according to the institution's protocol), continue to assess the need for continued catheter use <u>in order to remove the catheter as soon as it is no longer needed</u>] and ventilators (<u>elevate head-of-bed</u> 30-45 degrees, assess readiness to <u>wean off</u> ventilator at least daily, use breaks or <u>reductions in sedation use</u> if possible, consider <u>DVT prophylaxis</u>, use stress-ulcer prophylaxis <u>judiciously</u> and only in patients who meet requirements for use; refer to Intravenous Drugs chapter).

NPSG 01.01.01: Use at least two patient identifiers when providing care, treatment and services

There have been countless medication errors (and surgical misadventures) due to patient misidentification. Two identifiers (such as name and medical record number) must be verified prior to administering medications, blood or blood components, taking lab samples or providing any treatment or procedure. <u>The identifiers must be patient-specific – things like doctor's name, zip code or patient location should not be used.</u>

CONCLUSION

We are in an age where medication delivery is becoming more accountable and poor safety routines are no longer acceptable. Proactive assessment of safe medication use involves pharmacists at every step. Fortunately, we are over twenty years into the process and there is now a wide range of resources and information available to help us provide improved medication safety.

FDA DRUG APPROVAL AND THERAPEUTIC EQUIVALENCE

REFERENCE

http://www.fda.gov/drugs/developmentapprovalprocess/default.htm

We gratefully acknowledge the assistance of John An, PharmD, PhD, PPD Regulatory Intelligence Manager, in preparing this chapter.

OVERVIEW

The U.S. drug approval process is overseen by the Food and Drug Administration's (FDA) Center for Drug Evaluation and Research (CDER) for prescription and nonprescription or over-the-counter (OTC) drugs. There are four other FDA centers responsible for medical and radiological devices, food, and cosmetics, biologics, and veterinary drugs. The FDA is an important organization in safeguarding public health. A notable example that emphasizes this point was the refusal of Dr. Frances Oldham Kelsey, a FDA reviewer, to approve thalidomide as an antiemetic for use in pregnancy. In the 1950's and 60's thalidomide was given to pregnant women in other countries, and caused thousands of cases of severe birth defects including missing long bones. This case is considered one of the worst examples of medication-induced tragedy. Fortunately, the American consumer was largely protected by the heroic action of one FDA administrator.

Investigational products seeking medical claims must go through a review and approval process for both nonprescription (OTC) and prescription drugs, before they can be marketed. OTC drugs are defined as "drugs that are safe and effective for use by the general public without seeking treatment by a health professional" with less stringent regulations than prescription drugs. Manufacturers and sponsors seeking OTC drug designation can be approved through two routes; the New Drug Approval (NDA) process for new agents or indications or under the OTC monograph process. The OTC drug monograph is a "recipe book" of approved ingredients, doses, indications, formulations, and labeling requirements. If the drug and indication is already found in the OTC monograph, it may be marketed without further FDA review.

For prescription drugs, the drug approval process begins with pre-clinical (animal) research, which is followed by an Investigational New Drug (IND) application to conduct human clinical trials. [Or, if the company is requesting approval of a generic drug, they file an Abbreviated New Drug Application (ANDA)].

Current federal law requires that a drug be the subject of an approved marketing application before it is transported or distributed across state lines. Because an investigator will want to ship the investigational drug to clinical investigators in many states, they must seek an exemption from that legal requirement. The IND is the means through which the sponsor technically obtains this exemption from the FDA in order to conduct clinical trials. There are several phases of clinical trials performed to identify the drug's efficacy and safety. These phases are outlined in the chart on the following page. Note that each phase includes varying safety analysis.

Phase I studies focus on the safety and pharmacology of a compound. Low doses of the compound are given to a small group of healthy volunteers who are closely supervised. In cases of severe or life-threatening illnesses, volunteers with the disease may be used.

Phase II studies examine the effectiveness of a compound. Patients without complications and co-morbidities are often selected for a trial to reduce the number of confounding variables that may influence the trial results. Enrolling healthier individuals allows the potential benefit of the drug to be more clearly demonstrated. It is common in phase 2 trials to have 3 or 4 arms of the study; each investigating different doses for the best therapeutic benefit and minimal side effect profile.

After phase II, the manufacturer meets with the FDA to pave way for the "pivotal trials." Phase III trial designs must obtain FDA approval before enrollment can begin. During phase III, researchers try to confirm previous findings in a larger population. These studies usually last from 2 to 10 years and typically involve hundreds to thousands of patients across multiple sites.

After Phase III, the manufacturer files a New Drug Application (NDA). Once the NDA is filed, the FDA has one year to review all the data and provide its decision to the manufacturer/researcher. The NDA can either be approved or rejected, or the FDA may request further study before making a decision. Following acceptance, the FDA can also request that the manufacturer conduct additional post-marketing studies (AKA phase IV). Fast-track approval may be given to agents that show promise in treating serious, life-threatening medical conditions for which no other drug either exists or works well. Currently, the FDA is expected to make a decision within 6 months from submission if a drug is fast-tracked; however, this may change when PDUFA V is fully implemented.

IMPORTANCE OF PHASE IV

For some drugs the total drug approval process is limited to a few hundred patients – while in others, such as cardiovascular drugs, tens of thousands of subjects can be included. If a drug is tested in a relatively small number of patients, the complete safety profile may be missed. Even in larger trials, safety issues may be missed due to the exclusion of certain patient types. The FDA may request a post-marketing, or phase IV, study to examine the risks and benefits of the new drug in a different population or to conduct special monitoring in a high-risk population. The phase IV study can also be used to assess such issues as the longer term effects of drug exposure, to optimize the dose for marketing, to evaluate the effects in pediatric patients, or to examine the effectiveness of the drug for additional indications.

PHASE	PURPOSE	SUBJECTS	SCOPE	LENGTH OF TIME
I	Safety profile and dosing range, PK/PD, open label, often 1 center, may not be done in the US	Can be healthy volunteers or patients with illness	20-80 subjects	6-12 months
II	Safety and efficacy (dose response) IIa – proof of concept; pilot study, etc. IIb- well-controlled target population	Used in intended population	100-300 patients	1-2 years
III	Safety and efficacy at the dose and schedule you are seeking approval (package labeling) IIIb – post NDA –submission trial looking at additional indications	Subjects with indications the drug is seeking	Hundreds to thousands of patients	2-3 years
IV	New indications, QOL, surveillance studies	Subjects with indications the drug is seeking	Hundreds to thousands	1-5 years

For changes to an existing drug, the Supplemental New Drug Application (sNDA) is used. These changes include:

- Labeling changes
- New dose
- New strength
- New manufacturing process

Bioequivalence

Orange Book

- Can look up by active ingredient, proprietary name, applicant holder or applicant number.

- Published by the Food and Drug Administration (FDA) Center for Drug Evaluation and Research (CDER).

- Available at www.fda.gov/cder/ob

RATINGS

- **AA** Products in conventional dosage forms not presenting bioequivalence problems.

- **AB** Drugs that have been proven to meet the necessary bioequivalence requirements through in vivo and/or in vitro testing. AB is the most common designation. Drugs coded as AB are therapeutically equivalent and can be interchanged (brand to generic).

- The FDA may not have compared each generic to each brand of the same drug. For example, the Orange Book lists *Cardizem SR*, *Cardizem CD*, *Dilacor XR*, and *Tiazac* under the heading for diltiazem. These are not bioequivalent to each other; however, some have generic equivalents.

- For example, *Cardizem SR* and the generic formulations are "AB1," *Dilacor XR* is "AB2," The generic for *Cardizem CD* is "AB3." Products rated AB1 are bioequivalent to each other, products rated AB2 are bioequivalent to each other, and so forth.

- The 2nd letter can also refer to the dosage form:

- **AN** Solutions and powders for aerosolization

- **AO** Injectable oil solutions; these are considered to be pharmaceutically and therapeutically equivalent only when the active ingredient, its concentration, and the type of oil used as a vehicle are all identical.

- **AP** Injectable aqueous solutions

- **AT** Topical products, including those for dermatologic, ophthalmic, otic, rectal, and vaginal administration formulated as solutions, creams, ointments, gels, lotions, pastes, sprays, and suppositories

Biologic and Biosimilar Drug Formulations

Many drugs are _biologics_, including enzymes, vaccines, insulins, interferons, interleukins, erythropoietins, gonadotropins, granulocyte-colony stimulating factors, growth hormones, monoclonal antibodies and tissue plasminogen activators. _Biologics were first developed using recombinant technology_, using DNA grown in bacteria, yeast or mammalian cells. The drugs produced are more complex and larger than usual tablets and capsule formulations. For pharmacists, they require considerations for _storage_ (regarding refrigeration), _stability_ concerns (these do not last as long as more stable oral formulations) and _instructions for patients_ on administration and adverse effect management. These drugs have an overall higher risk of safety concerns, including higher incidence of severe reactions. Yet, they are very useful for many conditions. The growth in these agents has fueled the "specialty pharmacy" sector of our profession but many can be dispensed in the community pharmacy. These agents are much more <u>expensive</u> than typical drugs; for example: methotrexate for a year's supply for a patient with rheumatoid arthritis costs ~$750 and adalimumab costs about ~$50,000.

Patents are expiring for some of the common biologics and many "biosimilars" will become available. Biologics are approved under the Public Health Service Act (PHSA) and conventional drugs are approved under the Federal Food, Drug and Cosmetic Act (FDCA). The FDCA allows generic drug approvals via the Abbreviated New Drug Applications. Legislation under the Affordable Care Act established a regulatory pathway for biosimilars to allow approval for drugs that were considered "comparable" and "interchangeable" to the parent compound. Pharmacists look for bioequivalence ratings on drugs using the FDA's Orange Book. Enoxaparin was the first "biosimilar" but the FDA allowed approval of the "generic" using the ANDA and the "generic" formulations of enoxaparin can be found in the Orange Book. Yet, it could have been classified as a Biosimilar. Issues regarding biosimilar approvals and substitutions will continue until the legal issues are resolved. Enoxaparin has been the most costly item in hospital pharmacy budgets and this influenced the FDA's decision to allow approval as a generic drug, to the dismay of Sanofi, the manufacturer of Lovenox.

Patents and Exclusivity

Typically drugs are given patents from the date of filing (these are for twenty years) and exclusivity, which is exclusive marketing rights granted by the FDA upon approval of a new drug, which typically last for 5 years (on paper) but much longer in practice when the patents are tied up for years in court. Biologics, in contrast, are granted exclusivity for twelve years in order to compensate the manufacturer for the higher cost associated with development. Biosimilars do not need to be biologically identical to the original product and are not expected to be identical since differences in the manufacturing process alter the end product. To gain approval they need to demonstrate that they are not "clinically different" by providing data demonstrating that the biosimilar has no clinically significant differences in "safety, purity and potency." The FDA has considerable flexibility to decide, for each agent, what type of clinical data the manufacturer is required to submit. Since we are now on the "patent cliff" in which many biologics exclusivity is expiring the legality regarding biosimilar approval is expected to remain big drug news. Stay tuned.

NATURAL PRODUCTS & VITAMINS

REFERENCE

Natural Medicines Database, available at www.naturaldatabase.com

Shapiro, K. Natural Products: A Case-Based Approach for Health Care Professionals, APhA, Washington, D.C. 2007.

We gratefully acknowledge the assistance of Casey Whitaker, PharmD, in preparing this chapter.

BACKGROUND

Natural product use has a long history of traditional use among native cultures and has become popular today. Many patients supplement their diet or prescription medicines with vitamins or natural products. Natural product is an umbrella term that includes herbals (plant products), vitamins and many substances that are not plant-derived but exist in nature, such as glucosamine from shellfish.

Most natural products act as either mild drugs or are harmless. Pharmacists have accessible sources to check for drug interactions, safety concerns, dosage by indication, and quality. Some natural products pose health risks. A few top safety concerns include manufacturing quality, safety and effectiveness, and the use of a few select agents that can pose specific problems in certain patients:

<u>Manufacturing may not follow good manufacturing practices (GMP);</u> pharmacists need to help consumers choose a reputable product. In recent years quality companies have put in place programs that will put a seal of approval on products made by a company following good manufacturing practices. The website consumerlab.com is useful to help choose a reputable product – this is an independent testing service that analyzes the content of many popular supplements.

<u>A dietary supplement manufacturer does not have to prove a product's safety and effectiveness before it is marketed.</u> For example: late-night TV ads are promoting a thyroid product to help with low energy and fatigue. Perhaps some patients need a thyroid supplement, but this requires lab testing. If people who do not need thyroid hormone take it, they can become hyperthyroid and be subject to cardiovascular and other health risks. The product quality may

be poor – this can be a particular issue with thyroid hormone which may contain prions that can carry mad cow disease. Last but not least, the product used in this example is expensive. Generic levothyroxine, a safer alternative, is pennies per tablet.

Three areas of particular safety concern are natural products that increase bleeding risk, interactions between prescription drugs and St. John's wort and natural products that may be hepatotoxic.

- Ginkgo biloba and other agents that can ↑ bleeding risk

- Ginkgo biloba increases bleeding risk with no effect on the INR. Other natural products that can also pose a risk include bromelains, danshen, dong quai (this product may ↑ INR), vitamin E, evening primrose oil, high doses of fish oils, garlic, ginseng, glucosamine, grapefruit, policosanol, and willow bark.

- Enzyme induction by St. John's wort: this herbal is a "broad-spectrum" inducer and cannot be used with oral contraceptives, transplant drugs, warfarin, among others. St. John's wort induces 3A4 >> 2C9 > 1A2. See the Drug Interactions chapter. SJW causes photosensitivity and is serotonergic; caution with 5HT drugs.

- Natural products may be hepatotoxic (chaparral, comfrey, kava). If liver enzymes are elevated, check with the patient – sometimes the use of "tea blends" or mixtures can be contributory.

Safety/Financial Comments on Homeopathic Products and Medical Foods

Homeopathic Products: Homeopathy is based on "the law of similars" or the concept that "like is cured by like." This is the belief that giving very small amounts of the illness (so dilute that the original substance cannot be measured) will protect the patient or cure them of an illness. Most evidence does not support validity to homeopathy, however many adherents (including the Queen of England) are advocates. The remedies may be providing a placebo benefit, or, may actually be labeled as homeopathic but contain measurable concentrations of drugs. In 2010, *Hyland's Teething Tablets* were recalled due to cases of belladonna toxicity. The amount of belladonna could be measured and was unsafe. It is tempting to use the term "homeopathic" on a label. It sounds nice, and if a manufacturer labels a product "homeopathic," they are permitted to make health claims, while natural products are not allowed by law to claim benefit for particular conditions. There have been other recent examples of products labeled as homeopathic which actually were not. Check the ingredients.

Medical Foods: These are products that can also make health claims, since they are not FDA-approved drugs. Medical foods are supposed to meet a nutritional need for a group that cannot be met with usual foods, such as specific formulations of enteral nutrition. A recent medical food that many pharmacists will have seen is a formulation of folic acid called *Deplin* that is being marketed for help in treating depression. The ad for this product states that "*Deplin* is a medical food containing L-methylfolate,

VITAMINS	NAMES
Vitamin A	Retinol
Vitamin B1	Thiamine
Vitamin B12	Cobalamin
Vitamin B2	Riboflavin
Vitamin B3	Niacin
Vitamin B6	Pyridoxine
Vitamin B9	Folic Acid
Vitamin C	Ascorbic Acid

the active form of the vitamin, folate. It is the only folate that can be taken up by the brain where it helps balance the chemical messengers that affect mood (serotonin, norepinephrine and dopamine)." It is less expensive to use over-the-counter folic acid supplements and there is no evidence that this supplement would provide more benefit, however the manufacturer can make this claim since it is a medical food. In a medical food, all ingredients must be Generally Recognized as Safe (G.R.A.S.) or be approved food additives. Most of the medical foods have Rx-only on the label and have NDC numbers.

COMMONLY USED NATURAL PRODUCTS

CONDITION	TREATMENT
Anxiety	Valerian, lemon balm, glutamine, passion flower and hops (both as teas), chamomile tea, theanine and skullcap. Kava is used as a relaxant but can damage the liver and should not be recommended. Valerian may rarely be hepatotoxic (or some valerian products may have been contaminated with liver toxins); this is unclear at present. Passion flower is rated as "possibly effective" by the Natural Medicines Database. For most of the other agents the evidence is less robust but individual patients may get benefit from the various agents.
Sleep	Melatonin (also used for jet lag – carefully check doses for this use), valerian. Chamomile tea may help people relax. St. John's wort may help if the insomnia is due to depression (worry) but will lower levels of many other drugs. Kava is used but can damage the liver and should not be recommended.
ADHD	Fish oil supplements (which provide omega 3 fatty acids) with or without evening primrose oil (which provides omega-6 fatty acids) may be helpful in some patients.
Apthous Ulcers (canker sores)	Lysine
Cancer	Beta carotene, fish oil, black or green tea, garlic, soy, vitamins A and D Colon cancer: calcium Prostate cancer: lycopene (in cooked tomatoes)
Cholesterol	Fish oils (triglycerides), red yeast rice (monitor – may contain small amounts of an HMG CoA reductase inhibitor), plant sterols/stanols, certain probiotics
Depression	St. John's wort, SAMe (do not use with MAO Is), fish oils, 5-HTP, tryptophan, glutamine, inositol (for OCD and panic disorder). Caution with induction and substrates, with sun exposure and with other 5HT drugs – see above, L-methylfolate.
Colds and Flu	Echinacea (can cause mouth sores, heartburn, allergic reactions), elderberry, garlic, zinc, vitamin C. Caution for loss of smell (possibly permanent) with zinc nasal sprays and swabs.
Dementia/Memory	Ginkgo, huperzine A, vitamin E, phosphatidylserine, acetyl-L-carnitine. Caution with ginkgo for increased bleeding risk. Red palm oil is used for dementia and heart disease; unproven.
Diabetes	Bitter melon, gymnema, chromium, alpha lipoic acid, cinnamon, acetyl-l-carnitine (neuropathy). Green tea may lower DM risk.
Energy/Weight Loss	Bitter orange; caution with bitter orange (similar to ephedra, CVD risk) and guarana (caffeine, caution with excessive intake). Caffeine is in various "natural" weight loss products. A popular one in 2012-13 is "green coffee bean extract"-some products are decaffeinated. Another popular product is raspberry ketone, which is similar to synephrine.
UTI	Cranberry. Caution on the risk of kidney stones with cranberry supplements.

Commonly Used Natural Products Continued

CONDITION	TREATMENT
Gastrointestinal Distress	Peppermint oil, chamomile tea
IBD	Cascara, senna (stimulant laxatives) for constipation. For diarrhea, psyllium (in *Metamucil* and many other formulations) or other "bulk-forming" fiber products can be useful. Peppermint (oil, sometimes teas) can be useful as an antispasmodic. Some use chamomile tea. The probiotic Lactobacillus or bifidobacterium infantis may help reduce abdominal pain, bloating, urgency, constipation or diarrhea in some patients. Antibiotics and probiotics are not taken together; separate the dosing by at least two hours. Fish oils (for the EPA and DHA, omega fatty acid components) are being used, although the evidence for benefit is contradictory. Indian frankincense gum resin taken TID may be beneficial for UC, based on preliminary studies. Comfrey is used for GI issues but can damage the liver and should not be recommended.
Probiotics	Lactobacillus, bifidobacterium infantis etc – check the efficacy of the individual probiotic for the condition – they vary. Separate probiotics from antibiotics or they will get destroyed by the drug. These are used for many conditions, including diarrhea prevention with antibiotics, irritable bowel, cholesterol-lowering, and others. The type of probiotic needs to match the indication, based on efficacy.
Heart Health/Heart Failure	Coenzyme Q10, arginine (do not use with blood pressure meds – additive effect), fish oils, grape seed extract (grape seed extract used as a general health antioxidant and for atherosclerosis), garlic (mild decrease in blood pressure-caution for bleeding, may lower drug levels), hawthorne (caution – has additive effects with other drugs – can cause hypotension, dizziness with beta blockers, digoxin, calcium channel blockers, nitrates and PDE5-Is.)
Inflammation	Fish oils, willow bark (a salicylate)
Liver	Milk thistle
Menopausal Symptoms	Black cohosh (in popular menopause product *Remifemin*, generally safe, but reports of liver toxicity, some get GI upset), dong quai, red clover, evening primrose. Caution with dong quai and increased INR in patients using warfarin.
Migraine/Headache	Feverfew, willow bark, butterbur, guarana (a caffeine product), fish oils, magnesium, coenzyme Q10 and riboflavin. Combinations of these may be helpful.
Motion Sickness/Nausea	Ginger, peppermint
Osteoporosis	Soy, black cohosh, flax seed, evening primrose, calcium, vitamin D
Osteoarthritis	Glucosamine (may raise INR), Chondroitin, SAMe (do not use with MAO Is)
Prostate enlargement	Saw palmetto is used for BPH, but it is rated as "possibly ineffective" by The Natural Medicines Database. If men wish to try saw palmetto, they should be counseled to be seen first to rule out the possibility of prostate cancer and receive treatment, if needed. Pygeum and beta-sitosterol may provide benefit and are considered safe. Other products that may provide mild benefit are African wild potato extract and pumpkin seed. Rye grass pollen is used commonly in Europe. (Lycopene is used for prostate cancer prevention, however there is not good evidence for taking supplements for this purpose.)
Skin	Aloe vera, Tea tree oil is used for a variety of skin conditions. It can be useful for treating acne. It may be helpful for onychomycosis symptoms (depending on the dose and application schedule), but is not useful in eradicating the infection in most patients. Tea tree oil may also be useful for athlete's foot symptoms if the 10% oil is used (not tea tree cream). Higher concentrations (25 or 50%) can cure the infection in up to half of patients, but are not as effective as the recommended antifungal agents. This efficacy data is from the Natural Medicines Database.

VITAMIN SUPPLEMENTATION

People who consume an adequate diet do not require vitamin supplementation. However, many people eat poor diets. It is concerning to health care professionals that calcium and vitamin D intake remains insufficient for the majority of adults and children. Folic acid intake among women of child-bearing age can be insufficient. If thiamine (vitamin B1) is insufficient, this can cause Wernicke's encephalopathy. Symptoms of Wernicke's include ataxia, tremor and vision changes. A lack of vitamin B1 is common in alcoholism, and can be due to malabsorption, including from Crohn's, after obesity surgery, with advanced HIV and from a few other conditions. As the symptoms of Wernicke's fade, Korsakoff syndrome tends to develop (also called Korsakoff psychosis), which is permanent neurologic (mental) damage. Pharmacists are part of the solution to problems associated with vitamin deficiencies. Metformin can contribute to B12 deficiency, and there are other drugs with supplement recommendations (see table at end of chapter).

Calcium Supplementation

All prescription medicines for low bone density require adequate calcium and vitamin D supplementation taken concurrently (if dietary intake is inadequate). Dietary intake of calcium should be assessed first, and supplements used if insufficient. Over half of the US population has low calcium and vitamin D intake. Adequate calcium intake is required throughout life, and is critically important in children (who can build bone stores), in pregnancy (when the fetus can deplete the mother's stores if intake is insufficient) and during the years around menopause, when bone loss is rapid. Vitamin D is required for calcium absorption, and low levels contribute to various health conditions, including autoimmune conditions and cancer. In 2010 there were news reports that calcium supplementation may increase heart attack risk; at present, recommend that patients use the recommended levels and use calcium with vitamin D – the increased risk was seen in patients who did not use vitamin D with calcium. Keep in mind that increased vitamin D intake will increase calcium absorption, and this may affect the amount of calcium required. Dietary intake is preferred; supplements are used when this is insufficient.

NIH's Recommended Adequate Intakes (AIs) for Calcium (2010)

AGE	MALE	FEMALE	PREGNANT	LACTATING
0-6 months	210 mg	210 mg		
7-12 months	270 mg	270 mg		
1-3 years	500 mg	500 mg		
4-8 years	800 mg	800 mg		
9-13 years	1,300 mg	1,300 mg		
14-18 years	1,300 mg	1,300 mg	1,300 mg	1,300 mg
19-50 years	1,000 mg	1,000 mg	1,000 mg	1,000 mg
50+ years	1,200 mg	1,200 mg		

Notes on calcium selection & absorption

- Calcium absorption is saturable; doses should be divided.

- Dietary calcium is _preferred_ but is often not sufficient; most women need an additional 600-900 mg/day (2 to 3 dairy portions) to reach recommended levels.

- Calcium requires vitamin D for absorption (see below).

- Calcium citrate (_Citracal_, etc) has better absorption but is a larger pill to swallow and can be taken with or without food; usually tab has 315 mg calcium. It may be preferable with little or no stomach acid – such as with the use of H$_2$RAs and PPIs, which have been shown to increase fracture risk due to impaired calcium carbonate absorption (including dietary calcium.)

- Calcium carbonate (_Oscal, Tums_, etc) has acid-dependent absorption and should be taken with meals; usually tab is 500-600 mg.

- There is no known benefit of using more expensive formulations – recommend products made by reputable manufacturers, since lead may be present in untested products.

- Both forms come as chewables and in food products.

Vitamin D Supplementation

The NIH's recommended intake for vitamin D for people up to age 70 years is 600 IU daily, and 71+ years is 800 IU daily. However, these levels are currently controversial and many endocrinologists are recommending a higher intake of 800-2000 IU daily. This is based on the recognition that low vitamin D levels is associated with a variety of health conditions – and the fact that many Americans have low vitamin D levels. A few years ago vitamin D levels were not routinely ordered; this has become commonplace.

The 50,000 unit vitamin D2 supplement (the green capsules) are used in renal disease or short-term in adults with deficiency to replenish stores. Cholecalciferol, or vitamin D3, is the preferred source, although vitamin D2 is often the type in supplements and will provide benefit. For information on vitamin D supplementation in renal disease, refer to the renal chapter.

Folic Acid

Any woman planning to conceive (and all women of child-bearing age) should be taking a folic acid supplement (400 – 800 mcg/daily, which is 0.4-0.8 mg/daily) to help prevent birth defects of the brain and spinal cord (neural tube defects). Folic acid needs to be taken at least one month before pregnancy and continued for the first 2-3 months of pregnancy. Once pregnant, the woman is likely taking a prescription prenatal vitamin and this is continued throughout since it also contains calcium (not enough, about 200 mg) and some iron. Folic acid is in many healthy foods, including fortified cereals (some of which are not healthy), dried beans, leafy green vegetables and orange juice. Multivitamins usually contain an amount in the recommended range. Prescription prenatal vitamins usually contain 1000 mcg, or 1 mg, of folic acid. The newer birth control pill _Beyaz_ contains folate, however it is less expensive to use a different birth control pill with a supplement. _Beyaz_ contains the potassium-sparing progestin drospirenone, with ethinyl estradiol and folate.

Vitamin E

It is unusual to have a vitamin E deficiency, since it is present in many foods. Vitamin E in foods is considered healthy, but excess intake in supplements is considered a health risk (particularly CVD risk); <u>patients should not be exceeding 150 IU daily.</u>

Vitamin Requirements For Infants & Children

Most children do not need vitamins, except as listed per the American Academy of Pediatrics:

- <u>Exclusively breastfed infants or babies drinking less than 1 liter of baby formula need 400 IU of vitamin D daily (can use *Poly-Vi-Sol* or generic).</u>

- Older children who do not drink at least 4 cups of Vitamin D fortified milk also need Vitamin D supplements.

Iron Requirements For Infants & Children

0-4 months

- Supplemental iron not required.

4-6 months

- Formulas contain adequate iron; supplementation not required.

- <u>Breast-fed babies need 1 mg/kg/day from 4-6 months old and until consuming iron-rich foods.</u> At about 6 months most breast-fed babies get about half their calories from other foods.

6-12 months

- Need 11 mg/day of iron. Food sources are preferred; supplement as needed.

1-3 years old

- Need 7 mg/day of iron. Food sources are preferred; supplement as needed.

Adolescent girls

- <u>At risk of anemia once they begin menstruating.</u>

Iron-only supplements (generics available) – check bottle on iron drops because the iron mg/dropper ranges from 10-15 mg

- *Fer-In-Sol* Iron Supplement Drops

- *Feosol* Tablets and Caplets

Vitamin Supplements with Iron

- *Poly-Vi-Sol* Vitamin Drops With Iron: use if they need the vitamin D <u>and</u> iron

- Or others, such as: *Flintstones* Children's Chewable Multivitamin plus Iron, *Pokemon* Children's Multiple Vitamin with Iron, and store brands Supplements that May be Required with Certain Drugs

Supplements that May be Required with Certain Drugs

DRUG	DEPLETED NUTRIENT	CHAPTER
Metformin	Vitamin B12	Diabetes
Valproic Acid/Divalproex	Selenium, zinc, calcium, vitamin D	Epilepsy, Bipolar
Phenytoin	Selenium, zinc, calcium, vitamin D, folic acid	Epilepsy
Carbamazepine	Selenium, zinc (due to alopecia), calcium, vitamin D (due to bone loss)	Epilepsy
Oxcarbazepine	Selenium, zinc (due to alopecia)	Epilepsy
Lamotrigine	Selenium and Zinc (due to alopecia)	Epilepsy
Phenobarbital/Primidone	Selenium, zinc, calcium, vitamin D	Epilepsy
Zonisamide	Calcium and Vitamin D	Epilepsy
Topiramate	Calcium, vitamin D	Epilepsy, Weight Loss
Acetazolamide	Calcium, vitamin D	Epilepsy, Travelers
Bile Acid Sequestrants (Cholestyramine, Colsevelam, and Colestipol)	Multivitamin with A,D, E and K; separate, folic acid	Dyslipidemia
Orlistat	Multivitamin with A,D, E and K, beta-carotene; separate	Weight Loss
Methotrexate	Folic acid	Rheumatoid Arthritis, various
Loops	Potassium almost always, magnesium if needed	Hypertension and CHF
Aminoglycosides	Potassium, magnesium, calcium	Infectious Disease
Isoniazid	Vitamin B6	Infectious Disease
Trimethoprim (and *Bactrim*)	Folic acid (if used chronically)	Infectious Disease
Sulfasalazine	Folic acid due to impaired absorption	IBD
PPIs	Magnesium, calcium (possibly citrate)	GERD
Oral Contraceptives	Ferrous sulfate, folate	Contraception
Depo-Provera	Calcium, vitamin D	Contraception
Corticosteroids (used in excess)	Calcium, vitamin D	Various
Mineral Oil (possibly other laxatives used in excess)	Vitamins A, D, E, and K; separate	Constipation
Digoxin	Magnesium, potassium	Arrhythmias
Pemetrexed	Folic acid, vitamin B12	Oncology
Heparin (and possibly LMWH)	Calcium supplementation if long-term	Anticoagulation

Conditions that Require Supplements

CONDITION	REQUIRED SUPPLEMENT	CHAPTER
Alcoholism	Vitamin B1, folic acid	Hepatitis
Microcytic Anemia	Ferrous sulfate	Anemia
Macrocytic Anemia	Vitamin B12 and/or folic acid	Anemia
Pregnancy	Folic Acid, calcium, vitamin D, vitamin B6 if nausea	Pregnancy
Osteopenia/Osteoporosis	Calcium, vitamin D	Osteoporosis and Pregnancy
Osteomalacia (Rickets)	Calcium, vitamin D	Vitamin deficiency
Hyperparathyroidism and Chronic Kidney Disease	Calcium, vitamin D	Renal Disease and Bipolar Disorder (for Lithium side effect)
Scurvy	Vitamin C	Vitamin deficiency
Crohn's Disease (and possibly ulcerative colitis)	Patient specific-depends on levels; can require iron, zinc, folic acid, calcium, vitamin D, B vitamins	IBD
Cystic Fibrosis	Pancrealipase ↓ absorption of iron and ↓ concentration of vitamins A,D,E,K and folate	Cystic Fibrosis
Diabetes	Potassium, magnesium	Diabetes
Bariatric Surgery	Various; patient-specific, refer to chapter	Weight Loss
Heart Failure	Potassium, calcium, magnesium due to loop use	Heart Failure

Drugs that Require Supplementation to Work

DRUG	REQUIRED SUPPLEMENT	CHAPTER
Calcium	Vitamin D	Osteoporosis
All osteoporosis drugs	Calcium and Vitamin D	Osteoporosis
Epoetin alfa/Darbapoetin	Iron	Anemia

DRUG INTERACTIONS

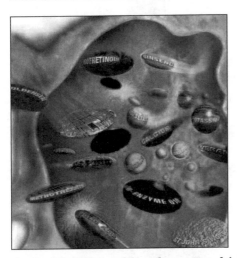

We gratefully acknowledge the assistance of Jeffrey Fudin, BS, PharmD, DAAPM, FCCP, www.paindr.com, Hannah R. Fudin, PharmD and Francis J. Zamora, PharmD, Virtua Health, in preparing this chapter.

BACKGROUND

The cytochrome P450 enzymes (abbreviated as CYP) contain many forms, but about a dozen of them are involved in the metabolism of most drugs. This discussion begins with the most common isoenzymes that are well known to pharmacists. Enzyme metabolism involves Phase I reactions (oxidation, reduction and hydrolysis), followed by Phase II, which normally terminates the activity of the drug. (Phase I provides a reactive functional group on the compound that permits the drug to be attacked by the Phase II enzymes.) Drugs are considered by the body to be foreign, similar to a toxin, which must be eliminated either through a pump that pushes the drug back into the gut (for elimination in the feces via the P-gp efflux pumps – efflux means "to flow out"), or in the bile (which eliminates through the gallbladder) or through the kidney via renal elimination. For most drugs to be excreted renally, they must be first converted (metabolized) into a more hydrophilic form, which occurs by the process of enzyme metabolism, described here.

CYP enzymes are found in many cells, but are primarily located in the liver and intestines. The majority of medications (75%) are metabolized by CYP 450 enzymes, and of these, greater than 80% are metabolized by CYP 450 <u>3A4</u> alone, or 3A4 <u>and</u> other enzymes.

<u>All enzymes in the body work using an enzyme-substrate system. The enzyme is a protein that performs some action. The substrate is a chemical that is acted upon.</u> Drug molecules, foods, and toxins are substrates for CYP enzymes. In the following figure, warfarin (the substrate) is joined with the CYP 2C9 enzyme in a manner similar to puzzle pieces. The enzyme converts the warfarin into an inactive metabolite (this is generally the case; however sometimes the conversion produces a toxic metabolite or an active or beneficial metabolite). The

metabolite is generally more water-soluble than the parent compound, which facilitates excretion (exit from the body) via filtration through the kidneys. Warfarin causes an increase in the INR (a pharmacologic action), but warfarin metabolites do not. Thus each time warfarin molecules pass through the liver, some are captured by the CYP 2C9 enzyme and converted into inactive metabolites, leaving less warfarin to elicit its beneficial effects of increasing the INR. Most of this reaction occurs during the "first pass" when the drug (substrate) passes through the gut wall and liver prior to reaching the systemic circulation.

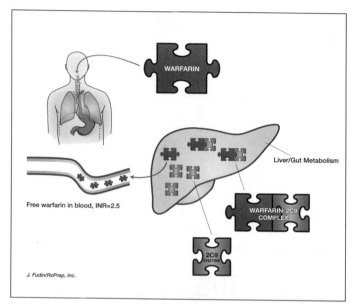

Inducers are compounds (many of which are drugs) that either increase the production of the enzyme (by increasing the expression of the gene sequence that codes for the enzyme), or, increase the activity of the enzyme. The net effect of an inducer is to increase the degree of drug metabolism, which results in lower blood levels of the substrate. In the figure to the right, rifampin has caused induction of the enzyme 2C9, which causes more of the enzyme to be present, resulting in more drug metabolism. The warfarin

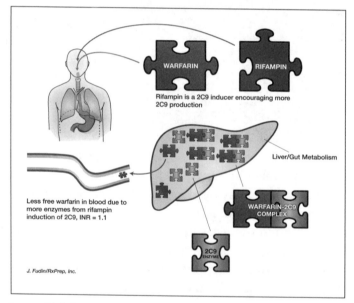

metabolism increases, less warfarin is available systemically, and the INR will decrease. Rifampin is used as an example here because it is one of the strongest inducers and induces many enzymes [1A2, 2C8, 2C9, 2C19, 3A4 and the P-glycoprotein (P-gp) pump]. If rifampin is given to a patient on warfarin the warfarin dose will need to be increased between 100-300% to keep the INR therapeutic.

In the case of prodrugs, the inducer can increase an enzyme that is responsible for converting the substrate into a more active form (instead of a less active or inactive form). Prodrug conversion is technically referred to as bioactivation.

Inhibitors are compounds (many of which are drugs) that inhibit the activity of the enzyme. The enzyme inhibition results in less drug metabolism. The drug serum level (and therapeutic effect) will increase. This can result in drug toxicity. In the figure, amiodarone, a 2C9 inhibitor is given to a patient using warfarin. Amiodarone inhibits metabolism of warfarin. The warfarin level in the serum will increase and there will be a corresponding increase in the INR. This interaction would cause a supratherapeutic INR with risk of bleeding. This

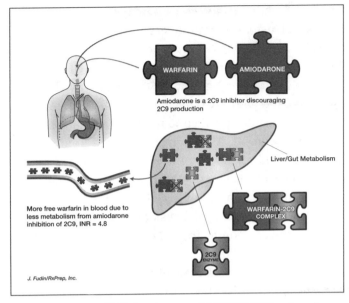

reaction is well known to pharmacists; when amiodarone is given to a patient who has been using warfarin (which is done commonly) the reaction is anticipated and the INR dose is decreased 30-50%. If they are started concurrently, a lower dose of warfarin will be given.

In the case of a prodrug, an inhibitor of the enzyme involved in bioactivation would block the production of the active form of the drug.

Prodrugs

As discussed above, inducers decrease the concentration of the substrate – except with prodrugs. Inhibitors increase the concentration of the substrate – except with prodrugs. Here, the opposite occurs because prodrugs are taken by the patient in an inactive form and are converted by bioactivation (enzyme conversion) into the active form. With prodrugs, inhibitors decrease the active form (the enzyme conversion is blocked) and inducers increase the

active form (more enzymes available to convert more of the drug).

In the figure, codeine is an inactive substrate that requires metabolism by the 2D6 enzymes to various metabolites, which include morphine. Much of the analgesic efficacy of codeine is due to the morphine metabolite. When codeine is dispensed to a patient who has not had a pharmacogenomic analysis the pharmacist will have no way of deducting the efficacy of the drug: the 2D6 enzyme is not inducible but is subject to a wide variabil-

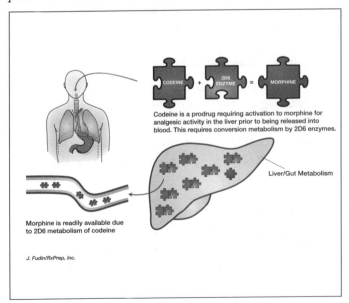

ity in 2D6 expression due primarily to ethnic variations in gene expression. Patients could be 2D6 ultrarapid metabolizers (UMs, producing a lot of the enzyme), extensive metabolizers (EMs, producing a lot of the enzyme but less than the UMs), intermediate metabolizers (IMs) or poor metabolizers (PMs). Even within ethnic groups there is wide variability in the gene expression. About 25% of drugs go through the 2D6 system, including many pain and psychiatric drugs. These two conditions, more than most others, typically involve multiple medications given concurrently for the same condition – which makes drug interaction analysis essential. Although diminished analgesic efficacy is a clinical concern, tragedies have occurred repeatedly because of the use of codeine in an UM, and resultant death from morphine overdose. In one case, a breastfeeding mother had taken codeine and (unknown to anyone) she was an UM of 2D6. Morphine passes readily into breast milk and the infant suffered fatal respiratory depression. Recently several children received a morphine overdose after receiving codeine for post-tonsillectomy pain.

In this figure the 2D6 inhibitor paroxetine inhibits the 2D6 enzymes which block the conversion of codeine to morphine, resulting in lower analgesia.

Practical Considerations: Discontinuation of an inhibitor or inducer can have dangerous consequences. If a patient is using methadone and the dose has been increased to compensate for induction and the inducer is stopped, the methadone level could become lethal. In the warfarin and rifampin example, if the rifampin is stopped the warfarin levels would become supratherapeutic – and potentially very dangerous.

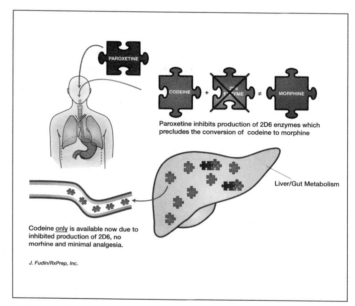

Paroxetine inhibits production of 2D6 enzymes which precludes the conversion of codeine to morphine

Liver/Gut Metabolism

Codeine only is available now due to inhibited production of 2D6, no morhine and minimal analgesia.

J. Fudin/RxPrep, Inc.

"Lag" time for Inhibition and Induction

Inhibition of an enzyme is fast and at most takes a few days to take effect and will end quickly when the inhibitor is discontinued. Induction most often requires additional enzyme production, which takes time. The full effect may not be present for up to two weeks. When the inducer is stopped it could take 2-4 weeks for the induction to disappear completely; the enzymes have been produced and will die off based on their half-lives.

P-glycoproteins (P-gp)

P-gp's are efflux transporters found in the gut and other organs. They pump drugs back into the gut (to exit out of the body). If a drug is subject to efflux, and the transporter is inhibited by a different drug, the substrate drug concentration will increase in the plasma. If an inducer is given that causes the production of more pumps, the blood levels of the substrate will decrease. The following figure is a schematic representation of this activity. Many of the P-gp drug interactions are not yet included in various pharmacy software packages, which warrants caution.

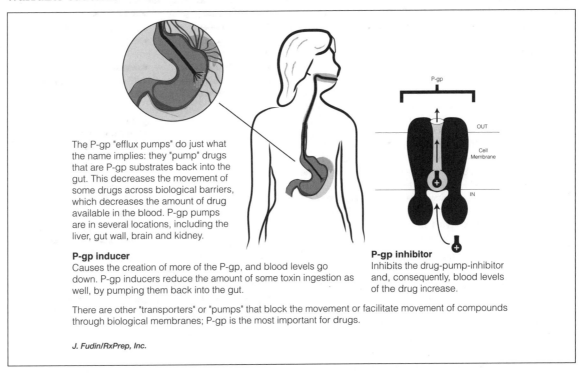

The P-gp "efflux pumps" do just what the name implies: they "pump" drugs that are P-gp substrates back into the gut. This decreases the movement of some drugs across biological barriers, which decreases the amount of drug available in the blood. P-gp pumps are in several locations, including the liver, gut wall, brain and kidney.

P-gp inducer
Causes the creation of more of the P-gp, and blood levels go down. P-gp inducers reduce the amount of some toxin ingestion as well, by pumping them back into the gut.

P-gp inhibitor
Inhibits the drug-pump-inhibitor and, consequently, blood levels of the drug increase.

There are other "transporters" or "pumps" that block the movement or facilitate movement of compounds through biological membranes; P-gp is the most important for drugs.

J. Fudin/RxPrep, Inc.

The following table provides a list of P-glycoprotein efflux pump substrates, inhibitors and inducers. This is not a complete list but includes many clinically important drugs.

P-gp Efflux Pump (Partial List)

STRONG INHIBITORS	STRONG INDUCERS	SUBSTRATES
Itraconazole	Rifampin	Aliskiren
Ketoconazole	Avasimibe	Colchicine
Verapamil	Carbamazepine	Dabigatran
Ritonavir	Phenytoin	Cyclosporine
Lopinavir/Ritonavir	St John's wort	Digoxin
Indinavir/Ritonavir	Tipranavir/Ritonavir	Fexofenadine
Conivaptan		Posaconazole
Clarithromycin		Ranolazine
Erythromycin		Rivaroxaban
Amiodarone		Saxagliptin
Quinidine		Tacrolimus

Cytochrome P 450 Substrates, Inducers, and Inhibitors (Partial List)

CLASS	SUBSTRATES	INDUCERS	INHIBITORS
3A4	alfentanil, alfuzosin, alprazolam, amiodarone, amlodipine, amprenavir, apixaban, aprepitant, atazanavir, apomorphine, aripiprazole, atazanavir, atorvastatin, buprenorphine, buspirone, carbamazepine, citalopram, clarithromycin, dapsone, delavirdine, diazepam, diltiazem, dronedarone, dutasteride, efavirenz, eplerenone, erythromycin, escitalopram, esomeprazole, estrogens, felbamate, fentanyl, fosamprenavir, haloperidol, hydrocodone, indinavir, ketoconazole, lansoprazole, levonorgestrel, lidocaine, lopinavir, losartan, lovastatin, mirtazapine, modafinil, nateglinide, nelfinavir, nevirapine, nifedipine, omeprazole, ondansetron, oxycodone, progesterone, propoxyphene, quinidine, rabeprazole, ranolazine, repaglinide, ritonavir, rivaroxaban, saquinavir, sildenafil, simvastatin, sirolimus, tadalafil, tipranavir, tramadol, trazodone, vardenafil, venlafaxine, verapamil, (R)-warfarin, zolpidem	carbamazepine, oxcarbazepine, phenytoin, phenobarbital, primidone, rifabutin, rifampin, rifapentine, smoking, St. John's wort	amiodarone, amprenavir, aprepitant, atazanavir, cimetidine, clarithromycin, cyclosporine, delavirdine, diltiazem, dronedarone, efavirenz, erythromycin, fluconazole, fluvoxamine, fosamprenavir, grapefruit juice, haloperidol, indinavir, isoniazid, itraconazole, ketoconazole, lidocaine, metronidazole, nefazodone, nelfinavir, nevirapine, posaconazole, propofol, quinidine, ranolazine, ritonavir, saquinavir, sertraline, telithromycin, verapamil, voriconazole
1A2	alosetron, amitriptyline, clozapine, cyclobenzaprine, duloxetine, estradiol, methadone, mirtazapine, olanzapine, pimozide, propranolol, rasagiline, ropinirole, theophylline, (R)-warfarin	carbamazepine, estrogen, phenobarbital, phenytoin, primidone, rifampin, ritonavir, smoking, St. John's wort	cimetidine, ciprofloxacin, clarithromycin, erythromycin, fluvoxamine, gemfibrozil, isoniazid, ketoconazole, zileuton
2C8	amiodarone, pioglitazone, repaglinide, rosiglitazone	carbamazepine, phenobarbital, phenytoin, rifampin	atazanavir, gemfibrozil, irbesartan, ritonavir
2C9	carvedilol, celecoxib, diazepam, fluvastatin, phenytoin, ramelteon, (S)-warfarin	aprepitant, carbamazepine, phenobarbital, phenytoin, primidone, rifampin, rifapentine, St. John's wort	amiodarone, cimetidine, trimethoprim/sulfamethoxazole, fluconazole, fluvoxamine, isoniazid, ketoconazole, metronidazole, voriconazole, warfarin, zafirlukast
2C19	clopidogrel, phenytoin, thioridazine, voriconazole	carbamazepine, phenobarbital, phenytoin, rifampin	cimetidine, esomeprazole, etravirine, efavirenz, fluoxetine, fluvoxamine, ketoconazole, modafinil, omeprazole, topiramate, voriconazole
2D6	amitriptyline, aripiprazole, atomoxetine, carvedilol, clozapine, codeine, desipramine, dextromethorphan, donepezil, doxepin, fentanyl, flecainide, haloperidol, hydrocodone, imipramine, lidocaine, meperidine, methadone, methamphetamine, mirtazapine, nortriptyline, oxycodone, propafenone, propoxyphene, propranolol, thioridazine, tramadol, trazodone, venlafaxine		amiodarone, cimetidine, darifenacin, duloxetine, fluoxetine, paroxetine, propafenone, quinidine, ritonavir, sertraline

QUICK STUDY TOOL FOR CYP INTERACTIONS
SEE MORE COMPLETE LIST OF INDUCERS AND INHIBITORS BELOW

PS PORCS (BIG INDUCERS)

Phenytoin

Smoking

Phenobarbital

Oxcarbazepine

Rifampin (and rifabutin, rifapentine)

Carbamazepine (and is an auto-inducer)

St. John's wort

G ♥ PACMAN (BIG INHIBITORS)

Grapefruit

♥

PIs Protease Inhibitors (don't miss ritonavir) but check all PIs since many are potent inhibitors

Azole antifungals, the agents that are used oral and IV: fluconazole, itraconazole, ketoconazole, posaconazole and voriconazole

C – cyclosporine and cimetidine, the H_2RA that is the most difficult to use due to DIs and androgen-blocking effects (that can cause gynecomastia – swollen, or painful breast tissue or impotence)

Macrolides (clarithromycin and erythromycin), not azithromycin, but DO include the related compound telithromycin

Amiodarone (and dronedarone)

Non-DHP CCBs diltiazem and verapamil

SELECT DRUGS WITH SIGNIFICANT INTERACTIONS – WATCH FOR THESE

This is only some, but not all of the common drug interactions – refer to the individual chapters.

Amiodarone

The following medications must have the doses ↓ 30-50% when starting amiodarone: digoxin, warfarin, quinidine and procainamide. Use lower doses of simvastatin, lovastatin and atorvastatin. Digoxin and warfarin are likely drugs to be given with amiodarone (for heart failure, and for arrhythmia). If the drugs are started concurrently the lower dose of the digoxin or warfarin is used. If warfarin or digoxin is on board first, the pharmacist must recognize the interaction and decrease the dose when amiodarone is started.

Digoxin

The digoxin level increases mostly due to a decline in renal function or hypokalemia. The drug interaction with amiodarone is described previously. Another consideration with digoxin is additive drugs that lower heart rate (< 60 BPM). These are primarily beta blockers and the non-DHP calcium channel blockers (diltiazem and verapamil). Other drugs that lower heart rate are amiodarone, dexmedetomidine (Precedex), clonidine and opioids. Bradycardia is one of the symptoms of organophosphate poisoning, which occurs most commonly with farm workers due to pesticide exposure.

Grapefruit Juice/Fruit Interactions

Concurrent use with grapefruit and some drugs (including simvastatin, lovastatin and atorvastatin and CCBs) will cause an increase in the drug concentration which may or may not be clinically relevant. With some drugs, it could be quite clinically relevant. For example, with rivaroxaban or ticagrelor there would be increased bleeding risk and with QT prolongers there would be risk of torsades (lurasidone, quinidine, many others). If there is any risk, safety is paramount. Counsel the patient to avoid grapefruit. This is not a "gut interaction" problem; the drug metabolizing enzymes are inactivated.

Lamotrigine & Valproate

This combination has high risk for severe rash and requires a careful titration with patient or parent monitoring. The interaction should not be missed by pharmacists because the rash may occur in children (seizures may require this combination) and the parents need to know that this is an emergency. Any inhibitor of lamotrigine will require a lower dose titration that is included in the package insert. Inducers require a higher dose; this would not cause as much risk with severe rash, but it would impair seizure control.

Monoamine Oxidase Inhibitors (MAO Is)

The non-selective MAO Is have drug interactions that can cause serotonin syndrome, hypertensive crisis, and potentially be fatal. Monoamines that would have reduced metabolism with monoamine oxidase inhibitors include dopamine, epinephrine, norepinephrine, serotonin (and tyramine, which is also a monoamine and thus the problem with foods rich in tyramine). This is mostly a risk with the antidepressants (which raise levels of the monoamines) and other agents that have a similar effect. There is some degree of risk with the Parkinson agents; refer to the chapter for specifics.

- Do not use MAO Is with ephedrine and analogs (pseudoephedrine, etc.), bupropion, buspirone, linezolid, lithium, meperidine, SSRIs, SNRIs, TCAs, tramadol, levodopa, mirtazapine, dextromethorphan, cyclobenzaprine (and other skeletal muscle relaxants), some of the triptans, St. John's wort, procarbazine, lorcaserin, and some others.

- The non-selective MAO Is, the selegiline patch (at the two higher doses) and rasagiline should not be used with tyramine-rich foods, which include aged cheeses, air-dried meats, certain wines and beers and other foods which have been aged, fermented, pickled or smoked.

Hydrocodone and Tramadol

Both of these opioids are metabolized by 2D6; patients without this enzyme (~10% of Caucasians, others) or those on 2D6 inhibitors (fluoxetine, paroxetine, others) would be at increased risk of respiratory depression and, at the least, have increased side effects.

Codeine

Codeine is a partial prodrug for morphine and undergoes conversion by the 2D6 enzyme. Patients who have a lot of 2D6 will produce morphine rapidly, which could be fatal to the patient, or to the infant if the mother is using codeine and is breastfeeding. Patients who lack 2D6 or those on 2D6 inhibitors would have a lack of analgesic efficacy from the drug.

Oxycodone and Methadone

Both of these drugs are metabolized by 3A4; patients on 3A4 inhibitors could suffer fatality. This is a black box warning for oxycodone (to avoid use with 3A4 inhibitors) and a product labeling warning for methadone. Using 3A4 inducers could cause a subtherapeutic response.

PDE5-Inhibitors

These are used for erectile dysfunction, pulmonary arterial hypertension, benign prostatic hypertrophy, and a few off label uses. They are contraindicated with nitrates due to severe hypotension. The nitrate most commonly used in the outpatient setting is the sublingual formulations, which are not dosed on a regular basis; it may be necessary to review further back in the dispensing history to find if the patient has the drug. Increasingly, patients use more than one pharmacy and the pharmacy computer will not contain the complete history unless it is collected at intake and entered manually.

These drugs cause orthostasis with headache and dizziness – and are used commonly in older men, who may also be taking alpha blockers for prostate enlargement – and which have similar side effects. The additive effect could be dangerous. When adding one class to another, it is done cautiously with lower dosing. Another complication would occur if too high a dose is given; the product labeling warns against using higher doses with 3A4 inhibitors as these are 3A4 substrates and this interaction would have the effect of providing a higher dose, with more dizziness, orthostasis, flushing and headache. These side effects are related to the action of the drug; blood is moving outward, towards the periphery.

Chelation Risk – Quinolones, Tetracyclines

Antacids, didanosine, sucralfate, bile acid resins, magnesium, aluminum, calcium, iron, zinc, multivitamins or any product containing these multivalent cations can chelate and inhibit absorption; the quinolone separation times vary. The tetracycline class (including doxycycline and minocycline) have the chelation interaction and require separation.

Statins

When the statin dose is increased, the risk is higher for muscle toxicity: muscle aches, soreness, or worse, including a rapid breakdown of muscle tissue (rhabdomyolysis), which can cause renal failure as the muscle "breakdown" products enter the blood and travel to the kidneys, causing damage. The statins that have the most risk for drug interactions are the ones that go through the highest degree of 3A4 metabolism: atorvastatin, simvastatin and lovastatin. Drugs that increase statin levels (including the inhibitor gemfibrozil, macrolides, others) will increase the risk.

Calcineurin Inhibitors (Tacrolimus & Cyclosporine)

The calcineurin inhibitors (CNIs) are important because they are the central immunosuppressants used chronically (with some combination of adjuvants) and they are subject to many drug interactions. Transplant patients are immune-suppressed and this results in illness: fungal infections may be treated with systemic azoles (which are inhibitors), bacterial infections may be treated with macrolides (most are inhibitors) or with rifampin (a strong inducer) or with aminoglycosides or other nephrotoxic drugs – and the calcineurin inhibitors themselves are nephrotoxic. Depression is common post-transplant; many of the SSRIs are inhibitors. Grapefruit juice is an absolute "do not take" with the CNIs. With transplant drugs the serum level needs to remain constant, around-the-clock, to reduce the risk of graft rejection.

ADDITIVE DRUG INTERACTIONS

These involve classes of drugs which may (or may not) pose a problem individually, but can become dangerous when used with other drugs that cause similar side effects. The MAO Is discussed previously could be placed in this section since the toxic effect is generally additive [for example, a patient using fluoxetine 60 mg Q daily, bupropion 150 mg BID and (due to a recent infection) is given linezolid 600 mg IV Q 12. Consider the additive effect with substantial doses.]

Bleeding risk

Anticoagulants (warfarin, dabigatran, rivaroxaban, heparin and others) and antiplatelets (aspirin, dipyridamole, clopidogrel, prasugrel, ticagrelor) _and_ other agents that increase bleeding risk have an additive effect: the more agents being used concurrently that increase bleeding risk, the higher the bleeding risk.

In some high-risk cases (such as a patient on warfarin who had a stroke) there may even be use of an anticoagulant with an antiplatelet (such as warfarin plus aspirin). However, the use of this combination may be inadvertent; the cardiologist may have prescribed the warfarin (or other anticoagulant) and the patient is using the aspirin OTC on their own – or is using it based on an old recommendation.

Other agents that increase bleeding risk which should be avoided in patients on the above agents, or at higher bleeding risk for other reasons (such as having had a previous bleed): OTC or prescription NSAIDs, SSRIs and SNRIs, natural products, including ginkgo biloba (commonly used agent that inhibits platelet activating factor and must be stopped in advance of surgery); ginkgo biloba increases bleeding risk with no effect on the INR. Other natural products that can also pose a risk include bromelain, danshen (can ↑ INR), dong quai (can ↑ INR), vitamin E, evening primrose oil, high doses of fish oils, garlic, glucosamine (can ↑ INR), grapefruit (can ↑ INR), policosanol, willow bark and wintergreen oil (can ↑ INR).

Hyperkalemia Risk

Potassium is renally cleared; severe renal disease causes hyperkalemia by itself. The largest increases among the drugs listed here would be expected from the aldosterone blockers (spironolactone and eplerenone) since aldosterone regulates potassium excretion; if aldosterone is blocked, hyperkalemia is a significant risk. The American Heart Association has issued recommendations to minimize the risk of hyperkalemia in patients treated with these agents, which includes avoiding use if the potassium is high at baseline (> 5 mEq/L), monitoring renal function and avoiding the use of concurrent NSAIDs. This is discussed further in the Heart Failure chapter.

- Additive potassium accumulation: ACEIs, ARBs, aliskiren, amiloride, triamterene, eplerenone, spironolactone, salt substitutes (KCl), and the drospirenone-containing oral contraceptives.

- Additional drugs that can cause or worsen hyperkalemia include the calcineurin inhibitors (tacrolimus and cyclosporine), canaglifozin and sulfamethoxazole/trimethoprim, due to the trimethoprim component.

CNS Depression

CNS side effects are caused by drugs that enter the CNS (lipophilic) and primarily involve drugs that cause sedation (somnolence), dizziness, confusion (↓ cognitive function) and altered consciousness. CNS side effects can be activating (such as with the use of stimulants), but are primarily sedating. CNS depressants that are legal and dispensed in the pharmacy are one of the top causes of automobile accidents. It is not only alcohol and illicit drug use that causes car crashes. In some cases, the two are mixed, such as the use of opioids and illicit drugs, or opioids taken with alcohol. Any agent will be worse if dosed higher and taken with other CNS depressants. Pain drugs, primarily opioids, cause more accidental death (by overdose) than deaths due to car accidents, whatever the cause. There is regional variance in the risk of death from opioids: this occurs everywhere, but the Southwest and Appalachia region are the hardest-hit. The rate of drug-related deaths more than quadrupled between 1999 and 2010 in several states, including Kentucky, Indiana and Iowa.

- Additive CNS effects: alcohol, most pain medications (all of the opioids, some of the NSAIDs, other pain drugs), skeletal muscle relaxants, anticonvulsants, benzodiazepines, barbiturates, hypnotics, mirtazapine, trazodone, dronabinol, nabilone, propranolol, clonidine, and others, and many illicit substances.

QT Prolongation & Torsade De Pointes (TdP)

QT risk drugs and QT risk conditions are listed in the Arrhythmia chapter. The risk of drug-induced TdP is low relative to other drug-induced effects, but the lethality is high. TdP is always preceded by QT prolongation; yet it is only within the last ten years that the FDA set a requirement that new drugs had to be tested for the effect on the QT interval. In some cases, the drug (alone) has high QT risk (such as with dofetilide and sotalol) but with many others with lower risk the danger develops when the risk is additive, especially in an at-risk patient, such as those with underlying cardiac disease or long QT syndrome. Most commonly, the effect is additive.

Ototoxicity

Many other additive interactions are described in the individual chapters, but ototoxicity is not described elsewhere and is included here. Ototoxicity is disturbing to patients: hearing loss can cause social isolation and impair relationships. Tinnitus can become chronic and cause a large decrease in the quality of life. A loss of equilibrium and dizziness, including increased falls, can decrease confidence and cause injury. The risk increases with concurrent ototoxic drugs, higher drug levels and the duration of exposure. Drugs with known ototoxic risk include:

- Salicylates, vancomycin, aminoglycosides, cisplatin and loop diuretics. If mefloquine (anti-malarial agent) causes tinnitus, it will be present with other symptoms of neurotoxicity.

Additive ototoxic drugs are given inpatient and audiology should be consulted to conduct a baseline hearing exam and throughout treatment on a scheduled basis. With some drugs an audiology consult is ordered after a certain period of time when damage would be expected.

Practice Questions

1. Drug A is a substrate of enzyme X. Drug B is an inducer of enzyme X. A patient has been using Drug A with good results. The patient has now started therapy with Drug B. What will happen to the concentration of Drug A?

    a. Increase

    b. Decrease

    c. Stay the Same

    d. There is not enough information given

    e. None of the above

2. Drug A is a substrate of enzyme X. Drug B is an inhibitor of enzyme X. A patient has been using Drug A with good results. The patient has now started therapy with Drug B. What will happen to the concentration of Drug A?

    a. Increase

    b. Decrease

    c. Stay the Same

    d. This is not enough information given

    e. None of the above

3. Drug A is a substrate of enzyme X. Drug A is also an inducer of enzyme Y. Drug B is a substrate of enzyme Y. Drug B is also an inhibitor of enzyme X. When these drugs are both administered, what will happen to the concentrations of Drug A and Drug B?

    a. Levels of both Drug A and Drug B will increase

    b. Levels of Drug A will increase and levels of Drug B will decrease

    c. Levels of Drug A will decrease and levels of Drug B will increase

    d. Levels of Drug A will increase and levels of Drug B will stay the same

    e. There is not enough information given.

4. A patient with heart failure is using many medications, including digoxin, warfarin and pravastatin. She is started on amiodarone therapy. Which statement is correct?

    a. The INR will increase; the warfarin dose will need to be reduced

    b. The digoxin will increase; the digoxin dose will need to be reduced

    c. The pravastatin level will increase; the pravastatin dose will need to be reduced

    d. A and B

    e. All of the above

5. A patient has been using warfarin for DVT treatment. She was hospitalized for afibrillation and started on amiodarone therapy. While hospitalized, she developed an infection and was prescribed trimethoprim/sulfamethoxazole and ketoconazole. Which of the following agents will increase the INR and could result in bleeding?

    a. Amiodarone

    b. Trimethoprim/sulfamethoxazole

    c. Ketoconazole

    d. A and B

    e. All of the above

6. The pharmacist is dispensing a prescription for ciprofloxacin. The only medication the patient is using is a daily multivitamin, which she takes with breakfast and an iron supplement, which she takes with dinner. She has yogurt or cheese every day with lunch. Which counseling statement is correct?

    a. She will need to separate the ciprofloxacin from the multivitamin

    b. She will need to separate the ciprofloxacin from the iron supplement

    c. She will need to separate the ciprofloxacin from the yogurt and cheese

    d. A and B

    e. All of the above

7. Drug A is a substrate of 2C9 and a potent 3A4 inhibitor. Drug B is a substrate of 2D6 and 1A2 as well as a potent inhibitor of 2C19. Drug C is a substrate of 3A4 and a potent inhibitor of 2D6. If all three drugs were given together, what would the expected levels of each drug to do?

   a. Drug A levels would stay the same, Drug B levels would increase, Drug C levels would increase.

   b. Drug A levels would increase, Drug B levels would decrease, Drug C levels would increase.

   c. Drug A levels would decrease, Drug B levels would decrease, Drug C levels would increase.

   d. Drug A levels would increase, Drug B levels would stay the same, and Drug C levels would decrease.

   e. Drug A, B, and C levels would all increase.

8. A major drug interaction can occur with the use of grapefruit juice and which of the following medications?

   a. Atorvastatin and Amiodarone

   b. Celecoxib and Felodipine

   c. Lovastatin and Lithium

   d. Levetiracetam and Topiramate

   e. Duloxetine and Mirtazapine

9. A patient has an estimated creatinine clearance of 18 mL/min. Her potassium level is 4.8 mEq/L. The following drugs will increase her risk of hyperkalemia and should be used with extreme caution:

   a. Enalapril

   b. Valsartan

   c. Eplerenone

   d. A and B only

   e. All of the above

10. A patient is at risk for afibrillation; she has had this afibrillation in the past. The medical team has asked the pharmacist to check for drugs on her profile which can increase her risk of arrhythmia. The pharmacist should include the following medications:

   a. Fluconazole

   b. Erythromycin

   c. Ziprasidone

   d. B and C only

   e. All of the above

Answers

1-b, 2-a, 3-b, 4-d, 5-e, 6-e, 7-a, 8-a, 9-e, 10-e

RENAL DISEASE & DOSING CONSIDERATIONS

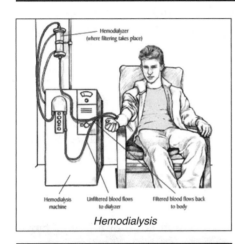

Hemodialyzer
(where filtering takes place)

Hemodialysis machine — Unfiltered blood flows to dialyzer — Filtered blood flows back to body

Hemodialysis

GUIDELINES/REFERENCES

National Kidney Foundation. KDOQI Clinical Practive Guidelines for Chronic Kidney Disease: Evaluation, Classification, and Stratification. *Am J Kidney Dis.* 2002;39(2 suppl 1):S1–266.

National Kidney Foundation. KDOQI Clinical Practice Guidelines on Hypertension and Antihypertensive Agents in Chronic Kidney Disease. *Am J Kidney Dis.*2004;43(suppl 1):S1-290.

National Kidney Foundation. KDOQI Clinical Practice Guidelines and Clinical Practice Recommendations for Anemia in Chronic Kidney Disease. *Am J Kidney Dis.*2006;47(suppl 3):S1-145.

National Kidney Foundation. KDOQI Clinical Practice Guidelines for Bone Metabolism and Disease in Chronic Kidney Disease. *Am J Kidney Dis.*2003;42(suppl 3):S1-201.

BACKGROUND

The prevalence of chronic kidney disease (CKD) has increased from 12.3% to 14% in the U.S. over the past twenty years. The most common causes of CKD are diabetes and hypertension with more than 35% of adults with diabetes and more than 20% of those with hypertension suffering from CKD. Patients with CKD have a higher risk of cardiovascular morbidity and mortality and therapies should be initiated to reduce the level of risk. The pharmacist's role in treating patients with CKD includes modifying medication regimens based on degree of renal functioning, initiating therapies to minimize disease progression, as well as treating the complications of CKD including anemia, bone and mineral metabolism, acid-base and electrolyte disturbances.

DIALYSIS

If the kidney disease progresses, then renal replacement therapy in the form of dialysis will be required to remove waste products, electrolytes and water. The two primary types of dialysis are hemodialysis (HD), and peritoneal dialysis (PD).

In HD, the patient is connected to a dialysis machine through a form of vascular access such as catheter or a more permanent form such as an arteriovenous fistula or graft. Blood leaves the patient's body and is pumped through the dialysis circuit in the machine. The blood enters the dialyzer and toxic waste products, electrolytes and water are removed through two processes; diffusion and convection. Solutes diffuse across the semiperme-

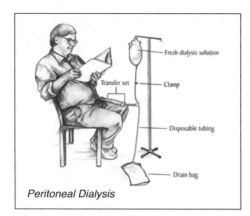

Peritoneal Dialysis

able membrane of the dialyzer and the cleansed blood is returned back to the patient. Convection is a process in which the pressure generated in the dialyzer generates filtration and allows for removal of water and solutes. HD is a 3-4 hour process, done several times (usually three times) per week. Increasingly, patients are choosing home HD, which is done more frequently (typically 5 times per week) with a portable device.

In PD, a glucose solution (the dialysate) is pumped into the peritoneal cavity, and the peritoneal membrane acts as the semipermeable membrane or the dialyzer. The solution is left in for a period of time, then drained and this cycle is repeated throughout the day, everyday. PD is performed by the patient at home. There are two types of PD: continuous ambulatory peritoneal dialysis (CAPD), which is done without a machine and automated peritoneal dialysis (ADP), where the patient uses a machine in the home to do the dialysis.

Factors Affecting Drug Removal during Dialysis

When a patient is on dialysis, the pharmacist needs to consider how much of the patient's medications are removed by dialysis in order to recommend a reasonable dosing regimen and/or schedule replacement dosing post-dialysis. The following factors determine the dialyzability of a drug:

Molecular Size

In HD, the pore size of the dialyzer determines the extent to which compounds can move across the membrane. High efficiency dialyzers are dialyzers with a large surface area whereas high flux dialyzers are those with larger pore sizes. The use of high flux dialyzers is more common and has contributed to the improved clearance of drugs such as vancomycin and daptomycin. Smaller molecules pass through more easily.

Protein Binding

Highly protein bound drugs will generally not be removed by dialysis procedures. The unbound fraction in the blood will determine how much is removed by the dialysis procedure. Examples of highly protein bound drugs include ceftriaxone and warfarin.

Volume of Distribution (VD)

Drugs with a large VD are distributed outside of the plasma space and in other tissues. Since the dialysis procedures removes drugs primarily in the blood, if a drug has a large VD, the dialysis procedure will not be effective at removing the drug. Examples of drugs that have a large VD are digoxin and amiodarone.

Plasma Clearance

The extent to which the drug is eliminated by renal clearance will determine the importance of the dialysis procedure towards drug removal. The dialysis procedure will likely not contribute much to the overall clearance of drugs with high hepatic clearance.

The Dialysis Membrane

As previously mentioned, the types of HD membrane vary. It is critical to consider the type of membrane when evaluating literature on drug removal. The membranes are characterized as low-flux (or conventional), medium-flux or high-flux. High-flux membranes have the largest pore size, and larger drugs are cleared with this method, such as vancomycin.

RENAL PHYSIOLOGY

The nephron is the functional unit of the kidney and there are roughly one million nephrons in each kidney. Blood is delivered into the glomerulus, a large filtering unit that is located within the Bowman's capsule.

Glomerulus

Substances with a molecular weight below 40,000 daltons can pass

HEMODIALYSIS AND DRUG DOSING – SUMMARY

Drug removal during dialysis depends primarily on:
- THE DRUG: VD, MW, size, protein-binding
- THE DIALYSIS: primarily due to the membrane (low or conventional, versus medium or high flux), & if HD or PD

Examples of Drug Removal in Dialysis
- L: likely significant amount of drug removed by High-Flux HD
- ND: No data
- Yes: Supplemental dosing usually required
- No: Supplemental dosing usually NOT required

DRUG	HEMODIALYSIS CONVENTIONAL, LOW-FLUX	HEMODIALYSIS, HIGH-FLUX	PERITONEAL DIALYSIS
Amikacin	Yes	L	Yes
Amiodarone	No	ND	No
Cefazolin	Yes	L	No
Cefepime	Yes	L	Yes
Ceftriaxone	No	ND	No
Cephalexin	Yes	L	No
Insulin	No	ND	No
Lithium	Yes	L	Yes
Meropenem	Yes	L	ND
Morphine	Yes	ND	No
Tobramycin	Yes	L	Yes
Vancomycin	No	Yes	No
Warfarin	No	ND	No

through the glomerular capillaries into the filtrate. Larger substances are not filtered and stay in the blood. If the filter is not damaged, large proteins such as albumin remain in the blood. If the glomerulus is damaged, some of the albumin passes into the urine. The level of albumin in the urine (micro or macroalbuminuria) can be used to gage the severity of kidney damage in patients with kidney disease or nephropathy. This is discussed further in the diabetes chapter.

Most drugs are small enough to pass through the filter. Exceptions are large protein compounds and drugs that are bound to albumin.

Creatinine, a waste product of muscle metabolism, is filtered through the glomerulus and secreted by the tubules. If the nephrons are damaged, the filtration of creatinine is reduced and the serum creatinine increases. The concentration of creatinine in the serum is used as a marker of renal function in various estimating equations. Estimates of kidney function using creatinine are not precise since the concentration of creatinine depends on the degree of muscle mass (and metab-

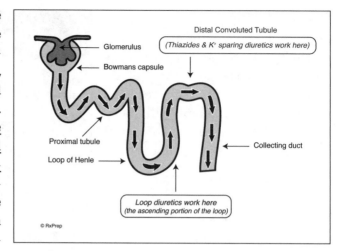

olism) in the patient. In addition, creatinine is filtered and secreted in the kidney and the contribution of tubular secretion to creatinine elimination increases with lower filtration rates.

There are more accurate markers to measure glomerular filtration rate (GFR) including inulin and radioactive substances but these markers are largely limited to the research setting.

Blood urea nitrogen (BUN) measures the amount of nitrogen that comes from the waste product urea. The BUN increases with renal impairment, however it cannot be used independently to measure declines in renal function since other factors affect the BUN, including the level of hydration.

Proximal Tubule
A primary function of the nephron is to control the concentration of water and Na+. The nephrons reabsorb what is needed (to go back into the circulation) and excrete the remainder as urine. This regulates the blood volume, and in turn, the blood pressure. "Proximal" means close to, and the proximal tubule is the closest part to the Bowman's capsule. Large amounts of water are reabsorbed here, along with Na+ and Cl-. The pH is regulated by exchange of hydrogen ions and bicarbonate ions. Water, Na+ and Cl- absorption also continues further along the nephron.

Loop of Henle
The loop of Henle has a descending limb and an ascending limb. As filtrate moves down the loop of Henle (the descending limb), water is reabsorbed, but sodium and chloride ions are not, thereby concentrating sodium and chloride in the lumen. As the filtrate moves up the loop of Henle (the ascending limb), sodium and chloride ions are reabsorbed but water is not. If antidiuretic hormone (ADH) is present, water will pass through the walls of the duct and, therefore, will not be eliminated. The more ADH present, the more water is absorbed back into the blood (anti-diuresis).

Loop diuretics inhibit the Na+-K+ pump in the ascending limb of the loop of Henle (the part that goes back up). About 25% of the sodium is reabsorbed here and inhibiting these pumps leads to a significant increase in the tubular concentration of sodium and less water reabsorption. By blocking the pump, the electrical gradient is altered and reabsorption of calcium decreases.

Distal Convoluted Tubule

Distal means farthest away and the distal convoluted tubule is the farthest away from the entry point to the nephron. The distal tubule is also involved in regulating K^+, Na^+, Ca^{2+} and pH.

Thiazide diuretics inhibit the Na-Cl pump in the distal tubule. Only about 5% of the sodium is reabsorbed at this point, which makes thiazides weaker diuretics than loops. Thiazides also increase calcium absorption by affecting the calcium pump in the distal convoluted tubule. Consequently, the long-term use of thiazide diuretics have a protective effect on bone.

Collecting Duct

The collecting duct is a network of tubules and ducts that connect the nephrons to the ureter. Urine passes from the ureter into the bladder, and from there out of the body via the urethra.

COMMON DRUGS & RENAL FUNCTION

COMMON DRUGS THAT REQUIRE DOSAGE REDUCTIONS OR INCREASED DOSING INTERVALS WITH DECREASED RENAL FUNCTION

Acyclovir, valacyclovir	NRTIs such as didanosine, lamivudine, stavudine, tenofovir, zidovudine
Allopurinol	
Amantadine	LMWHs: enoxaparin
Amphotericin	Macrolides such as clarithromycin, erythromycin
Aminoglycosides – increase dosing interval	
Azole antifungals, including fluconazole, etc.	Maraviroc
	Metoclopramide
Antiarrhythmics (digoxin, disopyramide, procainamide, sotalol)	Morphine and codeine: use lower starting dose
Anti-tuberculous medications such as ethambutol, pyrazinamide	Penicillins
	Quinolone antibiotics (most), including ciprofloxacin and levofloxacin
Aztreonam	Statins-most require dose adjustment
Beta-lactam antibiotics (most)	
Colchicine	Sulfamethoxazole/trimethoprim
Cyclosporine	Tramadol
Dabigatran	Vancomycin
Famotidine, ranitidine	Venlafaxine, desvenlafaxine
Gabapentin, pregabalin	Zoledronic Acid
Ganciclovir, valganciclovir	

The collecting duct is involved with water and electrolyte balance and is affected by levels of ADH and aldosterone. Aldosterone also works in the distal tubule. The primary function of aldosterone is to increase Na^+ and water retention and to lower K^+. By blocking aldosterone (with antagonists like spironolactone or eplerenone), serum potassium increases.

DRUGS AND RENAL CLEARANCE

Creatinine Clearance (CrCl) Estimation

A normal range of serum creatinine is approximately 0.6 to 1.2 mg/dL. A creatinine above this range indicates that the kidneys are not functioning properly. However, the values can appear normal when renal function is compromised. This is especially true in the elderly because the production and excretion of creatinine declines with age. This concern increases in frail

COMMON DRUGS THAT SHOULD NOT BE USED IN SEVERE RENAL IMPAIRMENT

Avanafil	Metformin
Bisphosphonates	Nitrofurantion
Chlorpropamide	NSAIDS
Cidofovir	Potassium-sparing diuretics
Dabigatran	Ribavirin
Dofetilide	Rivaroxaban
Duloxetine	Sotalol *(Betapace AF)*
Fondaparinux	Tadalafil
Foscarnet	Tenofovir
Glyburide	Tramadol ER
Lithium	Voriconazole IV
Meperidine	

patients who are bedridden and consequently have reduced muscle mass (creatinine concentration reflects muscle mass) and may lead to over-estimates of kidney function.

A review on how to use the Cockcroft-Gault equation is in the calculations chapter since this is the most commonly used method of estimating renal function. The Cockcroft-Gault formula may not be preferable in very young children, in end stage renal disease (ESRD) or when renal function is fluctuating rapidly. Cockcroft-Gault equation estimates are used to adjust medication regimens. Other equations such as the MDRD and CKD-EPI equations are more precise for estimating kidney function in CKD and are used to stage the severity of CKD as in the table below.

Stages of CKD

CKD STAGE	GFR (mL/min/1.73m²)
Stage 1	> 90
Stage 2	60-89
Stage 3	30-59
Stage 4	15-29
Stage 5	< 15 or dialysis dependent

Depending on the extent of renal impairment, drug regimens may need to be modified by reducing the dose and/or extending the dosing interval to avoid accumulation and potential toxicity while maintaining clinically effective serum drug concentrations. Dose reductions lead to reduced peak concentrations but maintain trough concentrations. This strategy is effective for drugs whose pharmacodynamic property is governed by a minimum concentration over the interval. Beta-lactams are a classic example of drugs that are dosed based on time above the minimum inhibitory concentration (MIC), exhibiting time-dependent killing properties. Extending the interval of a regimen maintains peak concentrations and reduces the trough concentration. This strategy is most useful for drugs such as quinolones and aminoglycosides that exhibit concentration-dependent kill of bacteria.

Impaired renal excretion – examples

Gabapentin (*Neurontin*), a drug commonly used for neuropathic pain, may cause CNS side effects such as dizziness and somnolence. Gabapentin is excreted renally and may accumulate in CKD. Gabapentin is dose adjusted when the CrCl is < 60 mL/min to minimize accumulation and the risk of sedation.

Metoclopramide (*Reglan*) is primarily used for nausea and poor GI motility. Metoclopramide is a dopamine-blocking agent and is renally cleared. In a patient with reduced renal clearance, the typical dose of 10 mg four times daily before meals and at bedtime would be too high and the patient could experience increased drowsiness, fatigue and extrapyramidal symptoms.

Proteinuria, Blood Pressure Control, and the Use of ACEIs and ARBs

Uncontrolled hypertension, diabetes and proteinuria are all risk factors for the progression of CKD. There is strong evidence to support the use of ACEIs or ARBs to prevent the progression of nephropathy in diabetic and non-diabetic patients with proteinuria. It is essential to control the blood pressure tightly. The goal blood pressure in kidney disease is < 130/80 mmHg. Glycemic control, if an issue, will also need to be tightly controlled to preserve kidney function.

ACEIs and ARBs help preserve renal function and reduce proteinuria, and provide cardiovascular protection. These drugs inhibit the renin-angiotensin-aldosterone system (RAAS), causing efferent arteriolar dilation. This is described in more detail in the hypertension chapter.

Note that the use of ACEIs and ARBs can cause a 30% rise in serum creatinine during the initiation of therapy. This rise is generally acceptable and not a reason to stop therapy. If the rise is greater than 30%, the therapy should be discontinued and the patient should be evaluated for hemodynamic factors that may need addressing. Additionally, ACEIs or ARBs may cause hyperkalemia in patients with CKD. It is important to counsel patients on adherence to potassium restricted diets in order to maximize their ACEI/ARB therapy. It is recommended that the serum creatinine and potassium be monitored 1-2 weeks after initiating ACEIs or ARBs in patients with CKD.

Anemia and bone metabolism problems in advanced renal disease

Anemia of Chronic Kidney Disease

Erythropoietin is produced by the kidneys and stimulates production of reticulocytes in the bone marrow. As kidney function declines, the production of erythropoietin declines and anemia results. In addition, chronic kidney disease is a pro-inflammatory condition that can result in anemia of chronic disease. Nutritional deficiencies may be present that could require iron, folate or vitamin B12 supplementation. Anemia identification and treatment is discussed in the anemia chapter.

Bone Metabolism Abnormalities

Patients with advanced kidney disease require screening for abnormalities associated with parathyroid hormone (PTH), phosphorus, calcium and vitamin D at regular intervals, according to the disease severity. Therapeutic targets for phosphorus, calcium and PTH is dependent on the severity of CKD. These targets are outlined in the table below.

Target Therapeutics Goals for Bone Mineral and Metabolism Disorders

CKD STAGE	iPTH (pg/mL)	Ca²⁺ (mg/dL)	PO4 (mg/dL)	Ca²⁺ x PO4 (mg/dL)
3	35-70	Normal range	2.7-4.6	< 55
4	70-110	Normal range	2.7-4.6	< 55
5	150-300	8.4-9.5	3.5-5.5	< 55

Treatment of Hyperphosphatemia

Bone metabolism abnormalities are initially caused by elevations in phosphorus, which is renally excreted. To compensate for hyperphosphatemia, the parathyroid gland increases the release of PTH. Elevated PTH concentrations over time leads to secondary hyperparathyroidism and high turnover bone disease. Treatment of secondary hyperparathyroidism is initially focused on controlling serum phosphorus by restricting dietary phosphorus. Eventually, phosphate binders may be required. There are three types of phosphate binders:

- Aluminum-based agents (*AlternaGel,* others): potent phosphate binders, but aluminum can accumulate in CKD and is toxic to the nervous system and bone. Should only be used short-term and are not currently used.

- Calcium-based agents (primarily calcium acetate and carbonate): effective first line agents for hyperphosphatemia in CKD. However, many renal patients are taking vitamin D (which raises calcium levels) and cannot tolerate additional calcium.

- Aluminum-free, calcium-free agents: effective at controlling phosphorus. Because they do not contain aluminum or calcium, they do not cause problems with excess aluminum or calcium load. They are the most expensive.

Phosphate binders bind meal-time phosphate in the gut that is coming from the diet. If a dose is missed and the food is absorbed, there is no point in taking it later or doubling up the next dose. Patients may be required to limit foods high in phosphate such as dairy products, dark colored sodas, chocolate and nuts.

PHOSPHATE BINDERS

DRUG	DOSE	SAFETY/SIDE EFFECTS/MONITORING

Aluminum-based: one of the most potent phosphate binders but due to risk of accumulation, the duration of therapy must be limited to 4 weeks.

| Aluminum hydroxide (*AlternaGel, Amphojel*, others) | 300-600 mg three times daily with meals | **SIDE EFFECTS**
Constipation, poor taste, nausea, aluminum intoxication and osteomalacia

MONITORING
Ca²⁺, phosphorus, serum aluminum concentrations, PTH |

Calcium-based: first line therapy for hyperphosphatemia of CKD.

| Calcium acetate (*PhosLo, Phoslyra*, others) | 667-1,334 mg three times daily with meals | **SIDE EFFECTS**
Constipation, nausea, hypercalcemia

MONITORING
Ca²⁺, phosphorus, serum calcium-phosphorus product, PTH |
| Calcium carbonate (*Tums*, store brands, others) | 500 mg three times daily with meals, chewable or not | **NOTES**
Calcium acetate binds more dietary phosphorus on an elemental calcium basis compared to calcium carbonate |

Aluminum-free, calcium-free

| Lanthanum carbonate (*Fosrenol*) | 500-1,000 mg three times daily with meals, chewable – must chew thoroughly | **CONTRAINDICATIONS**
Bowel obstruction, fecal impaction, ileus

SIDE EFFECTS
Nausea, vomiting, abdominal pain, constipation, diarrhea, and long term safety of lanthanum has not been determined.

MONITORING
Ca²⁺, phosphorus, PTH |

Sevelamer: a non-calcium, non-aluminum based phosphate binder that is not systemically absorbed. Also, has the benefit of lowering total cholesterol and LDL by 15-30%. Sevelamer carbonate may have the advantage over sevelamer hydrochloride of maintaining bicarbonate concentrations.

| Sevelamer carbonate (*Renvela*)

Sevelamer hydrochloride (*Renagel*) | 800-1,600 mg three times daily with meals | **CONTRAINDICATIONS**
Bowel obstruction

SIDE EFFECTS
Nausea, vomiting, diarrhea (all > 20%), constipation, abdominal pain

MONITORING
Ca²⁺, phosphorus, bicarbonate, Cl⁻, PTH |

Treatment of Vitamin D Deficiency AND SECONDARY HYPERPARATHYROIDISM

After contolling hyperphosphatemia, elevations in PTH are treated primarily through the use of vitamin D. Vitamin D deficiency results when the kidney is unable to hydroxylate

25-OH vitamin D to its final active form. Vitamin D deficiency can not only exacerbate bone disease but may also lead to poor immunity and cardiovascular disease.

Vitamin D occurs in two primary forms: vitamin D3 or cholecalciferol, which is synthesized in the skin after exposure to ultraviolet light, and vitamin D2 or ergocalciferol, which is produced from plant sterols and is the primary dietary source of vitamin D. Calcitriol *(Rocaltrol)* is the active form of vitamin D3 and is used in patients with CKD to increase calcium absorption from the gut, raise serum calcium concentrations and inhibit PTH secretion. Newer active vitamin D analogs such as paracalcitol and doxercalciferol are associated with less hypercalcemia than calcitriol. These agents are summarized in the table below.

Agents for the Treatment of Secondary Hyperparathyroidism

DRUG	DOSING	SAFETY/SIDE EFFECTS/MONITORING
Vitamin D analogs: increase intestinal absorption of Ca^{2+} and provide a negative feedback to the parathyroid gland		
Calcitriol *(Rocaltrol, Calcijex)* capsule, solution, injection	**CKD** 0.25 mcg PO three times weekly to daily **Dialysis** 0.5-1 mcg PO daily or 0.5-4 mcg IV three times weekly	**CONTRAINDICATIONS** Hypercalcemia, vitamin D toxicity **SIDE EFFECTS** Nausea, vomiting, diarrhea (>10%), hypercalcemia, hyperphosphatemia **MONITORING** Ca^{2+}, Phos, serum calcium-phosphorus product, PTH **NOTES** Take with food or shortly after a meal to ↓ GI upset
Doxercalciferol *(Hectorol)* capsule, injection	**CKD** 1 mcg PO three times weekly to daily **Dialysis** 2.5-10 mcg PO three times weekly; 1-4 mcg IV three times weekly	
Paricalcitol *(Zemplar)* injection, capsules	**CKD** 1 mcg PO three times weekly to daily **Dialysis** 2.8-7 mcg IV three times weekly; 2-4 mcg PO three times weekly	

Calcimimetic – ↑ sensitivity of calcium-sensing receptor on the parathyroid gland, thereby ↓ PTH, ↓ Ca^{2+}, ↓ Phos and preventing progressive bone disease

DRUG	DOSING	SAFETY/SIDE EFFECTS/MONITORING
Cinacalcet *(Sensipar)* tablets	30-180 mg PO daily with food	**CONTRAINDICATIONS** Hypocalcemia **SIDE EFFECTS** Hypocalcemia, nausea, vomiting, diarrhea **MONITORING** Ca^{2+}, Phos, PTH **NOTES** Take tablet whole, do not crush or chew

Supplementation of vitamin D2 may also be necessary in CKD. The dosing of vitamin D2 depends on the severity of the deficiency and is summarized in the table below. Treatment of vitamin D deficiency can result in hypercalcemia or hyperphosphatemia. These values must be monitored during treatment. Further information on vitamin D is contained in the natural products and vitamins chapter, and the osteoporosis chapter.

Treatment of Vitamin D Deficiency

SERUM 25(OH) VITAMIN D (NG/ML)	ERGOCALCIFEROL DOSE*	DURATION	COMMENT
< 5	50,000 units PO every week x 12 weeks, then every month	6 months	Measure levels after 6 months
5-15	50,000 units PO every week x 4 weeks, then every month	6 months	Measure levels after 6 months
16-30	50,000 units PO every month	6 months	Measure levels after 6 months

*alternative may supplement with cholecalciferol 2,000 units orally per day

Treatment of Hyperkalemia

A normal potassium level is 3.5-5 mEq/L. Hyperkalemia, depending on the source, can be defined as a potassium level above 5.3 or above 5.5 mEq/L, although most clinicians are concerned with any level above 5 mEq/L.

Potassium is the most abundant intracellular cation and is essential for life. Humans obtain potassium through the diet from many foods, including meats, beans and fruits. Daily intake through the GI tract is about 1 mEq/kg/day. Any excess intake is excreted partially via the gut and primarily via the kidneys. Potassium excretion is increased by aldosterone, diuretics (strongly by loops, weakly by thiazides), by a high urine flow (via osmotic diuresis), and by negatively charged ions in the distal tubule (via bicarbonate).

Even if a person intakes a very rich potassium load, the acute rise in potassium would be offset by the release of insulin, which would cause potassium to shift into the cells. Therefore, excessive intake is not normally a cause of hyperkalemia unless there is significant renal damage. The most common cause of hyperkalemia is decreased renal excretion due to renal failure. This may be in combination with a high potassium intake or can be partially due to the use of drugs that interfere with potassium excretion. Drugs that raise potassium levels include potassium-sparing diuretics, ACEIs, ARBs, NSAIDs, the oral contraceptives that contain drospirenone (Yaz, etc.), cyclosporine, tacrolimus, heparin, canaglifozin, pentamadine, trimethoprim /sulfamethoxazole, potassium supplements and potassium present in IV fluids, including TPN.

Patients with diabetes often have a diet high in sodium and low in potassium and are taking ACEIs or ARBs. They also have insulin deficiency, which reduces the ability to shift potassium into the cells. These factors make patients with diabetes higher risk for hyperkalemia. Hospitalized patients, primarily due to the use of drugs, are at higher risk of hyperkalemia than outpatients. Rarely, acute hyperkalemia can be due to tumor lysis, rhabdomyolysis or succinylcholine administration.

A patient with elevated potassium, depending on the level, may be asymptomatic or symptomatic. Muscle weakness and bradycardia may be present. Fatal arrhythmias can develop. The risk for severe, negative outcomes increases as the potassium level increases.

To Lower Potassium (↓ K⁺)

This does not lower potassium BUT an ECG may be needed to check for cardiotoxicity (monitor heart rhythm). If required, administer IV calcium to stabilize the cardiac tissue.

- Remove sources of potassium intake. This may require dietary changes.

- Enhance potassium uptake by the cells via:

  - Glucose (to stimulate insulin secretion – but not enough by itself).

  - Insulin, given with glucose (to prevent hypoglycemia).

- If metabolic acidosis is present, administer sodium bicarbonate.

- Consider beta-agonists, such as nebulized albuterol.

  - Monitor for tachycardia, chest pain.

- Increase renal excretion with a loop diuretic, such as furosemide.

  - Monitor volume status.

- Another option to increase renal excretion is fludrocortisone (*Florinef*), especially in a patient with hypoaldosteronism.

- Consider the use of the cation exchange resin, sodium polystyrene sulfonate (*Kayexelate*). This works within two hours and can decrease potassium by 2 mEq/L with a single enema. SPS is given orally or rectally. Rectal administration is preferred for high (emergency) treatment.

  - If using oral SPS, do NOT mix with sorbitol; in 2010 the FDA issued a warning against mixing the drug with sorbitol due to a risk of GI necrosis.

  - Common side effects include ↓ appetite, nausea, vomiting, or constipation (less commonly diarrhea).

- Emergency dialysis can be used if the hyperkalemia could be fatal or for patients with renal failure; setting up dialysis takes time.

TREATMENT OF METABOLIC ACIDOSIS OF CKD

The kidneys' ability to generate bicarbonate decreases as CKD progresses and may result in the development of metabolic acidosis. In the ambulatory care setting, treatment of metabolic acidosis is initiated when the serum bicarbonate concentration is < 22 mEq/L. Agents to replace bicarbonate are summarized below.

DRUG	DOSING	SAFETY/SIDE EFFECTS/MONITORING
Sodium bicarbonate Tablets, granules, powder	1-2 tabs PO 1-3 times a day	**CONTRAINDICATIONS** Alkalosis, hypernatremia, hypocalcemia, pulmonary edema **WARNINGS** Use caution in patients with HTN, cardiovascular disease, fluid retention problems **SIDE EFFECTS** Nausea, vomiting, diarrhea, $\uparrow$ Na^+ **MONITORING** Na^+, HCO_3^-
Sodium citrate/citric acid (*Bicitra, Cytra-2, Oracit, Shohl's solution*) Solution	10-30 mL PO with water after meals and at bedtime	**CONTRAINDICATIONS** Alkalosis, Na^+ restricted diet, hypernatremia **SIDE EFFECTS** Nausea, vomiting, diarrhea, $\uparrow$ Na^+ **MONITORING** Na^+, HCO_3^-, urinary pH **NOTES** Metabolized to bicarbonate by the liver, may not be effective in concomitant liver failure Avoid concurrent use with aluminum containing products (e.g., antacids) Take after meals to avoid laxative effect Chilled solution improves taste

13

DRUG USE IN PREGNANCY

FDA PREGNANCY CATEGORIES

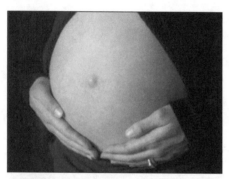

GUIDELINES (SELECTED)

CDC STD recommendations,
at www.cdc.gov

Department of Veteran Affairs, Department of Defense. VA/DoD clinical practice guideline for management of pregnancy. Washington (DC); 2009.

American College of Obstetricians and Gynecologists (ACOG) Practice Guidelines, various, available at www.guidelines.gov

Pregnancy Category A

Controlled studies in animals and women have shown no risk in the 1st trimester, and possible fetal harm is remote.

Pregnancy Category B

Either animal studies have not demonstrated a fetal risk but there are no controlled studies in pregnant women, or animal studies have shown an adverse effect that was not confirmed in controlled studies in women in the 1st trimester.

Pregnancy Category C

No controlled studies in humans have been performed and animal studies have shown adverse events, or studies in humans and animals are not available; give only if potential benefit outweighs the risk.

Pregnancy Category D

Positive evidence of fetal risk is available, but the benefits may outweigh the risk if life-threatening or serious disease.

Pregnancy Category X

Studies in animals or humans show fetal abnormalities; use in pregnancy is contraindicated.

As a General Rule: Try to avoid all drugs if possible during 1st trimester (organogenesis) and use lifestyle recommendations first, if reasonable.

Encourage Enrollment in the Pregnancy Registries

Pregnancy exposure registries exist for select disease states (cancer, autoimmune conditions, HIV, epilepsy) and for many individual drugs. They are designed to collect health information from women who take various drugs when they are pregnant and breastfeeding. Information is also collected on the newborn baby. This information is compared with women who have not taken medicine during pregnancy and the health of their babies.

The FDA pregnancy categories listed above do not always correctly define risk: consider that many drugs have had pregnancy categories changed recently in light of data that the drugs were not as safe as previously thought, including older drugs such as NSAIDs and SSRIs. Clinicians need real-life data on the effect of these drugs; only with this information can clinicians help parents make informed decisions. Search for "pregnancy registries" at www.fda.gov.

Common Teratogens

If a case indicates hCG+, the patient is pregnant and teratogenic drugs should be discontinued, if possible. Well-known teratogens include alcohol, ACE inhibitors, angiotensin receptor blockers, benzodiazepines, carbamazepine, ergot-derivatives, isotretinoin, leflunomide, lithium, methimazole, nafarelin, NSAIDs, paroxetine, phenytoin, phenobarbital, propylthiouracil, quinolones, ribavirin, tazarotene, tetracyclines, topiramate, valproic acid, misoprostol, methotrexate, statins, dutasteride, finasteride, warfarin, lenalidomide and thalidomide.

Many psychiatric drugs have risk in pregnancy. The drug's potential harm must be weighed against the risk of the condition not being treated adequately. In bipolar disorder, lithium and valproate are considered among the highest risk. The treatment of depression during pregnancy, and postpartum depression, has changed recently. Although SSRIs have historically been the preferred agents, in December of 2011 the FDA issued a warning regarding SSRI use during pregnancy and the potential risk of persistent pulmonary hypertension of the newborn (PPHN). Paroxetine is considered to have the highest risk in the class. Tricyclics, also pregnancy category C, are the second group most commonly used. Pregnancy-related depression and treatment is discussed further in the Depression chapter.

Folic Acid in Women of Child-Bearing Age

Whenever a young woman enters the pharmacy, the pharmacist can ask if she consuming adequate folic acid (400-800 mcg daily, which is 0.4-0.8 mg/day), calcium (1,000 mg daily) and vitamin D (600 IU daily).

It is a safe and reasonable recommendation to women planning to conceive (and all women of child-bearing age, since many pregnancies are not planned) to take a folic acid supplement (at least one month prior to pregnancy) to help prevent birth defects of the brain and spinal cord (neural tube defects). Folic acid should be continued for the first 2-3 months of pregnancy. Folic acid is in many healthy foods, including fortified cereals (some of which are not healthy), dried beans, leafy green vegetables and orange juice. An OTC prenatal vitamin that contains 600-800 mcg would supply the recommended amount. Prescription prenatal vitamins (*Prima-*

Care ONE, *Zenate*, others) usually contain 800 mcg. Folic acid at 1 mg and higher is prescription only, although there are prescription-only prenatal vitamins with lower amounts.

Common OTC-Treatable Conditions in Pregnancy

Nausea/Vomiting

First, recommend eating smaller, more frequent meals, avoiding spicy or odorous foods, taking more frequent naps, and reducing stress, including working long hours. If this does not work recommend pyridoxine, which is vitamin B6. This is the 1st line recommendation by ACOG, with or without first-generation antihistamine. A natural product which may be helpful is ginger, in tea form, or cooked, but do not recommend supplements. Dried, salted plums are used by certain ethnic groups. *Hyperemesis gravidarum* is severe N/V in pregnancy and causes weight loss, dehydration and electrolyte imbalance. It will be treated under the care of an obstetrician and may require hospitalization.

GERD/Heartburn/Gas Pains

First recommend eating smaller, more frequent meals, avoiding foods that worsen GERD, and if symptoms occur while sleeping, recommend elevating the head of the bed and not eating three hours prior to sleep. If this does not work, calcium antacids are first-line, such as calcium carbonate in *Tums* or store brands. This is a good antacid choice since calcium intake is often deficient in pregnancy. Use caution with excessive use of antacids containing aluminum or magnesium if renal disease is present. Do not recommend sodium bicarbonate or magnesium trisilicate (which comes in combination with aluminum hydroxide in *Gaviscon).*

If gas is a concern, simethicone is considered safe *(Gas-X, Mylicon)* – and the *Mylicon* infant drops are considered safe for infants. H2 antagonists *(Pepcid, Tagamet, Axid, Zantac)* are all pregnancy category B; many doctors recommend OTC or Rx doses. PPIs are B's or C's.

Constipation

First recommend increasing fluid intake, increasing fiber in the diet, increasing physical activity, such as walking. If this does not work fiber is 1st-line and psyllium is pregnancy category B *(Metamucil,* store brands).

Cough/Cold/Allergies

The first-generation antihistamines are the usual first-line recommendation. Chlorpheniramine (drug of choice) and diphenhydramine are pregnancy category B. The non-sedating 2nd generation agents loratadine and cetirizine are often recommended by obstetricians during the second and third trimesters. If nasal steroids are needed for chronic allergy symptoms, budesonide *(Rhinocort)* and beclomethasone *(Beconase AQ)* are considered safest; both are prescription only. Decongestants (pseudoephedrine, phenylephrine, oxymetazoline), the cough-suppressant dextromethorphan and the mucolytic guaifenesin are pregnancy category C, but may be recommended by the physician. The oral decongestants should not be recommended during the first trimester.

Pain

Acetaminophen is pregnancy category B and is the analgesic and antipyretic drug of choice during pregnancy. Ibuprofen is pregnancy category C/D > 30 weeks gestation, and naproxen is pregnancy category C; pharmacists should not recommend OTC NSAIDs in pregnancy. Codeine is considered unsafe in pregnancy and lactation. Most opioids are excreted in breast milk. While this use may be acceptable in small amounts, the risk to the infant must be considered. Do not dispense codeine (in *Tylenol #3*, others) to a woman who is breastfeeding since rapid metabolizers of the CYP 450 2D6 enzyme will produce excessive amounts of morphine rapidly, which could be fatal to the infant.

SELECT CONDITIONS AND FIRST-LINE TREATMENT

Vaccine Use During Pregnancy

- Influenza vaccine (shot, inactivated): each fall, whether pregnant or not – this is recommended in all stages of pregnancy.

- No live vaccines [MMR, varicella (chickenpox), live influenza nasal, etc.] one month before and during pregnancy.

- Pregnant women should receive Tdap between weeks 27-36, each pregnancy. If the woman has not been vaccinated or if the history is unclear, a 3-dose series is needed (one with Tdap, the other two with Td only). If the woman delivers and has not received vaccination, she should receive it post-delivery. Vaccination protects the baby (and the mother) from pertussis (whooping cough).

- Other vaccines may be needed in unusual circumstances, such as a need for a tetanus update, or foreign travel; refer to CDC guidelines.

Antibiotic Use During Pregnancy

Generally considered safe to use:

Penicillins (including amoxicillin and ampicillin, both B's) and cephalosporins, erythromycin and azithromycin (B's, but not clarithromycin, which is C)

Do not use during pregnancy:

Quinolones (due to cartilage damage) and tetracyclines (due to teeth discoloration)

Vaginal Fungal Infections

Use topical antifungals (creams, suppositories), at least 7 days.

Urinary Tract Infections

Beta lactams that cover the organism can be used, such as cephalexin (500 mg QID) or ampicillin. Nitrofurantoin 100 mg BID is used, but not in the last several weeks of pregnancy. Another option is fosfomycin (*Monurol*) 3 grams (1 packet, mixed with water) x 1. Must treat bacteriuria in pregnant women (for 7 days) even if asymptomatic with negative urinalysis. If not, the infection can lead to premature birth, pyelonephritis, and neonatal meningitis. In pregnant women, avoid quinolones (cartilage toxicity and arthropathies) and tetracyclines (teratogenic). SMX/TMP can cause hyperbilirubinemia and kernicterus in 3rd trimester, and is Pregnancy Category D.

Chlamydia

Azithromycin 1 g x 1, or amoxicillin 500 mg PO TID x 7 days.

Gonorrhea

Cephalosporin, or if contraindicated, azithromycin 2 g PO x 1

Bacterial Vaginosis

Clindamycin 300 mg PO BID or metronidazole (500 mg PO BID or 250 mg PO TID), all x 7 days. Topical (vaginal) therapy for bacterial vaginosis is not recommended during pregnancy.

Vaginal Trichomoniasis

2 g PO metronidazole x 1 (or 250 mg PO TID or 500 mg PO BID x 7d) at any stage of pregnancy. Treatment may be deferred after 37 weeks.

Asthma in Pregnancy

- Inhaled corticosteroids are first-line controller therapy for persistent asthma during pregnancy.

- Budesonide is the preferred inhaled corticosteroid for use during pregnancy (and is the preferred steroid for infants in the *Respules*, which are put in a nebulizer).

- Inhaled albuterol is the recommended rescue inhaler in pregnancy.

Venous Thromboembolism/Mechanical Valves

Heparin (UFH) or LMWH, convert to shorter half-life UFH during last month of pregnancy or if delivery appears imminent. Use pneumatic compression devices prior to delivery in women with thrombosis if they are getting a C-section. No warfarin during pregnancy (category X), the newer anticoagulants are category C and are not currently in the recommendations.

Hypothyroidism

Must test for and treat, with levothyroxine, which is pregnancy category A.

Hyperthyroidism

Mild cases will not require treatment. If drugs are needed, such as with Graves', both hyperthyroid drugs are pregnancy category D: propylthiouracil is used if trying to conceive and in 1st trimester, then it is generally reasonable to switch to methimazole. Both are high risk for liver injury and there is risk with either to the neonate: both of these drugs readily cross the placenta and cause congenital defects, however, uncontrolled maternal hyperthyroidism causes adverse neonatal outcomes, including premature delivery and low birth weight. This is why it is preferable to normalize the mother's thyroid function prior to pregnancy. Contraception should be used until the disease is controlled.

Anemia

Anemia due to iron deficiency can occur during pregnancy and will be treated with supplemental iron, in addition to prenatal vitamins (which contain some iron).

Do not use tobacco during pregnancy/encourage cessation: Smoking in pregnancy can cause adverse outcomes for the child, including spontaneous abortion, low birth weight and sudden infant death. If women smoke 5 or less cigarettes (occasional, "nervous" type smokers) they should be encouraged to quit with behavioral support. If they smoke more than 5 cigarettes daily, ACOG recommends bupropion (pregnancy category C), and other sources recommend nicotine replacement in pregnancy, however the efficacy is not as high in non-pregnant patients. All nicotine products are pregnancy category D except for the gum which is pregnancy category C.

Do not use alcohol during pregnancy/encourage cessation: No amount of alcohol is safe during pregnancy.

14

DRUG REFERENCES

BACKGROUND

Providing drug information to patients as well as other healthcare professionals is one of the critical functions of pharmacists, regardless of the practice setting. In order to perform this function effectively and efficiently, it is important to be able to choose the most appropriate and specific resources based on the type of information needed. The following section is intended to highlight some of the key resources based on the type of information needed. It is not intended to be a comprehensive review of drug information resources available, but should provide a basic understanding for licensure.

It is important to continually evaluate new drug information resources and technology, and incorporate them into your practice to insure the resources being reviewed are current, reflecting the most current information available.

It is also important to recognize that patients also have access to many of the same drug information resources. As healthcare providers, pharmacists need to be aware of what patients are reading and be able to provide context as-needed to clarify the information as it applied to their cases. Pharmacists must also be able to recognize when the medical information requested is outside the scope of normal pharmacy practice/expertise. These questions should be referred to the appropriate healthcare provider for follow up.

SOURCES, BY CATEGORY

General Drug Information

- American Hospital Formulary Service (AHFS) Drug Information

- Drug Information Handbook (LexiComp)

- Drug Topics: Red Book

  - Includes Average Wholesale Price (AWP) and the suggested retail price.

  - It is a useful resource to determine product presentations (i.e., dosage form, strength, and package size) and availability.

- Facts and Comparisons

- Food and Drug Administration: Drugs Home page
  www.fda.gov/Drugs

- Food and Drug Administration: Drugs@FDA
  www.accessdata.fda.gov/scripts/cder/drugsatfda

- Micromedex

- National Library of Medicine (NLM): Dailymed
  dailymed.nlm.nih.gov/dailymed

  - Database of Product Package Inserts

- National Library of Medicine (NLM): Drug Information Portal
  druginfo.nlm.nih.gov/drugportal

- Physician's Desk Reference (PDR)

  - Collection of Product Package Inserts

General Medical Information

- Centers for Disease Control and Prevention (CDC)
  www.cdc.gov

- Harrison's Principles of Internal Medicine

- National Cancer Institute (NCI)
  www.cancer.gov

- The Merck Manual

- Washington Manual of Medical Therapeutics

Consumer Medical and Drug Information

- Centers for Disease Control and Prevention (CDC): Diseases & Conditions
  www.cdc.gov/diseasesconditions

- Food and Drug Administration: Consumer page
  www.fda.gov/ForConsumers

- National Institutes of Health: MedlinePlus
  www.nlm.nih.gov/medlineplus

Medication Safety

(see Medication Safety Chapter for additional resources)

- Food and Drug Administration: Drug Safety Communications
  www.fda.gov/Drugs/DrugSafety

- Food and Drug Administration: Medication Guides
  www.fda.gov/Drugs/DrugSafety/ucm085729.htm

- Food and Drug Administration: MedWatch
  www.fda.gov/Safety/MedWatch

- Institute for Safe Medication Practices (ISMP)
  www.ismp.org

Reporting Adverse Drug Reactions

- FDA's MedWatch Program (AERS, for drugs/devices)
  www.fda.gov/medwatch or 1-800-FDA-1088 (1-800-332-1088).

- Vaccines: FDA's VAERS (see immunization section)

Reporting Medical Errors

In Hospital

- To the P&T Committee, at staff meetings (as defined by facility), to the Medication Safety Committee

In any setting

- ISMP's Medication Errors Reporting Program (MERP)

- FDA's MedWatch

- MedMARx program

Drug Interactions

- Drug Interaction Facts

- Hansten and Horn's Drug Interactions Analysis and Management

- Micromedex

- LexiComp Online Database

IV Stability/Compatibility

- AHFS Drug Information

- King's Guide

- Micromedex

- Package Inserts

- Trissel's Handbook on Injectable Drugs

Compounding and Manufacturing

- Allen's Compounded Formulations

- Handbook on Extemporaneous Formulations

- International Journal of Pharmaceutical Compounding

  - Bi-monthly publication

- Pediatric Drug Formulations

- Remington: The Science and Practice of Pharmacy

  - Includes a chapter on extemporaneous prescription compounding.

- Trissel's Stability of Compounded Formulations

- US Pharmacopoeia National Formulary (USP-NF)

  - Includes chapters on Pharmacy Compounding; Non-Sterile Compounding is USP Chapter 795.

  - USP sets standards for quality, purity, identity, and strength of medicines, food ingredients and dietary supplements manufactured.

Drug Identification

- Facts and Comparisons

- Ident-A-Drug

- Micromedex: IDENTIDEX

- Mosby's Drug Handbook

- Physician's Desk Reference (PDR)

- National Library of Medicine (NLM): PillBox
  pillbox.nlm.nih.gov

- United States Pharmacopoeia Drug Information (USPDI)

Foreign Drug Identification

- Diccionario de Especialidades Farmacéuticas

  ❏ Printed in Spanish

- European Drug Index

- International Drug Directory (Index Nominum)

- Martindales

- Micromedex

- USP Dictionary of USAN and International Drug Names

Natural Products/Alternative Medicine

- Micromedex

- Natural Medicines Comprehensive Database

- Natural Standard

- PDR for Herbal Medicines

- The Complete German Commission E Monograph (quite outdated, no updates since 1994; at one time was a reputable reference)

- US Pharmacopoeia

Travel Medicine

- Centers for Disease Control and Prevention (CDC): Travelers' Health
  www.cdc.gov/travel

- International Association For Medical Assistance To Travelers (IAMAT)
  www.iamat.org

- Travel Medicine Advisor at http://www.travelmedicineadvisor.com/

Pregnancy and Lactation

- Breastfeeding: A Guide for the Medical Profession

- Briggs' Drugs in Pregnancy and Lactation

- Centers for Disease Control and Prevention (CDC): Medications and Pregnancy
  www.cdc.gov/ncbddd/pregnancy_gateway/meds/index.html

- Medications and Mothers' Milk (Hales) at http://www.medsmilk.com/

- Micromedex

- National Library of Medicine (NLM): LactMed
  toxnet.nlm.nih.gov/cgi-bin/sis/htmlgen?LACT

Women's Health

- Centers for Disease Control and Prevention (CDC): Women's Health
  www.cdc.gov/women

- Department of Health and Human Services: Womenshealth.gov
  www.womenshealth.gov

- Food and Drug Administration: For Women
  www.fda.gov/ForConsumers/ByAudience/ForWomen

- National Library of Medicine (NLM): Women's health
  www.nlm.nih.gov/medlineplus/womenshealth.html

- World Health Organization (WHO): Women's health
  www.who.int/topics/womens_health/en

Geriatrics

- Food and Drug Administration: Medicines and You: A Guide for Older Adults
  www.fda.gov/Drugs/ResourcesForYou/ucm163959.htm

- Geriatric Dosage Handbook (LexiComp)

- National Institutes of Health: Senior Health
  nihseniorhealth.gov

- The American Geriatrics Society (AGS) Guidelines & Recommendations at

- http://www.americangeriatrics.org/health_care_professionals/clinical_practice/clinical_guidelines_recommendations/

Pediatrics

- AHFS Drug Information

- Centers for Disease Control and Prevention (CDC): Vaccines & Immunizations www.cdc.gov/vaccines

- Harriet Lane Handbook

- Micromedex

- Nelson: Textbook of Pediatrics

- Neofax

- Pediatric Dosage Handbook (LexiComp)

- Pediatric Injectable Drugs (ASHP)

Psychiatry

- Clinical Handbook of Psychotropic Drugs

- DSM-V (Diagnostic and Statistical Manual of Mental Disorders: Fifth edition)

Pharmacology

- Applied Therapeutics: The Clinical Use of Drugs (Koda-Kimble)

- Drugs of Choice from the Medical Letter

- Goodman and Gilman's: The Pharmacological Basis of Therapeutics

- Handbook of Nonprescription Drugs (OTC)

- Pharmacist's Letter

- Pharmacotherapy: A Pathophysiologic Approach (DiPiro)

- Sanford Guide (for ID)

Pharmaceutics

- Handbook of Pharmaceutical Excipients

- Merck Index

- Remington: The Science and Practice of Pharmacy

Guidelines

- National Guideline Clearinghouse
  www.guideline.gov

- Select Key Guidelines

  - National Cholesterol Education Project Adult Treatment Panel (NCEP ATP 3), Cholesterol

  - Joint National Commission (JNC) 7 (version 8 – pending) and American Heart Association (AHA) Update, Hypertension

  - American Diabetes Assoc (ADA) Clinical Practice Recommendations and American Association of Clinical Endocrinologists/American College of Endocrinology Consensus Statement (AACE), Diabetes

  - CHEST guidelines for antithrombotic therapy

- Also refer to Professional Organizations web sites

Clinical Trials

- National Institutes of Health: ClinicalTrials.gov
  www.clinicaltrials.gov

Professional Organizations

Select Professional Organizations

- American Academy of Pediatrics (AAP)
  www.aap.org

- American Cancer Society
  www.cancer.org

- American Diabetes Association (ADA)
  www.diabetes.org

- American Heart Association (AHA)
  www.heart.org/HEARTORG

- American Society of Clinical Oncology (ASCO)
  www.asco.org

- Infectious Diseases Society of America (IDSA)- http://www.idsociety.org/

For Additional Professional Organizations

- National Library of Medicine (NLM): Organizations
  www.nlm.nih.gov/medlineplus/organizations/all_organizations.html

Pharmacy Organizations

- Academy of Managed Care Pharmacy (AMCP)
  www.amcp.org

- American College of Clinical Pharmacy (ACCP)
  www.accp.com

- American Pharmacists Association (APhA)
  www.pharmacist.com

- American Society of Health-System Pharmacists (ASHP)
  www.ashp.org

Literature Search

- Excerpta Medica (EMBASE)

- International Pharmaceutical Abstracts (IPA)

- National Library of Medicine (NLM): PubMed
  www.ncbi.nlm.nih.gov/pubmed

Miscellaneous Resources

- National Library of Medicine (NLM): Gallery of Mobile Apps and Sites
  www.nlm.nih.gov/mobile

Legislative and Business Developments

- The Pink Sheet

- Pharmacist's Letter

- FDA Website

INN

- International Nonproprietary Names for Pharmaceutical Substances

NDC

- The National Drug Code (NDC) is the universal product identifier for human drugs.

DISPOSAL OF PRESCRIPTION DRUGS

PROPER DISPOSAL OF PRESCRIPTION DRUGS

Common prescription agents, including beta-blockers and ACE Inhibitors, can be measured in fish in the Pacific basin. This region is not alone; drug concentrations in the ocean are an environmental disaster. It is important to realize that proper disposal is critical, but only part of the solution. The majority of drugs and drug metabolites end up in the oceans from the patient's urine and stool – the best way to reduce this exposure is to improve the health of the population to reduce the amount of drugs people are using. The federal prescription drug disposal guidelines recommend (in the absence of a "take-back" program – described below) mixing unwanted drugs (including controlled drugs) with unpalatable substances and placing them in a non-descript container before discarding in the trash unless the prescribing information specifically states the drug is to be flushed down the toilet or sink (see list of "okay to flush" drugs at the end of this section). The list of drugs that are acceptable to flush include only certain controlled drugs.

Some environmental experts disagree with the FDAs recommendations for flushing certain high-risk drugs and instead advise consumers to dispose of unwanted medications in their original prescription containers with any identifying information removed, and to not flush any medications, even if the patient information instructs otherwise. Note that the FDA is particularly concerned with the risk of the wrong person getting or taking the controlled drug – and subsequent harm.

Instruct patients: Do not flush prescription drugs down the toilet or drain unless the label or accompanying patient information specifically instructs you to do so.

To dispose of prescription drugs not labeled to be flushed, patients should be advised to take advantage of community drug take-back programs or other programs, such as household hazardous waste collection events, that collect drugs at a central location for proper disposal. In 2010, the FDA started the first national "Take Back" day for unwanted drugs. Pharmacies have been involved, in all 50 states, in notifying patients where to take unused medications for destruction. These are annual events and have been very successful. The first three years of the program collected over a 1,000 tons of unused drugs; that's 2,000,000 pounds! They continue to grow.

The DEA's Take-Back events are a significant piece of the government's prescription drug abuse prevention strategy. Purging America's home medicine cabinets of unwanted or expired medications is one of four action items outlined in the strategy for reducing prescription drug abuse and diversion. The other action items include education of health care providers, patients, parents and youth; establishing prescription drug monitoring programs in all the states; and increased enforcement to address "doctor shopping" and pill mills.

Pharmacy Involvement in Taking Back Unwanted Drugs (this is ongoing, and not "Take Back Days" as described above)

In many states, pharmacies, and other designated sites, have the ability to help patients dispose of unwanted prescription and over-the-counter drugs – but not controlled substances, which must be returned only to law enforcement – without flushing them down the toilet or tossing them in the garbage. These are voluntary programs for community pharmacies.

The pharmacies can either:

- Use postage pre-paid envelopes so that consumers can return unwanted drugs to licensed waste disposal facilities, away from pharmacies where health care is provided, or

- Establish a collection bin for ongoing collection at pharmacies.

Drugs should not be reviewed by staff at a collection site (whether a pharmacy or community event) before being deposited into a secured collection bin. The patient or patient's agent should deposit the drugs themselves, thereby preventing staff from knowing what is being returned.

Drugs that are collected should be separated from their containers by patients or their agents before being placed in the collection bin, which reduces the disposal costs because the containers will not be part of the pharmaceutical waste.

Locking the "Take Back" Container

- There should be two separate locks on the secured collection bin: one key should be in the possession of the pharmacy, the other key in the possession of the licensed integrated waste hauler who will pick up what is now classified as "hazardous household waste."

- This dual lock ensures that the pharmacy cannot open the collection bin without the presence of the integrated waste hauler, and vice versa.

Some pharmacies do not participate in Take Back Programs, but offer services for disposal by mail, including the common "TakeAway" mailers that are processed by companies, such as Sharps, Inc.

The "TakeAway" mailers are popular in many pharmacies and include return shipping and handling. They are for Rx (not controlled) and OTC drugs. At the receiving end the products are processed by law enforcement. Pharmacies can also have bins for medication drop off in the store. These services can also be used by pharmacies for their own medical waste, such as syringes during flu season.

Patient either gives TakeAway envelope to US postal service or UPS driver, or store – this picture is a display box that contains the mailing envelopes

Or, the patient drops off in the box of a pharmacy that has the container – neither option is for controlled drugs

Some communities have locked boxes for controlled drugs – if putting medicine into this container, the drug name must be visible (but not patient info)

If the patient uses the mailer (rather than the drop-off box in a pharmacy) they put the medications into the brown mailing envelope, then put in the US mail or bring to a UPS store or driver. The return shipping is paid. Up to 4 ounces of liquids or gels can be put in a *Ziploc* bag into the envelope.

In the absence of a Take Back Program or access to mailers, instruct patients to follow local guidelines for Home Hazardous Waste (HHW) Collection.

Find the phone number of the local HHW collection site in the government section of the local white pages of the telephone directory. It is important for patients to know their local regulations. It may be that the locality requires drugs to be dropped off at certain sites, or be placed in the trash. If drugs are placed in the trash the following procedures should be followed:

- Keep medicine in its original child-resistant container. Scratch or mark out the patient information on the label.

- Place some water into solid medications, such as pills or capsules. Then add something nontoxic and unpalatable such as sawdust, kitty litter, charcoal, *Comet* or powdered spices (such as cayenne pepper).

- Close and seal the container lids tightly with packing or duct tape. If discarding blister packs of unused medicines, wrap in multiple layers of duct tape.

- Place medicine containers in durable <u>packaging that does not show what's inside</u> (such as a cardboard box).

- Place in the trash close to garbage pickup time.

SYRINGE DISPOSAL

Safe injection technique in a health care setting, including sharp disposal, is discussed in the Medication Safety chapter. This section is for patient (home) syringe disposal.

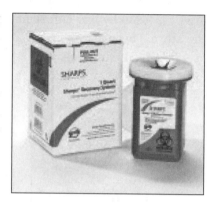

Improper management of discarded needles expose waste workers to potential needle stick injuries and infection risk when containers break open inside garbage trucks or needles are mistakenly sent to recycling facilities. Janitors, housekeepers and family members risk injury if loose sharps poke through plastic garbage bags. Used needles can transmit diseases, including HIV and hepatitis.

Options for Safe Syringe Disposal

Drop Box or Supervised Collection Sites

Sharps users can take their own sharps containers filled with used needles to appropriate collections sites: doctors' offices, hospitals, pharmacies, health departments, or fire stations. Services are free or have a nominal fee. Check the options in your area as they vary.

Mail-Back Programs

Sharps users place their used sharps in special containers and return the container by mail to a collection site for proper disposal. Fees depend on the size of the container. These are available in many pharmacies. Sharps, Inc. is a commonly used source for sharps mail-in containers, among others.

Syringe Exchange Programs (SEP)

Sharps users can exchange used needles for new needles. This is a proven method to decrease the transmission of blood-borne pathogens (HIV, hepatitis) by injection drug users. It is run by the North American Syringe Exchange Network at www.nasen.org. As of press time (at the end of 2013) the use of federal funds for syringe exchange has been banned. It is not clear if this will be overturned. In some states a small number of syringes can be purchased without a prescription.

At-Home Needle Destruction Devices

There are products patients use to destroy used needles at home. These devices sever, burn, or melt the needle. In general these are not recommended for places where others can be infected with a condition, because people can be pricked removing the needle. On the other hand, if the patient is in their own home and infection risk is low, this process reduces the cost of disposal because the plastic syringe can be disposed of in the trash if the needle has been removed. For example, this can be a cost-effective method for a patient injecting insulin several times daily.

Used Needle-Syringe Safety Tips

Disposable needles contaminated with drugs, chemicals or blood products should never be removed from their original syringes unless no other option is available. Throw the entire needle/syringe assembly (needle attached to the syringe) into the red plastic sharps container.

Never remove a needle by unscrewing it with your hands in a health care facility. At home, if infection risk is low, it may be possible to remove the needle by one of the devices described above.

Used disposable needles/sharps should be discarded immediately after use without recapping into a sharps container (a non-reusable plastic container that is puncture resistant, leak proof on the sides and bottom, properly labeled and closable).

Sharps containers should be easily accessible, replaced routinely, and not allowed to overfill. Never compress or "push down" on the contents of any sharps container.

If someone is stuck with a needle that someone else has used, they should be seen by a health care provider immediately to assess infection risk and consider prophylactic therapy.

This is the list from the FDA of unused or expired medicines that should be flushed down the sink or toilet in order to help prevent danger to people and pets in the home. Please note that there are other options for disposal, but the FDA feels that the risk permits the flushing of these medications only. These are all controlled substances and must be disposed of according to DEA law.

ACTIVE INGREDIENT	DRUG
Acetaminophen; Oxycodone Hydrochloride	*Percocet*, tablets *
Aspirin; Oxycodone Hydrochloride	*Percodan*, tablets *
Buprenorphine	*Butrans*, transdermal patch (extended release)
Buprenorphine Hydrochloride	Buprenorphine Hydrochloride, tablets (sublingual) *
Buprenorphine Hydrochloride; Naloxone Hydrochloride	Buprenorphine Hydrochloride; Naloxone Hydrochloride, tablets sublingual *Zubsolv*, tablets (sublingual)
Diazepam	*Diastat/Diastat AcuDial*, rectal gel
Fentanyl	*Abstral*, tablets (sublingual) *Duragesic*, patch (extended-release) *
Fentanyl Citrate	*Actiq*, oral transmucosal lozenge * *Fentora*, tablets (buccal) *Onsolis*, soluble film (buccal)
Hydromorphone Hydrochloride	Dilaudid, tablets * Dilaudid, oral liquid *Exalgo*, tablets (extended release)
Meperidine Hydrochloride	*Demerol*, tablets * *Demerol*, oral solution *
Methadone Hydrochloride	*Dolophine* Hydrochloride, tablets * Methadone Hydrochloride, oral solution * *Methadose*, tablets *
Methylphenidate	*Daytrana*, transdermal patch system
Morphine Sulfate	*Avinza*, capsules (extended release) *Kadian*, capsules (extended release) Morphine Sulfate, tablets (immediate release) * Morphine Sulfate, oral solution *MS Contin*, tablets (extended release)
Morphine Sulfate; Naltrexone Hydrochloride	*Embeda*, capsules (extended release)
Oxycodone Hydrochloride	*Oxecta*, tablets (immediate release) Oxycodone Hydrochloride, capsules Oxycodone Hydrochloride, oral solution *Oxycontin*, tablets (extended release)
Oxymorphone Hydrochloride	*Opana*, tablets (immediate release) *Opana ER*, tablets (extended release)
Sodium Oxybate	*Xyrem*, oral solution
Tapentadol	*Nucynta ER*, tablets (extended release)

* These medicines have generic versions available or are only available in generic formulations.

List revised: October 2013

INFECTIOUS DISEASES

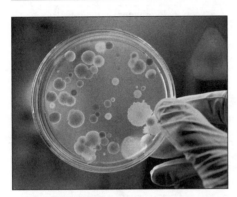

We gratefully acknowledge the assistance of Brett Heintz, PharmD, BCPS-ID, AAHIVE, Infectious Diseases/ Internal Medicine Pharmacist at Iowa City VA Medical Center and Associate Clinical Professor at University of Iowa College of Pharmacy, in preparing this chapter.

BACKGROUND

An infectious disease is caused by one or more pathogenic viruses, bacteria, fungi, protozoa, parasites, and aberrant proteins known as prions. Transmission of disease can occur through various pathways including through physical contact with an infected individual, food, body fluids, contaminated objects, airborne inhalation spread via a vector (carrier). Transmissible diseases, which occur through contact with an ill person or their secretions (or objects touched by them), are especially infective and are sometimes referred to as contagious diseases.

Bacterial Organism Identification

Bacterial organisms stain differently on a Gram stain depending if they are Gram-positive or Gram-negative organisms. Gram-positive organisms have a thick cell wall and stain purple, or bluish in color from the crystal violet stain, whereas Gram-negative organisms have a thin cell wall and take up the safranin counterstain and stain pink, or reddish in color. Empiric, broad-spectrum antimicrobial therapy (that covers any possible organism) should be changed to directed, definitive antimicrobial therapy as soon as possible (once gram stains, cultures and/or susceptibility data are available) in order to reduce the incidence of antibiotic resistance, toxicity and healthcare expenditures.

Bacterial Organism Classification

The results of a Gram stain will help to determine the appropriate antibiotic regimen for the infection. Gram-positive bacteria consist mainly of the following species: *Staphylococcus*, *Streptococcus*, *Enterococcus*, *Clostridium*, and *Listeria*. Following is a list of bacterial organisms.

Bacterial Organisms

CLASSIFICATION	ORGANISMS	
Gram-positive Cocci	Enterococcus (VRE)	Staphylococcus saprophyticus
	Peptostreptococcus sp.	Streptococcus agalactiae (Grp. B)
	Staphylococcus aureus (MSSA/MRSA)	Streptococcus bovis (Grp. D)
	Staphylococcus epidermidis (MSSE/MRSE)	Streptococcus pneumoniae (DRSP)
	Viridans group streptococcus	Streptococcus pyogenes (Grp. A)
Gram-positive Rods	Propionibacterium acnes	Corynebacterium jeikeium
	Bacillus anthracis	Listeria monocytogenes
	Clostridium difficile	Nocardia asteroids (branched)
	Clostridium perfringens	Actinomyces israelii (branched)
	Corynebacterium diphtheriae	Mycobacterium species (acid-fast)
Gram-negative Cocci	Neisseria gonorrhoeae	Neisseria meningitidis
	Neisseria gonorrhoeae (PRNG)	
Spirochetes	Borrelia burgdorferi	Leptospira interrogans
	Borrelia recurrentis	Treponema pallidum
Atypicals	Chlamydia/Chlamydophilia	Mycoplasma pneumoniae
	Mycoplasma hominis	Ureaplasma urealyticum
Gram-negative Coccobacillary	Acinetobacter sp.	Francisella tularensis
	Bartonella henselae	Moraxella catarrhalis
	Bordetella pertussis	Pasteurella multocida
	Family rickettsiaceae	
Gram-negative Rods	Aeromonas hydrophila	Helicobacter pylori (curved rod)
	Alcaligenes xylosoxidans	Klebsiella pneumoniae
	Bacteroides fragilis	Legionella pneumophilia
	Brucella sp.	Morganella morganii
	Burkholderia cepacia	Prevotella melaninogenica
	Campylobacter jejuni (curved rod)	Proteus mirabilis
	Citrobacter diversu	Proteus sp.
	Citrobacter freundii	Providencia sp.
	Eikenella corrodens	Pseudomonas aeruginosa
	Enterobacter cloacae	Salmonella sp.
	Enterobacter aerogenes	Samonella typhi
	Escherichia col	Serratia sp.
	Flavobacteriae	Shigella sp.
	Fusobacteriae	Stenotrophomonas maltophilia
	Gardnerella vaginalis)	Vibrio cholerae (curved rod)
	Haemophilus ducreyi	Yersinia enterocolitica
	Haemophilus influenzae	Yersinia pestis

(Bartlett. Johns Hopkins Antibiotic Guide: Diagnosis & Treatment of Infectious Diseases 3rd Ed. 2012)

KEY DEFINITIONS

- Minimum inhibitory concentration (MIC): lowest drug concentration that prevents visible microbial growth in 24 hours. Generally, the MIC required to inhibit the growth of 90% of microorganisms is used in practice (MIC_{90}).

- Breakpoint: the level of MIC at which a bacterium is deemed either susceptible or resistant to an antibiotic. Note that breakpoints vary for different antimicrobial classes. Breakpoints are established by the FDA and Clinical and Laboratory Standards Institute (CLSI) and can change based on clinical data, with the goal of optimizing antimicrobial therapy and patient outcomes.

- Minimum bactericidal concentration (MBC): lowest drug concentration that reduces bacterial density by 99.9% in 24 hours (kills bacteria).

- Synergy: effect of two or more agents produces a greater effect than each agent alone.

ANTIMICROBIAL STEWARDSHIP PROGRAMS (ASP)

- Antimicrobial stewardship has been defined as the optimal selection, dosage, and duration of antimicrobial treatment that results in the best clinical outcome for the treatment or prevention of an infection, with minimal toxicity to the patient and minimal impact on subsequent resistance. It aims to promote the appropriate use of antimicrobials – the right drug, duration, dose, and route of administration. Promoting the appropriate use of antimicrobials is intended to improve clinical outcomes by reducing the emergence of resistance, limiting drug-related adverse events, and minimizing risk of unintentional consequences associated with antimicrobial use.

- Antimicrobial stewardship programs are a joint venture that include infectious diseases physicians, infectious diseases pharmacists and staff from microbiology, infection control, and pharmacy departments.

- Most programs contain an auditing component to review prescribing habits of providers and an educational component to change poor prescribing habits and improve patient care. These programs often oversee guideline development with the goal of optimal antibiotic use.

- Other common aspects of an ASP include 1) a restriction and/or pre-authorization policy, 2) intravenous-to-oral switch, and 3) de-escalation or streamlining of therapy based on patient response and culture/susceptibility results.

ANTIBIOGRAM

An antibiogram is a chart that contains the susceptibility patterns of local bacterial isolates to antimicrobial agents at a single institution (hospital) over a specific period of time (generally 1 year). Antibiograms aid in selecting empiric antibiotic therapy and in monitoring resistance trends over time within an institution. They can also be used to compare susceptibility rates across institutions and track resistance trends in the community. An example of an antibiogram for Gram-negative organisms is on the following page.

Antibiogram Example (January 1, 2011 – December 31, 2011)

GRAM-NEGATIVE ORGANISM (#) – ALL SOURCES (EXCLUDING URINE)

MICROBIOLOGIC PATHOGEN (# OF ISOLATES)	AZTREONAM	CEFAZOLIN	BETA-LACTAMS CEFEPIME	CEFOTAXIME	CEFTAZIDIME	CEFTRIAXONE	PIPERACILLIN	CARBAPENEM MEROPENEM	B-LACTAM/B-LACTAMASE INHIBITOR COMBINATION AMPICILLIN/SULBACTAM	PIPERACILLIN/TAZOBACTAMC	FLUORO-QUINOLONES CIPROFLOXACIN	LEVOFLOXACIN	AMINOGLYCOSIDES AMIKACIN	GENTAMICIN	TOBRAMYCIN	OTHER TRIMETHOPRIM/SULFA
Acinetobacter baumannii (65)			71	8	68	38	0	94			69	86	85	71	82	85
Enterobacter cloacae (142)	72		92	70	70	68	64	100		74	95	95	98	96	91	85
Escherichia coli (431)	87	76	88	86	85	85	46	100	46	91	74	75	99	91	88	68
Klebsiella oxytoca (49)	96	67	96	96	96	96	80	100	61	98	92	92	100	100	100	85
Klebsiella pneumoniae (158)	87	87	87	87	87	87	77	100	75	90	91	97	98	98	87	86
Proteus mirabilis (84)	99	75	100	100	100	99		100		86	81	85	100	92	87	87
Pseudomonas aeruginosa (474)	64		74		80		87	88		88	79	79	99	92	96	
Serratia marcescens (104)	99		100	93	98	96	83	99		93	91	98	99	91	72	
Stenotrophomonas maltophilia (75)					29			0f				61				98

Data source: The Surveillance Network – hospital name has been intentionally deleted

Drug Therapy Considerations

FACTORS TO CONSIDER WHEN SELECTING A DRUG REGIMEN	MONITORING FOR THERAPEUTIC EFFECTIVENESS	LACK OF THERAPEUTIC EFFECTIVENESS
Etiology/epidemiology (community vs. hospital-acquired infection, exposures to pathogens) of infection Site/severity of infection Patient characteristics (age, body weight, renal/liver function, allergies, pregnancy status, immune function) Spectrum of activity and pharmacodynamics/pharmacokinetics of the drug regimen	Fever curve WBC count Radiographic findings Pain/inflammation – elevated markers of inflammation include procalcitonin levels (more specific to inflammation from bacterial infection), C-reactive protein, Erythrocyte Sedimentation Rate (ESR) Reduction in signs and symptoms of infection Gram stain, cultures and antimicrobial susceptibilities	Misdiagnosis (e.g., cancer, autoimmune disease, drug fever, etc.) Inappropriate drug regimen, including antimicrobial agent and/or dose, lack of penetration Drug resistance Non-adherence

Culture and Sensitivity Report

Once cultures and sensitivities are reported, the antimicrobial regimen will need to be evaluated and adjusted for appropriateness. For example, a hospitalized patient is experiencing urinary urgency and burning upon urination. She was started on *Unasyn* as empiric treatment. The patient has NKDA. The urine culture and sensitivities are now available and reported below. Based on the data below, what would be the best antibiotic regimen for this patient?

Sample Culture and Susceptibility Report

DRUG	ORGANISM 1 - *PSEUDOMONAS*	MIC (MG/L) FOR ORGANISM 1	ORGANISM 2 – *MORGANELLA*	MIC (MG/L) FOR ORGANISM 2
Ampicillin	-	-	R	> 16
Ampicillin/sulbactam	-	-	R	> 16
Cefazolin	-	-	R	> 16
Cefoxitin	-	-	R	> 16
Ceftazidime	S	2	I	16
Ceftriaxone	-	-	S	8
Cefuroxime	-	-	S	8
Ciprofloxacin	S	1	R	> 2
Ertapenem	-	-	S	2
Gentamicin	I	8	S	2
Imipenem	S	< 1	I	8
Levofloxacin	S	2	R	> 4
Meropenem	S	< 1	I	8
Nitrofurantoin	-	-	R	>
Piperacillin/tazobactam	S	8	R	> 16
Tobramycin	S	< 1	S	2
Trimethoprim-sulfamethoxazole	-	-	R	> 2/38

S = susceptible; I = intermediately susceptible; R = resistant

Antibiotic Regimen Considerations

■ If an infection is present or not. Often patients are just colonized and may not require antimicrobial therapy. Note that the urine culture report above does not determine the presence or absence of an infection. A urine analysis suggestive of pyuria/bacteruria and/or clinical signs and symptoms should be the determinant whether an infection is present.

■ Drug allergies, antibiotic use history and patient characteristics.

■ Location of infection. Lipophilic antimicrobials have enhanced tissue penetration. Hepatically cleared antimicrobials may not achieve adequate drug concentrations in the urine.

■ Drug regimen – ideally a single antimicrobial would be best for most infections (certain "mixed" infections may require more than one antimicrobial agent to target various pathogens). Other co-infections should also be taken into account. This could easily justify the use of more than one antibiotic.

■ Absence of susceptibility results reported as "-" does not mean resistance; it represents that the drug was not tested against the bacteria.

- If available, use MICs to guide definitive therapy. Generally, choose the most active antimicrobial agent to treat the infection; however, if the patient is responding to a less active agent based on MIC findings, it may be appropriate to continue that agent.

- To treat the urinary tract infection in the proceeding culture and sensitivity effectively, it is best to pick the narrowest spectrum antimicrobial to limit the spread of resistance (e.g., low dose tobramycin based on culture and susceptibility results and urinary source). Given the patient is in the hospital and can receive IV therapy, tobramycin is appropriate. If the patient was treated as an outpatient where oral therapy is used, ciprofloxacin targeting the *Pseudomonas* and cefuroxime targeting the *Morganella* would be the best choice.

ANTIMICROBIAL PRINCIPLES

The appropriate selection of an antimicrobial regimen requires an understanding of pharmacokinetic principles (absorption, distribution, metabolism and excretion) as well as pharmacodynamic principles (concentration-dependent or time-dependent killing). Refer to Pharmacokinetics chapter for a review on pharmacokinetic principles.

Antimicrobial Pharmacokinetics: Hydrophilic or Lipophilic Agents

Hydrophilicity or lipophilicity of the antimicrobial agent can be used to predict a number of pharmacokinetic features (see figure below). Lipophilic agents generally have enhanced penetration of bone, lung, and brain tissues.

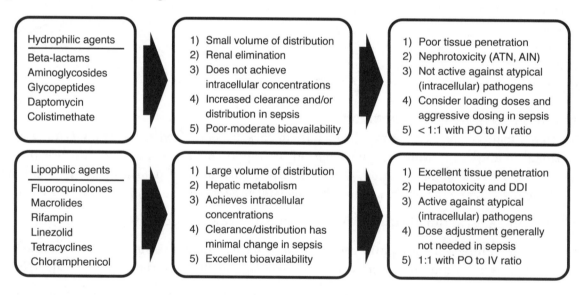

ATN = acute tubular necrosis, AIN = acute interstitial nephritis, PO = oral, IV = intravenous, DDI = drug-drug interaction

Antimicrobial Pharmacodynamics: Dose Optimization

Antimicrobial pharmacodynamics of selected antimicrobial agents is displayed in the following figure. Agents that exhibit time-dependent killing (such as beta-lactams) are generally dosed more frequently to maximize the time above the MIC, while concentration-dependent agents (such as aminoglycosides) are generally dosed as "high-dose once daily" to maximize the concentration above the MIC. Beta-lactam antibiotics may be maximized by extending the infusion time (such as over 4 hours) or given as a continuous infusion which can lead to

<u>greater time above the MIC</u>. Numerous studies have documented that extended/continuous infusion beta-lactam delivery can reduce length of stay, mortality, and costs particularly when treating Gram-negative pathogens, like *Pseudomonas*.

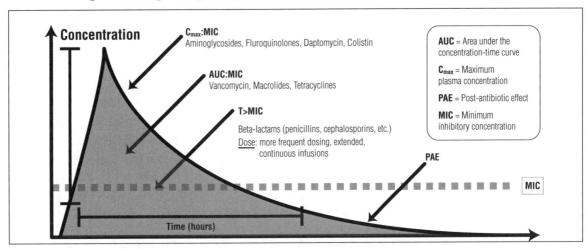

Antibacterial Mechanism of Action: Bacteriostatic or Bactericidal Activity

Knowledge of the mechanism of action generally predicts the bacteriostatic (bacterial inhibition by antimicrobial agent) or bactericidal (bacterial killing by antimicrobial agent) activity of antimicrobial agents (see figure below). However, it is important to note that for most mild infections bactericidal activity does not imply enhanced activity or improved patient outcomes in an immunocompetent host. Further, while bactericidal activity can be predicted by the mechanism of action, it is also dependent on a number of microbiologic, pharmacologic and host factors (culture and susceptibility results, achievable concentrations of the antimicrobial agent at the site of infection, duration of exposure, size of bacterium inoculums).

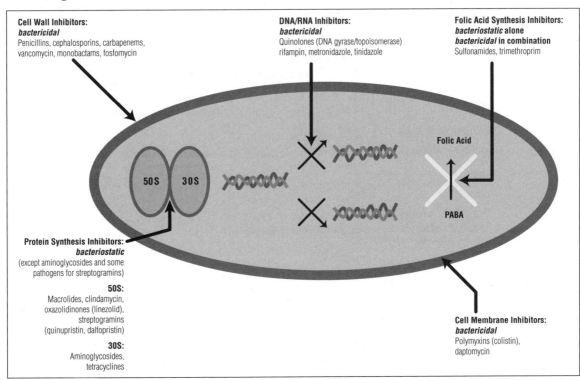

ANTIBACTERIAL AGENTS

All antibacterial agents carry a warning of the <u>risk of superinfection</u> with prolonged use including *C. difficile*-associated diarrhea (CDAD) and pseudomembranous colitis. It is important to optimize therapy with the right dose for a limited amount of time to reduce these complications.

Aminoglycosides (AMGs)

AMGs interfere with bacterial protein synthesis by binding to the 30S and 50S ribosomal subunits resulting in a defective bacterial cell membrane. AMGs exhibit <u>concentration-dependent killing</u> and have <u>a post-antibiotic effect</u> (PAE). The PAE is defined as the continued suppression of bacterial growth when antibiotic levels are below the MIC of the organism. Due to concentration-dependent killing activity and a long post-antibiotic effect, AMGs are generally dosed once daily (extended interval dosing) for Gram-negative organisms. Extended interval dosing has also been shown to <u>decrease nephrotoxicity</u> relative to traditional dosing.

- Coverage: Mainly active against Gram-negative bacteria (e.g., *Pseudomonas*); gentamicin and streptomycin are used for synergy in treating Gram-positive cocci (e.g., *Staphylococcus* and *Enterococcus endocarditis*) in combination with a beta-lactam or vancomycin.

DRUG	DOSING	SAFETY/SIDE EFFECTS/MONITORING
Gentamicin, Tobramycin, Amikacin – IV/IM Streptomycin – IM	<u>Dose on IBW</u>, unless total body weight (TBW) is less. Use AdjBW if TBW > 30% of IBW (morbidly obese) **Traditional Dosing** Gent/tobra: 1-3 mg/kg/dose [lower doses for Gram-positive infections; higher doses for Gram-negative infections] Amikacin: 5-7 mg/kg/dose CrCl > 60 mL/min: Q8H CrCl 40-60 mL/min: Q12H CrCl 20-40 mL/min: Q24H CrCl < 20 mL/min: give loading dose, then monitor levels **Extended Interval Dosing** Gent/tobra: 4-7 mg/kg Amikacin: 15-20 mg/kg Frequency determined by nomogram (example on next page)	**BLACK BOX WARNINGS (3)** AMGs may cause <u>neurotoxicity</u> (hearing loss, vertigo, ataxia); <u>nephrotoxicity</u> (particularly in renal impairment or with concurrent use of other nephrotoxic drugs); may cause fetal harm if given in pregnancy **WARNINGS** Neuromuscular blockade and respiratory paralysis especially when given soon after anesthesia or muscle relaxants **SIDE EFFECTS** Nephrotoxicity (acute tubular necrosis – ATN), hearing loss (early toxicity associated with high-pitched sounds). Use with caution in patients with impaired renal function, in the elderly, and those on other nephrotoxic drugs (amphotericin B, cisplatin, colistimethate, cyclosporine, loop diuretics, NSAIDs, radiocontrast dye, tacrolimus and vancomycin) **MONITORING** Renal function, urine output, hearing tests, and peak and trough levels if using traditional dosing or a random level with extended interval dosing Traditional dosing: Take trough level right before third dose, take a peak level ½ hour after the end of drug infusion Extended interval dosing: take random level per timing on the nomogram (example on next page) **NOTES** Pregnancy Category D May ↑ the respiratory depressant effect of neuromuscular blocking agents Tobramycin comes in an inhaled formulation, *TOBI, TOBI Podhaler* and *Bethkis*, used in Cystic Fibrosis (CF) Extended interval dosing is <u>less nephrotoxic</u> and <u>more cost-effective</u> Amikacin has the broadest spectrum of activity

Traditional Dosing Drug Concentrations

DRUG	PEAK	TROUGH
Gentamicin		
Gram-negative infection:	5-10 mcg/mL	< 2 mcg/mL
Gram-positive infection:	3-4 mcg/mL	< 1 mcg/mL
Tobramycin	5 – 10 mcg/mL	< 2 mcg/mL
Amikacin	20 – 30 mcg/mL	< 5 mcg/mL

Organism specific peak goals are typically 8-10 times the MIC of the bacteria causing the infection. (J. Infect. Dis. 155:93–99.)

Example of Extended Interval Dosing Nomogram

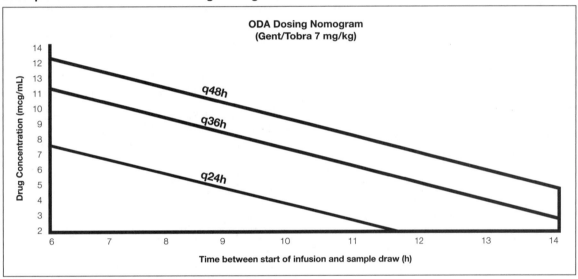

Antimicrob Agents Chemother. 1995 Mar;39(3):650-5

PENICILLINS (PCNs)

Penicillins are beta-lactams that <u>inhibit bacterial cell wall synthesis</u> by binding to one or more penicillin-binding proteins (PBPs), which in turn prevents the final transpeptidation step of peptidoglycan synthesis in bacterial cell walls. Penicillins exhibit <u>time-dependent killing and are bactericidal</u>, except against *Enterococci* species where aminoglycosides (gentamicin and streptomycin) are needed for bactericidal activity.

- Coverage: Mainly active against Gram-positive cocci (*Streptococcus*) and some Gram-negative bacilli coverage. No atypical coverage. Ampicillin, amoxicillin and piperacillin have activity against *Enterococci*. Nafcillin has enhanced activity against methicillin susceptible *Staphylococcus aureus* (MSSA). The addition of a beta-lactamase inhibitor adds additional Gram-negative coverage *(Proteus, E. coli, Klebsiella), H. influenzae,* MSSA and anaerobic coverage.

Select Penicillins

DRUG	DOSING	SAFETY/SIDE EFFECTS/MONITORING
Aminopenicillins: **Amoxicillin (Amoxil, Moxatag)** **+ clavulanate (Augmentin, Augmentin ES-600, Augmentin XR, Amoclan)** **Ampicillin** **+ sulbactam (Unasyn)**	Amoxicillin (PO): 250-500 mg Q8-12H or 500-875 mg Q12H *Moxatag:* 775 mg daily *H. pylori* treatment: 1,000 mg BID IE prevention: 2 grams 30-60 min before procedure	**WARNINGS** Anaphylaxis/hypersensitivity reactions **SIDE EFFECTS** GI upset, diarrhea, taste disturbance (oral), acute interstitial nephritis, rash/allergic reactions/anaphylaxis, bone marrow suppression with prolonged use, ↑ LFTs, seizures with accumulation **MONITORING** Renal function, symptoms of anaphylaxis with 1st dose, CBC, LFTs
Natural Penicillins: **Penicillin (Pen VK)** **Penicillin G Benzathine (Bicillin L-A)** Penicillin G Aqueous *(Pfizerpen-G)* Pen G Benzathine and Pen G Procaine *(Biciilin C-R)*	Pneumonia (CAP): 1,000 mg Q8H Amox/Clav (PO): 250-500 mg Q8H or 875-1,000 mg Q12H Pneumonia/Sinusitis: 2,000 mg Q12H Ampicillin (PO/IV): PO: 250-500 mg Q6H IV: 1-2 grams Q4-6H	**NOTES** Pregnancy Category B Test Interactions: can cause false (+) urinary glucose test *Augmentin* oral suspension must be refrigerated, *Amoxil* oral suspension is refrigerated to improve taste, but is stable for 14 days at room temperature Take *Moxatag* within 1 hour of finishing a meal Take extended release amox/clav tablets with food
Ureidopenicillins: **Piperacillin** **+ tazobactam (Zosyn)**	Amp/Sulbactam (IV): 1.5-3 grams Q6H *Unasyn* 3 g = 2 g of ampicillin and 1 g of sulbactam *Unasyn* 1.5 g = 1 g of ampicillin and 0.5 g of sulbactam Pen G Benzathine (IM): 1.2-2.4 MU x 1 (frequency varies) Penicillin G (IV): 2-4 MU Q4-6H	Take *Pen VK* on an empty stomach. *Pen VK* suspension should be refrigerated after reconstitution Take ampicillin PO on an empty stomach 1 hour before or 2 hours after meals Ampicillin IV is compatible with NS only; stable for 8 hours at room temperature (not suitable for continuous infusion) Nafcillin is a vesicant – if extravasation occurs, use cold packs and hyaluronidase injections. Administration through a central line is preferred
Carboxypenicillins: Ticarcillin + clavulanic acid *(Timentin)*	Penicillin VK (PO): 125-500 mg Q6-8H Piperacillin (IV): 3 grams Q4-6H Pip/Tazo (IV): 3.375-4.5 grams Q6-8H *(Zosyn* 3.375 g = 3 g of piperacillin and 0.375 g of tazobactam) Ticarcillin (IV): 3 grams Q4-6H Ticarcillin/Clav (IV): 3.1 grams Q4-6H *(Timentin* 3.1 g = 3 g of ticarcillin and 0.1 g of clavulanic acid)	Do not use in PCN-allergic patients Amoxicillin – DOC in acute otitis media, *H. pylori* regimen, pregnancy, prophylaxis for endocarditis Piperacillin and ticarcillin have activity against *Pseudomonas* Reduce dose and/or extend interval in renal impairment except for nafcillin, oxacillin and dicloxacillin When combined with a beta-lactamase inhibitor, suitable for treatment of mixed infections (intra-abdominal, diabetic foot, aspiration pneumonia, etc.)
Antistaphylococcal Penicillins: **Nafcillin**, oxacillin, and dicloxacillin	Nafcillin (IV): 1-2 grams Q4-6H Oxacillin (IV): 250 – 2,000 mg Q4-6H Dicloxacillin (PO): 125-500 mg Q6H	

Penicillin Drug Interactions

- Probenecid can ↑ levels of PCNs by interfering with renal excretion. This combination may be used to increase penicillin levels for severe infections.

- Penicillins can ↑ the serum concentration of methotrexate.

- Tetracyclines and other bacteriostatic agents may decrease the effectiveness of penicillins by slowing bacterial growth (penicillins work best against actively growing bacteria).

- Dicloxacillin and nafcillin can ↓ INR through increased metabolism of warfarin; other PCNs may increase anticoagulant effect of warfarin.

- Penicillins can ↓ serum concentrations of the active metabolite/s of mycophenolate due to impaired enterohepatic recirculation.

CEPHALOSPORINS

Cephalosporins are beta-lactams that inhibit bacterial cell wall synthesis by binding to one or more penicillin-binding proteins (PBPs), which in turn prevents the final transpeptidation step of peptidoglycan synthesis in bacterial cell walls. Cephalosporins exhibit time-dependent killing with bactericidal activity. The spectrum of activity is dependent upon the generation of the cephalosporin. For example, activity against *Staphylococci* generally decreases with each generation, while the activity of *Streptococci* and Gram-negative pathogens increases.

DRUG	DOSING	SAFETY/SIDE EFFECTS/MONITORING
1ˢᵗ Generation – Better *Staphylococci* activity, but lower *Streptococci* and Gram-negative activity compared to 2ⁿᵈ/3ʳᵈ generation; covers *Proteus mirabilis*, *E. coli* and *Klebsiella* species (PEK).		**WARNINGS** Anaphylaxis/hypersensitivity reactions Some agents may ↑ INR if patient is taking warfarin **SIDE EFFECTS** GI upset, diarrhea, rash/allergic reactions/anaphylaxis, acute interstitial nephritis, bone marrow suppression with prolonged use, ↑ LFTs, seizures with accumulation, drug fever
Cefadroxil	500-1,000 mg Q12H (PO)	
CeFAZolin *(Kefzol)*	250-2,000 mg Q8H (IV/IM)	
Cephalexin *(Keflex)*	250-1,000 mg Q6H (PO)	
2ⁿᵈ Generation – Better Gram-negative activity compared to 1ˢᵗ generation with similar Gram-positive activity including PEK, *Haemophilus* and *Neisseria* species (HNPEK). Cefotetan and cefoxitin have anaerobic activity (*Bacteroides fragilis*), but less Gram-positive activity.		**MONITORING** Renal function, signs of anaphylaxis with 1ˢᵗ dose, CBC, LFTs **NOTES** Cross sensitivity (< 10%) with PCN allergy – do not use in patients who have a type 1 mediated PCN allergy (swelling, angioedema, anaphylaxis)
Cefaclor	250-500 mg Q8H (PO)	
CefoTEtan	1-2 grams Q12H (IV/IM)	
CefOXitin	1-2 grams Q6-8H (IV/IM)	
Cefprozil	250-500 mg Q12-24H (PO)	
Cefuroxime *(Ceftin, Zinacef)*	250-1,500 mg Q8-12H (PO/IV/IM)	Pregnancy Category B Test Interactions – positive direct Coomb's test, false positive urinary glucose test
3ʳᵈ Generation – Better Gram-negative activity compared to 2ⁿᵈ generation, including HNPEK ± *Serratia* (HNPEKS) and some additional enteric Gram-negative rods; less *Staphylococcal* activity compared to 1ˢᵗ generation but enhanced *Streptococcal* activity. Note that ceftazidime has less Gram-positive activity, but enhanced Gram-negative activity including *Pseudomonas*.		Reduce dose and/or extend interval in renal impairment except for ceftriaxone Ceftriaxone can cause biliary sludging and should not be mixed (or given via Y-site) with calcium-containing solutions or used in neonates (cefotaxime preferred)
Cefdinir	300 mg Q12H or 600 mg daily (PO)	
Cefditoren *(Spectracef)*	200-400 mg Q12H (PO)	
Cefixime *(Suprax)*	400 mg divided every 12-24H (PO)	
Cefotaxime *(Claforan)*	1-2 grams Q4-12H (IV/IM)	Cefotetan contains a N-methylthiotetrazole (NMTT or 1-MTT) side chain, which can increase the risk of hypoprothrombinemia (bleeding) and a disulfiram-like reaction with alcohol ingestion.
Cefpodoxime	100-400 mg Q12H (PO)	
CefTAZidime *(Fortaz, Tazicef)*	1,000–2,000 mg Q8-12H (IV/IM)	
Ceftibuten *(Cedax)*	400 mg daily (PO)	Cefuroxime, cefpodoxime, and cefditoren tablets should be taken with food. Take ceftibuten suspension on an empty stomach.
CefTRIAXone *(Rocephin)*	1-2 grams Q12-24H (IV/IM)	
4ᵗʰ Generation – Best Gram-negative activity, including HNPEKS, *Citrobacter*, *Acinetobacter*, *Pseudomonas*, *Enterobacter* and *Serratia* species (CAPES) and Gram-positive activity similar to 3ʳᵈ generation.		
Cefepime *(Maxipime)*	1-2 grams Q8-12H (IV/IM)	
5ᵗʰ generation – Best Gram-positive activity; covers MRSA, some Gram-negative similar to ceftriaxone (no *Pseudomonas* coverage).		
Ceftaroline fosamil *(Teflaro)*	600 mg Q12H (IV)	

Cephalosporin Drug Interactions

■ Probenecid can ↑ levels of cephalosporins by interfering with renal excretion. This combination may be used to increase cephalosporin levels.

■ Cephalosporins may enhance the anticoagulant effect of warfarin by inhibiting the production of vitamin K-dependent clotting factors.

CARBAPENEMS

Carbapenems are beta-lactams that <u>inhibit bacterial cell wall synthesis</u> by binding to one or more penicillin-binding proteins (PBPs), which in turn prevents the final transpeptidation step of peptidoglycan synthesis in bacterial cell walls. Carbapenems exhibit <u>time-dependent killing with bactericidal activity</u>.

■ Coverage: Very broad spectrum with activity against most Gram-positive, Gram-negative, and anaerobic pathogens. They do not cover atypical pathogens, MRSA, VRE, *C. difficile* and *Stenotrophomonas*. <u>Ertapenem does not have activity against *Pseudomonas* or *Acinetobacter*.</u>

DRUG	DOSING	SAFETY/SIDE EFFECTS/MONITORING
Imipenem/ Cilastatin (*Primaxin*)	250-1,000 mg IV Q6-8H	**CONTRAINDICATIONS** Anaphylactic reactions to beta-lactam antibiotics **WARNINGS** Carbapenems have been associated with CNS adverse effects, including confusional states and seizures
Meropenem (*Merrem*)	500-2,000 mg IV Q8H	**SIDE EFFECTS** Diarrhea, rash, and seizures with higher doses and in patients with impaired renal function (mainly imipenem), bone marrow suppression with prolonged use, ↑ LFTs
Ertapenem (*Invanz*)	1,000 mg IV/IM daily Ertapenem is not active against *Pseudomonas* or *Acinetobacter*	**MONITORING** Renal function, symptoms of anaphylaxis with 1st dose, CBC, LFTs **NOTES** Pregnancy Category B/C (imipenem)
Doripenem (*Doribax*)	500 mg IV Q8H	Imipenem is combined with cilastatin to prevent drug degradation by renal tubular dehydropeptidase. Reduce dose and/or extend interval in renal impairment. Do not use in patients with PCN allergy, cross-reactivity has been reported to be as high as 50%, but newer studies show rates < 10%.

Carbapenem Drug Interactions

■ Probenecid can ↑ levels of carbapenems by interfering with renal excretion. This combination may be used to increase carbapenem levels.

■ Carbapenems can ↓ serum concentrations of valproic acid leading to a loss of seizure control.

■ Use with caution in patients at risk for seizures or with other agents known to lower seizure threshold (e.g., ganciclovir, fluoroquinolones, bupropion, tramadol, etc.). See Epilepsy chapter for a complete list.

FLUOROQUINOLONES (FQs)

Fluoroquinolones <u>inhibit bacterial DNA topoisomerase IV and inhibit DNA gyrase</u> (topoisomerase II). This prevents supercoiling of DNA and promotes breakage of double-stranded DNA. Fluoroquinolones exhibit <u>concentration-dependent killing</u> with bactericidal activity.

- Coverage: Extensive activity against Gram-negative, Gram-positive, and average to excellent atypical coverage (levofloxacin, moxifloxacin and gemifloxacin). Ciprofloxacin and levofloxacin have enhanced Gram-negative activity, including *Pseudomonas*, while moxifloxacin has enhanced Gram-positive and anaerobic activity and is often used for mixed infections alone (intra-abdominal infections). <u>Gemifloxacin, levofloxacin and moxifloxacin are often referred to as respiratory fluoroquinolones</u> due to enhanced coverage of *Streptococcus pneumoniae* and atypical coverage.

DRUG	DOSING	SAFETY/SIDE EFFECTS/MONITORING
Ofloxacin *Floxin* – otic Norfloxacin *(Noroxin)* **Ciprofloxacin *(Cipro, Cipro XR)*** *Ciloxan* – ophthalmic; *Cetraxal* and ***Ciprodex*** – otic **Levofloxacin *(Levaquin)*** *Iquix* and *Quixin* – ophthalmic Gatifloxacin (ophthalmic only) *Zymar* and *Zymaxid* – ophthalmic **Moxifloxacin *(Avelox, Avelox ABC Pack)*** *Moxeza* and ***Vigamox*** – ophthalmic Gemifloxacin *(Factive)*	Ofloxacin (PO): 200-400 mg Q12H CrCl < 30 mL/min: 400 mg Q24H Ciprofloxacin dosing (IV/PO): 250-750 mg PO or 200-400 IV Q8-12H CrCl 30-50 mL/min: Q12H CrCl < 30 mL/min: Q18-24H Levofloxacin dosing (IV/PO): 250-750 mg daily CrCl 20-49 mL/min (depends on the dose): 750 mg Q48H or 500 mg, then 250 mg daily or 250 mg daily CrCl < 20 mL/min: 750 mg, then 500 mg Q48H or 500 mg, then 250 mg Q48H or 250 mg Q48H Moxifloxacin dosing (IV/PO): 400 mg Q24H Gemifloxacin (PO): 320 mg daily	**BLACK BOX WARNINGS (2)** Tendon inflammation and/or rupture (most often in Achilles tendon) – risk may be increased with concurrent corticosteroid use, organ transplant patients, > 60 years of age May exacerbate muscle weakness related to myasthenia gravis **CONTRAINDICATIONS** Concurrent administration of tizanidine (with ciprofloxacin) **WARNINGS** Fluoroquinolones can prolong the QT interval; avoid use in patients at risk for QT prolongation. Use caution with agents that prolong QT interval including Class Ia and Class III antiarrhythmics Peripheral neuropathy (with oral and IV formulations) – may last months to years after the drug has been discontinued. In some cases, it may become permanent. If symptoms occur, stop the drug CNS effects: Tremor, restlessness, confusion, and very rarely hallucinations, increased intracranial pressure (including pseudotumor cerebri) or seizures may occur; use with caution in patients with known or suspected CNS disorder Fluoroquinolones can cause serious, and sometimes fatal, hypoglycemia Hepatotoxicity Photosensitivity/phototoxicity Children: Risk of arthropathy [use in children should be avoided due to concerns of musculoskeletal toxicity but may use if benefit outweighs the risk (such as anthrax) per the American Academy of Pediatrics] **SIDE EFFECTS** GI upset/diarrhea, headache, dizziness, insomnia, crystalluria and interstitial nephritis (rare) **NOTES** Pregnancy Category C – may cause cartilage damage in immature animals (benefit must outweigh risk) *Cipro Oral Susp* should not be given through a NG or other feeding tube (the oil based suspension adheres to the tubing). Shake vigorously for 15 seconds each time before use. Do not chew the microcapsules. Do not refrigerate the oral suspension. *Cipro IR* – can crush immediate release tablets, mix with water and give via feeding tube. Hold tube feedings at least 1 hour before and 2 hours after dose. IV levofloxacin should be protected from light. Take levofloxacin oral solution on an empty stomach (1 hour before or 2 hours after a meal); maintain adequate hydration to prevent crystalluria; store at room temperature. Extend interval (and may reduce dose) in renal impairment except for moxifloxacin. These agents can be used in PCN-allergic patients.

Quinolone Drug Interactions

- Antacids, didanosine, sucralfate, bile acid resins, magnesium, aluminum, calcium, iron, zinc, multivitamins or any product containing these multivalent cations can chelate and inhibit absorption. Separate as follows:

  - Give ciprofloxacin 2 hours before or 6 hours after these agents
  - Give levofloxacin 2 hours before or 2 hours after these agents
  - Give moxifloxacin 4 hours before or 8 hours after these agents

- Although it is usually recommended that concomitant intake of calcium-rich foods (dairy products) be avoided because of the potential for chelation, the actual influence of dairy products on fluoroquinolone absorption varies. In general, recommend to avoid administration with dairy products.

- Lanthanum *(Fosrenol)* can ↓ the serum concentration of quinolone; take oral quinolones at least 2 hours before or after lanthanum.

- Can ↑ the effects of warfarin, sulfonylureas/insulin and QT-prolonging drugs (moxifloxacin prolongs the QT interval the most).

- Probenecid and NSAIDs can ↑ FQ levels.

- Ciprofloxacin is a P-glycoprotein substrate and a 1A2 (strong) inhibitor and 3A4 (weak) inhibitor; ciprofloxacin can ↑ the levels of caffeine and theophylline by reducing metabolism.

- Levofloxacin is primarily renally cleared.

MACROLIDES

Macrolides bind to the 50S ribosomal subunit, resulting in inhibition of RNA-dependent protein synthesis with bacteriostatic activity related to total exposure of the drug (AUC/MIC).

- Coverage: Activity against Gram-positive pathogens, namely *Streptococci* species, and some Gram-negative pathogens, namely *Haemophilus, Neisseria* and *Moraxella* species, and good atypical coverage (*Legionella, Chlamydia, Mycoplasma* and some *Mycobacterium* species); suitable for treatment of upper and lower respiratory tract infections and certain sexually transmitted infections.

DRUG	DOSING	SAFETY/SIDE EFFECTS/MONITORING
Azithromycin *(Zithromax, Z-Pak, Zmax, Zithromax Tri-Pak, Azasite ophthalmic)* Better Gram-negative coverage compared to erythromycin	PO: 500 mg on day 1, then 250 mg on days 2-5 *(Z-Pak)* or 500 mg daily x 3 days or 1-2 grams x 1 IV: 250-500 mg daily	**CONTRAINDICATIONS** Concomitant use with pimozide, ergotamine or dihydroergotamine, lovastatin or simvastatin (with erythromycin) **WARNINGS** Macrolides have been associated with QT prolongation and ventricular arrhythmias, including torsade de pointes; use with caution in patients at risk of prolonged cardiac repolarization; avoid use in patients with uncorrected hypokalemia or hypomagnesemia, clinically significant bradycardia, and patients receiving Class Ia or Class III antiarrhythmic agents Hepatotoxicity
Clarithromycin *(Biaxin, Biaxin XL, **Biaxin XL Pac**)* Better Gram-positive coverage	250-500 mg PO Q12H or 1 gram PO daily CrCl < 30 mL/minute: ↓ dose by 50%	**SIDE EFFECTS** GI upset (diarrhea, abdominal pain and cramping especially with erythromycin), taste perversion, ↑ LFTs, ototoxicity (reversible and rare) **NOTES** Pregnancy Category B/C (clarithromycin) *Azasite* – viscous solution for ophthalmic use. Store at room temp once dispensed (cold makes solution more viscous). These agents can be used in PCN-allergic patients. Azithromycin and erythromycin do not require dose adjustments in renal impairment. Azithromycin ER suspension (*Zmax*) is not bioequivalent with *Zithromax* and should not be interchanged.
Erythromycin *(E.E.S., Ery-Tab, EryPed, Erythrocin)*	E.E.S.: 400-800 mg PO Q6-12H Erythromycin base/stearate: 250-500 mg PO Q6-12H IV: 500-1,000 mg Q6H (max 4 grams/day)	*Zmax* must be consumed within 12 hours of reconstitution on an empty stomach. Do not refrigerate azithromycin oral suspension *(Zmax).* Take *Biaxin XL* with food. Do not refrigerate *Biaxin* oral suspension (can gel). Must refrigerate erythromycin ethylsuccinate (E.E.S.) oral granule suspension and use within 10 days. Erythromycin powder suspension stable at room temperature x 35 days.

Macrolide Drug Interactions

- Erythromycin and clarithromycin are substrates of 3A4 (major) and 3A4 inhibitors (moderate/strong); use caution or avoid with many medications metabolized by 3A4 including apixaban, colchicine, conivaptan, cyclosporine, dabigatran, digoxin, quinidine, rivaroxaban, theophylline, warfarin and others. See Drug Interactions chapter for more information.

- Azithromycin is a substrate of 3A4 (minor) and inhibitor of 1A2 (weak) and P-gp; it does not have as many clinically significant drug interactions.

- All macrolides: do no use concurrently with agents that can prolong the QT interval.

TETRACYCLINES

Tetracyclines inhibit bacterial protein synthesis by reversibly binding to the 30S ribosomal subunit with bacteriostatic activity related to the total exposure of the drug (AUC/MIC). Doxycycline is used more often in practice due to improved tolerability and broader coverage, including for respiratory tract infections, tick-borne/rickettsial diseases, spirochetes and *Chlamydia* infections. Minocycline has enhanced Gram-positive coverage and is often preferred for skin infections, including acne. Tetracycline is rarely used in practice for treatment of infections, but is used as part of *H. pylori* regimens. Doxycycline is an option for the treatment of MRSA in mild skin infections and VRE in urinary tract infections.

- Coverage: Activity against many Gram-positive bacteria, including *Staphylococci, Streptococci, Enterococci, Nocardia, Bacillus* and *Propiobacterium* specius, Gram-negative bacteria, including respiratory tract flora *(Haemophilus, Moraxella,* atypicals) and other unique pathogens (e.g., spirochetes, rickettsial diseases, anthrax, syphilis, acne, *Chlamydia,* malaria, etc.).

DRUG	DOSING	SAFETY/SIDE EFFECTS/MONITORING
Doxycycline *(Vibramycin, Oracea, Doryx, Monodox, Atridox, Adoxa,* others)	100 mg PO/IV Q12H Take *Oracea* on an empty stomach (1 hr before or 2 hrs after meals). Take other forms with food to ↓ GI irritation	**WARNINGS** Children ≤ 8 years of age, pregnancy and breastfeeding (Preg Category D – suppresses bone growth and skeletal development, permanently discolors teeth) **SIDE EFFECTS** GI upset (nausea/vomiting/diarrhea), photosensitivity, rash;
Minocycline *(Minocin, Dynacin, Solodyn)*	50-100 mg PO/IV Q12-Q24H	exfoliative dermatitis, Drug Rash with Eosinophilia and Systemic Symptoms syndrome (DRESS), nephrotoxicity (Fanconi's syndrome), lupus-like syndrome, bone marrow suppression, hemolytic anemia (rare)
Tetracycline	250-500 mg PO Q6H Take on an empty stomach	**NOTES** Pregnancy Category D Take with 8 oz water to minimize GI irritation. Do not dose adjust doxycycline or minocycline in renal impairment (although some references recommend dose adjusting doxycycline when CrCl < 10 mL/min); extend interval with tetracycline in renal impairment. Doxycycline IV to PO ratio is 1:1. Doxycycline oral suspension should not be refrigerated. Doxycycline IV should be protected from light.

Tetracycline Drug Interactions

- Tetracycline absorption is impaired by antacids containing magnesium, aluminum, or calcium or medications that contain divalent cations such as iron-containing preparations, sucralfate, bile acid resins, or bismuth subsalicylate – separate doses (take 1-2 hours before or 4 hours after). Doxycycline and minocycline are less likely to be of clinical concern. These can be taken with food to reduce GI upset, but do not administer with dairy products (calcium). Do not eat or drink dairy products within 1 hour before or 2 hours after tetracycline products (except for *Doryx)*.

- Lanthanum *(Fosrenol)* can ↓ the concentration of tetracycline derivatives; take at least 2 hours before or after lanthanum.

- Tetracycline is a substrate of 3A4 (major) and 3A4 (moderate) inhibitor. Caution with the use of 3A4 inhibitors which ↑ levels and 3A4 inducers which ↓ levels.

- Doxycycline is a 3A4 (weak) inhibitor.

- Can enhance the anticoagulant effects in patients taking warfarin.

- Tetracycline derivatives can enhance the effects of neuromuscular blocking agents.

- Avoid concomitant use with retinoic acid derivatives due to the risk of pseudotumor cerebri.

- Tetracyclines can ↓ the effectiveness of penicillins by slowing bacterial growth (penicillins work best against actively growing bacteria).

SULFONAMIDES

Sulfamethoxazole (SMX) interferes with bacterial folic acid synthesis via inhibition of dihydrofolic acid formation from para-aminobenzoic acid and trimethoprim (TMP) inhibits dihydrofolic acid reduction to tetrahydrofolate resulting in inhibition of enzymes of the folic acid pathway. Individually they are bacteriostatic, however collectively they are bactericidal.

- Coverage: SMX/TMP has activity against Gram-positive bacteria, including *Staphylococci*/MRSA, and many Gram-negative bacteria, including *Haemophilus*, PEK, *Enterobacter, Acinetobacter, Shigella, Salmonella, Stenotrophomonas*; active against some opportunistic pathogens (*Nocardia, Pneumocystis, Toxoplasmosis*); but no *Pseudomonas, Enterococci,* atypical or anaerobic coverage.

DRUG	DOSING	SAFETY/SIDE EFFECTS/MONITORING
Sulfamethoxazole and trimethoprim *(Bactrim, Septra, Sulfatrim, others)* Single Strength (SS) = 400 mg SMX/80 mg TMP Double Strength (DS) = 800 mg SMX/160 mg TMP (Always a 5:1 ratio)	Adult female uncomplicated UTI: 1 DS tab BID x 3 days PCP prophylaxis: 1 DS or SS tab daily More severe infections: 10-20 mg/kg/day TMP (2 DS tabs BID-TID) PCP treatment: 15-20 mg/kg TMP IV/PO divided Q6-8H Other doses exist as well	**CONTRAINDICATIONS** Sulfa allergy, pregnancy (at term), breastfeeding, anemia due to folate deficiency, marked renal or hepatic disease, infants < 2 months of age **SIDE EFFECTS** GI upset (nausea, vomiting, diarrhea), skin reactions (rash, urticaria, SJS, TEN), crystalluria (take with 8 oz of water), interstitial nephritis, photosensitivity, bone marrow suppression with prolonged use, false elevations in SCr due to inhibition of tubular secretion of creatinine (pseudoazotemia), hyperkalemia, hypoglycemia, CNS (confusion, drug fever, seizures), ↑ LFTs, QT prolongation **NOTES** Pregnancy Category C/D (at term): risk for kernicterus and spinal cord defects Use caution with G6PD deficiency *Bactrim IV* – store at room temp, short stability (~6 hrs; however, the more concentrated the solution, the shorter the stability), dilute with D5W. Protect from light. Infuse over 60-90 minutes. *Bactrim susp* should be stored at room temp and protected from light. Reduce dose in renal impairment (CrCl < 30 mL/min) IV to PO ratio is 1:1

Sulfonamide Drug Interactions

- Sulfonamides are inhibitors of 2C8/9 (moderate/strong), caution with concurrent use of warfarin. See Drug Interactions chapter for more 2C8/9 substrates.

- May ↑ levels/effects of sulfonylureas, metformin, fosphenytoin/phenytoin, dofetilide, azathioprine, methotrexate, mercaptopurine and warfarin.

- Levels of SMX/TMP may be ↓ by 2C8/9 inducers and the therapeutic effects may be diminished by the use of leucovorin/levoleucovorin.

- ACE inhibitors, ARBs, aliskiren, potassium-sparing diuretics, drospirenone-containing oral contraceptives, cyclosporine, tacrolimus and canagliflozin will increase the risk for hyperkalemia when used concurrently; monitor.

- Additive QT prolongation with other agents that prolong the QT interval (refer to the Antiarrhythmics chapter for complete list).

ADDITIONAL AGENTS TO TREAT GRAM-POSITIVE INFECTIONS

Vancomycin

Inhibits bacterial cell wall synthesis by blocking glycopeptides polymerization by binding to the D-alanyl-D-alanine portion of cell wall precursor. Vancomycin exhibits time-dependent killing and is bactericidal.

- Coverage: Active against most Gram-positive bacteria, including *Staphylococci* (MRSA), *Streptococci* and *Enterococci* (not VRE) and *Clostridium difficile*.

DRUG	DOSING	SAFETY/SIDE EFFECTS/MONITORING
Vancomycin (*Vancocin*)	DOC for MRSA infections: 15-20 mg/kg Q8-12H IV Oral dosing for *C. Diff*: 125-500 mg QID x 10-14 days (higher if recurrent or severe, complicated disease) Extend interval in renal impairment: CrCl 20-49 mL/min: Q24H CrCL < 20 mL/min: give loading dose, then monitor levels	**SIDE EFFECTS** GI upset (oral route), infusion reaction/red man syndrome (maculopapular rash from too rapid of an infusion rate, hypotension, flushing, chills – give 30 min infusion for each 500 mg of drug), nephrotoxicity, bone marrow suppression (neutropenia/thrombocytopenia), drug fever, ototoxicity **MONITORING** Renal function, WBC, trough concentration at steady state (generally before the 4th dose) Troughs of 15-20 mcg/mL – pneumonia, endocarditis, osteomyelitis, meningitis, bacteremia Troughs of 10-15 mcg/mL for other infections. **NOTES** Pregnancy Category B (oral)/C (IV) Caution with the use of other nephrotoxic or ototoxic drugs (AMGs, cisplatin, others) Infuse peripheral IV at a concentration not to exceed 5 mg/mL Consider alternative agent when MIC of organism ≥ 2 mcg/mL

Vancomycin Drug Interactions

- Vancomycin can ↑ the toxicity of other nephrotoxic drugs (e.g., AMGs, amphotericin B, cisplatin, colistimethate, cyclosporine, loop diuretics, NSAIDs, radiocontrast dye, tacrolimus, vancomycin). Vancomycin can increase the toxicity of other ototoxic drugs (e.g., AMGs, cisplatin, loop diuretics, others).

- NSAIDs can ↑ the serum concentration of vancomycin.

- Vancomycin can enhance the effect of neuromuscular blocking agents.

Linezolid *(Zyvox)*

Oxazolidinone class – binds to the bacterial 23S ribosomal RNA of the 50S subunit inhibiting bacterial translation and protein synthesis and is mainly bacteriostatic.

- Coverage: Active against most Gram-positive bacteria, including MRSA, VRE *faecium* and *faecalis*. Approved for pneumonia and uncomplicated/complicated skin and soft-tissue infections including diabetic foot infections and infections caused by *Staphylococcus aureus* and *Streptococci* species and for VRE infections.

DRUG	DOSING	SAFETY/SIDE EFFECTS/MONITORING
Linezolid *(Zyvox)*	600 mg Q12H PO/IV	**CONTRAINDICATIONS** Concurrent use or within 2 weeks of MAO inhibitors **WARNINGS** Myleosuppression (duration related) Peripheral and optic neuropathy when treated > 28 days. A weak MAO inhibitor – can cause serotonin syndrome – caution in patients taking serotonergic or adrenergic drugs; avoid tyramine containing foods Hypoglycemia – cases of hypoglycemia have been reported in patients with diabetes mellitus receiving insulin or oral hypoglycemic agents **SIDE EFFECTS** Headache, diarrhea, nausea, insomnia, taste alteration, ↑ pancreatic enzymes, ↑ LFTs, neuropathy **NOTES** Pregnancy Category C IV to PO ratio is 1:1 No adjustment in renal impairment Store oral suspension at room temp and use within 21 days of reconstitution. Prior to administration mix gently by inverting bottle; do not shake.

Linezolid Drug Interactions

- Linezolid is a weak monoamine oxidase inhibitor. Avoid tyramine containing foods and serotonergic drugs. See Drug Interactions chapter.

Quinupristin/Dalfopristin *(Synercid)*

Streptogramin class – binds to different sites on the 50S bacterial ribosomal subunit inhibiting protein synthesis and is bactericidal.

- Coverage: Active against most Gram-positive bacteria, including MRSA, VRE *faecium* (not *E. faecalis*). Approved for complicated skin and soft-tissue infections caused by *Staphylococcus aureus* and *Streptococcus pyogenes*.

DRUG	DOSING	SAFETY/SIDE EFFECTS/MONITORING
Quinupristin/Dalfopristin *(Synercid)*	7.5 mg/kg IV Q8-12H	**SIDE EFFECTS** Arthralgias/myalgias (up to 47%), infusion reactions, including edema and pain at infusion site (up to 44%), phlebitis (40%), hyperbilirubinemia (up to 35%), GI upset, CPK elevations, ↑ LFTs **NOTES** Pregnancy Category B No adjustment in renal impairment Must be in a volume of 250 mL or greater (D5W only) to be given peripherally IV formulation should be refrigerated after reconstitution

Quinupristin/Dalfopristin Drug Interactions

- Quinupristin/Dalfopristin is a weak 3A4 inhibitor; can ↑ levels of CCBs, cyclosporine, dofetilide and others.

Daptomycin *(Cubicin)*

Cyclic lipopeptide class – binds to cell membrane components causing rapid depolarization, inhibiting all intracellular replication processes including protein synthesis. Daptomycin exhibits concentration-dependent killing and bactericidal activity.

- Coverage: Active against most Gram-positive bacteria, including MRSA, VRE *faecium* and *faecalis*. Approved for complicated skin and soft-tissue infections and *Staphylococus aureus* bloodstream infections, including right-sided endocarditis.

DRUG	DOSING	SAFETY/SIDE EFFECTS/MONITORING
DAPTOmycin *(Cubicin)*	4-6 mg/kg IV daily	**WARNINGS** May cause eosinophilic pneumonia – generally develops 2-4 weeks after therapy initiation Myopathy – discontinue in patients with signs and symptoms of myopathy in conjunction with an increase in CPK > 1,000 units/L (5 times ULN) or in asymptomatic patients with a CPK ≥ 2,000 units/L (10 times ULN) **SIDE EFFECTS** GI upset (constipation, diarrhea, vomiting), anemia, CNS (headache, dizziness, fever), ↑ CPK and myopathy, dyspnea, electrolyte disturbances (hypo- and hyperkalemia and hyperphosphatemia), ↑ LFTs **MONITORING** CPK level weekly (more frequently if on a statin); muscle pain/weakness **NOTES** Pregnancy Category B Extend interval in renal impairment (Q24H to Q48H) Do not use to treat pneumonia as it is inactivated by surfactant Compatible with NS (not D5W) Can cause false elevations in PT/INR (but no increase in bleeding risk)

Daptomycin Drug Interactions

- Daptomycin can have additive risk of muscle toxicity when used in conjunction with statins.

Telavancin *(Vibativ)*

<u>Lipoglycopeptide</u> and <u>derivative of vancomycin</u> – inhibits bacterial cell wall synthesis by blocking polymerization and cross-linking of peptidoglycan by binding to the D-Ala-D-Ala portion of the cell wall. Unlike vancomycin, the additional mechanism involves disruption of membrane potential and changes cell permeability due to the presence of a lipophilic side chain moiety. Telavancin exhibits concentration-dependent killing and is bactericidal.

- Coverage: Active against most Gram-positive bacteria, including MRSA, but not VRE strains. Approved for complicated skin and soft-tissue infections caused by Gram-positive organisms and for hospital acquired pneumonia (HAP) due to Gram-positive pathogens, including MRSA, when alternative treatments are not appropriate.

DRUG	DOSING	SAFETY/SIDE EFFECTS/MONITORING
Telavancin (*Vibativ*)	10 mg/kg IV daily	**BLACK BOX WARNINGS (3)** Fetal risk – obtain pregnancy test prior to starting therapy <u>Nephrotoxicity</u> – new onset or worsening renal impairment has occurred Patients with pre-existing moderate-to-severe renal impairment (CrCl ≤ 50 mL/minute) treated for hospital-acquired/ventilator-associated bacterial pneumonia (HABP/VABP) had increased mortality versus vancomycin **WARNINGS** May prolong the QT interval Infusion reactions: rapid IV administration may result in <u>red man syndrome</u> (flushing, rash, urticaria, and/or pruritus) – infuse over 60 minutes **SIDE EFFECTS** <u>Metallic taste, nausea, vomiting,</u> ↑ SCr, QT prolongation, red man syndrome **MONITORING** Renal function, pregnancy status **NOTES** Pregnancy Category C Reduce dose or extend interval in renal impairment Can interfere with coagulation tests MedGuide Required

Telavancin Drug Interactions

- Avoid in patients with congenital long QT syndrome, known QT prolongation, or uncompensated heart failure; caution with the use of other medications known to prolong the QT interval.

ADDITIONAL AGENTS TO TREAT GRAM-NEGATIVE INFECTIONS

Aztreonam

A monobactam that inhibits bacterial cell wall synthesis by binding to one or more of the penicillin-binding proteins (PBPs), which in turn inhibits the final transpeptidation step of peptidoglycan synthesis in bacterial cell walls, thus inhibiting cell wall synthesis; bactericidal. The monobactam structure makes cross-allergenicity with beta-lactams unlikely.

- Coverage: Active against many Gram-negative organisms, including *Pseudomonas*; no Gram-positive activity.

DRUG	DOSING	SAFETY/SIDE EFFECTS/MONITORING
Aztreonam **(Azactam IV,** *Cayston* – inhaled for CF)	500-2,000 mg IV Q6-12H	**SIDE EFFECTS** Similar to penicillins, including rash, diarrhea, nausea, vomiting, ↑ LFTs **NOTES** Pregnancy Category B Reduce dose in renal impairment Can be used in PCN-allergic patients

Colistimethate

Polymyxin antibiotic class – colistimethate is the inactive prodrug that is hydrolyzed to colistin, which acts as a cationic detergent and damages the bacterial cytoplasmic membrane causing leaking of intracellular substances and cell death. Colistimethate exhibits concentration-dependent killing and is bactericidal.

- Coverage: Covers Gram-negatives such as *Enterobacter, E. coli, Klebsiella pneumonia*, and *Pseudomonas aeruginosa* – used primarily in setting of multidrug resistant Gram-negative pathogens.

DRUG	DOSING	SAFETY/SIDE EFFECTS/MONITORING
Colistimethate sodium (Colistin, *Coly-Mycin M)* Colistin sulfate and Polymixin B are in the same class, but not used as commonly	2.5-5 mg/kg/day IV in 2-4 divided doses	**WARNING** Nephrotoxicity (dose-dependent) – monitor renal function/electrolytes closely **SIDE EFFECTS** Nephrotoxicity (proteinuria, ↑ SCr), neurologic disturbances (dizziness, tingling, numbness, paresthesia, vertigo) **NOTES** Pregnancy Category C Reduce frequency and extend interval in renal impairment

Colistimethate Drug Interactions

Other nephrotoxic agents (e.g., amphotericin B, AMGs, cisplatin, cyclosporine, loop diuretics, NSAIDs, radiocontrast dye, tacrolimus, vancomycin) can enhance the nephrotoxic effect of colistimethate.

ADDITIONAL BROAD SPECTRUM AGENTS

Chloramphenicol

Reversibly binds to the 50S ribosomal subunit of susceptible organisms inhibiting protein synthesis; bactericidal.

- Coverage: Activity against Gram-positives, Gram-negatives, anaerobes, and atypicals.

DRUG	DOSING	SAFETY/SIDE EFFECTS/MONITORING
Chloramphenicol Rarely used due to side effects	50-100 mg/kg/day in divided doses Q6H (max 4 g/day)	**BLACK BOX WARNING** Serious and fatal blood dyscrasias (aplastic anemia, thrombocytopenia) – must monitor CBC frequently **WARNINGS** Gray syndrome – characterized by circulatory collapse, cyanosis, acidosis, abdominal distention, myocardial depression, coma, and death; associated with high serum levels **SIDE EFFECTS** Myelosuppression (pancytopenia), aplastic anemia, dermatologic (angioedema, rash, urticaria) **MONITORING** CBC, liver and renal function, troughs (goal 5-15 mcg/mL) **NOTES** No adjustment in renal impairment but use with caution

Telithromycin *(Ketek)*

Ketolide class – inhibits bacterial protein synthesis by binding to 2 sites on the 50S ribosomal subunit (structurally related to macrolides). Telithromycin exhibits concentration-dependent killing and is bactericidal.

- Coverage: Activity against Gram-positives, primarily *Streptococci* species, including macrolide resistant strains, Gram-negatives, some anaerobes, and *Mycobacteria* atypicals; FDA approved for community acquired pneumonia only.

DRUG	DOSING	SAFETY/SIDE EFFECTS/MONITORING
Telithromycin *(Ketek)*	800 mg PO daily CrCl < 30 mL/min: 600 mg PO daily CrCl < 30 mL/min + cirrhosis: 400 mg PO daily	**BLACK BOX WARNING** Do not use in myasthenia gravis due to respiratory failure **CONTRAINDICATIONS** Allergy to macrolides, history of hepatitis or jaundice from macrolides, myasthenia gravis, concurrent use with colchicine (if patient has renal or liver impairment), lovastatin or simvastatin **WARNINGS** Acute hepatic failure (can be fatal), QT prolongation, visual disturbances (blurry vision, diplopia), syncope **SIDE EFFECTS** GI upset (diarrhea, vomiting), CNS (headache, dizziness, blurred vision), ↑ LFTs, rash **MONITORING** LFTs and visual acuity **NOTES** Pregnancy Category C Reduce dose in renal impairment

Telithromycin Drug Interactions

- Telithromycin is a substrate of 1A2 (minor), 3A4 (major) and an inhibitor of 2D6 (weak) and 3A4 (strong). Avoid with moderate/strong 3A4 inhibitors and substrates of 3A4 with a narrow therapeutic window or significant toxicity (e.g., simvastatin, lovastatin). Avoid with class Ia and class III antiarrhythmics and other major QT prolonging drugs. See Drug Interactions chapter for more information.

Tigecycline *(Tygacil)*

Glycylcyclines class – binds to the 30S ribosomal subunit inhibiting protein synthesis; structurally related to the tetracyclines. Tigecycline is bacteriostatic.

- Coverage: Activity against Gram-positives including MRSA, VRE *faecium* and *faecalis*, Gram-negatives, anaerobes, and atypicals. Among the Gram-negatives, tigecycline does not have activity against the "3 P's": *Pseudomonas, Proteus, Providencia* species. Tigecycline is approved for adults with complicated skin and soft-tissue infections/intraabdominal infections and for community acquired pneumonia; however, a recent FDA warning suggests to use it only when other alternatives are not possible.

DRUG	DOSING	SAFETY/SIDE EFFECTS/MONITORING
Tigecycline *(Tygacil)* Derivative of minocycline	100 mg IV x 1 dose, then 50 mg IV Q12H Severe hepatic impairment: 100 mg IV x 1, then 25 mg IV Q12H	**BLACK BOX WARNING** Increased risk of death for FDA-approved and non-approved uses – should only be used in situations when alternative treatments are not suitable **WARNINGS** Hepatotoxicity Pancreatitis Photosensitivity Children ≤ 8 years of age, pregnancy (Preg Category D – suppresses bone growth and skeletal development, discolors teeth permanently) **SIDE EFFECTS** GI upset (diarrhea, vomiting), CNS (headache, dizziness, insomnia), ↑ LFTs, pruritis/rash **NOTES** Pregnancy Category D Not to be used in children ≤ 8 years of age No adjustment in renal impairment Lower cure rates in ventilator-associated pneumonia Avoid for use in bloodstream infections as it does not achieve adequate concentrations in the central compartment (blood) due to its lipophilicity (concentrates in the peripheral compartment: tissues).

Tigecycline Drug Interactions

Tigecycline can ↑ INR in patient's taking warfarin.

OTHER ANTIBACTERIAL AGENTS

Clindamycin *(Cleocin)*

Reversibly binds to the 50S ribosomal subunit and inhibits bacterial protein synthesis; bacteriostatic.

- Coverage: Activity against most aerobic Gram-positives (not *Enterococcus*) and anaerobic Gram-negative and Gram-positives.

DRUG	DOSING	SAFETY/SIDE EFFECTS/MONITORING
Clindamycin *(Cleocin)* Topical: *Cleocin, Cleocin-T, Clindacin ETZ, Clindacin Pac, Clindacin-P, Clindagel, ClindaMax, Clindesse, Evoclin*	PO: 150-450 mg Q6-8H IV: 600-900 mg Q8H	**BLACK BOX WARNING** Can cause severe and possibly fatal colitis **SIDE EFFECTS** GI upset (nausea, vomiting, diarrhea); rash, urticaria, SJS, ↑ LFTs (rare) **NOTES** Pregnancy Category B No adjustment in renal impairment

Metronidazole *(Flagyl)* and Tinidazole *(Tindamax)*

Metronidazole causes a loss of helical DNA structure and strand breakage, which blocks translation and protein synthesis. Tinidazole damages DNA and blacks translation. Both are bactericidal.

- Coverage: Metronidazole has activity against anaerobes and protozoal infections; DOC for bacterial vaginosis, trichomoniasis, giardiasis, amebiasis and pseudomembranous colitis *(Clostridium difficile)*. Tinidazole has activity against protozoa (giardiasis, amebiasis), trichomoniasis and bacterial vaginosis organisms – structurally related to metronidazole.

DRUG	DOSING	SAFETY/SIDE EFFECTS/MONITORING
Metronidazole *(Flagyl, Flagyl ER, Metro)* Topical: *MetroCream, MetroGel, MetroGel Vaginal, MetroLotion, Noritate, Vandazole*	IV/PO: 500-750 mg Q8-12H or 250-500 mg Q6-8H 500 mg TID for 10-14 days for mild-to-moderate *C.diff* infections No adjustment in renal impairment (some sources say to adjust when CrCl < 10 mL/min)	**BLACK BOX WARNING** Possibly carcinogenic based on animal data **CONTRAINDICATIONS** Pregnancy (1ˢᵗ trimester); use of disulfiram within the past 2 weeks; use of alcohol during therapy or within 3 days of therapy discontinuation. **WARNINGS** CNS effects – aseptic meningitis, encephalopathy, seizures, and neuropathies (peripheral and optic) with high doses and chronic treatment **SIDE EFFECTS** GI upset, metallic taste, furry tongue, glossitis, darkened urine, rash, CNS (peripheral neuropathy, headache, ataxia, confusion, dizziness, seizures) **NOTES** Can take immediate release tablets with food to minimize GI effects Take extended release tablets on empty stomach IV to oral ratio is 1:1 Do not refrigerate metronidazole IV (crystals may form which may dissolve upon warming to room temp.) Pregnancy Category B (CI in 1ˢᵗ trimester)
Tinidazole *(Tindamax)*	2 grams PO daily, up to 5 days Take with food to minimize GI effects No adjustment in renal impairment	**BLACK BOX WARNING** Possibly carcinogenic based on animal data **CONTRAINDICATIONS** Pregnancy (1ˢᵗ trimester), breast-feeding **WARNINGS** CNS effects – aseptic meningitis, encephalopathy, seizures, and neuropathies (peripheral and optic) with high doses and chronic treatment **SIDE EFFECTS** GI upset, metallic taste, furry tongue, glossitis, darkened urine, rash, disulfiram-like reaction with alcohol, CNS (peripheral neuropathy, fatigue, headache, dizziness) **NOTES** Pregnancy Category C (CI in 1st trimester)

Metronidazole/Tinidazole Drug Interactions

- Metronidazole is a moderate 3A4 inhibitor and moderate 2C9 inhibitor whereas tinidazole is a minor 3A4 substrate.

- Metronidazole and tinidazole should not be used with alcohol (during and for 3 days after discontinuation of therapy) and can increase the INR if used with warfarin.

Rifaximin *(Xifaxan)*

Rifaximin inhibits bacterial RNA synthesis by binding to bacterial DNA-dependent RNA polymerase. It is structurally related to rifampin and is bactericidal. Rifaximin is indicated for treatment of traveler's diarrhea caused by non-invasive *E. coli* and prevention of hepatic encephalopathy.

DRUG	DOSING	SAFETY/SIDE EFFECTS/MONITORING
Rifaximin *(Xifaxan)*	Traveler's diarrhea: 200 mg PO TID x 3 days Hepatic encephalopathy: 550 mg PO BID	**SIDE EFFECTS** Flatulence, peripheral edema, dizziness, headache, GI upset, rash/pruritus **NOTES** Pregnancy Category C Not effective for systemic infections – absorption is minimal Take with or without of food No adjustment in renal impairment

Fosfomycin *(Monurol)*

Inhibits bacterial cell wall synthesis by inactivating the enzyme, pyruval transferase, which is critical in the synthesis of cell walls; bactericidal.

- Coverage: Single dose used to treat uncomplicated UTI (cystitis only) due to *E. coli* and *E. faecalis* (active against VRE).

DRUG	DOSING	SAFETY/SIDE EFFECTS/MONITORING
Fosfomycin *(Monurol)*	Uncomplicated UTI: 3 grams in 3-4 oz of water x 1	**SIDE EFFECTS** Headache, diarrhea, nausea **NOTES** Pregnancy Category B Mix with cold water (not hot). Stir to dissolve.

Nitrofurantoin *(Macrodantin, Macrobid, Furadantin)*

Bacterial cell wall inhibitor, hence bactericidal.

- Coverage: Used for uncomplicated UTI (cystitis only) due to *E. coli, S. aureus, Enterococcus, Klebsiella* and *Enterobacter*.

DRUG	DOSING	SAFETY/SIDE EFFECTS/MONITORING
Nitrofurantoin *(Macrodantin, Macrobid, Furadantin)*	*Macrodantin* 50-100 mg PO QID; 50-100 mg PO daily for prophylaxis *MacroBID* 100 mg PO BID	**CONTRAINDICATIONS** Patients with renal impairment (CrCl < 60 mL/min) due to concerns of inadequate urinary concentrations and risk for accumulation of neurotoxins; pregnancy (at term) **SIDE EFFECTS** Nausea, headache, hepatotoxicity (rare), peripheral neuropathy (rare). Pulmonary toxicity if used long term. **NOTES** Pregnancy Category B (contraindicated at term) Take with food to enhance absorption. May darken urine (dark yellow/brown color) during use (harmless)

Nitrofurantoin Drug Interactions

- Magnesium trisilicate-containing antacids can ↓ levels of nitrofurantoin; avoid.

- Probenecid can ↑ levels of nitrofurantoin by interfering with renal excretion; avoid.

Fidaxomicin *(Dificid)*

Inhibits RNA polymerase resulting in inhibition of protein synthesis and cell death; bactericidal.

- Coverage: Used for *Clostridium difficile* associated diarrhea. Currently used in select cases due to high cost (e.g., resistance and/or failure to vancomycin or metronidazole).

DRUG	DOSING	SAFETY/SIDE EFFECTS/MONITORING
Fidaxomicin *(Dificid)*	200 mg PO BID x 10 days	**SIDE EFFECTS** Nausea, vomiting, abdominal pain, GI bleeding, anemia **NOTES** Not effective for systemic infections – absorption is minimal Pregnancy Category B Can be given with or without food, no adjustment in renal impairment

ANTIBIOTIC REFRIGERATION AND RENAL INFORMATION

Antibiotics that need to be refrigerated

Amoxicillin/clavulanate *(Augmentin)*

Cefaclor

Cefadroxil

Cefpodoxime

Cefprozil

Cefuroxime *(Ceftin)*

Ceftibuten *(Cedax)*

Cephalexin *(Keflex)*

Erythromycin/benzoyl peroxide *(Benzamycin)*

Erythromycin ethylsuccinate/sulfi-soxazole

Penicillin VK

Refrigeration recommended

Amoxicillin *(Amoxil)* – improves taste

Do not refrigerate

Azithromycin *(Zmax)*

Cefdinir

Cefixime *(Suprax)*

Clarithromycin *(Biaxin)* – bitter taste and thickening/gels

Clindamycin *(Cleocin)* – thickening and may crystallize

Ciprofloxacin *(Cipro)*

Doxycycline *(Vibramycin)*

Fluconazole *(Diflucan)*

Levofloxacin *(Levaquin)*

Linezolid *(Zyvox)*

Sulfamethoxazole/trimethoprim *(Septra, Sulfatrim)*

Voriconazole *(VFEND)*

Common antibacterials that do not require renal dose adjustment

Azithromycin

Ceftriaxone

Chloramphenicol

Clindamycin

Dicloxacillin

Doxycycline

Erythromycin

Fidaxomicin

Linezolid

Metronidazole

Minocycline

Moxifloxacin

Nafcillin

Oxacillin

Quinupristin/dalfopristin

Rifaximin

Rifampin

Tigecycline

Tinidazole

DRUGS USED TO TREAT DIFFICULT PATHOGENS

Agents used for skin and skin structure infections caused by Community-Associated Methicillin-Resistant *Staphylococcus aureus* (CA-MRSA)

SMX -TMP *(Bactrim DS)* 1-2 DS tablets Q12H

Doxycycline 100 mg PO/IV Q12H

Minocycline 100 mg PO/IV Q12H

Clindamycin 600 mg PO/IV Q8H*

Linezolid 600 mg PO/IV Q12H

Daptomycin 4 mg/kg IV daily

Tigecycline 100 mg IV x 1, then 50 mg IV Q12H

Ceftaroline 600 mg IV Q12H

Vancomycin 10-15 mg/kg IV Q12H

Telavancin 10 mg/kg IV daily

Agents used to treat Nosocomial-Associated Methicillin-Resistant *Staphylococcus aureus*

Vancomycin (If VISA, then use agents listed below or consider agents below if MIC ≥ 2)

Linezolid

Quinupristin-dalfopristin

Daptomycin (not for pneumonia)

Ceftaroline

Telavancin

Tigecycline

Rifampin (combination therapy for prosthetic infections)

SMX/TMP

Agents used to treat VRE. *faecalis*

Pen G or ampicillin

Linezolid

Daptomycin

Tigecycline

Cystitis only per susceptibilities: nitrofurantoin, fosfomycin, doxy-cycline

Agents used to treat VRE. *faecium*

Daptomycin

Linezolid

Quinupristin-dalfopristin

Tigecycline

Cystitis only per susceptibilities: nitrofurantoin, fosfomycin, doxy-cycline

Agents used to treat *Pseudomonas aeruginosa*

Imipenem

Meropenem

Doripenem

Cefepime

Ceftazidime

Ciprofloxacin

Levofloxacin

Aztreonam

Ticarcillin/Clavulanic acid

Piperacillin

Piperacillin/Tazobactam

Colistimethate (colistin)

Amikacin

Tobramycin

Gentamicin

Agents used to treat Extended Spectrum Beta-Lactamase producing Enteric Gram-negative Rods (ESBL GNR) – *E. coli, Klebsiella pneumoniae, P. mirabilis*

Carbapenems

Cefepime (high dose)

Piperacillin/Tazobactam

Fluoroquinolones

Aminoglycosides (per susceptibilities)

Agents used to treat *Acinetobacter baumannii*

Imipenem

Meropenem

Doripenem

Ampicillin/Sulbactam

Colistimethate (colistin)

Minocycline

Tigecycline

Fluoroquinolones

SMX-TMP

Agents used to treat *Bacteroides fragilis*

Metronidazole

Carbapenems

Beta-lactam/Beta-lactamase inhibitor combos

Tigecycline

Cefoxitin

Cefotetan

Others but reduced activity: clindamycin, moxifloxacin

Agents used to treat *Clostridium difficile*

Metronidazole

Vancomycin (oral)

Fidaxomicin

---

* *Before using clindamycin, an induction test (D test) should be performed on isolates sensitive to clindamycin but resistant to erythromycin – look for a flattened zone between the disks → this signifies that inducible clindamycin resistance is present. Also, never use FQs regardless of susceptibility profile.*

Common Antimicrobial Drug-Drug Interactions, Toxicities and Pregnancy Categories

DRUG CLASS	P450 INHIBITION	HEPATIC TOXICITY	RENAL TOXICITY	OTHER	PREGNANCY CLASS B	C	D	X
Acyclovir			+		X			
Aminoglycosides			+++ (ATN)	↑ Neuromuscular blockers, ototoxic			X	
Beta-lactams			+ (AIN)	Seizures with accumulation; allergic reactions	X	imipenem		
Clindamycin		+		BBW: Colitis	X			
Colistin			+++ (ATN)			X		
Daptomycin				CPK levels; NS only	X			
Fluconazole	2C9 (weak-moderate), 2C19 (weak), 3A4 (moderate)	+		QT prolongation		150 mg	X	
Fosfomycin					X			
Linezolid				Serotonin syndrome (use with SSRI, MAO-I) and HTN crisis (sympathomimetics), BMS		X		
Macrolides	Erythro/clarithro 3A4 (mod/ strong)	++		Additive QT	X	Clarithromycin		
Metronidazole	3A4 (moderate); 2C9 (mod/strong)			Metallic taste, darkened urine, PN, no EtOH	X		Avoid 1st trimester	
Nitrofurantoin				CI when CrCl < 60 mL/min	X		at term	
Quinolones	Cipro – 1A2 (strong), 3A4 (weak)	+		BBW: tendonitis. Additive QT, photosensitivity, cations*, PN		X		
Quinupristin and dalfopristin	3A4 (weak)	+		Muscle toxicity, phlebitis, D5W only	X			
Rifampin	strong 450 inducer	+++		Red urine		X		
SMX/TMP	2C9 (mod/strong)		+	Allergic reactions, photosensitivity, additive QT, D5W only; room temp		X	(avoid 3rd trimester)	
Tetracycline	3A4 (weak/mod)	+		Cations* photosensitivity			X (bones)	
Vancomycin			+ (AIN)	Ototoxic, infusion reactions	oral	IV		

AIN = acute interstitial nephritis, ATN = acute tubular necrosis, BBW = black box warning, BMS = bone marrow suppression, CI = contraindicated, CPK = creatine phosphokinase, MAO-I = monoamine oxidase inhibitor, PN = peripheral neuropathy, QT = additive QT prolongation, SSRI = selective serotonin reuptake inhibitor, SMX/TMP = sulfamethoxazole-trimethoprim, + = not common, ++ = relatively common, +++ = very common

* Generally dose 1-2 hours before or 4-6 hours after administration of di/trivalent cations (e.g., magnesium, calcium, iron)

ANTIMICROBIAL AGENTS FOR SELECT INFECTIOUS DISEASE SYNDROMES

Background

Knowledge of the likely pathogens at the suspected site of infection helps the clinician choose the initial empiric therapy. When the specific pathogens and the sensitivities are identified, the antibiotics can be changed to directed therapy. Always consider the institutions resistance patterns and antibiotic use guidelines, and the patient characteristics.

COMMON BACTERIAL PATHOGENS FOR SELECTED SITES OF INFECTION

CNS/Meningitis
Streptococcus pneumoniae
Neisseria gonorrheoae
H. influenzae
Streptococci/*E. coli* (young)
Listeria (young/old)

Upper Respiratory
M. catarrhalis
H. influenzae
Streptococci

Bone & Joint
Staphylococcus aureus
Staphylococcus epidermidis
Streptococci
Neisseria gonorrhea
± GNR

Mouth/ENT
Peptostreptococcus
Actinomyces
Anaerobic GNRs
± *H. influenzae* and aerobic GNR

Skin/Soft Tissue
Staphylococcus aureus
Streptococcus pyogenes
Staphylococcus epidermidis
Pasteurella
± aerobic/anaerobic GNR (diabetics)

Intra-abdominal Tract
E. coli, Proteus, Klebsiella
Enterococci/Streptococci
Bacteroides species

Lower Respiratory (Community)
Streptococcus pneumoniae
H. influenzae
Atypicals: *Legionella, Mycoplasma*
Enteric GNRs (Alcoholics, IC, HCA)

Lower Respiratory (Hospital)
Enteric GNRs (*E. coli, Klebsiella, Proteus*)
Streptococcus pneumoniae
Pseudomonas aeruginosa
Enterobacter species
S. aureus, including MRSA

Urinary Tract
E. coli, Proteus, Klebsiella
Staphylococcus saprophyticus
Enterococci/Streptococci

CNS = central nervous system, ENT = ear, nose and throat, GNR = Gram-negative rods, HCA = healthcare associated, IC = immunocompromised

---

Surgical Antibiotic Prophylaxis

- A very brief course of an antimicrobial agent <u>initiated within 60 minutes before the incision</u> (or <u>120 minutes before the incision if using fluoroquinolones or vancomycin</u>) to obtain therapeutic levels in both serum and tissue.

- Maintain therapeutic levels throughout the surgery and until a few hours after the incision is closed (at most). Some surgeries may require longer duration (e.g., 48 hours post cardiac surgery). Most surgeries require < 24 hours of antibiotic coverage.

- A second dose of antibiotics may be needed <u>for longer procedures</u> (≥ 3-4 hours) or if there is <u>major blood loss</u> (≥ 1.5 L of blood).

- In general, first or second generation cephalosporins (e.g., <u>cefazolin/cefuroxime</u>) are the drugs of choice for most procedures. <u>In penicillin-allergic patients, a suitable alternative is vancomycin (given 2 hrs prior to surgical incision).</u>

- <u>Surgeries that involve parts of the bowel or put patients at risk of an anaerobic infection will commonly use antibiotics with broader coverage such as cefotetan, ertapenem or ceftriaxone with metronidazole.</u>

SURGICAL PROCEDURE	RECOMMENDED ANTIBIOTICS	IF BETA-LACTAM ALLERGY
CABG, other cardiac or vascular surgeries	Cefazolin, Cefuroxime	Vancomycin* or Clindamycin
Hip fracture repair/total joint replacement	Cefazolin	Vancomycin* or Clindamycin
Colon (colorectal)	Cefotetan, Cefoxitin, Ampicillin/ Sulbactam or Ertapenem or Cefazolin or Ceftriaxone + Metronidazole	Clindamycin + (Aminoglycoside or Quinolone or Aztreonam) or Metronidazole + (Aminoglycoside or Quinolone)
Hysterectomy	Cefotetan, Cefazolin, Cefoxitin or Ampicillin/Sulbactam	Clindamycin or Vancomycin* + (Aminoglycoside or Quinolone or Aztreonam) or Metronidazole + (Aminoglycoside or Quinolone)

For procedures and/or patients where MRSA is a likely pathogen consider using vancomycin.

Am J Health-Syst Pharm. 2013; 70:195-283

Meningitis

Meningitis is inflammation of the meninges (membranes) that cover the brain and spinal cord. The meninges swell, causing the "triad" of symptoms: severe headache, nuchal rigidity (stiff neck) and altered mental status. Other symptoms could include chills, vomiting and photophobia. Most cases are due to viral infections. Occasionally the causative pathogens are bacteria or fungi. Meningitis symptoms must be recognized quickly to avoid severe complications, including death.

- A lumbar puncture (LP) is mandatory for all suspected bacterial meningitis. The LP will help differentiate viral from bacterial meningitis as well as provide culture and sensitivity information.

- Gram stain is both rapid and sensitive for diagnosis of bacterial meningitis; however, the sensitivity decreases in patients who received prior antibiotic therapy.

- Antibiotic dosages must be maximized to optimize penetration of the CNS.

- The most likely organisms causing bacterial meningitis are *Streptococcus pneumonia*, *Neisseria meningitidis*, *Haemophilus influenza* and *Listeria monocytogenes*.

- Likely pathogens and empiric antimicrobial selection is dependent on the patient's age (see following table). Definitive therapy for the most common bacterial pathogen, *Streptococcus pneumoniae,* is dictated by the susceptibility results as follows:

ANTIBIOTIC	SUSCEPTIBLE (S)	INTERMEDIATE (I)	RESISTANT (R)
Penicillin	< 0.1 mcg/mL	0.1-1 mcg/mL	> 1 mcg/mL
Ceftriaxone	≤ 0.5 mcg/mL	1 mcg/mL	≥ 2 mcg/mL

- Penicllin-S: Penicllin/Ampicillin or Ceftriaxone

- Penicllin-I or -R and Ceftriaxone-S: Ceftriaxone

- Ceftriaxone-I or -R: Vancomycin + Ceftriaxone ± Rifampin

Generally, the duration of treatment is 7-14 days, but can vary based on the pathogen severity of infection and clinical response.

Acute Bacterial Meningitis

EMPIRIC THERAPY	NOTES

Treatment in Patients 2-50 Years Old (primarily *S. pneumoniae and N. meningitidis*)

Cefotaxime 2 grams IV Q4-6H or Ceftriaxone 2 grams IV Q12H or Meropenem 2 grams IV Q8H (alternative to 3rd gen. ceph) PLUS Vancomycin 30-45 mg/kg per day in divided doses ± Dexamethasone 0.15 mg/kg IV Q6H x 2-4 days	Give dexamethasone 15-20 min prior to or concomitantly with 1st dose of antibiotic Need high doses of vancomycin to penetrate CSF Add ampicillin 2 grams IV Q4H if age < 1 month or > 50 years, have impaired cellular immunity, if suspect *Listeria*

Treatment in Immunocompromised Patients or Those > 50 years old *(S. pneumoniae, N. meningitidis, L. monocytogenes)*

Vancomycin + ampicillin + ceftriaxone or Vancomycin + ampicillin + cefotaxime	

For Severe PCN Allergy

Chloramphenicol 4,000-6,000 mg per day in 4 doses PLUS Vancomycin 30-45 mg/kg per day in divided doses ± SMX/TMP 5 mg/kg IV Q6H	Chloramphenicol and vancomycin will provide adequate coverage for *Neisseria* and *Streptococcus pneumoniae*. SMX/TMP can be added for suspected *Listeria*.

Practice Guideline for Management of Bacterial Meningitis. Clin Infect Dis 2004; 39:1367-1289.

UPPER RESPIRATORY TRACT INFECTIONS
Acute Otitis Media (AOM)

AOM is the most common infection for which children in the United States receive antibiotic treatment. Signs and symptoms of the infection include bulging tympanic membrane, otorrhea (middle ear effusion/fluid), otalgia (ear pain), a rapid onset of symptoms, fever, crying and tugging or rubbing the ears. Many of the infections are viral (therefore, antibiotics will not work).

- Treat the pain with acetaminophen or ibuprofen. Can use topical benzocaine, procaine or lidocaine *(Auralgan, Americaine Otic)* in children > 5 years of age.

- Observation without antibiotics may be an option for non-severe AOM – depending on age, diagnostic certainty, and illness severity. The "observation" period is 48-72 hours and used to assess clinical improvement without antibiotics. The decision for observation should be a joint decision of the pediatrician and parents.

AGE	OTORRHEA WITH AOM	UNILATERAL OR BILATERAL AOM WITH SEVERE SYMPTOMS*	BILATERAL AOM WITHOUT OTORRHEA	UNILATERAL AOM WITHOUT OTORRHEA
6 months-2 years	Antibiotic therapy	Antibiotic therapy	Antibiotic therapy	Antibiotic therapy or additional observation
≥ 2 years	Antibiotic therapy	Antibiotic therapy	Antibiotic therapy or additional observation	Antibiotic therapy or additional observation

*Severe symptoms include otalgia > 48 hrs, temperature ≥ 39°C (102.2°F) in past 48 hrs

INITIAL TREATMENT		ANTIBIOTIC TREATMENT AFTER 48-72 HOURS OF FAILURE OF INITIAL THERAPY
Recommended First-line Treatment	Alternative Treatment (if penicillin allergic – non-type 1 allergy)	Recommended First-line Treatment
Amoxicillin 80-90 mg/kg/d in 2 divided doses or	Cefdinir 14 mg/kg/d in 1 or 2 doses	Amox/Clav* 90 mg/kg/day of amoxicillin in 2 divided doses or
Amox/Clav 90 mg/kg/d of amoxicillin in 2 divided doses	Cefuroxime 30 mg/kg/day in 2 divided doses	Ceftriaxone 50 mg IM/IV x 3 days
	Cefpodoxime 10 mg/kg/day in 2 divided doses	
	Ceftriaxone 50 mg IM/IV x 1 or 3 days	

*May be considered in patients who have received amoxicillin in the past 30 days

American Academy of Pediatrics Diagnosis and Management Acute Otitis Media; Pediatrics. 2013;131:e964-e999.

- Primary antibiotic treatment is high-dose amoxicillin (80-90 mg/kg/day) divided Q12H or amoxicillin/clavulanate *(Augmentin)* (90 mg/kg/day of amoxicillin) divided Q12H. The higher dose will cover most *S. pneumoniae*.

- Recommended agents in setting of amoxicillin failure include amoxicillin/clavulanate *(Augmentin)* 90 mg/kg/d of amoxicillin component x 5-10 days (see recommendations for duration below) or ceftriaxone 50 mg/kg IM/IV x 3 days.

- Recommended duration of treatment for amoxicillin, amox/clav and oral cephalosporins: < 2 years of age = 10 days; 2-5 years of age = 7 days; and ≥ 6 years of age = 5-7 days.

- Ceftriaxone (50 mg/kg) can be given IM/IV x 1-3 days (1-3 days for initial treatment or 3 days for treatment failure) for those who cannot tolerate oral medication (e.g., vomiting).

- *Prevnar 13,* the Pneumococcal Conjugate Vaccine (PCV) which contains 13 serotypes, is now given to all children 2-23 months. Children receive four doses of PCV13 intramuscularly at age 2, 4, 6, and 12 to 15 months old. *(Pneumovax* is the adult polyvalent vaccine which contains 23 serotypes).

- ACIP recommends the *Pneumovax* vaccine for children aged ≥ 24 months who are at increased risk for pneumococcal disease (children with sickle cell disease, HIV, and other immunocompromising or chronic medical conditions).

- Annual influenza vaccine should be given at ≥ 6 months of age and older.

- Clinicians should not prescribe prophylactic antibiotics to reduce frequency of AOM.

Overview of Upper Respiratory Tract Infection Management

The majority of upper respiratory tract infections are caused by viruses and antibacterials will have no benefit. In select cases of more severe/chronic symptoms and/or microbiologic/diagnostic evidence of a bacterial etiology antibacterials may be indicated in the setting of pharyngitis and sinusitis (see table below).

	COMMON COLD	INFLUENZA	PHARYNGITIS	SINUSITIS
Typical Etiology	Resp viruses: Rhinovirus Coronavirus RSV	Influenza virus	Resp viruses *S. pyogenes*	Resp viruses; *S. pneumoniae; H. influenzae; Moraxella catarrhalis; Staphylococci* species anaerobes, and Gram-negative rods may also be implicated in chronic sinusitis
Indications for Antibacterial Treatment	None	< 48 h post-Sx Risk factors for severe disease Outbreak scenario	Fever No cough Tonsil or LN swelling + RADT or cx for *Strep*	> 7-10 days of symptoms Tooth/face pain Nasal drainage/discharge Congestion or severe/worsening symptoms
Antibacterial Treatment	Symptomatic	Oseltamivir* Zanamavir* (Amantadine) (Rimantadine)	Penicillin Amoxicillin 1st/2nd generation cephalosporin Macrolides	**First Line** Amoxicillin; SMX/TMP; Doxycycline **Second Line if Failure to Above** Azithromycin; Amox/clav Oral 3rd generation cephalosporins Respiratory Fluoroquinolone
Adjunctive Treatment	Cough suppressants, decongestants, acetaminophen	Acetaminophen or NSAIDs, cough suppressants, throat lozenges/anesthetics, rest and fluids	Acetaminophen or NSAIDs, cough suppressants, throat lozenges/anesthetics	Nasal corticosteroids, decongestants, acetaminophen/NSAIDs
Duration	Per symptoms	5 days*	5-10 days	Variable depending on severity and chronicity Acute sinusitis: 7-14 days Chronic sinusitis: ≥ 21 days ± surgical intervention

cx = culture, dz = disease, LN = lymph nodes, RADT = rapid antigen diagnostic test, Sx = symptoms

* Active against Influenza A and B: not useful if used > 48 hours from symptom onset

CDC Get Smart Campaign

LOWER RESPIRATORY TRACT INFECTIONS

Bronchitis

Bronchitis, inflammation of the mucous membranes of the bronchi, can be divided into 2 categories: acute and chronic.

Acute Bronchitis

- Acute bronchitis is mainly caused by respiratory viruses and the disease is almost always self-limiting. Bacterial etiology should be considered for more severe cases of acute bronchitis and likely pathogens include *Mycoplasma pneumonia, Strep pneumonia, H. influenza, Bordetella pertussis*, and others.

- In mild-moderate disease, treatment is symptomatic and supportive with the use of fluids to prevent dehydration, antipyretics for fever, cough suppressants, vaporizers to thin secretions, etc. In more severe disease and/or bacterial, antibiotics are indicated. (see box)

- Signs and symptoms of acute bronchitis include cough (generally lasts 2 weeks), sore throat, coryza, malaise, headache, low-grade fever, and/or purulent sputum production.

Chronic Bronchitis – Acute Exacerbation of Chronic Bronchitis (AECB)

- Antibiotics are indicated in more severe cases of acute bronchitis, especially among patients with at least two of the following symptoms: increased dyspnea, increased sputum production, and increased sputum purulence. This is distinguished from acute bronchitis as acute exacerbation of chronic bronchitis (AECB).

BRONCHITIS NOTES & TREATMENT

Acute Bronchitis – expect cough to last 2 weeks
Mild-to-moderate disease:

- Usually viral – antibiotics not indicated. Recommend antitussive ± inhaled bronchodilators

Persistent Cough (> 14 days)/Pertussis (whooping cough)
Severe disease:

- Azithromycin 500 mg x 1, then 250 mg daily x 2-5 days or
- Erythromycin estolate 500 mg QID x 14 days or
- SMX/TMP DS 1 tab BID x 14 days or
- Clarithromycin 500 mg BID or 1 gm ER daily x 7 days

Acute Bacterial Exacerbation of Chronic Bronchitis (ABECB)
Mild-to-moderate disease:

- No antibiotic treatment or if used, choose: amoxicillin, doxycycline, SMX/TMP, or a cephalosporin

Severe disease with two or more of the following: increased dyspnea, increased sputum production, and increased sputum purulence:

- Inhaled anticholinergic bronchodilator plus oral corticosteroid, taper over 2 weeks.

- Role of antibiotic therapy debated even for severe disease. If used, choose: doxycycline or macrolide or SMX/TMP or 3rd generation cephalosporin or amoxicillin/clavulanic acid or antipneumococcal FQ (moxi, gemi or levo). In general, amox/clav or FQ should be reserved for patients at risk for drug-resistant *S. pneumoniae* (age > 65 years, multiple comorbidities, etc.). Treat 5-7 days or longer if needed.

Martinez FJ, et al. Appropriate outpatient treatment of acute bacterial exacerbations of chronic bronchitis. Am J Med. 2005;118:39S-44S.

COMMUNITY-ACQUIRED PNEUMONIA (CAP)

Community-acquired (occurring outside of health care facilities) pneumonia is one of the most common types of pneumonia. Causes could be bacterial, viral or fungal. The typical bacterial organisms causing 85% of bacterial cases are *Streptococcus pneumoniae, Haemophilus influenzae* and *Moraxella catarrhalis*. Patients present with fever, a productive cough (with purulent sputum) and pleuritic chest pain. Rales (crackling noises) can be heard over the infected lobe. If the patient requires hospitalization (ICU or non-ICU) the antibiotic regimen is different.

RECOMMENDED EMPIRICAL ANTIBIOTIC COVERAGE FOR CAP

Outpatient Treatment

Previously healthy and no use of antimicrobials within the past 3 months:

- Macrolide* (azithromycin, clarithromycin, erythromycin) or

- Doxycycline

At risk for drug-resistant *S. pneumonia* (comorbidities such as HF, DM, cancer, renal/liver dysfunction, alcoholism, asplenia, immunosuppression – and use of antibiotics within past 3 months):

- A respiratory fluoroquinolone (moxifloxacin, gemifloxacin,or levofloxacin [750mg]) or

- Beta-lactam PLUS a macrolide (high-dose amoxicillin or amoxicillin/clavulanate is preferred, alternatives include ceftriaxone, cefpodoxime, cefuroxime; doxycycline is an alternative to the macrolide)

Inpatient (non-ICU)

- Beta-lactam PLUS a macrolide (preferred beta-lactam agents include ceftriaxone, cefotaxime, ampicillin; doxycycline as an alternative to the macrolide) or

- Respiratory fluoroquinolone (moxifloxacin, gemifloxacin, or levofloxacin) – IV or PO (consider reserving fluoroquinolones for beta-lactam allergies)

Inpatient (ICU) – IV therapy preferred

- Beta-lactam (ceftriaxone, cefotaxime, ampicillin-sulbactam) PLUS azithromycin or a fluoroquinolone. For penicillin-allergic patients, a respiratory FQ and aztreonam are recommended.

If *Pseudomonas* is a consideration, use an antipneumococcal, antipseudomonal beta-lactam (piperacillin/tazobactam, cefepime, imipenem, meropenem or doripenem) plus either ciprofloxacin or levofloxacin

or

the above beta-lactam plus an aminoglycoside and (azithromycin or respiratory FQ)

If CA-MRSA is a consideration, add vancomycin or linezolid

preferred

MOST COMMON ETIOLOGIES OF CAP
Outpatient
Streptococcus pneumonia
Mycoplasma pneumonia
Haemophilus influenzae
Chlamydophila pneumonia
Respiratory viruses
Inpatient (non-ICU)
Streptococcus pneumonia
Mycoplasma pneumonia
Chlamydophila pneumonia
Haemophilus influenzae
Legionella sp.
Aspiration
Respiratory viruses
Inpatient (ICU)
Streptococcus pneumonia
Staphylococcus aureus
Legionella sp.
Gram-negative bacilli
Haemophilus influenzae

Oral Antibiotics for Community Acquired Pneumonia (CAP)

DRUG	USUAL ADULT DOSE
Cephalosporins	
Cefpodoxime	200 mg Q12H
Cefuroxime (*Ceftin*)	500 mg Q12H
Macrolides	
Azithromycin (*Zithromax*)	500 mg x 1, then 250 mg daily (days 2-5)
Clarithromycin (*Biaxin*) (*Biaxin XL*)	250-500 mg Q12H 1,000 mg daily
Erythromycin base (*E-mycin*)	250-500 mg Q6H
Fluoroquinolones	
Gemifloxacin (*Factive*)	320 mg daily
Levofloxacin (*Levaquin*)	750 mg daily
Moxifloxacin (*Avelox*)	400 mg daily
Tetracyclines	
Doxycycline (*Vibramycin*)	100 mg Q12H
Penicillins	
Amoxicillin (*Amoxil*)	1 grams Q8H
Amoxicillin/clavulanate (*Augmentin XR*)	2 grams Q12H

Duration

The duration of treatment can be as short as 5 days, or longer, depending on the patient's condition. Most are treated successfully in 5-10 days. If there is treatment failure the course will be longer.

Guidelines adapted from the Infectious Diseases Society of America/American Thoracic Society Consensus Guidelines on the Management of CAP in Adults. (Clin Infect Dis 2007;44 suppl 2:S27-72)

Hospital Acquired Pneumonia (HAP)/Ventilator Associated Pneumonia (VAP)

HAP is pneumonia that occurs during the hospital stay. Hospitalized patients are sick, and the organisms present in the hospital setting are highly pathogenic (i.e., deadly bugs). Many hospital infections are spread by health care workers. See the Medication Safety chapter for techniques to reduce transmission risk. Ventilated patients (on a respirator) are at high-risk. HAP is the leading cause of death in ICUs.

- In addition to proper hand-washing and coverage (gloves, gown, face mask), HAP can be reduced by elevating the head of bed by 30 degrees or more, wean off ventilator quickly, remove naso-gastric (NG) tube, and discontinue use of stress ulcer prophylaxis medication if not needed.

- HAP that occurs < 5 days (early onset) after admission are caused by pathogens similar to that of CAP except for the fact that the incidence of <u>enteric Gram-negative bacteria is more prevalent</u> and <u>atypical pathogens (e.g., *Legionella, Mycoplasma*) are less prevalent</u>. Nosocomial pathogens (<u>MRSA, *Pseudomonas*)</u> are more prevalent with hospitalization ≥ 5 days (late onset).

Overview of Hospital-Acquired Pneumonia (HAP) Management

ONSET	COMMON PATHOGENS	RECOMMENDED REGIMEN		
Early hospital-acquired pneumonia (< 5 days) and no risk factors for multidrug-resistant pathogens	*Streptococcus pneumonia* MSSA *Haemophilus influenzae* *E. coli, Proteus, Klebsiella*	Ceftriaxone or Ampicillin/sulbactam (*Unasyn*) or Ertapenem or Levofloxacin or moxifloxacin		
Late hospital-acquired pneumonia (≥ 5 days or risk for multidrug resistant pathogens)	Above pathogens PLUS MRSA *Pseudomonas aeruginosa* *Acinetobacter* species *Enterobacter* species + other nosocomial pathogens	Antipseudomonal Beta-lactam (choose 1) +	2nd Antipseudomonal Agent (choose 1) +	Anti-MRSA if patient has risk factors for MRSA (choose 1)
		Cefepime Ceftazidime Imipenem Meropenem Piperacillin/tazo	Gentamicin Tobramycin Amikacin Levofloxacin Ciprofloxacin	Vancomycin Linezolid

Am J Respir Crit Care Med Vol 171. pp 388–416, 2005

Severe Beta-lactam Allergy

- Early onset: Levofloxacin or Moxifloxacin

- Late onset: Aztreonam 2 grams IV Q8H + FQ or AMG + vancomycin or linezolid

Duration of Treatment

Treat for 7-8 days, except lactose negative Gram-negative rods (*Pseudomonas, Acineto-bacter*) or concomitant bloodstream infection (14 days recommended).

Tuberculosis (TB)

TB is caused by the bacterium *Mycobacterium tuberculosis* (aerobic, non-spore forming bacillus). It is transmitted by aerosolized droplets (via sneezing, coughing, talking, etc.) and is <u>highly contagious</u>. TB primarily attacks the lungs, and occasionally other organs. There are strains resistant to multiple drugs (MDR-TB) including INH and rifampin and these strains are on the rise. If not properly treated the disease is fatal.

- <u>Diagnosed by tuberculin skin test (TST), also called a PPD test. Look for induration (raised area) within 48-72 hours after injection.</u>

  - A TST test ≥ 5 mm is considered positive for patients with close contacts of recent TB cases or patients with significant immunosuppression (e.g., HIV).

  - A TST ≥ 10 mm is considered positive for recent immigrants, IV drug users, residents/employees of "high-risk congregate settings (e.g., healthcare workers or inmates) and patients with moderate immunosuppression.

  - A TST ≥ 15 mm is considered positive for patients with no risk factors.

  - Other tests used for diagnosis of latent or acute TB are sputum smears, cultures, polymerase chain reaction (PCR) assays, and interferon-gamma release assays (IGRAs such as QuantiFERON-TB Gold test). IGRAs are the preferred test for anyone who might not return to look for a reaction to the TST, and for those who received the BCG vaccine.

- <u>2 categories of TB; latent and active disease.</u>

  - <u>Latent Disease Treatment:</u>

    - Isoniazid (INH) 300 mg daily (or twice weekly) for 9 months (typical regimen, preferred for HIV+ or children),

    - Rifampin 400 mg daily for 4 months,

    - INH and Rifapentine once weekly for 12 weeks (not if HIV+ or in children) – The older recommendation of rifampin + pyrazinamide is no longer used due to hepatotoxicity.

  - <u>Active disease</u> is generally initiated with a <u>4-drug regimen of rifampin, isoniazid, pyrazinamide and ethambutol (RIPE)</u> and divided into two treatment phases (induction and continuation phases). When MDR-TB is of concern the addition of moxifloxacin is often added (RIPE becomes PRIME regimen).

TB Disease Treatment Regimens

PREFERRED REGIMEN

Initial Phase – Take all 4 drugs for ~8 weeks (when cultures and susceptibilities are available)

	Rifampin (RIF) + Isoniazid (INH) + Pyrazinamide + Ethambutol* (RIPE) for 56 daily doses (8 weeks)

Continuation Phase – Take once susceptibilities are known

If sensitive to INH + RIF	Continue INH and RIF daily or twice weekly (18 weeks)
	Total duration of therapy = 26 weeks (6 months)
If resistant to INH	RIF + Pyrazinamide + Ethambutol ± Moxifloxacin
	Total duration of therapy = 26 weeks (6 months)
If resistant to RIF	Isoniazid + Ethambutol + FQ + (Pyrazinamide x 2 months)
	Total duration of therapy = 12-18 months
If MDR-TB (resistant to 2 or more drugs including INH and RIF)	FQ + Pyrazinamide + Ethambutol + AMG (streptomycin/amikacin/kanamycin) ± alternative agent**
	Total duration of therapy = 18-24 months

* Ethambutol can be discontinued if drug susceptibility studies demonstrate susceptibility to first-line drugs. FQ = fluoro-quinolone (levofloxacin or moxifloxacin)

** Alternative agents include cycloserine, capreomycin, ethionamide and others

- <u>Use Direct Observed Therapy (DOT), if possible.</u> DOT regimens are preferred for regimens dosed 2 or 3 times per week instead of daily.

- <u>Many variations in dosing intervals exist; however daily dosing is strongly encouraged</u> unless DOT is possible.

- Patients with active TB should be in <u>isolated, single negative pressure rooms</u>!! Essential.

- <u>Recommended to add pyridoxine (vitamin B6) 25-50 mg PO daily to INH regimens to</u> ↓ risk of neuropathy.

- Rifabutin can be used instead of rifampin in cases of unacceptable drug-drug interactions with rifampin.

DRUG	MOA	DOSING	SAFETY/SIDE EFFECTS/MONITORING
Rifampin *(Rifadin)* + isoniazid *(Rifamate)* + isonazid + pyrazinamide *(Rifater)*	Inhibits RNA synthesis by blocking RNA transcription in susceptible isolates	10 mg/kg (max 600 mg) daily or 2-3x/wk Take 1 hour before or 2 hours after a meal on an empty stomach	**CONTRAINDICATIONS** Concurrent use with PIs (switch to rifabutin) **SIDE EFFECTS** ↑ LFTs, GI upset, rash/pruritus, orange-red discoloration of body secretions, flu-like syndrome **MONITORING** LFTs, CBC, mental status, sputum culture, chest X-ray **NOTES** Orange-red discoloration of body secretions – can stain contact lens and clothing Rifabutin dosed 5 mg/kg/day (300 mg) can replace rifampin to avoid significant drug-drug interactions (e.g., HIV patient on protease inhibitors).
Isoniazid (INH) + rifampin *(Rifamate)* + pyrazinamide/ rifampin *(Rifater)*	Inhibits cell wall synthesis of susceptible isolates	5 mg/kg (max 300 mg) daily or 15 mg/kg (max 900 mg) 2-3x/week Take 1 hour before or 2 hours after a meal on an empty stomach	**BLACK BOX WARNING** Severe (and fatal) hepatitis may occur; usually within first 3 months of treatment **CONTRAINDICATIONS** Active liver disease, previous severe adverse reaction to INH **SIDE EFFECTS** Headache, GI upset, ↑ LFTs, peripheral neuropathy, lupus-like syndrome, hyperglycemia, agranulocytosis, hemolytic and aplastic anemia, thrombocytopenia **MONITORING** LFTs, sputum culture, chest X-ray **NOTES** Add pyridoxine 25-50 mg/day to reduce risk of peripheral neuropathy Store oral solution at room temp.
Pyrazinamide + rifampin + isoniazid *(Rifater)*	Converts to pyrazinoic acid in susceptible strains of *Mycobacterium* which ↓ pH	20-25 mg/kg/day 40-55 kg: 1 g/d 56-75 kg: 1.5 g/d 76-90 kg: 2 g/d (max dose); 3-4 grams given 2-3x/week Extend interval for CrCl < 30 mL/min	**CONTRAINDICATIONS** Acute gout, severe hepatic damage **SIDE EFFECTS** GI upset, malaise, hepatotoxicity, arthralgias, myalgias, rash, hyperuricemia, gout **MONITORING** LFTs, uric acid, sputum culture, chest X-ray, SCr
Ethambutol *(Myambutol)*	Suppresses mycobacteria replication by interfering with RNA synthesis	15-20 mg/kg (max 1.6 grams) daily or 25-30 mg/kg (max 2.4 grams) 3x/week or 50 mg/kg (max 4 grams) 2x/week Take without regards to meals Extend interval for CrCl < 50 mL/min	**SIDE EFFECTS** Optic neuritis, ↓ visual acuity, scotoma and/ or color blindness (usually reversible); rash, headache, confusion, hallucinations, nausea, vomiting, abdominal pain **MONITORING** Routine vision tests (monthly), SCr

Tuberculosis Agents Continued

DRUG	MOA	DOSING	SAFETY/SIDE EFFECTS/MONITORING
Streptomycin	Binds to 30S ribosomal subunit and inhibits bacterial protein synthesis	15 mg/kg (max 1 gram) daily or 25-30 mg/kg (max 1.5 grams) 2-3x/week Extend interval for CrCl < 50 mL/min	**BLACK BOX WARNING** Neurotoxicity, nephrotoxicity, and neuromuscular blockade/respiratory paralysis **SIDE EFFECTS** Nephrotoxicity, ototoxicity (especially with IV) **MONITORING** Vestibular/audio tests, renal function and streptomycin levels
Bedaquiline (*Sirturo*) Indicated for MDR-TB	A diarylquinoline antimycobacterial that inhibits the proton transfer chain of mycobacterial ATP synthase required for energy generation in *M. tuberculosis*	Weeks 1-2: 400 mg once daily Weeks 3-24: 200 mg 3 times weekly (total weekly dose: 600 mg). Space doses at least 48 hours apart Take with food	**BLACK BOX WARNINGS (2)** May prolong QT interval Increased risk of death versus placebo; only use if no other effective treatment regimen is available. **SIDE EFFECTS** Nausea, arthralgia, headache, hemoptysis, chest pain, ↑ LFTs

Tuberculosis Agents Drug Interactions

- Rifampin – Potent inducer of 1A2, 2C8, 2C9, 2C19, 3A4 and P-glycoprotein. Avoid concomitant use with protease inhibitors, apixaban, dabigatran, dronedarone, lurasidone, mycophenolate, nilotinib, ranolazine, ticagrelor, voriconazole and alcohol. Can ↓ levels of warfarin (very large decrease in INR), antiretroviral agents, corticosteroids, quinidine, benzodiazepines, methadone, sulfonylureas, calcium channel blockers, digoxin, cyclosporine, amiodarone, and 100+ others. Rifampin will decrease the effectiveness of oral contraceptives and cannot be used together. Any other substrate of the above enzymes may be sub-therapeutic if given with rifampin. Rifabutin can replace rifampin to avoid significant drug-drug interactions such as HIV patients requiring protease inhibitors.

- INH – Inhibitor of 1A2 (weak), 2C19 (moderate), 2C9 (weak), 2D6 (moderate), and 3A4 (weak). Can ↑ levels of benzodiazepines, carbamazepine, citalopram, fosphenytoin/phenytoin, metoprolol, theophylline, and other 2C19 and 2D6 substrates; can ↓ effects of clopidogrel, codeine, tamoxifen and other drugs requiring conversion to active metabolite via pathways inhibiting by INH. Manufacturer recommends: avoiding tyramine and histamine containing foods (low clinical significance). ↑ dietary intake of folic acid, niacin, and magnesium while taking INH.

- Pyrazinamide – Can ↑ cyclosporine levels; can cause fatal hepatotoxicity with rifampin; monitor liver function tests and uric acid.

- Streptomycin – Can ↑ effects of neuromuscular blocking agents; ↑ nephrotoxicity with other nephrotoxic drugs.

Infective Endocarditis (IE)

IE is an infection of the inner tissue of the heart, which can include the heart valves. The majority of patients present with fever and heart murmur and is generally fatal if left untreated. The three most common organisms that cause IE are *Staphylococcus, Streptococcus*, and *Enterococcus* species. IE is diagnosed by the Modified Duke Criteria which includes an echocardiogram. Treatment is dependent on the pathogen, presence or absence of a prosthetic valve, and susceptibility results. In general, 4-6 weeks of treatment is required. Penicillin or ceftriaxone are preferred options for *Streptococci* IE. Nafcillin or cefazolin are preferred options for MSSA IE. Vancomycin is generally reserved for MRSA IE or for *Streptococci/MSSA/Enterococci* IE if the patient has a severe beta-lactam allergy. Prosthetic valve infective endocarditis is generally caused by *Staphylococci* species and requires the addition of rifampin. Gentamicin is often added to primary antimicrobial therapy for synergy for a varied duration depending on the pathogen (such as 4-6 weeks for *Enterococci)* and/or presence of a prosthetic valve (2 weeks). When gentamicin is used for synergy, target peak levels of 3-4 mcg/mL and trough levels < 1 mcg/mL. Do not use extended interval dosing for AMG when treating endocarditis.

American Heart Association guidelines. Circulation.2005;111:e394-e433.

Dental Procedures and IE Prophylaxis

The mouth contains bacteria that are released during dental work and travel in the bloodstream where they can settle on the heart lining, a heart valve or a blood vessel. IE is uncommon, but certain cardiac conditions increase the risk. Antibiotics are used before dental procedures only in patients with the highest risk of contracting IE. The antibiotics destroy the bacteria before they can settle in the heart. Patients with the following conditions should receive IE prophylaxis:

- An artificial (prosthetic) heart valve or who have had a heart valve repaired with artificial material.

- A history of endocarditis.

- A heart transplant with abnormal heart valve function.

- Certain congenital heart defects including:

  - Cyanotic congenital heart disease (birth defects with oxygen levels lower than normal), that has not been fully repaired, including children who have had surgical shunts and conduits.

  - A congenital heart defect that has been completely repaired with artificial material or a device for the first six months after the repair procedure.

  - Repaired congenital heart disease with residual defects, such as persisting leaks or abnormal flow at or adjacent to a prosthetic patch or prosthetic device.

AGENT	ADULTS	CHILDREN

Prophylactic Regimens: Take a single dose 30-60 minutes before dental procedure

Oral

AGENT	ADULTS	CHILDREN
Amoxicillin	2 grams	50 mg/kg

Unable to take oral medication

AGENT	ADULTS	CHILDREN
Ampicillin or	2 grams IM/IV	50 mg/kg IM/IV
Cefazolin or ceftriaxone	1 grams IM/IV	50 mg/kg IM/IV

Allergic to penicillins and can take oral medication

AGENT	ADULTS	CHILDREN
Cephalexin or cefadroxil* or	2 grams	50 mg/kg
Clindamycin or	600 mg	20 mg/kg
Azithromycin or clarithromycin	500 mg	15 mg/kg

Allergic to penicillins and unable to take oral medication

AGENT	ADULTS	CHILDREN
Cefazolin or Ceftriaxone or	1 grams IM/IV	50 mg/kg IM/IV
Clindamycin	600 mg IM/IV	20 mg/kg IM/IV

* *Cephalosporins should not be used in an individual with a history of anaphylaxis, angioedema, or urticaria with penicillins or ampicillin.*

Wilson W, Et Al. Prevention of Infective Endocarditis Guidelines. Circulation. 2007;116:1736-54.

Intra-Abdominal Infections

Intra-abdominal infections are a common cause of hospital admissions and the second most common cause of infectious mortality in ICUs. They are characterized as primary (spontaneous bacterial), secondary peritonitis and biliary tract infections (cholecystitis and cholangitis).

- Primary peritonitis is an infection of the peritoneal space and generally occurs in patients with liver disease. The most likely pathogens are *streptococci* and enteric Gram-negative organisms (PEK) and, rarely, anaerobes. The drug of choice is ceftriaxone for 5-7 days. Alternatives include ampicillin/gentamicin or a fluoroquinolone, among other options.

- Secondary peritonitis is caused by a traumatic event (ulceration, ischemia, obstruction or surgery). Any abscesses should be drained and damaged tissue may require surgery. The most likely pathogens are *Streptococci*, enteric Gram-negatives and anaerobes *(Bacteroides fragilis)*. In more severe cases (critically ill patients in the ICU), coverage of *Pseudomonas* and CAPES organisms may be necessary.

■ Cholecystitis is an infection of the gallbladder and is generally surgically managed (removal of gallbladder, or cholecysectomy). Likely pathogens and antimicrobial selection (if needed) is similar to primary peritonitis. Cholangitis is an infection of the biliary ductal system and is generally managed with bile decompression and antimicrobial therapy. Likely pathogens and antimicrobial selection is similar to secondary peritonitis.

Management of Secondary Peritonitis and Cholangitis

MILD-TO-MODERATE INFECTIONS	HIGH-SEVERITY INFECTIONS/ICU~,#
Cover PEK + anaerobes + *Streptococci* ± *Enterococci*	Cover PEK + CAPES + anaerobes + *Streptococcus* ± *Enterococci*

Single Agent Regimens: Duration of therapy is 7-14 days

Ticarcillin/clavulanate or	Imipenem or
Ertapenem or	Meropenem or
Cefoxitin or	Doripenem or
Tigecycline or	Piperacillin-tazobactam
Moxifloxacin	

Combination Regimens: Duration of therapy is 7-14 days

(Cefazolin or cefuroxime or ceftriaxone) + metronidazole	(Ceftazidime or cefepime) + metronidazole^
(Ciprofloxacin or levofloxacin) + metronidazole^	(Ciprofloxacin or levofloxacin) + metronidazole^
	(Aztreonam or AMG) + metronidazole^

AMG = aminoglycosides; CAPES (nosocomial GNRs) = Citrobacter, Acinetobacter, Pseudomonas, Enterobacter, Serratia; ICU = intensive care unit; PEK (enteric GNRs) = Proteus, E. coli, Klebsiella

~ High severity: ICU, APACHE > 15, advanced age, comorbidity and organ dysfunction, malignancy, lack of source control

^ Metronidazole may be substituted with clindamycin to improve Gram-positive coverage (e.g., with ciprofloxacin, ceftazidime, aztreonam, or AMG)

Solomkin JS, et al. Clin Infect Dis 2010; 50:133–64

Skin and Soft-Tissue Infections (SSTIs)

Skin and soft-tissue infections may involve any or all layers of the skin (epidermis, dermis, and subcutaneous fat), fascia, and muscle. Most primary infections, including cellulitis and impetigo, are superficial and mild. Secondary infections involve areas of previously damaged skin. Multiple organisms are usually involved.

Cellulitis affects all layers of the skin and is a serious type of SSTI. *S. pyogenes* and *S. aureus* are the most frequent pathogens, with community-acquired MRSA on the rise. Lesions are usually painful, erythematous, and feel hot and tender. The infected area has poorly defined margins and will spread. Non-pharmacologic treatment consists of elevation and immobilization of the area to decrease swelling and cool sterile saline dressings to decrease the pain. Mild to moderate infections without systemic symptoms may be treated with oral therapy. If possible, skin abscess should be incised and drained.

INFECTION	ADULT TREATMENT OPTIONS	COMMENTS

Empiric oral therapy options for purulent cellulitis. If non-purulent, treat with a beta-lactam (e.g., cephalexin)

Outpatient SSTI	Clindamycin 300-450 mg TID or SMX/TMP 1-2 DS tabs BID or Doxycycline 100 mg BID or Minocycline 200 mg x 1, then 100 mg BID or Linezolid 600 mg BID Duration of therapy = 5 to 10 days	Target Gram-positive organisms *(Staphylococci, Streptococci)* Primary treatment for cutaneous abscess is incision and drainage (I & D) Use IV antibiotics for severe infections, rapid progression, systemic illness, etc. For recurrent SSTIs, consider nasal decolonization with mupirocin *(Bactroban)* BID for 5 to 10 days and/or topical body decolonization with chlorhexidine for 5 to 14 days or dilute bleach baths twice weekly for 3 months

Empiric therapy options for <u>complicated</u> SSTIs (pending culture results)

Inpatient SSTI	Vancomycin 15 mg/kg IV Q12H (goal trough 10-15 mg/L) or Linezolid 600 mg IV/PO BID or Daptomycin 4 mg/kg/dose once daily or Telavancin 10 mg/kg/dose once daily or Clindamycin 600 mg IV Q8H or 300-450 mg PO Q6H Duration of therapy = 7 to 14 days	MRSA risk high compared to outpatient Broader spectrum therapy, including antipseudomonal coverage, may be required for immunocompromised patients and management of diabetic foot ulcers/infections, especially if severe and complicated ("limb-threatening."). See next chart for possible pathogens/regimens.

Stevens DL, et al. Practice guidelines for the diagnosis and management of skin and soft-tissue infections. Clin Infect Dis. 2005;41:1373-406.

Liu C, et al. Clinical Practice Guidelines for MRSA Infections. CID 2011;52:1-38.

Diabetic Foot Infections

Diabetes is high-risk for foot infections because of compromised (reduced) blood flow to the lower extremities (which make infections difficult to treat) and due to neuropathic damage (which can decrease the ability to feel pain from an injury) and (occasionally) due to changes in the shape of the feet. Amputations often result; it is imperative for patients to follow proper foot care and evaluation, as discussed in the Diabetes chapter.

ETIOLOGY	GRAM-POSITIVE	GRAM-NEGATIVE
Aerobic	*S. epidermidis* (including MRSE) *S. aureus* (including MRSA) *Group A Streptococcus* *Viridans Streptococcus*	*E. coli* *Klebsiella pneumoniae* *Proteus mirabilis* *Enterobacter cloacae* *Pseudomonas aeruginosa*
Anaerobic	*Peptostreptococcus* *Clostridium perfringens*	*Bacteroides fragilis* and other anaerobic Gram-negative

Treatment of Moderate-Severe ("Limb-threatening") Diabetic Foot Infections

TYPE OF REGIMEN	TREATMENT REGIMEN	COMMENTS
Combination	3rd or 4th generation cephalosporin + (metronidazole or clindamycin) ± vancomycin or Clindamycin + fluoroquinolone (ciprofloxacin or levofloxacin) or Vancomycin + ceftazidime + metronidazole or (Daptomycin or linezolid) + (aztreonam or aminoglycoside) + (metronidazole or clindamycin)	Consider adding vancomycin if MRSA is suspected Duration: 7-14 days More severe, deep tissue infection = treat for 2-4 weeks Severe, limb-threatening or bone/joint infection = treat 4-6 weeks Chronic osteomyelitis may require longer courses of therapy, including chronic suppressive therapy
Monotherapy	Ampicillin/sulbactam (*Unasyn*) or Piperacillin/tazobactam (*Zosyn*) or Ticarcillin/clavulanate (*Timentin*) or Imipenem/cilastatin or Meropenem or Doripenem or Ertapenem or Tigecycline or Moxifloxacin*	

Lipsky BA, Berendt AR, Deery HG, Embil JM et al. Diagnosis and treatment of diabetic foot infections. *Clin Infect Dis* 2012;54(12):132–173.

Urinary Tract Infection (UTI)

Most UTIs occur in the bladder (cystitis) and urethra, which is called the lower urinary tract. More severe infections can occur in the kidneys (pyelonephritis), or the upper urinary tract. UTIs are more common in females than males due to the shorter urethra and the shorter route for *E. coli* or other organisms to travel up into the urethra. Sexual intercourse can facilitate this movement and women who develop UTIs commonly after intercourse may be using antibiotics after sexual intercourse (post-coitus) prophylactically. UTIs are uncommon in younger males but increase in incidence with age. An infection in males is considered to be complicated because it is likely due to some type of abnormality or obstruction, such as an enlarged prostate. In females, the majority of infections are not associated with an abnormality or obstruction and are most often uncomplicated. Complicated infections result from a neurogenic bladder (e.g., spinal cord injury, stroke, multiple sclerosis) or obstruction (e.g., a stone, indwelling catheter). Both genders are at risk for catheter-associated infections; see the Medication Safety chapter for a discussion of ways to reduce this common type of (often preventable) infection.

- <u>Typical signs and symptoms of lower urinary tract infections (cystitis) are dysuria, urgency, frequency, burning, nocturia, suprapubic heaviness, and/or hematuria (fever is uncommon).</u> A positive urinalysis is considered when there is evidence of <u>pyuria</u> (positive leukocyte esterase or ≥ 10 WBC/mL) and <u>bacteriuria</u> (≥ 10^5 bacteria/mL in uncomplicated patients and ≥ 10^3 bacteria/mL in complicated patients, including in men).

- Typical signs and symptoms of upper urinary tract infections (pyelonephritis) are flank pain, abdominal pain, fever, nausea, vomiting, costovertebral angle pain, and malaise.

- <u>Must treat bacteriuria in pregnant women (for 7 days) even if asymptomatic with negative urinalysis.</u> If not, the infection can lead to premature birth, pyelonephritis, and neonatal meningitis. <u>In pregnant women, avoid quinolones (cartilage toxicity and arthropathies) and tetracyclines (teratogenic). SMX/TMP can cause hyperbilirubinemia and kernicterus in 3rd trimester (Pregnancy Category D near term); otherwise, category C.</u> Generally, beta-lactams are used (amox/clav, amoxicillin, cephalosporins) and, if penicillin-allergic, nitrofurantoin or fosfomycin can be used. See Drug Use in Pregnancy chapter for more information.

UTI Treatment

DIAGNOSIS	PATHOGENS	DRUGS OF CHOICE/GUIDELINES	COMMENTS
Acute uncomplicated cystitis in females of child bearing age (~15-45 years of age)	E. coli, Proteus, Klebsiella (PEK) S. saprophyticus, Enterococcus	Nitrofurantoin 100 mg BID x 5 days or SMX/TMP 1 DS tab BID x 3 days (avoid if resistance > 20% to E. coli or sulfa allergy) or Fosfomycin x 1 (3 grams in 4 oz water – lower efficacy) or If ≥ 20% local E. coli resistant to SMX/TMP or sulfa allergy: Cipro 250 mg BID x 3 days or Cipro ER 500 mg daily x 3 days or Levofloxacin 250 mg daily x 3 days	May add phenazopyridine 200 mg PO TID x 2 days to the regimen to relieve symptoms (dysuria) Usually empirically treated as an outpatient Prophylaxis: ≥ 3 episodes in 1 yr; use 1 SMX/TMP SS daily, nitrofurantoin 50 mg PO daily, or 1 SMX/TMP DS post coitus If no response on 3-day course, culture and treat for 2 weeks Do not recommend moxifloxacin (does not reach high levels in the urine) or gemifloxacin (poor to limited activity against normal UTI pathogens) Treat pregnant women for 7 days
Acute uncomplicated pyelonephritis	E. coli, Enterococci, P. mirabilis, K. pneumoniae, P. aeruginosa	Moderately ill outpatient (PO): For FQ resistance < 10%: Cipro 500 mg PO BID or Cipro ER 1,000 mg daily x 7 days or Levo 750 mg daily x 5 days For FQ resistance > 10%: Ceftriaxone 1 gram x 1 or 24 hours of AMG initially, followed by SMX/TMP (if susceptible) or beta-lactam (amox/clav, cefdinir, cefaclor, or cefpodoxime) – treat for 14 days Severe – hospitalized tx (IV): FQ, AMP + Gent, Pip/Tazo, or ceftriaxone, then stepdown to similar oral options above based on susceptibility results; treat for 14 days of total antibiotic duration (IV and PO)	Most require hospitalization Need urinalysis, urine and blood cultures If risk for or documented Pseudomonas infection, consider piperacillin/tazobactam or meropenem ± aminoglycoside

UTI Treatment Continued

DIAGNOSIS	PATHOGENS	DRUGS OF CHOICE/GUIDELINES	COMMENTS
Complicated UTI	*E.coli, Klebsiella, Enterobacter, Serratia, Pseudomonas, Enterococcus, Staph species*	Similar to options noted above for pyelonephritis or If ESBL producers are present, use carbapenems	Need urinalysis, urine and blood cultures May be due to obstruction, catheterization – remove or change catheter if possible Treat for 7 days if there is prompt symptom relief Treat for 10-14 days with delayed response regardless of catheterization or not

Clinical Infectious Diseases 2011;52;e103–e120; Clinical Infectious Diseases 2010; 50:625-663; Postgrad Med. 2010;122;:7-15.

Urinary Analgesic

Phenazopyridine may be given to reduce the symptoms of pain or burning with urination. It is occasionally given to reduce pain from vaginal procedures.

DRUG	DOSING	SAFETY/SIDE EFFECTS/MONITORING
Phenazopyridine (Azo, Uristat, Pyridium)	100-200 mg TID (OTC and Rx) x 2 days (max)	**CONTRAINDICATIONS** Do not use in patients with CrCl < 50 mL/min or liver disease **SIDE EFFECTS** Headache, dizziness, stomach cramps, body secretion discoloration **NOTES** Pregnancy Category B Take with or following food and 8 oz of water to minimize stomach upset May cause red-orange coloring of the urine and other body fluids. Contact lenses and clothes can be stained Can cause hemolytic anemia in patients with G6PD deficiency

Clostridium Difficile Infection (CDI)

The GI tract contains > 1,000 species of organisms; the use of antibiotics, particularly clindamycin, ampicillin, fluoroquinolones and cephalosporins, will eliminate much of the "healthy" bacteria, which causes an overgrowth of the *Clostridium difficile* bacteria. This organism releases toxins that attack the intestinal lining, causing colitis. Symptoms of CDI include abdominal cramps, bloody, soft or watery stool (frequent) and fever. Pseudomembraneous colitis occurs when the overgrowth has inflamed the colon. This infection is one of the causes (along with IBD) of toxic megacolon, which can be quickly fatal. Rates of CDI have nearly doubled in the past ten years. In addition to the antibiotic, other risk factors include previous CDI, advanced age, immune-compromised state and obesity.

Treatment principles of CDI include

- Discontinue the offending agent immediately, if possible.

- <u>Avoid antimotility agents</u> due to the risk of toxic megacolon.

- Wash hands with soap and water to prevent transmission. Hand sanitizers contain alcohol and do not kill *C. difficile* spores.

- Assign patients to contact precautions (single patient rooms, gloves, gowns).

- Metronidazole should not be used beyond the 1st recurrence or for long-term therapy due to the potential for cumulative neurotoxicity.

- Probiotics *(Lactobacillus)* are not beneficial for treatment, but may have some benefit for prophylaxis. The probiotic should be taken when the antibiotic is not in the gut.

Treatment of *C. difficile**

SEVERITY OF INFECTION	TREATMENT OF 1ST INFECTION	TREATMENT OF 2ND INFECTION (1ST RECURRENCE)	TREATMENT OF 3RD INFECTION (2ND RECURRENCE)
Mild-moderate disease	Metronidazole 500 mg PO TID x 10-14 days	Same as 1st infection if same severity	Vancomycin taper/pulse therapy 125 mg PO QID x 10-14 days, BID x 1 week, daily x 1 week, then 125 mg every 2-3 days/week for 2-8 weeks
Severe disease (WBC ≥ 15,000 or SCr > 1.5x premorbid level)	Vancomycin 125 mg PO QID x 10-14 days	Same as 1st infection if same severity	Vancomycin taper/pulse therapy
Severe, complicated disease (Hypotension, shock, ileus, or megacolon)	Vancomycin 500 mg PO QID + metronidazole 500 mg IV Q8H If complete ileus, add vancomycin per rectum (500 mg in 100 mL NS PR Q6H)	Same as 1st infection if same severity	Vancomycin taper/pulse therapy

* *In clinical trials, fidaxomicin was non-inferior to vancomycin oral therapy, but with lower recurrence rates. Consider fidaxomicin instead of vancomycin for patients at high risk of recurrence (patients receiving chemotherapy or immunosuppressed patients) – place in therapy not fully established. Cohen SH, et al. Infect Control Hosp Epidemiol 2010; 31(5).*

Traveler's Diarrhea (TD)

TD is the most common travel-related illness. Bacteria are the most common cause of TD (80% of cases), including enterotoxigenic *Escherichia coli*, followed by *Campylobacter jejuni*, *Shigella* spp., and *Salmonella* spp. Viral diarrhea can be caused by a number of pathogens, most commonly norovirus and rotavirus. Less commonly, protozoa including *Giardia*, *Entamoeba histolytica*, *Cryptosporidium* and *Cyclospora*, may result in TD. Bacterial and viral diarrhea presents with the sudden onset of symptoms, including mild cramps and urgent loose stools to severe abdominal pain, fever, vomiting, and bloody diarrhea. Protozoal diarrhea, such as that caused by *Giardia* or *E. histolytica*, generally has a more gradual onset of low-grade symptoms, with 2–5 loose stools per day.

The primary source of infection is ingestion of fecally contaminated food and water. Most cases are benign and resolve in 1-2 days without treatment. Preventive measures include:

- Avoid eating foods or drinking beverages from street vendors or other places of unhygienic conditions

- Avoid eating raw or undercooked meat/seafood

- Avoid eating raw fruits (e.g., oranges, bananas, avocados) and vegetables unless the traveler peels them

- Tap water, ice, unpasteurized milk and dairy products have an increased risk

A simple rule is "boil it, cook it, peel it, or forget it." Well-cooked and packaged foods are generally safe. Safe beverages include bottled, carbonated drinks, hot tea or coffee, beer, wine, boiled water or treated water (with iodine or chlorine).

<u>Prophylactic antibiotics are not recommended</u> due to concerns of toxicity, resistance, lack of activity against viral pathogens and the fact that most cases of TD are self-limiting without antimicrobial therapy. Bismuth subsalicylate (BSS) taken as either 2 tablets

TRAVELER'S DIARRHEA TREATMENT
Drug Therapy – FQs are the drugs of choice Ciprofloxacin 500 mg PO BID x 3 days or
Norfloxacin 400 mg BID x 3-5 days
Ofloxacin 300 mg BID x 3 days or
Levofloxacin 500 mg daily x 1-3 days or
Rifaximin 200 mg TID x 3 days or
Azithromycin 1,000 mg x 1 or 500 mg daily x 1-3 days – drug of choice for pregnancy and children
Bismuth subsalicylate 524 mg (2 tablets) every 30 minutes up to 8 doses/day x 2 days
PLUS
Loperamide 4 mg x 1, then 2 mg after each loose stool – max 16 mg/d (loperamide is not recommended if patient has signs of dysentery, high fever or blood in stool)
* Metronidazole, tinidazole, and nitazoxanide should be reserved for TD caused by Protozoa (e.g., Giardia or Cryptosporidia)

QID (or liquid) reduces the incidence of TD (not to be used longer than 3 weeks). BSS commonly causes blackening of the tongue and stool and may cause nausea, constipation, and rarely tinnitus. BSS should be avoided in those with an aspirin allergy, renal insufficiency, and by those taking anticoagulants, probenecid, or methotrexate. The role of probiotics for the prevention of TD is unclear at this time. The <u>most important treatment is oral rehydration therapy</u>, especially in <u>young children, elderly</u> or those with chronic medical conditions. A 1-3 day course of fluoroquinolones or macrolides are generally effective in treating TD (see table above). Adjunctive therapy, including antimotility agents (loperamide) provide symptomatic relief, but generally should be avoided for bloody diarrhea or for patients with a fever. Diphenoxylate is no longer recommended due to concerns of toxicity (risks > benefits).

Sexually Transmitted Infections (STIs)

INFECTION	DOC	DOSING/DURATION	ALTERNATIVES/NOTES
Syphilis – caused by *Treponema pallidum*, a spirochete Primary, secondary, or early latent (< 1 year duration)	Penicillin G benzathine *(Bicillin LA* – do not substitute with *Bicillin CR)*	2.4 million units IM x 1	Doxycycline 100 mg PO BID or Tetracycline 500 mg PO QID x 14 days Pregnant patients allergic to PCN should be desensitized and treated with PCN
Syphilis – Late latent (> 1 year duration), Tertiary (cardiovascular, gummas), or latent syphilis of unknown duration	Penicillin G benzathine *(Bicillin LA* – do not substitute with *Bicillin CR)*	2.4 million units IM weekly x 3 weeks (7.2 MU total)	Doxycycline 100 mg PO BID or Tetracycline 500 mg PO QID x 28 days Pregnant patients allergic to PCN should be desensitized and treated with PCN

Sexually Transmitted Infections (STIs) Continued

INFECTION	DOC	DOSING/DURATION	ALTERNATIVES/NOTES
Neurosyphilis (including ocular syphilis)	Penicillin G aqueous crystalline	3-4 million units IV Q4H or continuous infusion x 10-14 days (18-24 million units/day)	Penicillin G procaine 2.4 million units IM daily + probenecid 500 mg PO QID x 10-14 days
Congenital syphilis	Penicillin G aqueous crystalline	Newborns: 50,000 units/kg IV Q12H x 7 days, then Q8H for 10 days total Infants ≥ 1 month old: 50,000 units/kg IV Q4-6H x 10 days	Penicillin G procaine 50,000 units/kg IM daily x 10 days
Gonorrhea – caused by *Neisseria gonorrhea*, a Gram-negative diplococcus Urethral, cervical, rectal, pharyngeal	Ceftriaxone (*Rocephin*) PLUS Azithromycin (preferred) or Doxycycline – for co-infection with *Chlamydia**	250 mg IM x 1 1 gram PO x 1 100 mg PO BID x 7 days	*Ceftriaxone is most effective for pharyngeal infections If ceftriaxone is not available, can use Cefixime (*Suprax*) 400 mg PO x 1 + azithromycin (or doxycycline); test for cure in 1 week If severe cephalosporin allergy, azithromycin 2 g PO x 1 – effective for both gonorrhea and chlamydia but poorly tolerated (GI effects), more expensive and rapid emergence of resistance. Test for cure in 1 week
Chlamydial Infections – caused by *Chlamydia trachomatis*, intracellular obligate parasite	Azithromycin or Doxycycline PLUS Ceftriaxone for co-infection with Gonorrhea*	1 gram PO x 1 or 100 mg PO BID x 7 days	Erythromycin base 500 mg PO QID x 7 days or Levofloxacin 500 mg PO daily x 7 days or Ofloxacin 300 mg PO BID x 7 days
Bacterial Vaginosis – caused by many different organisms	Metronidazole or Metronidazole 0.75% gel or Clindamycin 2% cream	500 mg PO BID x 7 days 5 g intravaginally daily x 5 days 5 g intravaginally at bedtime x 7 days	Clindamycin 300 mg PO BID x 7 days or Clindamycin ovules 100 mg intravaginally at bedtime x 3 days or Tinidazole 2 g PO daily x 2 days or Tinidazole 1 g PO daily x 5 days
Trichomoniasis – caused by *Trichomonas vaginalis*, a flagellated protozoan	Metronidazole or Tinidazole	2 g PO x 1 2 g PO x 1	Metronidazole 500 mg PO BID x 7 days
Herpes Simplex Virus (HSV)			See Viral Section

* Coinfection with *C. trachomatis* frequently occurs among patients who have gonococcal infection (and vice versa); therefore, presumptive treatment for both pathogens is appropriate.

CDC. MMWR Recomm Rep. 2010;59(RR-12):1-110 and 2012 update.

<u>All sexual partners must also be treated concurrently to prevent re-infection</u>

Rickettsial Diseases

Rickettsia species are carried by many ticks, fleas, and lice and cause diseases in humans such as those found below. Rocky Mountain spotted fever is the most common and most fatal rickettsial illness in the U.S. Initial signs and symptoms include fever, headache, muscle pain followed by the development of a rash.

DISEASE	TREATMENT
Rocky Mountain Spotted Fever	Doxycycline 100 mg PO/IV BID x 7 days
Lyme Disease	Doxycycline 100 mg PO BID or amoxicillin 500 mg PO TID or cefuroxime axetil 500 mg PO BID x 10-21 days
Typhus	Doxycycline 100 mg PO/IV BID x 7 days
Ehrlichiosis	Doxycycline 100 mg PO/IV BID x 7-14 days
Tularemia	Gentamicin or tobramycin 5 mg/kg/d divided Q8H IV x 7-14 days

Reference: Wormser GP, et al. Clinical Infectious Diseases 2006; 43:1089–134

SYSTEMIC FUNGAL INFECTIONS

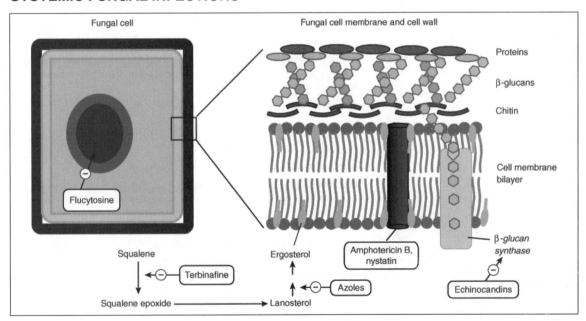

Background

- Certain types of fungi (including yeasts such as *Candida)* may colonize body surfaces and are considered to be normal flora in the intestine. They do not normally cause serious fungal infections unless the immune system is weakened, or compromised, by drugs or diseases.

- Invasive fungal infections are associated with high morbidity and mortality. For example, candidemia, the 4th most common nosocomial blood stream infection in the U.S., has mortality rates up to 30%.

- Some fungi reproduce by spreading microscopic spores. These spores are often present in the air, where they can be inhaled or come into contact with the skin; therefore, causing lung and skin infections and in some cases central nervous system infections.

- Some common fungal organisms include *Aspergillus* spp., *Blastomycosis* spp., *Candida* spp., *Crytococcosis* spp., *Coccidioidomycosis* spp., *and Histoplasmosis* spp. *Bastomycosis, Coccidioidomycosis* and *Histoplasmosis* are considered dimorphic fungi as they can exist in both mold (lower temperatures) and yeast forms (higher temperatures).

Pharmacologic Treatments

Amphotericin B

Amphotericin B binds to ergosterol, altering cell membrane permeability in susceptible fungi and causing cell death; fungicidal.

AMPHOTERICIN B FORMULATIONS	DOSING	SAFETY/SIDE EFFECTS/MONITORING
Amphotericin B (conventional) Broad spectrum: covers yeasts, molds, dimorphic fungi	0.25-1.5 mg/kg/ day	**BLACK BOX WARNING** Medication errors, including deaths, have resulted from confusion between lipid-based forms of amphotericin *(Abelcet, Amphotec, AmBisome)* and conventional amphotericin B for injection; conventional amphotericin B for injection doses should not exceed 1.5 mg/kg/day; verify product name and dosage if dose exceeds 1.5 mg/kg/day; overdose may result in cardiopulmonary arrest. **SIDE EFFECTS** Fever, chills, headache, malaise, rigors, hypokalemia, hypomagnesemia, nephrotoxicity, anemia, hypotension/hypertension, thrombophlebitis, nausea, vomiting *AmBisome* can cause back/chest pain with 1st dose **NOTES** Pregnancy Category B Compatible with D5W only; all products should be refrigerated
LIPID FORMULATIONS – Amphotericin B Lipid Complex *(Abelcet)* **Liposomal Amphotericin B *(AmBisome)*** Amphotericin B cholesteryl sulfate complex *(Amphotec)*	*Abelcet*: 5 mg/ kg/day *AmBisome*: 3-6 mg/kg/day *Amphotec*: 3-4 mg/kg/day	Lipid formulations reduce risk for infusion reactions and nephrotoxicity. Note, while lipid formulations are more expensive than conventional amphotericin B, most institutions use lipid formulations due to reduced toxicity and less dependency on premedication. Amphotericin B conventional – more infusion reactions and nephrotoxicity compared to lipid formulations. Premedication is generally necessary. Pre-medicate for infusion-related reactions with ampho B conventional (to minimize fever, chills, hypotension, nausea, etc.). Give 30-60 minutes prior to infusion: - Acetaminophen or NSAID - Diphenhydramine 25 mg IV and/or hydrocortisone 50-100 mg IV - Meperidine 25-50 mg IV for reducing the duration of severe rigors - Fluid boluses (500-1,000 mL) to reduce the risk of nephrotoxicity

Clin Infect Dis. 1998;27;603-18.

Amphotericin B Drug Interactions

■ Risk of nephrotoxicity with ampho B will be ↑ when used with other nephrotoxic agents such as AMGs, cisplatin, colistimethate, cyclosporine, flucytosine, loop diuretics, NSAIDs, radiocontrast dye, tacrolimus, vancomycin and others. Nephrotoxic effects are additive. May increase risk of digoxin toxicity due to hypokalemia.

■ Use caution with any agent that ↓ potassium or magnesium since amphotericin decreases both. Scheduled replacement of potassium or magnesium should be considered.

Flucytosine

Flucytosine penetrates fungal cells and is converted to fluorouracil which competes with uracil, interfering with fungal RNA and protein synthesis; fungicidal.

DRUG	DOSING	SAFETY/SIDE EFFECTS/MONITORING
Flucytosine (Ancobon, 5-FC) Spectrum: covers yeasts, including Candida and Cryptococcus with moderate Aspergillus activity.	25-37.5 mg/kg/dose PO Q6H Extend interval when CrCl < 50 mL/min	**BLACK BOX WARNINGS (2)** Use with extreme caution in patients with renal dysfunction Closely monitor hematologic, renal, and hepatic status **SIDE EFFECTS** Dose-related bone marrow suppression, many CNS effects, hypoglycemia, hypokalemia, aplastic anemia, hepatitis, ↑ bilirubin, ↑ SCr, ↑ BUN and others **NOTES** Avoid use as monotherapy due to rapid resistance Ampho B can ↑ effect of flucytosine; may be used for synergy with ampho B for certain fungal infections (Cryptococcus spp.)

Azole Antifungals

Azole antifungals decrease ergosterol synthesis and inhibit cell membrane formation and are typically fungistatic, but may be fungicidal for select fungal pathogens. Fluconazole is the drug of choice for oropharyngeal candidiasis (thrush) in HIV patients or in moderate-severe disease in non-HIV infected patients. Voriconazole is the drug of choice for *Aspergillus* infections.

DRUG	DOSING	SAFETY/SIDE EFFECTS/MONITORING
Itraconazole *(Sporanox, Sporanox PulsePak, Onmel)* Spectrum: covers yeasts, dimorphics, *Aspergillus*	200-400 mg daily-BID PO	**BLACK BOX WARNINGS** **Itraconazole** Use is contraindicated for treatment of onychomycosis in patients with ventricular dysfunction or a history of HF. Serious cardiovascular adverse events including, QT prolongation, ventricular tachycardia, torsade de pointes, cardiac arrest and/or sudden death have been observed due to itraconazole-induced increased serum concentrations of the following: Dofetilide, ergot alkaloids (dihydroergotamine, ergonovine, ergotamine, methylergonovine), felodipine, levomethadyl, lovastatin, methadone, midazolam (oral), nisoldipine, pimozide, quinidine, simvastatin, or triazolam; concurrent use contraindicated.
Ketoconazole *(Nizoral, Nizoral AD, Ketodan, Extina, Xolegel* – all brands are topicals)* Used more commonly for androgen related disorders due to anti-androgenic activity	200-400 mg PO daily	**Ketoconazole** Ketoconazole has been associated with hepatotoxicity, including fatal cases and cases requiring liver transplantation. Concomitant use with cisapride, dofetilide, pimozide, and quinidine is contraindicated due to the possible occurrence of life-threatening ventricular arrhythmias such as torsade de pointes. Use oral tablets only when other effective antifungal therapy is unavailable or not tolerated and the benefits of ketoconazole treatment are considered to outweigh the risks. **SIDE EFFECTS** Headache, nausea, abdominal pain, vomiting, rash/pruritus, ↑LFTs, hypertriglyceridemia, QT prolongation, hypokalemia, hypertension, edema; headache and dizziness with fluconazole; With ketoconazole shampoo, hair loss (or possible hair growth) and altered hair texture **NOTES** Itraconazole – capsules and oral solution are not interchangeable
Fluconazole *(Diflucan)* Spectrum: covers yeasts, including *Candida albicans* and *Cryptococcus* and dimorphic fungi	100-800 mg daily PO/IV Reduce dose when CrCl ≤ 50 mL/min	Capsule = take with food; solution = take on empty stomach *Sporanox PulsePak* should be taken in "pulses" of 200 mg PO BID for 1 week on and 3 weeks off (then repeat) for treatment of onychomycosis of the fingernails All azoles are cleared hepatically except fluconazole Only fluconazole and voriconazole penetrate the CNS adequately to treat fungal meningitis and are often associated with CNS toxicities (headache, dizziness, hallucinations or ocular toxicity as with voriconazole) Fluconazole IV should not be refrigerated. Fluconazole IV to PO ratio is 1:1 Pregnancy Category C (fluconazole 150 mg, others)/D (for fluconazole and voriconazole)

Azole Antifungals Continued

DRUG	DOSING	SAFETY/SIDE EFFECTS/MONITORING
Voriconazole (VFEND) Spectrum similar to itraconazole with enhanced mold coverage, drug of choice for *Aspergillosis*. No activity against *Mucormycosis* and *Zygomycosis*	IV: 6 mg/kg Q12H x 2 doses, then 4 mg/kg Q12H PO: 400 mg Q12H x 2 doses, then 200 mg Q12H. Take 1 hour before or 1 hour after meals (empty stomach) Avoid IV formulation for CrCl < 50 mL/min	**CONTRAINDICATIONS** Contraindicated with many 3A4 substrates (rifampin, rifabutin, ergot alkaloids, long-acting barbiturates, carbamazepine, pimozide, quinidine, sirolimus, St. John's wort) **WARNINGS** QT prolongation – correct K^+, Ca^{2+}, and Mg^{2+} prior to initiating therapy **SIDE EFFECTS** Visual changes (~20% – dose related – blurred vision, photophobia, altered color perception, altered visual acuity) ↑ LFTs, ↑ SCr, CNS toxicity (hallucinations, headache, dizziness), rash, photosensitivity **MONITORING** LFTs, renal function, electrolytes, visual function **NOTES** Caution driving at night due to vision changes. Avoid direct sunlight. In patients with CrCl < 50 mL/min, the IV vehicle, SBECD (sulfobutyl ether beta-cyclodextrin), may accumulate. Therefore, it is recommended to use oral dosing after the initial IV loading doses More active against *Aspergillus* species, *C. glabrata, C. krusei,* and *Fusarium* species compared to itraconazole/fluconazole
Posaconazole (Noxafil) Spectrum similar to voriconazole with *Mucormycosis* and *Zygomycosis* activity	200 mg PO Q6-8H or 400 mg PO Q12H 40 mg/mL suspension in a 4 oz. bottle packaged with dosing spoon; shake well before use Must be taken with a full meal (during or within 20 minutes following a meal)	**CONTRAINDICATIONS** Concurrent administration with ergot alkaloids, pimozide, quinidine, atorvastatin, lovastatin or simvastatin **WARNINGS** QT prolongation – correct K^+, Ca^{2+}, and Mg^{2+} prior to initiating therapy **SIDE EFFECTS** Diarrhea, nausea, vomiting, fever, headache, ↑ LFTs, rash, hypokalemia **MONITORING** LFTs, renal function, electrolytes, visual function

Azole Antifungals Drug Interactions

- All are 3A4 inhibitors (will ↑ concentration of 3A4 substrates). Itraconazole is an inhibitor of 3A4 (strong) and P-gp. Ketoconazole inhibits 1A2 (strong), 2C9 (strong), 2C19 (moderate), 2D6 (moderate), 3A4 (strong) and P-gp. Fluconazole is an inhibitor of 2C9 (strong), 2C19 (strong), and 3A4 (moderate). Voriconazole is an inhibitor of 2C9 (moderate), 2C19 (moderate) and 3A4 (strong). Posaconazole is an inhibitor of 3A4 (strong).

- Itraconazole and ketoconazole have pH-dependent absorption; ↑ pH causes ↓ absorption; avoid using with antacids, H_2RAs, PPIs.

- Voriconazole is metabolized by several CYP 450 enzymes (2C19, 2C9 and 3A4); the concentration of voriconazole can increase dangerously when given with drugs that inhibit voriconazole's metabolism or with small dose increases – it is 1st order, followed by Michaelis-Menten (non-linear) kinetics.

- Avoid concurrent use of voriconazole and the following drugs: alfuzosin, apixaban, barbiturates, carbamazepine, Copaxone, darunavir, dofetilide, dronedarone, eplererone, ergot derivatives, lopinavir, lovastatin, lurasidone, nilotinib, pimozide, quinidine, ranolazine, rifampin, rifabutin, ritonavir, rivaroxaban, simvastatin, St. John's wort, ticagrelor, thioridazine, and others.

- All azoles may increase the INR in patients on warfarin – greatest risk with fluconazole and voriconazole.

Echinocandins

Echinocandins inhibit synthesis of β(1,3)-D-glucan, an essential component of the fungal cell wall and are considered to be fungicidal. They are the drugs of choice for most systemic *Candida* infections, including non-albicans strains resistant to azole antifungals, hence the name echinoCANDINS.

DRUG	DOSING	SAFETY/SIDE EFFECTS/MONITORING
Caspofungin (*Cancidas*)	LD: 70 mg IV on day 1, then 50 mg daily Do not mix with dextrose-containing solutions Increase dose to 70 mg IV daily when used in combination with rifampin or other strong enzyme inducers	**WARNINGS** Rare: Histamine-mediated symptoms (rash, pruritus, facial swelling, flushing, hypotension) have occurred; anaphylaxis **SIDE EFFECTS** ↑ LFTs, hypotension, fever, diarrhea, hypokalemia, hypomagnesemia, rash, nausea, vomiting
Micafungin (*Mycamine*)	Candidemia 100 mg IV daily Esophageal candidiasis: 150 mg IV daily	**MONITORING** LFTs **NOTES** All 3 agents are given once daily and do not require dose adjustment in renal impairment. Very few drug interactions.
Anidulafungin (*Eraxis*)	Esophageal candidiasis: 100 mg IV on day 1, then 50 mg daily Candidemia: 200 mg IV on day 1, then 100 mg IV daily	Micafungin should be protected from light. Caution use of caspofungin with cyclosporine due to ↑ hepatotoxicity; Caution in hepatic impairment (use 35 mg of caspofungin for maintenance dose). Pregnancy Category C/B (anidulafungin)

Other Antifungal Agents

DRUG	DOSING	SAFETY/SIDE EFFECTS/MONITORING
Griseofulvin (*Grifulvin, Gris-PEG*) Griseofulvin binds to the keratin precursor cells which prevents fungal invasion; indicated for dermatomycosis and Tinea infections of skin, hair and nails	500-1,000 mg/day in 1-2 divided doses Take with a fatty meal to increase absorption or with food/milk to avoid GI upset	**CONTRAINDICATIONS** Severe liver disease, porphyria, pregnancy **SIDE EFFECTS** Headache, rash, urticaria, dizziness, photosensitivity, ↑ LFTs, agranulocytosis, severe skin reactions **MONITORING** LFTs, renal function, CBC **NOTES** Pregnancy Category X Cross reaction possible with PCN allergy

Other Antifungal Agents Caption

DRUG	DOSING	SAFETY/SIDE EFFECTS/MONITORING
Terbinafine *(Lamisil)* Inhibits squalene epoxidase, a key enzyme in sterol biosynthesis in fungi, resulting in a deficiency of ergosterol within the cell wall leading to cell death Topical forms (Rx, OTC)	250 mg in 1-2 divided doses without regards to meals Confirm fungal infection prior to use for onychomycosis	**WARNINGS** Taste disturbance (including loss of taste) may occur and severe cases resulting in weight loss. Depression has been reported. Loss of smell has been reported. Can exacerbate systemic lupus erythematosus **SIDE EFFECTS** Headache, skin rashes, diarrhea, dyspepsia, taste disturbance, ↑ LFTs **MONITORING** CBC and LFTs

Drug Interactions

- Griseofulvin: Induces 1A2, 2C9, 3A4 (all weak/moderate); griseofulvin may ↑ the metabolism of contraceptives; contraceptive failure is possible. Use an alternative, nonhormonal form of contraception.

- Terbinafine inhibits 2D6 (strong); induces 3A4 (weak/moderate)

Treatment Recommendations for Selected Fungal Pathogens

PATHOGEN	DISEASE	1ST-LINE	DURATION
Candida	Oropharyngeal (thrush)	Fluconazole or topicals (clotrimazole or nystatin)	7-14 days
	Esophageal	Fluconazole or echinocandins or ampho B	14-21 days
	Invasive	Echinocandins or fluconazole	14 days from first negative blood culture
Aspergillus	Pulmonary	Voriconazole	6-12 weeks or indefinite
Cryptococcus neoformans	Induction	Ampho + 5-FC	≥ 14 days
	Consolidation	Fluconazole	8-12 weeks
Coccidioides immitis	Meningitis	Fluconazole	Prolonged course
	Skin/Skeletal, Pulmonary	Fluconazole	≥ 3-6 months
Histoplasmosis capsulatum	Pulmonary, Disseminated	Itraconazole	≥ 14 days
Zygomycetes class	Rhinocerebral Disseminated	Amphotericin B ± posaconazole	Indefinite
Onychomycosis	Nail infections	Itraconazole, terbinafine, or fluconazole (confirm fungal infection prior to treatment)	Fingernail: ≥ 6 weeks Toenail: ≥ 12 weeks

Ampho: amphotericin B, 5-FC: flucytosine

VIRAL INFECTION OVERVIEW

Virus Replication Cycle

<u>Viruses are obligate intracellular parasites</u>: They depend on the host cell metabolic processes for survival.

Since they do not possess a cell wall or membrane, they do not respond to antibacterials. Antivirals treat viral infections by targeting viral specific steps in the replication process. As viruses depend on hosts for metabolism/replication, antivirals may injure or destroy the host cells.

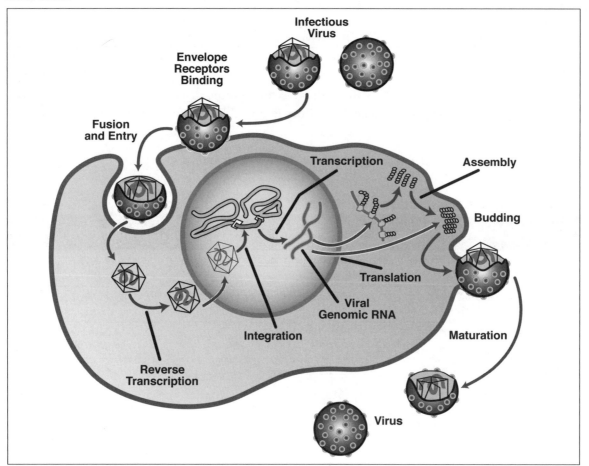

Steps to viral replication

1. Attachment of the virus to cell membrane

2. Penetration into the host cell

3. Uncoating of viral RNA/DNA

4. Transcription of viral proteins

5. Assembly of new virions (the infective form of the virus)

6. Budding of new, immature virions

7. Release of new virus

Antiviral Treatment of Patients with Influenza

- Check to see if there is *Tamiflu*-resistant flu in the area prior to solo treatment with neuraminidase inhibitor: if present, use zanamivir or oseltamivir plus rimantadine or amantadine.

- Neuraminidase inhibitors should be started within 48 hours of illness onset.

Neuraminidase inhibitors

Inhibits the neuraminidase enzyme which affects the release of viral particles, thereby reducing the amount of virus in the body. They are active against influenza A/B and the avian/swine flu.

DRUG	DOSING	SAFETY/SIDE EFFECTS/MONITORING
Oseltamivir (*Tamiflu*) 30, 45, 75 mg capsules 6 mg/mL (60 mL) suspension	Treatment – Adults: 75 mg BID x 5 days Prevention – Adults: 75 mg daily x 10 days Pediatric patients (2 weeks-12 years) are dosed on body weight CrCl < 30 mL/min: ↓ frequency to daily (for treatment) or ↓ frequency or dose (for prophylaxis)	**WARNINGS** CNS – rare side effects of neuropsychiatric events (sudden confusion, delirium, hallucinations, unusual behavior, or self-injury) **SIDE EFFECTS** Vomiting, nausea ("tummy-flu"), abdominal pain, diarrhea **NOTES** Pregnancy Category C Start within 48 hours of symptoms
Zanamivir (*Relenza Diskhaler*)	Treatment: 10 mg (two 5-mg inhalations) twice daily x 5 days Prevention: 10 mg (two 5-mg inhalations) once daily x 10 days	**WARNING** CNS – rare side effects of neuropsychiatric events (sudden confusion, delirium, hallucinations, unusual behavior, or self-injury) Bronchospasm risk: Do not use if asthma/COPD or with any breathing problem. Tell patient to stop if wheezing or breathing problems. **SIDE EFFECTS** Headache, throat pain, cough **NOTES** Pregnancy Category C The inhaler cannot be used by very young children or in patients with asthma/COPD; prophylaxis indicated for 5 years and older, treatment indicated for 7 years and older

OTHER ANTIVIRALS	DOSING	SAFETY/SIDE EFFECTS/MONITORING
Rimantadine (*Flumadine*) – for Influenza A only Amantadine can be used instead but has higher incidence adverse effects (↑ insomnia, dizziness, confusion, agitation, etc.) and greater dose reductions in renal impairment	Treatment/ Prevention: 100 mg BID CrCl < 30 mL/min: 100 mg daily	**WARNINGS** Seizures – use with caution in patients with a history of seizure disorder Psychosis – avoid use **SIDE EFFECTS** Nausea, vomiting, loss of appetite, dry mouth, insomnia, impaired concentration NOTES See Parkinson Disease chapter for further information on amantadine

Antivirals Used for Treatment of Herpes Simplex Virus (HSV), Varicella Zoster Virus (VZV) and Cytomegalovirus (CMV)

ANTIVIRAL	SPECTRUM	COMMON TREATMENT DOSING RANGE (ADULTS)*	SAFETY/SIDE EFFECTS/MONITORING
Acyclovir *(Zovirax)* PO, inj, topical	HSV, VZV	PO: 200-800 mg Q4-8H* IV: 5-10 mg/kg Q8H* Dose based on IBW in obese patients	**WARNINGS** Thrombocytopenic purpura/hemolytic uremic syndrome (TTP/HUS) – reported in immunocompromised patients Renal impairment – caution in patients with renal impairment, the elderly, and/or those receiving nephrotoxic agents; infuse over at least 1 hour to reduce risk of renal tubular damage
Valacyclovir *(Valtrex)* PO prodrug of acyclovir	HSV, VZV	500-1,000 mg daily-TID*	**SIDE EFFECTS** Malaise, headache, nausea, vomiting, diarrhea, rash, pruritus, ↑ LFTs, neutropenia; ↑ SCr and BUN (crystal nephropathy) and seizures especially with IV formulation; transient burning or stinging with topical formulation
Famciclovir *(Famvir)* PO prodrug of penciclovir	HSV, VZV	250-500 mg Q8-12H*	**MONITORING** BUN, SCr, LFTs, CBC **NOTES** Pregnancy Category B Infuse acyclovir IV over at least 1 hour and maintain adequate hydration to reduce risk of renal tubular damage. Limited stability with NS (use with caution) or consider using with D5W only. Take oral products with full glass of water Extend interval in renal impairment Store acyclovir IV at room temperature Store valacyclovir oral suspension in a refrigerator
Ganciclovir *(Cytovene IV, Vancyte, Zirgan* ophthalmic gel, *Vitrasert* ophthalmic implant) Inj, IO	CMV	5 mg/kg IV Q12H x 2 weeks, followed by 5 mg/kg IV daily or 1 gram PO TID	**BLACK BOX WARNINGS (2)** Myelosuppression; carcinogenic and teratogenic effects, and inhibition of spermatogenesis in animals **SIDE EFFECTS** Fever, nausea, vomiting, diarrhea, anorexia, thrombocytopenia, neutropenia, leukopenia, anemia, ↑ SCr, seizures (rare)
Valganciclovir *(Valcyte)* PO prodrug of ganciclovir	CMV, HSV, VZV	450-900 mg daily-BID* Take valganciclovir with food	**MONITORING** CBC with differential, PLT, SCr **NOTES** Pregnancy Category C Extend interval and reduce dose when CrCl < 60 mL/min Ganciclovir and valganciclovir are the drugs of choice for CMV

Antivirals Used for Treatment of HSV, VZV and CMV Continued

ANTIVIRAL	SPECTRUM	COMMON TREATMENT DOSING RANGE (ADULTS)*	SAFETY/SIDE EFFECTS/MONITORING
Cidofovir *(Vistide)* Inj.	CMV treatment in HIV patients only	5 mg/kg/wk x 2 weeks, then 5 mg/kg once every 2 weeks	**BLACK BOX WARNINGS (IN ADDITION TO ABOVE)** Dose-dependent nephropathy **CONTRAINDICATIONS** SCr > 1.5 mg/dL; CrCl < 55 mL/min; urine protein ≥ 100 mg/dL (> 2+ proteinuria); sulfa allergy; use with or within 7 days of other nephrotoxic drugs; direct intraocular injection **SIDE EFFECTS** Similar to ganciclovir with ↑ risk of nephrotoxicity and lower risk for bone marrow suppression **NOTES** Pregnancy Category C
Foscarnet *(Foscavir)* Inj.	Resistant CMV, HSV	90 mg/kg Q12H x 2 weeks, then 90-120 mg/kg/d*	**BLACK BOX WARNINGS** Renal impairment occurs to some degree in majority of patients; seizures due to electrolyte imbalances **SIDE EFFECTS** Electrolyte abnormalities (↓ K+, ↓ Ca²⁺, ↓ Mg²⁺, ↓ Phos), ↑ SCr, ↑ BUN **NOTES** Vesicant (use central line), handle as a chemotherapeutic agent

GI: gastrointestinal, INH: inhaled, IO: intraocular, PO: oral, Inj: intravenous, TTP/HUS: Thrombotic Thrombocytopenic Purpura and Hemolytic Uremic Syndrome

* *Depends on indication, phase of treatment (induction, recurrence, or suppressive therapy)*

Herpes Simplex Virus (HSV)

■ HSV-1 is most commonly associated with oropharyngeal disease, and HSV-2 is associated more closely with genital disease. However, each virus is capable of causing infections clinically indistinguishable in both anatomic areas.

■ Genital herpes is a chronic, life-long viral infection. 1 in 6 people in the U.S. have HSV-2.

■ The first episode of genital herpes usually begins within 2-14 days post exposure, but up to 50% of patients are asymptomatic. First episode symptoms can include flu-like symptoms, fever, headache, malaise, myalgias, and development of pustular or ulcerative lesions on external genitalia. Lesions usually begin as papules or vesicles that rapidly spread and clusters of lesions form, crust, and re-epithelialize. Lesions are described as painful. Itching, dysuria, and vaginal or urethral discharge are common symptoms.

■ Recurrent infections are not associated with systemic manifestations. Symptoms are localized to the genital area, milder, and of shorter duration. Patients typically experience a prodrome prior to symptoms. Must start treatment during prodrome or within 1 day of lesion onset for the patient to experience benefit.

■ Suppressive therapy reduces the frequency of genital herpes recurrences by 70-80% among patients who have frequent recurrences (e.g., > 6 recurrences/yr) and many report no symptomatic outbreaks.

■ Acyclovir *(Zovirax)* is usually the cheapest regimen. Valacyclovir *(Valtrex)* is a prodrug of acyclovir that results in higher concentrations than with oral acyclovir and less frequent dosing that may enhance adherence. If resistant to acyclovir, patient will be resistant to valacyclovir. Famciclovir *(Famvir)* is a pro-drug of penciclovir. Strains resistant to acyclovir are generally resistant to famciclovir.

Following is a table summarizing the treatment of herpes simplex virus infections.

Herpes Simplex Virus Treatment In Non-HIV Patients

HSV INFECTION	ACYCLOVIR	VALACYCLOVIR	FAMCICLOVIR
Primary – initial episode			
Genital HSV- Infection (1st episode)	200 mg PO 5x daily x 7-10 days or 400 mg PO TID x 7-10 days	1 g PO BID x 7-10 days	250 mg PO TID x 7-10 days
Oral HSV- initial infection	200 mg PO 5x daily or 400 mg TID x 7-10 days		
Recurrent episodes			
Genital HSV- recurrent episodic	400 mg PO TID x 5 days or 800 mg PO BID x 5 days or 800 mg PO TID x 2 days	500 mg PO BID x 3 days or 1 g PO daily x 5 days	125 mg PO BID x 5 days or 1g PO BID x 1 day
Oral HSV- recurrent episodic	200 mg PO 5x/d x 5 days or 400 mg PO TID x 5 days or 800mg PO BID x 5 days	1-2 g PO BID x 1 day	1.5 g PO x 1 dose
Chronic suppression (daily therapy)			
Genital HSV- recurrent-suppressive	400 mg PO BID	500 mg PO daily or 1 g PO daily	250 mg PO BID
Oral HSV- recurrent-suppressive	400 mg PO BID		

CDC. MMWR Recomm Rep. 2010;59(RR-12):1-110. Bartlett. Johns Hopkins Antibiotic Guide: Diagnosis & Treatment of Infectious Diseases 3rd Ed. 2012.

Herpes Varicella-Zoster (Chickenpox) Virus (Shingles)

Almost all adults in the U.S. have had chickenpox as a child. The virus can lie dormant for decades without causing any symptoms. An outbreak may occur as the patient ages, and is often due to acute stress. The rash is distinctive and painful. Pharmacists should be able to recognize a shingles rash and tell the patient to see a doctor that day; refer to the following image.

Therapy should be initiated at the earliest sign or symptom of shingles and is most effective when started within 72 hours of the onset of zoster rash.

Shingles vaccine (*Zostavax*) is not used for treatment, but can be given to patients who have experienced an outbreak. A study in 2012 questions whether this is useful, but the practice has been to give the vaccine in the hopes of reducing recurrent attacks. The vaccine is FDA-approved for use in 50+ years; the ACIP recommendation is for 60+ years; this may be lowered.

Antiviral therapy is in table below; pain can be treated with topical agents (*Lidoderm* patch, lidocaine viscous gel) or with pain agents with neuropathic efficacy (anticonvulsants, anti-depressants), and sometimes with NSAIDs or opioids. Most recover without long-term sequelae; 5-10% have chronic pain, which can be debilitating.

Shingles Treatment

DRUG	DOSING	DESCRIPTION
Acyclovir (*Zovirax*) or Famciclovir (*Famvir*) or Valacyclovir (*Valtrex*)	Acyclovir 800 mg PO 5 times daily for 7-10 days; Famciclovir 500 mg PO TID for 7 days; Valacyclovir 1,000 mg PO TID for 7 days	 A cluster of fluid-filled blisters, often in a band around one side of the waist or on one side of the forehead, or around an eye or on the neck (less commonly anywhere else on the body).

West Nile Virus

- Transmitted via mosquitos

- Most patients do not get very sick; only ~20% show symptoms of fever, headache, or other flu-like symptoms but < 1% can develop encephalitis or meningitis

- Antivirals do not really work and the best medicine is prevention

    □ Recommend using mosquito repellant with DEET, picaridin, oil of lemon eucalyptus (CDC recommended-products only) or IR3535

    □ Wear protective clothing (long sleeves and pants)

    □ Avoid/eliminate standing or stagnant water which are breeding grounds for mosquitos

MALARIA

Refer to Travelers Medicine chapter for background; this chapter discusses drug treatment options. Check for resistance patterns.

DRUG	DOSING	SAFETY/SIDE EFFECTS/MONITORING

Areas with chloroquine-resistant *Plasmodium falciparum*

DRUG	DOSING	SAFETY/SIDE EFFECTS/MONITORING
Atovaquone/ proquanil *(Malarone)*	**Adult Prophylaxis Dose** 250/100 mg PO once daily **Initiation (Pre Travel)** 1-2 days **Discontinue (Post Travel)** 7 days	**CONTRAINDICATIONS** Prophylaxis use when CrCl < 30 mL/min **SIDE EFFECTS** GI upset (abdominal pain, N/V), ↑ LFTs, headache, dizziness **MONITORING** LFTs, renal function (SCr, BUN) **NOTES** Must be taken with food or milk-based drink. If patient vomits within 1 hour of administration, repeat the dose. For patients who have difficulty swallowing the tablets, they can be crushed and mixed with condensed milk just prior to administration.
Mefloquine *(Lariam)*	**Adult Prophylaxis Dose** 250 mg PO once weekly **Initiation (Pre Travel)** 1-3 weeks **Discontinue (Post Travel)** 4 weeks Check for resistance	**BLACK BOX WARNINGS** Do not use for prophylaxis in patients with major psychiatric disorders. Neuropsychiatric effects, which can require drug discontinuation: ■ Psychiatric symptoms can include anxiety, paranoia, depression, hallucinations, and psychosis. ■ Neurologic symptoms of dizziness or vertigo, tinnitus, and loss of balance may occur and may be permanent. **CONTRAINDICATIONS** Hypersensitivity to mefloquine or related compounds (e.g., quinine and quinidine), prophylactic use in patients with a history of seizures or psychiatric disorder (including active or recent history of depression, generalized anxiety disorder, psychosis, schizophrenia, or other major psychiatric disorders) **SIDE EFFECTS** Loss of balance/dizziness, GI upset, chills, dizziness, fatigue, fever, headache, rash, tinnitus, psychiatric side effects (see warning above) **NOTES** Take with food and with at least 8 oz of water. If patient vomits within 30 minutes after the dose, repeat the full dose; if 30-60 minutes after dose, an additional half-dose should be given. Tablets may be crushed and suspended in a small amount of liquid. Acceptable for use in pregnancy (Pregnancy Category B) and children.
Doxycycline *(Vibramycin)*	**Adult Prophylaxis Dose** 100 mg PO daily **Initiation (Pre Travel)** 1-2 days **Discontinue (Post Travel)** 4 weeks	See details under tetracycline section earlier in this chapter.

Malaria Continued

DRUG	DOSING	SAFETY/SIDE EFFECTS/MONITORING
Quinine (Qualaquin)	**Adult Prophylaxis Dose** 648 mg PO Q8H – should be given with tetracycline, doxycycline or clindamycin	**BLACK BOX WARNINGS** Quinine is not recommended for the prevention/treatment of nocturnal leg cramps due to the potential for severe and/or life-threatening side effects (e.g., cardiac arrhythmias, thrombocytopenia, and HUS/TTP, severe hypersensitivity reactions). **CONTRAINDICATIONS** Hypersensitivity to quinine or related compounds (e.g., mefloquine and quinidine); prolonged QT interval; myasthenia gravis; optic neuritis; G6PD deficiency **SIDE EFFECTS** GI upset (abdominal pain, nausea, vomiting, diarrhea), visual changes (including blindess), hypersensitivity reactions including SJS/TEN, hypoglycemia, QT prolongation

Areas with chloroquine-sensitive *Plasmodium falciparum*

Chloroquine (Aralen)	**Adult Prophylaxis Dose** 500 mg PO once weekly **Initiation (Pre Travel)** 1-2 weeks **Discontinue (Post Travel)** 4 weeks	**CONTRAINDICATIONS** Hypersensitivity to 4-aminoquinoline compounds (e.g., chloroquine, hydroxychloroquine); retinal or visual field changes **WARNINGS** Retinopathy (dose and duration-related) and may be reversible if detected early. Rare hematologic reactions including agranulocytosis, aplastic anemia, and thrombocytopenia; monitoring (CBC) is recommended in prolonged therapy. May cause ECG changes, AV block, and cardiomyopathy (rare). Generally these are dose and/or duration dependent. May cause QT prolongation. **SIDE EFFECTS** GI upset (abdominal pain, nausea, vomiting, diarrhea), visual disturbances (blurred vision, difficulty of focusing or accommodation), photosensitivity, hair loss and bleaching of hair pigment, skeletal muscle myopathy or neuromyopathy leading to progressive weakness and atrophy, exacerbation of psoriasis **NOTES** May be taken with meals to decrease GI upset. Drug has bitter taste.

Areas with *Plasmodium vivax* and *P. ovale* with or without *P. falciparum*

Primaquine	**Adult Prophylaxis Dose** 30 mg PO daily **Initiation (Pre Travel)** 1 day **Discontinue (Post Travel)** 7 days Effective for *P. vivax*.	**CONTRAINDICATIONS** Concurrent use with other medications causing hemolytic anemia or myeloid bone marrow suppression **SIDE EFFECTS** GI upset (abdominal cramps, dyspepsia, nausea, vomiting), agranulocytosis, anemia, hemolytic anemia (in patients with G6PD deficiency) **NOTES** Take with meals to decrease adverse GI effects. Drug has a bitter taste. CDC requires screening for G6PD deficiency prior to initiating treatment.

Patient Counseling

Counseling That Applies to All Antibiotics

- Antibiotics only treat bacterial infections. They do not treat viral infections (e.g., the common cold and most cases of acute bronchitis and sinusitis unless certain criteria are met).

- Antibiotics work best when the amount of medicine in your body is kept at a constant level. Therefore, take this drug at evenly spaced intervals.

- Skipping doses or not completing the full course of therapy may decrease the effectiveness of treatment, cause the infection to return, and increase the likelihood that this medicine will not work for you in the future.

- If your symptoms worsen, contact your healthcare provider.

- All beta-lactams (and most other antibiotics) can cause rash. If the rash looks serious, the patient should be seen right away. Beta-lactams can cause severe skin rashes in rare cases.

- If using a suspension, all need shaking and most should be refrigerated (but not azithromycin, cefdinir, clarithromycin, clindamycin, ciprofloxacin, doxycycline, fluconazole, levofloxacin, linezolid, sulfamethoxazole/trimethoprim and voriconazole).

- Measure liquid doses carefully using a measuring device/syringe. These should be dispensed with the medicine if the patient does not have one already. Tell the patient not to use a household spoon because they may not get the correct dose.

- For all antibiotics, especially clindamycin and drugs with broad-spectrum coverage, instruct the patient to report symptoms of a C. *diff* infection, including watery diarrhea several times a day with (possible) mild abdominal cramping. This can occur during treatment, or weeks after the antibiotic treatment has finished. If present, the doctor should be contacted right away. Patients should be instructed not to self-treat this condition with anti-diarrheal medicine. Taking yogurt with active cultures, or certain probiotics, can help reduce the incidence, but should be taken at a time separate from the antibiotic.

Specific Counseling Points for Common Agents

Acyclovir *(Zovirax)* – Antiviral

- This medicine works best when taken at the first sign of an outbreak within the first day.

- The most common side effects are malaise, headache, nausea and diarrhea.

- Take this medication by mouth with or without food, usually 2 to 5 times daily, as directed. The intervals should be evenly spaced.

- Drink plenty of fluids while taking this medication.

- For the cream, side effects include temporary burning or stinging.

Amoxicillin products

- The most common side effects include an upset stomach and nausea. Be sure to take with plenty of water.

- Amoxicillin may be taken with food, usually every 8 or 12 hours. *Moxatag* is taken within 1 hour of finishing a meal. *Augmentin* is taken with food to increase absorption and decrease stomach upset. Amoxicillin/clavulanate extended release tablets should be administered with food.

- If you develop a rash, especially one that looks serious, you should be seen right away. This medicine can rarely cause serious skin rashes.

- The suspensions should be refrigerated (especially important for *Augmentin*).

Azithromycin *(Zithromax)*

- The most common side effect is upset stomach.

- Common dosing is two 250 mg tablets on day 1, followed by one 250 mg tablet daily on days 2-5 or 500 mg daily for 3 days.

- The tablets and immediate release oral suspension can be taken with or without food; extended release suspension should be taken on an empty stomach (1 hour before or 2 hours after a meal). The suspension should be stored at room temperature and should not be refrigerated.

Cefdinir/Cefuroxime *(Ceftin)*/Cephalexin *(Keflex)*

- Common side effects with this medication include diarrhea, nausea and vomiting. This medicine can rarely cause serious skin rashes. If you develop a rash, especially one that looks serious, you should be seen right away.

- Cefdinir: The suspension should **not** be refrigerated. Can be taken with or without food.

- Cefuroxime: Take this medication by mouth with a meal or snack every 12 hours. The suspension should be refrigerated.

- Cephalexin: Take this medication by mouth with or without a meal or snack every 6 hours. The suspension should be refrigerated.

Clarithromycin *(Biaxin)*

- Common side effects include abnormal (metallic) taste, diarrhea, abdominal pain and nausea.

- The tablets and oral suspension are taken with or without food and can be taken with milk twice daily.

- *Biaxin XL* tablets should be taken with food.

- The liquid suspension should not be refrigerated.

Ciprofloxacin *(Cipro)*

- The most common side effect is stomach upset. Rarely, seizures can occur, especially in those with seizure disorders (quinolones should be avoided with a seizure history).

- This medicine can make your skin more sensitive to the sun, and you can burn more easily. Use sunscreen and protective clothing, and try to avoid staying in the sun.

- This medicine can rarely cause a serious problem called tendon rupture or swelling of the tendon (tendinitis). If you notice, pain, swelling and inflammation of the tendons on the back of the ankle (Achilles), shoulder, hand or other sites, stop the medicine and be seen right away. This is uncommon, but occurs more frequently in people over age 60, and in patients who have had transplants and use steroid medicine, such as prednisone.

- This medicine can rarely cause weakness or tingling/painful sensations in the arms and legs. If this occurs, contact your healthcare provider immediately.

- This medicine should be taken 2 hours before or 6 hours after taking antacids, vitamins, magnesium, calcium, iron or zinc supplements, dairy products, bismuth subsalicylate or the medicines sucralfate or didanosine *(Videx)*.

- This is not a first choice medicine in patients under 18 years of age due to a risk of bone and joint problems. However, it is used occasionally on a short-term basis for certain conditions.

- Do not use this medicine if you take a different medicine called tizanidine *(Zanaflex)*. Please tell your pharmacist about all medicines you are using, since this medicine can interact with many others. The liquid suspension should not be refrigerated. Maintain adequate hydration to prevent crytalluria.

Clindamycin *(Cleocin)*

- The most common side effect is stomach upset.

- Take by mouth with or without food, 3-4 times a day.

- Take with a full glass of water.

- The liquid suspension should <u>not</u> be refrigerated.

Doxycycline *(Doryx*, others)

- The most common side effects are nausea and stomach upset.

- This medicine can make your skin more sensitive to the sun, and you can burn more easily. Use sunscreen and protective clothing, and try to avoid staying in the sun.

- Drink plenty of fluids while using this medicine.

- This medicine should be taken twice daily 1-2 hours before, or 4-6 hours after taking antacids, vitamins, magnesium, calcium, iron or zinc supplements, dairy products, bismuth subsalicylate.

- The liquid suspension should be stored at room temperature and not refrigerated.

- Do not use this medicine if you are pregnant, if you could become pregnant, or if you are breastfeeding.

Erythromycin *(EES)*

- May be administered with food to decrease GI upset.

- Common side effects are diarrhea, abdominal pain and stomach upset.

- The liquid suspension combination with sulfisoxazole should be refrigerated.

Fluconazole *(Diflucan)* [ketoconazole *(Nizoral)* and itraconazole *(Sporanox)*]

- Common side effects include headache, nausea and abdominal pain.

- Generally taken once daily with or without food (or given as a single 150 mg tablet for a vaginal fungal infection).

- Contact your healthcare provider right away if you are passing brown or dark-colored urine, have pale stools, feel more tired than usual or if your skin and whites of your eyes become yellow. These may be symptoms of liver damage.

- If you develop a rash, especially one that looks serious, you should be seen right away. This medicine can rarely cause serious skin rashes.

- If you have kidney disease, you will need to use a lower dose. Your healthcare provider or pharmacist will make sure the dose is correct.

- The liquid suspension should not be refrigerated.

- Ketoconazole tablets and itraconazole capsules should be taken with food (itraconazole solution should be taken on an empty stomach). Do not use with antacids (need two hour separation) and stop the use of PPIs or H_2RAs while using this medicine. These other medicines will reduce the amount of the antifungal medicine that gets absorbed.

Levofloxacin *(Levaquin)*

- This medication is taken once daily.

- The most common side effect is stomach upset.

- The tablets can be taken with or without food. The suspension is taken 1 hour before or 2 hours after eating. Maintain adequate hydration to prevent crystal formation in the urine.

- If you use blood sugar-lowering medicines, your blood sugar may get unusually low. Be sure to check your blood sugar level frequently and treat a low blood sugar if it occurs.

- If you have kidney disease, you will need to use a lower dose. Your healthcare provider will make sure the dose is correct.

- This medicine should be taken 2 hours before, or 2 hours after taking antacids, vitamins, magnesium, calcium, iron or zinc supplements, dairy products, bismuth subsalicylate or the medicines sucralfate *(Carafate)* or didanosine *(Videx)*.

- The liquid formulation should be stored at room temperature.

Metronidazole *(Flagyl)*

- Common side effects include nausea and unusual (metallic) taste.

- Do not use any alcohol products while using this medicine, and for at least 3 days afterward.

- Immediate-release tablets and capsules may be taken with food to minimize stomach upset. Take extended release tablets on an empty stomach (1 hour before or 2 hours after meals); do not split, crush, or chew.

Minocycline *(Minocin, Dynacin, Solodyn)*

- Common side effects with this medication include diarrhea, nausea and vomiting. This medicine can rarely cause serious skin rashes. If you develop a rash, especially one that looks serious, you should be seen right away.

- Take this medication with or without food, 1-2 times daily.

- Do not use this medication if you are pregnant, if you could become pregnant, or if you are breastfeeding.

Mupirocin *(Bactroban)*

- The most common side effects are burning, itching, and possibly a rash.

- The nasal ointment is used to prevent the spread of a bacteria known as MRSA and should be administered into each nostril twice daily for 5 days, or as directed by your healthcare provider.

Nitrofurantoin *(Macrodantin, Macrobid)*

- Take this medication with food to improve absorption and decrease side effects. Swallow the medication whole.

- Do not use magnesium trisilicate-containing antacids while taking this medication. These antacids can bind with nitrofurantoin, preventing its full absorption into your system.

- Continue to take this medication until the full prescribed amount is finished, even if symptoms disappear after a few days. Stopping the medication too early may allow bacteria to continue to grow, which may result in a return of the infection.

- Side effects including nausea and headache may occur.

- This medication may cause your urine to turn dark yellow or brown in color. This is usually a harmless, temporary effect and will disappear when the medication is stopped. However, dark brown urine can also be a sign of liver damage. Seek immediate medical attention if you notice dark urine along with any of the following symptoms: persistent nausea or vomiting, have pale stools, feel more tired than usual or if your skin and whites of your eyes become yellow.

■ This medication may rarely cause very serious (possibly fatal) lung problems. Lung problems may occur within the first month of treatment or after long-term use of nitrofurantoin (generally for 6 months or longer). Seek immediate medical attention if you develop symptoms of lung problems, including: persistent cough, chest pain, shortness of breath/trouble breathing, joint/muscle pain or bluish/purplish skin.

Nystatin

■ The most common side effects are nausea, vomiting, diarrhea, and stomach pain.

■ If you are using the suspension form of this medication, shake well before using. Be sure to swish the medication around in your mouth for several minutes before swallowing.

Oseltamivir *(Tamiflu)*

■ Treatment should begin within 2 days of onset of influenza symptoms.

■ Adult treatment dose is 75 mg twice daily for 5 days. Prophylaxis is 75 mg once daily for 10 days. Children (2 weeks-12 years) are dosed based on body weight.

■ The most common side effects are nausea and vomiting. Take with or without food. There is less chance of stomach upset if you take it with a light snack, milk, or a meal.

■ Please let your healthcare provider know if you have received the nasally administered influenza virus vaccine during the past two weeks (risk that drug may inhibit replication of the live virus vaccine).

■ People with the flu, particularly children and adolescents, may be at an increased risk of self-injury and confusion shortly after taking this medicine and should be closely monitored for signs of unusual behavior. Contact the healthcare provider immediately if the patient shows any signs of unusual behavior.

■ Vaccination is considered the first line of defense against influenza; this medicine does not replace an annual (fall) influenza vaccine.

Penicillin VK

■ Common side effects with this medication include diarrhea, nausea and vomiting. This medicine can rarely cause serious skin rashes. If you develop a rash, especially one that looks serious, you should be seen right away.

■ Take this medication by mouth one hour before or two hours after a meal, usually every 6 hours.

■ The suspension should be refrigerated.

Phenazopyridine *(Azo, Uristat, Pyridium)*

■ Common side effects include headache, dizziness, stomach cramps, and red-orange urine discoloration.

■ If there is no improvement in urinary symptoms after 2 days of treatment, you should be seen by your healthcare provider right away.

Sulfamethoxazole and Trimethoprim *(Bactrim, Septra)*

- Do not use this medication if you have an allergy to sulfa medicines.

- This most common side effects are nausea and rash.

- Take with a full glass of water to prevent crystal formation in the urine. Take with or without food. If stomach upset occurs, take with food or milk.

- Do not use this medication if you are pregnant, if you could become pregnant, or if you are breastfeeding.

- This medicine can make your skin more sensitive to the sun, and you can burn more easily. Use sunscreen and protective clothing, and try to avoid staying in the sun.

- If you develop a rash, especially one that looks serious, you should be seen right away. This medicine can rarely cause serious skin rashes.

- Shake the suspension prior to use. The suspension should be kept at room temperature.

Terbinafine *(Lamisil)*

- Terbinafine is used to treat certain types of fungal infections (e.g., fingernail or toenail). It works by stopping the growth of fungus.

- Take this medication by mouth with or without food, usually once a day. Dosage and length of treatment depend on the location of the fungus and the response to treatment.

- It may take several months after you finish treatment to see the full benefit of this drug. It takes time for your new healthy nails to grow out and replace the infected ones.

- Continue to take this medication until the full prescribed amount is finished. Stopping the medication too early may allow the fungus to continue to grow, which may result in a return of the infection.

- The most common side effect is headache. Diarrhea, stomach upset, skin rash or temporary change or loss of taste and appetite may occur. Tell your healthcare provider if any of these effects are bothersome or become severe.

- This drug has rarely caused very serious (and fatal) liver disease. Liver function tests may be monitored during the course of therapy. Tell your healthcare provider immediately if you develop symptoms of liver disease including persistent nausea, loss of appetite, severe stomach/abdominal pain, dark urine, yellowing of eyes/skin, or pale stools.

Valacyclovir *(Valtrex)* – for herpes simplex

- *Valtrex* used daily with the following safer sex practices can lower the chances of passing genital herpes to your partner.

  - Do not have sexual contact with your partner when you have any symptom or outbreak of genital herpes.

  - Use a condom made of latex or polyurethane whenever you have sexual contact.

- This medication does not cure herpes infections (cold sores, chickenpox, shingles, or genital herpes).

- This medication can be taken with or without food. If GI upset occurs, take with meals.

- Start treatment during prodrome or within 24 hours of the onset of symptoms. This medication is not helpful if you start treatment too late.

- Common side effects tiredness, include headache, nausea, stomach pain, vomiting, and and vomiting. These side effects are usually mild and do not cause patients to stop taking the medication.

- Store suspension in a refrigerator. Discard after 21 days.

Voriconazole *(VFEND)*

- Common side effects include eyesight changes, rash, and stomach upset. Vision changes are temporary and reversible.

- Avoid driving at night because this medicine may cause vision problems like blurry vision. If you have any change in your eyesight, avoid all driving or using dangerous machinery.

- Avoid sunlight. Your skin may burn more easily. Your eyes may hurt in bright sunlight.

- Discuss with the pharmacist if you have trouble digesting dairy products, lactose, or regular table sugar. The tablets contain lactose (milk sugar). The liquid contains sucrose (table sugar).

- Take this medication by mouth on an empty stomach, at least 1 hour before or 1 hour after meals, usually every 12 hours or as directed.

- The liquid suspension should not be refrigerated.

- There are many interactions with this drug and other medicines. Please discuss with your pharmacist to make sure this will not pose a problem.

- Do not use this medication if you are pregnant, if you could become pregnant, or if you are breastfeeding.

- Contact your healthcare provider right away if you are passing brown or dark-colored urine, feel more tired than usual or if your skin and whites of your eyes become yellow. These may be symptoms of liver damage.

Summary of Patient Counseling Points for Commonly Used Oral Antimicrobial Agents

ANTIBIOTIC	WITH H₂0	WITH FOOD	W/O FOOD	SUN SENS.	GI (N/V/D)	RASH	HA & CNS	OTHER
Amoxicillin(clav)		X			X	X		Refrigerate: amox/clav susp.
Azithromycin		X	ER susp.		X			Keep susp. at room temp
Cefdinir		X	X		X	X		Keep susp. at room temp
Cephalexin		X	X		X	X		Refrigerate susp.
Clarithromycin		X			X			*Biaxin XL:* Take with food Keep susp. at room temp
Clindamycin	X	X	X		X (↑D)			Keep susp. at room temp
Doxycycline	X		X (cations)	X	X		X	Keep susp. at room temp
Fluconazole		X	X		X	X	X	S/Sx of hepatotoxicity Keep susp. at room temp
Fluoroquinolone	X		X (cations)	X	X	X	X	Tendon Rupture Rare... Keep susp. at room temp
Metronidazole	X	X			X		X	Avoid alcohol, carcinogen
Nitrofurantoin		X			X		X	May darken urine, SOB
Oseltamivir		X	X		X			Start w/in 48h of Sx onset
Terbinafine		X	X		X (taste)			S/Sx of hepatotoxicity
TMP/SMX		X	X	X	X	X (sulfa)		Keep susp. at room temp
(Val)acyclovir	X	X	X		X		X	Start w/in 24h of Sx onset
Voriconazole			X	X	X	X	X/eye	S/Sx of hepatotoxicity Keep susp. at room temp

CNS=CNS toxicity (drowsy, confusion, ocular, activation, etc.), ER=extended release, H₂O=water, HA=headache, N/V/D=nausea/vomiting/diarrhea, S/Sx=signs/symptoms, SOB=shortness of breath, sun sens.=sensitivity, susp.=suspension, w/in = within, w/o=without

PRACTICE CASE

MJ is a 43 year old female who presents to the doctor with fever, runny nose, congestion, productive cough, and body aches. She tells you that she has been feeling this way for the past 36 hours and she needs to get better to return to work. She noticed a lot of people coughing on the bus she takes to work and figures that is where she picked it up.

CATEGORY	
PMH	Depression, GERD
Vitals	BP 164/81 HR 114 RR 24 Temp 102.3
Current medications	Fluoxetine 20 mg PO daily
	Ranitidine 150 mg PO BID
	Tums PRN
Labs	K+ 3.5 mEq/L, SCr 1.1 mg/dL
Allergies	Sulfa (major hives, extreme rash)

Questions

1. The doctor confirms by chest X-ray that MJ has community-acquired pneumonia. What is the most appropriate therapy for MJ?

    a. *Zithromax* 500 mg PO x 1, then 250 mg PO daily (days 2-5)

    b. *Avelox* 400 mg IV daily x 5-7 days

    c. *Levaquin* 500 mg PO x 1, then 250 mg PO daily x 5-7 days

    d. *Ceftin* 500 mg PO Q12H x 5-7 days

    e. *Bactrim* 1 DS tab PO Q12H x 5-7 days

2. MJ has accidentally lost the prescription and she cannot afford another office visit. She decides to tough it out and goes back to work. Two days later, MJ is admitted to the hospital due to worsening symptoms. What is the best agent(s) to treat her community-acquired pneumonia in the inpatient setting?

    a. Ciprofloxacin 500 mg PO daily

    b. Ceftriaxone 1 gram IV daily

    c. Ceftriaxone 1 gram IV daily + azithromycin 500 mg IV daily

    d. Vancomycin 1 gram IV Q12H + imipenem 500 mg Q6H

    e. Gemifloxacin 320 mg PO daily + clarithromycin 500 mg PO Q12H

3. While in the hospital, MJ develops a *Pseudomonal* infection in her lungs as well. Which of the following antibiotics would be an appropriate choice for coverage of *Pseudomonas*?

    a. Ampicillin

    b. Cubicin

    c. Invanz

    d. Doribax

    e. Tygacil

4. MJ's condition is not improving. She was placed on vancomycin a few days ago and now she has developed vancomycin-resistant *Enterococcus faecium*. The medical team puts her on linezolid. Which of the following statements regarding linezolid is correct?

    a. It is in a new class called cyclic lipopeptides.

    b. It is a MAO inhibitor and should be avoided with serotonergic agents.

    c. It is a combination product consisting of quinupristin and dalfopristin.

    d. It needs to be dose adjusted in patients with renal impairment.

    e. It is not effective for treating infections in the lung.

5. MJ has now been in the hospital for a month. She is still febrile, has an increased WBC count, and remains unable to wean from the ventilator. She has been on many intravenous antibacterial agents. The team decided to re-culture her and now they find *C. albicans* in the blood. They tried treating with fluconazole with no improvement. The team decides to treat with anidulafungin. Which of the following is correct regarding anidulafungin?

   a. This medication should be taken with meals for best absorption.

   b. This medication can cause an increase in liver transaminases.

   c. This medication is not effective for the treatment of candidemia.

   d. This medication needs to be dose adjusted in renal impairment.

   e. The brand name is *Cancidas*.

6. MJ has turned the corner and was discharged home a few weeks later. After about 3-4 months, she returns to the doctor complaining of intense burning on urination, dysuria, and frequency of bathroom visits. The doctor confirms that she has a urinary tract infection caused by *E. coli*, which is sensitive to everything. Which of the following is the best choice to treat MJ's UTI?

   a. *Bactrim* SS 1 tab PO BID x 3 days

   b. *Bactrim* DS 1 tab PO BID x 3 days

   c. Nitrofurantoin 100 mg PO BID x 3 days

   d. Nitrofurantoin 100 mg PO BID x 5 days

   e. Phenazopyridine 200 mg TID x 2 days

Questions 7-18 do not apply to the case

7. Which of the following statements regarding the intravenous formulation of *Bactrim* is/are correct? (Select **ALL** that apply.)

   a. *Bactrim* IV should be protected from light.

   b. *Bactrim* IV should be refrigerated.

   c. *Bactrim* IV is compatible with NS.

   d. *Bactrim* IV needs to be dose adjusted in patients with significant renal impairment.

   e. *Bactrim* IV can be converted to *Bactrim* PO in a 1:1 fashion.

8. You are working in the ER when an intern comes to you and asks how to treat the patient in room 4 who has a gonorrheal STD infection. What is the best recommendation to treat this patient?

   a. Levofloxacin 750 mg PO x 1

   b. Doxycycline 100 mg PO BID x 7 days

   c. Benzathine penicillin G 2.4 million units IM x 1

   d. Metronidazole 2 grams PO x 1

   e. Ceftriaxone 250 mg IM x 1 + azithromycin 1 gram PO x 1

9. The intern is back. This time to ask you about herpes simplex virus and *Valtrex*. Which of the following statements is correct regarding *Valtrex*?

   a. *Valtrex* is a prodrug of acyclovir and can be used as suppressive therapy in patients with herpes simplex virus.

   b. *Valtrex* is a prodrug of penciclovir and should not be used as suppressive therapy in patients with herpes simplex virus.

   c. *Valtrex* should only be used for herpes zoster virus.

   d. *Valtrex* needs to be taken with a fatty meal for best absorption.

   e. *Valtrex* is contraindicated in patients with a CrCl < 30 mL/min.

10. Tommy is taking isoniazid (INH) as part of his tuberculosis treatment. Which of the following is/are correct regarding INH? (Select **ALL** that apply.)

   a. INH should be taken 1 hour before or 2 hours after a meal on an empty stomach.

   b. INH is a potent enzyme inducer.

   c. INH is contraindicated in acute gout.

   d. INH can be used alone to treat latent TB.

   e. INH requires dose adjustments in renal impairment.

11. Which of the following medications will help prevent peripheral neuropathies in patients taking isoniazid?

   a. Pyrazinamide

   b. Pyridoxine

   c. *Pyridium*

   d. Pyridostigmine

   e. Pyrimethamine

12. A patient taking amphotericin B is at risk for which electrolyte abnormalities?

    a. Hypocalcemia and hypomagnesemia
    b. Hyponatremia and hypokalemia
    c. Hypernatremia and hyperkalemia
    d. Hypokalemia and hypernatremia
    e. Hypokalemia and hypomagnesemia

13. A patient comes into your clinic. She is 5 months pregnant and has a UTI. She is allergic to cephalexin. Which of the following regimens would be the best choice for her?

    a. *Bactrim* 1 DS tab BID x 3 days
    b. *Cipro ER* 500 mg PO daily x 7 days
    c. Nitrofurantoin 100 mg PO BID x 7 days
    d. Cefpodoxime 100 mg PO Q12H x 7 days
    e. Do not treat since she is pregnant.

14. Which of the following statements is/are correct regarding *VFEND*? (Select **ALL** that apply.)

    a. *VFEND* can cause visual changes and patients should be instructed not to operate heavy machinery while taking the medication.
    b. *VFEND* must be taken on an empty stomach.
    c. *VFEND* oral tablets should not be used in patients with poor renal function.
    d. *VFEND* oral suspension should be refrigerated.
    e. *VFEND* is a preferred agent for *Aspergillosis* infections.

15. Which of the following antibiotics do <u>not</u> require dose adjustment in renal impairment?

    a. Gentamicin
    b. Clarithromycin
    c. Cefixime
    d. Tigecycline
    e. Daptomycin

16. Which of the following antibiotics should be refrigerated?

    a. *Cipro*
    b. *Keflex*
    c. *Levaquin*
    d. *Septra*
    e. *Zithromax*

17. You should counsel a patient to use sunscreen when taking which of the following medication(s)? (Select **ALL** that apply.)

    a. *Cleocin*
    b. *Biaxin*
    c. *Avelox*
    d. *VFEND*
    e. *Tamiflu*

18. Which of the following antimicrobials in IV formulation is stable in and preferred to be reconstituted in normal saline (NS)?

    a. Quinupristin/dalfopristin
    b. Amphotericin B
    c. Ampicillin
    d. TMP/SMX
    e. Acyclovir

Answers

1-a, 2-c, 3-d, 4-b, 5-b, 6-d, 7-a,d,e, 8-e, 9-a, 10-a,d, 11-b, 12-e, 13-c, 14-a,b,e, 15-d, 16-b, 17-c,d, 18-c

IMMUNIZATION

We gratefully acknowledge the assistance of Jeannette Y. Wick, RPh, in preparing this chapter.

BACKGROUND

Immunizations in the United States over the past century are one of public health's greatest achievements. Since vaccines are medications, pharmacists should review immunization histories with patients. Vaccines prevent patients from acquiring serious or potentially fatal diseases. Many formerly prevalent childhood diseases (diphtheria, measles, meningitis, polio, tetanus) are rare because many children are vaccinated to prevent the illness, and others are protected by herd immunity (people around them are protected – thus they are less likely to catch the illness). If immunization rates drop below 85% to 95%, vaccine-preventable diseases may once again become common threats, as recent scattered pertussis outbreaks in the United States demonstrate.

GUIDELINES/REFERENCES

Immunization recommendations are written by the CDC Advisory Committee on Immunization Practices (ACIP) and the Committee on Infectious Diseases of the American Academy of Pediatrics (AAP). The pediatric and adult schedules are updated annually and published in January. Since the ACIP meets several times throughout the year to review new information, updates are published in Morbidity and Mortality Weekly Report (MMWR). Updated immunization schedules are available at www.cdc.gov.

The CDC's Pink Book, Epidemiology and Prevention of Vaccine Preventable Disease. is published every 2 years and is available at www.cdc.gov.

Helpful resources for immunizing pharmacists are available on the following three websites:

- www.pharmacist.com/imz (American Pharmacists Association)

- www.cdc.gov/vaccines (Centers for Disease Control and Prevention/Vaccines and Immunizations)

- www.immunize.org (Immunization Action Coalition)

Read through the background information before reviewing the individual vaccines. Immunization is currently taught in most pharmacy schools and has become standard pharmacy practice in many settings, especially in the community pharmacy. Principles of immunization should be well understood.

The CDC Advisory Committee on Immunization Practices (ACIP) develops written recommendations for the routine administration of vaccines to children and adults in the civilian population. The Immunization Action Coalition's website has useful information for clinicians, such as vaccine records and clinic tools.

Safety Concerns

Some parents withhold vaccines due to misconceptions about the risk of autism, a developmental disorder. There is no evidence that vaccines cause autism. Thimerosal, a mercury-containing preservative used in vaccines, was thought to be a possible cause since mercury has been linked to some brain disorders. Evidence does not suggest or prove that thimerosal poses a risk for or is linked to autism. Thimerosal has been removed from most childhood vaccines. Others thought the risk was due to providing multiple vaccines concurrently at an early age. Although the autism rates have not decreased among communities with a high rate of vaccine refusal, about 7% of parents remain concerned. This will likely continue to be an issue until the causes of autism are better understood. Promoting vaccination requires open communication and education.

Usually, vaccine side effects are minor and include mild fever and soreness or swelling at the injection site. Some vaccines cause headache, loss of appetite and dizziness – but these quickly dissipate. Very rarely (and mostly in children who have limited vaccine experience) anaphylaxis can occur. Anyone giving vaccines must screen for previous reactions and be prepared to treat a severe reaction. Some vaccines have specific contraindications to use, such as a true egg allergy with the some of the influenza vaccines (this has been "softened" in recent years; see allergy discussion in this chapter), and with yellow fever and rabies vaccine.

Federal law requires that patients receive the most up-to-date version of the Vaccine Information Statement (VIS) BEFORE EACH vaccine is administered. The VIS standardized forms describe the risk and benefit of the vaccines, purpose of the vaccine, who should receive it and who should not, and what the patient can expect for both mild and serious adverse effects. VISs are created by the CDC and updated versions are available on the CDC and IAC websites.

Pharmacist's Role in Immunization

Pharmacists in the community setting have increased immunization rates, particularly by providing influenza, meningococcal, pneumococcal, pertussis (in Tdap) and herpes zoster (shingles) vaccinations. Our role is expanding to include more vaccines and management of immunization clinics in health care settings. Pharmacists have become increasingly involved in pre-travel health services, providing travel advice, medications and immunizations per protocol for international travel. During comprehensive medication therapy management (MTM) sessions and in many inpatient and community pharmacy settings, pharmacists routinely screen and order vaccines (e.g., pneumococcal, Tdap, and seasonally, influenza), per protocols.

Principles of Immunity

Immunity is the ability of the human body to tolerate the presence of material indigenous to the body ("self"), and to eliminate foreign ("nonself") material. This discriminatory ability provides protection from infectious disease, since most microbes are identified as foreign by the immune system. Immunity to a microbe is usually indicated by the presence of antibody to that organism. There are two basic mechanisms for acquiring immunity, active and passive.

Active and Passive Immunity

Active immunity is protection that is produced by the person's own immune system. This type of immunity is usually permanent. One way to acquire active immunity is to survive an infection. Another way to produce active immunity is by vaccination. Passive immunity is protection by products produced by an animal or human and transferred to a human, usually by injection. This protection wanes with time, usually within a few weeks or months. The most common form of passive immunity is the antibodies an infant receives from the mother. Many types of blood products contain antibody, including intravenous immune globulin and plasma products.

Live Attenuated and Inactivated Vaccines

Live attenuated (weakened) vaccines are produced by modifying a disease-producing ("wild") virus or bacterium in a laboratory; they retain the ability to replicate (grow) and produce immunity, but usually do not cause illness. Administering live vaccines to immunocompromised patients may be contraindicated since uncontrolled replication of the pathogen could take place (see other chapters for immunization recommendations in specific populations, such as in diabetes). Live attenuated vaccines produce a strong immune response since the body's response to the vaccine is similar to actual disease.

Inactivated vaccines can be composed of either whole viruses or bacteria, or fractions of either. Antibody titers against inactivated antigens diminish with time. As a result, some inactivated vaccines may require periodic supplemental doses to increase, or "boost" antibody titers.

General rule

The more similar a vaccine is to the disease-causing form of the organism, the better the immune response to the vaccine.

Timing and Spacing of Vaccines

Vaccines and antibody products may require a separation period. The presence of circulating antibody to a vaccine antigen may reduce or completely eliminate the immune response to the vaccine. The amount of interference produced by circu-

SEPARATION TIME BETWEEN MEASLES AND VARICELLA *(VARIVAX)* VACCINES	
PRODUCT GIVEN FIRST	**ACTION**
Vaccine	Wait 2 weeks before giving antibody
Antibody	Wait 3 months or longer before giving vaccine
Except zoster vaccine	

lating antibody generally depends on the type of vaccine administered and the amount of antibody.

Inactivated antigens are generally not affected by circulating antibody, so they can be administered before, after, or at the same time as the antibody. Live vaccines, however, must replicate in order to cause an immune response and antibody against injected live vaccine antigen may interfere with replication. If the live vaccine is given first, it is necessary to wait at least 2 weeks (i.e., an incubation period) before giving the antibody.

The necessary interval between an antibody-containing blood product and MMR or varicella-containing vaccine (except zoster vaccine – this is not affected by circulating antibody) is always 3 months and may be up to 11 months. The specific blood product and dose administered determines the time interval. Consult "The Pink Book" to determine the specific recommended interval. During vaginal childbirth maternal antibodies are passed from the mother to the baby and may reduce the live vaccine response in the baby. This is why live vaccines are withheld until the child is 12 months. Inactivated vaccines are started at the age of 2 months, with the exception of Hepatitis B vaccine which can be started at birth.

Simultaneous administration of antibody (in the form of immune globulin) and vaccine is recommended for postexposure prophylaxis of certain diseases, such as hepatitis B, rabies and tetanus.

Simultaneous Administration

Administering the most common live or inactivated vaccines simultaneously (on the same day or at the same visit) does not decrease antibody responses and does not increase the rate of adverse reactions. Simultaneous administration of all vaccines for which a child is eligible is very important in childhood vaccination programs. It increases the probability that a child will be fully immunized at the appropriate age.

According to the ACIP, there are no contraindications to simultaneous administration of any of the vaccines currently available in the United States and every effort should be made to provide all necessary vaccinations at one visit.

Non-Simultaneous Administration of Different Vaccines

In some situations, vaccines that could be given at the same visit are not. If live parenteral (injected) vaccines (MMR, MMRV, varicella, zoster, and yellow fever) and live intranasal or influenza vaccine (LAIV) are not administered at the same visit, they should be separated by at least 4 weeks.

Intervals of Doses between Vaccines given in Series

Increasing the interval between doses of a multidose vaccine does not diminish the effectiveness of the vaccine after completion of all doses. It may, however, delay more complete protection. Decreasing the interval between doses of a multidose vaccine may interfere with antibody response and protection. Following a high risk exposure, a shorter interval may be used. In that situation either revaccinate after the recommended interval or check antibody titers.

INTERVAL FOR ADMINISTRATION OF LIVE VACCINES AND TB TEST

The skin test with purified protein derivative (PPD) of tuberculin and live vaccines can be administered on the same day and is the preferred method to avoid a false negative response to the skin test. If a live vaccine has been given recently (but not on the same day) as the PPD, wait 4 weeks before giving the PPD in order to avoid a false negative TB test result. False negative TB test results delay treatment of tuberculosis infection and are a significant risk to the patient and to public health. If the PPD test was given recently but not on the same day as the live vaccine, then wait 48-72 hours and determine the PPD results before administering the live vaccine.

Vaccine Side Effects or Adverse Reactions

Vaccine adverse reactions fall into three general categories: local, systemic, and allergic. Local reactions are generally the least severe and most frequent. Allergic reactions are the most severe and least frequent.

The most common type of adverse reactions are local reactions, such as pain, swelling and redness at the site of injection. Local reactions may occur with up to 80% of vaccine doses, depending on the vaccine type. Local reactions are most common with inactivated vaccines, particularly those, such as DTaP, that contain an adjuvant. These reactions generally occur within a few hours of the injection and are usually mild and self-limited. Rarely, local reactions may be very exaggerated or severe.

Systemic adverse reactions are more generalized events and include fever, malaise, myalgias (muscle pain), headache, loss of appetite, and others. These symptoms are common and non-specific; they may occur in vaccinated persons because of the vaccine or may be caused by something unrelated to the vaccine, such as a concurrent viral infection. Systemic adverse reactions following live vaccines are usually mild, and occur 7–21 days after the vaccine was given (i.e., after an incubation period of the vaccine virus). Intranasal LAIV is cold adapted, meaning it can replicate in the cooler temperatures of upper airways (nose and throat) but not in the higher temperatures of the lower airways and the lungs. Mild cold-like symptoms such as a runny nose may occur.

A third type of vaccine adverse reaction is a severe (anaphylactic) allergic reaction. The allergic reaction may be caused by the vaccine antigen itself or some other component of the vaccine, such as cell culture material, stabilizer, preservative, or antibiotic used to inhibit bacterial growth. Severe allergic reactions may be life-threatening. Fortunately, they are rare, occurring at a rate of less than one in half a million doses. The risk of an allergic reaction can be minimized by good screening prior to vaccination. A severe (anaphylactic) allergic reaction following a dose of vaccine will almost always contraindicate a subsequent dose of that vaccine. Anaphylactic allergies are those that are mediated by IgE, occur within minutes or hours of receiving the vaccine, and require immediate medical attention. Examples of symptoms and signs typical of anaphylactic reactions are generalized urticaria (hives), swelling of the mouth and throat, difficulty breathing, wheezing, abdominal cramping, hypotension, or shock. In the event of an anaphylactic reaction, the appropriate emergency protocols should be followed and epinephrine should be immediately accessible. Immunizations should never be administered if epinephrine is not available.

Providers should report clinically significant adverse events to the FDA's Vaccine Adverse Event Reporting System (VAERS) even if they are unsure whether a vaccine caused the event.

All providers who administer vaccines must have emergency protocols and supplies to treat anaphylaxis. If symptoms are generalized, a second person should activate the emergency medical system (EMS; e.g., call 911) and notify the on-call physician. The primary health care provider should remain with the patient, assessing the airway, breathing, circulation, and level of consciousness.

- Administer aqueous epinephrine 1:1000 dilution intramuscularly, 0.01 mg per kg of body weight per dose, up to a 0.5 mg maximum per dose.

- Most pharmacies use *EpiPens* or another epinephrine injection device are stocked, at least three adult (0.3 mg) should be available. should be available. Patients taking beta blockers may need higher or more frequent doses of epinephrine.

- In addition, for systemic anaphylaxis such as generalized urticaria, administer diphenhydramine either orally or by injection. Due to the risk of choking, no drug should be administered orally if the patient is exhibiting signs of mouth, throat or lip swelling or difficulty breathing.

- Monitor the patient closely until EMS arrives. Perform cardiopulmonary resuscitation (CPR), if necessary, and maintain the airway. Keep patient in a supine position (flat on back) unless he or she is having breathing difficulty. If breathing is difficult, the patient's head may be elevated, provided blood pressure is adequate to prevent loss of consciousness. If blood pressure is low, elevate legs. Monitor blood pressure and pulse every 5 minutes.

- If EMS has not arrived and symptoms are still present, repeat dose of epinephrine.

- Record all vital signs, medications administered to the patient, including the time, dosage, response, the name of the medical personnel who administered the medication and other relevant clinical information.

- Notify the patient's primary care physician.

- Report reaction to VAERS.

- Immunizing pharmacists should always maintain a current basic life support (BLS or CPR) certification.

Contraindications and Precautions

Contraindications and precautions to vaccination generally dictate circumstances when vaccines will not be given. Most contraindications and precautions are temporary, and the vaccine can be given at a later time.

A contraindication is a condition that greatly increases a potential vaccine recipient's chance of a serious adverse reaction. It is a condition related to the recipient, not with the vaccine per se. For instance, administering influenza vaccine (except *Flucelvax* or *Flubok*) to a person with a true anaphylactic allergy to egg could cause serious illness or death. In general, vaccines should not be administered when a contraindicated condition is present.

STEROID-INDUCED IMMUNOSUPPRESSION

CORTICOSTEROIDS
- 20 mg or more per day of prednisone
- 2 mg/kg or more per day of prednisone*
- NOT intra-articular injections, metered-dose inhalers, topical, alternate day or short course for less than 14 days

For 14 days or longer

Two conditions are absolute contraindications to vaccination with live vaccines: pregnancy and immunosuppression. Two conditions are temporary precautions to vaccination: moderate or severe acute illness (all vaccines), and recent receipt of an antibody-containing blood product. The latter precaution applies only to MMR and varicella-containing (except zoster) vaccines.

Immunosuppression

Live vaccines can cause severe or fatal reactions in immunocompromised people due to uncontrolled replication of the vaccine virus or reduced vaccine efficacy. Live vaccines should not be administered to severely immunosuppressed persons for this reason. Certain drugs may cause immunosuppression. For instance, anyone receiving cancer treatment with alkylating agents or antimetabolites or radiation therapy should not be given live vaccines. Live vaccines can be given after chemotherapy has been discontinued for at least 3 months. People or individuals receiving large doses of cortico-

---

INVALID CONTRAINDICATIONS TO VACCINATION
VACCINATIONS MAY BE GIVEN, IF REQUIRED & INDICATED

- Mild acute illness (slight fever, mild diarrhea)
- Antimicrobial therapy (exceptions are certain antiviral medications and oral typhoid vaccine)
- Local skin reactions (mild/moderate)
- Bird feather allergies
- Recent infectious disease exposure
- Penicillin allergy
- Disease exposure or convalescence
- Pregnant or immunosuppressive person in the household

- Breastfeeding
- Preterm birth
- Allergy to products not present in vaccine or allergy that is not anaphylactic
- Family history of adverse events
- Tuberculin skin test (see above for timing and spacing with live vaccines only)
- Multiple vaccines

steroids should not receive live vaccines (see the sidebar). Individuals infected with human immunodeficiency virus (HIV) may have no symptoms, or they may be severely immunosuppressed. Live vaccines are only contraindicated for HIV patients with CD4 T lymphocyte counts < 200 cells/mm³. In general, the same vaccination recommendations apply as with other types of immunosuppression. Live-virus vaccines are usually contraindicated, but the disease may indicate the need for certain inactivated vaccines such as pneumococcal. Transplant (adult) patients should receive receive PCV13 first, followed by PPSV23 at least 8 weeks later. Subsequent doses of PPSV23 should follow current PPSV23 recommendations for adults at high risk (5 years after the first PPSV23 dose). Some of the transplant centers recommend PPSV23 every 5 years.

VACCINATION OF PREGNANT WOMEN

- Live vaccines should not be administered to women 1 month before or during pregnancy

- In general, inactivated vaccines may be administered to pregnant women for whom they are indicated

- HPV vaccine should be deferred during pregnancy

- Pregnant women should receive the influenza vaccine (in season) and Tdap.

Vaccinations During Pregnancy

The most frequent vaccine administered to pregnant women is the influenza (shot, inactivated – not live) vaccine. It is indicated in all trimesters of pregnancy. Pregnant women should receive Tdap with each pregnancy. This includes female health care workers. The optimum time for Tdap vaccination is between weeks 27 and 36. If the woman has not been vaccinated or her vaccination history is unclear, a 3-dose series is needed; one Tdap then two Td doses at 1-2 months and 6 months. If the woman delivers and has not received vaccination, she should receive it post-delivery. Vaccination protects the baby (and the mother) from pertussis (whooping cough).

VACCINATIONS FOR HEALTHCARE PROFESSIONALS

Hepatitis B

If no documented evidence of a complete hepB vaccine series, or if without an up-to-date blood test that shows immunity to hepatitis B (i.e., no serologic evidence of immunity or prior vaccination) then the healthcare professional should:

- Get the 3-dose series (dose #1 now, #2 in 1 month, #3 approximately 5 months after #2).

- Get anti-HBs serologic tested 1–2 months after dose #3.

Flu (Influenza)

- Get 1 dose of influenza vaccine annually.

MMR (Measles, Mumps, & Rubella)

- If born in 1957 or later and have not had the MMR vaccine, or if lacking an up-to-date blood test showing immunity to measles, mumps, and rubella (i.e., no serologic evidence of immunity or prior vaccination), get 2 doses of MMR, 4 weeks apart. If varicella is needed, consider using MMRV.

Varicella (Chickenpox)

■ If no history of having had chickenpox (varicella), if no varicella vaccine received, or if without an up-to-date blood test showing immunity to varicella (i.e., no serologic evidence of immunity or prior vaccination) get 2 doses of varicella vaccine, 4 weeks apart.

Tdap (Tetanus, Diphtheria, Pertussis)

■ Get a one-time dose of Tdap as soon as possible if no Tdap previously (regardless of when previous dose of Td was received). Get Td boosters every 10 years thereafter. Pregnant health care workers need to get a dose of Tdap during each pregnancy.

Meningococcal

■ Those who are routinely exposed to isolates of *N. meningitidis* should get one dose.

Allergies to Vaccine Components

Anaphylaxis after a previous dose of the vaccine is a contraindication to the vaccine in the future. Egg allergy recommendations have changed in recent years for some vaccines. If a person can eat lightly cooked eggs without a reaction, or if the person experiences ONLY hives after eating egg-containing foods, inactivated influenza vaccine can be administered and the patient should be observed for a reaction for at least 30 minutes after administration. If a patient experiences cardiovascular changes, respiratory distress, or has symptoms of anaphylaxis after consuming eggs, refer to a physician with expertise in the management of allergic conditions. Some of the influenza vaccines can be administered by a specialist in the presence of an egg allergy. Yellow fever and rabies vaccines can provoke an allergic reaction in persons with an egg allergy, but they are sometimes given under medical supervision after testing for a reaction. Allergy to eggs is no longer considered a contraindication for giving MMR vaccine. Several vaccines are not absolute contraindications but caution is advised if the patient has a history of Guillian-Barré syndrome (tetanus containing vaccines, influenza, MCV). Both varicella vaccines (*Zostavax* and *Varivax*) and MMR should not be given to anyone with a true gelatin or neomycin allergy. Inactivated poliovirus vaccine (IPV) is contraindicated with streptomycin, polymyxin B and neomycin allergies. Check for contraindications for any vaccine in the CDC's Guide to Vaccine Contraindications and Precautions or by using the vaccine's package insert.

Screening Prior to Vaccine Administration

Use a screening form to rule out specific contraindications to the vaccine:

1. Are you sick today?

2. Do you have allergies to medications, food, a vaccine component, or latex?

3. Have you ever had a serious reaction after receiving a vaccination?

4. Do you have a long-term health problem with heart disease, lung disease, asthma, kidney disease, metabolic disease (e.g., diabetes), anemia, or other blood disorder?

5. Do you have cancer, leukemia, AIDS, or any other immune system problem?

6. Do you take cortisone, prednisone, other steroids, or anticancer drugs, or have you had radiation treatments?

7. Have you had a seizure or a brain or other nervous system problem?

8. Do you have cochlear implants or a cerebrovascular leak?

9. During the past year, have you received a transfusion of blood or blood products, or been given immune (gamma) globulin or an antiviral drug?

10. For women: Are you pregnant or is there a chance you could become pregnant during the next month?

11. Have you received any vaccinations in the past 4 weeks?

Immunization Registries

Immunization registries are computerized information systems that collect vaccination histories and help ensure correct and timely immunizations, especially for children. They are useful for healthcare providers who use the registries to obtain the patient's history, produce vaccine records, manage vaccine inventories, among other benefits. It helps the community at-large to identify groups who are not receiving vaccines in order to target outreach efforts. Some systems are able to notify parents if vaccines are needed.

Registries in one state or area may not be compatible with other registries, and information may have to be manually transferred between registries. Also, to protect personal information in registries, this information cannot be directly retrieved by individuals.

DRUG	ADMINISTER TO	STORAGE/ADMINISTRATION
Diphtheria Toxoid-, Tetanus Toxoid- and acellular Pertussis-Containing Vaccines		
DTaP: *DAPTACEL, Infanrix, Tripedia* DTaP-IPV: *KINRIX* DTaP-HepB-IPV: *Pediarix* DTaP-IPV/Hib: *Pentacel*	<u>DTaP series given to children younger than 7 years of age.</u>	Store in the refrigerator. Do not freeze. Shake the prefilled syringe or vial before use. Give IM.
Haemophilus influenzae type b-Containing Vaccines		
Hib: *ActHIB, Hiberix, PedvaxHIB* Hib-HepB: *Comvax* DTaP-IPV/Hib: *Pentacel*	Hib: Given to children. Sometimes in adults if HIV+, splenectomy, sickle cell disease, leukemia, or if they have not previously received Hib vaccine.	Store in the refrigerator. Do not freeze. Shake the prefilled syringe or vial before use. Give IM.

Vaccines Continued

DRUG	ADMINISTER TO	STORAGE/ADMINISTRATION

Hepatitis-Containing Vaccines

DRUG	ADMINISTER TO	STORAGE/ADMINISTRATION
HepA: *Havrix, Vaqta* **HepB:** *Engerix-B, Recombivax HB* **HepA-HepB:** *Twinrix* DTaP-HepB-IPV: *Pediarix* Hib-HepB: *Comvax*	Hep A is given to children > 1 year of age as a routine vaccination. Hep A in adults for men who have sex with men, IV drug abusers, chronic disease, travelers to countries with high Hep A incidence. Hep B Health care workers (required by OSHA), men who have sex with men, anyone who has sex with multiple partners, IV drug users, ESRD, chronic liver disease. Hep B is a 3-dose series given at 0, 1 and 6 months for adolescents and adults. Infants – dose 1: given at birth; dose 2: 1-2 months of age; dose 3: no earlier than 24 weeks (only if administering HBV vaccine by itself. Does not apply to pediatric combination products such as *Comvax)* If combined Hep A/Hep B vaccine (*Twinrix*) is used, administer 3 doses at 0, 1, and 6 months; a 4-dose *Twinrix* schedule is approved for accelerated dosing, administered on days 0, 7, and 21 to 30, followed by a booster dose at month 12.	Store in refrigerator. Do not freeze. Shake the vial or prefilled syringe before use. Give IM. HepA: Older than 18 years inject 1 mL intramuscularly. The two available brands can be used interchangeably. HepB: 20 years and older inject 1 mL intramuscularly. The two available brands have varying dosing indications. Check prior to administration.

Human Papillomavirus Vaccines: Prevents 70% of cervical cancers, as well as vulvar, vaginal, oropharyngeal, anal and penile cancers.

DRUG	ADMINISTER TO	STORAGE/ADMINISTRATION
HPV2: *Cervarix* Bivalent vaccine. Only provides immunity against the HPV strains that cause cervical cancer. **HPV4:** *Gardasil* Quadrivalent vaccine. Provides immunity against HPV strains responsible for causing cervical cancer, PAP smear abnormalities, and genital warts. Either vaccine recommended for females. Only *Gardasil* is indicated for males. Primary prevention of cervical CA is via vaccination, secondary prevention is via screening. Cervical CA has high mortality.	HPV vaccine is indicated for females age 9-26 years. ACIP recommends the 3 dose series between the age of 11-12 years, with catch-up vaccination at age 13-26 years. Vaccination can begin at age 9 years and ideally prior to sexual activity. Males 9-26 years to reduce the likelihood of genital warts or anal cancers. Requires 3 doses. The 2nd dose is 1–2 months after the 1st and the 3rd 6 months after the 1st.	Store in the refrigerator. Do not freeze. Protect from light. Shake the prefilled syringe or vial before use. Give IM.

Vaccines Continued

DRUG	ADMINISTER TO	STORAGE/ADMINISTRATION

Influenza Vaccines: Most illness occurs in young children, most severe illness occurs in people > 65 years or those with comorbid conditions.

Live attenuated influenza vaccine (LAIV): *FluMist Quadrivalent*

Inactivated influenza vaccine (IIV): *Afluria, Fluarix, Fluarix Quadrivalent, FluLaval Quadrivalent, Fluvirin, Fluzone, Fluzone Quadrivalent, Fluzone High-Dose, Fluzone Intradermal, Flucelvex*

RIV (egg-free): *FluBlok*

High-dose *(Fluzone)* licensed in 2010 for adults aged ≥ 65, trivalent like others but contains 60 mcg of each strain vs 15 mcg in others (4x hemagluttinin). ACIP has no preference for the high dose in elderly, but the prescriber (or patient) may request it.

Fluzone Intradermal (18-64 yrs only) uses smaller needle (30 gauge, 1.5 mm vs 22 to 25 gauge, 15.8- 38.1 mm). Smaller needle, but more redness, swelling, itching. Preg B (other influenza shots are Preg C)

Trivalent (3 strains) and Quadrivalent (4 strains)
Fluzone, Fluarix, FluLaval

Quadrivalent Only
FluMist

Trivalent Only
All other formulations

Completely Egg-Free
FluBlok (recombinant)

ACIP recommends influenza immunization for EVERYONE (starting at 6 months of age) every year. ALL children need 1 shot annually, regardless of history. EXCEPT: Previously unvaccinated children younger than 8 years old or those who have had < 2 shots since July 1, 2010 need two shots > 4 weeks apart.

■ 6 mos-35 mos, 0.25 mL/dose

■ 3+ yrs: 0.5 mL/dose.

People aged 2-49 years including healthcare personnel can receive the nasal spray, if healthy, and not pregnant.

Healthy, non-pregnant adults aged 2-49 years, without high-risk medical conditions can receive either LAIV or IIV (IM or intradermal).

Flu vaccine for 2013-2014 must be at a minimum, trivalent (3 strains):

■ an A/California/7/2009 (H1N1)pdm09-like virus;

■ an A(H3N2) virus antigenically like the cell-propagated prototype virus A/Victoria/361/2011;

■ a B/Massachusetts/2/2012-like virus.

The new, recently-licensed quadrivalent vaccines include an additional influenza B liniage (a B/Brisbane/60/2008-like virus).

Store all influenza vaccines in the refrigerator. Do not freeze.

Give vaccine as soon as it is available, even if it arrives in late summer and preferably before October. Offer throughout the influenza season; Outbreaks usually peak in February or later.

Revaccinate each year.

INACTIVATED INFLUENZA VACCINE
administer or *Fluzone Quadrivalent*

Two inactivated (shot) precautions:

1. Defer if patient has moderate-severe acute illness.

2. Refer to physician if patient had Guillain–Barré within 6 weeks of a prior dose of flu vaccine.

Those who can eat lightly cooked eggs without reactions or if they experience ONLY hives after eating eggs can receive inactivated vaccine and be observed for 30 minutes. See "Allergy to Vaccine Components" for details. (*FluBlok* is egg-free and approved for adults aged 18-49.)

Afluria: Note the product is labeled for children > 5 years old, but ACIP recommends giving it after age <u>9 years or older</u> due to reports of febrile illness in young children. If vaccine shortage occurs, discuss risks/benefits of using *Afluria* in younger children with parents.

Fluzone Intradermal is the only product that can be given intradermally (ID):

Have patient sitting, arm bent at elbow, hand on hip, straight down into deltoid.

Flumist Quadrivalent: is given as 0.2 mL, divided between the two nostrils. Guidelines in previously unvaccinated children are the same as for the inactivated shot, but only in children aged 2 to 9.

Vaccines Continued

DRUG	ADMINISTER TO	STORAGE/ADMINISTRATION

Measles, Mumps and Rubella-Containing Vaccine

MMR: M-M-RII MMRV: *ProQuad*	Given to children. Adults born before 1957 generally are considered immune to measles and mumps. Health care providers born before 1957 must prove immunity or receive 2 doses MMR vaccine at least 4 weeks apart. Live vaccine, not used in pregnancy.	MMR: Refrigerator or freezer MMRV: Freezer only due to varicella component. Always store diluents in refrigerator. Protect from light. Give SC.

Meningococcal Vaccines

MCV4: *Menactra, Menveo* MPSV4: *Menomune* Adults usually 1 dose but 2 doses for HIV+, asplenia, complement component deficiencies	Vaccinate: ■ 1 dose for 11-12 year old adolescents with one booster dose at age 16-18 ■ 1 dose at 13-18 years old if previously unvaccinated ■ 2-55 years old if in high risk, such as: College freshman in dormitories, asplenia, military service, immunodeficiencies, travelers to high-risk countries like the meningitis belt in sub Saharan Africa, lab workers with *N. meningitidis* exposure. People with continued risk of meningococcal disease should be revaccinated every five years. *Menomune:* use in ≥ 56 years old *Menactra:* 9 months-55 years *Menveo:* 2-55 years	Refrigerate. Protect from light. MCV give IM, MPSV give SC. Required by Saudi Arabia for annual travel during the period of the Hajj and Umrah pilgrimages, with proof of vaccination.

Vaccines Continued

DRUG	ADMINISTER TO	STORAGE/ADMINISTRATION

Pneumococcal Vaccines

13-valent pneumococcal conjugate vaccine (PCV13): *Prevnar 13* Minimum age at immunization: 6 weeks **23-serotype polysaccharide vaccine (PPSV23):** *Pneumovax 23* Minimum age at immunization: 2 years; PPSV23 does not invoke immunity in patients < 2 years old.	***PREVNAR13* (CONJUGATE)** **Children** Routine vaccination for all infants at 2, 4, 6 and 12-15 months. ■ 24 months-5 years get 1-2 doses if series has not been complicated and they have various conditions, including sickle cell disease, immunocompromised, others. ■ 6-18 years get single dose with sickle cell disease, HIV, or other immunocompromising condition, cochlear implant, or cerebrospinal fluid CSF leaks who have not previously received PCV13, regardless of whether they have previously PCV7 (the previous version) or PPSV23. **Adults** ■ 1 dose for non-pregnant adults 50 years of age and older ***PNEUMOVAX* (POLYSACCHARIDE)** **Recommended Patients** ■ All patients > 65 years x 1 dose ■ Patients aged 19-64 years who smoke or have asthma ■ Patients aged 2-64 years who have chronic illnesses **Revaccinate** ■ All adults with 1 dose age > 65 if 1st dose was 5 years earlier and < 65 years old. ■ Age 2-64 years if high risk of death from pneumococcal disease give 2nd dose 5 years after initial dose (sickle cell, immune compromised, asplenia). **Previously unvaccinated immunocompromised adults age 19 and older** ACIP expanded this definition to include patients with coclear implants or cerebrospinal leaks in addition to those traditionally considered immunocompromised. Give a single dose of PCV13 followed by a dose of PPSV23 at least 8 weeks later. Those who received at least one previous dose of PPSV23 should receive a single PCV13 dose no sooner than 1 year after the last PPSV23 dose. If patients require another PPSV23 dose, it should be administered no sooner than 8 weeks after PCV13 and 5 years after the last PPSV23 dose.	Store in refrigerator. Do not freeze. **PCV13** Shake the vial or prefilled syringe prior to use. Do not mix with other vaccines in the same syringe. Give IM. **PPSV23** Shake the vial or prefilled syringe prior to use. Do not mix with other vaccines in the same syringe. Give IM or SC.

Vaccines Continued

DRUG	ADMINISTER TO	STORAGE/ADMINISTRATION

Poliovirus-Containing Vaccine

DRUG	ADMINISTER TO	STORAGE/ADMINISTRATION
IPV: *IPOL* DTaP-HepB-IPV: *Pediarix* DTaP-IPV: *KINRIX* DTaP-IPV/Hib: *Pentacel*	Vaccine series to ALL children.	**Inactivated Poliomyelitis Vaccines (IPV)** Store in the refrigerator. Do not freeze. Shake the prefilled syringe or vial before use. Give IM or SC.

Rotavirus Vaccines

DRUG	ADMINISTER TO	STORAGE/ADMINISTRATION
RV1: *Rotarix* RV5: *RotaTeq*	Vaccine series to ALL children.	Oral suspensions. (Other oral vaccine is *Vivotif Berna* (typhoid) capsules that must be refrigerated)

Tetanus Toxoid Vaccine

DRUG	ADMINISTER TO	STORAGE/ADMINISTRATION
TT: *Tetanus Toxoid*		Tetanus Toxoid should not be stocked or administered by itself. Historically, this was used for wound management in emergency departments. Tetanus should always be administered with diphtheria toxoid. Tdap should always be administered if patient has not had a dose, otherwise, Td should be administered.

Tetanus Toxoid- and diphtheria toxoid-Containing Vaccines

DRUG	ADMINISTER TO	STORAGE/ADMINISTRATION
Td: *DECAVAC* DT: *Diphtheria and Tetanus Toxoid*	May be used in wound prophylaxis. If the patient has received 3 or more doses of tetanus, and the wound is NOT clean or minor, they may need revaccination with Td if more than 5 years since the last dose. They may also require tetanus immunoglobulin (TIG). If less than 3 doses or unclear history with serious wound, they may require both.	Used for primary series in infants and children < 7 years old who have a contraindication to the acellular pertussis antigen Give IM.

Vaccines Continued

DRUG	ADMINISTER TO	STORAGE/ADMINISTRATION
Tdap: *Adacel, Boostrix* See above for DTaP series, indicated for children 6 weeks to 6 years of age. Single Tdap dose for ages 7-10 years who were not fully vaccinated with DTaP series (missed dose in series). Tdap is the one time booster for ages 11-64 years with no previous record of Tdap, then one dose of Td every 10 years. Read recommendations to right to help reduce pertussis infections which have been epidemic in recent years.	Administer a one-time dose of Tdap to adults aged ≤ 65 years who have not received Tdap previously or for whom vaccine status is unknown to replace one of the 10-year Td boosters, and as soon as feasible to all 1) postpartum women, 2) close contacts of infants younger than age 12 months (e.g., grandparents and child-care providers), and 3) health-care personnel with direct patient contact. Adults aged 65 years and older who have not previously received Tdap and who have close contact with an infant aged less than 12 months should also be vaccinated. Other adults aged 65 years and older may receive Tdap. Tdap can be administered regardless of interval since the most recent tetanus or diphtheria-containing vaccine in order to administer the pertussis component since adults often infect children with pertussis. Pregnant women (weeks 27-36) should receive Tdap. If the woman has not been vaccinated or the history is unclear, a 3-dose series is needed (one with Tdap, the other 2 with Td only at 0, 1 month, and 6-12 months.). If the woman delivers and has not received vaccination, she should receive it post-delivery. Vaccination protects the baby (and the mother) from pertussis (whooping cough).	All tetanus, diphtheria, and pertussis containing vaccines: Store in the refrigerator. Do not freeze. Shake the prefilled syringe or vial before use. Give IM. The pediatric formulations (with the upper-case D, as in DTaP) have 3-5 times as much of the diphtheria component than the adult formulation. The adult formulations have a lower case d (Tdap, or Td).

Varicella containing vaccines

| VAR: *Varivax* (chickenpox)

ZOS: *Zostavax* (herpes zoster/shingles)

MMRV: *ProQuad* | Children get varicella at 12 months & again at 4 yrs.

All adults without evidence of immunity to varicella should receive 2 doses of varicella vaccine at least 4 weeks apart.

Varicella vaccines are live vaccines; do not use in pregnancy or if immunocompromised.

Herpes zoster vaccination (potency 14 times greater than varicella in order to elicit needed immune response)

In May, 2011 the FDA licensed zoster vaccine for adults 50 years of age and older. ACIP continues to recommend herpes zoster vaccine for patients 60 years and older. *Zostavax* is indicated for prevention of shingles and not for treatment of active case. Also reduces complications such as severity of postherpatic neuralgia following infections. Vaccinate even if history of zoster infection since you can get it again. | Varicella-containing vaccines have 2 components: vaccine & diluent.

Store vaccine in freezer & protect from light (keep in original container).

Store diluent in refrigerator or room temp.

LIVE vaccines: do not give if immuno-compromised, pregnant or if pregnancy is expected within 4 weeks.

Do not give if hypersensitivity to gelatin or neomycin.

Give SC. Reconstituted; reconstitute immediately upon removal from freezer and inject; short stability.

SC injection in adults for vaccines is in the fatty tissue at triceps; see diagram at end of chapter. |

Other Vaccines

DRUG	ADMINISTER TO	STORAGE/ADMINISTRATION
Japanese Encephalitis *Ixiaro*	Not recommended for all travelers to Asia. May be given if spending 1 month+ in endemic areas during transmission season, especially if travel will include rural areas.	2 doses 28 days apart, complete at least 1 week prior to potential exposure. Give IM.
Rabies *Imovax, RabAvert*	May be given preventively if high risk exposure (animal handlers, traveling to high risk area, etc.) or given with rabies exposure.	Reconstitute with provided diluent, 3 doses for prevention. If exposed to rabies with no rabies vaccination history: 4 doses vaccine + rabies immune globulin with 1st dose If exposed to rabies and had vaccination: 2 doses vaccine only. Give IM.
Smallpox	Eradicated; risk of use in bioterrorism. No specific treatment for infection. The U.S. government has vaccine stockpile.	
Tuberculosis BCG	Not used often in U.S. Often given to infants and small children in countries with higher TB incidence. Protection provided with vaccine poor versus other vaccines. Can cause (false) positive reaction to TB test.	
Typhoid *Vivotif Berna* (capsules, refrigerate) *Typhim Vi, Typherix* (Injections)	Typhoid fever caused by *Salmonella Typhi* exposure from food or drink beverages handled by infected person who is shedding or from contaminated sewage. Travelers from U.S. to Asia, Africa, and Latin America at risk. To reduce risk:"Boil it, cook it, peel it, or forget it."	4 capsules: 1 on alternate days (day 1, 3, 5 & 7); take on an empty stomach with cold or lukewarm water, complete at least 1 week prior to exposure.
Yellow Fever After vaccination provide International Certificate of Vaccination (yellow card) valid 10 days after vaccine for 10 years, may be required to enter endemic areas.	In tropical and subtropical areas South America and Africa. Transmitted by mosquito. Use insect repellent, wear protective clothing, and consider vaccination.	Give SC. Reconstituted. Contraindicated with a severe (life-threatening) allergy to eggs, chicken proteins, or gelatin; refer out for testing. Avoid donating blood for 2 weeks after receiving due to transmission risk.

Vaccine Storage/Name & misc. review information that is good to know

- If the wrong vaccine is chosen the patient is not covered for the intended disease.

- Review the brand name/components for vaccines that can be confused, including combos.

- If the vaccine is stored incorrectly, it may lose its potency and leave patients unprotected. Use vaccines quickly if removed from cold storage. Reconstituted vaccines have short stability.

VACCINE	NOTES
Most vaccines, including *Vivotif Berna* capsules	Refrigerate
Varicella vaccines *(Varivax, Zostavax, ProQuad, MMRV)*	Freezer (vaccine), diluent refrigerate or at room temp.
MMR	Refrigerate, or Freezer
Polio (IPV) SC or IM	Refrigerate
Influenza, all	
MMR (reconstituted, SC)	
Pneumococcal vaccines, *Pneumovax* is SC or IM	
Rotavirus vaccines (*Rotarix*), (*RotaTeq*)	
Most adult vaccines	IM
Fluzone Intradermal	Intradermal
Flumist	Nasal
MMR, MMRV, *Zostavax, Varivax*	SC
Pneumovax	SC or IM
Polio (IPV)	SC or IM
Menomune	SC
Menactra and Menveo	IM

Tips

- OHSA does not require gloves when giving vaccines, unless likely to come into exposure with bodily fluids. However, most wear gloves. If using gloves they must be changed between each patient.

- The CDC does NOT recommend using acetaminophen before or at vaccination as it may decrease the immune response. It can be used to treat pain and fever after vaccination.

- Never mix vaccines in the same syringe yourself – they have to come mixed.

- Do not aspirate. If this occurs, withdraw the needle, discard, and start over. This is an expensive waste so try not to aspirate. (this is when you see a flash of blood come up into the syringe)

- All vaccines can be given simultaneously. If a vaccine is missed, then any 2 live vaccines not given at the same time must be given at least 4 weeks apart.

- You can vaccinate through a tattoo.

STORAGE

Store refrigerated vaccines immediately upon arrival. Stand alone units are preferred but household combination units with separate exterior doors and thermostats can be used. Dormitory-style refrigerators should not be used. Keep a calibrated thermometer in the refrigerator and freezer. Post "Do Not Unplug" signs next electrical outlets and "Do Not Stop Power" signs near circuit breakers to maintain a consistent power source. Store vaccines on the shelves away from the walls. Vaccines should never be stored in the door of the freezer or refrigerator. The temperature there is unstable. Read and document refrigerator and freezer temperatures at least twice each workday: in the morning and before the end of the workday. Keep temperature logs for at least 3 years. Rotate stock so vaccine and diluent with the shortest expiration date is used first. Place vaccine with the longest expiration date behind the vaccine that will expire the soonest.

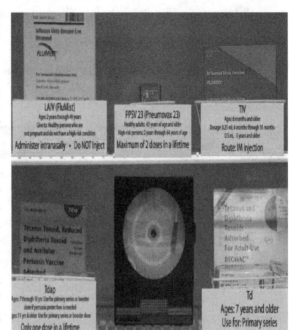

Staff can easily confuse the vaccines within the storage unit. Use labels & separate containers.

Store refrigerated vaccines between 35°F and 46°F (2°C and 8°C). Store frozen vaccines between -58°F and +5°F (-50°C and -15°C).

Administration

See the chart at the end of this chapter for injection technique. In adults intramuscular (IM) injections are given in the deltoid muscle at the central and thickest portion above the level of the armpit and below the acromion. Adults require a 1" syringe (or 5/8" for a person less than 130 lbs and a 1½" needle for women greater than 200 lbs or men greater than 260 pounds. Use a 22-25 gauge inserted at a 90 degree angle. (The higher the gauge, the thinner the needle.)

Subcutaneous (SC) vaccinations are given in the fatty tissue above the triceps with a 5/8", 23-25 gauge syringe at a 45 degree angle. The vaccines pharmacists administer in the community setting that are SC are varicella and zoster (shingles) and pneumococcal polysaccharide vaccine (PPSV23, *Pneumovax)* can be given either SC or IM.

Influenza (the Flu)

Influenza is the most common vaccine preventable illness in the U.S.

Make sure patients know:

- The influenza vaccine cannot cause the flu. They may get a sore arm, or mild systemic reactions that go away.

- The only patients who can use the nasal mist vaccine are healthy (no chronic disease) non-pregnant females and males from age 2 to 49 years. This is a live vaccine; the others are inactivated injections.

- Everyone 6 months and older should be vaccinated annually – patients at highest risk will get vaccinated first if there is a vaccine shortage; check the CDC vaccination website if a shortage is present.

- Pregnant women are at risk for severe disease and should be vaccinated.

- Individuals can and should be vaccinated for influenza even if it is late in the season.

Influenza A and B are the two types of influenza viruses that cause epidemic human disease. Influenza A viruses are further categorized into subtypes on the basis of two surface antigens: hemagglutinin and neuraminidase. Immunity to the surface antigens, particularly the hemagglutinin, reduces the likelihood of infection and severity of disease if infection occurs. Frequent development of antigenic variants through antigenic drift is the virologic basis for seasonal epidemics and the reason for the usual incorporation of one or more new strains in each year's influenza vaccine, which is made as a trivalent vaccine. More dramatic antigenic changes, or shifts, occur approximately every 30 years and can result in the emergence of a novel influenza virus with the potential to cause a pandemic.

The virus spreads from person to person, primarily through respiratory droplet transmission (e.g., when an infected person coughs or sneezes in close proximity to an uninfected person). If someone sneezes in their hands and touches something it is possible to spread illness.

Uncomplicated influenza illness is characterized by the abrupt onset of these symptoms: fever, myalgia, headache, malaise, non-productive cough, sore throat, and rhinitis. Among children, otitis media, nausea, and vomiting also are commonly reported with influenza illness.

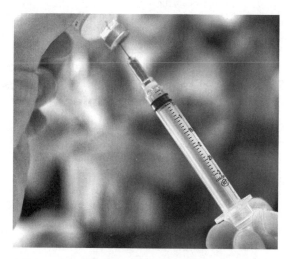

Influenza (inactivated) injection – annually, each fall

Uncomplicated influenza illness typically resolves after 3-7 days for the majority of persons, although cough and malaise can persist for more than 2 weeks. However, for certain people, influenza can exacerbate underlying medical conditions (e.g., pulmonary or cardiac disease), leading to secondary bacterial pneumonia or primary influenza viral pneumonia, or occur as part of a co-infection with other viral or bacterial pathogens.

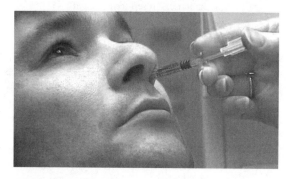

Influenza – live nasal vaccine, annually, each fall, if healthy, ages 2-49

Antiviral treatment of patients with influenza

■ See Infectious Disease chapter.

How to Administer IM and SC Vaccine Injections to Adults

Intramuscular (IM) Injections

Administer these vaccines via IM route:
Tetanus, diphtheria (Td), or with pertussis (Tdap); hepatitis A; hepatitis B; human papillomavirus (HPV); trivalent inactivated influenza (TIV); and quadrivalent meningococcal conjugate (MCV4). Administer polio (IPV) and pneumococcal polysaccharide vaccine (PPSV23) either IM or SC.

Injection site:
Give in the central and thickest portion of the deltoid—above the level of the armpit and below the acromion (see the diagram).

Needle size:
22–25 gauge, 1–1½" needle *(see note at right)*

Needle insertion:

• Use a needle long enough to reach deep into the muscle.
• Insert the needle at a 90° angle to the skin with a quick thrust.
• Separate two injections given in the same deltoid muscle by a minimum of 1".

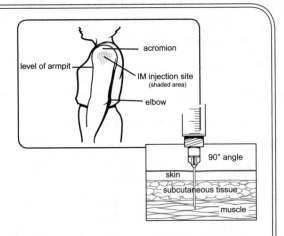

Note: A ½" needle is sufficient in adults weighing <130 lbs (<60 kg); a 1" needle is sufficient in adults weighing 130–152 lbs (60–70 kg); a 1–1½" needle is recommended in women weighing 152–200 lbs (70–90 kg) and men weighing 152–260 lbs (70–118 kg); a 1½" needle is recommended in women weighing >200 lbs (>90 kg) or men weighing >260 lbs (>118 kg). A ⅝" (16mm) needle may be used only if the skin is stretched tight, the subcutaneous tissue is not bunched, and injection is made at a 90-degree angle.

Subcutaneous (SC) Injections

Administer these vaccines via SC route:
MMR, varicella, meningococcal polysaccharide (MPSV4), and zoster (shingles). Administer polio (IPV) and pneumococcal polysaccharide vaccine (PPSV23) either SC or IM.

Injection site:
Give in fatty tissue over the triceps (see the diagram).

Needle size:
23–25 gauge, 5/8" needle

Needle insertion:

• Pinch up on the tissue to prevent injection into the muscle. Insert the needle at a 45° angle to the skin.
• Separate two injections given in the same area of fatty tissue by a minimum of 1".

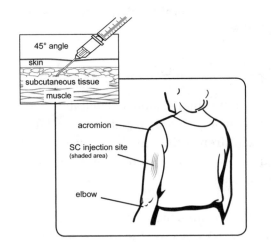

Adapted by the Immunization Action Coalition, courtesy of the Minnesota Department of Health

Technical content reviewed by the Centers for Disease Control and Prevention, November 2010.

www.immunize.org/catg.d/p2020A.pdf Item #P2020A (11/10)

Immunization Action Coalition • 1573 Selby Ave. • St. Paul, MN 55104 • (651) 647-9009 • www.immunize.org • www.vaccineinformation.org

TRAVELERS MEDICINE

BACKGROUND

International travel involves millions of people to all places in the world. Travelers often do not recognize the associated health risks and may not seek consultation with an appropriate health professional prior to travel. Pharmacists are in a good location to remedy the situation, and increasingly are doing just that. Pharmacists offer informal advice to the traveling public, provide vaccinations or other medications and, in some settings, charge for consultative services, which include awareness of country-specific risks and ways to prevent them.

Patients should be advised to <u>pack medications and medical supplies in carry-on luggage</u>, in the original prescription bottles. They should bring a copy of the prescriptions and a list of their medications and conditions. It is wise to have them check with their health insurance company to find out if the policy will cover medical care in another country or on board a ship. Travel health insurance information is available on the CDC's travel information website where the "<u>Yellow Book</u>" (the CDC's standard resource on travel information) and other travel health information is located. Travel advisories and visa requirements can be checked on the U.S. State Department website.

PREVENTABLE ILLNESS

Meningitis, yellow fever and typhoid vaccines are common travel-related vaccines and are discussed in detail here, with more information on these and other vaccines is in the Immunizations chapter. In addition to these three vaccines, travelers may require vaccination against hepatitis A (a food and water-borne illness), hepatitis B (transmitted by bodily fluids) and polio (for travelers going to certain parts of Africa and Asia; polio has been eliminated from most of the world but four countries remain endemic and travelers can transport infection). Malaria protection is provided by oral medications (rather than a vaccine), which must be started prior to travel; the choice of medication largely depends on the departure date. Vaccinations must also be given in advance to provide time for antibody levels to become sufficient. Vaccines need to be individualized after a risk assessment, taking into account both the traveler and the trip.

There are two vaccines that are required for specific regions: the meningococcal vaccine, required by the government of Saudi Arabia for annual travel during the period of the Hajj and Umrah pilgrimages, and the yellow fever vaccine, required for travel to certain parts of sub-Saharan Africa and South America.

Meningococcal Disease Prevention

Meningococcal vaccination is discussed first because unlike most other travel-related illness it is not transmitted by an insect, but is widely spread in parts of the world outside of the U.S. The vaccine is not required by other countries besides Saudi Arabia but is recommended by the CDC's Advisory Committee on Immunization Practices (ACIP) for people who travel to or reside in countries where *N. meningitidis* is hyperendemic or epidemic, particularly if contact with the local population will be prolonged. Hyperendemic regions include the meningitis belt of Africa during the dry season (December–June).

Bacterial meningitis has high fatality and is a medical emergency. Patients with symptoms of fever, severe, unrelenting headache, nausea, stiff neck and mental status changes require urgent treatment to avoid the risk of permanent brain damage and death. Patients at risk for meningitis can receive one of the three vaccines: *Menactra* (2-dose series for children 9–23 months, 1-dose for 2–55 years) or *Menveo* (2–55 years) or *Menomune* for ages 56 and older. Approximately 7–10 days are required after vaccination for development of protective antibody levels.

DISEASES TRANSMITTED BY INSECT BITES

Insects that transmit disease are vectors. The vector carries the disease to the individual, causing infection. A reservoir is any place (such as an animal, insect, soil or plant) in which the disease lives and can multiply. The primary insect that causes infection to travelers are various types of mosquitos, which carry parasites for Japanese encephalitis (vaccine available, used occasionally), yellow fever (vaccine available, may be required), dengue (no vaccine or prophylactic drugs) and malaria (no vaccine but prophylactic oral drugs available). The tsetse fly spreads African sleeping sickness (no vaccine or prophylactic drugs).

Mosquito-Borne Illness Prevention

The primary method (besides vaccination) of preventing mosquito-borne illness in most areas is to attempt to eliminate places where the mosquito lays her eggs. Travelers should use the following measures:

- Stay and sleep in screened or air-conditioned rooms.

- Cover exposed skin by wearing long-sleeved shirts, long pants and hats.

- Use a bed net, which can be pre-treated with mosquito repellant.

- Use proper application of mosquito repellents containing 20% to 30% <u>DEET</u> as the active ingredient on exposed skin and clothing. DEET also protects against ticks. Other insect repellants that can be used topically for mosquitos (but not for ticks) are picardin, oil of lemon eucalyptus or IR3535. <u>Permethrin</u> can be used to treat clothing, gear and bed nets but should not be applied directly to the skin.

Dengue: No Vaccine, Transmitted By Mosquito

Dengue (den' gee) is transmitted between people by the mosquitoes *Aedes aegypti* and *Aedes albopictus*. In many parts of the tropics and subtropics, dengue is endemic; it occurs every year, usually during a season when *Aedes* mosquito populations are high and rainfall is optimal for breeding. In rare cases dengue can be transmitted in organ transplants or blood transfusions from infected donors, and there is evidence of transmission from an infected pregnant mother to the fetus. But in the vast majority of infections, a mosquito bite is responsible. Sequential infections put people at greater risk for <u>dengue hemorraghic fever</u> and dengue shock syndrome, both of which can be fatal. <u>Protection from mosquito bites is essential</u>.

African Sleeping Sickness: No Vaccine, Transmitted By Tsetse Fly

The tsetse fly lives in sub-Saharan Africa and spreads African sleeping sickness (African trypanosomiasis). Tsetse fly protection is a different than mosquito protection. The insect can bite through thin fabric. Clothing should be medium-weight, and be neutral in color because the fly is attracted to bright colors, dark colors, metallic fabric and the color blue. Insect repellants described above should be used, but there is limited evidence they work against this insect.

Japanese Encephalitis

A vaccine that is occasionally recommended is the vaccine against Japanese Encephalitis (JE), which can cause asymptomatic infection, or can develop into encephalitis, with rigors and risk of seizures, coma and death. Transmission primarily occurs in rural agricultural areas, often associated with rice cultivation and flood irrigation. This is one of the conditions transmitted through mosquito bites and is best prevented by reducing exposure to mosquitos. The vaccine is recommended for travelers who plan to spend at least 1 month in endemic areas during the JE virus transmission season. The vaccine (*IXIARO*) is a two-dose series, with the doses spaced 28 days apart. The last dose should be given at least 1 week before travel.

Yellow Fever

Yellow fever is caused by a virus found in <u>tropical and subtropical areas in South America and Africa</u>. Transmission is by mosquitos and reducing the risk of exposure is essential. Most infections are asymptomatic. If symptoms develop, the initial illness presents as an influenza-like syndrome. Most patients improve after the initial presentation, but ~15% progress to a more toxic form of the disease characterized by jaundice, hemorrhagic symptoms and risk of shock and organ failure. There is no specific treatment for acute infection except symptomatic relief with fluids, analgesics and antipyretics. Aspirin and other NSAIDs cannot be used due to the increased risk for bleeding. Infected patients should be protected from further mosquito exposure (staying indoors or under a mosquito net) during the first few days of illness, or they will contribute to the transmission cycle.

The yellow fever vaccine is recommended for travelers to high-risk areas in South America and Africa. Some countries require proof of yellow fever vaccination for entry. The pharmacist who has given the vaccine can provide the patient with an "International Certificate of Vaccination or Prophylaxis", which is commonly referred to as the "yellow card." Yellow fever vaccine is contraindicated in infants < 6 months who are at higher risk for significant complications, and in patients with hypersensitivity to eggs, egg products, chicken proteins, or gelatin. Additional contraindications are a thymus disorder or myasthenia gravis. This is a live vaccine and cannot be used with immunosuppression, including HIV patients with a CD4+ count < 200/mm^3, anyone using strong immune-suppressants (TNF-inhibitors, high-dose systemic steroids, certain chemotherapy agents, and IL-1 and IL-6 antagonists).

ACIP recommends that a woman wait 4 weeks after receiving the yellow fever vaccine before conceiving. Yellow fever vaccine safety has not been tested during pregnancy and the CDC recommends advising pregnant women who would otherwise require vaccination to avoid travel to at-risk regions.

Medication-Preventable Illness

Malaria is transmitted by the bite of an infected *Anopheles* mosquito. It is endemic to tropical and subtropical areas of Asia, North and South America, the Middle East, North Africa, and the South Pacific. Travelers to sub-Saharan Africa have the greatest risk. The CDC website includes maps of malaria presence by country, the species of malaria and medication recommendations. *Plasmodium vivax* is the most common of four human malaria species (*P. falciparum, P. malariae, P. ovale,* and *P. vivax*). *P. vivax* causes up to 65% of malaria cases in India and is becoming increasingly resistant to malaria drugs. By contrast, *P. falciparum* is the most deadly species and the subject of most malaria-related research.

Several medications are available for malaria prophylaxis and some of these are used for treatment. When deciding on which drug to use for prevention, clinicians should consider the resistance, date of departure (some must be started longer in advance of travel), cost, allergies, pregnancy, if an infant or child, and concurrent conditions.

Mefloquine (*Larium*) is dosed once weekly. It is started 1-2 weeks prior to travel and is taken for 4 weeks post-travel. There is a high degree of resistance, which must be checked prior to dispensing. Neuropsychiatric effects, which can require drug discontinuation: psychiatric symptoms, which can include anxiety, paranoia, depression, hallucinations, and psychosis, and neurologic symptoms, which can include seizures, dizziness or vertigo, tinnitus, and loss of balance (could be permanent). It cannot be used with cardiac conditions. It is an option during pregnancy and for children.

Atovaquone/Proguanil (*Malarone*) is quick-acting and is dosed once daily. It is started 1-2 days before travel and is taken for 7 days post-travel. It is well tolerated but cannot be used during pregnancy.

Chloroquine is dosed once weekly. It is started 1-2 weeks before travel and is taken for 4 weeks post-travel. Chloroquine can cause visual problems (retinopathy), can exacerbate psoriasis, cause GI upset and is best avoided in pregnancy (although sometimes it is used) and with severe renal impairment. It should not be used in areas with high chloroquine or mefloquine resistance.

Primaquine is effective for *P. vivax*. It is dosed once daily. It is started 1-2 days before travel and taken for 7 days post-travel. It cannot be used in pregnancy or if G6PD deficiency or if not tested for G6PD deficiency. The CDC requires screening for G6PD deficiency prior to initiating treatment with primaquine.

Doxycycline is sometimes used and some patients may be using it for other conditions already, primarily for acne. For further discussion of malaria prophylaxis and treatment regimens refer to the Infectious Diseases chapter.

Typhoid Fever: Spread Through Contaminated Food or Water

Typhoid fever is potentially severe and can be life-threatening. Risk of contagion is highest for travelers to southern Asia. Other areas of risk include east and southeast Asia, Africa, the Caribbean, and Central and South America.

Humans are the only source of the bacteria, which is spread primarily through consumption of water or food that has been contaminated by feces of someone with an acute infection or from a chronic, asymptomatic carrier. Transmission through sexual contact, especially among men who have sex with men, can occur but is not the common cause of transmission.

The incubation period of typhoid (and paratyphoid infection, a similar disease) is 6–30 days. The onset of illness is insidious, with gradually increasing fatigue, fever, earache, malaise and anorexia, with possible hepatosplenomegaly. A transient, macular rash of rose-colored spots can occasionally be seen on the trunk. Intestinal hemorrhage or perforation can occur 2-3 weeks later and can be fatal.

Vaccines are recommended but are only 50-80% effective; this requires that even vaccinated travelers should follow safe food and water precautions and wash hands frequently. These precautions are the only prevention method for paratyphoid fever, for which there is no vaccine. There are two vaccines for typhoid: *Vivotif Berna*, taken as oral capsules, or *Typhim Vi*, an intramuscular injection.

Vaccination with *Vivotif Berna* consists of <u>4 capsules, 1 taken every other day</u>. The capsules are <u>refrigerated</u> (not frozen). Each capsule is <u>taken with cool liquid</u> (not warm), 1 hour before a meal. The regimen should be completed 1 week prior to travel. <u>Vaccination with the shot</u> is one 0.5-mL dose given <u>intramuscularly ≥ 2 weeks before expected exposure</u>.

Travelers' Diarrhea Prevention

Travelers' diarrhea is a common concern caused by unclean food and water. Most cases are bacterial and *E. coli* is the primary bacterial pathogen. Travelers to developing countries are at highest risk. Safe food and water habits will reduce risk. Diarrhea caused by a bacterial infection can be treated with antibiotics discussed in the Infectious Diseases chapter. Travelers should follow these precautions:

- Eat only food that is cooked and served hot. Avoid food that has been sitting on a buffet.

- Eat raw fruits and vegetables only if washed in clean water or peeled.

- Drink only beverages from factory-sealed containers, and avoid ice. Water should be purified.

- Keep hands clean; wash hands often with soap and water, especially after using the bathroom and before eating. If soap and water are not available, use an alcohol-based hand sanitizer. Keep hands out of the mouth.

If traveler's diarrhea develops, hydration is essential, especially for young children or adults with chronic illnesses. In serious cases of travelers' diarrhea, oral rehydration solution – available online or in pharmacies in developing countries – can be used for fluid replacement. Oral rehydration solution can be prepared by mixing 1 liter of purified water with 1 teaspoon of salt and 8 teaspoons of sugar. Over-the-counter loperamide (*Imodium*) can be used to decrease the frequency and urgency of bowel movements, and can make it easier for a person with diarrhea to ride on a bus or airplane while waiting for an antibiotic to take effect. It should not be used in children < 2 years old without a physician's authorization due to the risk of toxic megacolon. Another option to firm stool is bismuth subsalicylate. This should not be used by anyone using anticoagulants or with a salicylate allergy, or in children who may have a viral infection due to the risk of Reye's syndrome. It turns the tongue (and possibly stool) black, which resolves with drug discontinuation. If used excessively or with other salicylates, toxicity could present as tinnitus.

Deep Vein Thrombosis Prevention

Travelers are at increased risk for deep vein thrombosis (DVT) and pulmonary embolism (PE) due to limited movement with long-term immobility, such as with an intercontinental plane flight. Wearing compression stockings during long trips reduces risk; these can be sold in the pharmacy. Travelers should follow these additional precautions:

- Get up occasionally and walk around. Choosing an aisle seat is helpful.

- Perform exercises while sitting, with repetitions of each: Raise and lower heels while keeping toes on the floor. Raise and lower toes while keeping heels on the floor. Tighten and release leg muscles.

Patients should know symptoms of DVT or PE and be instructed to seek immediate medical care if suspected. DVT risk factors, symptoms and prophylaxis are discussed in the Anticoagulation chapter.

Motion Sickness, Altitude Sickness, Jet Lag

Motion Sickness is common among travelers and is discussed in the Motion Sickness chapter. Acute mountain sickness (AMS) is a common type of altitude sickness that occurs when people climb rapidly to a high altitude. It occurs commonly above 8,000 feet and is more likely in persons who live close to sea level or have had a previous bout with AMS. Primary symptoms are dizziness, headache, tachycardia and shortness of breath. The primary prophylactic medication is acetazolamide *(Diamox Sequels)* 125 mg twice daily, beginning either the day before (preferred) or on the day of ascent. Higher doses (500-1,000 mg) are used for treatment. This can improve breathing, but is not without side effects (polyuria, taste alteration, risk of dehydration, photosensitivity, urticaria and a possibility of severe skin rashes). Acetazolamide is contraindicated with a sulfa allergy. Patients should be instructed to use sun protection and keep well hydrated. In acute cases, the patient may require oxygen, inhaled beta-agonists and dexamethasone to reduce cerebral edema.

Travelers often consult with pharmacists regarding ways to manage jet lag; this is discussed in the Natural Products chapter.

19

HUMAN IMMUNODEFICIENCY VIRUS (HIV)

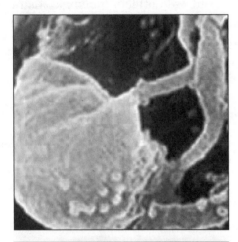

We gratefully acknowledge the assistance of Jenana Halilovic, PharmD, BCPS, University of the Pacific Thomas J Long School of Pharmacy and Health Sciences and Brett Heintz, PharmD, BCPS-ID, AAHIVE, Infectious Diseases/Internal Medicine Pharmacist at Iowa City VA Medical Center and Associate Clinical Professor at University of Iowa College of Pharmacy, in preparing this chapter.

GUIDELINES

Panel on Antiretroviral Guidelines for Adults and Adolescents. Guidelines for the Use of Antiretroviral Agents in HIV-1 Infected Adults and Adolescents. Department of Health and Human Services. Last updated on Feb. 12, 2013 Available at http://aidsinfo.nih.gov/contentfiles/lvguidelines/adultandadolescentgl.pdf. (accessed 2013 Nov. 21)

BACKGROUND

Since the first cases of the Human Immunodeficiency Virus (HIV)/Acquired Immunodeficiency Syndrome (AIDS) were reported in 1981, the Centers for Disease Control now estimates that there are 1.2 million people in the United States living with HIV. HIV is a RNA retrovirus that attacks the immune system, mainly the CD4+ T cells, causing a progressive decrease in the CD4+ T cell count. Once CD4+ cell counts fall below a critical level, the person becomes more susceptible to opportunistic infections due to the loss of cell-mediated immunity. CD4+ counts are the major laboratory indicator of immune function in patients infected with HIV and serve as a key factor in determining both the urgency of antiretroviral therapy (ART) initiation and the need for prophylaxis against opportunistic infections. Plasma HIV-1 RNA (viral load) should be measured in all HIV-1 infected patients at baseline and on a regular basis thereafter, especially in patients who are on treatment, because viral load is the most important indicator of response to antiretroviral therapy. The viral load quantifies the degree of viremia by measuring the amount of HIV RNA in the blood and is used to assess disease progression and possible drug resistance.

TRANSMISSION

HIV may be spread through infected <u>blood</u>, <u>semen</u>, and <u>vaginal secretions</u>. Unprotected intercourse and sharing needles with HIV positive individuals are the two most common means of HIV transmission. The entry of the virus is facilitated through the presence of sores or cuts in the vagina, penis, rectum, or mouth. Vertical transmission may also occur, either during <u>pregnancy</u>, <u>at birth</u>, or through <u>breastfeeding</u>.

ANTIRETROVIRAL THERAPY

Treatment for HIV requires combination therapy known as antiretroviral therapy (ART). <u>ART has dramatically reduced HIV-associated morbidity and mortality</u> and has transformed HIV disease into a chronic, manageable condition. Without treatment, the vast majority of HIV-infected individuals will eventually develop progressive immunosuppression (as evident by low CD4+ count), leading to AIDS-defining illnesses and premature death. <u>The primary goals of ART are to: restore and preserve the immune system, suppress HIV viral load to undetectable levels, reduce HIV-associated morbidity, prolong survival, and prevent HIV transmission.</u>

<u>ART is recommended in ALL HIV-infected individuals</u> but the strength of the recommendation varies depending on the patient's baseline CD4+ count and/or presence of certain co-morbid conditions. The conditions that favor more rapid initiation of therapy are pregnancy, lower CD4+ counts, or history of an AIDS-defining illness, including HIV-associated dementia, HIV-associated nephropathy (HIVAN), hepatitis B virus (HBV), hepatitis C virus (HCV) and acute/recent HIV infection. Acute HIV infection is the phase of the HIV disease immediately after infection during which the initial burst of viremia in newly infected patients occurs; anti-HIV antibodies are undetectable at this time while HIV RNA and p24 antigen are present. Recent infection generally is considered the phase up to 6 months after infection during which anti-HIV antibodies are detectable. <u>ART is also recommended for HIV-infected individuals for the prevention of HIV transmission including to sexual partners.</u>

Patients starting ART should be willing and able to commit to treatment and should understand the benefits and risks of therapy and the importance of adherence. Patients may choose to postpone therapy, and providers, on a case-by-case basis, may elect to defer therapy on the basis of clinical and/or psychosocial factors. Patients need to be advised that they need to have <u>an adherence rate of 95% or higher in order for their ART regimen to be effective long-term.</u>

Below is a diagram of the <u>HIV replication cycle</u>. <u>It is very important to understand the steps involved in viral replication and know where each drug class works</u>.

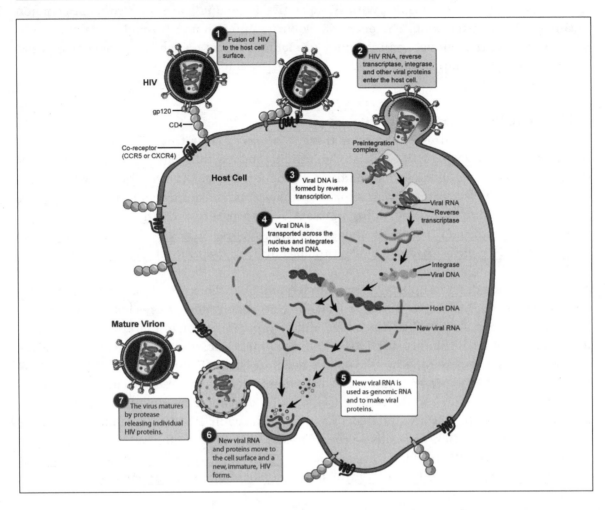

Source: DHHS-NIH website http://www.niaid.nih.gov/topics/HIVAIDS/Understanding/Biology/pages/hivreplicationcycle.aspx

HIV Replication Cycle Steps and the Sites of Action of Antiretrovirals

1. Fusion of the HIV cell to the host cell surface (e.g., Fusion inhibitor and CCR5 antagonist).

2. HIV RNA, reverse transcriptase, integrase, and other viral proteins enter the host cell.

3. Uncoating of the viral core exposes the viral RNA which is then converted to viral DNA by reverse transcriptase (e.g., NRTIs and NNRTIs).

4. Viral DNA is transported across the nucleus and integrates into the host DNA (e.g., Integrase Strand Transfer Inhibitors).

5. New viral RNA is used as genomic RNA and to assemble viral proteins.

6. New viral RNA and proteins move to cell surface and a new, immature, HIV virus forms.

7. The virus matures by protease releasing individual HIV proteins (e.g., PIs).

Initial Evaluation and Monitoring

The initial evaluation should include a discussion on the benefits of antiretroviral therapy for the patient's health and to prevent transmission. It is recommended that the following laboratory parameters be measured for all HIV-infected individuals:

- CD4+ count and HIV RNA viral load (an increase in viral load generally indicates drug resistance and/or inadequate treatment response while a decrease in the CD4+ count is a predictor of disease progression) – prior to ART initiation or modification, 2-8 weeks post initiation, then every 3-6 months thereafter

- Drug resistance testing – at entry into care regardless of ART initiation, at ART initiation and at ART modification

- Lipid panel, blood chemistry, CBC with differential – prior to ART initiation or modification and every 6-12 months thereafter

Some Common Complications of Art

<u>Lactic acidosis and severe hepatomegaly with steatosis</u>: suspend treatment in any patient who develops clinical or laboratory findings suggestive of lactic acidosis or hepatotoxicity (transaminase elevation may/may not accompany hepatomegaly and steatosis). Most commonly associated with NRTIs.

<u>Immune reconstitution inflammatory syndrome (IRIS or IRS)</u>: A paradoxical worsening of a <u>preexisting</u> opportunistic infection when ART is initiated. Since ART leads to an improvement in immune function, an inflammatory reaction may occur at the site of the preexisting infection. Patients at highest risk for IRIS are those with low CD4 counts and high viral loads. IRIS generally develops between 1-3 months of ART initiation. Commonly found pathogens associated with IRIS include *M. tuberculosis*, *M. avium*, *Pneumocystis jiroveci* pneumonia (PCP), Herpes Simplex Virus (HSV), Herpes zoster, cytomegalovirus (CMV), *Cryptococcus*, and Hepatitis B.

Management of IRIS:

- Start or continue therapy for the underlying opportunistic pathogen.

- Continue ART if the patient is currently receiving ART. Among patients newly diagnosed with HIV with an opportunistic infection (OI), ART may be intentionally delayed while treating the OI to minimize risk for IRIS. However, ART should always be started for PCP and generally for *M. tuberculosis* secondary to mortality benefits.

- In select circumstances, the addition of corticosteroids may be appropriate.

<u>Lipodystrophy/lipoatrophy</u>: Loss of subcutaneous fat in the face, arms, legs and buttocks – most commonly associated with PIs and stavudine

<u>Fat redistribution/lipohypertrophy</u>: Fat accumulation in the upper back (buffalo hump) and abdominal area and increased breast size in females and males – most commonly associated with PIs and stavudine

<u>Diarrhea</u>: Diarrhea is a common side effect of ART. Crofelemer was recently approved for treatment of <u>non-infectious diarrhea</u> in adult patients with HIV/AIDS on ART. It works by inhibiting cyclic adenosine monophosphate (cAMP)-stimulated cystic fibrosis transmembrane conductance regulator (CFTR) chloride ion channel and calcium activated chloride ion channels at the enterocyte luminal membrane. This regulates fluid secretion and water loss (high volume) due to diarrhea, normalizing chloride ion and water flow in the GI tract. All ARTs have been associated with GI toxicity, however protease inhibitors (PIs) are generally the most problematic: Especially nelfinavir and lopinavir/ritonavir.

DRUG	DOSING	SAFETY/SIDE EFFECTS/MONITORING
Crofelemer *(Fulyzaq)*	125 mg BID	**SIDE EFFECTS** URTIs, bronchitis, cough, flatulence and increased bilirubin

INITIAL COMBINATION REGIMENS FOR THE ANTIRETROVIRAL-NAÏVE HIV PATIENTS

Selection of a regimen should be individualized based on virologic efficacy, toxicity, pill burden, dosing frequency, drug-drug interaction potential, resistance testing results, and comorbid conditions. The regimens in each category are listed in alphabetical order.

REGIMENS	COMMENTS

Preferred Regimens – Regimens with optimal and durable efficacy, favorable tolerability and toxicity profile, and ease of use. The preferred regimens for non-pregnant patients are arranged by chronological order of FDA approval of components other than nucleosides and, thus, by duration of clinical experience.

NNRTI-BASED REGIMEN Efavirenz/tenofovir/emtricitabine	Atazanavir should not be used in patients who require > 20 mg omeprazole equivalent per day. Tenofovir should be used with caution in patients with renal insufficiency. Elvitegravir/cobicistat/tenofovir/emtricitabine should only be initiated in patients with CrCL ≥ 70 mL/min and should not be used with other antiretroviral therapy or with other nephrotoxic drugs.
PI-BASED REGIMENS Atazanavir + ritonavir + tenofovir/emtricitabine Darunavir + ritonavir + tenofovir/emtricitabine	
INSTI-BASED REGIMEN Raltegravir + tenofovir/emtricitabine Elvitegravir/cobicistat/tenofovir/emtricitabine Dolutegravir + abacavir/lamivudine Dolutegravir + tenofovir/emtricitabine	

Initial Combination Regimens for the Antiretroviral-Naïve HIV Patients Continued

REGIMENS	COMMENTS

Preferred Regimen for Pregnant Women

REGIMENS	COMMENTS
PI-BASED REGIMEN Lopinavir/ritonavir + zidovudine/lamivudine Atazanavir + ritonavir + zidovudine/lamivudine **NNRTI-BASED REGIMEN** Nevirapine + zidovudine/lamivudine	Efavirenz is not recommended to women who are planning or at risk of becoming pregnant (Pregnancy category D). Because the risk of neural tube defects is restricted to the first 5 to 6 weeks of pregnancy and pregnancy is rarely recognized before 4 to 6 weeks of pregnancy, efavirenz can be continued in pregnant women who present for antenatal care in the first trimester, provided the regimen produces virologic suppression. Do not use once daily dosing of lopinavir/ritonavir in pregnant women. Always use twice daily dosing.

Alternative Regimens

REGIMENS	COMMENTS
NNRTI-BASED REGIMENS Efavirenz + abacavir/lamivudine Rilpivirine/tenofovir/emtricitabine Rilpivirine + abacavir/lamivudine **PI-BASED REGIMENS** Atazanavir + ritonavir + abacavir/lamivudine Darunavir + ritonavir + abacavir/lamivudine Fosamprenavir + ritonavir + either [abacavir/lamivudine or tenofovir/emtricitabine] Lopinavir + ritonavir + either [abacavir/lamivudine or tenofovir/emtricitabine] **INSTI-BASED REGIMEN** Raltegravir + abacavir/lamivudine	Rilpivirine in not recommended in patients with pretreatment HIV RNA > 100,000 copies/mL. Use of proton pump inhibitors is contraindicated with rilpivirine. Once daily lopinavir/ritonavir is not recommended in pregnant women. Abacavir should not be used in patients who test positive for HLA-B*5701. Use abacavir with caution in patients with high risk of cardiovascular disease or with pretreatment HIV-RNA > 100,000 copies/mL.

NUCLEOSIDE/TIDE REVERSE TRANSCRIPTASE INHIBITORS (NRTIs)

NRTIs work by binding to the catalytic site of reverse transcriptase, interfering with HIV viral RNA-dependent DNA polymerase and resulting in inhibition of viral replication (see Step #3 in the HIV diagram).

DRUG	REGIMEN PREFERENCE	DOSING	SAFETY/SIDE EFFECTS/MONITORING
Entire Class			**BLACK BOX WARNING** Lactic acidosis and severe hepatomegaly with steatosis, sometimes fatal, have occurred especially with stavudine, didanosine and zidovudine
Abacavir, ABC **(Ziagen)** Tablet, oral solution (20 mg/mL) **+ lamivudine (Epzicom)** + lamivudine and zidovudine (Trizivir)	Preferred	300 mg BID or 600 mg daily 1 tab daily (for Epzicom) 1 tab BID (for Trizivir) No renal dose adjustments required	**BLACK BOX WARNING** Serious, sometimes fatal, hypersensitivity reaction – look for fever, skin rash, respiratory symptoms (dyspnea, cough) and/or GI symptoms (nausea, vomiting, diarrhea, abdominal pain); discontinue drug and do not re-challenge Must screen for the HLA-B*5701 allele prior to starting abacavir therapy – if positive, ↑ risk for hypersensitivity reaction so do not use. Record as abacavir allergy in patient record. **SIDE EFFECTS** N/V, headache, rash, ↑ LFTs, hypersensitivity reaction **MONITORING** LFTs, signs and symptoms of hypersensitivity **NOTES** Avoid alcohol (increases AUC)
Didanosine, ddI (Videx, Videx EC) Caspule, solution (10 mg/mL)	Avoid if possible	≥ 60 kg: 400 mg daily < 60 kg: 250 mg daily *Videx EC* – Take on an empty stomach (1 hour before or 2 hours after a meal); *Videx* (oral soln) – Take on empty stomach (30 minutes before or 2 hours after a meal) ↓ dose when CrCl < 60 mL/min Oral soln: Stable for 30 days if refrigerated	**BLACK BOX WARNINGS** Pancreatitis (sometimes fatal) **CONTRAINDICATIONS** Concurrent use with allopurinol or ribavirin **SIDE EFFECTS** Peripheral neuropathy, diarrhea, ↑ LFTs, insulin resistance/diabetes, non-cirrhotic portal HTN, retinal changes and optic neuritis (rare) **MONITORING** LFTs, eye exam, CBC, blood chemistry, renal function, amylase and lipase (with pancreatitis) **NOTES** Avoid didanosine and stavudine combination due to increased risk of pancreatitis, peripheral neuropathy, and hyperlactatemia. Avoid use with tenofovir due to resistance and virologic failure as well as increased didanosine concentrations.

Nucleoside/tide Reverse Transcriptase Inhibitors (NRTIs) Continued

DRUG	REGIMEN PREFERENCE	DOSING	SAFETY/SIDE EFFECTS/MONITORING
Emtricitabine, FTC (*Emtriva*) Capsule, oral solution (10 mg/mL) **+ tenofovir (*Truvada*)** **+ efavirenz and tenofovir (*Atripla*)** + tenofovir and rilpivirine (*Complera*) + tenofovir and elvitegravir and cobicistat (*Stribild*)	Preferred	Cap: 200 mg daily Soln: 240 mg daily (stable for 3 months at room temp) ↓ dose when CrCl < 50 mL/min One tab daily for *Truvada, Atripla, Complera* and *Stribild*. Take *Atripla* on an empty stomach, preferably at bedtime. Take *Complera* with a meal. Take *Stribild* with food.	**BLACK BOX WARNING** May exacerbate Hepatits B once drug is discontinued or HBV resistance may develop **SIDE EFFECTS** Hyperpigmentation primarily of palms and/or soles (mainly in children), N/V/D, rash, ↑ CPK, ↑ LFTs **MONITORING** LFTs, renal function **NOTES** Avoid combining with lamivudine (no benefit) as both are cytosine analogs: FTC and 3TC). MedGuide Required
LamiVUDine, 3TC (*Epivir*) Tablet, oral solution (10 mg/mL) + zidovudine (*Combivir*) **+ abacavir (*Epzicom*)** + abacavir and zidovudine (*Trizivir*)	Preferred Preferred in pregnancy when combined with zidovudine	150 mg BID or 300 mg daily ↓ dose when CrCl < 50 mL/min Caution with solution in diabetic patients 1 tab daily for *Epzicom* 1 tab BID for *Combivir* and *Trizivir*	**BLACK BOX WARNINGS (2)** Do not use *Epivir-HBV* for treatment of HIV (contains lower doses of lamivudine) May exacerbate Hepatitis B once drug is discontinued or Hep B resistance may develop **SIDE EFFECTS** Headache, N/V/D, fatigue, insomnia, myalgias, ↑ LFTs, rash **MONITORING** LFTs, renal function **NOTES** Avoid combining with emtricitabine (no benefit) as both are cytosine analogs: FTC and 3TC).
Stavudine, d4T (*Zerit*) Capsule, oral solution (1 mg/mL)	Avoid if possible	≥ 60 kg: 40 mg Q12H < 60 kg: 30 mg Q12H ↓ dose when CrCl < 50 mL/min Oral soln: Stable for 30 days in refrigerator	**BLACK BOX WARNING** Pancreatitis (sometimes fatal) has occurred during combinations with didanosine **SIDE EFFECTS** ↑LFTs, insulin resistance/diabetes, peripheral neuropathy, lipoatrophy/lipodystrophy, hyperlipidemia, pancreatitis **MONITORING** LFTs, renal function, signs and symptoms of peripheral neuropathy, lipids **NOTES** Avoid stavudine and didanosine combination due to increased risk of pancreatitis, peripheral neuropathy, and hyperlactatemia. Do not combine with zidovudine (antagonist effect on HIV as both are thymidine analogs: d4T and AZT)

Nucleoside/tide Reverse Transcriptase Inhibitors (NRTIs) Continued

DRUG	REGIMEN PREFERENCE	DOSING	SAFETY/SIDE EFFECTS/MONITORING
Tenofovir, TDF *(Viread)* Tablet, oral powder (40 mg/g) **+ emtricitabine** *(Truvada)* **+ emtricitabine and efavirenz** *(Atripla)* + emtricitabine and rilpivirine *(Complera)* + emtricitabine and elvitegravir and cobicistat *(Stribild)*	Preferred	300 mg daily ↓ dose when CrCl < 50 mL/min One tab daily for *Truvada, Atripla, Complera* and *Stribild*. Take *Atripla* on an empty stomach, preferably at bedtime. Take *Complera* with a meal. Take *Stribild* with food. Dispense in original container	**BLACK BOX WARNING** May exacerbate Hepatitis B once drug is discontinued or HBV resistance may develop **SIDE EFFECTS** Fanconi syndrome, renal insufficiency, osteomalacia and ↓ bone density, GI upset (N/V/D), ↑ LFTs **MONITORING** LFTs, CBC, renal function, phosphorus, urinalysis, bone density (long term) **NOTES** Avoid use with didanosine due to resistance and virologic failure as well as increased didanosine concentrations. Powder should be mixed with 2-4 oz of soft food (applesauce, yogurt) to avoid bitter taste. Consider vitamin D and calcium supplementation.
Zidovudine, ZDV or AZT *(Retrovir)* Capsule, tablet, oral solution (10 mg/mL), inj. + lamivudine *(Combivir)* + abacavir and lamivudine *(Trizivir)*	Less satisfactory, except preferred in pregnancy	300 mg BID ↓ dose when CrCl < 15 mL/min 1 tab BID for *Combivir* and *Trizivir*	**BLACK BOX WARNINGS (2)** Hematologic toxicities (neutropenia and anemia) especially in advanced HIV Prolonged use has been associated with symptomatic myopathy and myositis **SIDE EFFECTS** N/V, nail hyperpigmentation, myopathy, lipoatrophy, ↑ LFTs insulin resistance/diabetes, hyperlipidemia, bone marrow suppression, macrocytic anemia **MONITORING** CBC, LFTs, mean corpuscular volume (MCV), CPK, lipids **NOTES** Avoid combining with stavudine (antagonist effect on HIV as both are thymidine analogs: d4T and AZT); Erythropoetin is indicated to manage ZDV-induced anemia. IV zidovudine should be administered in the setting of labor for HIV+ women, unless viral load is < 400 copies/mL

Nucleoside/Tide Reverse Transcriptase Inhibitor Drug Interactions

NRTIs do not undergo hepatic transformations via the CYP metabolic pathway, therefore, they have fewer significant drug interactions compared to PIs and NNRTIs. Some NRTIs have other mechanisms of drug interactions. Here are a few notable drug interactions:

- Ribavirin may ↑ levels of all NRTIs (combo ↑ risk lactic acidosis).

- Avoid didanosine (ddI) and stavudine (d4T) combination due to increased risk of pancreatitis, peripheral neuropathy, and hyperlactatemia.

- Avoid didanosine and tenofovir combination due to resistance and virologic failure as well as increased didanosine concentrations.

- Avoid emtricitabine and lamivudine combination (no benefit as both cytosine analogs: FT<u>C</u> and 3T<u>C</u>).

- Avoid zidovudine and stavudine (antagonist effect on HIV-1 as both are thymidine analogs: d4<u>T</u> and AZ<u>T</u>).

NON-NUCLEOSIDE REVERSE TRANSCRIPTASE INHIBITORS (NNRTIs)

NNRTIs work by binding to reverse transcriptase and blocking the RNA-dependent and DNA-dependent DNA polymerase activities including HIV-1 replication (see Step #3 in the HIV diagram).

DRUG	REGIMEN PREFERENCE	DOSING	SAFETY/SIDE EFFECTS/MONITORING
Entire Class			**SIDE EFFECTS** Rash (SJS/TEN) – Monitor for erythema, facial edema, skin necrosis, blisters, tongue swelling Hepatotoxicity – monitor LFTs
Delavirdine, DRV (*Rescriptor*) Tablet	Avoid if possible	400 mg TID Patients with achlorhydria should take with acidic beverage; separate dose from antacids by 1 hour	**CONTRAINDICATIONS** Concurrent use of alprazolam, ergot alkaloids, midazolam, rifampin and triazolam **SIDE EFFECTS** Nausea, headache, depression, rash, ↑ LFTs **NOTES** Rarely used due to TID dosing and suboptimal response (compared to other antiretrovirals)
Efavirenz, EFV *(Sustiva)* Capsule, tablet **+ emtricitabine and tenofovir** *(Atripla)*	Preferred	600 mg daily Take on an empty stomach, preferably at bedtime	**CONTRAINDICATIONS** Concurrent use of ergot alkaloids, midazolam, pimozide, triazolam, and St. John's Wort **SIDE EFFECTS** CNS (impaired concentration, drowsiness, vivid dreams – usually resolve within 2-4 weeks) and psychiatric symptoms (depression, paranoia, mania, suicide), hyperlipidemia **MONITORING** Lipids, psychiatric effects, ↑ LFTs **NOTES** Pregnancy Category D – use other ARV agents in women of childbearing potential who are planning to become pregnant or who are sexually active and not using effective contraception. For women who present in the first trimester already on an efavirenz-containing regimen and who have adequate viral suppression, efavirenz may be continued; changing regimens may lead to loss of viral control and increase the risk of perinatal transmission Capsule contents may be sprinkled onto 1-2 teaspoons of food
Etravirine, ETR *(Intelence)* Tablet	For treatment-experienced patients	200 mg BID after meals	**SIDE EFFECTS** Rash, ↑ cholesterol, hyperglycemia and peripheral neuropathy

Non-Nucleoside Reverse Transcriptase Inhibitors (NNRTIs) Continued

DRUG	REGIMEN PREFERENCE	DOSING	SAFETY/SIDE EFFECTS/MONITORING
Nevirapine, NVP (*Viramune, Viramune XR*) Tablet, oral suspension (10 mg/mL)	Avoid if possible Preferred NNRTI in pregnancy	200 mg daily x 14 days; then 200 mg BID (*Viramune*) or 400 mg daily (*Viramune XR*) <u>Need 14 day lead-in period</u>	**BLACK BOX WARNINGS (2)** <u>Severe hepatotoxic reactions may occur (liver failure, death)</u> – risk highest during the first 6 weeks of therapy but may be seen out to 18 weeks (or more); more common in women and with higher CD4 counts as noted below <u>Severe, life-threatening skin reactions (SJS/TEN)</u> – risk highest during the first 18 weeks of therapy **CONTRAINDICATIONS** Moderate-to-severe hepatic impairment, post-exposure prophylaxis regimens **SIDE EFFECTS** GI (nausea, diarrhea), ↑ <u>LFTs</u>, rash (more common with this agent) **NOTES** Do not initiate therapy in women with CD4+ counts > 250 cells/mm^3 and in men with CD4+ counts > 400 cells/mm^3 due to ↑ risk of hepatotoxicity
Rilpivirine, RPV (*Edurant*) Tablet + emtricitabine and tenofovir (*Complera*)	Alternative	25 mg daily <u>with a meal</u> Keep in original container; protect from light 1 tab daily <u>with a meal</u> (*Complera*)	**CONTRAINDICATIONS** All PPIs, rifabutin, rifampin, rifapentine, dexamethasone, carbamazepine, oxcarbazepine, phenobarbital, phenytoin, St. John's Wort due to significant drug-drug interactions **SIDE EFFECTS** CNS (depression, mood changes, suicidal ideation, insomnia), headache, rash **NOTES** Higher rates of failure have been seen in patients with HIV-RNA levels > 100,000 at treatment initiation. Use of H$_2$RAs should only be administered at least 12 hours before or at least 4 hours after rilpivirine. Antacids should be given at least 2 hours before or 4 hours after rilpivirine.

Non-Nucleoside Reverse Transcriptase Inhibitor Drug Interactions

All NNRTIs are cleared non-renally and metabolized in the liver via the CYP 450 system and have MANY drug interactions. They are all 3A4 substrates and may also be an inducer (neviripine and etravirine), inhibitor (delavirdine) or both inducer and inhibitor (efavirenz). Many of the NNRTIs inhibit other isoenzymes. You should always run a drug interaction check on all patients receiving NNRTIs. Below are some notable drug interactions:

- Delavirdine: Strong inhibitor of 2C9, 2C19, 2D6 and 3A4 and major 3A4 substrate.

- Efavirenz: Moderate inhibitor of 2C9, 2C19 and 3A4 and strong inducer of 3A4 and a major substrate of 3A4. Avoid use with boceprevir, clopidogrel, dronedarone, ergot derivatives, midazolam, nilotinib, pimozide, ranolazine, rivaroxaban, St. John's wort, triazolam and others.

- Etravirine: Moderate inhibitor of 2C9, 2C19, and p-glycoprotein and strong inducer of 3A4 and major substrate of 3A4, 2C9, and 2C19. Do not co-administer with carbamazepine, oxcarbazepine, phenobarbital, phenytoin, rifampin, and St. John's Wort.

- Nevirapine: Strong 3A4 inducer and major 3A4 substrate. Watch for strong 3A4 inhibitors.

- Rilpivirine: Contraindicated with strong 3A4 inducers (carbamazepine, oxcarbazepine, phenobarbital, phenytoin, rifampin, rifabutin, St. John's wort) and proton pump inhibitors. Use of H_2RAs should only be administered at least 12 hours before or at least 4 hours after rilpivirine. Antacids should be given at least 2 hours before or 4 hours after rilpivirine.

PROTEASE INHIBITORS (PIs)

PIs work by inhibiting HIV-1 protease and rendering the enzyme incapable of cleaving the Gag-Pol polyprotein, resulting in the production of immature, noninfectious virions (see Step #7 in the HIV diagram).

DRUG	REGIMEN PREFERENCE	DOSING	SAFETY/SIDE EFFECTS/MONITORING
PI Class			**CONTRAINDICATIONS** Concurrent use of alfuzosin, amiodarone, cisapride, ergot derivatives, flecainide, lovastatin, midazolam (oral), pimozide, propafenone, quinidine, sildenafil (when used for the treatment of pulmonary arterial hypertension), simvastatin, St. John's wort, triazolam, and voriconazole (when ritonavir ≥ 800 mg/day). **SIDE EFFECTS** Hyperglycemia/insulin resistance/ diabetes, lipoatrophy, fat maldistribution, hyperlipidemia (lowest with atazanavir and darunavir), hepatitis and hepatic decompensation (highest with tipranavir), immune reconstitution syndrome **MONITORING** Glucose, LFTs, lipid panel, bilirubin

Protease Inhibitors (PIs) Continued

DRUG	REGIMEN PREFERENCE	DOSING	SAFETY/SIDE EFFECTS/MONITORING
Atazanavir, ATV **(Reyataz)** Capsule	Preferred, including in pregnancy	300 mg + 100 mg ritonavir daily 400 mg daily if therapy-naïve and unable to tolerate ritonavir Take with food and water (better absorption)	**SIDE EFFECTS** PR interval prolongation, indirect hyperbilirubinemia (leading to jaundice or scleral icterus – referred to as "bananavir"), rash, nephrolithiasis [taking with 48 oz (1.5 L) of water may reduce risk], cholelithiasis **NOTES** Caution with acid-suppressive agents as they can reduce the levels of atazanavir **With H$_2$RAs** Atazanavir alone (unboosted): take at least 2 hours before or 10 hours after H$_2$RA Atazanavir with ritonavir: take together or at least 10 hours after H$_2$RA **With Antacids** Atazanavir should be taken at least 2 hours before or 1 hour after antacids **With PPIs** Atazanavir with ritonavir: take at least 12 hours after PPIs. The dose should not be > 20 mg of omeprazole (or equivalent) per day (PPIs are not recommended if atazanavir unboosted or in treatment-experienced patients) **MONITORING** ECG in at-risk patients
Darunavir, DRV **(Prezista)** Tablet, oral suspension (100 mg/mL)	Preferred	Treatment naïve: 800 mg + 100 mg ritonavir daily Treatment-experienced: 600 mg + 100 mg ritonavir BID Take with food. Swallow whole. Must be given with ritonavir.	**SIDE EFFECTS** Nausea, diarrhea, rash (including SJS/TEN) **WARNINGS** Use caution in patients with a sulfa allergy
Fosamprenavir, FPV *(Lexiva)* Tablet, oral suspension (50 mg/mL)	Alternative	Treatment naïve: 1,400 mg ± 100-200 mg ritonavir daily or 700 mg + 100 mg ritonavir BID Treatment-experienced: 700 mg + 100 mg ritonavir BID Oral suspension: take without food (adults) Tablets: Take without regards to meals	**SIDE EFFECTS** N/V/D, rash (including SJS/TEN), nephrolithiasis **WARNING** Use caution in patients with a sulfa allergy

Protease Inhibitors (PIs) Continued

DRUG	REGIMEN PREFERENCE	DOSING	SAFETY/SIDE EFFECTS/MONITORING
Indinavir, IDV *(Crixivan)* Capsule	Avoid if possible	Without ritonavir: 800 mg every 8 hours. Take 1 hour before or 2 hours after a meal With ritonavir: 800 mg BID + 100-200 mg ritonavir BID. <u>Take with food and water</u> Swallow whole, do not break, crush, or chew	**SIDE EFFECTS** <u>Nausea, nephrolithiasis</u> [taking with 48 oz (1.5 L) of water may reduce risk] and indirect hyperbilirubinemia **NOTES** <u>Must dispense in the original container with the desiccant to protect from moisture.</u>
Nelfinavir, NFV *(Viracept)* Tablet	Avoid if possible	750 mg TID or 1,250 mg BID <u>Take with food</u>	**SIDE EFFECTS** <u>Diarrhea</u> (~17%), rash **NOTES** Boosting with ritonavir not recommended due to significantly increased levels and risk for toxicity.
Ritonavir, RTV *(**Norvir**)* Capsule, tablet, oral solution (80 mg/mL) Primarily used as a booster agent and not as a sole PI.	Perferred	<u>100-400 mg/d – booster dose</u> <u>Take with food</u> <u>Capsules: Keep refrigerated; can be left at room temperature if used within 30 days</u> Tablets: store at room temp; should be swallowed whole; do not break, crush, or chew <u>Solution: contains 43% alcohol; do not refrigerate</u>	**BLACK BOX WARNING** Ritonavir may interact with many medications, including antiarrhythmics, ergot alkaloids, and sedatives/hypnotics, resulting in potentially serious and/or life-threatening adverse events **SIDE EFFECTS** <u>N/V/D, paresthesias, asthenia, altered taste, PR prolongation</u>
Lopinavir + Ritonavir, LPV/r *(**Kaletra**)* Tablet, oral solution (80 mg lopinavir + 20 mg ritonavir/mL)	Alternative Preferred in pregnancy	Treatment naïve: <u>800 mg lopinavir/200 mg ritonavir daily or 400/100 mg BID</u> Treatment-experienced: 400/100 mg BID <u>Take oral soln with food. Take tablets without regard to meals.</u> Solution: <u>Refrigerate</u>. Good for 2 months if left at room temperature. Contains 42% alcohol. Tabs: Store at room temperature; swallow whole, do not break, crush, or chew.	**SIDE EFFECTS** N/V/D, pancreatitis, asthenia, abdominal pain, prolongation of PR and QT interval **NOTES** Avoid once daily dosing with carbamazepine, phenytoin, phenobarbital and in pregnant women
Saquinavir, SQV *(Invirase)* Capsule, tablet	Avoid if possible	1,000 mg + ritonavir 100 mg BID <u>Take within 2 hours of a full meal</u> Must be given with ritonavir	**CONTRAINDICATIONS** Severe hepatic impairment, prolonged QT interval and refractory hypokalemia or hypomagnesemia **SIDE EFFECTS** N/V/D, PR and QT interval prolongation (avoid use if QT > 450 msec) **MONITORING** ECG (baseline and ongoing)

Protease Inhibitors (PIs) Continued

DRUG	REGIMEN PREFERENCE	DOSING	SAFETY/SIDE EFFECTS/MONITORING
Tipranavir, TPV *(Aptivus)* Capsule, oral solution (100 mg/mL)	Avoid if possible	500 mg + ritonavir 200 mg BID Caps: Refrigerate. Can store at room temp up to 60 days; need to discard 60 days after opening bottle Solution: Store at room temperature (do not refrigerate); need to discard 60 days after opening bottle Take with food Swallow whole, do not break, crush, or chew	**BLACK BOX WARNINGS (2)** In combination with ritonavir, can cause hepatitis (sometimes fatal) and intracranial hemorrhage **WARNING** Use caution in patients with a sulfa allergy **CONTRAINDICATIONS** Moderate or severe hepatic impairment **SIDE EFFECTS** Diarrhea, rash, ↑ CPK, hepatotoxicity, intracranial hemorrhage (rare)

Protease Inhibitor Drug Interactions

All PIs are metabolized in the liver via the CYP 450 system and have many drug interactions. All PIs are 3A4 substrates and most are strong inhibitors of 3A4. Ritonavir is a potent 3A4 inhibitor used at low doses to increase, or boost, the level of other PIs. The drug interaction list below highlights the most important interactions and contraindications and is not all-inclusive.

■ Avoid concomitant use with alfuzosin, amiodarone, cisapride, ergot derivatives, flecainide, lovastatin, midazolam (oral), pimozide, propafenone, quinidine, sildenafil (when used for the treatment of pulmonary arterial hypertension), simvastatin, St John's wort, triazolam, and voriconazole (when ritonavir ≥ 800 mg/day). Many of the PIs should not be used with boceprevir or telaprevir.

■ Caution with the use of 3A4 inducers as they can lower the concentration of PIs.

■ PIs can alter the INR (mainly ↓) in patients taking warfarin; the INR should be closely monitored.

■ PIs increase the levels of trazodone and many tricyclic antidepressants. Titrate anti-depressant doses based upon clinical response.

■ Atazanavir: caution with the use of acid-suppressive agents. See chart above.

FUSION INHIBITORS

Fusion inhibitors block the attachment (or fusion) of the HIV-1 virus with the CD4 cells by blocking the conformational change in gp41 required for membrane fusion and entry into CD4 cells. They are also known as cell entry inhibitors (see Step #1 in the HIV diagram).

DRUG	REGIMEN PREFERENCE	DOSING	SAFETY/SIDE EFFECTS/MONITORING
Enfuvirtide, T20 (Fuzeon) – Salvage Therapy	For treatment-experienced patients	90 mg SC BID	**SIDE EFFECTS** Local injection site reactions in almost 100% of patients (pain, erythema, induration, nodules and cysts, pruritus, ecchymosis); ↑ risk of bacterial pneumonia **NOTES** Reconstituted solution should be refrigerated and used within 24 hours No significant drug interactions

CCR5 ANTAGONIST

CCR5 inhibitors bind to the CCR5 co-receptor on the CD4 cells and prevent the conformational change required for HIV cell entry (see Step #1 in the HIV diagram).

DRUG	REGIMEN PREFERENCE	DOSING	SAFETY/SIDE EFFECTS/MONITORING
Maraviroc, MVC (Selzentry) Tablet	For treatment-experienced patients	300 mg BID Take without regard to meals ↓ dose when CrCl < 30 mL/min	**BLACK BOX WARNING** Hepatotoxicity with allergic type features **CONTRAINDICATIONS** Patients with severe renal impairment (CrCl < 30 mL/min) who are taking potent 3A4 inhibitors or inducers **SIDE EFFECTS** Upper respiratory tract infections, fever, rash (including SJS), cough, abdominal pain, musculoskeletal symptoms, hepatotoxicity, dizziness, orthostatic hypotension (especially in renal impairment) **MONITORING** Prior to starting therapy, patients must undergo a screening test (Trofile), preferably with a phenotypic tropism assay, to determine the tropism of their HIV since this agent will only work for patients with CCR5-tropic disease

CCR5 Antagonist Drug Interactions

Maraviroc is a P-glycoprotein and major 3A4 substrate. Maraviroc concentrations can be significantly increased in the presence of strong 3A4 inhibitors and reduced with 3A4 inducers. Avoid use with St. John's wort.

INTEGRASE STRAND TRANSFER INHIBITORS (INSTIs)

Integrase inhibitors block the integrase enzyme needed for viral DNA to enter into the host nucleus (see Step #4 in the HIV diagram).

DRUG	REGIMEN PREFERENCE	DOSING	SAFETY/SIDE EFFECTS/MONITORING
Raltegravir, RAL *(Isentress)* Tablet (including chewable)	Preferred	400 mg BID Take without regard to meals	**SIDE EFFECTS** Nausea, diarrhea, headache, insomnia, pyrexia, CPK elevation, myopathy and rhabdomyolysis, rash (including SJS) **MONITORING** CPK
Dolutegravir, DTG *(Tivicay)* Tablet	Preferred	50 mg PO daily (not indicated for weight < 40 kg) Take without regard to meals	**CONTRAINDICATION** Coadministration with dofetilide due to risk for significantly increased dofetilide concentration resulting in increased toxicity **SIDE EFFECTS** Insomnia, headache, diarrhea, rash, CPK elevation, ↑ LFTs among Hep B/C patients **MONITORING** CPK, LFTs (Hep B/C patients)
Elvitegravir (EVG), cobicistat (COB), emtricitabine, tenofovir *(Stribild)* Tablet	Preferred	1 tablet daily with food Do not initiate if CrCl < 70 mL/min; discontinue when CrCl < 50 mL/min Dispense in original container	**BLACK BOX WARNINGS (2)** Lactic acidosis with severe hepatomegaly with steatosis and acute exacerbation of HBV in patients who are co-infected. **CONTRAINDICATIONS** Concurrent use of alfuzosin, cisapride, ergot derivatives, lovastatin, midazolam (oral), pimozide, rifampin, sildenafil (when used for pulmonary arterial hypertension), simvastatin, St. John's wort and triazolam **WARNINGS** New onset or worsening renal impairment and decreases in bone mineral density **SIDE EFFECTS** Proteinuria (39%), nausea and diarrhea **NOTES** Cobicistat is a booster similar to ritonavir It is recommended to separate the dosing from antacids by at least 2 hours. H$_2$RAs and PPIs do not pose an interaction.

Integrase Strand Transfer Inhibitor Drug Interactions

- Dolutegravir: Should be taken 2 hours before or 6 hours after taking cation-containing antacids or laxatives, sucralfate, iron supplements, calcium supplements or buffered medication.

- Raltegravir: Metabolized by the UGT1A1-mediated glucuronidation pathway. Rifampin, a strong inducer of UGT1A1, will ↓ levels of raltegravir. When given concurrently with rifampin, use raltegravir 800 mg BID. Avoid St. John's wort. PPIs can ↑ levels of raltegravir.

- *Stribild:* Cobicistat, a component of *Stribild*, is an inhibitor of CYP3A, CYP2D6 and p-glycoprotein. Elvitegravir is a modest inducer of CYP2C9 and may decrease the plasma concentrations of CYP2C9 substrates.

COMBINATION PRODUCTS

GENERIC NAME	BRAND NAME	DOSE
Emtricitabine 200 mg + tenofovir 300 mg	*Truvada*	1 tab daily
Lamivudine 150 mg + zidovudine 300 mg	*Combivir*	1 tab BID
Abacavir 600 mg + lamivudine 300 mg	*Epzicom*	1 tab daily
Abacavir 300 mg + lamivudine 150 mg + zidovudine 300 mg	*Trizivir*	1 tab BID
Emtricitabine 200 mg + tenofovir 300 mg + efavirenz 600 mg	*Atripla*	1 tab daily on empty stomach
Emtricitabine 200 mg + tenofovir 300 mg + rilpivirine 25 mg	*Complera*	1 tab daily with food
Emtricitabine 200 mg + tenofovir 300 mg + elvitegravir* 150 mg + cobicistat* 150 mg	*Stribild*	1 tab daily with food

*   Elvitegravir (integrase inhibitor) and cobicistat (boosting agent) are not (yet) FDA-approved as sole agents and are only available as a combination product with emtricitabine/tenofovir.

PRE-EXPOSURE PROPHYLAXIS (PrEP)

PrEP is a new HIV prevention method in which people who do not have HIV take <u>emtricitabine/tenofovir (Truvada) 1 tab PO daily</u> to reduce their risk of becoming infected. PrEP is recommended for both homosexual and heterosexual individuals who are at very high risk for sexual exposure to HIV.

Before Initiating PrEP

■ Confirm HIV negative status through HIV antibody test

■ Confirm CrCl ≥ 60 mL/min

■ Confirm patient very high risk for acquiring HIV

■ Screen for Hep B and STDs

Once PrEP is initiated, follow-up visits are needed every 2-3 months with the following recommendations during EACH visit:

■ HIV test and document negative result

■ Provide no more than 90-day supply at a time (renew Rx only once HIV negative status is confirmed)

ADMINISTRATION

With food	Without food
Atazanavir	*Atripla*
Complera	Didanosine
Darunavir	Efavirenz (or small amount of food)
Etravirine (after meals)	Fosamprenavir (oral suspension)
Indinavir – boosted	Indinavir – unboosted
Kaletra oral soln	Tenofovir powder (to avoid bitter taste)
Nelfinavir	
Rilpivirine	
Ritonavir	
Saquinavir	
Stribild	
Tipranavir	

- Pregnancy test

- Counseling on PrEP adherence and safe sex practices

- Every 6 months, check SCr and calculate CrCl, and test for bacterial STDs (regardless of symptoms)

NONOCCUPATIONAL POSTEXPOSURE PROPHYLAXIS (nPEP)

Nonoccupational exposure is the use of ART prophylaxis after sexual, injection drug use, or some other nonoccupational exposure to HIV.

Nonoccupational Postexposure Prophylaxis (nPEP) Recommendations

PREFERRED REGIMENS	CRITERIA TO QUALIFY	DURATION
NNRTI-BASED Efavirenz + (Lamivudine or emtricitabine) + (Zidovudine or tenofovir) **PI-BASED** Lopinavir/ritonavir + (Lamivudine or emtricitabine) + Zidovudine	≤ 72 hours since exposure Known HIV (+) status (If HIV status unknown, then case-by-case determination)	28 days

OCCUPATIONAL POSTEXPOSURE PROPHYLAXIS RECOMMENDATIONS (PEP)

Occupational exposure refers to exposure of health care personnel to blood and body fluids that may potentially be contaminated with HIV. ART prophylaxis for occupational exposure is generally only recommended if the source of contaminated blood or body fluid is known to be HIV positive. If the source patient's HIV status is unknown, the HIV status should be determined, if possible, to guide need for HIV PEP. Therapy should be started right away, ideally within 72 hours, when treatment is indicated. Per the updated guidelines a three drug regimen including raltegravir + tenofovir/emtricitibine *(Truvada)* for a 4-week course is the preferred regimen.

Reference: Infect Control Hosp Epidemiol. 2013 Sep;34(9):875-92

Over-the-Counter HIV Testing

There are 2 over-the-counter HIV tests that patients can do in their home. *Express HIV-1 Test System* is a blood test where the patient collects the sample of blood, ships the sample in a pre-paid overnight envelope, and obtains results the next day (excluding weekends and holidays). The *OraQuick* test is an oral swab test where results are obtained in 20-40 minutes. Individuals who get a positive result do need to get a confirmatory test at their physician's office (usually a Western blot). These are HIV antibody tests, meaning they detect the presence of HIV antibodies which can take up to 3 months after infection to develop. Testing sooner than 3 months after the risk event can lead to a false negative reading. Patients should wait at least 3 months after the risk event to test.

How to take the *OraQuick* test:

1. Do not eat, drink, or use oral care products at least 30 min before taking the test. Remove dental products such as dentures that cover your gums.

2. Tear open the packet labeled "Test Tube". There is liquid in this tube so be careful upon opening not to spill out the liquid. POP off the cap – do NOT twist.

3. Open the packet labeled "Test Stick". Do not touch the pad with your fingers. Gently swipe the pad along your upper gums once and your lower gums once. You may use either side on the flat pad. Make sure you swipe each gum only once or your results could be wrong (do not swab the roof of the mouth, inside of the cheek, or the tongue).

4. Insert the test stick into the test tube which contains liquid at the bottom. Write down your start time. Then add 20 minutes and write down this number, which is your read time.

5. Read the results after 20 minutes but not later than 40 minutes.

6. If there is one line next to "C" and no line next to "T", your test result is negative. If there are 2 lines, one next to "C" and any line next to "T" (even a faint one), your test result is positive for HIV. The test is considered invalid if no line appears next to "C" or no lines appear at all.

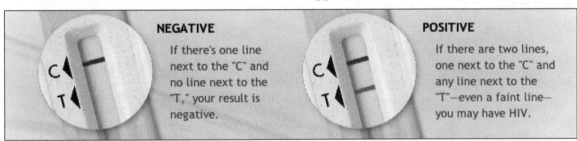

NEGATIVE

If there's one line next to the "C" and no line next to the "T," your result is negative.

POSITIVE

If there are two lines, one next to the "C" and any line next to the "T"—even a faint line— you may have HIV.

Strategies to Improve Adherence to Antiretroviral Therapy

STRATEGIES	EXAMPLES
Utilize a multidisciplinary team approach	Nurses, social workers, pharmacists, and medication managers
Provide an accessible, trusting health care team	
Establish a trusting relationship with the patient	
Establish patient readiness to start ART	
Assess and simplify the regimen, if possible	
Identify potential barriers to adherence prior to starting ART	Psychosocial issues
	Active substance abuse or at high risk of relapse
	Low literacy
	Low numeracy
	Busy daily schedule and/or travel away from home
	Nondisclosure of HIV diagnosis
	Skepticism about ART
	Lack of prescription drug coverage
	Lack of continuous access to medications
Provide resources for the patient	Referrals for mental health and/or substance abuse treatment
	Resources to obtain prescription drug coverage
	Pillboxes, reminder tools
Involve the patient in ARV regimen selection	For each option, review regimen potency, potential side effects, dosing frequency, pill burden, storage requirements, food requirements, and consequences of nonadherence
Assess adherence at every clinic visit	Use a simple checklist that the patient can complete in the waiting room
	Ensure that other members of the health care team also assess adherence
	Ask the patient open-ended questions (e.g., In the last 3 days, please tell me how you took your medicines.)
Identify the type of nonadherence	Failure to fill the prescription(s)
	Failure to take the right dose(s) at the right time(s)
	Nonadherence to food requirements
Identify reasons for nonadherence	Adverse effects from medications
	Complexity of regimen – pill burden, dosing frequency, etc.
	Difficulty swallowing large pills
	Forgetfulness
	Failure to understand dosing instructions
	Inadequate understanding of drug resistance and its relationship to adherence
	Pill fatigue
	Other potential barriers
If resources allow, select from among available effective interventions	See http://www.cdc.gov/hiv/topics/research/prs/ma-good-evidence-interventions.htm

PRIMARY PROPHYLAXIS OF OPPORTUNISTIC INFECTIONS IN PATIENTS WITH HIV

PATHOGEN	INDICATION	PRIMARY PROPHYLAXIS REGIMEN	CRITERIA FOR DISCONTINUING PRIMARY PROPHYLAXIS
Pneumocystis pneumonia (PCP)	CD4+ count < 200 cells/mL or oropharyngeal candidiasis	Preferred: TMP/SMX 1 DS tab PO daily or 1 SS PO daily Alternative: TMP/SMX 1 DS PO TIW or dapsone 100 mg PO daily or 50 mg PO BID, or (dapsone + pyrimethamine + leucovorin), or aerosolized pentamidine, or atovaquone	CD4+ count > 200 for 3 months on ART
Toxoplasma gondii	Toxoplasma IgG positive patients with CD4+ count < 100 cells/mL	Preferred: TMP/SMX 1 DS tab PO daily Alternative: TMP/SMX 1 DS PO TIW or 1 SS PO daily or (dapsone 50 mg PO daily + pyrimethamine 50 mg PO weekly + leucovorin 25 mg PO weekly)	CD4+ count > 200 for 3 months on ART
Mycobacterium avium complex (MAC)	CD4+ count < 50 cells/mL after ruling out active disseminated MAC disease	Preferred: Azithromycin 1,200 mg PO weekly or clarithromycin 500 mg PO BID or azithromycin 600 mg PO twice weekly	CD4+ count ≥ 100 for 3 months on ART

TREATMENT OF OPPORTUNISTIC INFECTIONS

PATHOGEN	FIRST LINE TREATMENT	ALTERNATIVE TREATMENT	SECONDARY PROPHYLAXIS
Cryptococcal Meningitis	Liposomal amphotericin B + flucytosine	Amphotericin B deoxycholate + flucytosine or fluconazole + flucytosine or fluconazole alone	Fluconazole (low dose)
Cytomegalovirus (CMV) retinitis	Valganciclovir or ganciclovir	Foscarnet or cidofovir	Continue same agent at reduced dose (usually valganciclovir)
Mycobacterium avium complex infection	Clarithromycin or azithromycin + ethambutol ± rifampin/rifabutin	Replace one agent with moxifloxacin	Same agents at same doses
Pneumocystis pneumonia (PCP)	TMP/SMX ± corticosteroids	Atovaquone or (clindamycin + primaquine) or pentamidine IV or (dapsone + trimethoprim)*	TMP/SMX or dapsone or (dapsone + pyrimethamine) or atovaquone or inhaled pentamidine
Toxoplasmosis meningoencephalitis	Pyrimethamine** + sulfadiazine	TMP/SMX, (pyrimethamine** + clindamycin or azithromycin), (atovaquone alone or with sulfadiazine or pyrimethamine**)	Same agents at reduced dose

* Selection of alternative therapy for PCP is dependent on severity of illness and patient specific factors (allergies and G6PD deficiency). For example, atovaquone, clindamycin + primaquine or pentamidine are all potential options in the setting of sulfa allergy, however only atovaquone (mild disease) and pentamadine (moderate-severe disease) are available in the setting of G6PD deficiency.

** Leucovorin added as rescue therapy to reduce risk for bone marrow suppression associated with pyrimethamine.

PATIENT COUNSELING

All HIV Medications

- This medication is not a cure for HIV and it does not prevent the spread of HIV to others through sexual contact or blood contamination (such as sharing used needles).

- It is very important to continue taking this medication (and other HIV medications) exactly as prescribed by your doctor. <u>Do not skip any doses</u>. Do not stop taking it (or other HIV medicines) even for a short time unless directed to do so by your doctor. Skipping or stopping your medication without approval from your doctor may cause the amount of virus to increase and make the infection more difficult to treat (resistant). Refill your medication before you run out.

NRTIs Patient Counseling

- This medication can cause changes in your body fat distribution. Changes include increased amount of fat in the upper back and neck, breast and around the main part of the body (belly area). Loss of fat from the legs, arms and face may also happen.

- Rarely, this medication can cause severe (sometimes fatal) liver problems. Tell your doctor immediately if you develop symptoms of liver problems such as persistent nausea, loss of appetite, stomach/abdominal pain, pale stools, dark urine, yellowing eyes/skin, or unusual tiredness.

- Rarely, this medication can cause a build-up of acid in your blood; report any symptoms such as stomach pain, nausea, vomiting, troubled breathing, feeling tired or weak, muscle pain, or cold skin. These serious side effects may occur more often in women, obese patients, or those taking this medication for a long time.

- If you have hepatitis B infection and are taking lamivudine, emtricitabine, or tenofovir, your hepatitis symptoms may get worse or become very serious if you stop taking any of these medications. Talk with your doctor before stopping this medication. Your doctor will monitor liver tests for several months after you stop this medication. Tell your doctor immediately if you develop symptoms of worsening liver problems.

For Emtricitabine

- Rarely, this medication can cause darkening skin color on the palms of hands and on the soles of feet. Notify your doctor if this is problematic to you.

For Tenofovir

- Tell your doctor immediately if any of these rare but serious side effects occur: signs of kidney problems such as a change in the amount of urine, unusual thirst, muscle cramps/weakness, bone pain, or easily broken bones.

- Tenofovir powder: This medication comes with a dosing scoop; <u>use only the dosing scoop to measure the oral powder</u>. Mix the <u>oral powder with soft foods</u> that can be swallowed without chewing (e.g., applesauce, baby food or yogurt). <u>Do not mix the oral powder with liquid</u>. The powder may float to the top even after stirring. <u>Give the entire dose right away after mixing</u> to avoid a bad taste.

Efavirenz

- Take this medication by mouth <u>on an empty stomach, without food, usually once daily at bedtime</u> or as directed by your doctor. Swallow this medication with water. Taking efavirenz with food increases the blood level of this medication, which may increase your risk of certain side effects.

- Efavirenz can cause side effects that may impair your thinking or reactions. Be careful if you drive or do anything that requires you to be awake and alert.

- Avoid drinking alcohol. It can increase some of the side effects of efavirenz.

- Dizziness, trouble sleeping, drowsiness, unusual dreams, and trouble concentrating may frequently occur. These side effects may begin 1-2 days after starting this medication and usually go away in 2-4 weeks. They are also reduced by taking efavirenz on an empty stomach at bedtime.

- Tiredness, headache, nausea, vomiting, and diarrhea may also occur. If any of these effects persist or worsen, tell your doctor or pharmacist promptly.

- Infrequently, serious psychiatric symptoms may occur during efavirenz treatment, although it is unclear if they are caused by efavirenz. These effects may be seen especially in people who have mental/mood conditions. Tell your doctor immediately if any of these unlikely but serious side effects occur: mental/mood changes (such as depression, rare thoughts of suicide, nervousness, angry behavior, or hallucinations).

- Tell your doctor immediately if you develop persistent nausea/vomiting, stomach/abdominal pain, severe tiredness, yellowing eyes/skin, or dark urine as those can be signs of liver problems.

- Efavirenz can commonly cause a rash that is usually not serious. A rash may occur in the first 2 weeks after starting treatment and if it is not serious, it will usually resolve in 4 weeks. However, you may not be able to tell it apart from a rare rash that could be a sign of a severe reaction. Therefore, seek immediate medical attention if you develop any rash.

- Efavirenz can speed up or slow down the removal of many other medications from your body, which may affect how they work. Make sure that your doctor and/or pharmacist are aware of all medications that you are taking, including over-the-counter medicines and herbal supplements.

- This medication may decrease the effectiveness of hormonal birth control such as pills, patch, or ring. This could cause pregnancy. However, to reduce the risk of spreading HIV to others, use barrier protection during all sexual activity.

- This medication can cause harm to an unborn baby. Do not use efavirenz without your doctor's consent if you are pregnant. Use two forms of birth control, including a barrier form (such as a condom or diaphragm with spermicide gel) while you are taking efavirenz, and for at least 12 weeks after your treatment ends. Tell your doctor if you become pregnant during treatment.

PI Patient Counseling

- Diarrhea, nausea, vomiting, heartburn, stomach pain, loss of appetite, headache, dizziness, tiredness, weakness, or changes in taste may occur. If any of these effects persist or worsen, tell your doctor or pharmacist promptly.

- A mild rash (redness and itching) may occur within the first few weeks after the medicine is started and usually goes away within 2 weeks with no change in treatment.

- If a severe rash develops with symptoms of fever, body or muscle aches, mouth sores, shortness of breath, or swelling of the face, contact your doctor immediately.

- Tell your doctor immediately if any of these unlikely but serious side effects occur: persistent nausea/vomiting, stomach/abdominal pain, dark urine, yellowing eyes/skin, mental/mood changes (such as depression or anxiety), joint pain, muscle weakness/cramps/aches, increased urination (especially at night), or increased thirst.

- Before using this medication, tell your doctor or pharmacist your medical history, especially of: diabetes, heart problems (coronary artery disease, heart attack), hemophilia, high cholesterol/triglycerides, gout/high uric acid in the blood, liver problems (such as hepatitis B or hepatitis C) and/or pancreatitis.

- If you have diabetes, this product may increase your blood sugar levels. Check your blood sugar levels regularly as directed by your doctor. Tell your doctor immediately if you have symptoms of high blood sugar, such as increased thirst, increased urination, confusion, drowsiness, flushing, rapid breathing, or fruity breath odor. Your doctor may need to adjust your diabetes medication.

- Changes in body fat may occur while you are taking this medication (such as increased fat in the upper back and stomach areas and decreased fat in the arms and legs). The cause and long-term effects of these changes are unknown. Discuss the risks and benefits of treatment with your doctor, as well as the possible use of exercise to reduce this side effect.

- If you are taking HIV medications for the first time, you may experience symptoms of an old infection. This may happen as your immune system begins to work better. Contact your doctor immediately if you notice any of the following symptoms: new cough, trouble breathing, fever, new vision problems, new headaches or new skin problems.

- This medication interacts with many medications. Your doctor or pharmacist may already be aware of any possible drug interactions and may be monitoring you for them. Do not start, stop or change the dosage of any medicine before checking with your doctor or pharmacist first.

For Atazanavir

- Take this medication once daily with food.

- If you are taking antacids or a buffered form of didanosine (e.g., chewable/dispersible buffered tablets), take atazanavir 2 hours before or 1 hour after these medicines.

- Also, other acid-lowering medications for indigestion, heartburn, or ulcers (e.g., prescription or over-the-counter medications such as famotidine or omeprazole) may prevent your HIV drugs from working. Ask your doctor or pharmacist how to use these medications safely.

- Seek immediate medical attention if any of these rare but serious side effects occur: symptoms of a heart attack (such as chest/jaw/left arm pain, shortness of breath or unusual sweating), change in heart rhythm, dizziness, lightheadedness, severe nausea or vomiting, severe stomach pain, extreme weakness (especially in arms and legs), trouble breathing or signs of a kidney stone (e.g., pain in side/back/abdomen, painful urination or blood in the urine).

For Darunavir

- Take darunavir with ritonavir at the same time(s) each day with food.

- If you have a sulfonamide allergy, tell your doctor or pharmacist right away.

20

HEPATITIS & LIVER DISEASE

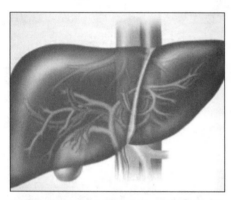

We gratefully acknowledge the assistance of Brett Heintz, PharmD, BCPS-ID, AAHIVE, Infectious Diseases/ Internal Medicine Pharmacist at Iowa City VA Medical Center and Associate Clinical Professor at University of Iowa College of Pharmacy, in preparing this chapter.

BACKGROUND

The term hepatitis means inflammation of the liver. There are many possible causes of hepatitis, including viral hepatitis and liver inflammation due to drugs, including alcohol.

GUIDELINES

Ghany MG, Nelson DR, Strader DB, et al. An Update on Treatment of Genotype 1 Chronic Hepatitis C Infection: 2011 Practice Guideline by the American Association for the Study of Liver Diseases. Hepatology 2011;54:1433-1444.

Alcoholic Liver Disease. American Association for the Study of Liver Diseases and the American College of Gastroenterology. Hepatology 2010;307-328.

Chronic Hepatitis B: Update 2009: Practice Guidelines by the American Association for the Study of Liver Diseases. Hepatology 2009;50:661-699.

Symptoms of Liver Disease

Symptoms can include nausea, loss of appetite, vomiting, diarrhea, malaise, abdominal pain in the upper right quadrant (of the abdomen), yellowed skin and yellowed whites of the eyes (jaundice), darkened urine and/ or lightened color (white or clay-colored) stool caused by low bile in the stool due to decreased production or a blocked bile duct.

Objective Criteria

Alanine aminotransferase (ALT) and asparatate aminotransferase (AST) are liver enzymes. The ALT normal range is 7-55 units per liter (units/L), and the AST normal range is 8-48 units/L. There is some slight variance in these ranges on different lab reports. In general, the higher the values, the worse the liver disease. Clinical signs of liver disease, in addition to ↑ ALT and ↑ AST, include ↓ albumin (protein produced by the liver; normal range 3.5-5.5 g/dL), ↑ alkaline phosphatase (Alk Phos), ↑ total bilirubin (Tbili), ↑ lactate dehydrogenase (LDH), and ↑ in

DRUGS THAT CAN CAUSE LIVER DAMAGE

Below are some drugs in which patients should monitor for symptoms of liver disease. Patients may require blood tests to check on their liver function.

Acarbose

Acetaminophen (acute, high doses)

Amiodarone

Atomoxetine

Azathioprine

Bicalutamide, flutamide

Bosentan

Carbamazepine

Dronedarone

Estrogen

Etanercept and other TNF-blockers

Febuxostat

Felbamate

Fenofibrates

Flutamide

Gemfibrozil

Griseofulvin

Imatinib & other "ibs"

Interferons

Isoniazid

Isotretinoin

Ketoconazole (highest risk), other azoles

Ketorolac

Leflunomide and Teriflunomide

Lomitapide

Macrolides

Maraviroc

Metaxolone

Methimazole

Methotrexate

Methyldopa

Mipomersen

Mycophenolate

Nefazodone

Niacins

NNRTIs (highest risk with nevirapine)

NRTIs (highest risk with didanosine, stavudine, zidovudine)

Oxymorphone

Phenobarbital/ Primidone

Phenytoin

Pioglitazone, Rosiglitazone

PIs (highest risk with tipranavir)

Propylthiouracil

Pyrazinamide

Quinidine

Ribavirin

Rifampin

Tamoxifen

Telithromycin

Terbinafine

Testosterone

Tigecycline

Tizanidine

Tolcapone

Tolvaptan

Valproic acid

Zileuton

Natural products
Comfrey, Flavocoxid *(Limbrel)*, a medical food

Kava

prothrombin time (PT). Albumin and PT/INR are markers of synthetic (production ability) liver function. Liver disease can be classified as hepatocellular ($\uparrow$ ALT and $\uparrow$ AST), cholestatic ($\uparrow$ Alk Phos and $\uparrow$ Tbili), or mixed ($\uparrow$ALT, AST, Alk Phos and Tbili).

Severity of Liver Disease

It is important to assess the severity of the cirrhosis as it serves as a predictor of patient survival, surgical outcomes, and the risk of complications such as variceal bleeding. The Child-Pugh classification system is widely used which has a scoring ranging from 0-15. Class A (mild disease) is defined as a score < 7; Class B (moderate disease) is a score of 7-9, and Class C (severe disease) is a score of 10-15. Model for end-stage liver disease (MELD) is another scoring system ranging from 0-40 with higher numbers indicating a greater risk of dying within 3 months than patients with a lower score. Unlike in the setting of renal failure, little data is available to guide drug dosing of hepatically cleared agents in the setting of liver failure. In general, caution is advised when using hepatically cleared agents in severe liver disease (Class C) and, in select cases, dose adjustment may be necessary.

Natural Product

Milk thistle, an extract derived from a member of the daisy family, is often used by patients with liver disease. Per the AALSD guidelines, milk thistle does not significantly influence the course of patients with alcoholic liver disease. The Natural Medicines database states there is insufficient evidence to rate milk thistle for alcoholic liver disease, hepatitis B and C. Milk thistle does not appear to be harmful and a possible side effect is mild diarrhea.

Drug-Induced Liver Damage

If a drug is damaging the liver, the primary treatment (in most cases) is to <u>stop the drug</u>. Many drugs that are hepatotoxic are discontinued when the liver enzymes are > 3 times the upper limit of normal (> 150 ALT or AST), however clinical judgment is warranted. Rechallenging with the potential agent can be considered if clinically necessary.

ALCOHOLIC LIVER DISEASE

Alcoholic liver disease is a term that encompasses the hepatic manifestations of alcohol over-consumption, including fatty liver, alcoholic hepatitis, and chronic hepatitis with hepatic fibrosis or cirrhosis. Individuals who consume a large quantity of alcoholic beverages over a long period of time develop fatty deposition in the hepatocytes (or fatty liver known as steatosis). This process is transient and reversible as long as scarring, or fibrosis, has not occurred. Of all chronic heavy drinkers, only 15–20% develop hepatitis or cirrhosis, which can occur simultaneously or in succession.

The longer the alcohol use has occurred and the more alcohol that was consumed, the greater the likelihood of developing liver disease. Women are more at risk of developing liver disease due to alcohol than men. Alcohol-induced liver disease is the most common type of drug-induced liver disease. Treatment programs use mainly benzodiazepines for alcohol withdrawal in an inpatient environment whereas anticonvulsants are used for outpatients. Naltrexone *(ReVia)*, acamprosate *(Campral)* and disulfiram *(Antabuse)* are used to prevent relapses. Other therapies have been tried off label for reducing relapses.

Chronic consumption of alcohol results in the secretion of pro-inflammatory cytokines (TNF-alpha, IL-6 and IL-8), oxidative stress, lipid peroxidation, and acetaldehyde toxicity. These factors cause inflammation, apoptosis and eventually fibrosis of liver cells resulting in many complications, including portal hypertension, ascites, variceal bleeding and hepatic encephalopathy (discussed in the next sections). Drinking habits of patients need to be routinely screened by providers.

Treatment

The most important part of treatment is alcohol cessation. If liver cirrhosis has not yet occurred, the liver can regenerate even when a majority of the hepatocytes are dead.

An alcohol rehabilitation program and a support group whose members share common experiences and problems are extremely helpful in breaking the addiction to alcohol.

Proper nutrition is essential to help the liver recover. Vitamins and trace minerals, including vitamin A, vitamin D, thiamine (vitamin B1), folate, pyridoxine (vitamin B6) and zinc, can help reverse malnutrition. <u>Thiamine is used to prevent and treat Wernicke-Korsakoff syndrome.</u> Wernicke's encephalopathy and Korsakoff syndrome are different conditions that are both due to brain damage caused by a <u>lack of vitamin B1</u>. Last, avoidance of hepatotoxic agents and/or adjusting/limiting the dose of hepatotoxic agents should be utilized.

COMPLICATIONS OF LIVER DISEASE

Portal Hypertension and Variceal Bleeding

Portal hypertension, or increased blood pressure in the portal vein, can cause further complications including the development and bleeding of varices. Non-selective beta-blockers (such as nadolol and propranolol) or endoscopic variceal ligation (EVL) are used for primary prevention. Beta-blockers reduce portal pressure by reducing portal venous inflow by 2 mechanisms: 1. decreasing cardiac output (via beta-1 blockade) and 2. decreasing splanchnic blood flow by vasoconstriction (via beta-2 blockade and unopposed alpha activity). The beta-blocker should be titrated to the maximal tolerated dose (target HR 55-60 BPM) and continued indefinitely.

DRUG	DOSING	SAFETY/SIDE EFFECTS/MONITORING
Nadolol *(Corgard)*	20-40 mg PO daily	**BLACK BOX WARNING** Beta-blockers should not be withdrawn abruptly (particularly in patients with CAD), gradually taper over 1-2 weeks to avoid acute tachycardia, HTN, and/or ischemia. **CONTRAINDICATIONS** Sinus bradycardia, 2nd or 3rd degree heart block, sick sinus syndrome (unless patient has a functioning artificial pacemaker), cardiogenic shock, severe hyperactive airway disease. **SIDE EFFECTS** ↓ HR, hypotension, fatigue, dizziness, depression, ↓ libido, impotence, hyperglycemia (non-selective agents can decrease insulin secretion in type 2 diabetes), hypertriglyceridemia, ↓ HDL
Propranolol *(Inderal LA, InnoPran XL)*	20 mg PO BID	**MONITORING** HR (55-60 BPM), BP, SCr (renally cleared) **NOTES** Avoid abrupt discontinuation – must taper Caution in diabetes with recurrent hypoglycemia, asthma, severe COPD or resting limb ischemia Caution: IV doses are not equivalent to oral doses (usually IV is much lower)

Managing Acute Variceal Bleeding

Patients with acute variceal bleeding should be stabilized by providing supportive therapy such as blood volume resuscitation/blood products, mechanical ventilation, correction of coagulopathy, and attempts to stop the bleeding and preventing rebleeding. Band ligation or sclerotherapy are recommended first-line treatments for bleeding varices. In addition, vasoactive therapy is used to stop or minimize the bleeding by decreasing portal blood flow and pressure by splanchnic vasoconstriction. Octreotide is selective for the splanchnic vessels whereas vasopressin is non-selective. Surgical interventions may be considered if the patient is not responding to treatment or to prevent future rebleeding episodes. Common surgical procedures include balloon tamponade (may help control current bleeding) or transjugular intrahepatic portosystemic shunt (TIPS). In general, the addition of antimicrobial therapy (ceftriaxone) for 5 days to prevent subsequent infection and albumin (1.5 mg/kg IV on day 1 and 1 mg/kg IV on day three) are recommended as they are both associated with mortality benefits. Non-selective beta-blockers should be added after resolution of variceal bleeding for secondary prevention of variceal bleeding recurrence.

DRUG	DOSING	SAFETY/SIDE EFFECTS/MONITORING
Octreotide (SandoSTATIN) (analogue of somatostatin – has greater potency and longer duration of action)	25-50 mcg IV bolus, followed by 25-50 mcg/hr continuous IV infusion x 2-5 days	**SIDE EFFECTS** Bradycardia, chest pain, fatigue, headache, pruritus, hyperglycemia, hypoglycemia (highest risk in type 1 diabetes), diarrhea, nausea, hypothyroidism **MONITORING** Blood glucose, HR, ECG
Vasopressin (Pitressin) antidiuretic hormone analog Not 1st line (usually used with nitroglycerin IV to prevent myocardial ischemia)	0.2-0.4 units/min (max 0.8 units/min) IV continuous infusion for max of 24 hours	**SIDE EFFECTS** Arrhythmias, chest pain, MI, ↓ cardiac output, ↑ BP, nausea, vomiting **MONITORING** BP, HR, ECG, fluid balance

Hepatic Encephalopathy

Hepatic encephalopathy (HE) is a syndrome of neuropsychiatric abnormalities caused by acute or chronic hepatic insufficiency. Symptoms include musty odor of the breath and/or urine, changes in thinking, confusion, forgetfulness, mood changes, poor concentration, drowsiness, disorientation, worsening handwriting and hand tremor (asterixis), sluggish movements, and many others, including risk of coma. The symptoms of HE result from an accumulation of gut-derived nitrogenous substances in the blood (such as ammonia, glutamate, others) due to decreased hepatic functioning and shunting through the porto-systemic collaterals, which by-pass the liver. Treatment includes identifying and treating precipitating factors and reducing blood ammonia levels through diet (limiting the amount of protein) and drug therapy.

Patients should get a daily protein intake of 1-1.5 g/kg. Vegetable and dairy sources of protein are preferred to animal sources due to the lower calorie to nitrogen ratio. Branched-chain amino acids (BCAAs) (e.g., leucine, isoleucine, valine) are favored over aromatic amino acids (AAAs); they interfere with AAAs ability to cross the blood-brain barrier and increase hepatocyte growth factor synthesis.

Drug therapy consists of nonabsorbable disaccharides (such as lactulose) and antibiotics (rifaximin, neomycin, others) for acute and chronic therapy. Lactulose is first line therapy for both acute and chronic (prevention) therapy, followed by rifaximin. Lactulose works by converting ammonia produced by intestinal bacteria to ammonium, which is polar and therefore cannot readily diffuse into the blood. Lactulose also enhances diffusion of ammonia into the colon for excretion. Antibiotics work by inhibiting the activity of urease-producing bacteria, which decreases the ammonia production. Probiotics that are lactic acid bacteria (lactobacilli, lactococci, bifidobacterium) may also be used for treatment and prevention. Zinc (220 mg PO BID) is increasingly being used; it can serve as a cofactor for enzymes of the urea cycle and further decrease ammonia concentrations and correct a zinc deficiency.

DRUG	DOSING	SAFETY/SIDE EFFECTS/MONITORING
Lactulose (Constulose, Enulose, Generlac)	Treatment: 30-45 mL (or 20-30 g powder) PO every hour until evacuation; then 30-45 mL (20-30 g powder) PO 3-4 times/day titrated to produce 2-3 soft bowel movements daily Enema: given Q4-6H PRN Prevention: 30-45 mL (or 20-30 g powder) PO 3-4 times/day titrated to produce 2-3 soft bowel movements daily	**SIDE EFFECTS** Flatulence, diarrhea, dyspepsia, abdominal discomfort, dehydration, hypernatremia, hypokalemia **MONITORING** Mental status, bowel movements, ammonia, fluid status, electrolytes
Neomycin (Neo-Fradin)	500-2,000 mg PO Q6-8H	**BLACK BOX WARNINGS (3)** Neurotoxicity, (hearing loss, vertigo, ataxia); nephrotoxicity (particularly in renal impairment or with concurrent use of other nephrotoxic drugs); may cause neuromuscular blockade and respiratory paralysis especially when given soon after anesthesia or with muscle relaxants **SIDE EFFECTS** GI upset, ototoxicty, nephrotoxicity **MONITORING** Mental status, renal function, hearing, ammonia
Rifaximin (Xifaxan)	Treatment (off-label): 400 mg PO Q8H x 5-10 days Prevention: 550 mg PO BID	**SIDE EFFECTS** Peripheral edema, dizziness, fatigue, nausea, ascites, flatulence, headache **MONITORING** Mental status, ammonia
Metronidazole (Flagyl ER, Metro) off-label	250 mg PO Q6-12H Do not use long term due to peripheral neuropathies	**BLACK BOX WARNING** Possibly carcinogenic based on animal data **CONTRAINDICATIONS** Pregnancy (1st trimester); use of disulfiram within the past 2 weeks; use of alcohol during therapy or within 3 days of therapy discontinuation **WARNINGS** CNS effects – aseptic meningitis, encephalopathy, seizures, and neuropathies (peripheral and optic) with high doses and chronic treatment **SIDE EFFECTS** GI upset, metallic taste, furry tongue, glossitis, darkened urine, rash, CNS (peripheral neuropathy, headache, ataxia, confusion, dizziness, seizures) **MONITORING** Mental status, ammonia **NOTES** Can take immediate release tablets with food to minimize GI effects Take extended release tablets on empty stomach

Ascites

Ascites is fluid accumulation within the peritoneal space that can lead to the development of spontaneous bacterial peritonitis (SBP) and hepatorenal syndrome (HRS). Ascites is a common occurrence when the portal hypertension leads to an increase in systemic and splanchnic vasodilation, which results in increased arterial pressure, sodium and water retention, and renal vasoconstriction.

There are many treatment approaches to managing ascites, which depend on the severity. Patients with ascites due to portal hypertension should restrict dietary sodium intake to < 2 grams/day, avoid sodium-retaining medications (including NSAIDs), and use diuretic therapy to increase fluid loss. Restriction of fluid is recommended only in patients with symptomatic severe hyponatriemia (serum Na^+ < 120 mEq/L).

Diuretic therapy with a combination of furosemide and spironolactone should be initiated for acute and chronic ascites. The drugs should be titrated to a maximal weight loss of 0.5 kg/day with a ratio of 40 mg furosemide to 100 mg spironolactone to maintain potassium balance, if possible. All patients with cirrhosis and ascites should be considered for liver transplantation. In severe cases therapeutic abdominal paracentesis may be needed to directly remove ascitic fluid. Large volume paracentesis (removal of > 5 L) has been associated with significant fluid shifts and the addition of albumin is recommended to prevent progression to hepatorenal syndrome.

Spontaneous Bacterial Peritonitis (SBP)

SBP is an acute infection of the ascitic fluid. Diagnosis is guided by cell and microbiologic analysis. In general, targeting *Streptococci* and enteric Gram-negative pathogens with ceftriaxone (or equivalent) for 5-7 days is recommended. Primary prophylaxis with norfloxacin or trimethoprim-sulfamethoxazole to prevent SBP is indicated in select cases. The same agents are used to prevent SBP recurrence.

Hepatorenal Syndrome (HRS)

HRS is the development of renal failure in patients with advanced cirrhosis. HRS is the result of renal vasoconstriction mediated by activation of the renin-angiotensin-aldosterone system (RAAS) and the sympathetic nervous system (SNS) through a feedback mechanism known as hepatorenal reflux. Appropriately treating the various stages and complications of cirrhosis helps prevent progression to HRS; however HRS can be directly treated with renal vasodilators such as fenoldopam or dopamine.

VIRAL HEPATITIS

Viruses that damage the liver include hepatitis A through E (most cases of viral hepatitis are caused by hepatitis A, B and C), along with herpes, CMV, Epstein-Barr virus, and adenoviruses.

Hepatitis A virus (HAV) is a vaccine preventable disease that causes an acute, self-limiting illness. Transmission is primarily via the fecal-oral route through improper hand washing after exposure with an infected person or via contaminated food/water. The hepatitis A vaccine *(Havrix, Vaqta)* is given to children beginning at one year of age (2 shots are required), and to older persons if risk factors are present: homosexual (male-male intercourse), prostitution, IVDA, if someone lives in or travels to areas with high prevalence, if liver disease is present, if receiving blood products, or if working with HIV-A infected animals. <u>Treatment of hepatitis A is supportive and no antiviral agents are needed.</u> Immunoglobulin (IgG) can be given for post-exposure prophylaxis in select cases.

<u>Hepatitis B virus (HBV) is a vaccine preventable disease that causes acute illness and may lead to chronic infection</u>, cirrhosis (scarring) of the liver, liver cancer, liver failure, and death. Transmission requires contact with infectious blood, semen, or other body fluids by having sex with an infected person, sharing contaminated needles to inject drugs, or from an infected mother to her newborn (perinatal transmission). The vaccination schedule for adults and children is typically three IM injections, the second and third administered 1 and 6 months after the first, respectively (using *Engerix-B)*. *Recombivax H* is given in a two dose schedule for ages 11-15 years. *Twinrix* has also been approved as a four dose accelerated schedule. <u>Many antivirals (NRTIs) and interferons are used for chronic therapy of HBV which generally requires one year of treatment.</u>

<u>Hepatitis C virus (HCV) is a non-vaccine preventable disease that can cause acute disease, but more commonly is silent until chronic disease emerges</u>, with consequences similar to hepatitis B. Transmission is the same (requires body fluid transfer) but is most commonly transmitted in the United States via intravenous drug use. <u>There are 3 different genotypes</u> for hepatitis C; genotype 1 which requires 48 weeks of treatment and is the most difficult to treat, and genotypes 2 and 3 which require 24 weeks of treatment. Depending on the genotype, treatment options include peginterferons, ribavirin, protease inhibitors and/or the new agent, sofosbuvir.

INTERFERON ALFA

Interferon alfas are indicated for treatment of HBV and HCV. The pegylated forms (*Pegasys* or *PEG-Intron*) have polyethylene glycol added to the interferon via pegylation, which prolongs the half-life, reducing the dosing frequency from three-times weekly to once weekly. Interferons are naturally-produced cytokines that have antiviral, antiproliferative, and immunomodulatory effects. They inhibit cell growth, alter cellular differentiation, alter surface antigen expression, interfere with oncogene expression, and augment cytotoxicity of lymphocytes for target cells.

DRUG	DOSING	SAFETY/SIDE EFFECTS/MONITORING
Interferon-α-2b (*Intron A*) – for HBV, HCV, many cancers Pegylated interferon–α-2b (*PegIntron*) – for HCV Pegylated interferon–α-2a (*Pegasys*) – for HBV and HCV Interferon Alfacon-1 (*Infergen*) – for HCV Combo product: Interferon-α-2b and ribavirin (*Rebetron*) Interferon-βs are used for Multiple Sclerosis; see Autoimmune chapter	Dosing varies based on indication. HCV dosing example: *Intron A:* 3 million units SC 3 times weekly *PegIntron:* 1.5 mcg/kg SC weekly *Pegasys:* 180 mcg SC weekly + ribavirin (different doses depending on interferon type used) Treatment duration depends on the genotype (which determines disease severity) Dose reduction required in the setting of thrombocytopenia and neutropenia (withhold treatment when ANC < 500/mm³ or platelets < 25,000/mm³) and for renal dysfunction (CrCl < 50 for *PegIntron* and CrCl < 30 for *Pegasys*)	**BLACK BOX WARNINGS (4)** May cause or exacerbate autoimmune disorders; may cause or aggravate infectious disorders; may cause or aggravate ischemic and hemorrhagic cerebrovascular events; combination treatment with ribavirin may cause birth defects and/or fetal mortality and/or hemolytic anemia. **CONTRAINDICATIONS** Autoimmune hepatitis, decompensated liver disease in cirrhotic patients, infants and neonates **WARNINGS** Neuropsychiatric events, cardiovascular events, endocrine disorders (aggravates hypo/hyperthyroidism, hypo/hyperglycemia), ophthalmologic disorders (retinopathy, decrease in vision), pancreatitis, myelosuppression and serious skin reactions **SIDE EFFECTS** Interferons can cause <u>many</u> adverse effects. Flu-like syndrome 1-2 hrs after administration (fever, chills, headache, malaise, arthralgia, myalgia, diaphoresis – can last 24 hrs) – can pre-treat with acetaminophen, antihistamine; CNS effects (fatigue, anxiety, depression, weakness), GI upset (nausea, vomiting, anorexia, weight loss), ↑ LFTs (5-10x ULN during treatment), myelosuppression, mild hair loss **MONITORING** CBC with differential and platelets, LFTs, uric acid, SCr, electrolytes, triglycerides, thyroid function tests, serum HBV DNA or HCV-RNA levels **NOTES** MedGuide must be dispensed with each new prescription and refill.

Interferon Alfa Counseling

Injection Technique for Interferon Injections

■ Keep the pre-filled syringes in refrigerator (never frozen). Avoid exposure to direct sunlight. Patients get 4 prefilled syringes/pack (or vials with empty syringes for reconstitution).

- Like insulin and other protein injectables, always instruct patient to check for discoloration and expiration date.

- Attach needle to pre-filled syringes. If drawing up from a vial, the instruction is similar to insulin vials.

- <u>Interferons are injected in the abdomen (but not if patient is too thin), the top of the thigh, or the outer surface of the upper arm; rotate sites.</u>

- Interferons should not be injected IV; avoid areas where you can see veins. When you inject, pull the plunger of the syringe back very slightly and see if you get blood in the syringe. If you see blood in the syringe, do not inject.

- Tap syringe to push bubbles to top, inject out the bubbles (by pressing slightly). Make sure the edge of the stopper is at the correct dose. Patients may have to discard excess medicine, depending on the dose.

- Pinch a fold of skin and inject at 45- to 90-degree angle. Insert needle as far as it will go and press plunger. Press the needle into the safety sleeve to prevent needlestick injuries. If the patient is using syringes they fill from a vial, they should also have a safety sleeve. Due to the risk of contracting hepatitis, only syringes with safety tops are used.

- You will likely experience flu-like symptoms after injection; these can be reduced by taking acetaminophen and an antihistamine.

Tell your doctor if any of the following occurs:

- You become pregnant or your female partner becomes pregnant
- New or worsening mental health problems such as thoughts about hurting or killing yourself or others
- Decreased vision
- Trouble breathing or chest pain
- Severe stomach or lower back pain
- Bloody diarrhea or bloody bowel movements
- High fever
- Easy bruising or bleeding

NUCLEOSIDE REVERSE TRANSCRIPTASE INHIBITORS

- These agents inhibit HBV replication by inhibiting HBV polymerase resulting in DNA chain termination; <u>for hepatitis B only</u>.

DRUG	DOSING	SAFETY/SIDE EFFECTS/MONITORING
Entire Class	↓ in CrCl < 50 mL/min	**BLACK BOX WARNINGS (2)** <u>Lactic acidosis and severe hepatomegaly with steatosis, which may be fatal</u> <u>Exacerbations of hepatitis B may occur upon discontinuation, monitor closely</u> **SIDE EFFECTS** Headache, fatigue, nausea, vomiting, diarrhea, abdominal pain, ↑ LFTs, ↑ bilirubin, rash **MONITORING** LFTs, CBC with differential, renal function, HBV DNA, signs and symptoms of HBV relapse/exacerbation upon discontinuation
LamiVUDine *(Epivir HBV)*	100 mg PO daily 150 mg BID if co-infected with HIV CrCl < 50 mL/min: ↓ dose	**BLACK BOX WARNINGS (3)** <u>Do not use *Epivir HBV* for treatment of HIV</u> (contains lower doses of lamivudine) **SIDE EFFECTS** Headache, N/V/D, fatigue, insomnia, myalgias, ↑ LFTs, rash
Adefovir *(Hepsera)*	10 mg PO daily CrCl < 50 mL/min: ↓ frequency	**BLACK BOX WARNINGS (4)** May cause HIV resistance in patients with unrecognized or untreated HIV infection <u>Use caution in patients with renal impairment or those at risk of renal toxicity (including concurrent nephrotoxic agents or NSAIDs)</u> **SIDE EFFECTS** Headache, weakness, abdominal pain, hematuria, rash, nephrotoxicity
Tenofovir *(Viread)* 1st line agent	300 mg PO daily CrCl < 50 mL/min: ↓ dose	**SIDE EFFECTS** <u>Fanconi syndrome, renal insufficiency, osteomalacia and ↓ bone density</u>, GI upset, ↑ LFTs
Entecavir *(Baraclude)* 1st line agent	Nucleoside-treatment naïve: 0.5 mg PO daily Lamivudine-resistant: 1 mg PO daily <u>Take on empty stomach</u> CrCl < 50 mL/min: ↓ dose or frequency	**BLACK BOX WARNINGS (3)** May cause HIV resistance in patients with unrecognized or untreated HIV infection **SIDE EFFECTS** Peripheral edema, pyrexia, ascites, ↑ LFTs, hematuria, nephrotoxicity **NOTES** Food reduces AUC by 20%; take on an empty stomach (2 hours before or after a meal)
Telbivudine *(Tyzeka)*	600 mg PO daily CrCl < 50 mL/min: ↓ frequency	**SIDE EFFECTS** ↑ CPK, fatigue, headache, ↑ LFTs **MONITORING** CPK

Nucleoside Reverse Transcriptase Inhibitor Drug Interactions

- Ribavirin can ↑ hepatotoxic effects of all NRTIs

- Lamivudine: SMX/TMP can ↑ lamivudine levels due to reduced excretion

- Tenofovir: Avoid concomitant treatment with didanosine due to increased risk of virologic failure and potential for increased side effects.

Nucleoside Reverse Transcriptase Inhibitor Counseling

- *EPIVIR-HBV* tablets and oral solution are not interchangeable with *Epivir* tablets and solution (which have higher doses).

- Entecavir: Food reduces AUC by 20%; take on an empty stomach (take 2 hours before or after a meal).

- Some people (rarely) have developed a serious condition called lactic acidosis (a buildup of an acid in the blood). Lactic acidosis is a medical emergency and must be treated in the hospital. Be seen right away if you feel very weak or tired, have unusual muscle pain, have trouble breathing, have stomach pain with nausea and vomiting, and feel dizzy or light-headed.

- Lamivudine: Some people (rarely) have developed pancreatitis, which is a medical emergency and must be treated in the hospital. Be seen right away if you have upper abdominal pain that radiates to your back, or abdominal pain that feels worse after eating with or without nausea or vomiting.

RIBAVIRIN

Ribavirin is an antiviral agent that inhibits replication of RNA & DNA viruses. It is indicated for hepatitis C virus (HCV) in combination with interferon alfa.

DRUG	DOSING	SAFETY/SIDE EFFECTS/MONITORING
Ribavirin *(Copegus, Rebetol, Ribasphere, RibaPak, Virazole)* 200 mg caps, 40 mg/mL soln, and 20 mg/mL for nebulization	MedGuide must be dispensed with each new prescription and refill. Dose (400-600 mg PO BID) varies based on indication, patient weight and genotype (which determines severity). Stop ribavirin if there has not been an early viral response (EVR) by week 12. Take with food (better tolerated). Not recommended in patients with CrCl < 50 mL/min Dose reductions are needed for hemoglobin < 10 g/dL (avoid for hemoglobin < 8.5 g/dL).	**BLACK BOX WARNINGS (4)** Significant teratogenic effects (avoid in pregnancy or women wishing to become pregnant) Monotherapy not effective for HCV and should not be used alone Hemolytic anemia (primary toxicity of oral therapy mostly occurring within 1-2 weeks of therapy) Caution with inhalation formulation in patients on a ventilator (precipitation of drug may interfere with ventilation) **CONTRAINDICATIONS** Pregnancy, women of childbearing age who will not use contraception reliably, male partners of pregnant women, hemoglobinopathies, CrCl < 50 mL/min, autoimmune hepatitis, concomitant use with didanosine **SIDE EFFECTS** Hemolytic anemia – primary toxicity, can worsen cardiac disease and lead to MIs; do not use with unstable cardiac disease. Fatigue, headache, insomnia, nausea, anorexia, myalgias, hyperuricemia **MONITORING** CBC with differential and PLTs, electrolytes, uric acid, bilirubin, LFTs, serum HCV-RNA levels, TSH, monthly pregnancy tests. **NOTES** Highly teratogenic; Pregnancy Category X Can stay in body for as long as 6 months. Avoid pregnancy in female patients and female partners of male patients during therapy and for 6 months after completing therapy. At least two reliable forms of effective contraception must be utilized during treatment and during the 6-month post-treatment follow-up period.

Ribavirin Drug Interactions

- Do not use with didanosine due to cases of fatal hepatic failure, peripheral neuropathy and pancreatitis.

- Ribavirin can ↑ hepatotoxic effects of nucleoside reverse transcriptase inhibitors.

- Zidovudine can enhance the adverse effect of anemia from ribavirin.

Ribavirin Patient Counseling

- Ribavirin can cause birth defects or death of an unborn child. If you are pregnant or your sexual partner is pregnant, do not use. If you could become pregnant, you must not become pregnant during therapy and for 6 months after you have stopped therapy. During this time, you must use 2 forms of birth control, and you must have pregnancy tests that show that you are not pregnant.

- Female sexual partners of male patients being treated must not become pregnant during treatment and for 6 months after treatment has stopped. Therefore, you must use 2 forms of birth control during this time.

- If you or a female sexual partner becomes pregnant, you should tell your health care provider. There is a Ribavirin Pregnancy Registry that collects information about pregnancy outcomes in female patients and female partners of male patients exposed to ribavirin. You or your doctor should contact the Registry at 1-800-593-2214. All information is confidential.

- If using the oral solution, wash the measuring cup or spoon to avoid swallowing of the medicine by someone other than the person to whom it was prescribed.

- This medicine can cause a dangerous drop in your red blood cell count, called anemia. Your healthcare provider should check your red blood cell count before you start therapy and often during the first 4 weeks of therapy. Your red blood cell count may be checked more often if you have any heart or breathing problems.

- Do not take ribavirin alone to treat hepatitis C infection. Ribavirin is used in combination with interferon for treating hepatitis C infection.

PROTEASE INHIBITORS

These direct-acting antiviral agents (DAA) are indicated for the treatment of chronic hepatitis C genotype 1 infection when used in combination with peginterferon alfa and ribavirin in adult patients. These agents bind reversibly to protein 3 (NS 3) serine protease and inhibit replication of the hepatitis C virus.

DRUG	DOSING	SAFETY/SIDE EFFECTS/MONITORING
Boceprevir (*Victrelis*)	800 mg 3 times/day (every 8 hours) with food (a meal or light snack) starting on week 5 of peginterferon alfa plus ribavirin for 24-44 weeks With compensated cirrhosis – treat for 44 weeks Without cirrhosis – treat for 24 to 44 weeks	**CONTRAINDICATIONS** All contraindications to peginterferon alfa and ribavirin also apply since must be administered with these agents. Due to co-administration with ribavirin, pregnancy (use of 2 non-hormonal contraceptives and negative pregnancy test before use and monthly is required) and men whose female partner is pregnant. Concurrent administration of drugs dependent on 3A4 for clearance where ↑ concentrations result in serious or life-threatening events and concurrent use of 3A4 inducers. **SIDE EFFECTS** Fatigue, anemia (requiring ESA use), neutropenia, taste distortion (dysgeusia), nausea, headache **MONITORING** CBC with differential (to monitor anemia and neutropenia) at baseline and every 4 weeks, HCV-RNA levels, electrolytes, monthly pregnancy tests **NOTES** Never reduce the dose or interrupt therapy as treatment failure may result. Never use as monotherapy; must always be combined with peginterferon and ribavirin. If HCV-RNA >100 units/mL at week 12 or detectable at week 24 (treatment futility), discontinue treatment (boceprevir, peginterferon alfa, and ribavirin).

Protease Inhibitors Continued

DRUG	DOSING	SAFETY/SIDE EFFECTS/MONITORING
Telaprevir (*Incivek*)	750 mg 3 times/day (every 8 hours) with food (containing ~20 grams of fat) plus peginterferon alfa plus ribavirin for 12 weeks (interferon and ribavirin are continued for an addition 12-36 weeks for a total of 24 or 48 weeks based on virologic response)	**CONTRAINDICATIONS** All contraindications to peginterferon alfa and ribavirin also apply since must be administered with these agents. Due to co-administration with ribavirin, pregnancy (use of 2 non-hormonal contraceptives and negative pregnancy test before use and monthly is required) and men whose female partner is pregnant. Concurrent administration of drugs dependent on 3A4 for clearance where ↑ concentrations result in serious or life-threatening events and concurrent use of 3A4 inducers. **SIDE EFFECTS** Serious skin rash (discontinue all treatment if progressive or severe), fatigue, itching, taste distortion (dysgeusia), anemia, anorectal disorders, nausea, diarrhea **MONITORING** CBC with differential (to monitor anemia) at baseline and every 4 weeks, HCV-RNA levels, electrolytes, bilirubin, uric acid, monthly pregnancy tests **NOTES** Never reduce the dose or interrupt therapy as treatment failure may result. Never use as monotherapy; must always be combined with peginterferon and ribavirin. If HCV-RNA level >1,000 units/mL at treatment weeks 4 or 12, or detectable at week 24 (treatment futility), discontinue treatment (telaprevir, peginterferon alfa and ribavirin).
Simeprevir (*Olysio*)	150 mg PO daily with food	**CONTRAINDICATIONS** All contraindications to peginterferon alfa and ribavirin also apply since must be adminsterd with these agents. Due to co-administration with ribavirin, pregnancy (use of 2 non-hormonal contraceptives and negative pregnancy test before use and monthly is required) and men whose female partner is pregnant. **SIDE EFFECTS** Rash (photosensitivity), pruritus and nausea **NOTES** Screening patients with HCV genotype 1a infection for the presence of virus with the NS3 Q80K polymorphism at baseline is strongly recommended. Patients with this polymorphism will not respond and alternative therapy should be given. If HCV-RNA level ≥ 25 units/mL at treatment weeks 4 or 12 (treatment futility), discontinue treatment (simeprevir, peginterferon alfa and ribavirin). Never use as monotherapy; must always be combined with peginterferon and ribavirin.

Protease Inhibitor Drug Interactions

- Boceprevir and telaprevir are CYP3A4 inhibitors (strong) and 3A4 substrates (strong) as well as P-glycoprotein inhibitors. Strong 3A4 inhibitors and inducers are contraindicated with the use of these agents. There are many drug interactions.

- Simeprevir mildly inhibits CYP1A2 activity and intestinal 3A4 activity, but does not affect hepatic 3A4 activity.

- Simeprevir is a CYP3A4 substrate; do not administer with moderate or strong CYP3A4 inhibitors or inducers.

SOFOSBUVIR

Sofosbuvir is an inhibitor of the HCV NS5B RNA-dependent RNA polymerase, which is essential for viral replication. Sofosbuvir is a nucleotide prodrug and is <u>indicated for hepatitis C only</u>.

DRUG	DOSING	SAFETY/SIDE EFFECTS/MONITORING
Sofosbuvir *(Sovaldi)*	400 mg PO daily with or without food HCV Genotype 1 & 4: give with peginterferon alfa + ribavirin x 12 weeks HCV Genotype 2: give with ribavirin x 12 weeks HCV Genotype 3: give with ribavirin x 24 weeks	**CONTRAINDICATIONS** All contraindications to peginterferon alfa and ribavirin also apply when administered with these agents. Due to co-administration with ribavirin, pregnancy (use of 2 non-hormonal contraceptives and negative pregnancy test before use and monthly is required) and men whose female partner is pregnant. **SIDE EFFECTS** Fatigue, headache, nausea, insomnia, anemia **MONITORING** CBC with differential, HCV-RNA levels, electrolytes, monthly pregnancy tests **NOTES** Can use without interferon alfa in genotypes 2 & 3 and in genotype 1 patients who are interferon ineligible (treat for 24 weeks)

Sofosbuvir Drug Interactions

- Sofosbuvir is a substrate of drug transporter P-gp; avoid with potent intestinal P-gp inducers (e.g., St. John's wort, rifampin). Avoid co-administration with carbamazepine, oxcarbazepine, phenobarbital, phenytoin, rifapentine, rifabutin and tipranavir/ritonavir.

PRACTICE CASE

PATIENT PROFILE

Patient Name	Patrick Mally
Address	18 Santa Rosa

Age	44	**Sex**	Male	**Race**	White	**Height**	5'11"	**Weight**	185 lbs.

Allergies	None known

DIAGNOSES

Hepatitis C

Depression

Insomnia

MEDICATIONS

Date	No.	Prescriber	Drug & Strength	Quantity	Sig	Refills
7/12/13	64538	Kroner	Ribivarin 200 mg	150	6 A.M., 6 P.M.	
7/12/13	64537	Kroner	Intron A 18 MU multidose #2	2	3 MU TIW	3
5/11/13	56825	Beebee	Citalopram 40 mg	30	1 daily	3
5/11/13	56826	Beebee	Zolpidem 10 mg	30	1 PO QHS	3

LAB/DIAGNOSTIC TESTS

Test	Normal Value	Results Date 7/10/13	Date	Date
Protein, T	6.2-8.3 g/dL			
Albumin	3.6-5.1 g/dL			
Alk Phos	33-115 u/L			
AST	10-35 u/L	127 u/L		
ALT	6-40 u/L	168 u/L		
CH, T	125-200 g/dL			
TG	<150 g/dL			
HDL	g/dL			
LDL	g/dL			
GLU	65-99 mg/dL			
Na	135-146 mEq/L			
K	3.5-5.3 mEq/L			
Cl	98-110 mEq/L			
HCO3-	22-28 mg/dL			
BUN	7-25 mg/dL	14		
Creatinine	0.6-1.2 mg/dL	0.9		
Calcium	8.6-10.2 mg/dL			
WBC	4-11 cells/mm³			
RBC	3.8-5.1 mL/mm³			
Hemoglobin	Male: 13.8- 17.2 g/dL Female: 12.1-15.1 g/dL			
Hematocrit	Male: 40.7-50.3% Female: 36.1- 44.3%			
MCHC	32-36 g/dL			
MCV	80-100 µm			
Platelet count	140-400 x 10³/mm³			

ADDITIONAL INFORMATION

Date	Notes
7/12/13	Recent diagnosis Hepatitis C infection. HIV negative. Patient states previous IVDA; none currently. Smokes 1 PPD; occasional alcohol. Counseled to discontinue alcohol. Nurse to instruct on injection technique & safe needle disposal. Return to clinic 4 weeks. Significant anxiety. Case mgmt to ensure safe needle storage, patient support.

Questions

1. The patient is receiving interferon therapy. Which of the following side effects can occur during therapy? (Select **ALL** that apply.)

   a. Depression

   b. Hypersalivation

   c. Flu-like syndrome

   d. Anorexia

   e. Hypothyroidism

2. The patient is receiving ribavirin therapy. He is in a sexual relationship with a female partner. Which of the following statements is correct?

   a. No precautions are required since she is not using ribavirin.

   b. Female sexual partners of male patients being treated must not become pregnant during treatment and for 6 months after treatment has stopped. Therefore, 2 forms of birth control are required during this time.

   c. Female sexual partners of male patients being treated must not become pregnant during treatment and for 60 days after treatment has stopped. Therefore, 2 forms of birth control are required during this time.

   d. If she becomes pregnant, she should notify the Centers for Disease Control.

   e. If she becomes pregnant, the baby will be fine, however, the mom will develop anemia.

3. The patient requires counseling for ribavirin therapy. Which is the most serious and primary toxicity of this drug?

   a. Hemolytic anemia

   b. Hemorrhagic cystitis

   c. Pancreatitis

   d. Agranulocytosis

   e. Gastrointestinal hemorrhage

4. Patrick has been on his current hepatitis medication regimen for nearly 4 weeks. Which of the following medications would be appropriate to add to Patrick's current regimen given his diagnosis?

   a. Lactulose

   b. *Viread*

   c. Boceprevir

   d. Lamivudine

   e. *Rebif*

Questions 5-10 do not apply to the case

5. A patient with liver failure presents with acute hepatic encephalopathy. Which of the following is considered first-line treatment for acute hepatic encephalopathy?

   a. Decreasing protein intake to < 1 gram/kg/day

   b. Lactulose

   c. Furosemide

   d. Neomycin

   e. Octreotide

6. What is the rationale behind adding polyethylene glycol to interferons?

   a. Reduce incidence of bone marrow suppression

   b. Decrease administration time

   c. Decrease administration frequency

   d. Reduce ischemic complications

   e. All of the above

7. Which of the following medications can lead to renal insufficiency and osteomalacia?

   a. Telaprevir

   b. Tenofovir

   c. Boceprevir

   d. Lamivudine

   e. Entecavir

8. Which of the following statements is correct regarding syringes for interferon self-injection?

    a. Safety tips are required to prevent accidental needle-stick injuries
    b. The syringes should be at least 1-inch long
    c. This medication cannot be self-injected
    d. A and B
    e. None of the above

9. A patient seen in hepatology clinic today has ascites, portal hypertension and a serum sodium of 138 mg/dL and potassium of 4.1 mEq/dL. Which of the following should be recommended for this patient to treat his ascites? (Select **ALL** that apply.)

    a. Restrict his fluid intake
    b. Restrict sodium intake to < 2 grams/day
    c. Initiate hydrochlorothiazide
    d. Initiate furosemide
    e. Initiate spironolactone

Answers

1-a,c,d,e, 2-b, 3-a, 4-c, 5-b, 6-c, 7-b, 8-a, 9-b,d,e

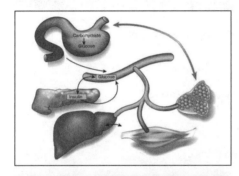

DIABETES

We gratefully acknowledge the assistance of Eric Ip, PharmD, BCPS, CSCS, CDE, Chair and Associate Professor, Pharmacy Practice Department Touro University California College of Pharmacy, in preparing this chapter.

GUIDELINES

American Diabetes Association (ADA) Position Statement. Standards of Medical Care in Diabetes – 2013. Diabetes Care 2013; 36: Supplement 1. S11- S66.

American Association of Clinical Endocrinologists (AACE)/American College of Endocrinology Consensus Panel on Type 2 Diabetes Mellitus: An Algorithm for Glycemic Control. Endocrine Practice 2013;19:327-336.

BACKGROUND

Diabetes is the most common endocrine disorder in the United States, affecting 8.3% of the population. Diabetes is characterized by high blood glucose, or hyperglycemia. Glucose is the body's main source of energy. High blood glucose indicates that the glucose cannot get into the cell or cannot be properly stored. Insulin is a hormone that moves glucose into muscle and other tissue cells. In diabetes, there is a deficiency in insulin production, insulin action, or both. Continued hyperglycemia leads to many complications including organ and nerve damage. Acutely, hypoglycemia puts patients at risk for injury and death. In addition to type 1 and 2 diabetes, described below, the disease could be due to other causes, such as genetic defects in β-cell function, genetic defects in insulin action, diseases of the exocrine pancreas (such as cystic fibrosis) or be drug- or chemical-induced (such as in the treatment of HIV/AIDS or after organ transplantation). Gestational diabetes mellitus (GDM, described later in the chapter) may or may not continue after pregnancy.

DIAGNOSIS/DEFINITIONS

Prediabetes: Focus on Preventing or Delaying Type 2 Diabetes

The 2013 guidelines emphasize prevention with the presence of elevated blood glucose or an A1C of 5.7–6.4%. Patients should be referred to a support program targeting weight loss of 7% of body weight and increasing physical activity to at least 150 min/week of moderate activity such as walking. Metformin therapy may be considered in these patients, especially for those with a BMI > 35, less than 60 years of age and in women with a history of GDM. These patients should be monitored at least yearly and assisted with methods to reduce CVD risk factors.

Type 1 Diabetes

Type 1 diabetes affects ~5% of patients with diabetes and is caused by a cellular-mediated <u>autoimmune destruction of the beta cells in the pancreas</u>, leading to absolute insulin deficiency. Family history is less of a risk factor than with type 2 diabetes. Patients may present (initially) with diabetic ketoacidosis (DKA), which is a life-threatening condition. This type of diabetes usually presents in younger, thinner patients. Therapy must include insulin replacement.

Type 2 Diabetes

Type 2 diabetes accounts for about 95% of patients diagnosed with diabetes and is characterized by a combination of insulin resistance and relative insulin deficiency, with progressively lower insulin secretion over time. Type 2 diabetes may be treated with lifestyle modifications, oral medications, and/or injections, including insulin. Type 2 diabetes is strongly associated with obesity, physical inactivity, and a family history of diabetes. Lifestyle factors can be altered to reduce the risk of disease. <u>Risk factors</u> for type 2 diabetes include:

- First-degree relative with diabetes

- Race/Ethnicity (Native American, African-American, Asian-American, Hispanic, Pacific Islander)

- Overweight (BMI ≥ 25 kg/m²)

- Physical inactivity

- Hypertension or taking medications for hypertension

- HDL < 35 mg/dL and/or TG > 250 mg/dL

DRUGS THAT CAN ALTER BLOOD GLUCOSE LEVELS

Drugs that Can Cause Hyperglycemia*
Corticosteroids

Protease Inhibitors

Atypical antipsychotics (e.g., olanzapine, clozapine, quetiapine)

Niacin

Thiazide and Loop diuretics

Statins

Octreotide (in type 2)

Fluoroquinolones

Beta-agonists

Carvedilol and Propranolol and possibly other beta-blockers

Cyclosporine, Tacrolimus

Interferons

Diazoxide (*Proglycem*-used for low BG due to certain diseases)

Cough syrups (sugar content usually modest)

* The drug may be required in which case the resultant hyperglycemia would need to be treated.

Drugs that Can Cause Hypoglycemia
Fluoroquinolones

Octreotide (in type 1)

Propranolol

Lorcaserin (*Belviq*)

Quinine

Many anti-diabetic drugs, primarily insulin and insulin secretagogues

- History of CVD

- A1C ≥ 5.7%, IGT, IFG on previous testing

- Women who delivered a baby weighing > 9 lbs or had GDM

- Women with polycystic ovary syndrome

- Other clinical conditions associated with insulin resistance (e.g severe obesity, acanthosis nigricans)

Screening and Testing

Testing to detect type 2 diabetes and prediabetes should be considered in adults of any age who are overweight or obese and who have one or more risk factors. Without risk factors, testing should begin at 45 years. Children have increased incidence of type 2 diabetes and testing is now recommended in overweight children with 2 or more risk factors.

Clinical Signs and Symptoms

Hyperglycemia commonly results in polyuria, polyphagia, polydipsia, blurred vision, and fatigue. Type 1 patients may also present with <u>weight loss</u>. Symptoms of hyperglycemia may gradually worsen in type 2 patients, and these patients may attribute the symptoms to other causes, such as environmental changes or older age. To avoid missing cases the screening recommendations should be followed.

Long-Term Complications

Long-term complications of diabetes are classified as microvascular and macrovascular.

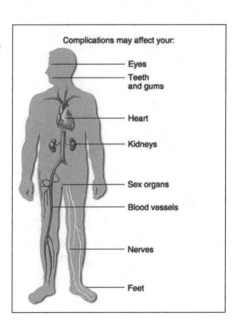

Microvascular Disease

- Retinopathy (most common)

- Nephropathy (may progress to ESRD)

- Peripheral neuropathy (increased risk for foot infections and amputations)

- Autonomic neuropathy (erectile dysfunction, gastroparesis, loss of bladder control/UTIs)

Macrovascular Disease

- Coronary artery disease (e.g., HTN, MI, HF)

- Cerebrovascular disease (e.g., TIA/stroke)

- Peripheral artery disease (PAD)

TREATMENT GOALS – THE ABC'S OF DIABETES

A – A1C

While a glucometer measures the blood glucose at that given moment, the A1C measures the average blood glucose over the past 2-3 months. The AIC should be measured:

- At least quarterly in patients are not controlled (at goal)
- Twice per year if at goal and have stable control

Use of Point of Care (POC) testing allows timely treatment changes.

MEASUREMENT	TARGET

ADA Treatment Guidelines

A1C	< 7.0%*
Preprandial capillary plasma glucose	70-130 mg/dL
Postprandial capillary plasma glucose (1-2 hours after the start of a meal)	< 180 mg/dL

AACE Treatment Guidelines

A1C	≤ 6.5%*
Preprandial capillary plasma glucose	< 110 mg/dL
Postprandial capillary plasma glucose	< 140 mg/dL

* *Must individualize target goals. Per the ADA, a more stringent A1C goal (such as < 6.5%) may be appropriate for younger adult patients not experiencing hypoglycemia, those with long life expectancy and no significant CVD. A less stringent A1C goal (such as < 8%) may be appropriate for people with severe hypoglycemia, limited life expectancy, extensive comorbid conditions, advanced complications, or longstanding diabetes where the goal is difficult to attain despite optimal efforts.*

Estimated average glucose (eAG) refers to the mean plasma glucose concentrations over 2-3 months, and may be easier for patients to understand over A1C. The eAG goal is < 154 mg/dL per the ADA guidelines.

Correlation of A1C with Average Glucose (estimated)

A1C (%)	MEAN PLASMA GLUCOSE (MG/DL)
6	126
7	154
8	183
9	212
10	240
11	269
12	298

B – Blood Pressure

Goal blood pressure for patients with diabetes is < 140/80 mmHg. A lower systolic target (such as < 130 mmHg) may be appropriate for certain individuals such as younger patients, if it can be reached without undue treatment burden, or in patients at high risk of stroke. ACE inhibitors or ARBs should be chosen first-line since they reduce the development or progression of diabetic nephropathy. One or more of the antihypertensive medications should be given at bedtime. Most patients with diabetes will require 2 or more medications to control their blood pressure. Choice of additional agents will depend on the patient's comorbidities. Thiazide-like diuretics and dihydropyridine calcium channel blockers are generally the drugs used for additional BP control in most patients.

C – Cholesterol

LDL cholesterol should be < 100 mg/dL in patients without overt CVD. In patients with overt CVD, a LDL goal < 70 mg/dL may be preferred. Triglycerides should be < 150 mg/dL. HDL should be > 40 mg/dL in men and > 50 mg/dL in women. Statin therapy should be added, regardless of baseline lipid levels for patients with diabetes when they have overt CVD or without CVD and the patient is > 40 years old and has one or more CVD risk factors (family history of CVD, hypertension, smoking, dyslipidemia, or albuminuria). Please note, according to the ATP IV lipid guidelines, patients with diabetes who are 40-75 years of age and have a LDL of 70 mg/dL or higher should be taking moderate or high-intensity statin.

GESTATIONAL DIABETES MELLITUS (GDM)

GDM (diabetes of pregnancy) carries risk for adverse maternal, fetal and neonatal outcomes. Treatment for GDM should keep blood glucose at levels <u>equal to those of pregnant women who do not have GDM</u> (this means tighter blood glucose control). In pregnancy, the preprandial blood glucose should be ≤ 95 mg/dL, postprandial either ≤ 140 mg/dL 1 hour postmeal or ≤ 120 mg/dL 2 hours post meal, and the A1C should be < 6%, assuming it can be achieved without excessive hypoglycemia.

<u>Nutritional therapy is the standard of care</u> for both the needs of the pregnancy and to maintain proper blood glucose levels. SMBG must be done regularly to see if the changes in diet are adequate. If

DIAGNOSIS OF DIABETES AND PRE-DIABETES

Criteria for the Diagnosis of Diabetes
- Classic symptoms of hyperglycemia crisis (polyuria, polydipsia and unexplained weight loss) or hyperglycemic crisis AND a random plasma glucose ≥ 200 mg/dL
  or
- FPG ≥ 126 mg/dL – fasting is defined as no caloric intake for at least 8 hours*
  or
- 2-hr plasma glucose of ≥ 200 mg/dL during a 75 g oral glucose tolerance test (OGTT)*
  or
- A1C ≥ 6.5%*

Categories of Risk for Diabetes (Pre-Diabetes)
- Fasting plasma glucose (FPG) 100-125 mg/dL
  or
- 2-hr plasma glucose in the 75-g oral glucose tolerance test (OGTT) of 140-199 mg/dL
  or
- A1C 5.7-6.4%

* *In the absence of unequivocal hyperglycemia, result should be confirmed by repeat testing*

not, insulin is often used, but some pregnant women may be taking oral diabetes medications.

LIFESTYLE MODIFICATIONS

Lifestyle modifications should be used in <u>combination</u> with any medication therapy for all patients with diabetes. Some patients may be able to control their blood glucose using lifestyle modifications alone or can slow disease progression.

Weight Loss

Overweight or obese patients with diabetes or pre-diabetes should be encouraged to lose weight. A deficit of 3,500 kcal will produce a weight loss of 1 pound. For patients who need to lose weight, decrease body weight at a relatively slow and progressive rate of 0.5-2 lbs/week. A 300-500 kcal/day reduction in caloric intake will translate roughly to a weight loss of 0.5-1.0 pound/week in those patients with a BMI > 25. <u>Patients should also maintain a waist circumference < 35 inches for females and < 40 inches for males</u>.

Diet

Weight loss is recommended for all overweight or obese individuals who have or are at risk for diabetes. For weight loss, either low-carbohydrate, low-fat calorie-restricted, or Mediterranean diets may be effective in the short-term (up to 2 years). For patients on low-carbohydrate diets, monitor lipid profiles, renal function, and protein intake (in those with nephropathy) and adjust hypoglycemic therapy as needed. Physical activity and behavior modification are important components of weight loss programs and are most helpful in maintenance of weight loss.

Carbohydrates and Postprandial Levels

Monitoring carbohydrate intake has been used to maintain glycemic control, and many patients with diabetes match the prandial (meal-time) insulin dose to the carbohydrate intake. At the present time, there is controversy regarding the utility of this approach, but it may still be useful to know that a carbohydrate serving is measured as 15 grams. A serving is approximately one small piece of fruit, 1 slice of bread, 1/3 cup of cooked rice/pasta, or ½ cup of oatmeal.

Fat Intake

The ADA recommends limiting saturated fat intake to <7% of total calories to help reduce cardiovascular risk. Reducing intake of *trans* fat lowers LDL cholesterol and increases HDL; therefore, intake of *trans* fat should be minimized. Please note these recommendations are different from the obesity guideline recommendations (see Weight Loss chapter for more information).

Exercise

Aerobic exercise of moderate-intensity should be performed for at least 30 minutes, 5 days per week (or 150 minutes per week). Resistance training is recommended 2 days per week.

Smoking

All patients who smoke should receive cessation counseling and other forms of treatment as a routine component of diabetes care.

COMPREHENSIVE CARE

Primary Prevention of Cardiovascular Disease

Aspirin therapy should be considered for primary prevention in patients with type 1 and type 2 diabetes and an increased CV risk (10-year risk > 10%). This includes men > 50 years of age and women > 60 years of age with at least one additional major risk factor (e.g., family history of CVD, HTN, smoking, dyslipidemia, or albuminuria). The dose of aspirin should be 75-162 mg daily (usually 81 mg EC) if there is no contraindication (aspirin allergy, bleeding, etc.). If the patient has an aspirin allergy, then other antiplatelet agents may be considered.

Nephropathy Screening/Treatment

Diabetic nephropathy is the leading cause of end-stage renal disease (ESRD). An annual urine test for albumin is required for patients with diabetes. Any protein in the urine indicates renal disease and optimizing glycemic and blood pressure control helps to slow the progression of diabetic nephropathy. Microalbuminuria is defined as a urine protein level of 30-299 mg/day and macroalbuminuria is a urine protein level > 300 mg/day.

Screening

- Done annually

- Looking for the presence of microalbuminuria (urine albumin excretion of 30-299 mg/day)

- Type 1 diabetes: Annual testing starting 5 years after diagnosis

- Type 2 diabetes: Annual testing starting at the time of diagnosis

Treatment

- Optimize glucose and blood pressure control.

- Antihypertensive treatment should include an ACE inhibitor or ARB as first-line therapy. Additional agents are added if further control is needed.

Retinopathy Screening

Diabetic retinopathy is the leading cause of blindness in adults. An annual dilated, comprehensive eye exam is recommended in patients with diabetes. A longer interval (every 2-3 years) may be acceptable in patients who have had one or more normal eye exams and if their diabetes is well controlled. The comprehensive eye exam should be performed by an ophthalmologist or optometrist. More frequent exams may be advised if retinopathy is progressing.

Screening

- Type 1 diabetes: Annual beginning within 5 years of diagnosis in patients ≥ 10 years old

- Type 2 diabetes: Annual beginning soon after diagnosis

Foot Care

All adult patients with diabetes should have a comprehensive foot exam, performed by a podiatrist, at least once per year. The podiatrist examines the skin of the feet for dryness/ cracking and for signs of infection, ulcers, bunions, calluses, and any deformities such as claw toes. Pedal pulses are assessed (looking for signs of peripheral arterial disease). Tests, such as the 10-gram monofilament test, are performed to assess loss of sensation and presence of peripheral neuropathy.

All patients with diabetes should inspect their feet daily (or have a family member do so if they are unable). Patients should have their feet inspected at every visit to a physician as well. Daily self-care of the feet include:

- Wash feet daily and inspect them for any changes (red spots, cuts, blisters, cracks, etc.). Be sure to look between the toes. Use a mirror, if needed, to inspect the bottom of the feet.

- Dry feet completely, particularly in between the toes. Rub a thin coat of skin lotion over to the tops and bottoms of dry feet, but not between toes due to increased risk of tinea pedis.

- Trim toe nails carefully – straight across – and file with an emery board to the contour of the toe.

- Callouses may be filed with a pumice stone or emery board. Patients should never use any instruments to cut hardened skin on the feet.

- Avoid walking barefoot.

- Use soft cotton or synthetic blend socks to absorb moisture.

- Wear properly fitting, comfortable, supportive shoes (with orthotics if needed). Use caution when "breaking in" new shoes. May need to select extra-wide to accommodate any deformities (bunions, hammertoes).

- Inspect shoes for foreign objects before inserting feet.

- Keep the blood flowing to feet. Put feet up when sitting. Wiggle toes and move ankles up and down for 5 minutes, 2-3 times/day. Do not cross your legs for long periods of time.

- Remove socks and shoes at each physician visit to allow for visual inspection.

- Patients should test bathtub water with another part of their body to prevent burns. Also, keep feet away from the fireplace. Avoid electric blankets and heating pads on the feet.

Vaccinations for Adults with Diabetes

<u>Do NOT share insulin pens</u> (even if needle is changed) due to risk of hepatitis transmission, and possibly other conditions. Multi-dose vials should be labeled for one patient only.

Required

- Hepatitis B: If 19-59 years of age and have never completed series

- Influenza: annually

- PPSV23 *(Pneumovax):* At 2-64 years of age and again at 65 years if > 5 years since previous vaccination

- Tetanus, diphtheria, pertussis (TdaP): Once

    ◦Afterwords: Td every 10 years, more frequent if deep or dirty wound

Possibly Required

- May require if at risk or at recommended age; see immunizations chapter: Hepatitis A, PCV13 *(Prevnar),* Varicella, Zoster, Meningococcal, MMR, HPV

ADA TREATMENT GUIDELINES FOR TYPE 2 DIABETES

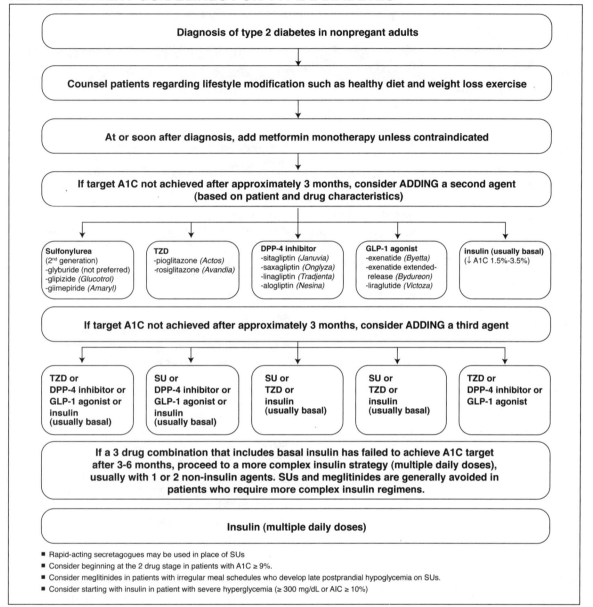

Diagnosis of type 2 diabetes in nonpregant adults

Counsel patients regarding lifestyle modification such as healthy diet and weight loss exercise

At or soon after diagnosis, add metformin monotherapy unless contraindicated

If target A1C not achieved after approximately 3 months, consider ADDING a second agent (based on patient and drug characteristics)

| **Sulfonylurea**
(2nd generation)
-glyburide (not preferred)
-glipizide (Glucotrol)
-giimepiride (Amaryl) | **TZD**
-pioglitazone (Actos)
-rosiglitazone (Avandia) | **DPP-4 inhibitor**
-sitagliptin (Januvia)
-saxagliptin (Onglyza)
-linagliptin (Tradjenta)
-alogliptin (Nesina) | **GLP-1 agonist**
-exenatide (Byetta)
-exenatide extended-release (Bydureon)
-liraglutide (Victoza) | **insulin (usually basal)**
($\downarrow$ A1C 1.5%-3.5%) |

If target A1C not achieved after approximately 3 months, consider ADDING a third agent

| TZD or
DPP-4 inhibitor or
GLP-1 agonist or
insulin
(usually basal) | SU or
DPP-4 inhibitor or
GLP-1 agonist or
insulin
(usually basal) | SU or
TZD or
insulin
(usually basal) | SU or
TZD or
insulin
(usually basal) | TZD or
DPP-4 inhibitor or
GLP-1 agonist |

If a 3 drug combination that includes basal insulin has failed to achieve A1C target after 3-6 months, proceed to a more complex insulin strategy (multiple daily doses), usually with 1 or 2 non-insulin agents. SUs and meglitinides are generally avoided in patients who require more complex insulin regimens.

Insulin (multiple daily doses)

- Rapid-acting secretagogues may be used in place of SUs
- Consider beginning at the 2 drug stage in patients with A1C ≥ 9%.
- Consider meglitinides in patients with irregular meal schedules who develop late postprandial hypoglycemia on SUs.
- Consider starting with insulin in patient with severe hyperglycemia (≥ 300 mg/dL or AIC ≥ 10%)

The AACE guidelines agree with the ADA in recommending <u>metformin as initial therapy</u> (unless insulin is required or the patient cannot use metformin) – but they differ in 2nd line treatment options. The ADA lists sulfonylureas (SUs) as a second-line option whereas AACE does not favor SUs due to the risks of hypoglycemia, weight gain, and loss of efficacy over time. The AACE treatment algorithm recommends evaluating the initial A1C and, based on the value, initiating single, double or triple drug therapy. The AACE goal for A1C is ≤ 6.5% for healthy patients without concurrent illness and at a low hypoglycemic risk.

BIGUANIDE

Metformin works primarily by ↓ hepatic glucose production. Metformin also decreases intestinal absorption of glucose and improves insulin sensitivity.

DRUG	DOSING	SAFETY/SIDE EFFECTS/MONITORING
Metformin *(Glucophage, Glucophage XR, Fortamet, Glumetza)* **Immediate release: 500, 850, 1,000 mg** **Extended release 500, 750, 1,000 mg** *Riomet liquid* (500 mg/5 mL) + glipizide *(Metaglip)* + glyburide *(Glucovance)* + pioglitazone *(Actoplus Met, Actoplus Met XR)* + rosiglitazone *(Avandamet)* **+ sitagliptin *(Janumet, Janumet XR)*** + saxagliptin *(Kombiglyze XR)* + linagliptin *(Jentadueto)* + repaglinide *(PrandiMet)* + alogliptin *(Kazano)*	↓ A1C 1-2% Start IR 500 mg daily-BID or 850 mg daily Start ER 500-1,000 mg with dinner. Titrate to 1.5-2 g daily, although higher doses are sometimes used. Max daily dose: 2,550 mg. First line therapy for type 2 treatment, and may be used for prevention. Extended release: Swallow whole; do not crush, break, or chew.	**BLACK BOX WARNING** Lactic acidosis **CONTRAINDICATIONS** Contraindicated with SCr ≥ 1.5 mg/dL (males) or ≥ 1.4 mg/dL (females) or abnormal creatinine clearance (CrCl < 60 mL/min), metabolic acidosis. Temporarily discontinue in patients receiving intravascular iodinated contrast media. **WARNINGS** Metformin should be stopped in any case of hypoxia, such as decompensated heart failure, respiratory failure, acute MI or sepsis. Avoid in patients with hepatic impairment due to increased risk for lactic acidosis. **SIDE EFFECTS** Diarrhea, nausea, vomiting, flatulence; vitamin B12 deficiency long term. weight neutral (few patients may lose weight), little-to no risk of hypoglycemia (when used as monotherapy). **MONITORING** FBG, A1C, SCr, BUN **NOTES** Pregnancy Category B. Hold prior to use of IV contrast dye and wait 48 hours after the procedure and restart only once renal function has been confirmed as normal. The ER formulations may appear in the stool. See counseling section.

Metformin Drug Interactions

- Alcohol can increase risk for lactic acidosis, especially with renal impairment and advanced heart disease.

- Iodinated contrast dye increases risk of lactic acidosis – hold x 48 hours and recheck renal function prior to restarting metformin.

- Metformin ↓ vitamin B-12 absorption (and possibly folic acid): this can lead to neuropathy. Consider vitamin supplement.

Metformin Counseling

- Some people have developed a very rare, life-threatening condition called lactic acidosis while taking metformin. Get emergency medical help if you have any of these symptoms of lactic acidosis: weakness, increasing sleepiness, slow heart rate, cold feeling, muscle pain, shortness of breath, stomach pain, feeling light-headed, and fainting.

- If you need to have any type of X-ray or CT scan using a contrast dye that is injected into your vein, you may need to temporarily stop taking metformin. Be sure the physician knows ahead of time that you are using metformin.

- Take metformin twice daily with your morning and evening meals (daily with evening meal if ER). Taking with food will also help decrease stomach upset.

- Do not crush, chew, or break an extended-release tablet. Swallow the pill whole. It is specially made to release medicine slowly in the body. Breaking the pill would cause too much of the drug to be released at one time.

- Diarrhea, nausea, vomiting, abdominal discomfort, and flatulence may occur; it often goes away. If the immediate dose is used, it should be given twice daily with meals. The stomach upset may be worse if taken on an empty stomach. You may find relief with the extended release formulation which is taken with dinner.

- If using *Glumetza, Fortamet,* or *Glucophage XR*, you may see a shell of the medicine in the stool. This is not a problem; the medicine is in your body and the tablet is empty.

SULFONYLUREAS

Sulfonylureas work by stimulating insulin secretion from the pancreatic beta cells. <u>Do not use with meglitinides due to similar MOA.</u>

DRUG	DOSING	SAFETY/SIDE EFFECTS/MONITORING
Chlorpropamide *(Diabinese)* Acetohexamide Tolazamide Tolbutamide	↓ A1C 1-2% These older agents should not be used	**WARNING:** Sulfa allergy (not likely to cross-react – please see cautionary statement in drug allergy chapter) **SIDE EFFECTS** Hypoglycemia, weight gain
Glipizide *(Glucotrol, Glucotrol XL, Glipizide XL)* + metformin *(Metaglip)*	IR 5-10 mg BID XL 5-10 mg daily, max 20 mg daily	**MONITORING** FBG, A1C **NOTES** ↓ efficacy after long-term use
Glimepiride *(Amaryl)* + pioglitazone *(Duetact)* + rosiglitazone *(Avandaryl)*	1-2 mg, max 8 mg daily	First generation agents (chlorpropamide, tolazamide, tolbutamide) can cause long-lasting hypoglycemia. Glyburide has a partially active metabolite that is renally cleared; it accumulates with renal dysfunction and should be avoided in patients with a CrCl < 50 mL/min. Glyburide is not a recommended agent.
Glyburide *(DiaBeta)* Micronized glyburide *(Glynase)* + metformin *(Glucovance)*	2.5-5 mg daily, max 20 mg/d *Glynase* 1.5-3 mg daily; max 12 mg/d CrCl < 50 mL/min: avoid	Regular tablets cannot be used interchangeably with micronized tablet formulations. Micronized glyburide has better absorption than glyburide; 3 mg micronized glyburide = 5 mg of glyburide Pregnancy Category C

Sulfonylurea Drug Interactions

- Primary interaction is with insulin because both can cause hypoglycemia; sulfonylureas should be discontinued when insulin is initiated, per AACE.

- Use caution with drugs that can cause hypoglycemia; see table at the beginning of the chapter.

- Sulfonylurea dose reduction may be required when a TZD, GLP-1 agonist, DPP-4 inhibitor, or canagliflozin is initiated.

- These agents are CYP2C9 substrates; use caution with drugs that are 2C9 inducers or inhibitors.

Sulfonylurea Counseling

- Do not crush, chew, or break an extended-release tablet. Swallow the pill whole. It is specially made to release medicine slowly in the body. Breaking the pill would cause too much of the drug to be released at one time.

- Keep away from children; even 1 tablet can be dangerous.

- Glipizide XR is taken with the first meal of the day, the IR is either 30 minutes before breakfast and dinner, or if once daily 30 minutes before first meal. Glimepiride is once daily, with the first meal.

- If the patient is made NPO or plans to reduce caloric intake, may need to hold the dose.

- This medicine can cause low blood sugar. Be able to recognize the symptoms of low blood sugar including shakiness, irritability, hunger, headache, confusion, drowsiness, weakness, dizziness, sweating, and fast heartbeat. Very low blood sugar can cause seizures (convulsions), fainting, or coma. Always keep a source of sugar available in case you have symptoms of low blood sugar.

MEGLITINIDES

Meglitinides work by stimulating insulin secretion from the pancreatic beta cells. Do not use with sulfonylureas due to similar MOA.

DRUG	DOSING	SAFETY/SIDE EFFECTS/MONITORING
Repaglinide *(Prandin)* + metformin (*PrandiMet*)	↓ A1C 0.5-1.5%; used for ↓ postprandial BG A1C < 8%: 0.5 mg before each meal (TID) A1C ≥ 8%: 1-2 mg before each meal (TID); max 16 mg daily Take 15-30 minutes before meals	**SIDE EFFECTS** Hypoglycemia, mild weight gain, upper respiratory tract infection **MONITORING** FBG, A1C **NOTES** Nateglinide is slightly less effective than repaglinide Pregnancy Category C
Nateglinide *(Starlix)*	60 mg before each meal (TID) if near goal A1C, otherwise 120 mg before each meal (TID) Take 1-30 minutes before meals	

Meglitinides Drug Interactions

- Primary interaction is with insulin because both can cause hypoglycemia.

- Meglitinide dose reduction may be required when a TZD, GLP-1 agonist, DPP-4 inhibitor, or canagliflozin is initiated.

- Gemfibrozil increases *Prandin* concentrations and can ↓ BG: recommend fenofibrate instead.

- Use caution with drugs that can cause hypoglycemia; see table at the beginning of the chapter.

Meglitinides Counseling

- Take 1-30 minutes prior to meals. If you forget to take a dose until after eating, skip that dose and take only your next regularly scheduled dose, before a meal.

- If you plan to skip a meal, skip the dose for that meal. (Some patients will be told to increase dose if they eat significantly more food at a meal.)

- This medicine can cause low blood sugar. Be able to recognize the symptoms of low blood sugar including shakiness, irritability, hunger, headache, confusion, drowsiness, weakness, dizziness, sweating, and fast heartbeat. Very low blood sugar can cause seizures (convulsions), fainting, or coma. Always keep a source of sugar available in case you have symptoms of low blood sugar.

- Keep away from children; even 1 tablet can be dangerous.

THIAZOLIDINEDIONES (TZDs)

Thiazolidinediones are peroxisome proliferator-activated receptor gamma (PPARγ) agonists causing ↑ peripheral insulin sensitivity (↑ uptake and utilization of glucose by the peripheral tissues; insulin sensitizers).

DRUG	DOSING	SAFETY/SIDE EFFECTS/MONITORING
Pioglitazone *(Actos)* + metformin *(Actoplus Met, Actoplus Met XR)* + glimepiride *(Duetact)* + alogliptin *(Oseni)*	↓ A1C 0.5-1.4% 15-30 mg daily; max 45 mg daily	**BLACK BOX WARNING** May cause or exacerbate heart failure in some patients; do not initate therapy in patients with NYHA Class III/IV heart failure. **WARNINGS** Do not use pioglitazone in patients with active bladder cancer
Rosiglitazone *(Avandia)* + metformin *(Avandamet)* + glimepiride *(Avandaryl)*	4-8 mg daily Not in any guidelines. Previous restrictions required patients to be enrolled in the *Avandia*-Rosiglitazone Medication Access Program- REMS Program. Restrictions were lifted November 2013.	**SIDE EFFECTS** Peripheral edema, weight gain, URTIs; macular edema, CHF, ↑ fracture risk, ↑ LFTs, pioglitazone has ↑ risk of bladder cancer when used beyond 1 year Good: ↑ HDL, ↓ TGs and ↓ total cholesterol (pioglitazone) **MONITORING** LFTs, FBG, A1C, and signs and symptoms of heart failure **NOTES** Pregnancy Category C

Glitazone Drug Interactions

- These agents can reduce the amount of insulin or insulin secretagogue required. Monitor blood glucose closely after initiation of therapy.

- These agents are CYP2C8 substrates; use caution with drugs that are 2C8 inducers (e.g., rifampin) or inhibitors (e.g., gemfibrozil).

Glitazone Counseling

- May take several weeks for the drug to lower blood sugar; monitor your levels carefully.

- Take once daily, with or without food.

- Contact your doctor right away if you are passing dark-colored urine, have pale stools, feel more tired than usual or if your skin and/or whites of your eyes become yellow. These may be signs of liver damage.

- This drug can cause water retention and can cause your ankles to swell. You may develop trouble breathing. If this happens, inform your doctor right away.

- Women may also be more likely than men to have bone fractures in the upper arm, hand, or foot while taking pioglitazone. Talk with your doctor if you are concerned about this possibility.

- Before taking pioglitazone, tell your doctor if you have congestive heart failure or heart disease, fluid retention, a history of bladder cancer, a history of heart attack or stroke, or liver disease.

ALPHA-GLUCOSIDASE INHIBITORS

These agents cause reversible inhibition of membrane-bound intestinal alpha-glucosidases which hydrolyze oligosaccharides and disaccharides to glucose and other monosaccharides in the brush border of the small intestine. In patients with diabetes, this enzyme inhibition results in delayed glucose absorption and lowering of postprandial hyperglycemia.

DRUG	DOSING	SAFETY/SIDE EFFECTS/MONITORING
Acarbose *(Precose)* Miglitol *(Glyset)*	↓ A1C 0.5-0.8%; used to ↓ postprandial BG Both acarbose and miglitol are started at 25 mg with the first bite of each main meal; ↑ by 25 mg every 1-2 months, max 300 mg/d, divided. CrCl < 25 mL/min: not recommended	**CONTRAINDICATIONS** Inflammatory bowel disease (IBD), colonic ulceration, partial or complete intestinal obstruction **SIDE EFFECTS** GI effects (flatulence, diarrhea, abdominal pain) – so titrate slowly. Weight neutral **MONITORING** Postprandial BG, A1C and LFTs with acarbose Acarbose can rarely ↑ liver enzymes; check LFTs every 3 months during 1st year **NOTES** Pregnancy Category B

Alpha-Glucosidase Inhibitor Counseling

- Take with a full glass of water with your first bite of food; the medicine needs to be in the stomach with your food. If you plan to skip a meal, you do not need to take the dose for that meal.

- This medicine will cause flatulence (gas), diarrhea and abdominal pain, but this usually goes away with time. The dose may be increased as you get over these side effects.

- These agents, by themselves, do not cause low blood sugar. If you get low blood sugar after taking acarbose or miglitol, you cannot treat it with sucrose (present in fruit juice) or with table sugar or candy. If you are using this agent with a drug that causes low blood sugar (such as insulin, a sulfonylurea or a meglitinide), you will need to purchase glucose tablets or gel to have on-hand to treat any hypoglycemic episode.

- This medicine does not cause any weight gain.

DPP-4 INHIBITORS

Dipeptidyl peptidase IV (DPP-4) inhibitors prevent the enzyme DPP-4 from breaking down incretin hormones, glucagon-like peptide-1(GLP-1) and glucose-dependent insulinotropic polypeptide (GIP). These hormones help to regulate blood glucose levels by increasing insulin release from the pancreatic beta cells and decreasing glucagon secretion from pancreatic alpha cells. A reduction in glucagon results in decreased hepatic glucose production. These are *incretin enhancers*.

DRUG	DOSING	SAFETY/SIDE EFFECTS/MONITORING
Sitagliptin *(Januvia)* **+ metformin *(Janumet, Janumet XR)*** + simvastatin *(Juvisync)*	↓ A1C 0.5-0.8%, ↓ (primarily) postprandial BG 100 mg daily CrCl 30-49 mL/min: 50 mg daily CrCl < 30 mL/min: 25 mg daily	**SIDE EFFECTS** Nasopharyngitis, upper respiratory tract infections, UTIs, peripheral edema, rash and hypoglycemia. Rarely can cause acute pancreatitis. Weight neutral
Saxagliptin *(Onglyza)* + metformin *(Kombiglyze XR)*	5 mg daily CrCl < 50 mL/min or with strong CYP 3A4 inhibitors: 2.5 mg daily *Kombiglyze XR* is given daily with evening meal	**MONITORING** FBG, A1C, renal function **NOTES** Pregnancy Category B
Linagliptin *(Tradjenta)* + metformin *(Jentadueto)*	5 mg daily No renal dose adjustment	
Alogliptin *(Nesina)* + metformin *(Kazano)* + pioglitazone *(Oseni)*	25 mg daily CrCl 30-59 mL/min: 12.5 mg daily CrCl < 30 mL/min: 6.25 mg daily	

DPP-4 Inhibitor Drug Interactions

- These agents can reduce the amount of insulin or insulin secretagogue required. Monitor blood glucose closely after initiation of therapy.

- Saxagliptin (*Onglyza*) is a major 3A4 substrate: Use the lower 2.5 mg dose with strong CYP 3A4 inhibitors including ketoconazole, atazanavir, clarithromycin, indinavir, itraconazole, nefazodone, nelfinavir, ritonavir, saquinavir and telithromycin.

- Linagliptin (*Tradjenta*) is a major 3A4 and P-glycoprotein substrate. Linagliptin levels are decreased by strong inducers (carbamazepine, efavirenz, phenytoin, rifampin, St. John's wort).

DPP-4 inhibitor Counseling

- Take once daily in the morning, with or without food.

- If you have trouble breathing, or any kind of rash, see the doctor at once.

- Counsel patients to be seen right away if they develop symptoms of pancreatitis, which include severe stomach pain that does not go away, with or without vomiting. The pain can radiate from the abdomen through to the back.

SODIUM GLUCOSE CO-TRANSPORTER-2 INHIBITOR

Sodium glucose co-transporter-2 (SGLT2), expressed in the proximal renal tubules, is responsible for the majority of the reabsorption of filtered glucose from the tubular lumen. Canagliflozin is an inhibitor of SGLT2. By inhibiting SGLT2, canagliflozin reduces reabsorption of filtered glucose and lowers the renal threshold for glucose, which increases urinary glucose excretion.

DRUG	DOSING	SAFETY/SIDE EFFECTS/MONITORING
Canagliflozin (*Invokana*) 100, 300 mg tablets	100 mg daily, taken before the first meal of the day; can ↑ to 300 mg daily CrCl 45-60 mL/min: 100 mg max dose CrCl < 45 mL/min: do not use	**CONTRAINDICATIONS** Severe renal impairment (CrCl < 30 mL/min), ESRD, or on dialysis **SIDE EFFECTS** Female genital mycotic infections, UTIs, hyperkalemia, ↑ urination, renal insufficiency, hypovolemia, hypotension, ↑ thirst, hypoglycemia **MONITORING** CrCl, renal function, K⁺ **NOTES** Pregnancy Category C Consider a lower dose of insulin or insulin secretagogue when used in combo with canagliflozin to reduce risk of hypoglycemia

SGLT2 Drug Interactions

- These agents can reduce the amount of insulin or insulin secretagogue required. Monitor blood glucose closely after initiation of therapy.

- UGT inducers (e.g., rifampin) can reduce level of canagliflozin; consider dose increase to 300 mg.

- Monitor digoxin levels if taking digoxin concurrently due to ↑ AUC of digoxin.

GLUCAGON-LIKE PEPTIDE-1 (GLP-1) AGONISTS

These agents are analogs of glucagon-like peptide-1 (GLP-1) which ↑ insulin secretion, ↓ glucagon secretion, slow gastric emptying, improve satiety, and may result in weight loss. These are *incretin mimetics*.

DRUG	DOSING	SAFETY/SIDE EFFECTS/MONITORING
Exenatide *(Byetta)* 5 mcg, 10 mcg pens **Exenatide extended-release *(Bydureon)*** 2 mg extended release powder for injection A synthetic version of exendin, a substance found in Gila monster saliva Can be used as mono- or combination therapy only in type 2 diabetes	↓ A1C 0.5-1%, primarily ↓ postprandial BG Exenatide IR: Start at 5 mcg SC BID for 1 month; then 10 mcg SC BID Should be given within 60 minutes (usually 30) before the morning and evening meal Exenatide ER: Inject 2 mg SC once every 7 days. May inject without regard to meals. Must be reconstituted immediately prior to injection. Abdomen is preferred SC injection site, but can use thigh or upper arm. Count to 5 before withdrawing syringe Can be stored at room temperature for up to 30 days	**BLACK BOX WARNING – FOR *BYDUREON*** Thyroid C-cell carcinomas seen in rats – unknown if this could happen in humans. Contraindicated in patients with a personal or family history of medullary thyroid carcinoma (MTC) or patients with Multiple Endocrine Neoplasia syndrome type 2 (MEN2) **WARNINGS** Pancreatitis (fatal and non-fatal) can occur, but occurs most commonly in patients with risk factors (history of pancreatitis, gallstones, alcoholism, or high triglycerides). This is in the required MedGuide. Use caution with moderate renal impairment, avoid in severe impairment (CrCl < 30 mL/min) Not recommended in severe GI disease **SIDE EFFECTS** Nausea (primary side effect), vomiting, diarrhea, constipation, anti-exenatide antibodies, hypoglycemia (all > 10%), weight loss – different for all patients, usually ~5 pounds. Can cause pancreatitis Exenatide ER: may cause nodule at injection site. Nodule usually resolves without intervention. **MONITORING** FBG, A1C, renal function **NOTES** Pregnancy Category C

Glucagon-Like Peptide-1 (GLP-1) Agonists

DRUG	DOSING	SAFETY/SIDE EFFECTS/MONITORING
Liraglutide (*Victoza*) Can be used as mono- or combination therapy only in type 2 diabetes	↓ A1C 0.5-1.1% 0.6, 1.2, or 1.8 mg SC daily – available in prefilled pens Start with 0.6 mg SC daily x 1 wk, then 1.2 mg SC daily x 1 wk. Can ↑ to 1.8 mg SC daily, if needed. Given without regard to meals Can be stored at room temperature for up to 30 days	**BLACK BOX WARNING** Thyroid C-cell carcinomas seen in rats and mice – unknown if this could happen in humans. Contraindicated in patients with a personal or family history of medullary thyroid carcinoma (MTC) or Multiple Endocrine Neoplasia syndrome type 2 (MEN 2). **WARNINGS** Pancreatitis, reports of acute renal failure and worsening of chronic renal failure Use caution in moderate renal impairment, use is not recommended in severe renal impairment (CrCl < 30 mL/min) **SIDE EFFECTS** Nausea (28%), diarrhea, vomiting, anti-liraglutide antibodies, more weight loss and less hypoglycemia than with exenatide; pancreatitis **MONITORING** FBG, A1C **NOTES** Pregnancy Category C

GLP-1 Agonist Drug Interactions

- These agents can reduce the amount of insulin or insulin secretagogue required. Monitor blood glucose closely after initiation of therapy.

- These drugs slow gastric emptying and can reduce the extent and rate of absorption of orally administered drugs. Caution is warranted.

Byetta

- Oral contraceptive levels may be decreased in patients taking *Byetta*. Patients should be advised to take oral contraceptives at least 1 hour before *Byetta* injection.

- May enhance the anticoagulant effects of warfarin: monitor INR.

GLP-1 Agonist Counseling

- Pancreatitis, or inflammation of the pancreas, can rarely happen with the use of this drug. Be seen right away if you develop stomach pain that does not go away, with or without vomiting. The pain can radiate from the abdomen through to the back. Alcohol consumption should be limited.

- If you develop nausea, which is common when starting therapy, you must be careful to consume adequate fluids. If you are vomiting or have diarrhea, take fluid replacement drinks and contact your doctor. Nausea generally decreases over time.

- Administer (using a fresh needle) by SC injection in stomach area (abdomen – preferred), upper leg (thigh), or the back of the upper arm. Count to 5 before withdrawing the syringe.

- Store in the refrigerator; stable at room temperature for up to 30 days. Never freeze.

- Keep pens and needles out of the reach of children.

Byetta

- Inject two times each day, within 60 minutes before the morning and evening meals (or before the 2 main meals of the day but they need to be 6 hours or more apart).

- Never inject after a meal due to the risk of hypoglycemia.

- After 1 month, if the nausea is manageable, the dose will be increased from 5 mcg twice daily to a more concentrated pen that provides a 10 mcg dose twice daily.

- Do not store your *Byetta* Pen with the needle attached. If the needle is left on, *Byetta* may leak from the pen and air bubbles may form in the cartridge (same for *Victoza)*.

- After 30 days of use, throw away the *Byetta* Pen, even if it is not completely empty. Mark the date when you first used your pen and the date 30 days later. *Byetta* should not be used after the expiration date printed on the pen label (same for *Victoza)*.

Bydureon and Victoza

- Do not take this medication if you or any family members have had thyroid cancer, especially medullary thyroid cancer.

- While taking this medication, tell your doctor if you get a lump or swelling in your neck, hoarseness, trouble swallowing, or shortness of breath. These may be symptoms of thyroid cancer.

- *Bydureon:* This medication is taken once every 7 days (weekly). If a dose is missed, it should be administered as soon as noticed, provided the next regularly scheduled dose is due at least 3 days later.

- *Bydureon:* Must be injected right after it is mixed.

- *Victoza:* This medication is injected 1 time each day. Your dose should be increased after 1 week of starting therapy.

PRAMLINTIDE

Pramlintide is a synthetic analog of the human neuroendocrine hormone, amylin. Amylin is produced by pancreatic beta cells to assist in postprandial glucose control. Amylin helps slow gastric emptying, prevents an increase in serum glucagon following a meal, and increases satiety. This is an amylinomimetic agent.

DRUG	DOSING	SAFETY/SIDE EFFECTS/MONITORING
Pramlintide *(Symlin)* *SymlinPen 120* *SymlinPen 60* **Can use in both Types 1 and 2 DM:** ↓ rapid-acting, short-acting, and fixed-mix insulins by 50% when starting this drug.	Type 1: Start at 15 mcg immediately prior to meals – can titrate at 15 mcg increments up to 60 mcg if no significant nausea. Type 2: Start at 60 mcg prior to meals – can increase to 120 mcg if no significant nausea. Administered SC in abdomen or thigh prior to each meal (≥ 250 kcal or ≥ 30 grams of carbohydrates).	**BLACK BOX WARNING** Co-administration with insulin may induce severe hypoglycemia (usually within 3 hours following administration) **CONTRAINDICATIONS** Gastroparesis, hypoglycemia unawareness **SIDE EFFECTS** Hypoglycemia (when starting therapy, reduce meal-time insulins by 50% to ↓ risk of hypoglycemia), nausea (30%), anorexia (15%), weight loss **MONITORING** FBG, A1C **NOTES** Pregnancy Category C Refrigerate pens not in use. Can be stored at room temperature for up to 30 days. If skipping meal or consuming < 250 calories or < 30 grams of carbohydrates skip the dose. Do not mix with the insulin injection.

Pramlintide Drug Interactions

- These drugs slow gastric emptying and can reduce the extent and rate of absorption of orally administered drugs. Caution is warranted.

BILE ACID BINDING RESINS

Resins work by binding bile, blocking reabsorption. Bile is produced from cholesterol and cholesterol levels decrease. The mechanism by which colesevelam improves glycemic control in unknown.

DRUG	DOSING	SAFETY/SIDE EFFECTS/MONITORING
Colesevelam *(Welchol)* 625 mg tabs or 3.75 gram and 1.875 gram packets for oral solution	Take 6 tabs daily or 3 tabs BID WITH a meal AND liquid or take one 3.75 gram packet daily or 1.875 gram packet BID [dissolved in ½ to 1 cup (4-8 oz.) of water] Approved for lipids (↓ LDL ~20%) and DM 2 (↓ A1C 0.5%, ↓ postprandial BG)	**CONTRAINDICATIONS** History of bowel obstruction, TG > 500 mg/dL, history hypertriglyceridemia-induced pancreatitis **SIDE EFFECTS** Constipation (> 10%), dyspepsia, nausea, bloating. Can ↑ TGs (~5%) **MONITORING** FBG, A1C, LDL, TG **NOTES** Pregnancy Category B ↓ absorption of other drugs; see below *Welchol* has less GI SEs than the other agents in this class that are used for lipid-lowering

Colesevelam Drug Interactions

■ The following medications should be taken 4 hours prior to *Welchol*: cyclosporine, glimepiride, glipizide, glyburide, levothyroxine, olmesartan, phenytoin and oral contraceptives containing ethinyl estradiol + norethindrone.

■ With warfarin, monitor INR frequently during initiation.

■ Take bile acid resins 4-6 hours before *Niaspan*.

Colesevelam Counseling

■ Check for other constipating drugs or constipation, and counsel appropriately (laxative, such as senna, or the stool softener docusate, if appropriate). Adequate fluid intake is required.

■ May take a multivitamin at other time, due to possible risk of ↓ A, D, E and K (mostly K) absorption.

BROMOCRIPTINE

Bromocriptine is indicated as an adjunct to diet and exercise to improve glycemic control in adults with type 2 diabetes. It is a dopamine agonist but it improves glycemic control by working in the CNS to decrease insulin resistance.

DRUG	DOSING	SAFETY/SIDE EFFECTS/MONITORING
Bromocriptine (*Cycloset*), *Parlodel* is used for Parkinson's 0.8 mg tabs	1.6-4.8 mg daily – take with food to ↓ nausea Start at 0.8 mg daily within 2 hours of waking. If miss a dose, do not take later in the day. Titrate in 0.8 mg increments weekly ↓ A1C by 0.5%	**CONTRAINDICATIONS** Patients allergic to ergot-related drugs, patients with syncopal migraines, and nursing women **SIDE EFFECTS** Nausea, dizziness due to orthostasis (requires slow dose titration), fatigue, headache, vomiting, rhinitis, risk of psychiatric effects **MONITORING** FBG, A1C **NOTES** Pregnancy Category B

Bromocriptine Drug Interactions

- Bromocriptine is extensively metabolized by CYP 450 3A4 (substrate); inducers or inhibitors of 3A4 can lower or raise the bromocriptine concentration.

- Do not use with other ergot medications. May increase ergot-related side effects or reduce ergot effectiveness for migraines if co-administered within 6 hours of ergot-related drug.

- Monitor for hypoglycemia if patient is using a sulfonylurea – may need dose adjustment.

INSULIN

Insulin is a hormone that muscle and adipose tissue require for glucose uptake. Insulin also has a role in regulating fat storage and inhibits the breakdown of fat for energy. Commercially available insulins differ in their onset and duration of action. All insulins have a concentration of 100 units/mL, except *Humulin R* U-500 which has a concentration of 500 units/mL.

U-500 INSULIN

All insulins have a concentration of 100 units/mL, except *Humulin R* U-500 which has a concentration of 500 units/mL. This concentration of insulin is for patients requiring a large volume of insulin (> 200 units/day). *Humulin R* U-500 has an onset of action of 30 minutes, has a peak similar to U-100 regular insulin, and has a relatively long duration of action (up to 24 hrs after a single dose) compared to U-100 regular insulin. The prescribed dose of *Humulin R* U-500 should be expressed in actual units of *Humulin R* U-500 along with corresponding markings on the syringe the patient is using (e.g., a U-100 syringe or tuberculin syringe). ISMP recommends the use of tuberculin syringes when administering *Humulin R* U-500 insulin [e.g., 200 units (0.4 mL)]. *Humulin R* U-500 is available in 20 mL vials.

BOLUS OR MEAL-TIME OR PRANDIAL INSULIN

Rapid-acting Insulin

Aspart *(NovoLog, NovoLog FlexPen)*, Glulisine *(Apidra, Apidra SoloStar)*, Lispro *(Humalog, Humalog KwikPen)*

These are injected when the person sits down to eat, up to 15 minutes prior to eating, or may be injected immediately after a meal. They are designed to last for a meal, and usually are gone in 3-5 hours. In some patients they last an hour or two longer. The duration of action is shorter than regular insulin.

Rapid-acting insulin is dosed for the amount of carbohydrates in a meal, or is given on a fixed regimen for typical-sized meals. They are clear and can be mixed with NPH insulin, but they are usually given by themselves with meals or in mixes with a longer-acting insulin. They come in pre-filled injection syringes (pens) in mixes and in 10 mL vials, and are used in insulin pumps and for sliding scales in hospitals (as is regular insulin).

Regular, or "short-acting" Insulin

Regular insulin *(Humulin R, Novolin R)*

Regular insulin should be injected 30 minutes before a meal. The onset of action is at least 30 minutes. Regular insulin lasts around 6-10 hours. Regular insulin is clear, and comes in pens and vials, and in mixes with intermediate acting (N, or NPH).

Baseline, or "basal" Insulin

NPH, or "intermediate" Insulin: NPH *(Humulin N, Novolin N)*

NPH insulin is typically given once or twice daily. The onset of action is 1 to 2 hours, with a peak of 4-8 hours, and a duration of up to 24 hours. The variable pharmacokinetics of NPH insulin between patients make it more difficult to predict glycemic response, and the insulin usually "peaks" during mid-afternoon (when dosed in the morning) and early morning hours (when dosed in the evening) when the patient is not eating. It is not a good match for physiological insulin, but it is used by some patients. NPH insulin is cloudy, and any mixed insulin preparation containing NPH is cloudy. It comes in pens, vials, and in mixes.

Long-acting Insulin: Insulin Detemir *(Levemir, Levemir FlexPen)*, Insulin Glargine *(Lantus, Lantus SoloStar)*

The baseline insulins are dosed once or twice daily. The onset and duration is patient specific, and for both the onset is around 1-2 hours. Both last ~24 hours and do not peak. This is important because when insulin peaks, it can increase the risk of hypoglycemia in some patients. If there is hypoglycemia with a long-acting agent, it can last a long time and may require re-treatment. Detemir and glargine should not be mixed with other insulins in the same syringe.

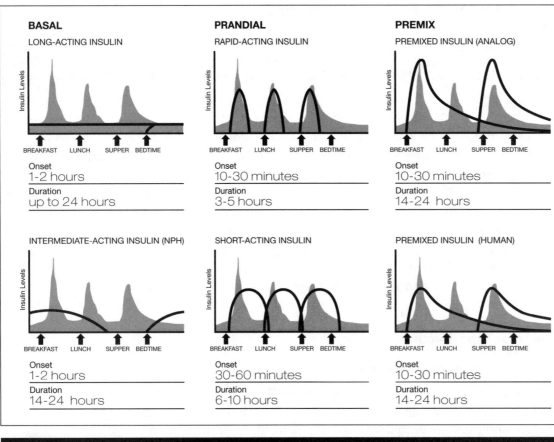

INSULIN	ONSET	PEAK	DURATION
Rapid-acting Insulin			
Insulin aspart (*NovoLOG, NovoLOG FlexPen*) **Insulin glulisine (*Apidra, Apidra SoloStar*)** **Insulin lispro (*HumaLOG, HumaLOG KwikPen*)**	10-30 minutes	0.5-2.5 hours	3-5 hours
Short-acting Insulin (OTC)			
Regular (*HumuLIN R, NovoLIN R*)	30-60 minutes	1-3.5 hours	6-10 hours
Intermediate-acting Insulin (OTC)			
NPH (*HumuLIN N, NovoLIN N*)	1-2 hours	4-8 hours	14-24 hours
Insulin NPH/Insulin Regular (*HumuLIN 70/30, NovoLIN 70/30*)	30 minutes	2-12 hours	14-24 hours
Long-acting Insulin			
Insulin detemir (*Levemir, Levemir FlexPen*)	1-2 hours	–	14-24 hours
Insulin glargine (*Lantus, Lantus SoloStar*)	1-2 hours	–	24 hours

Premixed Insulins

Premixed Insulin Analogs

INSULIN	ONSET	PEAK	DURATION
Insulin aspart protamine suspension and insulin aspart *(NovoLOG Mix 70/30, NovoLOG Mix 70/30 Flexpen)*	10-30 minutes	varies	14-24 hours
Insulin lispro protamine suspension and insulin lispro *(HumaLOG Mix 50/50, HumaLOG Mix 50/50 Kwikpen, HumaLOG Mix 75/25, HumaLOG Mix 75/25 Kwikpen)*	10-30 minutes	varies	14-24 hours

NPH-Regular Combinations (OTC)

Insulin NPH suspension and insulin regular solution *(HumuLIN 70/30, NovoLIN 70/30)*	30 minutes	varies	14-24 hours

Insulin Side Effects

- Hypoglycemia, weight gain, and local skin reactions (to avoid, rotate the injection site). Insulin glargine *(Lantus)* may sting a little when injecting (minor).

Mixing Insulins

NPH can be mixed with regular and rapid acting insulins. Some patients mix their own insulins to provide specific doses. They do this by first drawing up the clear insulin into a syringe (regular or rapid-acting insulin) and then drawing up the cloudy insulin (NPH). It may be helpful to remember that "clear before cloudy" is alphabetical. There are some commercial preparations of pre-mixed insulins as well. These include either NPH with regular, or aspart protamine or lispro protamine with the rapid-action insulin. The pre-mixed insulins are also cloudy due to the longer-acting component. They come in varying proportions, including 70/30, 75/25 and 50/50. In a mix, the first number is the percentage of the longer-acting intermediate insulin (N, also written as NPH, or aspart protamine or lispro protamine), followed by the percentage of the shorter-acting insulin (R, for regular, or rapid-acting aspart or lispro). They are named after the regular or rapid-acting insulin (example: *NovoLOG* 70/30 contains insulin aspart protamine). Pre-mixed insulins are available in vials and pens.

Insulin Vials, Pens, and Pumps

Most insulin vials contain 10 mL. *Humulin R* U-100 insulin comes in both 3 mL and 10 mL vials. *Humulin R* U-500 insulin comes in a 20 mL vial. All insulin pen cartridges contain 3 mL. In general, pens are easier to use and cause fewer dosing errors if used correctly. They are easier to use for patients with dexterity problems such as tremor, or with arthritis or with vision difficulty. Insulin pumps are devices that consist of a pump, an insulin reservoir, tubing, and a cannula. The devices can be programmed to mimic the insulin secretion of the pancreas. Insulin pumps infuse a basal rate of insulin throughout the day, and boluses of insulin are taken when the patient eats. The pumps are very small devices (about the size of a deck of cards, or smaller) and can use regular or rapid acting insulins. Pumps are most often used by type 1 patients but are increasingly used by type 2 patients.

INSULIN DOSING

Initiating Insulin Therapy for Patients with Type 1 Diabetes

Typical starting dose: 0.6 units/kg/day. This is the total daily dose (TDD) of insulin.

If using basal-bolus insulins, take 50% of TDD for the basal insulin dose and 50% for the bolus (mealtime) insulin. The bolus insulin is divided evenly among the 3 meals (or can give more for a larger meal or less for a smaller meal).

If using NPH and regular, take 2/3 of the TDD as the intermediate acting (NPH) dose and 1/3 as the regular acting (generally dosed BID).

Patients on meal time insulin may be counting carbohydrates to better adjust the insulin dose for that meal. These adjustments are made using an insulin-to-carbohydrate ratio (ICR). One way to determine ICR is by the Rule of 500 (for rapid-acting insulins) and Rule of 450 (for regular insulin):

$$\frac{500}{\text{total daily dose of insulin (TDD)}} = \text{grams of carbohydrate covered by 1 unit of rapid-acting insulin}$$

$$\frac{450}{\text{total daily dose of insulin (TDD)}} = \text{grams of carbohydrates covered by 1 unit of regular insulin}$$

Patients with diabetes should know their correction dose, or how much additional insulin is needed to keep their blood glucose in range. For example, a patient is going to a wedding and they want to enjoy a piece of cake at the wedding. Knowing how to calculate a correction dose will allow the patient to accurately dose the "additional" insulin needed for the extra carbohydrate load.

Correction Factor – 1,800 Rule (Rapid-acting Insulin)

$$\frac{1,800}{\text{total daily dose of insulin (TDD)}} = \text{correction factor for 1 unit of rapid-acting insulin}$$

Correction Factor – 1,500 Rule (Regular Insulin)

$$\frac{1,500}{\text{total daily dose of insulin (TDD)}} = \text{correction factor for 1 unit of regular insulin}$$

Correction Dose

$$\frac{(\text{Blood glucose now}) - (\text{target blood glucose})}{\text{correction factor}} = \text{correction dose}$$

Initiation and Adjustment of Insulin for Patients with Type 2 Diabetes

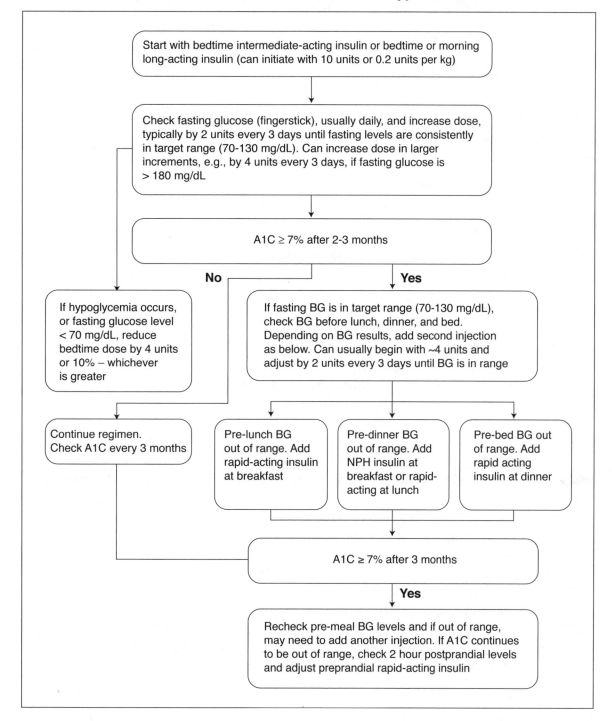

Insulin Conversion Calculations

NPH to Glargine

- Once-daily NPH to glargine: 1:1 conversion (same dose), unless adjustment is warranted

- Twice-daily NPH to glargine: reduce daily dose 20% and give once daily

Example: A patient has been using NPH 20 units before breakfast and 10 units at bedtime. Convert the NPH to *Lantus*, given once daily.

Solution: Add up the daily dose of NPH (20 + 10 = 30 units). Reduce dose by 20%: 30 units x 0.80 = 24 units.

NPH to Detemir

1:1 conversion (same dose), unless adjustment is warranted

Glargine to Detemir (or vice versa)

1:1 conversion (same dose), unless adjustment is warranted.

Regular or rapid-acting to another rapid-acting, or rapid-acting to regular

1:1 conversion (same dose), unless adjustment is warranted, and may be dosed to carbohydrate intake.

Premixed to Premixed

Intermediate/regular (70% NPH/30% Regular – *HumuLIN, NovoLIN, ReliOn 70/30)* to intermediate/rapid-acting *(HumaLOG 75/25* or *NovoLOG 75/25 or 70/30)* or vice-versa,

OR

Intermediate/regular (50% NPH/50% Regular, *HumuLIN 50/50)* to intermediate/rapid-acting *(HumaLOG 50/50)* or vice versa: 1:1 conversion (same dose), unless adjustment is warranted.

The regular is usually dosed twice daily. The rapid-acting insulin can be dosed similarly if in a mix or split according to carbohydrate intake.

Example: A patient has been using 70/30 NPH/Regular twice daily, 11 units before breakfast and 11 units before dinner. Reported preprandial blood glucose ranges are within 85-109 mg/dL and postprandial ranges are 108-138 mg/dL. Convert the 70/30 NPH/R to *Humalog Mix 75/25* given twice daily. Solution: The patient appears well-controlled. *Humalog Mix 75/25* is dosed once or twice daily. In this case, the dosing can stay the same except it will be dosed 15 minutes before meals, or immediately after eating, rather than 30 minutes prior to meals.

Insulin Stability

For all Insulins: Do not freeze; if frozen, discard. Check for discoloration or particulates; if present, discard. If needle is attached for use, discard used needle after use; do not keep on device. Do not store under direct sunlight or heat. If the insulin is placed into an admixture the stability is shorter and will depend (also) if additional components. If refrigerated and unopened use, expiration date on label.

INSULIN	STABILITY AT ROOM TEMP*	NOTES

Rapid-Acting Insulin

Apidra, Humalog, Novolog (vials and pens)	28 days (vials and pens)	

Regular Insulin

Humulin R (U-100, U-500 vial)	31 days	
Novolin R (U-100 vial)	42 days	

NPH Insulin

Humulin N (vial)	28 days	
Humulin N and *Novolin N* (pens)	14 days	
Novolin N (vial)	42 days	

Mixed Insulin

Humalog 50/50, 75/25, *Humulin* 70/30 and *Novolog* 70/30	28 days (vials)	
Humalog 50/50, 75/25 and *Humulin* 70/30	10 days (pens)	Do not refrigerate opened pens, store at room temp ≤ 30°C (≤ 86°F).
Novolin 70/30 (vial)	42 days	
Novolog 70/30 (pen)	14 days(2)	

Long-Acting Insulin and Other Injectables

Lantus	28 days (vials and pens)	*Lantus* is all 28 days if opened (vials/cartridges) except 3 mL cartridge once inserted in the *OptiClik* pen is at room temp only; do not refrigerate.
Levemir	42 days (vials and pens)	*Levemir* is all 42 days if opened (vials/cartridges) except in use cartridges and pens are at room temp only; do not refrigerate.
Byetta	30 days	*Byetta* pens stored in refrigerator; in-use pen can be kept at room temp if ≤ 25°C (≤ 77°F).
Bydureon	28 days	*Bydureon* vials stored in refrigerator; vials can be kept at room temp if ≤ 25°C (≤ 77°F).
Victoza	30 days	*Victoza* pens stored in refrigerator; in-use pen can be kept at room temp if ≤ 30°C (≤ 86°F).
Symlin	30 (vials and pens)	*Symlin* vials/pens stored in refrigerator; in-use pen or vial can be kept at room temp if ≤ 30°C (≤ 86°F).

* when in use

Insulin Sliding Scales

In the hospital setting, insulin is often dosed as 1-2 basal injections, plus either regular or rapid-acting insulin, dosed according to a sliding scale. Or, patients can use sliding scales to adjust their own insulin at home.

Sliding Scale Example

BLOOD SUGAR READING (MG/DL)	INSTRUCTION
BS < 60	Hold insulin; contact MD
150-200	Give 2 units of insulin
201-250	Give 4 units of insulin
251-300	Give 6 units of insulin
301-350	Give 8 units of insulin
351-400	Give 10 units of insulin
401-450	Call MD

Insulin Administration

- Keep unused vials or cartridges in the refrigerator. <u>Vials or pens in current use are good at room temperature if a certain period of time (e.g., 28 days, 42 days, etc.).</u> Please see stability information above.

- Wash hands and lay out all supplies.

- Check insulin for any discoloration, crystals, or lumps.

- If insulin is a suspension, roll bottle gently between hand (do not shake). If pen, invert 4-5 times.

- Clean injection site area (the skin) and wipe the top of the insulin vial with an alcohol swab.

- Inject an equal volume of air into the vial that is going to be taken out so not to create negative pressure in the vial. Make sure to limit the bubbles in the syringe.

- The abdomen is the preferred injection site. For alternate sites, see the diagram on the following page. Do not inject within 1 inch of the navel.

- Alternating injection sites around the abdomen should be done regularly to prevent inflammation and atrophy.

- To inject subcutaneously, pinch a layer of skin tissue outward and insert the needle all the way at a 90 degree (or 45 degree if very thin). If using a syringe, inject insulin and remove needle slowly. If using an insulin pen, inject insulin and count to 5 seconds slowly before removing the needle.

■ Proper needle disposal: Place the needle or entire syringe in a sharps container. These containers can be brought to any proper disposal site (e.g., public health clinic or local needle exchange). Ask the local health department for guidelines or check out the website www.safeneedledisposal.org.

Insulin Injection Sites

Absorption is fastest and most predictable form the abdomen followed by the posterior upper arm, the superior buttocks area, and the lateral thigh area. (The absorption of long-acting insulin is not affected by the site of injection.) Because of these variations, the injections should be rotated within a specific region to limit fluctuations in blood glucose.

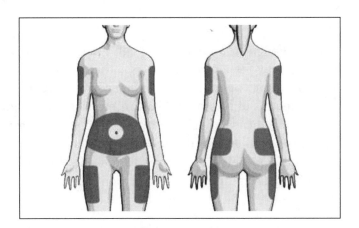

Hypoglycemia

Normal fasting blood glucose (in a person without diabetes) is 70-99 mg/dL. Hypoglycemia occurs when blood glucose falls below this level, or < 70 mg/dL. The lower the level, the more symptomatic the patient. At a blood glucose < 20 mg/dL, seizures, coma and death can occur.

Diabetes Drugs That Cause Hypoglycemia

Insulin is the #1 drug that can cause hypoglycemia; it is used, after all, to lower BG, and is potent. The drugs that make the body secrete more insulin are also high-risk because the patient will have more insulin; these are the sulfonylureas and the meglitinides.

The GLP-1 agonists, the DPP-4 inhibitors, the thiazolidinediones (such as pioglitazone) and the new agent canagliflozin (Invokana) can increase the risk of hypoglycemia, primarily in patients using a hypoglycemic agent (that is, insulin or an insulin secretagogue), which may necessitate a dose reduction due to hypoglycemic risk. Pramlintide is used with insulin, at mealtimes (injected separately); with this agent, hypoglycemia is a large risk if the mealtime insulin dose is not reduced as the patient's insulin requirements will be lower. These drugs reduce the requirement for insulin; if the insulin dose is not well-managed there will be risk for hypoglycemia. Other drugs may list hypoglycemia as possible, but it is generally due to the medical condition rather than the agent. These are isolated cases.

Hypoglycemic Symptoms

Hypoglycemic symptoms include dizziness, headache, anxiety, shakiness, diaphoresis (sweating), excessive hunger, confusion, clumsy or jerky movements, tremors, palpitations or fast heart rate, and blurred vision.

Beta-blockers can cover up (or mask) the symptoms of shakiness, palpitations, and anxiety (but not sweating or hunger). That is why the beta-blocker propranolol is used for stage freight. This is important to know, but keep in mind that this is most notable with the non-cardioselective agents (such as carteolol, carvedilol, propranolol, others). The cardio-selective beta-blockers (atenolol, metoprolol) are used more commonly.

Hypoglycemia Treatment

Recommended treatment of hypoglycemia in a conscious individual is 15-20 g of glucose, although any form of carbohydrate that contains glucose may be used including: ½ cup (4 oz) of any juice or regular (non-diet) soda, 1 cup (8 oz) milk, 1 tablespoon of sugar or honey, 2 tablespoons of raisins, 4-5 saltine crackers, 3 or 4 glucose tabs, or 1 serving of glucose gel. The blood glucose should be retested 15 minutes after treatment to see if it has reached a safe level. If the level still shows continued hypoglycemia, the treatment should be repeated. Once the blood glucose returns to normal, the patient should eat a meal (if close to meal-time), or a reasonable snack, to prevent recurrence.

Patients often overeat when the blood glucose is low, which causes unnecessary weight gain

Glucagon should be prescribed for all patients at significant risk of severe hypoglycemia, and caregivers and family members should be instructed on its administration. Glucagon administration is not limited to health care professionals. Glucagon is only used if the patient is unconscious or not conscious enough to self-treat the hypoglycemia. Glucagon 1 mg is given by SC, IM, or IV injection, or glucose can be given intravenously (Dextrose 25%, Dextrose 50%). The patient does not need to be unconscious to receive glucose intravenously.

After treating the low blood glucose, check the BG in 15 minutes. If the BG < 70 mg/dL or if the patient is still symptomatic, repeat the treatment and check the BG again in 15 minutes. All episodes of hypoglycemia are dangerous and should be reported to the physician. Hypoglycemia unawareness or one or more episodes of severe hypoglycemia should trigger re-evaluation of the treatment regimen.

Self-Monitoring Blood Glucose (SMBG)

This is important to prevent hypo- and hyperglycemia, and complications. Patients on multiple-dose insulin (MDI) or insulin pump therapy should do SMBG at least prior to meals and snacks, occasionally post-prandial, at bedtime, prior to exercise, when they suspect low blood sugar, after treating low blood sugar until they are normoglycemic, and prior to critical tasks such as driving. For patients using less frequent insulin injections, non-insulin therapies or medical nutrition therapy, SMBG may be useful as a guide to the success of therapy.

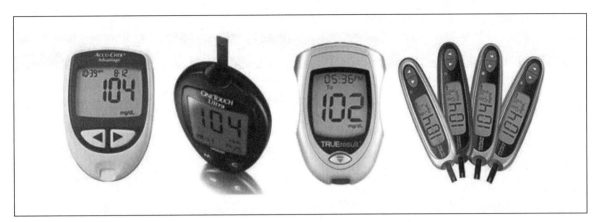

Various Glucometers

Glucometers

- Some machines require calibration before the 1st use, if a new package of strips is opened, machine is left in extreme conditions, machine is dropped, or if the level does not match how the patient is feeling.

- Check the expiration date on the strips container.

- Close the lid of the strips container after every use, as air and moisture can destroy the strips and affect results.

- Thoroughly wash hands vigorously with warm water and mild soap to cleanse the site and increase circulation at the fingertip. Try to warm the hand to get an adequate sample of blood.

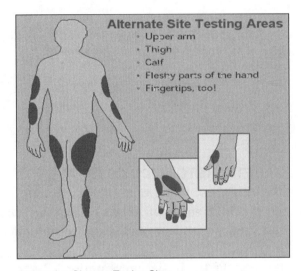

Alternative Glucose Testing Sites

- Dry hands thoroughly since water can affect the blood sample and create an error/false reading.

- Let arm hand down at the side of the body for 30 seconds to allow blood to pool in the fingertips.

- In order to minimize pain, lance the finger on the side where there are fewer nerves, instead of on the finger pads. Keep hand below the level of the heart.

- Make sure you have a large enough drop of blood as directed by the meter.

- Clean meter regularly.

- Some meters are approved for testing on other areas, such as the forearm.

- With regards to testing from alternate areas, measurements may be different, such as after meals when BG levels are changing rapidly. A finger may have faster blood flow than other areas. Therefore, alternate testing is best used for fasting BG values.

Errors That Can Occur with Glucometers

PROBLEM	RESULTS	RECOMMENDATION
Test strip not fully inserted into meter	false low	always be sure test strip is fully inserted in meter
Patient sample site (for example, the fingertip) is contaminated with sugar	false high	always clean and dry test site before sampling
Not enough blood applied to strip	false low	repeat test with a new sample
Batteries low on power	error codes	change batteries and repeat sample collection
Test strips/Control solutions stored at temperature extremes	false high/low	store kit and components according to directions
Patient is dehydrated	false high	stat venous sample on main lab analyzer
Patient in shock	false low	stat venous sample on main lab analyzer
Squeezing fingertip too hard because blood is not flowing	false low	repeat test with a new sample from a new stick
Sites other than fingertips	high/low	results from alternative sites may not match finger stick results
Test strip/Control solution vial cracked	false high/low	always inspect package for cracks, leaks, etc.
Anemia/decrease hematocrit	false high	venous sample on main lab analyzer
Polycythemia/increased hematocrit	false low	venous sample on main lab analyzer

DIABETIC KETOACIDOSIS (DKA)

DKA can occur when there is not enough insulin and the body breaks down fat to make energy. The breakdown of fats causes the concentration of ketones in the blood to increase. DKA can lead to coma, and if not treated quickly, can result in death.

DKA may be the initial presentation of type 1 diabetes, or can be due to a person stopping insulin therapy (running out, cutting the dose due to weight gain, etc.) Acute illness such as infection, pancreatitis, myocardial infarction and stroke can precipitate DKA. Symptoms develop rapidly.

- DKA Symptoms: Hyperglycemia, polyuria, polyphagia, polydipsia, blurred vision, metabolic acidosis (fruity breath, dyspnea) and dehydration (dry mouth, excessive thirst, poor skin turgor, fatigue).

- DKA Lab Abnormalities: Glucose > 300 mg/dL, ketones present in urine and blood, pH < 7.2, bicarb < 15 mEq/L, WBC 15-40 cells/mm^3

- DKA Treatment: Treatment involves giving IV fluids and insulin → closely monitoring and replacing electrolytes. This typically involves using NS, followed by ½ NS, and correcting potassium to bring the level > 3.5 mEq/L.

  ▫ Potassium, even if high initially, should be expected to drop as insulin is administered. It may be necessary to replace potassium as the insulin drives the potassium into the cells (intracellular).

  ▫ It may be required to administer an anticoagulant to prevent DVT – the hospitalized patient should be considered at high risk for clotting.

PRACTICE CASE

Irma is a 44 y/o Hispanic female with dyslipidemia, depression, and type 2 diabetes. Her father is on dialysis, due to uncontrolled hypertension and diabetes. Her mother and brother have diabetes. Irma is concerned about her family history and wants to "control my sugars better." She has been to a diabetes education class and received instruction in healthy eating and exercise. She has just joined a local exercise club and plans to start soon; until now, she has not had any type of regular physical activity. She has been to the podiatrist and had her feet checked. She has lost some sensation in both feet, but does not have any open cracks or wounds. Her annual vision exam with the ophthalmologist was normal. Her only surgical procedures involved a caesarean section, with sterilization procedure, after the birth of her third child. She does not smoke or drink.

CATEGORY	
Vitals	Blood pressure last visit (1 month ago): 134/74 mmHg, today 136/78 mmHg
	Height 5 feet, 3 inches, weight 172 pounds, BMI 30
Current medications	Metformin extended-release 1,000 mg x 2, with dinner
	Simvastatin 20 mg QHS
	Niacin extended-release 1,000 mg x 2 QHS
	Duloxetine 30 mg BID, for nerve pain in feet
	Sertraline 100 mg once daily
	Multivitamin daily
Labs	Lipid panel: CH 150, HDL 55, LDL 68, TG 131
	AST 22, ALT 16, BUN/SCr 12/0.8
	A1C 8.2%
	Urine test for albumin negative

Questions

1. Based on the patient's current A1C, choose the correct statement:

   a. The A1C is elevated; it should be less than 7%, according to the ADA guidelines.

   b. The A1C is elevated; it should be less than 5%, according to the ADA guidelines.

   c. The A1C is well-controlled.

   d. The A1C is a little high, but is acceptable due to her age.

   e. None of the above.

2. Which of the following risk factors for diabetes are present in this patient? (Select **ALL** That Apply.)

   a. Ethnicity

   b. Obese

   c. Family history

   d. Low physical activity

   e. Number of births

3. Which lifestyle modification still needs to be discussed with Irma?

   a. Exercise

   b. Weight loss

   c. Smoking cessation

   d. A and C

   e. None of the above

4. Which microvascular complication of diabetes is present in this patient?

   a. Retinopathy

   b. Nephropathy

   c. Peripheral neuropathy

   d. A and B only

   e. All of the above

5. Irma has brought her fasting blood glucose recordings into the clinic. In the morning before breakfast, she has recorded a range of 135-143 mg/dL. Her postprandial blood glucose (after lunch) recordings have a range of 190-236 mg/dL. Using the American Diabetes Association (ADA) recommendations for blood glucose control, choose the correct statement:

   a. Her morning fasting blood glucose levels are controlled.
   b. Her morning fasting blood glucose levels are not controlled.
   c. Her lunch time postprandial blood glucose levels are not controlled.
   d. A and C
   e. B and C

6. According to the ADA guidelines, which of the following medications should be started for the patient's blood pressure?

   a. Enalapril
   b. Furosemide
   c. Losartan
   d. A or C
   e. No medication is necessary

7. What immunizations should Irma receive?

   a. Influenza
   b. Hepatitis A
   c. Pneumococcal
   d. A and C
   e. A, B and C

8. Per the ADA guidelines, which therapy should be added to treat Irma's diabetes?

   a. Bromocriptine
   b. Pramlintide
   c. Glimepiride
   d. Acarbose
   e. Cholestyramine

9. Which mechanism of action describes Irma's current diabetes therapy?

   a. Increases pancreatic insulin secretion
   b. Decreases hepatic glucose output
   c. Replaces endogenous insulin
   d. Enhances the action of incretins
   e. Alpha glucosidase inhibitor

Questions 10-13 do not apply to the case.

10. A patient currently uses 30 units of *Lantus* daily and 10 units of *Humalog* with breakfast, lunch, and dinner. She is going to be started on pramlinitide and needs to be counseled on how to adjust her dose of insulin. Select the correct adjustments.

    a. Reduce *Lantus* to 15 units and *Humalog* to 5 units with meals
    b. Reduce *Lantus* to 10 units and *Humalog* to 5 units with meals
    c. Reduce *Lantus* to 15 units and keep *Humalog* at 10 units with meals
    d. Do not adjust *Lantus* and reduce *Humalog* to 5 units with meals
    e. Do not adjust *Lantus* or *Humalog*

11. A patient is taking *Humalog* 70/30, 10 units twice a day. How many units of insulin lispro does the patient inject in the morning?

    a. 20 units
    b. 10 units
    c. 7 units
    d. 6 units
    e. 3 units

12. Which of the following insulins has the shortest duration?

    a. Glulisine
    b. Detemir
    c. Regular
    d. Glargine
    e. NPH

13. A patient is prescribed *Glucovance*. What are the individual components?

    a. Metformin/glyburide
    b. Metformin/pioglitazone
    c. Metformin/sitagliptin
    d. Metformin/repaglinide
    e. Metformin/glipizide

Answers

1-a, 2-a,b,c,d, 3-b, 4-c, 5-e, 6-e, 7-d, 8-c, 9-b, 10-d, 11-e, 12-a, 13-a.

AUTOIMMUNE CONDITIONS:
RA, SLE, MS, CELIAC DISEASE
& SJÖGREN'S SYNDROME

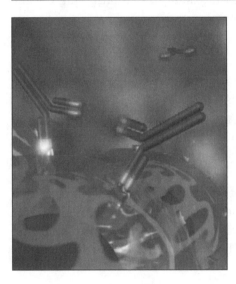

BACKGROUND

Autoimmune diseases are illnesses that occur when the body's tissues are attacked by the person's own immune system. The immune system is a complex organization of cells and antibodies designed to "seek and destroy" invaders of the body, particularly infections.

Rheumatoid arthritis (RA), systemic lupus erythematosus (SLE), multiple sclerosis (MS), celiac disease and Sjögren's syndrome are discussed in this chapter. Other autoimmune diseases include type 1 diabetes (discussed in the Diabetes chapter), Hashimoto's thyroiditis and Graves disease (discussed in the Thyroid chapter) and a few others.

Vaccination in Autoimmune Disease

Patients can be immune (or immuno-) compromised due to any one of the following:

- Disease states which destroy key components of the immune response (primarily, HIV patients with a CD4 T lymphocyte count < 200 cells/microliter);

- Steroids (oral or injectable only) taken 14 days or longer at a dose of either 2 mg/kg/day or 20 mg prednisone, or prednisone-equivalent dose;

- Oncology treatment that destroys white blood cells;

- Transplant drugs that depress the immune system;

- Asplenia (lack of a functioning spleen) increases the risk for certain types of infections;

- And, the use of the strong immune suppressants described in this chapter.

LABS THAT MAY BE ASSOCIATED WITH AUTOIMMUNE DISEASE

C-reactive protein (CRP)

Erythrocyte sedimentation rate (ESR)

Rheumatoid factor (RF)

Anti-nuclear antibodies (ANA)

These labs can be elevated by a number of diseases, both autoimmune and not; therefore, the presence or absence of one or more of these is not enough to make the diagnosis of a specific autoimmune disease; each requires a certain number of criteria.

The drugs described here are used to dampen the immune response; this is necessary with autoimmune disease, but the use of strong immune-suppressants (primarily, the biologics – these are the stronger agents and are used when others are not sufficient) will increase the risk of conditions <u>due to</u> the strong depression of the immune system. These include:

- Tuberculosis and hepatitis B (if present) re-activation; testing (and treatment if needed) must be done prior to the start of the immune-suppressing agent.

- Viruses; if the virus can be prevented by a live vaccine, the vaccine must be given prior to the start of treatment.

- Lymphomas and certain skin cancers: these cancer types are normally suppressed by the immune system.

- Infections of various types; this requires CBC monitoring, symptom monitoring (by the patient) and may require infection control mechanisms.

Vaccines for Immune-Compromised Patients

<u>Live vaccines</u>: If needed these must be given <u>prior</u> to the start of immunosuppressive drugs. Live vaccines include measles, rubella, varicella and zoster. Zoster should be given at age 60 and older prior to the start of strong immunosuppressive drugs. Yellow fever vaccine is live, and may be requested for travel, but cannot be given to anyone with severe immune suppression; advise these patients to avoid travel to endemic regions.

<u>Inactivated vaccines</u>: Annually, each patient should get an influenza vaccine (inactivated shot). Tdap is given if needed, pneumococcal (both types, see Immunizations chapter for schedule), and the HPV vaccine for men and women up to the age of 26 years. Patients with asplenia, a damaged spleen or terminal complement deficiency require the meningococcal vaccine (either MPSV4 or MC4).

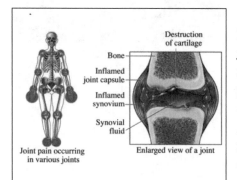

Joint pain occurring in various joints

Enlarged view of a joint

RHEUMATOID ARTHRITIS

Rheumatoid arthritis (RA) causes inflammation of the joints and other organs in the body, including the kidneys, eyes, heart and lungs. This is a <u>chronic, symmetrical, systemic</u> and <u>progressive</u> disease – although the disease course is variable and some have much more aggressive disease than others. RA typically presents first in the hands and feet. Macrophages, cytotoxins, and free oxygen radicals promote cellular damage and inflammation. The inflammation leads to cartilage and bone destruction, resulting in the <u>classic symptoms of RA: joint swelling, stiffness, pain and eventually, bone deformity</u>.

2012 Update of the 2008 American College of Rheumatology Recommendations for the Use of Disease-Modifying Antirheumatic Drugs and Biologic Agents in the Treatment of Rheumatoid Arthritis. Arthritis Care and Research, 2012;64(5):625-639.

American College of Rheumatology 2008 Recommendations for the Use of Nonbiologic and Biologic Disease-Modifying Antirheumatic Drugs in Rheumatoid Arthritis. Arthritis and Rheumatism, 2008;59(6):762-784.

DIAGNOSIS

Criteria 1-4 must be present for ≥ 6 weeks and 4 or more criteria must be present.

Diagnostic Criteria

1. Morning stiffness around joints lasting > 1 hour

2. Soft tissue swelling (arthritis) in 3 or more joints

3. Swelling (arthritis) of hand, foot, or wrist joints

4. Symmetric involvement

5. Rheumatoid nodules

6. Positive serum rheumatoid factor (about 70% of patients)

7. Radiographic erosions or periarticular osteopenia in hand or wrist joints

Clinical Presentation

The disease process is highly variable, progressing rapidly in some and slow in others. Many symptoms are constitutional, such as morning fatigue, fever, weakness, loss of appetite, and joint and muscle pain. Patients experience articular manifestations (affecting the joints) that are almost always <u>polyarticular</u> and <u>symmetrical</u>. Any synovial joint can be involved, but the finger joints of the hand are most often affected. The wrists, knees and toe joints are also frequently involved. Morning stiffness, swelling, redness, edema, pain, decreased range of motion, muscle atrophy, weakness, and deformity are typical articular symptoms of RA. Morning stiffness is a clue for RA and may last for up to 2 hours. <u>Osteoarthritis (OA) does not cause prolonged stiffness.</u>

Patients may also experience extra-articular manifestations, including firm lumps, called rheumatoid nodules, which are subcutaneous nodules in places such as the elbow or hands. Other extra-articular symptoms may include vasculitis, pulmonary complications (fibrosis, effusions, nodules), lymphadenopathy, splenomegaly, eye inflammation, dry eyes and/or mouth from a related condition (Sjögren's syndrome), pericarditis/myocarditis, and atherosclerosis.

Non-Pharmacologic Treatment

Non-Pharmacologic treatments include rest, physical therapy, occupational therapy, exercise, diet and weight control, and surgical intervention (e.g., a joint replacement).

Pharmacologic Treatment

The goal is to have the patient on a Disease-Modifying Antirheumatic Drug (DMARD) <u>within 3 months of diagnosis</u>. DMARDs work via various mechanisms to slow down the disease and help prevent further joint damage. In addition, patients may require <u>bridging therapy</u> (short-term) or, in some cases, long-term use of anti-inflammatory medications such as <u>NSAIDs</u> or <u>steroids</u>. NSAIDs and steroids have significant health risks when used long-term. NSAIDs are further discussed in the Pain chapter; steroids are further discussed in the Asthma chapter.

Patients with milder symptoms may be able to live acceptably on non-biologic DMARDs (including methotrexate, hydroxychloroquine, leflunomide, sulfasalazine, and minocy-

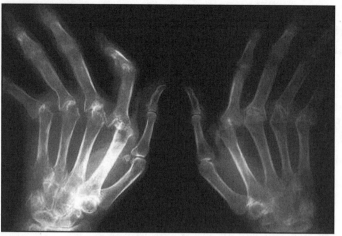

Degenerative joint damage with nodules

cline). These DMARDs can be used as monotherapy or as combination therapy consisting of 2 or 3 drugs.

For patients with more severe disease, treatment can include newer biologic agents that antagonize tumor necrosis factor (TNF) or work via other mechanisms. Anti-TNF agents include adalimumab, certolizumab pegol, etanercept, golimumab, and infliximab. Non-TNF agents include abatacept, rituximab and tocilizumab. Certain biologic agents are given with methotrexate. Biologic agents have adverse effects, require special monitoring, are costly and do not work well for everyone. However, for many patients they significantly reduce symptoms associated with RA, increase mobility and improve quality of life.

Agents Used for Pain and Inflammation

DRUG	DOSING

Non-Selective NSAIDs – for more complete information, see Pain chapter

Ibuprofen *(Motrin, Advil* and others)	Rx 800 mg Q6-8H; max 3,200 mg/day Moderate pain or inflammation, such as with RA.

COX-2 Selective Inhibitor – for more complete information, see Pain chapter

Celecoxib *(Celebrex)*	100-200 mg BID

Steroids, using prednisone as an example–for more complete information, see Asthma chapter

Prednisone *[Prednisone Intensol* (solution), *Rayos* (delayed release tablet), generics-oral]	Initial dose 5-60 mg daily, some use Alternate Day Therapy (ADT) dosing regimen in which twice the usual daily dose is given every other day to ↓ adrenal suppression. Indicated for acute inflammation/pain and as bridge therapy while waiting for DMARDs to take effect. Steroids are not supposed to be used long-term. However, some patients may use chronically (≤ 10 mg daily) due to severe disease.

Disease-Modifying Anti-Rheumatic Drugs (DMARDs)

DRUG	DOSING	SAFETY/SIDE EFFECTS/MONITORING
Methotrexate *(Rheumatrex, Trexall, Otrexup)*	7.5-25 mg/week Low weekly doses are used for RA (the weekly dose can be split into smaller doses taken over 12-36 hours); never dose daily for RA If patient is not using the *Rheumatrex* dose-pack, be sure to counsel the patient to take weekly. Numerous incidences of hepatotoxicity have occurred due to patients receiving a 90-day supply and taking daily	**BLACK BOX WARNINGS** Hepatitis, renal, pneumonitis, bone marrow suppression, mucositis/stomatitis, dermatologic reactions, others – renal and lung toxicity more likely when using oncology doses. **CONTRAINDICATIONS** Pregnancy and breastfeeding, alcoholism, chronic liver disease, blood dyscrasias, immunodeficiency syndrome **SIDE EFFECTS** Nausea, vomiting, ↑ LFTs, stomatitis, alopecia, photosensitivity **MONITORING** LFTs, and SCr (baseline and every 2-4 weeks for first 3 months, then less frequently). Also: chest X-ray, hepatitis B and C at baseline. Pulmonary function tests if lung-related symptoms. **NOTES** Pregnancy Category X Folic acid can be given to decrease the side effects associated with methotrexate—commonly given 5 mg PO weekly on the day following methotrexate administration. May take up to 12 weeks to see full benefit *Otrexup* was approved for RA by the FDA in 2013 – it allows patients to self-administer methotrexate SC once weekly using an auto-injector.
Hydroxychloroquine *(Plaquenil)*	400-600 mg/day initially, then 200-400 mg/day for maintenance dose Take with food or milk	**SIDE EFFECTS** Nausea, diarrhea, rashes, pigmentation of skin and hair, weakness, vision changes (rare) **MONITORING** CBC at baseline and periodically, LFTs. Eye exam at baseline and every 3 months during prolonged therapy. **NOTES** Pregnancy Category C May take 4-6 weeks to respond Used in mild RA
SulfaSALAzine *(Azulfidine, Azulfidine EN-tabs, Sulfazine, Sulfazine EC)*	500 – 1,000 mg BID (max 3 grams/day)	**CONTRAINDICATIONS** Patients with a sulfa or salicylate allergy, GI or GU obstruction, porphyria **SIDE EFFECTS** Headache, anorexia, dyspepsia, GI upset (N/V/D), oligospermia (reversible), rash (all > 10%), folate deficiency, arthalgias, crystalluria **MONITORING** CBC, LFTs **NOTES** Can cause yellow-orange coloration of skin/urine Impairs folate absorption, may give 1 mg/day folate supplement Take with food and 8 oz of water to prevent crystalluria

Disease-Modifying Anti-Rheumatic Drugs (DMARDs) Continued

DRUG	DOSING	SAFETY/SIDE EFFECTS/MONITORING
Minocycline *(Minocin, Dynacin, Solodyn)*	50-100 mg Q12-Q24H	**WARNINGS** Children ≤ 8 years of age, pregnancy (Preg Category D – suppresses bone growth and skeletal development, permanently discolors teeth) **SIDE EFFECTS** GI upset (nausea/vomiting/diarrhea), photosensitivity, rash; exfoliative dermatitis, Drug Rash with Eosinophilia and Systemic Symptoms syndrome (DRESS), nephrotoxicity (Fanconi's syndrome), lupus-like syndrome, bone marrow suppression, hemolytic anemia (rare) **NOTES** Pregnancy Category D Take with 8 oz water to minimize GI irritation Do not dose adjust in renal impairment
Leflunomide *(Arava)*	100 mg x 3 days, then 20 mg daily (may omit loading dose if at higher risk of liver or hematologic toxicity)	**BLACK BOX WARNINGS (2)** Women of childbearing potential should not receive leflunomide until pregnancy has been excluded. Hepatotoxicity **CONTRAINDICATION** Pregnancy **SIDE EFFECTS** Hepatotoxicity, diarrhea, upper respiratory tract infections (URTIs), alopecia, rash, hypertension, blood dyscrasias **MONITORING** LFTs and CBC at baseline and monthly for first 6 months, BP at baseline and regularly. Screen for TB and pregnancy prior to starting therapy. **NOTES** Pregnancy Category X Must have negative pregnancy test before starting this medication and use 2 forms of birth control. If pregnancy is desired, must wait 2 years after discontinuation or give cholestyramine to eliminate drug. Can use +/- methotrexate

Disease-Modifying Anti-Rheumatic Drugs (DMARDs) Continued

DRUG	DOSING	SAFETY/SIDE EFFECTS/MONITORING
Tofacitinib *(Xeljanz)*	5 mg PO BID Do not use with strong CYP 450 inducers; reduce dose to 5 mg daily with strong 3A4 and 2C19 inhibitors	**BLACK BOX WARNINGS (3)** Increased risk for serious infections (interrupt therapy if serious infection develops). Risk for developing active tuberculosis. Screen for latent TB and treat prior to using tofacitinib. Increased risk for lymphomas and other malignancies, invasive fungal, viral, bacterial or opportunistic infections. **WARNINGS** GI perforation, not recommended in severe hepatic impairment, and should not be given concurrently with live vaccines. **SIDE EFFECTS** Bone marrow suppression, infections (URTIs), diarrhea, headache, increased lipids **MONITORING** CBC, signs of infection, LFTs, lipids, Hgb **NOTES** Pregnancy Category C Can be used as monotherapy or with non-biologic DMARDs Do not use with biologic DMARDs or potent immunosuppressants REMS drug – must dispense MedGuide

Methotrexate Drug Interactions

- Methotrexate should not be taken with alcohol; this combination increases the risk of liver toxicity.

- Active transport renal elimination is decreased by aspirin, beta lactams, probenecid and NSAIDs, resulting in toxicity. Avoid concurrent use.

- Sulfonamides and topical tacrolimus increase the adverse effects of methotrexate. Avoid concurrent use.

- Methotrexate may reduce the effectiveness of loop diuretics; loop diuretics may increase the methotrexate concentration. Use caution if using these agents concomitantly.

- Methotrexate and cyclosporine concentrations will both increase when used concomitantly, leading to toxicity; avoid this combination.

Methotrexate Counseling

- Patients should be encouraged to read the patient instruction sheet within the dose pack. Prescriptions should not be written or refilled on a PRN basis.

- If you are receiving this medicine for rheumatoid arthritis or psoriasis, the dosage is usually given <u>once weekly</u>. Some patients are told to divide the once weekly dose in half and take it over two days per week. <u>Do not use this medicine daily</u> or double-up on doses. Serious side effects could occur if it is used more frequently than directed. Choose a day of the week to take your medicine that you can remember.

- Methotrexate has caused birth defects and death in unborn babies (Pregnancy Category X). <u>If you are pregnant or have a chance of becoming pregnant, you should not use this medicine.</u> Use an effective form of birth control, whether you are a man or a woman. Tell your healthcare provider if you or your sexual partner become pregnant during treatment.

- Do not use methotrexate if you are breast-feeding.

- If you have kidney problems or excess body water (ascites, pleural effusion), you must be closely monitored and your dose may be adjusted or stopped by your healthcare provider.

- Your healthcare provider will perform periodic blood tests to measure your liver function to ensure it stays healthy.

- Methotrexate (usually at high dosages) has rarely caused severe (sometimes fatal) bone marrow suppression (decreasing your body's ability to fight infections) and stomach/intestinal disease (e.g., bleeding) when used at the same time as non-steroidal anti-inflammatory drugs (NSAIDs). Therefore, NSAIDs should not be used with high-dose methotrexate. Caution is advised if you also take aspirin. NSAIDs/aspirin may be used with low-dose methotrexate such as for the treatment of rheumatoid arthritis if directed by your healthcare provider. If you are using low-dose aspirin (81-325 milligrams per day) for heart attack or stroke prevention, continue to take it unless directed otherwise. Consult your healthcare provider regarding safe use of these drugs (e.g., close monitoring by your healthcare provider, maintaining stable doses of NSAIDs). Do not use additional OTC NSAIDs (such as ibuprofen or naproxen).

- In rare instances, this drug may cause liver problems when it is used for long periods of time. If you are using methotrexate long-term, a liver biopsy may be recommended.

- Do not drink alcohol when using this medicine; alcohol can also damage the liver.

- Methotrexate use has rarely resulted in serious (sometimes fatal) side effects, such as lung problems, lung infections (*Pneumocystis* pneumonia), skin reactions, diarrhea, and mouth sores (ulcerative stomatitis).

- Tell your healthcare provider right away if you develop any new or worsening symptoms, including black, tarry stools; dry, nonproductive cough; mouth sores; red, swollen, or blistered skin; severe or persistent diarrhea or vomiting; shortness of breath or trouble breathing; signs of infection (e.g., fever, chills, cough, change in sputum, pain, sore throat); stomach pain; unusual bruising or bleeding; unusual tiredness or weakness; or yellowing of the skin or eyes.

Biologic Agents

Tumor Necrosis Factor (TNFα) Inhibitors (Anti-TNF biologics)

DRUG	DOSING	SAFETY/SIDE EFFECTS/MONITORING
Etanercept **(Enbrel, Enbrel SureClick)**	50 mg SC weekly, or 25 mg SC twice/week (separated by 72-96 hours)	**BLACK BOX WARNINGS (3)** Serious infections (some fatal) – discontinue treatment if patient develops a severe infection; lymphomas and other malignancies; Reactivation of latent TB or new infections; perform test for latent TB prior to starting therapy **CONTRAINDICATIONS** Active systemic infection, dose > 5 mg/kg in mod-severe heart failure (infliximab)
Adalimumab **(Humira, Humira Pen)**	40 mg SC every other week (if not taking methotrexate, can ↑ dose to 40 mg SC weekly)	**WARNINGS** TNF inhibitors can cause demyelinating disease, hepatitis B reactivation, heart failure, hepatotoxicity, lupus-like syndrome, and severe infections. They should not be used with other TNF inhibitors or immunosuppressive biologics, or live vaccines. **SIDE EFFECTS** Infections and injection site reactions (redness, rash, swelling, itching, or bruising), positive anti-nuclear antibodies, headache, nausea
Infliximab **(Remicade)** – given only in combination with methotrexate in RA	3 mg/kg IV at weeks 0, 2, and 6, and then every 8 weeks (can ↑ dose to 10 mg/kg based on need but ↑ infection risk) Infusion reactions: hypotension, fever, chills, pruritus (may benefit w/pre-treatment w/acetaminophen, antihistamine, steroids) Delayed hypersensitivity reaction 3-10 days after administration (fever, rash, myalgia, HA, sore throat)	**MONITORING** TB test (prior to administration and annually), signs and symptoms of infection, CBC, LFTs, HBV (prior to initiation), HF, malignancies **NOTES** Do not shake. Requires refrigeration (biologics will denature if hot). Etanercept may be stored at room temperature for a maximum of 14 days. Do not freeze. Allow to reach room temperature before injecting (15-30 min).
Certolizumab pegol (*Cimzia*, *Cimzia* Prefilled)	400 mg SC at weeks 0, 2, and 4. Then, 400 mg every 4 weeks (or 200 mg every other week)	Usually, methotrexate is used 1st-line and these agents are add-on therapy. However, if the initial presentation is severe, these can be started as initial therapy. Do not use more than one biologic concurrently. Do not use live vaccines if using these drugs. Antibody induction can occur and will ↓ usefulness of drug Use with caution in patients with existing heart failure. **Dispense MedGuide** All TNF inhibitors carry a black box warning for risk of serious infections, including tuberculosis, and invasive fungal and other opportunistic infections. All patients should be evaluated for TB before starting these drugs. Patients with latent TB should start prophylactic treatment. Retest TB annually.
Golimumab **(Simponi, Simponi Aria)** – given only in combination with methotrexate in RA	50 mg SC monthly *(Simponi)* 2 mg/kg IV at weeks 0, 2, and 4. Then, 2 mg/kg IV every 8 weeks *(Simponi Aria)*	It is recommended that RA patients receive pneumococcal, influenza shot, hepatitis B, HPV (if applicable), and herpes zoster (shingles) prior to starting DMARDs. Do not give herpes zoster (or any live vaccine) to patients already receiving biologic agents.

Other Biologics (Also known as Non-TNF Biologics)

Rituximab

Depletes CD20 B cells. B cells are believed to have a role in RA development and progression.

DRUG	DOSING	SAFETY/SIDE EFFECTS/MONITORING
RiTUXimab *(Rituxan)* – given with methotrexate in RA	1 gram IV on day 1 and 15 in combination with methotrexate for 2 doses. Can repeat treatment if needed. Need to pre-medicate with a steroid Start infusion at 50 mg/hr; can ↑ to 400 mg/hr if no reaction	**BLACK BOX WARNINGS (4)** Severe and fatal infusion-related reactions, usually with the first infusion Progressive multifocal leukoencephalopathy (PML) due to JC virus infection Tumor lysis syndrome leading to acute renal failure and dialysis may occur following the first dose (when used to treat NHL) Severe and fatal mucocutaneous reaction (e.g., SJS, TEN) can occur **WARNINGS** Can cause serious infections, discontinue if serious infection develops. Screen for latent TB prior to initiating therapy. Do not give with other biologics or live vaccines. **SIDE EFFECTS** Fever, chills, headache, pain, rash, pruritus, angioedema, abdominal pain, bone marrow suppression, infusion-related reactions **MONITORING** Cardiac monitoring during and after infusion, vital signs, infusion reactions, CBC, CD20+ cells, renal function

Anakinra

IL-1 receptor antagonist. IL-1 mediates immunologic reactions in RA (degrades cartilage, increases bone resorption).

DRUG	DOSING	SAFETY/SIDE EFFECTS/MONITORING
Anakinra *(Kineret)*	100 mg SC daily	**WARNINGS** Can cause serious infections, discontinue if serious infection develops. Screen for latent TB prior to initiating therapy. Do not give with other biologics or live vaccines. **SIDE EFFECTS** Headache, injection site reactions, infections, bone marrow suppression **MONITORING** CBC, SCr, signs of infection

Abatacept

Selective T cell costimulator; inhibits T cell activation by binding to CD80 and CD86 on cells that present these antigens (activated cells are detected in the synovium of RA joints).

DRUG	DOSING	SAFETY/SIDE EFFECTS/MONITORING
Abatacept *(Orencia)*	500 mg – 1,000 mg IV based on body wt; given IV over 30 min. Give at 0, 2, and 4 weeks, then every 4 weeks thereafter or can give the first infusion dose, followed by 125 mg SC within 24 hours, then 125 mg SC weekly	**WARNINGS** Increased risk for serious infections, discontinue if serious infection develops. <u>Screen for latent TB</u> prior to initiating therapy. Do not give with other biologics or live vaccines. **SIDE EFFECTS** Headache, injection site reactions, infections **MONITORING** Signs of infection, CBC **NOTES** Caution in those with COPD– may worsen symptoms

Tocilizumab

IL-6 receptor antagonist. IL-6 mediates immunologic reactions in RA.

DRUG	DOSING	SAFETY/SIDE EFFECTS/MONITORING
Tocilizumab *(Actemra)*	4 mg/kg IV every 4 weeks given over 60 min (may ↑ to 8 mg/kg based on clinical response). Max 800 mg	**BLACK BOX WARNING** Risk of serious infections; <u>screen for latent TB</u> prior to initiating therapy **WARNINGS** Increased risk for serious infections, discontinue if serious infection develops. GI perforation, do not give with other biologics or live vaccines. Do not give if ALT or AST is > 1.5 times ULN. **SIDE EFFECTS** ↑ LFTs, infections, bone marrow suppression, GI perforation, ↑ LDL **MONITORING** CBC and LFTs (every 4-8 weeks), LDL, signs of infection, lipids

Pointers for All Immune Modulators

If hypersensitivity to a drug develops, further use is contraindicated (this is true for other drugs as well but these drugs cause more hypersensitivity). Consider varicella vaccination prior to the start of treatment. The patients should monitor for infections and for liver damage (see the counseling section). If you dispense a self-injectable, counseling must include how to store the medication, reconstitute (if a powder), and where to inject (<u>these medications should be injected into the upper middle thigh or abdomen</u>). All above SC biologics are to be <u>kept refrigerated</u> (except etanercept, which may be stored at room temperature for up to 14 days) and the patient should <u>wait until the drug is at room temperature before injecting</u> (cold injections are painful). Tell patients not to use external heat sources for warming the product; holding the medication or slowly rolling it in the hand is acceptable (except for golimumab, which should simply be left sitting at room temperature). Do not shake.

Patient Counseling

Biologic Agents

■ Read the medication guide that comes with this medicine. You will be given a medication guide the first time you get the medicine, and with each refill.

■ This medication is used alone or in combination with an immunosuppressant (such as methotrexate) to treat certain types of arthritis (e.g., rheumatoid, psoriatic, and ankylosing spondylitis), as well as a skin condition called psoriasis. These conditions are caused by an overactive immune system (autoimmune disease).

■ People taking this medicine should not get live vaccines. Make sure your vaccines are up-to-date before taking this medicine. You can continue to take the annual influenza shot (but not the nasal mist vaccine, since this is a live vaccine).

■ Because this medicine works by blocking the immune system, it may lower your ability to fight infections. This may make you more likely to get a serious (rarely fatal) infection or can make any infection you have worse. You should be tested for tuberculosis (TB skin test or chest X-ray) before and during treatment with this medicine. If you have been exposed to TB (but do not have active disease) you will need to start taking a daily TB medicine to prevent TB before starting therapy. Tell your healthcare provider immediately if you have any signs of infection such as a fever of 100.5°F (38°C) or higher, chills, very bad sore throat, ear or sinus pain, a cough or more sputum or a change in the color of sputum.

■ This medicine has a possibility of causing liver damage. Call your healthcare provider right away if you have any of these symptoms: feel very tired, skin or eyes look yellow, poor appetite or vomiting, pain on the right side of your stomach (abdomen).

■ This medicine may worsen congestive heart failure (CHF). Notify your healthcare provider if you experience sudden weight gain or shortness of breath.

■ Common side effects include injection site reactions such as redness, swelling, itching, or pain. These symptoms usually go away within 3 to 5 days. If you have pain, redness or swelling around the injection site that doesn't go away or gets worse, call your healthcare provider.

■ Other side effects can include upper respiratory infections (sinus infections), headache, dizziness or coughing.

■ This medicine is injected subcutaneously (SC) under the skin of the thigh, abdomen, or upper arm, exactly as prescribed by your healthcare provider (once weekly for etanercept, every 2 weeks for adalimumab, every 4 weeks for certolizumab, monthly for golimumab).

■ Store the medication (single-use syringes or multiple-use vials) in the refrigerator (etanercept may be stored at room temperature for a maximum of 14 days). Allow the medicine to warm to room temperature before injecting (takes 15-30 minutes). Do not shake the medicine. Before using, check for particles or discoloration. If either is present, do not use the medicine.

- Before injecting each dose, clean the injection site with rubbing alcohol. It is important to change the location of the injection site each time you use this drug to prevent problems under the skin. New injections should be given at least 1 inch (2.5 centimeters) from the last injection site. Do not inject into areas of the skin that are sore, bruised, red, or hard.

- For adalimumab *(Humira)*: Inject into abdomen, thigh, or upper arm. A loud click is heard when the plum-colored activator button is pressed. Continue to hold injector against the skin until the yellow marker fully appears in the window view and stops moving (may take 10 seconds).

- For etanercept *(Enbrel)*: Inject into abdomen, thigh, or upper arm. A loud click is heard when injection begins, continue to hold autoinjector against skin for 15 seconds. You may hear a second click as the purple button pops back up, indicating all of the medicine has been injected.

- For golimumab *(Simponi)*: Do not warm to room temperature any other way than letting the product sit at room temperature outside the carton for 30 minutes. Inject into abdomen, thigh, or upper arm. A loud click is heard when injection begins, continue to hold autoinjector against skin until second click is heard (3-15 seconds)

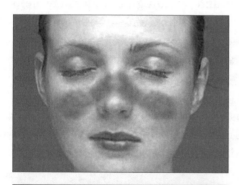

GUIDELINE

Hahn BH, McMahon MA, Wilkinson A, et al. American College of Rheumatology guidelines for screening, treatment, and management of lupus nephritis. Arth Care Res 2012;64(6):797-808.

SYSTEMIC LUPUS ERYTHEMATOSUS (SLE)

Background

Systemic lupus erythematosus (SLE), or lupus, is a multisystem autoimmune disease that affects roughly 250,000 Americans, with a female-to-male ratio of 10:1. The disease predominantly occurs in persons 15-45 years of age, and it is more common in women of African-American and Asian descent. Patients experience flare-ups to varying degrees as well as periods of disease remission. As the disease progresses, symptoms may manifest in almost every organ system, with the heart, lungs, kidneys, and brain being most affected.

The hallmark of SLE is the development of auto-antibodies by B cells to cellular components that leads to chronic inflammation and tissue damage. This abnormal auto-antibody formation can attack multiple types of cells in various organ systems, leading to a highly-variable disease process with multiple organ involvement. Many antibodies can be produced, including antinuclear antibodies and antiphospholipid antibodies. These are often present many years before the diagnosis of SLE.

Clinical Presentation

Patients with SLE can develop different combinations of symptoms and organ involvement. The most common symptoms include fatigue, fever, anorexia, weight loss, muscle aches, arthritis, rash (butterfly rash), photosensitivity, and joint pain and stiffness. Over half of the

<table>
<tr><td>

PRIMARY AGENTS ASSOCIATED WITH DRUG-INDUCED LUPUS

Drug-induced lupus has been most commonly associated with the following agents:

Procainamide

Hydralazine (alone, and in *BiDil*)

Isoniazid

Quinidine

Methyldopa

Propylthiouracil

Methimazole

Terbinafine

Anti-TNF agents

</td></tr>
</table>

people with SLE develop a characteristic red, flat facial rash over the bridge of their nose and cheeks. Because of its shape, it is frequently referred to as the SLE "butterfly rash." The rash is painless and does not itch. The facial rash, along with inflammation in other organs, can be precipitated or worsened by exposure to sunlight. Arthritis and cutaneous manifestations are most common, but renal, hematologic and neurologic manifestations contribute largely to morbidity and mortality. Lupus nephritis develops in over 50% of patients with SLE.

Treatment

Non-pharmacologic therapy consists of rest and proper exercise to manage the fatigue these patients experience. Also, smoking cessation is encouraged since tobacco smoke can be a trigger for disease. Many patients experience photosensitivity, therefore, using sunscreens and avoiding sunlight may help better manage their disease. Drug therapy for SLE consists of immunosuppressants, cytotoxic agents, and/or anti-inflammatory agents. Treatment approaches emphasize using a combination of drugs to minimize chronic exposure to corticosteroids. The goal of therapy is to suppress the immune system to avoid disease flares and keep the patient in remission.

Patients with mild disease may do well on an NSAID (dosed at anti-inflammatory doses) but use caution as these patients are more sensitive to the GI and renal side effects. Concurrent use with a PPI is generally recommended to reduce GI side effects of NSAIDs. Other agents are discussed below.

Agents Used in Lupus

DRUG	DOSING	SAFETY/SIDE EFFECTS/MONITORING
Antimalarial agents – impair complement-dependent antigen-antibody reactions		
Hydroxychloroquine	200–400 mg daily	Hydroxychloroquine is safer (preferred); takes 6 months to see maximal effect
		Effective for cutaneous symptoms and arthralgias, fatigue and fever – used for mild disease; chronic (not acute) therapy
		See more information in RA section above
Chloroquine	250–500 mg daily	

Agents Used in Lupus Continued

DRUG	DOSING	SAFETY/SIDE EFFECTS/MONITORING

Corticosteroids

DRUG	DOSING	SAFETY/SIDE EFFECTS/MONITORING
PredniSONE (or **methylprednisolone** IV if life-threatening disease)	1–2 mg/kg/day PO; then taper 500–1,000 mg/day IV for 3-6 days (acute flare)	Used acutely to control flares at higher doses; taper to lower doses for chronic, suppressive therapy More complete information can be found in the Asthma chapter.

Cytotoxic agents – used in severe disease

DRUG	DOSING	SAFETY/SIDE EFFECTS/MONITORING
Cyclophosphamide	500–1,000 mg/m² IV monthly for 6 months, then every 3 months for 2 years; or 1-3 mg/kg daily if using PO	**SIDE EFFECTS** Bone marrow suppression, infections, hemorrhagic cystitis (give mesna therapy and keep patient well hydrated), malignancy, sterility, and teratogenesis **MONITORING** CBC and urinalysis monthly **NOTES** Pregnancy Category D Can use IV or oral therapy; used for flares as induction therapy; very toxic for chronic therapy
AzaTHIOprine *(Azasan, Imuran)*	2 mg/kg PO daily	**BLACK BOX WARNINGS (2)** Chronic immunosuppression can ↑ risk of neoplasia (especially lymphomas) Hematologic toxicities (leukopenia, thrombocytopenia) and mutagenic potential **SIDE EFFECTS** GI upset (N/V), rash, ↑ LFTs, bone marrow suppression **MONITORING** LFTs, CBC, renal function **NOTES** Pregnancy Category D Patients with genetic deficiency of thiopurine methyltransferase (TPMT) will be more sensitive to myelosuppressive effects and may require a lower dose
Mycophenolate mofetil *(CellCept)*	1–3 grams PO daily, can be divided BID	**BLACK BOX WARNINGS (3)** ↑ risk of infection; ↑ development of lymphoma and skin malignancies; ↑ risk of congenital malformations and spontaneous abortions when used during pregnancy **SIDE EFFECTS** Diarrhea, GI upset, vomiting, hypo- and hypotension, edema, tachycardia, pain, hyperglycemia, hypo and hyperkalemia, hypomagnesemia, hypocalcemia, hypercholesterolemia, tremor, acne, infections **MONITORING** CBC, LFTs, SCr, signs of infection **NOTES** Pregnancy Category D; lowers efficacy of birth control pills See more information in the Transplant chapter

Agents Used In Lupus Continued

DRUG	DOSING	SAFETY/SIDE EFFECTS/MONITORING
Cyclosporine *(Neoral, Sandimmune)*	Initial: 2.5 mg/kg/day, divided twice daily Dose may be increased by 0.5-0.75 mg/kg/day after 8 and/or 12 weeks, up to a maximum of 4 mg/kg/day.	**BLACK BOX WARNINGS (7)** Renal impairment (with high doses); ↑ risk of lymphoma and other malignancies; ↑ risk of skin cancer; ↑ risk of infection, may cause hypertension; dose adjustments should only be made under the direct supervision of an experienced physician; cyclosporine (modified – Gengraf/Neoral) has ↑ bioavailability compared to cyclosporine (non-modified – Sandimmune) and cannot be used interchangeably. **CONTRAINDICATIONS** Renal dysfunction, uncontrolled hypertension, malignancies **SIDE EFFECTS** Hypertension, nephropathy, hirsutism, ↑ triglycerides, nausea, tremor **NOTES** Discontinue if no benefit is seen by 16 weeks of therapy Discontinue if persistent hypertension in a patient with no previous history of hypertension See Transplant chapter for more complete information

IgG1-lambda monoclonal antibody that prevents the survival of B lymphocytes by blocking the binding of soluble human B lymphocyte stimulator protein (BLyS) to receptors on B lymphocytes. This reduces the activity of B-cell mediated immunity and the autoimmune response.

DRUG	DOSING	SAFETY/SIDE EFFECTS/MONITORING
Belimumab *(Benlysta)*	10 mg/kg IV at 2 week intervals for the first 3 doses, then 4 week intervals thereafter, infuse over 1 hour	**SIDE EFFECTS** Higher risk of infection, depression, anaphylaxis and infusion reactions, malignancy **NOTES** Consider giving premedication for infusion reactions and hypersensitivity reactions Live vaccines should not be given 30 days prior or concurrently with therapy

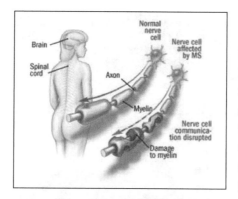

GUIDELINE

Disease Modifying Therapies in Multiple Sclerosis, TTA/AAN/MS Council, available at: http://advocacyforpatients.org/pdf/ms/ms_aan.pdf (accessed 2013 Dec 15).

MULTIPLE SCLEROSIS

Background

Multiple sclerosis (MS) is a chronic, progressive auto-immune disease in which the patient's immune system attacks the myelin peptide antigens, destroying the fatty myelin sheaths that surround the axons in the brain and spinal cord (CNS). As demyelination progresses, the symptoms worsen because the nerves can no longer properly conduct electrical transmission. Most patients experience periods of disease activity followed by intervals of remission. The presentation is highly variable with some patients having a much more aggressive course while others have occasional discrete attacks.

Early symptoms include weakness, tingling, numbness and blurred vision. As the condition worsens, a variety of physical and psychological issues can make life very challenging, including deterioration of cognitive function, fatigue, muscle spasms, pain, incontinence, depression, heat sensitivity, sexual dysfunction, difficulty walking and gait instability, weakness and visual disturbances. If left untreated, about 30% of patients will develop significant physical disability. Up to 10% of patients have a milder phenotype in which no significant physical disability develops, although these patients may develop mild cognitive dysfunction. Male patients with primary progressive MS generally have the worst prognosis. Symptoms for MS are characterized as primary (due to demyelination, such as muscle weakness), secondary (which result from primary symptoms, such as incontinence due to muscle impairment) and tertiary, which involve psychological and social concerns, such as depression.

MS occurs in both men and women, but is more common in women. The typical age of onset is between 20 to 40 years old. Regretfully this is not an uncommon condition; MS is one of the most frequent neurologic disorders in young adults. Over two million people suffer with MS around the world, with about 500,000 cases in the U.S.

The cause of MS is unknown. Current research is investigating whether certain viruses can be causative, or whether viruses were more likely to have occurred in patients who develop MS due to an immune system that was not functioning properly.

In addition to the personal suffering caused by this condition, MS inflicts a heavy financial burden on individuals and society. A primary goal of therapy must be prevention of disease progression; what is lost in neuronal function cannot be regained. The newer agents that can modify disease progression are costly. The beta interferons cost about $40,000/year. The newer oral immune modulator fingolimod costs about $48,000/year. The newest agent, dimethyl fumarate, costs upwards of $60,000/year.

Pharmacologic Treatment

Mitoxantrone is a chemotherapeutic agent that is sometimes used for MS and is approved for this condition; a review of mitoxantrone can be found in the Oncology chapter. Steroids are used to help with exacerbations. In addition to using disease-modifying drugs to prevent disease progression, the clinician must be focused on symptom control. The drugs used for various related symptoms are summarized at the end of this chapter, and detailed information on these agents can be found in other chapters of this text. Many chemotherapeutics are used in MS treatment off-label for their anti-inflammatory properties. These include cyclophosphamide, azathioprine, intravenous immunoglobulin, and alemtuzumab.

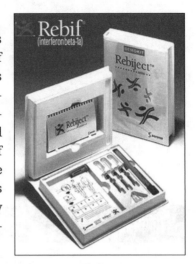

Disease Modifying Drugs

Interferon beta formulations (*Betaseron, Avonex, Rebif, Extavia*) and glatiramer acetate (*Copaxone*) have been the mainstay of treatment for patients with relapsing forms of MS. Fingolimod (*Gilenya*) and teriflunomide *(Aubagio)* were the first oral disease-modifying agents to be approved for MS. In 2013, a third oral agent, dimethyl fumarate *(Tecfidera)* was approved.

Natalizumab (*Tysabri*) is a humanized monoclonal antibody that targets the α4-integrin, which interferes with the infiltration of activated T cells across the blood-brain barrier into the CNS. Results from clinical trials with natalizumab show a

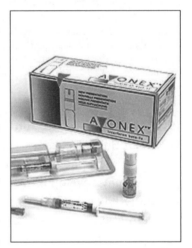

larger reduction in relapse rates; however, it is used only in patients who could not tolerate or had poor response to other agents because it is associated with an increased risk of progressive multifocal leukoencephalopathy (PML), a rare, opportunistic, viral brain infection that can cause death or severe disability.

If the drug is a powder that is reconstituted, the drug powder may be required to be refrigerated or be kept at room temperature (they vary). If a drug is reconstituted, it has to be used right away (at most within a few hours; a few reconstituted injections permit short storage in the refrigerator; others do not). Some of the powders that are reconstituted contain albumin and some patients will not wish to or cannot use albumin-containing products.

DRUG	DOSING	SAFETY/SIDE EFFECTS/MONITORING

Glatiramer acetate is an immune modulator, mechanism not well-defined.

| Glatiramer acetate *(Copaxone)* | 20 mg SC daily, single use syringe | **SIDE EFFECTS**
Injection site reactions (inflammation, erythema, pain, pruritus, mass), infection, pain, flushing, diaphoresis, chest pain, weakness, anxiety, rash, nausea

NOTES
Pregnancy Category B

Check solution for color discoloration; if present, discard.

Can be kept at room temperature for up to one month, or in the refrigerator. If cold, let it reach room temp prior to injecting.

Inject at the same time each day, into the fatty skin (SC). |

Interferons have antiviral and antiproliferative effects. Reduce antigen presentation and T-cell proliferation, alter cytokine and matrix metalloproteinase (MMP) expression, and restore suppressor function. Refer to the Hepatitis chapter for more complete information about the interferons.

| Interferon beta-1a *(Avonex)*

Interferon beta-1a *(Rebif, Rebif Rebidose)*

Interferon beta-1b *(Betaseron, Extavia)* | *Avonex*
IM: 30 mcg weekly

Powder (for reconstitution), pre-filled syringes and pens – refrigerate

Rebif
SC: 22 mcg or 44 mcg three times per week (at least 48 hours apart). Pre-filled syringes – refrigerate

Betaseron, Extavia
SC: 0.25 mg every other day. Powder (for reconstitution) – store at room temperature | **WARNINGS**
Depression/suicide, injection site necrosis, bone marrow suppression, ↑ LFTs, thyroid dysfunction, infections, anaphylaxis worsening cardiovascular disease

SIDE EFFECTS
Flu-like reaction following administration, usually lasting minutes or hours, usually dissipates with continued treatment. Some patients will take acetaminophen or NSAIDs prior to injection.

Injection site reactions: range from mild erythema to severe skin necrosis.

MONITORING
LFTs, CBC (at 1, 3 and 6 months, then periodically); thyroid function every 6 months (in patients with pre-existing abnormalities and/or clinical indications)

NOTES
Do not shake

Pregnancy Category C

For the SC injections: Pinch skin, inject into SC tissue in abdomen, left arm, right arm, thighs, buttocks, rotate sites, see counseling. If refrigerated, let stand to room temp prior to injection. Do not expel small air bubble in pre-filled syringes because dose may be reduced.

Some formulations contain albumin – risk of Creutzfeldt-Jakob disease transmission (rare); avoid in albumin-sensitive patients. |

Multiple Sclerosis Drugs Continued

DRUG	DOSING	SAFETY/SIDE EFFECTS/MONITORING

Natalizumab is a recombinant humanized monoclonal antibody.

DRUG	DOSING	SAFETY/SIDE EFFECTS/MONITORING
Natalizumab *(Tysabri)*	300 mg IV given over 1 hour, every 4 weeks	**BLACK BOX WARNING** Can cause progressive multifocal leukoencephalopathy (PML), an opportunistic brain viral infection. PML is associated with several factors including anti-JC virus antibodies, treatment duration and prior immunosuppressant use **CONTRAINDICATIONS** History of PML **SIDE EFFECTS** Fatigue, headache, infections, depression, pain in extremity, abdominal discomfort **NOTES** REMS: Only available through the TOUCH prescribing program; requires patient, physician and pharmacist registration as well as a MedGuide. Pregnancy Category C

Oral Immune Modulators

DRUG	DOSING	SAFETY/SIDE EFFECTS/MONITORING
Fingolimod (*Gilenya*)	0.5 mg capsule daily	**CONTRAINDICATIONS** Recent (within the last 6 months) MI, unstable angina, stroke, TIA, HF requiring hospitalization, or NYHA Class III/IV HF; history of 2nd or 3rd degree heart block or sick sinus syndrome (without a functional pacemaker), QTc interval $\geq$ 500 msec, concurrent use of Class Ia or III anti-arrhythmics **WARNINGS** Decrease in heart rate (must monitor), macular edema, infections, $\downarrow$ pulmonary function tests, $\uparrow$ LFTs **SIDE EFFECTS** Headache, diarrhea, influenza, back pain, $\uparrow$ LFTs, cough **MONITORING** CBC (baseline and periodically thereafter); ECG (baseline; repeat after initial dose observation period); heart rate, blood pressure and signs and symptoms of bradycardia [hourly for 6 hours following first dose; continued observation (until resolved) required if 6-hour postdose heart rate is either < 45 BPM, is lowest post-baseline measurement, or new-onset second degree or higher AV block occurs on repeat ECG]; continuous (until symptoms resolved) ECG monitoring if postdose symptomatic bradycardia occurs (overnight continuous ECG in a medical facility and repeat observation period for second dose if pharmacologic intervention for bradycardia necessary) **NOTES** Pregnancy Category C Avoid live vaccines until 2 months after stopping treatment Blister packs; protect from moisture

Multiple Sclerosis Drugs Continued

DRUG	DOSING	SAFETY/SIDE EFFECTS/MONITORING
Teriflunomide *(Aubagio)* active metabolite of leflunomide	7 mg or 14 mg PO daily	**BLACK BOX WARNINGS (2)** Severe liver toxicity and teratogenicity **CONTRAINDICATIONS** Severe hepatic impairment, pregnancy, current leflunomide treatment **SIDE EFFECTS** ↑ LFTs, alopecia, diarrhea, influenza, nausea, paresthesia, hypophosphatemia Rare: renal impairment, hyperkalemia, peripheral neuropathy **MONITORING** LFTs, SCr, BUN, K⁺, BP, CBC **NOTES** Pregnancy Category X
Dimethyl fumarate *(Tecfidera)*	120 mg BID for 7 days, then 240 mg BID	**SIDE EFFECTS** Flushing, abdominal pain, diarrhea, nausea, infection, ↓ WBC **MONITORING** CBC **NOTES** Can give aspirin 30 minutes prior to prevent flushing Do not crush, chew, or sprinkle capsule contents on food Pregnancy Category C

Ampyra: **Potassium channel blocker, may increase nerve signal conduction.**

Dalfampridine *(Ampyra)*	10 mg BID, extended-release tablets	**CONTRAINDICATIONS** History of seizures, CrCl < 50 mL/min **WARNINGS** Can cause seizures (especially with higher doses), anaphylaxis **SIDE EFFECTS** Urinary tract infections, insomnia, dizziness, headache, nausea, weakness, back pain **NOTES** Pregnancy Category C Take tablets whole; do not crush, chew, divide, or dissolve Most do not respond; monitor for improvement, takes up to 6 weeks, if effective, it primarily improves walking.

Interferon Counseling

- Read the medication guide that comes with this medicine. You will be given a medication guide the first time you get the medicine, and with each refill.

- This medication may lower your ability to fight infections. This may make you more likely to get a serious (rarely fatal) infection or can make any infection you have worse. Tell your healthcare provider immediately if you have any <u>signs of infection</u> such as fever of 100.5°F (38°C) or higher, chills, very bad sore throat, cough, sputum or change in the color of sputum, sweating or pain.

- This medicine has a possibility of causing liver damage. Call your healthcare provider right away if you have any of these symptoms: feel very tired, skin or eyes look yellow, poor appetite or vomiting, pain on the right side of your stomach (abdomen).

- For injections: common side effects include injection site reactions such as redness, swelling, itching, or pain. If you have pain, redness or swelling around the injection site that doesn't go away or gets worse, call your healthcare provider. (Refer to drug-specific administration instructions in the table. Do not shake the medicine.)

- Before using, check for particles or discoloration. If either is present, do not use the medicine.

- Before injecting each dose, clean the injection site with rubbing alcohol. It is important to change the location of the injection site each time you use this drug to prevent problems under the skin. New injections should be given at least 1 inch (2.5 centimeters) from the last injection site. Do not inject into areas of the skin that are sore, bruised, red, or hard.

- Some people have severe allergic reactions which can lead to trouble breathing and swallowing. Significant swelling of the mouth and tongue may occur with these severe allergic reactions. These reactions can happen quickly. Less severe allergic reactions such as rash, itching, skin bumps or minor swelling of the mouth and tongue can also happen. If you think you are having an allergic reaction, stop taking the drug and contact your healthcare provider immediately.

- If you become pregnant while taking this drug contact your healthcare provider. (see specific agent risk above). If the drug has a pregnancy registry, please register. This is important for the public health.

Drugs Used for Symptom Control

Patients with MS may be using <u>a variety of medications for symptom control</u>. The individual agents used can be found in the different chapters in this book. Commonly used symptom-control agents for MS include anticholinergics for incontinence, laxatives for constipation (or loperamide if diarrhea), skeletal muscle relaxants for muscle spasms/spasticity, or various pain agents for muscle spasms and pain. For localized pain and spasms botulinum toxin (*Botox*) injections can provide relief for up to three months. Propranolol can help with tremor. For depression many antidepressants are used; if an SNRI is chosen these may help both neuropathic pain and depression. Fatigue is often treated with modafinil or similar agents, or stimulants used for ADHD, such as methylphenidate. Meclizine and scopolamine are used for dizziness and vertigo. Acetylcholinesterase inhibitors, including donepezil, are used to

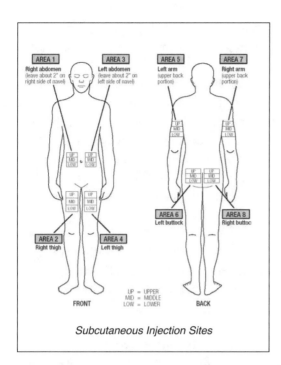

AREA 1
Right abdomen
(leave about 2" on
right side of navel)

AREA 3
Left abdomen
(leave about 2" on
left side of navel)

AREA 5
Left arm
(upper back
portion)

AREA 7
Right arm
(upper back
portion)

UP
MID
LOW

AREA 6
Left buttock

AREA 8
Right buttoc

AREA 2
Right thigh

AREA 4
Left thigh

UP = UPPER
MID = MIDDLE
LOW = LOWER

FRONT   BACK

Subcutaneous Injection Sites

help cognitive function. Erectile dysfunction can be treated with the phosphodiesterase inhibitors.

Notice that the drugs used for symptom control can worsen other symptoms. For example, anticholinergics can mildly worsen cognitive function (not all of them do, and this is patient-specific), but it happens. The vertigo agents can worsen cognitive function. Propranolol can worsen cognitive function, depression and cause problems with sexual performance. The SSRI and SNRI antidepressants will worsen sexual concerns, particularly by reducing libido or affecting the ability to sustain an erection or complete orgasm. Opioids, if used for pain, will worsen constipation, can decrease cognition and have dependence concerns. Managing the various medications used for MS requires competent pharmacists.

CELIAC DISEASE

Background

Celiac disease (celiac sprue) is an immune response to eating gluten, a protein found in wheat, barley and rye. The primary and effective treatment is to avoid gluten entirely. Gluten is present in many foods and food additives and in many drug excipients. Pharmacists assist patients in avoiding gluten-containing drugs completely; even a small exposure will trigger a reaction. To emphasize this point, the FDA permits food products to be labeled "gluten-free' only if the food contains less gluten than 20 parts per million.

The common symptoms of celiac disease are diarrhea, abdominal pain, bloating and weight loss. Patients with any of these symptoms that last longer than two weeks should be referred to a physician to rule out celiac disease or possibly another serious condition.

GUIDELINES

ACG clinical guidelines: diagnosis and management of celiac disease. Am J Gastroenterol. 2013;108(5):656-76.

King, AR. Gluten Content of the Top 200 Medications: Follow-Up to the Influence of Gluten on a Patient's Medication Choices. Hosp Pharm. 2013;48:736-743.

Gluten Free Drugs. www.gluten-freedrugs.org (accessed 2013 Nov 7).

Constipation (rather than diarrhea) can be present, and is more common in children. Symptoms can be atypical and sublime and diagnosis might occur only after a secondary problem is identified, such as growth problems in children or iron-deficiency anemia at any age. Vitamin deficiencies are common due to decreased absorption in the small intestine. Other complications include nutritional deficiencies (primarily anemia and osteoporosis), small bowel ulcers, amenorrhea and infertility, and increased risk of cancer (primarily lymphomas). Ninety-five percent of cases will respond well to dietary changes, although avoiding gluten entirely is not a simple task.

The risk for disease occurrence is higher in Caucasians, in females (2:1 incidence versus males), and with presence in a first-degree relative. Other autoimmune conditions can occur concurrently, including Sjögren's syndrome, autoimmune thyroid disease (hyper and hypo) and type 1 diabetes. The incidence is ~1% in the general population, but in type 1 diabetes the incidence of celiac disease is 3-5%. The incidence with Down syndrome is 10%; parents of children with Down's have a heavy responsibility with the care of their child and celiac should be identified if present since it responds well to dietary measures. Otherwise, the child will have chronic symptoms that are avoidable.

Dermatitis herpetiformis is an extremely itchy, blistery skin rash with chronic eruptions that is present in 20-25% of celiac patients, and occurs more often in males. The rash can be present with or without overt intestinal symptoms. The rash is often mistaken for eczema or psoriasis – which leads to a delay in diagnosis and treatment.

Serologic assays [tissue transglutaminase antibody (tTG; IgA) and endomysial antibody (EMA; IgA)] are used to select patients for biopsy and to support the diagnosis. Specific antibodies in celiac disease are present in ~95% of cases. If a gluten-free diet has been followed the antibodies will have dissipated; the diet must be reviewed prior to the initiation of diagnostic tests. Results from serologic testing are confirmed by biopsy, which must include a duodenal bulb sample with at least several other tissue samples.

If the diagnosis is confirmed, a dietician should be involved in assessing the diet and in food education. Pharmacists must be knowledgeable in assisting patients in avoiding gluten in over-the-counter and prescription drugs.

Non-Pharmacologic Treatment
The problem with identifying gluten content in drugs is due to the fact that while the FDA has strict regulations regarding the active ingredients in drugs they provide little oversight for the excipients. Drugs themselves are gluten-free; it is the excipients that may be a problem. And, it is not safe to assume that the generic formulations will ontain the same excipients as the brand; there is no legal requirement to match the excipients.

The first place to look for excipient content is the package insert, which may, or may not, contain the excipient components. The key word to look for is "starch" which will be either corn, potato, tapioca or wheat. If the package insert lists "starch" alone then the manufacturer must be consulted to find out if the starch is wheat. The manufacturer may report that they do not use gluten in the manufacturing process, but they cannot state whether the excipients purchased from outside vendors are gluten-free; there may be cross-contamination. The risk of cross-contamination is low, but not absent, and this information should be provided to the patient who ultimately must decide, hopefully in consult with the prescriber, whether to take the drug or not.

There are resources that are helpful. A clinical pharmacist maintains the website *Gluten Free Drugs*, and the journal *Hospital Pharmacy* and the American Pharmacists Association have published lists of gluten content in common medications. The University of Kansas Drug Information Center has published a list of the gluten content in the Top 200 list.

If the information is not known and the manufacturer needs to be consulted, the phone number for the Drug Information line can be obtained from the product's website, or can be found in the *Red Book* or in *Facts & Comparisons*. It is imperative to check due to the very small quantity of gluten that can trigger an immune response.

OTC drugs can be more challenging. Some of the larger chains have begun to list gluten content on the OTC packaging. Nutritional supplements are simpler; these are considered "food" products and fall under the FDA regulations for requirements for gluten-free labeling.

"Gluten-free" labels are increasingly common on foods, and on OTC medicines. It appears that the incidence of celiac disease is increasing, but it may be that the awareness has led to more diagnoses coupled with the many patients who are avoiding gluten for help with other conditions entirely, which are varied. This necessitates a fuller understanding of the gluten content in drugs.

SJÖGREN'S SYNDROME

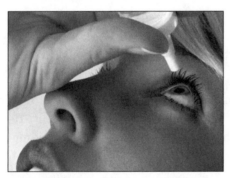

Sjögren's syndrome is an autoimmune disease, most often characterized by severe dry eyes and dry mouth. Many other symptoms can be associated with Sjögren's, including thyroiditis, Raynaud's phenomenon, neuropathy, and lymphadenopathy. Sjögren's syndrome can be primary or secondary, associated with another autoimmune disease such as RA or SLE. Dry mouth and dry eyes are a source of significant morbidity for these patients and can lead to complications such as dental caries, corneal ulceration and chronic oral infections. There is no known cure for Sjögren's; therefore, treatment focuses on reducing the symptoms of dry eyes and dry mouth.

Dry Eyes

The use of artificial teardrops is the primary treatment for dry eye. Popular artificial teardrops available over the counter are *Systane, Refresh, Clear Eyes* and *Liquifilm*.

It may be necessary to try a couple of different OTC eye drops before finding one that provides the most comfort. If the preservative is irritating (likely benzoyl peroxide) most artificial tear drops come in individual use containers that are preservative-free. If the eyes dry out while sleeping an ointment may be preferable.

Cyclosporine eye drops *(Restasis)* can be used in patients who do not get satisfactory relief from other measures, including ductal occlusion (lacrimal duct plugs). *Restasis* provides benefit for a small percentage of users and is expensive – patients should be instructed to monitor a reduction in symptoms and a reduction in the use of OTC eye drops and to use properly to avoid infection, which is more likely due to the dry eye state. Counsel patients that it may take up to 3-6 months to notice an increase in tear production.

Cyclosporine Emulsion Eye Drops

DRUG	DOSING	SAFETY/SIDE EFFECTS/MONITORING
Cyclosporine Emulsion Eye Drops *(Restasis)*	1 drop to each eye twice daily (~12 hours apart)	**SIDE EFFECTS** (unusual) Burning, stinging, redness, pain, or itching eye Blurred vision, feeling as if something is in the eye, or eye discharge may also occur **NOTES** Requires MedGuide which states: The emulsion from one individual single-use vial is to be used immediately after opening for administration to one or both eyes, and the remaining contents should be discarded immediately after administration. Do not allow the tip of the vial to touch the eye or any surface, as this may contaminate the emulsion. Do not administer while wearing contact lenses. (may be reinserted 15 mins afterwards.)

Dry Mouth

Non-pharmacologic treatment for dry mouth includes salivary stimulation, using sugar-free chewing gum (with xylitol) and lozenges, as well as daily rinses with antimicrobial mouth-wash. Salivary substitutes are available in lozenges, rinses, sprays, and swabs *(Plax, Ora-lube, Salivart)*. These may contain carboxymethylcellulose or glycerin. If OTC treatments do not provide sufficient relief, prescription muscarinic agonists such as pilocarpine or cevime-line *(Evoxac)* can be used.

Muscarinic Agonists Used for Dry Mouth

DRUG	DOSING	SAFETY/SIDE EFFECTS/MONITORING
Pilocarpine *(Salagen)* Pilocarpine opthalmic *(Isopto Carpine, Pilopine HS)* is used for glaucoma	5 mg four times daily	**CONTRANDICATIONS** Uncontrolled asthma, narrow-angle glaucoma, severe hepatic impairment **SIDE EFFECTS** Diaphoresis, flushing, nausea, urinary frequency **NOTES** Avoid taking with a high-fat meal
Cevimeline *(Evoxac)*	30 mg three times daily	**CONTRAINDICATIONS** Uncontrolled asthma, narrow-angle glaucoma, acute iritis **SIDE EFFECTS** Diaphoresis, nausea, sinusitis, rhinitis, URI

PRACTICE CASE

PATIENT PROFILE

Patient Name	Gina Calderon
Address	1954 Milton Drive, San Gabriel
Age 44	**Sex** Female **Race** Hispanic **Height** 5'3" **Weight** 140 lbs
Allergies	None known

DIAGNOSES

Rheumatoid Arthritis	Poor exercise tolerance
Hypertension	
Depression	
Chronic fatigue	

MEDICATIONS

Date	No.	Prescriber	Drug & Strength	Quantity	Sig	Refills
4/20/13	55287	Casey	Lisinopril 20 mg	30	1 PO daily	11
4/20/13	55288	Casey	Methotrexate 7.5 mg	8	2 tabs Q weekly	3
4/20/13	55289	Casey	Prednisone 10 mg	45	1 PO daily	3
4/20/13	55292	Casey	Alendronate 70 mg	4	1 PO Q weekly	3
		(OTC)	Calcium 500+ D 400 IU		1 tab Q AM	

LAB/DIAGNOSTIC TESTS

Test	Normal Value	Results Date 5/12/13	Date	Date
Rheum Fact	< 40 IU/mL	88 IU/mL		
ESR	≤ 30 mm/hr	81.1 mm/hr		
Alk Phos	33-115 u/L			
AST	10-35 IU/L	48 IU/L		
ALT	6-40 IU/L	76 IU/L		
GLU	65-99 mg/dL			
Na	135-146 mEq/L			
K	3.5-5.3 mEq/L			
Cl	98-110 mEq/L			
HCO3-	22-28 mEq/L			
BUN	7-25 mg/dL			
Creatinine	0.6-1.2 mg/dL			
Calcium	8.6-10.2 mg/dL			
WBC	4-11 cells/mm^3	5.8 cells/mm^3		
TB test, PPD		Negative		

ADDITIONAL INFORMATION

Date	Notes
7/31/13	BP 122/78 mmHg. Patient reports morning stiffness for past 2 months which improves as the day progresses. Reports that wrists, arms and leg joints are swollen and tender. States she is physically exhausted. No chest pain, breathing problems.

Questions

1. The physician is deciding whether to change the dose of methotrexate to daily therapy or begin etanercept. Choose the correct response:

   a. The methotrexate can be increased safely to 50 mg daily for rheumatoid arthritis.

   b. The methotrexate can be increased safely to 100 mg daily for rheumatoid arthritis.

   c. The methotrexate can be increased safely to 150 mg daily for rheumatoid arthritis.

   d. The methotrexate can be increased safely to 200 mg daily for rheumatoid arthritis.

   e. Methotrexate is not given daily for this condition.

2. The pharmacist will counsel the patient on her methotrexate therapy. She should include the following counseling points: (Select **ALL** that apply.)

   a. Common side effects include GI upset, nausea and diarrhea.

   b. She should not get pregnant while using this medication.

   c. Her liver will need to be checked periodically with a blood test.

   d. Choose a day of the week that you will remember to take the medicine.

   e. She should be taking leucovorin as well.

3. The patient is using prednisone 10 mg daily and weekly bisphosphonate therapy. Choose the correct statement:

   a. She does not need supplemental calcium and vitamin D with the alendronate.

   b. The prednisone may improve her blood pressure control.

   c. If she is able, her healthcare provider should try and help her decrease the prednisone dose.

   d. Prednisone is not bad for bones; in fact, it builds strong bones.

   e. A, B and C.

4. The physician decides to begin etanercept therapy. Choose the correct administration route for this medication:

   a. Oral tablets

   b. Suppository

   c. Subcutaneous injection

   d. Intramuscular injection

   e. Intravenous infusion

5. The pharmacist will counsel the patient on the etanercept therapy. She should include the following counseling points:

   a. Store the medication at room temperature.

   b. Inject subcutaneously in the deltoid muscle.

   c. This medication can activate latent tuberculosis; you will need to have a TB test prior to starting therapy.

   d. This medication does not cause increased risk of infections, except for tuberculosis.

   e. You can receive live vaccines, but not the annual influenza vaccine.

6. A physician has written a prescription for *Humira*. Choose the appropriate therapeutic interchange:

   a. Adalimumab

   b. Etanercept

   c. Rituximab

   d. Anakinra

   e. Infliximab

7. A physician has written a prescription for *Remicade*. Choose the appropriate therapeutic interchange:

   a. Adalimumab

   b. Etanercept

   c. Rituximab

   d. Anakinra

   e. Infliximab

Answers

1-e, 2-a,b,c,d, 3-c, 4-c, 5-c, 6-a, 7-e

THYROID DISORDERS

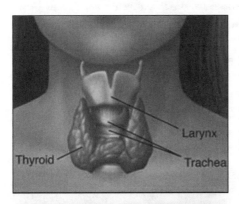

Thyroid — Larynx — Trachea

BACKGROUND

The thyroid gland is a butterfly-shaped organ composed of two symmetrical lobes, one on each side of the windpipe, connected by the isthmus. The thyroid gland synthesizes and releases thyroid hormones. Thyroid hormones affect metabolism, brain development, respiration, cardiac and nervous system functions, body temperature, muscle strength, skin dryness, menstrual cycles, body weight, and cholesterol levels. The thyroid gland is one of the largest organs within the body's endocrine system and is the only organ which contains cells that have the ability to absorb iodine. Hyperthyroidism (overactive thyroid) and hypothyroidism (underactive thyroid) are the most common problems of the thyroid gland. Hypothyroidism occurs more commonly in women, and its incidence increases with age.

PATHOPHYSIOLOGY

The thyroid gland produces two thyroid hormones, triiodothyronine (T_3) and thyroxine (T_4). Iodine and tyrosine are used to form both T_3 and T_4. Less than 20% of T3 is produced by the thyroid gland; T_3 is primarily formed from the breakdown of T_4 by peripheral tissues. T_3 is more potent than T_4 but has a much shorter half-life. Thyroid hormone production is regulated by thyroid-stimulating hormone (TSH or thyrotropin), which is made by the pituitary gland in the brain. Elevations in T_4 levels will inhibit the secretion of TSH, and create a negative feedback loop. Since T_3 and T_4 are transported in the blood and bound by proteins, it is important to measure the free T_4 (FT_4) levels as this is the active form.

In hypothyroidism, there is a deficiency in T_4, and consequently an elevation in TSH. In hyperthyroidism, there is over-secretion of T_4, and consequently a low level of TSH.

HYPOTHYROIDISM

In hypothyroidism, the decrease in thyroid hormone causes the body to slow down and the classic symptoms of low metabolism appear (fatigue, weight gain). The most common cause of hypothyroidism is Hashimoto's disease, an autoimmune condition in which a patient's antibodies attack their own thyroid gland. Drugs can also cause hypothyroidism (listed in the chart to the right) and may require monitoring of thyroid function tests. When hypothyroidism decompensates or goes untreated for a long period, myxedema coma can result. Myxedema coma is a life-threatening emergency characterized by poor circulation, hypothermia and hypometabolism. Due to unpredictable absorption of oral thyroid hormone from the gastrointestinal tract, intravenous thyroid hormone products should be administered.

Diagnosis

Low free thyroxine ($\downarrow$ FT_4) (normal range 0.7-1.9 ng/dL)

High thyroid stimulating hormone ($\uparrow$ TSH) (normal range 0.3 – 3.0 mIU/L)

Monitoring Parameters

Check free T_4 and TSH levels every 6-8 weeks until levels are normal, then 6 months later, then yearly. It is important to monitor as the person ages; they may need a dose reduction. Over-dosing levothyroxine in elderly patents leads to atrial fibrillation and fractures.

HYPOTHYROIDISM NOTES

Causes of Hypothyroidism
Hashimoto's disease – most common cause

Pituitary failure

Surgical removal of part or all of the thyroid gland

Congenital hypothyroidism

Thyroid gland ablation with radioactive iodine

External irradiation

Iodine deficiency

Drugs (e.g., amiodarone, interferons, lithium, nitroprusside, tyrosine kinase inhibitors – most notably sunitinib)

Clinical Signs and Symptoms
Cold intolerance

Dry skin

Fatigue

Weight gain

Hoarseness

Coarseness or loss of hair

Heavier than normal menstrual periods (menorrhagia)

Memory and mental impairment

Goiter (possible, can be due to low iodine intake)

Myalgias

Weakness

Depression

Constipation

Bradycardia

Complications
Cardiovascular disease (cardiomyopathy, HF, hyperlipidemia, CAD)

Goiter

Depression

Infertility

Myxedema – intense cold intolerance, drowsiness, unconsciousness

Pregnancy and Hypothyroidism

Levothyroxine is FDA pregnancy category A. Pregnant women with thyroid hormone deficiency or TSH elevation during pregnancy may have children at risk of impairment in their intellectual function and motor skills, unless properly treated. Pregnant women being treated with thyroid hormone replacement will require a 30-50% increase in the levothyroxine dose throughout the course of their pregnancy. The mother will need an elevated dose for several months after giving birth. In 2011 new guidelines called for more aggressive control of hypothyroidism in pregnancy. Preferably, treatment should start prior to pregnancy.

Pharmacologic Treatment

The goal of therapy is to achieve and maintain a euthyroid (normal) state by both clinical signs and symptoms as well as laboratory values. Counsel the patient regarding clinical symptoms for both hypo- and hyperthyroidism as the dose will be titrated to the individual's needs. Per the guidelines, levothyroxine (T_4) is the drug of choice and current recommendations encourage the use of a consistent preparation for the patient to minimize variability from refill to refill. There are patients who state they just do not "feel right" on T_4 alone, and may be supplementing with other formulations, such as liothyronine (T_3, *Cytomel* and *Triostat*) or desiccated thyroid (T_3 and T_4, *Armour Thyroid*). Desiccated thyroid is not favored since the preparations can contain variable amounts, although newer formulations have become standardized. This is called "natural thyroid" and it is dosed in "grains." Some patients choose to use these alternatives alone.

It is important that patients take their thyroid replacement in the morning, first thing, on an empty stomach at least 30 minutes before breakfast.

Iodine supplementation, including kelp or other iodine-containing functional foods, is not recommended in the management of hypothyroidism in iodine-sufficient areas.

Potassium Iodide Use After Exposure to Radiation

Potassium iodide (KI) blocks the accumulation of radioactive iodine in the thyroid gland; thus preventing thyroid cancer. Potassium iodide should be taken as soon as possible after radiation exposure, at the right dose, but not with an over-dose. The doses below are for 24 hours. If the radiation exposure is longer, refer to the CDC website for repeat-dose instructions. Iodized salt and foods do not contain enough iodine to block radioactive iodine and are not recommended.

- Birth – 1 month: 16 mg KI

- Infants and children between 1 month–3 years: 32 mg KI

- Children 3 -18 years: 65 mg KI

- Adults and children > 68 kg: 130 mg KI

Hypothyroid Treatment

DRUG	DOSING	SAFETY/SIDE EFFECTS/MONITORING
Levothyroxine (T₄) *(Synthroid, Levothroid, Levoxyl, Unithroid, Tirosint)* Check AB-rating of a generic to a brand. Not all generic levothyroxine formulations are AB-rated to various brands. If you change formulations, check signs and symptoms and <u>levels in 6-8 weeks</u>. Capsule, tablet, inj.	25, 50, 75, 88, 100, 112, 125, 137, 150, 175, 200, 300 mcg Start 50 mcg/day in patients > 50 years or if < 50 years of age with underlying cardiac disease. Start 12.5-25 mcg/day in patients > 50 years with cardiac disease. Titrate in 12.5-25 mcg increments every 4-8 weeks, as needed. Usual dose: 0.5 mcg/kg/day for elderly; see starting dose above 1.7 mcg/kg/day in younger patients (< 50 years of age) **TABLETS** 25 mcg – orange 50 mcg – white 75 mcg – violet 88 mcg – olive 100 mcg – yellow 112 mcg – rose 125 mcg – brown 137 mcg – turquoise 150 mcg – blue 175 mcg – lilac 200 mcg – pink 300 mcg – green	**BLACK BOX WARNING** Thyroid supplements are ineffective and potentially toxic when used for the treatment of obesity or for weight reduction, especially in euthyroid patients. High doses may produce serious or even life-threatening toxic effects particularly when used with some anorectic drugs (e.g., sympathomimetic amines). **CONTRAINDICATIONS** Acute MI, thyrotoxicosis, uncorrected adrenal insufficiency **WARNINGS** Use with caution and reduce dosage in patients with cardiovascular disease; chronic hypothyroidism predisposes patients to coronary artery disease **SIDE EFFECTS** If patient is euthyroid, no side effects should exist. If dose is too high, patient will experience hyperthyroid symptoms such as ↑ HR, palpitations, sweating, weight loss, arrhythmias, irritability, others. **MONITORING** Check TSH levels (rarely free T₄) and clinical symptoms every 6-8 weeks until levels are normal, then 6 months later, then yearly. It is important to monitor as the person ages; they may need a dose reduction. Over-dosing levothyroxine in elderly patents leads to atrial fibrillation and fracture. **NOTES** Pregnancy Category A Highly protein bound (> 99%) Levothyroxine is the drug of choice due to chemical stability, once-daily dosing, inexpensiveness, and is free of antigenicity and has more uniform potency. Take on an empty stomach, at least 30 minutes before breakfast, with a full glass of water
Thyroid, Desiccated USP (T₃ and T₄) *(Armour Thyroid, Nature-Throid, Westhroid, NP Thyroid, WP Thyroid)* Tablet	Start 15-30 mg daily (15 mg in cardiac disease and elderly); titrate in 15 mg increments. Usual dose is 60-120 mg daily	**Levothyroxine IV** Must be given upon reconstitution. IV to PO ratio is 1:2 **Thyroid USP** Natural porcine-derived thyroid that contains both T₃ and T₄; less predictable potency and stability. Not preferred, but some feel better using it
Liothyronine (T₃) *(Cytomel, Triostat)* Tablet, inj.	Start 25 mcg daily; titrate in 12.5-25 mcg increments. Usual dose is 25-75 mcg daily	**Liothyronine** Shorter t ½ leading to fluctuations in T₃ levels
Liotrix (T₃ and T₄ in 1:4 ratio) *(Thyrolar)* Tablet	Start 25 mcg levothyroxine/6.25 mcg liothyronine – usual dose is 50-100 mcg levothyroxine/12.5-25 mcg liothyronine.	

Drug Interactions

Drugs that decrease thyroid hormone levels:

- Aluminum (antacids), calcium, cholestyramine, iron, magnesium, multivitamins (containing ADEK, folate, iron), orlistat *(Xenical, Alli)*, sevelamer, sodium polystyrene *(Kayexalate)*, sucralfate: all ↓ absorption; separate doses by 4 hours

- Separate doses of lanthanum by 2 hours from thyroid replacement therapy

- Estrogen and hepatic inducers (e.g., carbamazepine, phenobarbital, phenytoin, rifampin, others): ↓ thyroid hormone levels

- Beta-blockers, amiodarone, glucocorticoids, and PTU may decrease the effectiveness of levothyroxine by decreasing the conversion of T_4 to T_3

- SSRIs can decrease thyroid levels

- Thyroid hormone is highly-protein bound (>99%). Drugs that may cause protein-binding site displacement include salicylates (> 2 g/d), heparin, phenytoin, NSAIDs, others.

Thyroid hormone can change concentrations/effects of these drugs:

- ↑ effect of anticoagulants (e.g., increased PT/INR with warfarin)

- ↓ digoxin levels

- ↓ theophylline levels

- ↓ effect of antidiabetic agents

Patient Counseling for Levothyroxine

- Levothyroxine is a replacement for a hormone that is normally produced by your body to regulate your energy and metabolism. Levothyroxine is given when the thyroid does not produce enough of this hormone on its own.

- There are many medicines that can alter levothyroxine effects; tell the pharmacist about all medications you are taking. This includes over-the-counter vitamins, supplements and heartburn medications.

- Different brands of levothyroxine may not work the same. If you get a prescription refill and your new pills look different, ask the pharmacist.

- This medicine is safe to use while you are pregnant. It is also safe to use while you are breast-feeding a baby. It does pass into breast milk, but it is not harmful to a nursing infant.

- Tell your doctor if you become pregnant during treatment; it is likely that your dose will need to be increased during pregnancy or if you plan to breast-feed.

- Take on an empty stomach with a full glass of water at least 30 minutes before breakfast.

- Some patients will notice a slight reduction in symptoms within 1 to 2 weeks, but the full effect from therapy is often delayed for a month or two before people start to feel normal.

- Even if you feel well, you still need to take this medicine every day for the rest of your life to replace the thyroid hormone your body cannot produce.

- To be sure the dose being used is optimal for you, your blood will need to be tested on a regular basis (at least annually).

HYPERTHYROIDISM (THYROTOXICOSIS)

Hyperthyroidism (overactive thyroid) occurs when there is over-production of thyroid hormones. Instead of low FT_4 and high TSH, you have <u>high FT_4 and low TSH</u> and nearly opposite symptoms as compared to hypothyroidism. Hyperthyroidism can significantly accelerate the metabolism, causing sudden weight loss, a rapid or irregular heartbeat, sweating, nervousness, irritability, diarrhea and insomnia. Goiter and exopthalmus can occur. Without treatment, hyperthyroidism can lead to tachycardia, arrhythmias, heart failure and osteoporosis. No one should be using thyroid hormone to lose weight – they will be irritable and can end up with severe cardiac complications. Interestingly, older cats often get hyperthyroidism (more frequently than dogs) and pharmacists occasionally fill scripts for patients with names like Kitty.

Causes

The most common cause of hyperthyroidism is <u>Graves' disease</u>, which tends to occur in females in their 30's and 40's. Graves' disease is an autoimmune disorder (like Hashimoto's) but instead of destroying the gland, the antibodies stimulate the thyroid to produce too much T_4. Less commonly, a single nodule is responsible for the excess hormone secretion. Thyroiditis (inflammation of the thyroid) can also cause hyperthyroidism. <u>Drugs that can cause hyperthyroidism include iodine, amiodarone and interferons</u>. Hyperthyroidism can also occur in patients who take excessive doses of any of the available forms of thyroid hormone.

Treatment involves anti-thyroid medications, destroying part of the gland via radioactive

HYPERTHYRODISM NOTES

Causes of Hyperthyroidism
Graves' disease – most common cause

Toxic Multinodular Goiter

Toxic Adenoma

Thyroiditis

Drugs (e.g., iodine, amiodarone, interferons, too much thyroid hormone)

Clinical Signs and Symptoms
Heat intolerance or increased sweating

Weight loss (or gain)

Agitation, nervousness, irritability, anxiety

Palpitations and tachycardia

Fatigue and muscle weakness

Frequent bowel movements or diarrhea

Insomnia

Light or absent menstrual periods

Goiter (possible)

Thinning hair

Tremor

Exopthalmos (exophthalmia), diplopia

iodine (RAI-131) or surgery. <u>RAI-131 is the treatment of choice in Graves' disease.</u> With any option, the patient can be treated with <u>beta blockers first for symptom control (to reduce palpitations, tremors and tachycardia).</u> PTU or methimazole can be used as a temporary measure until surgery is complete. <u>Initially, when treating with drugs, it takes 1-3 months at higher doses to control symptoms, at which point the dose is reduced to prevent hypothyroidism from occurring.</u>

Hyperthyroid Treatment

DRUG	DOSING	SAFETY/SIDE EFFECTS/MONITORING

Thionamides – inhibit synthesis of thyroid hormones by blocking the oxidation of iodine in the thyroid gland; PTU also inhibits peripheral conversion of T_4 to T_3

DRUG	DOSING	SAFETY/SIDE EFFECTS/MONITORING
Propylthiouracil (PTU) (*Propyl-Thyracil*)	50-150 mg Q8H initially (or higher) until euthyroid, followed by dose reduction	**BLACK BOX WARNING** Severe liver injury and acute liver failure (with PTU) **SIDE EFFECTS** GI upset, headache, rash, itching, fever, constipation, loss of taste/taste perversion, SLE-like syndrome, lymphadenopathy Hepatitis, agranulocytosis (rare): see MD at once if develop yellow skin, abdominal pain, high fever, or severe sore throat. **MONITORING** CBC, LFTs, PT and thyroid function tests (TSH, FT_4, total T_3) every 4-6 weeks until euthyroid **NOTES** Pregnancy Category D – PTU preferred in 1st trimester – change to methimazole for 2nd and 3rd trimesters due to increased risk of liver toxicity from PTU PTU is preferred in thyroid storm
Methimazole (*Tapazole*)	5-20 mg Q8H initially until euthyroid, then 5-10 mg daily	Take with food to reduce GI upset Patient must monitor for liver toxicity (abdominal pain, yellow skin/eyes, dark urine, nausea, weakness) PTU is not a first line treatment for hyperthyroidism except in patients who cannot tolerate other options or conditions where other antithyroid therapies are contraindicated.

Hyperthyroid Treatment Continued

DRUG	DOSING	SAFETY/SIDE EFFECTS/MONITORING

Iodides – temporarily inhibit secretion of thyroid hormones; T_4 and T_3 levels will be reduced for several weeks but effect will not be maintained

| Potassium Iodide and Iodine solution (*Lugol's solution*) Off label | 4-8 drops Q8H | **CONTRAINDICATIONS** Hypersensitivity to iodide or iodine; dermatitis herpetiformis; hypocomplementemic vasculitis, nodular thyroid condition with heart disease

SIDE EFFECTS Rash, metallic taste, sore throat/gums, GI upset, urticaria, hypo/hyperthyroidism with prolonged use |
| Saturated solution of potassium iodide (SSKI, *ThyroShield*) | 1-2 drops Q8H | **MONITORING** Thyroid function tests, signs and symptoms of hyperthyroidism

NOTES Pregnancy Category D

Dilute in a glassful of water, juice, or milk. Take with food or milk to reduce GI upset |

Drug Interactions with Thionamides

- May decrease the anticoagulant effect of warfarin; monitor.

THYROID STORM

Thyroid storm is a life-threatening medical emergency characterized by decompensated hyperthyroidism that can be precipitated by infection, trauma, surgery, radio-active iodine treatment or non-adherence to antithyroid medication. The following treatment measures mentioned below must be implemented promptly.

Treatments

- Antithyroid drug therapy (PTU is preferred; 900-1,200 mg PO daily – divided every 4-6 hrs) <u>PLUS</u>

  - Can crush tablets and administer through NG-tube if needed

  - Given 1 hour before iodide to block synthesis of thyroid hormone

- Inorganic iodide therapy such as SSKI 3-5 drops PO Q8H or Lugol's solution 5-10 drops PO Q8H <u>PLUS</u>

- Beta-adrenergic blockade (e.g., propranolol 40-80 mg PO Q6H) <u>PLUS</u>

- Corticosteroid therapy (e.g., dexamethasone 2-4 mg PO Q6H) <u>PLUS</u>

- Aggressive cooling with acetaminophen and cooling blankets and other supportive treatments (e.g., antiarrhythmics, insulin, fluids, electrolytes, etc.)

THYROID STORM SIGNS & SYMPTOMS
Fever (> 103 degrees Fahrenheit)
Tachycardia
Tachypnea
Dehydration
Profuse sweating
Agitation
Delirium
Psychosis
Coma

PRACTICE CASE

MT is a 45 year old female who comes to the clinic complaining of more fatigue than normal and constipation. On exam, you notice the patient has some dry skin patches and looks a bit depressed. Her past medical history is significant for GERD for which she takes *Dexilant* 30 mg daily and *Maalox*. You order some blood work and it is reported below.

CATEGORY	
Vitals	BP 139/82 mmHg, HR 62 BPM, Temp. 38.0, RR 15 BPM
Labs	TSH: 44 mIU/L (normal range 0.3 – 3.0 mIU/L)
	Free T$_4$: 0.5 ng/dL (normal range 0.8-1.7 ng/dL)

Questions

1. The physician is considering starting thyroid medication for MT. Which of the following options is considered most appropriate for initial therapy?

   a. *Levoxyl*

   b. *Armour Thyroid*

   c. *Thyrolar*

   d. RAI 131

   e. Propranolol

2. What is a reasonable starting dose of *Synthroid*?

   a. 12.5 mcg daily

   b. 25 mg daily

   c. 75 mg daily

   d. 50 mcg daily

   e. 2.5 mg daily

3. Which of the following medications can decrease the levels of levothyroxine?

   a. Magnesium – Aluminum hydroxide *(Maalox)*

   b. Iron

   c. Warfarin

   d. A and B only

   e. A, B, and C

4. Propylthiouracil is associated with which of the following serious adverse effects?

   a. Pregnancy

   b. Liver failure

   c. Renal failure

   d. Rhabdomyolysis

   e. Priapism

5. What is the most common cause of hypothyroidism?

   a. Graves' disease

   b. Hashimoto's disease

   c. Surgery

   d. Amiodarone

   e. Lithium

6. A patient is beginning levothyroxine therapy. Patient counseling points should include the following:

   a. You should feel all better by this afternoon or tomorrow morning.

   b. Your doctor will need to recheck your thyroid hormone levels in 6-8 weeks.

   c. If you get pregnant, stop using this medicine.

   d. A and C only

   e. All of the above

7. Which of the following are symptoms of hypothyroidism?

    a. Fatigue
    b. Weight gain or increased difficulty losing weight
    c. Diarrhea
    d. A and B only
    e. All of the above

8. The pharmacist should instruct the patient to take levothyroxine in this manner:

    a. The first thing in the morning, with food
    b. The first thing in the morning, about 30 minutes before food or other medicines
    c. With the largest meal to reduce nausea
    d. With dinner since levothyroxine is sedating
    e. At bedtime

9. A pregnant female is being started on levothyroxine therapy. Levothyroxine has the following pregnancy rating:

    a. Pregnancy Category A
    b. Pregnancy Category B
    c. Pregnancy Category C
    d. Pregnancy Category D
    e. Pregnancy Category X

10. What is the most common cause of hyperthyroidism?

    a. Hashimoto's disease
    b. Pituitary failure
    c. Lithium
    d. Amiodarone
    e. Graves' disease

Answers

1-a, 2-d, 3-d, 4-b, 5-b, 6-b, 7-d, 8-b, 9-a, 10-e

TRANSPLANT/ IMMUNOSUPPRESSION

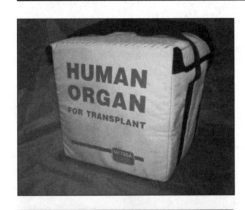

GUIDELINES

Resources available at: http://www.kidney.
org/professionals/(accessed 2013 Dec 2).

KDIGO clinical practice guideline for the
care of kidney transplant recipients. Am J
Transplant. 2009 Nov;9(Suppl 3):S1-155.

BACKGROUND

Transplantation medicine is one of the most challenging and complex areas of modern medicine. Some of the key areas for medical management are the problems of transplant rejection, during which the body has an immune response to the transplanted organ, possibly leading to transplant failure and the need to immediately remove the organ from the recipient. When possible, transplant rejection can be reduced through serotyping to determine the most appropriate donor-recipient match and through the use of immunosuppressant drugs. Although other organs can be transplanted (primarily kidney, liver, heart, lung, and pancreas), the majority of transplant cases are kidney (1st) and liver (2nd). Prior to any transplant, tissue typing or cross-matching is performed to assess donor-recipient compatibility for human leukocyte antigen (HLA) and ABO blood group. A mismatch in either would lead to a fast, acute rejection. This is followed by a Panel Reactive Antibody (PRA) test that is taken to gage the degree to which the recipient is "sensitized" to foreign (or "non-self") proteins. A high score correlates with the likelihood of graft rejection and could necessitate some type of desensitization protocol prior to the transplant.

An allograft is the transplant of an organ or tissue from one individual to another of the same species with a different genotype. This can also be called an allogenic transplant or homograft. A transplanted organ from a genetically identical donor (such as an identical twin) is called an isograft. An autograft is when a tissue is a transplant from one site to another on the same patient, also termed autologous transplant (or autologous stem cell transplant). Hyperacute rejection occurs in the operating room within hours of the transplant and is due to some type of mismatch; no treatment exists, and the transplanted organ will be removed.

<u>Induction immunosuppressant therapy</u> most often consists of a short course of very effective intravenous (IV) agents. The induction agents provide an immunologic cover (to prevent rejection) during the time the graft needs to stabilize in order to be able to tolerate a calcineurin inhibitor (CNI) at a therapeutic dose. The most commonly used induction agent is basiliximab, an interleukin-2 (IL-2) receptor antagonist. The IL-2 receptor is expressed on activated T lymphocytes and is a critical pathway for activating cell-mediated allograft rejection. Higher risk patients will receive (in addition) the lymphocyte-depleting agent rabbit antithymocyte globulin. In some cases induction can be achieved with higher doses of the same drugs used for maintenance. Induction agents may not be required if the transplant is from an identical twin.

<u>Maintenance immunosuppressant</u> therapy is generally provided by the combination of:

- A calcineurin inhibitor (tacrolimus is the 1st line CNI) plus

- An antiproliferative agent (mycophenolate is 1st line in most protocols), or everolimus, sirolimus, belatacept or azathioprine.

- +/- steroids (typically prednisone).

If the patient is low immunological risk the steroids will be discontinued; otherwise, they are not and the long-term adverse effects will need to be considered. Attacking the immune system via <u>multiple mechanisms through different drug classes</u> is designed to both lower toxicity risk and to reduce the risk of graft rejection.

> **AVOIDING AN "ABO MISMATCH" OR INCOMPATIBILITY REACTION**
>
> Type A blood will react against type B or type AB blood.
>
> Type B blood will react against type A or type AB blood.
>
> Type O blood will react against type A, type B, or type AB blood.
>
> Type AB blood will not react against type A, type B, or type AB blood.
>
> Type O blood does not cause an immune response when it is received by people with type A, type B, or type AB blood. This is why type O blood cells can be given to patients of any blood type. People with type O blood are called "universal donors."
>
> However, type O can only receive type O blood.

Cardiovascular Disease: The Common Cause of Death in Transplant Patients

A concerted effort must be made to reduce risk factors for heart disease. This is challenging considering that the patient is using transplant-rejection drugs that cause metabolic syndrome. Nonetheless, these patients are among the highest risk for CVD and blood pressure, blood glucose, cholesterol and weight must be tightly controlled. In a renal transplant patient the blood pressure goal is the same as for renal insufficiency (< 130/80 mmHg). Blood glucose is managed to the ADA guidelines and cholesterol to the NCEP guidelines. Weight is measured at each visit, with reduction programs used as-needed. Refer to the individual chapters.

Cancer: Higher Risk in Transplant Patients

Cancer risk is higher compared to the general population. Some cancer types are viral-mediated and related to immune suppression – causing increased cancer incidence similar to that seen with the use of the stronger agents used for autoimmune conditions. Screening for common cancers should be routine, along with lifestyle measures to reduce risk. Skin cancer is common with transplant and sunscreen must be used routinely, along with sun avoidance or sun protection with clothing. In a ddition, CNIs cause photosensitivity. The skin should be assessed professionally at least annually.

Monitoring by the Patient & Health Care Team is Essential

In addition to drug toxicity symptoms, patients will need to monitor for symptoms of organ rejection. Common symptoms of an acute rejection include flu-like symptoms, such as chills, body aches, nausea, cough, and shortness of breath <u>and</u> organ-specific symptoms (for example, heart failure symptoms with a heart transplant rejection or a decrease in urine output/fluid retention/edema/blood pressure elevation with a kidney transplant rejection).

All immunosuppressive agents require <u>careful monitoring</u> (including drug trough levels) to minimize toxicities and decrease the incidence of rejection. Keep in mind which maintenance agents have the highest nephrotoxicity (<u>tacrolimus, cyclosporine</u>), the most likely to worsen diabetes or cause new-onset diabetes (<u>tacrolimus, steroids, cyclosporine,</u> and the mTor inhibitors everolimus and sirolimus), which are the most likely to worsen lipid parameters (<u>mTor inhibitors</u>, steroids, cyclosporine) and which are the highest risk for blood pressure elevations (<u>steroids, cyclosporine</u>, tacrolimus).

TRANSPLANT DRUGS: WHAT'S USED, WHEN

Induction Drugs, to avoid acute early rejection are either:
Basilixumab is an interleukin-2 (IL-2) receptor antagonist and is the primary induction agent.

Patients at highest risk of rejection may be receiving antithymocyte globulin.

Or, the maintenance drugs at higher doses.

Primary Immunosuppressive Drugs
The calcineurin inhibitors (CNIs), which are tacrolimus (primarily) or cyclosporine.

Adjuvant Agents (given with the primary drugs), also called Antiproliferative or Antimetabolite Agents
Given with the CNI (to enable lower doses of the CNI to reduce nephrotoxicity risk), and include steroids, azathioprine or mycophenolate mofetil (*CellCept*). The majority of transplant patients use a CNI +/- steroids + *CellCept*. Or, patients may be using one of the drugs that bind to the mTOR protein (such as everolimus) to reduce the CNI nephrotoxicity risk. This class may act synergistically with the CNIs.

With the use of adjuvants, adequate immunosuppression can be achieved while decreasing the dose and toxicity of the individual agents.

Infection Risk Reduction
There are others; these are infections in which prophylaxis or treatment is available. Vaccines discussed in a separate sidebar.

Candida: Oral and esophageal prophylaxis with oral clotrimazole lozenges, nystatin or fluconazole used commonly 1-3 months post-transplant.

Cytomegalovirus: valganciclovir (pro-drug of ganciclovir) is the usual drug of choice for prophylaxis, which may be required.

Herpes simplex: prophylaxis or treatment with acyclovir, valacyclovir or famciclovir.

Varicella zoster (vaccine prior to transplant): if shingles appear, it is treated with IV or oral acyclovir or valacyclovir.

Pneumocystis jirovecii pneumonia: Daily trimethoprim-sulfamethoxazole for 3-6 months post-transplant.

Tuberculosis: if positive, same prophylaxis as general population.

All patients using strong immunosuppressants or with any condition that suppresses the immune system should <u>self-monitor for symptoms of infection</u>: fever of 100.5°F (38°C) or higher (or lower if elderly), chills, sore throat, ear or sinus pain, cough, more sputum or change in color of sputum, pain with passing urine, mouth sores, wound that will not heal, or anal itching or pain.

Reducing Infection Risk

The use of potent drugs has made solid organ transplant widely available and successful. However, the use of these agents is _interrelated to the development of infection_. The majority of infections that occur in organ transplant recipients are opportunistic and are a major cause of death in the immunocompromised patient. Opportunistic infections are caused by organisms that are ubiquitous in the environment, but rarely cause disease in the immunocompetent host. Infection prophylaxis is essential; review the basics in the sidebar. Infection control must include reducing risk from transmission, such as proper hand-washing techniques (see Medication Safety chapter), air filtration systems, keeping the mouth clean, and keeping away from dusty, crowded areas and sick people. One of the sidebars discusses drugs used for common infections. Often the prophylaxis drugs are the same used for treatment, in larger doses and possibly given IV. Or, other drugs or a combination is required for treatment. Vaccine-preventable illness is an important consideration pre-transplant since live vaccines cannot be given post-transplant.

VACCINE-PREVENTABLE ILLNESS

Required vaccines should be given pre-transplant if the recipient is not current. The inactivated vaccines can be given post-transplant if needed; live vaccines cannot be given post-transplant. Influenza (inactivated, not live) annually (recurring, each October-November) should be given when the vaccine is available.

Pneumococcal vaccine in adults ≥ 19 years who are immunocompromised receive PCV13 first, followed by PPSV23 at least 8 weeks later. Subsequent doses of PPSV23 should follow current PPSV23 recommendations for adults at high risk (5 years after the first PPSV23 dose). Some of the transplant centers recommend PPSV23 every 5 years.

Transplant patients are at high risk for serious varicella infections, with a very high risk of disseminated disease with a primary infection. The best protection is to vaccinate the close contacts (in addition to the recipient pre-transplant). Although there is a small risk that transmission could occur (from the vaccine recipient to the transplant recipient) ACIP states "the benefits of vaccinating susceptible household contacts of immunocompromised persons outweigh the potential risk for transmission of vaccine virus to immunocompromised contacts."

If the vaccinated household contact develops a rash post-vaccine they should avoid contact with the transplant recipient; they are contagious – and should report to their physician. If the transplant patient develops a rash they will need to be seen right away.

INDUCTION AGENTS

DRUG	SAFETY/SIDE EFFECTS/MONITORING

Antibodies – reverse rejection by binding to antigens on T-lymphocytes (killer cells) and interfering with their function

Antithymocyte Globulin *(Atgam-Equine)* *(Thymocyte-Rabbit)*	**BLACK BOX WARNING** Should be administered under the supervision of a physician experienced in immunosuppressive therapy. Adequate laboratory and supportive medical resources must be readily available (e.g., epinephrine). **SIDE EFFECTS** Anaphylaxis (intradermal skin testing recommended prior to 1st dose), fever, chills, pruritus, rash, leukopenia, chest pain, hypertension, edema and others **MONITORING** Lymphocyte profile (T-cell count), CBC with differential, vital signs during administration **NOTES** May need to pre-medicate (diphenhydramine, acetaminophen and steroids). Epinephrine and resuscitative equipment should be nearby.

Interleukin 2 (IL-2) receptor antagonist – Chimeric (murine/human) monoclonal antibody that inhibits the IL-2 receptor on the surface of activated T-lymphocytes preventing cell-mediated allograft rejection

Basiliximab *(Simulect)*	**BLACK BOX WARNING** Should only be used by physicians experienced in immunosuppressive therapy. **SIDE EFFECTS** Hypertension, fever, weakness, stomach upset/nausea/vomiting/cramping, peripheral edema, dyspnea/upper respiratory irritation/infection, cough, tremor, painful urination; side effects listed are rated as severe and >10%, others are >10% and rated less severe **MONITORING** Signs and symptoms of hypersensitivity and infection

MAINTENANCE MEDICATIONS

DRUG	DOSING	SAFETY/SIDE EFFECTS/MONITORING

Corticosteroids – naturally occurring hormones that prevent or suppress inflammation and humoral immune responses

DRUG	DOSING	SAFETY/SIDE EFFECTS/MONITORING
PredniSONE, others	2-5-5 mg PO daily, or on alternate days	**SHORT-TERM SIDE EFFECTS** Fluid retention, stomach upset, emotional instability (euphoria, mood swings, irritability), insomnia, ↑ appetite, weight gain, acute rise in blood glucose and blood pressure with high dose **LONG-TERM SIDE EFFECTS** Adrenal suppression/Cushing's syndrome, impaired wound healing, hypertension. See Asthma chapter for further information on chronic steroid use.

Maintenance Medications Continued

DRUG	DOSING	SAFETY/SIDE EFFECTS/MONITORING

Antiproliferative Agents – inhibit T-lymphocyte proliferation by altering purine synthesis

DRUG	DOSING	SAFETY/SIDE EFFECTS/MONITORING
Mycophenolate Mofetil (*CellCept*) **Mycophenolic Acid (*Myfortic*)**	1-1.5 g PO BID, depending on transplant type	**BLACK BOX WARNINGS (3)** ↑ risk of infection; ↑ development of lymphoma and skin malignancies; ↑ risk of congenital malformations and spontaneous abortions when used during pregnancy **SIDE EFFECTS** Diarrhea, GI upset, vomiting, hypo- and hypotension, edema, tachycardia, pain, hyperglycemia, hypo and hyperkalemia, hypomagnesemia, hypocalcemia, hypercholesterolemia, tremor, acne, infections **MONITORING** CBC, renal, liver, signs of infection **NOTES** *CellCept* and *Myfortic* should not be used interchangeably due to differences in absorption. *Myfortic* is enteric coated which helps to ↓ diarrhea. Should be taken on an empty stomach to avoid variability in absorption. Pregnancy Category D, and decreases efficacy oral contraceptives.
AzaTHIOprine (*Azasan, Imuran*)	1-3 mg/kg PO daily, for maintenance	**BLACK BOX WARNINGS (2)** Chronic immunosuppression can ↑ risk of neoplasia (esp. lymphomas) Hematologic toxicities (leukopenia, thrombocytopenia) and mutagenic potential **SIDE EFFECTS** GI upset (N/V), rash, ↑ LFTs, bone marrow suppression **MONITORING** LFTs, CBC, renal function **NOTES** Pregnancy Category D Patients with genetic deficiency of thiopurine methyltransferase (TPMT) will be more sensitive to myelosuppressive effects and may require a lower dose

Maintenance Medications Continued

DRUG	DOSING	SAFETY/SIDE EFFECTS/MONITORING

Calcineurin inhibitors – suppresses cellular immunity by inhibiting T-lymphocyte activation

Tacrolimus *(Prograf, Astagraf XL)* *Protopic* – topical for eczema	Initial: 0.1-0.2 mg/kg/day (depending on transplant type) in 2 divided doses, given every 12 hours Trough level varies, dependent on: 1. Transplant type 2. Number of months since transplant 3. Concurrent medications Example: trough level with mycophenolate and IL-2 receptor antagonist at months 1-12: 4-11 ng/mL	**BLACK BOX WARNINGS (4)** ↑ susceptibility to infection; possible development of lymphoma; not recommended in liver transplantation; should be administered under the supervision of a physician experienced in organ transplantation in a facility appropriate for monitoring and managing therapy **SIDE EFFECTS** Hypertension, nephrotoxicity, hyperglycemia, tremor, hyperkalemia, hypomagnesemia, edema, chest pain, headache, insomnia, generalized pain, dizziness, rash/pruritus, diarrhea, abdominal pain, nausea, dyspepsia, anorexia, constipation, urinary tract infection, anemia, leukopenia, leukocytosis, thrombocytopenia, elevated liver enzymes, paresthesia, arthralgia, hypophosphatemia, hyperlipidemia, hypokalemia, QT prolongation **MONITORING** Trough levels, serum electrolytes, renal function, hepatic function if liver transplant, blood pressure, blood glucose, electrolytes (especially potassium), lipid profile **NOTES** Should be taken on an empty stomach to avoid variability in absorption. If taking with food, take consistently. (Higher fat food decreases absorption the most.) Do not interchange XL to immediate release. Conversion IV to PO immediate-release is 1:4. Start oral dosing 8-12 hours after last IV dose. Most drugs will affect the tacrolimus level; this is a CYP 450 3A4 and P-gp substrate. Avoid alcohol.
CycloSPORINE *(Neoral, Gengraf, SandIMMUNE)* *Restasis* – for dry eyes	Dose depends on transplant type and formulation Cyclosporine (modified): Renal: 9 ± 3 mg/kg/day, divided twice daily Liver: 8 ± 4 mg/kg/day, divided twice daily Heart: 7 ± 3 mg/kg/day, divided twice daily Cyclosporine (non-modified): 3-10 mg/kg/day for maintenance Conversion to cyclosporine (modified) from cyclosporine (non-modified): Start with daily dose previously used and adjust to obtain pre-conversion cyclosporine trough concentration; monitor every 4-7 days and dose adjust as necessary Trough 100-400 ng/mL (nephrotoxicity can occur at any level)	**BLACK BOX WARNINGS (7)** Renal impairment (with high doses); ↑ risk of lymphoma and other malignancies; ↑ risk of skin cancer; ↑ risk of infection, may cause hypertension; dose adjustments should only be made under the direct supervision of an experienced physician; cyclosporine (modified – *Gengraf/Neoral)* has ↑ bioavailability compared to cyclosporine (non-modified – *Sandimmune)* and cannot be used interchangeably. **SIDE EFFECTS** Hypertension, nephropathy, hirsutism, gingival hyperplasia, edema, hyperglycemia, headache, paresthesia, abdominal discomfort/nausea/diarrhea, hypertrichosis, photosensitivity, increased triglycerides, urinary tract infection, viral infections, tremor, QT prolongation **MONITORING** Trough levels, serum electrolytes, renal function, hepatic function if liver transplant, blood pressure, blood glucose, electrolytes (especially potassium), lipid profile **NOTES** Most drugs will affect the cyclosporine level; this is a CYP 450 3A4 and P-gp substrate. Avoid alcohol.

Maintenance Medications Continued

DRUG	DOSING	SAFETY/SIDE EFFECTS/MONITORING

Mammalian target of rapamycin (mTOR) kinase inhibitor which inhibits T-lymphocyte activation and proliferation; may be synergistic with CNIs

Everolimus *(Zortress, Afinitor)* Tablets *(Afinitor, Zortress)* and tablets for oral suspension *(Afinitor Disperz)* are not interchangeable; *Afinitor Disperz* is only indicated for the treatment of subependymal giant cell astrocytoma (SEGA)	Initial: 0.75-1 mg PO twice daily; adjust maintenance dose if needed to reach serum level of 3-8 ng/mL	**BLACK BOX WARNINGS (5)** ↑ risk of infection; ↑ risk of lymphoma and skin cancer; reduced doses of cyclosporine are recommended when used concomitantly; ↑ risk of renal thrombosis may result in graft loss; not recommended in heart transplant **SIDE EFFECTS** Peripheral edema, constipation, hypertension, hyperglycemia, hyperlipidemia, delayed wound healing, pneumonitis, fatigue, fever, headache, seizures, behavioral changes (anxiety/ aggression), insomnia, dizziness, rash/pruritus, cellulitis, xeroderma, acne, onychoclasis (nail disease), hyperglycemia/ new onset diabetes, hypertriglyceridemia, decreased serum bicarbonate, hypophosphatemia, hypocalcemia, decreased serum albumin, hypoglycemia, hypokalemia, hyponatremia, hypomagnesemia, abdominal discomfort, nausea, stomatitis, diarrhea, amenorrhea, dysgeusia, weight loss, xerostomia, dysuria, anemia, prolonged PTT, lymphocytopenia, thrombocytopenia **MONITORING** Trough levels, renal function, liver function, lipids, blood glucose, BP, CBC, signs of infection
Sirolimus *(Rapamune)*	Usually 2-5 mg/day Serum drug concentrations should be determined 3-4 days after loading doses and 7-14 days after dosage adjustments; approximate range 4-12 ng/mL, level dependent on concurrent drug use, including potent inhibitors or inducers of CYP3A4 or P-gp.	**BLACK BOX WARNINGS (4)** ↑ risk of infection; ↑ risk of lymphoma; not recommended for use in liver transplantation; not recommended for use in lung transplantation **SIDE EFFECTS** Delayed wound healing, pneumonitis/bronchitis, cough, hyperglycemia, hyperlipidemia, peripheral edema, hypertension, headache, pain, insomnia, acne, constipation, abdominal pain, diarrhea, nausea, urinary tract infection, anemia, thrombocytopenia, arthralgia, nephrotoxicity **MONITORING** Trough levels, liver function, renal function, blood glucose, lipids, BP, CBC **NOTES** Tablets and oral solution are not bioequivalent due to differences in absorption

Maintenance Medications Continued

DRUG	DOSING	SAFETY/SIDE EFFECTS/MONITORING

Mammalian target of rapamycin (mTOR) kinase inhibitor which inhibits T-lymphocyte activation and proliferation

Belatacept *(Nulojix)* Administer with silicone-free disposable syringe (comes with drug)	Initial: 10 mg/kg/day Maintenance: 5 mg/kg/day Round doses to the nearest 12.5 mg, dose using TBW	**BLACK BOX WARNINGS (5)** Increased risk post-transplant lymphoproliferative disorder (PTLD); recipients without immunity to Epstein-Barr Virus (EBV) are at highest risk; use in EBV seropositive patients only. Increased susceptibility to infection and malignancies. Avoid use in liver transplant patients due to risk of transplant rejection and death. Should be administered under the supervision of a physician experienced in immunosuppressive therapy. **WARNINGS** Increased risk opportunistic infections, sepsis, and/or fatal infections. Increased risk tuberculosis (TB); test patients for latent TB prior to initiation, and treat latent TB infection prior to use. **SIDE EFFECTS** Headache, anemia, leukopenia, constipation, diarrhea, nausea, peripheral edema, hypertension, cough, photosensitivity, insomnia, urinary tract infection, pyrexia, hypo/hyperkalemia **MONITORING** New-onset or worsening neurological, cognitive, or behavioral signs/symptoms; signs/symptoms of infection, TB screening prior to therapy initiation, EBV seropositive verification prior to therapy initiation

Drug Interactions

Transplant drugs affect the levels of each other and the following interactions must be considered: Cyclosporine will ↓ mycophenolate and ↑ sirolimus and everolimus (and will increase some of the statins, which transplant patients are usually taking) and the mTor inhibitors (sirolimus and everolimus) are enzyme inhibitors and increase cyclosporine levels. Both cyclosporine and tacrolimus are CYP 450 3A4 and P-gp substrates. Inducers of either enzyme will decrease the CNI concentration, and inhibitors will increase the CNI concentration. Both will interact with the majority of drugs. Consistency is essential; the drug dose will be adjusted to the trough level. Tacrolimus absorption is decreased by food; take with or without, but consistently.

- Azathioprine – allopurinol, aspirin, ACE Is and sulfamethoxazole/trimethoprim may ↑ levels of azathioprine.

- Mycophenolate – can ↓ levels of hormonal contraception; mycophenolate levels can be ↓ by antacids and multivitamins, cyclosporine, metronidazole, proton pump inhibitors, fluoroquinolones, sevelamer, bile acid resins, and rifampin and derivatives. Acyclovir, valganciclovir and ganciclovir will ↑ mycophenolate.

- Avoid grapefruit juice and St. Johns wort with either CNI.

- Caution with additive drugs that are <u>nephrotoxic</u> with <u>tacrolimus and cyclosporine</u>.

- Caution with additive drugs that <u>raise blood glucose</u> with <u>tacrolimus, steroids, cyclosporine and the mTor inhibitors</u> (everolimus/sirolimus).

- Caution with additive drugs that worsen lipids with the <u>mTor inhibitors, steroids and cyclosporine</u>.

- Caution with additive drugs that <u>raise blood pressure</u> with <u>steroids, cyclosporine and tacrolimus</u>.

Patient Counseling for All Immunosuppressants

- Take the medication <u>exactly</u> as prescribed by your doctor. It is important that you take your medication at the same time every day. Also, <u>stay consistent</u> on how you take your medication.

- Never change or skip a dose of medication. Remember, if you stop taking your immunosuppressive medications, your body will reject your transplanted organ.

- Monitor your health at home and keep <u>daily</u> records of your <u>temperature, weight, blood pressure</u>, and glucose (if diabetes is present).

- Do <u>not</u> take any NSAIDs (e.g., *Advil, Naprosyn, Aleve)* as these drugs could cause harm to your kidneys.

- Do <u>not</u> take any over-the-counter, herbal, or alternative medications without consulting with your health care provider.

- Protect and cover your skin from the sun. Be sure to use sunscreen with a SPF of 30 or higher. Avoid using tanning beds or sunlamps. People who take immunosuppressive agents have a higher risk of getting skin cancer.

- Do not get immunizations/vaccinations without the consent of your doctor. The use of <u>live vaccines should definitely be avoided</u>. Avoid contact with people who have recently received oral polio vaccine or nasal flu vaccine.

- Patients are vulnerable to developing infections (severe infections) due to their suppressed immune system. Avoid contact with people who have the flu or other contagious illness. Practice infection control techniques such as good hand washing.

- Chronic immunosuppression has been associated with an increased risk of cancer, particularly lymphoma and skin cancer.

- If getting a blood test to measure the drug level, take your medication <u>after</u> you had your blood drawn (not before). It is important to measure the lowest (trough) level of drug in your blood.

Patient Counseling for Mycophenolate

- Take <u>exactly</u> as prescribed, every 12 hours (8 AM and 8 PM). It is important that you take your medication at the same time every day.

- If you miss a dose and it is <u>less than 4 hours after the scheduled dose, take the missed dose</u> and continue on your regular schedule. If you miss a dose and it is <u>more than 4 hours after your scheduled dose, skip the missed dose</u>, and return to your regular dosing schedule. Never take 2 doses at the same time. Record any missed doses.

- Take capsules, tablets and oral suspension <u>on an empty stomach</u>, either 1 hour before or 2 hours after a meal.

- Do not open or crush tablets or capsules. If you are not able to swallow tablets or capsules, your healthcare provider may prescribe an oral suspension. Your pharmacist will mix the medicine before giving it to you.

- Do not mix the oral suspension with any other medicine.

- This medication can cause <u>diarrhea</u>. Call your healthcare provider right away if you have diarrhea. Do not stop the medication without first talking with your healthcare provider. Other side effects include nausea, vomiting, abdominal pain/cramping, headache, and decreased white blood cells and platelets.

- Do not get pregnant while taking this medication. Women who take this medication during pregnancy have a higher risk of losing a pregnancy (miscarriage) during the first 3 months (first trimester), and a higher risk that their baby will be born with birth defects. Birth control pills do not work as well with this drug.

- <u>Do not take with antacids or multivitamins concurrently. Separate the doses by 2 hours. Avoid use with bile acid resins.</u>

- <u>Limit the amount of time you spend in sunlight.</u> Avoid using tanning beds or sunlamps. Use sunscreen with a SPF of 30 or higher. People who take this medicine have a higher risk of getting skin cancer.

- <u>Mycophenolic acid *(Myfortic)* and mycophenolate mofetil *(CellCept)* are not interchangeable. Do not switch between products unless directed by your healthcare provider. These medicines are absorbed differently. This may affect the amount of medicine in your blood.</u>

Patient Counseling for Tacrolimus

- Take this medication as directed by your doctor, usually every 12 hours. It is best to take on an empty stomach for best absorption. However it is taken, you must be consistent (with food or without food) and take this medication the same way everyday so that your body always absorbs the same amount of drug.

- It is important to take all doses on time to keep the amount of medicine in your body at a constant level. Remember to take it at the same times each day. Patients should be informed of the need for repeated appropriate laboratory tests while they are receiving tacrolimus. They should be given complete dosage instructions, advised of the potential risks during pregnancy, and informed of the increased risk of neoplasia. Patients should be informed that changes in dosage should not be undertaken without first consulting their physician.

- If you miss a dose and it is <u>less than 4 hours after the scheduled dose, take the missed dose</u> and continue on your regular schedule. If you miss a dose and it is <u>more than 4 hours after your scheduled dose, skip the missed dose</u>, and return to your regular dosing schedule. Never take 2 doses at the same time. Record any missed doses.

- As with other immunosuppressive agents, owing to the potential risk of malignant skin changes, exposure to sunlight and ultraviolet (UV) light should be limited by wearing protective clothing and using a sunscreen with a SPF of 30 or higher.

- <u>Avoid eating grapefruit or drinking grapefruit juice</u> while being treated with tacrolimus. Grapefruit can increase the amount of tacrolimus in your bloodstream.

- Tacrolimus may cause your blood pressure to increase. You may be required to check your blood pressure periodically and/or take another medication to control your blood pressure.

- Side effects of tacrolimus also include tremors/shaking, headache, diarrhea, nausea/vomiting, upset stomach, loss of appetite, tingling of the hands/feet, increased blood pressure, increased cholesterol, increased blood sugar, and increase in potassium levels.

- <u>Tacrolimus may cause diabetes.</u> Tell your doctor or pharmacist if you experience any of the following symptoms of high blood sugar: increased thirst/hunger or frequent urination.

- Tacrolimus may cause a condition that affects the heart rhythm (QT prolongation). QT prolongation can infrequently result in serious fast/irregular heartbeat and other symptoms (such as severe dizziness, fainting) that require immediate medical attention. The risk of QT prolongation may be increased if you have certain medical conditions or are taking other drugs that may affect the heart rhythm. Before using tacrolimus, tell your doctor or pharmacist if you have any of the following conditions: certain heart problems (heart failure, slow heartbeat, QT prolongation in the ECG), family history of certain heart problems (QT prolongation or sudden cardiac death).

- High (or low) levels of potassium or magnesium in the blood may also increase your risk of QT prolongation. This risk may increase if you use certain drugs (such as diuretics/"water pills") or if you have conditions such as severe sweating, diarrhea, or vomiting. This drug may increase your potassium levels.

Patient Counseling for Cyclosporine (using *Neoral* as an example)

- Because different brands deliver different amounts of medication, <u>do not switch brands of cyclosporine without your doctor's permission and directions.</u>

- Patients should be advised to take *Neoral* on a consistent schedule with regard to time of day and relation to meals. <u>Grapefruit and grapefruit juice affect metabolism</u>, increasing blood concentration of cyclosporine, thus <u>should be avoided.</u>

- If you miss a dose and it is <u>less than 4 hours after the scheduled dose, take the missed dose</u> and continue on your regular schedule. If you miss a dose and it is <u>more than 4 hours after your scheduled dose, skip the missed dose</u>, and return to your regular dosing schedule. Never take 2 doses at the same time. Record any missed doses.

- Patients should be informed of the necessity of repeated laboratory tests while they are receiving cyclosporine. Laboratory tests (e.g., kidney function tests, blood tests) may be performed to monitor your progress. If getting a blood test to measure the drug level, take your medication <u>after</u> you had your blood drawn.

- Patients should be given careful dosage instructions. *Neoral* Oral Solution (cyclosporine oral solution, USP) Modified should be diluted, preferably with orange or apple juice that is at room temperature. Do not administer oral liquid from plastic or styrofoam cup. The combination of *Neoral* Oral Solution (cyclosporine oral solution, USP) Modified with milk can be unpalatable. *(Sandimmune* may be diluted with milk, chocolate milk, or orange juice). Avoid changing diluents frequently. Mix thoroughly and drink at once. Use syringe provided to measure dose, mix in glass container and rinse container with more diluent to ensure total dose was taken.

- Cyclosporine can also cause <u>high blood pressure</u> and <u>kidney problems</u>. The risk of both problems increases with higher doses and longer treatment with this drug.

- Side effects of cyclosporine also include increased cholesterol, headache, nausea, vomiting, diarrhea, stomach upset, increased hair growth on the face/body, tremor, swollen/red/painful gums, and acne. If any of these effects persist or worsen, notify your doctor or pharmacist promptly.

- This drug may increase your risk for developing skin cancer. Avoid prolonged sun exposure, tanning booths and sunlamps. Use a sunscreen, SPF 30 or higher, and wear protective clothing when outdoors.

- This medication <u>may cause swelling and growth of the gums (gingival hyperplasia).</u> Brush your teeth and floss daily to minimize this problem. See your dentist regularly.

OSTEOPOROSIS & HORMONE THERAPY

GUIDELINE

American College of Obstetricians and Gynecologist's Clinical Management Guideline for Osteoporosis, 2012; 120(3):718-729.

BACKGROUND

Osteoporosis, which means "porous bones," causes bones to become weak and brittle. Falls can cause a bone to fracture. If the bones are extremely porous, coughing or rolling over in bed can cause fractures. The most common location of a fracture is the lower (lumbar) spine. These vertebrae turn over more rapidly (higher rate of cell turnover) than hip bones, and are holding the weight of the upper spine and head.

Hip fractures occur with more severe disease (or bad falls) and can be debilitating. A hip fracture in a woman has a 25% risk of mortality at one year, and is higher in men, since men with osteoporosis are often using long-term steroids or androgen blockers and may be sicker at baseline. Hip fractures, if not fatal, can lead to loss of independence and/or chronic pain. Wrist fracture, which appears often in younger woman, may be an early warning sign of poor bone health.

DIAGNOSIS/DEFINITIONS

Osteoporosis is defined by a T-score <-2.5. Osteopenia is lower bone density than normal, but not as low as osteoporosis. Osteopenia is defined by a T-score between -1 and -2.5.

Notice that the scores are negative; a T-score from -1 and higher indicates normal bone density. A higher number correlates with stronger (denser) bones, which are less likely to fracture. The T-score is calculated by comparing the woman's bone mineral density (BMD) to the average peak BMD of a normal, young adult of the same gender. Z-scores compare the patient's bone mineral density (BMD) to the mean BMD of women her age and are sometimes included in the report.

Osteoblasts are the cells involved in bone formation, and osteoclasts break-down bone; that is, they are involved in resorption. Bone is not "dead tissue"; it is living and constantly re-models, although some types of bone remodels very slowly, and others remodel at a faster rate. The older medications (estrogen, raloxifene, bisphosphonates) slow down bone break-down, or resorption. Newer agents that both prevent bone break-down and help to build bone are the strongest agents and are reserved for higher-risk patients.

A bone scan is performed by a dual energy x-ray absorptiometry (DEXA, or DXA) machine. The results are reported for several high-risk locations, including hips and the lumbar vertebrae. Ultrasound devices are not optimal, yet they are less expensive and do not emit radiation. An ultrasound reading provides bone density in one location, such as the heel. An ultrasound reading, if low, should encourage the patient to get a DEXA scan. All women at age 65 should receive a DEXA, and in women younger than 65 years, bone density can be determined earlier if there is a history of a fragility fracture, low BMI, medical or drug-induced bone loss, parental history of hip fracture, current smoker, alcoholism or rheumatoid arthritis. In addition to monitoring the BMD over time, biochemical markers of bone turnover are also useful.

Fracture Risk Assessment Tool (FRAX)

The FRAX tool estimates the risk of fracture in the next 10 years (http://www.sheffield.ac.uk/FRAX/). It has been well-validated and use is recommended in the ACOG guidelines to determine if medication therapy is warranted. FRAX is a computer-aided program. The patient's age, sex, BMI, previous fragility fracture, parental hip fracture, current smoking status, steroid use (greater than 5 mg prednisolone per day for three months), alcohol intake and a few other measures are entered to assess the usefulness (risk/benefit) of drug therapy.

Phases of Bone Loss

Bone accumulates until approximately age 30. After that, the initial phase of bone loss occurs throughout life. Men lose bone at a rate of 0.2-0.5%

RISK FACTORS FOR LOW BONE DENSITY

GENETIC factors are most important, with Caucasian and Asian American women at highest risk
Advanced age

Low bone mineral density (usually evidenced by the T-score)

Previous fracture as an adult (other than skull, facial bone, ankle, finger or toe)

More than 2 alcoholic drinks per day

Oral or IM glucocorticoid use for > 3 months at a daily dose of 5 mg prednisone equivalent, or greater.

Body weight < 127 pounds
or low BMI < 21 kg/m²

A decline in adult estrogen levels, from menopause, anorexia nervosa, lactation, hypogonadism

Rheumatoid arthritis and Lupus

Low level of physical activity and adequate nutrition – low over the life span

Calcium and vitamin D – low intake over life span

Smoking

DRUGS AND OSTEOPOROSIS RISK

Steroid use, long-term, is the major drug-contributing factor to poor bone health (≥5 mg/d of prednisone equivalent for ≥3 months). Other medications that lower bone density include:

Depot medroxyprogesterone acetate

Anticonvulsants (carbamazepine, fosphenytoin, phenobarbital, phenytoin, primidone)

Warfarin and heparin

Excess thyroid hormone

Loop diuretics

Aromatase inhibitors used for breast CA

Nafarelin (Synarel) – used for endometriosis

Androgen blockers used for prostate CA

Proton pump inhibitors used chronically (↓ calcium absorption due to ↓ gastric pH)

per year, unless they use drugs that accelerate bone loss (such as long-term steroids) or prostate cancer agents. Women lose bone slowly after peak bone growth, and then at an increased rate in the 10 years from menopause (1-5% bone loss per year) and then at a slower rate thereafter.

Fall Risk/Fall Prevention Measures

If the bone density is low, care must be taken to avoid falls. Factors that put a patient at increased fall risk include the use of drugs that cause CNS depression or cause falls by another mechanism (such as SSRIs), any condition that causes physical instability or tremor, impaired vision, dementia, poor health/frailty, low physical activity and a history of recent falls. The ACOG guidelines recommend checking that lighting is appropriate, floors are safe (throw rugs/clutter/cords have been removed), storage is at reasonable heights, bathrooms have safety bars and nonskid floors, handrails are present on all stairs, and the stairs are well-lit with non-skid treads or carpet.

Additional "Lifestyle" Recommendations

In addition to the changes in the environment listed above, all patients with low bone density should be encouraged to perform weight-bearing exercise (such as walking), taking adequate vitamin D and calcium, stopping smoking and avoiding secondhand smoke, reducing alcohol intake and adopting fall prevention strategies.

Preventing falls requires measures to improve muscle strength, balance and vision. Adequate corrective lenses, safe shoes and appropriate clothing (that will not cause falls) are required. If a disability is present, canes or walkers should be strongly recommended.

OSTEOPOROSIS IN MEN

When men get an osteoporotic fracture, they are generally sick, such as men with prostate cancer (on androgen-blocking agents) or with COPD (receiving series of systemic steroids), with rheumatoid arthritis, or other bone-debilitating conditions. In these patients, fractures have high fatality as the patient is weak. Recently, there has been increased emphasis on preventing and treating osteoporosis in men.

Typically, bisphosphonates are used. It is still necessary to limit treatment duration (3-5 years), as is done with females. High-risk agents *(Forteo, Prolia)* are other options, depending on the risk and condition. Men, as with women, will require adequate calcium and vitamin D.

CALCIUM & VITAMIN D

All prescription medications for low bone density require adequate calcium and vitamin D taken concurrently. Dietary intake of calcium should be assessed first and is preferred, and supplements used if insufficient. Over half of the US population has low calcium and vitamin D intake. Adequate calcium intake is required throughout life, and is critically important in children (who can build bone stores), in pregnancy (when the fetus can deplete the mother's stores if intake is insufficient) and during the years around menopause, when bone loss is rapid. <u>Vitamin D is required for calcium absorption, and low levels contribute to various health conditions, including autoimmune conditions and cancer.</u> <u>Vitamin D deficiency in children causes rickets</u>, and in <u>adults causes osteomalacia</u> (softening of the bone, with low levels of collagen and calcium). In 2010 there were news reports that calcium supplementation may increase heart attack risk; at present, recommend that patients use the recommended levels and <u>use calcium with vitamin D</u> – the increased risk was seen in patients who did not use vitamin D with calcium. If possible obtain calcium from food sources.

NIH's Recommended Adequate Intakes (AIs) for Calcium (2010)

AGE	MALE	FEMALE	PREGNANT	LACTATING
0-6 months	210 mg	210 mg		
7-12 months	270 mg	270 mg		
1-3 years	500 mg	500 mg		
4-8 years	800 mg	800 mg		
9-13 years	1,300 mg	1,300 mg		
14-18 years	1,300 mg	1,300 mg	1,300 mg	1,300 mg
19-50 years	1,000 mg	1,000 mg	1,000 mg	1,000 mg
50+ years	1,200 mg	1,200 mg		

Notes on calcium selection & absorption

- <u>Calcium absorption is saturable; doses should be divided.</u>

- Dietary calcium is generally not sufficient; most women need an additional 600-900 mg/day (2 to 3 dairy portions) to reach recommended levels.

- Calcium requires vitamin D for absorption.

- Calcium citrate *(Citracal,* others) has better absorption but is a larger tablet to swallow and can be taken with or without food; usually tab has 315 mg calcium. It may be preferable with little or no stomach acid – such as with the use of PPIs, which have been shown to increase fracture risk due to impaired calcium carbonate absorption (including the dietary calcium).

- Calcium carbonate *(Oscal, Tums,* others) has acid-dependent absorption and should be taken with meals; usually tab is 500-600 mg.

- There is no known benefit of using more expensive formulations – recommend products made by reputable manufacturers, since lead may be present in untested products.

- Both forms come as chewables and in food products.

NOTES ON VITAMIN D SELECTION

- The NIH's recommended intake for vitamin D for people up to age 70 years is 600 IU daily, and 71+ years is 800 IU daily. However, these levels are currently controversial and many endocrinologists are recommending a higher intake of 800-2,000 IU daily. The Institute of Medicine has a recommended upper intake of 4,000 IU daily for adolescents and adults. The recent ACOG guidelines recommend the same amounts. A few years ago vitamin D levels were not routinely ordered; this has become commonplace. A serum vitamin D level of 20 ng/mL (50 nmol/L) is adequate for most people.

- The 50,000 unit vitamin D2 supplement (the green capsules) are used in renal disease or short-term in adults with deficiency to replenish stores. Cholecalciferol, or vitamin D3, is the preferred source, although vitamin D2 is often the type in supplements and will provide benefit. In the renal chapter calcitriol and vitamin D analogs are discussed, which are used in advanced renal disease.

DRUG TREATMENT

Bisphosphonates are used first-line in most patients. They increase bone density more than estrogen and raloxifene, and reduce fracture risk. Patients with gastrointestinal problems with oral bisphophonates may prefer an injectable bisphosphonate. Or, adherence issues may make an annual infusion of zoledronic acid preferable.

Duration of bisphosphonate therapy: Due to the risk of atypical femur fracture, esophageal cancer and osteonecrosis of the jaw, bisposphonates should be stopped after 3-5 years. The patient should be switched to a completely different class of drug, such as denosumab, although atypical fractures and osteonecrosis of the jaw has also been reported with this drug class. Alternatively, a younger woman in her 50's may begin with estrogen or the estrogen agonist/antagonist raloxifene (if no contraindications) and then switch to a bisphosphonate in her 60's when the risk for hip fracture and venous thrombosis increase.

Teriparatide injection *(Forteo)* is used in patients with osteoporosis who are at high risk for having fractures, or have already had an osteoporotic fracture, or have OP and need to take long-term steroids, or who cannot tolerate bisphosphonates. The newer agent denosumab *(Prolia)* is difficult to administer (it must be given in a doctor's office) and is expensive; it is also reserved for those with high risk.

Estrogen is no longer used first-line for osteoporosis because of health risks. However, if used for menopausal symptoms, estrogen does increase bone density. Estrogen may be appropriate short-term in younger women without contraindications and can be useful due to time limits currently being used for bisphosphonates. Raloxifene can be used similarly, and is used most commonly in women who are at risk or have fear of breast cancer. Calcitonin is used less often than in previous years since the evidence of benefit for bone density improvement is poor.

Osteoporosis Treatment & Prevention Options

DRUG	DOSING	SAFETY/SIDE EFFECTS/MONITORING

Bisphosphonates work by inhibiting osteoclast activity. Used for prevention (osteopenia), treatment (osteoporosis), Paget's disease, glucocorticoid-induced osteoporosis (and zoledronic acid is also used for hypercalcemia of malignancy.)

DRUG	DOSING	SAFETY/SIDE EFFECTS/MONITORING
Alendronate *(Fosamax, Binosto)* Bisphosphonates are 1st line for most patients	5 mg PO daily prevention; 10 mg PO daily treatment 35 mg PO weekly for prevention; 70 mg PO weekly alone or with vit D3 2,800 or 5,600 IU (cholecalciferol) or 70 mg/75 mL solution – after drink at least 2 oz plain water (tablets need to be taken with 6-8 oz of plain water) GIO-induced OP: 5 mg PO daily or 10 mg PO daily if postmenopausal female not on estrogen Paget's disease: 40 mg PO daily x 6 months	**CONTRAINDICATIONS** Inability to stand or sit upright for at least 30 minutes (60 minutes with once-monthly *Boniva*) Hypocalcemia Creatinine clearance < 35 mL/min (some are < 30 mL/min) **WARNINGS** FDA Warning: Due to the risk of atypical femur fracture, esophageal cancer and osteonecrosis of the jaw, bisposphonates should be stopped after 3-5 years. Bone, joint or muscle pain, which may be severe. Esophagitis, dysphagia, esophageal ulcers, esophageal erosions and esophageal stricture (rare). Osteonecrosis of the jaw; risk increases with dental surgery, poor dental hygiene, cancer.
Risedronate *(Actonel, Atelvia)* *Actonel + Calcium:* 35 mg weekly and Ca²⁺ carb 500 mg x 6 days *Atelvia* is long-acting risedronate that is taken after breakfast, with 4 oz water	5 mg PO daily, or 35 mg PO weekly or 75 mg PO on 2 consecutive days/ month 150 mg PO/once once monthly	**SIDE EFFECTS** Hypocalcemia (mild, transient), back pain, arthralgias, dyspepsia, N/V, dysphagia, heartburn, esophagitis (may ↑ esophageal cancer risk long-term, much higher with Paget's dose), – if GI issues consider injectable bisphosphonate **NOTES** With *Atelvia*, no H₂RAs or PPIs. Separate calcium, iron and magnesium supplements (separate time)
Ibandronate *(Boniva)*	150 mg PO monthly 3 mg IV every 3 months	Due to risk of jaw decay/necrosis – get dental work done before starting therapy Due to transient hypocalcemia when initiating check calcium and vitamin D levels prior to start

Osteoporosis Treatment & Prevention Options Continued

DRUG	DOSING	SAFETY/SIDE EFFECTS/MONITORING

Injectable Bisphosphonate

| **Zoledronic Acid *(Reclast)***

 Zometa – for hypercalcemia of malignancy | 5 mg infusion yearly for treatment, every 2 years for prevention (chemo dose is 4 mg) | **SIDE EFFECTS**
 No GI problems (bypasses gut), but can cause all others, and TPS (transient post-dose syndrome) in 25-40% of patients on days 2-3 post-injection: flu-like symptoms such as achiness, runny nose, headache, taking NSAIDs prior and afterwards can ↓ symptoms

 NOTES
 Do not use in patients with CrCl < 35 mL/min |

Raloxifene is an Estrogen Agonist/Antagonist, Also Called a Selective Estrogen Receptor Modulator (SERM) and ↓ bone resorption

| **Raloxifene *(Evista)***

 Used often in women at risk (or have fear of) breast CA | 60 mg PO daily

 Favorable lipid effects (↓ CH and LDL; no effect on HDL and TGs) | **BLACK BOX WARNINGS (2)**
 ↑ risk of thromboembolic events (DVT, PE, MI, stroke)

 The risk of death due to stroke may be increased in women with coronary heart disease or in women at risk for coronary events

 SIDE EFFECTS
 Hot flashes, peripheral edema, hot flashes, arthralgia, leg cramps/muscle spasms, flu-like syndrome, infection, amenorrhea, vaginal bleeding/discharge, skin changes

 NOTES
 Pregnany Category X |

Calcitonin Nasal Spray and Injection – inhibits osteoclastic bone resorption

| Calcitonin *(Miacalcin, Fortical)*

 Not in current guidelines as recommended agent | Inhale 1 spray (200 IU) daily (alternate nostril daily)

 Or SC or IM: 100 IU every other day | **CONTRAINDICATIONS**
 Allergy to calcitonin-salmon

 SIDE EFFECTS
 Rhinitis

 NOTES
 Keep unused bottles refrigerated.

 Possible antibody development to salmon that reduces efficacy.

 Not recommended agent in current guidelines. |

Teriparatide Injection – stimulates new bone formation and depresses osteoclast activity; recombinant human PTH 1-34

| **Teriparatide *(Forteo)***

 For patients who are at very high risk for fracture, or who have already had a fracture due to osteoporosis, or for GIO, or if cannot take other medications | 20 mcg SC inj daily for max of 2 years

 If bone pain with bisphosphonates it is less risky (although painful) than with teriparatide; bone pain from this drug could be bone cancer | **BLACK BOX WARNING**
 Osteosarcoma (bone cancer)

 WARNINGS
 Orthostatic hypotension, use cautiously if Hx or current urolithiasis (kidney stones)

 SIDE EFFECTS
 Orthostasis/dizziness, ↑ HR (especially with 1st few doses), injection site pain, hypocalcemia (transient, post-dose)

 NOTES
 28-day pen, keep refrigerated, inject in thigh or abdomen, sit or lie down due to tachycardia, dizziness post-shot |

Osteoporosis Treatment & Prevention Options Continued

DRUG	DOSING	SAFETY/SIDE EFFECTS/MONITORING

Monoclonal Antibody that binds to nuclear factor-kappa ligand (RANKL) and prevents interaction between RANKL and RANK, preventing osteoclast formation; leads to decreased bone resorption and increased bone mass

Denosumab *(Prolia)* *Xgeva* – for hypercalcemia of malignancy High Risk, or cannot use other agents	60 mg SC inj (in MD's office) every 6 months	**CONTRAINDICATIONS** Hypocalcemia-check levels prior to using drug **WARNINGS** Esophagitis, dysphagia, esophageal ulcers, esophageal erosions and esophageal stricture (rare), osteonecrosis of the jaw; risk increases with dental surgery or poor dental hygiene, cancer, atypical femur fractures, dermatitis/eczema/rash, anaphylaxis risk, hypocalcemia-monitor levels, use cautiously if hypoparathyroidism or thyroid surgery or infection **SIDE EFFECTS** Fatigue, hypocalcemia (correct), eczema, rash, weakness, arthralgia/weakness/limb pain, nausea, dyspnea, cough

Bisphosphonate Counseling

- Take first thing in the morning before you eat or drink anything else except 6-8 ounces (1 cup) of plain water. If you are using formulations that are not once daily (such as weekly), choose the day of the week that is easy to remember (such as Sunday if you going to church, or bridge day, etc.)

- Take the medicine while you are sitting up or standing and stay upright for at least 30 minutes (60 minutes with monthly *Boniva)*. During this time, you cannot eat or drink anything else except more plain water. You cannot take any other medicines or vitamins. Nothing but plain water!

- This medicine must be swallowed whole, and washed down with water. Do not crush or chew the tablet or keep it in your mouth to melt or dissolve.

- This medicine does not work well if you are not taking enough calcium and vitamin D. Some formulations contain calcium or vitamin D. Discuss with your pharmacist if you need to use calcium or vitamin D supplements.

- If you are using a proton pump inhibitor for heartburn, discuss with your pharmacist. These drugs may increase fracture risk. You may need to use a calcium citrate tablet, with adequate vitamin D.

- Your bone and muscle strength will improve faster if you are doing exercise. Your physician should discuss with you safe and healthy ways to exercise.

- Common side effects include GI upset, joint pain, back pain, dyspepsia or heartburn.

- Stop taking the medicine if you develop difficult or painful swallowing, have chest pain, have very bad heartburn that doesn't get better, or have severe pain in the bones, joints or muscles.

- Some patients have developed serious <u>jaw-bone problems</u> after using this medicine, which may include infection and slower healing after teeth are pulled. Tell your healthcare providers, including your dentist, right away if you have these symptoms. <u>If you have dental work due now, you should have it done before starting the medicine.</u>

Atelvia: This is a long-acting form of risedronate. Take the medicine <u>after breakfast</u>. Sit or stand upright for thirty minutes or longer after taking. <u>Do not use</u> acid suppressing "heartburn" therapy with this medicine. Do not take Calcium, iron, magnesium or multivitamin supplements until later in the day.

Bisphosphonate Missed Doses

- If on weekly schedule and missed one dose, take the following morning (but not 2 doses in 1 day).

- If on daily schedule missed one dose, skip until next dose.

- If on monthly *Boniva* and miss a dose, take it as soon as you remember (in the morning before eating) except if it is less than one week to the next dose, skip it (can't take 2 doses in one week).

For *Reclast* Injection

- Make sure patient is not using *Zometa* (used for hypercalcemia of malignancy) since it is the same drug. Immediately after injection, low serum calcium can occur. This is aggravated if on aminoglycosides, and these should not be used concurrently.

- It is necessary to take 1,500 mg calcium in divided doses (2-3 doses daily) for the 2 weeks after the injection and 1,200 mg the rest of the year, and 800 IU vitamin D throughout the year.

Teriparatide Counseling

- Please read the Medication Guide. During the drug testing process, *Forteo* caused some rats to develop a bone cancer called osteosarcoma. Osteosarcoma has been reported rarely in people who took *Forteo*. The warning states that it is not known if people who use *Forteo* have a higher chance of getting osteosarcoma.

- <u>You may feel dizzy or have a fast heartbeat after the first few doses</u>. In case you experience these symptoms, <u>inject this medication where you can sit or lie down right away if necessary</u>; most people sit on the side of the bed to inject.

- Inform your doctor if you develop bone or joint pain.

- The medicine comes in a prefilled injection pen that lasts 28 days. Each injection provides a 20-mcg dose. You should change the needle each day.

- The pen should be kept in the <u>refrigerator</u> and re-capped after each use. <u>After 28 days, the pen should be discarded</u> even if some medicine remains. There is a place at the end of the user manual to mark the date when the pen is started and the date (28 days later) when the pen should be thrown away.

- Inject one time each day in your <u>thigh or abdomen</u> (lower stomach area). The injection sites must be rotated.

- Do not transfer the medicine from the delivery device to a syringe. The injection pen is set at the right dose and does not require any dose adjustment.

- You can inject at any time of the day. Take it at about the same time each day.

- If you forget or cannot take the medicine at your usual time, take it as soon as you can on that day. Do not take more than one injection in the same day.

- <u>Do not exceed 2 years of use</u>.

- This medicine does not work well if you are not taking enough calcium and vitamin D. Discuss with your pharmacist if you need to use calcium or vitamin D supplements.

- If you are using a proton pump inhibitor for heartburn, discuss with your pharmacist. <u>These drugs may increase fracture risk</u>. You may need to use a calcium citrate tablet, with adequate vitamin D.

Calcitonin Nasal Spray Counseling

- This medicine is sprayed in one nostril daily. The other nostril is used the following day.

- A common side effect you may experience are nasal symptoms, including nasal irritation.

- Keep unused bottles in the refrigerator, but not the one being used. When a new bottle is removed it should be allowed to reach room temperature prior to priming. To prime the pump, hold the bottle upright and press the 2 white side arms toward the bottle until a faint spray is seen. Once the pump is primed, it does not have to be re-primed if the bottle is stored in an upright position.

- Before using, allow the product to reach room temperature.

- To use the nasal spray, remove the protective cap, keep head upright and insert the tip into a nostril. Press down firmly on the pump to deliver the medication. Use the other nostril the next day.

- After 30 doses, the pump may not deliver the correct amount of medicine with each spray and should be discarded.

- The bottle should last for 30 doses (even though there may still be product in the bottle after 30 days, subsequent sprays may not deliver full doses). Store the bottle you are using at room temperature and store extra bottles in the refrigerator.

- This medicine does not work well if you are not taking enough calcium and vitamin D. Some formulations contain calcium or vitamin D. Discuss with your pharmacist if you need to use calcium or vitamin D supplements.

- If you are using a proton pump inhibitor for heartburn, discuss with your pharmacist. These drugs may increase fracture risk. You may need to use a calcium citrate tablet, with adequate vitamin D.

Hormone Therapy (HT)

HT is used for women who are in the peri-menopause, or what is commonly referred to as menopause (menopause technically means that menses has ceased for 12 months.) Peri-menopause normally occurs between the ages of 45 and 55. Many women experience vaso-motor symptoms as their ovaries produces less estrogen. A decrease in estrogen causes an increase in luteinizing hormone (LH), which can result in hot flashes and night sweats (hot flashes that occur during sleep). Sleep can be disturbed, and mood changes may be present. Due to a decline in estrogen in the vaginal mucosa, vaginal dryness, burning and painful intercourse may be present.

Some women remain largely asymptomatic during menopause. In others the symptoms can be quite bothersome. Women who have had their ovaries removed, or are receiving anti-estrogen therapy for cancer may experience similar symptoms, but more acutely initially due to a sudden, rather than gradual, estrogen decline.

Estrogen-Progestin Use: Health Risks/Considerations For Use

The most effective therapy for vasomotor symptoms (hot flashes, night sweats) is estrogen, which causes a decrease in LH, and, consequently, more stable temperature control. Estrogen improves bone density and has historically been used to prevent postmenopausal osteoporosis. Estrogen is not a strong enough bone density agent to be used for treatment.

In women with a uterus, estrogen should not be given alone. This will put the woman at elevated risk for endometrial cancer – the risk is 5 times higher if using estrogen alone for 3+ years. Progestins can cause mood disturbances in some women, and may be hard to tolerate. If given intermittently, such as with *Premphase*, spotting can be a nuisance.

Several years ago the data from large trials on hormone therapy became available – these were the Women's Health Initiative (WHI) postmenopausal hormone therapy trials. At first, the news was scary and led to several black box warnings on the use of HT, including warnings for increased risk of stroke, heart attacks and probable risk of dementia.

As the data was reanalyzed, it became apparent that the majority of risk was highest in older women. Currently, the following considerations for use should be followed:

- Hormone therapy is safest around the time of menopause, and can be used in younger women, without contraindications, such as cancer or clotting history. The hormone therapy will likely be discontinued as the woman gets older (typically after 7-10 years use), at which time the risk for complications, such as thrombosis, increase.

- The "lowest possible dose for the shortest possible time" should be chosen.

- Estrogen with progestin increases breast cancer risk, and the use of this combination should be limited to 3-5 years. Recall that women with a uterus need a progestin to reduce the risk of endometrial cancer.

- Bioidentical Hormone Replacement Therapy (BHRT, discussed below) may or may not be safer; the risk/benefit profile is unknown, at present.

Bioidentical Hormone Replacement Therapy (BHRT), other "Natural" Formulations

The warnings for HT therapy are based on the analysis of the WHI data and do not distinguish between hormone type. In the future, when more information is available, these warnings should be refined. At present it is safest to assume that known risk for one estrogen formulation applies to others. Some women will prefer to use compounded formulations.

In the WHI trial, the estrogen component was *Premarin*, or conjugated estrogens made from desiccated mare (horse) urine. Many clinicians (and patients) prefer to use "natural" hormones such as estradiol, a hormone made by human females. It is interesting to note that estradiol is made by pre-, rather than post-menopausal women.

The term "bioidentical" generally refers to compounds that have the same chemical and molecular structure as hormones that are produced in the human body. Many woman, physicians and compounding pharmacists believe that BHRT is safer, but keep in mind that there are no well-designed studies to confirm risk or benefit. If a woman is using BHRT products and feels better, this is important. She should understand the risks that may be present (it is safest to assume risks known from available trial data (above) for any hormone therapy, until proven otherwise.)

Natural Products Used for Vasomotor Symptoms

Natural products used for vasomotor symptoms include black cohosh, red clover, soy, flaxseed and evening primrose. The mild "plant estrogens," such as soy, are called phytoestrogens; phyto means plant. These natural products may help a little bit with mild symptoms, but would not provide the benefit of estrogen due to the strong feedback inhibition on LH.

Estrogen in any form has the following contraindications:

- Undiagnosed abnormal genital bleeding

- Active or past breast cancer

- Known or suspected estrogen-dependent cancer

- Active or past deep vein thrombosis or pulmonary embolism

- Active or recent arterial thromboembolic disease (e.g., stroke, myocardial infarction)

- Liver dysfunction or disease

- Known or suspected pregnancy

Formulation Considerations

Topical formulations, given as a patch, gel or emulsion, bypass first dose metabolism, and lower doses can be used. Topical formulations usually cause less nausea and may expose the woman to lower systemic estrogen. Estrogen use is generally well tolerated, but can cause nausea, dizziness, bloating and breast tenderness/fullness.

Vaginal products are most useful for patients who have vaginal symptoms (dryness, painful intercourse) only, and expose the woman to less risk than from systemic estrogen. Due to bypassing the liver, topical formulations do not affect cholesterol levels.

Estrogen typically ↑ TG and ↑ HDL. In some women the use of estrogen can ↑ TGs about 25% and may put them into a danger zone, but in others the ↑ HDL may be beneficial.

SSRI to Reduce Hot Flashes

Paroxetine (*Brisdelle*) is the first non-hormonal treatment to reduce moderate-severe hot flashes associated with menopause. This will be used in older women who have higher incidence of warfarin and tamoxifen use and *Brisdelle* should not be used with either. As an SSRI, it will increase the risk of bleeding, and as a CYP450 2D6 inhibitor, it will block the effectiveness of tamoxifen and will block the metabolism of warfarin, causing bleeding risk. Women in the perimenopause may have accidental pregnancy as the menstrual cycle has become irregular; they should be counseled to use effective birth control. *Brisdelle* is Pregnancy Category X (other forms of paroxetine are pregnancy category D, due to cardiovascular risks in the newborn, and with paroxetine specifically, a high risk of withdrawal effects in the newborn post-delivery.

DRUG	DOSING	SAFETY/SIDE EFFECTS/MONITORING
PARoxetine *(Brisdelle)* *Paxil, Pexeva, Paxil CR*-for depression	7.5 mg PO QHS	**BLACK BOX WARNING** Antidepressants increase the risk of suicidal thinking and behavior in children, adolescents, and young adults (18-24 years of age) with major depressive disorder (MDD) and other psychiatric disorders; consider risk prior to prescribing. **CONTRAINDICATIONS/WARNINGS** Same as with other use; see Depression chapter (wash-out required between paroxetine and MAO Is, serotonergic, slow taper with discontinuation, hyponatremia, QT prolongation). **SIDE EFFECTS** Sexual side effects same as with other use, and in the *Brisdelle* trials > 10% incidence for sedation, insomnia, restlessness, tremor, dizziness/weakness, nausea, xerostomia, constipation, diaphoresis **NOTES** Lag time to effect (~4 weeks) Preg Category X Do not use with warfarin (↑ bleeding risk) or tamoxifen (↓ efficacy tamoxifen)

Common HRT Products (Not Complete List – There Are Many)

DRUG	COMPONENTS	SAFETY/SIDE EFFECTS/MONITORING
Activella	estradiol/norethindrone PO	**CONTRAINDICATIONS** For further discussion see Contraception chapter Undiagnosed abnormal vaginal bleeding, any clotting incident or disorder (DVT, PE, MI, CVA, etc.), liver disease, pregnancy, any hormone-dependent cancer
Vivelle, Vivelle-Dot	estradiol transdermal system Twice-weekly patch	
Alora	estradiol patch	
Climara	estradiol patch	**SIDE EFFECTS** Nausea, dizziness, bloating, breast tenderness/fullness, increased triglycerides, increased HDL., and if patch, redness/irritation at the application site
Climara Pro	estradiol/levonorgestrel patch	
CombiPatch	estradiol/norethindrone patch	**NOTES** Some formulations come in patches – for all patches check if the patch must be removed during MRI or the skin can be burned.
Estraderm	estradiol patch	
Estrace	17-beta-estradiol micronized tablet	Patch summary table in Pharmacokinetics chapter, *Vivelle-Dot* is applied twice weekly; counseling at end of this chapter.
Estrace vaginal cream	17-beta-estradiol cream	
Estrasorb	estradiol topical emulsion	
Estring	17-beta-estradiol vaginal ring	
Femhrt	ethinyl estradiol/norethindrone acetate PO	
Generic	estradiol	0.5, 1, 2 mg oral tab, 10 mcg vaginal tab
Femring	estradiol acetate vaginal ring	For vaginal symptoms
Provera	medroxyprogesterone	2.5, 5, 10 mg
Premarin	conjugated estrogens tablet	0.3, 0.45, 0.625, 0.9, 1.25 mg
Premarin vaginal cream	conjugated estrogens cream	0.625 mg/gram
Premphase	conjugated estrogens/medroxyprogesterone acetate tablet – <u>P component changes (phasic)</u>	0.625 mg conjugated E continuously + 5 mg medroxyprogesterone (MPA) taken on days 15-28 only
Prempro	conjugated estrogens/medroxyprogesterone acetate tablet <u>(P component stable)</u>	0.3-0.625 conjugated E+1.5-5 MPA
Estratest	esterified estrogens/ methyltestosterone tablets (with testosterone – ↑ risk CVD)	

Estrogen Counseling

- <u>This product does not contain a progestin, which should be dispensed to a woman with a uterus.</u> Estrogens increase the chances of getting cancer of the uterus.

- Report any unusual <u>vaginal bleeding right away</u> while you are taking estrogen. Vaginal bleeding after menopause may be a warning sign of cancer of the uterus (womb). Your healthcare provider should check any unusual vaginal bleeding to find out the cause.

- Do not use estrogens, with or without progestins, to prevent heart disease, heart attacks, or strokes.

- Using estrogens with or without progestins <u>may increase your chances</u> of getting heart attacks, strokes, breast cancer, and blood clots. Using estrogens may increase your risk of dementia. You and your healthcare provider should talk regularly about whether you still need treatment with this product.

- <u>Estrogen use is primarily for menopausal symptoms, and should not be continued indefinitely</u>. When you are ready to stop discuss with your physician the best way to stop the medicine – it will need to be decreased slowly.

- Estrogen can help keep your bones healthy. Ask your pharmacist for help in figuring out if you need to take calcium and vitamin D – these are important for healthy bones.

Vivelle-Dot Patch Application

- Your *Vivelle-Dot* (estradiol transdermal system) individual carton contains a calendar card printed on its inner flap. <u>Mark the two-day schedule</u> you plan to follow on your carton's inner flap.

- If you forget to change your patch on the correct date, apply a new one as soon as you remember.

- <u>Apply patch to lower abdomen, below the waistline</u>. Avoid the waistline, since clothing may cause the patch to rub off.

VIVELLE dot®
(estradiol transdermal system)
Change your patch only on these two days:
- ☐ Sun / Wed   ☐ Thu / Sun
- ☐ Mon / Thu   ☐ Fri / Mon
- ☐ Tue / Fri   ☐ Sat / Tue
- ☐ Wed / Sat

- The area must be clean, dry, free of powder, oil or lotion. <u>This applies to all patches</u>. And never apply a patch to cut or irritated skin (unless it is a bandage!)

- <u>Do not apply patch to breasts</u>. (Never apply any estrogen patch to the breasts.)

- If any adhesive residue remains on your skin after removing the patch, allow the area to dry for 15 minutes. Then, gently rub the area with oil or lotion to remove the adhesive from your skin.

TESTOSTERONE THERAPY

Hypogonadism (low testosterone) is due to diseases, procedures, or to a normal age-related decline in men. If testosterone replacement is due to a medical procedure, that is considered acceptable therapy. Increasingly, older males are requesting testosterone therapy for <u>improved sexual interest</u> (↑ libido) and performance, increased muscle mass, increased bone density, sharpened memory and concentration, and increased energy. The use of testosterone replacement is controversial: the primary risk is whether the use of testosterone increases <u>prostate cancer risk</u>. Testosterone can <u>also increase cholesterol levels and cause liver damage</u>.

<u>An accepted use for testosterone replacement is in men with low prostate cancer risk who have a low testosterone level and a related condition, such as low muscle mass</u>. It should not be used routinely for normal aging until the health risks are better quantified. [Another

reason for the increase in testosterone prescriptions has been due to the restriction on PDE 5 I's in the Medicare Part D formulary – which led men and their physicians to consider other options.] If testosterone is used, levels should be monitored. Liver function and cholesterol should be checked prior to start of treatment. The topical testosterone products require a MedGuide, primarily due to the risk of drug transfer from Dad (or Grandpa) to others in the household, including risk to young male children.

Reports of virilization of children due to testosterone exposure are serious and proper counseling is required. Men at high risk of prostate cancer should not use testosterone products. BPH symptoms would be expected to worsen with testosterone treatment. If dispensing a 5-α-reductase inhibitor for BPH that blocks the conversion of testosterone to its active form it would not make much sense to dispense another drug that provides testosterone directly.

Testosterone Products: C III

TESTOSTERONE	COUNSELING	SAFETY/SIDE EFFECTS/MONITORING
AndroGel 1%, 1.62% Meter-dose pumps (# of pumps depends on dose) or foil packets of 2.5 g or 5 g gel *Testim* gel 1% Unit dose tubes with 50 mg testosterone in 5 g of gel	See additional counseling that follows. *AndroGel* 1.62% is applied to the area of the upper arms and shoulders, but not the abdomen; with the 1% the abdomen can be used. Wash hands, dry, dress. Flammable when wet. Air dry before getting dressed. If woman and child comes into accidental contact wash fast with soap and water. Do not apply to genitals. Do not use if Hx breast or prostate CA. Do not apply *Testim* to abdomen.	**BLACK BOX WARNINGS** Children should avoid contact with unwashed or unclothed application sites in men using testosterone products. Healthcare providers should advise patients to strictly adhere to recommended instructions for use. Secondary exposure to testosterone in children and women can occur with use of testosterone. Cases of secondary exposure resulting in virilization of children have been reported. Women and children should avoid contact with any unwashed or unclothed application sites in men using testosterone gel. **WARNINGS** Patients with benign prostatic hyperplasia (BPH) treated with androgens are at an increased risk for worsening of signs and symptoms of BPH.
Androderm patch 2 mg, 4 mg patch Remove patches during MRI: can burn skin	Apply to back, abdomen, thighs or upper arms. Apply each evening between 8pm and midnight. For 4 mg/day do not use two 2 mg/day patches, use 4 mg patch.	**CONTRAINDICATIONS** Breast or prostate cancer. Never apply to breast or genitals. **SIDE EFFECTS** Increased appetite, increased creatinine, sensitive nipples, acne, gynecomastia, dyslipidemia, edema, increases PSA, increased risk of hepatotoxicity
Striant buccal tabs 30 mg to the gum region BID	30 mg to the gum region BID	
Testosterone solution *(Axiron)* Testosterone gel *(Fortesta)* *Testopel* pellets, given SC every 3-6 months *Depo-Testosterone*, given IM every 2-4 weeks	Applied to underarms. Applied to thighs. Application to thighs, underarms can help reduce accidental exposure	**MONITORING** Testosterone levels, PSA, liver function, cholesterol, some products recommend checking hematocrit

AndroGel Patient Counseling

Pump

- Before using the pump for the first time, you will need to prime the pump. To prime *AndroGel*, fully push down on the pump 3 times. Do not use any *AndroGel* that came out while priming. Wash it down the sink or throw it in the trash to avoid accidental exposure to others.

- The doctor or pharmacist will tell you the number of times to press the pump for each dose.

Packets

- Tear open the packet completely at the dotted line.

- Squeeze all of the *AndroGel* out of the packet into the palm of your hand. Squeeze from the bottom of the packet to the top.

For Both

- This medication should not be used by women or children. Testosterone can cause birth defects in unborn babies. A pregnant woman should avoid coming into contact with testosterone topical gel, or with a man's skin areas where a testosterone topical patch has been worn or the gel has been applied. If contact does occur, wash with soap and water right away.

- Topical testosterone is absorbed through the skin and can cause side effects or symptoms of male features in a child or woman who comes into contact with the medication. Call your doctor if a person who has close contact with you develops enlarged genitals, premature pubic hair, increased libido, aggressive behavior, male-pattern baldness, excessive body hair growth, increased acne, irregular menstrual periods, or any signs of male characteristics.

- The testosterone transdermal patch may burn your skin if you wear the patch during an MRI (magnetic resonance imaging). Remove the patch before undergoing such a test.

How to apply (1+ push from pump/day or 1 packet/day), or topical gels

- Apply the medication as directed to clean, dry skin of the shoulders/upper arms and/or domen (1% only to abdomen) once daily in the morning. Apply only to areas that would be covered if you were to wear a short sleeve t-shirt. Avoid applying this medication to broken, irritated skin. Do not apply to genitals (penis or scrotum). Do not let others apply this medication to your body.

- After applying, wash your hands thoroughly with soap and water to reduce the risk of accidentally spreading it from your hands to other people. Before dressing, wait a few minutes for the application site to dry completely. Be sure to always wear clothing (such as a t-shirt) to cover the application site until you wash the areas well with soap and water.

- If you expect to have skin-to-skin contact with another person, first wash the application area well with soap and water. For best effect, wait at least 2 to 6 hours before showering.

- This medication is <u>flammable</u> until dry. Let the gel dry before smoking or going near an open flame.

- *Axiron* gel (applied to underarms): Apply deodorant first.

CONTRACEPTION & INFERTILITY

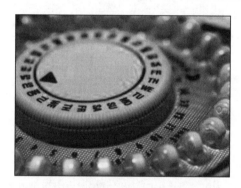

GUIDELINES

EC: Emergency contraception.
2010 May. NGC:007753 American College of Obstetricians and Gynecologists – Medical Specialty Society.

Websites for general contraception information:
Association of Reproductive Health Professionals (ARHP)
www.arhp.org/healthcareproviders/resources/contraceptionresources/

Planned Parenthood
www.plannedparenthood.org
For referrals of women with low income/lack of insurance to get contraception (pills, patch, ring, injections, IUD) at reduced cost (sliding scale based on income).

The Alan Guttmacher Institute (AGI)
www.guttmacher.org/sections/contraception.php

BACKGROUND

There are 62 million U.S. women in their childbearing years. Seven in 10 women of reproductive age (43 million) are sexually active and do not want to become pregnant, but could become pregnant if they or their partner fails to use a contraceptive method. The typical U.S. woman wants only two children. To achieve this goal, she must use contraceptives for roughly three decades. (source: Guttmacher Institute)

Among the 43 million women who do not want to become pregnant, 89% are practicing contraception. Sixty-three percent of reproductive-age women who practice contraception use nonpermanent methods, including hormonal methods (such as the pill, patch, implant, injectable and vaginal ring), the IUD and condoms. The remaining women rely on female or male sterilization.

Contraceptive choices vary markedly with age. For women younger than 30 years old, the pill is the leading method. Among women aged 30 and older, more rely on sterilization, which is often performed post-partum. Pharmacists have an important role in providing contraceptive health information. We recommend OTC products, including the use of condoms if a risk of sexually transmitted infection (STI) transmission is present, make emergency contraception services available in the community and provide referral services for pregnancy prevention and STI treatment.

Many women are not aware that birth control pills provide health benefits, including decreased blood loss and a lower incidence of iron-deficiency anemia, reduced cramps, ovarian cysts, ectopic pregnancy, less noncancerous breast cysts/lumps, less acute pelvic inflammatory disease and a decreased risk of endometrial and ovarian cancer. The combination pill also protects against bone thinning.

MENSTRUAL CYCLE PHASES/TEST KITS

A normal menstrual cycle ranges from 23-35 days (average 28 days). Menstruation starts on day 1 and typically lasts a few days.

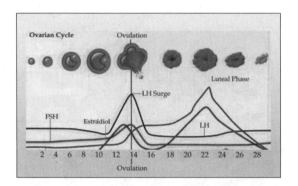

Ovulation

The mid-cycle luteinizing hormone (LH) surge results in release of the oocyte (egg) from the ovary into the fallopian tube.

If the oocyte is not fertilized, it is washed out through menstruation. Ovulation kits test for LH and are positive if LH is present. They predict the best time for a patient to have intercourse in order to try to conceive (get pregnant).

Pregnancy

A female has the highest chance to become pregnant on days 8-16 of her cycle, although pregnancy can occur during any time – no time is considered 100% "safe". Pregnancy test kits are positive if hCG (human chorionic gonadotropin) is in the urine.

If a case indicates hCG+, the patient is pregnant and teratogenic drugs should be discontinued, if possible. Well-known teratogens include alcohol, ACE inhibitors, angiotensin receptor blockers, benzodiazepines, carbamazepine, ergot-derivatives, isotretinoin, leflunomide, lithium, methimazole, nafarelin, NSAIDs, paroxetine, phenytoin, phenobarbital, propylthiouracil, quinolones, ribavirin, tazarotene, tetracyclines, topiramate, valproic acid, misoprostol, methotrexate, statins, dutasteride, finasteride, warfarin, lenalidomide and thalidomide. Refer to the Drug Use in Pregnancy chapter for a further discussion of teratogenic drugs.

Any woman planning to conceive (and all women of child-bearing age) should be taking a folic acid supplement (400-800 mcg/day) to help prevent birth defects of the brain and spinal cord (neural tube defects). Folic acid should be taken at least one month before pregnancy, since it takes time to build up adequate body stores. Folic acid is in many healthy foods, including fortified cereals, dried beans, leafy green vegetables and orange juice. A couple of the newer pill formulations contain folic acid – see chart of formulations later in this chapter.

HORMONAL CONTRACEPTIVES

These contain progestin only (pill or injectable) or estrogen/progestin combinations (in pills, a patch, and a ring). Contraceptives work primarily by preventing the release of the egg (blocking ovulation).

Progestin-only pill (POPs): The use of POPs as a contraceptive method is mostly recommended for lactating (breastfeeding) women, because estrogen reduces the milk production. They are sometimes used for women who cannot tolerate or have a contraindication to estrogen.

Estrogen and progestin combination oral contraceptives (COCs) inhibit the production of both follicle stimulating hormone (FSH) and LH, which prevents ovulation. Contraceptives also may prevent pregnancy by altering the endometrial lining, altering cervical mucus, interfering with fertilization or transport of an egg, or preventing implantation. COCs are used for various indications, including pregnancy prevention, dysmenorrhea, PMS, perimenopausal symptoms (hot flashes, night sweats, as well as pregnancy protection), anemia due to excessive period-related blood loss, and acne (in females). They are sometimes used for reduction in premenstrual migraine (a common migraine in women). The POPs are useful for this purpose, and are safest for migraines with aura (in this type of migraine estrogen should not be used due to stroke risk.)

Adverse Effects Due to Estrogen

Estrogen can cause nausea, breast tenderness/fullness, bloating, weight gain or elevated blood pressure. If low-dose estrogen pills are used, or if there is insufficient estrogen (the patient may be a fast metabolizer, or be using an enzyme inducer), then mid-cycle breakthrough bleeding can occur (days 14-21) and may require a higher estrogen dose. Many women are affected by nausea. Counsel patients that it should help to take the pill in the evening or at bedtime.

Serious adverse effects are rare but can include thrombogenic disorders, including heart attack, stroke, DVT/PE. The risk for clotting disorders increases as the woman ages, if she smokes, if she has diabetes or hypertension, if she requires prolonged bedrest, and if she is overweight. (See table on contraindications to estrogen use.) The progestin drospirenone, present in *YAZ, Gianvi, YASMIN, Ocella, Syeda, Zarah, Beyaz* and *Safyral*, as well as the *Ortho Evra* patch (due to a higher systemic estrogen level) are linked to a higher risk of blood clots and are best avoided in at-risk women. Higher estrogen formulations have higher risk.

DO NOT USE ANY FORM OF ESTROGEN WITH THESE CONDITIONS
History of blood clot disorders (DVT, PE)
History of stroke or heart attack
Heart valve disease with complications
Severe hypertension
Diabetes that causes blood vessel problems
Poorly controlled diabetes
Severe headaches (for example, migraines – some forms helpful)
Recent major surgery with prolonged bed rest
Breast cancer
Liver cancer or disease
Uterine cancer or other known or suspected estrogen-dependent cancers
Unexplained abnormal bleeding from the uterus
Jaundice during pregnancy or jaundice with prior hormonal contraceptive use
Known or possible pregnancy
If > 35 years old and smokes > 15 cigarettes/day

Adverse Effects Due to Progestin

Progestin can cause breast tenderness, headache, fatigue or changes in mood. If late cycle breakthrough bleeding occurs (after day 21) a higher progestin dose may be required.

Birth control pills do not provide protection from STIs. (Condoms provide some protection.)

CLOTTING RISK! WATCH FOR HIGH RISK PATIENTS

3 things to keep in mind (in addition to the patient's risk factors):

- Higher estrogen dose, higher clotting risk.

- FDA Safety Announcement [4-10-2012] Drospirenone-containing birth control pills may be associated with a higher risk for blood clots than other progestin-containing pills.

- *Ortho Evra* patch: higher systemic estrogen exposure than most COC pills.

FORMULATION CONSIDERATIONS

Breastfeeding
Choose progestin only pill.

Elevated Clotting Risk
Avoid drospirenone-containing COC pills, including *YAZ, Gianvi, Yasmin, Ocella, Syeda, Zarah, Beyaz, Vestura* and *Safyral.*

Avoid the *Ortho Evra* patch.

Use lower dose estrogen content.

Choose progestin-only pill.

Estrogen contraindication, including clotting risk
Choose progestin-only pill.

Estrogenic side effects
Use low estrogen formulation.

Spotting/"breakthrough bleeding"
(This is more common with *Seasonale, Seasonique* and *Lybrel.*) When starting the conventional formulations, wait for three cycles before switching. If persists use higher estrogen and progestin if mid-cycle spotting (days 14-21) or more progestin if spotting occurs later in cycle.

Avoiding monthly cycle
Use longer formulation *Seasonale* or *Seasonique* (every 3 months) or *Lybrel* (continuous).

Migraine
Choose among various formulations, if with aura choose POP.

Fluid retention/bloating
Choose a product containing drospirenone, if low clotting risk. Progestin component helps reduce water retention.

The progestin component is a mild diuretic. It retains potassium, and is contraindicated with renal or liver disease. Check potassium, renal function and use of other potassium-retaining agents.

Premenstrual dysphoric disorder
Choose *Yaz* or sertraline or fluoxetine *(Sarafem)* – see Depression chapter.

Acne
Can use most formulations; COCs approved for acne include *Ortho Tri-Cyclen, Estrostep,* and *Yaz.*

Heavy Menstrual Bleeding
Any oral contraceptive will decrease monthly blood loss. The COC *Natazia* is indicated for this condition (menorrhagia). IUDs decrease blood loss a lot; *Mirena* is preferred because it decreases blood loss ~75%; *Mirena* releases a low dose of levonorgestrel into the uterine lining (which reduces cramping.) Tranexamic acid *(Lysteda)*, which slows clot breakdown, is indicated for menorrhagia. It is not more effective than COC's, and has clotting risk – do not use with estrogen-containing products. Used for up to 5 days when bleeding. Visual changes could be due to clotting in retina – counsel. The bleeding loss is slight with the injectable and implant progestin birth control options *(Depo-Provera, Implanon, Nexplanon)* and with IUDs.

Drug Interactions that can Decrease Efficacy of Hormonal Contraceptives

Use back-up while taking the antibiotics listed (with rifampin, use other form of birth control since the induction will last – if switching back, a back-up method needs to be used for 1½ months after rifampin is stopped). Rifapentine and rifabutin are also strong inducers. A strong inducer, used long-term, will require an alternate form of birth control, such as condoms/spermicide, an IUD or the *Depo-Provera* injection. *Depo-Provera* does not have drug interactions (although it does lower bone density and should be avoided in women at risk for osteoporosis.)

Decreases Hormone Efficacy

- Antibiotics (rifampin, rifapentine, rifabutin)

- Anticonvulsants (barbiturates, carbamazepine, oxcarbazepine, phenytoin, topiramate and felbamate)

- St John's wort

- Several protease inhibitors (PIs) and non-nucleoside reverse transcriptase inhibitors (NNRTIs) – ↑ or ↓ contraceptives

- Bosentan *(Tracleer)*, Mycophenolate *(CellCept)*

- Smoking

ORAL CONTRACEPTIVE TYPES (REPRESENTATIVE LIST)

High dose Monophasic COCs: all active pills contain the same level of the hormones throughout the 3 active weeks:
50 mcg ethinyl estradiol, with various progestins: *Ogestrel 0.5/50-28, Ovcon-50, Zovia 1/50-28*

Biphasic or Triphasic (also called Multiphasic, where: the dose of the hormones changes over the course of 21 days
Various, including: *Cyclessa, Estrostep FE, Kariva, Mircette, Nortrel 7/7/7, Necon 7/7/7, Ortho-Novum 7/7/7 Tri-Cyclen Lo, Tri Lo Sprintec*

1 formulation is four-phasic *(Natazia)*, with four phases of estradiol valerate and the progestin dienogest

Low Estrogen COCs (20-30 mcg estrogen, compared to 35 mcg) – Used to ↓ withdrawal symptoms (emotional/ physical) and bleeding
Ethinyl estradiol/levonorgestrel *(Aviane-28, Falmina, Lessina, Lutera, Orsythia, Sronyx)*

Ethinyl estradiol/desogestrel *(Apri, Desogen, Emoquette, Ortho-Cept, Reclipsen, Solia)*

Ethinyl estradiol/levonorgestrel *(Altavera, Kurvelo, Levora, Marlissa, Nordette-28, Portia-28)*

Ethinyl estradiol/norethindrone *(Gildess Fe 1.5/30, Junel 1.5/30, Junel Fe 1.5/30, Loestrin 1.5/30-21, Loestrin Fe 1.5/30, Microgestin 1.5/30, Microgestin Fe 1.5/30, Generess FE, chewable)*

Ethinyl estradiol/drospirenone *(Ocella, Safyral, Syeda, Zarah, Yasmin)*

Ethinyl estradiol/norgestrel *(Gildess Fe 1.5/30, Junel 1.5/30, Junel Fe 1.5/30, Loestrin 1.5/30-21, Loestrin Fe 1.5/30, Microgestin 1.5/30, Microgestin Fe 1.5/30)*

Extended Cycle COCs
Norethindone/ethinyl estradiol *(Loestrin Fe 24)* – 24 vs 21 day active pills

Levonorgestrel/Ethinyl Estradiol *(Seasonale)* – 3 months

Levonorgestrel/Ethinyl Estradiol *(Seasonique)* – 3 months, shorter placebo period (and for PMDD)

Estradiol valerate/dienogest *(Natazia)* – 24 vs 21 day active pills, estradiol may be better tolerated

Ethinyl estradiol/drospirenone *(YAZ 24, Gianvi, Loryna, Vestura)* – 24 vs 21 day with 20 mcg ethinyl estradiol, The ones with folic acid are called *Beyaz or Safyral*

Levonorgestrel/Ethinyl Estradiol *(Lybrel)* – 12 months

Ethinyl estradiol/levonorgestrel *(Amethyst)* is continuous (no placebo or stop)

Levonorgestrel/ethinyl estradiol *(LoSeasonique)* – 3 months, with 20 mcg EE

Progestin Only Mini-Pills (POPs) include:
Norethindrone 35 mcg *(Camila, Errin, Heather, Jolivette, Micronor, Nor-QD, Nora-BE – some names include "nor")*

- Check the package insert for new drugs you are dispensing to a patient on birth control pills since you don't want to miss counseling on an interaction that could decrease the pill's efficacy.

POP Start Day Options

- Start at any time. Use another method of birth control for the first 48 hours of progestin-pill use – protection begins after two days. All come in 28-day packs and all pills are active.

- POPs need to take exactly around the same time of day everyday; if 3 hours have elapsed from the regular scheduled time, back up is needed for 48 hours after taking the late pill. If a dose is missed, patient could be pregnant and EC may be suitable.

COC Start Day Options

- Start on the Sunday following the onset of menses (will menstruate during the week – most common start is a Sunday start.)

- Start on 1st day of menses – if COCs are started within five days after the start of the period, no back up method of birth control is needed; protection is immediate. If not within 5 days, use back-up for first week of use.

Missed COC Pills – Instructions for Typical Formulations

Missed pills (particularly if the seven-day hormone-free interval is extended on either end) are a common cause of contraceptive failure. Check the package insert of the formulation dispensed; the instructions vary.

PILLS MISSED	NOTES
Single Pill Missed	If a single pill is missed anywhere in the packet, the forgotten pill needs to be taken when noticed and the next pill is taken when it is due, which may mean taking two pills on the same day. No additional contraception is required.
2+ Pills Missed	Back-up contraception is generally needed if two or more consecutive hormonal pills are missed.
	Women should take one of the missed active (hormonal) pills as soon as possible and then continue taking one pill each day as prescribed. Depending on when she remembers her missed pill, she may take two pills on the same day.
	If the two or more pills are missed in the first week of the cycle and unprotected intercourse occurs during this week, use of emergency contraception could decrease the risk of pregnancy.
	If pills were missed in the last week of hormone pills, days 15 to 21 of a 28-day pack, omit the hormone-free week by finishing the hormone pills in current pack and start a new pack the next day. If unable to start a new pack, use back-up until hormonal pills from a new pack are taken for seven consecutive days.

Select Different Formulation Overview, Start Day, Gap in Treatment

Seasonale and Seasonique are three month birth control pill formulations:

- They both have a 91-day pill regimen with 84 active pills. The difference is the placebo week: Seasonale has 7 days of placebo, and Seasonique has 7 days of low dose estrogen. This is not the only formulation where the placebo week has been replaced with low dose estrogen, to ↓ symptoms and bleeding.

- *Seasonale* and *Seasonique* must be started on the Sunday after the period starts, even if the patient is still bleeding. If the period began on Sunday, they should start that same day.

- They must use another method of birth control (such as condom or spermicide) as a back-up method if they have sex anytime from the Sunday they start until the next Sunday (the first 7 days). These formulations require that the pill be taken at the same time each day.

Continuous Pills With No Monthly Cycle *(Lybrel, Generic is Amethyst)*

- *Lybrel* comes in 28 day packets of all active (yellow) pills, with no placebo pills; the packets are taken continously. When empty, start the next pack.

- With this formulation, it can be difficult to tell if a woman is pregnant.

- It is important to take at the same time each day. Have the patient pick the time of day preferred.

- There is a higher discontinuation rate with the continuous formulations than with other COCs, due to spotting; counsel patients that the spotting should decrease over time.

- *Lybrel* must be started within 24 hrs of start of period if patient had not been on previous contraception. If on COCs begin on day 1 of the placebo week. If using a POP, begin at any time. Back-up contraception for 7 days is needed only after switching from a POP.

- 1 tablet missed: Take as soon as remembered and take the next tablet at the regular time (2 tablets in 1 day). Pregnancy is possible if sex during the 7 days after restarting; it is important to use back-up for 7 days to avoid pregnancy. 2 pills missed: Take the 2 tablets as soon as remembered and continue with one the next day. Pregnancy is possible if sex during the 7 days after restarting; it is important to use back-up for 7 days to avoid pregnancy. 3+ pills missed: Continue to take 1 tablet daily; do not take the missed pills. EC may be required. Pregnancy is possible if sex during the 7 days after restarting; it is important to use back-up for 7 days to avoid pregnancy.

Drospirenone Formulations: YAZ, Gianvi, Yasmin, Ocella, Syeda, Zarah, Beyaz, Vestura, Safyral, Loryna

These are popular COCs, since they <u>decrease</u> bloating, PMS symptoms and weight gain. This is due to the progestin drospirenone, which is a potassium-sparing diuretic.

- Drospirenone-containing formulations have a risk of increased K^+ and caution must be used with K^+-sparing agents, including aldosterone antagonists, potassium supplements, salt substitutes (KCl), ACE inhibitors, angiotensin receptor blockers, heparin, canaglifozin and calcineurin inhibitors.

- <u>Avoid use if kidney, liver, or adrenal gland disease</u>. On a case, <u>check the potassium level</u>. It should be in the safe range of 3.5-5 mEq/L.

- This type of progestin puts the patients at a <u>slightly higher risk of clotting</u>, and should be avoided in women with clotting risk.

Ortho Evra COC Contraceptive Patch

- Thin, beige, plastic patch placed on clean, dry skin of buttocks, stomach, upper arm, or upper torso <u>once a week for 21 out of 28 days</u>. Do not apply to breasts.

- Start on either Day 1 (no back-up needed) or Sunday (back-up 7-days if not day 1).

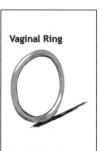

Contraceptive Patch

- If patch becomes loose or falls off <u>> 24 hours</u> during the 3 weeks of use or if > 7 days have passed during the 4th week where no patch is required, there is a risk of pregnancy; thus a back-up method should be used for 1 week while a new patch is put in place.

- Has the same side effects, contraindications and drug interactions as the pills except that the patch causes a <u>higher systemic estrogen exposure</u> (60% more than a 35 mcg pill), which can increase clotting risk; avoid carefully in anyone with clotting risk factors.

- <u>Less effective in women > 198 pounds</u>. Do not use if smoker and over 35 years old.

NuvaRing Vaginal Contraceptive Ring

- Small flexible ring inserted into the vagina <u>once a month</u>.

- Similar to OCs in that the ring is inserted <u>in place for 3 weeks</u> and taken out for 1 week before replacement with a new ring.

- For starting: insert the ring between day 1 and day 5 of menses.

- Exact position of ring in vagina does not matter.

Vaginal Ring

- If ring is out > 3 hours during week 1, rinse with cool to luke-warm water and reinsert; use back-up method for 1 week while the ring is in place, consider EC if intercourse within last 5 days.

- If ring is out < 3 hours during week 2 or 3, rinse and re-insert ring.

- If ring is out <u>> 3 hours</u> during week 2 or 3, rinse and re-insert ring and use back-up for 7 days.

- If starting 1st cycle of birth control, use back-up method for the 1st week.

- Has the same side effects, contraindications and drug interactions as the pills.

- Patient can store for up to 4 months at room temperature – refrigerated at pharmacy.

Combination Oral Contraceptives Patient Counseling

- Forgetting to take pills considerably increases the chances of pregnancy.

- <u>The FDA requires that the Patient Package Insert (PPI) be dispensed with oral contraceptives – they are in the product packaging</u>. Tell the patient that the PPI has important safety information and instructions how to use them properly and what to do if pills are missed.

- For the majority of women, oral contraceptives can be taken safely. But there are some women who are at high risk of developing certain serious diseases that can be life-threatening or may cause temporary or permanent disability or death. The risks associated with taking oral contraceptives increase significantly if you:

  - Have or have had clotting disorders, heart attack, stroke, angina pectoris, cancer of the breast or sex organs, jaundice, or malignant or benign liver tumors.

- You should not take the pill if you suspect you are pregnant or have unexplained vaginal bleeding.

- Cigarette smoking increases the risk of serious adverse effects on the heart and blood vessels from oral contraceptive use. This risk increases with age and with heavy smoking and is quite marked in women over 35 years of age. Women who use oral contraceptives should not smoke.

- Most side effects of the pill are not serious. The most common such effects are nausea, vomiting, bleeding between menstrual periods, weight gain, and breast tenderness. These side effects, especially nausea and vomiting may subside within the first three months of use. Many women have nausea, and some have spotting or light bleeding, during the 1st three months.

- For any estrogen containing product and for any containing the progestin drospirenone, counsel to watch for severe pain in leg/calf, severe abdominal pain, chest pain/shortness of breath/cough, blurred or loss of vision – all due to clotting risk. Clotting is rare with current dosages; look at the preceeding table for women at highest risk (overweight, on bed-rest, smokers) Any previous clotting history means that estrogen, in any form, is contraindicated.

- Make sure to discuss with your pharmacist if you start any new medicines, including over-the-counter products, or short-term antibiotics for illness.

- If any of this information is unclear, consult the Patient Information Leaflet or your pharmacist. Your pharmacist will also discuss whether to start your pill on the 1st Sunday following your period (which is done most commonly) or on a different day.

ADDITIONAL METHODS OF BIRTH CONTROL AND "SAFE" OR "SAFER SEX"

Abstinence is the only 100% way to prevent pregnancy and STIs. Safer sex recommendations:

- Alcohol and other drugs can make people forget safer sex; avoid use when in high-risk situations.

- Condoms form a barrier between the penis and anus, vagina or mouth. The barrier keeps one partner's fluids from getting into or on the other. And condoms reduce the amount of skin-to-skin contact. Latex (not natural) condoms must be used.

- Oral sex is safer than vaginal or anal sex to reduce HIV risk, but will still put the person at risk for herpes, syphilis, hepatitis B, gonorrhea, and HPV. The *Sheer Glyde* dam is FDA-approved for safer sex; it blocks passage of infectious organisms during oral contact.

- Lubricant is important for safer sex because it makes condoms and dams slippery and less likely to break, and reduces dry friction. Never recommend oil-based lubricant (called "lube") with a latex or non-latex rubber condom; only recommend water or silicone-based lubricant.

Condoms

- Male condoms are a thin latex or plastic sheath to be worn around the penis, thus acting as a barrier to sperm. Female condoms are inserted deep into the vagina; collects semen thus keeping sperm from entering further into the vagina; obtainable OTC, suitable as a back-up method.

- Condoms help protect against many STIs (not plastic condoms).

- Can increase birth control effectiveness of condom with <u>nonoxynol-9 spermicide.</u>

- Do not use spermicide with anal sex. It is irritating and can increase the risk of STIs. Some of the condoms are lubricated with nonoxynol-9.

OTC contraceptive methods (and some condoms) all contain the spermicide <u>nonoxynol-9.</u>

- Available as foams, film, creams, suppositories, and jellies.

- Place deep into the vagina right before intercourse where they melt (except for foam, which bubbles).

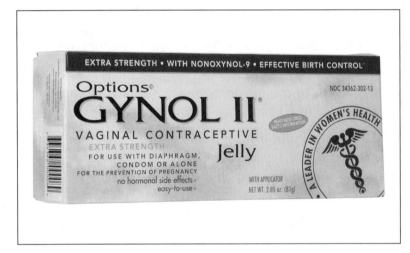

Diaphragm, Caps & Shields

These 3 options are soft latex or silicone barriers that cover the cervix and prevent sperm passage.

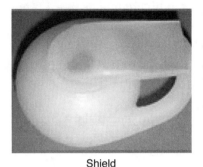
Shield

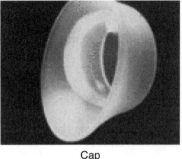
Cap

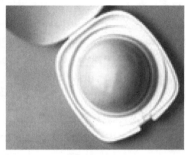
Diaphragm

Diaphragm Directions for Use

- Wash hands thoroughly.

- Place 1 tablespoon of spermicide in the diaphragm and disperse inside and to rim.

- Pinch the ends of the cup and insert the pinched end into the vagina.

- Diaphragms should not be in place greater than 24 hours.

- Leave in for six hours after intercourse.

- Reapply spermicide if intercourse is repeated, by inserting jelly with applicator.

- Wash with mild soap and warm water after removal, air dry.

- Needs refitting after a greater than 20% weight change and after pregnancy.

Other Forms of Contraception not Dispensed by Pharmacists

- Intrauterine device *(Mirena, Skyla)* are both hormonal IUDs. These cause light bleeding and minor or no cramping. *Mirena* lasts up to 5 years and *Skyla* up to 3 years. The copper-T IUD *(ParaGard)* can be used for EC, and lasts up to 10 years, but has more bleeding and cramping.

- Subdermal rod *(Implanon, Nexplanon)* – contains the progestin etonogestrel.

- Injection *(Depo-Provera, Depo-subQ Provera)* – medroxyprogesterone acetate, a progesterone given by IM or SC injection every 3 months.

Emergency Contraception (EC)

Emergency contraception (the "morning after pill") is a form of contraception that prevents pregnancy up to 72 hours (3 days) for levonorgestrel EC and up to 120 hours (5 days) after sexual intercourse for *Ella*. Another option to prevent pregnancy is the copper IUD insertion *(ParaGard)*.

Higher-than-normal doses of regular daily oral contraceptives can be used, but are not preferred and are used when the recommended EC products are not available, such as 5 tablets of *Aviane* or *Alesse* x 2 doses, taken 12 hours apart. A reference list of common contraceptive pill brands and the numbers needed to prevent pregnancy is available at http://ec.princeton.edu/questions/dose.html#dose

The two available formulations are *Plan B One Step* and generics, which come as one 1.5 mg tab and or two separate 0.75 mg tabs of levonorgesterol. This formulation of EC reduces the risk of pregnancy by 89 percent when started within 72 hours after unprotected intercourse. The sooner it is started, the higher the efficacy. EC has been available for 30 years and there have been no reports of serious complications or birth defects.

EC can be an important resource after unprotected sex, such as from missed pills, a condom breaking during intercourse, a diaphragm or cap that moved out of place during intercourse, or if a woman may have been sexually assaulted.

[Note that EC is not the same as abortion; abortion is used to interrupt an established pregnancy while EC is used to prevent one. This follows the FDA definition of pregnancy as a fertilized egg implanted in the uterine wall. If a person believes that pregnancy occurs at the point of conception (from the time of sexual intercourse) they may not want to use EC. Some pharmacists and patients do not wish to dispense, or use, the EC formulation ulipristal (*Ella*), which is a chemical cousin to misoprostol (*Mifeprex*), one of the components in the "abortion pill" RU-486. They are not the same drugs and are used differently. In RU-486, misoprostol is used to expel the uterine contents (which is why it is pregnancy category X because it causes uterine contractions). In EC, ulipristal is used at a lower dose to delay or inhibit ovulation. It may also prevent implantation and this is a cause of concern for some. All forms of EC, whether ulipristal or levonorgestrel, do not interfere with the fertilized egg after implantation.]

If sexual assault has occurred the woman may require STI treatment, including HIV prevention. Pharmacists should have referrals for other providers available to suggest to patients. Referrals may be needed for regular contraception care.

If a patient vomits within 2 hours of taking the pill/s, they should consider repeating the dose. If easily nauseated, recommend an OTC antiemetic (1 hour prior to use, and caution if driving home due to sedation).

Occasionally women may be using EC after sex as a means of birth control; this may be done when a woman has occasional (not regular) sexual activity. This is not preferred due to a lower efficacy than regular birth control pills and changes in the menstrual cycle due to the high, intermittent levonorgestrel doses. Depending on insurance coverage, it may also be more expensive.

Levonorgestrel EC

Plan B One-Step is over-the-counter with no age or other restrictions. The pharmacy does not need to be open to sell this product. Per the FDA, *Plan B One-Step* should be placed in the OTC aisles with the other family-planning products, such as condoms and spermicides. One-pill generics *(My Way and Next Choice One Dose)* will be available OTC in 2014 (next to *Plan*

B One-Step), but for these the purchaser must be 17 and older to purchase (ID required). The generics cost $35-$45, about $10 less than the brand. Two-pill generics (levonorgestrel 0.75 mg tablets) are still available only behind the counter without a prescription for ages 17 or older; ages 16 and under still need a prescription. Both sexes require proof of age if getting behind the counter OTC. There is no reason to use a prescription with the formulations available OTC (unless someone wanted the 2 pill formulation) except to use insurance coverage.

If the EC is coming from behind the counter, there is no requirement for purchasers to sign a registry. They can receive multiple packets and ACOG recommends an additional packet for future use, if needed, since EC is more effective the sooner it is used.

Levonorgestrel Formulations

- <u>Mechanism of action</u>: similar to other hormonal contraceptives. All of them act by one or more of the following mechanisms: altering the endometrial lining, altering cervical mucus, interfering with fertilization or transport of an egg, or preventing implantation. There is evidence that <u>levonorgestrel primarily works by preventing or delaying ovulation</u>, but other mechanisms may be involved.

- This type of EC is indicated for up to 3 days (the sooner, the better) after unprotected intercourse (and is used longer off-label).

- Take 1.5 mg as a single dose *(Plan B One Step)*, or in two divided doses (0.75 mg) separated by 12 hours.

- Primary side effect is nausea, which occurs in 23% of women, and 6% have vomiting. If the women is easily nauseated OTC anti-emetics should be recommended to avoid losing the dose.

- If the period is more than a week late, a pregnancy test should be taken.

Ulipristal *(Ella)*

- Requires a prescription or ordered through an online site for $42, which includes next-day shipping.

- Works primarily by delaying ovulation. May also prevent implantation in the uterus – this mechanism is more controversial than levonorgestrel.

- Indicated for up to 5 days after unprotected intercourse.

- Primary side effects are headache, nausea and abdominal pain. Some women have changes in their menstrual cycle, but all should get their period within a week. If the period is more than a week late, they should get a pregnancy test. If they have severe abdominal pain, they may have an ectopic pregnancy (outside of the uterus) and need immediate medical attention.

- Use contraception the rest of the cycle as ovulation may occur later than normal.

Resuming Contraception after EC

Regular hormonal contraceptives (OCs, the shot, the ring, or the patch), should be started on the following day after completing the last EC dose. The patch and the ring can also be started on the first day of menses.

INFERTILITY

Infertility affects 10-15% of persons trying to conceive, or over 2 million American couples annually. One in sixteen babies are now conceived by women using fertility medications. From a business perspective, the sale of infertility medications is profitable. Detailed knowledge of this topic is a "specialty" area; this section provides "basic competency" knowledge.

The chance of pregnancy in couples attempting pregnancy is about 25% per month, and most will become pregnant within a year. If pregnancy has not occurred at one year's time, the couple should be referred for medical consultation. Infertility can be due to either the male or female. Males can be contributory due to various problems with sperm production. Females could have one or more contributory factors, including congenital defects, infectious pathogens (including damage from chlamydia or trichomoniasis), abdominal conditions, ectopic pregnancy, scarring from previous surgeries, hypothyroidism or polycystic ovary syndrome (PCOS).

In the beginning part of this chapter there is a brief description of ovulation kits; these are a reasonable place to start, prior to outside referral. Ovulation kits test for luteinizing hormone (LH), which is present in the urine and surges 24-48 hours prior to ovulation. The LH surge triggers the release of an egg from an ovary (ovulation). Ovulation is the most fertile time of the cycle. The three days immediately from the positive result is the highest chance for pregnancy. The kits are simple to use and require either running the test stick under the urine stream, or collecting the urine in a small container and dipping the test strip.

There are other more complex ways to assess ovulation, including testing body temperature, cervical mucus, and using fertility monitors. Any women trying to conceive should have possible teratogens discontinued, if possible. The pharmacist should check the woman's OTC and Rx medication use and consult with the prescriber. It may also be necessary to eliminate medications from the male partners regimen. Possible teratogens are discussed in more detail in the Drug Use in Pregnancy chapter.

Patient-Specific Infertility Treatment Goals

- Address any underlying medical condition.

- Increase quantity of quality sperm

- Increase number of eggs

- In-vitro fertilization (IVF)

If medications are used they are either oral or injectable. The table below provides a summary of the common fertility medications.

DRUG	DOSING	SAFETY/SIDE EFFECTS/MONITORING
Oral		
Clomiphene *(Clomid, Serophene)* GnRH → ↑ FSH & ↑ LH, to ↑ <u>ovulation</u> <u>Selective Estrogen Receptor Modulator</u> (SERM)	50 mg x 5 days, taken on days 3, 4 or 5 after period starts. Can increase to 150 mg, 5 days/cycle.	**CONTRAINDICATIONS** Liver disease, pregnancy, uncontrolled adrenal or thyroid disorders **SIDE EFFECTS** <u>Hot flashes, ovarian enlargement, abdominal bloating/ discomfort</u>, blurred vision, headache, fluid retention. Can ↑chance of multiple births (but less than injectables), ovarian enlargement, <u>thrombosis risk</u>
Injectable		
Human Chorionic Gonadotropin (hCG) (*Pregnyl, Novarel*), IM **Gonadotropins** Follitropin Beta (*Follistim AQ*), IM, SC **Urofollitropin** (*Bravelle*), IM, SC **Follitropin Alpha** (*Gonal-F*), SC **Menotropins** (*Menopur, Repronex*), IM, SC **Gonadotropin Releasing Hormone Agonist (GnRH agonist)** Sometimes used: leuprolide (*Lupron*), Goserelin (*Zoladex*), Nafarelin (*Synarel*), IM, SC **Gonadotropin Releasing Hormone Antagonist (GnRH antagonist)** Cetrorelix (*Cetrotide*), SC	These come in either prefilled syringes, or as pens that may be preloaded, or pens with prefilled cartridges, or in ampules that are reconstituted, with supplied diluent. If reconstituting: insert syringe needle into vial, invert, slowly draw entire contents into syringe. Make sure tip of needle is not sticking through the solution or it will not be pulled into the syringe. Remove needle and syringe, replace syringe with injection needle. If air bubbles they can be tapped out. Some multiple dose pens require priming – these pens have dose counters on them and the instructions will designate the priming dose. The pen is primed when liquid appears at the tip. All SC injections: keep needle in skin for at least 5 seconds; some are longer, to avoid the drug "popping" out onto the skin. If multiple use, recap. Otherwise, discard entire device without recapping into appropriate container (sharps container, milk container, unbreakable plastic container).	**SIDE EFFECTS** Injection site pain, CNS (depression, fatigue, headache), ovarian hyperstimulation syndrome (ovaries become enlarged and tender, small risk multiple pregnancies). **NOTES** SC: abdomen is generally preferred due to a more even absorption, or other SC sites. Instructions will indicate either 45 or 90 degrees. See immunization chapter for more details: these are short needles (½" or less). For IM: Upper outer quadrant is often used, as marked in this picture. These are 1" or longer needles; more information on injections in the Immunization chapter. 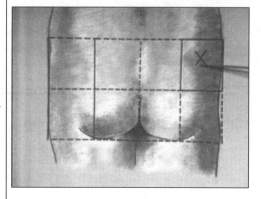

27

PAIN

We gratefully acknowledge the assistance of Lori Reisner, PharmD, Health Sciences Associate Clinical Professor of Pharmacy and Clinical Pharmacist, University of California, San Francisco, School of Pharmacy, in preparing this chapter.

BACKGROUND

Pain is an unpleasant sensory and emotional experience. It is due to tissue damage, either actual or potential, or both. Pain can be acute (usually due to a recent injury, such as a cut), or chronic, which lasts beyond the expected time of tissue healing.

Chronic pain can be attributed to an injury or can be due to disease, such as chronic back or joint pain related to cancer or diabetes. Many patients, especially elderly patients, live with daily chronic pain, and some may die with uncontrolled pain. This is a tragic but avoidable problem in medicine. Pharmacists and prescribers are concerned about inadequate pain treatment <u>as well as</u> the abuse potential of some of these medicines <u>and</u> side effect management.

<u>Joint Commission standards require that pain be treated in the same manner as vital signs making it compulsory for health care professionals in accredited facilities to inquire about, measure and treat pain</u> as they would blood pressure, pulse or respiratory rate. Pain has become recognized as the "fifth vital sign."

GUIDELINES

Many resources, including guidelines, at the American Pain Society Website: www.ampainsoc.org. Selected resources include:

American Pain Society's Principles of Analgesic Use in the Treatment of Acute Pain and Cancer Pain, 6th Edition, 2008.

Chou R, Fanciullo GJ, Fine PG, et al. Clinical guidelines for the use of chronic opioid therapy in chronic noncancer pain. J Pain 2009;10:113–130.

Evidence-Based Guideline: Treatment of Painful Diabetic Neuropathy. Neurology 2011; 2011;43(6):910-917.

PHARMACIST'S ROLE IN PAIN MANAGEMENT

The pharmacy profession provides pain management consultation and care to patients in various settings, including hospitals, skilled nursing facilities (SNFs), community pharmacies and in dedicated pain management clinics.

In community settings, the use of OTC products requires careful consideration – these drugs can be toxic, and overdose or use in the wrong patient population must be avoided. On the other hand, proper use of OTC agents can enhance pain management and is generally more affordable than comparative prescription agents. In clinical settings pharmacists are in-

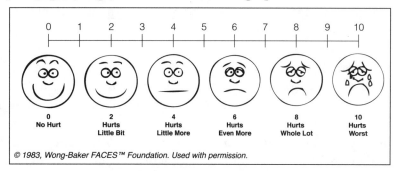

© 1983, Wong-Baker FACES™ Foundation. Used with permission.

volved in selection of appropriate medications, or combinations of medicines, and in assisting with monitoring and side effect management. They can also assist with risk reduction and management of tolerance via opioid conversions and dose adjustments. Pharmacists also help with cost management via conversion to more affordable agents, or provide assistance with applications for patient assistance programs. Most importantly, they provide essential counseling regarding the benefits and risks of opioids and other prescription drugs.

TREATMENT PRINCIPLES

Non-experimental pain is subjective, and thus the primary measurement for assessing pain is the <u>patient's</u> own report. Patients should be taught to monitor and document their pain. This will enable the clinician to adjust medications more precisely. Pain scales (as shown here) can be used as guides to assess pain severity. The patient should record the pain level or severity, pain type or quality (using words such as burning, shooting, stabbing, aching, etc.) and the time of day that pain is better or worse. Timing is important; the frequency of breakthrough pain medication use can indicate the need for a higher scheduled (long-acting) pain medication dose.

It is preferable to <u>treat severe pain at initial onset</u> since delays may require a higher total analgesic dose. The lowest dose that adequately reduces the pain is the appropriate dose. Using medicines with multiple mechanisms of action can produce better responses via additive effects or synergism. Opioid agents in particular can be difficult to manage even for the patient who needs them, and an appropriate goal may be to try and reduce or avoid the use of opioids, if reasonable for the pain type. The addition of <u>non-opioids to a regimen can often reduce the total opioid dose required while providing superior analgesia</u>. Additionally, access to non-medication techniques and modalities, such as physical therapy or directed exercise, is essential.

OPIOID TERMINOLOGY

Patients taking opioids chronically, including tramadol and tapentadol, which have dual mechanisms of action, will develop physiological adaptation and ultimately may live "dose to dose." Such patients will suffer withdrawal symptoms including anxiety, tachycardia, shakiness, shortness of breath or GI symptoms if a dose is missed or late.

It is important to distinguish between physiological adaptation and addiction. All patients, including addicts, become physiologically adapted to opioids after repeated exposure. By contrast, addiction involves a strong desire or compulsion to take the drug despite harm, and is manifested by drug-seeking behaviors such as prescription theft or exaggerated (or fake) physical problems.

Occasionally, patients are observed who exhibit a phenomenon known as "pseudo-addiction." The patient is often anxious about running out of drug and may have used up the medication too quickly – signs which can be mistaken for addiction, but may actually be due to poorly treated pain. The response to this type of patient is not to scold – but to determine which aspects of their pain are inadequately controlled, and counsel them to return to their pain management provider for reassessment and additional help in developing a tailored proper pain management regimen. Often, the drug being used too frequently is a short-acting agent such as a hydrocodone/acetaminophen combination. In such cases, if continuation of opioids is appropriate, consideration of conversion to a long-acting agent is warranted. Overuse of combination agents will put the patient at risk of hepatotoxicity or nephrotoxicity.

Tolerance to opioids develops over time and necessitates a higher dose to produce the same analgesic response. It is important to distinguish whether the condition causing the pain has worsened (e.g., cancer), as opposed to a decrease in effectiveness of the medication. Is it tolerance, a worsening of disease, or both? It has been proposed that opioid agonists have no maximal upper dose (no ceiling effect), although recent studies have demonstrated that average pain reduction – regardless of dose – is approximately 0-50% in non-malignant pain syndromes. Thus, there is a limit to what can be expected from opioids and they may not be sufficient for controlling pain as monotherapy. More importantly, there is mounting evidence in some patients that chronic opioid use can worsen pain sensitivity, a phenomenon known as opioid hyperalgesia. In cases where this is suspected it is prudent to switch patients to a different opioid to mitigate tolerance or to consider weaning off the opioids and substituting other analgesics in the pain management regimen.

"Break-through" pain (BTP) is acute pain that occurs despite use of a long-acting or scheduled opioid. It is treated with a fast relief agent – such as an immediate release opioid. In practice BTP is often treated with generic hydrocodone/acetaminophen or similar agents. Oral absorption of these can require up to 60 minutes but they are generally more cost-effective than faster-acting sublingual or injectable formulations. If repeat doses of BTP medication are required, then the baseline opioid dose should be increased or substituted with a different opioid. New or adjusted baseline opioids should be dispensed with a BTP medication until the dose of the scheduled opioid is stabilized. Constipation prophylaxis is an essential component of a chronic opioid regimen. Inpatients on intravenous opioids must be <u>monitored for sedation</u>; sedation is the <u>most important predictor of respiratory depression</u>, the usual cause of <u>fatality</u> with an <u>opioid overdose</u>.

PHARMACOTHERAPY

Analgesics can be chosen based on <u>severity</u> and <u>type of the pain target</u>. Severity is usually categorized as mild, moderate or severe. <u>Mild pain can be self-treated at the pharmacy and usually responds to acetaminophen, or an NSAID. Moderate pain is often treated with combination agents, such as hydrocodone or oxycodone with acetaminophen. Severe pain may require opioids, although neuropathic pain syndromes may respond adequately to non-opioids such as duloxetine or pregabalin.</u> However, multimodal therapies may be required for moderate and severe pain. Non-opioid medications for pain, other than acetaminophen or NSAIDs, primarily consist of antidepressants and anticonvulsants, but may also include muscle relaxants or other agents. Adjuvants and non-opioid analgesics can reduce the total daily dose of opioids required to control the pain.

Specifying the pain type is important in choosing the right therapy. For neuropathic pain, an antidepressant such as amitriptyline or duloxetine and/or an anticonvulsant, such as pregabalin may be considered, with or without other classes of agents. For severe pain due to an injury, cancer, or other indications, the patient might need to start on an opioid.

Mild Pain Agents, Available Rx and OTC: Acetaminophen and NSAIDs

Acetaminophen inhibits the synthesis of prostaglandins in the CNS and peripherally blocks pain impulse generation. Note that IV acetaminophen (similar to IV ibuprofen) can be used when oral routes are not available and can enable lower opioid doses.

Acetaminophen

DRUG	DOSING	SAFETY/SIDE EFFECTS/MONITORING
Acetaminophen *(Tylenol,* **"Non-Aspirin" pain reliever, others)** **+ hydrocodone** *(Vicodin, Norco, Lortab)* + oxycodone *(Percocet, Endocet)* + codeine: *(Tylenol #2, 3, 4)* + tramadol *(Ultracet)* … and many OTC combos + diphenhydramine *(Tylenol PM)* And in multiple cough and cold products IV Acetaminophen *(Ofirmev)* – used inpatient to enable lower opioid doses, and can be used when oral routes are not available	Keep below 4,000 mg/day 325 mg, max 2 tabs Q4-6H, NTE 10 tabs per 24 hours (3,250 mg) 500 mg, max 2 tabs Q6H, NTE 6 tabs per 24 hours (3,000 mg) 650 ER, max 2 tabs Q8H, NTE 6 tabs per 24 hours (3,900 mg) Children's Dosing 10-15 mg/kg Q4-6H, max 5 doses/d Children's *Feverall* rectal supp 120 mg Infant drops are now the same concentration as the children's suspension (160 mg/5 mL) to ↓ dosing confusion and thus ↓ toxicity risk CONSIDERATIONS: Use dosing syringe or cup provided with the medicine Do not use "APAP" on labels so that patients understand that they are getting acetaminophen. Caution with dosing IV acetaminophen in infants: Solution is 10 mg/mL, in 100 mL vials. Use caution that doses ordered in mg are not dispensed as mL (for example, a 75 mg dose is not 75 mL, it is 7.5 mL). Do not permit nurses to prepare doses in the units. All IV acetaminophen doses should be prepared in the pharmacy.	**BLACK BOX WARNING** Acetaminophen may cause severe hepatotoxicity, potentially requiring liver transplant or resulting in death; hepatotoxicity is usually associated with excessive acetaminophen intake (> 4 g/day). **SIDE EFFECTS** Hepatotoxicity: with overdose can be fatal. Heavy drinkers or patients with known hepatitis should not exceed 2 g/day All do not exceed 3,000-3,900 mg/day FDA requested manufacturers not to exceed 325 mg APAP in combo drugs to ↓ toxicity risk (Jan 2011) – they have until 2014 to comply DOC for pain in pregnancy (Rare) but cases of severe skin rash: SJS, TEN, AGEP. Stop drug, seek immediate medical help. Nephrotoxicity: rare renal damage but generally safer than NSAIDs in renal disease **Antidote for Overdose** N- Acetylcysteine (NAC, oral and IV) MOA: Restores intracellular glutathione (acts as a glutathione substitute) NAC should be administered immediately, even before the results of APAP level are obtained; within 8 hours of ingestion. Oral loading dose is 140 mg/kg PO, followed by 70 mg/kg Q4H x 17 doses, unless the APAP level is non-toxic. Has an odor of rotten eggs and often causes nausea. IV form *(Acetadote)* can be used as an alternative, but is more costly; does not require oral ingestion.

Acetaminophen Drug Interactions

■ Considered drug of choice for use with warfarin; however, if used chronically, can alter INR – monitor accordingly.

■ Avoid or limit alcohol use due to the risk of hepatotoxicity – see counseling section.

Acetaminophen Counseling

- Contact your doctor right away for any condition that is being self-treated if the condition worsens, if it lasts for more than two days, if there is a high fever (> 102.5 °F), or with rash, nausea, vomiting or blood in the stool. These are true also for children. Infants should be seen by the pediatrician.

- Many products contain acetaminophen, including prescription pain medicines and over-the-counter pain and cough-and-cold products. The name may be written as acetaminophen, *Tylenol*, APAP, non-aspirin pain reliever, etc. The total daily dose of all products should not exceed the limits above.

- Too much acetaminophen can cause kidney damage, and can permanently harm the liver. This can be exacerbated by the use of too much alcohol. Women should not exceed more than 1 drink per day, and men should not exceed more than 2 drinks per day.

Aspirin/NSAIDs

Mechanism of Action and Function

NSAIDs inhibit the activity of cyclooxygenase enzymes. These enzymes catalyze the production of prostaglandins (PG) and thromboxane from arachidonic acid. Aspirin irreversibly, and other NSAIDs reversibly, block the activity of thromboxane and prostaglandins. PGs have various functions, including facilitating inflammation. By suppressing PG formation, NSAIDs thereby decrease inflammation. Both acetaminophen and NSAIDs treat pain and fever, while NSAIDs also treat inflammation. Cyclooxygenase (COX)-1 inhibition increases bleeding risk. The COX-2 selective agents have lower bleeding risk, but may have greater cardiovascular risk, than non-selective NSAIDs that block both COX-1 and COX-2 activity.

NSAID Black Box Warnings (3)

CV: NSAIDs may cause ↑ risk of serious CV thrombotic events, MI, and stroke, which can be fatal. Risk may be ↑ with duration of use. Patients with CV disease or risk factors for CV disease may be at greater risk.

GI: NSAIDs cause an increased risk of serious GI adverse events including bleeding, ulceration, and perforation of the stomach or intestines, which can be fatal. These events can occur at any time during use and without warning. Elderly patients, those with previous history of GI bleed, patients taking corticosteroids, and those taking concurrent SSRIs or SNRIs are at greater risk for serious GI events.

CABG: Contraindicated for peri-operative pain management in the setting of CABG surgery

All NSAIDs, even OTC that arrived at the pharmacy on a prescription, require a MedGuide for warnings above.

NSAIDs, Salicylates

DRUG	DOSING	SAFETY/SIDE EFFECTS/MONITORING
Aspirin – Acetylsalicylic Acid primarily used for cardioprotection (81-162 mg) **Bayer, Bayer "Advanced" Aspirin** (dissolves slightly faster), **Ascriptin, Bufferin** (↓ stomach upset), **Ecotrin, Excedrin** (Aspirin + Acetaminophen + Caffeine) EC (enteric-coated) and buffered products ↓ nausea	Analgesic dosing: 325-650 mg All NSAIDs: known risk factors for GI bleeding: Elderly, previous bleed, chronic or high dose use, hypoxic gut – check for dark, tarry stool, stomach upset, weakness, coffee-ground emesis (indicates a more serious, fast GI bleed) Also increases GI risk: concomitant anticoagulants or steroids, SSRIs/SNRIs, smoking, "poor health" Ibuprofen and naproxen are relatively lower risk for GI complications, but have risk, especially if high doses taken chronically	**BLACK BOX WARNINGS** See preceeding page **CONTRAINDICATIONS** Pregnancy category: most are C/D (avoid, esp 3rd trimester) Avoid with NSAID hypersensitivity (past reaction with trouble breathing), nasal polyps, asthma Avoid aspirin (not other NSAIDs) in children (< 16 y/o) with any viral infection due to potential risk Reye's syndrome (symptoms include sleepiness, nausea, lethargy, confusion) **SIDE EFFECTS** Dyspepsia, heartburn (more common with aspirin – EC or buffered products can reduce symptoms) – take NSAIDs with food to ↓ nausea! Blood pressure may increase (monitor) GI irritation/bleeding, renal (caution in patients with renal impairment), CNS effects (fatigue, confusion, dizziness), photosensity (Rare) but cases of severe skin rash: SJS, TEN. Stop drug, seek immediate medical help. **NOTES** Due to antiplatelet effects, stop all NSAIDs at least a week prior to elective surgery. Patients may be using PPIs to protect the gut with chronic NSAID use. If done, consider the risk from chronic PPIs (decreased bone density, increased infection risk). **Salicylate Specific** Overdose can manifest with tinnitus. Take with food or water or milk to minimize GI upset. All NSAIDs recommend to take with food; note that the salicylates usually cause more nausea & this counseling is important.
Salsalate	Up to 3 grams/day, divided BID-TID	Similar to aspirin, lower risk GI toxicity than aspirin, can cause tinnitus with overdose
Magnesium Salicylate *(Doans, Doans ES, Momentum, Keygesic)*	ES: 500 mg/caplet 2 caplets Q 6 hours, max 8 caplets/day	Similar to aspirin Not a contraindication, but NSAIDs (except aspirin) are unsafe if heart attack; try to avoid use. Avoid with heart failure.
Choline Magnesium Trisalicylate	500 mg-1.5 g 2-3 times/day or 3 g at bedtime	
Diflunisal	500 mg-1.5 g 2-3 times/day or 3 g at bedtime	
Salicylate salts *(Arthropan, Asproject, Magan, Mobidin, Rexolate, Tusal)*	No longer commonly used	
Topical Salicylates		See end of chapter

NSAIDs, Others

DRUG	DOSING	SAFETY/SIDE EFFECTS/MONITORING
Ibuprofen (Motrin, Advil) IV *Caldolor*, also for mild-mod pain, can ↓ opioid dose, and can be used when oral routes are not available	OTC 200-400 mg Q4-6H, max 1.2 g/day, limit self-Tx to 10 days or less OTC: mild-mod pain, fever, dysmenorrhea Rx 400-800 mg Q6-8H, max 3.2 g/day Rx: moderate pain or inflammation	Similar to aspirin
Naproxen Na⁺ *Treximet* (Sumatriptan-Naproxen 85-500 mg) *Vimovo* (Naproxen-Esomeprazole) – the PPI is used to protect the gut from damage caused by the NSAID	All given BID OTC Typical pain, OTC: 500 mg, then 250 mg (or 220 mg, if naproxen Na⁺) Q6-8H; maximum: 1,250 mg/day naproxen base Inflammation, mild-mod pain, Rx: 500-1,000 mg/day in 2 divided doses; may increase to 1.5 g/day of naproxen base Rx *Naprosyn* 250-375-500 mg *Naprosyn EC* 375-500 mg *Naprelan* 375-500 mg *Anaprox* 275 mg *Anaprox DS* 550 mg	Prescribers and patients sometimes prefer naproxen since it is BID dosing. Relatively lower cardiac risk than some of the other NSAIDs.

Other Non-Selective NSAIDs

DRUG	DOSING	SAFETY/SIDE EFFECTS/MONITORING
Diclofenac (Cataflam, Voltaren XR) *Arthrotec* (50 mg-200 mcg misoprostol) *Voltaren* gel *Flector* patch (topical formulations)	50-75 mg BID	**BLACK BOX WARNING** Same as other NSAIDs, plus: *Arthrotec:* not to be used in women of childbearing potential unless woman is capable of complying with effective contraceptive measures **NOTES** In addition to increasing uterine contractions (which can terminate pregnancy), misoprostol component causes cramping and diarrhea Misoprostol is used to replace the gut-protective prostaglandin to reduce the risk of GI damage from the NSAID. This used to be a more popular agent before the advent of PPIs. Topical forms of diclofenac for mild pain, possible risk GI/renal issues
Indomethacin *(Indocin IR, CR)*	IR 25-50 mg CR 75 mg Approved for gout; others can be used	High risk for CNS SEs (avoid in psych conditions) and GI toxicity
Piroxicam *(Feldene)*	10-20 mg daily	High risk for GI toxicity and severe skin reactions, including SJS/TEN Use for inflammatory conditions if failed other NSAIDs, and may need agent to protect gut (PPI, misoprostol)

NSAIDs, Others Continued

DRUG	DOSING	SAFETY/SIDE EFFECTS/MONITORING
Ketorolac *(Toradol, Sprix NS)*	10-20 mg (oral) Always start IV, IM or nasal spray and continue with oral, if necessary. Not to be used in any situation with increased bleeding risk. Start with injection and switch to oral for 5-days total maximum treatment.	Can cause severe adverse effects including GI bleeding and perforation, post-op bleeding, acute renal failure, liver failure and anaphylactic shock. For short-term moderate to severe acute pain (max 5 days in adults), usually in post-op setting and never pre-op.
Other less-commonly used NSAIDs include: meclofenamate *(Meclomen)*, tolmectin *(Tolectin)*, sulindac *(Clinoril* –may be preferred with reduced renal function if an NSAID required), oxaprozin *(Daypro* – caution similar to piroxicam – higher risk side effects).		

COX-2 Selective – Lower risk for GI complications (but still present), ↑ risk MI/stroke (avoid with CVD risk – which is dose related, do not use higher doses in CVD-risk patients), same risk for renal complications

Celecoxib *(Celebrex)*	50-400 mg OA: 100 BID or 200 daily RA: 100-200 BID Indications: OA, RA, juvenile RA, acute pain, primary dysmenorrhea, ankylosing spondylitis	Highest COX-2 selectivity Contraindicated with sulfonamide allergy Same Black Box Warnings as NSAIDs above Pregnancy Category C prior to 30 weeks gestation; Category D starting at 30 weeks gestation
Meloxicam *(Mobic)*	7.5-15 mg/day	Agents that have some COX-2 selectivity (but less relative selectivity than celecoxib)
Etodolac *(Lodine)*	300-500 mg Q6-8H	
Nabumetone *(Relafen)*	1,000-2,000 mg daily (can be divided BID)	

NSAID Drug Interactions

- Caution for additive bleeding risk with the use of concurrent agents with antiplatelet activity, such as aspirin, clopidogrel *(Plavix)*, prasugrel *(Effient)*, ticagrelor *(Brilinta)*, dipyridamole *(Persantine)* and with warfarin, dabigatran, rivaroxaban, ginkgo biloba, and others.

- There is no reason to use two different NSAIDs concurrently (exception: low dose aspirin for cardioprotection but the cardioprotective effects may be blocked by ibuprofen and other NSAIDs).

- NSAIDs can increase the level of lithium (avoid concurrent use) and methotrexate.

- Caution with use of aspirin and other ototoxic agents (aminoglycosides, IV loop diuretics, etc.)

NSAID Counseling

- Take with food if this medicine upsets your stomach.

- This medicine may increase the chance of a heart attack or stroke that can lead to death. The risk increases in people who have heart disease. If you have heart disease, please discuss using this medicine with your doctor.

- Do not use this medicine before any elective surgery.

- Do not use after coronary heart surgery, unless you have been instructed to do so by your doctor.

- This medicine can cause ulcers and bleeding in the stomach and intestines at any time during treatment. The risk is highest if you use the drugs at higher doses, and when used longer-term. To help reduce the risk, limit alcohol use while taking this medicine, and use the lowest possible dose for the shortest possible time. This medicine should not be used with medicines called "steroids" (such as prednisone) and "anticoagulants" (such as warfarin, *Pradaxa* or *Xarelto)*. [There are some exceptions in very high risk (clotting) patients who use both aspirin and warfarin. In general, using them together is not recommended.]

- The risk of bleeding with these medicines is also higher with many antidepressants, including fluoxetine, paroxetine, sertraline, citalopram, escitalopram, venlafaxine and others.

- Do not use this medicine if you have experienced breathing problems or allergic-type reactions after taking aspirin or other NSAIDs.

- This medicine can raise your blood pressure. If you have high blood pressure, you will need to check your blood pressure regularly. You may have to stop using this medicine if your blood pressure increases too much.

- This medicine can cause fluid and water to accumulate, particularly in your ankles. If you have heart disease, discuss the use of this medicine with your doctor and monitor your weight. (Pharmacists, note: NSAIDs are best avoided if history of heart attack, and if heart failure-unsafe!)

- Photosensitivity: Limit sun exposure, including tanning booths, wear protective clothing, use sunscreen that blocks both UVA and UVB (this actually applies to some of the NSAIDs, but there is a class risk).

- Do not use this medicine if you are pregnant.

Opioids

Opioids in combination (such as with acetaminophen) are used for moderate pain, and strong opioid agents are used for severe pain. Codeine, fentanyl, hydrocodone, hydromorphone, methadone, morphine, oxycodone, and oxymorphone are classified as pure opioid receptor agonists. The primary receptor for pain relief is the mu receptor. Full agonists are used for acute and chronic pain and have no true "ceiling effect" – the dose can be increased – but they have a limitation to how much pain relief they can offer. However, opioids at high doses should be rotated with other opioids to reduce the risk of tolerance.

On July 9, 2012, the FDA approved a risk evaluation and mitigation strategy (REMS) for extended-release (ER) and long-acting (LA) opioid medications-including *Nucynta ER*. Primary components of the REMS: Education for the prescribers, and requirement that the prescribers counsel the patients.

DRUG	DOSING	SAFETY/SIDE EFFECTS/MONITORING
Morphine (long-acting brands: *MS Contin, Avinza, Kadian, Oramorph SR, Roxanol*) C II Morphine/Naltrexone *(Embeda)* **OPIOID AUX LABELS** Controlled substance: do not share with others. May cause dizziness or drowsiness. Do not operate machinery. Do not share: can be fatal to others. Keep away from children and animals. If long-acting: Do not crush or chew – swallow whole. Do not drink alcoholic beverages. Take with food or milk. Do not write MSO4 or MS for morphine or magnesium – due to risk of errors	Common dosing IR 10-30 mg Q4H PRN ER 15, 30, 60, 100, 200 mg Q8-12H *Avinza* daily *Kadian* daily or BID Do not crush or chew any long-acting or controlled-release opioids *Avinza*: No alcohol, can shorten long-acting duration. Can sprinkle on applesauce, soft food. *Kadian*: can be opened and can sprinkle on applesauce, soft food. If renally impaired, start at a lower dose, or avoid morphine, oxycodone or tapentadol which are all primarily renally cleared.	**BLACK BOX WARNING** Fatal respiratory depression has occurred with administration with the highest risk at initiation and with dosage increases. Proper dosing and titration should be done by a healthcare professional who is knowledgeable in the use of potent opioids for chronic pain management. Instruct patient about proper administration to prevent rapid release and absorption of long-acting products. Crushing, dissolving, or chewing of the long acting products can cause the delivery of a potentially fatal dose. **SIDE EFFECTS** **GI effects** Constipation, nausea, vomiting (May need anti-emetics, such as prochlorperazine, ondansetron, etc.) **CNS effects** Sedation (somnolence), dizziness, changes in mood, confusion, delirium **Skin reactions** Flushing, pruritus, diaphoresis – may need antihistamine (more likely with IV dosing), impotence possible with chronic use **NOTES** **Constipation** Tolerance usually develops to opioid side effects except constipation. When opioids are ATC, constipation will likely require stimulant laxatives (senna, bisacodyl) or osmotic laxatives (e.g., MOM). Rarely, docusate alone may be enough, or docusate + stimulant laxative. Methylnaltrexone (*Relistor*) is a laxative for constipation due to opioids (it blocks gut opioid-receptors). The patient must have failed DSS + laxative (senna, bisacodyl). Administered SC every other day. Cost-effective alternative: oral naloxone solution **Respiratory depression** Caused by opioid overdose or combination with other sedatives and CNS depressants, and can be fatal (see opioid antagonist section that follows) **Allergy Information** Cross-reactivity with these agents (if allergy to 1 of the following, do not use another: morphine, oxymorphone, codeine, hydrocodone, hydromorphone, oxycodone – and less commonly used agents: nalbuphine, buprenorphine, butorphanol, or levorphanol) If morphine-group allergy, choose (if appropriate): fentanyl, meperidine, methadone, tramadol, tapentadol (meperidine and fentanyl cross react) Opioid Allergy Symptoms (rare, but dangerous if present): Difficulty breathing, severe drop in BP, serious rash, swelling of face, lips, tongue, larynx – use an agent in a different chemical class

Opioids Continued

DRUG	DOSING	SAFETY/SIDE EFFECTS/MONITORING
Fentanyl _(Duragesic)_ C II Fentanyl injection _Actiq_ SL lozenge on a stick "lollipop": always start with 200 mcg, can titrate to 4 BTP episodes/day. Only for cancer BTP. **_Abstral, Fentora_ SL pills** _Onsolis_ SL film, _Subsys_ SL spray _Lazanda_ nasal spray -keep in child-resistant box. -empty unused drug into carbon lined pouch. Fentanyl transmucosal forms (all of them except patch and injection) are REMS drugs and pharmacies must be enrolled in REMS to dispense. These products are only for patients who need BTP control, who are on scheduled opioids, and who are the minimum age (16 or 18 years). Primarily for cancer BTP.	Patch: 12 (delivers 12.5 mcg/hr), 25, 50, 75, 100 mcg/h transdermal patch – change patch Q 3 days (occas. Δ Q48H – do not ↑ dose if pain is controlled but doesn't last long enough – in this case you shorten the interval, as you would do with any long-acting opioid. Otherwise, you risk overdose or higher degree of side effects.) Fentanyl, in any form, is for chronic pain management only: can transfer patient who has been using morphine 60 mg daily or equivalent x at least 7 days – not used PRN and not used as initial opioid agent PATCH Analgesic effect of patch can be seen 8-16 hrs after application – do not stop other analgesic at first (decrease dose 50% for the first 12 hrs). Do not apply > 1 patch each time and do not heat up patch or skin area before applying. Do not cover with heating pad or any bandage. Caution with fever (tell patient to call doctor if they have a fever). Do not cover with heating pads. Some need to be removed prior to MRI. Apply to hairless skin (cut short if necessary) on flat surface (chest, back, flank, upper arm) and change every 72 hrs. Press in place for 30 seconds.	**BLACK BOX WARNINGS (2)** May cause potentially life-threatening hypoventilation, respiratory depression, and/or death; only for opioid-tolerant patients (not injection). Risk of respiratory depression increased in elderly patients, debilitated patients, and patients with conditions associated with hypoxia or hypercapnia; usually occurs after administration of initial dose in nontolerant patients or when given with other drugs that depress respiratory function. Use with strong or moderate CYP3A4 inhibitors may result in increased effects and potentially fatal respiratory depression. **NOTES** Cannot use in opioid-naïve patients – especially the potent SL forms; these are for cancer-related BTP. The SL forms are REMS drugs (_Onsolis Focus_ program, etc.) Cut off stick and flush unused/unneeded _Actiq_. Do not switch generic fentanyl patches – try to use the same one. Do not use soap, alcohol, or other solvents to remove transdermal gel if it accidentally touches skin. Use large amount of water. Dispose patch in toilet or cut it up and put it in coffee grounds. Keep away from children and animals, including used patches. Alfentanil _(Alfenta)_, remifentanil _(Ultiva)_, sufentanil _(Sufenta):_ same chemical class, IV only.
Hydromorphone _(Dilaudid)_ _Exalgo_ (hydromorphone extended release) REMS drug C II	2, 4, 8 mg _Exalgo_ contraindicated in opioid-naïve patients. 2 week washout required between _Exalgo_ and MAO-is. Potent!! High risk for overdose May cause less nausea, itching	**BLACK BOX WARNING** May cause potentially life-threatening respiratory depression even with therapeutic use, especially with initiation or dose increases; instruct patients on proper administration of extended-release tablets. The use of ethanol, other opioids, and other CNS depressants may increase the risk of adverse outcomes, including death. **NOTES** Opioid-naïve patients should start with no more than 2 to 4 mg orally or 1 to 2 mg by injection every four to six hours Potent; start low, convert carefully Caution with 3A4 Inhibitors, use lower doses initially

Opioids Continued

DRUG	DOSING	SAFETY/SIDE EFFECTS/MONITORING
Oxycodone **IR: oxycodone,** *Oxenta* **CR:** *OxyContin,* *OxyContin OP* ***Endocet, Percocet,*** ***Roxicet* (oxycodone/** **acetaminophen),** also comes with ibuprofen *(Combunox)* C II – full opioids and oxycodone combos CR formulations are REMS drugs.	IR – 5-30 mg CR – 10-80 mg (60, 80 mg only for opioid-tolerant patients) Avoid high fat meals with higher doses	**BLACK BOX WARNINGS (2)** Report abuse, misuse and diversion. Avoid use with 3A4 inhibitors – will increase oxycodone levels. **NOTES** Due to abuse potential, prescribers receive training. New formulation called *"OxyContin OP"* contains polyethylene oxide to deter abuse – substance forms a gel when mixed with water. *Oxenta* is IR form that cannot be crushed into powder and contains nasal irritant (also to deter abuse)
Oxymorphone *(Opana,* ***Opana ER,*** *Opana* *Injectable)* C II	*Opana ER* 5-30 mg BID *Opana IR* 5-10 mg PRN Take on empty stomach (most other analgesics are with food to help avoid stomach upset) No alcohol with ER formulation	**BLACK BOX WARNINGS (3)** *Opana ER* is an extended release oral formulation of oxymorphone and is not suitable for use as an "as needed" analgesic. Tablets should not be broken, chewed, dissolved, or crushed; tablets should be swallowed whole. *Opana ER* is intended for use in long-term, continuous management of moderate-to-severe chronic pain. The coingestion of ethanol or ethanol-containing medications with *Opana ER* may result in accelerated release of drug from the dosage form, abruptly increasing plasma levels, which may have fatal consequences. Healthcare provider should be alert to problems of abuse, misuse, and diversion. **NOTES** Do not use with moderate-to-severe liver impairment. Use low doses in elderly, renal or mild liver impairment; there will be higher drug concentrations in these patients.
Methadone *(Dolophine)* ***(Methadose*-** liquid) C II	Start at 2.5-10 mg Q8-12H Methadone 40 mg is indicated for detox and maintenance treatment of opioid-addicted patients. Useful for detox because it relieves opioid craving and blocks euphoric effects of abusable opioids.	**BLACK BOX WARNINGS (2)** QTc interval prolongation and serious arrhythmias (e.g., torsade de pointes) have occurred during treatment. Most cases involve patients being treated for pain with large, multiple daily doses. Fatal respiratory depression has occurred with the highest risk at initiation and with dosage increases. Should be prescribed by professionals who know requirements for safe use. **NOTES** Due to variable half-life (it varies widely and can range from 15-55 hours) methadone is hard to dose safely AND has a risk of QT prolongation (pro-arrhythmic) – which will be aggravated if dosed incorrectly. Can ↓ testosterone, contribute to sexual dysfunction (others can, this one noteable). In combo with other drugs, it is serotonergic and can raise risk of serotonin syndrome

Opioids Continued

DRUG	DOSING	SAFETY/SIDE EFFECTS/MONITORING
Meperidine *(Demerol)* C II	50-150 mg Q2-4H Short duration of action (pain control for max 3 hrs) Avoid as agent for chronic pain management and do not use at all chronically, even short-term in elderly. Okay drug for short-term acute or single use (e.g., sutures in ER).	**WARNING** Renal impairment/elderly at risk for CNS toxicity **NOTES** Normeperidine (metabolite) is renally cleared and can accumulate and cause CNS toxicity, including seizures. In combo with other drugs, it is serotonergic and can raise risk of serotonin syndrome ISMP discourages use as analgesic – especially in elderly and renally impaired.

Opioids used primarily in combination

DRUG	DOSING	SAFETY/SIDE EFFECTS/MONITORING
Hydrocodone **+ acetaminophen** ***Lorcet, Lortab, Vicodin***, *Zydone, Anexsia, Co-Gesic,* **Norco (325 mg APAP – safer combo)** + chlorpheniramine *(Tussicaps)* + chlorpheniramine and pseudoephedrine *(Zutripro)* + pseudoephedrine *(Rezira)* + homatropine *(Tussagon)* + ibuprofen *(Vicoprofen, Reprexain)*	2.5, 5, 7.5, 10 mg in combo with APAP Watch for acetaminophen max dosing – higher doses of acetaminophen can result in liver toxicity; acetaminophen doses higher than 325 mg being phased out – should be gone mid-2012 *Vicodin* 5 mg HC, *Vicodin ES* 7.5 mg, *Vicodin HP* 10 mg; have variable amounts acetaminophen. The brands will drop to 300 mg acetaminophen and most of the generics will have 325 mg.	Hydrocodone is C II, combos (w/acetaminophen, ibuprofen) are C III; All hydrocodone formulations are expected to be reclassified as C II. Check prior to your law exam. Some states are C II currently.
Hydrocodone ext-release *(Zohydro ER)* C II	Start 10 mg Q 12 (opioid-naïve) Range 10-50 mg	**BLACK BOX WARNINGS** Significant respiratory depression, acute or severe bronchial asthma or hypercarbia, suspected of having paralytic ileum. **NOTES** New formulation, C II, long-acting formulation of hydrocodone alone. Use lower doses with CYP 3A4 Inhibitors.
Codeine **+ acetaminophen** ***(Tylenol #2, 3, 4)*** Codeine is C II, combos (w/acetaminophen) are C III Used as antitussive (anti-cough) agent – codeine cough syrups are C V	Usually 30 mg Q4-6H PRN, range 15-120 mg	**BLACK BOX WARNING** Respiratory depression and death have occurred in children who received codeine following tonsillectomy and/or adenoidectomy and were found to have evidence of being ultra-rapid metabolizers of codeine due to a CYP2D6 polymorphism. Deaths have also occurred in nursing infants after being exposed to high concentrations of morphine because the mothers were ultra-rapid metabolizers. Use is contraindicated in the postoperative pain management of children who have undergone tonsillectomy and/or adenoidectomy. **NOTES** Codeine has a high degree of GI side effects: constipation, nausea

Combination Opioid Agonists/Norepinephrine Reuptake Inhibitors – and Tramadol Also Inhibits 5HT Reuptake

DRUG	DOSING	SAFETY/SIDE EFFECTS/MONITORING
Tramadol *(Ultram, Ultram ER, Conzip IR/ER)* Not controlled by DEA, but C IV in many states. DEA may reclassify. **+ acetaminophen *(Ultracet)***	50 mg, or with APAP 37.5-325 mg 1-2 Q4H PRN, max 400 mg/d (300 mg/day for ER forms) Reduce if renal impairment, tramadol ER contraindicated if CrCl < 30 mL/min	**WARNING** ↑ seizure risk – avoid in patients with seizure history, head trauma **SIDE EFFECTS** Dizziness, nausea, constipation, loss of appetite, flushing insomnia (some patients find tramadol sedating but for most it is not sedating; this can be an advantage over hydrocodone), possible headache, ataxia. Lower severity of GI side effects versus strong opioids. **NOTES** Respiratory depression (rare), like opioids, can cause physiological dependence Serotonin syndrome risk if used in combination with others, such as SSRIs, etc. and is dose-dependent Avoid tramadol with 2D6 Inhibitors (requires conversion)
Tapentadol *(Nucynta, Nucynta ER)* C II	IR: 50-100 mg Q4-6H PRN ER: 50-250 mg BID	**BLACK BOX WARNINGS (2)** Respiratory depression, possibly fatal, may occur. Proper dosing, titration, and monitoring are essential. Extended release tablets must be swallowed whole and should NOT be split, crushed, broken, chewed, or dissolved in order to avoid rapid release and potential for fatal dose. No alcohol with ER formulation. **SIDE EFFECTS** Dizziness, drowsiness, nausea but lower severity of GI side effects than stronger opioids **NOTES** Like opioids, can cause physiological dependence, risk 5HT additive toxicity. No alcohol with ER formulation; alcohol may increase tapentadol systemic exposure which may lead to possible fatal overdose.

Opioid Drug Interactions

- Caution with use of concurrent CNS depressants: Additive sleepiness (somnolence), dizziness, confusion, increased risk of respiratory depression. These include alcohol, hypnotics, benzodiazepines, muscle relaxants, etc.

- Increased risk of hypoxemia with underlying respiratory disease (e.g., COPD) and sleep apnea.

- With methadone, caution with agents that worsen cardiac function or increase arrhythmia risk. Caution with other serotonergic agents.

- With meperidine, caution with agents that worsen renal function, elderly and those with seizure history. Caution with other serotonergic agents.

- With tramadol and tapentadol *(Nucynta):*, caution with other agents that lower seizure threshold. Caution with other serotonergic agents. Avoid tramadol with 2D6 Inhibitors (requires conversion). Possibility of increased INR with warfarin; monitor. Tapentadol may enhance the adverse/toxic effect of MAO Inhibitors; avoid concurrent use.

- All opioids: No alcohol, special warning to avoid alcohol with *Opana ER, Nucynta ER* and *Avinza.*

Opioid Counseling

- Do not crush, chew, break, or open controlled-release forms. Breaking them would cause too much drug to be released into your blood at one time.

- *Avinza* and *Kadian* must be swallowed whole or may be opened and the entire bead contents sprinkled on a small amount of applesauce immediately prior to ingestion. The beads must NOT be chewed, crushed, or dissolved due to the risk of exposure to a potentially toxic dose of morphine. *Avinza* can be put down a G-tube.

- *Opana*: take on empty stomach (1 hour before, 2 hours after eating).

- All Opioids, special warning for *Avinza* and *Opana ER, Nucynta ER*: No alcohol.

- To ensure that you get a correct dose, measure liquid forms with a special dose-measuring spoon or cup, not with a regular tablespoon. If you do not have a dose-measuring device, ask your pharmacist.

- This medicine will cause drowsiness and fatigue. Avoid alcohol, sleeping pills, antihistamines, sedatives, and tranquilizers that may also make you drowsy, except under the supervision of your doctor.

- Take with a full glass of water. Take with food or milk if it upsets your stomach.

- Do not stop taking suddenly if you have been taking it continuously for more than 5 to 7 days. If you want to stop, your doctor will help you gradually reduce the dose.

- This medicine is constipating. Increase the amount of fiber and water (at least six to eight full glasses daily) in your diet to prevent constipation (if not fluid restricted due to heart failure). Your pharmacist or doctor will recommend a stronger agent for constipation if this is not adequate. (If asked, recommend stool softener if hard stool, stimulants for most scheduled opioid patients.)

- Do not share this medication with anyone else.

- Never take more pain medicine than prescribed. If your pain is not being adequately treated, talk to your doctor.

Opioid Dose Conversions

The correct dose is the lowest dose that provides effective pain relief. If the dose has been increased and the pain relief is not adequate or if the side effects are intolerable (patients react differently to different opioids) <u>or</u> if the drug is unaffordable or not included on formulary, then switch. Switch safely (and always be on the watch for hyperalgesia, which should be suspected when opioids increase pain (rather than decreasing pain) due to a paradoxical situation. This happens occasionally, and if so, increasing the dose will not work. <u>If switching to morphine</u> and the patient has renal insufficiency, a 50% deduction in the total daily dose or similar would be wise; morphine has an active metabolite that is renally cleared, thus a lower dose is required. <u>Always</u> use breakthrough medication, as-needed, when converting.

For opioid conversions (not methadone) you can use ratio conversion to solve. Make sure the units <u>and</u> route in the numerator match, and the units <u>and</u> route in the denominator match. You can technically convert with fentanyl (note no oral dose conversion as fentanyl is not absorbed orally) but it is sometimes done differently using a dosing table. Some clinicians use this estimation: morphine 60 mg total daily dose = 25 mcg/hr fentanyl patch. If converting fentanyl using the chart, remember that you are finding the total daily dose in mg, <u>and will then need to convert it to mcg (multiply by 1,000) and then divide by 24 to get the patch dose; fentanyl is dosed in mcg per hour.</u>

When converting one opioid to another, estimate down (don't round up) and use breakthrough doses for compensation. A patient may respond better to one agent than another (likely due to less tolerance) and estimating lower will reduce the risk of overdose.

DRUG	IV/IM (MG)	ORAL (MG)
Morphine	10	30
Hydromorphone	1.5	7.5
Oxycodone	–	20
Hydrocodone	–	30
Codeine	130	200
Fentanyl	0.1	–
Meperidine	75	300

<u>If the medicine works, but runs out too fast, do not increase the dose</u>. This will cause a risk of respiratory depression. Rather, shorten the dosing interval.

To convert

- Calculate total 24 hour dose requirement of the current drug.

- Use ratio-conversion to calculate the dose of the new drug: make sure the numerators and denominators match in both drug and route of administration.

- Calculate 24 hr dose of new drug and <u>reduce dose at least</u> 25%. (If the problem on the exam does not tell you to reduce it but just to find the equivalent dose then don't reduce it.)

- Divide to attain appropriate interval and dose for new drug.

- Always have breakthrough pain (BTP) medication available while making changes. Guideline recommendation for BTP dosing ranges from 5-17% of the total daily baseline opioid dose.

Example of Opioid Conversion:

A hospice patient has been receiving 12 mg/day of IV hydromorphone. You are instructed to convert the hydromorphone to morphine extended-release, to be given Q12 H. The hospice policy for opioid conversion is to reduce the new dose by 50%, and to use 5-17% of the total daily dose for breakthrough pain.

The conversion factors (the left fraction) are taken from the above table. The right fraction has the patient's current total daily IV dose of hydromorphone in the denominator, and you are calculating the total daily dose of morphine in the numerator.

$$\frac{30 \text{ mg oral morphine}}{1.5 \text{ mg IV hydromorphone}} = \frac{X \text{ mg oral morphine}}{12 \text{ mg IV hydromorphone}}$$

Multiply the top left numerator (30) by the bottom right denominator, and then divide by the left denominator. This will give a total daily dose of morphine (PO) of 240 mg. Reduce by 50%, as instructed. The correct dose of morphine extended-release would be 60 mg BID.

Morphine IR can be given for BTP as 10 mg Q4H PRN. Other agents commonly used for BPT include the combo agents, such as acetaminophen/hydrocodone. In an inpatient setting, injections can be given – injections will have a faster onset and since BTP is typically severe, it may be preferable. However, if the patient does not have a port, the injection itself will cause discomfort. In real life, morphine IR may not be available. Hydrocodone-Acetaminophen is often used for breakthrough pain. The hydrocodone dose is roughly the same as the morphine dose. If the patient is using acetaminophen alone for more mild pain, and the combination if moderate, the total daily acetaminophen intake will need to be counted. Keep in mind that any drug that requires oral absorption will take time; if the patient has cancer pain (in which case the breakthrough pain is likely to be quite severe) a sublingual form of fentanyl may be used, which has faster onset.

Example of Conversion to Fentanyl Patch using a Fentanyl Patch Conversion Table

Myron has been using *Oxycontin* 40 mg BID and *Endocet* 5-325 mg as-needed for breakthrough pain. He uses the breakthrough pain medication 2-3 times weekly. Using the *Oxycontin* dose only select the fentanyl patch strength that should be chosen for this patient, using the following table.

DOSAGE COVERSIONS TO FENTANYL PATCH STRENGTHS

DRUG	25 mcg/hour	50 mcg/hour	75 mcg/hour	100 mcg/hour
Oral Morphine	60-134	135-224	225-314	315-404
IM/IV Morphine	10-22	23-37	38-52	53-67
Oral Oxycodone	30-67	67.5-112	112.5-157	157.5-202
IM/IV Oxycodone	15-33	33.1-56	56.1-78	78.1-101
Oral Codeine	150-447	448-747	748-1,047	1,048-1,347
Oral Hydromorphone	8-17	17.1-28	28.1-39	39.1-51
IV Hydromorphone	1.5-3.4	3.5-5.6	5.7-7.9	8-10
IM Meperidine	75-165	166-278	279-390	391-503
Oral Methadone	20-44	45-74	75-104	105-134
IV Methadone	10-22	23-37	38-52	53-67

SOLUTION:

Oxycodone 80 mg daily is in the range of 67.5-112 mg daily which correlates to the 50 mcg/h patch.

Methadone Conversion: Not straight-forward; should be done by pain specialists

Methadone conversion from morphine ranges from 1-20:1; this is highly variable due to patient tolerance and duration of therapy. The half-life of methadone varies widely. There are separate conversion charts for pain specialists to estimate methadone dosing. This should be done only by specialists with experience in using methadone. In addition to the variable half-life, methadone is pro-arrhythmic and has other safety issues. Methadone is used for both treatment of addiction (heroin and other opioid addiction) and for general use in chronic pain by those familiar with this agent.

Buprenorphine and Naloxone Formulations: For Pain, Addiction or Overdose.

Buprenorphine is an opioid agonist and naloxone is an opioid antagonist. Higher doses of buprenorphine are used to treat addiction, lower doses used to treat pain. Given by itself, naloxone is used for opioid overdose. As an opioid antagonist, it replaces the opioid on the mu receptor.

DRUG	DOSING	SAFETY/SIDE EFFECTS/MONITORING
Naloxone Nalmefene Naltrexone is an opioid blocker normally used to help treat alcoholism; the IV form *(Vivitrol)* is used for alcohol and opioid dependence	Naloxone-Initially, 0.4 mg-2 mg Q 2-3 min or IV infusion at 100 mL/hr (0.4 mg/hr) Repeat dosing may be required (opioid may last longer than blocking agent) Will cause an acute withdrawal syndrome (pain, anxiety, tachypnea) in patients physically dependent on opioids	**ACUTE OVERDOSE SIGNS AND SYMPTOMS** Somnolence, respiratory depression with shallow breathing, cold and clammy skin and constricted (pinpoint, miosis) pupils. Can lead to coma and death. **NOTES** Highest risk of respiratory depression in opioid-naïve patients (new users), if dose is ↑ too rapidly, and in illicit substance abuse (e.g., heroin). Due to low bioavailability, can be given orally to prevent opioid-induced constipation (off-label).
Buprenorphine + naloxone (to block opioid if used) *(Suboxone* tabs and sublingual film – slightly higher concentration, not bioequivalent to tabs) Buprenorphine transdermal *(Butrans)* – only for mod-severe pain in patients who need ATC opioid Buprenorphine *(Buprenex* Inj) C III Buprenorphine formulations are REMS drugs	*Suboxone:* Used as alternative for methadone (so patients can get from a regular doctor and filled at any pharmacy and can get over opioids since withdrawal Sx are reduced). Used daily for addiction. To prescribe *Suboxone:* Prescribers need Drug Addiction Treatment Act (DATA 2000) waiver. If they have it, the DEA number will start with X. **PATCH APPLICATION** Apply to upper outer arm, upper chest, side of chest, upper back. Change weekly. Do not use same site for at least 3 weeks. Disposal: Fold sticky sides together, flush or put in disposal unit that comes with drug.	***BUTRANS* BLACK BOX WARNING (PATCH)** Do not exceed a one 20 mcg/hr patch due to risk of QT prolongation. **SIDE EFFECTS** Sedation, dizziness, headache, confusion, mental and physical impairment QT prolongation, respiratory depression: dose-dependent Side effects from patch: nausea, headache, application site pruritis/rash, dizziness, constipation, somnolence, vomiting, application site erythema, dry mouth. **NOTES** Do not expose to patch to heat. Buprenorphine reduces patients' opioid cravings and withdrawal symptoms. In addition, buprenorphine may discourage use of nonprescribed opioids by binding to the mu receptor, thereby blocking other opioids' effects.

Buprenorphine Drug Interactions

- Caution with use of concurrent CNS depressants: Additive sedation (somnolence), dizziness, confusion. These include alcohol, hypnotics, benzodiazepines, skeletal muscle relaxants, etc.

- Prolongs the QT interval – do not use with other QT-prolonging agents or in patients at risk of arrhythmia.

MUSCLE RELAXANT/SPASTICITY AGENTS

Muscle Relaxant mechanism: Various; some work as sedatives (carisoprodol, chlorzoxazone, metaxalone, methocarbamol) and others via effects on spinal reflexes.

DRUG	DOSING	SAFETY/SIDE EFFECTS/MONITORING

Antispasmodics with analgesic effects

DRUG	DOSING	SAFETY/SIDE EFFECTS/MONITORING
Baclofen *(Lioresal)* **AUX LABELS** May cause drowsiness. Do not operate machinery….	5-20 mg TID-QID, PRN	**BLACK BOX WARNING** Avoid abrupt withdrawal of the drug; abrupt withdrawal of intrathecal baclofen has resulted in severe sequelae (hyperpyrexia, obtundation, rebound/exaggerated spasticity, muscle rigidity, and rhabdomyolysis), leading to organ failure and some fatalities. **SIDE EFFECTS** For all muscle relaxants Excessive sedation, dizziness, confusion **FOR ALL OF THE SKELETAL MUSCLE RELAXANTS:** Excessive sedation, dizziness, confusion **NOTES** Do not overdose in elderly (e.g., start low, titrate carefully), watch for additive side effects
Cyclobenzaprine *(Flexmid, Amrix* ER) Flexeril	5-10 mg TID, PRN ER: 15-30 mg once daily	*[handwritten: Dry Mouth]* Xerostomia. May have efficacy with fibromyalgia Serotonergic: should not be combined with other serotonergic agents. May precipitate or exacerbate cardiac arrhythmias; caution in elderly or those with heart disease (similar to tricyclics)
Tizanidine *(Zanaflex)*	2-4 mg Q6-8H, PRN (max 3/d)	Central alpha-1-agonist: hypotension, dizziness, xerostomia, weakness

Drugs that exert their effects by sedation

DRUG	DOSING	SAFETY/SIDE EFFECTS/MONITORING
Carisoprodol *(Soma)* C IV (due to dependence, withdrawal symptoms, and diversion and abuse)	250-350 mg QID, PRN	Drowsiness Poor CYP 2C19 metabolizers will have higher carisoprodol concentrations (up to 4-fold)
Metaxalone *(Skelaxin)*	800 mg TID-QID, PRN	Decreased cognitive/sedative effects; hepatotoxic; monitor
Methocarbamol *(Robaxin, Robaxin-750)*	1,500-2,000 mg QID, PRN	Hypotension; monitor BP

Rarely used muscle relaxants include dantrolene *(Dantrium* – sometimes used for malignant hyperthermia), chlorzoxazone *(Parafon Forte)*, orphenadrine *(Norflex)*

Muscle Relaxant Drug Interactions

- Caution with use of concurrent agents that are CNS depressants: Additive sedation (somnolence), dizziness, confusion. These include alcohol, hypnotics, benzodiazepines, opioids, etc.

- Carisoprodol: Poor CYP 2C19 metabolizers will have higher carisoprodol concentrations (up to 4-fold).

- Tizanidine: contraindicated with ciprofloxacin and fluvoxamine due to elevated tizanidine levels.

Muscle Relaxant Counseling

- This medicine will cause <u>drowsiness and fatigue</u> and can impair your ability to perform mental and physical activities. Do not drive when using this medicine.

- <u>Avoid alcohol</u>, sleeping pills, antihistamines, sedatives, pain pills and tranquilizers that may also make you drowsy, except under the supervision of your doctor.

Common Neuropathic Pain Agents

For a fuller discussion, see Epilepsy and Depression chapters.

DRUG	DOSING	SAFETY/SIDE EFFECTS/MONITORING
Pregabalin *(Lyrica)* Diabetic neuropathic pain, postherpetic neuralgia, fibromyalgia, spinal cord damage, adjunctive therapy for adult patients with partial onset seizures C V Capsule, solution	Initial: 75 mg BID Maximum: 600 mg/day ↓ dose and ↑ interval if CrCl < 60 mL/min	**SIDE EFFECTS** Dizziness, somnolence, peripheral edema, weight gain, ataxia, diplopia, blurred vision, xerostomia, mild euphoria
Duloxetine *(Cymbalta)* Peripheral neuropathic pain Fibromyalgia Chronic musculoskeletal pain Depression Generalized Anxiety Disorder	30-60 mg/day	**SIDE EFFECTS** **Common to all SNRIs** ↑ BP, HR, sexual side effects (20-50%) include ↓ libido, ejaculation difficulties, anorgasmia, increased sweating (hyperhydrosis), restless leg (see if began when therapy was started) Possibility of mood changes – requires MedGuide and monitoring **Duloxetine-Specific Side Effects** Nausea, Dry mouth; somnolence, fatigue, ↓ appetite
Gabapentin *(Neurontin)* *Gralise* – indicated for postherpetic neuralgia *Horizant* – indicated for postherpetic neuralgia and restless leg syndrome Capsule, tablet, solution	Initial: 300 mg TID Maximum: 3,600 mg/day ↓ dose and ↑ interval if CrCl < 60 mL/min	**SIDE EFFECTS** Dizziness, somnolence, ataxia, peripheral edema, weight gain, diplopia, blurred vision, xerostomia **NOTES** Used more often for off-labeled uses such as fibromyalgia, pain, headache, peripheral neuropathy, drug abuse, alcohol withdrawal Take extended release formulation with food
Amitriptyline *(Elavil)*	10-50 mg QHS, sometimes higher	**SIDE EFFECTS** Are uncommon with low doses used for pain, but could include: **Cardiotoxicity** (QT-prolongation) with overdose – can be used for suicide- counsel carefully Orthostatic hypotension, tachycardia, anticholinergic – dry mouth, blurred vision, urinary retention, constipation, delirium in elderly

Fibromyalgia Agents

DRUG	DOSING/INDICATIONS	SAFETY/SIDE EFFECTS/MONITORING
Milnacipran *(Savella)* Selective Serotonin Reuptake Inhibitor (SNRI)	Day 1: 12.5 mg daily Days 2-3: 12.5 mg BID Days 4-7: 25 mg BID Then 50 mg BID (CrCl < 30 mL/min, max dose is 25 mg BID)	**BLACK BOX WARNINGS** Milnacipran is a serotonin/norepinephrine reuptake inhibitor (SNRI) similar to SNRIs used to treat depression and other psychiatric disorders. Antidepressants increase the risk of suicidal thinking and behavior in children, adolescents, and young adults (18-24 years of age) with major depressive disorder (MDD) and other psychiatric disorders (not approved for depression). **CONTRAINDICATIONS** Concomitant use or within 2 weeks of MAO inhibitors; uncontrolled narrow-angle glaucoma **SIDE EFFECTS** Nausea, headache, constipation, dizziness, insomnia, hot flashes **DRUG INTERACTIONS** Digoxin: Milnacipran may enhance the adverse/toxic effect of Digoxin. The risk of postural hypotension and tachycardia may be increased, particularly with IV digoxin. Do not use IV digoxin in patients receiving milnacipran. Do not use with methylene blue or linezolid. Increased bleeding risk with anticoagulants or antiplatelets.
Pregabalin *(Lyrica)*	See above neuropathic pain section	
Duloxetine *(Cymbalta)*	See above neuropathic pain section	

Topical Pain Agents, For Localized Pain

DRUG	DOSING/NOTES	SAFETY/SIDE EFFECTS/MONITORING
Lidocaine 5% patches *(Lidoderm)* Lidocaine viscous gel (Rx) *LidoPatch*, OTC, 3.99%	Apply to affected area 1-3 patches/day for up to 12 hrs/day (5% patch) Approved for postherpetic neuralgia (shingles)	**SIDE EFFECTS** Minor topical burning, itching, rash **NOTES** Can cut into smaller pieces (before removing backing). Do not apply more than 3 patches at one time. Caution with used patches; can harm children and pets; fold patch in half and discard safely. Do not cover with heating pads/electric blankets.
Capsaicin 0.025% and 0.075% *(Zostrix, Zostrix HP)* *Qutenza 8% – Rx* capsaicin patch	Apply to affected area TID-QID ↓ TRPV1-expressing nociceptive nerve endings (↓ substance P)	**SIDE EFFECTS** Topical burning, which dissipates with continued use **NOTES** *Qutenza* is given in the doctor's office only – it causes topical burning and requires pre-treatment with lidocaine – applied for 1 hour and lasts for months – works in ~ 40% of patients to reduce pain, indicated for post-herpetic neuralgia (PHN) pain.

Topical Pain Agents, For Localized Pain Continued

DRUG	DOSING/NOTES	SAFETY/SIDE EFFECTS/MONITORING
Diclofenac topical *Voltaren* gel *Flector* patch	Apply to affected area TID-QID NSAIDs, for OA	**NOTES** *Flector* patch: apply to most painful area, twice daily. Remove if bathing/showering. Remove for MRI.
Methyl salicylate topical OTCs (*BenGay, Icy Hot, Precise, SalonPas, Thera-Gesic*, store brands) Methyl salicylate plus other ingredients	Patches, creams	**NOTES** OTC counseling: contact healthcare provider if rash, itching, or excessive skin irritation occurs, or symptoms persist for > 7 days. Do not apply over wounds or damaged skin. Occasionally the topicals have caused first to third-degree burns, mostly in patients with neuropathic damage: Discontinue use and seek medical attention if signs of skin injury (pain, swelling, or blistering) occur following application.

Lidoderm Patient Counseling

- Patches may be cut into smaller sizes with scissors before removal of the release (plastic) liner.

- Safely discard unused portions of cut patches where children and pets cannot get to them.

- Apply up to three (3) patches at one time to cover the most painful area. Apply patches only once for up to 12 hours in a 24-hour period (12 hours on and 12 hours off).

- Remove patch if skin irritation occurs.

- Fold used patches so that the adhesive side sticks to itself and safely discard used patches or pieces of cut patches where children and pets cannot get to them. Even a used patch contains enough medicine to harm a child or pet.

- Do not use on broken, abraded, severely burned or skin with open lesions (can significantly increase amount absorbed).

Capsaicin Patient Counseling

- Apply a thin film of cream to the affected area and gently rub in until fully absorbed.

- Apply 3 to 4 times daily.

- Best results typically occur after 2 to 4 weeks of continuous use. Do not use as-needed, since frequent, long-term use is required for benefit.

- Unless treating hands, wash hands thoroughly with soap and water immediately after use.

- If treating hands, leave on for 30 minutes, then wash hands as above.

- Do not touch genitals, nasal area, mouth or eyes with the medicine; it will burn the sensitive skin.

- The burning pain should dissipate with continual use; starting at the lower strength will help.

- Never cover with bandages or a heating pad; serious burning could result.

PRACTICE CASE

PATIENT PROFILE

Patient Name	Gene Schneider						
Address	11188 Countryclub Drive						
Age	50	**Sex** Male	**Race** White	**Height** 5'6"		**Weight** 239lbs	
Allergies	SULFA						

DIAGNOSES

Hypertension

Osteoarthritis

MEDICATIONS

Date	No.	Prescriber	Drug & Strength	Quantity	Sig	Refills
12/13	57643	Suhlbach	Atenolol 100 mg	30	1 PO daily	11
12/13	57647	Suhlbach	Amlodipine 5 mg	30	1 PO daily	11
12/13	57648	Suhlbach	HCTZ 25 mg	30	1 PO daily	11
OTC			Acetaminophen 500 mg		1-2 PO prn, 4-5x daily	
OTC			Capsaicin cream 0.025%		Apply QID	

LAB/DIAGNOSTIC TESTS

Test	Normal Value	Results Date 12/11/2013	Date	Date
GLU	65-99 mg/dL	118		
Na	135-146 mEq/L	130		
K	3.5-5.3 mEq/L	3.7		
Cl	98-110 mEq/L	104		
C02	21-33 mmHg	28		
BUN	7-25 mg/dL	26		
Creatinine	0.6-1.2 mg/dL	1.5		

ADDITIONAL INFORMATION

Date	Notes
12/15/2013	BP today 152/92, Pt reports pain at 5-7 throughout day, describes knee as "grating." Capsaicin and APAP used regularly; asking for stronger pain medicine.

Questions

1. Gene's wife asks if OTC ibuprofen would be useful when the pain is not relieved with acetaminophen. You counsel Gene and his wife that this may be unsafe due to the following reason/s. (Select **ALL** that apply).

   a. It could cause acute kidney problems.

   b. It could cause his blood pressure to increase.

   c. It could cause an interaction with the acetaminophen.

   d. Ibuprofen is contraindicated with a sulfa allergy.

   e. Ibuprofen is not safe to use with concurrent capsaicin.

2. Gene's physician prescribes *Ultracet*. This drug contains the following ingredients:

   a. Tramadol-acetaminophen

   b. Tramadol-ibuprofen

   c. Hydrocodone-acetaminophen

   d. Hydrocodone-ibuprofen

   e. Codeine-acetaminophen

3. Gene's wife uses *Percocet*, and she suggests that this might help Gene. Which of the following statements is correct?

   a. This drug contains an NSAID.

   b. It is no more effective for pain than aspirin and can be dangerous.

   c. There are no significant side effects.

   d. It is more effective for pain than acetaminophen alone.

   e. It may raise blood pressure.

4. Gene fills a prescription for *Ultracet*, and finds that the pain relief is satisfactory for about one year. After this time, the physician tries *MS Contin*, and eventually switches Gene over to the *Duragesic* patch. You call the physician and suggest the following:

   a. *Duragesic* is the brand name for hydromorphone.

   b. This is a poor choice due to his degree of renal insufficiency.

   c. This medication can only be used in patients who have dysphagia.

   d. The correct dosing frequency is one patch daily.

   e. The correct dosing frequency is one patch every 3 days.

Questions 5-11 are NOT based on the above case.

5. Tramadol is not a safe choice in a patients with this condition in their profiles:

   a. Renal insufficiency

   b. Aspirin allergy

   c. Seizures

   d. Peptic ulcer disease

   e. Gout

6. A physician has called the pharmacist. He has a patient on morphine sulfate extended-release who is having difficulty with regular bowel movements. The patient is using docusate sodium 100 mg BID. The patient reports that his stools are difficult to expel, although they are not particularly hard or condensed. Which of the following recommendation is most appropriate to prevent the constipation?

   a. Senna

   b. Bismuth subsalicylate

   c. *Relistor*

   d. Mineral oil

   e. Phosphate soda

7. A patient with cancer is using the fentanyl patch along with the *Actiq* transmucosal formulation for breakthrough pain. Which statement is correct?

   a. The starting dose of *Actiq* is 400 mcg.

   b. No more than 4 BTP episodes per day should be treated with *Actiq*; if more are required, the patient should consult with his/her physician.

   c. A patient who is not taking an extended-release version of an opioid may still use *Actiq* for occasional, breakthrough cancer pain.

   d. This drug should not be given with *MS Contin* at doses greater than 100 mg daily.

   e. This drug is contraindicated in patients older than 65 years of age.

8. Which of the following brand-generic combinations is correct?

   a. Celecoxib *(Mobic)*
   b. Naproxen *(Motrin)*
   c. Morphine *(Opana)*
   d. Hydromorphone *(Dilaudid)*
   e. Methadone *(Demerol)*

9. Choose the correct statement regarding the pain medication *Celebrex*:

   a. This may be a safer option for patients with GI bleeding risk.
   b. This may be a safer option for patients with reduced renal function.
   c. This is a non-selective NSAID, and has a better safety profile.
   d. This drug is safe to use in patients with any type of sulfonamide allergy.
   e. The maximum dose for inflammatory conditions, such as RA, is 200 mg daily.

10. A pain patient with poor control has been taking hydrocodone-acetaminophen 10mg-500mg 8 tablets daily. The physician will convert the patient to *Avinza* to provide adequate pain relief and to reduce the risk of acetaminophen toxicity. Using the hydrocodone component only, calculate the total daily dose of *Avinza* that is equivalent to the hydrocodone dose, and then reduce the dose by 25% (to lessen the possibility of excessive side effects from the initial conversion). The final daily dose of *Avinza* is:

    a. 10 mg *Avinza*
    b. 40 mg *Avinza*
    c. 60 mg *Avinza*
    d. 80 mg *Avinza*
    e. 110 mg *Avinza*

11. Which is the correct antidote for acetaminophen toxicity?

    a. Flumazenil
    b. N- Acetylcysteine
    c. Pyridoxine
    d. Physostigmine
    e. Atropine

Answers

1-a,b, 2-a, 3-d, 4-e, 5-c, 6-a, 7-b, 8-d, 9-a, 10-c, 11-b

MIGRAINE

GUIDELINES

Treatment: Evidence-Based Guidelines for Migraine Headache in the Primary Care Setting: Pharmacologic Management for Prevention of Migraine, American Academy of Neurology. Available at www.aan.com

ICSI Health Care Guideline: Diagnosis and Treatment of Headache, 2011. Available at: http://www.icsi.org/headache/headache__diagnosis_and_treatment_of_2609.html

BACKGROUND

Headache treatment is a common concern in the community pharmacy, one of the most common patient complaints in neurologists' offices and the most common pain complaint seen in family practice. Most headaches are migraine and tension-type headaches.

Migraines are chronic headaches that can cause significant pain for hours or days. In addition to severe pain, most migraines cause nausea, vomiting, and sensitivity to light and sound. Some migraines are preceded or accompanied by sensory warning symptoms or signs (auras), such as flashes of light, blind spots or tingling in the arms or legs. Most migraines do not have an aura.

Rarely, a migraine could be occurring with a serious cardiovascular, cerebrovascular or infectious event. Patients should be seen at once if the headache is accompanied with fever, stiff neck, rash, mental confusion, seizures, double vision, weakness, numbness, chest pain, trouble breathing or trouble speaking.

MIGRAINE CAUSES

Migraines may be caused by changes in the trigeminal nerve and imbalances in neurotransmitters, including serotonin, which decreases during a migraine causing a chemical release of neuropeptides that trigger vasodilation in cranial blood vessels. Triptan drugs are serotonin-receptor agonists and cause vasoconstriction of cranial blood vessels.

The cause of migraines is not well-understood but "trigger" identification can be useful to help the patient avoid triggers and reduce migraine incidence.

TREATMENT

A common type of migraine is a menstrual-associated migraine in women. These may be treated with oral contraceptives to decrease migraine frequency. Another option is NSAIDs or Triptans, started 2d prior to the menses and continued for 5-7 days.

Children get migraines and may ask the pharmacist for advice. OTC agents, usually ibuprofen, are used first. Triptans are used in children.

Non-pharmacologic interventions involve avoiding triggers, mental relaxation, stress management, or applying cold compresses to the head.

Pharmacologic interventions include OTC medicines (such as *Advil Migraine*, which is plain ibuprofen), *Excedrin migraine* (aspirin, acetaminophen and caffeine) or other agents, including store brands of these options. Some patients get more relief from OTC products, some from triptans or other prescription agents (including hydrocodone or other opioid combos or tramadol) and others need to use combinations of both OTC and prescription agents.

If a patient uses acute treatments more than twice per week, or if the migraines decrease their quality of life, an agent can be used to decrease migraine frequency. These agents can be antidepressants, anticonvulsants, vitamins or natural products, and should be tried at a reasonable dose for 2-6 months. All prophylactic agents can ↓ frequency by 50%, but a patient may need to try several options before finding an agent (or combination of agents) that works for them.

The pharmacist should understand which drugs are useful for both treating an acute attack and which drugs are used for preventing further attacks (prophylaxis).

Natural Products

Feverfew, willow bark (a salicylate), butterbur, magnesium, and riboflavin may be helpful, alone or in combination.

COMMON MIGRAINE TRIGGERS

Hormonal changes in women
Fluctuations in estrogen trigger headaches in many women. Some women will use monophasic birth control pill formulations to keep estrogen levels more constant and help reduce pre-menstrual migraines, the most common type of female migraine. ACOG recommends progestin-only bcp's for women with migraine with aura, due to stroke risk with estrogen-containing contraceptives.

Foods
Common offending agents include alcohol, especially beer and red wine, aged cheeses, chocolate, aspartame, overuse of caffeine, monosodium glutamate (MSG), salty foods and processed foods.

Stress
Stress is a major instigator of migraines.

Sensory stimuli
Bright lights, sun glare, loud sounds and scents (which may be pleasant or unpleasant odors).

Changes in wake-sleep pattern
Either missing sleep or getting too much sleep (including jet lag).

Changes in the environment
A change of weather or barometric pressure.

Acute Treatment

Triptans are used commonly for migraines but some patients find better relief with NSAIDs or *Excedrin Migraine* or generics (acetaminophen+aspirin+caffeine). OTC agents, in some patients, are the best option. Other patients find that using an NSAID and triptan together provides stronger relief.

TRIPTANs: are 5HT$_1$ receptor agonists. Blood vessels in the brain become dilated during a migraine attack and the triptans, by binding to 5HT$_1$-receptors, causes cranial vessel constriction, inhibiting neuropeptide release and ↓ pain transmission.

DRUG	DOSING	SAFETY/SIDE EFFECTS/MONITORING
Naratriptan *(Amerge)*	1 and 2.5 mg, can repeat x 1 after 4 hr	**CONTRAINDICATIONS** Serious but rare cerebrovascular and cardiovascular events can occur; because of this, triptans are contraindicated in patients with cerebrovascular disease or uncontrolled hypertension.
Almotriptan *(Axert)*	6.25 and 12.5 mg, can repeat x 1 after 2 hr Max 25 mg/day	A few are contraindicated with MAOIs (see below). All must be used with caution with concurrent use of other serotonergic drugs.
Frovatriptan *(Frova)*	2.5 mg, can repeat x 1 after 2 hr Max 7.5 mg/day	**SIDE EFFECTS** Somnolence, nausea, paresthesias (tingling/numbness), throat/neck pressure, dizziness, hot/cold sensations, chest pain/tightness
SUMAtriptan ***(Imitrex, Alsuma)*** Needleless sumatriptan injection *(Sumavel DosePro*- 6 mg – injection by air pressure – may hurt)* ***Imitrex STATdose* SC injection** ***Imitrex* nasal spray** SUMAtriptan + naproxen 85-500 mg*(Treximet)* *Zecuity* transdermal	PO: 25, 50 and 100 mg, can repeat x 1 after 2 hr Nasal Spray: 5, 20 mg, can repeat x 1 after 2 hr SC inj: 4, 6 mg, can repeat x 1 after 1 hr *Treximet* max 2 tabs/24 hr	Triptan sensations include pressure in the chest or heaviness or pressure in the neck region and usually dissipate after administration. **NOTES** **Formulations** ■ All of the triptans are available in tablet formulation. ■ Rizatriptan and zolmitriptan also have disintegrating tablets that dissolve on the tongue: *good if N/V, dysphagia.* Sumatriptan has a nasal spray and a SC injection – fast onset for migraines that come on quickly, and avoids oral route. Zolmitriptan has an intranasal spray (and the disintegrating tablet).
Rizatriptan *(Maxalt,* ***Maxalt-MLT* disint tabs)**	5 mg and 10 mg, can repeat x 1 after 2 hr *Maxalt MLT* 5 mg, no water needed Max 30 mg/day	
Eletriptan *(Relpax)*	20 mg and 40 mg, can repeat after 2 hr Max 80 mg/day	**Duration of Action** The longest-acting triptans (longer acting, but slower onset) are frovatriptan (the longest – has 26 hr t½ – and naratriptan. Choose if HA recurs after dosing, lasts a long time. Can use agents with shorter durations of action if fast onset required. The ones with a shorter half-life have a faster onset: almotriptan, eletriptan, rizatriptan, sumatriptan and zolmitriptan.
ZOLMItriptan *(Zomig,* *Zomig-ZMT* disint tabs) *Zomig* nasal spray (NS)	PO: 2.5 and 5 mg, can repeat after 2 hr NS: 5 mg, can repeat after 2 hr *Zomig-ZMT* dissolving tabs 2.5, 5 mg, no water needed	Study: eletriptan *(Relpax)* 40 mg was more effective than sumatriptan *(Imitrex)* 100 mg in relieving pain.

Triptan Drug Interactions

- FDA warning about combining triptans with serotonergic drugs such as SSRIs and SNRIs. Counsel patients on both medications to report restlessness, sweating, poor coordination, confusion, hallucinations. However, many patients take both types together. It may present a problem when another serotonergic agent is added to the combination.

- *Imitrex, Maxalt* and *Zomig* are contraindicated with MAO-Is, the others are not.

- Eletriptan *(Relpax)* is contraindicated with strong CYP 3A4 inhibitors.

Patient Counseling for Triptans

- Side effects that you may experience include sleepiness, nausea, numbness, throat or neck pressure, dizziness, hot or cold sensations, and a heaviness or pressure in the chest or neck region. These usually occur after the drug is taken and go away shortly.

- If nausea prevents you from swallowing or holding down your medicine, your doctor can prescribe a tablet that dissolves in your mouth or an injection or nasal spray.

- If you have migraines that come on very quickly, a nasal spray or SC injection will provide faster relief.

- Serious, but rare, side effects such as heart attacks and strokes have occurred in people who have used this type of medicine; because of this, triptans cannot be used in patients who have had a stroke, have heart disease or have blood pressure that is not well-controlled. If any of this applies to you, please let your pharmacist know so the doctor can be contacted.

- With *Imitrex, Maxalt* and *Zomig*: There is a chance of serotonin syndrome when using this drug with some drugs for low mood (depression) or weight loss. The syndrome is caused by too much serotonin in the body. Signs include agitation, changes in blood pressure, loose stools, a fast heartbeat, hallucinations, upset stomach and throwing up, change in balance, and change in thinking clearly and with logic.

- Take the medicine with or without food, at the first sign of a migraine. The migraine treatment will not work as well if you wait to use it.

- If you use the orally disintegrating tablets *(Maxalt-MLT* and *Zomig-ZMT)*, peel open the blister pack and place the orally disintegrating tablet on your tongue, where it will dissolve and be swallowed with saliva. You do not need to use water with the medicine. These formulations should not be used in patients with phenylketonuria, due to the sweetener.

- If your symptoms are only partly relieved, or if your headache comes back, you may take a second dose in the time period explained to you by the pharmacist.

- If you use migraine treatments more than twice a week or if they are severe, you should be using a daily medicine to help reduce the number of migraines. Please discuss using a "prophylaxis" medicine with your doctor if you are not using one.

Imitrex Injection Counseling using the STATdose system

Imitrex injections can be administered by prefilled SC syringe, or commonly using the STAT-dose injection device. *Alsuma* is a pre-filled auto injector. Protect all from light.

- Inject the medication just below the skin (always SC, never IM or IV) as soon as the symptoms of your migraine appear.

- Use the STATdose system to administer your injection. This system includes a carrying case and two syringes which will assist you in taking your subcutaneous shot. The shot is relatively mild as it is not a large needle.

- Clean the area of skin, usually in the upper outside arm, with rubbing alcohol prior to administering the injection.

- Open the *Imitrex* injection carrying case and pull off the tamper-proof packaging from one of the cartridge packs. Open the lid of the cartridge. Pull the unused STATdose cartridge from the carrying case.

- Load the STATdose pen by inserting it into the cartridge and turning it clockwise. The cartridge is loaded when you are no longer able to turn the pen clockwise.

- Gently pull the loaded pen out of the carrying case. The blue button on the side triggers the injection. There is a safety feature that does not allow the injection to be triggered unless it is against your skin

- Hold the loaded pen to the area that you have cleaned to receive the shot. Push the blue button on the side of the pen. To make sure you receive all of the medicine, you must hold the pen still for 5 seconds.

- Follow safety procedures and return the used injection needle to the cartridge. Insert the pen once again into the cartridge. This time turn it counterclockwise to loosen the needle. Remove the empty STATdose pen from the cartridge and store it in the carrying case.

- Replace the cartridge pack after both doses of have been used. Discard the pack and insert a new refill.

Zomig Nasal Spray Counseling

- Blow your nose gently before use.

- Remove the protective cap.

- Hold the nasal sprayer device gently with your fingers and thumb as shown in the picture to the right.

- There is only one dose in the nasal sprayer. Do not try to prime (test) the nasal sprayer or you will lose the dose.

- Do not press the plunger until you have put the tip into your nostril or you will lose the dose. Insert into nose about a half an inch, close your mouth, press the plunger, keep head level for 10-20 seconds, gently breathe in through your mouth.

- *Zecuity* sumatriptan patch: This is a transdermal patch that runs on lithium batteries. The red light indicates the drug is being released. Use on upper arm or thigh (dry, clean, relatively hair-free). Remove for MRI. Most common side effect is application site irritation.

OTC MIGRAINE AGENTS

If recommending an OTC product, any OTC NSAID such as *Advil Migraine* (ibuprofen only, or generics), or *Excedrin Migraine* (acetaminophen+aspirin+caffeine) are reasonable options. Aspirin would not be a good choice due to nausea. Always ask the patient what they have tried in the past, and if it was useful.

Less Commonly Used Acute Migraine Medications

Acetaminophen/butalbital/caffeine (*Fioricet*), also comes *Fioricet* with codeine, C III, *Fiorinal* is aspirin/butalbital/caffeine.

- *Fioricet* generic is popular drug. It contains a barbiturate and if using regular, and long-term, must taper off or patient will get worsening of headache, tremors, and be put at risk of delirium and seizures.

- If using codeine formulation, counsel on possible nausea, constipation.

- Do not mix with alcohol.

- Do not exceed safe doses of acetaminophen.

Can also use hydrocodone/APAP combinations *(Vicodin* etc)*, or other opioid combo products.

Butorphanol *(Stadol NS)*, C IV, intranasal spray may provide fast and effective relief of migraine. Onset in 15 mins.

Ergotamine Products

- Pregnancy Category X Black Box Warning: Do not use with strong/moderate CYP 3A4 Inhibitors due to risk of cerebral ischemia with higher levels of the ergotamine drug.

- Ergoloid mesylates *(Ergomar, Ergostat)*, ergotamine/caffeine *(Cafergot,* generics), Dihydroergotamine *(DHE-45, Migranal Nasal Spray)*.

- Ergotamine side effects include nausea/vomiting, muscle pain, tingling in periphery, angina-like pain, weakness in legs, tachycardia, bradycardia.

Migraine Prophylaxis

Consider using a prophylactic if the patient uses acute treatments more than twice per week, or if the migraines decrease their quality of life. This is an agent taken daily. Typically, the reduction in migraines is ~50%, but a patient may have to try more than one agent to find one that works well for them. A full trial, at a reasonable dose, should be 2-6 months. Topiramate is being used commonly since it has a better side effect profile than most of the other agents, and causes weight loss. The efficacy data is similar; choose the prophylactic agent based on the patient and the side effect profile. If hypertension, using a beta-blocker may be the most practical. If weight loss is desirable, topiramate may be chosen. Valproate works, but is often chosen last due to the side-effect profile. In young women, valproate can cause polycystic ovary syndrome (PCOS), due to an increase in testosterone levels. Young women often get migraines, and for this reason (along with weight gain), valproate is avoided, if possible, in this population.

First-line therapies for migraine prophylaxis in adults include:

■ Beta-blockers: best evidence with propranolol *(Inderal)*, timolol *(Blocadren)*, metoprolol, valproate, and topiramate *(Topamax)*. Extended-cycle oral contraceptives if pre-menstrual migraine, or start NSAIDs or triptan 2 days prior to menses, continue for 5-7 days.

Second-line therapy for migraine prophylaxis include:

■ Other beta-blockers, ACE Inhibitors, antidepressants, natural products (see introduction section), birth control pills (for premenstrual migraine) and botulinum toxin type A *(Botox)* injections – *Botox* is for CHRONIC migraines only (lasts 15 or more days/month.) Amitryptiline is lower than for depression. This is why venlafaxine is often used first, but amitryptiline can be added on as a low dose QHS for migraine if the patient is using an SSRI.

First-line agents for migraine prophylaxis

DRUG	TYPICAL DOSING RANGE	COMMENTS/SIDE EFFECTS
Beta-blockers		
Propranolol (*Inderal*)	40-120 mg, divided BID	Fatigue, ↓ HR, possible depression with propranolol (most lipophilic); complete discussion in Hypertension chapter.
Timolol (*Blocadren*)	10-15 mg twice daily	Both propranolol and timolol are non-selective beta-blockers; do not use in COPD, emphysema, complete discussion in Hypertension chapter.
Metoprolol (*Lopressor*, if long acting: *Lopressor XL, Toprol XL*)	100-200 mg daily	Metoprolol is beta1-selective. Caution with all beta-blockers if low HR (they will ↓ HR), monitor for hypotension, dizziness; complete discussion in Hypertension chapter.
Anticonvulsants		
Divalproex (*Depakote*), Valproate (*Depakene*) Preg D: Avoid in women of childbearing age	250-500 mg twice daily	Liver toxicity, pancreatitis, sedation, weight gain, tremor, teratogenicity, thrombocytopenia, alopecia, nausea (less with divalproex), polycystic ovarian syndrome; complete discussion in Epilepsy chapter.
Topiramate (*Topamax*) Preg D: Avoid in women of childbearing age	Start 25 mg QHS, titrate to 50 mg BID	Nephrolithiasis, open angle glaucoma, hypohydrosis (children), depression, metabolic acidosis, 6-8% weight loss, reduced efficacy of oral contraceptives, cognitive impairment; complete discussion in Epilepsy chapter.

Medication-overuse ("rebound") headaches

These result from overuse of most headache medicines: NSAIDs, opioids, the butalbital-containing drugs, any analgesic combination products, triptans, and ergotamines (except DHE). Pharmacists are in a position to see many patients who are chronically using headache medicines, and have daily headaches. It may be best to discuss this with a doctor if the patient seems at risk or is unlikely to try and cut down analgesic use independently. To prevent medication-overuse headaches, educate patients to limit acute treatment medications to 2 or 3 times per week, at most. The most important thing is to stop the "over-used" medication. If the drug is an opioid or contains butalbital *(Fioricet, Fiorinal)* they will require a slow taper to discontinue.

GOUT

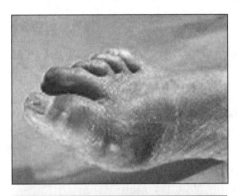

GUIDELINE

Khanna D, Fitzgerald JD, Khanna PP, et al. 2012 American College of Rheumatology Guidelines for Management of Gout. Arthritis Care and Research 2012;64(10):1431-1461.

BACKGROUND

Gout is a disease that usually presents with recurrent attacks of acute inflammatory arthritis. Gout attacks are sudden with severe pain, burning, and swelling. Gout typically occurs in one joint, which is most often the metatarsophalangeal joint (MTP, the big toe). If left untreated, the attacks can occur over and over, and will eventually damage the joints, tendons and other tissues.

CAUSES

Uric acid is produced as an end-product of purine metabolism (see production of uric acid diagram). Under normal conditions, uric acid is excreted ⅔ renally and ⅓ by the GI tract. When uric acid builds up in the blood, the patient may remain asymptomatic (many people with high uric acid, or hyperuricemia, never get gout) or the uric acid can crystallize in the joints, resulting in a severe, painful gout attack. Gout typically strikes after many years of persistent hyperuricemia.

Risk Factors

Risk factors for gout include male sex, obesity, excessive alcohol consumption (particularly beer), hypertension, chronic kidney disease, lead intoxication, advanced age and using medications that increase uric acid. To reduce the risk of recurrent gout attacks patients should avoid organ meats, high-fructose corn syrup and alcohol. Servings of fruit juices, table sugar, sweetened drinks and desserts, salt, beef, lamb, pork and seafood with high purine content (sardines, shellfish) should be limited. Low-fat dairy products, vegetables, hydration, weight loss and exercise are encouraged and may reduce the risk for gout attacks.

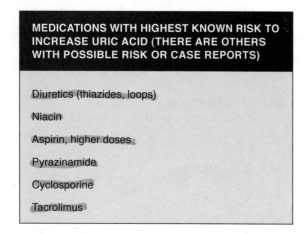

MEDICATIONS WITH HIGHEST KNOWN RISK TO INCREASE URIC ACID (THERE ARE OTHERS WITH POSSIBLE RISK OR CASE REPORTS)

Diuretics (thiazides, loops)

Niacin

Aspirin, higher doses

Pyrazinamide

Cyclosporine

Tacrolimus

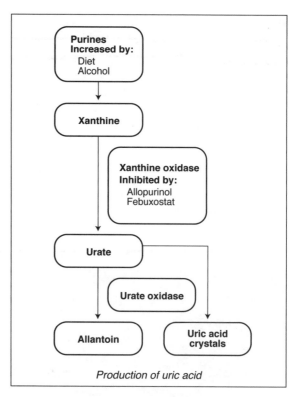

Purines
Increased by:
Diet
Alcohol

Xanthine

Xanthine oxidase
Inhibited by:
Allopurinol
Febuxostat

Urate

Urate oxidase

Allantoin

Uric acid
crystals

Production of uric acid

Laboratory Parameters

A normal serum uric acid level is ~2.0 – 7.2 mg/dL. If you are given a case with elevated uric acid, do not choose treatment unless a gout attack has occurred. Asymptomatic hyperuricemia is not treated.

PHARMACOLOGIC THERAPY

The goal of treatment is to treat acute attacks, prevent future flare-ups, and reduce UA levels. Note that the drugs used to treat an acute attack (colchicine, NSAIDs, steroids) are different than the drugs used to prevent attacks. Colchicine or NSAIDs, however, are recommended during the initiation of prophylactic therapy to reduce the risk of acute attacks which can occur when uric acid is lowered rapidly.

First-line therapy for an acute gout attack can be either colchicine, a NSAID, systemic corticosteroids or a combination of these agents. Any of these drugs can be supplemented with topical ice therapy as needed. If patients were taking chronic urate-lowering therapy (allopurinol, febuxostat), they should continue to take without interruption. Steroids can be administered PO or intra-articularly (injected into the joint). Intra-articular administration should be considered when the gout attack involves only 1-2 large joints. If the patient is NPO, steroids can be given by IM, IV or subcutaneous administration.

Chronic prophylactic therapy should be started in patients with ≥ 2 acute attacks/year or who have tophi. Chronic therapy may also be considered in patients with CKD. First-line agents for chronic prophylactic therapy are the xanthine-oxidase (XO) inhibitors (allopurinol or fubuxostat). These agents are titrated up (slowly for allopurinol) to lower the uric acid level to a target of < 5-6 mg/dL. Probenecid can be used if XO inhibitors are contraindicated or not tolerated or can be added when the uric acid level is not at goal despite maximal doses of XO inhibitors (but only in patients with adequate renal function). Pegloticase is reserved for severe, refractory disease.

Acute Gout Attack Treatment

DRUG	DOSING	SAFETY/SIDE EFFECTS/MONITORING

Colchicine

DRUG	DOSING	SAFETY/SIDE EFFECTS/MONITORING
Colchicine *(Colcrys)*	1.2 mg orally (this is two 0.6 mg tablets) followed by 0.6 mg in 1 hour (do not exceed a total of 1.8 mg) This regimen can be followed by a prophylaxis regimen of 0.6 mg BID starting 12 hours later and continued at least until the acute attack resolves	**CONTRAINDICATIONS** Concomitant use of a P-gp or strong CYP3A4 inhibitor in the presence of renal or hepatic impairment **WARNINGS** Clearance decreased in renal or hepatic impairment **SIDE EFFECTS** Nausea, vomiting, diarrhea (~80% of patients) Myelosuppression, myopathy, neuropathy (dose-related) **NOTES** Recommended only when treatment is started within 36 hours of onset of symptoms. Do not use if patient is on prophylactic colchicine and has received acute regimen in the last 14 days.

NSAIDs

DRUG	DOSING	SAFETY/SIDE EFFECTS/MONITORING
Indomethacin *(Indocin)*	50 mg TID until attack resolved	See Pain chapter for more complete information. **NOTES** Avoid use in severe renal disease (uric acid is renally cleared and patients with gout may have renal insufficiency); consider risk of bleeding (however risk of GI bleeding is less due to short duration of therapy), CVD risk (most with celecoxib).
Naproxen *(Naprosyn, others)*	750 mg x 1, then reduce to 250 mg Q8H until attack resolved	
Sulindac *(Clinoril)*	300-400 mg daily until attack resolved	Indomethacin was the 1st NSAID approved and is the traditional DOC; however, it is more toxic than ibuprofen (increased risk for GI toxicity) and has psychiatric side effects including confusion, depression, psychosis.
Celecoxib *(CeleBREX)*	Off-label	

Steroids: Can be given PO, IM, IV, intra-articular or via ACTH (adrenocorticotropic hormone) which triggers endogenous glucocorticoid secretion.

DRUG	DOSING	SAFETY/SIDE EFFECTS/MONITORING
PredniSONE (orally)	0.5 mg/kg/day for 5-10 days (no taper) or 0.5 mg/kg/day for 2 days, then taper (reduce dose by 5 mg each day) over 7-10 days	See Asthma chapter for more complete information. **NOTES** Acute side effects of steroids (e.g., hyperglycemia, hypertension, nervousness, insomnia, increased appetite, edema) are not common when injected into a joint.
MethylPREDNISolone *(Medrol, Solu-Medrol)* Triamcinolone	Intra-articular: Dose depends on joint size; can be combined with oral steroid Oral: Methylprednisolone dose pack IM: Triamcinolone 60 mg, then start PO prednisone	Repeated injections may increase risk of joint damage.

Colchicine Drug Interactions

- Colchicine is a substrate of CYP 3A4 and the efflux transporter P-glycoprotein (P-gp). Fatal toxicity can occur if colchicine is combined with strong 3A4 inhibitors, such as clarithromycin or a strong inhibitor of P-gp, such as cyclosporine. Check for inhibitors prior to dispensing drug. If using a moderate 3A4 inhibitor, the maximum dose for acute treatment is 1.2 mg (2 tablets).

- Myopathy and rhabdomyolysis have been reported in patients taking colchicine with a statin or fibrate; try not to use with gemfibrozil and have patients monitor muscle pain/soreness.

Colchicine Counseling

- At the first sign of an attack, take 2 tablets. You can take 1 more tablet in one hour. Do not use more than this amount. Taking too much colchicine can lead to serious side effects.

- You should not take the 2nd dose if you have upset stomach, nausea or diarrhea.

- Report any serious nausea, vomiting, diarrhea, fatigue, unusual bleeding or tingling in your fingers or toes, to your healthcare provider.

- Wait at least 3 days before initiating another acute course of therapy.

Prophylactic Treatment

Allopurinol and febuxostat are xanthine oxidase inhibitors (block UA production). Probenecid inhibits reabsorption of uric acid in the proximal tubule of the nephron, thus promoting uric acid excretion. Pegloticase is a recombinant uricase enzyme, which converts uric acid to an inactive, water-soluble metabolite that can be easily excreted.

Chronic UA – Lowering Therapy

DRUG	DOSING	SAFETY/SIDE EFFECTS/MONITORING
Use colchicine at daily dose of 0.6 mg once or twice daily or NSAIDs for at least 6 months to reduce the risk of acute flares when beginning UA-lowering acid therapy.		

Xanthine Oxidase Inhibitors

| Allopurinol *(Zyloprim)* | Initial: 50-100 mg daily, then slowly titrate up until UA target reached (doses > 300 mg may be necessary and can be used even in patients with CKD so long as patients are being monitored for toxicity) | **WARNINGS** Hypersensitivity reactions can occur, including severe rash (SJS/TEN). Can test for HLA-B*5801 prior to starting treatment (recommended in Koreans with stage 3 or worse CKD, and Han Chinese or Thai irrespective of renal function) Hepatotoxicity, caution in patients with liver impairment **SIDE EFFECTS** Rash, acute gout attacks, ↑ LFTs **MONITORING** LFTs, presence of rash (especially important in patients with renal dysfunction) **NOTES** Maximum starting dose of 50 mg daily in patients with CKD |

Chronic UA – Lowering Therapy Continued

DRUG	DOSING	SAFETY/SIDE EFFECTS/MONITORING
Febuxostat *(Uloric)*	40-80 mg daily	**CONTRAINDICATIONS** Concomitant use with azathioprine or mercaptopurine **WARNINGS** Hepatotoxicity, use with caution in patients with liver impairment and discontinue therapy if LFTs > 3x ULN Possible increase in thromboembolic events **SIDE EFFECTS** ↑ LFTs, rash **MONITORING** LFTs at 2 months, 4 months, then periodically **NOTES** Very expensive compared to allopurinol (~$2,000/year) No dose reduction necessary in renal impairment Reduced risk for hypersensitivity reactions compared to allopurinol

Uricosuric

DRUG	DOSING	SAFETY/SIDE EFFECTS/MONITORING
Probenecid	500-1,000 mg BID	**CONTRAINDICATIONS** Concomitant aspirin therapy, uric acid kidney stones, initiation during an acute gout attack, blood dyscrasias **WARNINGS** Increased risk of hemolytic anemia in patients with G6PD deficiency
Colchicine-Probenicid	0.5/500 mg daily for 1 week, then BID (for starting probenecid, to reduce risk acute attack)	**SIDE EFFECTS** Hypersensitivity reactions, hemolytic anemia **NOTES** Requires adequate renal function; not recommended as monotherapy in patients with CrCl < 50 mL/min; avoid use in patients with CrCl < 30 mL/min

Chronic UA – Lowering Therapy Continued

DRUG	DOSING	SAFETY/SIDE EFFECTS/MONITORING

Uricase

Pegloticase (*Krystexxa*) – injection, costly, <u>refractory cases only</u>	8 mg IV every 2 weeks	**BLACK BOX WARNING** <u>Anaphylactic reactions</u> can occur during infusion; patients should be monitored by healthcare personnel and <u>premedicated with antihistamines and corticosteroids.</u> Risk is highest if UA level is > 6 mg/dL. <u>Consider discontinuing treatment if UA is > 6 mg/dL.</u> **CONTRAINDICATIONS** G6PD deficiency **WARNINGS** Acute gout flares may occur upon initiation of therapy; an NSAID or colchicine should be given as prophylaxis (1 week prior to infusion; continue for at least 6 months) **SIDE EFFECTS** <u>Antibody formation, gout flare, infusion reactions, nausea, bruising, urticaria, erythema, pruritus</u> **NOTES** Very expensive (~$6,500/dose) <u>Do not use in combination with allopurinol</u> (increased risk of anaphylaxis)

Probenecid Drug Interactions

■ Probenecid may decrease the renal clearance of other medications taken concurrently, including aspirin, methotrexate, theophylline and pencillins.

■ Probenecid used to be given with penicillins to ↑ the penicillin plasma concentrations; this will ↑ adverse reactions associated with the beta-lactam.

Allopurinol Counseling

■ Take once daily with a meal to reduce stomach upset (higher doses can be divided).

■ It may take up to several weeks for this medicine to have an effect and you may have more gout attacks for several months after starting this medicine while the body removes extra uric acid. If this happens, you can use different medicine for the acute attack.

■ If you get a rash, notify your healthcare provider. The rash could become serious. If the rash looks serious, you should be seen quickly.

PRACTICE CASE

Brian is a 62 year-old male with hypertension. His blood pressure has a daily range of 155-178/88-98 mmHg. He is using amlodipine 10 mg daily, lisinopril 10 mg daily and HCTZ 25 mg daily. He takes several OTC products, including aspirin EC 81 mg daily, fish oils and coenzyme Q10. He reports "weekend" alcohol use (3-4 beers on Saturday/Sunday). No past or present history of tobacco use. Brian is presenting at the clinic with pain described as 10/10. He is trying to avoid putting weight on his right foot. Physical exam reveals a swollen, tender, enlarged big toe.

CATEGORY	
Vitals/Labs	Height 5'11", weight 255" AST 12 U/L, ALT 14 U/L, BUN/SCr 22/1.4, Uric Acid 18.3 mg/dL

Questions

1. What is Brian's creatinine clearance (in mL/min), using the Cockcroft-Gault equation and his ideal body weight?

   a. 89
   b. 71
   c. 58
   d. 34
   e. 11

2. The physician is considering allopurinol therapy to treat the acute attack. Choose the correct statement:

   a. This is not appropriate therapy for an acute attack.
   b. He should receive a starting dose of 50 mg daily.
   c. He should receive a starting dose of 75 mg daily.
   d. He should receive a starting dose of 100 mg daily.
   e. He should receive a starting dose of 150 mg daily.

3. Brian will receive a short-course of prednisone therapy, with taper, that will last less than 2 weeks. Which of the following adverse effects are possible and should be explained to Brian?

   a. Growth suppression
   b. Insomnia/spaciness
   c. Osteoporosis
   d. Cataracts
   e. All of the above

4. Choose the correct dosing regimen for colchicine for an acute gout attack:

   a. 1.2 mg followed by 0.6 mg every 2 hours, not to exceed 6 tablets/24 hours
   b. 1.2 mg followed by 0.6 mg every 2 hours, not to exceed 8 tablets/24 hours
   c. 1.2 mg followed by 0.6 mg in 2-4 hours (total 1.8 mg)
   d. 1.2 mg followed by 0.6 mg in 1 hour, then as-needed for 3 additional doses (total 3.6 mg)
   e. 1.2 mg followed by 0.6 mg in 1 hour (total 1.8 mg)

5. A pharmacist receives a prescription for *Zyloprim*. Which medication is an acceptable alternative?

   a. Probenecid
   b. Colchicine
   c. Allopurinol
   d. Naproxen
   e. Febuxostat

6. Which of the following are true regarding pegloticase? (Select **ALL** that apply.)

   a. The brand name is *Krystexxa*
   b. The recommended dose is 8 mg PO daily
   c. It should not be given in combination with allopurinol
   d. It is a first-line treatment for acute gout
   e. Patients must be monitored for anaphylactic reactions when receiving this agent

7. Which of the following side effects are likely to occur with colchicine therapy?

   a. Nausea
   b. Stomach upset
   c. Mental confusion
   d. A and B only
   e. All of the above

8. A pharmacist has just attended an education program on the use of febuxostat *(Uloric)*. He wants to present the main points about this drug to his pharmacy colleagues. He should include the following points:

   a. Febuxostat (like allopurinol) is a xanthine oxidase inhibitor.
   b. Febuxostat appears to have lower risk of hypersensitivity reactions than allopurinol, including less of a risk of serious rash.
   c. Febuxostat costs much more than generic allopurinol and provides little extra benefit in the majority of patients.
   d. A and B only.
   e. All of the above.

9. A pharmacist is going to counsel a patient beginning allopurinol therapy. Which counseling statement should be included?

   a. This medication should be taken on an empty stomach.
   b. Allopurinol can cause blood pressure changes; hold onto the bed or rail when changing from a sitting to a standing position.
   c. If you notice a rash, contact your doctor at once. If the rash looks serious, you should not use the medicine and should be seen right away.
   d. A and C.
   e. All of the above.

10. The patient in this case has several known risk factors for gout. Which of the following risk factors increase his risk of gout?

   a. Consuming alcohol, especially beer
   b. His weight
   c. His hypertension history, and the use of HCTZ
   d. A and B only
   e. All of the above

Answers

1-c, 2-a, 3-b, 4-e, 5-c, 6-a,c,e, 7-d, 8-e, 9-c, 10-e

HYPERTENSION

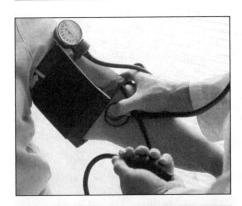

BACKGROUND

Nearly 1 in 3 adults have hypertension. If left untreated, the patient is at increased risk of heart disease, stroke and kidney disease. Hypertension is largely asymptomatic, and often is untreated. Only when the blood pressure is very high (such as with hypertensive crisis) are symptoms (throbbing headache, fatigue and shortness of breath) likely to appear. Pharmacists should help patients identify if they have hypertension and advise hypertensive patients to adhere to medication therapy. One in four patients discontinue antihypertensive therapy within 6 months. Beta-blockers can cause fatigue (and sometimes sexual problems), diuretics can increase urination and ACE inhibitors can cause cough. Some patients get edema from calcium channel blockers, especially if high doses are used. These side effects can each lead to discontinuation, but the major cause of patients stopping their medicines is a lack of understanding of the necessity for treatment and cost. If a brand is prescribed, see if a generic can be used.

Counseling should include recommendations to follow healthy lifestyle measures that can decrease blood pressure, such as sodium restriction, a healthy diet, physical activity, maintaining a healthy weight, smoking cessation, etc. Recommending a home blood pressure monitoring device can help the patient get involved and improve motivation and success of therapy.

PATHOPHYSIOLOGY

Most cases of hypertension are essential hypertension, which means they are not known to be caused by an identifiable factor, although poor lifestyle and genetics are contributory. Secondary hypertension is linked to a specific cause, such as renal disease, adrenal disease and/or drug-induced hypertension.

Classification of Blood Pressure in Adults According to JNC 7

CLASSIFICATION	SYSTOLIC BP/DIASTOLIC BP (mmHg)
Normal	Less than 120/80
Pre-hypertension	120-139/80-89
Stage 1	140-159/90-99
Stage 2	≥ 160/≥ 100

Compelling Indication And Treatment Choice per JNC-7

INDICATION	TREATMENT CHOICE
Heart Failure	ACEI, ARB, BB, diuretic, aldosterone antagonist
S/P MI	ACEI, BB, aldosterone antagonist
High risk of CAD	ACEI, BB, diuretic, CCB
Diabetes	ACEI, ARB, BB, CCB, diuretic
CKD	ACEI, ARB
Recurrent stroke prevention	ACEI, diuretic

DRUG THAT CAN CAUSE OR WORSEN HYPERTENSION

ACTH

Alcohol (excessive)

Amphetamines (e.g., ADHD drugs)

Appetite suppressants

Caffeine

Calcineurin antagonists (cyclosporine, tacrolimus)

Corticosteroids

Decongestants (e.g., pseudoephedrine)

Erythropoietin Stimulating Agents

Estrogen

Herbals [bitter orange, ephedra (ma-huang), ginseng, guarana, St. John's Wort].

Mirabegron (Myrbetriq)

NSAIDs

Oncology drugs [e.g. bevacizumab (Avastin), sorafenib (Nexavar), others]

SNRIs (e.g., duloxetine and venlafaxine – at higher doses)

Thyroid hormone (if given too much)

BP TREATMENT PER STAGE

If Stage 1 HTN, consider thiazide-type diuretics for most. May consider ACEI, ARB, BB, CCB, or combo.

If Stage 2 HTN, start with two drugs (usually thiazide-type diuretic and ACEI, or ARB, or BB, or CCB).

Beta-blockers are not 1st line for general coronary artery disease (CAD) prevention.

High risk is defined as having diabetes mellitus, chronic kidney disease (CKD), known CAD or CAD equivalent (carotid artery disease, peripheral arterial disease, abdominal aortic aneurysm), or a 10-year Framingham risk score > 10%.

Lifestyle modification is recommended at ALL levels.

BP goal per JNC-7 is < 140/90 mmHg, unless patient has DM or CKD, then BP goal is < 130/80 mmHg.

Treatment Based on AHA Guidelines

CONDITION	GOAL (mmHg)	DRUG CHOICE
General CAD prevention	< 140/90	Any drug or combo
High CAD risk	< 130/80	ACEI or ARB or CCB or thiazide diuretic or combo
Stable angina	< 130/80	Beta-Blocker and ACEI or ARB
Unstable Angina/NSTEMI	< 130/80	Beta-Blocker (if patient is hemodynamically stable) and ACEI or ARB
STEMI	< 130/80	Beta-Blocker (if patient is hemodynamically stable) and ACEI or ARB
LVD	< 120/80	ACEI or ARB and beta-blocker and aldosterone antagonist and thiazide or loop diuretic and hydralazine/isosorbide dinitrate (black patients)

LIFESTYLE MODIFICATIONS

ALWAYS ENCOURAGE IF NEEDED!

Weight
Maintain normal BMI and waist circumference

Eating
Recommend the Dietary Approaches to Stop HTN (DASH) eating plan, which is high in fruits and veg-etables, and recommends low-fat dairy products with reduced saturated and total fat

Reduce Sodium Intake
Should limit sodium to ≤ 2.4 grams/day; lower may be more beneficial

Increase Physical Activity
Engage in regular aerobic physical activity such as brisk walking (at least 30 min per day, most days of the week)

Moderate Alcohol Consumption
Alcohol should be limited to 1 drink/day (most women) and 2 drinks/day (most men)

Smoking Cessation
Pharmacists should be able to recommend how to quit and assist with therapy (nicotine replacement, gum, etc.)

Control Blood Glucose And Lipids To Reduce Cardiovascular Disease Risk!

DIURETICS

- Thiazides (HCTZ, others) are inexpensive, effective, have mild side effects and are often used as first-line or second-line agents (in many combination pills).

- Loop diuretics (furosemide, others) are used mostly in heart failure. Loops cause more sodium excretion, and are thus more potent fluid depletors (greater water loss), which provides benefit in HF. They also waste much more potassium than thiazides and run a risk of ototoxicity (auditory damage/hearing loss). Loops usually require K^+ supplements (potassium ext-release, or *Klor-Con* – see Heart Failure chapter for information on K^+ supplements). If used long-term, they can lower bone density.

- Thiazides work on the distal convoluted tubule of the nephron, however the long-term blood pressure lowering effect is thought to be due to vasodilation ($\downarrow$ resistance). Loops work on the ascending loop by blocking sodium reabsorption – this causes water to follow sodium into the urine, resulting in volume depletion.

- Potassium-sparing diuretics (triamterene, others) are not as effective and are not used as monotherapy for BP, but they are commonly used in combination with HCTZ *(Maxzide/ Dyazide)* to counter the thiazide's mild potassium loss and help (a little) with BP. If any potassium-retaining agent is used, there will be a risk of hyperkalemia, especially with reduced renal function. Spironolactone and eplerenone are used for HF (and HTN) and $\uparrow$ K^+ is a considerable risk with these agents.

Thiazides

Thiazides and thiazide-type diuretics inhibit Na^+ reabsorption in the distal convoluted tubules causing increased excretion of Na^+ and water as well as K^+ and H^+ ions.

DRUG	DOSING	SAFETY/SIDE EFFECTS/MONITORING
Chlorothiazide *(Diuril)*	125-500 mg/day	**CONTRAINDICATIONS** Hypersensitivity to sulfonamide-derived drugs, anuria, and renal decompensation
Chlorthalidone *(Thalitone)*	12.5-25 mg, max 100 mg/day (although not much clinical benefit seen > 25-50 mg/day)	**WARNINGS** Sulfa allergy (not likely to cross-react – please see cautionary statement in Drug Allergy chapter); electrolyte disturbances; gout can be precipitated in those with a history
Hydrochlorothiazide (*Microzide* – capsule, *Oretic* – tablet)	12.5-25 mg, max 100 mg/day (although not much clinical benefit seen > 25-50 mg/day)	**SIDE EFFECTS** Hypokalemia (can usually be avoided with regular intake of potassium rich foods), hyperuricemia ($\uparrow$ UA), elevated lipids ($\uparrow$ CH, $\uparrow$ TG), hyperglycemia ($\uparrow$ BG), hypercalcemia ($\uparrow$ Ca^{2+}), hyponatremia, hypomagnesemia, dizziness, photosensitivity, rash. Rarely, can cause hypochloremic alkalosis.
Indapamide	1.25-5 mg/day	
Metolazone *(Zaroxolyn)*	2.5-5 mg, max 20 mg/day	**NOTES** Thiazides may not be effective if CrCl < 30 mL/min, except metolazone. Metolazone may work in patients with reduced renal function.
Methyclothiazide	2.5-5 mg/day	Pregnancy Category B

Loop Diuretics

Loops inhibit reabsorption of Na^+ and Cl^- in the thick ascending loop of Henle, interfering with the chloride-binding co-transport system thus causing increased excretion of water, Na^+, Cl^-, Mg^{2+}, and Ca^{2+}. Loop diuretics are used more for edema (for fluid depletion) particularly in heart failure.

DRUG	DOSING	SAFETY/SIDE EFFECTS/MONITORING
Furosemide (Lasix) PO, IV Most patients take divided doses: take 2nd dose early in the afternoon	Oral: 20-80 mg daily or divided, can go higher with all loops Oral loop dose equivalency = 40 mg	**BLACK BOX WARNING** Can lead to profound diuresis resulting in fluid and electrolyte depletion **CONTRAINDICATIONS** Anuria **WARNINGS** Sulfa allergy (not likely to cross-react – please see cautionary statement in Drug Allergy chapter) – this warning does not apply to ethacrynic acid
Bumetanide PO, IV	Oral: 0.5-2 mg daily or divided Oral loop dose equivalency = 1 mg	**SIDE EFFECTS** Hypokalemia, orthostatic hypotension, $\downarrow Na^+$, $\downarrow Mg^{2+}$, $\downarrow Cl^-$, $\downarrow Ca^{2+}$ (different than thiazides which $\uparrow Ca^{2+}$), metabolic alkalosis, hyperuricemia ($\uparrow$ UA), hyperglycemia ($\uparrow$ BG), $\uparrow$ TGs, $\uparrow$ total cholesterol, photosensitivity, ototoxicity (MORE with ethacrynic acid) including hearing loss, tinnitus and vertigo **MONITORING** Renal function (SCr, BUN), fluid status (in's and out's, weight), BP, electrolytes, hearing with high doses or rapid IV administration
Torsemide (Demadex) PO, IV	Oral: 5-10 mg daily Oral loop dose equivalency = 20 mg	**NOTES** IV formulations of furosemide and bumetanide are light sensitive (in amber bottles). Furosemide IV:PO ratio is 1:2 (furosemide 20 mg IV = furosemide 40 mg PO). Store at room temp (refrigeration causes precipitation – warming may dissolve crystals). IV:PO ratio for torsemide and bumetanide is 1:1.
Ethacrynic Acid (Edecrin) PO, IV	Oral: 25-100 mg daily or divided Oral loop dose equivalency = 50 mg	

Potassium-Sparing Diuretics

These agents compete with aldosterone at the receptor sites in the distal convoluted tubule and collecting ducts, increasing Na⁺, and water excretion while conserving K⁺ and H⁺ ions.

DRUG	DOSING	SAFETY/SIDE EFFECTS/MONITORING
AMILoride *(Midamor)*	5-20 mg daily	**BLACK BOX WARNINGS** Tumor risk with spironolactone; tumorigenic in chronic rat toxicity studies. Avoid unnecessary use. **CONTRAINDICATIONS** Renal impairment (CrCl < 30 mL/min), hyperkalemia; concomitant use of strong 3A4 inhibitors (with eplerenone)
Triamterene *(Dyrenium)* **+ HCTZ (Maxzide, Maxzide-25, Dyazide)**	50-100 mg daily	**SIDE EFFECTS** Hyperkalemia, ↑ serum creatinine. For spironolactone, gynecomastia, breast tenderness, impotence. Rare: hyperchloremic metabolic acidosis.
Spironolactone *(Aldactone)*	HF: 12.5-25 mg daily HTN: 25-50 mg daily	**MONITORING** Check K⁺ before starting and frequently thereafter; BP, SCr/BUN
Eplerenone *(Inspra)*	HF: 25-50 mg daily HTN: 50-100 mg daily	

Diuretic Drug Interactions

- All antihypertensives can potentiate the therapeutic effect of other blood pressure lowering drugs; always carefully monitor BP when adding-on therapy.

- Loop diuretics can increase the ototoxic potential of other ototoxic drugs, such as aminoglycosides and vancomycin, especially in the presence of impaired renal function. This combination should be avoided if alternative treatments are available.

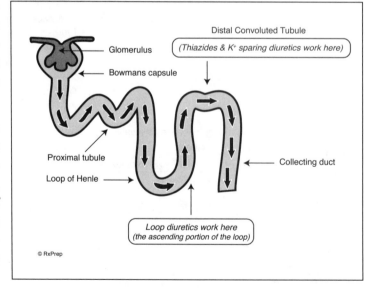

- Do not use ethacrynic acid with other loop diuretics due to the risk of additive ototoxicity.

- Diuretics may ↓ lithium's renal clearance and ↑ risk of lithium toxicity.

- Patients with hypertension should not be routinely using agents that can cause Na^+ and H_2O retention, such as NSAIDS. These agents lower the effectiveness of diuretics.

- Eplerenone is a CYP3A4 substrate; use with strong 3A4 inhibitors is contraindicated.

- Potassium-sparing diuretics have a risk of hyperkalemia. Monitor K^+ and renal function frequently and be careful of other medications that can increase potassium (see Drug Interactions chapter).

RENIN-ANGIOTENSIN ALDOSTERONE SYSTEM (RAAS) INHIBITORS

- RAAS inhibitors reduce vasoconstriction, ↓ aldosterone release, and some agents have shown benefit in renal protection and heart failure. If patients are taking two RAAS inhibitors (ACE inhibitor ± ARB ± aliskiren) together, the renal function, BP and K^+ should be carefully monitored. Potassium should remain within the safe level of 3.5-5 mEq/L.

- ARBs are typically given if a patient is intolerant to an ACE inhibitor (e.g., cough that is dry, intermittent), and are also used first-line.

- Angioedema is more common in black patients. Although angioedema is more likely with ACE inhibitors than ARBs or aliskiren, if a person has had angioedema with these classes of agents, all others are contraindicated since angioedema can quickly be fatal. Counsel to report any swelling of lips, mouth, tongue, face, or neck immediately.

- Patients on these medicines should be careful with salt substitutes that contain potassium chloride (instead of NaCl).

- Captopril has more side effects than other agents (taste disturbances, rash). It is not an optimal agent due to frequent dosing (BID or TID). The others are daily or BID.

- When used in pregnancy, fetal/neonatal morbidity/mortality can occur with any drug class that directly acts on the renin-angiotensin system (ACE inhibitor, ARB, direct renin inhibitor); discontinue drug as soon as possible when pregnancy is detected.

Angiotensin-Converting Enzyme Inhibitors (ACE Inhibitors)

These agents inhibit the angiotensin converting enzyme, preventing the conversion of angiotensin I (Ang I) to angiotensin II (Ang II), a potent vasoconstrictor, thereby reducing BP.

DRUG	DOSING	SAFETY/SIDE EFFECTS/MONITORING
Benazepril (Lotensin)	10-40 mg daily – BID	**BLACK BOX WARNING** Can cause injury and death to developing fetus; discontinue as soon as pregnancy is detected **CONTRAINDICATIONS** Angioedema. Do not use in bilateral renal artery stenosis; renal function will worsen. Cannot use concurrently with aliskiren in patients with diabetes. **WARNINGS** Concomitant use of an ARB or aliskiren is associated with an increased risk of hypotension, hyperkalemia, and renal dysfunction. Concomitant use with aliskiren should be avoided in patients with GFR < 60 mL/minute. **SIDE EFFECTS** Cough, hyperkalemia, angioedema (if occurs, drug is CI), hypotension, dizziness and acute renal insufficiency. Captopril has more SEs (taste perversion, rash). **MONITORING** BP, K⁺, renal function **NOTES** Pregnancy Category D Patients inadequately treated with once daily dosing may be treated with twice daily dosing.
Captopril (Capoten)	25-50 mg BID-TID Take 1 hour before meals	
Enalapril, Enalaprilat IV injection (Vasotec)	5-40 mg daily – BID	
Fosinopril	20-80 mg daily	
Lisinopril (Prinivil, Zestril)	5-40 mg daily	
Moexipril (Univasc)	7.5-30 mg daily – BID Take on an empty stomach	
Perindopril (Aceon)	4-16 mg daily	
Quinapril (Accupril)	10-80 mg daily	
Ramipril (Altace)	2.5-20 mg daily	
Trandolapril (Mavik)	2-8 mg daily	

Angiotensin Receptor Blockers (ARBs)

ARBs block angiotensin II from binding to the angiotensin II type-1 (AT$_1$) receptor on vascular smooth muscle, preventing vasoconstriction.

DRUG	DOSING	SAFETY/SIDE EFFECTS/MONITORING
Valsartan *(Diovan)*	80-320 mg daily	**BLACK BOX WARNING** Can cause injury and death to developing fetus; discontinue as soon as pregnancy is detected **CONTRAINDICATIONS** Angioedema. Do not use in bilateral renal artery stenosis; renal function will worsen. Cannot use concurrently with aliskiren in patients with diabetes.
Losartan *(Cozaar)*	25-100 mg daily	**WARNINGS** Concomitant use of an ACE inhibitor or aliskiren is associated with an increased risk of hypotension, hyperkalemia, and renal dysfunction. Concomitant use with aliskiren should be avoided in patients with GFR < 60 mL/minute.
Irbesartan *(Avapro)*	150-300 mg daily	Olmesartan only: Sprue-like enteropathy – severe, chronic diarrhea with substantial weight loss has been reported in patients taking olmesartan months to years after drug initiation. **SIDE EFFECTS** Hyperkalemia, angioedema (if occurs, drug is CI), hypotension, dizziness and acute renal insufficiency
Candesartan *(Atacand)*	8-32 mg daily	**MONITORING** BP, K$^+$, renal function
Olmesartan *(Benicar)*	20-40 mg daily	**NOTES** Pregnancy Category D
Telmisartan *(Micardis)*	40-80 mg daily	
Eprosartan *(Teveten)*	400-800 mg daily	
Azilsartan *(Edarbi)*	40-80 mg daily	

Direct Renin Inhibitor

Aliskiren directly inhibits renin which is responsible for the conversion of angiotensinogen to angiotensin I (Ang I), a potent vasoconstrictor, thereby reducing BP.

DRUG	DOSING	SAFETY/SIDE EFFECTS/MONITORING
Aliskiren *(Tekturna)*	150-300 mg daily Avoid high fat foods. Take with or without food and take the same way each day.	**BLACK BOX WARNING** Can cause injury and death to developing fetus; discontinue as soon as pregnancy is detected **CONTRAINDICATIONS** Do not use concurrently with ACE inhibitors or ARBs in patients with diabetes; Angioedema. Do not use in bilateral renal artery stenosis – renal function will worsen. **WARNINGS** Avoid concomitant use with ACE inhibitors or ARBs in patients with GFR < 60 mL/min **SIDE EFFECTS** Hyperkalemia, angioedema (if occurs, drug is CI), hypotension. **MONITORING** BP, K+, renal function **NOTES** Pregnancy Category D

RAAS Inhibitor Drug Interactions

- All RAAS inhibitors ↑ the risk of hyperkalemia. Monitor K+ and renal function frequently.

- Dual inhibition of the renin-angiotensin system leads to increased risks of renal impairment, hypotension, and hyperkalemia; avoid.

- ACE inhibitors or ARBs should not be used in combination with aliskiren in patients with diabetes.

- RAAS inhibitors can ↓ lithium's renal clearance and ↑ the risk of toxicity.

- Aliskiren is metabolized by CYP3A4; concentration is affected by 3A4 inducers and inhibitors. Do not use with cyclosporine due to increased aliskiren levels. Atorvastatin ↑ aliskiren levels.

- Aliskiren ↓ the level of furosemide; monitor effectiveness.

BETA-BLOCKERS, BETA-BLOCKERS WITH ALPHA-BLOCKING ACTIVITY AND BETA-BLOCKER WITH NITRIC OXIDE PRODUCTION

- Beta-blockers are used for HTN, post-MI, angina, HF and migraine prophylaxis. 1st-line use for HTN is now being discouraged; risk may be higher with atenolol (currently unknown).

- The primary alpha- and beta-blocking agent (carvedilol) is used for HF and HTN; note different dosing/titration schedules for the indications and formulation. Metoprolol XL is also commonly used for HF and HTN.

- Nebivolol, the beta-blockers/nitric oxide agent, is indicated for HTN.

- Beta-blockers with intrinsic sympathomimetic activity (ISA): CAPP (carteolol, acebutolol, penbutolol, pindolol). ISA beta-blockers can show antagonism (blocker) and low level agonist (stimulate) activity at the beta receptor. These agents are useful in patients with excessive bradycardia who need beta-blocker therapy.

- $Beta_1$- selective agents include: AMEBBA (atenolol, metoprolol, esmolol, bisoprolol, betaxolol, acebutolol).

- Propranolol has high lipid solubility (lipophilic); therefore, more CNS side effects since it crosses the blood brain barrier. CNS side effects include sedation, depression, cognitive effects and others.

- Take carvedilol with food (even the CR version).

- Carvedilol CR is less bioavailable than carvedilol IR, therefore, dose conversions are not mg per mg.

- Labetolol is often used 1st-line for HTN in pregnancy. Nifedipine is also used. Methyldopa can be used and was used historically, but has many side effects.

- Beta-blockers can cover up the symptoms of shakiness, palpitations and anxiety with hypoglycemia; this occurs mostly with the non-selective agents. This is why the beta-blocker propranolol is used for stage fright. They do not, however, cover up sweating (diaphoresis) and hunger.

- Use caution in patients with breathing problems (asthma, COPD). Choose $Beta_1$- selective agents and keep at lower (selective) dosing.

Beta-Blockers

Beta-blockers inhibit the effects of catecholamines (especially norepinephrine) at the $beta_1$- and $beta_2$- adrenergic receptors, causing BP and HR reduction.

DRUG	DOSING	SAFETY/SIDE EFFECTS/MONITORING

Beta$_1$- selective Blockers

DRUG	DOSING	SAFETY/SIDE EFFECTS/MONITORING
Acebutolol *(Sectral)* ISA	200-800 mg daily	**BLACK BOX WARNING** Beta-blockers should not be withdrawn abruptly (particularly in patients with CAD), gradually taper over 1-2 weeks to avoid acute tachycardia, HTN, and/or ischemia. **CONTRAINDICATIONS** Sinus bradycardia, 2nd or 3rd degree heart block, sick sinus syndrome (unless patient has a functioning artificial pacemaker) or cardiogenic shock. Do not initiate in patients with active asthma exacerbation.
Atenolol *(Tenormin)* Preg Cat D	25-100 mg daily	**SIDE EFFECTS** ↓ HR, hypotension, fatigue, dizziness, depression, ↓ libido, impotence, hyperglycemia (non-selective agents can ↓ insulin secretion in type 2 diabetes), hypertriglyceridemia, ↓ HDL; weight gain and edema with carvedilol
Betaxolol	5-40 mg daily	**MONITORING** HR, BP, titrate every 2 weeks (as tolerated); ↓ dose if HR < 55
Bisoprolol *(Zebeta)*	2.5-20 mg daily	**NOTES** Avoid abrupt discontinuation – must taper Caution in diabetes with recurrent hypoglycemia, asthma, severe COPD or resting limb ischemia Take metoprolol immediate-release tablets with food. Metoprolol extended-release tablets are taken without regard to meals.
Metoprolol tartrate *(Lopressor)*, Metoprolol succinate extended release *(Toprol XL)*	HTN: 25-400 mg daily IR BID; XL daily HF: Start 12.5-25 mg daily (max 200 mg daily)	Pregnancy Category C/D (atenolol) Caution: IV doses are not equivalent to oral doses (usually IV is much lower)

Beta$_1$- selective Blocker and Nitric Oxide-Dependent Vasodilation

DRUG	DOSING	SAFETY/SIDE EFFECTS/MONITORING
Nebivolol *(Bystolic)*	5-40 mg daily With a CrCl < 30 mL/min or moderate liver impairment, start at 2.5 mg daily	**SIDE EFFECTS** Headache, fatigue, dizziness, diarrhea, nausea, bradycardia, hypertriglyceridemia, ↓ HDL **NOTES** Nitric oxide causes peripheral (arterial) vasodilation; clinical benefit unclear

Beta-Blockers Continued

DRUG	DOSING	SAFETY/SIDE EFFECTS/MONITORING

Beta$_1$- and Beta$_2$-Blockers (non-selective)

DRUG	DOSING	SAFETY/SIDE EFFECTS/MONITORING
Carteolol ISA	2.5-10 mg/day	ISA Agents – acebutolol, carteolol, penbutolol, pindolol (CAPP): Do not ↓ HR as much as other beta-blockers.
Nadolol *(Corgard)*	20-320 mg/day	
Penbutolol *(Levatol)* ISA	10-80 mg/day	
Pindolol ISA	10-60 mg/day	
Propranolol *(Inderal LA, InnoPran XL)*	40-480 mg/day	
Timolol	10-60 mg/day	

Non-selective Alpha- and Beta-Blockers

DRUG	DOSING	SAFETY/SIDE EFFECTS/MONITORING
Carvedilol **(Coreg, Coreg CR)**	HTN: Start IR 6.25 mg BID (max: 25 mg BID) or CR 20 mg daily (max: 80 mg daily) HF: Start IR 3.125 mg BID (max 50 mg BID if > 85 kg; 25 mg BID if < 85 kg) or CR 10 mg/day (max 80 mg)	Same as above – more weight gain and edema side effects Take carvedilol – all forms – with food Pregnancy Category C Dosing conversion from *Coreg* to *Coreg CR:* *Coreg* 3.125 mg BID = *Coreg CR* 10 mg daily *Coreg* 6.25 mg BID = *Coreg CR* 20 mg daily *Coreg* 12.5 mg BID = *Coreg CR* 40 mg daily *Coreg* 25 mg BID = *Coreg CR* 80 mg daily
Labetalol *(Trandate)*	200-2,400 mg/day	

Beta-Blocker Drug Interactions

- Beta-blockers can enhance the effects of insulin and oral hypoglycemic agents (sulfonylureas, etc.) – monitor BG carefully.

- Caution in patients with diabetes. Beta-blockers mask the symptoms of shakiness, palpitations and anxiety with hypoglycemia – this occurs mostly with the non-selective agents. However, sweating and hunger are not masked.

- Use caution when administering other drugs that slow HR; see Drug Interactions chapter.

- Carvedilol is a substrate of CYP2D6; 2D6 inhibitors may increase carvedilol levels and rifampin may decrease carvedilol levels.

- Carvedilol can increase digoxin and cyclosporine levels; may require dose adjustments.

- Nebivolol should be used with caution in patients taking 2D6 inhibitors.

CALCIUM CHANNEL BLOCKERS (CCBs)

There are 2 types of CCBs: the dihydropyridines and the non-dihydropyridines. With CCBs, be careful to check the orange book since there is such a variety of long-acting formulations; choose a generic that is AB-rated to the brand.

Dihydropyridines

The dihydropyridines end in "pine" and include amlodipine, nifedipine, felodipine, and others. They are used for HTN and angina (Prinzmetal's).

Dihydropyridine CCBs

These agents inhibit Ca^{2+} ions from entering the "slow" channels or voltage-sensitive areas of vascular smooth muscle resulting in peripheral arterial vasodilation and decreasing peripheral vascular resistance. The dihydropyridines cause peripheral vasodilation, which may lead to reflex tachycardia, headache, flushing, and peripheral edema. Some agents are worse than others: amlodipine is used commonly since it does not commonly cause these effects.

DRUG	DOSING	SAFETY/SIDE EFFECTS/MONITORING
AmLODIPine *(Norvasc)*	2.5-10 mg/day	**SIDE EFFECTS** Peripheral edema, headache, flushing, tachycardia/reflex tachycardia, gingival hyperplasia
Felodipine *(Plendil)*	2.5-10 mg/day	
Isradipine ER (daily) Isradapine IR (BID)	5-10 mg/day	**MONITORING** BP, HR, peripheral edema
NIFEdipine ER *(Adalat CC, Procardia XL, Afeditab CR),* NIFEdipine IR *(Procardia)*	30-90 mg/day	**NOTES** Do not use sublingual nifedipine – may ↑ risk of MI *Covera HS, Adalat CC,* and *Sular* have capsular shells that can be seen in feces (ghost shells).
Nisoldipine ER *(Sular)*	8.5-34 mg/day	
Nisoldipine ER	20-60 mg/day	
NiCARdipine ER *(Cardene SR)* NiCARdipine IR *(Cardene)* is TID **NiCARdipine IV** *(Cardene)*	30-60 mg (BID)	

Inpatient Acute Care Dihydropyridine CCB

DRUG	DOSING	SAFETY/SIDE EFFECTS/MONITORING
Clevidipine *(Cleviprex)* IV only Other IV CCBs are used acutely: diltiazem, verapamil, niCARdipine	1-21 mg/hr	**CONTRAINDICATIONS** Do not use in soy or egg allergy, acute pancreatitis, severe aortic stenosis **SIDE EFFECTS** Headache, nausea/vomiting. Rare: hypertriglyceridemia, infections **MONITORING** BP, HR **NOTES** In a lipid emulsion (provides 2 kcal/mL); it is milky-white in color. Risk of infection and hypertriglyceridemia. Use strict aseptic technique upon administration. Maximum hang-time per vial/bottle is 12 hours.

Non-dihydropyridines

The non-dihydropyridines consist of verapamil and diltiazem. These agents are used primarily for arrhythmias to control/slow HR, and sometimes for HTN and angina. Diltiazem and verapamil are negative inotropes (↓ contraction force) and negative chronotropes (↓ HR). The dihydropyridines do not have these properties.

Non-dihydropyridine CCBs

These agents inhibit Ca²⁺ ions from entering the "slow" channels or voltage-sensitive areas of vascular smooth muscle and myocardium, resulting in coronary vasodilation.

DRUG	DOSING	SAFETY/SIDE EFFECTS/MONITORING
Diltiazem *(Cardizem, Cardizem CD, Cardizem LA, Dilacor XR, Dilt-CD, Dilt-XR, Diltzac, Cartia XT, Tiazac, Taztia XT)*	QD is 120-420 mg BID is 60-240 mg TID is 30-120 mg	**CONTRAINDICATIONS** Severe hypotension (SBP < 90 mmHg), 2nd or 3rd degree heart block, sick sinus syndrome (unless the patient has a functioning artificial pacemaker), cardiogenic shock, acute MI and pulmonary congestion
Verapamil *(Calan, Calan SR, Covera HS, Verelan, Verelan PM)*	QD is 100-300 mg BID is 120-180 mg TID is 40-120 mg	**SIDE EFFECTS** Edema, headache, AV block, bradycardia, hypotension, arrhythmias, HF, constipation (more with verapamil), gingival hyperplasia **MONITORING** BP, HR, ECG

Calcium Channel Blocker Drug Interactions

- Diltiazem and verapamil are both CYP3A4 substrates and moderate 3A4 inhibitors. They will raise the concentration of many other drugs, and 3A4 inducers and inhibitors will affect their concentration; check for interactions prior to dispensing. Avoid grapefruit juice.

CENTRALLY-ACTING ALPHA-2 ADRENERGIC AGONISTS

- Clonidine is used commonly for resistant hypertension and in patients who can not swallow (due to dysphagia, dementia) since it comes as a patch formulation. Since the patch is changed weekly, it can help with adherence.

- Clonidine has many side effects, including sedation, dizziness, lethargy, dry mouth, and can aggravate depression and contribute to sexual dysfunction. If it is used first-line without a valid reason, it may be inappropriate prescribing.

- Clonidine is sometimes used off-label for opioid withdrawal to block nervousness, anxiety and help with sleep.

- If stopped abruptly, especially at higher doses, a withdrawal syndrome with a very high blood pressure, headache, anxiety, and tremors will result. Must taper over 2-5 days.

Centrally-Acting Alpha₂ Agonists

Stimulate alpha₂-adrenergic receptors in the brain which results in reduced sympathetic outflow from the CNS.

DRUG	DOSING	SAFETY/SIDE EFFECTS/MONITORING
CloNIDine (Catapres, Catapres-TTS patch, Duraclon inj) Kapvay – for ADHD	0.1-0.3 mg BID Catapres-TTS-1 = 0.1 mg/24 hr Catapres-TTS-2 = 0.2 mg/24 hr Catapres-TTS-3 = 0.3 mg/24 hr	**SIDE EFFECTS** Bradycardia, dry mouth, drowsiness, sedation, lethargy, hypotension, depression, psychotic reactions, nasal stuffiness, sexual dysfunction
Guanabenz	4 and 8 mg tabs	Methyldopa has same as above plus hypersensitivity reactions, hepatitis, myocarditis, hemolytic anemia, positive Coombs test, drug-induced fever and lupus-like syndrome **MONITORING** BP, HR, mental status
GuanFACINE (Tenex) **Intuniv** – for ADHD	0.5 – 2 mg daily	**NOTES** Clonidine patch is applied weekly. Apply patch to a hairless area on upper, outer arm or on upper chest. Place white round adhesive cover over patch to hold it in place. Rotate application site. Remove patch before MRI.
Methyldopa	250 mg BID-TID; max 3 grams/day	Rebound hypertension (with sweating/anxiety/tremors), if stopped abruptly (less likely with the patches). Do not stop abruptly, must taper. Skin irritation (with patches)

Direct Vasodilators

Cause direct vasodilation of arterioles with little effect on veins.

DRUG	DOSING	SAFETY/SIDE EFFECTS/MONITORING
HydrALAZINE	10-75 mg PO QID (max 300 mg/day) 10-20 mg IV Q4-6H PRN	**SIDE EFFECTS** Headache, reflex tachycardia, palpitations, anorexia; rare: lupus-like syndrome (dose and duration related-report fever, joint/muscle aches, fatigue) **MONITORING** HR, BP
Minoxidil	2.5-40 mg/day	**SIDE EFFECTS** Fluid retention, tachycardia, aggravation of angina, pericardial effusion, hirsutism (used for hair growth)

Alpha Blockers

Alpha blockers bind to alpha$_1$-adrenergic receptors which results in vasodilation of arterioles and veins; used mostly for BPH; not first-line therapy for HTN.

DRUG	DOSING	SAFETY/SIDE EFFECTS/MONITORING
Prazosin (Minipress)	1-5 mg BID-TID	**SIDE EFFECTS** Orthostatic hypotension, syncope with 1st dose, dizziness, fatigue, headache, fluid retention, priapism
Terazosin (Hytrin)	1-20 mg QHS	**NOTES** Caution with concurrent use with the PDE-5 inhibitors (sildenafil, tadalafil, vardenafil and avanafil) due to additive effects on BP, dizziness
Doxazosin (Cardura, Cardura XL)	1-16 mg QHS	

Combination Products

SELECT COMBO AGENTS	BRAND NAME	GENERIC DRUGS
ACE-I and CCB	*Lotrel*	**Amlodipine and benazepril**
	Tarka	Trandolapril and verapamil
ARB and CCB	*Twynsta*	Amlodipine and telmisartan
	Exforge	Amlodipine and valsartan
	Azor	Amlodipine and olmesartan
DRI and CCB	*Tekamlo*	Aliskiren and amlodipine
DRI and diuretic	*Tekturna HCT*	Aliskiren and HCTZ
DRI, CCB, and diuretic	*Amturnide*	Aliskiren, amlodipine and HCTZ
ACE-I and diuretic	*Lotensin HCT*	Benazepril and HCTZ
	Capozide	Captopril and HCTZ
	Vaseretic	Enalapril and HCTZ
	Prinzide, Zestoretic	**Lisinopril and HCTZ**
	Uniretic	Moexipril and HCTZ
	Accuretic	Quinapril and HCTZ
ARB's and diuretic	*Atacand HCT*	Candesartan and HCTZ
	Edarbyclor	Azilsartan and chlorthalidone
	Teveten HCT	Eprosartan and HCTZ
	Avalide	Irbesartan and HCTZ
	Hyzaar	**Losartan and HCTZ**
	Micardis HCT	Telmisartan and HCTZ
	Diovan HCT	**Valsartan and HCTZ**
	Benicar HCT	**Olmesartan and HCTZ**
Beta-blocker and diuretic	*Tenoretic*	Atenolol and chlorthalidone
	Ziac	**Bisoprolol and HCTZ**
	Inderide	Propranolol and HCTZ
	Lopressor HCT	Metoprolol and HCTZ
	Corzide	Nadolol and bendroflumethiazide
Diuretic and diuretic	*Aldactazide*	Spironolactone and HCTZ
	Dyazide, Maxzide	**Triamterene and HCTZ**
Vasodilator and diuretic	*Hydra-zide*	Hydralazine and HCTZ
CCB and ARB and diuretic	*Exforge HCT*	Amlodipine, valsartan and HCTZ
	Tribenzor	Amlodipine, olmesartan and HCTZ

Hypertensive Urgencies and Emergencies

	URGENCY: NOT LIFE-THREATENING	EMERGENCY: POTENTIALLY LIFE-THREATENING
Definition	BP (generally ≥ 180/110-120) without acute target organ damage	BP (generally ≥ 180/110-120) with acute target organ damage (such as encephalopathy, MI, unstable angina, pulmonary edema, eclampsia, stroke, aortic dissection, etc).
Treatment	Oral medication with an onset of action of 15-30 minutes; reduce BP gradually over 24-48 hrs.	Reduce MAP by no more than 25% (within minutes to 1 hour), then if stable, to 160/100-110 mmHg within the next 2-6 hours. Use IV medication.

Drugs Used in Hypertensive Urgencies*

DRUG	DOSE	SIDE EFFECTS
Captopril (Capoten)	25 mg, repeat in 1-2 hrs PRN	Hypotension, ↑ K+, angioedema
CloNIDine (Catapres)	0.1-0.2 mg, repeat in 1-2 hrs PRN	Hypotension, drowsiness, sedation, dry mouth, etc.
Labetalol (Trandate)	100-400 mg, repeat in 2-3 hrs PRN	Hypotension, heart block, bronchoconstriction

*   Of note, do not use nifedipine SL for HTN urgency!

Drugs Used in Hypertensive Emergencies

DRUG	MOA
Clevidipine (Cleviprex) *	DHP-CCB
Sodium Nitroprusside (Nitropress)	Arteriole and Venous Vasodilator – nitrate
NiCARdipine (Cardene)	DHP-CCB
Fenoldopam (Corlopam)	Dopamine-1 receptor agonist
Nitroglycerin **	Venous vasodilator – nitrate
Enalaprilat (Vasotec IV)	ACEI
HydrALAZINE	Arteriole vasodilator
Labetalol (Trandate)	Alpha and beta-blocker
Esmolol (Brevibloc)	Beta-blocker

*   Cleviprex comes in a lipid emulsion (milky white in color), therefore, maintain strict aseptic technique. Vials in use need to be discarded after 12 hours.

** Nitroglycerin (by injection) will absorb into plastic. Keep in glass bottles and do not use PVC tubing.

Patient Counseling

All Hypertension Medications

- Hypertension often has no symptoms, so you may not even feel that you have high blood pressure. Continue using this medicine as directed, even if you feel well. You may need to use blood pressure medication for the rest of your life. If cost prevents you from obtaining the medicine, please ask the pharmacist for help finding a lower priced alternative.

- To be sure this medication is helping your condition, your blood pressure will need to be checked on a regular basis. It is important that you do not miss any scheduled visits to your healthcare provider.

- This medicine is only part of a complete program of treatment for hypertension that also includes diet, exercise, and weight control. Follow your diet, medication, and exercise routines very closely if you are being treated for hypertension.

Diuretics

- This medication will cause you to urinate more throughout the day. This is expected from your medication.

- This medicine may make you feel dizzy and lightheaded when getting up from a sitting or lying position. Get up slowly. Let your feet hang over the bed for a few minutes before getting up. Hang on to the bed or nearby dresser when standing from a sitting position.

- Be sure that all objects are off the floor as you make your way to the bathroom. It is best to prevent any risks of falls.

- Potassium supplements may be needed while you are on this medication to ensure you have enough potassium for your heart. (not for potassium-sparing diuretics)

- If you have diabetes, your blood sugar may have to be monitored more frequently in the beginning as this medication can affect your blood sugar.

ACE Inhibitors, ARBs, and Aliskiren

- Do not use this medicine without telling your healthcare provider if you are pregnant or planning a pregnancy. This medicine could cause birth defects in the baby if you take the medication during pregnancy. Use an effective form of birth control. Stop using this medication and tell your healthcare provider right away if you become pregnant during treatment.

- Take the missed dose as soon as you remember. If it is almost time for your next dose, skip the missed dose and take the medicine at the next regularly scheduled time. Do not take extra medicine to make up the missed dose.

- Do not use salt substitutes or potassium supplements while taking this medication, unless your healthcare provider has told you to do so. Be careful of your potassium intake.

- Get emergency medical help if you have any of these signs of an allergic reaction: hives; difficulty breathing; swelling of your face, lips, tongue, or throat.

- Tell your healthcare provider if you develop a bothersome, dry occasional cough while taking this medicine (with ACE inhibitors only).

Beta-Blockers

- Remember to take at the same time every day.

- This medication can cause a few side effects, including dizziness and fatigue and can contribute to sexual dysfunction. If the side effects bother you, please let your healthcare provider know.

- Do not skip doses. If you miss a dose, take the missed dose as soon as you remember. If your next dose is less than 8 hours away, skip the missed dose and take the medicine at the next regularly scheduled time.

- Do not discontinue your medication without consulting your physician. Stopping this medicine suddenly may make your condition worse.

- Avoid operating automobiles and machinery or engaging in other tasks requiring alertness until you are use to the medicine's effects.

- Contact your healthcare provider if you experience any difficulty in breathing (for nonselective beta-blockers).

- If taking carvediolol *(Coreg/Coreg CR)*, take with food.

- If taking immediate-release metoprolol *(Lopressor)*, take with food.

Clonidine

- Do not stop clonidine suddenly; this can cause your blood pressure to become dangerously high. Make sure you do not run out of medicine.

- Clonidine can cause a variety of side effects, including sedation, dizziness, fatigue, dry mouth, and can aggravate depression and contribute to sexual dysfunction. If the side effects bother you, please let your healthcare provider know.

- The clonidine patch *(Catapres-TTS)* is changed weekly: Apply the patch to a hairless area of the skin on the upper outer arm or chest every 7 days. Do not use on broken or irritated skin. After 7 days, remove the used patch and apply a new patch to a different area than the previous site to avoid skin irritation.

PRACTICE CASE

FP is a 58 year old black male who comes to your clinic for a routine follow up visit. He states that he feels fine and does not understand why he has to take any medications.

CATEGORY	
PMH	Chronic lower back pain, Hypertension
Vitals	BP 162/95 mmHg, HR 88 BPM, RR 18 BPM, Temp 38.0 Pain 3/10
Current medications	*Lortab* 1-2 tabs NTE 8 tabs/day *Prinzide* 20/25 mg 1 tab daily
Labs	Na+ 141 mEq/L, K+ 3.8 mEq/L, BUN 35 mg/dL, SCr 1.2 mg/dL Glucose (non-fasting) 180 mg/dL

Questions

1. Which of the following medication combinations is *Prinzide*?

    a. Benazepril and hydrochlorothiazide

    b. Enalapril and hydrochlorothiazide

    c. Irbesartan and hydrochlorothiazide

    d. Lisinopril and hydrochlorothiazide

    e. Triamterene and hydrochlorothiazide

2. FP has a risk factor for developing angioedema. Which of the following increases his risk?

    a. Age

    b. Gender

    c. Ethnicity

    d. Concurrent medications

    e. Electrolyte profile

3. FP needs better BP control. Which of the following medications would be the best recommendation to add to his profile?

    a. *Lasix*

    b. *Zaroxolyn*

    c. *Hytrin*

    d. *Avalide*

    e. *Norvasc*

Questions 4-10 do not apply to the above case.

4. What is the mechanism of action for *Bystolic*? (Select **ALL** that apply.)

    a. Beta 2- selective blocker

    b. Beta-1 selective blocker

    c. Increases nitric oxide production

    d. Alpha-1 selective blocker

    e. Alpha-2 agonist

5. Choose the correct statement(s) concerning *Coreg CR*: (Select **ALL** that apply.)

    a. The generic name is nebivolol.

    b. The starting dose for hypertension is 12.5 mg BID.

    c. The drug is a non-selective beta and alpha blocker.

    d. The drug decreases heart rate.

    e. The drug should be taken without food.

6. A 77 year old patient comes into the pharmacy and takes their BP reading. It is 155/105 mmHg. She mentions her BP has been around that reading for a while. What is the best recommendation to give this patient?

   a. You should have your BP checked by your healthcare provider and it is likely you will need to be started on 2 medications to control your BP.

   b. You should have your BP checked by your healthcare provider and it is likely you may need to be started on 1 medication to control your BP.

   c. You should go to the urgent care center since you are in hypertensive urgency and need immediate treatment.

   d. Your BP is within normal range.

   e. As long as you are not symptomatic, you do not need to treat your BP with medicine.

7. A patient comes in with a new prescription for *Exforge*. Which of the following medications are the correct match for this prescription?

   a. Aliskiren and hydrochlorothiazide

   b. Aliskiren and valsartan

   c. Amlodipine and benazepril

   d. Valsartan, amlodipine, and hydrochlorothiazide

   e. Amlodipine and valsartan

8. A patient develops angioedema while taking *Altace*. Which of the following medications would be appropriate as an alternative agent?

   a. *Tenormin*

   b. *Atacand*

   c. *Lotrel*

   d. *Mavik*

   e. *Tekturna*

9. Which one of the following beta-blockers has intrinsic sympathomimetic activity (ISA)?

   a. Atenolol

   b. Acebutolol

   c. Carvedilol

   d. Timolol

   e. Nadolol

10. A patient is prescribed diltiazem. Choose the correct statement:

   a. Heart rate would be expected to slow.

   b. The correct reference to check for an AB-rated generic is the *Red Book*.

   c. Diltiazem is an enzyme inducer.

   d. Diltiazem is a beta-blocker.

   e. Diltiazem is a dihydropyridine calcium channel blocker.

Answers

1-d, 2-c, 3-e, 4-b,c, 5-c,d, 6-a, 7-e, 8-a, 9-b, 10-a

DYSLIPIDEMIA

We gratefully acknowledge the assistance of Renu F. Singh, PharmD, BCACP, CDE, Associate Clinical Professor at the University of California San Diego Skaggs School of Pharmacy and Pharmaceutical Sciences, in preparing this chapter.

GUIDELINES

Stone NJ, Robinson J, Lichtenstein AH, et al. 2013 ACC/AHA Guideline on the Treatment of Blood Cholesterol to Reduce Atherosclerotic Cardiovascular Risk in Adults. JACC, doi:10.1016/j.jacc.2013.11.002.

Eckel RH, Jakicic JM, Ard JD, et al. 2013 AHA/ACC Guideline on Lifestyle Management to Reduce Cardiovascular Risk. JACC, doi:10.1016/j.jacc.2013.11.003.

Goff Jr DC, Lloyd-Jones DM, Bennett G, et al. 2013 ACC/AHA Guideline on the Assessment of Cardiovascular Risk. JACC, doi:10.1016/j.jacc.2013.11.005.

BACKGROUND

Cholesterol is needed for cell membrane formation and function, hormone synthesis, and fat soluble vitamin production. Production of cholesterol occurs in the liver, intestines, adrenal glands, and reproductive organs and it is absorbed from certain foods including dairy products (whole milk), eggs, meat, and many types of prepared food. Cholesterol is recycled; the liver excretes cholesterol in a non-esterified form (via bile) in the digestive tract, of which 50% gets reabsorbed back into the bloodstream. Lipids, being water immiscible, are not present in the free form in the plasma, but rather circulate as lipoproteins. Abnormalities of plasma lipoproteins can result in a predisposition to coronary, cerebrovascular, and peripheral arterial disease and is considered a <u>major risk factor for the development of coronary heart disease (CHD)</u>. Elevated concentrations of oxidized LDL particles are associated with atheroma formation in the walls of the arteries, leading to atherosclerosis. Premature coronary atherosclerosis, leading to the manifestations of ischemic heart disease, is the most common and significant consequence of dyslipidemia. Other dyslipidemias can exist, including elevated triglycerides, which pose other risks, primarily acute pancreatitis and myocardial infarction.

CLASSIFICATION OF DYSLIPIDEMIA

Primary (or Familial)

■ Familial hyperlipidemias are classified according to the Fredrickson classification

Secondary (or Acquired)

■ Mimic primary forms of hyperlipidemia and can have similar consequences. Some common causes of secondary dyslipidemia are listed in the table below. Secondary causes of severe elevations of LDL ≥ 190 mg/dL and triglycerides ≥ 500 mg/dL often contribute to the magnitude of the hyperlipidemia and should be evaluated and treated appropriately.

Secondary Causes of Hyperlipidemia Most Commonly Seen in Practice

SECONDARY CAUSE	ELEVATED LDL	ELEVATED TRIGLYCERIDES
Diet	Saturated or *trans* fats, weight gain, anorexia	Weight gain, very low-fat diets, high intake of refined carbohydrate, excessive alcohol intake
Drugs	Diuretics, cyclosporine, tacrolimus, glucocorticoids, amiodarone	Oral estrogen, glucocorticoids, bile acid resins, protease inhibitors, retinoic acid, anabolic steroids, sirolimus, raloxifene, tamoxifen, beta blockers (not carvedilol), thiazides, atypical antipsychotics, alpha interferons, propofol
Diseases	Biliary obstruction, nephrotic syndrome	Nephrotic syndrome, chronic renal failure, lipodystrophies
Disorders and altered states of metabolism	Hypothyroidism, obesity, pregnancy	Diabetes (poorly controlled), hypothyroidism, obesity, pregnancy

Cholesterol (Lipoprotein) Types and Normal Values

Many clinicians will recommend checking lipoprotein levels after a 9-12 hour fast (if patient did not fast, the TG level may be falsely elevated). You may need to calculate LDL if it is not given using the Friedewald equation: LDL = Total CH – HDL – (TG/5). This formula can not be used when the TGs are > 400 mg/dL.

Natural Products

Red yeast rice is the product of yeast grown on rice that contains naturally occurring HMG-CoA reductase inhibitors and is commercially available in capsules. The amount of statin in each product can vary. Both myalgias and myopathy have been reported with the use of the product and it would be prudent to apply the same precautions, interactions and monitoring parameters that are recommended for statins. Garlic may have a very small beneficial effect on cholesterol. Over-the-counter fish oils (to ↓ TGs in patients with TG ≥ 500) and plant sterols/stanols may provide additional benefit.

TREATING DYSLIPIDEMIAS

In November 2013, new national guidelines for the treatment of high cholesterol were released (Guideline on the Treatment of Blood Cholesterol – ATP IV). While the previous ATP III guidelines focused on specific LDL and non-HDL cholesterol target goals, the new guidelines identify <u>four</u> key patient groups who should be initiated with appropriate statin intensity to obtain relative reductions in LDL-cholesterol. The recommendations aim to simplify treatment guidelines based on evidence from large randomized controlled trials. Of note, nonstatin therapies are not recommended unless statins are not tolerated, and treating to specific LDL goals is no longer advised.

> **KEY POINT**
>
> The new guidelines state that there is no evidence to support continued use of specific LDL or HDL treatment targets. Statins (primarily), dosed at the appropriate intensity, are used in at-risk patients.

Identification of 4 Statin Benefit Groups

The following 4 groups of patients should be initiated on statin therapy:

1. Clinical atherosclerotic cardiovascular disease (ASCVD), including coronary heart disease (ACS, S/P MI, stable or unstable angina, coronary or other arterial revascularization), stroke, TIA, or peripheral arterial disease thought to be of atherosclerotic origin

2. Primary elevations of LDL ≥ 190 mg/dL

3. Diabetes and 40-75 years of age with LDL between 70-189 mg/dL

4. 40-75 years of age with LDL between 70-189 mg/dL and estimated 10-year ASCVD risk of ≥ 7.5% (using the Global Risk Assessment Tool)

> **ADDITIONAL FACTORS***
>
> If after quantitative risk assessment, a risk-based treatment decision is uncertain, additional factors may be considered to assist with decision making. These factors include:
>
> - LDL ≥ 160 mg/dL or other evidence of genetic hyperlipidemia
>
> - Family history of premature ASCVD with onset < 55 years in a first degree male relative or < 65 years in a first degree female relative
>
> - High-sensitivity C-reactive protein > 2 mg/L
>
> - Coronary Artery Calcium score ≥ 300 Agatston units or ≥ 75 percentile for age, sex and ethnicity
>
> - Ankle Brachial Index < 0.9
>
> * These factors support revising risk assessment upward

Global Risk Assessment Tool

The race- and gender-specific Pooled Cohort Equations to predict 10-year risk for a first hard ASCVD event should be used in non-Hispanic African Americans and non-Hispanic whites, 40-79 years of age (other populations may be considered as well). This tool assesses the risk of an initial cardiovascular event in patients without ASCVD. The clinician inputs information on gender, age, race, total cholesterol, HDL, systolic blood pressure, whether antihypertensive treatment is used, presence of diabetes, and smoking status. A 10-year ASCVD score of ≥ 7.5% is an indication to start statin therapy. This risk assessment should be repeated every 4-6 years in persons who are found to be at low 10-year risk (< 7.5%).

The tool can be downloaded and completed at: http://my.americanheart.org/cvriskcalculator

Determining Appropriate Statin Treatment Intensity Based on Patient Risk

PREVENTION LEVEL	STATIN TREATMENT

Primary Prevention

Primary elevation of LDL ≥ 190 mg/dL	High-intensity*
Diabetes and 40-75 years with LDL between 70-189 mg/dL with estimated 10-year ASCVD risk < 7.5%	Moderate-intensity
Diabetes and 40-75 years with LDL between 70-189 mg/dL with estimated 10-year ASCVD risk ≥ 7.5%	High-intensity*
Ages 40-75 years with LDL between 70-189 mg/dL with estimated 10-year ASCVD risk < 7.5%	Consider risk benefit
Ages 40-75 years with LDL between 70-189 mg/dL with estimated 10-year ASCVD risk ≥ 7.5%	Moderate-to-high intensity

Secondary Prevention

Clinical atherosclerotic cardiovascular disease (ASCVD) ≤ 75 years	High-intensity*
Clinical atherosclerotic cardiovascular disease (ASCVD) > 75 years	Moderate-intensity

Use moderate-intensity statin if not candidate for high-intensity

Statin Therapy Intensity Definitions and Selection Options

HIGH-INTENSITY	MODERATE-INTENSITY	LOW-INTENSITY
DAILY DOSE ↓ LDL ≥ 50%	**DAILY DOSE ↓ LDL 30%-49%**	**DAILY DOSE ↓ LDL < 30%**
Atorvastatin 40-80 mg daily	Atorvastatin 10-20 mg daily	Simvastatin 10 mg daily
Rosuvastatin 20-40 mg daily	Rosuvastatin 5-10 mg daily	Pravastatin 10-20 mg daily
	Simvastatin 20-40 mg daily	Lovastatin 20 mg daily
	Pravastatin 40-80 mg daily	Fluvastatin 20-40 mg daily
	Lovastatin 40 mg daily	Pitavastatin 1 mg daily
	Fluvastatin XL 80 mg daily	
	Fluvastatin 40 mg BID	
	Pitavastatin 2-4 mg daily	

NON-PHARMACOLOGIC THERAPY

In all patients with dyslipidemia, lifestyle changes are recommended (see below). These recommendations apply to adults < 80 years old with and without cardiovascular disease (CVD) and should be emphasized, monitored and reinforced.

- Consume a dietary pattern that emphasizes intake of vegetables, fruits and whole grains; includes low-fat dairy products, poultry, fish, legumes, nontropical vegetable oils and nuts; and limits intake of sweets, sugar-sweetened beverages and red meats. Adapt to appropriate calorie requirements, food preferences and nutritional therapy for other conditions. Can use plans such as the DASH, USDA Food Pattern or AHA diet.

- Aim for 5-6% of calories from saturated fat; reduce % of calories from *trans* fat.

- Aerobic physical activity 3-4 sessions per week, lasting 40 minutes/session and involving moderate-to-vigorous intensity (can reduce LDL 3-6 mg/dL).

- Maintain a healthy weight (BMI 18.5-24.9 kg/m^2).

- Avoid tobacco products.

Please note these recommendations are different from the obesity guideline recommendations (see Weight Loss chapter for more information).

PHARMACOLOGIC THERAPY

Statins are the drugs of choice in treating elevated LDL due to the extensive data showing a reduction in cardiovascular endpoints. The appropriate statin intensity is based on the patient's level of risk. In individuals who are candidates for statin therapy but are completely statin intolerant, it is reasonable to use nonstatin cholesterol-lowering drugs that have been shown to reduce ASCVD events in randomized controlled trials. Note: Many of the drug classes used for cholesterol management are potentially hepatotoxic (statins, niacin, potentially fibrates and ezetimibe). Liver enzymes should be monitored and the drug stopped if AST (8-48 units/L) or ALT (7-55 units/L) become > 3 times the upper limit of normal. Increases in liver transaminases are similar to the general population; however, LFTs should be monitored at baseline and periodically thereafter. Newer agents, lomitapide and mipomerson,

MANAGEMENT OF MILD-TO-MODERATE MUSCLE SYMPTOMS ASSOCIATED WITH STATIN USE
Discontinue the statin and evaluate symptoms
Evaluate patient for other conditions that may increase the risk for muscle damage
If muscle symptoms resolve, and if no contraindication, restart same statin at the same or lower dose
If myalgias return, discontinue original statin. Once muscle symptoms resolve, use a low dose of a different statin
If low dose of a different statin is tolerated, gradually increase the dose as tolerated

are effective in treating homozygous familial hypercholesterolemia (HoFH), which is a rare genetic disorder resulting in very high LDL levels. Although some of the statins are indicated for HoFH, they are only minimally effective and this condition usually requires additional lipid lowering therapies.

STATINS

Statins inhibit the enzyme 3-hydroxy-3-methylglutaryl coenzyme A (HMG-CoA) reductase preventing the conversion of HMG-CoA to mevalonate (the rate-limiting step in cholesterol synthesis). Extensive evidence exists that the appropriate intensity of statin therapy be used to reduce ASCVD risk in those most likely to benefit.

DRUG	DOSING	SAFETY/SIDE EFFECTS/MONITORING
Atorvastatin (*Lipitor*) + amlodipine (*Caduet*) + ezetimibe (*Liptruzet*)	10-80 mg daily Equiv dose = 10 mg	**CONTRAINDICATIONS** Active liver disease (including any unexplained elevations in hepatic transaminases), pregnancy, breastfeeding; concurrent use of strong 3A4 inhibitors – with simvastatin and lovastatin
Simvastatin (*Zocor*) **+ ezetimibe** (***Vytorin***) + niacin (*Simcor*) + sitaGLIPtin (*Juvisync*)	10-40 mg daily in the evening Equiv dose = 20 mg	**WARNINGS** Skeletal muscle effects (e.g., myopathy, including risk of rhabdomyolysis) – risk ↑ with higher doses and concomitant use of certain medicines. Predisposing factors include advanced age (≥ 65), female gender, uncontrolled hypothyroidism, and renal impairment. Patients should be advised to report promptly any unexplained and/or persistent muscle pain, tenderness, or weakness
Rosuvastatin (***Crestor***)	5-40 mg daily Equiv dose = 5 mg	Diabetes – can ↑ A1C and fasting blood glucose; benefits of statin therapy far outweigh the risk of hyperglycemia Immune-mediated necrotizing myopathy (IMNM) – an autoimmune-mediated myopathy presenting as proximal muscle weakness with elevated CPK levels, which persists despite discontinuation of the statin; immunosuppressive therapy (e.g., corticosteroids, azathioprine) may be used for treatment
Pravastatin (*Pravachol*)	10-80 mg daily Equiv dose = 40 mg	Liver enzyme abnormalities – persistent elevations in hepatic transaminases can occur (rare)
Lovastatin (*Mevacor, Altoprev*) + niacin (*Advicor*)	20-80 mg *Mevacor* (immediate release) is taken with evening meal *Altoprev* (extended release) is taken at bedtime Equiv dose = 40 mg	**SIDE EFFECTS** Myalgias, arthralgias, myopathy, diarrhea, ↑ CPK, rhabdomyolysis (↑ risk with higher doses), cognitive impairment (memory loss, confusion – reversible), ↑ blood glucose, ↑ A1C, possible ↑ risk of cataracts, ↑ LFTs
Fluvastatin (*Lescol, Lescol XL*)	20-80 mg at bedtime with immediate release (anytime with XL) Equiv dose = 80 mg	**MONITORING** LFTs at baseline and as clinically indicated thereafter; obtain a lipid panel 4-12 weeks after initiation or up titration of therapy; then every 3-12 months thereafter
Pitavastatin (*Livalo*)	1-4 mg daily Most potent statin Equiv dose = 2 mg	**NOTES** Pregnancy Category X Can take *Crestor, Lipitor, Livalo, Lescol XL* and *Pravachol* at any time of day. Use lower doses if CrCl < 30 mL/min, except with *Lescol* and *Lipitor*. With *Livalo*, use lower doses when CrCl < 60 mL/min. **Lipid Effects** ↓ LDL ~20-55% ↑ HDL ~5-15% ↓ TG ~10-30%

Statin Drug Interactions

All Statins

- Concomitant lipid-lowering therapies: use with fibrates (esp. gemfibrozil – which should be avoided with statins) and niacin products containing ≥ 1 gram ↑ the risk of myopathies.

- Cases of myopathy, including rhabdomyolysis, have been reported with HMG-CoA reductase inhibitors coadministered with colchicine.

Simvastatin, Lovastatin & Atorvastatin

- Simvastatin, lovastatin and atorvastatin are major 3A4 substrates. Simvastatin and lovastatin undergo extensive first-pass metabolism by CYP 3A4. Atorvastatin undergoes less first-pass metabolism by 3A4; therefore, most 3A4 inhibitors cause a smaller ↑ in plasma concentration than with simvastatin and lovastatin.

- Simvastatin: do not use simvastatin 80 mg/day due to ↑ risk of myopathy. Restrict use to only patients taking simvastatin 80 mg/day chronically (e.g., for 12 months or more) without evidence of muscle toxicity. Avoid with strong 3A4 inhibitors (see box). Do not exceed simvastatin 10 mg/day with verapamil, diltiazem or dronedarone. Do not exceed simvastatin 20 mg/day with amiodarone, amlodipine or ranolazine.

- Lovastatin: avoid with strong 3A4 inhibitors (see box). Do not exceed lovastatin 20 mg/day with danazol, diltiazem, dronedarone or verapamil. Do not exceed lovastatin 40 mg/day with amiodarone.

- Atorvastatin: avoid with cyclosporine, tipranavir plus ritonavir or telaprevir. Do not exceed atorvastatin 20 mg/day with clarithromycin, itraconazole, lopinavir + ritonavir, darunavir + ritonavir, fosamprenavir ± ritonavir. Do not exceed atorvastatin 40 mg/day with nelfinavir and boceprevir.

- Digoxin levels may ↑ with these agents; monitor.

Rosuvastatin

- Rosuvastatin is a substrate of 2C9 (minor) and 3A4 (minor): may ↑ INR in patients taking warfarin; monitor.

- Cyclosporine may ↑ rosuvastatin; do not exceed 5 mg/day of rosuvastatin.

- Ritonavir-boosted lopinavir or atazanavir: do not exceed 10 mg/day of rosuvastatin.

Pravastatin

- Cyclosporine can ↑ pravastatin; do not exceed pravastatin 20 mg/day.

- Clarithromycin can ↑ pravastatin; do not exceed pravastatin 40 mg/day.

Fluvastatin

- Fluvastatin inhibits 2C9 (moderate): may ↑ INR in patients taking warfarin; monitor.

- Cyclosporine and fluconazole can ↑ fluvastatin.

- Fluvastatin can enhance the levels of glyburide and phenytoin, monitor.

Pitavastatin

- Minimal CYP450 metabolism. Contraindicated with cyclosporine. Limit dose to 1 mg daily with erythromycin and 2 mg daily with rifampin. Monitor PT/INR in patients taking warfarin.

Statin Patient Counseling

For <u>all</u> cholesterol medicines: Your healthcare provider should start you on lifestyle changes including a heart healthy food pattern and exercise.

- Contact your healthcare provider right away if you have muscle weakness, tenderness, aching, cramps, stiffness or pain that happens without a good reason, especially if you also have a fever or feel more tired than usual. These may be symptoms of muscle damage.

- Contact your healthcare provider right away if you are passing brown or dark-colored urine, have pale stools, feel more tired than usual or if your skin and/or whites of your eyes become yellow. These may be symptoms of liver damage.

- Grapefruit and grapefruit juice may interact with this medicine. This could lead to higher amounts of drugs in your body. Do not consume grapefruit products without discussing with your healthcare provider (for lovastatin, simvastatin, atorvastatin).

- <u>Do not use</u> if pregnant or if you think you may be pregnant. This drug may harm your unborn baby. If you get pregnant, stop taking and call healthcare provider right away.

STRONG 3A4 INHIBITORS – AVOID WITH SIMVASTATIN AND LOVASTATIN
Itraconazole
Ketoconazole
Posaconazole
Voriconazole
Erythromycin
Clarithromycin
Telithromycin
HIV protease inhibitors
Boceprevir
Telaprevir
Nefazodone
Cyclosporine
Gemfibrozil
Danazol (with simvastatin)
Grapefruit juice

EZETIMIBE

Inhibits absorption of cholesterol at the brush border of the small intestine.

DRUG	DOSING	SAFETY/SIDE EFFECTS/MONITORING
Ezetimibe *(Zetia)* **+ simvastatin *(Vytorin)*** + atorvastatin *(Liptruzet)*	10 mg daily	**WARNING** Avoid use in moderate-or-severe hepatic impairment Skeletal muscle effects (e.g., myopathy, including risk of rhabdomyolysis) when combined with a statin **SIDE EFFECTS** URTIs, diarrhea, arthralgias, myalgias, pain in extremities, sinusitis **MONITORING** When used with a statin and/or fibrate, obtain liver function tests at baseline and as clinically indicated thereafter **NOTES** Pregnancy Category C Clinical trial results showed a ↓ in LDL, but no reduction in clinical outcomes If CrCl < 60 mL/min, do not exceed simvastatin 20 mg/day when using combination product *(Vytorin)* **Lipid Effects** ↓ LDL 18-23% ↑ HDL 1-3% ↓ TG 8-10%

Ezetimibe Drug Interactions

- When ezetimibe and cyclosporine are given together, the concentration of both can ↑; monitor levels of cyclosporine.

- Concomitant bile acid resins ↓ ezetimibe; give ezetimibe 2 hours before or 4 hours after bile acid resin.

- Can ↑ risk of cholelithiasis when used with fenofibrate; avoid use with gemfibrozil.

- If using warfarin, monitor INR/bleeding.

Ezetimibe Patient Counseling

- <u>Especially if taken with statin</u>: Contact your healthcare provider right away if you are passing brown or dark-colored urine, have pale stools, feel more tired than usual or if your skin and/or whites of your eyes become yellow. These may be symptoms of liver damage. Contact your healthcare provider right away if you have muscle weakness, tenderness, aching, cramps, stiffness or pain that happens without a good reason, especially if you also have a fever or feel more tired than usual. These may be symptoms of muscle damage.

- Take this medicine once daily, with or without food.

BILE ACID SEQUESTRANTS/BILE ACID BINDING RESINS

Binds bile acids in the intestine forming a complex that is excreted in the feces. This non-systemic action results in a partial removal of the bile acids from the enterohepatic circulation, preventing their reabsorption.

DRUG	DOSING	SAFETY/SIDE EFFECTS/MONITORING
Cholestyramine (*Questran, Questran Light, Prevalite*) Also approved for pruritus due to increased levels of bile acids	4 grams initially (max 24 grams), divided BID with meals – mix the powder with water or other non-carbonated liquid (2-6 oz.)	**CONTRAINDICATIONS** Cholestyramine – Complete biliary obstruction Colesevelam – Bowel obstruction, TG > 500 mg/dL, history of hypertriglyceridemia-induced pancreatitis **SIDE EFFECTS** Constipation (may need dose reduction or laxative), dyspepsia, nausea, abdominal pain, cramping, gas, bloating, hypertriglyceridemia, esophageal obstruction, ↑ LFTs.
Colesevelam *(Welchol)* 625 mg tablet, 3.75 g packet Also approved for DM Type 2 (↓ A1C~ 0.5%)	3.75 grams (6 tabs or 1 packet daily or 3 tabs BID) with a meal and liquid	**NOTES** Pregnancy Category B *(Welchol)*/C (others) ATP IV guidelines do not recommend using these agents when TGs are ≥ 300 mg/dL. Cholestyramine – Sipping or holding the resin suspension in the mouth for prolonged periods may lead to changes in the surface of the teeth resulting in discoloration, erosion of enamel or decay; good oral hygiene should be maintained.
Colestipol *(Colestid)*	Tablets: 2 g daily or BID (max 16 g/day) Granules: 5 g daily or BID (max 30 g/day)	Colesevelam packet – Empty 1 packet into a glass; add 1/2-1 cup (4-8 ounces) of water, fruit juice, or a diet soft drink and mix well. Colestipol: Add granules to at least 90 mL of liquid and stir until completely mixed. **Lipid Effects** ↓ LDL ~10-30% ↑ HDL ~3-5% No change or ↑ TG (~5%)

Bile Acid Sequestrants Drug Interactions

- Colesevelam has less drug interactions than the other 2 bile acid sequestrants and is more commonly used. For cholestyramine or colestipol, separate all other drugs by 1-4 hours before or 4-6 hours after the bile acid sequestrants.

- The following medications should be taken 4 hours prior to colesevelam: cyclosporine, oral contraceptives, levothyroxine, olmesartan, phenytoin, sulfonylureas and tetracyclines. Consider separation with other drugs as well. Colesevelam ↑ levels of metformin extended release.

- With warfarin, monitor INR frequently during initiation.

- Bile acid sequestrants may ↓ absorption of fat-soluble vitamins (A, D, E, K), folic acid and iron. Separate administration times with concurrent multivitamin use as noted above.

FIBRATES

Fibrates are peroxisome proliferator receptor alpha (PPARα) activators. By activating PPARα, there is enhanced elimination and ↓ synthesis of VLDL (causing ↓ TGs) and an ↑ in HDL – this causes an increase in apolipoprotein lipase, which may ↓ LDL – however, when TGs are high, reducing TGs can ↑ LDL – be careful to monitor LDL when reducing TGs. The ACCORD Lipid Study showed no significant difference in experiencing a major cardiac event between patients treated with fenofibrate plus simvastatin compared with simvastatin alone. In addition, worsening of renal function occurred more commonly in patients taking a fenofibrate.

DRUG	DOSING	SAFETY/SIDE EFFECTS/MONITORING
Fenofibrate, Fenofibric Acid *(Antara, Fenoglide, Fibricor, Lipofen, Lofibra,* **TriCor**, *Triglide,* **Trilipix**, generics)*	**FORMULATIONS** Micronized formulations and other modes are used to improve bioavailability – to get more TG reduction (which is dose dependent). If a generic is needed, it may be necessary to call the prescriber for a close mg strength – and try to match one with a similar delivery technology, using the Orange Book. *Antara:* 30, 43, 90, 130 mg *Fenoglide* (with meals): 40, 120 mg *Fibricor:* 35, 105 mg *Lofibra* (micronized capsules – with meals; tablets with or without food): 67, 134, 200 mg *Lipofen* (with meals): 50, 150 mg *TriCor:* 48, 145 mg *Triglide:* 50, 160 mg *Trilipix:* 45, 135 mg	**CONTRAINDICATIONS** Severe liver disease including primary biliary cirrhosis Severe renal disease (CrCl < 30 mL/min) Gallbladder disease Nursing mothers **WARNINGS** Myopathy, including the risk of rhabdomyolysis, has been reported in patients taking fibrates; the risk is higher when fibrates are co-administered with a statin particularly in elderly patients and patients with diabetes, renal failure, or hypothyroidism Fenofibrates increase cholesterol excretion into the bile, leading to risk of cholelithiasis Reversible ↑ SCr (> 2 mg/dL) has been observed with use; clinical significance unknown **SIDE EFFECTS** ↑ LFTs (dose related), abdominal pain, ↑ CPK, dyspepsia, URTIs
Gemfibrozil *(Lopid)*	600 mg BID, 30 minutes before breakfast and dinner	**MONITORING** LFTs, renal function **NOTES** Pregnancy Category C Reduce dose if CrCl 30-80 mL/min with fenofibrates (max dose 54 mg/day). **Lipid Effects** ↓ TGs ~20-50% ↑ HDL ~15% ↓ LDL ~5-20% (but can ↑ LDL when TG are high)

Fibrate Drug Interactions

- When used in combination with statins, fibrates can ↑ the risk of myopathies and rhabdomyolysis, especially with gemfibrozil. <u>Only *Trilipix*</u> has the indication for use with a statin although others (except gemfibrozil – avoid if on a statin) may have a similar safety profile. Monitor liver enzymes with all fibrates, statins, and when the 2 drug classes are used in combination.

- Fibrates may ↑ cholesterol excretion into the bile, leading to cholelithiasis.

- Colchicine can ↑ the risk of myopathy when coadministered with fenofibrate.

- Gemfibrozil is contraindicated with repaglinide as it may increase hypoglycemic effects.

- Fibrates may increase the effects of sulfonylureas and warfarin.

NIACIN

Decreases the rate of hepatic synthesis of VLDL (↓ TGs) and LDL; may also ↑ rate of chylomicron TG removal from plasma. Also known as <u>nicotinic acid or vitamin B3</u>, although doses for cholesterol reduction are much higher than doses found in multivitamin products.

DRUG	DOSING	SAFETY/SIDE EFFECTS/MONITORING
Immediate-Release (crystalline) niacin (*Niacor*) – OTC	250 mg with dinner; can ↑ every 4-7 days to max dose 6 g daily, divided in 2-3 doses	**CONTRAINDICATIONS** Active liver disease, active PUD, arterial bleeding **WARNINGS** Use with caution in patients with unstable angina or in the acute phase of an MI Hepatotoxicity **SIDE EFFECTS** Flushing, pruritus (itching), nausea, vomiting, diarrhea, GI distress, hyperglycemia, hyperuricemia (or gout), increased cough, hepatotoxicity, orthostatic hypotension, hypophosphatemia
Extended-Release Niacin (*Niaspan*) **500, 750, 1,000 mg** + lovastatin (*Advicor*) + simvastatin (*Simcor*)	500 mg QHS x 4 weeks Can ↑ every 4 weeks to a max dose of 2 g daily	**MONITORING** Check LFTs at the start (baseline), every 6 to 12 weeks for the first year, and periodically thereafter (e.g., at approximately 6-month intervals); blood glucose (if have diabetes); uric acid (if have gout); INR (if on warfarin) **NOTES** Pregnancy Category C Immediate-release niacin has poor tolerability due to flushing/itching. Extended-release forms (CR and SR) have less (but still significant) flushing but more hepatotoxicity. Therefore, the best clinical choice is *Niaspan* with less flushing and less hepatotoxicity – but it is the most expensive.
Controlled-(or sustained) Release Niacin (*Slo-Niacin, OTC*) 250, 500, 750 mg	500 mg QHS x 4 weeks Can ↑ every 4 weeks to a max dose of 2 g daily	Formulations of niacin (regular release versus extended release) are not interchangeable. Flush-free niacins (inositol hexaniacinate or hexanicotinate), niacinamide or nicotinamide are not effective. Take with food, avoid hot beverages and spicy food. **Lipid Effects** ↓ LDL 5-25% ↑ HDL 15-35% ↓ TG 20-50%

Niacin Drug Interactions

- <u>Watch for other drugs that are potentially hepatotoxic being used concurrently. This includes use with statins – stick to lower statin doses.</u> The combination drug lovastatin/niaspan *(Advicor)* has a max dose of 2,000/40 mg and simvastatin/niaspan *(Simcor)* has a max dose of 2,000/40 mg.

- <u>Take niacin 4-6 hours after bile acid sequestrants.</u>

FISH OILS

Not completely understood; may be due to reduction of hepatic synthesis of TGs. These are indicated as an adjunct to diet in patients with TGs ≥ 500 mg/dL. Also known as omega-3 fatty acids.

DRUG	DOSING	SAFETY/SIDE EFFECTS/MONITORING
Omega-3 Acid Ethyl Esters (*Lovaza*) 1 g capsule contains 465 mg EPA (eicosapentaenoic acid) and 375 mg DHA (docosahexaenoic acid)	Start 2 capsules daily, can ↑ to 4 caps daily	**WARNINGS** Use with caution in patients with known hypersensitivity to fish and/or shellfish. *Lovaza* may ↑ levels of LDL; monitor. There is a possible association between *Lovaza* and more frequent recurrences of symptomatic atrial fibrillation or flutter in patients with paroxysmal or persistent atrial fibrillation, particularly within the first months of initiating therapy. **SIDE EFFECTS** Eructation (burping), dyspepsia, taste perversions *(Lovaza)*; arthalgias *(Vascepa)* **MONITORING** LFTs (in patients with hepatic impairment) periodically during therapy
Icosapent ethyl *(Vascepa)* contains 1 gram of icosapent ethyl, an ethyl ester of omega-3 fatty acid eicosapentaenoic acid (EPA)	2 capsules twice daily with food	**NOTES** Pregnancy Category C There are many OTC omega-3 fatty acid products marketed as dietary supplements. Only *Lovaza* and *Vascepa* (both Rx) are FDA approved for TG lowering when TG ≥ 500 mg/dL in addition to diet. Stop prior to elective surgeries due to increased risk of bleeding. **Lipid Effects** ↓ TGs up to 45% ↑ HDL ~9% Can ↑ LDL up to 44% (only with *Lovaza*; no ↑ seen with *Vascepa*)

Fish Oil Drug Interactions

- Omega-3-acids may prolong bleeding time. Monitor INR if patients are taking warfarin. Caution with other medications that can ↑ bleeding risk.

Fish Oil Patient Counseling

- This medication is taken in addition to a healthy diet.

- Can take once daily, or split BID.

- Take with or without food, but you may find it more comfortable to take with food.

- This medicine does not usually cause side effects, but may cause indigestion (stomach upset), burping, or a distorted sense of taste *(Lovaza)* or joint pain *(Vascepa)*.

NEW AGENTS FOR HOMOZYGOUS FAMILIAL HYPERCHOLESTEROLEMIA (HoFH)

Lomitapide

Lomitapide binds to and inhibits microsomal triglyceride transfer protein (MTP) in the endoplasmic reticulum. MTP inhibition prevents the assembly of apo-B containing lipoproteins in enterocytes and hepatocytes resulting in reduced production of chylomicrons and VLDL and subsequently reduced plasma LDL concentrations.

DRUG	DOSING	SAFETY/SIDE EFFECTS/MONITORING
Lomitapide (Juxtapid)	5-60 mg daily Initiate at 5 mg daily. If tolerated, increase after 2 weeks to 10 mg daily; increase at 4 week intervals to a max of 60 mg Take whole with water and without food, at least two hours after the evening meal	**BLACK BOX WARNING** Hepatotoxicity **CONTRAINDICATIONS** Pregnancy; concomitant use with moderate or strong CYP3A4 inhibitors; moderate or severe hepatic impairment; active liver disease including unexplained persistent elevations of serum transaminases **WARNINGS** GI side effects occur in majority of patients and may affect absorption of concomitant oral medications **SIDE EFFECTS** Diarrhea, nausea, vomiting, dyspepsia, abdominal pain, constipation, flatulence, ↑ LFTs, chest pain, back pain **MONITORING** ALT, AST, alkaline phosphatase, total bilirubin and pregnancy test in females of reproductive potential at baseline; measure transaminases prior to any increase in dose or monthly (whichever occurs first) during the first year, and then every 3 months and prior to dosage increases **NOTES** Pregnancy Category X Due to the risk of hepatotoxicity, this agent is only available through a Juxtapid Risk Evaluation and Mitigation Strategy (REMS) program.

Lomitapide Drug Interactions

- Strong and moderate CYP3A4 inhibitors are contraindicated with lomitapide. Refer to the Drug Interactions chapter for a complete list of moderate and strong 3A4 inhibitors.

- If using weak CYP3A4 inhibitors concomitantly, do not exceed 30 mg/day of lomitapide. These include amiodarone, atorvastatin, cyclosporine, fluoxetine, fluvoxamine, isoniazid, oral contraceptives, ranitidine, ranolazine and others.

- Warfarin: ↑ INR; monitor.

- Simvastatin, lovastatin; concomitant use may increase risk of myopathy. Do not exceed simvastatin 20 mg/day (may use 40 mg/day if patients have previously tolerated simvastatin 80 mg/day for 12 months or more without evidence of muscle toxicity). Lovastatin dose should also be reduced when starting lomitapide concomitantly.

- Lomitapide is an inhibitor of P-glycoprotein, which may increase drugs that are P-glycoprotein substrates, such as aliskiren, ambrisentan, colchicine, dabigatran, digoxin, everolimus, fexofenadine, imatinib, lapatinib, maraviroc, nilotinib, posaconazole, ranolazine, saxagliptin, sirolimus, sitagliptin, tolvaptan and topotecan. Dose reduction of the P-glycoprotein substrates should be considered when used concomitantly.

- Watch for other drugs that are potentially hepatotoxic being used concurrently. This includes isotretinoin, amiodarone, high dose acetaminophen, methotrexate, tetracyclines, and tamoxifen.

- Lomitapide reduces absorption of fat soluble vitamins from the small intestine.

- Separate dosing from bile acid sequestrants by 4 hours.

Mipomersen

Mipomersen is an oligonucleotide inhibitor of apo B-100 synthesis. ApoB is the main component of LDL and very low density lipoprotein (VLDL), which is the precursor to LDL.

DRUG	DOSING	SAFETY/SIDE EFFECTS/MONITORING
Mipomersen (Kynamro)	200 mg SC once weekly Maximal LDL reduction seen after ~ 6 months	**BLACK BOX WARNING** Hepatotoxicity **CONTRAINDICATIONS** <u>Liver disease</u> (including unexplained elevations in hepatic transaminases) **WARNINGS** Can cause hepatotoxicity, with elevations in transaminases and/or hepatic steatosis **SIDE EFFECTS** Injection site reactions, flu-like symptoms, nausea, headache, ↑ ALT **MONITORING** ALT, AST, total bilirubin, alkaline phosphatase at baseline; then monthly for the first year of treatment, then every 3 months thereafter **NOTES** Pregnancy Category B Due to the risk of hepatoxicity, this agent is only available through a *Kynamro* Risk Evaluation and Mitigation Strategy (REMS) program.

Mipomersen Drug Interactions

- Watch for other drugs that are potentially hepatotoxic being used concurrently. This includes isotretinoin, amiodarone, high dose acetaminophen, methotrexate, tetracyclines, and tamoxifen.

Niacin Patient Counseling

- *Niaspan*: Take at bedtime after a low-fat snack. Other niacins: Take with food.

- With long-acting formulations: Do not crush or chew.

- Contact your healthcare provider right away if you are passing brown or dark-colored urine, feel more tired than usual or if your skin and/or whites of your eyes become yellow. These may be symptoms of liver damage.

- Flushing (warmth, redness, itching and/or tingling of the skin) is a common side effect that may subside after several weeks of consistent use. Pretreatment with 325 mg aspirin (or 200 mg of ibuprofen) 30-60 minutes before the dose (for a few weeks) may help to ↓ flushing. With *Niaspan*, flushing will occur mostly at night; use caution if awakened due to possible dizziness.

- Avoid using alcohol or hot beverages or eating spicy foods around the time of taking this medicine to help reduce flushing.

- If you have diabetes, check your blood sugar when starting this medicine because there may be a mild increase.

Bile Acid Sequestrant Patient Counseling

See notes section in chart for instructions regarding food/fluid intake for specific agents.

- Take this medication at mealtime with plenty of water or other liquid. Never take dry.

- Check for other constipating drugs or constipation itself and counsel appropriately (laxative, such as senna, or the stool softener docusate, if appropriate). Maintain adequate fluid and fiber intake.

- Separate the dose of this medication from multivitamin dosing due to ↓ absorption of vitamins A, D, E and K (mostly K), folic acid and iron. Supplementation with a multivitamin (esp. in women and children) may be needed while taking this medication.

Fibrate Patient Counseling

- *Antara, Fibricor, TriCor, Triglide* and *Trilipix*: Take once daily, with or without food.

- *Fenoglide, Lofibra* (micronized capsules) *and Lipofen*: Take once daily, with food.

- *Lopid*: Take twice daily, 30 minutes before breakfast and dinner.

- Do not crush or chew. Contact your healthcare provider if you experience muscle aches.

- Contact your healthcare provider right away if you experience abdominal pain, nausea or vomiting. These may be signs of inflammation of the gallbladder or pancreas.

- Contact your healthcare provider right away if you are passing brown or dark-colored urine, feel more tired than usual or if your skin and/or whites of your eyes become yellow. These may be signs of liver damage.

PRACTICE CASE

PATIENT PROFILE

Patient Name David Armistead

Address 1882 Peekaborn

Age 57   **Sex** Male   **Race** White   **Height** 5'11"   **Weight** 246 lbs

Allergies NKDA

DIAGNOSES

Coronary Heart Disease, stent placement 7/13

Dyslipidemia

Hypertension

Diabetes Type 2

MEDICATIONS

Date	No.	Prescriber	Drug & Strength	Quantity	Sig	Refills
5/15/13	77328	Gallagher	*Actos* 45 mg	#30	1 PO daily	2
5/15/13	73768	Gallagher	Metformin 1000 mg	#60	1 PO BID	2
5/15/13	73554	Gallagher	Lisinopril-HCT 20-25 mg	#30	1 PO daily	2
			Fish oils 1000 mg cap		1 PO BID	
			Aspirin 81 mg EC		1 PO daily	
			Multivitamin		1 PO daily	

LAB/DIAGNOSTIC TESTS

Test	Normal Value	Results Date 5/12/13	Date	Date
Protein, T	6.2-8.3 g/dL			
Albumin	3.6-5.1 g/dL			
Alk Phos	33-115 units/L			
AST	10-35 units/L	32		
ALT	6-40 units/L	20		
CH, T	125-200 g/dL	224		
TG	<150 g/dL	248		
HDL	g/dL	36		
LDL	g/dL			
GLU	65-99 mg/dL	114		
Na	135-146 mEq/L	131		
K	3.5-5.3 mEq/L	3.8		
Cl	98-110 mEq/L	105		
HCO3-	22-28 mEq/L	25		
BUN	7-25 mg/dL	18		
Creatinine	0.6-1.2 mg/dL			
Calcium	8.6-10.2 mg/dL			
WBC	4-11 cells/mm³	4.6		
RBC	3.8-5.1 mL/mm³			
Hemoglobin	Male: 13.8- 17.2 g/dL Female: 12.1-15.1 g/dL	14.2		
Hematocrit	Male: 40.7-50.3% Female: 36.1- 44.3%	38		
MCHC	32-36 g/dL			
MCV	80-100 µm			
Platelet count	140-400 x 10³/mm³	210		
TSH	0.4-4.0 mIU/L			
FT4	4.5- 11.2 mcg/dL			
Hgb A1c	4-6%	7.2%		

ADDITIONAL INFORMATION

Date	Notes
11/11/13	Patient reports walking more since heart procedure. He has lost 13 lbs in last 5 months by decreasing "donuts and sugar." No EtOH, no tobacco use (past Hx smoking). Patient states he prefers not to take more pills, and is scared about his heart. BP today is 145/88.

Questions

1. What is David's calculated LDL?

   a. 188
   b. 176
   c. 138
   d. 105
   e. 99

2. David needs to be placed on statin therapy. According to the ATP IV Treatment of Blood Cholesterol Guideline, which would be the most appropriate statin regimen for David?

   a. Pravastatin 40 mg daily
   b. Rosuvastatin 20 mg daily
   c. Lovastatin 40 mg daily
   d. Atorvastatin 20 mg daily
   e. Pitavastatin 4 mg daily

3. David returns to the clinic for follow up and complains of pain in his legs with occasional weakness. The statin therapy is stopped and the pain resolves. What is the best course of action to take for treatment of David's dyslipidemia according to the ATP IV Treatment of Blood Cholesterol Guideline?

   a. Restart the same statin at a lower dose
   b. Switch to a different statin
   c. Consider the patient unable to tolerate statin therapy and start a nonstatin cholesterol medication
   d. Recommend angiography to evaluate the leg for claudication
   e. Recommend a venous ultrasound to evaluate the leg for a DVT

Questions 4-8 do not relate to the case.

4. Which of the following cholesterol medicines should be taken with dinner?

   a. Niaspan
   b. Mevacor
   c. Zetia
   d. Zocor
   e. Altoprev

5. A patient is going to be started on *Niaspan* therapy. Which of the following statements is correct?

   a. *Niaspan* is immediate release niacin.
   b. *Niaspan* has a higher degree of hepatotoxicity than all the other niacin formulations.
   c. *Niaspan* must be taken on an empty stomach.
   d. *Niaspan* is taken with breakfast.
   e. *Niaspan* causes less flushing than immediate release niacin.

6. A physician has called the pharmacist. He has a patient on phenytoin who cannot tolerate statins. He wishes to begin *Welchol*. Which of the following statements is correct?

   a. The phenytoin should be given 4 hours before *Welchol*.
   b. He cannot use this class of drugs with phenytoin.
   c. *Questran* would be a better option due to a lower risk of drug interactions.
   d. The dose of *Welchol* is 5 g twice daily, with food and water.
   e. There is no drug interaction between phenytoin and *Welchol*.

7. Which of the following drug classes can significantly reduce triglycerides by > 10%? (Select **ALL** that apply.)

   a. Fibrates
   b. Fish oils
   c. Bile Acid Resins
   d. Ezetimibe
   e. Niacin

8. Which of the following generic/brand combinations is correct?

   a. Amlodipine/Atorvastatin (*Vytorin*)
   b. Fenofibric Acid (*Trilipix*)
   c. Amlodipine/Rosuvastatin (*Caduet*)
   d. Fluvastatin (*Mevacor*)
   e. Pitavastatin (*Lescol*)

Answers

1-c, 2-b, 3-a, 4-b, 5-e, 6-a, 7-a,b,e, 8-b

32

HEART FAILURE

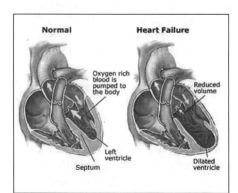

Normal — **Heart Failure**

Oxygen rich blood is pumped to the body

Reduced volume

Left ventricle

Septum

Dilated ventricle

GUIDELINES

Yancy CW, Jessup M, Bozkurt B, et al. 2013 ACCF/AHA guideline for the management of heart failure: a report of the American College of Cardiology Foundation/American Heart Association Task Force on Practice Guidelines. J Am Coll Cardiol 2013 June 5.

Executive Summary: HFSA 2010 Comprehensive Heart Failure Practice Guideline. Journal of Cardiac Failure. June 2010;16(6):475-539.

We gratefully acknowledge the assistance of Tien Ng, PharmD, FCCP, BCPS (AQ-C), Associate Professor at the University of Southern California School of Pharmacy, in preparing this chapter.

BACKGROUND

Heart failure is a syndrome where the heart is not able to supply sufficient blood flow (or cardiac output) to meet the metabolic needs of the body. Most commonly, heart failure is caused by a reduced ability of the heart to eject blood, known as low-output heart failure. Low cardiac output can be a consequence of impaired ability of the left ventricle to eject blood [systolic dysfunction; heart failure with a reduced ejection fraction (HFrEF)] or impaired ability of the left ventricle to fill with blood [diastolic dysfunction; heart failure with a preserved ejection fraction (HFpEF)]. Generally, systolic dysfunction (HFrEF) is characterized by a left ventricular ejection fraction less than 40%, whereas diastolic dysfunction (HFpEF) patients have only mildly reduced (40-50%) or normal left ventricular ejection fraction. Many patients with low-output heart failure have components of both systolic and diastolic dysfunction. Less commonly, the reason for the mismatch in blood flow and metabolic need is due to supra-physiologic metabolic needs (e.g., thyrotoxicosis, sepsis), a condition known as high-output heart failure. For the purposes of this chapter, the term "heart failure" will refer to systolic heart failure, or HFrEF.

The heart failure syndrome is characterized by high mortality, frequent hospitalizations, and reduced quality of life. Heart failure is a leading cause of hospitalizations in the elderly. Patients hospitalized for new-onset or worsening heart failure symptoms are referred to as having acute heart failure or acute decompensated heart failure, respectively. Although some hospitalizations are unavoidable due to disease progression or association with an acute cardiac event, many are attributable to non-adherence to medications and/or lifestyle modifications such as sodium and fluid restriction. This is a major cause of increased health care expenditure, and consequently, it presents an opportunity for clinicians to impact this syndrome. Studies have shown that pharmacists can positively impact the outcome of heart failure patients by providing education on dietary and lifestyle measures, and to ensure optimization of the complex medication regimens that are used to improve patient outcomes. Heart failure is one of the most important conditions to include lifestyle counseling and the requirements for strict medication adherence.

CAUSES OF SYSTOLIC HEART FAILURE

Heart failure can be classified by the underlying etiology as either an ischemic or non-ischemic cardiomyopathy. Ischemic cardiomyopathy results from myocardial damage sustained during an acute myocardial infarction, resulting in a loss of contractile function. Non-ischemic cardiomyopathies encompass a variety of conditions that ultimately increase the workload of cardiomyocytes, accelerating cell death, and lead to a thin-walled dilated left ventricle with reduced contractile function. Longstanding hypertension is the leading cause of non-ischemic cardiomyopathy, with other less common causes being valvular disease, excessive alcohol intake or illicit drug use, congenital heart defects, viral infections, diabetes, and cardiotoxic drugs. The most common causes of heart failure in North America are ischemic heart disease (myocardial infarction) and hypertension.

PATHOPHYSIOLOGY

Some important hemodynamic parameters are worth reviewing prior to discussing the pathophysiology and treatment of heart failure. Cardiac output is the volume of blood (expressed in liters) pumped by the heart in one minute. It is a function of heart rate and stroke volume (the amount of blood ejected from the left ventricle during one cardiac cy-

---

DRUGS THAT CAUSE OR WORSEN HEART FAILURE

Some chemotherapeutic agents, particularly anthracyclines [doxorubicin (Adriamycin, Doxil), daunorubicin (Cerubidine, DaunoXome), etc.] and some tyrosine kinases inhibitors such as lapatinib (Tykerb) and sunitinib (Sutent). Also, trastuzumab (Herceptin), imatinib (Gleevec) and docetaxol (Taxotere) can cause fluid retention.

Amphetamines and other sympathomimetics.

Routine use of calcium channel blockers in systolic HF.

Anti-arrhythmic drugs (lower risk with amiodarone and dofetilide). Do NOT use class I antiarrhythmic agents (mexiletine, tocainide, procainamide, quinidine, disopyramide, flecainide and propafenone).

Avoid itraconazole for non-life threatening infections (such as onychomycosis).

Immunomodulators, including interferons, TNF inhibitors (can worsen heart failure), rituximab and others.

NSAIDs, including the selective COX-2 inhibitor celecoxib (Celebrex) – avoid use of NSAIDs especially if advanced renal disease – use can cause renal dysfunction, fluid retention and worsen heart failure.

Glucocorticoids can worsen heart failure.

Triptan migraine drugs (contraindicated with history of cardiovascular disease or uncontrolled hypertension).

Thiazolidinediones – particularly rosiglitazone (Avandia); and pioglitazone (Actos) due to increased risk of edema.

Excessive alcohol use: modest use may have mild cardiovascular benefit, but excessive use does not.

Heart valve disease can be caused by these drugs: fenfluramine (Pondimin), dexfenfluramine (Redux), ergot derivatives including ergotamine (Ergostat), dihydroergotamine (Migranal), methysergide (Sansert), and others.

cle). It can be represented by the equation: CO = HR x SV. Stroke volume is determined by the volume of blood in the ventricle (preload), the resistance to forward flow in the arterial vessels (afterload), and how hard the ventricle squeezes during systole (contractility). Cardiac index is the CO/BSA.

Heart failure is a progressive syndrome, meaning that regardless of the initial etiology of myocardial damage, over time left ventricular systolic function will continue to decline. In simple terms, initial damage to the heart leads to a reduction in cardiac output. To compensate, several acute adaptations occur, including structural changes in the shape and composition of the myocardium, and activation of neurohormonal systems. Activation of the sympathetic nervous system and the renin-angiotensin-aldosterone system [endothelin and vasopressin (anti-diuretic hormone) are also activated] results in vasoconstriction, or increased systemic vascular resistance (SVR). This vasoconstriction helps maintain blood pressure and perfusion to vital organs. Sympathetic (adrenergic) activation also increases heart rate and contractility which augments cardiac output. Aldosterone release results in sodium and water retention which increases preload in an attempt to augment stroke volume and thus cardiac output (CO). While sodium and water retention leads to increases in blood volume to maintain CO, it can cause edema. The excess fluid causes the body to become "congested" and the classic symptoms of "congestive" heart failure appear, including dyspnea (shortness of breath), fatigue, and peripheral edema.

Although short-term these adaptations result in improved cardiac output, they have deleterious effects such as increased myocardial workload, increased risk of arrhythmias, and accelerated myocardial cell death. Therefore, chronic activation of these neurohormonal systems results in a further decline in cardiac systolic function, and hence a vicious cycle of neurohormonal activation and reduced cardiac function ensues. The pathophysiology of heart failure also involves alterations at the genetic and molecular level, inflammation, and oxidative stress, however, the neurohormonal model of heart failure remains important as currently the only pharmacologic therapies that have been shown to slow the progressive decline in cardiac function and improve survival in heart failure patients antagonize these neurohormonal systems.

Clinical Presentation and Assessment

Symptoms of heart failure are generally a result of either congestion behind the failing ventricle or hypoperfusion due to the reduced cardiac output. As the left or right ventricle

---

SIGNS AND SYMPTOMS OF HEART FAILURE

General
Dyspnea at rest or on exertion

Weakness/fatigue

Shortness of breath (SOB)

Reduction in exercise capacity

LVH

↑ BNP (B-type Natriuretic Peptide): normal < 100 pg/mL

↑ NT-proBNP (N-terminal pro B-type Natriuretic Peptide): normal < 300 pg/mL

Left-sided HF
Orthopnea

Paroxysmal nocturnal dyspnea (PND) or nocturnal cough

Bibasilar rales

S3 gallop

EF < 40%

Right-sided HF
Edema

Ascites

Jugular venous distention (JVD)

Hepatojugular reflux (HJR)

Hepatomegaly

weakens, blood volume and pressure increase in the chamber resulting in a "back-up" of the circulatory system. This leads to signs and symptoms of congestion which can be categorized as right-sided or left-sided failure symptoms (see table on previous page). In addition, a reduction in cardiac output may result in hypoperfusion or "underfilling" of essential organ systems leading to common symptoms of exercise intolerance, fatigue, dizziness or weakness, and reduced renal function.

Heart failure patients can be categorized by the presence or severity of symptoms. The American College of Cardiology and American Heart Association (ACC/AHA) recommends categorizing patients by heart failure stage (see table below). The staging system is used to help practitioners optimize the management of patients in order to slow the development of symptoms in asymptomatic patients (stages A and B) or slow the progression of the syndrome (stages C and D). Heart failure patients can also be classified by their level of physical functional limitation or New York Heart Association (NYHA) functional class (see table below). Functional class is an important prognostic indicator for heart failure patients. With proper treatment, it is possible for a given patient's functional classification to improve.

ACC/AHA STAGING SYSTEM		NYHA FUNCTIONAL CLASS	
A	At high risk for development of HF, but without structural heart disease or symptoms of HF (i.e., patients with HTN, CHD, DM, obesity, metabolic syndrome)		No corresponding category
B	Structural heart disease present, but without signs or symptoms of HF (i.e., LVH, low EF, valvular disease, previous MI)	I	No limitations of physical activity. Ordinary physical activity does not cause symptoms of HF (i.e., fatigue, palpitations, dyspnea).

Clinical Diagnosis of HF

C	Structural heart disease with prior or current symptoms of HF (i.e., patients with known structural heart disease, SOB and fatigue, reduced exercise tolerance)	I	No limitations of physical activity. Ordinary physical activity does not cause symptoms of HF (i.e., fatigue, palpitations, dyspnea).
		II	Slight limitation of physical activity. Comfortable at rest, but ordinary physical activity results in symptoms of HF.
		III	Marked limitation of physical activity. Comfortable at rest but minimal exertion (bathing, dressing) causes symptoms of HF
D	Advanced structural heart disease with symptoms of HF at rest despite maximal medical therapy (Refractory HF requiring specialized interventions)	IV	Unable to carry on any physical activity without symptoms of HF, or symptoms of HF at rest.

Non-Pharmacologic Therapy
Patients with heart failure should be instructed to:

- Monitor and document body weight daily. This should be done preferably in the morning before eating and after voiding.

- Notify their provider if heart failure symptoms worsen or when weight increases. For example, sudden increases, such as 3 or more pounds in one day or 5 or more pounds in 1 week.

- Sodium restriction is reasonable for patients with symptomatic heart failure – less than 1,500 mg/d appears to be appropriate for most patients with HF.

- Consider daily multivitamin due to dietary restrictions and diuretic therapy.

- Fluid restriction (1.5-2 L/d) is reasonable in stage D, especially in patients with hyponatremia, to reduce congestive symptoms.

- Stop smoking. Limit alcohol intake. Avoid illicit drug use.

- Obtain pneumococcal polysaccharide and annual influenza vaccination; may consider Tdap and zoster (60 years and older); other vaccines may be required in younger patients.

- Consider weight reduction to BMI < 30. Weight reduction is important to reduce workload on the failing heart.

- Exercise 30 minutes/day, 3-5 days a week as tolerated. Patients with greater limitations in exercise tolerance should seek professional assistance (e.g., cardiac rehab program).

OTC and Alternative Medications

- Omega-3 polyunsaturated fatty acid (PUFA) supplementation is reasonable to use as adjunctive therapy in patients with NYHA class II-IV symptoms to reduce mortality and cardiovascular hospitalizations.

- Avoid using products containing ephedra (ma huang) or ephedrine.

- Avoid NSAIDS, including COX-2 inhibitors, due to the risk of renal insufficiency and fluid retention.

- Hawthorn and coenzyme Q10 may improve heart failure symptoms based on small studies. Patients should consult with their provider before beginning these alternative medications.

PHARMACOTHERAPY
The cornerstones of heart failure therapy are diuretics to control fluid volume, angiotensin antagonists [Angiotensin Converting Enzyme (ACE) inhibitors or Angiotensin Receptor Blockers (ARBs)] and beta-blockers to delay or halt the progression of cardiac dysfunction and improve survival. These medications should be utilized in everyone with heart failure who does not have a contraindication or intolerance to their use. ACE inhibitors are considered first line therapy over ARBs, however, ARBs are equivalent in terms of clinical benefit.

As the syndrome progresses, additional therapies may provide added symptomatic (digoxin) and/or survival advantages [aldosterone receptor antagonists (ARAs) and combination of hydralazine and an oral nitrate].

Diuretics

Loop diuretics are the most common diuretics used to manage the fluid volume status of heart failure patients. Loop diuretics block sodium and chloride reabsorption in the thick ascending limb of the loop of Henle, interfering with the chloride-binding co-transport system, thus causing increased excretion of water, sodium, chloride, magnesium, and calcium. They are used to reduce congestive symptoms (reduction in preload) and restore euvolemia (or "dry" weight). Diuretics have not been shown to alter the survival of heart failure patients, so the lowest effective dose should be used. Care must be taken not to over-diurese patients which can result in symptomatic hypotension or worsening renal function. Some heart failure patients may not respond adequately to escalating doses of loop diuretics, in which case they may be combined with thiazide-type diuretics such as metolazone.

DRUG	DOSING	SAFETY/SIDE EFFECTS/MONITORING

Loops

DRUG	DOSING	SAFETY/SIDE EFFECTS/MONITORING
Furosemide *(Lasix)* Most patients take divided doses: take 2nd dose early in the afternoon	Oral: 20-80 mg daily or divided, can go higher with all loops Oral loop dose equivalency = 40 mg	**BLACK BOX WARNING** Can lead to profound diuresis resulting in fluid and electrolyte depletion **CONTRAINDICATIONS** Anuria **WARNINGS** Sulfa allergy (not likely to cross-react – please see cautionary statement in Drug Allergy chapter) – this warning does not apply to ethacrynic acid
Bumetanide	Oral: 0.5-2 mg daily or divided Oral loop dose equivalency = 1 mg	**SIDE EFFECTS** Hypokalemia, orthostatic hypotension, ↓ Na+, ↓ Mg²⁺, ↓ Cl⁻, ↓ Ca²⁺ (different than thiazides which ↑ Ca²⁺), metabolic alkalosis, hyperuricemia (↑ UA), hyperglycemia (↑ BG), ↑ TGs, ↑ total
Torsemide *(Demadex)*	Oral: 10-20 mg daily Oral loop dose equivalency = 20 mg	cholesterol, photosensitivity, ototoxicity (more with ethacrynic acid) including hearing loss, tinnitus and vertigo **MONITORING** Renal function (SCr, BUN), fluid status (in's and out's, weight), BP, electrolytes, hearing with high doses or rapid IV administration
Ethacrynic Acid *(Edecrin)*	Oral: 50-200 mg daily or divided Oral loop dose equivalency = 50 mg	**NOTES** IV formulations of furosemide and bumetanide are light-sensitive (in amber bottles), all available in IV and PO formulations. Furosemide IV:PO ratio is 1:2 (furosemide 20 mg IV = furosemide 40 mg PO). Store at room temp (refrigeration causes precipitation – warming may dissolve crystals). IV:PO ratio for torsemide and bumetanide is 1:1

Loop Diuretic Drug Interactions

- Can acutely lower blood pressure. Always carefully monitor BP when adding-on therapy.

- Loop diuretics can increase the ototoxic potential of other ototoxic drugs, such as aminoglycosides and vancomycin, especially in the presence of impaired renal function. This combination should be avoided if alternative treatments are available.

- Diuretics may ↓ lithium's renal clearance and ↑ risk of lithium toxicity.

- Do not use NSAIDs in patients with HF. NSAIDs can cause sodium and water retention and reduce the effect of the loop diuretics.

- The combination of a loop and a thiazide-type diuretic may increase diuretic response, however, electrolyte abnormalities are also more common and serum chemistries must be monitored closely.

ACE Inhibitors and Angiotensin Receptor Blockers

ACE inhibitors block the conversion of angiotensin I to angiotensin II by inhibiting the angiotensin converting enzyme. ACE inhibitors also prevent the degradation of bradykinin, which is thought to contribute to the vasodilatory effect. ARBs block the angiotensin II receptor, AT_1, which is responsible for the vasoconstrictive, aldosterone stimulating, and remodeling effects of angiotensin II. Overall, these agents decrease renin-angiotensin-aldosterone system (RAAS) activation, specifically reducing the effects of angiotensin II and aldosterone. This results in a decrease in preload and afterload. In addition, these agents reduce pathologic cardiac remodeling, improve left ventricular function, and reduce morbidity and mortality. The clinical benefits appear to be a drug class effect. The use of an ACE inhibitor (or ARB if intolerant to ACE inhibitors) is indicated for all heart failure patients regardless of symptoms (NYHA FC I-IV). Other important points include:

- The target doses for these agents are the doses used in clinical trials demonstrating their benefit or the maximum tolerated dose for a given patient. Titrate the drug to target doses, if possible. Titrate dose to reduce symptoms, not BP.

- The combination of ACE inhibitor and ARB has been shown to reduce hospitalizations for heart failure, however, it is not used frequently as it is more common to combine one of these agents with a aldosterone receptor antagonist (e.g., spironolactone). Triple combination of ACE inhibitor/ARB/aldosterone receptor antagonist is not recommended due to elevated risk of hyperkalemia and increased incidence of renal insufficiency.

- There is an increased incidence of angioedema in black patients. Angioedema is more likely with ACE inhibitors than ARBs, but if a person had angioedema with either class of agents (or aliskiren), these agents should not be used since angioedema can be fatal. Counsel to report any swelling of lips, mouth, tongue, face or neck immediately.

- Patients on these medicines should be careful using salt substitutes (which contain KCl rather than NaCl) or potassium supplements.

DRUG	DOSING	SAFETY/SIDE EFFECTS/MONITORING

ACE Inhibitors – only those mentioned in the guidelines (See complete list in Hypertension chapter)

DRUG	DOSING	SAFETY/SIDE EFFECTS/MONITORING
Captopril *(Capoten)*	6.25-50 mg TID Target dose: 50 mg TID Take 1 hour before meals	**BLACK BOX WARNING** Can cause injury and death to developing fetus; discontinue as soon as pregnancy is detected
Enalapril *(Vasotec)*	5-40 mg/d Target dose: 10 mg BID	**CONTRAINDICATIONS** Angioedema; Do not use in bilateral renal artery stenosis; renal function will worsen. Cannot use concurrently with aliskiren in patients with diabetes.
Fosinopril	10-80 mg/d Target dose: 80 mg daily	**WARNINGS** Concomitant use of an ARB or aliskiren is associated with increased risks of hypotension, hyperkalemia and renal dysfunction. Concomitant use with aliskiren should be avoided in patients with GFR < 60 mL/minute.
Lisinopril *(Prinivil, Zestril)*	5-40 mg/d Target dose: 20 mg daily	
Quinapril *(Accupril)*	20-80 mg/d Target dose: 80 mg daily	**SIDE EFFECTS** Cough, hyperkalemia, angioedema (if occurs, drug is CI), hypotension, dizziness and acute renal insufficiency. Captopril has more SEs (taste perversion, rash).
Ramipril *(Altace)*	2.5-20 mg/d Target dose: 10 mg daily	**MONITORING** BP, K⁺, renal function; signs and symptoms of HF
Trandolapril *(Mavik)*	2-8 mg/d Target dose: 4 mg daily	**NOTES** Pregnancy Category D

Angiotensin Receptor Blockers (ARBs) – only those mentioned in the guidelines (See complete list in Hypertension chapter)

DRUG	DOSING	SAFETY/SIDE EFFECTS/MONITORING
Candesartan *(Atacand)*	8-32 mg/d Target dose: 32 mg daily	**BLACK BOX WARNING** Can cause injury and death to developing fetus; discontinue as soon as pregnancy is detected **CONTRAINDICATIONS** Angioedema; Do not use in bilateral renal artery stenosis; renal function will worsen. Cannot use concurrently with aliskiren in patients with diabetes.
Losartan *(Cozaar)* – benefit in clinical trials but no FDA indication	25-100 mg/d Target dose: 50-150 mg daily	**WARNINGS** Concomitant use of an ACE inhibitor or aliskiren is associated with increased risks of hypotension, hyperkalemia and renal dysfunction. Concomitant use with aliskiren should be avoided in patients with GFR < 60 mL/minute. **SIDE EFFECTS** Hyperkalemia, angioedema (if occurs, drug is CI), hypotension, dizziness and acute renal insufficiency
Valsartan *(Diovan)*	80-320 mg/d Target dose: 160 mg BID	(Note: side effects same as for ACE inhibitors except lack of cough) **MONITORING** BP, K⁺, renal function; signs and symptoms of HF **NOTES** Pregnancy Category D

ACE Inhibitor/ARB Drug Interactions

- All RAAS inhibitors ↑ the risk of hyperkalemia (most significant side effect). Monitor K^+ and renal function frequently.

- Dual inhibition of the renin-angiotensin system with ACE inhibitors and ARBs leads to increased risks of renal impairment, hypotension, and hyperkalemia; avoid.

- The triple combination of ACE inhibitor, ARB, and aldosterone receptor antagonist is not recommended due to high risk of hyperkalemia and increased incidence of renal insufficiency.

- ACE inhibitors or ARBs should not be used in combination with the renin inhibitor, aliskiren, in patients with diabetes.

- All RAAS inhibitors can have additive antihypertensive effects – monitor BP.

- RAAS inhibitors may ↓ lithium's renal clearance and ↑ risk of lithium toxicity.

Beta-Blockers

Beta-adrenergic receptor antagonists, or simply beta-blockers, antagonize the effects of catecholamines (especially norepinephrine) at the $beta_1$ and $beta_2$-adrenergic receptors. Beta-blockers reduce vasoconstriction, and although intrinsically negative inotropes, these agents improve ventricular systolic function when used chronically. Overall, these agents reduce morbidity and mortality in heart failure. A beta-blocker is recommended for all heart failure patients, especially those in functional class II-IV. Unlike ACE inhibitors (or ARBs), the clinical benefits of beta-blockers are not considered a class effect. Only carvedilol, metoprolol succinate extended-release and bisoprolol are recommended in the guidelines. The target doses for these agents are the doses used in clinical trials demonstrating their benefit or the maximum tolerated dose for a given patient. Beta-blockers with intrinsic sympathomimetic activity (ISA) should be avoided.

DRUG	DOSING	SAFETY/SIDE EFFECTS/MONITORING

Beta-blockers – only those mentioned in the guidelines (See complete list in Hypertension chapter)

Bisoprolol *(Zebeta)* – benefit in clinical trials but no FDA indication	Start 1.25-2.5 mg/d Target dose: 10 mg daily	**BLACK BOX WARNING** Beta-blockers should not be withdrawn abruptly (particularly in patients with CAD), gradually taper over 1-2 weeks to avoid acute tachycardia, HTN, and/or ischemia.
Metoprolol succinate extended-release *(Toprol XL)*	Start 12.5-25 mg/d [Metoprolol tartrate *(Lopressor)]* is not recommended by guidelines) Target dose: 200 mg daily	**CONTRAINDICATIONS** Sinus bradycardia, 2nd or 3rd degree heart block, sick sinus syndrome (unless patient has a functioning artificial pacemaker) or cardiogenic shock; do not initiate in patients with active asthma exacerbation. **SIDE EFFECTS** ↓ HR, hypotension, fatigue, dizziness, depression, ↓ libido, impotence, hyperglycemia (non-selective agents can decrease insulin secretion in type 2 diabetes), hypertriglyceridemia, ↓ HDL; weight gain and edema with carvedilol **MONITORING** HR, BP, titrate every 2 weeks (as tolerated); ↓ dose if HR < 55 BPM; signs and symptoms of HF **NOTES** Avoid abrupt discontinuation – must taper Caution in diabetes with recurrent hypoglycemia, asthma, severe COPD or resting limb ischemia Caution: IV doses are not equivalent to oral doses (usually IV is much lower)

Non-selective Alpha- and Beta-Blocker

Carvedilol *(Coreg, Coreg CR)*	Start IR 3.125 mg BID or CR 10 mg/d Target dose IR: 25 mg BID or 50 mg BID if patient > 85 kg Target dose CR: 80 mg daily	**NOTES** Same as above Take carvedilol – all forms – with food Dosing conversion from *Coreg* to *Coreg CR:* *Coreg* 3.125 mg BID = *Coreg CR* 10 mg daily *Coreg* 6.25 mg BID = *Coreg CR* 20 mg daily *Coreg* 12.5 mg BID = *Coreg CR* 40 mg daily *Coreg* 25 mg BID = *Coreg CR* 80 mg daily

Beta-Blocker Drug-Drug and Drug-Disease Interactions

- Caution in patients with diabetes: beta-blockers can mask the symptoms of shakiness, palpitations and anxiety with hypoglycemia – this occurs mostly with the non-selective agents. However, sweating (diaphoresis) and hunger are not masked.

- Beta-blockers can enhance the effects of insulin and oral hypoglycemic agents (sulfonyl-ureas, etc) – monitor BG carefully.

- Use caution when administering other drugs that slow HR; see Drug Interactions chapter.

- Carvedilol is a substrate of CYP450 2D6; 2D6 inhibitors may increase carvedilol levels and rifampin may decrease carvedilol levels.

- Carvedilol can ↑ digoxin and cyclosporine levels; may require dose adjustments.

Aldosterone Receptor Antagonists (ARAs)

Spironolactone is a non-selective aldosterone receptor blocker (also blocks androgen and progesterone receptors). Eplerenone is a selective aldosterone blocker and does not exhibit the endocrine side effects. These agents compete with aldosterone at the receptor sites in the distal convoluted tubule and collecting ducts, increasing Na$^+$ and H$_2$O excretion while conserving K$^+$ and H$^+$ ions. Clinically, these effects lead to a reduction in sodium and water retention, cardiac remodeling (especially myocardial fibrosis), and risk of sudden cardiac death. Overall, ARAs reduce morbidity and mortality. An ARA should be added to standard therapy in patients who have progressed to functional class III or IV. Some emerging data suggest that they may have some benefit if initiated early (functional class II) as well, although this is currently not recommended in all heart failure guidelines.

DRUG	DOSING	SAFETY/SIDE EFFECTS/MONITORING

Aldosterone Receptor Antagonists – only those mentioned in the guidelines (See complete list in Hypertension chapter)

DRUG	DOSING	SAFETY/SIDE EFFECTS/MONITORING
Spironolactone (*Aldactone*)	12.5-25 mg daily Target dose: 25 mg daily	**BLACK BOX WARNING** Tumor risk with spironolactone; tumorigenic in chronic rat toxicity studies. Avoid unnecessary use. **CONTRAINDICATIONS** Renal impairment (CrCl < 30 mL/min), hyperkalemia; concomitant use of strong 3A4 inhibitors (eplerenone) **WARNINGS** Do not initiate therapy in patients with K$^+$ > 5.0 mEq/L; SCr > 2.0 mg/dL (females) or SCr > 2.5 mg/dL (males) (HF warning only) **SIDE EFFECTS** Hyperkalemia, ↑ SCr. For spironolactone, gynecomastia, breast tenderness, impotence. Rare: hyperchloremic metabolic acidosis **MONITORING** Check K$^+$ before starting and frequently thereafter. BP, SCr/BUN; signs and symptoms of HF
Eplerenone (*Inspra*)	25-50 mg daily Target dose: 50 mg daily	**NOTES** To minimize risk of hyperkalemia in patients treated with aldosterone blockers: Higher risk if ↓ renal function (CI if CrCl < 30mL/min) Do not start if K$^+$ > 5 mEq/L Use low doses – and must start low. Higher risk when concurrent ACE inhibitors or ARBs used at higher doses. Do not use NSAIDs concurrently (which should be avoided in HF anyway). Monitor frequently Counsel patient about ↑ risk if dehydration occurs (due to vomiting, diarrhea or ↓ fluid intake)

ARA Drug Interactions

- Eplerenone is a CYP3A4 substrate; use with strong 3A4 inhibitors is contraindicated.

- All RAAS inhibitors ↑ the risk of hyperkalemia (most significant side effect). Monitor K⁺ and renal function frequently.

- The triple combination of ACE inhibitor, ARB, and ARA is not recommended due to high risk of hyperkalemia and renal insufficiency.

- All RAAS inhibitors can have additive antihypertensive effects – monitor BP.

- RAAS inhibitors may ↓ lithium's renal clearance and ↑ risk of lithium toxicity.

Hydralazine/Nitrate

Hydralazine is a direct arterial vasodilator which reduces afterload. Nitrates are venous vasodilators and reduce preload. The combination of hydralazine and an oral nitrate also acts by increasing the availability of nitric oxide which provides vasodilatory effects. Hydralazine may also attenuate the development of nitrate tolerance. The combination of hydralazine and isosorbide dinitrate has been shown to improve the survival of heart failure patients, although not as much as ACE inhibitors. Therefore, this combination is used as alternative therapy for patients who cannot tolerate ACE inhibitors or ARBs due to poor renal function, angioedema, or hyperkalemia. The combination may also be added to standard therapy in black patients based on a study demonstrating improved survival. The combination product, *BiDil*, is indicated in self-identified black patients with functional class III or IV heart failure who are symptomatic despite optimal therapy with ACE inhibitors and beta-blockers. Hydralazine or oral nitrates may be used as monotherapy in heart failure patients for other indications, however, they have not individually been shown to affect heart failure outcomes. Isosorbide dinitrate was the oral nitrate used in clinical trials – there are no data with isosorbide mononitrate although it is used in practice. As with ACE inhibitors or ARBs, the target doses are those shown to be beneficial in clinical trials.

DRUG	DOSING	SAFETY/SIDE EFFECTS/MONITORING
Isosorbide dinitrate/hydrALAZINE (*BiDil*)	20/37.5 mg tablets Start 1 tablet TID, to 2 tablets TID (target dose), as tolerated. No nitrate tolerance Target dose: 40 mg ISDN/75 mg hydralazine TID	**CONTRAINDICATIONS** CI with PDE-5 Inhibitors **SIDE EFFECTS** Headache, dizziness, hypotension; rare: lupus-like syndrome (dose and duration related – report fever, joint/ muscle aches, fatigue) **MONITORING** HR, BP; signs and symptoms of HF
HydrALAZINE	37.5 mg QID Target dose: 75 mg QID	**SIDE EFFECTS** Headache, reflex tachycardia, palpitations, anorexia; rare: lupus-like syndrome (dose and duration related – report fever, joint/muscle aches, fatigue) **MONITORING** HR, BP; signs and symptoms of HF

Hydralazine/Nitrate Continued

DRUG	DOSING	SAFETY/SIDE EFFECTS/MONITORING
Isosorbide mononitrate *(Monoket)* Isosorbide dinitrate *(Isordil, Dilatrate SR)*	Given daily or BID (mononitrate) or TID-QID (dinitrate) Target dose: 40 mg TID-QID (dinitrate)	**CONTRAINDICATIONS** CI with PDE-5 Inhibitors **SIDE EFFECTS** Headache, dizziness, lightheadedness, flushing, hypotension, tachyphylaxis (need 10-12 hour nitrate free interval), syncope **MONITORING** HR, BP; signs and symptoms of HF

Hydralazine/Nitrate Drug Interactions

- Must avoid administration within 12 hours of avanafil, within 24 hours of sildenafil or vardenafil and within 48 hours of tadalafil.

Digoxin

Digoxin inhibits the Na^+/K^+ ATPase pump which results in a positive inotropic effect ($\uparrow$ in CO). It also exerts a parasympathetic effect which provides a negative chronotropic effect ($\downarrow$ HR). Digoxin is added in patients who remain symptomatic despite receiving standard therapy, including ACE inhibitors and beta-blockers. Digoxin has been shown to improve symptoms, exercise tolerance, and QOL. Overall, digoxin does not improve survival of heart failure patients, but it does appear to reduce hospitalizations for heart failure. Dosing should take into account the patient's renal function, body size, age and gender (lower dose for renal insufficiency, smaller, older, female), with the majority of patients being on no more than 0.125 mg daily. Serum digoxin concentrations should be maintained < 1.0 ng/mL (range 0.5-0.9 ng/mL) for heart failure patients.

DRUG	DOSING	SAFETY/SIDE EFFECTS/MONITORING
Digoxin *(Lanoxin)* Tablet, solution, injection	0.125-0.25 mg daily Loading doses not used in HF $\downarrow$ dose when CrCl < 50 mL/min; can be given 0.125 mg every other day, or even less frequently Therapeutic range for HF = 0.5-0.9 ng/mL (higher range for A. Fib) Watch for renal impairment $\downarrow$ dose when CrCl < 50 mL/min; can be given 0.125 mg every other day or less frequently $\downarrow$ 20-25% when going from oral tabs to IV Antidote: *DigiFab*	**CONTRAINDICATIONS** 2nd or 3rd degree heart block without a functional pacemaker, Wolff-Parkinson-White syndrome (WPW) with A. Fib. **SIDE EFFECTS** Dizziness, headache, diarrhea, nausea, vomiting, anorexia, mental disturbances **MONITORING** HR, BP, electrolytes (K^+, Ca^{2+}, Mg^{2+}), renal function; ECG and drug level (if suspected toxicity) **TOXICITY** First signs of toxicity are nausea/vomiting, loss of appetite and bradycardia. Other signs of toxicity include blurred/double vision, altered color perception, greenish-yellow halos around lights or objects, abdominal pain, confusion, delirium, arrhythmia (prolonged PR interval, accelerated junctional rhythm, bidirectional ventricular tachycardia).

Digoxin Drug-Drug and Drug-Disease Interactions

- Use caution when administering other drugs that slow HR (such as beta-blockers); see common side effects/adverse drug reactions chart.

- Digoxin is mostly renally cleared and partially cleared hepatically. Decreased renal function requires a ↓ digoxin dose. In acute renal failure, digoxin is held.

- Digoxin is a P-glycoprotein and 3A4 substrate. Digoxin levels ↑ with amiodarone, dronedarone, quinidine, verapamil, erythromycin, clarithromycin, itraconazole, cyclosporine, propafenone, and many other drugs. Reduce digoxin dose by 50% if patient is on amiodarone.

- Digoxin levels may ↓ with bile acid resins (check separation times), St. John's wort and others.

- Hypokalemia (K^+ < 3.5 mEq/L), hypomagnesemia, and hypercalcemia ↑ risk of digoxin toxicity.

- Hypothyroidism can ↑ digoxin levels.

Potassium Oral Supplementation

Potassium supplementation is an important aspect of managing heart failure as many of the heart failure drugs affect potassium levels. Most heart failure patients require loop diuretics which waste K^+. Maintenance of serum and body potassium levels is essential to reduce the proarrhythmic risk of digoxin, especially as heart failure increases arrhythmia risk. There are different formulations (tablets, capsules and liquids) and they vary by salt form (K^+ acetate, K^+ bicarbonate, K^+ citrate, K^+ chloride, K^+ gluconate and K^+ phosphate). The salt used depends on patient factors such as acid-base status and deficiency of other electrolytes such as phosphate. Potassium chloride is used most commonly.

Potassium levels should be monitored with the frequency dependent on the stability of the renal function, medication regimen, and the clinical status. Check levels after any change in diuretic, ACE inhibitor, ARB or ARA dose. It should also be checked if a patient's renal function changes. Magnesium deficiency aggravates hypokalemia. The magnesium level may need to be checked and should be corrected prior to correcting the potassium level.

Supplementation may not be needed in patients who are able to supplement their intake of potassium through dietary sources (e.g., bananas, potatoes, orange juice, beans, dark leafy greens, apricots, peaches, avocados, white mushrooms and some varieties of fish). Some cases, particularly those with mild heart failure (Class I and II), may be able to maintain K^+ through dietary sources. The usual range of K^+ is 3.5-5 mEq/L. Patients on digoxin should keep a potassium level of 4-5 mEq/L (depending on the normal range of the laboratory).

DRUG	DOSING	SAFETY/SIDE EFFECTS/MONITORING
Potassium chloride (K-Tab, Klor-Con, Klor-Con M10, Klor-Con M15, Klor-Con M20, Micro-K, Micro-K 10, others)	Prevention of hypokalemia: 20-40 mEq/day in 1-2 divided doses Treatment of mild hypokalemia: Generally 40-100 mEq/day in 2-4 divided doses; additional amounts as needed based on laboratory values No more than 20-25 mEq should be given as a single dose to avoid GI discomfort	**CONTRAINDICATIONS (3)** Severe renal impairment, hyperkalemia Oral solid dosage forms are contraindicated in patients with delayed or obstructed passage through the GI tract. **WARNINGS** Caution in patients with mild-moderate renal impairment; patients with disorders that alter K+ (untreated Addison's disease, heat cramps, severe tissue trauma/burns), and in patients taking other medications that $\uparrow$ K+ **SIDE EFFECTS** Diarrhea, nausea, vomiting, abdominal pain, flatulence, hyperkalemia **MONITORING** Serum potassium, glucose, chloride (chloride salts), pH, urine output **NOTES** Take with meals and a full glass of water or other liquid to minimize the risk of GI irritation. Caution when used in patients on ACE inhibitors, ARBs, ARAs or other medications that $\uparrow$ K+. Caution if using potassium supplement and salt substitutes, as many salt substitutes contain potassium. *Micro-K:* capsules may be opened and contents sprinkled on a spoonful of applesauce or pudding and immediately swallowed without chewing. *Klor-Con, K-Tab:* Swallow whole, do not crush, cut, chew, or suck on tablet. *Kor-Con M:* Swallow whole, do not crush, chew, or suck on tablet. Tablet may be cut in half and swallowed separately, or can dissolve the whole tablet in 4 oz. of water – drink immediately.

Acute Decompensated Heart Failure (ADHF)

Heart failure patients may experience episodes of worsening symptoms such as sudden weight gain, inability to lie flat without becoming short of breath, decreasing functionality (e.g., unable to perform their daily routine), increasing shortness of breath and fatigue. Patients in ADHF are generally hospitalized.

Clinical Presentation and Assessment

ADHF is often a result of disease progression. However, in many instances a precipitating cause can be identified, such as myocardial infarction, arrhythmias, valvular disease, uncontrolled hypertension and myocarditis. Non-cardiac causes include non-adherence with medications or dietary restrictions, worsening renal function, thyroid disease, infection, alcohol binging, illicit drug use and certain medications (e.g., initiation of negative inotropic drugs, sudden use of NSAIDs/COX-2 inhibitors, drugs which promote fluid retention, and direct cardiotoxic drugs). Identification and treatment of reversible causes remains an important aspect of returning heart failure patients to a compensated state.

Patients in ADHF should have their hemodynamic profile assessed to determine whether they are presenting with congestion and/or hypoperfusion. This is done primarily through assessment of clinical symptomology and diagnostic tests. Evidence of congestion includes elevated jugular venous pulsation, lower extremity or pulmonary edema, rales, and ascites. Evidence of hypoperfusion include cool extremities, hypotension, decreased renal function, and impaired mental function. The majority of ADHF patients present primarily with worsening congestion.

In all ADHF cases, reinforcement of medication adherence is addressed and drug doses are optimized, if possible. Beta-blockers should only be stopped if hypotension or hypoperfusion is present.

Treating Congestion

Congestion is treated with diuretics and possibly IV vasodilators. Loop diuretics are initially given IV since congestion may affect absorption. If diuretic resistance develops, the dose can be increased or a thiazide-type diuretic (e.g., metolazone, chlorothiazide) may be added in combination with the loop diuretic. Intravenous vasodilators include nitroglycerin, nitroprusside, and nesiritide. Frequent blood pressure monitoring is required ($\downarrow$ dose if hypotensive or worsening renal function).

Treating Hypoperfusion

In hypoperfusion or cardiogenic shock, intravenous vasodilators are contraindicated. In these patients, it may become necessary to initiate therapy with an IV inotropic drug such as dobutamine, dopamine or milrinone. Dobutamine is a beta$_1$ and beta$_2$-adrenergic agonist which $\uparrow$ cardiac output in a dose-dependent manner. Dobutamine has some vasodilatory effect (beta$_2$) and is used if SBP > 90 mmHg. Milrinone is a phosphodiesterase-3 inhibitor that $\uparrow$ CO in a dose-dependent manner. Milrinone also has profound vasodilatory effects and can only be used if blood pressure is adequate. Milrinone requires dose adjustment in renal insufficiency. Dopamine has dose-dependent effects (dopaminergic receptor agonist at low doses, beta$_1$ at moderate doses, alpha$_1$ at higher doses) and is used as an inotrope and vasopressor. Dopamine is the inotrope of choice in heart failure patients with SBP < 90 mmHg. Inotropes are associated with worse outcomes and should be discontinued once the patient is stabilized. See Intravenous Drugs, Fluids, and Antidotes chapter for more information on dobutamine, dopamine, and milrinone.

VASODILATORS

Vasodilators used in ADHF are nitroglycerin, nitroprusside, and nesiritide. With all three, blood pressure must be monitored closely.

Nitroglycerin is more of a venous vasodilator, particularly at low doses, but is an effective arterial vasodilator at higher doses. To achieve a desirable effect, the dose should be titrated up. Nitroglycerin may be preferred in ADHF with active myocardial ischemia or uncontrolled hypertension, but its effectiveness may be limited after 2-3 days.

Nitroprusside is an equal arterial and venous vasodilator at all doses. Nitroprusside has a greater effect on blood pressure than nitroglycerin, and unlike nitroglycerin, its use is discouraged in the setting of active myocardial ischemia as it may cause a phenomenon of "coronary steal" or shunting of blood away from areas with diseased coronary arteries. Nitroprusside metabolism results in the formation of thiocyanate and cyanide, both of which can cause toxicity (especially in the setting of renal and hepatic insufficiency, respectively). Therefore, nitroprusside may be a desirable choice in patients with uncontrolled hypertension, but renal and hepatic function must be monitored closely. Although tachyphylaxis does not occur with nitroprusside, prolonged administration is discouraged due to increased risk of toxicity. Hydroxycobalamin can be administered to reduce the risk of thiocyanate toxicity, whereas, sodium thiosulfate may be used treat cyanide toxicity.

Nesiritide (Natrecor) is a recombinant B-type natriuretic peptide that binds to vascular smooth muscle, increasing cGMP resulting in smooth muscle cell relaxation, and hence vasodilation. Nesiritide provides both arterial and venous vasodilation, and has been shown to indirectly ↑ CO. Nesiritide has a longer half-life than nitroglycerin or nitroprusside. Nesiritide is also the only intravenous vasodilator that has been evaluated in prospective acute heart failure studies, which demonstrated neither an increase nor decrease in mortality and rehospitalization, and has no discernable effect on risk of worsening renal function compared to standard therapy with diuretics with or without another intravenous vasodilator.

DRUG	DOSING	SAFETY/SIDE EFFECTS/MONITORING
Nesiritide *(Natrecor)*	Draw bolus only from prepared (reconstituted) infusion bag: give 2 mcg/kg IV bolus followed by a continuous infusion at 0.01 mcg/kg/min; max 0.03 mcg/kg/min. Limited experience with infusion lasting longer than 96 hours.	**CONTRAINDICATIONS** Persistent SBP < 100 mmHg prior to therapy **SIDE EFFECTS** Hypotension, SCr **MONITORING** BP, SCr, BUN, urine output
Nitroglycerin	Continuous IV infusion due to short t ½. Prepare in glass bottles, PAB™, EXCEL™ (polyolefin) containers. Soft plastic-like PVC can cause adsorption of drug. Use administration sets intended for NTG.	**CONTRAINDICATIONS** SBP < 90 mmHg, CI with PDE-5 Inhibitors, ↑ intracranial pressure **SIDE EFFECTS** Hypotension, headache, lightheadedness, tachycardia, tachyphylaxis **MONITORING** BP, HR, SCr, BUN, urine output

Vasodilators Continued

DRUG	DOSING	SAFETY/SIDE EFFECTS/MONITORING
Nitroprusside *(Nitropress)*	Need to protect infusion bag from light (cover with opaque material or aluminum foil). A blue-color solution indicates degradation to cyanide – do not use.	**BLACK BOX WARNINGS (3)** Keep infusion doses at < 2 mcg/kg/min (or < 400 mcg/min) due to ↑ cyanide toxicity risk Can cause excessive hypotension Do not give solution undiluted **CONTRAINDICATIONS** SBP < 90 mmHg, CI with PDE-5 Inhibitors, ↑ intracranial pressure **SIDE EFFECTS** Hypotension, headache, tachycardia, thiocyanate/cyanide toxicity (especially in renal and hepatic impairment) **MONITORING** BP, HR, SCr, BUN, urine output, thiocyanate/cyanide toxicity, acid-base status

Preventing Heart Failure Readmissions

Reducing readmissions is becoming a larger priority for healthcare professionals. As the United States transitions from a fee-for-service model to an accountable care organization (ACO) model, providers and healthcare systems will become increasingly responsible for the costs associated with treating their patients. Heart failure is one of the disease states that insurers are focusing on because it is a very high-cost condition. Medicare has already started penalizing hospitals for excessive readmissions due to heart failure exacerbations. This has led most organizations to devote additional resources to preventing readmissions... including pharmacists! If health-systems spend a little more up front to provide these preventative services and reduce readmissions (which are very expensive), they will improve the quality of care provided to patients with heart failure as well as save money. Below are some of the ways pharmacists (and other healthcare professionals) can help reduce readmissions in patients with heart failure.

- Use a transitional care nurse or pharmacist to help ensure a smooth transition between levels of care (e.g., inpatient to outpatient). This will include medication reconciliation.

- Educate patients about their disease. This should include identifying the signs/symptoms of worsening heart failure, recording daily weights, avoiding foods that may worsen their condition and the importance of medication adherence.

- Schedule regular medication management appointments with patients to offer counseling and answer medication-related questions the patients may have.

- Ensure the appropriate, evidence-based medications are prescribed (ACE inhibitors/ARBs, beta-blockers, spironolactone, loop diuretics, etc).

- Ensure dose of each agent is titrated to target dosing for heart failure (e.g., lisinopril 20 mg daily).

- Attempt to reduce or eliminate medications that can worsen heart failure (e.g., NSAIDs, TZDs, diltiazem, verapamil).

Patient Counseling

All Heart Failure Patients

- Monitor body weight daily, preferably in the morning before eating and after using the restroom. Weight should be documented.

- Patients should have instructions on what to do if HF symptoms worsen and what to do when body weight increases.

- Follow a sodium restricted diet. Foods high in sodium include:

  - prepared sauces and condiments (such as soy sauce, BBQ sauce, Worcestershire sauce or salsa)

  - canned vegetables and soups

  - frozen dinners

  - deli meats (sandwich meats, bacon, ham, hot dogs, sausage or salami)

  - salty foods (pickles, olives, cheese, nuts, chips or crackers).

- Patients are encouraged to take nutrition classes and learn to read nutrition labels. Patients should choose "no sodium added" or "low sodium" options. Healthy ways of cooking include broiling, baking, poaching, and steaming without added salt.

- Avoid cigarette smoking, alcohol, and illicit drug use.

- Do not use NSAIDs or COX-2 inhibitors (or negative inotropic drugs such as verapamil, diltiazem, etc.) unless you check with your doctor first. Also, do not use nutritional supplements for HF without discussion of safety with your health-care provider.

- Stay compliant with all medications – discuss with the pharmacist if cost-barriers exist. Remind patients that non-compliance to medications and food restrictions often lead to worsening of HF and possible hospitalizations. Patients may need extra support during celebrations and holiday seasons.

Beta-Blockers in HF

- Do not stop taking the medication unless your doctor tells you to do so.

- If you miss a dose, take your dose as soon as you remember, unless it is time to take your next dose. Do not double the dose.

- This medication can cause you to feel dizzy, tired, or faint. Do not drive a car, use machinery, or do anything that requires you to be alert until you adjust to the medication and the symptoms subside.

- This medication may make you feel more tired and dizzy at first. These effects will go away in a few days. However, call your doctor if the symptoms feel severe, or you have weight gain or increased shortness of breath.

- This medication can cover up some of the signs and symptoms of low blood sugar (hypoglycemia); make sure to test your blood sugar often, and take a fast-acting sugar source if needed.

- This medication may cause worsening symptoms of peripheral vascular disease like pain, numbness and cold legs/feet.

- Medications used to treat severe allergic reactions may not work as well while taking this medication.

Toprol XL

- If your doctor has instructed you to cut the *Toprol XL* or its generic equivalent tablet in half, you must use a pill cutter and cut only at the score line. Otherwise, the medicine will enter your body too quickly. Swallow the ½ tablet whole. The tablets cannot be crushed or chewed.

Coreg CR

- Take with food, to help reduce dizziness by delaying absorption.

- Swallow *Coreg CR* capsules whole. Do not chew or crush the capsules. If you have trouble swallowing *Coreg CR* whole:

  - The capsule may be carefully opened and the beads sprinkled over a spoonful of applesauce which should be taken right away. The applesauce should not be warm. Do not use other foods…only applesauce.

Digoxin

- This medicine helps make the heart beat stronger and with a more regular rhythm. Keep taking as directed, even if you feel well.

- Do not stop taking this medicine without talking to your doctor. Stopping this medication suddenly may make your condition worse.

- Avoid becoming overheated or dehydrated as an overdose can more easily occur if you are dehydrated.

- Symptoms of overdose may include nausea, vomiting, diarrhea, loss of appetite, vision changes (such as blurred or yellow/green vision), uneven heartbeats, and feeling like you might pass out. If any of these occur, see a doctor right away.

- There are many medications that can interact with digoxin. Check with your physician or pharmacist before starting any new medicines, including over the counter, vitamin, and/ or herbal products.

- To be sure that this medication is not causing harmful effects, your blood may need to be tested on a regular basis. Your kidney function will also need to be monitored.

PRACTICE CASE

Janice is a 74 year old white female (60 kg) who presents to the hospital with acute decompensated heart failure. Per her husband's report, Janice had been doing well over the past few months with her heart failure regimen. Her symptoms started on Easter night after she ate ham, canned vegetables, and other dishes. She mentioned her weight was up about 7 pounds and she noticed being more short of breath, but thought these symptoms would go away on their own. She states her feet and legs are puffy by midday. She used to be able to walk many blocks without trouble, but now gets short of breath after only 1 block, but has no symptoms while resting.

CATEGORY	
PMH	HF (LVEF 35%)
	Hypertension
	Diabetes, Type 2 (controlled by diet)
	Depression
Vitals	BP:97/62 HR:104 RR:23 Temp:38.4°C
Test Results	

Item	Normal Range	Patient Value
Glucose	70-110 mg/dL	218
Na^+	135-145 mEq/L	134
K^+	3.5-5.0 mEq/L	4.7
Cl^-	96-106 mEq/L	104
HCO_3	22-28 mEq/L	23
BUN	10-24 mg/dL	45
Creatinine	0.6-1.2 mg/dL	1.8

Digoxin level: 1.8 ng/mL

ECG: sinus tachycardia

Medications prior to hospitalization	
	Lasix 40 mg PO daily
	Lisinopril 40 mg PO daily
	Digoxin 0.25 mg PO daily
	Toprol XL 100 mg PO daily
	Citalopram 20 mg PO daily

Questions

1. Which of the following correctly describes Janice's NYHA functional class at the time of hospital admission?

    a. FC 0
    b. FC I
    c. FC II
    d. FC III
    e. FC IV

2. Based on ACC/AHA heart failure staging, what is the correct classification for Janice's heart failure?

    a. Stage A
    b. Stage B
    c. Stage C
    d. Stage D
    e. Stage E

3. While in the hospital, Janice is started on furosemide IV to remove some fluid that has accumulated around her lungs. Choose the correct statement concerning Janice's furosemide therapy:

a. If Janice experiences ototoxicity, she should be switched to ethacrynic acid.

b. Furosemide is not effective as a diuretic if the creatinine clearance is < 30 mL/min.

c. The furosemide will increase her risk of hyperkalemia.

d. A and B only.

e. None of the above.

4. Janice is ready to be discharged home. She is restarted on all of her previous medications at the same doses before hospitalization. Which of the following counseling points are correct? (Select **ALL** that apply.)

a. If you lose your appetite, become nauseated, have mental disturbances, and/or lightheadedness, contact your doctor immediately – this may indicate that the digoxin level is too high.

b. Stop all use of potassium supplements while taking digoxin as potassium supplements will cause digoxin toxicity.

c. Digoxin therapy can cause you to be more symptomatic at first, but this will resolve within a week.

d. Digoxin therapy is best taken at night, after dinner.

e. Taking digoxin can improve your symptoms and increase your quality of life.

5. Which of the following medications should Janice generally avoid as they may worsen her heart failure? (Select **ALL** that apply.)

a. Celecoxib

b. Verapamil

c. Amiodarone

d. Pioglitazone

e. Naproxen

6. Janice has been home for 1 month and goes in for her first doctor's appointment since her hospitalization. She is taking all her medications which include lisinopril 40 mg daily, *Lasix* 40 mg daily and *Toprol XL* 100 mg daily. She is following a sodium restricted diet and monitoring her weight but she still gets fatigued quite easily. The doctor decides to increase her *Toprol XL* dose to 200 mg daily. Which of the following patient counseling points should be discussed with Janice regarding this change? (Select **ALL** that apply.)

a. The increase in medication may make you feel more tired and dizzy at first. These effects will likely improve in a few days – if they do not, contact the doctor.

b. This increase in medication can cause a loss of appetite, blurred vision, lightheadedness, and/or visual changes.

c. This medication may be cut in half (if directed to do so) with a pill cutter, but do not crush or chew the tablets.

d. This medication can be taken without regards to food.

e. The increase in medication will cause an increase in your heart rate. Call your doctor if you feel your heart racing.

Questions 7-10 do not pertain to the above case.

7. A 70 kg patient is beginning carvedilol therapy for heart failure. The starting dose is 3.125 mg BID. What should the target dose for carvedilol be in this patient?

a. 6.25 mg BID

b. 12.5 mg BID

c. 25 mg BID

d. 50 mg BID

e. 100 mg BID

8. A 75 year-old patient comes to the emergency department with acute decompensated heart failure. He presents with pulmonary congestion, altered mental status and poor urine output. His vital signs are BP 80/57, HR 112, RR 24 and oxygen saturation of 93%. He is started on bumetanide 1mg IV Q12 hours. Which of the following medications is most appropriate to initiate in this patient at this time?

    a. Dopamine

    b. Nitroprusside

    c. Metolazone

    d. Nitroglycerin

    e. Milrinone

9. What is the trade name for eplerenone?

    a. Invega

    b. Invanz

    c. Invirase

    d. Isuprel

    e. Inspra

10. The medical team will start a dobutamine drip on a 60 kg patient at 10 mcg/kg/min. The standard concentration of dobutamine in the pharmacy is a 250 mg/250 mL bag. Calculate how many hours the bag will last at the prescribed infusion rate.

    a. 3 hours

    b. 5 hours

    c. 7 hours

    d. 10 hours

    e. 15 hours

Answers

1-d, 2-c, 3-e, 4-a,e, 5-a,b,d,e, 6-a,c,d, 7-c, 8-a, 9-e, 10-c

ANTICOAGULATION

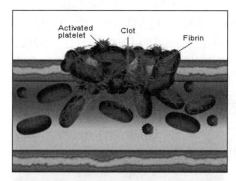

GUIDELINES

Executive Summary of Antithrombotic Therapy and Prevention of Thrombosis, 9th ed: American College of Chest Physicians Evidence-Based Clinical Practice Guidelines. CHEST 2012;141(2):7S-47S.

ISMP has many resources on safe use of anticoagulants available at www.ismp.org

BACKGROUND

Anticoagulants are used to prevent blood clots from forming and to keep existing clots from becoming larger or expanding. They do not break down existing clots (that is done by drugs such as tissue plasminogen activator, or tPA). Anticoagulant therapy must be intensively monitored as the risks of not using anticoagulants correctly can lead to patient harm. A deep vein thrombosis (DVT) is a blood clot (thrombus) in a vein. DVTs can occur anywhere in the body but are most frequently found in the deep veins of the legs, thighs, and pelvis. When a clot forms in a deep vein, a piece of the clot can break off, travel to the heart and be pumped into the arteries of the lung. This can cause a pulmonary embolism (PE). Patients with atrial fibrillation or patent foramen ovale (PFO) can form clots in the heart which can travel to the brain causing a transient ischemic attack (TIA) or ischemic stroke. A blood clot which has traveled from its point of origin is called an embolus (plural emboli). Anticoagulants are used for the prevention and treatment of venous thromboembolism (DVT/PE), for the prevention of stroke, and in the treatment of acute coronary syndrome (ACS).

CLOT FORMATION

Coagulation is the process by which blood forms clots. A number of factors can lead to activation of the coagulation process such as blood vessel injury, blood stasis, and certain conditions (e.g., cancer). The coagulation process involves activation of platelets and the clotting cascade which lead to fibrin formation and a stable clot. The goal of the clotting cascade is to form fibrin. All of the clotting factors have an inactive and an active form. Once activated, the clotting factor will serve to activate the next clotting factor in the sequence un-

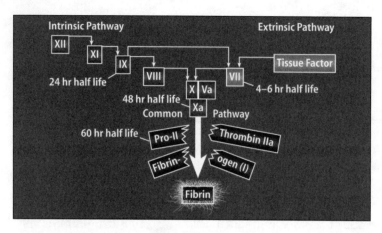

til fibrin is formed. The coagulation cascade has two pathways which lead to fibrin formation: the contact activation pathway (or the intrinsic pathway) and the tissue factor pathway (or the extrinsic pathway). Anticoagulants are used to inhibit the clotting cascade, thereby reducing clot formation.

PHARMACOLOGIC TREATMENT

Anticoagulants work by various mechanisms. Unfractionated heparin, low molecular weight heparins (LMWHs), and fondaparinux work by binding to antithrombin (AT) causing a conformational change which increases ATs activity 1,000-fold. AT inactivates thrombin and other proteases involved in blood clotting, including factor Xa. LWMHs inhibit factor Xa more specifically than unfractionated heparin. Fondaparinux (Arixtra) is a synthetic pentasaccharide that requires AT binding to selectively inhibit Factor Xa.

Direct thrombin inhibitors (which block thrombin directly, as the name suggests) decrease the amount of fibrin available for clot formation. The intravenous direct thrombin inhibitors have been very important clinically since they do not cross-react with heparin-induced thrombocytopenia (HIT) antibodies. Once HIT develops from the use of heparin (or less commonly from LMWHs), the injectable direct thrombin inhibitors are the drugs of choice (e.g., argatroban). The oral direct thrombin inhibitor, dabigatran (Pradaxa), does not require blood tests to monitor for effectiveness, is not subject to food interactions and has few drug interactions; these are advantages over warfarin. It does, however, cause significant dyspepsia/gastritis and has an increased risk of GI bleeding compared to other oral anticoagulants.

Rivaroxaban (Xarelto) and apixaban (Eliquis) work by inhibiting Factor Xa. These oral agents are taken once or twice daily and require no laboratory monitoring for efficacy. Dabigatran, rivaroxaban and apixaban should not be used in patients with prosthetic heart valves and they do have some drug interactions (although fewer than warfarin).

RISK FACTORS FOR THE DEVELOPMENT OF VENOUS THROMBOEMBOLISM

Surgery

Major trauma or lower extremity injury

Immobility

Cancer or chemotherapy

Venous compression (tumor, hematoma, arterial abnormality)

Previous venous thromboembolism

Increasing age

Pregnancy and postpartum period

Estrogen-containing medications or selective estrogen receptor modulators

Erythropoietin-stimulating agents

Acute medical illness

Inflammatory bowel disease

Nephrotic syndrome

Myeloproliferative disorders

Paroxysmal nocturnal hemoglobinuria

Obesity

Central venous catheterization

Inherited or acquired thrombophilia

Warfarin is a vitamin K antagonist. Vitamin K is required for the carboxylation of clotting factors II, VII, IX, and X. Without adequate vitamin K, the liver produces the factors – but they have reduced coagulant activity. Warfarin requires careful patient monitoring – with frequent blood tests to measure the INR (international normalized ratio), the test used to measure warfarin's effectiveness. Warfarin has a narrow therapeutic range and the INR is highly variable and is affected greatly by many drugs or changes in dietary vitamin K intake.

Treatment Safety Concerns & the Pharmacist's Role

All of the anticoagulants can cause significant bleeding and are classified as "High Alert" medications by the Institute for Safe Medication Practices (ISMP). Bleeding events associated with anticoagulants put the patient at risk for increased mortality, including higher risk for stroke and myocardial infarction. Ten percent of all adverse drug events treated in the emergency room are due to anticoagulants. The Joint Commission's National Patient Safety Goals require the implementation of policies and protocols to properly initiate and manage anticoagulant therapy. Patients receiving anticoagulants should receive individualized care through a defined process that includes standardized ordering, dispensing, administration, monitoring and patient/caregiver education (for treatment doses). When pharmacists are involved in managing anticoagulants, patient care and outcomes are improved and costs are decreased. Pharmacists are also involved with ensuring that patients who need anticoagulants for DVT prophylaxis – such as orthopedic and cardiac surgical patients – receive them.

Heparin-Induced Thrombocytopenia (HIT) Overview

Heparin-induced thrombocytopenia is an immune-mediated (IgG) drug reaction that is associated with a high risk of venous and arterial thrombosis. The immune system forms antibodies against heparin when it binds to platelet factor 4 (PF 4). These IgG antibodies form a complex with heparin and PF 4. In HIT, this complex binds to the Fc receptors on platelets, which leads to further platelet activation, and causes a release of PF 4 and other pro-coagulant microparticles from platelet granules. If left untreated, HIT can lead to a pro-thrombotic state causing many complications such as venous and arterial thrombosis (HITT) resulting in amputations, post-thrombotic syndrome, and/or death. The estimated incidence of HIT is ~3% of those patients exposed to heparin for more than four days. It is lower with a shorter duration of treatment. Typical onset of HIT occurs 5-14 days after the start of heparin or within hours if a patient has been recently exposed to heparin (within the last 3 months). A diagnosis is made by a profound, unexplained drop in platelet count (defined as > 50% drop) from baseline and laboratory confirmation of antibodies or platelet activation by heparin. Although thrombocytopenia is the most common presenting feature of HIT, in up to 25% of patients with HIT, the development of thrombosis precedes the development of thrombocytopenia. Pharmacists should check platelets at baseline and routinely monitor platelets in patients who are receiving heparin therapy.

Management of HIT Complicated by Thrombosis (HITT) Per the CHEST 2012 Guidelines

- If HIT is suspected/confirmed, <u>stop</u> all forms of heparin and LMWH [including heparin flushes (use regional citrate) and heparin-coated catheters]. If the patient is on warfarin and diagnosed with HIT, the warfarin should be discontinued and vitamin K should be administered. Although the patient is at a high risk of thrombosis, warfarin use with a low platelet count has a high correlation with warfarin-induced necrosis.

- In patients with HIT, nonheparin anticoagulants are recommended, in particular, <u>argatroban</u>, over the further use of heparin or LMWH or initiation/continuation of vitamin K antagonists. Argatroban is also favored in patients with renal impairment.

- Do not start warfarin therapy until the platelets have recovered to at least $150,000/mm^3$. Warfarin should be initiated at lower doses (5 mg maximum). Overlap warfarin with a nonheparin anticoagulant for a minimum of 5 days and until the INR is within target range for 24 hours.

- If patients require urgent cardiac surgery or PCI, bivalirudin is the preferred anticoagulant.

UNFRACTIONATED HEPARIN (UFH)

UFH binds to antithrombin (AT) and inactivates thrombin (Factor IIa) and Factor Xa (as well as factors IXa, XIa, XIIa, and plasmin) and prevents the conversion of fibrinogen to fibrin.

DRUG	DOSING	SAFETY/SIDE EFFECTS/MONITORING
Heparin (AKA unfractionated heparin) Heparin Treatment Many strengths and volumes (ranging from 1 unit/mL-20,000 units/mL), including total units of 5,000, 10,000, 12,500, 20,000, 25,000 & others. Usual infusion for treatment is 25,000 units in 250 mL (concentration: 100 units/mL) in D5W (or available in ½ NS or NS) Line Flush 10 units/mL, 100 units/mL syringes (in 3, 5 & 6 mL-6 mL may be in 10 mL syringe) **SAFETY NOTE** Heparin "lock-flushes" (HepFlush) are used to keep IV lines open (patent). They are not used for anticoagulation. There have been fatal errors made by choosing the incorrect heparin strength. (Heparin injection 10,000 units/mL and heparin flushes 10 or 100 units/mL have been confused with each other). Using a higher dose to flush a line could cause significant bleeding, including fatal hemorrhage. Many of the dosing errors have occurred in neonates. Refer to the Medication Safety chapter for recommendations on the safe use of antithrombotics.	**Prophylaxis of VTE** 5,000 units SC Q8-12H **Treatment of VTE** 80 units/kg IV bolus followed by 18 units/kg/hr infusion (70 units/kg IV bolus followed by 15 units/kg/hr infusion for cardiac and stroke patients) or a fixed dose of 5,000 units IV bolus followed by 1,000 units/hr infusion. If treating as an outpatient, give 333 units/kg x 1 dose SC, then 250 units/kg SC Q12H **Treatment of ACS/STEMI** 60 units/kg IV bolus (max 4,000 units); 12 units/kg/hr (max 1,000 units/hr) infusion Use actual body weight for dosing Onset – IV: immediate; SC: 20-30 min t½ = 60-90 min HIT type II (IgG mediated) – heparin antibody complexes form and bind to platelets, causing aggregation and clots. Look for a drop in platelet count of > 50% from baseline. HIT has cross-sensitivity with LMWHs Antidote: Protamine – 1 mg protamine will reverse ~100 units of heparin; max dose 50 mg	**BLACK BOX WARNING** Some products contain benzyl alcohol as a preservative: use of these products is contraindicated in neonates and infants **CONTRAINDICATIONS** Uncontrolled active bleed, severe thrombocytopenia, ICH, history of HIT, hypersensitivity to pork products **WARNING** Do not give IM due to hematoma risk **SIDE EFFECTS** Bleeding (epistaxis, ecchymosis, gingival, GI, etc.), thrombocytopenia, heparin induced thrombocytopenia (HIT), hyperkalemia and osteoporosis (with long-term use) **MONITORING** Heparin is monitored via the aPTT (or anti-Xa level: 0.3-0.7 units/mL) aPTT is taken 6 hours after initiation and every 6 hrs until the the therapeutic range of 1.5-2.5 x control (patient's baseline) is reached; also check aPTT at every rate change; then daily Platelet count, Hgb, Hct at baseline and daily to monitor for thrombocytopenia and bleeding **NOTES** Pregnancy Category C Unpredictable anticoagulant response – has variable and extensive binding to plasma proteins and cells

Heparin Drug Interactions

- Most drug interactions are due to additive effects with other agents that can ↑ bleeding risk (e.g., anticoagulants, antiplatelet drugs, ginkgo and other natural products, dextran, NSAIDs, SSRIs, SNRIs, thrombolytics and others). See Drug Interactions chapter for more information on drugs that can increase bleeding risk.

- Drugs that increase clotting risk (including estrogen and SERMS) should likely be discontinued if heparin is required. This applies to other anticoagulants; pro-coagulant agents are high risk in patients requiring anticoagulants.

LOW MOLECULAR WEIGHT HEPARINS (LMWHs)

LMWHs work similar to heparin except that the inhibition is much greater for Factor Xa than Factor IIa.

DRUG	DOSING	SAFETY/SIDE EFFECTS/MONITORING
Enoxaparin (Lovenox) Comes in multidose vials (300 mg/3 mL) or these prefilled syringes: 30 mg/0.3 mL, 40 mg/0.4 mL, 60 mg/0.6 mL, 80 mg/0.8 mL, 100 mg/mL, 120 mg/0.8 mL, 150 mg/mL 1 mg = 100 units Anti-Xa activity	**Prophylaxis of VTE** 30 mg SC Q12H or 40 mg SC daily CrCl < 30 mL/min: 30 mg SC daily **Treatment of VTE and UA/NSTEMI** 1 mg/kg SC Q12H or 1.5 mg/kg SC daily CrCl < 30 mL/min: 1 mg/kg SC daily **Treatment for STEMI** In patients < 75 years: 30 mg IV bolus plus a 1 mg/kg SC dose followed by 1 mg/kg SC Q12H (max 100 mg for the 1st two doses only) In patients ≥ 75 years: 0.75 mg/kg SC Q12H (no bolus – max 75 mg for the first two doses only) CrCl < 30 mL/min: 1 mg/kg SC daily In patients managed with percutaneous coronary intervention (PCI): if the last SC dose was given 8-12 hours before balloon inflation, give 0.3 mg/kg IV bolus	**BLACK BOX WARNING** Patients receiving neuraxial anesthesia (epidural, spinal) or undergoing spinal puncture are at risk of hematomas and subsequent paralysis **CONTRAINDICATIONS** History of HIT, active major bleed, hypersensitivity to pork **SIDE EFFECTS** Bleeding, thrombocytopenia, hyperkalemia, anemia, injection site reactions **MONITORING** Anti-Xa levels can be used to monitor, but monitoring is not routine in most patients. Monitoring is recommended in pregnancy and in patients with mechanical heart valves. Monitoring may be done in renal insufficiency or in morbidly obese patients. aPTT is not used. Obtain peak anti-Xa levels 4 hours post dose. When treating VTE with enoxaparin daily, the anti-Xa level should be 1-2 anti-Xa units/mL. If using enoxaparin twice daily for VTE treatment, the level should be 0.6-1 anti-Xa units/mL. Monitor platelet count, Hgb, Hct at baseline and every 2-3 days (if inpatient); stool occult blood tests, SCr **NOTES** Pregnancy Category B
Dalteparin (Fragmin)	**Prophylaxis of VTE** 2,500-5,000 units SC daily **Treatment of UA/NSTEMI** 120 units/kg (max 10,000 units) Q12H	More predictable anticoagulant response (therefore, do not need to monitor anti-Xa levels in most cases). Less monitoring and more cost effective, even though the actual drug costs more than unfractionated heparin. Do not expel air bubble from syringe prior to injection. Do not administer IM. Store at room temperature. No true antidote.

LMWH Drug Interactions

- Most drug interactions are due to additive effects with other agents that can ↑ bleeding risk (e.g., anticoagulants, antiplatelet drugs, ginkgo and other natural products, dextran, NSAIDs, SSRIs, SNRIs, thrombolytics and others). See Drug Interactions chapter for more information on drugs that can increase bleeding risk.

FACTOR Xa INHIBITORS

Fondaparinux *(Arixtra)* is a synthetic pentasaccharide that selectively inhibits Factor Xa via antithrombin (AT). Therefore, it is an indirect inhibitor of Factor Xa.

DRUG	DOSING	SAFETY/SIDE EFFECTS/MONITORING

Injectable Indirect Factor Xa Inhibitor (SC)

DRUG	DOSING	SAFETY/SIDE EFFECTS/MONITORING
Fondaparinux *(Arixtra)* Comes in prefilled syringes: 2.5 mg, 5 mg, 7.5 mg, 10 mg	**Prophylaxis of VTE** 2.5 mg SC daily for ≥ 50 kg patients **Treatment of VTE** < 50 kg: 5 mg SC daily 50–100 kg: 7.5 mg SC daily > 100 kg: 10 mg SC daily	**BLACK BOX WARNING** Patients receiving neuraxial anesthesia (epidural, spinal) or undergoing spinal puncture are at risk of hematomas and subsequent paralysis **CONTRAINDICATIONS** Severe renal impairment (CrCl < 30 mL/min), active major bleed, bacterial endocarditis, thrombocytopenia with positive test for anti-platelet antibodies in presence of fondaparinux, or body weight < 50 kg (for prophylaxis only) **SIDE EFFECTS** Bleeding (epistaxis, ecchymosis, gingival, GI, etc.), local injection site reactions (rash, pruritus, bleeding), thrombocytopenia, anemia, nausea **MONITORING** Platelet count, Hgb, Hct at baseline and daily to monitor for thrombocytopenia and bleeding; SCr, stool occult blood testing **NOTES** Pregnancy Category B Do not expel air bubble from syringe prior to injection No antidote Do not administer IM. Store at room temperature.

Factor Xa Inhibitors Continued

DRUG	DOSING	SAFETY/SIDE EFFECTS/MONITORING

Oral Direct Factor Xa Inhibitors

Rivaroxaban (Xarelto)

Switching patients from warfarin to rivaroxaban: discontinue warfarin and start rivaroxaban when INR < 3.0

Switching from LMWH/heparin to rivaroxaban: start rivaroxaban ≤ 2 hrs before the next dose of LMWH or at the time of discontinuation of heparin infusion.

Missed doses – administer the dose as soon as possible on the same day as follows:

For patients receiving 15 mg twice daily: take rivaroxaban immediately to ensure intake of 30 mg rivaroxaban per day. In this particular instance, two 15 mg tablets may be taken at once. Then continue with the regular 15 mg twice daily intake as recommended on the following day.

For patients receiving 20, 15 or 10 mg once daily: take the missed rivaroxaban dose as soon as possible on the same day; otherwise skip..

Non-valvular A. Fib
CrCl > 50 mL/min: 20 mg PO daily with the evening meal

CrCl 15-50 mL/min: 15 mg PO daily with the evening meal

CrCl < 15 mL/min: avoid use

Treatment of DVT/PE
15 mg PO BID with food x 21 days, then 20 mg PO daily with food.

CrCL < 30 mL/min: avoid use

Prophylaxis for DVT (after knee/hip replacement)
10 mg PO daily – without regards to meals

Do not use in CrCl < 30 mL/min

First dose given 6-10 hours after surgery

Take for 35 days after hip replacement surgery; take for 12 days after knee replacement surgery

BLACK BOX WARNINGS (2)
Patients receiving neuraxial anesthesia (epidural, spinal) or undergoing spinal puncture are at risk of hematomas and subsequent paralysis

Premature discontinuation of rivaroxaban increases the risk of thrombotic events

CONTRAINDICATIONS
Active major bleeding; avoid use in patients with moderate to severe hepatic impairment or with any degree associated with coagulopathy; avoid use in severe renal impairment [DVT treatment and prophylaxis (CrCl < 30 mL/min) and A. Fib (CrCl < 15 mL/min)]; avoid use in prosthetic heart valves

SIDE EFFECTS
Bleeding

NOTES
Pregnancy Category C

No antidote

No monitoring of efficacy required

Apixaban (Eliquis)

Switching from warfarin to apixaban: discontinue warfarin and start apixaban when the INR < 2.0.

Switching from apixaban to anticoagulants other than warfarin: Discontinue apixaban and start the other anticoagulant at the next scheduled dose.

Missed dose – the dose should be taken as soon as possible on the same day and twice daily administration should be resumed. The dose should not be doubled to make up for a missed dose.

Non-valvular A. Fib
5 mg BID

If have at least 2 of the following: age ≥ 80 years, body weight ≤ 60 kg, or SCr ≥ 1.5 mg/dL, give 2.5 mg BID

Do not use in CrCl < 15 mL/min

BLACK BOX WARNING
Discontinuing apixaban in patients without adequate continuous anticoagulation increases risk of stroke

CONTRAINDICATIONS
Active pathological bleed, severe hepatic impairment, prosthetic heart valves

SIDE EFFECTS
Bleeding, anemia

NOTES
Pregnancy Category B

No antidote

No monitoring of efficacy required

Factor Xa Inhibitor Drug Interactions

- Rivaroxaban is a major 3A4 substrate; 3A4 inhibitors can increase rivaroxaban levels and 3A4 inducers can decrease rivaroxaban levels. Avoid concomitant use with drugs that are combined P-gp AND strong 3A4 inducers (e.g., carbamazepine, phenytoin, rifampin, St. John's wort) OR strong 3A4 inhibitors (e.g., ketoconazole, itraconazole, lopinavir/ritonavir, ritonavir, indinavir/ritonavir, and conivaptan). Use caution in patients with CrCl 15-50 mL/min who are receiving concomitant combined P-gp and weak to moderate 3A4 inhibitors.

- Apixaban is a major 3A4 substrate; 3A4 inhibitors can increase apixaban levels and 3A4 inducers can decrease apixaban levels. Avoid concomitant use with drugs that are combined P-gp AND strong 3A4 inducers (e.g., carbamazepine, phenytoin, rifampin, St. John's wort). The dose of apixaban should be reduced to 2.5 mg BID when coadministered with combined P-gp and strong 3A4 inhibitors (e.g., clarithromycin, itraconazole, ketoconazole, or ritonavir). If the patient is taking 2.5 mg BID, then avoid these inhibitors.

- The prothrombotic effects of some estrogens and progestin-estrogen combinations may counteract the anticoagulant effects of these medications; best to avoid.

DIRECT THROMBIN INHIBITORS

These agents directly inhibit thrombin (Factor IIa); they bind to the active thrombin site of free and clot-associated thrombin.

DRUG	DOSING	SAFETY/SIDE EFFECTS/MONITORING
Direct Thrombin Inhibitors (IV or SC)		
Argatroban HIT with thrombosis and patients undergoing PCI who are at risk for HIT **Bivalirudin (Angiomax)** For patients with ACS undergoing PTCA and are at risk for HIT	Initial: 2 mcg/kg/min – titrate to target aPTT. Max: 10 mcg/kg/min Intravenous drugs given as a bolus followed by an infusion; all are weight-based Used in patients with a history of HIT Argatroban – reduce dose in hepatic impairment Bivalirudin – reduce dose in renal impairment (CrCl < 30 mL/min)	**CONTRAINDICATIONS** Active major bleeds **SIDE EFFECTS** Bleeding, anemia, hematoma **MONITORING** aPTT, and/or ACT (for bivalirudin); platelets, Hgb, Hct, SCr **NOTES** Pregnancy Category B No cross-reaction with HIT No antidote Argatroban can increase the INR; if starting on warfarin concurrently do not use a loading dose of warfarin; dose cautiously.

Direct Thrombin Inhibitors Continued

DRUG	DOSING	SAFETY/SIDE EFFECTS/MONITORING
Desirudin *(Iprivask)* Indicated for VTE prevention after hip arthroplasty	15 mg SC Q12H Reduce dose in renal impairment (CrCl < 60 mL/min)	**BLACK BOX WARNING** Patients receiving neuraxial anesthesia (epidural, spinal) or undergoing spinal puncture are at risk of hematomas and subsequent paralysis **MONITORING** aPTT, SCr, stool occult blood test **NOTES** Pregnancy Category C No antidote

Direct Thrombin Inhibitor (oral)

Dabigatran *(Pradaxa)* Reduce the risk of stroke and systemic embolism in patients with non-valvular atrial fibrillation 75, 150 mg caps Switching from warfarin to dabigatran: discontinue warfarin and start dabigatran when INR < 2.0. Switching from LMWH/heparin to dabigatran: start dabigatran ≤ 2 hrs before the next scheduled dose of parenteral drug, like *Lovenox*, or at the time of discontinuation of heparin infusion.	**Non-Valvular A.FIB** 150 mg BID; 75 mg BID if CrCl 15-30 mL/min Swallow capsules whole. Do not break, chew, crush or open. Do not put in NG tube. Take missed dose ASAP unless it is within 6 hours of next scheduled dose; do not double up Keep in original container. Discard 4 months after opening the original container. Keep bottle tightly closed to protect from moisture. Blister packs are good until the date on the pack (usually 6-12 months)	**BLACK BOX WARNING** Discontinuing dabigatran places patients at an increased risk of thrombotic events. If dabigatran must be discontinued for a reason other than pathological bleeding, consider the use of another anticoagulant during the time of interruption. **CONTRAINDICATIONS** Active pathological bleed and patients with mechanical prosethetic heart valve(s) **SIDE EFFECTS** Dyspepsia, gastritis-like symptoms, bleeding (including more GI bleeding) **MONITORING** Renal function at baseline and yearly in patients > 75 years of age or in patients with a CrCl < 50 mL/min **NOTES** Pregnancy Category C Dabigatran prevents 5 more strokes per 1,000 patients/year than warfarin (therefore preferred by CHEST guidelines for stroke prevention in non-valvular A. Fib). These guidelines came out before rivaroxaban and apixaban were approved; therefore, there are no published recommendations for these agents. Discontinue if going for invasive surgery (1-2 days before if normal renal function, 3-5 days before if CrCl < 50 mL/min). No antidote No monitoring of efficacy required Store in a cool, dry place; not in bathrooms.

Dabigatran Drug Interactions

- Dabigatran is a substrate of P-gp. Avoid concomitant use with P-gp inducers such as rifampin; rifampin will cause the dose to become subtherapeutic.

- In moderate renal impairment (CrCl 30-50 mL/min), reduce dose to 75 mg BID when given with the P-gp inhibitors dronedarone or systemic ketoconazole. In severe renal impairment (CrCl 15-30 mL/min), concomitant use of P-gp inhibitors should be avoided.

- Use of P-gp inhibitors (verapamil, amiodarone, quinidine and clarithromycin) does not require a dose reduction of dabigatran.

- See Drug Interactions chapter for more information on drugs that can increase bleeding risk.

WARFARIN (COUMADIN, JANTOVEN)

Warfarin competitively inhibits the C1 subunit of the multi-unit vitamin K epoxide reductase (VKORC1) enzyme complex, thereby reducing the regeneration of vitamin K epoxide and causing depletion of active clotting factors II, VII, IX and X and proteins C and S.

DRUG	DOSING	SAFETY/SIDE EFFECTS/MONITORING
Warfarin (Coumadin, Jantoven) Racemic mixture of R- and S-enantiomers with the S- enantiomer being more potent (2.7-3.8x more potent)	Healthy outpatients should be started on warfarin 10 mg daily for 1st 2 days, then adjust dose per INR values. Doses of ≤ 5 mg may be an appropriate starting dose for those who are elderly, malnourished, taking drugs which can ↑ warfarin levels, liver disease, heart failure, or have a high risk of bleeding 1 mg (pink) 2 mg (lavender) 2.5 mg (green) 3 mg (tan) 4 mg (blue) 5 mg (peach) 6 mg (teal) 7.5 mg (yellow) 10 mg (white) 5 mg/mL inj. Highly protein bound (99%)	**BLACK BOX WARNING** May cause major or fatal bleeding **CONTRAINDICATIONS** Hemorrhagic tendencies (cerebrovascular hemorrhage, bacterial endocarditis, pericarditis, pericardial effusions), blood dyscrasias, pregnancy, uncontrolled hypertension, a non-compliant patient and others. **SIDE EFFECTS** Bleeding, skin necrosis, purple toe syndrome **MONITORING** PT/INR should be 2.0-3.0 for most indications (DVT, A. fibrillation, bioprosthetic mitral valve, mechanical aortic valve, antiphospholipid syndrome) and should be 2.5-3.5 for some high-risk indications such as a mechanical mitral valve or mechanical heart valves in both the aortic and mitral position. INR monitoring to begin after the initial 2 or 3 doses, or if on a chronic, stable dose of warfarin, monitor at intervals up to 12 weeks. Hct, Hgb, signs of bleeding **NOTES** Pregnancy Category X/D (women with mechanical heart valves) Antidote: vitamin K Take at the same time each day. Missed doses – take the dose as soon as possible on the same day; do not double the dose the next day to make up for a missed dose. Dental cleanings and single tooth extraction do not generally require a change in warfarin dosing if INR is in therapeutic range.

Warfarin Pharmacogenomics

The presence of variant alleles, CYP2C9*2 and CYP2C9*3, as well as polymorphisms to the VKORC gene can increase the risk of bleeding from warfarin. Patients with these polymorphisms may require lower doses of warfarin therapy. ~~Genetic testing is not routinely recommended at this time.~~

Warfarin Use – Key Points from CHEST 2012 Guidelines

- In healthy outpatients, the initial starting dose of warfarin should be 10 mg daily for the first 2 days, then adjust per INR values.

- For patients with stable therapeutic INRs presenting with a single subtherapeutic INR value, routinely bridging with heparin is not recommended.

- Routine pharmacogenomic testing is not recommended at this time.

- For patients with consistently stable INRs on warfarin therapy, INR testing can be done up to every 12 weeks rather than every 4 weeks.

- For patients with previously stable therapeutic INRs who present with a single out-of-range INR of ≤ 0.5 below or above therapeutic, continue current dose and obtain another INR within 1-2 weeks.

- Routine use of vitamin K supplementation is not recommended in patients taking warfarin.

- Start warfarin therapy the same day as parenteral therapy and continue anticoagulation for a minimum of 5 days and until the INR is 2.0 or above for at least 24 hrs.

- Warfarin is highly protein bound; caution with other highly protein bound drugs that may displace warfarin (e.g., phenytoin, valproic acid, furosemide, bumetanide, spironolactone, metolazone, doxycycline, glipizide, glyburide, ibuprofen, naproxen, diphenhydramine, others)

Warfarin – Pharmacokinetic Drug Interactions

- Warfarin is a substrate of CYP 2C9 (major), 1A2 (minor), 2C19 (minor) and 3A4 (minor) and an inhibitor of 2C9 (weak) and 2C19 (weak). Avoid use with tamoxifen.

- 2C9 inducers – including aprepitant, bosentan, carbamazepine, phenobarbital, phenytoin, primidone, rifampin (large ↓ INR), licorice and St. John's Wort – may ↓ INR.

- 2C9 inhibitors – including amiodarone, azole antifungals (e.g., fluconazole, ketoconazole, voriconazole), capecitabine, etravirine, fluvastatin, fluvoxamine, macrolide antibiotics, metronidazole, tigecycline, TMP/SMX and zafirlukast – may ↑ INR. See Drug Interactions chapter.

- Antibiotics: Penicillins, including amoxicillin, some cephalosporins, fluoroquinolones, macrolides, TMP/SMX and tetracyclines may enhance the anticoagulant effect of warfarin – monitor INR.

- Check for 1A2, 2C19 and 3A4 interactions; these occur, but usually have less of an effect on INR.

- When starting amiodarone, decrease the dose of warfarin by 30-50%.

Warfarin – Pharmacodynamic Drug Interactions

- The most common pharmacodynamic interactions are with NSAIDs (e.g., aspirin, ibuprofen, celecoxib and others), antiplatelet agents, other anticoagulants, SSRIs and SNRIs. These interactions ↑ bleeding risk, but the INR may be in the usual range or slightly elevated.

- Nutritional products, including drinks and supplements, can include vitamin K (e.g., alfalfa and green tea). Any additions of vitamin K will lower the INR. Check the product for vitamin K content. Alfalfa, American ginseng, green tea and coenzyme Q-10 can reduce the effectiveness of warfarin.

- Stay consistent with the amount of vitamin K consumed through the diet (see foods high in vitamin K below).

Herbal/Natural Product Drug Interactions

- Ginkgo biloba increases bleeding risk with no effect on the INR. Other natural products that can pose an increased bleeding risk include bromelain, danshen (can ↑ INR), dong quai (can ↑ INR), vitamin E, evening primrose oil, echinacea, high doses of fish oils, garlic, glucosamine (can ↑ INR), goldenseal, grapefruit (can ↑ INR), policosanol, willow bark and wintergreen oil (can ↑ INR). There are other herbal products that can increase the bleeding risk with warfarin.

Use of Vitamin K for High (Supratherapeutic) INRs

Variable INRs are a norm of clinical practice. Elevated INRs can scare the clinician due to increased risk of bleeding. It is important to know how to treat patients with high INR values. Bleeding, at any INR, will warrant more serious intervention.

Oral formulations of vitamin K (generally at doses of 2.5-5 mg) are preferred in patients without significant or major bleeding. For more serious bleeds, the subcutaneous route (SC) has a slower onset and can produce a variable response; therefore, SC injections of vitamin K should not be used. The intramuscular route should also be avoided due to the risk of hematoma formation. Intravenous administration should be given only when the patient is experiencing major (or serious) bleeding. IV injection is reported to cause anaphylaxis in 3 of out 100,000 patients, resulting in advice to infuse slowly.

FOODS HIGH IN VITAMIN K	
Broccoli	Lettuce (red leaf or butterhead)
Brussels sprouts	Mustard greens
Cabbage	Parsley
Canola oil	Soybean Oil
Cauliflower	Spinach
Chickpeas	Swiss chard
Cole Slaw	Tea (green or black)
Collard Greens	
Coriander	Turnip greens
Endive	Watercress
Green kale	

When vitamin K is used, if a stat reversal is not required, oral is the preferred formulation.

Use of Vitamin K for Overanticoagulation

SYMPTOMS/INR VALUE	WHAT TO DO
INR above therapeutic range but < 4.5	Reduce or skip warfarin dose. Monitor INR. Resume warfarin when INR therapeutic. Dose reduction may not be needed if only slightly above therapeutic range.
For patients with a supratherapeutic INR of 4.5-10 without bleeding	Routine use of vitamin K is NOT recommended if no evidence of bleeding. Hold 1-2 doses of warfarin. Monitor INR. Resume warfarin at lower dose when INR therapeutic. Vitamin K can be used if urgent surgery needed (≤ 5 mg, with additional 1-2 mg in 24 hours if needed) or bleeding risk is high (1-2.5 mg).
For patients with INR > 10 without bleeding	Hold warfarin. Give oral vitamin K 2.5-5 mg even if not bleeding. Monitor INR. Resume warfarin at a lower dose when INR is therapeutic.
For patients with major bleeding from warfarin	Hold warfarin therapy. Give vitamin K 5-10 mg by slow IV injection and four-factor prothrombin complex concentrate (PCC). PCC suggested over fresh frozen plasma (FFP) due to risks of allergic reactions, infection transmission, longer preparation time, slower onset and higher volume.

Anticoagulant Antidotes

Protamine combines with strongly acidic heparin to form a stable complex (salt) neutralizing the anticoagulant activity of both drugs. Phytonadione provides an essential vitamin for liver synthesis of clotting factors (II, VII, IX, X). *Kcentra* is a newer product available as a single-use vial containing coagulation Factors II, VII, IX and X, and antithrombotic proteins C and S as a lyophilized concentrate. It is indicated for the urgent reversal of warfarin.

ANTIDOTE*	DOSING	SAFETY/SIDE EFFECTS/MONITORING

For Heparin reversal (may partially reverse LMWH)

Protamine 10 mg/mL (5 mL, 25 mL)	1 mg protamine will reverse ~ 100 units of heparin – reverse the amount of heparin given in the last 2-2.5 hours; max dose: 50 mg Administer slow IVP (50 mg over 10 minutes). Inject without further dilution over 1-3 minutes	**BLACK BOX WARNING** Hypotension, cardiovascular collapse, non-cardiogenic pulmonary edema, pulmonary vasoconstriction, and pulmonary hypertension may occur **SIDE EFFECTS** Hypotension, bradycardia, flushing, anaphylaxis **NOTES** For I.V. use only. Rapid I.V. infusion causes hypotension.

Anticoagulant Antidotes Continued

ANTIDOTE*	DOSING	SAFETY/SIDE EFFECTS/MONITORING

For Warfarin reversal

ANTIDOTE*	DOSING	SAFETY/SIDE EFFECTS/MONITORING
Vitamin K or Phytonadione *(Mephyton)* 5 mg tablets 1 mg/0.5 mL, 10 mg/mL inj.	1-10 mg PO/IV If given IV, infuse slowly; rate of infusion should not exceed 1 mg/minute	**BLACK BOX WARNING** Severe reactions resembling hypersensitivity reactions (e.g., anaphylaxis) have occurred rarely during or immediately after I.V. administration (even with proper dilution and rate of administration); some patients had no previous exposure to phytonadione. **SIDE EFFECTS** Anaphylaxis **NOTES** To reduce the incidence of anaphylactoid reaction upon I.V. administration, dilute dose in a minimum of 50 mL of compatible solution and administer using an infusion pump over at least 20 minutes SC route not recommended due to variable absorption IM route not recommended due to risk of hematoma Discontinue orlistat and mineral oil during vitamin K administration (decreases vitamin K absorption).
Four Factor Prothrombin Complex Concentrate (Human) *(Kcentra)* Factors II, VII, IX, X, Protein C, Protein S	Based on patient's INR and body weight – given IV Do not let drug back-up into line; will clot Refrigerate. Reach room temp prior to administration. Protect from light.	**CONTRAINDICATIONS** Disseminated intravascular coagulation and known heparin-induced thrombocytopenia (contains heparin) **WARNINGS** Arterial and venous thromboembolic complications have been reported Made from human blood and may carry risk of transmitting infectious agents (e.g., viruses) **SIDE EFFECTS** Headache, nausea, vomiting, arthralgia, hypotension and thrombotic events **NOTES** Do not repeat dose Administer vitamin K concurrently
Three Factor Prothrombin Complex Concentrates (Human) *(Bebulin, Profilnine)* Off label	Weight-based dosing given IV slowly Given with Fresh Frozen Plasma (FFP) or Factor VIIa	**WARNING** *Bebulin* and *Profilnine* contain Factors II, IX and X but low or nontherapeutic levels of factor VII and should not be confused with Prothrombin Complex Concentrate (Human) [(Factors II, VII, IX, X), Protein C, Protein S] *(Kcentra)* which contains therapeutic levels of factor VII. **SIDE EFFECTS** Chills, fever, flushing, nausea, headache, risk of thrombosis **NOTES** Due to ADRs may need to slow infusion and give antihistamine
Factor VIIa Recombinant *(NovoSeven RT)* Off label	10-20 mcg/kg IV bolus over 5 minutes	**WARNING** Serious thrombotic events are associated with the use of factor VIIa outside labeled indications.

*There are no available antidotes for dabigatran, rivaroxaban, or apixaban; however, drug-specific antidotes for each drug have been developed and are in clinical trials – FDA-approval may come as early as 2014.

Perioperative Management of Patients on Warfarin

- Stop warfarin therapy approximately 5 days before major surgery. In patients with a mechanical heart valve, A. Fib, or VTE at high risk for thromboembolism, bridging therapy with LMWH or UFH is recommended. Discontinue therapeutic-dose SC LMWH 24 hours before surgery (4-6 hours before surgery if using UFH IV).

- If INR is still elevated 1-2 days before surgery, give low-dose vitamin K (1-2 mg).

- If reversal of warfarin is needed in a patient requiring an urgent surgical procedure, give low-dose (2.5-5 mg) IV or oral vitamin K.

- Resume warfarin therapy 12-24 hours after the surgery, when there is adequate hemostasis.

- In patients who are receiving bridge therapy with SC LMWH and are undergoing high-bleeding risk surgery, resume therapeutic dose of LMWH therapy 48-72 hours after surgery, when there is adequate hemostasis. If low bleeding risk, may resume therapeutic dose LMWH therapy 24 hours after surgery.

- Continue warfarin or aspirin in patients undergoing minor dental, dermatologic, or cataract surgery.

- Antiplatelet therapies (such as clopidogrel or prasugrel) may need to be stopped 5-10 days prior to major surgery. The risks/benefit of stopping therapy must be evaluated on a case-by-case basis.

Anticoagulation for Patients with Atrial Fibrillation (Per the Chest Guidelines 2012)

Anticoagulation for patients with A. Fib. who are going to undergo cardioversion:

- For patients with A. Fib of > 48 hours or unknown duration, anticoagulation (if warfarin, target INR 2.0-3.0) is recommended for at least 3 weeks prior to and 4 weeks after cardioversion (regardless of method – electrical or pharmacologic) when normal sinus rhythm is restored.

- For patients with A. Fib ≤ 48 hours duration undergoing elective cardioversion, start full therapeutic anticoagulation at presentation, do cardioversion, and continue full anticoagulation for at least 4 weeks while patient is in normal sinus rhythm.

- For patients staying in atrial fibrillation, chronic anticoagulation therapy is needed for stroke prevention. Treatment depends on the number of risk factors present. See following tables.

CHADS$_2$ SCORING SYSTEM

Each risk factor = 1, except for stroke/TIA which = 2. Add up the total number of risk factors for a given patient.

C – CHF

H – HTN

A – Age (> 75)

D – Diabetes

S$_2$ – prior Stroke/TIA

Antithrombotic Therapy for Patients with Atrial Fibrillation

RISK CATEGORY	RECOMMENDED THERAPY
CHADS$_2$ score = 0	No therapy. For patients wanting anticoagulant therapy, ASA 75-325 mg daily should be used over oral anticoagulation or combination therapy with ASA and clopidrogrel.
CHADS$_2$ score = 1	Oral anticoagulation* rather than ASA 75 mg–325 mg daily or combination therapy with ASA and clopidogrel. For patients unable to take oral anticoagulants, ASA and clopidogrel should be used.
CHADS$_2$ score ≥ 2	Oral anticoagulation*. For patients unable to take oral anticoagulants, ASA and clopidogrel should be used.

Oral anticoagulation favors dabigatran 150 mg BID rather than adjusted-dose warfarin therapy (target INR 2.0-3.0).

Options for Patients Who Cannot Receive Anticoagulation (Due to a Contraindication)

Graduated compression stockings (GCS) and intermittent pneumatic compression (IPC) devices are 2 non-pharmacologic measures used to prevent venous thromboembolism.

Patient Counseling: For All Anticoagulants

- This medication can interact with many other drugs. Check with your doctor or pharmacist before taking any other medication, including over the counter medications, vitamins, and herbal products.

- This medication can cause you to bruise and/or bleed more easily. Report any unusual bleeding, bruising, or rashes to your physician.

- Tell physicians and dentists that you are using this medication before any surgery is performed.

- Call your healthcare provider right away if you fall or injure yourself, especially if you hit your head. Alcoholic drinks should be avoided.

- Do not start, stop, or change any medicine without talking with your healthcare provider.

- This medication is very important for your health, but it can cause serious and life-threatening bleeding problems.

- Call your healthcare provider right away if you develop any of these symptoms:

  - Unexpected pain, swelling, or discomfort

  - Headaches, dizziness, or weakness

  - Unusual bruising (bruises that develop without known cause or grow in size)

  - Nose bleeds that happen often

  - Unusual bleeding gums

  - Bleeding from cuts that take a long time to stop

  - Menstrual bleeding or vaginal bleeding that is much heavier than normal

  - Pink or brown urine

  - Red or black stools (looks like tar)

  - Coughing up blood or blood clots

  - Vomiting blood or material that looks like coffee grounds

Enoxaparin

- First, wash and dry hands.

- Choose an area on the right or left side of your abdomen, at least 2 inches from the belly button. Most people lie down so they can look up and see the area around the sides of their belly button.

- Clean the injection site with an alcohol swab. Let dry.

- Remove the needle cap by pulling it straight off the syringe and discard it into a sharps container (do not twist the cap off as this can bend the needle).

- <u>Do not expel the air bubble in the syringe prior to injection (unless your doctor has advised you to do so).</u>

- With your other hand, pinch an inch of the cleansed area to make a fold in the skin. Insert the full length of the needle straight down – at a 90 degree angle – into fold of skin.

- Press the plunger with your thumb until the syringe is empty.

- Pull the needle straight out at the same angle that it was inserted.

- Point the needle down and away from yourself and others, and push down on the plunger to activate the safety shield.

- Do not rub the site of injection as this can lead to bruising. Place the used syringe in the sharps collector.

Dabigatran

- Do not stop taking dabigatran without talking to your prescriber. Stopping dabigatran increases your risk of having a stroke.

- Swallow dabigatran capsules whole. Do not break, chew, or empty the pellets from the capsule. It is fine to take with or without food.

- Common side effects of dabigatran include indigestion, upset stomach or stomach burning and/or pain.

- Only open 1 bottle of dabigatran at a time. Finish your opened bottle of dabigatran before opening a new bottle. After opening a bottle of dabigatran, use within 4 months.

- Keep dabigatran in the original bottle or blister package to keep it dry (protect the capsules from moisture). Do not put dabigatran in pill boxes or pill organizers.

- Tightly close your bottle of dabigatran right away after you take your dose.

- If you miss a dose of dabigatran, take it as soon as you remember. If your next dose is less than 6 hours away, skip the missed dose. Do not take two doses of dabigatran at the same time.

- Dabigatran is not for patients with artificial heart valves.

Rivaroxaban

- Rivaroxaban is not for patients with artificial heart valves.

- If you take rivaroxaban for atrial fibrillation: Take rivaroxaban 1 time a day with your evening meal.

  ❑ If you miss a dose of rivaroxaban, take it as soon as you remember on the same day. Take your next dose at your regularly scheduled time.

- If you take rivaroxaban for blood clots in the veins of your legs or lungs: Take rivaroxaban once or twice a day as prescribed with food at the same time each day.

  ❑ If you miss a dose of rivaroxaban and take rivaroxaban 2 times a day: Take rivaroxaban as soon as you remember on the same day. You may take 2 doses at the same time to make up for the missed dose. Take your next dose at your regularly scheduled time.

  ❑ If you miss a dose of rivaroxaban and take rivaroxaban 1 time a day: Take rivaroxaban as soon as you remember on the same day. Take your next dose at your regularly scheduled time.

- If you take rivaroxaban for hip or knee replacement surgery: Take rivaroxaban 1 time a day with or without food.

  ❑ Take rivaroxaban 1 time a day with or without food.

  ❑ If you miss a dose of rivaroxaban, take it as soon as you remember on the same day. Take your next dose at your regularly scheduled time.

Warfarin

- Take warfarin at the same time every day as prescribed by your doctor. You can take warfarin either with food or on an empty stomach.

- Warfarin lowers the chance of blood clots forming in your body.

- If you miss a dose, take the dose as soon as possible on the same day. Do not take a double dose the next day to make up for a missed dose.

- You will need to have your blood tested frequently to monitor your response to this medication. This test is called an INR. Your dose may be adjusted to keep you INR in a target range.

- Do not make changes in your diet, such as eating large amounts of green, leafy vegetables. Be consistent with the amount of leafy green vegetables and other foods rich in vitamin K.

- Do not change your weight by dieting, without first checking with your healthcare provider.

- Avoid drinking alcohol.

- Other side effects besides bleeding include purple toe syndrome that can cause your toes to become painful and purple in color. Also, death of skin tissue can occur. Report any unusual changes or pain immediately to your health care professional.

PRACTICE CASE

Alice is a 47 year old female (5' 6", 176 lbs.) who has been admitted to the hospital with shortness of breath, problems breathing, chest pain, coughing, and sweating. She may have a pulmonary embolism so the medical team started her on heparin therapy.

CATEGORY	
Past Medical History	Atrial Fibrillation HTN – Stage 1
Vitals	BP 155/89 HR 155 RR 25 Temp 38°
Labs	SCr 1.8 mg/dL; K 4.2 mEq/L; Glucose 241 mg/dL
Current Medications	Amiodarone 200 mg daily ASA 325 mg daily
Allergies	Sulfites

Questions

Heparin protocol for St. Mary's Hospital

INDICATION	INITIAL REGIMEN
Treatment of DVT/PE	80 units/kg (max 10,000 units bolus); 18 units/kg/hr (max 2,300 units/hr)

APTT (SEC.)	DOSE ADJUSTMENT
< 35	80 units/kg bolus, then ↑ infusion by 4 units/kg/hr
35-50	40 units/kg bolus, then ↑ infusion by 2 units/kg/hr
51-70	No change
71-90	Decrease infusion by 2 units/kg/hr
> 90	Hold infusion for 1 hour, then ↓ by 3 units/kg/hr

1. The medical team asks you to dose the heparin for Alice per hospital protocol. The protocol is to the left. What should the correct bolus and infusion rate of heparin be for Alice?

   a. 10,000 units bolus, followed by 2,300 units/hr infusion

   b. 14,000 units bolus, followed by 3,500 units/hr infusion

   c. 7,000 units bolus, followed by 1,400 units/hr infusion

   d. 6,400 units bolus, followed by 1,440 units/hr infusion

   e. None of the above

2. The bolus and infusion are given. After 6 hours, the aPTT comes back at 48 sec. What is the correct dose adjustment to make to the heparin according to the protocol?

   a. Give a 6,400 unit bolus now and increase the infusion rate to 1,900 units/hr

   b. Give a 3,200 unit bolus now and increase the infusion rate to 1,600 units/hr

   c. Make no change to the dose

   d. Do not give a bolus and reduce the infusion rate to 1,500 units/hr

   e. None of the above

3. The pulmonary embolism was confirmed. It is Alice's third day in the hospital, and the medical team would like her discharged. She is going to be transitioned to warfarin. She receives 5 mg of warfarin at her bedside. Which of the statements is true regarding warfarin? (Select **ALL** that apply.)

   a. Warfarin is a direct thrombin inhibitor that helps to prevent clot formation.

   b. Warfarin has a high risk of bleeding. Careful monitoring is advised.

   c. Warfarin should be taken with a low fat meal and never double up on the dose.

   d. Warfarin is a racemic mixture and the R-isomer is more potent than the S-isomer.

   e. Warfarin should overlap the heparin therapy until she is at the therapeutic INR for 24 hours.

4. Alice needs another medication as a "bridge" therapy until her warfarin becomes therapeutic. Select the appropriate agent, route of administration, and dose for Alice's treatment of PE.

   a. *Lovenox* 30 mg SC daily

   b. *Lovenox* 30 mg SC Q12H

   c. *Lovenox* 80 mg SC Q12H

   d. *Lovenox* 80 mg SC daily

   e. *Lovenox* 180 mg SC daily

5. Alice will need proper counseling on subcutaneous administration of enoxaparin. List the steps in order that the patient should take to administer the drug.

   a. Place injection in the abdomen at least 2" from the navel.

   b. Insert full length of the needle at a 90 degree angle.

   c. Place the used syringe in a sharps container.

   d. Wash hands thoroughly.

   e. The patient should clean the injection site with alcohol.

6. Alice should be careful not to take other products that can increase the bleeding risk while taking warfarin. Which of the following would *not* increase her risk of bleeding? (Select **ALL** that apply.)

   a. Calcium with Vitamin D

   b. Large amounts of garlic

   c. Dong quai

   d. Fidaxomicin

   e. Ginkgo biloba

Questions 7-10 do not relate to the case.

7. Which of the following medications can significantly interact with warfarin? (Select **ALL** that apply.)

   a. Amiodarone

   b. Morphine

   c. Rifampin

   d. Levetiracetam

   e. Fluconazole

8. A patient comes to the hospital with a DVT. He has developed HIT with thrombosis in the past. Which of the following agents is considered first line treatment in this patient?

   a. *Arixtra*

   b. Argatroban

   c. *Xarelto*

   d. *Fragmin*

   e. Desirudin

9. Which of the following is a side effect of heparin therapy? (Select **ALL** that apply.)

   a. Xerostomia

   b. Thrombocytopenia

   c. Osteoporosis

   d. Hyperkalemia

   e. Bleeding

10. Which of the following parameters need to be monitored during heparin therapy?

    a. Hematocrit, hemoglobin, platelets, AST, and ALT

    b. Hematocrit, hemoglobin, platelets, and aPTT

    c. Hematocrit, hemogloblin, platelets, and PT

    d. CBC and Chem 7 panel

    e. Chem 7 panel and aPTT

Answers

1-d, 2-b, 3-b,e, 4-c, 5-d,e,a,b,c, 6-a,d, 7-a,c,e, 8-b, 9-b,c,d,e, 10-b

CHRONIC STABLE ANGINA

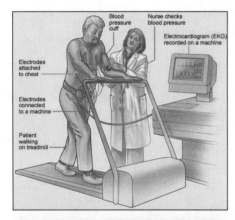

Blood pressure cuff
Nurse checks blood pressure
Electrocardiogram (EKG) recorded on a machine
Electrodes attached to chest
Electrodes connected to a machine
Patient walking on treadmill

GUIDELINES

2012 ACCF/AHA/ACP/AATS/PCNA/SCAI/STS Guideline for the Diagnosis and Management of Patients with Stable Ischemic Heart Disease. Circulation. 2012 Dec 18;126(25):e354-471.

We gratefully acknowledge the assistance of Cynthia Jackevicius, BScPhm, PharmD, MSc, FCSHP, BCPS, Western University, School of Pharmacy and Eric Ip, PharmD, BCPS, CSCS, CDE, Chair and Associate Professor, Pharmacy Practice Department, Touro University California College of Pharmacy, in preparing this chapter.

BACKGROUND

Angina is chest pain, pressure or discomfort. The chest pain is described as "squeezing," "grip-like," "heavy," or "suffocating," and typically does not vary with position or respiration. The patient presenting with angina must be categorized as having stable angina or unstable angina (UA). UA is defined as new onset, increasing (in frequency, intensity or duration), or occurring at rest and is a medical emergency. Stable angina, also known as stable ischemic heart disease (SIHD), is associated with predictable chest pain often brought on by exertion or emotional stress and relieved within minutes by rest (or with nitroglycerin), but can recur with additional activity or stress. Stable angina is due to plaque build up on the inner walls of the coronary arteries (atherosclerosis), causing narrowing in the arteries and reduced blood flow to the heart.

Angina can also be present in patients with normal coronary arteries, where symptoms are the result of vasospasm in the arteries. This type of angina is known as Prinzmetal's (variant or vasospastic) angina.

Some patients (women, elderly and those with diabetes) may not develop the classic symptoms of angina and may not recognize they have cardiac risk and need medical attention.

NON-PHARMACOLOGIC TREATMENT

Patients should be encouraged to follow a heart healthy lifestyle (saturated fats < 7% of total calories and trans fat < 1% of total calories, intake of fresh fruits and vegetables, low-fat dairy products, etc.). Encourage patients to stop smoking and avoidance of secondhand smoke, maintain a BMI of 18.5-24.9 kg/m², and maintain a waist circumference < 35 inches in females and < 40 inches in males. Encourage physical activity, 30-60 minutes of moderate-intensity aerobic activity, at least 5 days and preferably 7 days per week, supplemented by an increase in daily lifestyle activities (e.g., walking breaks at work, gardening) to improve cardiopulmonary fitness. Medically supervised programs such as cardiac rehabilitation, and physician-directed, home-based programs are recommended for at-risk patients at first diagnosis. Please note these recommendations are different from the obesity guideline recommendations (see Weight Loss chapter for more information).

TYPES OF ANGINA

Stable Angina
Decreased myocardial O_2 supply due to reduced blood flow from narrowed arteries by atherosclerotic plaque

Symptoms have been occurring for weeks but without worsening

Prinzmetal's Angina
Decreased myocardial O_2 supply due to vasospasm of the artery

Silent Ischemia
Transient myocardial ischemia without symptoms of angina

Unstable Angina
Severe, crushing chest pain unrelieved by rest; acute medical care is needed

PHARMACOLOGIC TREATMENT

The treatment goals for chronic angina are to reduce the risk of an acute coronary syndrome (unstable angina/myocardial infarction) and provide symptomatic relief from the angina pain. An antiplatelet agent and an antianginal regimen are used together for this purpose. Aspirin is the antiplatelet agent recommended; clopidogrel (Plavix) is used in patients with an allergy or other contraindication to aspirin. Beta blockers are first line therapy for the treatment of chronic stable angina. Calcium channel blockers or long-acting nitrates should be utilized when beta blockers are contraindicated or when additional symptomatic relief is needed. Ranolazine can also be utilized as a substitute or in addition to beta blocker therapy. Sublingual nitroglycerin or nitroglycerin spray is recommended for immediate relief of angina. All patients with stable chronic angina should be on moderate or high dose statin therapy regardless of LDL values. For patients who cannot tolerate statins, bile acid sequestrants or niacin or both is reasonable. Patients should be aggressively managed if they have hypertension, heart failure and diabetes with the guideline-driven therapies for each of these disease states. An annual influenza vaccine is recommended. The acronym below summarizes the non-pharmacologic and pharmacologic therapies in chronic angina:

DIAGNOSTIC PROCEDURES

History and physical

Labs

CBC, CK-MB, troponin (T or I), aPTT, PT/INR, lipid panel, glucose

ECG (at rest and during chest pain)

Exercise tolerance test

Stress imaging

Cardiac catheterization/angiography

A – Antiplatelet and antianginal drugs

B – Blood pressure and beta-blockers

C – Cholesterol (statins) and cigarettes

D – Diet and diabetes

E – Exercise and education

ANTIPLATELET AGENTS

Aspirin binds irreversibly to cyclooxygenase-1 and 2 (COX-1 and 2) enzymes which results in decreased prostaglandin (PG) and thromboxane A_2 (TxA_2) production; TxA_2 is a potent vasoconstrictor and facilitates platelet aggregation. Aspirin has anti-platelet, antipyretic, analgesic and anti-inflammatory properties. Clopidogrel inhibits P2Y$_{12}$ ADP-mediated platelet activation and aggregation.

DRUG	DOSING	SAFETY/SIDE EFFECTS/MONITORING
Aspirin *(Bayer, Ascriptin, Bufferin*, others) See Pain chapter for further information on aspirin	75-162 mg daily	**CONTRAINDICATIONS** Allergy or hypersensitivity; active bleeding **SIDE EFFECTS** Dyspepsia, heartburn, GI upset, GI bleed/ulceration, bleeding, renal impairment, hypersensitivity **MONITORING** Signs and symptoms of bleeding **NOTES** Shown to decrease incidence of MI, CV events, and death; to be used in all acute and chronic ischemic heart disease patients indefinitely EC aspirin must be chewed if patient is having ACS
Clopidogrel *(Plavix)*	75 mg daily	**BLACK BOX WARNING** Effectiveness depends on the activation to an active metabolite mainly by CYP2C19. Poor metabolizers exhibit higher cardiovascular events than patients with normal CYP2C19 function. Tests to check CYP 2C19 genotype can be used as an aid in determining a therapeutic strategy. Consider alternative treatment strategies in patients identified as 2C19 poor metabolizers. The CYP2C19*1 allele corresponds to fully functional metabolism while the CYP2C19*2 and *3 alleles are nonfunctional. **CONTRAINDICATIONS** Active pathological bleed (e.g., PUD, ICH) **SIDE EFFECTS** Bleeding, bruising, rash, TTP (rare) Thrombotic thrombocytopenic purpura (TTP) – rare but serious – have patients report fever, weakness, extreme skin paleness, purple skin patches, yellowing of the skin or eyes, or neurological changes **MONITORING** Symptoms of bleeding; Hgb/Hct as necessary **NOTES** Do not start in patients likely to undergo CABG surgery and discontinue 5 days prior to any major surgery Used in patients with a contraindication to aspirin

Aspirin Drug Interactions

- Most drug interactions are due to additive effects with other agents that can ↑ bleeding risk (e.g., anticoagulants, other antiplatelet drugs, ginkgo and other natural products, dextran, NSAIDs, SSRIs, SNRIs, thrombolytics and others). See Drug Interactions chapter for more information on drugs that can increase bleeding risk.

- NSAIDs (like aspirin) can increase the level of lithium (avoid concurrent use) and methotrexate.

- Caution with use of aspirin and other ototoxic agents (vancomycin, loop diuretics, others).

Clopidogrel Drug Interactions

- Most drug interactions are due to additive effects with other agents that can ↑ bleeding risk (e.g., anticoagulants, other antiplatelet drugs, ginkgo and other natural products, dextran, NSAIDs, SSRIs, SNRIs, thrombolytics and others). See Drug Interactions chapter for more information on drugs that can increase bleeding risk.

- Clopidogrel is a prodrug metabolized mainly by CYP450 2C19. Avoid concomitant use with strong or moderate 2C19 inhibitors (cimetidine, fluconazole, ketoconazole, voriconazole, fluoxetine, fluvoxamine and others). Avoid concomitant use with omeprazole and esomeprazole as these agents may reduce the effectiveness of clopidogrel due to 2C19 inhibition.

ANTI-ANGINAL THERAPY

DRUG	MECHANISM	CLINICAL NOTES
Beta Blockers Used 1st line See Hypertension chapter for a complete review of these agents	Reduce myocardial oxygen demand by ↓ HR (negative chronotropic effect); ↓ contractility (negative inotropic effect) and ↓ LV wall tension with long term use. Improves oxygen supply by greater coronary perfusion.	Start low, go slow; titrate to resting HR of 50-60 BPM; avoid abrupt withdrawal. Do not use a beta blocker with intrinsic sympathomimetic activity (ISA). More effective than nitrates and CCBs in silent ischemia; avoid use in Prinzmetal's angina; effective as monotherapy or in combination with CCBs, nitrates, and/or ranolazine.
Calcium Channel Blockers Preferred agent for Prinzmetal's (variant) angina See Hypertension chapter for a complete review of these agents	Produces vasodilation, ↓ SVR and BP and improves myocardial oxygen supply; reduces oxygen demand by ↓ contractility and SVR	Used when beta blockers are contraindicated or as add on therapy. Slow-release or long-acting dihydropyridine and nondihydropyridine CCBs are effective; avoid short-acting CCBs (e.g., nifedipine IR).

Anti-Anginal Therapy Continued

DRUG	MECHANISM	CLINICAL NOTES
Nitrates	Reduces cardiac oxygen demand by ↓ left ventricular pressure and preload; causes vasodilation of veins and arteries	**SL tablets or spray** Used for fast relief of angina. Call 911 if chest pain does not go away after the first dose of SL tabs or spray. **For long-acting nitrates** Used for chronic anginal therapy. Requires a nitrate-free interval with dosing. See dosing below. Long-acting nitrates are not used alone for chronic therapy but can be used in combination with beta-blockers and CCBs as add on therapy
Ranolazine *(Ranexa)*	Selectively inhibits the late Na^+ current; ↓ intracellular Na^+ and Ca^{2+}; may ↓ myocardial O_2 demand 500 mg BID (max 1,000 mg BID)	**CONTRAINDICATIONS** Hepatic cirrhosis, concurrent use of strong 3A4 inhibitors and inducers **WARNING** Can cause QT prolongation **SIDE EFFECTS** Dizziness, constipation, headache, nausea **MONITORING** ECG, BP, K^+ **NOTES** Has little to no clinical effects on HR or BP More effective in males than females Do not crush, break, or chew.

Nitrate Drug Interactions

- Avoid concurrent use with PDE-5 inhibitors; use caution with other antihypertensive medications and alcohol as these can potentiate the hypotensive effect and cause a significant drop in blood pressure.

Ranolazine Drug Interactions

- Ranolazine is a substrate of 3A4 (major), 2D6 (minor) and P-gp and an inhibitor of 3A4 (minor), 2D6 (minor) and P-gp. Do not use with strong 3A4 inhibitors (e.g., itraconazole, ketoconazole, clarithromycin, nefazodone, nelfinavir, ritonavir, indinavir, saquinavir). Limit the dose to 500 mg BID in patients taking moderate CYP3A4 inhibitors (e.g., diltiazem, verapamil, erythromycin, fluconazole, and grapefruit juice). Limit simvastatin to 20 mg/day if used concurrently. Do not use with CYP3A4 inducers.

NITROGLYCERIN FORMULATIONS	SAFETY/SIDE EFFECTS/MONITORING
Nitroglycerin SL tabs *(Nitrostat)* 0.3, 0.4, 0.6 mg	**CONTRAINDICATIONS** Hypersensitivity to organic nitrates, concurrent use with PDE-5 inhibitors; increased intracranial pressure; severe anemia
Nitroglycerin sublingual spray 0.4 mg/spray *(Nitromist, Nitrolingual Pump Spray)*	**SIDE EFFECTS** Headache, dizziness, lightheadedness, flushing, hypotension, tachyphylaxis, syncope
Nitroglycerin IV	**MONITORING** BP (continuously if receiving IV), HR, chest pain **NOTES** Counsel patients to dose the medication so they have a 10-12 hour nitrate-free period to ↓ tolerance (some products require longer than 12 hours of a nitrate-free interval).
Nitroglycerin ointment 2%	**Nitroglycerin IV** Prepare in glass bottles or polyolefin bags (non-PVC) due to sorption of the drug in PVC. Use administration sets intended for nitroglycerin (non-PVC as well)
Nitroglycerin transdermal patches *(Nitro-Dur, Minitran)*	**Nitroglycerin patch** On for 12-14 hours, off for 10-12 hours; rotate sites
Nitroglycerin extended release caps *(Nitro-Time, generics)*	**Nitroglycerin ointment 2%** Dosed BID, 6 hours apart with 10-12 nitrate-free interval
Isosorbide mononitrate IR/ER tabs/caps *(Monoket)*	**Isosorbide mononitrate** Dosed daily or BID. Immediate release (IR) is BID; given 8 A.M. and 1 P.M. (or similar). Extended release is the same (if divided) or daily in the morning.
Isosorbide dinitrate IR/ER *(Isordil, Dilatrate-SR)* – preferred for systolic HF	**Isosorbide dinitrate** IR is dosed BID-TID. If TID, give at 7 A.M., 12 P.M. and 5 P.M. for a 14 hour nitrate-free interval (or similar). SR/ER is daily in the morning or divided BID for an 18 hour nitrate-free interval.

Patient Counseling

Sublingual or Spray Nitroglycerin

- Nitroglycerin sublingual tablet should not be chewed, crushed or swallowed. Take one tablet at the first sign of chest pain. (This medication may also be taken prophylactically 5-10 minutes before activities that bring on chest pain). The tablet should be placed under the tongue or in the buccal pouch.

- Patients should take the medicine while sitting down to avoid dizziness, lightheadedness or fainting which may be associated with use. Patients should not eat, drink, or smoke for at least 5-10 minutes after use of the product or while experiencing chest pain.

- **Contact EMS immediately if chest pain/angina persists after one dose of sublingual NTG.** You can continue to take additional doses (up to 3) at 5 minute intervals while waiting for the ambulance to arrive. Explain to patients that many of the patient inserts provided with sublingual NTG products may not reflect these updated recommendations.

- **Patients should be reminded that the reformulated NTG tablets have extended potency and stability.** If NTG products are stored at room temperature and properly handled; the tablets should be stable until the manufacturer provided expiration date.

- If the tablets start to get powdery, instruct patients to get a new bottle.

- You may feel a slight burning or stinging in your mouth when you use this medication. However, this sensation is not a sign of how well the medication is working. Do not use more medication just because you do not feel a burning or stinging sensation. Newer formulations of these products are less likely to have this side effect.

- Nitroglycerin SL tablets should be kept in the original amber glass bottle, which is kept tightly capped.

- For the *Nitrolingual Pump Spray:* The pump must be sprayed 5 times into the air to prime the pump before use. If not used within 6 weeks, prime the pump with 1 spray before use. Do not shake. Press the button firmly with the forefinger to release the spray onto or under the tongue. Close your mouth after the spray. Do not inhale the spray and try not to swallow too quickly afterwards. Do not eat or drink or rinse the mouth for 5-10 minutes after the dose. You can use 1 spray every 5 minutes but no more than 3 sprays in 15 minutes.

- If a patient has recently used a PDE-5 inhibitor like sildenafil *(Viagra, Revatio)*, tadalafil *(Cialis, Adcirca)*, vardenafil *(Levitra, Staxyn)*, or avanafil *(Stendra)*, he/she should avoid using nitroglycerin and inform medical professionals of PDE-5 inhibitor use immediately.

Nitroglycerin Patches

- Remove the patch from its pouch and peel off the protective clear liner as directed. Usually, you will wear the patch on the upper arm or chest. Keep the patch above the elbows when wearing on the arm. If placing on the legs, keep patch above the knees.

- Apply the patch to a clean, dry, and hairless area. Hair in the area may be clipped, but not shaved. Avoid areas with cuts or irritation. Do not apply the patch immediately after bathing or showering. Wait until your skin is completely dry. However, you may bathe, shower, and swim while wearing the patch.

- Press the patch firmly in place with the palm of your hand. Wash your hands after applying the patch.

- You will usually use 1 patch a day and wear it for 12 to 14 hours or as directed. The dosage is based on your medical condition and response to treatment.

- For the medicine to work well, there must be a 10-12 hour "patch free" interval between patches (where the patch is left off).

- To reduce skin irritation, apply each new patch to a different area of skin. After removing the old patch, fold it in half with the sticky sides together, and discard out of the reach of children and pets.

- This drug should not be used with the following medications: sildenafil *(Viagra, Revatio)*, tadalafil *(Cialis, Adcirca)*, vardenafil *(Levitra, Staxyn)* or avanafil *(Stendra)*. A dangerous drop in blood pressure could occur.

Isosorbide Mononitrate

- Take this medication by mouth, once or twice daily or as directed by your healthcare provider. Take the first dose of the day when you wake up, then take the second dose 5 hours later. It is important to take the drug at the same times each day. Do not change the dosing times unless directed by your healthcare provider.

- Side effects can include headache (can be severe), dizziness, lightheadedness, redness, mild warmth, or nausea. The redness and mild warmth is called flushing and this will go away when your body adjusts to the medicine. Headache is often a sign that this medication is working. Your healthcare provider may recommend treating headaches with an over-the-counter pain reliever (such as acetaminophen). The headache also should become less bothersome as your body gets used to the medicine. If the headaches continue or become severe, tell your healthcare provider promptly.

- This drug may make you dizzy. Do not drive, use machinery, or do any activity that requires alertness until you are sure you can perform such activities safely. Limit alcoholic beverages.

- To reduce the risk of dizziness and lightheadedness, get up slowly when rising from a sitting or lying position. Hold onto the side of the bed or chair to avoid falling.

- This drug should not be used with the following medications: sildenafil *(Viagra, Revatio)*, tadalafil *(Cialis, Adcirca)*, vardenafil *(Levitra, Staxyn)* or avanafil *(Stendra)*. A dangerous drop in blood pressure could occur.

Ranolazine

- Ranolazine is used to decrease the number of times you may get chest pain. Relieving symptoms of angina can increase your ability to exercise and perform more strenuous work.

- Ranolazine works differently than other drugs for angina, so it can be used with your other angina medications (e.g., nitrates, calcium channel blockers such as amlodipine, beta blockers such as metoprolol). It is thought to work by improving how well the heart uses oxygen so that it can do more work with less oxygen.

- Take this medication by mouth, usually twice daily with or without food or as directed by your healthcare provider. Swallow the tablet whole. Do not crush or chew the tablets.

- Use this medication regularly in order to get the most benefit from it. Take it at the same times each day. This medication must be taken regularly to be effective. It should not be used to treat chest pain when it occurs. Use other medications (e.g., sublingual nitroglycerin) to relieve an angina attack as directed by your healthcare provider.

- Inform your healthcare provider if your condition does not improve or if it worsens (e.g., your chest pain happens more often).

- Dizziness, headache, lightheadedness, nausea, tiredness, and constipation may occur. If any of these effects persist or worsen, notify your healthcare provider or pharmacist promptly.

- Avoid eating grapefruit or drinking grapefruit juice while being treated with this medication. Grapefruit can increase the amount of certain medications in your blood.

- Ranolazine may cause a condition that affects the heart rhythm (QT prolongation). This heart rhythm can infrequently result in serious fast/irregular heartbeat and other symptoms (such as severe dizziness, fainting) that require immediate medical attention. The risk may be increased if you are taking other drugs that may affect the heart rhythm. Check with your healthcare provider or pharmacist before using any herbal, over the counter or other medication.

ACUTE CORONARY SYNDROMES

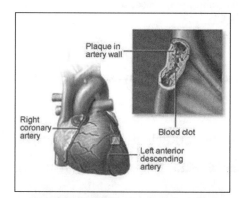

Plaque in
artery wall

Right
coronary
artery

Blood clot

Left anterior
descending
artery

We gratefully acknowledge the assistance of Cynthia Jackevicius, BScPhm, PharmD, MSc, FCSHP, BCPS, Western University, School of Pharmacy, in preparing this chapter.

BACKGROUND

Acute Coronary Syndrome (ACS) refers to a set of clinical disorders that result from an imbalance between myocardial oxygen demand and supply. This imbalance is most often a complication of plaque build-up in the coronary arteries. These plaques are made up of fatty deposits and cause the arteries to narrow, making blood flow more difficult. When a plaque ruptures, a clot forms and the reduction in blood flow leads to ischemia, compromising proper cardiac functioning. This ischemia leads to a release of biochemical markers into the bloodstream, mainly troponins I and T and creatine kinase (CK) myocardial band (MB).

Acute coronary syndrome encompasses the clinical conditions of unstable angina (UA), non-ST segment elevation myocardial infarction (NSTEMI), and ST segment elevation myocardial infarction (STEMI). With UA/NSTEMI, there can be transient ST-segment depression, T-wave inversion, or no changes at all seen on the electrocardiogram (ECG).

When a patient first experiences symptoms of ACS (chest pain that feels like pressure or tightness, shortness of breath, pain in other areas such as the left upper arm or jaw) they should immediately call 9-1-1. The emergency medical personnel should immediately perform a 12-lead ECG

GUIDELINES

2013 ACCF/AHA Guideline for Management of ST-Elevation Myocardial Infarction: A Report of the American College of Cardiology Foundation/American Heart Association Task Force on Practice Guidelines. Circulation. 2013; 127:e362-e425.

2012 ACCF/AHA Focused Update of the Guideline for the Management of Patients with Unstable Angina/Non-ST-Elevation Myocardial Infarction (Updating the 2007 Guideline and Replacing the 2011 Focused Update). Circulation. 2012; 126:875-910.

2007 ACC/AHA Guidelines for the Management of Patients with Unstable Angina/Non-ST-Elevation Myocardial Infarction. Circulation. 2007;116:e148-e304.

at the site of first medical contact. The patient should then be urgently transported to a hospital with percutaneous coronary intervention (PCI) capability. Coronary heart disease is the leading cause of death in men and women in the United States.

Classic Signs and Symptoms of ACS

- Chest pain/discomfort (with or without radiation to the arms, back, neck, jaw, or epigastrium), diaphoresis, nausea, weakness, shortness of breath, or lightheadedness

- Precipitating factors include: exercise, cold weather, extreme emotions, stress, and sexual intercourse

- Pain is usually not relieved by nitroglycerin sublingual tablets or spray or rest

RISK FACTORS
Age (men > 45 years of age, women > 55 years of age or had early hysterectomy)
Family history of coronary event before 55 years of age (men) or 65 years of age (women)
Smoking
Hypertension
Hyperlipidemia
Diabetes
Chronic angina
Known coronary artery disease

Diagnosis

- UA: chest pain; cardiac enzymes are negative; no or transient ECG changes

- NSTEMI: chest pain + positive cardiac enzymes (troponins, CK-MB); no or transient ECG changes

- STEMI: chest pain + positive cardiac enzymes + ST segment changes or new left bundle branch block (LBBB) on ECG (≥ 0.1 mV of ST segment elevation in 2 or more contiguous ECG leads)

PHARMACOLOGIC TREATMENT

Acute treatment of patients with ACS is aimed at stabilizing the patient's condition, relieving pain from ischemia and reducing myocardial damage and further ischemia. To stabilize the patient and treat the pain, a combination of morphine, oxygen, nitroglycerin and aspirin are given upon presentation to the ED (acronym MONA). Antithrombotic therapy is then initiated to reduce myocardial damage and prevent further ischemia. This typically includes a combination of dual oral antiplatelet therapy (e.g., clopidogrel plus aspirin) and anticoagulation with heparin, low-molecular weight heparin or bivalirudin. Additionally a GP IIb/IIIa antagonist (eptifibatide, tirofiban, abciximab) may be given in select patients. All patients without contraindications should receive a beta blocker and an ACE inhibitor within 24 hours of presentation. For patients presenting with STEMI, a fibrinolytic may be administered; however, this should only be done when the patient cannot be immediately transferred to a percutaneous coronary intervention (PCI) capable hospital.

Treatment of Unstable Angina/Non-ST segment Elevation Myocardial Infarction (UA/NSTEMI)

Treatment acronym is MONA + GAP-BA (see chart below).

Summary of Drugs Used Acutely for ACS

DRUG	MOA	CLINICAL COMMENTS
MONA (acronym)		
Morphine	Produces arterial and venous dilation; prompts a ↓ in myocardial O_2 demand; pain relief	Morphine sulfate (2 to 8 mg IV repeated at 5- to 15-minute intervals PRN) may be used in patients with ongoing chest discomfort despite NTG therapy. Side effects: hypotension, bradycardia, N/V, sedation, and respiratory depression. Antidote: naloxone *(Narcan)*. More information in the Pain chapter.
Oxygen		Supplemental oxygen should be administered to patients with arterial oxygen desaturation ($SaO_2 < 90\%$), or who are in respiratory distress.
Nitrates	Dilates coronary arteries and improves collateral blood flow; ↓ cardiac oxygen demand by ↓ preload	NTG (SL tabs or spray) followed by IV for immediate relief of ischemia and associated chest pain. Take 1 dose (e.g., 0.4 mg of SL NTG) every 5 minutes, up to a total of 3 doses. If chest pain/discomfort is not improved or worsening 5 minutes after the first dose, call 911. NTG IV is indicated for relief of ongoing ischemic discomfort, control of hypertension, or management of pulmonary congestion. Do not use NTG if patient's SBP < 90 mmHg, HR < 50 BPM, or tachycardic (> 100 BPM). NTG or other nitrates should not be administered to patients receiving PDE-5 inhibitors for erectile dysfunction within 24 hrs of sildenafil/vardenafil or 48 hrs of tadalafil use (or 12 hrs for avanafil). More information on nitrates in Chronic Stable Angina chapter.
Aspirin	Inhibits platelet aggregation by inhibiting TxA_2	Aspirin given immediately and continued indefinitely (162-325 mg initially followed by 81 mg daily). Take 162-325 mg and chew the aspirin for the initial dose. If intolerant to aspirin, take loading dose followed by daily maintenance dose of either clopidogrel, prasugrel or ticagrelor.
GAP-BA (acronym)		
GP IIb/IIIa receptor antagonists	Blocks fibrinogen binding to the GPIIb/IIIa receptors on platelets, preventing PLT aggregation	Can be used in medical management or for those going for an intervention (PCI +/- stent). Agents include abciximab, eptifibatide, or tirofiban. Abciximab should only be given to patients in whom PCI is planned.
Anticoagulants	Clotting factor inhibitors	Used to prevent further clotting. Agents include heparin, LMWH (enoxaparin, dalteparin), fondaparinux, bivalirudin. More information in Anticoagulation chapter.
$P2Y_{12}$ inhibitors	Inhibitor of the $P2Y_{12}$ receptor on platelets	Clopidogrel or prasugrel (only if going for PCI) or ticagrelor for all patients (loading dose followed by a maintenance dose) unless patient is going for CABG surgery.

Summary of Drugs Used Acutely for ACS Continued

DRUG	MOA	CLINICAL COMMENTS
Beta Blockers	Decrease O_2 demand due to reductions in BP, HR, and contractility; may reduce the magnitude of infarction	In UA/NSTEMI, oral beta blocker therapy should be initiated within the first 24 hours for patients who do not have 1 or more of the following: 1) signs of HF, 2) evidence of a low-output state 3) increased risk for cardiogenic shock, 4) other relative contraindications to beta blockade (e.g., PR interval > 0.24 sec, 2nd or 3rd degree heart block, etc.). IV beta blocker therapy may be reasonable especially if ongoing ischemia or hypertension is present. In STEMI, beta blockers should be administered promptly without a contraindication. Oral long-acting non-dihydropyridine calcium antagonists are reasonable to use in patients with recurrent ischemia without condraindications after beta blockers and nitrates have been fully used. See Hypertension chapter for more information.
ACE Inhibitors	Inhibits Angiotensin Converting Enzyme and blocks the production of Angiotensin II; prevents cardiac remodeling; ↓ preload and afterload	Oral ACE inhibitors should be administered within the first 24 hours to patients without hypotension (SBP < 100) or other contraindications. If a patient is intolerant of ACE inhibitors, it may be reasonable to give an ARB. Do not use an IV ACE inhibitor within the first 24 hours due to the risk of hypotension. See Hypertension chapter for more information.

Medications to Avoid in the Acute Setting

- NSAIDs (except for aspirin), whether nonselective or COX-2-selective agents, should not be administered during hospitalization due to ↑ risk of mortality, reinfarction, hypertension, cardiac rupture, renal insufficiency and heart failure associated with their use.

- Immediate-release form of a dihydropyridine calcium channel blocker (e.g., nifedipine) should not be used.

- Do not use IV fibrinolytic therapy unless patient has ST-segment elevation or a new left bundle branch block (which is a STEMI equivalent).

Glycoprotein IIb/IIIa Receptor Antagonists

Bind to and inhibit the platelet glycoprotein IIb/IIIa receptor, the binding site for fibrinogen, von Willebrand factor, and other ligands. Eptifibatide and tirofiban reversibly block platelet aggregation, preventing thrombosis. Abciximab irreversibly blocks platelet aggregation.

DRUG	DOSING	SAFETY/SIDE EFFECTS/MONITORING
Abciximab **(ReoPro)**	LD: 0.25 mg/kg IV bolus MD: 0.125 mcg/kg/min (max 10 mcg/min) IV infusion	**CONTRAINDICATIONS** Thrombocytopenia (platelets < 100,000/mm³) History of bleeding diathesis (predisposition) Active internal bleeding Recent (within 6 weeks) of major surgery ↑ prothrombin time History of stroke within 2 years (abciximab); History of stroke within 30 days or any history of hemorrhagic stroke (eptifibatide/tirofiban) Severe uncontrolled HTN Hypersensitivity to murine proteins (abciximab)
Eptifibatide **(Integrilin)**	LD:180 mcg/kg IV bolus (max 22.6 mg) followed 10 min later by second IV bolus of 180 mcg/kg (omit second bolus if patient not undergoing PCI) MD: 2 mcg/kg/min (max 15 mg/hour) IV infusion started after the first bolus Reduce infusion dose by 50% in patients with CrCl < 50 mL/min	**SIDE EFFECTS** Bleeding, thrombocytopenia (esp. abciximab), hypotension **MONITORING** Hgb, Hct, platelets, signs and symptoms of bleeding, SCr **NOTES** Do not shake vials upon reconstitution Must filter abciximab with administration Platelet function returns in 24-48 hours after discontinuing abciximab, 2-4 hours after stopping eptifibatide and 4-8 hours after stopping tirofiban
Tirofiban *(Aggrastat)*	UA/NSTEMI dose: 0.4 mcg/kg/min IV over 30 minutes, followed by 0.1 mcg/kg/min IV infusion PCI dose: LD: 25 mcg/kg IV bolus MD: 0.15 mcg/kg/min IV infusion Reduce infusion dose by 50% in patients with CrCl < 30 mL/min	

P2Y$_{12}$ Inhibitors

Inhibitors of platelet activation and aggregation through the binding to the P2Y$_{12}$ subunit on the ADP receptors on platelets. Clopidogrel and prasugrel are prodrugs and have irreversible binding to the receptor. Ticagrelor is not a prodrug (therefore faster onset) and has reversible binding to the receptor (therefore faster offset).

DRUG	DOSING	SAFETY/SIDE EFFECTS/MONITORING
Clopidogrel *(Plavix)*	LD: 300-600 mg (600 mg for PCI) MD: 75 mg PO daily Alternative dosing per guidelines: Give LD of 600 mg, followed by 150 mg daily for 6 days, then 75 mg daily (if not high risk for bleeding) If managed medically without stenting, no loading dose is recommended.	**BLACK BOX WARNING** Effectiveness depends on the activation to an active metabolite mainly by CYP 2C19. Poor metabolizers exhibit higher cardiovascular events than patients with normal CYP 2C19 function. Tests to check CYP 2C19 genotype can be used as an aid in determining a therapeutic strategy. Consider alternative treatment strategies in patients identified as 2C19 poor metabolizers. The CYP2C19*1 allele corresponds to fully functional metabolism while the CYP2C19*2 and *3 alleles have reduced function. **CONTRAINDICATIONS** Active pathological bleed (e.g., PUD, ICH) **SIDE EFFECTS** Bleeding, bruising, rash, TTP (rare) Thrombotic thrombocytopenic purpura (TTP) – rare but serious – have patients report fever, weakness, extreme skin paleness, purple skin patches, yellowing of the skin or eyes, or neurological changes. **MONITORING** Signs of bleeding. Hgb/Hct as necessary **NOTES** Do not start in patients likely to undergo CABG surgery and discontinue 5 days prior to any major surgery.
Prasugrel *(Effient)* Indicated for the reduction of thrombotic events in patients with ACS who are to be managed with PCI	LD: 60 mg MD: 10 mg PO daily (5 mg daily if patient < 60 kg)	**BLACK BOX WARNING (3)** Can cause significant, sometimes fatal, bleeding In patients ≥ 75 years, prasugrel is generally not recommended due to ↑ risk of fatal and intracranial bleeding and uncertain benefit, except in high risk patients (DM and prior MI). Do not start in patients likely to undergo CABG surgery and discontinue 7 days prior to any major surgery. **CONTRAINDICATIONS** Active pathological bleed; patients with a history of TIA or stroke **SIDE EFFECTS** Bleeding (more than clopidogrel), TTP (rare) **NOTES** Once PCI is planned, give the dose promptly and no later than 1 hour after the PCI

P2Y$_{12}$ Inhibitors Continued

DRUG	DOSING	SAFETY/SIDE EFFECTS/MONITORING
Ticagrelor (*Brilinta*) Indicated for reduction of thrombotic events in patients with ACS	LD: 180 mg MD: 90 mg PO BID (use with a daily aspirin dose of 75-100 mg) If managed medically without stenting, no loading dose is recommended.	**BLACK BOX WARNINGS (2)** Can cause significant, sometimes fatal, bleeding Maintenance doses of aspirin above 100 mg reduce the effectiveness of ticagrelor and should be avoided. After any initial dose, use with aspirin 75-100 mg daily. **CONTRAINDICATIONS** Active pathological bleed, history of ICH, severe hepatic impairment **SIDE EFFECTS** Bleeding, dyspnea (> 10%); ↑ SCr, ↑ uric acid, bradyarrhythmias **NOTES** Do not start in patients likely to undergo CABG surgery and discontinue 5 days prior to any major surgery.

Drug Interactions

- With all P2Y$_{12}$ inhibitors: Avoid use, if possible, with other agents that ↑ bleeding risk, including other antiplatelets (although P2Y$_{12}$ inhibitors are used with low-dose aspirin), NSAIDs, anticoagulants, SSRIs, ginkgo and others. See Drug Interactions chapter for drugs that can ↑ bleeding risk. If a patient does bleed on a P2Y$_{12}$ inhibitor, manage bleeding without discontinuing the P2Y$_{12}$ inhibitor, if possible. Stopping the P2Y$_{12}$ inhibitor (particularly within the first few months after ACS) increases the risk of subsequent cardiovascular events.

- Clopidogrel is a prodrug metabolized mainly by CYP2C19. Avoid concomitant use with strong or moderate 2C19 inhibitors (cimetidine, fluconazole, ketoconazole, voriconazole, fluoxetine, fluvoxamine and others). Avoid omeprazole and esomeprazole as these agents may reduce the effectiveness of clopidogrel due to 2C19 inhibition.

- Ticagrelor is an inhibitor of 3A4 and P-glycoprotein and major substrate of 3A4 – avoid use with strong 3A4 inhibitors and inducers. See drug interactions chapter for more information. Avoid simvastatin and lovastatin doses greater than 40 mg/d. Monitor digoxin levels with initiation of or any change in ticagrelor dose.

Treatment of ST Segment Elevation Myocardial Infarction (STEMI)

MONA + GAP-BA + PCI or fibrinolytic therapy (PCI is preferred if facilities are available).

Fibrinolytics

These agents cause fibrinolysis by binding to fibrin in a thrombus (clot) and converting entrapped plasminogen to plasmin. Most patients receive PCI without the use of fibrinolytics. Fibrinolytic use is recommended when a hospital cannot perform PCI within 90 minutes (door-to-balloon time) and should be initiated within 30 minutes from time of arrival to the hospital (door-to-needle time). The STEMI guidelines find fibrinolytic use still beneficial when given 12-24 hours out from symptom onset of STEMI.

DRUG	SAFETY/SIDE EFFECTS/MONITORING
Alteplase *(t-PA, rt-PA, Activase)*	**CONTRAINDICATIONS** Active internal bleeding or bleeding diathesis History of stroke Recent intracranial or intraspinal surgery or trauma (last 3 months) Intracranial neoplasm, arteriovenous malformation, or aneurysm Aortic dissection
Tenecteplase *(TNKase)*	Ischemic stroke within past 3 months **Relative Contraindications** Severe uncontrolled HTN (SBP > 185 mmHg or DBP > 110 mmHg) For streptokinase/anistreplase: prior exposure (past year) or prior allergic reaction to these agents; uncommonly used due to allergy risk in ACS, (and streptokinase not used for stroke due to hemorrhage risk)
Reteplase (r-PA) *(Retevase)*	Pregnancy Active peptic ulcer Current use of anticoagulants **SIDE EFFECTS** <u>Bleeding, hypotension, intracranial hemorrhage, fever</u>
Streptokinase *(Streptase)*	**MONITORING** Hgb, Hct, signs and symptoms of bleeding **NOTES** Door-to-needle time should be < 30 minutes (for thrombolytics) Door-to-balloon time should be < 90 minutes (for PCI)

Long-Term Medical Management in Patients S/P MI (Secondary Prevention)

TREATMENT	CONSIDERATIONS
Aspirin	Use indefinitely unless there is a contraindication or allergy. For patients who receive a stent and do not have an aspirin contraindication (bleeding, inherited bleeding disorders, allergy, inflammatory breathing difficulty/nasal polyps, children less than 16 years old with viral infection), use aspirin 162 mg – 325 mg daily for: ■ 1 month for bare metal stent ■ 3 months for sirolimus-eluting stent ■ 6 months for paclitaxel-eluting stent Then aspirin 81 mg daily indefinitely (use this dose if no stent placed).
P2Y$_{12}$ inhibitor	Clopidogrel 75 mg daily, prasugrel 10 mg daily, ticagrelor 90 mg BID for at least 1 month and up to 1 year if patients are not at high risk of bleeding. Continuation beyond 12 months may be considered in patients following drug eluting stent placement.
Nitroglycerin	SL tabs or spray PRN.

Long-Term Medical Management in Patients S/P MI (Secondary Prevention) Continued

TREATMENT	CONSIDERATIONS
Beta blocker	Daily for 3 years per ACC/AHA secondary prevention guidelines.
ACE inhibitor	Daily, particularly if patient has EF < 40%, HTN, CKD, or diabetes.
Statin	Use high-intensity statin therapy daily (atorvastatin 80 mg is preferred).
Warfarin (if required)	Target INR for warfarin alone: 2.5-3.5
	Target INR for warfarin + aspirin or warfarin + aspirin + $P2Y_{12}$ inhibitor: 2.0-2.5 if not at high bleeding risk.
Pain relief	Use acetaminophen, aspirin, tramadol or short-term narcotic analgesics. Non-acetylated salicylates can be used. <u>NSAIDs are not recommended in post-MI patients due to the risk of reinfarction and death.</u>
Lifestyle	Control other conditions (HTN, DM, smoking cessation)
	Physical activity (30-60 minutes/day, 5-7 days/wk)
	Dietary therapy for all patients should include reduced intake of saturated fats (< 7% of total calories), cholesterol (< 200 mg/day) and trans fat (< 1% of energy). Please note the 2013 obesity guidelines do not say to limit fat intake, but recommend weight loss to lower elevated levels of total cholesterol, LDL-cholesterol, and triglycerides, and to raise low levels of HDL-cholesterol in overweight and obese patients with dyslipidemia.

Patient Counseling for Clopidogrel

- Take this medication once daily. Clopidogrel can be taken with or without food

- Clopidogrel helps prevent platelets from sticking together and forming a clot that can block an artery.

- It is important to take this medication every day. Do not stop taking clopidogrel without talking to your healthcare provider who prescribed it for you. If you stop taking this medication, you can put yourself at risk of developing a clot which can be life-threatening.

- If you miss a dose, take as soon as you remember. If it is almost time for your next dose, skip the missed dose. Take the next dose at your regular scheduled time. Do not take 2 doses at the same time unless instructed by your doctor.

WHAT MEDICATIONS TO STOP/CONTINUE WHEN PATIENT GOES FOR CABG SURGERY

Continue
Aspirin

UFH

Discontinue
Clopidogrel and ticagrelor 5 days before elective CABG.

Prasugrel 7 days before elective CABG. More urgent surgery, if necessary, may be performed by experienced surgeons if the incremental bleeding risk is considered acceptable.

Eptifibatide/tirofiban 4 hours before CABG; 12 hours before CABG for abciximab

Enoxaparin 12-24 hours before CABG and dose with UFH

Fondaparinux 24 hours before CABG and dose with UFH

Bivalirudin 3 hours before CABG and dose with UFH

- You may bleed and bruise more easily, even from a minor scrape. It may take longer for you to stop bleeding.

- Call your healthcare provider at once if you have black or bloody stools, or if you cough up blood or vomit that looks like coffee grounds. These could be signs of bleeding in your digestive tract.

- One rare but serious side effect is thrombotic thrombocytopenic purpura (TTP). Seek prompt medical attention if you experience any of these symptoms that cannot otherwise be explained: fever, weakness, extreme skin paleness, purplish spots or skin patches (called purpura), yellowing of the skin or eyes (jaundice), or mental status changes.

- Avoid drinking alcohol while taking clopidogrel. Alcohol may increase your risk of bleeding in your stomach or intestines.

- If you need to have any type of surgery or dental work, tell the surgeon or dentist ahead of time that you are using clopidogrel. You may need to stop using the medicine for at least 5 days before having surgery, to prevent excessive bleeding.

- While you are taking clopidogrel, do not take aspirin, other NSAIDs (non-steroidal anti-inflammatory drugs) or acid-reducing medications without your healthcare provider's advice.

ANTIARRHYTHMICS

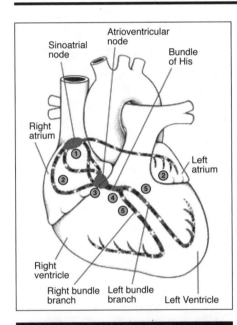

Sinoatrial node
Atrioventricular node
Bundle of His
Right atrium
Left atrium
Right ventricle
Right bundle branch
Left bundle branch
Left Ventricle

GUIDELINES

2011 ACCF/AHA/HRS Focused Update on the Management of Patients With Atrial Fibrillation (Updating the 2006 Guideline). Circulation 2011;123:104-123.

ACC/AHA/ESC 2006 Guidelines for the Management of Patients with Atrial Fibrillation – Executive Summary. Circulation 2006;114:700-752.

We gratefully acknowledge the assistance of Tien Ng, PharmD, FCCP, BCPS (AQ-C), Associate Professor at the University of Southern California School of Pharmacy, in preparing this chapter.

BACKGROUND

A normal heart beats in a regular, coordinated way because electrical impulses traveling down the cardiac conduction system trigger a sequence of organized contractions. Arrhythmias are caused by abnormalities in the formation and/or conduction of these electrical impulses. Heart rate describes the frequency of depolarization of the ventricles. Arrhythmias can result in the heart rate being slow (bradyarrhythmias) or fast (tachyarrhythmias). Normally the resting heart rate in adults is 60 to 100 beats per minute. An arrhythmia can be silent (asymptomatic) which may only detected during a routine physical exam. However, most patients experience symptoms. The common complaints of patients experiencing an arrhythmia are: palpitations (feeling like there is fluttering or racing), dizziness, lightheadedness, shortness of breath, chest pain, fatigue, and in severe cases can lead to syncope, heart failure, and death.

PATHOPHYSIOLOGY OF ARRHYTHMIAS

Activation of the heart in the normal sequence through the cardiac conduction system, and at the usual rate of 60 to 100 beats per minute, is called normal sinus rhythm (NSR). The diagram above traces the normal sequence of formation and conduction of an electrical impulse in the heart. The sinoatrial (SA) node (1) initiates an electrical impulse that spreads throughout the right and left atria (2), resulting in atrial contraction. The electrical impulse reaches the atrioventricular (AV) node (3), where its conduction is slowed. Once through the atrioventricular node, the impulse travels down the bundle of HIS (4), which divides into the right bundle branch for the right ventricle (5) and the left bundle branch for the left ventricle (5). The impulse then spreads through the ventricles via Purkinje fibers, resulting in a coordinated and rapid contraction of both ventricles. Any disruption in the normal sequence of impulse formation or conduction can result in an arrhythmia.

Many factors can contribute to the development of arrhythmias in a given patient. The most common etiology of arrhythmias is myocardial ischemia or infarction secondary to coronary artery disease. Other conditions resulting in damage to cardiac tissue, such as heart valve disorders, hypertension and heart failure, also are causes of arrhythmias. Non-cardiac conditions can also trigger or predispose to arrhythmias. Electrolyte imbalances, especially those involving <u>potassium, magnesium, sodium and calcium</u> (since these are important to cardiac electrophysiology), can result in arrhythmias. Elevated sympathetic states, such as hyperthyroidism and infection, can also contribute. <u>Drugs can cause or worsen arrhythmias; this includes the drugs used to treat arrhythmias.</u> Many drugs can affect conduction and/or prolong repolarization through effects on ion currents in the heart. Drug-induced slowing of repolarization, as indicated by prolongation of the QT interval on an electrocardiogram, can result in a particularly dangerous ventricular tachyarrhythmia called Torsade de Pointes (TdP).

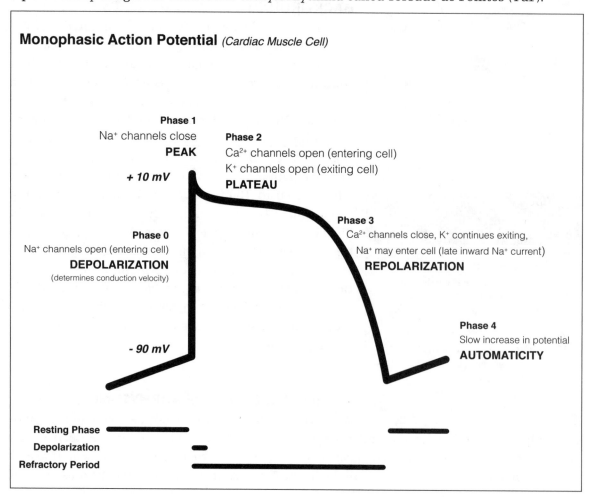

Monophasic Action Potential *(Cardiac Muscle Cell)*

Phase 1
Na+ channels close
PEAK

Phase 2
Ca²⁺ channels open (entering cell)
K+ channels open (exiting cell)
PLATEAU

+ 10 mV

Phase 3
Ca²⁺ channels close, K+ continues exiting,
Na+ may enter cell (late inward Na+ current)
REPOLARIZATION

Phase 0
Na+ channels open (entering cell)
DEPOLARIZATION
(determines conduction velocity)

Phase 4
Slow increase in potential
AUTOMATICITY

- 90 mV

Resting Phase
Depolarization
Refractory Period

CLASSIFICATION OF ARRHYTHMIAS

Arrhythmias are generally classified based on their location of origin into two broad categories: supraventricular (originating above the atrioventricular node) or ventricular (originating below the atrioventricular node). Common supraventricular tachyarrhythmias include sinus tachycardia, atrial fibrillation, atrial flutter, focal atrial tachycardias, and supraventricular re-entrant tachycardias (formerly known as paroxysmal supraventricular tachycardias or PSVTs). Common ventricular arrhythmias include premature ventricular contractions (PVCs), ventricular tachycardia and ventricular fibrillation.

Atrial fibrillation (AFib) is the most common supraventricular arrhythmia. AFib results from multiple waves of electrical impulses in the atria, resulting in an irregular and usually rapid ventricular response. The rapid ventricular rate can result in hypotension, and worsen underlying ischemia and heart failure. Due to the disorganized depolarization of the atria, coordinated atrial contraction is impaired, which increases the risk of thromboembolism and stroke. Therefore, the management of atrial fibrillation usually involves anticoagulation (see Anticoagulation chapter), and antiarrhythmics to slow the ventricular rate and/or terminate the atrial fibrillation to restore normal sinus rhythm.

Atrial flutter is caused by one or more rapid circuits in the atrium. Atrial flutter is usually more organized and regular than atrial fibrillation. This arrhythmia occurs most often with heart disease, and in the first week after heart surgery. Atrial flutter often converts to AFib.

Premature ventricular contractions (PVCs) are among the most common arrhythmias and occur in people with and without heart disease. This is a "skipped heartbeat" everyone will occasionally experience. These electrical impulses are generated from within the ventricular tissue. In some people, it can be related to stress, too much caffeine or nicotine, or too much exercise. A series of PVCs in a row resulting in a heart rate of greater than 100 beats per minute is known as ventricular tachycardia. Ventricular tachycardia is further classified based on the presence or absence of a detectable peripheral pulse. Ventricular tachycardia with a pulse is treated with certain antiarrhythmics, whereas, ventricular tachycardia without a pulse is a medical emergency. Untreated ventricular tachycardia can degenerate into ventricular fibrillation (complete disorganized electrical activation of the ventricles) which is always a medical emergency.

QT Prolongation & Torsade De Pointes (TdP)

Prolongation of the QT interval is a risk factor for Torsade de Pointes, a particularly lethal ventricular tachyarrhythmia which is most commonly associated with drugs and can result in sudden cardiac death. The QT interval is measured from the beginning of the QRS complex to the end of the T wave. It reflects ventricular depolarization and repolarization. Drug-induced QT interval prolongation is dose-dependent (concentration-dependent). Combining different drugs that can cause QT interval prolongation can have additive effects, and the benefit-risk of using multiple QT interval prolonging medications must be assessed carefully. Reduced drug clearance or drug interactions which result in increased concentrations of QT interval prolonging drugs will also accentuate the effect on the QT interval and risk for TdP. Therefore, if a patient is using low dose of amitriptyline for neuropathic pain, this may not be considered a particularly risky drug due to the low dose, although the risk may be additive with other drugs or if the elimination of the drug is impaired.

Additive QT Prolongation

The following QT interval prolonging drugs must be used with caution in patients with any arrhythmia risk (including those with any pre-existing cardiac condition or history of arrhythmia, electrolyte abnormalities or those taking other proarrhythmic drugs).

- Any pre-existing cardiac condition (or history of arrhythmia)

- <u>Class Ia and Class III antiarrhythmics</u> (amiodarone, disopyramide, dofetilide, dronedarone, ibutilide, procainamide, quinidine, sotalol), flecainide and others

- Antibiotics including <u>quinolones</u> (ciprofloxacin, levofloxacin, moxifloxacin, norfloxacin, ofloxacin, gemifloxacin, and sparfloxacin), <u>macrolides</u> (azithromycin, erythromycin, clarithromycin and telithromycin), telavancin, sulfamethoxazole/trimethoprim, amantadine, foscarnet, bedaquiline and others

- Azole antifungals (fluconazole, itraconazole, ketoconazole, posaconazole and <u>voriconazole</u>)

- Anticancer agents (arsenic, bosutinib, crizotinib, dasatinib, lapatinib, <u>nilotinib</u>, pazopanib, sorafenib, sunitinib, tamoxifen, others)

- Protease inhibitors (saquinavir, ritonavir, atazanavir) and rilpivirine

- Antidepressants including tricyclics (amitriptyline, nortriptyline, doxepin, desipramine, imipramine), SSRIs (<u>citalopram</u>, escitalopram, fluoxetine, paroxetine, sertraline) and SNRIs (venlafaxine and desvenlafaxine) and trazodone. Do not exceed 40 mg/d with citalopram, or 20 mg/d if patients are 60+ years, have liver impairment, HF, S/P MI, a 2C19 poor metabolizer, on 2C19 inhibitors, or taking QT prolonging drugs. Similar but lower risk with escitalopram at > 20 mg/d. Do not exceed 10 mg/d in elderly. If cardiac risk, avoid citalopram. Sertraline is preferred in cardiac patients.

- Antiemetic agents including the <u>5-HT$_3$-receptor antagonists</u> (dolasetron, ondansetron, granisetron, palonosetron) and droperidol and promethazine

- <u>Antipsychotics</u> (chlorpromazine, <u>thioridazine</u>, pimozide, haloperidol, ziprasidone, risperidone, paliperidone, iloperidone, quetiapine, clozapine and asenapine)

- Other agents: alfuzosin, solifenacin, ranolazine, quinine, apomorphine, chloroquine, galantamine, <u>methadone</u>, pentamidine, others

PHARMACOLOGIC TREATMENT

Antiarrhythmic drugs are used for two main purposes in the treatment of cardiac arrhythmias. Some antiarrhythmic drugs are used to terminate the arrhythmia and restore and maintain normal sinus rhythm (class I and III antiarrhythmics). Other agents are used to slow the ventricular rate during a supraventricular arrhythmia (class II and IV antiarrhythmics, digoxin).

Antiarrhythmics work by affecting the electrical conduction in the heart. By blocking the movement of ions in different phases of the cardiac action potential (see figure), select drugs can reduce conduction velocity and/or automaticity, or prolong the refractory period which can slow or terminate abnormal electrical activity which results in arrhythmias. They can also occasionally worsen the existing arrhythmia or cause other arrhythmias. All patients should be instructed to be seen if they suspect they have "worse heartbeat problems" or have an increase in their symptoms. <u>Prior to starting any medication for a non-life-threatening arrhythmia, be sure to always check the patient's electrolytes and run a toxicology screen.</u>

Vaughan Williams Classification of Antiarrhythmics

The Vaughan Williams classification system is the most commonly used classification system for antiarrhythmic drugs. Here the drugs are split into categories based on their dominant electro-physiologic effect. It has the virtue of simplicity, although many drugs overlap into more than one category.

CLASS	DRUGS
Ia	Quinidine, Procainamide, Disopyramide
Ib	Lidocaine, Mexiletine, (Phenytoin)
Ic	Flecainide, Propafenone
II	Beta-blockers (e.g., esmolol, propranolol)
III	Amiodarone, Dofetilide, Dronedarone, Ibutilide, Sotalol
IV	Verapamil, Diltiazem

CLASS I ANTIARRHYTHMICS

Class I antiarrhythmics are sodium channel blockers. They are further sub-classified based on the duration of time they bind to the sodium channel. Class Ia drugs are intermediate sodium channel blockers and they also block the potassium channels. Class Ib drugs are fast sodium channel blockers. Class Ic are long sodium channel blockers.

The Cardiac Arrhythmia Suppression Trial (CAST) was a negative study in which patients with premature ventricular contractions (PVCs) after a MI randomized to flecainide or ecainide resulted in an increase in mortality compared to patients randomized to placebo. This led to a black box warning on many of the Class I antiarrhythmics, particularly the Class Ic agents.

Class Ia Antiarrhythmics

Class Ia antiarrhythmics block both sodium channels and potassium channels. Quinidine and disopyramide also have strong anticholinergic effects. Procainamide is metabolized by acetylation to N-acetyl-procainamide. Class Ia antiarrhythmic drugs ↓ conduction velocity, ↑ refractory period, and ↓ automaticity.

DRUG	DOSING	SAFETY/SIDE EFFECTS/MONITORING
QuiNIDine Injection, oral	IR: 200-400 mg PO Q6H ER: 300-324 mg PO Q8-12H Take with food or milk to ↓ GI upset	**BLACK BOX WARNING** Quinidine may ↑ mortality in treatment of AFib or flutter; control AV conduction before initiating. Antiarrhythmic drugs have not been shown to enhance survival in non-life-threatening ventricular arrhythmias and may increase mortality; the risk is greatest in patients with structural heart disease. **CONTRAINDICATIONS** Concurrent use of quinolones that prolong the QT interval, amprenavir, ritonavir; 2nd/3rd degree heart block or idioventricular conduction delays (unless patient has a functional artificial pacemaker), thrombocytopenia, thrombocytopenic purpura **SIDE EFFECTS** Diarrhea (35%), stomach cramping (22%), QT prolongation, nausea, vomiting, anorexia, lightheadedness, cinchonism (tinnitus, hearing loss, blurred vision, headache, delirium), thrombocytopenia, pruritus, rash **MONITORING** ECG (QT interval, QRS duration), electrolytes, BP, CBC, LFTs, renal **NOTES** Different salt forms are not interchangeable (267 mg of gluconate = 200 mg of sulfate form) Avoid changes in Na+ intake. ↓ Na+ intake can ↑ quinidine levels Alkaline foods may ↑ quinidine levels
Procainamide Injection	Has active metabolite, N-acetyl procainamide (NAPA) which is renally cleared Therapeutic levels: Procainamide: 4-10 mcg/mL NAPA: 15-25 mcg/mL Combined: 10-30 mcg/mL Draw levels 6-12 hours after IV infusion has started	**BLACK BOX WARNINGS (3)** Potentially fatal blood dyscrasias (e.g., agranulocytosis) → monitor patient closely in the first 3 months of therapy and periodically thereafter. Long-term use leads to positive antibody (ANA) test in 50% of patients which may result in drug-induced lupus erythematosus-like syndrome (in 20-30% of patients) In the Cardiac Arrhythmia Suppression Trial (CAST), recent (> 6 days but < 2 years ago) myocardial infarction patients with asymptomatic, non-life-threatening ventricular arrhythmias did not benefit and may have been harmed by attempts to suppress the arrhythmia with flecainide or encainide. **CONTRAINDICATIONS** 2nd/3rd degree heart block (unless patient has a functional artificial pacemaker), SLE, torsade de pointes, procaine or other ester-type local anesthetics **SIDE EFFECTS** Hypotension, rash, lupus-like syndrome, QT prolongation, agranulocytosis **MONITORING** ECG (QT interval, QRS duration), electrolytes, BP, renal function, signs of lupus (butterfly rash, stabbing chest pain, joint pain), procainamide and NAPA levels, CBC

Class Ia Antiarrhythmic Agents Continued

DRUG	DOSING	SAFETY/SIDE EFFECTS/MONITORING
Disopyramide (*Norpace*, Norpace CR)	IR: 150 mg PO Q6H CR: 300 mg PO Q12H CrCl ≤ 40 mL/min: Decrease frequency of IR and do not use CR formulation Take on an empty stomach	**BLACK BOX WARNING** In the Cardiac Arrhythmia Suppression Trial (CAST), recent (> 6 days but < 2 years ago) myocardial infarction patients with asymptomatic, non-life-threatening ventricular arrhythmias did not benefit and may have been harmed by attempts to suppress the arrhythmia with flecainide or encainide. **CONTRAINDICATIONS** 2nd/3rd degree heart block (unless patient has a functional artificial pacemaker), cardiogenic shock, congenital QT syndrome, sick sinus syndrome, BPH/urinary retention/narrow-angle glaucoma, myasthenia gravis (due to anticholinergic effects) **SIDE EFFECTS** Anticholinergic effects (xerostomia, constipation, urinary retention > 10%), hypotension, QT prolongation, HF exacerbation and others **MONITORING** ECG (QT interval, QRS duration), electrolytes, BP, signs of heart failure **NOTES** Anticholinergics worsen myasthenia gravis.

Class IA Antiarrhythmic Drug Interactions

- Quinidine is a substrate of 3A4 (major), 2C9 (minor) and P-glycoprotein; inhibits 2D6 (strong), 2C9 (weak), 3A4 (weak) and P-glycoprotein. Avoid concurrent use with alfuzosin, azole antifungals, dronedarone, eplerenone, grapefruit juice, PIs, pimozide, nilotinib, ranolazine, salmeterol, silodosin, tamoxifen, inducers (phenytoin, phenobarbital), others. Some major drug interactions with quinidine include digoxin (↓ digoxin dose by 50%), warfarin (↑ INR), verapamil, diltiazem, erythromycin and others.

- Procainamide is a substrate of 2D6 (major). Moderate and strong 2D6 inhibitors will ↑ levels of procainamide.

- Disopyramide is a substrate of 3A4 (major). Inhibitors of 3A4 and anticholinergics may ↑ risk of side effects. 3A4 inducers may ↓ the effects of disopyramide.

- All Class Ia antiarrhythmic agents can have additive QT prolongation with other agents that also prolong the QT interval.

Class Ib Antiarrhythmics

Class Ib antiarrhythmics are pure sodium channel blockers. They are only useful for ventricular arrhythmias (no efficacy for supraventricular arrhythmias such as atrial fibrillation). They can all cross the blood-brain-barrier and, therefore, can cause CNS adverse effects. Class Ib antiarrhythmic drugs have little effect on conduction velocity at normal heart rates but will have greater effects on ↓ conduction at higher heart rates, little effect on ↓ refractory period, and ↓ automaticity.

DRUG	DOSING	SAFETY/SIDE EFFECTS/MONITORING
Lidocaine *(Xylocaine)* Injection	1-1.5 mg/kg IV bolus; can repeat bolus 0.5-0.75 mg/kg up to 3 mg/kg (cumulative dose); followed by 1-4 mg/min IV infusion. Reduce dose in patients with HF or hepatic dysfunction Can be given via endotracheal tube (need higher dose – 2-2.5x the IV dose)	**CONTRAINDICATIONS** 2nd/3rd degree heart block (unless patient has a functional artificial pacemaker), Wolff-Parkinson-White syndrome, Adam-Stokes syndrome, allergy to corn or corn-related products or amide type anesthetic **SIDE EFFECTS** Lightheadedness, dizziness, incoordination, nausea, vomiting, tremor, CNS (hallucinations, disorientation, confusion)
Mexiletine	200 mg PO Q8H; max 1.2 g/d Take with food. Reduce dose in hepatic impairment.	**MONITORING** ECG, BP, LFTs **NOTES** Caution in patients with severe hepatic dysfunction, elderly

Class IB Antiarrhythmic Drug Interactions

■ Lidocaine is a substrate of 3A4 (major), 1A2 (major), and 2C9 (minor); inhibits 1A2 (weak). Amiodarone, beta-blockers, 3A4 inhibitors (e.g., diltiazem, verapamil, grapefruit juice, erythromycin, clarithromycin, itraconazole, ketoconazole, PIs, etc.) may ↑ lidocaine levels.

■ Mexiletine is a substrate of 1A2 (major) and 2D6 (major); inhibits 1A2 (strong).

Class Ic Antiarrhythmics

Class Ic antiarrhythmic agents are sodium channel blockers. Propafenone also has significant beta-adrenergic receptor blocking effects. These drugs are absolutely contraindicated in patients with heart failure or have just experienced an acute myocardial infarction. Class Ic antiarrhythmic drugs significantly ↓ conduction velocity, have little effect on refractory period, and ↓ automaticity.

DRUG	DOSING	SAFETY/SIDE EFFECTS/MONITORING
Flecainide	100 mg PO Q12H; max 400 mg/d CrCl ≤ 50 mL/min: ↓ dose by 50%	**BLACK BOX WARNINGS (3)** When treating atrial flutter, 1:1 atrioventricular conduction may occur; pre-emptive negative chronotropic therapy (e.g., digoxin, beta-blockers) may lower the risk. Pro-arrhythmic effects – not recommended for patients with chronic atrial fibrillation. In the Cardiac Arrhythmia Suppression Trial (CAST), recent (> 6 days but < 2 years ago) myocardial infarction patients with asymptomatic, non-life-threatening ventricular arrhythmias did not benefit and may have been harmed by attempts to suppress the arrhythmia with flecainide or encainide. Do not use in patients with structural heart disease (HF, S/P MI) **CONTRAINDICATIONS** 2nd/3rd degree heart block (unless patient has a functional artificial pacemaker), cardiogenic shock, coronary artery disease (heart failure, myocardial infarction), concurrent use of amprenavir or ritonavir **SIDE EFFECTS** Dizziness, visual disturbances, headache, dyspnea, proarrhythmic **MONITORING** ECG, BP, HR, electrolytes
Propafenone *(Rythmol, Rythmol SR)*	IR: 150-300 mg PO Q8H SR: 225-425 mg PO Q12H	**BLACK BOX WARNING** In the Cardiac Arrhythmia Suppression Trial (CAST), recent (> 6 days but < 2 years ago) myocardial infarction patients with asymptomatic, non-life-threatening ventricular arrhythmias did not benefit and may have been harmed by attempts to suppress the arrhythmia with flecainide or encainide. Do not use in patients with structural heart disease (HF, S/P MI). **CONTRAINDICATIONS** 2nd/3rd degree heart block (unless patient has a functional artificial pacemaker), sinus bradycardia, cardiogenic shock, hypotension, coronary artery disease (heart failure, myocardial infarction), bronchospastic disorders, concurrent use of ritonavir **SIDE EFFECTS** Taste disturbance (metallic), nausea, vomiting, new or worsening arrhythmia, dyspnea, dizziness, bronchospasm, worsening HF **MONITORING** ECG, BP, HR, electrolytes

Class IC Antiarrhythmics Drug Interactions

- Flecainide is a substrate of 2D6 (major) and 1A2 (minor); inhibits 2D6 (weak).

- Propafenone is a substrate of 2D6 (major), 3A4 (minor) and 1A2 (minor); inhibits 1A2 and 2D6 (weak).

Class II Antiarrhythmic Agents

Class II antiarrhythmic drugs block beta receptors and indirectly block calcium channels in the SA and AV nodes, resulting in decreased automaticity and conduction velocity in the nodes. These drugs are used to slow the ventricular rate in supraventricular tachyarrhythmias.

DRUG	DOSING	SAFETY/SIDE EFFECTS/MONITORING
Esmolol *(Brevibloc)* Injection Beta-1 selective	0.5–1 mg/kg–followed by 50-150 mcg/kg/min; max 300 mcg/kg/min	**CONTRAINDICATIONS** 2nd/3rd degree heart block (unless patient has a functional artificial pacemaker), sinus bradycardia, sick sinus syndrome, cardiogenic shock, decompensated heart failure, severe hyperactive airway disease (asthma or COPD with propranolol) **SIDE EFFECTS** Hypotension, bradycardia, hyperkalemia, hypo- and hyperglycemia **MONITORING** ECG, BP, HR, electrolytes **NOTES** Esmolol is a vesicant; monitor IV site
Propranolol *(Inderal LA, InnoPran XL)* Injection, oral Non-selective beta-blocker	Dose varies Oral: 10-30 mg Q6-8H IV: 1-3 mg slow IVP (5 mg max initially)	

For drug interactions/counseling of beta-blockers, refer to the Hypertension chapter.

Class III Antiarrhythmic Agents

Class III antiarrhythmic drugs block mainly K+ channels resulting in a significant ↑ in refractory period. Ibutilide is the exception, and works by activating the late inward sodium current which results in a significant ↑ in refractory period. Amiodarone and dronedarone also block alpha- and beta-adrenergic receptors, and calcium and sodium channels. Sotalol also has significant beta-adrenergic receptor blocking activity.

DRUG	DOSING	SAFETY/SIDE EFFECTS/MONITORING
Amiodarone *(Cordarone, Pacerone, Nexterone)* Injection, oral	**IV dosing** Pulseless VT/VF = 300 mg IV push x 1, may repeat 150 mg x 1 if needed VT with pulse = 150 mg IV bolus, 1 mg/min x 6 hours, then 0.5 mg/min x 18 hours or longer **Atrial fibrillation** 1.2-1.8 g/d for a 10 gram loading dose, followed by 200-400 mg/d **Ventricular arrhythmias** 800-1,600 mg/d x 1-3 weeks, then 600-800 mg/d x 4 weeks, then 400 mg/d Mean daily doses > 2.1 g/day are associated with hypotension	**BLACK BOX WARNINGS (4)** Only for life-threatening arrhythmias due to toxicity; patients should be hospitalized when therapy is initiated Pulmonary toxicity may occur without symptoms Liver toxicity Proarrhythmic: exacerbation of arrhythmias making them more difficult to tolerate or reverse **CONTRAINDICATIONS** Severe sinus-node dysfunction, 2nd/3rd degree heart block (unless patient has a functional artificial pacemaker), bradycardia causing syncope, cardiogenic shock, hypersensitivity to iodine **SIDE EFFECTS** Hypotension (IV), GI upset, hypothyroidism/hyperthyroidism (more hypo), dizziness, bradycardia, peripheral neuropathy/paresthesias, ataxia, tremor, corneal microdeposits, optic neuritis, pulmonary fibrosis, photosensitivity, ↑ LFTs, slate blue (blue-grayish) skin discoloration **MONITORING** Pulmonary (including chest X-ray), thyroid, and liver function tests at baseline and periodically thereafter; ECG, BP, HR, electrolytes, regular ophthalmic exams, during infusion monitor hypotension/ bradycardia **NOTES** Pregnancy Category D Infusions longer than 2 hours must be administered in a non-polyvinyl chloride (PVC) container such as polyolefin or glass. Use a 0.22 micron filter, incompatible with heparin (flush with saline). Recommended to be added to D5W. Administer IV according to protocol. Premixed IV bag advantages: longer stability, PVC bag not an issue (both fine with PVC tubing), available in most commonly used concentrations. If hypotension occurs, can slow rate or discontinue. t½ = 40-60 days. Recommended as a drug of choice in patients with concomitant heart failure. MedGuide required.

Class III Antiarrhythmic Agents Continued

DRUG	DOSING	SAFETY/SIDE EFFECTS/MONITORING
Dronedarone *(Multaq)*	400 mg PO BID with meals t½ = 13-19 hrs (less lipophilic than amiodarone)	**BLACK BOX WARNINGS (2)** HF (Class IV or any class with a recent hospitalization) and in patients with permanent AFib. **CONTRAINDICATIONS** 2nd/3rd degree heart block (unless patient has a functional artificial pacemaker), symptomatic heart failure, HR < 50, concomitant use of strong 3A4 inhibitors, concomitant use of drugs that prolong the QT interval, QTc ≥ 500 msec, PR interval > 280 msec, lung or liver toxicity related to previous amiodarone use, severe hepatic impairment, pregnancy, nursing mothers **WARNINGS** Hepatic failure (esp. in the first 6 months), lung toxicity (pneumonitis, pulmonary fibrosis) **SIDE EFFECTS** QT prolongation, bradycardia, ↑ SCr (and possibly BUN), diarrhea, nausea, hypokalemia, hypomagnesemia **MONITORING** LFTs (especially in the first 6 months), ECG, K+, Mg2+, SCr, BUN, HR, ECG **NOTES** Pregnancy Category X Only used in patients who can be converted to normal sinus rhythm MedGuide required
Sotalol *(Betapace, Betapace AF, Sorine)* Injection, oral	80 mg PO BID; can increase to 160 mg PO BID (monitor QT interval and renal function closely) CrCl ≤ 60 mL/min: ↓ frequency Non-selective beta-blocker	**BLACK BOX WARNINGS (4)** Initiation (or reinitiation) and dosage increase should be done in a hospital with continuous monitoring and staff familiar with recognizing and treating life-threatening arrhythmias Adjust dosing interval based on creatinine clearance to decrease risk of proarrhythmia, QT prolongation is directly related to sotalol concentration Sotalol injection can cause life-threatening ventricular tachycardia and QT prolongation *Betapace* should not be substituted with *Betapace AF* since *Betapace AF* is distributed with educational information specifically for patients with AFib/Atrial flutter. **CONTRAINDICATIONS** 2nd/3rd degree heart block (unless patient has a functional artificial pacemaker), congenital or acquired long QT syndrome, sinus bradycardia, uncontrolled HF, cardiogenic shock, asthma For *Betapace AF* and injectable: QTc > 450 msec, CrCl < 40 mL/min, K+ < 4 mEq/L, sick sinus syndrome **SIDE EFFECTS** Bradycardia, dizziness, lightheadedness, fatigue, dyspnea, hypotension, chest pain, palpitation, weakness, nausea/vomiting, torsades, HF, bronchoconstriction **MONITORING** ECG, K+, Mg2+, HR, BP, SCr, BUN

Class III Antiarrhythmic Agents Continued

DRUG	DOSING	SAFETY/SIDE EFFECTS/MONITORING
Ibutilide *(Corvert)* Injection	1 mg IV over 10 min, may repeat x 1 (after 10 minutes)	**BLACK BOX WARNINGS (2)** Potentially fatal arrhythmias can occur Patients with chronic AFib may not be the best candidates since they often revert back **SIDE EFFECTS** Ventricular tachycardias (e.g., torsades), hypotension, increased QT interval
Dofetilide *(Tikosyn)*	500 mcg PO BID if CrCl > 60 mL/min; reduce dose in renal impairment and/or if QT interval increases REMS program – available to prescribers and hospitals through *Tikosyn* Education Program. This program provides comprehensive education about the importance of in-hospital treatment initiation and individualized dosing. T.I.P.S. *(Tikosyn* In Pharmacy System) – designated to allow retail pharmacies to stock and dispense *Tikosyn*; must be enrolled and staff must be educated. Pharmacists must verify that the hospital/prescriber is a confirmed participant before drug is dispensed.	**BLACK BOX WARNING** Must be initiated (or reinitiated) in a setting with continuous ECG monitoring for a minimum of 3 days or 12 hrs after cardioversion, whichever is greater **CONTRAINDICATIONS** Concurrent use of HCTZ, itraconazole, ketoconazole, megestrol, prochlorperazine, trimethoprim, verapamil; HR < 50, CrCl < 20 mL/min, QTc > 440 msec, hypokalemia, hypomagnesemia **SIDE EFFECTS** Headache, dizziness, ventricular tachycardias (e.g., torsades), increased QT interval **MONITORING** ECG, renal function, K+, Mg2+, HR, BP in the first few days. Then monitor QTc interval and CrCl every 3 months (discontinue if QTc > 500 msec) **NOTES** MedGuide required

Class III Antiarrhythmic Drug Interactions

- Avoid co-administration of drugs that prolong the QT interval (e.g., tricyclic antidepressants, fluoroquinolones, macrolides, azoles antifungals and other antiarrhythmics) due to risk of torsade de pointes.

- All Class III antiarrhythmic agents can have additive QT prolongation with other agents that also prolong the QT interval.

- Use extreme caution with other negative chronotropes (e.g., beta-blockers, verapamil, diltiazem) which can ↑ risk of bradycardia with sotalol, amiodarone, and dronederone.

- Electrolyte abnormalities (K⁺, Na⁺, Ca²⁺, Mg²⁺, etc.) should be corrected before any antiarrhythmic therapy is initiated or the risk of arrhythmia is increased (true for all antiarrhythmics).

- Do not use grapefruit juice/products.

- Avoid ephedra and St. John's wort (P-glycoprotein inducer).

Amiodarone Drug Interactions

- Amiodarone is a moderate inhibitor of 2C9, 2D6, 3A4 and P-glycoprotein; major substrate of 3A4 and 2C8 and P-glycoprotein. Strong/moderate inhibitors of 3A4, 2C8/9 and P-gp will increase the levels of amiodarone and strong/moderate inducers of 3A4, 2C8/9 and P-gp will decrease the levels of amiodarone.

- Avoid many medications while taking amiodarone such as any major QT prolonging medications, azole antifungals, macrolides, conivaptan, tolvaptan, fingolimod, grapefruit juice, PIs, silodosin, and others.

- When starting amiodarone, ↓ dose of digoxin by 50% and ↓ dose of warfarin by 30-50%. Use lower doses of simvastatin, lovastatin and atorvastatin.

Dronedarone Drug Interactions

- Dronedarone is a moderate inhibitor of 2D6, 3A4, and P-glycoprotein; major substrate of 3A4. Avoid use with strong inhibitors and inducers of 3A4 and other other drugs that can prolong the QT interval. If using digoxin, reduce dose of digoxin by 50%. Caution with the use of statins at higher doses (see above under amiodarone).

- Monitor INR after initiating dronedarone in patients taking warfarin.

Dofetilide Drug Interactions

- Dofetilide is a minor 3A4 substrate. Avoid concomitant use with many medications including azole antifungals, fingolimod, hydrochlorothiazide, itraconazole, ketoconazole, megestrol, prochlorperazine, trimethoprim, verapamil, others. Avoid with other QT prolonging agents.

Class IV Antiarrhythmic Agents

Class IV antiarrhythmic drugs block L-type calcium channels, slowing SA and AV nodal conduction velocity. These drugs are used to slow the ventricular rate in supraventricular tachyarrhythmias.

DRUG	DOSING	SAFETY/SIDE EFFECTS/MONITORING
Diltiazem *(Cardizem, Cardizem CD, Cardizem LA, Diltzac, Dilacor XR, Dilt-CD, Dilt-XR, Cartia XT, Tiazac, Taztia XT)* Injection, oral	Oral: 120-480 or 540 mg/day depending on the max dose of the product	**CONTRAINDICATIONS** 2nd/3rd degree heart block, sick sinus syndrome, severe hypotension (systolic < 90 mmHg), cardiogenic shock, acute MI and pulmonary congestion **SIDE EFFECTS** Edema, headache, AV block, bradycardia, hypotension, arrhythmias, HF, constipation (more with verapamil), gingival hyperplasia **MONITORING** ECG, BP, HR, electrolytes **NOTES** Only non-dihydropyridine CCBs are used as antiarrhythmics May be preferred over beta-blockers if co-existing asthma/ COPD
Verapamil *(Calan, Calan SR, Verelan, Verelan PM, Covera HS)* Injection, oral	Oral: 240-480 mg/day	

For drug interactions/counseling of calcium channel blockers, please see Hypertension chapter.

Agents Not Included In Vaughan Williams Classification

- Adenosine slows conduction through the AV node via activation of adenosine-1 receptors. Adenosine is used to restore normal sinus rhythm (NSR) in supraventricular re-entrant tachyarrhythmias.

- Digoxin causes direct AV node suppression, ↑ refractory period and ↓ conduction velocity. Digoxin enhances vagal tone, resulting in decreased ventricular rate in atrial tachyarrhythmias.

DRUG	DOSING	SAFETY/SIDE EFFECTS/MONITORING
Adenosine *(Adenocard)* Injection	Used in paroxysmal supraventricular tachycardia (PSVTs) and not for converting AFib/Atrial flutter or ventricular tachycardia 6 mg IV push (may increase to 12 mg if not responding) t½: less than 10 sec	**SIDE EFFECTS** Transient new arrhythmia, facial flushing, headache, chest pain/pressure, neck discomfort, dizziness, GI distress, transient decrease in blood pressure, dyspnea
Digoxin *(Lanoxin)* Injection, oral (tablet, solution)	0.125-0.25 mg daily (or less) Loading dose [called total digitalizing dose (TDD)] is 1.0-1.5 mg. Give ½ of the TDD as the initial dose, followed by ¼ of the TDD in 2 subsequent doses at 6-8 hour intervals. Therapeutic range for AFib = 0.8 – 2 ng/mL (lower therapeutic range in heart failure) Watch for renal impairment ↓ dose when CrCL < 50 mL/min; can be given 0.125 mg every other day or less frequently ↓ 20-25% when going from oral tabs to IV Antidote: *DigiFab*	**CONTRAINDICATIONS** 2nd or 3rd degree heart block without a pacemaker, Wolff-Parkinson-White syndrome (WPW) with A Fib **SIDE EFFECTS** Dizziness, headache, diarrhea, nausea, vomiting, anorexia, mental changes **MONITORING** HR, BP, electrolytes (K^+, Ca^{2+}, Mg^{2+}), renal function. ECG and drug level (if suspect toxicity) **Toxicity** First signs of toxicity are nausea/vomiting, loss of appetite and bradycardia. Other signs of toxicity include blurred/double vision, altered color perception, greenish-yellow halos around lights or objects, abdominal pain, confusion, delirium, arrhythmia (prolonged PR interval, accelerated junctional rhythm, bidirectional ventricular tachycardia). **NOTES** Pregnancy Category C Digoxin is not given alone; used in combination with a beta-blockers or CCB.

Digoxin Drug-Drug and Drug-Disease Interactions

- Use caution when administering other drugs that slow HR (such as beta-blockers); see Drug Interactions chapter.

- Digoxin is mostly renally cleared and partially cleared hepatically. Decreased renal function requires a ↓ digoxin dose. In acute renal failure, digoxin is held.

- Digoxin is a P-glycoprotein and 3A4 substrate. Digoxin levels ↑ with amiodarone, dronedarone, quinidine, verapamil, erythromycin, clarithromycin, itraconazole, cyclosporine, propafenone, and many other drugs. Reduce digoxin dose by 50% if patient is on amiodarone.

- Digoxin levels may ↓ with bile acid resins (check separation times), St. John's wort and others.

- Hypokalemia (K^+ < 3.5 mEq/L), hypomagnesemia, and hypercalcemia ↑ risk of digoxin toxicity.

- Hypothyroidism can ↑ digoxin levels.

Amiodarone Patient Counseling

- Dispense Medication Guide.

- This medication is used to treat certain types of serious (possibly fatal) irregular heart-beat problems called arrhythmias. It is used to restore the normal heart rhythm and maintain a regular, steady heartbeat. Amiodarone works by blocking certain electrical signals in the heart that can cause an irregular heartbeat. This medication has not been shown to help people with these arrhythmias live longer.

- Take this medication by mouth, usually once or twice daily or as directed by your doctor. You may take this medication with or without food, but it is important to choose one way and take the same way with every dose.

- Severe (sometimes fatal) lung or liver problems have infrequently occurred in patients using this drug. Tell your doctor immediately if you experience any of these serious side effects: cough, fever, chills, chest pain, difficult or painful breathing, coughing up blood, severe stomach pain, fatigue, yellowing eyes or skin, or dark urine, and new shortness of breath.

- Like other medications used to treat irregular heartbeats, amiodarone can infrequently cause them to become worse. Seek immediate medical attention if your heart continues to pound or skips a beat.

- This drug may infrequently cause serious vision changes. Tell your doctor immediately if you develop any vision changes (such as seeing halos or blurred vision). You will need to have your eyes checked before and during the time you are taking amiodarone. You will also need to have your blood checked, and possibly a chest X-ray during treatment.

- You may develop "pins and needles" or numbness in your legs, hands and feet, or muscle weakness, or trouble walking. Discuss with your healthcare provider if this happens.

- This drug can change how your thyroid gland works, and may cause your metabolism to speed up or slow down. Tell your doctor if you develop any symptoms of low or overactive thyroid including cold or heat intolerance, unexplained weight loss/gain, thinning hair, unusual sweating, nervousness, irritability, or restlessness. Please discuss this with your doctor and tests can be ordered to check your thyroid function.

- This drug may cause your skin to be more sensitive to the sun. Stay out of the sun during the mid-day and use protective clothing and broad spectrum sunscreen (see Skin chapter) .Infrequently, this medication has caused the skin to become a blue-gray color. This effect is not harmful and usually goes away after the drug is stopped.

- Do not consume grapefruit or drink grapefruit juice while using this medication. Grape-fruit juice can increase the amount of medication in your blood.

- This drug can interact with other medicines. Before starting a new medicine, discuss with your pharmacist if it is safe to use with amiodarone.

- If you miss a dose, do not take a double dose to make up for the dose you missed. Continue with your next regularly scheduled dose.

Digoxin Patient Counseling

- This medicine helps make the heart beat with a more regular rhythm. Keep taking as directed, even if you feel well.

- Do not stop taking this medicine without talking to your doctor. Stopping suddenly may make your condition worse.

- Avoid becoming overheated or dehydrated as an overdose can more easily occur if you are dehydrated.

- Symptoms of overdose may include nausea, vomiting, diarrhea, loss of appetite, vision changes (such as blurred or yellow/green vision), uneven heartbeats, and feeling like you might pass out. If any of these occur, see a doctor right away.

- There are many medications that can interact with digoxin. Check with your physician or pharmacist before starting any new medicines, including over the counter, vitamin, and/or herbal products.

- To be sure that this medication is not causing harmful effects, your blood may need to be tested on a regular basis. Your kidney function will also need to be monitored.

PRACTICE CASE

Arnie is a 57 year-old male who comes into your pharmacy with a new prescription for amiodarone 200 mg PO daily. He tells you that he went to the doctor because his heart felt like it was racing and he was feeling dizzy. The doctor told him he has atrial fibrillation. He is concerned that this will affect his life span.

CATEGORY	
PMH	Smoker
	HF – NYHA Class 3
	HTN – Stage 2
Current medications	Digoxin 0.25 mg PO daily
	Lasix 40 mg PO daily
	Spironolactone 12.5 mg PO daily
	Coreg CR 20 mg PO daily
	Lisinopril 40 mg PO daily
Labs	K$^+$ = 5.2 mEq/L
	SCr = 1.4 mg/dL
	BUN = 43 mg/dL

Questions

1. Before the prescription for amiodarone is filled, the pharmacist should call the doctor to decrease the dose of which of Arnie's medications?

    a. Digoxin
    b. Lasix
    c. Spironolactone
    d. Coreg CR
    e. Lisinopril

2. When counseling Arnie on the use of amiodarone, he should be told to expect periodic monitoring of these organ systems:

    a. Liver, kidney, and eyes
    b. Liver, colon, and kidney
    c. Kidney, gall bladder, and CNS
    d. Thyroid, kidney, and liver
    e. Thyroid, liver, and lungs

3. Which of the following are side effects of amiodarone? (Select **ALL** that apply.)

    a. Skin discoloration
    b. Corneal deposits
    c. Lung damage
    d. Taste perversions
    e. Hypothyroidism

4. Arnie develops thyroid dysfunction. His doctor switches him to Multaq to try and alleviate the problem. Choose the correct therapeutic equivalent for Multaq:

    a. Mexiletine
    b. Flecainide
    c. Lidocaine
    d. Dronedarone
    e. Dofetilide

Questions 5-10 do not apply to the above case.

5.   A patient is beginning digoxin 0.125 mg daily. The patient has mild renal insufficiency. After a few weeks, the patient develops an infection with nausea and vomiting. She is weak and dehydrated. The patient is admitted to the hospital to treat the infection and to check for digoxin toxicity. Choose the correct statement:

   a. The digoxin may have become toxic due to decreased renal function.

   b. An elevated digoxin level can worsen nausea and vomiting.

   c. Mental confusion may be due to an elevated digoxin level.

   d. A and B.

   e. All of the above.

6.   A patient was using furosemide 40 mg twice daily (at 8 am and 12 noon) for heart failure. The doctor forgot to call in a prescription for potassium when he called the pharmacy to order the furosemide. The patient's other medications include carvedilol, digoxin and aspirin. What clinical scenario would be most likely to occur?

   a. Digoxin toxicity

   b. Carvedilol toxicity

   c. Aspirin toxicity

   d. Furosemide toxicity

   e. Spiked T waves on ECG

7.   What class of antiarrhythmic is disopyramide in the Vaughan Williams classification system?

   a. IA

   b. IB

   c. IC

   d. III

   e. IV

8.   A patient has a long QT interval. She is at risk for fatal arrhythmias. Which of the following medications will increase her risk of further QT prolongation? (Select **ALL** that apply.)

   a. Quinidine

   b. Ketorolac

   c. Docusate

   d. Amiodarone

   e. Sotalol

9.   A patient is slightly bradycardic. The physician does not wish to further lower the heart rate. Choose the agent that will least likely cause the patient's heart rate to drop any lower:

   a. Verapamil

   b. Sotalol

   c. Digoxin

   d. Amlodipine

   e. Diltiazem

10. A patient is using digoxin. The doctor must make sure that the potassium level stays within a safe range. This safe range is defined as:

   a. 0.8-2 ng/mL

   b. 2.5-5 ng/dL

   c. 3.5-5 mEq/L

   d. 3.5-5 mEq/mL

   e. 7.8-10 mEq/mL

Answers

1-a, 2-e, 3-a,b,c,e, 4-d, 5-e, 6-a, 7-a, 8-a,d,e, 9-d, 10-c

PULMONARY ARTERIAL HYPERTENSION (PAH)

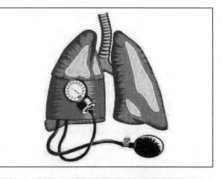

We gratefully acknowledge the assistance of Heather R. Bream-Rouwenhorst, PharmD, BCPS, Clinical Assistant Professor, University of Iowa College of Pharmacy, in preparing this chapter.

GUIDELINE

ACCF/AHA 2009 Expert Consensus Document on Pulmonary Hypertension. J Am Coll Cardiol. 2009;53:1573-1619.

CLINICAL CLASSIFICATION OF PULMONARY HYPERTENSION

1. Pulmonary arterial hypertension (PAH)

Includes idiopathic PAH, heritable, drug and toxin induced, PAH associated with connective tissue diseases, HIV infection, portal hypertension, and persistent pulmonary hypertension of a newborn

2. Pulmonary hypertension owing to left heart disease

3. Pulmonary hypertension owing to lung diseases and/or hypoxia

4. Chronic thromboembolic pulmonary hypertension (CTEPH)

5. Pulmonary hypertension with unclear multifactorial mechanisms

BACKGROUND

Pulmonary Arterial Hypertension (PAH) is characterized by continuous high blood pressure in the pulmonary artery. The average blood pressure in a normal pulmonary artery (called pulmonary artery pressure) is about 14 mmHg when a person is resting. A mean pulmonary artery pressure (PAP) greater than 25 mmHg in the setting of normal fluid status defines PAH. Other hemodynamic parameters are affected as well.

CLASSIFICATION

Pulmonary hypertension (PH) may occur with various disease states. The World Health Organization (WHO) classifies it into five groups.

Group 1 is PAH, which may arise from genetic inheritance, connective tissue disease, advanced liver disease, and HIV among others. Some patients have no identifiable cause of the disease – this is primary, or idiopathic, PAH (versus secondary, which has a known cause). Less commonly, medications can be the causative factor, including the diet drugs dexfenfluramine *(Redux)* and Fen/Phen or from the chronic use of cocaine and methamphetamine. Recently, dasatinib *(Sprycel)* has been linked to causing PAH. Selective serotonin reuptake inhibitor (SSRI) use during pregnancy increases risk of persistent pulmonary hypertension of the newborn (PPHN). <u>PH treatments discussed in this chapter have only been approved for the treatment of PAH with the exception of riociguat *(Adempas)*.</u>

Treatment of the other PH groups is aimed at the underlying causes. Group 2 is pulmonary venous hypertension, which arises from left-sided heart disease. Group 3 is PH from hypoxia or chronic lung disease, such as chronic obstructive pulmonary disease or interstitial lung disease. Group 4 is chronic thromboembolic PH (CTEPH), which occurs in a minority of PE survivors. Warfarin anticoagulation to an INR goal of 2-3 is recommended given the history of a clot, and for patients who are not thrombectomy candidates, riociguat *(Adempas)* is an approved treatment. Group 5 is PH due to causes that do not fit in the above categorization (e.g., sarcoidosis).

The pathology of PAH stems from an imbalance of vasoconstrictor/vasodilator substances and an imbalance of proliferation and apoptosis. The vasoconstrictor substances such as endothelin-1 and thromboxane A_2 (TxA_2) are increased in PAH, whereas the vasodilators (e.g., prostacyclins, others) are decreased. The vasoconstriction results in reduced blood flow and high pressure within the pulmonary vasculature. The walls of the pulmonary arteries thicken as the amount of muscle increases and scar tissue can form on the artery walls (vasoproliferation). As the walls thicken and scar, the arteries become increasingly narrower. These changes make it hard for the right ventricle to pump blood through the pulmonary artery and into the lungs due to the increased pressure. As a result of the heart working harder, the right ventricle becomes enlarged and right heart failure can result. Heart failure is the most common cause of death in people who have PAH.

The biochemical changes mentioned above ($\uparrow TxA_2$, $\downarrow$ prostacyclin), along with other altered pathways, lead to a pro-thrombotic state and anticoagulation is suggested to prevent blood clots from forming. <u>Warfarin, titrated to an INR of 1.5 – 2.5, is recommended in PAH.</u>

Symptoms of PAH include fatigue, dyspnea, chest pain, syncope, edema, tachycardia and/or Raynaud's phenomenon. In Raynaud's, the reduced blood supply causes discoloration and coldness in the fingers, toes, and occasionally other areas.

There is no cure for PAH, but in the last decade, the knowledge of PAH has increased significantly and many more treatment options have become available. Without treatment, life expectancy is three years. In some cases, a lung or heart-lung transplant may be an option, at least for younger patients.

NON-PHARMACOLOGIC TREATMENT

Patients with PAH should follow a sodium restricted diet (< 2.4 grams/day) and manage volume status, especially if they have right ventricular failure. Routine immunizations against influenza and pneumococcal pneumonia are advised. Exposure to high altitudes may contribute to hypoxic pulmonary vasoconstriction and may not be tolerated by patients. Oxygen is used to maintain oxygen saturation above 90%.

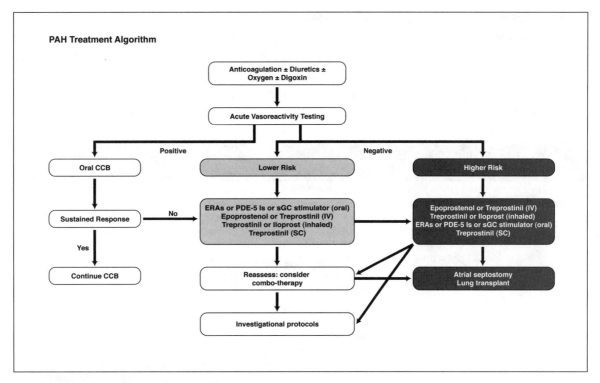

PAH Treatment Algorithm

PHARMACOLOGIC TREATMENT

Approximately 10 percent of patients respond to and are candidates for calcium channel blocker therapy, although only half have a sustained response. The calcium channel blockers used most frequently are long acting nifedipine, diltiazem, and amlodipine. The use of verapamil is not recommended due to its more pronounced negative inotropic effects relative to diltiazem. Digoxin is sometimes used in patients with right heart failure and a low cardiac output and in patients with atrial arrhythmias.

For most cases, drug therapy will reduce symptoms. Parenteral prostacyclin therapy appears to prolong life. Medications include prostacyclin analogues which cause vasodilation. These drugs may be given by continuous IV infusion, infusion under the skin, or as inhaled therapy. Endothelin receptor antagonists block endothelin, a vasoconstrictor. Phosphodiesterase-5 inhibitors (the same drugs used for erectile dysfunction – but with different brand names and doses) and a soluble guanylate cyclase (sGC) stimulator relax the blood vessels in the lungs. Some patients may benefit from combination therapy.

Prostacyclin Analogues (or Prostanoids)

Prostacyclin analogues act as potent vasodilators (on both pulmonary and systemic vascular beds). They are also inhibitors of platelet aggregation. Prostacyclin synthase is reduced in PAH resulting in inadequate production of prostacyclin I_2, which normally stimulates cAMP, a vasodilator with antiproliferative effects, in pulmonary artery smooth muscle cells. Drugs which decrease prostaglandins – nonsteroidal antiinflammatory drugs (NSAIDs) – should be avoided in patients with PAH.

DRUG	DOSING	SAFETY/SIDE EFFECTS/MONITORING
Epoprostenol *(Flolan, Veletri)* AKA prostacyclin and PGI$_2$	Start at 2 ng/kg/min and increase by 1 ng/kg/min in at least 15 minute increments. Normal dose is 25-40 ng/kg/min (may be up to 200 ng/kg/min) via continuous IV infusion	**SIDE EFFECTS** During Dose Titration – vasodilation (hypotension, headache, flushing; dose-limiting; if this happens, reduce the dose of the drug), nausea, vomiting, diarrhea, anxiety, chest pain/palpitations, tachycardia, edema, and jaw claudication With Chronic Use – Anxiety, flu-like symptoms, jaw pain, thrombocytopenia, neuropathy in addition to those seen during dose titration Treprostinil (inhaled) and iloprost: cough (in addition to above side effects) **NOTES** Avoid interruptions in therapy. Immediate access to back up pump, infusion sets and medication is essential to prevent treatment interruptions (epoprostenol half-life ~ 5 minutes vs. treprostinil half-life ~ 4 hours).
Treprostinil *(Remodulin* is SC/IV, *Tyvaso* is inhaled)	*Remodulin:* start at 1.25 ng/kg/min and increase by 1.25 ng/kg/min at weekly intervals for the first month and 2.5 ng/kg/min increments thereafter up to 40-160 ng/kg/min via continuous SC or IV infusion Inhalation form *(Tyvaso)* is given 4 times/day	Avoid large, sudden reductions in dose *Flolan:* pump needs to be on ice packs for proper cooling *Veletri:* thermostable (no need for ice packs) *Remodulin:* SC very painful (85% of patients), may need analgesic to tolerate. Also thermostable – no ice packs needed The parenteral agents are considered the most potent of all PAH medications. Patients must be instructed on central catheter maintenance to reduce infections and to avoid interruption of therapy – both which can be fatal.
Iloprost *(Ventavis)*	2.5-5 mcg/inhalation given 6-9 times/day	

Prostacyclin Analogue Drug Interactions

- May increase the effects of antihypertensive and antiplatelet agents.

Endothelin Receptor Antagonists (ERAs)

These agents block endothelin receptors on pulmonary artery smooth muscle. Endothelin is a vasoconstrictor with cellular proliferative effects.

DRUG	DOSING	SAFETY/SIDE EFFECTS/MONITORING
Bosentan *(Tracleer)* This is one of the REMS drugs (Risk Evaluation and Mitigation Strategies)	62.5 mg BID (for 4 wks) then 125 mg BID	**BLACK BOX WARNINGS (2)** Hepatotoxicity Use in pregnancy is contraindicated (Pregnancy Category X) Because of the risks of hepatic impairment and possible teratogenic effects, bosentan is only available through the *Tracleer* Access Program (T.A.P.). Prescribers and pharmacists must be certified and enroll patients in T.A.P. **CONTRAINDICATIONS** Pregnancy; concurrent use of cyclosporine or glyburide **WARNINGS** Avoid use in moderate-to-severe hepatic impairment **SIDE EFFECTS** Headache, ↓ Hgb (usually in first 6 weeks of therapy), ↑ LFTs (dose related), upper respiratory tract infections, edema (all > 10%) Spermatogenesis inhibition (25%) leading to male infertility (with bosentan only) **MONITORING** Monitor LFTs and bilirubin at baseline and every month thereafter. Monitor hemoglobin and hematocrit at baseline and at 1 month and 3 months, then every 3 months thereafter. **NOTES** Women of childbearing potential must have a negative pregnancy test prior to initiation of therapy and monthly thereafter (prior to shipment of the monthly refill). Barrier techniques of contraception are recommended.
Ambrisentan *(Letairis)* This is one of the REMS drugs (Risk Evaluation and Mitigation Strategies)	5 or 10 mg daily	**BLACK BOX WARNING** Use in pregnancy is contraindicated (Pregnancy Category X) Because of the risk of possible teratogenic effects, ambrisentan is only available through the *Letairis* Education and Access Program (LEAP) restricted distribution program. Prescribers and pharmacists must be certified and enroll patients in LEAP. **CONTRAINDICATIONS** Pregnancy **SIDE EFFECTS** Peripheral edema, headache, ↓ Hgb, flushing, palpitations, and nasal congestion **MONITORING** Monitor hemoglobin and hematocrit at baseline and at 1 month, then periodically thereafter. **NOTES** Women of childbearing potential must have a negative pregnancy test prior to initiation of therapy and monthly thereafter (prior to shipment of the monthly refill). Monitoring of LFTs was removed from the package insert on March 4, 2011 (FDA)

Endothelin Receptor Antagonists (ERAs) Continued

DRUG	DOSING	SAFETY/SIDE EFFECTS/MONITORING
Macitentan (*Opsumit*) This is one of the REMS drugs (Risk Evaluation and Mitigation Strategies)	10 mg daily	**BLACK BOX WARNING** Use in pregnancy is contraindicated (Pregnancy Category X) Because of the risk of possible teratogenic effects, macitentan is only available through the *Opsumit* restricted distribution program. Prescribers and pharmacists must be certified and enroll patients in the *Opsumit* REMS program. **CONTRAINDICATIONS** Pregnancy **SIDE EFFECTS** ↓ Hgb, headache, pharyngitis, bronchitis (all > 10%) **MONITORING** Monitor hemoglobin, hematocrit, and LFTs at baseline and repeat as clinically indicated. **NOTES** Women of childbearing potential must have a negative pregnancy test prior to initiation of therapy and monthly thereafter (prior to shipment of the monthly refill).

Endothelin Receptor Antagonist Drug Interactions

■ Avoid use with St. John's wort or grapefruit juice.

■ Bosentan is a substrate of 3A4 (major) and 2C9 (minor) and an inducer of 3A4 (weak/moderate) and 2C9 (weak/moderate); monitor for drug interactions. Levels of bosentan may ↑ with 2C8/9 and 3A4 inhibitors. Bosentan may decrease the effectiveness of hormonal birth control and is contraindicated with glyburide and cyclosporine.

■ Ambrisentan is a substrate of 3A4 (major), 2C19 (minor), P-glycoprotein and other pathways. The dose should not exceed 5 mg/d when given concomitantly with cyclosporine.

■ Macitentan is a substrate of 3A4 (major) and 2C19 (minor). Strong 3A4 inhibitors and inducers should be avoided with macitentan.

Phosphodiesterase-5 Inhibitors (PDE-5 Inhibitors)

These agents inhibit phosphodiesterase type 5 (PDE-5) in smooth muscle of pulmonary vasculature. PDE-5 is responsible for the degradation of cyclic guanosine monophosphate (cGMP). Increased cGMP concentrations lead to pulmonary vasculature relaxation and vasodilation.

DRUG	DOSING	SAFETY/SIDE EFFECTS/MONITORING
Sildenafil *(Revatio)*	IV: 10 mg IV 3 TID Oral: 20 mg TID, taken 4-6 hours apart	**CONTRAINDICATIONS** Concurrent use of nitrates. Avoid using sildenafil for PAH in patients taking PI-based HAART regimens. **SIDE EFFECTS** Dizziness, sudden drop in blood pressure, headache, flushing, dyspepsia, back pain *(Adcirca)*, and epistaxis. Priapism (< 2%) – if erection lasts for > 4 hours, get medical help right away.
Tadalafil *(Adcirca)*	40 mg daily (two, 20 mg tabs) (20 mg daily if mild to moderate renal/hepatic impairment)	Sudden vision loss in one or both eyes – seek medical help right away. May cause permanent vision loss. Other visual problems (blurred vision, increased sensitivity to light, bluish haze, or temporary difficulty distinguishing between blue and green) may occur. Sudden decrease or loss of hearing has been reported, usually in one ear. Tinnitus is another rare, but possible, side effect. **NOTES** Avoid use in severe hepatic impairment. With tadalafil, avoid use when CrCl < 30 mL/min.

PDE-5 Is Drug Interactions

- Do not give with PDE-5 inhibitors used for erectile dysfunction. Avoid concurrent use of nitrates, itraconazole, and ketoconazole. Avoid grapefruit juice.

PDE-5 Is are Contraindicated With Nitrates!

- Concurrent use of nitrate medications (any nitroglycerin-containing drug including [*Nitro-DUR, Nitrolingual, Nitrostat,* isosorbide dinitrate/hydralazine *(BiDil)*, others], increases the potential for excessively low blood pressure. Taking nitrates is an absolute contraindication to the use of these medicines. These include the illicit drugs such as amyl nitrate and butyl nitrate ("poppers").

- If a patient with ED has taken a PDE-5 inhibitor and then develops angina, nitroglycerin should not be used until after 12 hours has elapsed for avanafil, 24 hours has elapsed for sildenafil and vardenafil or 48 hours has elapsed for tadalafil. Other anti-anginal and anti-ischemic therapies may be used – such as beta blockers, calcium channel blockers, aspirin, morphine, heparin, statins and percutaneous coronary intervention. (Sometimes nitrates are used in an acute emergency, despite this warning, with careful monitoring.)

Caution with PDE-5 Inhibitors and Concurrent Alpha Blocker Therapy

■ Caution is advised when PDE-5 inhibitors are co-administered with alpha blockers. PDE-5 inhibitors and alpha-adrenergic blocking agents are both vasodilators with BP lowering effects. When vasodilators are used in combination, an additive effect on BP may be anticipated. In some patients, concomitant use of these two drug classes can lower BP significantly leading to symptomatic hypotension (e.g., dizziness, light headedness, fainting).

■ Patients should be stable on alpha-blocker therapy before PDE-5 inhibition and use the lowest dose of the PDE-5 inhibitor when initiating therapy. Conversely, if a patient is already taking an optimal dose of PDE-5 inhibitor and an alpha blocker needs to be started, the alpha blocker should be started at the lowest dose, and preferably the alpha-1a selective agents are chosen (tamsulosin, silodosin, others).

Soluble Guanylate Cyclase (sGC) Stimulator

Increasing conversion of GTP to cGMP leads to increased relaxation and antiproliferative effects in the pulmonary artery smooth muscle cells. Riociguat is approved for use in both PAH and CTEPH.

DRUG	DOSING	SAFETY/SIDE EFFECTS/MONITORING
Riociguat *(Adempas)* This is one of the REMS drugs (Risk Evaluation and Mitigation Strategies)	0.5-1 mg TID, increasing by 0.5 mg TID every 2 weeks to target 2.5 mg TID	**BLACK BOX WARNING** Use in pregnancy is contraindicated (Pregnancy Category X) Because of the risk of possible teratogenic effects, riociguat is only available through the *Adempas* restricted distribution program. Prescribers and pharmacists must be certified and enroll patients in the *Adempas* REMS program. **CONTRAINDICATIONS** Pregnancy; concomitant use of PDE-5 inhibitors or nitrates **SIDE EFFECTS** Headache, dyspepsia, dizziness, hypotension, nausea, vomiting, and diarrhea (all > 10%). Bleeding appears to be more common with riociguat than placebo.

sCG Stimulator Drug Interactions

■ Smoking increases riociguat clearance; the dose may need to be decreased with smoking cessation.

■ Separate from antacids by > 1 hour.

■ Strong enzyme inhibitors (e.g., ketoconazole, ritonavir) may warrant a lower starting dose.

ASTHMA

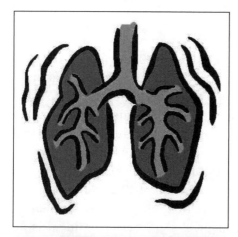

GUIDELINES

Expert Panel Report 3. Guidelines for
the Diagnosis and Management of
Asthma. National Heart, Lung and Blood
Institute, August 2007. Available at
http://www.nhlbi.nih.gov/guidelines/
asthma (accessed 2013, Nov. 8)

The Global Strategy for Asthma
Management and Prevention, Global
Initiative for Asthma (GINA) 2012. Available from: http://www.ginasthma.org/
(accessed 2013, Nov. 8)

BACKGROUND

Asthma is characterized by a predisposition to chronic inflammation of the lungs in which the airways (bronchi) are reversibly narrowed. Asthma affects 8% of the population of the United States. During asthma attacks (exacerbations of asthma), the smooth muscle cells in the bronchi constrict, the airways become inflamed and swollen, and breathing becomes difficult.

The National Heart, Lung and Blood Institute defines asthma as a common chronic disorder of the airways characterized by variable and recurring symptoms, airflow obstruction, bronchial hyperresponsiveness (bronchospasm), and underlying inflammation. Asthma is a chronic inflammatory disorder of the airways in which many cells and cellular elements play a role, in particular, mast cells, eosinophils, neutrophils, T lymphocytes, macrophages, and epithelial cells. This inflammation causes recurrent episodes of the classic signs and symptoms of asthma: wheezing, breathlessness, chest tightness, and coughing; particularly at night or early in the morning. These episodes are generally associated with variable airflow obstruction that is often reversible spontaneously or with treatment. Airway remodeling can occur consisting of fibrosis and increased goblet (mucus-producing) cells.

COMMON TRIGGERS OF ASTHMA

TRIGGERS	EXAMPLES
Allergens	Airborne pollens (grass, trees, weeds), house-dust mites, animal dander (cats, dogs, horses, rabbits, rats, mice), cockroaches, fungal spores
Drugs	Aspirin, NSAIDs, sulfites, beta-blockers (non-selective)
Environmental	Cold air, fog, ozone, sulfur dioxide, nitrogen dioxide, tobacco smoke, wood smoke
Exercise	Cold air or humid, hot air
Occupational	Bakers (flour dust), farmers (hay mold), spice and enzyme workers; painters (arabic gum), chemical workers (azo dyes, toluene diisocyanates, polyvinyl chloride); plastics, rubber, and wood workers (formaldehyde, dimethyethanolamine)
Respiratory Infections	Respiratory syncytial virus (RSV), rhinovirus, influenza, parainfluenza, *Mycoplasma pneumonia*, *Chlamydia*

PHARMACOLOGIC TREATMENT

Drugs used to treat asthma are classified as <u>controllers</u> or <u>relievers</u>. <u>Controllers</u> are taken on a chronic, <u>daily basis to keep asthma under control, primarily by reducing inflamma-tion</u>. <u>Relievers are used as-needed to quickly reverse bronchoconstriction</u>, or preventively for <u>exercise-induced bronchospasm</u> (EIB). Asthma drugs come in oral, inhaled and injectable formulations. <u>Inhaled forms</u> deliver drugs directly into the lungs, have reduced toxicity, and are the <u>preferred</u> delivery vehicle. <u>Inhaled steroids</u> (glucocorticosteroids) are the <u>most effec-tive</u> and <u>preferred controller</u> medication. <u>Rapid-acting beta$_2$-agonists</u> (primarily <u>albuterol</u>) is the preferred reliever for acute bronchospasm, and for prevention of EIB, in both adults, children and during pregnancy. Increased use of a reliever medication indicates worsening asthma control, and indicates the need to reassess treatment. The primary treatment is an increase in the inhaled steroid dose. Steroids can be given by injection in acute cases, and oral steroids are used for severely uncontrolled asthma, but the use of steroids in other for-mulations than inhaled is limited by the risk of adverse effects. Theophylline can be helpful in some cases, but has significant adverse effects and drug interactions. Cold air, pollutants and other "triggers" can worsen asthma control. Patients should attempt to identify what triggers their exacerbations and reduce trigger exposure.

"RESCUERS" – THESE AGENTS ARE COMMONLY USED IN ASTHMA EXACERBATIONS	"CONTROLLERS" – OR LONG-TERM, MAINTENANCE THERAPY
Short-acting beta$_2$-agonists	Inhaled steroids
Systemic steroids (inj. or oral)	Long-acting beta$_2$-agonists (taken with steroids)
Anticholinergics	Leukotriene Modifying Agents
	Theophylline
	Omalizumab *(Xolair)*

Beta$_2$-agonists

Bind to beta$_2$ receptors causing relaxation of bronchial smooth muscle resulting in bronchodilation – inhaled route is the preferred route of administration.

DRUG	DOSING	SAFETY/SIDE EFFECTS/MONITORING

Short-Acting Beta$_2$-Agonists (SABAs)

DRUG	DOSING	SAFETY/SIDE EFFECTS/MONITORING
Racepinephrine *(Asthmanefrin atomizer)* OTC	Should not be used; not beta$_2$ selective	**SIDE EFFECTS** Tremor, shakiness, lightheadedness, cough, palpitations, hypokalemia, tachycardia, hyperglycemia **MONITORING** Number of days of use of SABA, symptom frequency, peak flow, BP, HR, blood glucose, and K$^+$ **NOTES** Pregnancy Category C With MDIs, shake well before use. Prime prior to first use (3-4 sprays into the air away from face) and again if inhaler has not been used for > 2 weeks Prefer a beta-2 selective agent and the inhaled route. These are rescue medications used PRN in asthma. If using SABA > 2 days/week, then need to ↑ maintenance therapy
Albuterol *(Ventolin HFA, Proventil HFA, ProAir HFA,* AccuNeb, VoSpire ER)	1-2 inhalations Q4-6H PRN (MDI) 2.5 mg Q4-8H PRN (neb) 2-4 mg Q4-6H PO PRN	
Levalbuterol *(Xopenex, Xopenex HFA)*	1-2 inhalations Q4-6H PRN (MDI) 0.63 mg or 1.25 mg Q6-8H PRN (neb)	
Pirbuterol *(Maxair Autohaler)*	1-2 inhalations Q4-6H PRN (MDI)	Short acting beta-2 agonists are the drugs of choice for exercise-induced bronchospasm (EIB) Levalbuterol contains R-isomer of albuterol

Long-Acting Beta$_2$-Agonists (LABAs)

DRUG	DOSING	SAFETY/SIDE EFFECTS/MONITORING
Salmeterol *(Serevent Diskus)* + fluticasone *(Advair Diskus, Advair HFA)* *Advair Diskus* – 100, 250, 500 mcg fluticasone + 50 mcg salmeterol/inh (ages ≥ 4 years) *Advair HFA* – 45, 115, 230 mcg fluticasone + 21 mcg salmeterol/inh (ages ≥ 12 years)	1 inhalation BID *(Diskus)* 2 inhalations BID (HFA)	**BLACK BOX WARNING** ↑ risk of asthma-related deaths. Do not use LABA as monotherapy in patients with persistent asthma; should only be used in asthma patients as adjunctive therapy in patients who are currently receiving but are not adequately controlled on a long-term asthma control medication (e.g., an inhaled corticosteroid) Once asthma control is achieved and maintained, assess the patient at regular intervals and step down therapy (e.g., discontinue LABA) if possible without loss of asthma control Similar side effects and monitoring as SABAs **NOTES** Pregnancy Category C *Foradil* Refrigerate capsules in the pharmacy, patient can keep at room temp. for 4 months
Formoterol *(Foradil Aerolizer)* **+ budesonide *(Symbicort)* *Symbicort* – 80, 160 mcg budesonide + 4.5 mcg formoterol/inh (ages ≥ 12 years)**	1 capsule via *Aerolizer* BID 2 inhalations BID	

Corticosteroids

Inhibit the inflammatory response, depress migration of polymorphonuclear (PMN) leukocytes, fibroblasts; reverses capillary permeability and lysosomal stabilization at the cellular level to prevent or control inflammation.

Inhaled Corticosteroids

DRUG	DOSING	SAFETY/SIDE EFFECTS/MONITORING
Beclomethasone HFA (QVAR) – solution, do not need to shake	Low dose: 80-240 mcg/d Medium dose: > 240-480 mcg/d High dose: > 480 mcg/d	**CONTRAINDICATIONS** Primary treatment of status asthmaticus or acute episodes of asthma (not for relief of acute bronchospasm) **SIDE EFFECTS (INHALED)** Dysphonia, oral candidiasis (thrush), cough, hoarseness, URTI's, hyperglycemia, ↑ risk of fractures and pneumonia (with high dose, long-term use), growth retardation (in children with high doses)
Budesonide (Pulmicort Flexhaler, Pulmicort Respules) **+ formoterol (Symbicort)**	Low dose: 180-600 mcg/d Medium dose: > 600-1,200 mcg/d High dose: > 1,200 mcg/d Pulmicort Respules – suspension for nebulization (ages 1-8 years)	**MONITORING** Use of SABA, symptom frequency, growth (adolescents) and signs/symptoms of HPA axis suppression/adrenal insufficiency; signs/symptoms of oral candidiasis; peak flow
Ciclesonide (Alvesco) – do not need to shake	80-320 mcg BID	**NOTES** To prevent oral candidiasis, rinse mouth and throat with warm water and spit out or use a spacer device Inhaled steroids are first-line for long term control for all ages with persistent asthma
Flunisolide HFA (Aerospan HFA) – has built-in spacer	Low dose: 320 mcg/d Medium dose: > 320-640 mcg/d High dose: > 640 mcg/d	Systemic steroids have a rapid onset of action and are used as "pulse" therapy – for up to 15 days after an asthma attack QVAR and Alvesco – do not have to shake before use Pregnancy Category C/B (budesonide) To ↓ fracture risk: avoid smoking, exercise, use lowest, effective steroid dose, recommend Ca^{2+} and vitamin D, use prescription therapies if needed and get regular bone density screening.
Fluticasone (Flovent HFA, Flovent Diskus) **+ salmeterol (Advair Diskus, Advair HFA)**	**For MDI:** Low dose: 88-264 mcg/d Medium dose: 264-440 mcg/d High dose: > 440 mcg/d **For Diskus:** Low dose: 100-300 mcg/d Medium dose: > 300-500 mcg/d High dose: > 500 mcg/d	
Mometasone (Asmanex Twisthaler) + formoterol (Dulera) Dulera – 100, 200 mcg mometasone + 5 mcg formoterol/inh (ages ≥ 12 years)	Low dose: 220 mcg/d Medium dose: 440 mcg/d High dose: > 440 mcg/d	

STEROIDS

The two types of steroids are glucocorticoids, produced by the body as a reaction to stress or given exogenously, and mineralocorticoids (fludrocortisone), which regulates sodium and water balance. Mineralocorticoids are used to raise sodium levels and to replace some of the function of aldosterone in Addison's disease.

Steroids (glucocorticoids) are used clinically primarily to reduce inflammation, which can require high doses. In some cases the dose is given quickly and then stopped, such as with a methylprednisolone injection. In other cases the dose is started high and then "tapered" down to avoid the patient crashing or experiencing a rebound attack. This is not always necessary but is done with either a de-escalating dose of a drug such as prednisone, or with the methylprednisolone (Medrol) or dexamethasone (Decadron) dose packs. The doses are sequentially decreased, which is called a taper.

This is different than what is typically called a steroid "taper", which is a steady reduction in dose for patients using steroids for longer than 14 days. (Some state to taper if used longer than 10-14 days.) This taper is designed to give the patient's body time to increase their own endogenous cortisol production, which would have decreased during the extended period using systemic steroids. A taper is not required for inhaled steroid use.

LONG-TERM SIDE EFFECTS OF SYSTEMIC STEROIDS

Cushing Syndrome
A condition due to the pituitary gland producing large amounts of endogenous cortisol production; here, it is due to exogenous steroid use

Central redistribution of fat (fat deposits in the abdomen)

Moon facies (fat deposits in the face)

Buffalo hump (fat deposits between the shoulders)

Impaired wound healing

Dermal thinning/bruising

Other conditions in this table

Psychiatric disturbances (mood swings, delirium, psychoses)

Sodium and water retention/hypertension

Hypokalemia
Hyperglycemia/diabetes

Increased appetite/weight gain

Immunosuppression
Impaired wound healing

Glaucoma/cataracts

Growth retardation

Amenorrhea
Osteoporosis/fractures

Hirsutism (in women)

Acne
Dermal thinning/bruising

Insomnia/nervousness
GI bleeding/esophagitis/ulcers (do not use with NSAIDs due to ↑ risk)

ORAL STEROIDS – DOSE EQUIVALENTS

Short-acting
Cortisone – 25 mg
Hydrocortisone – 20 mg

Intermediate-acting
Methylprednisolone/Triamcinolone – 4 mg
Prednisone/Prednisolone – 5 mg

Long-acting
Betamethasone – 0.6 mg
Dexamethasone – 0.75 mg

Mineralcorticoids
Fludrocortisone – no anti-inflammatory effect

Oral Corticosteroids

DRUG	DOSING	SAFETY/SIDE EFFECTS/MONITORING
Cortisone	Dosing varies by disease severity and patient response Used as pulse therapy for acute exacerbations; used for maintenance therapy in very severe disease (Step 6) at doses of 5-60 mg daily or every other day	**CONTRAINDICATIONS** Live vaccines, systemic fungal infections, varicella **SIDE EFFECTS** Short-term side effects (used < 1 month): ↑ appetite/weight gain, fluid retention, emotional instability (euphoria, mood swings, irritability), insomnia, indigestion, bitter taste. Higher doses ↑ in BP and ↑ blood glucose. Long term side effects are below.
Hydrocortisone [*Cortef* (oral), *Solu-CORTEF* (injectable)]		**MONITORING** BP, weight, appetite, mood **NOTES** Cortisone is a prodrug for cortisol. Prednisone is a prodrug for prednisolone. Prednisolone is used most commonly in children (comes in many formulations).
MethylPREDNISolone [*Medrol* and *Medrol Dosepak* (both orals), *Solu-MEDROL, A-Methapred, Depo-Medrol* (all injections)]		Steroids should be given between 7-8am to mimic the body's diurnal release of cortisol. If taking longer than 10-14 days, must taper slowly due to suppression of the hypothalamic-pituitary-adrenal axis
PredniSONE [*PredniSONE Intensol* (solution), *Rayos* (delayed release tablet) generics – oral]		
PrednisoLONE [*Millipred* and *Orapred* (tablets, ODT and solution), *Pediapred, Veripred* (both solutions), *Prelone* (syrup), *Flo-Pred* (suspension)]		Tapering dose packs available for acute inflammation – this is to provide high doses to quickly reduce the inflammation
Triamcinolone *Aristospan, **Kenalog,** Trivaris* (all injections)		

Relative antiinflammatory potency: betamethasone/dexamethasone > fludrocortisone > methylprednisolone/triamcinolone > prednisone/prednisolone > hydrocortisone > cortisone

Fludrocortisone has the highest mineralcorticoid potency causing Na^+ and H_2O retention – used for hyponatremia

Leukotriene Modifying Agents

Zafirlukast and montelukast are leukotriene-receptor antagonists (LTRAs) of leukotriene D4 (LTD4 – both drugs) and E4 (LTE4 – just zafirlukast). Zileuton is a 5-lipoxygenase inhibitor which inhibits leukotriene formation. All agents help ↓ airway edema, constriction and inflammation.

DRUG	DOSING	SAFETY/SIDE EFFECTS/MONITORING
Zafirlukast (*Accolate*)	20 mg BID (empty stomach) Children 5-11 years: 10 mg BID	**CONTRAINDICATIONS** Hepatic impairment – zafirlukast Active liver disease or LFTs ≥ 3 x ULN – zileuton **WARNINGS** Neuropsychiatric events; monitor for signs of aggressive behavior, hostility, agitation, depression, suicidal thinking Hepatotoxicity
Montelukast (*Singulair*)	10 mg daily in the evening Age 1-5 years: 4 mg daily Age 5-14 years: 5 mg daily	Systemic eosinophilia, sometimes presenting with clinical features of vasculitis consistent with Churg-Strauss syndrome. Churg-Strauss is associated with a ↓ in steroids while this class of medications are added (rare)
Zileuton (*Zyflo, Zyflo CR*)	*Zyflo*: 600 mg QID *Zyflo CR*: 1,200 mg BID within 1 hour of morning and evening meals Children: not recommended	**SIDE EFFECTS** Headache, dizziness, abdominal pain, ↑ LFTs, URTIs, pharyngitis, sinusitis **MONITORING** Zileuton – need to monitor LFTs every month for first 3 months, every 2-3 months for the rest of the first year of therapy; use of SABAs **NOTES** Zafirlukast is taken 1 hour before or 2 hours after meals Pregnancy Category B/C (zileuton)

Leukotriene Modifying Agents Drug Interactions

- Zafirlukast: substrate of 2C9 (major); inhibitor of 1A2 (weak), 2C9 (moderate), 2C19 (weak), 2D6 (weak) and 3A4 (weak) – may ↑ levels of carvedilol, pimozide, theophylline, warfarin and 2C9 substrates. Levels of zafirlukast may be ↓ by erythromycin, theophylline, and food (↓ bioavailability by 40%) – take 1 hour before or 2 hours after meals

- Montelukast: substrate of 3A4 (major) and 2C9 (major); inhibitor of 2C8/9 (weak)

- Zileuton: substrate of 1A2 (minor), 2C9 (minor), 3A4 (minor); inhibitor of 1A2 (weak) – may ↑ levels of pimozide, propranolol, theophylline, and warfarin

Theophylline

Blocks phosphodiesterase causing ↑ cyclic adenosine monophosphate (cAMP) which promotes release of epinephrine from adrenal medulla cells. This results in bronchodilation, diuresis, CNS and cardiac stimulation and gastric acid secretion. Theophylline may help as add-on therapy in some patients, but it is not most effective and drug interactions and adverse effects limit its use.

DRUG	DOSING	SAFETY/SIDE EFFECTS/MONITORING
Theophylline Immediate Release *(Elixophyllin)* Extended Release *(Theolair, Theo-24, Theochron)* active metabolites are caffeine and 3-methylxanthine	200-600 mg daily Therapeutic range: <u>5-15 mcg/mL</u> (measure <u>peak</u> level after 3 days of oral dosing, at steady state)	**WARNINGS** Caution in patients with cardiovascular disease, hyperthyroidism, PUD and seizure disorder since use may exacerbate these conditions **SIDE EFFECTS** <u>Nausea, loose stools</u>, headache, tachycardia, insomnia, tremor, and nervousness Signs of toxicity – persistent and repetitive vomiting, ventricular tachycardias, seizures **MONITORING** Theophylline levels, use of SABA, HR, CNS effects **NOTES** Dosing is based on IBW. LD = 5 mg/kg (if not previously on theophylline) LD = (Cp-Co)(Vd) (if taking theophylline), where Vd = 0.5 L/kg; Cp = desired theophylline concentration; Co = initial theophylline concentration If <u>using IV aminophylline</u>, then <u>divide by 0.8</u> (aminophylline contains 80% theophylline) Pregnancy Category C

Theophylline Drug Interactions

Theophylline is a substrate of 1A2 and 3A4 (both major), 2C9 (minor) and 2D6 (minor) and an inhibitor of 1A2 (weak). It has first order kinetics, followed by Michaelis-Menten (or saturable) kinetics (similar to phenytoin and voriconazole). A small increase in dose can result in a large increase in the theophylline concentration.

- <u>Drugs that may ↑ theophylline levels</u> due to 1A2 inhibition: ciprofloxacin, fluvoxamine, propranolol, zafirlukast, zileuton and possibly others

- <u>Drugs that may ↑ theophylline levels</u> due to 3A4 inhibition: clarithromycin, conivaptan, erythromycin and possibly others

- <u>Drugs that may ↑ theophylline levels</u> due to other mechanisms: alcohol, allopurinol antithyroid agents, disulfiram, estrogen containing oral contraceptives, methotrexate, pentoxifylline, propafenone, verapamil and possibly others. Also conditions such as acute pulmonary edema, CHF, cirrhosis or liver disease, cor-pulmonale, fever, hypothyroidism or shock can ↓ clearance.

- <u>Drugs that may ↓ theophylline levels</u>: carbamazepine, fosphenytoin, phenobarbital, phenytoin, primidone, rifampin, ritonavir, tobacco/marijuana smoking, St. John's wort, thyroid hormones (levothyroxine), high-protein diet and charbroiled meats. Conditions such as hyperthyroidism and cystic fibrosis can ↑ clearance.

- <u>Theophylline will ↓ lithium</u> (theophylline ↑ renal excretion of lithium) and will ↓ zafirlukast

Anticholinergics

Mainly used with other medications in the emergency department for bronchodilation in acute attacks. See COPD chapter for more information on these drugs.

Omalizumab *(Xolair)*

IgG monoclonal antibody that inhibits <u>IgE binding</u> to the IgE receptor on mast cells and basophils. Omalizumab is indicated for moderate to severe persistent, <u>allergic asthma</u> in patients with a positive skin test to perennial aeroallergen and inadequately controlled symptoms on inhaled steroids (Step 5 or 6 per guidelines).

DRUG	DOSING	SAFETY/SIDE EFFECTS/MONITORING
Omalizumab *(Xolair)*	Dose and frequency based on pretreatment total IgE serum levels and body weight – given SC every 2 or 4 weeks <u>Drug should always be given in the doctor's office</u>	**BLACK BOX WARNING** <u>Anaphylaxis</u>, including delayed-onset, can occur. Anaphylaxis has occurred after the first dose but also has occurred beyond 1 year after beginning treatment. Closely observe patients for an appropriate period of time after administration and be prepared to manage anaphylaxis that can be life-threatening. **SIDE EFFECTS** Injection site reactions, arthralgias, pain, dizziness, fatigue, leg pain, arm pain, pruritus, dermatitis, bone fracture **MONITORING** Baseline IgE, FEV_1, peak flow **NOTES** Pregnancy Category B Doses > 150 mg should be divided over more than one injection site

SPECIAL POPULATIONS

Exercise-Induced Bronchospasm (EIB)

- Pretreatment before exercise with SABAs, LABAs or montelukast is recommended. SABAs are the drugs of choice generally.

- SABAs can be taken 5-15 minutes before exercise and have a duration of 2-3 hours.

- If longer duration of symptom control is needed, LABAs can be used but need to take 15 minutes prior to exercise (for formoterol) or 30 minutes prior to exercise (for salmeterol). If already using for asthma maintenance, then should not use additional doses for exercise-induced bronchospasm. <u>Remember LABAs should not be used as monotherapy in patients with persistent asthma.</u>

- Montelukast must be taken 2 hours prior to exercise and it lasts up to 24 hours. However, it only works in 50% of patients. Daily administration to prevent exercise-induced bronchoconstriction has not been evaluated. Patients receiving montelukast for asthma or another indication should not take an additional dose to prevent exercise-induced bronchoconstriction.

Pregnancy

- Albuterol is the preferred short-acting beta$_2$-agonist.

- Budesonide is the preferred inhaled corticosteroid due to more data in pregnancy.

- Monitor asthma as it may get worse. It is safer to be treated with asthma medications than to have poorly controlled asthma to ensure oxygen supply to the fetus.

Classifying Asthma Severity & Initiating Treatment In Youths ≥ 12 Years Of Age and Adults

Components of Severity		Classification of Asthma Severity ≥12 years of age			
				Persistent	
		Intermittent	Mild	Moderate	Severe
Impairment Normal FEV₁/FVC: 8–19 yr 85% 20–39 yr 80% 40–59 yr 75% 60–80 yr 70%	Symptoms	≤2 days/week	>2 days/week but not daily	Daily	Throughout the day
	Nighttime awakenings	≤2x/month	3–4x/month	>1x/week but not nightly	Often 7x/week
	Short-acting beta₂-agonist use for symptom control (not prevention of EIB)	≤2 days/week	>2 days/week but not daily, and not more than 1x on any day	Daily	Several times per day
	Interference with normal activity	None	Minor limitation	Some limitation	Extremely limited
	Lung function	• Normal FEV₁ between exacerbations • FEV₁ >80% predicted • FEV₁/FVC normal	• FEV₁ >80% predicted • FEV₁/FVC normal	• FEV₁ >60% but <80% predicted • FEV₁/FVC reduced 5%	• FEV₁ <60% predicted • FEV₁/FVC reduced >5%
Risk	Exacerbations requiring oral systemic corticosteroids	0–1/year (see note)	≥2/year (see note) ⟶		
		⟵ Consider severity and interval since last exacerbation. ⟶ Frequency and severity may fluctuate over time for patients in any severity category. Relative annual risk of exacerbations may be related to FEV₁.			
Recommended Step for Initiating Treatment (See figure 4–5 for treatment steps.)		Step 1	Step 2	Step 3	Step 4 or 5
					and consider short course of oral systemic corticosteroids
		In 2–6 weeks, evaluate level of asthma control that is achieved and adjust therapy accordingly.			

Key: FEV₁, forced expiratory volume in 1 second; FVC, forced vital capacity; ICU, intensive care unit

Notes:

■ The stepwise approach is meant to assist, not replace, the clinical decisionmaking required to meet individual patient needs.

■ Level of severity is determined by assessment of both impairment and risk. Assess impairment domain by patient's/caregiver's recall of previous 2–4 weeks and spirometry. Assign severity to the most severe category in which any feature occurs.

■ At present, there are inadequate data to correspond frequencies of exacerbations with different levels of asthma severity. In general, more frequent and intense exacerbations (e.g., requiring urgent, unscheduled care, hospitalization, or ICU admission) indicate greater underlying disease severity. For treatment purposes, patients who had ≥2 exacerbations requiring oral systemic corticosteroids in the past year may be considered the same as patients who have persistent asthma, even in the absence of impairment levels consistent with persistent asthma.

Stepwise Approach For Managing Asthma In Youths ≥ 12 Years Of Age and Adults

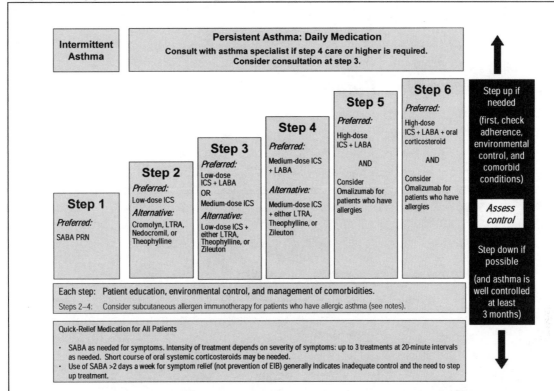

Key: **Alphabetical order is used when more than one treatment option is listed within either preferred or alternative therapy.** EIB, exercise-induced bronchospasm; ICS, inhaled corticosteroid; LABA, long-acting inhaled beta$_2$-agonist; LTRA, leukotriene receptor antagonist; SABA, inhaled short-acting beta$_2$-agonist

Notes:

■ The stepwise approach is meant to assist, not replace, the clinical decisionmaking required to meet individual patient needs.

■ If alternative treatment is used and response is inadequate, discontinue it and use the preferred treatment before stepping up.

■ Zileuton is a less desirable alternative due to limited studies as adjunctive therapy and the need to monitor liver function. Theophylline requires monitoring of serum concentration levels.

■ In step 6, before oral systemic corticosteroids are introduced, a trial of high-dose ICS + LABA + either LTRA, theophylline, or zileuton may be considered, although this approach has not been studied in clinical trials.

■ Step 1, 2, and 3 preferred therapies are based on Evidence A; step 3 alternative therapy is based on Evidence A for LTRA, Evidence B for theophylline, and Evidence D for zileuton. Step 4 preferred therapy is based on Evidence B, and alternative therapy is based on Evidence B for LTRA and theophylline and Evidence D for zileuton. Step 5 preferred therapy is based on Evidence B. Step 6 preferred therapy is based on (EPR—2 1997) and Evidence B for omalizumab.

■ Immunotherapy for steps 2–4 is based on Evidence B for house-dust mites, animal danders, and pollens; evidence is weak or lacking for molds and cockroaches. Evidence is strongest for immunotherapy with single allergens. The role of allergy in asthma is greater in children than in adults.

■ Clinicians who administer immunotherapy or omalizumab should be prepared and equipped to identify and treat anaphylaxis that may occur.

Sample Asthma Action Plan (Adult)

ENGLISH

My Asthma Action Plan

Patient Name: _____

Medical Record #: _____

Physician's Name: _____   DOB: _____

Physician's Phone #: _____   Completed by: _____   Date: _____

Long-Term-Control Medicines	How Much To Take	How Often	Other Instructions
		_____ times per day **EVERY DAY!**	
		_____ times per day **EVERY DAY!**	
		_____ times per day **EVERY DAY!**	
		_____ times per day **EVERY DAY!**	

Quick-Relief Medicines	How Much To Take	How Often	Other Instructions
		Take ONLY as needed	NOTE: If this medicine is needed frequently, call physician to consider increasing long-term-control medications.

Special instructions when I feel ● good, ○ not good, and ● awful.

GREEN ZONE

I feel *good.*
(My peak flow is in the GREEN zone.)

My Personal Best Peak Flow

PREVENT asthma symptoms everyday:

☐ Take my long-term-control medicines (above) every day.

☐ Before exercise, take _____ puffs of _____

☐ Avoid things that make my asthma worse like: _____

YELLOW ZONE

I do *not* feel *good.*
(My peak flow is in the YELLOW zone.)

My symptoms may include one or more of the following:
- Wheeze
- Tight chest
- Cough
- Shortness of breath
- Waking up at night with asthma symptoms
- Decreased ability to do usual activities
- _____

80% Personal Best

CAUTION. I should continue taking my long-term-control asthma medicines every day AND:

☐ Take _____

If I still do not feel good, or my peak flow is not back in the **Green Zone** within 1 hour, then I should:

☐ Increase _____

☐ Add _____

☐ Call _____

RED ZONE

I feel *awful.*
(My peak flow is in the RED zone.)

Warning signs may include one or more of the following:
- It's getting harder and harder to breathe
- Unable to sleep or do usual activities because of trouble breathing

50% Personal Best

Liters/Min.

Peak Flow Meter

MEDICAL ALERT! *Get help!*

☐ Take _____ until I get help immediately.

☐ Take _____

☐ Call _____

Danger! Get help immediately!   Call 9–1–1 if you have trouble walking or talking due to shortness of breath or lips or fingernails are gray or blue.

PEAK FLOW METERS

Introduction

Peak flow meters are devices that measure a patient's peak expiratory flow rate (PEFR) – the greatest velocity attained during a forced expiration starting from fully inflated lungs. The patient's best PEFR is known as a Personal Best (PB) and is determined by spirometry, taking into account the patient's height, gender, and age. The PEFR and hence, the patient's PB, is effort-dependent. Peak flow meters are beneficial in patient's with frequent exacerbations of asthma. These devices can identify exacerbations early (even before the patient is symptomatic) allowing the patient to initiate treatment sooner. A treatment plan, called an action plan, is developed by the health care practitioner so the patient may be able to avoid hospitalizations due to an exacerbation.

Technique

- Use the peak flow meter every morning when you wake up, before you take any asthma medications. <u>Proper technique and best effort are essential</u>. Less than <u>best effort</u> can lead to false 'exacerbation' and unnecessary medication treatment.

- Move the indicator to bottom of numbered scale. Stand up straight. Exhale comfortably.

- Inhale as deeply as you can. Place lips firmly around mouthpiece, creating a tight seal.

- Blow out as <u>hard</u> and as <u>fast</u> as possible. Write down the PEFR.

- Repeat steps two more times, allowing enough rest in between. Record the highest value.

Zones

<u>Green zone (80-100% of personal best)</u>

- Indicates "all clear" – good control

- Patients are instructed to follow routine maintenance plan

<u>Yellow zone (50-80% of personal best)</u>

- Indicates "caution" – indicative of worsening lung function

- Patient-specific intervention required (action plan) – usually an increase in beta$_2$-agonist use and the addition or increase in other medications

<u>Red zone (< 50% of personal best)</u>

- Indicates medical <u>alert</u> and patient needs to seek medical attention – action plan includes use of SABA, possibly steroids and go to the emergency department

Peak Flow Meter Care

- Always use the same brand of peak flow meter.

- Peak flow meters should be cleaned once a week at least; if patient has an infection, they should clean more frequently. Wash peak flow meters in warm water with mild soap. Rinse gently but thoroughly. Do not use brushes to clean inside the peak flow meters. Do not place peak flow meters in boiling water. Allow to air dry before taking next reading.

SPACERS

- Some spacer devices and chambers greatly enhance the coordination necessary to administer inhaled medication from a MDI.

- Spacer devices help prevent thrush from inhaled corticosteroids and can reduce cough associated with some inhalers.

- Need to clean at least once a week in warm, soapy water.

- Do not share spacer devices with anyone.

ASTHMA MEDICATION COUNSELING

Albuterol MDI (e.g., *ProAir HFA)*

- This medication provides quick relief of acute asthma symptoms. This is your rescue medication and should be taken as needed when breathing becomes difficult or during an asthma attack.

- Check each time to make sure the canister fits firmly in the plastic actuator. Remove the cap off the mouthpiece. Look into mouthpiece to make sure there are no foreign objects there, especially if the cap is not being used to cover the mouthpiece.

- Prime the inhaler before you use it for the first time or if you have not used it for > 14 days. To prime, spray it into the air away from your face. Shake and spray the inhaler 2 more times to finish priming it.

- <u>Shake the inhaler well before each spray.</u>

- Hold the inhaler with the mouthpiece down. <u>Breathe out fully through your mouth</u>. Put the mouthpiece in your mouth and close your lips around it.

- <u>Push the top of the canister all the way down while you breathe in deeply and slowly through your mouth</u>. Right after the spray comes out, take your finger off the canister. After you have inhaled in all the way, take the inhaler out of your mouth and close your mouth.

- <u>Hold your breath as long as you can</u>, up to 10 seconds, then breathe normally.

- If your doctor has prescribed more sprays, wait 1 minute and <u>shake</u> the inhaler again. Repeat.

- Put the cap back on the mouthpiece after every time you use the inhaler.

- <u>Throw the inhaler away</u> when you have used 200 sprays. You should not keep using the inhaler after 200 sprays (when the dose counter says 0) even though the canister may not be completely empty because you cannot be sure you will receive any medicine.

- Side effects of this medication can include chest pain, racing or pounding heart, shakiness, nervousness, low potassium levels, sore throat and/or cough.

- <u>Do not use the inhaler</u> after the expiration date, which is on the packaging it comes in.

- Wash the actuator at least 1 time each week.

- The inhaler should be stored at room temperature. Do not leave it in extreme temperatures.

Advair Diskus

- This medication is used to reduce the inflammation and promote bronchodilation in your lungs. <u>This is not a rescue medication for asthma attacks</u>.

- Take *Advair Diskus* out of the box and foil pouch. Write the "Pouch opened" and "Use by" dates on the label on top of the device. The "Use by" date is 1 month from date of opening the pouch.

- The dose indicator on the top of the device tells you how many doses are left. After you have used 55 doses from the device, the numbers 5 to 0 will appear in red to warn you that there are only a few doses left.

- Hold the *Diskus* in one hand and put the thumb of your other hand on the thumbgrip. Push your thumb away from you as far as it will go until the mouthpiece appears and snaps into position.

- Hold the *Diskus* in a level, flat position with the mouthpiece towards you. Slide the lever away from you as far as it will go until it clicks. The *Diskus* is now ready to use.

- Breathe out (exhale) fully while holding the *Diskus* level and away from your mouth. <u>Remember, never breathe out into the mouthpiece</u>.

- Breathe in quickly and deeply through the *Diskus*. Do not breathe in through your nose.

- Remove the *Diskus* from your mouth. Hold your breath for about 10 seconds, or for as long as is comfortable. Breathe out slowly.

- <u>Rinse your mouth with water after your dose of medicine. Spit the water out. Do not swallow</u>.

- Close the *Diskus* when you are finished by putting your thumb on the thumbgrip and slide the thumbgrip back towards you as far as it will go and the device clicks shut. The lever will automatically return to its original position.

- Never breathe into the *Diskus*.

- Never take the *Diskus* apart.

- Always ready and use the *Diskus* in a level, flat position.

- Do not use the *Diskus* with a spacer device.

- Never wash the mouthpiece or any part of the *Diskus*. Keep it dry.

- Always keep the *Diskus* in a dry place.

- Never take an extra dose, even if you did not taste or feel the medicine.

Flovent HFA

- This medication is used to reduce the inflammation in your lungs. <u>This is not a rescue medication for asthma attacks.</u>

- Common side effects of this medication include upper respiratory infections, sore throat, cough and hoarseness.

- Take your *Flovent* inhaler out of the moisture-protective foil pouch just before you use it for the first time. Safely throw away the foil pouch and the drying packet that comes inside the pouch.

- Before you use *Flovent* for the first time, you must prime the inhaler so that you will get the right amount of medicine when you use it. To prime the inhaler, take the cap off the mouthpiece and shake the inhaler well for 5 seconds. Then spray the inhaler into the air away from your face. Avoid spraying in eyes. Shake and spray the inhaler like this 3 more times to finish priming it. The counter should now read 120.

- You must prime the inhaler again if you have not used it in more than 7 days or if you drop it. Take the cap off the mouthpiece and shake the inhaler well for 5 seconds. Then spray it 1 time into the air away from your face.

- Take the cap off the mouthpiece of the actuator.

- Look inside the mouthpiece for foreign objects. Make sure the mouthpiece is clean and free of debris. Make sure the canister fits firmly in the actuator.

- Shake the inhaler well for 5 seconds.

- Hold the inhaler with the mouthpiece down. Breathe out through your mouth and push as much air from your lungs as you can. Put the mouthpiece in your mouth and close your lips around it.

- Push the top of the canister all the way down while you breathe in deeply and slowly through your mouth.

- Right after the spray comes out, take your finger off the canister. After you have breathed in all the way, take the inhaler out of your mouth and close your mouth.

- Hold your breath as long as you can, up to 10 seconds. Then breathe normally.

- After you finish taking this medicine, rinse your mouth with water. Spit out the water. Do not swallow it.

- Put the cap back on the mouthpiece after each time you use the inhaler. Make sure it snaps firmly into place.

- Clean the inhaler at least once a week after your evening dose. It is important to keep the canister and plastic actuator clean so the medicine will not build-up and block the spray.

- Take the cap off the mouthpiece. The strap on the cap will stay attached to the actuator. Do not take the canister out of the plastic actuator.

- Use a clean cotton swab dampened with water to clean the small circular opening where the medicine sprays out of the canister. Gently twist the swab in a circular motion to take off any medicine. Repeat with a new swab dampened with water to take off any medicine still at the opening.

- Wipe the inside of the mouthpiece with a clean tissue dampened with water. Let the actuator air-dry overnight.

- Put the cap back on the mouthpiece after the actuator has dried.

- When the counter reads 020, you should refill your prescription. When the counter reads 000, throw the inhaler away. You should not keep using the inhaler because you will not receive the right amount of medicine.

- Do not use the inhaler after the expiration date, which is on the packaging it comes in.

Symbicort HFA

- This medication is used to reduce the inflammation and promote bronchodilation in your lungs. <u>This is not a rescue medication for asthma attacks</u>.

- Take 2 puffs in the morning and 2 puffs in the evening every day.

- Rinse your mouth with water and spit the water our after each dose (2 puffs) of *Symbicort*. Do not swallow the water. This will help lessen the chance of getting a fungus infection (thrush) in your mouth.

- *Symbicort* does not relieve sudden symptoms and should never be used as a rescue inhaler. Always have a rescue inhaler with you to treat sudden symptoms.

- Throw away *Symbicort* when the counter reaches zero or 3 months after you take *Symbicort* out if its foil pouch, whichever comes first.

- Take the inhaler out of the moisture-protective foil pouch before you use it for the first time. Write the date that you open the foil pouch on the box.

- A counter is attached to the top of the metal canister. This counter will count down each time you release a puff of *Symbicort*. The arrow points to the number of inhalations left in the canister.

- Use the *Symbicort* canister only with the red *Symbicort* inhaler supplied.

- Shake your *Symbicort* inhaler well for 5 seconds right before each use. Remove mouthpiece cover and check for foreign objects.

- Prime your inhaler before you use it. Shake for 5 seconds and release a test spray, shake again for 5 seconds and release another test spray. Your inhaler is now ready to use.

- If you do not use your *Symbicort* inhaler for more than 7 days or if you drop it, you will need to prime again.

- Do proper inhaler technique (mentioned under *Flovent HFA).*

- Clean the inhaler every 7 days. To clean, remove mouthpiece cover, wipe inside and outside the mouthpiece with a clean, dry cloth. Replace mouthpiece cover. Do not put *Symbicort* inhaler into water.

Singulair

For adults and children 12 months of age and older with asthma:

- Take this medication once a day in the evening.

- Take every day for as long as your doctor prescribes it, even if you have no asthma symptoms.

- You may take this medication with food or without food.

- If your asthma symptoms get worse, or if you need to increase the use of your inhaled rescue medicine for asthma attacks, call your doctor right away.

- Do not take this medication for the immediate relief of an asthma attack. If you have an asthma attack, you should follow the instructions your doctor gave you for treating asthma attacks. Always have your inhaled rescue medicine for asthma attacks with you.

- Do not stop taking or lower the dose of your other asthma medicines unless your doctor instructed you to do so.

- The most common side effects with this medication include: stomach pain, upper respiratory infections, headache, flu and sinus infection.

- Rarely, this medication has been associated with behavior and mood changes including aggressive behavior, hostility, anxiousness, depression and/or suicidal thoughts and actions. Please report any of the symptoms to your healthcare provider immediately.

For patients 6 years of age and older for the prevention of exercise-induced asthma:

- Take this medication at least 2 hours before exercise.

- Always have your inhaled rescue medicine with you for asthma attacks.

- If you are taking *Singulair* daily for chronic asthma or allergies, do not take another dose to prevent exercise-induced asthma. Talk to your healthcare provider about your treatment of exercise-induced asthma.

- Do not take an additional dose of *Singulair* within 24 hours of a previous dose.

- *Singulair* 4-mg oral granules can be given:

    ❏ directly in the mouth;

- ❑ dissolved in 1 teaspoonful (5 mL) of cold or room temperature baby formula or breast milk;

- ❑ mixed with 1 spoonful of one of the following soft foods at cold or room temperature:

  - ◆ applesauce, mashed carrots, rice, or ice cream. Give the child all of the mixture right away (within 15 minutes).

- ■ <u>Important:</u> Never store any oral granules mixed with food, baby formula, or breast milk for use at a later time. Throw away any unused portion. Do not mix *Singulair* oral granules with any liquid drink other than baby formula or breast milk.

PRACTICE CASE

Terri is a 22 year-old female patient with Step 3 asthma who comes to your pharmacy and asks for a refill on all her asthma medications. You ask her how she is doing and she states that she has been using her *Maxair* inhaler 4 times/week for chest tightness and shortness of breath. She asks you to recommend a good sleep agent to help her fall back asleep. You notice that she is also picking up ferrous sulfate tablets, aspirin, *Dexatrim*, *Sucrets* lozenges, and *Maalox*. Terri is a college student and lives with her parents.

MEDICATIONS
Maxair 1-2 puffs Q4-6H PRN (last refilled 18 days ago)
Flovent Diskus 100 mcg/inh – take 2 inh BID (last refilled 27 days ago)
Singulair 10 mg daily (last refilled 27 days ago)
Aciphex 20 mg daily (last refilled 27 days ago)
Advil 200 mg TID PRN headaches
Ferrous Sulfate 325 mg daily

Questions

1. Terri seems to be exhibiting signs of uncontrolled asthma. Which of the following would be the <u>best</u> recommendation for better control?

   a. Take *Maxair* on a scheduled basis.

   b. Change the *Flovent Diskus* to 3 inhalations BID.

   c. Take *Singulair* 10 mg BID.

   d. Go to the emergency room as she is having an acute asthma attack.

   e. Elevate the head of the bed by 30 degrees when she sleeps.

2. Terri states that she doesn't understand why her asthma is worsening. Which of the following could be a trigger for her symptoms?

   a. Living in the same place for many years

   b. NSAID use

   c. Ferrous sulfate use

   d. *Aciphex* use

   e. She could be sleeping on her stomach more

3. Terri asks you if the *Sucrets* lozenges will help the sore throat. She was told by her doctor that she has signs of thrush. Which of the following recommendations would you give that would help prevent this from happening in the future? (Select **ALL** that apply.)

   a. Take the *Sucrets* lozenges because they will help with her sore throat and cure thrush.

   b. Recommend that she switch to *Symbicort* instead of *Flovent*.

   c. Recommend that she rinse her mouth after her *Flovent Diskus*, if not already doing so.

   d. Tell her to save her money; *Sucrets* will not work for treating thrush.

   e. Tell her to purchase a spacer device for the *Flovent Diskus*.

4. Terri comes back to your pharmacy with a prescription for *Foradil*. Which of the following statements is correct?

   a. The patient can store the medication at room temperature.
   b. This medication needs to be taken with 8 oz of water.
   c. This medication is not recommended in Step 3 asthma.
   d. This medication is taken once daily.
   e. This medication will interact with *Aciphex*.

5. Which of the following side effects is most likely to occur when using *Foradil* therapy?

   a. Neuropsychiatric behavior
   b. Palpitations
   c. Stomach upset
   d. Enuresis
   e. Depression

6. Terri comes to you 2 days after a severe asthma exacerbation. She is currently taking dexamethasone 3 mg PO daily. Convert her to an equivalent dose of prednisone. Choose the correct dose of prednisone:

   a. 20 mg
   b. 12 mg
   c. 3.75 mg
   d. 2 mg
   e. 0.75 mg

7. Terri is placed on theophylline therapy for treatment of her asthma. Which of the following can decrease theophylline levels? (Select **ALL** that apply.)

   a. Ciprofloxacin
   b. Carbamazepine
   c. Erythromycin
   d. Cirrhosis
   e. High protein diet

Questions 8-11 do not relate to the above case.

8. Omalizumab has a black box warning for:

   a. Increased risk of MI
   b. Stevens-Johnson syndrome
   c. Thrombocytopenia
   d. GI ulcers
   e. Anaphylaxis

9. A patient with asthma has been prescribed *Advair Diskus*. Which of the following statements is correct?

   a. *Advair Diskus* contains fluticasone, a long-acting beta$_2$ agonist.
   b. *Advair Diskus* contains flunisolide, an inhaled corticosteroid.
   c. *Advair Diskus* is usually dosed 2 inhalations once daily.
   d. *Advair Diskus* treats both airway constriction and inflammation.
   e. *Advair Diskus* contains formoterol, an anticholinergic agent.

10. Carla is a 10 year old girl with asthma. The physician wants to give her montelukast, but is not sure of the correct dose. Choose the correct dose of montelukast for a 10-year old child:

   a. A 5 mg chewable tablet taken BID
   b. A 5 mg chewable tablet taken once daily
   c. A 10 mg chewable tablet taken once daily
   d. A 10 mg chewable tablet taken BID
   e. A 4 mg packet of granules mixed with milk

11. The therapeutic range for theophylline is:

   a. 10-20 mcg/mL
   b. 5-10 mcg/mL
   c. 5-15 mg/mL
   d. 8-12 mg/mL
   e. 5-15 mcg/mL

Answers

1-b, 2-b, 3-c,d, 4-a, 5-b, 6-a, 7-b,e, 8-e, 9-d, 10-b, 11-e

39

COPD

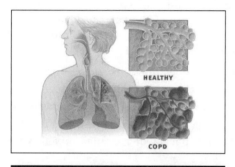

HEALTHY

COPD

GUIDELINE

Global Strategy for the Diagnosis, Management and Prevention of COPD, Global Initiative for Chronic Obstructive Lung Disease (GOLD) 2013 update. Available at: http://www.goldcopd. org/uploads/users/files/GOLD_Report_2013_Feb20.pdf (accessed 2013 Oct 14).

BACKGROUND

Chronic obstructive pulmonary disease (COPD) is a common preventable and somewhat treatable disease characterized by persistent airflow limitation that is usually progressive and associated with an enhanced chronic inflammatory response in the airways to noxious particles or gases. In contrast to asthma, the limitation of airflow is not fully reversible and generally worsens over time. COPD is the 4th leading cause of death in the world and the incidence is increasing, primarily due to tobacco use and secondhand smoke.

COPD is caused by inhalation of cigarette smoke and other noxious particles or gas (such as from biomass fuels) which triggers an abnormal inflammatory response in the lungs. This chronic inflammatory response can lead to lung tissue destruction (resulting in emphysema), and alter normal repair and defense mechanisms (resulting in small airway narrowing and fibrosis). These changes lead to air trapping and worsening airflow limitation, and to the breathlessness and other classic symptoms of COPD.

A clinical diagnosis of COPD should be considered in any patient who has dyspnea (shortness of breath, which is chronic and progressive), chronic cough or sputum production, and a history of exposure to risk factors for the disease, especially cigarette smoke. Spirometry (ways to measure breathing) is required to make the diagnosis; the presence of a post-bronchodilator $FEV_1/FVC < 0.70$ confirms the presence of persistent airflow limitation and thus of COPD. Smoking cessation is the only management strategy proven to slow progression of disease. Other important management strategies include vaccinations, pulmonary rehabilitation programs, and drug therapy (often using inhalers). Some patients go on to requirelong-term oxygen therapy, either given in the hospital for acute exacerbations, or used chronically outpatient with the use of portable oxygen systems. Uncommonly, lung transplantation is used.

RISK FACTORS

The major risk factors for developing COPD include <u>smoking or smoke exposure</u>, alpha-1 antitrypsin deficiency, occupational dusts and chemicals (chemical agents and fumes), and indoor and outdoor air pollution.

ASSESSMENT OF COPD

The goals of COPD assessment are to determine the severity of disease, its impact on the patient's health status and the risk of future events (exacerbations, hospital admissions, death) in order to guide therapy. Assess the following aspects of the disease separately:

- Symptoms

- Degree of airflow limitation (using spirometry)

- Risk of exacerbations

- Comorbidities

Symptoms

Symptoms can be assessed using validated questionnaires such as the COPD Assessment Test (CAT) or the Modified British Medical Research Council (mMRC) breathlessness scale.

Degree of Airflow Limitation

Degree of airflow limitation is assessed using spirometry. Please see table below for classification of severity.

Classification of Severity of Airflow Limitation in COPD (Based on Post-Bronchodilator FEV_1)

CLASSIFICATION	SEVERITY	AIRFLOW
In patients with $FEV_1/FVC < 0.70$		
GOLD 1	Mild	$FEV_1 \geq 80\%$ predicted
GOLD 2	Moderate	$50\% \leq FEV_1 < 80\%$ predicted
GOLD 3	Severe	$30\% \leq FEV_1 < 50\%$ predicted
GOLD 4	Very Severe	$FEV_1 < 30\%$ predicted

Risk of Exacerbations

An exacerbation of COPD is defined as an acute event characterized by a worsening of the patient's respiratory symptoms that is beyond normal day-to-day variations and leads to a change in medication. The best predictor of having frequent exacerbations (2 or more per year) is a history of previous treated events. The risk of exacerbations will also increase as airflow limitation worsens.

Comorbidities

Comorbid conditions such as cardiovascular diseases, osteoporosis, depression and anxiety, skeletal muscle dysfunction, metabolic syndrome, and lung cancer may influence mortality and hospitalizations, and should be looked for routinely and treated appropriately.

The combined assessment of COPD takes into account the symptoms, airflow limitation and exacerbation risk of the patient (see table below).

Combined Assessment of COPD

When assessing risk, choose the <u>highest risk</u> according to GOLD grade or exacerbation history.

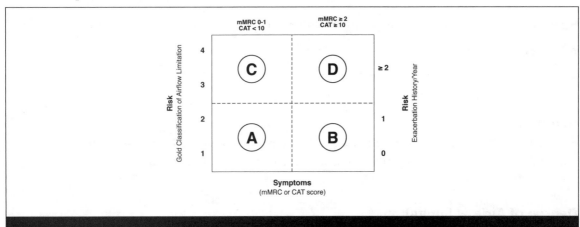

PATIENT	CHARACTERISTIC	SPIROMETRIC CLASSIFICATION	EXACERBATIONS PER YEAR	mMRC	CAT
A	Low Risk Less Symptoms	GOLD 1-2	≤ 1	0-1	< 10
B	Low Risk More Symptoms	GOLD 1-2	≤ 1	≥ 2	≥ 10
C	High Risk Less Symptoms	GOLD 3-4	≥ 2	0-1	< 10
D	High Risk More Symptoms	GOLD 3-4	≥ 2	≥ 2	≥ 10

CAT: COPD Assessment Test, mMRC: Modified British Medical Research Council

Pharmacologic Therapy for Stable COPD*

PATIENT GROUP	RECOMMENDED FIRST CHOICE	ALTERNATIVE CHOICE	OTHER POSSIBLE TREATMENTS**
A	SA anticholinergic PRN or SA beta$_2$-agonist PRN	LA anticholinergic or LA beta$_2$-agonist or SA beta$_2$-agonist and SA anticholinergic	Theophylline
B	LA anticholinergic or LA beta$_2$-agonist	LA anticholinergic and LA beta$_2$-agonist	SA beta$_2$-agonist and/or SA anticholinergic Theophylline
C	ICS + LA beta$_2$-agonist or LA anticholinergic	LA anticholinergic and LA beta$_2$-agonist or LA anticholinergic and PDE-4 inhibitor or LA beta$_2$-agonist and PDE-4 inhibitor	SA beta$_2$-agonist and/or SA anticholinergic Theophylline
D	ICS + LA beta$_2$-agonist and/or LA anticholinergic	ICS + LA beta$_2$-agonist and LA anticholinergic or ICS + LA beta$_2$-agonist and PDE-4 inhibitor or LA anticholinergic and LA beta$_2$-agonist or LA anticholinergic and PDE-4 inhibitor	Carbocysteine SA beta$_2$-agonist and/or SA anticholinergic Theophylline

Medications in each box are mentioned in alphabetical order and therefore not necessarily in order of preference

** *Medications in this column can be used alone or in combination with other options in the First and Alternative Choice columns*

SA: short-acting, LA: long-acting, ICS: inhaled corticosteroid, PDE-4: phosphodiesterase-4, PRN: when necessary

Pharmacologic Management

No medication used in COPD has been shown to modify the long-term decline in lung function that is the hallmark of COPD. Therefore, pharmacotherapy is used to decrease symptoms and/or complications. Carbocysteine is a mucolytic that has shown a small benefit in patients with viscous sputum. Bronchodilators (beta$_2$-agonists, anticholinergics) are used as-needed or on a regular basis, depending on symptom severity. If used on a regular basis, long-acting inhaled bronchodilators are more effective and more convenient than treatment with short-acting inhaled bronchodilators. Combining bronchodilators of different Pharmacologic classes may improve efficacy and decrease the risk of side effects compared to increasing the dose of a single agent. Long-term monotherapy with oral or inhaled corticosteroids is not recommended in COPD. PDE-4 inhibitors reduce inflammation by inhibiting the breakdown of intracellular cyclic AMP and should always be used in combination with at least one long-acting bronchodilator. Treatment with theophylline is not recommended unless other long-term treatment bronchodilators are unavailable or unaffordable.

Influenza (each fall) and pneumococcal (PPSV23, *Pneumovax*) (x 1, repeat when 65 years or older, and if received vaccine more than 5 years ago) should be given to patients with COPD, unless contraindications exist. Vaccines are used to prevent infections and reduce the risk of acute exacerbations.

If patients have severe hereditary alpha-1 antitrypsin deficiency, they may be placed on an alpha-1 proteinase inhibitor *(Prolastin, Aralast, or Zemaira)* for chronic augmentation therapy. These agents are very expensive, given as weekly IV infusions and are associated with many side effects, including anaphylaxis.

For treatment of acute COPD exacerbations, see the infectious disease section. Outside of antibiotics, an inhaled anticholinergic bronchodilator plus oral steroids (tapered over 2 weeks) are effective treatments. The use of azithromycin 250 mg/d reduces the risk of acute exacerbations due to its anti-inflammatory and immunomodulatory properties; however, treatment is not recommended because of an unfavorable balance between benefits and side effects (e.g., decreased hearing).

PHARMACOLOGIC AGENTS

DRUG	DOSING	SAFETY/SIDE EFFECTS/MONITORING

Anticholinergics – block the action of acetylcholine [and ↓ cyclic guanosine monophosphate (cGMP)] at parasympathetic sites in bronchial smooth muscle causing bronchodilation.

Short-acting anticholinergics		**WARNINGS** Use with caution in patients with myasthenia gravis, narrow-angle glaucoma, urinary retention, benign prostatic hyperplasia, or bladder neck obstruction
Ipratropium bromide *(Atrovent HFA)*	2 inhalations QID (MDI) 0.5 mg TID-QID (neb)	
		SIDE EFFECTS Dry mouth (much more common with tiotropium), upper respiratory tract infections, nasopharyngitis, sinusitis, cough and bitter taste
+ albuterol *(Combivent Respimat, DuoNeb)*	1 inhalation QID 0.5 mg QID (neb)	
Long-acting anticholinergics		**MONITORING** Signs and symptoms at each visit, smoking status, COPD questionnaires, spirometry yearly
Aclidinium *(Tudorza Pressair)*	1 inhalation BID (DPI)	
		NOTES Avoid spraying in the eyes
		Do NOT swallow capsules of tiotropium
Tiotropium *(Spiriva HandiHaler)*	1 capsule (18 mcg) inhaled daily via the *HandiHaler* device (requires 2 puffs)	*Combivent Respimat* – Discard 3 months from when cartridge is inserted into device. *Tudorza* – Discard product 45 days after opening pouch, when device locks out, or when dose indicator displays "0", whichever comes first.

Pharmacologic Agents Continued

DRUG	DOSING	SAFETY/SIDE EFFECTS/MONITORING

Beta$_2$-agonists – bind to beta$_2$ receptors causing relaxation of bronchial smooth muscle, resulting in bronchodilation – inhaled route is the preferred route of administration. For short-acting beta$_2$-agonists, see asthma section.

DRUG	DOSING	SAFETY/SIDE EFFECTS/MONITORING
Long-acting Beta$_2$ -agonists		**BLACK BOX WARNING** Long-acting beta$_2$-agonists (LABAs) increase the risk of asthma-related deaths and should only be used in asthma patients who are currently receiving but are not adequately controlled on a long-term asthma control medication (e.g., inhaled corticosteroid)
Salmeterol *(Serevent Diskus)*	1 inhalation BID	
+ fluticasone *(Advair Diskus)*	1 inhalation BID (100/50, 250/50, 500/50 – mcg fluticasone/mcg salmeterol)	**SIDE EFFECTS** Tachycardia, tremor, shakiness, lightheadedness, cough, palpitations, hypokalemia and hyperglycemia
Formoterol *(Foradil Aerolizer, Perforomist)*	12 mcg capsule via *Aerolizer* BID 20 mcg BID (neb)	**MONITORING** Signs and symptoms at each visit, smoking status, COPD questionnaires, spirometry yearly
+ budesonide (Symbicort)	2 inhalations BID (80/4.5, 160/4.5 – mcg budesonide/mcg formoterol)	**NOTES** Bronchodilators are used on a PRN or scheduled basis to reduce symptoms Long-acting inhaled bronchodilators are more effective and convenient
Arformoterol *(Brovana)*	15 mcg BID (neb)	Combination therapy with inhaled steroids can ↑ the risk of pneumonia, however, the combination showed a ↓ in exacerbations and improvement in lung function when compared to the individual components Arformoterol contains R-isomer of formoterol Do NOT swallow capsules of indacaterol All steroid-containing inhalers – rinse mouth with water after use and spit.
Indacaterol *(Arcapta Neohaler)*	75 mcg capsule via *Neohaler* device daily	*Advair* – discard device 1 month after removal from pouch *Symbicort* – discard inhaler after the labeled number of inhalations have been used or within 3 months after removal from foil pouch *Serevent Diskus/Breo Ellipta* – discard device 6 weeks after removal from the foil tray or when the dose counter reads "0" (whichever comes first).
Vilanterol/fluticasone *(Breo Ellipta)*	1 inhalation daily (25 mcg vilanterol/100 mcg fluticasone)	

Pharmacologic Agents Continued

DRUG	DOSING	SAFETY/SIDE EFFECTS/MONITORING

Phosphodiesterase 4 inhibitor – PDE-4 inhibitor that ↑ cAMP levels, leading to a reduction in lung inflammation.

Roflumilast *(Daliresp)*	500 mcg PO daily	**CONTRAINDICATIONS** Moderate to severe liver impairment **SIDE EFFECTS** Diarrhea, weight loss, nausea, ↓ appetite, insomnia, depression and psychiatric events including suicidality **MONITORING** Signs and symptoms at each visit, LFTs, smoking status, COPD questionnaires, spirometry yearly **NOTES** Use only in severe COPD due to modest benefit

See asthma section for details on theophylline and inhaled corticosteroids

Drug Interactions with Roflumilast

Roflumilast is a substrate of 3A4 and 1A2. Use with strong enzyme inducers (carbamazepine, phenobarbital, phenytoin, rifampin) is not recommended. Use with 3A4 inhibitors or dual 3A4 and 1A2 inhibitors (erythromycin, ketoconazole, fluvoxamine, cimetidine) will ↑ roflumilast levels.

Patient Counseling for *Atrovent HFA*

- Insert the metal canister into the clear end of the mouthpiece. Make sure the canister is fully and firmly inserted into the mouthpiece.

- The *Atrovent HFA* canister is to be used only with the *Atrovent HFA* mouthpiece.

- Do not use the *Atrovent HFA* mouthpiece with other inhaled medicines.

- Remove the green protective dust cap. If the cap is not on the mouthpiece, make sure there is nothing in the mouthpiece before use. For best results, the canister should be at room temperature before use.

- Breathe out (exhale) deeply through your mouth. Put the mouthpiece in your mouth and close your lips. Keep your eyes closed so that no medicine will be sprayed into your eyes. If sprayed into the eyes, *Atrovent HFA* can cause blurry vision and other vision abnormalities, eye pain or discomfort, dilated pupils, or narrow-angle glaucoma or worsening of this condition. If any combination of these symptoms develops, you should consult your physician immediately.

- Breathe in (inhale) slowly through your mouth and at the same time spray the *Atrovent HFA* into your mouth.

- Hold your breath for ten seconds and then take the mouthpiece out of your mouth and breathe out slowly.

- Replace the green protective dust cap after use.

- Keep the mouthpiece clean. At least once a week, wash the mouthpiece, shake it to remove excess water and let it air dry all the way.

- There are approximately 40 actuations (sprays) left when the dose indicator displays "40," where the background changes from green to red. This is when you need to refill your prescription or ask your doctor if you need another prescription for *Atrovent HFA* inhalation aerosol. Discard the inhaler once the dose indicator displays "0".

Patient Counseling for *Combivent Respimat*

- *Combivent Respimat* may increase eye pressure which may cause or worsen some types of glaucoma. Do not get the spray into your eyes.

- *Combivent Respimat* may cause difficulty with urination.

- If you have vision changes or eye pain or if you have difficulty with urination, stop taking *Combivent Respimat* and call your doctor right away.

- Dizziness and blurred vision may occur with *Combivent Respimat*. Should you experience these symptoms, use caution when engaging in activities such as driving a car or operating appliances or other machines.

- Do not use *Combivent Respimat* more often than your doctor has directed. Deaths have been reported with similar inhaled medicines in asthma patients who use the medicine too much.

- Allergic reactions may occur, including itching, swelling of the face, lips, tongue, or throat (involving difficulty in breathing or swallowing), rash, hives, bronchospasm (airway narrowing), or anaphylaxis. Some of these may be serious. If you experience any of these symptoms, stop taking *Combivent Respimat* at once and call your doctor or get emergency help.

- Tell your doctor about all your medical conditions, especially if you have narrow-angle glaucoma, prostate or urinary problems, a history of heart conditions (such as irregular heartbeat, high blood pressure), seizures, thyroid disorder, diabetes, low potassium levels, or kidney or liver disease. Also tell your doctor if you are pregnant or nursing.

- Tell your doctor about all medicines you are taking, especially heart medications or drugs to treat depression.

- The most common side effects reported with use of *Combivent Respimat* include infection of the ears, nose, and throat, runny nose, cough, bronchitis, headache, and shortness of breath.

Directions for using your medication daily:

1. Hold the inhaler upright with the orange cap closed to avoid accidental release of dose. <u>TURN</u> the clear base in the direction of the white arrows on the label until it clicks (half turn).

2. Flip the orange cap until it snaps fully <u>OPEN</u>. Breathe out slowly and fully, and then close your lips around the end of the mouthpiece without covering the air vents.

3. Point your inhaler to the back of your throat. While taking in a slow, deep breath through your mouth, <u>PRESS</u> the dose-release button and continue to breathe in slowly for as long as you can. Hold your breath for 10 seconds or for as long as comfortable. Close the orange cap until you use your inhaler again.

Patient Counseling for *Spiriva*

- Do not swallow *Spiriva* capsules. *Spiriva* capsules should only be used with the *HandiHaler* device. *Spiriva HandiHaler* should only be inhaled through your mouth (oral inhalation).

- Do not open the *Spiriva* capsule before you insert it into the *HandiHaler* device.

- Open the dust cap by pressing the green piercing button.

- Pull the dust cap upwards to expose the mouthpiece.

- Open the mouthpiece by pulling the mouthpiece ridge upwards away from the base.

- Always store *Spiriva* capsules in the sealed blisters. Remove only one *Spiriva* capsule from the blister right before use. Do not store *Spiriva* capsules in the *HandiHaler* device. Inhale the contents of the *Spiriva* capsule using the *HandiHaler* device right away after the blister packaging of an individual *Spiriva* capsule is opened, or else it may not work as well.

- If more *Spiriva* capsules are opened to air, they should not be used and should be thrown away

- Insert the *Spiriva* capsule in the center chamber of the *HandiHaler* device. It does not matter which end of the *Spiriva* capsule you put in the chamber.

- Close the mouthpiece until you hear a click, but leave the dust cap open.

- Be sure that you have the mouthpiece sitting firmly against the gray base.

- Hold the *HandiHaler* device with the mouthpiece upright. It is important that you hold the *HandiHaler* device in an upright position when pressing the green piercing button.

- Press the green piercing button until it is flat against the base and release. This is how you make holes in the *Spiriva* capsule so that you get the medicine when you breathe in.

- Do not press the green button more than once.

- Breathe out completely. Do not breathe into the mouthpiece of the *HandiHaler* device at any time. Hold the *HandiHaler* device by the gray base. Do not block the air intake vents.

- Raise the *HandiHaler* device to your mouth and close your lips tightly around the mouthpiece.

- Keep your head in an upright position. The *HandiHaler* device should be in a horizontal position.

- Breathe in slowly and deeply so that you hear or feel the *Spiriva* capsule vibrate.

- Breathe in until your lungs are full.

- Hold your breath as long as is comfortable and at the same time take the *HandiHaler* device out of your mouth. Breathe normally again.

- To make sure you get the full dose, you must breathe out completely, and inhale again.

- If you do not hear or feel the *Spiriva* capsule vibrate, do not press the green piercing button again. Instead, hold the *HandiHaler* device in an upright position and tap the *HandiHaler* device gently on a table. Check to see that the mouthpiece is completely closed. Then, breathe in again.

- After you finish taking your daily dose of *Spiriva HandiHaler*, open the mouthpiece again. Tip out the used *Spiriva* capsule and throw it away.

- Close the mouthpiece and dust cap for storage of your *HandiHaler* device.

- Do not store used or unused *Spiriva* capsules in the *HandiHaler* device.

- Clean the *HandiHaler* device one time each month or as needed.

  - Open the dust cap and mouthpiece. Open the base by lifting the green piercing button.

  - Look at the center chamber for *Spiriva* capsule fragments or powder residue.

  - Rinse the *HandiHaler* device with warm water.

  - Do not use cleaning agents or detergents.

  - Do not place the *HandiHaler* device in the dishwasher for cleaning.

  - Dry the *HandiHaler* device well by tipping the excess water out on a paper towel. Air-dry afterwards, leaving the dust cap, mouthpiece, and base open.

  - Do not use a hair dryer to dry the *HandiHaler* device.

  - It takes 24 hours to air dry, so clean the *HandiHaler* device right after you use it so that it will be ready for your next dose.

  - Do not use the *HandiHaler* device when it is wet. If needed, you may clean the outside of the mouthpiece with a clean damp cloth.

40

SMOKING CESSATION

GUIDELINES/REFERENCES

Treating Tobacco Use and Dependence. 2008 Update. April 2009. U.S. Public Health Service. Agency for Healthcare Research and Quality. Available at http://www.ahrq.gov/clinic/(accessed 2013 Dec 1)

FDA Drug Safety Communication: Safety review update of Chantix (varenicline) and risk of neuropsychiatric adverse events, Available at: http://www.fda.gov/Drugs/DrugSafety/ucm276737.htm (accessed 2013 Dec 1)

The American College of Obstetricians and Gynecologists – Committee Opinion: Smoking Cessation During Pregnancy. Number 471, November 2010 (Reaffirmed 2013).

BACKGROUND

Tobacco dependence is a chronic disease that often requires repeated intervention and multiple attempts to quit. Effective treatments exist that can significantly increase rates of long-term abstinence. It is essential that clinicians and healthcare delivery systems consistently identify and document tobacco use status and treat every tobacco user seen in a healthcare setting.

Counseling and medication are more effective when used together than either modality used alone. Two counseling components that are especially effective are practical counseling (problem-solving/skills training) and social support delivered as part of treatment. There is a strong correlation between counseling intensity and quitting success (counseling sessions should be > 10 minutes in length and number of sessions should be ≥ 4).

Smoking accounts for more than 435,000 deaths per year in the U.S. It is a known cause of multiple cancers, heart disease, stroke, complications of pregnancy, COPD, and many other diseases. Still, roughly 20% of adult Americans smoke representing ~45 million current adult smokers.

Numerous effective medications (5 nicotine and 2 nonnicotine) are available for treating tobacco dependence and clinicians should encourage their use by all patients attempting to quit smoking except when medically contraindicated. Use a combination of two nicotine products (use extreme caution if any underlying cardiovascular condition due to additive side effects) or combination with bupoprion, if a single agent is not enough (e.g., patch + gum or nasal spray or inhaler or bupropion SR + patch). Bupropion plus a nicotine product is sometimes used initially; however, there is less evidence of benefit with this combination versus using two nicotine agents. There is benefit (and increased side effects) with the use of bupropion and two nicotine products. Do not use varenicline with nicotine products due to increased side effects.

Recently, electronic cigarettes (e-cigarettes) have gained popularity as an alternative to traditional cigarettes and as a potential smoking cessation aid. E-cigarettes use an electronic delivery system to aerosolize nicotine without the traditional carcinogenic toxins present in cigarettes. They reduce the user's desire to smoke traditional cigarettes and thus, are sometimes recommended to help smoking cessation. The FDA has not approved the use of any e-cigarettes thus far, citing potential safety concerns (e.g., potential for toxic ingestion in children, rising use in adolescents).

THE "5 A'S" MODEL FOR TREATING TOBACCO USE AND DEPENDENCE

Ask about tobacco use
Identify and document tobacco use status for every patient at every visit.

Advise to quit
In a clear, strong, and personalized manner, urge every tobacco user to quit.

Assess
For current tobacco user, is the tobacco user willing to make a quit attempt at this time?

For the ex-tobacco user, how recent did you quit and are there any challenges to remaining abstinent?

Assist
For the patient willing to make a quit attempt, offer medication and provide or refer for counseling or additional behavioral treatment to help the patient quit.

For patients unwilling to quit at this time, provide motivational interventions designed to increase future quit attempts.

For the recent quitter and any with remaining challenges, provide relapse prevention.

Arrange
All those receiving the previous A's should receive follow up.

Smoking causes an induction of some isoforms of the CYP450 system. Therefore, smokers who quit can experience side effects from supratherapeutic drug levels of caffeine, estrogens (oral), theophylline, fluvoxamine, olanzapine, quetiapine and clozapine. High levels of clozapine have increased risk for agranulocytosis. Ensure that smokers get required vaccines, including pneumococcal (*Pneumovax 23*) and an annual (fall) influenza vaccine. If no local programs are available smokers can get free assistance by calling the U.S. national quit-line network at 1-800-QUIT-NOW (1-800-784-8669). The help line has services available in multiple languages.

Smoking in Pregnancy

Smoking in pregnancy can cause adverse outcomes for the child, including spontaneous abortion, low birth weight and sudden infant death. If women smoke 5 or less cigarettes daily (occasional, "nervous" type smokers), they should be encouraged to quit with behavioral support. If they smoke more than 5 cigarettes daily, more intensive therapy along with bupropion (Pregnancy Category C) may be used, although evidence to support its use in pregnant patients is lacking. Nicotine products may also be considered; however, the efficacy is not as high as it is in non-pregnant patients. All nicotine products are Pregnancy Category D, except the gum and lozenge are Pregnancy Category C.

Vaccinations in Smokers

Smokers 19-64 years old should receive the pneumococcal polysaccharide vaccine (PPSV23, *Pneumovax*). If 65 and older and it's been more than 5 years since vaccination a 2nd dose is needed. Everyone should receive the influenza vaccine in the fall, including people who smoke. The ACIP has no recommendation on vaccine use with e-cigarettes. See Immunizations chapter for further discussion.

Nicotine Replacement Therapy (NRT)

DRUG	DOSING	SAFETY/SIDE EFFECTS/MONITORING
Nicotine gum (*Nicorette, Nicorelief, Thrive*) OTC	If < 25 cigs/day, use 2 mg gum If ≥ 25 cigs/day, use 4 mg gum 1 gum Q1-2H x 6 wks, then 1 gum Q2-4H x 3 wks, then 1 gum Q4-8H hrs x 3 wks; max 24 pieces/day Use up to 12 weeks	**CONTRAINDICATIONS** Recent MI (within 2 weeks), life-threating arrhythmia, severe or worsening angina, pregnancy **SIDE EFFECTS** Headache, dizziness, nervousness, insomnia, dyspepsia (all products) Local irritation in the mouth and throat, coughing, rhinitis (inhaler) Nasal irritation, transient changes in taste and smell (nasal spray) Application site reaction, local erythema (patch) **NOTES** Nicotine patch has highest adherence rate; however, may need additional product for acute cravings Patients must show identification for proof of age prior to purchase of nicotine products since the FDA prohibits sale of nicotine products to individuals younger than 18 years of age (REMS). Gum has been shown to reduce or delay weight gain – review gum counseling at end of this section. Inhaler has a hand to mouth use; mimics smoking action, providing a coping mechanism Nasal spray has the fastest delivery system; useful for rapid relief of withdrawal; highest dependence potential among NRTs. Avoid in severe reactive airway disease Patch is typically worn for 24 hours; however, can remove at bedtime to avoid insomnia Pregnancy Category C (gum, lozenge)/D (all others)
Nicotine Inhaler (*Nicotrol Inhaler*) Rx	6-16 cartridges daily; taper frequency of use over the last 6-12 weeks Use up to 6 months	
Nicotine nasal spray (*Nicotrol NS*) Rx	1 dose = 2 sprays (1 spray in each nostril), give 1-2 doses per hour, ↑ PRN for symptom relief; max: 5 doses/hr or 40 doses/day Use 3-6 months	
Nicotine patch (*NicoDerm CQ*) OTC	7 mg/day, 14 mg/day, 21 mg/day; apply upon waking on quit date If > 10 cigs/day, use 21 mg x 6 wk, then 14 mg x 2 wk, then 7 mg x 2 wk If ≤ 10 cigs/day, use 14 mg x 6 wk, then 7 mg x 2 wk	
Nicotine Lozenge (*Commit, Nicorelief, Nicorette*) OTC	1st cigarette smoked > 30 min after waking up: use 2 mg lozenge 1st cigarette smoked within 30 min of waking up: use 4 mg lozenge Do not exceed 20 lozenges/day Minimum of 9 lozenges/day 1 lozenge Q1-2H x 6 wks, then 1 lozenge Q2-4H x 3 wks, then 1 lozenge Q4-8H x 3 wks.	

Oral Prescription Agents

Bupropion blocks neural re-uptake of dopamine and/or norepinephrine and blocks nicotinic acetylcholinergic receptors. Varenicline is a partial neuronal α4-β2 nicotinic receptor agonist. It also stimulates dopamine activity, resulting in reduced withdrawal symptoms, including cravings.

DRUG	DOSING	SAFETY/SIDE EFFECTS/MONITORING
BuPROPion SR *(Zyban, Buproban)*	150 mg QAM for 3 days, then 150 mg BID. Start 1 week before quit date	**BLACK BOX WARNINGS** Serious neuropsychiatric events, including depression, suicidal thoughts and suicide have been reported in patients taking bupropion; not approved for use in children; not approved for bipolar; ↑ risk of suicidal thinking and behavior in young adults (18-24 years) with depression or other psychiatric disorders **CONTRAINDICATIONS** Seizure disorder; history of anorexia/bulimia; patients undergoing abrupt discontinuation of ethanol or sedatives, including benzodiazepines; use of MAO inhibitors or MAO inhibitors intended to treat psychiatric disorders (concurrently or within 14 days of discontinuing either bupropion or the MAO inhibitor); initiation of bupropion in a patient receiving linezolid or intravenous methylene blue; patients receiving other dosage forms of bupropion **WARNINGS** Use with caution in patients with underlying psychiatric disorders and while driving or operating machinery, traffic accidents have occurred. Avoid use in pilots, air traffic controllers, commercial truckers, bus drivers. **SIDE EFFECTS** Dry mouth, insomnia, headache/migraine, weight loss, nausea/vomiting, constipation, and tremors/seizures (dose-related), possible blood pressure changes (more hypertension than hypotension – monitor) No effects on 5HT and therefore no sexual dysfunction **NOTES** Can be used in combination with NRT Delays weight gain, can be used with CVD risk Do not exceed 450 mg/day due to seizure risk Pregnancy Category C (but used in pregnancy) MedGuide required

Oral Prescription Agents Continued

DRUG	DOSING	SAFETY/SIDE EFFECTS/MONITORING
Varenicline *(Chantix)*	Start one week before the quit date Days 1-3: 0.5 mg daily Days 4-7: 0.5 mg BID Days 8 (quit date) and beyond: 1 mg BID	**BLACK BOX WARNING** Serious neuropsychiatric events including depression, suicidal ideation, suicide attempt and completed suicide have been reported in patients taking varenicline. Stop taking this medication if patients become hostile, agitated, depressed, or have changes in behavior or thinking that are not typical for the patient. **WARNINGS** Angioedema, hypersensitivity rxns, and serious skin reactions have occurred. Use with caution in patients with underlying psychiatric disorders and while driving or operating machinery, traffic accidents have occurred. Avoid use in pilots, air traffic controllers, commercial truckers, bus drivers. **SIDE EFFECTS** Nausea (~30% and dose dependent), insomnia, abnormal dreams, constipation, flatulence, vomiting **NOTES** To reduce nausea, can use lower dosage and/or take with food and a full glass of water. To reduce insomnia, take 2nd dose at dinner rather than bedtime. CrCl < 30 mL/min: dose 0.5 mg daily If patient has cardiovascular disease they can use if stable but need to stop smoking as varenicline may exacerbate CVD, but at this point it is thought that risk may be worth the benefit. Pregnancy Category C MedGuide required

Nicotine Replacement Counseling

Counseling with the Nicotine Gum

- Gum should be chewed slowly until a "peppery" or "flavored" taste emerges, then "parked" between cheek and gum to facilitate nicotine absorption through the oral mucosa. Gum should be slowly and intermittently chewed and parked for about 30 minutes or until the taste dissipates.

- Acidic beverages (e.g., coffee, juices, soft drinks) interfere with the buccal absorption of nicotine, so eating and drinking anything except water should be avoided for 15 minutes before or during chewing.

- Patients often do not use enough gum to obtain optimal clinical effects. Instruct to use at least 1 piece Q1-2 hours.

Counseling with Inhaler

- Frequent, continuous puffing for 20 minutes is advised with each cartridge. Once a cartridge is opened, it is only good for one day. Peak effect is achieved within 15 minutes. After your dose is established, it is generally maintained for 3 months and then gradually tapered during the following 3 months. Clean mouthpiece with soap and water regularly. Delivery of nicotine from the inhaler declines significantly below 40°F. In cold weather, the inhaler and cartridge should be kept in an inside pocket or other warm area.

■ Acidic beverages (e.g., coffee, juices, soft drinks) interfere with the buccal absorption of nicotine, so eating and drinking anything except water should be avoided for 15 minutes before or during the use of the nicotine inhaler.

Counseling with the Lozenge

■ The lozenge should be allowed to <u>dissolve in the mouth</u> rather than chewing or swallowing it.

■ Acidic beverages (e.g., coffee, juices, soft drinks) interfere with the buccal absorption of nicotine, so eating and drinking anything except water should be avoided for 15 minutes before or during use of the nicotine lozenge.

■ Patients often do not use enough PRN nicotine replacement medications to obtain optimal clinical effects. <u>Generally, patients should use 1 lozenge every 1-2 hours</u> during the first 6 weeks of treatment, using a minimum of 9 lozenges/day, then decrease over time.

Counseling with Nasal Spray

■ Patients should not sniff, swallow, or inhale through the nose while administering doses, as this increases irritating effects. The spray is best delivered with the <u>head tilted slightly back</u>.

Counseling with the Nicotine Patch

■ At the start of each day, place the patch on a relatively hairless location, typically between the neck and waist, rotating the site to reduce local skin irritation.

■ Patches should be applied <u>as soon as the patient wakes on the quit day</u>. With patients who experience sleep disruption, have the patient remove the 24-hour patch prior to bedtime, or use the 16 hour patch.

■ Up to 50% of patients using the nicotine patch will experience a <u>local skin reaction</u>. Skin reactions usually are mild and self-limiting, but occasionally worsen over the course of therapy. Local treatment with hydrocortisone cream (1%) or triamcinolone cream (0.5%) and rotating patch sites may ameliorate the reaction. Fewer than 5% of patients discontinue patch treatment due to skin reactions.

Bupropion Counseling

■ It takes about 1 week for the medication to start working. For your best chance of quitting, you should not stop smoking until you have been taking for 1 week. Set a date to stop smoking during the second week of starting this medication.

■ The most common side effects are dry mouth and trouble sleeping. These side effects are generally mild and often disappear after a few weeks.

■ Some people have severe allergic reactions to bupropion. Stop taking and call your healthcare provider right away if you get a rash, itching, hives, fever, swollen lymph glands, painful sores in your mouth or around your eyes, swelling of your lips or tongue, chest pain, or have trouble breathing. These could be signs of a serious allergic reaction.

- Do not take if have a seizure disorder, are taking other forms of bupropion, or have taken an MAO inhibitor within the last 14 days or had an eating disorder.

- Do not chew, cut, or crush the tablets. If you do, the medicine will be released into your body too quickly. If this happens you may be more likely to get side effects including seizures. Tablets must be swallowed whole. Do not exceed 450 mg daily, or 150 mg at each dose if using the IR formulation, due to seizure risk.

- Take the doses at least 8 hours apart.

- If you, your family, or caregiver notice agitation, hostility, depression or changes in behavior or thinking that are not typical for you, or you develop any of the following symptoms, stop taking the medication and call your healthcare provider right away:

  - thoughts about suicide or dying, or attempts to commit suicide

  - new or worse depression, anxiety or panic attacks

  - feeling very agitated or restless

  - acting aggressive, being angry, or violent

  - acting on dangerous impulses

  - an extreme increase in activity and talking (mania)

  - abnormal thoughts or sensations

  - seeing or hearing things that are not there (hallucinations)

  - feeling people are against you (paranoia)

  - feeling confused

  - other unusual changes in behavior or mood

Varenicline Counseling

- Choose a quit date to stop smoking.

- Start taking the medication 1 week (7 days) before the quit date. This allows the medication to build up in the body. You may continue to smoke during this time. Try to stop smoking on the quit date. If it doesn't happen, try again. Some people need to take the medication for a few weeks to work best.

- Take the medication after eating and with a full glass (8 ounces) of water.

- Most people will take this medicine for up to 12 weeks. If quit smoking by 12 weeks, another 12 weeks of therapy may helpful to stay cigarette-free.

- Symptoms of nicotine withdrawal include the urge to smoke, depressed mood, trouble sleeping, irritability, frustration, anger, feeling anxious, difficulty concentrating, restlessness, decreased heart rate, and increased appetite or weight gain.

- Before taking this medication, tell your healthcare provider if you have ever had depression or other mental health problems.

- **If you, your family, or caregiver notice agitation, hostility, depression or changes in behavior or thinking** that are not typical for you, or you develop any of the following symptoms, stop taking the medication and call your healthcare provider right away:

  - thoughts about suicide or dying, or attempts to commit suicide

  - new or worse depression, anxiety or panic attacks

  - feeling very agitated or restless

  - acting aggressive, being angry, or violent

  - acting on dangerous impulses

  - an extreme increase in activity and talking (mania)

  - abnormal thoughts or sensations

  - seeing or hearing things that are not there (hallucinations)

  - feeling people are against you (paranoia)

  - feeling confused

  - other unusual changes in behavior or mood

- Some people can have allergic reactions to this medication. Some of these allergic reactions can be life-threatening and include: swelling of the face, mouth, and throat that can cause trouble breathing. If these symptoms occur, stop taking the medication and get medical attention right away.

- Some people can have serious skin reactions while taking this medication. These can include rash, swelling, redness, and peeling of the skin. Some of these reactions can become life-threatening. If a rash with peeling skin or blisters in your mouth occurs, stop taking the medication and get medical attention right away.

- Tell your pharmacist about all your other medicines including prescription and nonprescription medicines, vitamins and herbal supplements.

- Use caution driving or operating machinery until you know how this medication may affect you. Some people may become sleepy, dizzy, or have trouble concentrating, that can make it hard to drive or perform other activities safely.

41

ALLERGIC RHINITIS, COUGH & COLD

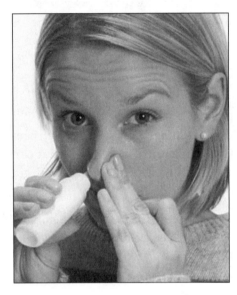

We gratefully acknowledge the assistance of Jeannette Y. Wick, RPh, in preparing this chapter.

BACKGROUND

<u>Allergic Rhinitis (sometimes known as "hay fever")</u> is the 6th most prevalent chronic disease. It represents an opportunity for pharmacists to help patients select self care products OTC, and to use prescription medication correctly. Allergic rhinitis is a major reason for decreased work productivity, or lost work or school days each year. Rhinitis is an inflammation of the membrane linings in the nose. Symptoms include sneezing, itchy nose, eyes or throat, watery eyes, rhinorrhea, nasal congestion, and postnasal drip.

NON-PHARMACOLOGIC MANAGEMENT

Environmental control is required to minimize allergic symptoms and involves <u>avoiding exposure to allergens</u>, if possible. Ventilation systems with high-efficiency particulate air (HEPA) filters can help with some allergens (pollen, mold), however, these systems are expensive and ineffective for some patients. Vacuuming carpets, drapes, and upholstery with a HEPA vacuum cleaner weekly or more often will reduce household allergens. Removing carpets, upholstered furniture, encasing mattresses, pillows and boxsprings in allergen-impermeable covers, and washing bedding and soft toys in hot water every 1-2 weeks reduces dust mite allergens. Nasal wetting agents (Saline, propylene, and polyethylene glycol sprays) or nasal irrigation with warm saline (isotonic or hypertonic) may reduce symptoms. Keeping an environment that is "too clean" reduces exposure to microbes and helminths and may not be ideal: children need exposure to various "germs" to build a healthy immune system.

PHARMACOLOGIC MANAGEMENT

Selecting appropriate pharmacologic management depends on the illness's severity and symptoms. Intranasal corticosteroids are first line for chronic, moderate-to-severe rhinitis. Milder, intermittent symptoms can be treated with oral antihistamines. Decongestants are used for congestion (if present) and come in nasal and oral formulations. Agents for itchy eyes can be found in the ophthalmic chapter. A variety of other agents can be modestly useful.

Intranasal Corticosteroids

Intranasal corticosteroids work by decreasing inflammation. They are the most effective medication class in controlling symptoms of chronic allergic rhinitis and are considered 1st line treatment for moderate-severe rhinitis. Note: steroids used to treat chronic allergic rhinitis have different names and delivery vehicles than those used to treat asthma. Do not mix up the brand names. There is a table with a blank column at the end of this chapter where you can test yourself on the asthma drug names. For example, fluticasone for nasal allergy relief is *Flonase* (nase for nose) and for asthma is *Flovent*. During pregnancy budesonide (in the nasal formulation *Rhinocort Aqua*) is preferred for nasal allergy symptoms.

DRUG	DOSING	SAFETY/SIDE EFFECTS/MONITORING
Beclomethasone (Qnasi)	2 sprays in each nostril daily	**WARNINGS** Delayed wound healing, avoid use if recent nasal septal ulcers, nasal surgery, or nasal trauma until healing has occurred.
Beclomethasone (Beconase AQ)	1 to 2 sprays in each nostril daily or BID Pediatrics: 1 to 2 sprays in each nostril BID	
Budesonide (Rhinocort Aqua)	1 to 4 sprays in each nostril daily Pediatrics: 1 to 2 sprays in each nostril daily	Pediatrics: may cause a reduction in growth velocity in pediatric patients (~1 centimeter per year [range 0.3-1.8 cm per year] and related to dose and duration of exposure). To minimize, use lowest effective dose. Monitor growth.
Ciclesonide (Omnaris, Zetonna)	2 sprays in each nostril daily (Omnaris); 1 spray in each nostril daily (Zetonna) Ages ≥ 6 use adult dose	
Flunisolide	2 sprays in each nostril BID to TID Pediatrics: 2 sprays in each nostril BID or 1 spray in each nostril TID	**SIDE EFFECTS** Headache, pharyngitis, epistaxis
Fluticasone (Flonase, Veramyst) + azelastine (Dymista)	2 sprays in each nostril daily Pediatrics: 1 spray in each nostril daily Dymista: 1 spray in each nostril BID	**NOTES** Budesonide is Pregnancy Category B and is the preferred inhaled steroid in pregnancy.
Mometasone (Nasonex)	2 sprays in each nostril daily Pediatrics: 1 spray in each nostril daily	
Triamcinolone (Nasacort AQ)	1 to 2 sprays in each nostril daily Pediatrics: 1 to 2 sprays in each nostril daily	

Oral Antihistamines

Oral antihistamines are considered first line agents for patients with mild-moderate disease. They are effective in reducing symptoms of itching, sneezing, and rhinorrhea, but have little effect on nasal congestion. Antihistamines work by blocking histamine at the histamine-1 (H1) receptor site. The second-generation agents are generally preferred since they cause less sedation and cognitive impairment. Antihistamines can help if symptoms of allergic conjunctivitis (itchy, red eyes) are present. Antihistamine eye drops discussed later would help if needed.

Oral & Intranasal Antihistamines: block histamine at the H1-receptor

DRUG	ADULT DOSE	SAFETY/SIDE EFFECTS/MONITORING

First Generation Oral Antihistamines

DRUG	ADULT DOSE	SAFETY/SIDE EFFECTS/MONITORING
Clemastine *(Tavist)*	1.34-2.68 mg PO Q8-12H (max: 8.04 mg/d)	**CONTRAINDICATIONS** Carbinoxamine: Do not use in children < 2 years, lactation, use of MAO Inibitors. **WARNINGS** Due to strong anticholinergic effects, avoid use in elderly (Beers criteria), caution with cardiovascular disease, prostate enlargement, glaucoma, asthma, pyloroduodenal obstruction, thyroid disease. Caution for excessive sedation.
DiphenhydrAMINE *(Benadryl)*	25-50 mg PO Q4-6H (max: 300 mg/d) 12.5 mg/5 mL liquid	**SIDE EFFECTS** Sedation, cognitive impairment, strong anticholinergic effects (dry mouth, blurred vision, urinary retention, constipation), and seizures/arrhythmias in higher doses
Carbinoxamine extended-release *(Karbinal ER)*	4 mg/5 mL liquid	**NOTES** Ethanolamine antihistamines (clemastine, diphenhydramine, doxylamine) are highly sedating as are the phenothiazines (promethazine) whereas the alkylamines (brompheniramine, chlorpheniramine, others) are moderately sedating. In general, first generation antihistamines are considered safe in pregnancy; chlorpheniramine is first-line. All of the others (including diphenhydramine, the most common OTC second-generation agent) are Pregnancy Category B except promethazine and carbinoxamine, which are Pregnancy Category C.
Chlorpheniramine *(Chlor-Trimeton)*	4 mg PO Q4-6H or 8-12 mg PO SR Q6-8H (max: 24 mg/d)	
Promethazine *(Phenergan)*	12.5-25 mg PO Q4-6H PRN (max: 100 mg/d)	**BLACK BOX WARNING** Promethazine: Do not use in children < 2 years due to risk of respiratory failure. Subcutaneous administration is contraindicated (can cause gangrene); preferred route of administration is intramuscular, but any route of injectable administration can cause severe tissue injury; discontinue with burning/pain, avoid extravasation. **SIDE EFFECTS** Sedation, strong anticholinergic effects, hypotension, dystonic and akathisia reactions, QT risk, parkinsonism, tardive dyskinesia

Oral & Intranasal Antihistamines: block histamine at the H1-receptor Continued

DRUG	ADULT DOSE	SAFETY/SIDE EFFECTS/MONITORING

Second Generation Oral Antihistamines

DRUG	ADULT DOSE	SAFETY/SIDE EFFECTS/MONITORING
Cetirizine (ZyrTEC, ZyrTEC D)	5-10 mg PO daily	**WARNINGS** Caution with cardiovascular disease, diabetes, glaucoma, prostate enlargement, renal impairment, seizure disorder, thyroid disorder.
Desloratadine (Clarinex, Clarinex D, Clarinex RediTabs)	5 mg PO daily	**SIDE EFFECTS** Sedation can still be seen occasionally with the 2nd generation agents (more with cetirizine and levocetirizine)
Fexofenadine (Allegra, Allegra D 12H, Allegra D 24H, Children's Allegra ODT)	60 mg PO BID or 180 mg daily	**NOTES** Onset: cetirizine and levocetirizine work faster than other 2nd generation agents – onset in ~1 hour. Orange, grapefruit and apple juice and antacids containing aluminum or magnesium ↓ GI absorption of fexofenadine (Allegra), separate by 2 hours. Ketoconazole and erythromycin ↑ GI absorption of fexofenadine. Avoid this combination. These products are indicated for children 2 years and up.
Levocetirizine (Xyzal)	5 mg PO QHS	
Loratadine (Claritin, Claritin-D 24 hour, Claritin RediTabs, Alavert)	5 mg PO BID or 10 mg daily	

Intranasal Antihistamines

DRUG	ADULT DOSE	SAFETY/SIDE EFFECTS/MONITORING
Azelastine (Astelin, Astepro) + fluticasone (Dymista)	1-2 sprays each nostril BID	**SIDE EFFECTS** Bitter taste, headache, somnolence, nasal irritation, minor nosebleed, sinus pain
Olopatadine (Patanase)	2 sprays each nostril BID	**NOTES** Helps with nasal congestion as well. Oloptadine is indicated for 6 years and older. Azelastine is indicated for 5 years and older.

Decongestants

These agents are effective in reducing sinus and nasal congestion. Decongestants are alpha-adrenergic agonists (sympathomimetics) that work by causing vasoconstriction. If a product contains a D after the name (such as *Mucinex D* or *Robitussin D*), it usually contains a decongestant (phenylephrine or pseudoephedrine).

DRUG	ADULT DOSE	SAFETY/SIDE EFFECTS/MONITORING

Systemic (oral)

DRUG	ADULT DOSE	SAFETY/SIDE EFFECTS/MONITORING
Phenylephrine HCL *(Sudafed PE)*	10 mg PO Q4H PRN (max: 60 mg/d)	**CONTRAINDICATIONS** Do not use within 14 days of MAOIs **WARNINGS** Use with caution in patients with CV disease and hypertension (can ↑ BP), hyperthyroidism (can worsen), diabetes (can ↑ blood glucose), bowel obstruction, glaucoma (can ↑ IOP), BPH (can cause urinary retention), and in the elderly **SIDE EFFECTS** Cardiovascular stimulation (tachycardia, palpitations, ↑ BP), CNS stimulation (anxiety, tremors, insomnia, nervousness, restlessness), dizziness, headache, anorexia **NOTES** Pregnancy Category C Phenylephrine has low bioavailability (~38%); pseudoephedrine is the more effective agent, but has dose limitations (refer to boxed information) Onset of 30-60 minutes
Pseudoephedrine *(Sudafed)*	60 mg PO Q4-6H PRN (max: 240 mg/d)	

Topicals (Intranasal)

DRUG	ADULT DOSE	SAFETY/SIDE EFFECTS/MONITORING
Naphazoline 0.05% *(Privine)*	1-2 sprays Q6H PRN	**SIDE EFFECTS** Stinging, burning, sneezing, dryness (vehicle-related), trauma from the tip of the device, rhinitis medicamentosa (rebound congestion if used longer than 3 days)
Oxymetazoline 0.05% *(Afrin, Neo-Synephrine Nighttime 12-Hour)*	2-3 sprays Q12H PRN	**NOTES** Effective with a fast onset of 5-10 minutes Limit use to ≤ 3 days to prevent rebound congestion
Phenylephrine 0.25%, 0.5%, 1% *(Neo-Synephrine 4-Hour)*	2-3 sprays Q4H PRN	
Tetrahydrozoline 0.05%, 0.1% *(Tyzine)* – Rx	3-4 sprays Q3-4H PRN	
Xylometazoline 0.05%, 0.1% *(Otrivin)*	2-3 sprays Q8-10H PRN	

Additional Allergy Agents

Intranasal cromolyn *(Nasalcrom)*

- Takes 4-7 days to see symptom relief; up to 2-4 weeks of continued use for maximal effect. Must administer regularly (no more often than every 4 hours and as infrequently as every 6 hours), not as-needed, and start at onset of allergy season.

- Not as effective as other agents.

- Due to its safety profile, is used in young children and pregnancy.

Intranasal ipratropium bromide *(Atrovent Nasal Spray)*

- Effective in reducing rhinorrhea but no effect on other nasal symptoms (can cause nasal dryness).

- Usually used in combination with other agents when rhinorrhea is the predominant symptom.

Oral antileukotrienes (Montelukast – *Singulair*)

- No more effective than antihistamines or pseudoephedrine. Full information in Asthma chapter.

- Dose: 10 mg daily (15 years and up), 5 mg chewable tablet (ages 6-14 years), 4 mg chewable tablet (ages 2-5 years), or one packet of 4 mg oral granules (ages 6 months-5 years).

Nasal Irrigation and Wetting Agents

A neti pot looks like a small genie lamp or teapot. It is used to hold salt water (saline solution) that is poured into one nostril and allowed to drain out of the other nostril. This technique may help with sinus symptoms. It can clear out nasal passages and reduce swelling. Neti pots are safe for children and pregnant women. Instruct to use distilled water (not tap) in neti pots. The most common side effects are nasal burning or stinging. Nasal irrigation can also be done with nasal

COMBAT METHAMPHETAMINE EPIDEMIC ACT 2005

Pseudoephedrine (PSE) is located behind pharmacy counters as part of the "Combat Meth Act" (CMEA), under the Patriot Act, to crack down on the methamphetamine epidemic. Meth use has decreased among younger users since the restrictions were put into place, but it remains a high use street drug, particularly in certain regions. It is relatively inexpensive. It is a highly addictive substance, and tolerance develops quickly. Unfortunately, meth use causes unpredictable and often violent behavior. The waste created in the production is very toxic and is usually dumped illegally. The act applies to pseudoephedrine, phenylpropanolamine and ephedrine, all of which can be converted rather easily into methamphetamine. To sell these products (primarily PSE, the others are not easily available), stores must keep a logbook of sales (exception is the single dose package that contains a maximum of 60 mg – this is 2 of the 30 mg tablets.)

For any sale above this amount, customer must show photo ID issued by the State (e.g., license, ID card, expired or unexpired US passport, unexpired foreign passport or employment authorization document, and a few less common options-refer to training).

Customers record their name, date and time of sale – store staff must verify the name matches the photo ID and that the date and time are correct. Record the address. (Some stores can swipe the drivers license to get the name and address recorded.) The store staff must record what the person received [max 3.6 grams or 120 of the 30 mg tablets, and 9 grams (300 tablets) in a 30-d period.] The customer has to sign the logbook. Keep log for at least 2 years. The logbook has to be kept secured and the information in it cannot be shared with the public. (Inspectors, law enforcement only.)

This includes combo products with PSE, such as cough/cold tablets and syrups. Any product containing PSE must be kept behind the counter or in a locked cabinet. They often are, but do not need to be, located in the pharmacy. It does not apply to prescription products. Certification to sell is completed online through the Department of Justice (DOJ) website at https://www.deadiversion.usdoj.gov/webforms/jsp/cmea/forms/menu.jsp

Many states now have their own restrictions in addition to the federal restriction, such as age restrictions, prescription required or stricter limits.

sprays/drops containing saline or sodium chloride 0.65% (hypotonic saline) drops/sprays. These solutions rinse allergens out of nasal passages. Nasal gels with petrolatum *(Allergen Block)* can be applied around the nostrils to physically block pollens and allergens from entering the nose.

COUGH AND COLD AGENTS

Background

Most colds, as well as influenza, are transmitted primarily by mucus secretions via patient's hands. It is essential to clean surfaces such as telephones and keyboards, and to wash hands often. Viruses are also transmitted through the air by coughing or sneezing. Coughing or sneezing into the elbow or into a tissue is preferable over coughing into a hand, which can then touch surfaces and spread illness. About half of all colds are caused by rhinoviruses. Other viruses (coronavirus, others) cause the remainder. Refer to the Medication Safety chapter for correct hand washing technique. Refer to the Infectious Diseases chapter for a table that compares the flu, other viral infections and bacteria infections that have similar characteristics, with differences.

Natural Products used for Colds

Zinc, in various formulations including lozenges, is used for cold prevention and treatment. There is little efficacy data for cold prevention, but zinc lozenges may slightly decrease cold duration if used correctly (taken every 2 hours while awake, starting within 48 hours of symptom onset). For this purpose zinc supplements are rated as "possibly effective" by the Natural Medicines Database. Do not recommend zinc nasal swabs or sprays due to the risk of loss of smell. Vitamin C supplements are commonly used, with some efficacy for cold prevention. They might decrease the duration of the cold by 1-1.5 days and are rated as "possibly effective" for cold treatment by the Natural Medicines Database. Echinacea is also rated as "possibly effective" for cold treatment. With any of these products it is important to use the correct dose in a reputable formulation. Drugs, including mild natural products, have dose-response relationships. *Airborne* is a popular product that contains a variety of ingredients, including vitamins C, E, zinc and echinacea. It is costly and has no known benefit in the combinations provided.

Cough and Cold Use During Pregnancy

Any pregnancy can result in some birth defect, although most are correctable, and it is always best, if possible to treat conditions without medications. Pharmacists can recommend first-line ACOG recommendations; see the Drug Use in Pregnancy chapter. Many symptoms of a cold can be resolved with warm water or teas (to loosen phlegm) and the use of humidifiers to counteract dry air in homes that are heated during cold weather. Nasal saline and neti-pots, to moisten and wash out irritants, can be useful. Decongestants may be recommended by the obstetrician, but are not first-line during pregnancy and should not be recommended in the pharmacy. Guaifenesin and dextromethorphan are both Pregnancy Category C. Do not recommend guaifenesin in the first trimester. Although dextromethorphan is considered likely safe it should be left to the physician to recommend use. Liquid OTC products may contain alcohol; no amount of alcohol intake during pregnancy is considered safe. Most importantly, never dispense codeine in any form to a woman who is breastfeeding. If the mother is a 2D6 ultra rapid metabolizer (which the pharmacist would likely not know) the mother will produce excessive morphine which rapidly crosses into breast milk and could produce fatal respiratory depression in the infant.

Dextromethorphan (DM)

Dextromethorphan is the most commonly used cough suppressant. It is in a multitude of cough and cold preparations in a variety of formulations (syrup, tablets, gel caps and others). The most common brand name is *Delsym*. If a product contains DM at the end of the name, such as *Robitussin DM*, it contains dextromethorphan.

DM has several mechanisms. For coughs, it blocks the cough reflex center in the brain. DM acts as a serotonin reuptake inhibitor, and there is a risk of serotonergic syndrome if taken in high doses along with other serotonergic medications. Cases of serotonergic syndrome are due to an additive effect. A dose of fluoxetine and normal dosing of DM should not pose a problem, but DM (referred to as DXM) is also a drug of abuse when taken in large quantities. It acts as an NMDA-receptor blocker, which gives it euphoric, hallucinogenic properties similar to PCP. The toxic dose is highly variable – symptoms are generally observed at doses > 10 mg/kg. DM is used in some of the recipes for the illicit combination "purple drank." Cough suppressant adult dose: 10-20 mg Q4H PRN, or 30 mg Q6-8H PRN, or 60 mg Q12H PRN (max 120 mg/d).

Delsym contains dextromethorphan (DM), which provides benefit as a cough suppressant. It is also a drug of abuse (hallucinogenic) if taken in very high doses. In 2012, California became the first state to ban the sale of dextromethorphan to minors < 18 years of age. This was in response to the large numbers of adolescents abusing dextromethorphan. Cashiers must request identification from anyone purchasing an OTC medication containing dextromethorphan in California. A few other states have followed, some with more stringent requirements.

Guaifenesin

Guaifenesin is an expectorant used to decrease the phlegm viscosity (thickness) in the lower respiratory tract. It may also increase secretions in the upper respiratory tract to help move the phlegm upwards and out (so that the patient can cough out the phlegm). The most common brand name is *Mucinex*, which comes in various formulations, including pills and liquid. It is also present in some cough and cold combination products. It is unclear if guaifenesin provides a useful benefit.

Mucinex contains guaifenesin, an expectorant, which has very mild, if any, benefit. Drinking liquids such as warm tea can also provide a mild benefit.

Some patients find it useful and singers sometimes use guaifenesin to help preserve their voice during long performances or in dry weather. May be added to dextromethorphan formulations to prevent abuse as it causes nausea in high doses. Adult Dose: 200-400 mg Q4H PRN, or 600-1,200 mg XR Q12H (max: 2,400 mg/d).

Select Cough and Cold Products

DRUG	ADULT DOSING	SAFETY/SIDE EFFECTS/MONITORING
Benzonatate *(Tessalon)*	100-200 mg PO TID PRN (max: 600 mg/d)	Sedation, confusion and visual hallucinations. Chemically related to local anesthetic procaine and can cause numbness of mouth if chewed. Avoid in children < 10 years.
GuaiFENesin/Codeine syrup *(Cheratussin AC, Robitussin AC)* C V	400-100 mg/10-20 mg PO codeine Q4-6H PRN (max: 120 mg/d of codeine)	Caution with use of codeine in children after tonsillectomy or adenoidectomy as it may cause fatal respiratory depression; avoid use in lactation. Sedation, constipation (from codeine component, dose-dependent)
GuaiFENesin/ Codeine/Pseudoephedrine *(Cheratussin DAC, Robitussin DAC)* C V	100 mg/10 mg/30 mg/5 mL; 10 mL Q4H PRN (max: 40 mL/d)	
Promethazine/ codeine/phenylephrine (Promethazine VC) C V	6.25 mg/10 mg/5 mg/5 mL; 5 mL Q4-6 H PRN (max: 30 mL/d)	Sedation, dizziness Promethazine, codeine warnings apply for all drugs that include them as components.
Chlorpheniramine and hydrocodone *(Tussionex)* C III	8 mg/10 mg ER/5 mL; 5 mL Q12H PRN (max: 10 mL/d)	Hydrocodone can cause respiratory and CNS depression and risk of dependence. Is a more potent antitussive than codeine.
Brompheniramine/pseudo ephedrine/dextromethorph an *(Bromfed DM)*	4 mg/60 mg/30 mg/5 mL; 5 mL Q4-6H PRN (max: 20 mL/d)	Dizziness, drowsiness, dry mouth, nose or throat, loss of appetite, nausea
Dextromethorphan/ promethazine *(Promethazine DM)*	15 mg/6.25 mg/5 mL; 5 mL Q4-6H (max: 30 mL/d)	Dizziness, drowsiness, dry mouth, nausea, stomach upset
Clophedianol and pseudoephedrine *(Clofera)*	12.5 mg/30 mg/5 mL; 10 mL Q6-8 H PRN (max: 40 mL/d)	Less effective antitussive than dextromethorphan; may be unavailable in 2014. Dizziness, drowsiness, stomach upset, restlessness

Cough and Cold Products in Children

OTC cough and cold products should NOT be used in children under age 4. Combination cough and cold products should not be used in children under 2 years old per the FDA (under 6 years old per the American Academy of Pediatrics). The FDA recommendation includes a warning not to use antihistamines (such as diphenhydramine) to make children sleepy. Do not use promethazine in any form in children less than 2 years old. The FDA advises against the use of promethazine with codeine cough syrups in children younger than 6 years of age, due to the risk of respiratory depression, cardiac arrest and neurological problems.

If a young child has a cold, it is safe and useful to recommend nasal bulbs for gentle suctioning, saline drops/sprays (*Ocean* and generics), vaporizers/humidifiers, and ibuprofen and acetaminophen. Parents should be told that OTC cough and cold medications have not been shown to work in young children and they can be dangerous. Symptoms of the common cold usually resolve in a few days (up to 2 weeks). If symptoms worsen or do not go away, the child should be seen by a pediatrician. Do not use aspirin in children due to the risk of Reye's syndrome; ibuprofen (5-10 mg/kg every 6-8 hours) and acetaminophen (10-15 mg/kg every 4-6 hours) are safe to use, if kept to safe doses, in young children.

If the child is a small infant, or seems seriously ill, instruct the patient to have the child seen by a medical professional quickly. Always recommend adequate hydration. No combination products in young children. Over the past year there have been cases of severe skin reactions in patients using acetaminophen and NSAIDs. This risk is very uncommon, but the complications are significant. Parents should not over-use analgesics to help limit all toxicity risk.

Tips

- If you dispense any oral liquid to a child (or adult), always dispense a calibrated oral syringe (if the package does not contain one) or a dosing cup and counsel parents not to use "teaspoons" used for eating because they come in different sizes.

- Do not use aspirin in children due to risk of Reye's syndrome.

- Advise patients to keep well hydrated.

- Menthol and camphor used topically, such as in *Vick's VapoRub*, do not work well and should not be used in children less than 2 years. The risk with these agents is ingestion – do not apply to nostrils or leave out where young children can ingest. (Menthol can result in aspiration and cardiac and CNS toxicity if ingested, and camphor may rarely be unsafe – this is being debated.) *Vick's BabyRub* contains petrolatum, eucalyptus oil, lavendar oil, rosemary oil and aloe extract and is not thought to be harmful but lacks evidence of efficacy.

- Humidifiers and vaporizers, on the other hand, are useful. The hot water types can cause burns in children if spilled, otherwise, they work just as well. Keep them clean – dirty mist can worsen colds, allergies or asthma.

Acetaminophen & Ibuprofen in Children

If a parent purchases OTC infant drops for acetaminophen or ibuprofen (let pediatrician recommend if under age 4), remind them to use the dropper that came with the bottle and do not mix and match dosing devices or overdose can occur.

- Acetaminophen infants or children's liquid suspensions: 160 mg/5 mL Q4-6H PRN. If the older concentrated infant drops (80 mg/0.8 mL) are in the home they should be discarded.

- Ibuprofen infant drops: 50 mg/1.25 mL (10-15 mg/kg) Q6-8H PRN

- Ibuprofen children's liquid suspensions: <u>100 mg/5 mL</u> Q4-6H PRN

- Some doctors recommend alternating so as not to risk acetaminophen toxicity (and sometimes, due to feared stomach upset from ibuprofen).

Patient Counseling for *Flonase* (Fluticasone Nasal Inhaler)

Before using

- Shake the bottle gently and then remove the dust cover

- It is necessary to prime the pump into the air the first time it is used, or when you have not used it for a week or more. To prime the pump, hold the bottle with the nasal applicator pointing away from you and with your forefinger and middle finger on either side of the nasal applicator and your thumb underneath the bottle. When you prime the pump for the first time, press down and release the pump 6 times. The pump is now ready for use. If the pump is not used for 7 days, prime until a fine spray appears.

Using the spray

- Blow your nose to clear your nostrils.

- Close one nostril. Tilt your head forward slightly and, keeping the bottle upright, carefully insert the nasal applicator into the other nostril.

- Start to breathe in through your nose, and while breathing in, press firmly and quickly down once on the applicator to release the spray. To get a full actuation, use your forefinger and middle finger to spray while supporting the base of the bottle with your thumb. Avoid spraying in eyes. Breathe gently inwards through the nostril.

- Breathe out through your mouth.

- If a second spray is needed in that nostril, repeat the above 3 steps. Repeat the above 3 steps in the other nostril.

- Wipe the nasal applicator with a clean tissue and replace with dust cover.

- Do not use the bottle for more than the labeled number of sprays even though the bottle is not completely empty.

- Do not blow your nose right after using the nasal spray

MEMORY PRACTICE

DRUG	FILL IN THE NAME OF THE ASTHMA DRUG HERE FOR PRACTICE
Beclomethasone *(Beconase, Beconase AQ)*	
Budesonide *(Rhinocort Aqua)*	
Ciclesonide *(Omnaris, Zetonna)*	
Flunisolide	
Fluticasone furoate *(Veramyst)*	
Fluticasone propionate *(Flonase)*	
Mometasone *(Nasonex)*	
Triamcinolone *(Nasacort AQ)*	

42

CYSTIC FIBROSIS

We gratefully acknowledge the assistance of Paul Beringer, PharmD, Associate Professor of Clinical Pharmacy and Clinical Medicine, University of Southern California, in preparing this chapter.

GUIDELINES

Cystic Fibrosis Pulmonary Guidelines: Chronic Medications for Maintenance of Lung Health. Am J Respir Crit Care Med. 2013;187:680–689.

Cystic Fibrosis Pulmonary Guidelines: Treatment of Pulmonary Exacerbations. Am J Respir Crit Care Med. 2009; 180:802–808.

BACKGROUND

Cystic fibrosis (CF) is an autosomal recessive genetic disorder that leads to abnormal transport of chloride, bicarbonate, and sodium ions across the epithelium, leading to thick, viscous secretions. The thick mucus mostly affects the lungs, pancreas, liver and intestine, primarily causing difficulty breathing and lung infections as well as digestive complications. The name cystic fibrosis refers to the characteristic scarring (fibrosis) and cyst formation that occurs within the pancreas.

CF is caused by a mutation in the gene for the protein cystic fibrosis transmembrane conductance regulator (CFTR). This protein is required to regulate the components of sweat, digestive juices, and mucus. CFTR regulates the movement of chloride, bicarbonate, and sodium ions across epithelial membranes and mutations can lead to a chronic cycle of lung infection, inflammation, and obstruction which results in a progressive loss of pulmonary function and eventual respiratory failure. CFTR dysfunction also leads to pancreatic insufficiency, infertility, biliary cirrhosis as well as a range of other defects.

CLINICAL PRESENTATION

The classic symptoms of CF are salty tasting skin, poor growth and poor weight gain despite adequate food intake, thick and sticky mucus production, frequent chest infections, coughing and shortness of breath. Digital clubbing is often present. Digestive symptoms include steatorrhea, malnutrition due to poor absorption of nutrients, including fat-soluble vitamins, and a failure to thrive if not treated.

PHARMACOLOGIC TREATMENT

An early diagnosis of CF and a comprehensive treatment plan can improve both survival and quality of life. Specialty clinics for cystic fibrosis are helpful and are found in many communities.

Treatment for Lung Problems

- Inhaled bronchodilators to help open the airways.

- Hypertonic saline *(HyperSal)* for hydrating the airway mucus secretions and facilitating mucociliary clearance.

- DNAse enzyme to breakdown extracellular DNA from accumulated neutrophils. DNAse therapy is designed to thin mucus and facilitate mucociliary clearance.

- Inhaled antibiotics to prevent and treat lung and sinus infections.

- Oral azithromycin to reduce airway inflammation and disrupt *P. aeruginosa* biofilm formation.

- Transplantation, in patients with end-stage lung disease.

Treatment for Intestinal and Nutritional Problems

- A high-fat and calorically-dense diet to help with nutrition.

- Pancreatic enzyme replacement to optimize growth and nutritional status and promote healthy bowels.

- Proton pump inhibitors to prevent degradation of pancreatic enzymes in the stomach and for treatment of GERD.

- Vitamin supplements, especially the fat-soluble vitamins A, D, E, and K.

- Insulin for treatment of CF-related diabetes mellitus.

Controlling Infections in the Lungs

Intermittent Infection

- Impaired mucociliary clearance predisposes patients with CF to lung infections. The most common organisms early in the disease are *Staphylococcus aureus* and *Haemophilus influenzae* followed by *P. aeruginosa* in adolescents and adults. Acute pulmonary exacerbations characterized by an increase in cough, sputum production with a change in sputum color (greenish), shortness of breath, a rapid decline in FEV1, loss of appetite and weight are a frequent complication of CF. Treatment often includes an extended course of antibiotics (2-4 weeks), modalities to increase airway clearance and nutritional therapies.

- If the patient has a *P. aeruginosa* infection, 2 drugs given IV are recommended to provide potential synergy and prevent resistance. These include aminoglycosides, beta lactams, quinolones, and others that cover *P. aeruginosa*. See infectious diseases chapter for a complete discussion on treatment of *P. aeruginosa*. Doses tend to be larger than normal due to the need to obtain a therapeutic concentration in lung tissue and the reduced susceptibility of the bacteria chronically colonizing the airways of these patients.

- Lung infections occur intermittently at first, but eventually become chronic. In particular, chronic lung infections with *P. aeruginosa* are associated with more rapid decline in pulmonary function. Inhaled antibiotics may be used to eradicate *P. aeruginosa* from the lungs. See agents below. If patient is using a bronchodilator and/or mucolytic, make sure these are given prior to the antibiotic inhalation.

Chronic Infection

Inhaled antibiotics are recommended for patients with chronic *P. aeruginosa* lung infections to reduce the bacterial burden. Treatment is associated with an improvement in lung function and a reduction in the frequency of acute pulmonary exacerbations. The frequency of acute pulmonary exacerbations is strongly associated with lung function decline and shortened survival in CF.

DRUG	DOSE/INDICATION	SAFETY/SIDE EFFECTS/MONITORING
Antibiotics, Inhaled		
Tobramycin Inhaled Solution (*TOBI*) Ready to use ampules	300 mg via nebulizer Q12H x 28 days, followed by 28 days off cycle Indicated in CF patients ≥ 6 years who are colonized with *P. aeruginosa* to reduce infection/hospitalization	**SIDE EFFECTS** Ototoxicity, tinnitus, voice alteration, dizziness, bronchospasm **NOTES** Little systemic absorption Use with *PARI LC Plus* reusable nebulizer and DeVilbiss *Pulmo-Aide* air compressor Doses should be taken at least 6 hours apart Recommended to store in refrigerator; can be kept at room temperature up to 28 days In foil to protect from light
TOBI Podhaler Tobramycin Inhalation powder: 28 mg capsules Blister card	112 mg (4 caps) via podhaler Q12H x 28 days, followed by 28 days off cycle. Indicated in CF patients ≥ 6 years who are colonized with *P. aeruginosa* to reduce infection/hospitalization	**SIDE EFFECTS** Ototoxicity, tinnitus, voice alteration, dizziness, bronchospasm **NOTES** Little systemic absorption Use with *Podhaler* Doses should be taken at least 6 hours apart Store capsules at room temperature in dry place
Bethkis Tobramycin inhalation solution	300 mg in 4 mL ampule, taken BID x 28 days, followed by 28 days off cycle Indicated in CF patients ≥ 6 years who are colonized with *P. aeruginosa* to reduce infection/hospitalization	**SIDE EFFECTS** Similar to above **NOTES** Use with *PARI LC* nebulizer and *Vios* air compressor Not for use if FEV1 < 40% or > 80% predicted, or if colonized with *Burkholderia cepacia*.

Chronic Infection Continued

DRUG	DOSE/INDICATION	SAFETY/SIDE EFFECTS/MONITORING
Aztreonam Lysine Inhalation Solution (*Cayston*)	75 mg TID x 28 days, followed by 28 days off cycle Indicated in CF patients ≥ 7 years with *P. aeruginosa* in the lungs	**SIDE EFFECTS** Allergic reactions (may be severe), bronchospasm, fever, wheezing, cough, chest discomfort **NOTES** Doses should be taken at least 4 hours apart Use with *Altera* nebulizer system Need to reconstitute with 1 mL of sterile diluent (provided); give immediately Recommend to refrigerate; can be kept at room temperature up to 28 days Protect from light

Antibiotic, Oral

Azithromycin	< 40 kg: 250 mg 3 times/week > 40 kg: 500 mg 3 times/week Used to decrease inflammation and reduce exacerbations; not an FDA-indicated use.	**SIDE EFFECTS** Of note in CF patients: Tinnitus, nausea, risk of QT prolongation **NOTES** Do not use as monotherapy in individuals with nontuberculous mycobacteria lung infections

Select Patient Instructions on Using *TOBI Podhaler*

- *TOBI* should be taken using the *Podhaler* device.

- Do not swallow the capsules.

- Use a new *Podhaler* device every 7 days.

- Each dose of 4 *TOBI Podhaler* capsules should be taken as close to 12 hours but no less than 6 hours apart.

- Make sure to finish the whole dose of *TOBI*. Do not leave any medication in the capsules.

- *TOBI* comes in 4 weekly packs containing 7 blister cards of 8 capsules each (4 for each morning and evening) and 2 *Podhaler* devices. Store capsules at room temperature in a dry place.

- Only remove 1 capsule at a time immediately before administration.

- If you are taking several medications, the recommended order is as follows: bronchodilator, hypertonic saline, dornase alfa, chest physiotherapy, then inhaled antibiotics.

Agents to Promote Mucus Clearance

DRUG	DOSING	SAFETY/SIDE EFFECTS/MONITORING
Albuterol (*AccuNeb; Proventil HFA*, others)	Prior to other agents: 2-4 times daily	Well-tolerated if taken correctly; refer to Asthma chapter for complete information
Hypertonic saline (*HyperSal*)	4 mL via a nebulizer 2-4 times daily	Hypertonic saline is a high-alert drug; risk concerns IV administration; here, the use is small ampules that are <u>delivered via a nebulizer.</u>
Dornase alfa (*Pulmozyme*)	2.5 mg single use ampule taken once daily with recommended nebulizer and compressor system	**CONTRAINDICATIONS** Hypersensitivity to Chinese Hamster Ovary (CHO) products **SIDE EFFECTS** Chest pain, fever, rash, rhinitis, laryngitis, voice alteration, throat irritation **NOTES** <u>Store the ampules in the refrigerator (do not expose to room temperature ≥ 24 hours)</u> <u>Do not mix with any other drug in the nebulizer</u> <u>Protect from light</u>

ADEQUATE NUTRITION

Dietary measures must ensure adequate nutrition and include high calorie, high protein, and high fat diets with liberal use of salt to encourage normal weight and growth. The needs are high due to the extra work involved with breathing and a hyper-metabolic state associated with bronchial infection. Due to poor fat absorption, patients use <u>1-2 multivitamins</u> daily (with <u>A, D, E and K</u>), and some require additional doses.

Pancreatic Enzyme Products (PEPs)

The thick mucus obstructs pancreatic enzyme flow, resulting in a paucity of these enzymes reaching the gastrointestinal tract. Frequently, greasy, foul-smelling stools are manifestations of pancreatic insufficiency. Most CF patients need to supplement their diet with appropriate amounts of pancreatic enzyme supplements.

Pancrelipase is a natural product harvested from porcine pancreatic glands which contains a combination of <u>lipase, amylase, and protease</u>. PEPs are formulated to dissolve in the more basic pH of the duodenum so they can act locally to break down fat, starches and protein. The dose is individualized for each patient and is based on the <u>lipase</u> component. Once enzyme therapy is started, the dose is adjusted every 3-4 days <u>until stools are normalized</u>. Do not use doses > 6,000 units/kg/meal of lipase due to colonic stricture risk.

Enzymes are given prior to meals and snacks: full doses are given before meals and 50% of the mealtime dose is given with snacks. Meals with high fat content require higher doses. Counsel patients not to chew or crush the capsules. If a patient cannot swallow them whole, the microsphere-contents can be sprinkled on soft food with a low pH that does not require chewing (such as applesauce, gelatin, baby food, etc.). Do not mix with milk-based foods, such as yogurt or pudding since these have a higher pH. There is also a powder formulation. Take the entire dose at the beginning of each meal or snack. Take with a generous amount of liquid. Retention in the mouth before swallowing may cause mucosal irritation and stomatitis.

Do not substitute pancreatic enzyme products. This is an FDA recommendation. They do not require refrigeration. They do degrade; check the expiration date. If infants spit them out, immediately follow with liquid until they are swallowed.

DRUG	DOSING	SAFETY/SIDE EFFECTS/MONITORING
Pancrelipase *(Creon, Lip-Prot-Amyl, Pancreaze, Pertzye, Ultresa, Viokace, Zenpep)*	**Initial:** Age < 4 years: Lipase 1,000 units/kg/meal Age > 4 years: Lipase 500 units/kg/meal **Max:** Lipase ≤ 2,500 units/kg/meal or ≤ 10,000 units/kg/day. Doses > 6,000 units/kg/meal are associated with colonic stricture. Take before or with food, avoid foods with high pH (e.g., dairy). Use 1/2 meal-time dose with snacks.	**WARNING** Caution for risk of (rare) fibrosing colonopathy: Symptoms include severe abdominal pain, bloating, difficulty passing stools, nausea, vomiting, diarrhea. Risk higher with doses > 10,000 lipase units/kg/day. **SIDE EFFECTS** Mucosal irritation, abdominal pain, nausea, headache, neck pain **MONITORING** Abdominal symptoms, nutritional intake, weight, height (children), stool, fecal fat **NOTES** *Viokace* is the only formulation not enteric coated and needs to be given with PPI. All formulations are porcine derived and are not interchangeable. Do not crush or chew contents of capsules. Delayed-release capsules with enteric coated microspheres or microtablets may be opened and sprinkled on soft, acidic foods (pH ≤ 4.5).

Pancreatic Enzyme Counseling (Children)

- This medication comes with an extra patient fact sheet called a Medication Guide. Read it carefully. The Medication Guide discusses a rare, but serious allergic reaction that can happen with some people.

- This medication is taken with meals and snacks, right before eating. At snacks give half the meal-time dose.

- Have your child swallow whole. Do not let your child chew or crush or hold in the mouth or the medicine will cause the mouth to become sore.

- If it is difficult to swallow the capsules the contents can be sprinkled on a spoonful of soft food such as applesauce, pureed bananas or pears. Once the medicine is sprinkled on the food it needs to be used right away. Do not have the child chew it, just swallow. (Do not mix with baby formula or breast milk; sprinkle into the child's mouth or mix with a small amount of applesauce.)

- <u>Do not mix with dairy</u> products such as milk or yogurt.

- Have your child <u>drink lots of non-caffeinated liquids</u> every day.

- It is important to <u>follow the diet plan</u> you received for your child to get adequate nutrition and to keep as healthy as possible.

- <u>Common side effects</u> can include stomach pain, nausea, headache, and neck pain.

- If you forget to give the medicine before the meal <u>give it as soon you remember</u>, but <u>if it is close to time for the next dose, skip it</u> and go back to the usual schedule.

Targeting the G1551D-CFTR Protein Defect

Ivacaftor has recently been approved for CF in patients 6 years and older who have a G551D mutation in the cystic fibrosis transmembrane conductance regulator (CFTR) gene. There are an estimated 30,000 people in the U.S. with CF and ~4-5% of these patients have 1 copy of the G551D mutation of the CFTR gene (most common CFTR mutation, F508del, accounts for 70% of the CFTR alleles). Ivacaftor works by increasing the time CFTR channels remain open, augmenting chloride transport activity.

DRUG	DOSING/INDICATIONS	SAFETY/SIDE EFFECTS/MONITORING
Ivacaftor *(Kalydeco)* CFTR Potentiator	150 mg PO Q12H With CYP450 3A4 moderate inhibitors or moderate-severe hepatic impairment: 150 mg daily With CYP450 3A4 strong inhibitors: 150 mg twice weekly Indicated in patients ≥ 6 years with at least one G551D CFTR mutation	**SIDE EFFECTS** Headache, URTIs, nasal congestion, oropharyngeal pain, abdominal pain, rash **MONITORING** LFTs (baseline, Q 3 months for 1 year, then annually) **NOTES** Take with <u>high-fat</u> containing food.

PRACTICE CASE

Ginny is a 6-year-old female patient with cystic fibrosis who presents to the clinic with a recent history of mild cough and sputum production. Her pulmonary function tests are at her baseline. Her sputum cultures reveal *Staphylococcus aureus*. Current medications include a multivitamin once daily, pancreatic enzymes with meals, and albuterol twice daily.

Questions

1. Which one of the following is the best pharmacologic intervention for management of Ginny's airway disease at this time?

   a. Tobramycin via *Podhaler* 112 mg twice daily for 28 days

   b. Aztreonam 75 mg via *Altera nebulizer* three times daily for 28 days

   c. Dornase alfa 2.5 mg once daily via nebulizer

   d. Increase albuterol to four times daily

   e. Decrease albuterol to once daily

2. Ginny returns to clinic 2 weeks later and her parents report that her symptoms are not improved. Her pulmonary function tests are reduced by 10%. Based on the above culture only, which of the following represents the best pharmacologic intervention at the present time?

   a. Cephalexin 500 mg 4 times/day

   b. Tobramycin via *Podhaler* 112 mg twice daily for 28 days

   c. Dornase alfa 2.5 mg once daily via nebulizer

   d. Aztreonam 75 mg via *Altera* nebulizer three times daily for 28 days

   e. Imipenem 500 mg IV Q 6 hours

3. Which of the following is a correct patient counseling recommendation for pancreatic enzyme replacement therapy?

   a. If the patient has difficulty swallowing the capsules the microspheres can be crushed and sprinkled over food.

   b. The enzymes should be taken with meals.

   c. The enzyme products are equivalent and can be interchanged, depending on formulary requirements.

   d. *Viokace* should be administered with an acidic liquid such as orange juice.

   e. Pancreatic enzymes should not be taken if the meal contains little or no fat content.

Questions 4-9 do not apply to the above case.

4. Which of the following are potential adverse effects associated with *TOBI* therapy? (Select **ALL** that apply.)

   a. Voice alteration

   b. Bronchospasm

   c. Ototoxicity

   d. Tinnitus

   e. Pulmonary infiltrates

5. Which of the following is an appropriate counseling recommendation for *TOBI Podhaler* therapy?

   a. Store capsules in the refrigerator.

   b. Capsules should be taken orally on an empty stomach.

   c. Take twice daily; doses may be taken 4 hours apart.

   d. Remove only 1 capsule at a time immediately before administration.

   e. Instruct the patient to thoroughly chew (or crush) the tablets.

6. Which therapy is indicated only for cystic fibrosis patients with the CFTR genotype G551D/F508del?

   a. Ivacaftor

   b. *Pulmozyme*

   c. Ipratropium

   d. Fluticasone

   e. *HyperSal*

7. Which of the following therapies are used in promoting mucus clearance in patients with cystic fibrosis?

   a. Pseudoephedrine

   b. Hypertonic saline

   c. Tiotroprium

   d. Inhaled aztreonam

   e. Inhaled tobramycin

8. Which of the following are correct statements regarding dosing considerations for ivacaftor? (Select **ALL** that apply.)

    a. The brand name is *Kaleidoscope XR*.
    b. Ivacaftor should be administered with a high fat containing meal.
    c. Dosage adjustment is necessary when co-administered with CYP450 3A4 inhibitors.
    d. Ivacaftor is nephrotoxic and is contraindicated in severe renal insufficiency.
    e. The normal dose is 150 mg by mouth every 12 hours.

9. Which of the following are correct statements regarding the dosing of pancreatic enzymes in patients with cystic fibrosis? (Select **ALL** that apply.)

    a. Doses should not exceed 6,000 lipase units/kg/meal.
    b. Enzymes are not taken with snacks.
    c. Doses > 10,000 units/kg/day have been associated with colonic stricture.
    d. The dose is based on the lipase component.
    e. Pancreatic enzyme products are not interchangeable.

Answers

1-c, 2-a, 3-b, 4-a,b,c,d, 5-d, 6-a, 7-b, 8-b,c,e, 9-a,c,d,e

ONCOLOGY I:
OVERVIEW, PREVENTION, SCREENING & SIDE EFFECT MANAGEMENT

We gratefully acknowledge the assistance of Muoi Gi, PharmD, BCPS, BCOP, Oncology Pharmacy Residency Director, VA San Diego Healthcare System and D. Raymond Weber, PharmD, BSPharm, BCOP, BCPS, RPh, Associate Professor, University of Maryland Eastern Shore School of Pharmacy and Health Professions (rweberpharmd@umes.edu), in preparing this chapter.

GUIDELINES

National Comprehensive Cancer Network (NCCN) website (www.nccn.org – by cancer type) and through the American Society of Clinical Oncology (ASCO) website (www.asco.org).

WARNING SIGNS

The American Cancer Society lists seven warning signs of cancer in an adult. Any of these warning signs should warrant referral to a physician:

Change in bowel or bladder habits

A sore that does not heal

Unusual bleeding or discharge

Thickening or lump in breast or elsewhere

Indigestion or difficulty swallowing

Obvious change in wart or mole

Nagging cough or hoarseness

BACKGROUND

Cancer is a group of diseases characterized by uncontrolled growth and spread of abnormal cells. If the spread is not controlled, it can result in death. Cancer is caused by both external factors [such as chemicals, radiation and infectious organisms (some bacteria and viruses)] and internal factors (heredity, hormones, immune disorders, and genetic mutations). Growing older is certainly contributory. Sunlight exposure, tobacco use, excessive alcohol intake, obesity, a poor diet and low physical activity level increase the risk for certain types of cancer.

CLASSIFICATION

Malignancies are classified based on the tissue type as epithelial, connective, lymphoid or nerve. A sample of tissue should be taken for diagnosis along with X-rays, CT scans, MRIs and other diagnostic tools to evaluate the cancer's stage. Lab work is required for blood chemistries and tumor markers.

749

CANCER SCREENING RECOMMENDATIONS

Cancer Screening Guidelines

CANCER	ACS GUIDELINES	NCCN GUIDELINES	USPSTF
Breast	Age: 20-39 (CBE every 3 years) Age: ≥ 40 (CBE + Mammography yearly)	Age: 25-39 (CBE every 1-3 years) Age: 40-74 (CBE + mammography yearly)	Age: 40s (start discussion) Age: 50-74 (mammography every 2 years)
Colon	Age: ≥ 50 (annual FOBT or FIT; and 1 of the following: every 5 years sigmoidoscopy, contrast enema, CT scan, or colonoscopy (every 10 years)	Age: ≥ 50 (annual FOBT or FIT; and/or 1 of the following: every 5 years sigmoidoscopy or every 10 years colonoscopy)	Age: 50-75 (annual FOBT, every 5 years sigmoidoscopy, or colonoscopy every 10 years)
Cervical	Age: 21-29 (Pap smear only every 3 years) Age: 30-65 [Pap only every 3 years or Pap + HPV testing (preferred) every 5 years]	Same as ACS guidelines	Same as ACS guidelines
Prostate	Age: 50s (start discussion) (if treated: PSA with or without DRE)	Age: 40s (start discussion) (if treated: PSA with or without DRE)	Recommend against screening for prostate cancer
Lung (High Risk)	Age: 55-74 (in fairly good health) with ≥ 30 pack year smoking Hx and are either still smoking or have quit for < 15 years (low dose CT scan)	Age: 55-74 with ≥ 30 pack year smoking Hx and quit for < 15 years Age: ≥ 50 with ≥ 20 pack year smoking Hx and 1 additional risk factor (other than 2nd hand smoke)	Recommend against screening for lung cancer

ACS: American Cancer Society; CBE: Clinical Breast Exam; DRE: Digital Rectal Exam; FIT: Fecal Immunochemical Test; FOBT: Fecal Occult Blood Test; HPV: Human Papilloma Virus; NCCN: National Comprehensive Cancer Network; PSA: Prostate-Specific Antigen; USPSTF; United States Preventive Services Task Force

Everyone should be encouraged to control their health to reduce cancer risk:

- Stay away from tobacco (enroll in smoking cessation program if needed).

- Stay at a healthy weight.

- Get moving with regular physical activity.

- Eat healthy with plenty of fruits and vegetables.

- Limit how much alcohol you drink (if you drink at all).

- Protect your skin.

- Know yourself, your family history, and your risks.

- Have regular check-ups and cancer screening tests.

TREATMENT OVERVIEW

Cancer can be treated with surgery, radiation, chemotherapy, hormone therapy, biological therapy, targeted therapy, immunotherapy and/or vaccines. Treatment decisions are based on the cancer type and stage. For most cancers (including breast, lung, prostate and colon cancer), the stage is based on the size of the tumor and whether the cancer has spread to lymph nodes or elsewhere. The treatment decisions also consider patient characteristics, such as age, performance status, tumor markers and ethnicity. Goals depend on prognosis. The plan may attempt to achieve remission (with curative intent) or be palliative (to reduce tumor size and symptoms). Most cancers will not relapse if a patient remains cancer free for 5 years. These patients may be "cured" but are really considered cancer free survivors. Response to treatment is classified as complete (no evidence of disease for at least 1 month) or partial ($\geq 50\%$ tumor size decrease). Stable disease means less than a 25% decrease or increase in tumor size, and progression is $\geq 25\%$ tumor growth or tumor growth in a new site.

Often, the primary treatment modality is surgery (that is, if the cancer is resectable). Neoadjuvant therapy (e.g., radiation or chemotherapy) may be used prior to surgery to shrink the tumor initially. Adjuvant therapy (may include radiation and/or chemotherapy) is given after surgery in an attempt to eradicate residual disease and decrease recurrence.

Sometimes, surgery is not an option for initial treatment and the treatment regimen begins with chemotherapy. This is called primary induction chemotherapy.

Chemotherapeutic regimens are usually designed for synergism. Drugs with different mechanisms of action that complement each other are chosen. Synergy will not work unless each drug is active on the tumor independently. Most drugs work on rapidly dividing DNA since they work by damaging the DNA. They may work on different phases of the cell cycle (described below) or are phase non-specific. The success or failure of previous treatments is an important consideration in recurrent disease.

Chemotherapeutic regimens can be highly toxic and preventing adverse events is part of the treatment plan. Just as different mechanisms of action are desired, as noted above, different toxicities are desired in combination chemotherapy so as to avoid a single intolerable toxicity. The goal is to maintain a high quality of life for the patient. The majority of adverse effects are due to damaging effects on cells that divide more rapidly than others, but are not cancerous. Chemotherapy affects fast growing cells in the GI tract, hair follicles and bone marrow (blood cells). Thus, nausea and vomiting, alopecia, and myelosuppression are common side effects of most chemotherapy. Patient specific factors affect treatment choice, and can include the patient's age and co-morbidities. Sometimes, a patient's condition will lead the clinician and family to recommend palliative measures (to reduce the symptoms) over a more aggressive treatment plan with side effects that could be prohibitive for the patient. Since chemotherapy can have severe side effects, the patient's quality of life must be assessed. Common rating systems for monitoring quality of life include the Karnofsky, Zubrod and the ECOG (Eastern Cooperative Oncology Group) toxicity and performance status scales.

CHEMOTHERAPEUTICS

Chemotherapeutic regimens are designed to complement each other (with different mechanisms of action, toxicities, and cell cycle specificity). This makes it important to note where in the cell cycle the agents work in order to target tumor cells which will be at different stages in the cycle.

Danger During Pregnancy & Breastfeeding

Chemotherapy should be avoided during pregnancy and breastfeeding, although some patients treated while pregnant have delivered healthy children. Counsel both the male and female to avoid conceiving during treatment. Some of the medications can cause sterility long-term.

Summary of Toxicities

For studying purposes, it's best to group drugs based on the side effects. In this text monitoring is not included with the individual oncology agents; in most cases the drugs cause similar issues (such as myelosuppression) and it is best to focus on the differences among agents, along with the significant toxicities.

- Myelosuppression (decreased red blood cells, white blood cells and platelets): requires monitoring the complete blood cell count (CBC), ordered with the differential (includes the segs and bands needed to calculate the absolute neutrophil count). Most oncology drugs cause myelosuppression; the few that do not include asparaginase, bleomycin and vincristine.

- Neuropathy: platinum agents, proteosome inhibitors, taxanes and vinca alkaloids.

- Cardiotoxicity: requires ECG or ECHO or MUGA monitoring. Chest radiation causes cardiac damage; in combination with a cardiotoxic drug, the damage is more severe. Cardiotoxic agents include the anthracyclines, CML drugs (such as imatinib, nilotinib, and dasatinib), and breast cancer drugs (such as trastuzumab and lapatinib).

- Pulmonary toxicity: may require pulmonary function tests if a high-risk agent, including the alkylators (such as busulfan, carmustine, and lomustine), bleomycin, and methotrexate.

- Nephrotoxicity/Bladder toxicity (cystitis): requires monitoring the BUN and SCr, urinalysis and urine output. Hydration is used to flush the drug out and prevent bladder or renal toxicity. Nephrotoxic agents include ifosfamide, cyclophosphamide, arsenic, bevacizumab, methotrexate, and platinum agents (such as cisplatin and carboplatin). Amifostene (Ethyol) may be used to reduce the risk of cisplatin-induced renal toxicity. Cyclophosphamide and ifosfamide cause bladder toxicity. Mesna (Mesnex) is always given with ifosfamide to prevent hemorrhagic cystitis. However, mesna is only recommended with high-doses of cyclophosphamide.

- Acneiform rash: cetuximab, erlotinib, panitumumab, sorafenib, sunitinib (all agents with an EGFR inhibition MOA).

- Mucositis (painful inflammation of the GI tract): if concentrated in the mouth it is referred to as oral mucositis. The inflammation can develop into painful (burning) ulcers. High risk agents include 5-fluorouracil, capecitabine, irinotecan, and methotrexate.

- Hand-foot syndrome: occurs with many oral chemotherapy agents, including capecitabine, pazopanib, sorafenib, sunitinib and vemurafenib, and the IV agents, 5-fluorouracil, liposomal doxorubicin and cytarabine.

- Hepatotoxicity: requires monitoring of liver enzymes and symptoms. Hepatotoxic agents include antiandrogens, the folate and pyrimidine analog antimetabolites (including methotrexate), aromatase inhibitors, busulfan, ixabepilone, SERMs, taxanes, some tyrosine kinase inhibitors and the vinca alkaloids.

- Clotting risk: monitor for DVT/PE with the SERMs and some immunomodulators (thalidomide, lenalidamide, pomalidomide).

- Alopecia: thinning of hair can occur with many agents and some cause complete hair loss. Most notably the taxanes and anthracyclines cause hair loss in nearly 100% of patients including loss of the eyebrows, eyelashes and pubic hair. Other agents that cause alopecia include carboplatin, cyclophosphamide, etoposide, ifosfamide and the vinca alkaloids.

- Extravasation: is leakage of the drug from a vein into the extravascular space; "vesicants" are drugs known to cause tissue necrosis with extravasation, which can require surgical debridement and skin grafting. Each oncology agent should have an extravasation protocol; follow it. Minimally, stop the infusion, elevate the limb, use cold compresses (except with the vinca alkaloids and etoposide use warm compresses – with these agents cold worsens tissue ulceration). There is high-risk of damage with extravasation with these agents: anthracyclines, ixabepilone, mitomycin, teniposide and the vinca alkaloids. Common antidotes used if the drug extravasates include:

  - Dimethyl sulfoxide (DMSO) or dexrazoxane *(Totect)* for the anthracyclines or mitoxantrone (one or the other but not both).

  - Hyaluronidase for the vinca alkaloids.

  - Sodium thiosulfate for mechlorethamine.

MANAGEMENT OF SIDE EFFECTS & COMORBIDITIES

Chemotherapeutic agents are toxic – to the tumor and to the rest of the patient. Many pharmacists are directly involved with cancer treatment and assist patients with the complications of chemotherapy. All pharmacists should be able to assist with the related therapies while specialists are required to help manage the chemotherapeutic regimens.

This section discusses the treatment of myelosuppression (primarily anemia, neutropenia and thrombocytopenia), nausea/vomiting, mucositis, hand-foot syndrome and hypercalcemia of malignancy. Weight loss/gain is a separate chapter, and the drugs used for tumor lysis syndrome are discussed in the Gout chapter.

Myelosuppression Overview

Myelosuppression (↓ in bone marrow activity resulting in fewer red blood cells, white blood cells, and platelets) is a complication with the use of most chemotherapic agents. Neutrophils and platelets are often affected since these cells have a short lifespan, and consequently, have rapid turnover. If white blood cells decrease, the patient is at increased risk of infection and will have trouble fighting an infection. If red blood cells decrease, the patient becomes anemic – with weakness and fatigue. If platelets decrease, there is an increased risk of severe bleeding.

The lowest point that the white blood cells (WBC) and platelets reach (the nadir) occurs about 7-14 days after chemotherapy, although some agents have a delayed effect. Red blood cell nadir occurs much later due to their long life span (~120 days). The cell lines generally recover 3-4 weeks post treatment. The next dose of chemotherapy is given after the cells have returned to a safe level. It may be necessary to help restore blood cell counts with medications. Severe cases might require a transfusion (providing the missing cell line directly, such as giving packed red blood cells for severe anemia). All agents used for myelosuppression discussed here are usually given by SC (subcutaneous) injection, either by the patient, caregiver or medical provider.

Anemia: Assessment & Treatment with Transfusions or ESAs

Until recently, anemia was routinely treated with an erythropoiesis stimulating agent (ESA). However, most anemias are not life-threatening and there is now awareness that the ESAs can shorten survival and increase tumor progression in some cancers. This has resulted in much less frequent use of the ESAs. To make sure that patients are aware of the risks, MedGuides are dispensed with each prescription/filling. For cancer, the use of ESAs must fulfill the requirements of the ESA APPRISE Oncology program. This is a REMS (Risk Evaluation and Mitigation Strategies) program whose purpose is to make sure the healthcare providers are trained and that the patient has received proper counseling on risks and benefits.

Hemoglobin (Hgb) levels are used to assess anemia. Anemia may recover on its own, or be treated with a transfusion or with the use of ESAs. Normal Hgb levels are within 12-16 g/dL for females and 13.5-18 g/dL for males (hematocrit is 36-46% females; 38-50% males). Serum ferritin, transferrin saturation (TSAT) and total iron-binding capacity (TIBC) may be ordered to assess iron storage and transport since the ESAs will not work well to correct anemia if iron levels are inadequate. Levels of folate and vitamin B-12 may need to be evaluated, especially if there is a poor response to the ESA. Anemia may also be treated with red blood cell transfusions.

ESAs are associated with major warnings. The black box warnings for ESA use in cancer:

- ESAs shortened overall survival and/or increased the risk of tumor progression or recurrence in clinical studies of patients with breast, head and neck, lymphoid, non-small cell lung, and cervical cancers.

- Prescribers and hospitals must enroll in and comply with the ESA APPRISE Oncology Program to prescribe and/or dispense these agents to patients with cancer. The patient must sign a form that states they have received counseling about risks and benefits.

- The patient must receive the ESA MedGuide when ESA therapy begins and at least monthly, if continuing.

- Use the lowest dose necessary to avoid the need for RBC transfusions. ESAs should only be used if the hemoglobin level is < 10 g/dL prior to therapy and if there is a minimum of 2 additional months of chemotherapy planned. Discontinue the ESA if no response after 8 weeks, if transfusions are still required, or after the completion of chemotherapy course.

- ESAs are not indicated for patients receiving myelosuppressive chemotherapy when the anticipated outcome is to cure, since the tumor may progress and there is thrombosis risk.

DRUG	DOSING	SAFETY/SIDE EFFECTS/MONITORING
Epoetin alfa (Epogen, Procrit)	150 units/kg SC three times per week or 40,000 units SC once weekly	**BLACK BOX WARNINGS (SEE ABOVE)** **WARNING WITH ALL ESA USE** Increased risk cardiovascular events, thromboembolic events, stroke, and mortality when Hgb levels > 11 g/dL; a rapid rise in hemoglobin (> 1 g/dL over 2 weeks) may contribute to these risks. **CONTRAINDICATIONS** Uncontrolled hypertension, pure red cell aplasia (PRCA) that begins after treatment, multidose vials containing benzyl alcohol contraindicated in neonates, infants, pregnancy and lactation. **SIDE EFFECTS** Hypertension, fever, headache, arthralgia/bone pain, pruritus/rash, nausea, cough, injection site pain, thrombosis, edema, chills, dizziness
Darbepoetin (Aranesp)	300-500 mcg SC usually every 2-3 weeks	**MONITORING** Hgb, Hct, transferrin saturation, serum ferritin, BP **NOTES** Store in refrigerator The doses of ESAs for chemotherapy-induced anemia are much higher than the doses used for anemia due to chronic renal disease. A medication guide must be dispensed with every fill. If Hgb increases > 1 g/dL in any 2-week period, reduce dose by 25% for epoetin alfa and decrease dose by 40% for darbepoetin alfa. MedGuide required

Neutropenia: Assessment & Treatment with Colony Stimulating Factors (CSFs)

Low neutrophil count increases infection risk and make it difficult to fight an infection should one develop. The more neutropenic the patient is the higher the risk of infection.

Neutropenia Definition

CATEGORY	ANC
Neutropenia	< 1,000 mmol/L
Severe Neutropenia	< 500 mmol/L
Profound Neutropenia	< 100 mmol/L

Know how to calculate the ANC; this is reviewed in the Calculations chapter.

The CSFs are called "myeloid growth factors." Myeloid refers to the granulocyte precursor cell, which differentiates into neutrophils, eosinophils, and basophils. These agents are expensive and have not been shown to improve overall survival outcomes. They do shorten the time that a patient is at risk for infection due to neutropenia and they reduce mortality from infections when given prophylactically in patients at a high risk of febrile neutropenia. Consequently, the use is usually limited to conditions outlined in an institution's protocol which define criteria for use. There are three types: GM-CSF (sargramostatin), G-CSF (filgrastim) and pegylated G-CSF (pegfilgrastim). GM-CSF is limited to use in stem cell transplantation. Both forms of G-CSF are indicated in febrile neutropenia.

The NCCN recommends all patients with > 20% chance of developing febrile neutropenia receive myeloid growth factors. The use of growth factors in intermediate-risk patients is more controversial.

DRUG	DOSING	SAFETY/SIDE EFFECTS/MONITORING
Sargramostim (Leukine) GM-CSF Limited to use in stem cell transplantation	250 mcg/m²/day given IV/SC daily; treat through post-nadir recovery	**SIDE EFFECTS** Filgrastim/pegfilgrastim: bone pain, fever, generalized rash Sargramostim: Fever, bone pain, arthralgias, myalgias, rash, dyspnea, peripheral edema, pericardial effusion, cardiovascular edema, HTN, chest pain
Filgrastim (Neupogen) G-CSF	5-10 mcg/kg/day given IV/SC daily (round to the nearest 300 mcg or 480 mcg vial size); treat through post-nadir recovery	**MONITORING** CBC with differential, pulmonary function, weight, vital signs **NOTES** Store in refrigerator
Pegfilgrastim (Neulasta) Pegylated G-CSF Long acting: relatively equivalent to 14 daily doses of filgrastim	1 prefilled syringe (6 mg) SC once per chemotherapy cycle	Administer first dose 24-72 hours after the end of the chemotherapy Patients should report any signs of enlarged spleen (pain in left upper stomach or respiratory distress syndrome) Must document when pegfilgrastim was given

Thrombocytopenia

Low platelets (thrombocytes) can result in spontaneous, uncontrolled bleeding. The normal range for platelets is 150,000-450,000/mm³. Chemotherapy may be placed on hold until the platelet count recovers or there may be a dose reduction in the offending agent (to minimize the toxicity). Platelet transfusions are generally indicated when the count falls below 10,000/mm³ (or 20,000/mm³ if a patient has an active bleed).

Chemotherapy-Induced Nausea and Vomiting (CINV): Prevention is Essential

Nausea and vomiting are common with chemotherapy. Patient factors which increase the risk of nausea and vomiting include female gender, < 50 years of age, dehydration, history of motion sickness, and history of nausea and vomiting with prior regimens. For chemotherapy-induced nausea and vomiting (CINV), give anti-emetics at least 30 minutes prior to chemotherapy and provide take-home anti-emetic medication (such as ondansetron, prochlorperazine, or metoclopramide) for breakthrough nausea and vomiting.

Emetic Risk Potential

HIGH EMETIC RISK	MODERATE EMETIC RISK	LOW EMETIC RISK	MINIMAL EMETIC RISK
> 90% frequency of emesis	30%-90% frequency of emesis	10%-30% frequency of emesis	< 10% frequency of emesis
IV Cisplatin AC combination (doxorubicin or epirubicin w/cyclophosphamide) Epirubicin > 90 mg/m² Ifosfamide ≥ 2 g/m² per dose Cyclophosphamide > 1,500 mg/m² Doxorubicin ≥ 60 mg/m²	**IV** Aldesleukin > 12-15 million unit/m² Bendamustine Interferon alfa ≥ 10 million unit/m² Epirubicin ≤ 90 mg/m² Idarubicin Carboplatin Arsenic trioxide Ifosfamide < 2 g/m² per dose Cyclophosphamide ≤ 1,500 mg/m² Doxorubicin < 60 mg/m² Daunorubicin Oxaliplatin **ORAL** Cyclophosphamide ≥ 100 mg/m²/day, temozolomide (> 75 mg/m²/day), etoposide, crizotinib, procarbazine, vismodegib	**IV** Aldesleukin ≤ 12 million unit/m² Cabazitaxel Carfilzomib Docetaxel 5-FU Gemcitabine Paclitaxel Pemetrexed Etoposide Ixabepilone Mitoxantrone Oxaliplatin **ORAL** Majority of the TKIs (imatinib, nilotinib, dasatinib, erlotinib, sunitinib, sorafenib), immunomodulators (lenalidomide, pomalidomide, thalidomide), capecitabine	**IV** Majority of the monoclonal antibodies (bevacizumab, cetuximab, ipilimumab, panitumumab, pertuzumab, rituximab, trastuzumab) Bleomycin Vinca alkaloids

Anti-Emetic Regimens for Acute Nausea & Vomiting

DRUG	DAY 1	DAY 2	DAY 3	DAY 4
Aprepitant and (IV = fosaprepitant*)	125 mg PO or 150 mg IV	80 mg PO –	80 mg PO –	– –
Dexamethasone and	12 mg PO/IV 12 mg PO/IV*	8 mg PO 8 mg PO*	8 mg PO 8 mg PO BID*	8 mg PO 8 mg PO BID*
Ondansetron or	16-24 mg PO or 8-16 mg IV	–	–	–
Granisetron or	2 mg PO or 0.01 mg/kg IV (max 1 mg) or *Sancuso* patch	–	–	–
Dolasetron† or	100 mg PO	–	–	–
Palonosetron	0.25 mg IV (preferred)	–	–	–

+/- Lorazepam 0.5-2 mg PO/IV/SL Q4-6H on days 1-4

+/- H₂RA or proton pump inhibitor

* Fosaprepitant 150 mg IV once on Day 1 (lasts 5 days, thus oral aprepitant is not needed), but oral dexamethasone dosing is now 8 mg PO on day 2, then 8 mg PO BID days 3 and 4.

† Dolasetron IV is contraindicated in CINV due to incidence of QT prolongation

Note: Use this regimen for patients receiving combination of an anthracycline and cyclophosphamide and select patients receiving other chemotherapies of moderate emetic risk (e.g., carboplatin, cisplatin, doxorubicin, epirubicin, ifosfamide, irinotecan or methotrexate).

Olanzapine-Containing Regimen

May be used as an alternative in the highly and moderately emetogenic regimens

DRUG	DAY 1	DAY 2	DAY 3	DAY 4
Olanzapine and	10 mg PO	10 mg PO –	10 mg PO –	10 mg PO –
Dexamethasone and	20 mg IV	–	–	–
Palonosetron	0.25 mg IV	–	–	–

+/- Lorazepam 0.5-2 mg PO/IV/SL Q4-6H on days 1-4

+/- H₂RA Blocker or proton pump inhibitor

Moderate Emetic Risk Chemotherapy

Typically, a 2-drug combination is used (steroid and a 5-HT$_3$ antagonist) with or without a neurokinin 1 antagonist (for selected patients, where appropriate).

Low Emetic Risk Chemotherapy

Typically, a 1-drug regimen is used (either a 5-HT$_3$ antagonist, dexamethasone, prochlorperazine or metoclopramide).

Delayed emesis (defined as vomiting ocurring > 24 hours after chemotherapy) can be prevented with dexamethasone, aprepitant or palonosetron, alone or in combination depending on the risk and severity (note that palonosetron is the only 5-HT$_3$ receptor antagonist with proven efficacy in delayed CINV). At any point, an adjunct such as lorazepam *(Ativan)* may be added for anxiety/amnestic response or a H₂RA or PPI if upper GI symptoms similar to GERD are present. For moderate emetogenic chemotherapy regimens, give a combination of a steroid and a 5-HT$_3$-receptor antagonist (gold standard). Chemotherapy that is low emetogenic risk may require a single antiemetic such as dexamethasone, prochlorperazine or metoclopramide.

Prochlorperazine or similar phenothiazine-like agent, antihistamines (diphenhydramine or others), or metoclopramide *(Reglan)* are sometimes used, however each has safety concerns. Phenothiazines and metoclopramide are dopamine-blocking agents and could cause or worsen movement disorders. Both classes are sedating and can cause cognitive dysfunction. Metoclopramide requires a reduced dose with renal dysfunction. When overdosed, the side effect profile is worsened. Centrally-acting antihistamines such as diphenhydramine can cause central and peripheral anticholinergic side effects, which may be intolerable in elderly patients (refer to discussion in the Overactive Bladder chapter).

Dronabinol *(Marinol)* and nabilone *(Cesamet)* can be used as second line agents. These are synthetic analogs of delta-9-tetrahydrocannabinol, a naturally occurring component of Cannabis sativa (marijuana). The DEA classifies *Cannabis*, (marijuana, used in the plant form) as a schedule I drug, however it can be purchased for medical and nonmedical use in some states, and in some jurisdictions can be purchased for medical use only.

Antiemetic Agents

DRUG	DOSING	SAFETY/SIDE EFFECTS/MONITORING

5-HT₃-receptor antagonists: Work by blocking serotonin, both peripherally on vagal nerve terminals and centrally in the chemoreceptor trigger zone

DRUG	DOSING	SAFETY/SIDE EFFECTS/MONITORING
Ondansetron *(Zofran, Zuplenz film)* IV, PO, ODT, solution	High risk: 16 mg IV on day(s) of chemo Moderate risk: 8 mg IV on day(s) of chemo 4-8 mg IM/IV/PO Q6H PRN breakthrough nausea Single max IV dose is 16 mg; 24 mg max for PO	**CONTRAINDICATIONS** Concomitant use of apomorphine *(Apokyn)*; do not use dolasetron IV for acute CINV (due to QT prolongation) **SIDE EFFECTS** Headache, fatigue, dizziness, constipation **NOTES** Pregnancy Category B
Granisetron *(Granisol solution, Sancuso transdermal patch)* IV, PO, solution	High risk: 2 mg oral or 1 mg IV on day(s) of chemo 2 mg PO or 1 mg IV Q12H PRN breakthrough nausea Sancuso patch 3.1 mg/24 hr	*Zofran ODT*: With dry hands, peel back the foil backing of 1 blister and gently remove the tablet and immediately place on top of the tongue where it will dissolve in seconds, then swallow with saliva. *Sancuso patch* (3.1 mg/24 hr): useful if sores in mouth (mucositis), dysphagia or if expected to need up to 5 days nausea prevention (apply on the upper arm the day before chemo and leave on at least 24 hr after last session – lasts up to 7 days). Avoid sunlight near patch site.
Dolasetron *(Anzemet)*	High risk only: 100 mg PO once on day 1 of chemo	Risk of prolonged QT interval (torsades de pointes) with all 5-HT₃ antagonists; correct Mg²⁺ and K⁺ and monitor ECG. Due to the long half-life (~40 hrs) of IV palonosetron, it is indicated for acute and delayed nausea/vomiting (up to 7 days). Caution when using additional 5-HT₃ antagonists for 1 week after palonosetron administration. Consider using prochlorperazine or metoclopramide instead. IV and oral 5-HT₃ antagonists are equally efficacious. If a patient failed one 5-HT₃ antagonist, try switching to another 5-HT₃ antagonist. Give 30 minutes prior to chemotherapy for CINV.
Palonosetron *(Aloxi)*	High and moderate risk: 0.25 mg IV once on day 1 of chemotherapy.	

Phenothiazines: work by blocking dopamine receptors in the CNS, including the chemoreceptor trigger zone (among other mechanisms)

DRUG	DOSING	SAFETY/SIDE EFFECTS/MONITORING
Prochlorperazine *(Compro)*	5-10 mg IM/IV/PO Q6H PRN May give 25 mg suppository PR Q12H PRN	**CONTRAINDICATIONS** Do not use in children < 2 years old and use dosing guidelines for older children. Do not administer promethazine via the SC route.
Chlorpromazine *(Thorazine)*	10-25 mg PO Q4-6H PRN 25-50 mg IM Q4-6H PRN	**WARNINGS** I.V. administration is not the preferred route; severe tissue damage may occur. Solution for injection should be administered in a maximum concentration of 25 mg/mL (more dilute solutions are recommended). Administer through a large bore vein (not hand or wrist).
Promethazine *(Phenergan, Phenadoz, Promethegan)*	IV, IM, PR 12.5-25 mg Q4-6H PRN	**SIDE EFFECTS** Sedation, lethargy, hypotension, neuroleptic malignant syndrome (NMS), QT prolongation, acute EPS (common in children – antidote is diphenhydramine or benztropine), can lower seizure threshold, strong anticholinergic side effects

Antiemetic Agents Continued

DRUG	DOSING	SAFETY/SIDE EFFECTS/MONITORING

Corticosteroid

Dexamethasone (Decadron) IV, PO	High risk: 12 mg PO/IV on day 1 of chemotherapy, then 8 mg PO/IV days 2-4 Moderate risk: 8 mg PO/IV on day 1 of chemotherapy, then 8 mg PO/IV day 2-3 Low risk: 8 mg PO/IV day 1 of chemotherapy Breakthrough: 12 mg PO/IV daily up to 3 days	**SIDE EFFECTS** Short-term side effects include ↑ appetite/weight gain, fluid retention, emotional instability (euphoria, mood swings, irritability, acute psychosis), insomnia, GI upset. Higher doses can cause ↑ in BP and blood glucose (especially in patients with diabetes).

Cannabinoids

Dronabinol (Marinol) Refrigerate capsules C III	5-10 mg PO TID or QID	**SIDE EFFECTS** Drowsiness, euphoria, increased appetite, orthostatic hypotension
Nabilone (Cesamet) BID No refrigeration needed C II	1-2 mg PO BID, continue for up to 48H after last chemotherapy dose	

Substance P/Neurokinin-1 receptor antagonist – For acute and delayed nausea

Aprepitant (Emend) **Fosaprepitant (Emend for injection)** – prodrug of aprepitant IV	PO: 125 mg given 1 hour before chemo, then 80 mg daily x 2 days or IV: 150 mg given 30 minutes before chemo as single dose only (lasts up to 5 days)	**SIDE EFFECTS** Dizziness, fatigue, constipation, hiccups. **NOTES** Drug interaction: reduce dose of dexamethasone by ~50%.

Mucositis

Inflammation and sores in the mouth, esophagus and lower GI tract can cause pain, ulceration and considerable suffering. There are many agents used to prevent and treat mucositis ("Magic Mouthwash", chlorhexidine rinse, etc) but only one FDA approved agent: palifermin (Kepivance) which is restricted to high dose chemo prior to stem cell transplant. Patients at risk for mucositis should be counseled to use a saline rinse several times daily. Use of agents containing viscous lidocaine are effective in numbing the local affected area. Patient can swish and spit the suspension.

Hand-Foot Syndrome

Hand-foot syndrome (also known as palmar-plantar erythrodysesthesia) can occur following the chemotherapy drugs listed previously. Small amounts of the drug leak out of the capillaries and into the palms of the hands and the soles of feet. Exposure of the hands and feet to heat as well as friction increases the amount of drug in the capillaries. This leakage results in redness, swelling, tenderness, pain, blisters and possibly peeling of the palms and soles.

Blisters may appear. Dose reductions or delays in treatment are recommended if symptoms do not improve. Pyridoxine (vitamin B6) is no longer recommended as prophylaxis or treatment (it was found to be no better than placebo).

Prevention is very important in trying to reduce the development of hand-foot syndrome and includes:

- Limit daily activities to reduce friction and heat exposure to hands and feet [for 1 week after IV medication (e.g., 5-Fluorouracil) or during the duration of oral exposure (e.g., capecitabine)].

- Avoid long exposure to hot water (washing dishes, showers). Take short showers in tepid water.

- Do not wear dishwashing gloves as the rubber will hold in the heat.

- Avoid increased pressure on soles of feet (no jogging, aerobics, power walking, jumping).

- Avoid increased pressure on palms of hands (do not use garden tools, screwdrivers, knives for chopping or performing other tasks that require squeezing hand(s) on a hard surface).

Cooling procedures provide temporary relief of pain and tenderness. Using cold compresses like ice packs or frozen peas may reduce the severity of the pain (alternate cold packs on and off for 15-20 minutes at a time). Emollients such as petrolatum, *Udderly Smooth Cream* and *Bag Balm* provide excellent moisturizing for hands and feet; lotions do not provide adequate protection. Corticosteroids and pain medications may be used to help alleviate inflammation and pain.

HYPERCALCEMIA OF MALIGNANCY

Prior to the therapeutic use of bisphosphonates in metastatic bone cancer, hypercalcemia occurred in ~25% of cancer patients and was the most common metabolic complication of breast cancer. It also occurs commonly with lung cancer and multiple myeloma. The bone destruction that results in hypercalcemia causes significant symptoms for the patient, including nausea, vomiting, fatigue, dehydration and mental status changes. Bone pain can be significant, and the complication carries a high risk of long-term skeletal damage (fractures, spinal cord compression, etc.) which is why bisphosphonates or denosumab *(Xgeva)* are used early in metastatic disease to prevent skeletal-related events. Denosumab blocks the interaction between RANKL and RANK (a receptor located on osteoclast surfaces), preventing osteoclast formation and leading to decreased bone resorption. Denosumab is also indicated for osteoporosis under the brand name *Prolia*; do not get *Xgeva* (120 mg SC monthly) and *Prolia* (60 mg SC every 6 months) confused (see Osteoporosis chapter for further information).

Zoledronic also comes as two brand names for different indications. *Reclast* (5 mg/year) is used for osteoporosis compared to 4 mg monthly with *Zometa*. The bisphosphonates require adjustment for renal insufficiency whereas denosumab, a monoclonal antibody, does not. All these have a risk of osteonecrosis of the jaw (ONJ) for which discontinuation of therapy is required. Treatment for hypercalcemia of malignancy is summarized in the following table.

Hypercalcemia of Malignancy Treatment

TREATMENT	MOA	ONSET	DURATION	DEGREE OF HYPERCALCEMIA *
Hydration with normal saline	Dilutional effect and increased renal calcium excretion	Minutes to hours	Only during length of infusion	Mild Moderate Severe
Loop Diuretics	Increased renal calcium excretion (only with hydration)	Hours	Only during length of therapy	Mild Moderate Severe
Calcitonin	Inhibits bone resorption, increased renal calcium excretion	4-6 hours	48 hours max (quickly develop tachyphylaxis)	Moderate Severe
IV Bisphosphonates zoledronic acid (Zometa) 4 mg pamidronate (Aredia) 30-90 mg	Inhibits bone resorption by stopping osteoclast function	24-72 hours	2-4 weeks	Mild Moderate Severe

*Mild: corrected calcium < 12 mg/dL, Moderate: corrected calcium 12-14 mg/dL, Severe: corrected calcium > 14 mg/dL

Safe Handling of Hazardous Agents

Chemotherapy agents are hazardous drugs that are considered carcinogenic, mutagenic, and teratogenic. To limit exposure to these agents, pharmacies should have written procedures for handling these drugs safely. The United States Pharmacopeia (USP) chapter 797 regulates the preparation of extemporaneously compounded sterile preparations and should be used by centers that prepare chemotherapy. Refer to the Medication Safety chapter for further information.

Routes of exposure include inhalation, ingestion, dermal contact, and accidental injections. The most common type of accidental exposure is inhalation of the aerosolized drug. A class II biologic safety cabinet should be used at all times in addition to chemo-gowns and chemo-block gloves (preferably double gloving). The gowns should be made of lint-free, low-permeability fabric with a solid front, long sleeves, and tight-fitting elastic cuffs. Negative-pressure techniques should be employed during drug preparation. Chemotherapy spill kits should be readily available and located in areas of the institution in which chemotherapy is handled. Cytotoxic waste should be disposed of properly, IV bags should be labeled "Chemotherapeutic: Dispose of Properly" or similar, and patients should be informed of proper methods of disposing of potentially contaminated body waste (such as flushing the toilet twice).

Timing of Vaccinations

Vaccination during chemotherapy should be avoided because the antibody response is suboptimal. When chemotherapy is being planned, vaccination should precede the initiation of chemotherapy by ≥ 2 weeks. The administration of live vaccines to immunocompromised patients should be avoided.

ONCOLOGY II:
COMMON CANCER TYPES
& TREATMENT

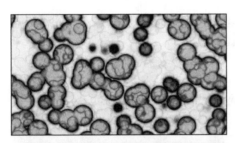

We gratefully acknowledge the assistance of Muoi Gi, PharmD, BCPS, BCOP, Oncology Pharmacy Residency Director at the VA San Diego Healthcare System and D. Raymond Weber, PharmD, BSPharm, BCOP, BCPS, RPh, University of Maryland Eastern Shore, School of Pharmacy and Health Professions (rweberpharmd@umes.edu), in preparing this chapter.

GUIDELINES

National Comprehensive Cancer Network (NCCN). www.nccn.org (accessed 2013 Dec 1)

American Society of Clinical Oncology (ASCO). www.asco.org (accessed 2013 Dec 1)

CHEMOTHERAPY REGIMENS AND DOSING

In the preceeding section an overview of cancer treatment and management of major side effects were discussed. Cancer treatment depends on multiple factors, including cancer type, staging and patient factors. When chemotherapy is used, the regimens are usually in combinations chosen for efficacy, synergy and to target cells with different resistance mechanisms and in different stages of replication. There are many regimens; for example, the ABVD regimen used for Hodgkin's lymphoma [<u>A</u>driamycin (doxorubicin), <u>B</u>leomycin, <u>V</u>inblastine, <u>D</u>acarbazine] and the FOLFOX regimen used for colorectal cancer [<u>FOL</u>inic acid (leucovorin), <u>F</u>luorouracil, <u>OX</u>aliplatin], among many others.

Often the regimen is administered in cycles involving one or more drugs, given once, or multiple times, such as over several consecutive days, followed by days or weeks without treatment. The break in treatment will give the patient, including the patient's cell lines, time to recover.

Dosing, Body Surface Area (BSA) Calculations

Chemotherapy dosing may be in mg, mg/kg, or by the patient's body surface area (BSA). There are four BSA formulas: 1. DuBois and DuBois, 2. Mosteller, 3. Haycock, and 4. Gehan and George. These formulas may produce slightly different BSAs and, consequently, a different drug dosage. The one most commonly used in adult oncology practice is the DuBois and DuBois formula. Oncology pharmacists will use a "plug-in" to get the result as the formula is complex. You may wish to work out the calculation, as shown here. This is followed by the Mosteller formula, which is also used in adults. The weight that is commonly used for calculating the dose in oncology is the actual weight; sometimes the adjusted weight is used if the patient is overweight. Use the actual weight unless instructed by the oncologist to use another weight or if instructed to use a specific weight on the exam. In practice, note the weight that was used, since the weight changes the dose.

Dubois And Dubois

$$BSA\ (m^2) = 0.007184 \times Height(cm)^{0.725} \times Weight(kg)^{0.425}$$

Example

A patient has a weight of 175 lbs and height of 6'1". Calculate the patient's BSA using the DuBois and DuBois formula. Round to the nearest hundredth.

Convert weight in pounds to kilograms by dividing by 2.2: 175/2.2 = 79.5 kg
Convert height in inches to centimeters by multiplying by 2.54: 73" x 2.54 = 185.4 cm

$$BSA\ (m^2) = 0.007184 \times Height(cm)^{0.725} \times Weight(kg)^{0.425}$$

$$BSA\ (m^2) = 0.007184 \times (185.4)^{0.725} \times (79.5)^{0.425}$$

$$BSA\ (m^2) = 2.03$$

Mosteller

$$BSA\ (m^2) = \sqrt{\frac{Ht\ (cm) \times Wt\ (kg)}{3,600}}$$

Example

A patient has a weight of 175 lbs and height of 6'1". Calculate the patient's BSA using the Mosteller formula. Round to the nearest hundredth.

Convert weight in pounds to kilograms by dividing by 2.2: 175/2.2 = 79.5 kg
Convert height in inches to centimeters by multiplying by 2.54: 73" x 2.54 = 185.4 cm

$$BSA\ (m^2) = \sqrt{\frac{185.4(cm) \times 79.5(kg)}{3,600}} = 2.02$$

- If you do not wish to use the square root key, it can be calculated using the y^x key since any number raised to the ½ power will produce that number's square root. Enter the number for which the square root is required, press y^x, then enter 0.5 as the exponent.

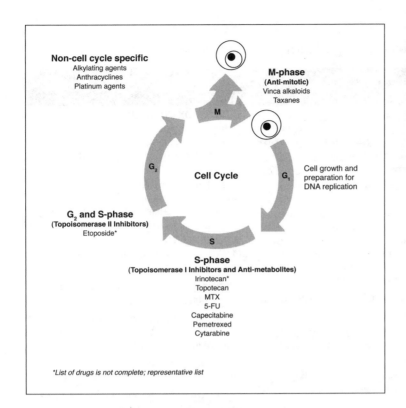

Non-cell cycle specific
Alkylating agents
Anthracyclines
Platinum agents

M-phase
(Anti-mitotic)
Vinca alkaloids
Taxanes

Cell growth and preparation for DNA replication

Cell Cycle

G₂ and S-phase
(Topoisomerase II Inhibitors)
Etoposide*

S-phase
(Topoisomerase I Inhibitors and Anti-metabolites)
Irinotecan*
Topotecan
MTX
5-FU
Capecitabine
Pemetrexed
Cytarabine

List of drugs is not complete; representative list

PHASES OF THE CELL CYCLE

M
Mitosis – cell divides into 2 daughter cells

G₀
Resting phase post mitosis – no cell division occurs

G₁
Post-mitotic phase – where enzymes and proteins are synthesized

S
DNA synthesis and duplication occurs

G₂
Pre-mitotic phase – RNA and topoisomerase I and II are produced to prepare for cell division

CONVENTIONAL CHEMOTHERAPY

In the following sections the agents are listed in relative order of importance for general adult oncology practice. Specific areas of oncology (pediatrics, urology, transplantation) would place a higher level of importance on less common agents and there are also regional differences in which agents may be considered more important.

The initial groups of chemotherapy agents that follow are commonly used in a multitude of cancers and have many overlapping toxicities. These are followed by more targeted agents accompanied by brief descriptions of some of the more common cancers they treat. This review focuses on the medications and does not go into detail on the actual cancers or treatments which are generally protocol based.

Alkylators

Non-cell cycle specific: Cross-links DNA, preventing cell replication.

DRUG	UNIQUE CONCERNS	SAFETY/SIDE EFFECTS/MONITORING
Cyclophosphamide *(Cytoxan)* Ifosfamide *(Ifex)* Temozolomide *(Temodar)* Dacarbazine *(DTIC)* Bendamustine *(Treanda)* Melphalan *(Alkeran)* – tablets require refrigeration Busulfan *(Myleran)* Lomustine *(CeeNU)* Carmustine *(BiCNU, Gliadel* wafer for brain CA) Procarbazine *(Matulane)* Chlorambucil *(Leukeran)* – requires refrigeration Mechlorethamine *(Mustargen)* Streptozocin *(Zanosar)* Altretamine *(Hexalen)* Thiotepa *(Thioplex)*	Bladder toxicity with high-dose cyclophosphamide and all doses of ifosfamide – give mesna *(Mesnex)* to protect against hemorrhagic cystitis and also ensure adequate hydration Temozolomide can cross the blood brain barrier. Used primarily in brain cancers (such as glioblastoma multiforme). Best taken on an empty stomach or at bedtime to decrease nausea. Prophylaxis against *Pneumocystis* pneumonia is important while on temozolomide + radiation. Lomustine PO is dosed QHS with an antiemetic. Procarbazine is a monoamine oxidase inhibitor; avoid interacting drugs/foods. Carmustine: use non-PVC bag and tubing due to leaching of DEHP.	**BLACK BOX WARNINGS** Hemorrhagic cystitis (ifosfamide, cyclophosphamide), severe bone marrow suppression, secondary malignancy **CONTRAINDICATIONS** Pregnancy, severe bone marrow suppression, bladder or urinary obstruction **SIDE EFFECTS** Myelosuppression, nausea/vomiting, alopecia Pulmonary toxicity (busulfan, carmustine, lomustine) Neurologic toxicity such as seizures, encephalopathy (chlorambucil, ifosfamide, temozolamide, thiotepa) Skin pigmentation changes (busulfan, carmustine) Dacarbazine is highly emetogenic and can cause flu-like symptoms Impairs fertility

Anthracyclines

Non-cell cycle specific: Work by several mechanisms, including intercalcation into DNA, inhibiting topoisomerase II, and creating oxygen-free radicals that damage cells.

DRUG	UNIQUE CONCERNS	SAFETY/SIDE EFFECTS/MONITORING
DOXOrubicin *(Adriamycin)* DOXOrubicin liposomal *(Doxil)* Epirubicin *(Ellence)* Idarubicin *(Idamycin)* DAUNOrubicin *(Cerubidine)* DAUNOrubicin liposomal *(DaunoXome)* Mitoxantrone *(Novantrone)* Valrubicin *(Valstar)* intravesicular bladder irrigation only	Very effective but use limited by cardiac toxicity and N/V. Vesicants: High risk of severe tissue damage with extravasation: antidote is dexrazoxane *(Totect)* or dimethyl sulfoxide. Do not use both. Serial monitoring of cardiac output is necessary at baseline and with anthracycline doses exceeding: 250 mg/m² doxorubicin; 320 mg/m² daunorubicin. The liposomal products are associated with a higher incidence of hand-foot syndrome and allergic reactions. Cardiotoxicity: ↓ risk by not exceeding max lifetime dose: Doxorubicin = 450-550 mg/m² (450 mg/m² with mediastinal radiation). The cardioprotective agent dexrazoxane *(Zinecard)* should be considered when doxorubicin doses are anticipated to continue beyond 300 mg/m². Mitoxantrone is an anthracenedione similar to anthracyclines in toxicity but a three rather than four membered ring structure and turns body fluids blue rather than red as with the other anthracyclines.	**BLACK BOX WARNINGS** Irreversible myocardial toxicity may occur as total dosage approaches cumulative max doses Secondary malignancy (AML or MDS) Severe myelosuppression in patients with impaired hepatic function Potent vesicant – avoid extravasation **CONTRAINDICATIONS** HF, MI or arrhythmias; pre-existing bone marrow suppression (ANC < 1,500), previous therapy with high cumulative doses of anthracyclines, severe liver impairment **SIDE EFFECTS** Myelosuppression, alopecia, N/V, mucositis, injection site extravasation, radiation recall, hepatitis, red urine and body secretions (blue with mitoxantrone)

Anthracycline and Mitoxantrone Maximum Lifetime Doses

DRUG	LIFETIME DOSE
Doxorubicin	450-550 mg/m²
	450 mg/m² with chest radiation
Daunorubicin	400-550 mg/m²
Epirubicin	800-900 mg/m²
Idarubicin	120-150 mg/m²
Mitoxantrone	140 mg/m²

Platinum-Based Compounds

Non-cell cycle specific: Cross-links DNA, leading to apoptosis (programmed cell death)

DRUG	UNIQUE CONCERNS	SAFETY/SIDE EFFECTS/MONITORING
Cisplatin *(Platinol)*	Nephrotoxicity – vigorous hydration and sometimes mannitol are used to prevent renal failure; electrolyte wasting requiring magnesium and potassium supplementation. Amifostine *(Ethyol)* may also be used prophylactically for renal protection. Ototoxicity may occur (recommend audiograms prior to each cycle). Severe N/V, acute and delayed (use 3 drug combination antiemetic regimen).	**BLACK BOX WARNINGS** Doses > 100 mg/m² Q 3-4 weeks are rarely used and should be verified (cisplatin). Cumulative renal toxicity may be severe. Dose-related myelosuppression, nausea and vomiting. Hearing impairment, anaphylactic-like reactions. **CONTRAINDICATIONS** Pre-existing renal impairment, hearing impairment (cisplatin), myelosuppression
Carboplatin *(Paraplatin-AQ)*	Calvert Formula: Carboplatin Dose (total in mg) = Target AUC X (GFR + 25). Target AUC ranges from 1 to 7 with 1-2 as a radiosensitizer (makes cancer cells sensitive to radiation therapy); 4-6 in combination therapy and 7 as a single agent. Commonly used max GFR for calculating carboplatin dose = 125 mL/min.	**SIDE EFFECTS** Myelosuppression, neuropathy (cumulative, dose-dependent) Hypersensitivity reactions (including anaphylaxis); may respond to pretreatment with steroids and antihistamines.
Oxaliplatin *(Eloxatin)*	Anaphylaxis, pancreatitis, pulmonary toxicity, hepatotoxicity. Neuropathy exacerbated by exposure to cold; infusion of calcium and magnesium (1 gram each) prior to oxaliplatin reduces neuropathy by ~ 50%.	

Folate Antimetabolites

Cell cycle specific, S-phase: Prevent DNA synthesis.

DRUG	UNIQUE CONCERNS	SAFETY/SIDE EFFECTS/MONITORING
Methotrexate *(Trexall, Rheumatrex)* Lower doses used in RA and psoriasis	High-dose provides a dose increase 10-100 fold higher increasing the amount of methotrexate that penetrates the blood-brain barrier and overcomes relative resistance in malignancies (osteosarcoma). High-dose requires leucovorin (or levoleucovorin) rescue to ↓ toxicity. Leucovorin is the active form of folic acid, which bypasses the enzyme block of dihydrofolate reductase by methotrexate. Active transport renal elimination ↓ by aspirin, beta lactams, probenecid and NSAIDs, resulting in toxicity (avoid concurrent use). Maintain hydration. Drink fluids. Alkalinize urine (by giving bicarb IV) to reduce toxicity.	**BLACK BOX WARNINGS (MANY)** Pregnancy, hepatic disease, ascites (third space), diarrhea, exfoliative dermatitis, infection, renal impairment, tumor lysis syndrome, stomatitis, pulmonary disease, lymphoma, preserved formulation for intrathecal administration, radiation therapy (if is used as a radiation sensitizer, it may cause more soft tissue or bone necrosis) **CONTRAINDICATIONS** Pregnancy, hepatic disease, AIDS, immunosuppression, alcoholism, bone marrow suppression **SIDE EFFECTS** Myelosuppression, mucositis, hepatic and renal toxicity (renal is dose-related), pulmonary toxicity (rare), tumor lysis syndrome Red-tender palms and feet (hand-foot syndrome)
Pemetrexed *(Alimta)*	To reduce side effects (hematologic, mucositis, diarrhea, dermatologic): give folic acid supplements (1 mg PO daily), vitamin B12 (cyanocobalamin) plus dexamethasone.	**SIDE EFFECTS** Renal toxicity, bone marrow suppression, dermatologic toxicity, mucositis, N/V/D
Pralatrexate *(Folotyn)*	Similar to above, use B12 and folate to reduce toxicity. Avoid renal transport inhibitors as with methotrexate.	**SIDE EFFECTS** Myelosuppression, mucositis, anemia, renal toxicity, hepatic toxicity, tumor lysis syndrome, fetal harm

Pyrimidine Analog Antimetabolites

Cell cycle specific, S-phase: Inhibits pyrimidine synthesis.

DRUG	UNIQUE CONCERNS	SAFETY/SIDE EFFECTS/MONITORING
Capecitabine *(Xeloda)* prodrug of 5-fluorouracil PO take with meal	Pharmacogenomic testing for dihydropyrimidine dehydrogenase (DPD) – deficiency increases risk of severe toxicity. Capecitabine can ↑ INR up to 91% due to 2C9 inhibition – dose modification based on severity of the interaction.	**BLACK BOX WARNING** ↑ INR during and up to 1 month after discontinuation; reduce warfarin dose, monitor carefully; fatal bleeding can occur. **CONTRAINDICATIONS** Dihydropyrimidine dehydrogenase (DPD) deficiency, renal impairment (CrCl < 30 mL/min) **SIDE EFFECTS** Hand-foot syndrome (more than 5-fluorouracil), diarrhea, mucositis, gastritis, N/V, dermatitis, cardiotoxicity, edema, myelosuppression
Cytarabine *(Ara-C, Cytosar)* Cytarabine liposomal *(DepoCyt)*: for intrathecal administration	"Ara-C syndrome" includes fever, general weakness, fatigue, skin rash, reddened eyes, bone, muscle, joint and/or chest pain – responds to corticosteroids.	**BLACK BOX WARNING** Bone marrow suppression **SIDE EFFECTS** Mucositis, myelosuppression, hepatotoxicity, pulmonary toxicity, encephalopathy, severe N/V and peripheral neuropathy at high doses, hand-foot syndrome

Pyrimidine Analog Antimetabolites Continued

DRUG	UNIQUE CONCERNS	SAFETY/SIDE EFFECTS/MONITORING
Fluorouracil (5-FU, *Adrucil)* *Efudex* is topical formulation for wrinkles, *Carac* and *Fluoroplex* are topical for actinic keratosis	Pharmacogenomics same as *Xeloda* above Given with leucovorin to increase efficacy of 5-FU	**BLACK BOX WARNINGS (2)** Bone marrow suppression, GI bleed **CONTRAINDICATIONS** Dihydropyrimidine dehydrogenase (DPD) deficiency, bone marrow suppression, infection, malnutrition, pregnancy **SIDE EFFECTS** Myelosuppression, mucositis, dermatitis, diarrhea, cardiotoxicity, hand-foot syndrome (with continuous infusions), photosensitivity
Gemcitabine *(Gemzar)*	Flu-like syndrome during first 24 hours: use acetaminophen for treatment. Prolonged infusion time may increase toxicities; use infusion rates per protocol.	**SIDE EFFECTS** Myelosuppression, hepatotoxicity, arthralgia, rash, fatigue, headache, N/V/D, stomatitis, radiation recall, peripheral edema, dyspnea

Taxanes

M-phase specific: Inhibit microtubule function and angiogenesis (dysfunctional microtubule bundling). Elimination of taxanes is reduced when given immediately after administration of cisplatin or carboplatin. Give taxanes first.

DRUG	UNIQUE CONCERNS	SAFETY/SIDE EFFECTS/MONITORING
Paclitaxel *(Taxol)* Paclitaxel albumin-bound *(Abraxane):* less hypersensitivity reactions	Anaphylaxis, hypersensitivity reaction (78%) due to polyoxyethylated castor oil solvent system; can be severe in 2-4% of patients. Symptoms include dyspnea, hypotension, angioedema, and generalized urticaria. Pretreat with dexamethasone, diphenhydramine and H₂RA (not needed with *Abraxane).* All taxanes: Use non-PVC IV bag and tubing due to leaching of DEHP. Do not extravasate. Will ↑ INR if on warfarin; monitor closely.	**BLACK BOX WARNING** Neutropenia **CONTRAINDICATIONS** Neutropenia **SIDE EFFECTS** Myelosuppression, peripheral neuropathy, anaphylactoid reaction, alopecia (can be entire body), fever, skin reaction, cardiotoxicity, hepatotoxicity, myalgia/arthralgia, N/V, radiation recall
Docetaxel *(Taxotere)*	Hypersensitivity (40-50%) due to polysorbate 80 solvent system. Cardio-Pulmonary: Fluid retention, pericardial effusion, pleural effusion and edema (41-70%). Pretreatment with dexamethasone 8 mg BID x 3 days starting the day prior to docetaxel to decrease fluid retention. All taxanes: Use non-PVC IV bag and tubing due to leaching of DEHP.	**BLACK BOX WARNINGS (4)** Neutropenia, edema, hepatic disease, lung cancer **CONTRAINDICATIONS** Neutropenia **SIDE EFFECTS** Myelosuppression, fluid retention, peripheral neuropathy, anaphylactoid reaction, cutaneous reactions, N/V/D, mucositis, myalgias, arthralgias, fatigue

Taxanes Continued

DRUG	UNIQUE CONCERNS	SAFETY/SIDE EFFECTS/MONITORING
Cabazitaxel *(Jevtana)*	Hypersensitivity reaction (40-50%) due to polysorbate 80 solvent system; premedicate with antihistamines and corticosteroids. All taxanes: Use non-PVC IV bag and tubing due to leaching of DEHP.	**BLACK BOX WARNING** Neutropenia **CONTRAINDICATIONS** Neutropenia **SIDE EFFECTS** Myelosuppression, peripheral neuropathy, anaphylactoid reaction, N/V/D, hepatic and renal failure, peripheral edema, fatigue, alopecia, myalgias, arthralgias, stomatitis

Vinca Alkaloids

M-phase specific: Inhibit microtubule function (destabilizers).

DRUG	UNIQUE CONCERNS	SAFETY/SIDE EFFECTS/MONITORING
VinCRIStine **(Vincasar, Oncovin)** Max single dose: 2 mg Vincristine liposomal (Marqibo)	These agents are vesicants. Best to administer with a central line. Avoid extravasation as tissue damage will occur. Use warm compress and hyaluronidase as treatment. IV only; Do not administer intrathecally – fatal Causes only mild myelosuppression	**BLACK BOX WARNINGS (2)** Extravasation, intrathecal administration (fatal) **SIDE EFFECTS** Cumulative (dose-dependent) nerve damage/ peripheral neuropathy (paresthesias, gastroparesis/constipation, paralytic ileus, ↑ risk of falls), alopecia, rash, SIADH, tumor lysis syndrome
VinBLASTine **(Velban)** **VinORELbine** **(Navelbine)**	These agents are vesicants. Best to administer these agents via a central line. Avoid extravasation as tissue damage may occur. Use warm compress and hyaluronidase as treatment. IV only; Do not administer intrathecally – fatal	**BLACK BOX WARNINGS (3)** Neutropenia, extravasation, intrathecal administration (fatal) **CONTRAINDICATIONS** Bone marrow suppression, infection **SIDE EFFECTS** Myelosuppression, peripheral neuropathy (less than vincristine), gastroparesis/constipation, tumor lysis syndrome

Topoisomerase I Inhibitors

S-phase specific: Block the coiling and uncoiling of the DNA helix. Topoisomerase I facilitates single stand breaks followed by religation (putting the DNA strands back together).

DRUG	UNIQUE CONCERNS	SAFETY/SIDE EFFECTS/MONITORING
Irinotecan **(Camptosar)**	Acute diarrhea is a cholinergic symptom: treat with atropine. Delayed diarrhea is treated with loperamide (up to 24 mg daily). Pharmacogenomic testing: Those who are homozygous for the UGT1A1*28 allele are at an ↑ risk for neutropenia and other toxicities.	**BLACK BOX WARNINGS (2)** Bone marrow suppression, diarrhea **SIDE EFFECTS** Diarrhea, myelosupresion, mucositis, Acute cholenergic syndrome (rhinitis, hypersalivation, sweating, etc), N/V, asthenia, fever, pain, headache, chills, pulmonary reactions (dyspnea, cough), hepatic enzymes, alopecia

Topoisomerase I Inhibitors Continued

DRUG	UNIQUE CONCERNS	SAFETY/SIDE EFFECTS/MONITORING
Topotecan *(Hycamtin)*	Used typically as a second line agent for cervical, ovarian or small cell lung cancer	**BLACK BOX WARNING** Bone marrow suppression **SIDE EFFECTS** Myelosuppression, N/V/D, alopecia; dyspnea, flu-like symptoms, infertility

Topoisomerase II Inhibitors

G2-phase specific: Block the coiling and uncoiling of the DNA helix by facilitating single stand breaks followed by religation.

DRUG	UNIQUE CONCERNS	SAFETY/SIDE EFFECTS/ MONITORING
Etoposide (VePesid) *VePesid capsules require refrigeration*	Etoposide IV can cause hypotension or bronchospasm if infusion rate is too fast. Bioavailability of oral etoposide capsule is ~50%. Double the IV dose and round dose to the nearest 50 mg capsule. If total dose is > 400 mg, then divide dose to twice daily. IV piggyback concentrations greater than 0.4 mg/mL may precipitate; use large volume infusion. Vesicant: use hyaluronidase and warm compresses to treat.	**BLACK BOX WARNINGS (3)** Bone marrow suppression, bleeding, infection **SIDE EFFECTS** Myelosuppression, hypotension, bronchospasm, anaphylactoid reaction, neuropathy, hepatotoxicity, alopecia, N/V, mucositis
Teniposide *(Vumon)*	Use non-PVC IV bag and tubing due to leaching of DEHP. Vesicant: use hyaluronidase and warm compresses to treat. Teniposide can cause hypotension if infusion rate is too fast. Do not run IVPB faster than 30 minutes.	**BLACK BOX WARNINGS (2)** Hypersensitivity to castor oil, bone marrow suppression **CONTRAINDICATIONS** Hypersensitivity to castor oil **SIDE EFFECTS** Myelosuppression, hypersensitivity reaction (hypotension, bronchospasm), mucositis, N/V/D, secondary malignancy, alopecia

Epothilone

M-phase specific: Microtubule stabilizer enhancing polymerization of tubules halting cell division; mechanism similar to taxanes.

DRUG	UNIQUE CONCERNS	SAFETY/SIDE EFFECTS/MONITORING
Ixabepilone *(Ixempra)*	Similar mechanism to taxanes but retains efficacy in taxane-resistant breast cancer. Hypersensitivity due to *Cremophor EL* (polyoxethylated castor oil solvent) requiring antihistamines +/- steroids, acetaminophen. Use 0.2 – 1.2 micron filter. Use non-PVC IV bag and tubing due to leaching of DEHP.	**BLACK BOX WARNING** Hepatic disease **CONTRAINDICATIONS** Hypersensitivity to castor oil, neutropenia, thrombocytopenia, hepatic disease **SIDE EFFECTS** Myelosuppression, neuropathy, hypersensitivity reaction (flushing, rash, dyspnea, bronchospasm), fatigue, asthenia, mucositis, N/V/D, alopecia, hand foot syndrome, alopecia

Miscellaneous Agents

DRUG	UNIQUE CONCERNS	SAFETY/SIDE EFFECTS/MONITORING
Tretinoin (All-trans Retinoic Acid, ATRA Vesanoid) Decreases cell proliferation and promotes apoptosis. First line therapy for acute promyelocytic leukemia (APL)	Retinoids (vitamin A analogues) Pregnancy Category D Retinoic Acid-Acute Promyelocytic Leukemia (RA-APL) differentiation syndrome: fever, dyspnea, weight gain, edema, pulmonary infiltrates, pericardial or pleural effusions – treat with dexamethasone.	**BLACK BOX WARNINGS (3)** RA-APL differentiation syndrome, leukocytosis, pregnancy **CONTRAINDICATIONS** Hypersensitivity to paraben or retinoid **SIDE EFFECTS** Leukocytosis, RA-APL differentiation syndrome, QT prolongation, N/V/D, skin/mucous membrane dryness, hyperlipidemia, GI bleeding
Arsenic trioxide (Trisenox) Induces terminal differentiation of cells or apoptosis Second line therapy for acute promyelocytic leukemia (APL)	QT prolongation: monitor ECG, avoid concurrent QT prolonging agents, keep Mg^{2+} and K^+ within normal range. "APL Differentiation Syndrome" (see above). If acute vasomotor reactions (lightheadedness, dizziness, or hypotension) occur, prolong infusion.	**BLACK BOX WARNINGS (5)** RA-APL differentiation syndrome, AV block, electrolyte imbalance, leukocytosis, QT prolongation **SIDE EFFECTS** Leukocytosis, APL differentiation syndrome, QT prolongation, N/V/D, GI bleeding, stomatitis, electrolyte imbalance, acute vasomotor reactions (lightheadedness, dizziness, or hypotension), fatigue, edema, headache, insomnia, anxiety, infection
L-Asparaginase (Elspar): Derived from Escherichia coli Asparaginase (Erwinaze): Derived from Erwina chrysanthemi Pegaspargase PEG- (polyethylene glycol) modified form: (Oncaspar)	Deprives leukemia cells of asparagine: essential amino acid in leukemia. Erwinaze is FDA approved for patients who develop allergic reactions to the E. coli derived asparaginase. The pegylated form allows for every 2 week dosing and a lower incidence of allergic reactions. Anaphylaxis: requires test dose.	**CONTRAINDICATIONS** Hypersensitivity to E. coli or L-asparaginase; bleeding, pancreatitis **SIDE EFFECTS** Hypersensitivity reactions, pancreatitis, hyperglycemia, hepatotoxicity, CNS toxicity (lethargy, somnolence), N/V, encephalopathy, prolonged prothrombin time (PT/INR) and thrombin time (TT)
Bleomycin Intercalating agent blocking topoisomerase II	Due to risk of anaphylactoid reaction, a test dose may be given to lymphoma patients. May pre-medicate with acetaminophen to decrease incidence of fever or chills. Increased risk of pulmonary fibrosis when given with G-CSF (filgrastim). Recommended to not use G-CSF on days of bleomycin administration. Not myelosuppressive. Maximum lifetime dose of 400 units (400 mg) due to pulmonary toxicity risk.	**BLACK BOX WARNINGS (2)** Pulmonary fibrosis, fever **SIDE EFFECTS** Hypersensitivity reaction, Pulmonary reactions (10%) – such as pneumonitis, which may progress to pulmonary fibrosis, mucositis, hyperpigmentation, fever, chills, N/V (mild)
Mitomycin (Mutamycin) Derived from Streptomyces caespitosus Free radical formation and alkylator	Vesicant – do not extravasate. Antidote is dimethyl sulfoxide (DMSO) and cool compresses. Mitomycin IV solutions are a purple/blue-gray color.	**BLACK BOX WARNINGS (5)** Pulmonary fibrosis, thrombocytopenia, bone marrow suppression, leukopenia, hemolytic-uremic syndrome **CONTRAINDICATIONS** Thrombocytopenia, coagulopathy, bleeding, pregnancy **SIDE EFFECTS** Leukopenia, thrombocytopenia, N/V, fatigue, skin toxicity, cystitis or dysuria (from intravesical administration into bladder)

Nomenclature: Monoclonal Antibodies

MAB = MONOCLONAL ANTIBODY, TU = TUMOR	SOURCE
U-mab	H<u>u</u>man
O-mab	M<u>o</u>use
Xi-mab	Chimeric = human and animal source
Zu-mab	Humaniz<u>e</u>d

COMMON MABs	TARGET
Bevacizumab *(Avastin)*	Binds to VEGF-A
Cetuximab *(Erbitux)*	Binds to EGFR
Trastuzumab *(Herceptin)*	Binds to HER-2/neu
Rituximab *(Rituxan)*	Binds to CD-20
Ipilimumab *(Yervoy)*	Binds to Cytotoxic T-lymphocyte antigen-4 (CTL4) receptor

Monoclonal Antibodies

Over-expression targeted: Inhibit growth factors that are promoting cancer cell growth.

DRUG	UNIQUE CONCERNS	SAFETY/SIDE EFFECTS/MONITORING
Bevacizumab *(Avastin)* Binds to VEGF-A Angiogenesis inhibitor: Limit tumor's blood supply.	Impairs wound healing: stop at least 28 days before elective surgery and may restart bevacizumab 28 days after surgery. Used with other agents in numerous types of cancer but a high cost for modest benefit resulting in debate on the benefit-cost ratio.	**BLACK BOX WARNINGS (3)** Bleeding, GI perforation, wound dehiscence **SIDE EFFECTS** Bleeding, hypertension, HF, thrombosis (including DVT, PE and stroke), GI perforation, wound dehiscence, nephrotic syndrome, proteinuria, exfoliative dermatitis
Trastuzumab *(Herceptin)* **HER2/neu over-expression required for use** Added efficacy with some chemotherapeutics but avoid use with anthracyclines due to additive cardiotoxicity.	Pharmacogenomics: trastuzumab binds to and reverses effects of overactive HER2 receptors; HER2 gene is over-expressed in ~25% of early-stage breast tumors. Must be ≥ 2+ by immunohistochemical (IHC) testing to respond/use this drug. Not interchangeable with ado-trastuzumab emtansine.	**BLACK BOX WARNINGS (4)** Heart failure, severe reactions (including hypersensitivity, infusion reactions or pulmonary); may give acetaminophen, diphenhydramine, corticosteroids or meperidine for management. **SIDE EFFECTS** Cardiomyopathy (HF, ↓ LVEF), infusion reaction, weakness, pain, chills, fever, cough, pulmonary toxicity, N/V/D, rash, edema

Monoclonal Antibodies Continued

DRUG	UNIQUE CONCERNS	SAFETY/SIDE EFFECTS/MONITORING
Ado-Trastuzumab Emtansine *(Kadcyla)* HER2/neu over-expression required for use	*Kadcyla* is a conjugate of trastuzumab linked to DM-1, a highly potent anti-microtubule derivative of maytansine and provides targeted delivery of drug. Use 0.22 micron filter. Do not confuse with conventional trastuzumab; not interchangeable.	**BLACK BOX WARNINGS (3)** Heart failure, hepatotoxicity, embryo-fetal death and birth defects; ado-trastuzumab emtansine and conventional trastuzumab are not interchangeable **SIDE EFFECTS** Cardiac dysfunction, constipation, nausea, headache, thrombocytopenia, ↑ LFTs, pain (musculoskeletal), fatigue, N/V/D
Pertuzumab *(Perjeta)* HER2/neu over-expression required for use	Pharmacogenomics: HER2 gene over-expression.	**BLACK BOX WARNINGS (2)** Embryo-fetal death and birth defects; cardiac failure **SIDE EFFECTS** Cardiomyopathy (HF, ↓ LVEF), alopecia, rash, N/V/D, anemia, asthenia, fatigue, anaphylaxis, peripheral neuropathy
Cetuximab *(Erbitux)* EGFR positive expression correlates with better response rates. K-ras mutation indicates poor response; requires EGFR positive and K-ras negative.	Pharmacogenomics: Must test for EGFR and K-ras mutations before treatment. Premedicate with diphenhydramine for at least the first dose.	**BLACK BOX WARNINGS (2)** Severe infusion reactions, cardiopulmonary arrest. **SIDE EFFECTS** Acne-like rash onset in 1st few weeks of treatment, severe rash possible. Presence of rash correlates with a higher survival rate. N/V/D, fatigue, magnesium and calcium wasting
Panitumumab *(Vectibix)* Same EGFR and K-ras issues as cetuximab	Pharmacogenomics: Must test for K-ras mutations before treatment.	**BLACK BOX WARNINGS (2)** Severe infusion reactions, dermatologic toxicities **SIDE EFFECTS** Acne-like rash onset in 2 weeks of treatment, severe rash possible. Presence of rash correlates with a higher survival rate; infusion reactions (can be fatal); N/V/D, fatigue, magnesium and calcium wasting

Cell Surface Marker Targeted Therapies

DRUG	UNIQUE CONCERNS	SAFETY/SIDE EFFECTS/MONITORING
RiTUXimab *(Rituxan)* Targets CD-20 antigen on B lymphocytes killing the cancer and releasing cytokines Infusions must be given in hospital or clinic since they can be fatal. Severe reactions typically occur during the first infusion with time to onset of 30-120 minutes. Administer diphenhydramine and acetaminophen prior to infusion.	Rituximab-induced cytokine release infusion reactions and sequelae include urticaria, hypotension, angioedema, hypoxia, bronchospasm, pulmonary infiltrates, acute respiratory distress syndrome, myocardial infarction, ventricular fibrillation, cardiogenic shock, anaphylaxis, and/or death.	**BLACK BOX WARNINGS (4)** Severe infusion reactions, hepatitis B reactivation, fatal mucocutaneous reactions, progressive multifocal leukoencephalopathy (PML) from JC virus **SIDE EFFECTS** Infusion reaction (chills, rigors, fever) Tumor lysis syndrome, rash, pruritus, toxic epidermal necrolysis. Myelosuppression with prolonged immune suppression increases the risk of opportunistic infections and reactivation of hepatitis B

Immunotherapy: Stimulates the Patient's Immune System

DRUG	UNIQUE SIDE EFFECTS/NOTES	SAFETY/SIDE EFFECTS/MONITORING
Ipilimumab *(Yervoy)* Blocks the Cytotoxic T-lymphocyte antigen-4 (CTL4) receptor, which effectively takes the brake off T-cell activation. Activated T-cells then can recognize melanoma cells for removal but at a risk of autoimmune activity	Primarily autoimmune system unchecked	**BLACK BOX WARNING** Fatal immune-mediated reactions (enterocolitis, hepatitis, dermatitis) – discontinue drug and start high doses of steroids. **SIDE EFFECTS** Dermatologic (rash, pruritus), gastrointestinal (diarrhea, colitis, esophagitis, gastritis, jejunitis, ulcers), endocrine (hypophysitis, hypothyroidism, hypoadrenalism, hyponatremia, pancreatitis), neuropathies, hepatitis, uveitis, and nephritis

PROSTATE CANCER

1 out of 6 males may get prostate cancer in his lifetime. After surgery or radiation therapy have been considered, oral or injectable agents for prostate cancer are used. Typically, "castration sensitive" patients are started on Luteinizing Hormone-Releasing Hormone (LHRH) agonists for chronic suppression of testosterone. Antiandrogens are started 1-4 weeks prior (to help mitigate the tumor flare) to the LHRH agonists. Many clinicians will discontinue the anti-androgens after starting the LHRH agonists. PSA levels are checked routinely as a marker of treatment response. IV chemotherapy (with docetaxel/prednisone) or abiraterone (a more potent oral antiandrogen) are used in metastatic disease.

Antiandrogens: Block Androgens at the Receptor Site

DRUG	UNIQUE CONCERNS	SAFETY/SIDE EFFECTS/MONITORING
Bicalutamide *(Casodex)* 50 mg PO daily **Flutamide *(Eulexin)*** 250 mg PO Q8H Nilutamide *(Nilandron)* 300 mg PO daily x 30 days, then 150 mg PO daily	Used 1-4 weeks prior to starting LHRH agonists to mitigate tumor flare	**SIDE EFFECTS** Hot flashes, edema, pain, asthenia, heart failure, hepatotoxicity, gynecomastia, N/V/D, visual disturbances **NOTES** Used less due to night blindness (nilutamide)

Antiandrogen-Antiestrogen: LHRH (Luteinizing Hormone-Releasing Hormone) Agonists

Used for prostate cancer in males and for endometriosis, fibroids and breast cancer in females: initially increase the production of androgens and estrogens, which can cause an initial tumor flare; followed by down regulation through a negative feedback loop resulting in suppressed gonadotropin release, LH, and FSH, resulting in a chemical castration/oophorectomy.

DRUG	UNIQUE CONCERNS	SAFETY/SIDE EFFECTS/ MONITORING
Goserelin (Zoladex) **Leuprolide (Lupron,** Eligard, Viadur) Histrelin (Vantas) Triptorelin (Trelstar) Given SQ or IM monthly or less frequently (up to once/yr) depending on formulation and indication.	↓ bone density and ↑ risk for osteoporosis: consider calcium and vitamin D supplementation, weight bearing exercise and DEXA screening. Typically patients should start an anti-androgen at least 1 week prior to mitigate "tumor flare".	**CONTRAINDICATIONS** Pregnancy, breast feeding, vaginal bleeding **SIDE EFFECTS** Hot flashes, bone pain, impotence, injection site pain/swelling, dyslipidemia, QT prolongation, gynecomastia (men), peripheral edema

Antiandrogen, GRH Antagonist: Gonadotropin-Releasing Hormone (GRA) Antagonist Used in Prostate Cancer

DRUG	UNIQUE CONCERNS	SAFETY/SIDE EFFECTS/MONITORING
Degarelix (Firmagon)	Similar efficacy/toxicity to LHRH agonists (above) but true blockade of GRH so does not cause increased testosterone with tumor flare. No need for concomitant antiandrogens.	Hypersensitivity reactions, QT prolongation, hot flashes

Antiandrogen: Inhibits the Production of Androgen (Testosterone)

A pregnenolone analog that irreversibly inhibits CYP450 C17, the rate limiting enzyme in androgen production in the testes, adrenal gland and prostate without causing adrenal insufficiency.

DRUG	UNIQUE CONCERNS	SAFETY/SIDE EFFECTS/MONITORING
Abiraterone acetate (Zytiga) 1,000 mg (4 x 250 mg tabs) PO once daily Take on an empty stomach	Substrate of CYP3A4 and inhibitor of CYP2D6 requires caution with inhibitors/substrates. Taken in combination with prednisone 5 mg PO BID or 10 mg PO daily.	**CONTRAINDICATION** Pregnancy **SIDE EFFECTS** Mineralocorticoid elevation with fluid retention, hypertension, hypokalemia hepatotoxicity, joint swelling, hot flashes, diarrhea, nocturia, osteoporosis (fractures)

Antiandrogen: Receptor-Signaling Pathway Inhibitor

Blocks the downstream transfer of information from the activated receptor. Used in patients with castration-resistant metastatic prostate cancer who failed docetaxel chemotherapy.

DRUG	UNIQUE CONCERNS	SAFETY/SIDE EFFECTS/MONITORING
Enzalutamide (Xtandi) 160 mg (4 x 40 mg caps) PO once daily without regard to food	CYP2C8 and CYP3A4 substrate; avoid use with inhibitors. If concurrent with a strong CYP2C8 inhibitor it is necessary to reduce dose to 80 mg daily. CYP2C9, CYP3A4 and CYP2C19 inhibitor so caution with substrates.	**CONTRAINDICATION** Pregnancy **SIDE EFFECTS** Fatigue, insomnia, weakness, diarrhea, edema, pulmonary infections, dizziness, flushing, neutropenia, seizures (~1%).

Vaccine: Re-Programs the Immune System Against Advanced Prostate Cancer; see below.

DRUG	UNIQUE CONCERNS	SAFETY/SIDE EFFECTS/MONITORING
Sipuleucel-T *(Provenge)*	Infusion of CD 54+ antigen presenting cells obtained through leukapheresis. Patient's own WBCs are harvested and activated against PAP (prostatic acid phosphatase) to target prostate cells. Requires premedication with acetaminophen and diphenhydramine due to acute flu-like infusion reactions.	**SIDE EFFECTS** Acute infusion reactions, nausea, vomiting, hypersensitivity, back pain, hypertension

BREAST CANCER

1 out of 8 females may get breast cancer in her lifetime. Approximately 1% of all breast cancer patients are male patients. Risk factors include: family history (BRCA 1 or BRCA 2 mutations), early menarche or late menopause (which increases the woman's lifetime exposure to estrogen), late pregnancy (age > 30 years old), nulliparity (no pregnancy), smoking, obesity and lack of exercise. Typically, breast cancer patients will get conventional chemotherapy for a limited number of cycles (in the adjuvant setting) or until disease progression (in the metastatic setting).

To prevent recurrence, hormonal therapy is recommended for the following patients:

1. ER/PR+ (pre-menopausal) will receive oral hormonal therapy (SERM agent for 5-10 years; tamoxifen is the first line agent). After 2 years, if the patient becomes post-menopausal, switch from a SERM to an aromatase inhibitor (AI) (due to better tolerability and efficacy).

2. ER/PR+ (post-menopausal) will receive AI agent for 5-10 years; anastrozole is typically the first line agent. If intolerable side effects to anastrozole, can switch to another AI, tamoxifen or fulvestrant.

3. ER/PR (negative) – do not have benefit with hormonal agents.

4. Male breast cancer patients with ER/PR+ will receive oral hormonal therapy (SERM agent for 5-10 years; tamoxifen is typically the first line agent).

In the metastatic setting, standard IV chemotherapy combinations may be used. However, in HER2/neu positive patients, the first line combination includes pertzumab, trastuzumab and docetaxel. Second line therapies can also use other standard IV chemotherapy combinations. However, if oral therapy is preferred, lapatinib with capecitabine is a viable option.

Antiandrogen-Antiestrogen: Aromatase Inhibitors – All Oral

Blocks conversion to active estrogen/androgen/corticosteroid/mineralocorticoid to reduce cell growth in breast, prostate and/or adrenal cancer. These agents are approved for post-menopausal women and are not FDA-approved for men with breast cancer.

DRUG	UNIQUE CONCERNS	SAFETY/SIDE EFFECTS/MONITORING
Anastrozole (Arimidex) 1 mg PO daily **Letrozole (Femara)** 2.5 mg PO daily **Exemestane (Aromasin)** 25 mg PO daily Mitotane (Lysodren) non-selective	↓ bone density and ↑ risk for osteoporosis: consider calcium and vitamin D supplementation, weight bearing exercise, DEXA screening. ↑ cardiovascular disease risk compared to SERMs. Mitotane is a non-selective aromatase inhibitor requiring glucocorticoid and mineralocorticoid supplementation.	**CONTRAINDICATION** Pregnancy **SIDE EFFECTS** Arthralgia, edema, lethargy/fatigue, rash, menopausal symptoms/hot flashes, hepatotoxicity, nausea, vomiting, weakness, joint pain, bone pain, HTN, depression

Antiestrogens/SERMs

Selective Estrogen Receptor Modulators (SERMs) are estrogen antagonists (blockers) in breast tissue, but act as estrogen agonists in some other tissues, including bone. These are used for breast cancer in hormone receptor + tumors (estrogen/progesterone). Used in post-menopausal women, except tamoxifen, which is indicated for pre- and post- menopausal women and in men.

DRUG	UNIQUE CONCERNS	SAFETY/SIDE EFFECTS/MONITORING
Tamoxifen (Soltamox) 20 mg PO daily **Fulvestrant (Faslodex)** 500 mg IM days 1, 15, 29, then monthly **Raloxifene (Evista)** Used for osteoporosis in women at risk of breast cancer 60 mg PO daily Toremifene (Fareston)	Tamoxifen increases risk of endometrial cancers: others decrease risk. Tamoxifen CYP2D6 polymorphism *4/*5 results in shorter disease free survival. Consider alternative therapy (aromatase inhibitor). Tamoxifen is a substrate of CYP3A4, CYP2C9 and CYP2D6. Watch for drug-drug interactions (especially with agents used for hot flashes). Recommend venlafaxine for hot flashes (over fluoxetine and paroxetine) for patients on tamoxifen. Fulvestrant: osteoporosis, hyperlipidemia; Note: other SERMs increase bone density and are beneficial for cholesterol.	**BLACK BOX WARNINGS (3)** Uterine malignancy, stroke, ↑ risk of thromboembolic events (DVT, PE, MI, stroke) with all SERMs **CONTRAINDICATIONS** DVT/PE, concomitant warfarin therapy, endometrial cancer (tamoxifen) **SIDE EFFECTS** DVT/PE, menopausal symptoms, hot flashes, flushing, N/V, edema, weight gain, increased blood pressure, mood changes, amenorrhea, vaginal bleeding/discharge, skin changes, cataracts (tamoxifen) **NOTES** Pregnancy Category D (tamoxifen, fulvestrant) Pregnancy Category X (raloxifene)

Tyrosine Kinase Inhibitors (TKIs) Targeting HER-2 neu

All TKIs are substrates of CYP3A4 and have many drug-drug interactions – some of which require dose modification. HER-2 neu is a tyrosine kinase that regulates cell proliferation and survival in over-expressed cancers (~25% of breast cancer). Blocking this results in a halt to cancer cell growth and possibly apoptosis. Requires testing for HER-2 neu positivity.

DRUG	UNIQUE CONCERNS	SAFETY/SIDE EFFECTS/MONITORING
Lapatinib *(Tykerb)* 1,250 mg (5 x 250 mg) PO on empty stomach	Inhibits HER-2/neu (ErbB2) and EGFR (Erb1) tyrosine kinases. Used in metastatic breast cancer.	**BLACK BOX WARNING** Hepatotoxicity **SIDE EFFECTS** Myelosuppression, hand-foot syndrome, acneiform rash, N/V/D, fatigue, ↑ LFTs, interstitial lung disease hepatotoxicity, HF, <u>decreased LVEF</u> and QT-prolongation

RENAL CELL CANCER (RCC)

RCC is the most common type of kidney cancer in adults (~80% of the cases). Risk factors include smoking, obesity and hypertension. Primary therapy is surgery (radical or partial nephrectomy) and is for curative intent. RCC is fairly resistant to radiation therapy and chemotherapy. Below is a list of targeted cancer therapies.

Tyrosine Kinase Inhibitors (TKIs) Targeting Multiple Kinases

DRUG	UNIQUE CONCERNS	SAFETY/SIDE EFFECTS/MONITORING
Sunitinib *(Sutent)* 50 mg PO daily for 4 weeks on and 2 weeks off Dosing varies depending on indication Not affected by food	Inhibits multiple tyrosine kinases: PDGF; VEGF R 1/2; SCF R; cKIT and others.	**BLACK BOX WARNING** Hepatotoxicity **SIDE EFFECTS** <u>Rash, hand-foot syndrome</u>, N/V/D, mucositis/stomatitis, dyspepsia, anorexia, taste disturbance, skin discoloration, alopecia, neutropenia, anemia, thrombocytopenia, lymphopenia, hypertension, edema, <u>HF, ↓ LVEF, QT prolongation</u>, fatigue, electrolyte imbalance, ↑ LFTs, elevated lipase, hypothyroidism
Pazopanib *(Votrient)* 800 mg PO without food (1 hour before or 2 hours after a meal), do not crush	Inhibits PDGF-R alpha and beta; VEGF R 1/2/3; FGFR 1/3, cKit; and others.	**BLACK BOX WARNING** Hepatotoxicity **SIDE EFFECTS** ↑ LFTs, hyperglycemia, hypothyroidism, electrolyte loss (phosphorus, Na⁺, Mg²⁺) fatigue, diarrhea, weight loss, <u>hypertension</u>, anorexia, nausea, vomiting, headache, dysguesia, dyspnea, <u>prolongs QT interval</u>, thromboembolic events, hemorrhagic events, color changes in skin and hair
Sorafenib *(Nexavar)* 400 mg PO BID on an empty stomach (1 hour before or 2 hours after a meal)	Inhibits raf-mek pathway kinases (CRAF, BRAF); PDGF; EGFR; VEGF R 2/3; SCF R; cKIT; FLT-3.	**CONTRAINDICATIONS** Combination with carboplatin and paclitaxel (squamous cell lung cancer) causing aplastic anemia **SIDE EFFECTS** <u>Fatigue, hypertension, hand-foot syndrome, diarrhea,</u> N/V, mucositis/stomatitis, dyspepsia, GI bleed, acneiform rash, alopecia, neutropenia, anemia, thrombocytopenia, lymphopenia, electrolyte imbalance, ↑ LFTs, ↑ lipase/amylase, impaired wound healing (dehiscence), interstitial pneumonitis, hair color changes

Tyrosine Kinase Inhibitors (TKIs) Targeting VEGF

The VEGF family of protein kinases regulate angiogenesis which is blocked by these TKIs resulting in a limit to the tumor's blood supply.

DRUG	UNIQUE CONCERNS	SAFETY/SIDE EFFECTS/MONITORING
Axitinib *(Inlyta)* 5 mg PO Q12H After 2 weeks, may increase to 7 mg PO Q12H, and further to 10 mg Q12H (If tolerated)	Inhibits: VEGF receptors 1, 2 and 3. CYP-3A4/5 substrate: caution with inhibitors.	**BLACK BOX WARNING** Hepatotoxicity **SIDE EFFECTS** Hypertension, hand-foot syndrome, dysphonia, weight loss, anorexia, fatigue, asthenia, nausea, vomiting, diarrhea, constipation, thromboembolic events, hemorrhagic events, hypothyroidism, and ↑ LFTs

mTOR Inhibitors

Inhibit downstream regulation of VEGF reducing cell growth, metabolism, proliferation and angiogenesis

DRUG	UNIQUE CONCERNS	SAFETY/SIDE EFFECTS/MONITORING
Everolimus *(Afinitor)* 10 mg PO daily with or without food Various doses used for other cancers and in <u>transplantation</u>	CYP3A4 inhibitor/ substrate	**BLACK BOX WARNINGS (2)** Malignancy (lymphoma), infection (additional warnings applicable to transplant; see Transplant chapter) **CONTRAINDICATIONS** Hypersensitivity to rapamycin derivatives **SIDE EFFECTS** <u>Dyslipidemia</u>, hyperglycemia, myelosuppression, <u>rash</u>, pruritus, hand-foot syndrome, <u>stomatitis</u>, fatigue, N/V/D, peripheral edema, <u>interstitial lung disease</u>, elevated creatinine with decreased renal function, ↑ LFTs
Temsirolimus *(Torisel)* 25 mg IVPB over 30-60 minutes once weekly	CYP3A4 inhibitor/ substrate Pre-medicate with diphenhydramine. <u>Use non-PVC bag & tubing</u> due to leaching of DEHP.	**CONTRAINDICATION** Hepatotoxicity **SIDE EFFECTS** <u>Dyslipidemia, hyperglycemia, myelosuppression, interstitial lung disease</u>, acute hypersensitivity reactions (polysorbate 80 solvent system), N/V/D, peripheral edema, pain, dyspnea, cough, fever, asthenia, rashes, acne

CHRONIC MYELOID LEUKEMIA (CML)

Chronic myelogenous (or myeloid) leukemia (CML) is a type of myeloproliferative disease of mature granulocytes (neutrophils, eosinophils and basophils) with a characteristic chromosomal translocation called the Philadelphia chromosome (bcr-abl fusion gene). CML is primarily treated with oral tyrosine kinase inhibitors (TKIs), which have led to dramatically improved long term survival rates (mean 47 months to over 10 years) since the introduction of imatinib in 2001.

Tyrosine Kinase Inhibitors (TKIs) Targeting BCR-ABL

A fusion gene is created when the ABL gene on chromosome 9 is translocated to the Breakpoint Cluster Region (BCR) gene on chromosome 22 resulting in cancer cell growth, replication and immortality. Blocking this results in a halt to cancer cell growth and likely apoptosis. <u>Use of TKIs requires pharmacogenomic testing for the presence of bcr-abl fusion gene.</u>

DRUG	UNIQUE CONCERNS	SAFETY/SIDE EFFECTS/MONITORING
Imatinib *(Gleevec)* 400-600 mg daily PO, with water and full meal	Indications: Philadelphia-chromosome positive (Ph+) chronic myelogenous leukemia (CML) or cKIT (CD117)-positive gastrointestinal stromal tumors (GIST).	**SIDE EFFECTS** <u>Fluid retention, skin rash, diarrhea</u>, edema, leukopenia, thrombocytopenia, N/V, HF, muscle spasms
Nilotinib *(Tasigna)* 300-400 mg BID PO, on an empty stomach: 1 hour before, 2 hours after meal	Maintains clinical activity in CML resistant to imatinib but more expensive as first line therapy.	**BLACK BOX WARNINGS (3)** QT prolongation – contraindicated with hypomagnesemia, hypokalemia, or long QT syndrome; give on empty stomach; avoid with strong CYP3A4 inhibitors **CONTRAINDICATIONS** Hypomagnesemia, hypokalemia, long QT syndrome **SIDE EFFECTS** <u>Prolongs QT interval</u>, hypo- and hyperkalemia, hypomagnesemia, leukopenia, thrombocytopenia, N/V/D, fluid retention, edema, skin rashes, pruritus, alopecia
Dasatinib *(Sprycel)* 100-180 mg daily PO with or without food Needs acid for absorption; avoid PPIs and H$_2$RAs	Maintains clinical activity in CML resistant to imatinib but more expensive as first line therapy. Approximately 300 times more potent than imatinib. Also inhibits cKit, PDGFR, SCF, SRC tyrosine kinases.	**SIDE EFFECTS** <u>Pleural effusions, fluid retention, edema</u>, leukopenia, thrombocytopenia, N/V/D, skin rash, headache, musculoskeletal pain
Bosutinib *(Bosulif)* 500-600 mg PO once daily with food	Maintains clinical activity in CML in ~ 33% of imatinib resistant and ~ 27% of dasatinib or nilotinib resistant patients. CYP3A4 and P-gp substrate; avoid use with inhibitors.	**BLACK BOX WARNINGS (2)** Thrombotic events, hepatotoxicity **SIDE EFFECTS** <u>Diarrhea</u>, fluid retention (pleural effusions, pericardial effusion, pulmonary edema, and/or peripheral edema), anemia, rash, fever, fatigue, ↑ LFTs, nausea, vomiting, abdominal pain, thrombocytopenia, neutropenia

NON-SMALL CELL LUNG CANCER

Lung cancer is the most common cause of cancer-related death in men and women. The most important risk factor is smoking. About 80–90% of lung cancers are caused by long-term exposure to tobacco smoke. Nonsmokers account for 10–15% of lung cancer cases. Other risk factors include genetic factors, radon gas, asbestos, and second-hand smoke. Treatment options include surgery, radiation and chemotherapy. Non-small cell lung cancer (NSCLC) is sometimes treated with surgery. Small cell lung cancer (SCLC) usually responds better to chemotherapy and radiation.

Tyrosine Kinase Inhibitors (TKIs) Targeting EGFR

Epidermal growth factor receptors (1, 2, 3 and 4) control cell growth, angiogenesis, invasion, metastasis and resistance to apoptosis. Inhibition of EGFR results in a halt to cancer cell growth and possibly apoptosis (programmed cell death, in which the cells self-destruct). Pharmacogenomic testing for the EGFR mutation in the adenocarcinoma NSCLC subtype is required. An EGFR mutation predicts response.

DRUG	UNIQUE CONCERNS	SAFETY/SIDE EFFECTS/MONITORING
Erlotinib *(Tarceva)* 150 mg daily PO – Take 1 hour before or 2 hours after meal Various doses used for other cancers	Works best in patients with EGFR mutation positive, adenocarcinoma histology, non-smoker, Asian, female patients. Dose reductions by 50 mg are based on toxicities.	**SIDE EFFECTS** Acneiform rash, diarrhea, hepatotoxicity, GI perforation, severe skin reactions, eye damage, nephrotoxicity, stomatitis, interstitial lung disease, cough, headache, fatigue, fever
Afatinib *(Gilotrif)* 40 mg PO daily on an empty stomach – Take 1 hour before or 2 hours after meal	Inhibits EGFR 1, 2, 4. Approved for patients with metastatic NSCLC with known EGFR exon 19 deletions or exon 21 substitution mutations detected by FDA-approved test (EGFR, RGQ, PCR, Kit).	**SIDE EFFECTS** Acneiform rash, diarrhea, stomatitis, dry skin, paronychia, ↓ appetite, pruritus

Tyrosine Kinase Inhibitors (TKIs) Targeting ALK

In ALK-positive lung cancer (~1-7% of NSCLC), the ALK fusion protein is responsible for tumor growth. By inhibiting ALK, crizotinib causes stabilization or regression of tumors. ALK is prevalent in non-smokers or those with a history of light smoking and an adenocarcinoma subtype.

DRUG	UNIQUE CONCERNS	SAFETY/SIDE EFFECTS/MONITORING
Crizotinib *(Xalkori)* Primary target is ALK but also inhibits cMET (Mesenchymal Epithelial Transition Factor) 250 mg PO BID with or without food	Must be ALK positive to use this drug (pharmacogenomic testing required).	**SIDE EFFECTS** Swelling (edema), N/V/D, constipation, vision disturbances (visual impairment, flashes of light, blurred vision, floaters, double vision, sensitivity to light, visual field defects), interstitial pneumonitis

MELANOMA

Melanoma is usually caused by damage from UV light from the sun or tanning beds. Symptoms can be non-specific and include loss of appetite, nausea, vomiting and fatigue. The primary treatment is surgery. If melanoma is found early, surgery has a high cure rate. For melanomas that return or spread, treatments include surgery, radiation, chemotherapy or immunotherapy. Stage IV (metastatic) melanoma can spread to the brain, bone, liver, abdomen or distant lymph nodes. Early signs of melanoma are summarized by the mnemonic "ABCDE":

- Asymmetry

- Borders (irregular)

- Color (variegated – with different colors)

- Diameter [greater than 6 mm (0.24 in), about the size of a pencil eraser]

- Evolving over time

These classifications do not, however, apply to the most dangerous form of melanoma, nodular melanoma, which has its own classifications:

- Elevated above the skin surface

- Firm to the touch

- Growing

Tyrosine Kinase Inhibitors (TKIs) Targeting BRAF: BRAF Protein Kinase Mutation

DRUG	UNIQUE CONCERNS	SAFETY/SIDE EFFECTS/MONITORING
Vemurafenib (Zelboraf) 960 mg PO twice daily without regards to food	Pharmacogenetic testing required. Use only in BRAF positive melanoma with the V600E mutation (~50% of patients). Inhibitor of CYP1A2, 2A6, 2C9, 2C19, 2D6 and 3A4/5; Substrate of CYP3A4/5.	**CONTRAINDICATIONS** BRAF wild types as vemurafenib paradoxically activates the MAPK pathway promoting tumor growth. **SIDE EFFECTS** Dermatologic disorders (rashes, photosensitivity, alopecia, pruritus, SJS/TEN), prolonged QT syndrome, N/V/D, constipation, anorexia, weight loss, dysguesia arthralgias, arrhythmias, headache, uveitis, fatigue, asthenia, ↑ liver enzymes
Dabrafenib (Tafinlar) 150 mg PO BID on an empty stomach (1 hour before or 2 hours after food)	For metastatic melanoma patients with BRAF V600E mutation. Less skin toxicities compared with vemurafenib.	**CONTRAINDICATIONS** Not recommended in BRAF wild types **SIDE EFFECTS** Pyrexia, hyperglycemia, hypophosphatemia, alopecia, hand-foot syndrome, headache, arthralgia

Inhibitor of Mitogen-Activated Extracellular Signal Kinase 1 and 2 (MEK1 and MEK2).

DRUG	UNIQUE CONCERNS	SAFETY/SIDE EFFECTS/MONITORING
Trametinib (Mekinist) 2 mg PO daily on an empty stomach (1 hour before or 2 hours after food)	For metastatic melanoma patients with BRAF V600E or V600K mutations.	**CONTRAINDICATIONS** Not recommended in BRAF wild types **SIDE EFFECTS** Hand foot syndrome, ↑ LFTs, diarrhea, anemia, lymphedema, stomatitis, bleeding cardiomyopathy, hypertension, rhabdomyolysis, infection, skin rashes, interstitial lung disease (can be fatal)

MULTIPLE MYELOMA

In multiple myeloma, abnormal plasma cells accumulate in the bone marrow. A mneumonic used to remember the common tetrad of multiple myeloma is CRAB: C = Calcium (elevated), R = Renal failure, A = Anemia, B = Bone lesions. Most cases of myeloma have high levels of paraprotein (also known as M protein) – an abnormal antibody that can cause renal failure.

Myeloma is generally incurable but highly treatable. With conventional treatment, median survival is 3–4 years, which may be extended to 5–7 years or longer with advanced treatments. Remission can be induced with steroids, chemotherapy, proteasome inhibitors, immunomodulators, and stem cell transplant.

Immunomodulators

The immunomodulatory drugs are thalidomide or thalidomide-derivatives; the primary toxicity is severe birth defects and patients must not get pregnant using these drugs. All three have strict REMS programs designed to prevent pregnancy. They block angiogenesis and kill abnormal cells in the bone marrow while stimulating the bone marrow to produce normal healthy cells.

DRUG	UNIQUE CONCERNS	SAFETY/SIDE EFFECTS/MONITORING
Lenalidomide *(Revlimid)* 25 mg PO once daily for 21 days and 7 days off	<u>Pregnancy Category X</u> <u>Severe birth defects (similar to thalidomide in animal studies). Only available under restricted distribution program: patient, prescriber and pharmacist must be registered with *Revlimid* REMS program.</u> Consider prophylactic anticoagulation due to increased VTE risk.	**BLACK BOX WARNINGS (4)** Fetal risk/pregnancy, hematologic toxicity, thrombosis-DVT/PE, only available through REMS program **CONTRAINDICATIONS** Pregnancy **SIDE EFFECTS** Neutropenia, thrombocytopenia, constipation or diarrhea, fatigue, fever, cough, pruritus, rash, arthralgias, back pain. DVT and PE: <u>seek medical care if develop shortness of breath, chest pain, or arm or leg swelling</u>
Pomalidomide *(Pomalyst)* 4 mg PO once daily for 21 days and 7 days off For relapsed multiple myeloma after at least 2 prior therapies (including lenalidomide and bortezomib)	<u>Pregnancy Category X</u> <u>Severe birth defects (similar to thalidomide in animal studies). Only available under restricted distribution program: patient, prescriber and pharmacist must be registered with *Pomalyst* REMS program.</u> Consider prophylactic anticoagulation due to increased VTE risk.	**BLACK BOX WARNINGS (4)** Fetal risk/pregnancy, hematologic toxicity, thrombosis-DVT/PE, only available through REMS program **CONTRAINDICATIONS** Pregnancy **SIDE EFFECTS** Similar to above, plus peripheral edema, hypercalcemia, N/V
Thalidomide *(Thalomid)* 100-400 mg PO once daily PO, take at least 1 hr after a meal Various doses are used for other cancers	<u>Pregnancy Category X</u> <u>Severe birth defects (limb defects, cardiac, GI, ear, eye, GU). Only available under restricted distribution program *Thalomid* REMS program.</u> Consider prophylactic anticoagulation due to VTE risk.	**BLACK BOX WARNINGS (4)** Fetal risk/pregnancy, hematologic toxicity, thrombosis-DVT/PE, only available through REMS program **CONTRAINDICATIONS** Pregnancy **SIDE EFFECTS** Similar to lenalidomide plus somnolence, neuropathy, dizziness

Proteasome Inhibitors

Proteasomes are large protein complexes responsible for degrading intracellular proteins, enzymes and transcription factors. This maintains protein homeostasis upon which cancer cells are highly dependent. The <u>26S proteasome inhibitors</u> block this pathway, inhibiting cell cycle progression and inducing apoptosis.

DRUG	UNIQUE CONCERNS	SAFETY/SIDE EFFECTS/MONITORING
Bortezomib *(Velcade)* Very active drug for multiple myeloma (typically part of first line regimen) SC administration has less neuropathy than IV administration 1.3 mg/m² SC/IV or 1.5mg/m² IV Various doses and frequencies used for other cancers	Interactions: Substrate/Inhibitor of CYP1A2, 2C9, 2C19, 2D6, 3A4 <u>Give acyclovir to prevent zoster reactivation.</u>	**CONTRAINDICATIONS** Hypersensitivity to boron or mannitol; intrathecal administration (fatal) **SIDE EFFECTS** <u>Peripheral neuropathy</u>, psychiatric disturbances, insomnia, weakness, paresthesias, arthralgias/myalgias, cardiotoxicity, pulmonary toxicity, hypotension, thrombocytopenia, neutropenia, N/V/D, tumor lysis syndrome

Proteasome Inhibitors Continued

DRUG	UNIQUE CONCERNS	SAFETY/SIDE EFFECTS/MONITORING
Carfilzomib *(Kyprolis)* Cycle 1: 20 mg/m² once daily for 2 days Cycle 2 and on: 27 mg/m² once daily for 2 days IVPB For relapsed multiple myeloma after at least 2 prior therapies	More specific for the 26S-proteasome so maintains activity in some patients refractory to bortezomib. Premedicate with dexamethasone and fluids. An increase in alkaline phosphatase correlates with efficacy.	**SIDE EFFECTS** Peripheral neuropathy (but less than bortezomib), fatigue, pulmonary toxicity, acute renal failure, tumor lysis syndrome, hepatic toxicity, anemia, thrombocytopenia, nausea, diarrhea, pyrexia, cardiotoxicity

Prevalent Toxicities of Common Chemotherapy

B **Bleomycin, Busulfan, Carmustine, Lomustine**
Pulmonary Fibrosis

C **Cisplatin, Carboplatin**
Nephro/ototoxic

D **Doxorubicin & other anthracyclines**
Cardiotoxic

M **Methotrexate**
Mucositis

N **Nitrosoureas (lomustine, carmustine)**
Neurotoxic (cross blood brain barrier)

IP **Ifosfamide & Cyclophosphamide**
Hemorrhagic Cystitis

V
T **Vinca Alkaloids (Vincristine, Vinblastine & Vinorelbine)**
Taxanes (Paclitaxel, Docetaxel)
Peripheral Neuropathy

B
M **Bone marrow suppression is a common toxicity of many chemotherapy agents including: alkylators, anthracyclines, folate antagonists, platinum based compounds (cisplatin), purine antimetabolites, pyrimidine antimetabolites, taxanes, topoisomerase I and II inhibitors, antimetabolites and vinca alkaloids (vinblastine and vinorelbine)**
S

© RxPrep

Patient Counseling Examples

Patient Counseling for SERMs (Using Tamoxifen as an Example)

- This medication can be used to reduce your chance of getting breast cancer, reduce the spread of breast cancer or be used to treat breast cancer.

- Swallow the tablet whole, with water or another non-alcoholic liquid. You can take it with or without food.

- Take your medicine every day. It may be easier to remember if you take it at the same time each day.

- If you forget a dose, take it when you remember, then take the next dose as usual. If it is almost time for your next dose or you remember at your next dose, do not take extra tablets to make up the missed dose.

- Do not become pregnant while taking this medication or for 2 months after you stop. This medication can stop hormonal birth control methods from working correctly (birth control pills, patches, injections, rings and implants). Therefore, while taking this medication, another method of contraception should be used, such as condoms, diaphragms with spermicide, or IUDs.

- If you get pregnant, stop taking this medication right away and call your healthcare provider.

- Be sure to have regular gynecology check-ups ("female exams"), breast exams and mammograms. Your healthcare provider will tell you how often. These will check for signs of breast cancer and cancer of the endometrium (lining of the uterus).

- This medication can cause some serious, but rare, adverse effects such as <u>endometrial cancer</u>, strokes, or a <u>blood clot</u>. This medication can also increase the risk of getting <u>cataracts</u>.

- The most common side effects include hot flashes, hypertension, peripheral edema, mood changes, depression, skin changes, and vaginal discharge.

- You should call your healthcare provider right away if you develop:

  - vaginal bleeding or bloody discharge that could be a rusty or brown color, change in your monthly bleeding, such as in the amount or timing of bleeding or increased clotting, or pain or pressure in your pelvis (below your belly button).

  - sudden chest pain, shortness of breath, coughing up blood, pain, tenderness, or swelling in one or both of your legs.

  - sudden weakness, tingling, or numbness in your face, arm or leg, especially on one side of your body; sudden confusion, trouble speaking or sudden trouble seeing in one or both eyes, sudden trouble walking, dizziness, loss of balance or coordination, or sudden severe headache with no known cause.

  - signs of liver problems like lack of appetite and yellowing of your skin or whites of your eyes.

- For *Evista* – discontinue at least 72 hours prior to and during prolonged immobilization (e.g., post-surgical recovery, prolonged bed rest), and patients should be advised to avoid prolonged restrictions of movement during travel because of the increased risk of thromboembolic event (blood clots).

Aromatase Inhibitors

- This medication is to treat breast cancer in women who have <u>finished menopause</u>. This medication does not work in women who have not finished menopause.

- Take exactly as prescribed by your healthcare provider.

- Can be taken with or without food.

- If you miss a dose, take it as soon as you remember. If it is almost time for your next dose, skip the missed dose. Take your next regularly scheduled dose. Do not take two doses at the same time.

- Common side effects include hot flashes, weakness, <u>joint pain</u>, bone pain, <u>osteoporosis</u>, mood changes, high blood pressure, depression, and rash.

- This medication can cause rare, but serious, adverse effects such as heart disease, increased cholesterol, skin reactions, allergic reactions, and liver problems.

- Call your healthcare provider right away if you develop:

  ❑ chest pain, shortness of breath.

  ❑ any skin lesions, ulcers, or blisters.

  ❑ swelling of the face, lips, tongue, or throat, trouble swallowing, or trouble breathing.

  ❑ a general feeling of not being well with yellowing of the skin or whites of the eyes or pain on the right side of your abdomen.

- Tell your healthcare provider or pharmacist about all the medicines you take, including prescription and non-prescription medicines, vitamins, and herbal supplements. This medication should not be taken with tamoxifen or any medicines containing estrogen including pills, patches, creams, rings, or suppositories.

Leuprolide (for men with prostate cancer)

- This medication will lower sex hormones (testosterone and estrogen) produced by the body.

- Patients may experience worsening of their prostate cancer upon initiation of the LHRH agonist due to "tumor flare". To mitigate this side effect, typically an anti-androgen (such as bicalutamide) is started at least 1 week prior to leuprolide injection.

- Common side effects include hot flashes and impotence.

- During the first few weeks of treatment you may experience increased bone pain and increased difficulty in urinating.

- If you have a change in strength on one side of your body that is greater than the other side, trouble speaking or thinking, change in balance, or blurred eyesight you will need to see a healthcare provider right away.

Ondansetron

- Ondansetron is used to prevent or treat nausea and vomiting caused by chemotherapy or after surgery.

- Take this medicine by mouth with a glass of water. It may be taken only when needed or have scheduled times to take a dose. Follow the directions on your prescription label. Do not take your medicine more often than directed.

- Do not take this medicine if you are taking apomorphine.

- Inform your provider if you have a heart condition.

- Common side effects of this medication include headache, constipation, fatigue and dizziness.

- If you are prescribed the oral disintegrating tablets (ODT): Do not attempt to push the tablets through foil backing. With <u>dry hands</u>, peel back the foil of 1 blister and remove the tablet. Place tablet on the tongue; it will dissolve in seconds. Once dissolved, the patient may swallow with saliva. Administration with liquid is not necessary. Wash hands after administration.

- If you are prescribed the oral soluble film *(Zuplenz)*: with dry hands, fold the pouch along the dotted line to expose the tear notch. While still folded, tear the pouch carefully along the edge and remove the oral soluble film just prior to dosing.

- Place the film on the tongue; it will dissolve in a few seconds.

- Once dissolved, the tablet can be swallowed with saliva. Administration with liquid is not necessary.

- When administering oral soluble films successively to reach a desired dose (i.e., 16 mg given as two 8 mg films) allow each film to dissolve completely before administering the next one.

- The maximum oral dose of ondansetron is 24 mg/day.

Administration and Safe Handling of Oral Chemotherapeutic Agents

GENERIC (BRAND)	ADMINISTRATION	SPECIAL HANDLING
Imatinib *(Gleevac)* Capecitabine *(Xeloda)* Thalidomide* *(Thalomid)*	Take with food or within 1 hour after a meal	Pregnancy Category D *Pregnancy Category X Thalidomide female patients of reproductive potential must have negative pregnancy tests and use 2 forms of birth control. This REMS drug is only available through a specialty pharmacy.
Nilotinib *(Tasigna)*, Erlotinib *(Tarceva)*, Sorafenib *(Nexavar)*, Pazopanib *(Votrient)*, Temozolomide *(Temodar)*, Abiraterone* *(Zytiga)*, Pomalidomide* *(Pomalyst)*	Take on an empty stomach (1 hour before or 2 hours after food)	Pregnancy Category D *Pregnancy Category X Pomalidomide female patients of reproductive potential must have negative pregnancy tests and use 2 forms of birth control. This REMS drug is only available through a specialty pharmacy.
Dasatinib *(Sprycel)*, Sunitinib *(Sutent)*, Tamoxifen *(Nolvadex)*, Anastrozole* *(Arimidex)*, Bicalutamide* *(Casodex)*, Lenalidomide* *(Revlimid)*	Take without regards to food	Pregnancy Category D *Pregnancy Category X Lenalidomide female patients of reproductive potential must have negative pregnancy tests and use 2 forms of birth control. This REMS drug is only available through a specialty pharmacy.

REMS program requires prescribers and pharmacists to be certified and patients to enroll and comply with all of the requirements for each program.

PRACTICE CASE

Tommy is a 53 year old male (height 5'10", weight 200 lbs) who is receiving the following medication regimen for the treatment of non-Hodgkin's lymphoma. His past medical history is significant for mild stage 1 HF. He is to receive 6 cycles of "CHOP" chemotherapy.

CATEGORY	
Chemotherapy Regimen	Cyclophosphamide 750 mg/m² IV on day 1
	Doxorubicin 50 mg/m² IV on day 1
	Vincristine 1.4 mg/m² IV on day 1
	Prednisone 100 mg PO on days 1-5 given first

Questions

Questions 1-5 refer to the above case.

1. The pharmacist must first calculate the patient's BSA and will use the Dubois and Dubois equation: $BSA(m^2) = 0.007184 \times$ [weight $(kg)^{0.425}$] x [height $(cm)^{0.725}$] The patient's BSA is:

    a. 1.15 m²
    b. 1.03 m²
    c. 2.09 m²
    d. 2.18 m²
    e. 3.15 m²

2. What is the correct milligram dose of doxorubicin that the patient should receive on Day 1?

    a. 104.5 mg
    b. 510 mg
    c. 949.5 mg
    d. 948.5 mg
    e. 300 mg

3. The physician wants to know if there are any medications that can reduce the likelihood of cardiotoxicity with doxorubicin therapy. Which of the following would you suggest?

    a. Totect
    b. Zinecard
    c. Lasix
    d. Epogen
    e. Mesna

4. What is the dose limiting toxicity of vincristine?

    a. Neuropathy
    b. Nephrotoxicity
    c. Hypersensitivity reaction
    d. Ototoxicity
    e. Pulmonary toxicity

Questions 5-13 do not relate to the above case.

5. A patient is using apomorphine *(Apokyn)* injections for advanced Parkinson disease. The patient has been suffering from nausea. Which of the following antiemetics is contraindicated with apomorphine?

    a. Lorazepam
    b. Metoclopramide
    c. Prochlorperazine
    d. Granisetron
    e. All of the above

6. A patient will begin raloxifene therapy. Choose the correct counseling points: (Select **ALL** that apply.)

    a. This drug can increase your risk of breast cancer.
    b. Avoid long periods of immobility, such as during long airplane flights – get up and move when you can.
    c. This medication can cause weakened bones and fractures.
    d. This medication should only be used by men.
    e. This drug should be taken once daily.

7. Which of the following medications should be taken with food? (Select **ALL** that apply.)

    a. *Gleevec*

    b. *Xeloda*

    c. *Nexavar*

    d. *Votrient*

    e. *Zytiga*

8. An antidote for toxicity from high-dose methotrexate is:

    a. Folic acid

    b. Leucovorin

    c. Vitamin B12

    d. Cholestyramine

    e. Vitamin D

9. A pharmacist received a prescription for *Gleevec*. An appropriate generic interchange is:

    a. Aprepitant

    b. Imatinib

    c. Temozolomide

    d. Anastrozole

    e. Capecitabine

10. A pharmacist received a prescription for *Arimidex*. An appropriate generic interchange is:

    a. Aprepitant

    b. Anastrozole

    c. Exemestane

    d. Letrozole

    e. Tamoxifen

11. A patient is receiving dronabinol for nausea. Appropriate counseling points should include:

    a. The capsules should be kept in the refrigerator.

    b. Your appetite may increase.

    c. This medication cannot be shared with others.

    d. A and B only.

    e. A, B and C.

12. A patient has chemotherapy-induced anemia. She states she is weak. The pharmacist has access to her labs and finds that the current hemoglobin level is 11 g/dL. Ferritin, serum iron, TIBC, folate and vitamin B12 are all at acceptable levels. Her oncologist has prescribed *Procrit*. The patient has brought the *Procrit* prescription to the pharmacy. Choose the correct statement:

    a. The prescription can be filled after the pharmacist confirms that the patient is registered with the ESA APPRISE program.

    b. The generic name of *Procrit* is darbepoetin.

    c. The patient should be aware that they may experience euphoria and increased appetite.

    d. The prescription should not be filled; the pharmacist should contact the prescriber.

    e. A and B only.

13. A patient with end stage breast cancer has been experiencing fatigue and dehydration. She has a corrected calcium of 11.5 mg/dL. What is most appropriate for treating her hypercalcemia?

    a. Instruct patient to drink 8 glasses of water

    b. IV hydration, loop diuretic, and zoledronic acid

    c. Calcitonin

    d. Vitamin D

    e. No treatment is necessary since her calcium is within the normal range

Answers

1-c, 2-a, 3-b, 4-a, 5-d, 6-b,e, 7-a,b, 8-b, 9-b, 10-b, 11-e, 12-d, 13-b

ANEMIA

Normal amount of red blood cells Anemic amount of red blood cells

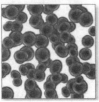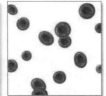

GUIDELINES/REFERENCES

Kidney Disease: Improving Global Outcomes (KDIGO) Anemia Work Group. KDIGO Clinical Practice Guideline for Anemia in Chronic Kidney Disease. Kidney International. Suppl 2012;2:279-335.

FDA Drug Safety Communication: Modified dosing recommendations to improve the safe use of erythropoiesis-stimulating agents in chronic kidney disease. www.fda.gov/Drugs/DrugSafety/ucm259639.htm (accessed 2013 Dec 1).

National Institute of Health Dietary Supplement Fact Sheet: Iron. http://ods.od.nih.gov/factsheets/Iron-HealthProfessional/ (accessed 2013 Dec 1).

Note: Iron requirements for infants, per the American Pediatric Association, are in the Natural Products and Vitamins chapter.

BACKGROUND

Anemia is the most common disorder of the blood and is characterized by a decrease in either hemoglobin or the volume of red blood cells (RBCs). Red blood cells (erythrocytes) are the most common type of blood cell. Hemoglobin is the protein in red blood cells that carries oxygen. Normally, a red blood cell has a lifespan of about 120 days after which they are removed from circulation. The decrease in Hgb or RBC volume results in a decreased oxygen carrying capacity of the blood. The main causes of anemia can be classified as impaired RBC production, increased RBC destruction (hemolysis), and blood loss. It can be a sign of many medical disorders, including chronic renal disease and malignancy; therefore, rapid diagnosis of the cause is essential.

SYMPTOMS OF ANEMIA

In anemia, since the tissues are not getting enough oxygen-rich blood, most of the symptoms are due to tissue hypoxia. Most patients with mild anemia or in the beginning stages are generally asymptomatic. As the anemia worsens, the patient may experience some of the classic symptoms such as <u>fatigue, malaise, weakness, shortness of breath, headache, dizziness, and/or pallor</u>. More severe symptoms, usually due to acute blood loss, may include chest pain, angina, fainting, palpitations and tachycardia. <u>Glossitis</u> (an inflamed, sore tongue), <u>koilonychias</u> (thin, concave, spoon-shaped nails) or <u>pica</u> (craving and eating non-foods such as chalk or clay) may develop in iron deficiency anemia.

A decreased oxygen supply can cause ischemic damage to many organs. Anemia is most notable in causing heart damage if it persists long-term; the heart will try to compensate for low oxygen levels by pumping faster (tachycardia) and by increasing the mass of the ventricular wall; this can eventually lead to heart failure.

TYPE OF ANEMIA

Anemia is characterized by low hemoglobin (Hgb) and low hematocrit (Hct) levels. The most common way to classify the type of anemia is by the mean corpuscular volume (MCV), or the average volume of RBCs. While the symptoms may be similar for both macrocytic and microcytic anemia, the MCV will differ. The MCV is small (< 80 μm^3) in microcytic anemia due to a small cell size from a lack of iron. The MCV is large (> 100 μm^3) in macrocytic (AKA megaloblastic) anemia due to folate or vitamin B12 deficiency. Anemias can also have a normal MCV (80-100 μm^3) and are therefore called normocytic anemia. These anemias can result from acute blood loss (surgery or trauma), hemolysis, bone marrow failure, or anemia of chronic disease. Certain genetic conditions cause dysfunctional RBCs resulting in anemia, such as sickle cell anemia. Please refer to the Sickle Cell Disease chapter for more information.

Patients with chronic kidney disease (CKD) generally have insufficient endogenous erythropoietin which can be due to loss of renal erythropoietin production capacity or a derangement in oxygen sensing as recently proposed. Erythropoietin is a hormone secreted by the kidneys that increases the rate of production of red blood cells in response to falling levels of oxygen in the tissues. In addition, iron stores can be low especially if the patient is on hemodialysis. Iron is essential for hemoglobin formation. The iron values are important to assess prior to the initiation of erythropoietin therapy. If the iron stores are low, erythropoietin-stimulating agents (ESAs) will not be able to work. Iron therapy and ESAs are the mainstay of anemia treatment in patients with CKD. Patients with chronic kidney disease may have poor iron absorption and may be receiving iron by injection. The majority of patients who need iron replacement are able to use oral supplementation. The majority of patients who receive iron by injection are on hemodialysis since hemodialysis results in losses of 6-7 mg of iron per day of dialysis and is further compounded by physiologic and venipuncture losses.

TEST	NORMAL ADULT RANGE
Hemoglobin (Hgb)	Males: 13.5-18 g/dL
	Females: 12-16 g/dL
Hematocrit (Hct)	Males: 38-50%
	Females: 36-46%
Mean Corpuscular Volume (MCV)	80-100 μm^3
Total Iron-Binding Capacity (TIBC)	250-400 mcg/dL
Serum Ferritin	Males: 30-300 ng/mL
	Females: 10-200 ng/mL
Transferrin Saturation (TSAT)	Males: 15-50%
	Females: 12-45%

MICROCYTIC ANEMIA DUE TO IRON DEFICIENCY

The most common type of anemia is <u>iron-deficiency anemia</u>. Causes of iron deficiency in adults include increased iron loss (e.g., acute/chronic hemorrhage, blood donation), decreased iron in the diet (e.g., vegetarian diet, malnutrition, dementia, psychiatric illnesses), decreased iron absorption (e.g., antacid therapy or high gastric pH, celiac disease, partial gastrectomy), or increased iron requirements (e.g., pregnancy and lactation). Iron deficiency results when the iron demand by the body is not met by iron absorption from the diet. Dietary iron is available in two forms; heme iron (found in meat) and nonheme iron (found in plant and dairy foods). Absorption of heme iron is minimally affected by dietary factors and is much more absorbable than nonheme iron. The bioavailability of nonheme iron requires gastric acid and varies greatly depending on the concentration of enhancers (e.g., meat, ascorbate) and inhibitors (tannins found in tea, calcium, phytates found in legumes and whole grain) in the diet. Vegetarians may or may not require iron supplementation; even if the intake is adequate, the absorption can be decreased by concurrent foods. <u>Microcytic anemia is diagnosed by a low hemoglobin and a low mean corpuscular volume (MCV) < 80 μm^3</u>. Other abnormal laboratory findings include a low ferritin level, low transferrin saturation, low serum iron and high TIBC. Iron deficiency anemia is generally treated with oral ferrous sulfate and takes months to adequately replete iron stores.

At-Risk Patients

Pregnant women, pre-term and low birth weight infants, older infants and toddlers, teenage girls, women with heavy menstrual periods, and renal failure patients are at increased risk for iron deficiency. Gastrointestinal diseases, including Crohn's, celiac disease and weight loss surgery, can reduce absorption and require replacement therapy. Total dietary iron intake in vegetarian diets may meet recommended levels; however, that iron is less available (non-heme iron) for absorption than in diets that include meat (heme-containing iron). As stated above, vegetarians may need iron replacement.

Women taking hormonal contraception experience less bleeding during their periods and therefore have a lower risk of developing an iron deficiency. A pharmacist may occasionally dispense contraception to a female (mostly younger – since younger women tend to have heavier blood loss) that is being used to reduce anemia.

The CDC recommends routine low-dose iron supplementation (30 mg/day) for all pregnant women, beginning at the first prenatal visit. Commonly, the low iron dose is provided in the prenatal vitamin. When a low hemoglobin or hematocrit is confirmed by testing, larger doses of iron are required.

TREATMENT OF IRON DEFICIENCY ANEMIA

Oral Iron Therapy

- <u>Oral iron therapy (ferrous sulfate) is usually used first-line for patients with iron-deficiency anemia</u>, except in those patients on hemodialysis (discussed in parenteral iron therapy section).

- Ferrous iron (Fe^{2+}) is absorbed more readily than the ferric (Fe^{3+}) form.

- An increase in Hgb level by 1 g/dL should occur every 2-3 weeks on iron therapy. Treatment should continue for 3-6 months after the anemia is resolved to allow for iron stores to return to normal and to prevent relapse.

- Sustained-release formulations or enteric coated formulations of iron are not recommended as initial therapy because they reduce the amount of iron that is present for absorption in the duodenum.

- Absorption of iron is enhanced in an acidic gastric environment. Ascorbic acid (vitamin C 200 mg), taken concurrently, may enhance absorption, to a minimal extent.

- Food will decrease the absorption of iron. It is best to take iron at least 1 hour before meals. However, many patients must take iron with food because they experience GI upset (nausea) when iron is administered on an empty stomach.

Oral Iron Therapy

DRUG	DOSING	SAFETY/SIDE EFFECTS/MONITORING
Ferrous sulfate **Infant Drops** *Fer-In-Sol* Iron Supplement Drops *Poly-Vi-Sol With Iron* Vitamin Drops – use if they need the vitamin D and iron **Children** *Flintstones* Children's Chewable Multivitamin, Tablets, plus Iron *Pokemon* Children's Multiple Vitamin with Iron, Chewable Tablets	325 mg PO daily to TID (65 mg elemental iron) 1st line therapy	Ferrous sulfate – 20% elemental iron Ferrous sulfate, exsiccated – 30% elemental iron Ferrous fumarate – 33% elemental iron Ferrous gluconate – 12% elemental iron Carbonyl iron, polysaccharide iron complex – 100% elemental iron **WARNING** Accidental overdose of iron-containing products is a leading cause of fatal poisoning in children under 6. Keep iron out of reach of children. In case of accidental overdose, go to ED or call poison control center immediately. **SIDE EFFECTS** Nausea, stomach upset, constipation (dose related), dark and tarry stools
Ferrous fumarate (*Ferretts*, *Hemocyte*, generic)	324 mg PO daily to TID (other doses available) (106 mg elemental iron)	**MONITORING** Hgb, serum iron, TIBC, ferritin, transferrin
Ferrous gluconate (*Fergon*, generic)	324 mg PO daily to TID (other doses available) (38 mg elemental iron)	**NOTES** Enteric coated and delayed-release products are not recommended due to decrease in iron absorption by delaying time of release [Less iron is absorbed since it passes the duodenum (site of maximal absorption) and is released into the ileum of the small intestine]
Ferrous sulfate, dried (exsiccated) Controlled Release (*Slow Fe, Feosol*)	160 mg PO daily to TID	Although fiber is 1st line treatment for constipation, a stool softener such as docusate is often recommended for iron-induced constipation
Carbonyl iron (*Feosol with Carbonyl Iron, Ferracap, Ferralet 90*)	varies	Highest amount of iron (100% elemental iron); no clear advantage over other forms of iron, but may be better tolerated by some patients

Iron Drug Interactions

- Antacids and agents that raise pH (H$_2$RAs, PPIs) decrease iron absorption by increasing pH. Thus, patients should take iron 2 hours prior to, or 4 hours after antacids.

- Antibiotics, primarily tetracycline (less of a concern with doxycycline and minocycline) and quinolones, can decrease iron absorption through chelation. Take iron 1-2 hours before or 4 hours after tetracycline; 2 hours before or 6 hours after ciprofloxacin; 2 hours before or 2 hours after levofloxacin; 4 hours before or 8 hours after moxifloxacin.

- Vitamin C increases acidity thus increases the absorption of iron; little benefit with low doses (need ~200 mg of ascorbic acid).

- Food decreases absorption as much as 50%; try to take on an empty stomach. If unable to tolerate, take with a small amount of food. If taken with food, it will take longer to correct the anemia.

- Iron can interact and decrease the levels of the following medications: levodopa, methyldopa, levothyroxine, cefdinir, bisphosphonates and mycophenolate. Separate the doses by 2-4 hours.

Iron: Toxic in Overdose!

Accidental iron poisoning is the leading cause of poisoning deaths among young children. As little as 5 tablets in a small child can lead to overdose. The child can appear asymptomatic (initially) or have already developed severe nausea, vomiting, gastrointestinal bleeding (most often vomiting blood), and diarrhea. If a parent suspects their child took iron pills or liquid, they should be directed to the nearest emergency room immediately – whether symptomatic or not. Left untreated, iron overdose will damage most organs, including the brain, and can be fatal. The antidote for iron overdose is deferoxamine. (Deferiprone *(Ferriprox)* is for transfusional iron overload unresponsive to chelation therapy).

Parenteral Iron Therapy

Parenteral iron therapy is as effective but can be more dangerous and is much more expensive than oral therapy. The following clinical situations can warrant IV administration:

- Hemodialysis (most common use of IV iron) – the National Kidney Foundation (NKF) guidelines state that to achieve and maintain a hemoglobin level of 11 g/dL (and hematocrit of 33-36%), most hemodialysis patients will require IV iron on a regular basis.

- Unable to tolerate iron given orally; or losing iron too fast for oral replacement.

- Intestinal malabsorption, such as Crohn's.

- Patients donating large amounts of blood for autoinfusion.

Intravenous (Parenteral) Iron Supplementation

DRUG	SAFETY/SIDE EFFECTS/MONITORING
Iron Dextran *(INFeD, Dexferrum)*	**Black Box Warning with Iron Dextran only** Risk of anaphylactic reactions. A test dose should be given to all patients prior to first therapeutic dose. Fatal reactions have occurred even in patients who tolerated the test dose. History of drug allergy and/or concomitant use of ACE inhibitor may ↑ risk.
Sodium Ferric Gluconate *(Ferrlecit,* Nulecit)	**SIDE EFFECTS** Hypotension, chest tightness, peripheral edema, risk of anaphylaxis with all agents (greatest risk with iron dextran – test dose required only for iron dextran)
Iron Sucrose *(Venofer)*	**MONITORING** Hgb, serum ferritin, serum iron, transferrin saturation, TIBC, vital signs, electrolytes, anaphylaxis **NOTES** Give by slow IV injection to ↓ risk of hypotension
Ferumoxytol *(Feraheme)*	
Ferric carboxymaltose *(Injectafer)*	

MACROCYTIC ANEMIA

Macrocytic anemia is due to either a vitamin B12 or folate deficiency, or both. If macrocytic anemia continues long-term, the patient is at risk for serious neurological consequences – including cognitive dysfunction (dementia) and peripheral nerve damage. Pernicious anemia is a type of macrocytic anemia that results in low B12 levels due to a lack of intrinsic factor, which is required for adequate B12 absorption in the small intestine. Since gut absorption is impaired in those who lack intrinsic factor, pernicious anemia requires lifelong vitamin B12 replacement therapy. Some patients can get enough supplementation with high-dose tablets of oral vitamin B12, but many clinicians prefer injections since macrocytic anemia can lead to neurological complications.

Alcoholism, Crohn's disease and celiac disease are other causes of macrocytic anemia. Macrocytic anemia is diagnosed by a low hemoglobin and a high mean corpuscular volume (MCV) > 100 mm³. Vitamin B12 and/or serum folate levels will be low. The Schilling test can diagnose vitamin B12 deficiency due to lack of intrinsic factor.

Treatment of Macrocytic Anemia

Treatment may start with vitamin B12 injections and follow with oral supplements. Injections are preferred for anyone with a severe deficiency or with neurological symptoms.

DRUG	DOSING	SAFETY/SIDE EFFECTS/MONITORING
Cyanocobalamin (vitamin B12) Injection: *Physicians EZ Use B-12, Vibisone* Nasal spray: *Nascobal* Oral: vitamin B12 generics	IM or deep SC: 100-1,000 mcg (dose and frequency depend on the regimen followed); can be given daily/weekly/monthly Oral/Sublingual: 1,000-2,000 mcg/day for mild-moderate deficiencies Intranasal *(Nascobal)*: 500 mcg in one nostril once weekly	**CONTRAINDICATIONS** Cobalt allergy **SIDE EFFECTS** Pain with injection **MONITORING** Hgb, Hct, vitamin B12, folate, iron Do not use sustained-release B12 supplements as the absorption is not adequate.
Folic Acid (folate)	0.4 – 1 mg daily 0.4, 0.8 mg tab (OTC) 1 mg tab (Rx)	**SIDE EFFECTS** Bronchospasm, flushing, rash, pruritus **MONITORING** Hgb, Hct, folate, vitamin B12, iron

Drug Interactions

Vitamin B12

- Chloramphenicol, colchicine, ethanol and long-term treatment with metformin may ↓ B12 absorption.

Folic Acid

- Folic acid decreases the efficacy of raltitrexed; avoid concurrent use.

ANEMIA OF CHRONIC KIDNEY DISEASE

Chronic kidney disease causes anemia due to a deficiency in erythropoietin, or EPO, a hormone produced by healthy kidneys. Erythropoietin stimulates the bone marrow to produce RBCs. In chronic kidney disease, the deficiency results in the bone marrow making fewer red blood cells. Erythropoietin can be given by injection; however, it is important to check that the anemia warrants the use. In recent years, the use of erythropoietin has narrowed due to safety concerns but it is still used frequently for this indication.

For chronic renal failure, ESAs should be used at the lowest possible dose that reduce the need for blood transfusions. Start when hemoglobin is < 10 g/dL and reduce or stop therapy when the hemoglobin is near 11 g/dL. Transferrin saturation should be at least 20%, and ferritin should be at least 100 ng/mL prior to starting ESA treatment. Levels of folate and vitamin B12 may also be assessed, especially if there is a poor response to the ESA.

DRUG	DOSING	SAFETY/SIDE EFFECTS/MONITORING
Epoetin alfa *(Epogen, Procrit)*	IV/SC: 50-100 units/kg 3 times weekly initial, then individualize maintenance dose (CKD dose) Can be given 150 units/kg 3 times weekly or 40,000 units once weekly in cancer patients	**BLACK BOX WARNINGS** ESAs increased the risk of serious cardiovascular eents, thromboembolic events, stroke and mortality in clinical studies when administered to target hemoglobin levels > 11 g/dL. **Chronic Kidney Disease** Patients experienced greater risks for death, serious cardiovascular events, and stroke when administered ESAs to target a hemoglobin level > 11 g/dL. No trial has identified a Hgb target level, ESA dose, or dosing strategy that does not increase these risks. Use the lowest dose sufficient to reduce the need for RBC transfusions. **Cancer** ESAs shortened overall survival and/or increased the risk of tumor progression or recurrence in clinical studies of patients with breast, head and neck, non-small cell lung, lymphoid, and cervical cancers. Prescribers and hospitals must enroll in and comply with the ESA APPRISE Oncology Program to prescribe and/or dispense these agents to patients with cancer. Use ESAs only for anemia from myelosuppressive chemotherapy. Use the lowest dose to avoid RBC transfusions. ESAs should only be used if the hemoglobin level is < 10 g/dL. ESAs are not indicated when the anticipated outcome is cure. Discontinue following completion of a chemotherapy course.
Darbepoetin *(Aranesp)*	IV/SC: 0.45 mcg/kg weekly or 0.75 mcg/kg every 2 weeks (for patients on dialysis) or 0.45 mcg/kg given once every 4 weeks (for non dialysis patients) Can be given 2.25 mcg/kg weekly or 500 mcg every 3 weeks in cancer patients	**Perisurgery** Due to increased risk of deep venous thrombosis (DVT), DVT prophylaxis is recommended. **CONTRAINDICATIONS** Uncontrolled HTN, pure red cell aplasia (PRCA) that begins after treatment; multidose vials containing benzyl alcohol contraindicated in neonates, infants, pregnancy and lactation. **SIDE EFFECTS** Hypertension, fever, headache, arthralgia/bone pain, pruritus/rash, nausea, cough, injection site pain, thrombosis, edema, chills, dizziness **MONITORING** Hgb, Hct, transferrin saturation, serum ferritin, BP **NOTES** IV route is recommended for patients on hemodialysis Store in refrigerator. Do not administer additional doses if Hgb is above 11.5 (CKD); 11 (cancer). If Hgb increases > 1 g/dL in any 2-week period, reduce dose by 25% for epoetin alfa and decrease dose by 40% for darbepoetin alfa.

Iron Patient Counseling

- This medication will work faster if taken on an empty stomach. If taking it on an empty stomach is too nauseating, it can be taken with food, but this will mean that it will take more time to correct the anemia.

- Limit consumption of tannins, calcium, polyphenols, and phytates (found in legumes and whole grains), as these can decrease iron absorption.

- This medication needs to be taken for at least a few months after your anemia symptoms have improved; do not stop until directed by your doctor.

- Iron can cause your stool to become dark. This is expected.

- If you develop constipation, ask your pharmacist for a recommendation for a stool softener, such as docusate and a fiber product such as psyllium.

ESA Patient Counseling

- This drug can increase your risk of life-threatening heart or circulation problems, including heart attack or stroke. This risk will increase the longer you use this drug. Seek emergency medical help if you have symptoms of heart or circulation problems, such as: chest pain or heavy feeling, pain spreading to the arm or shoulder, nausea, sweating, general ill feeling, feeling short of breath, even with mild exertion.

- Less serious side effects may include dizziness, mild headache, fever, sore throat, body aches, nausea, vomiting, diarrhea, or pain or tenderness where you injected the medication.

- This drug may shorten remission time in patients with breast cancer, non-small cell lung cancer, head and neck cancer, cervical cancer, or lymphoid cancer. Talk with your doctor about your individual risk.

- Your doctor may occasionally change your dose to make sure you get the best results from this medication.

- Do not shake the medication vial (bottle). Vigorous shaking will ruin the medicine. Do not draw up the drug dose into a syringe until you are ready to give yourself an injection. Do not use the medication if it has changed colors or has any particles in it. Use each disposable needle only one time. Throw away used needles in a puncture-proof container (ask your pharmacist where you can get one and how to dispose of it). Keep this container out of the reach of children and pets.

- Do not inject into an area that is tender, red, bruised, hard, or has scars or stretch marks. Recommended sites for injection are the outer area of the upper arms, the abdomen (except for 2 inches around the navel), the front of the middle thighs, and the upper outer area of the buttocks. See shaded areas for injection below.

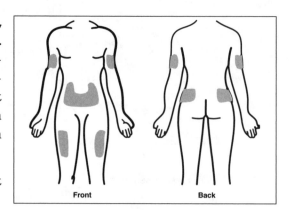

- Store this drug in the refrigerator and do not allow it to freeze.

- To be sure this medication is helping your body produce red blood cells, your blood will need to be tested on a regular basis. You may also need to check your blood pressure during treatment. Do not miss any scheduled appointments.

SICKLE CELL DISEASE

We gratefully acknowledge the assistance of Kimberly B. Tallian, PharmD, BCPP, FASHP, FCCP, FCSHP, Assistant Dean and Chair for Clinical and Administrative Sciences, Professor at Keck Graduate Institute, School of Pharmacy, Claremont Colleges, in preparing this chapter.

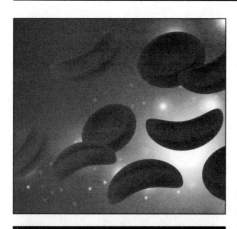

GUIDELINES

The Management of Sickle Cell Disease. NIH Publication 02-2117, 4th Ed. 2000: 1-188.

Benjamin LJ, Dampier CD, Jacox AK et al. Guideline for the management of acute and chronic pain in sickle-cell disease. Glenville, IL: APS Clinical Practice Guideline Series, No. 1, 1999.

BACKGROUND

Sickle cell disease (SCD) is a group of disorders that affects the hemoglobin in red blood cells (RBCs). The hemoglobin molecule has an alpha chain and a beta chain. Patients with SCD have a single base substitution on chromosome 11 in the DNA sequence of the gene encoding the beta chain. Sickle cell hemoglobin is designated HbS, and normal hemoglobin is designated HbA. This causes the hemoglobin to be misshapen, which makes the RBCs rigid with a concave "sickle" shape. The irregularly shaped RBCs are unable to transport oxygen effectively and get stuck in smaller blood vessels. When the tissue is deprived of oxygen-rich blood it is ischemic, and painful. Acute episodes of ischemic pain is called sickle cell crisis or vaso-occlusive crisis and is the hallmark of sickle cell disease. These are severe painful episodes that usually begin at night, are most common in the lower back, legs, hips, abdomen and chest, and last from 3 to 14 days. If the pain is in the chest it is called acute chest syndrome (ACS), which is very painful and can be life-threatening. ACS is the leading cause of illness in SCD and is the most common condition at the time of death. Other common conditions with SCD include:

- Infections: 35% of infants with sickle cell die from infections most commonly due to *Streptococcus pneumoniae* and *Haemophilus influenza*. Infections are also common in children and young adults, with a higher prevalence of *Chlamydia* and *Mycoplasma pneumonia* infections.

- Pulmonary hypertension: 30% of patients with SCD have pulmonary hypertension, which leads to *cor pulmonale*, (increase in size in the right side of the heart), which can lead to heart failure.

- Stroke: is a common killer in SCD, primarily due to blockages of coronary blood vessels. Multiple aneurysms are common.

- Anemia: sickle cell anemia (SCA) is caused when sickled cells collect in the spleen. Chronic hemolytic anemia develops due to the shortened lifespan of the RBCs; the bone marrow is not able to replace the damaged RBCs as quickly as they are destroyed. The chronic anemia is a major contributor to overall poor health and heart failure.

- Kidneys: are chronically infected, urination problems are common, including uncontrolled urination during sleep, and there is high-risk for renal medullary carcinoma.

- Priapism: occurs in over 30% of male patients and must be treated.

- Liver enlargement: is present in over half of SCD patients and acute liver damage is common during hospitalization. In previous years there was a high risk of hepatitis infections from chronic transfusions; this risk has decreased in recent years due to screening procedures.

- Gallstones: are common, which are asymptomatic or painful.

- Spleen: the spleen becomes nonfunctional due to recurrent episodes of oxygen deprivation. Spleen injury increases the risk for serious infections. Acute splenic sequestration crisis (sudden spleen enlargement) occurs when the spleen suddenly becomes enlarged from trapped blood.

- Other concerns: excessive production of blood cells causes the bones to grow abnormally, resulting in long legs and long arms. Sickled cells that block oxygen to bone cause severe bone pain, and sickled cells in the small capillaries cause painful hand-foot syndrome (described in the Oncology I chapter). Eye problems can develop. Pregnancies in women with SCD have high risk of miscarriage, premature birth and low birth weight.

Children with severe sickle cell disease have been cured with <u>bone marrow transplant</u> after undergoing a regimen in which their own marrow was completely destroyed with chemotherapy first, followed by the healthy donor marrow replacement. This regimen is considered too toxic for adults who have accumulated organ damage. Some adults have been successfully treated in recent years with a partial bone marrow transplant in combination with immune-suppressants.

PHARMACOLOGIC TREATMENT

The primary drug classes used in SCD are <u>immunizations and antibiotics</u> (primarily <u>penicillin</u>) to reduce infection risk, <u>analgesics</u> to control pain, <u>folic acid</u> to help control anemia, <u>hydroxyurea</u> to reduce the frequency of pain episodes and acute chest syndrome, and iron chelation therapy.

Blood transfusions are often essential for treating SCD. Transfusions protect against many of the life-threatening complications by providing healthy red blood cells. These are given either chronically or for acute episodes. The goal hemoglobin level is <u>no higher than 10 g/dL</u> post-infusion. Transfusions carry risk, including iron overload. <u>Chelation therapy and drugs used for iron overload</u> are discussed in the last section.

Immunizations and Antibiotics

<u>The major cause of death for children with SCD under 5 years of age is infection</u>. Due to the repetitive sickling and infarctions, the spleen becomes fibrotic and eventually shrinks in size. <u>Bacteria proliferates and causes increased risk of infection, including septicemia with encapsulated bacteria</u> (*S. pneumonia, H. influenza, Salmonella spp.*)

Children under the age of 2 years are at highest risk for invasive pneumococcal disease and should receive the pneumococcal conjugate vaccine. SCD children older than 2 years, with either surgical splenectomy or functional asplenia, should receive the <u>pneumococcal poly-saccharide vaccine</u> and the <u>meningococcal conjugate vaccine</u>. <u>Prophylactic penicillin</u> has been shown to dramatically reduce the mortality associated with invasive pneumococcal infection in young children and should be <u>initiated at age 2 months and continued minimally until age 5 years.</u> If invasive pneumococcal infection develops despite antibiotic prophy-laxis, indefinite antibiotic prophylaxis should be used.

AGE	VACCINATIONS*
< 2 years	13-valent pneumococcal conjugate vaccine (*Prevnar 13*) *H. influenza* vaccine
≥ 2 years	23-valent pneumococcal polysaccharide vaccine (*Pneumovax*) x 2 Administer at ≥ 2 years (at least 2 months apart from *Prevnar 13*) and at 5 years Meningococcal conjugate vaccine x 2, given between 2-6 years and 5-9 years

* In addition to normal childhood vaccine schedule (see Immunizations chapter)

PNEUMOCOCCAL PROPHYLAXIS	DRUGS AND DOSE
Penicillin	Penicillin V Potassium 125 mg PO BID, to age 3, then 250 mg PO BID until at least 5 years or Benzathine penicillin 600,000 million units IM Q 4 weeks in nonadherent patients from 6 months to 6 years
Penicillin Allergy	Erythromycin 10 mg/kg PO BID

(see Infectious Disease chapter for further information on the antibiotics)

Pain Management

Mild to moderate pain can often be managed at home with rest, fluids, application of warm compresses applied to affected areas, and the use of NSAIDs or acetaminophen. For severe pain, opioids are recommended. Hospitalization may be indicated.

Anemia Management

Folic acid is recommended in children with SCD with chronic hemolytic anemia at a dose of 0.1 mg/day up to age 1 year, 0.3 mg/day from 1-4 years, and 0.4-1 mg/day from 4 years through adolescence.

Hydroxyurea to Stimulate HbF Production

Fetal hemoglobin, or HbF, is the form of hemoglobin present in the fetus and young infants. Fetal hemoglobin blocks the sickling action of red blood cells, which is why infants with SCD do not develop symptoms until HbF levels have dropped. Hydroxyurea reduces the severity of sickle cell disease by stimulating production of HbF, by blocking the enzyme ribonucleotide reductase. This reduces the frequency of acute pain crises and episodes of ACS.

DRUG	DOSE	SAFETY/SIDE EFFECTS/MONITORING
Hydroxyurea (Droxia, Hydrea)	Initiate: 15 mg/kg PO daily (round to nearest capsule), max 35 mg/kg/day (divide higher doses)	**BLACK BOX WARNING** Serious and life-threatening adverse events may occur. Should be administered under the supervision of a physician experienced in the treatment of SCD (or in cancer chemotherapy). **CONTRAINDICATIONS** Significant bone marrow suppression: WBC < 2,500/mm³ or platelet count < 100,000/mm³ or severe anemia **SIDE EFFECTS** Leukopenia, anemia, thrombocytopenia, anorexia, nausea, diarrhea, constipation, hyperpigmentation, scaling, headache, dizziness, rash, skin and nail atrophy **MONITORING** HgF levels, CBC with differential; monitor for toxicity every 2 weeks; if toxicity, withhold until bone marrow recovers, then restart with dose reduction. If no toxicity, then can increase dose to maximum tolerated. **NOTES** Pregnancy Category D Wear gloves when handling and wash hands before and after contact

Hydroxyurea Drug Interactions

- Hydroxyurea can increase the effects of clozapine, didanosine, natalizumab, pimecrolimus, stavudine, tacrolimus (topical), tofacitinib, and live vaccines. Concomitant use should be avoided. Concurrent treatment with antiretrovirals (including didanosine and stavudine), is higher risk for potentially fatal pancreatitis, hepatotoxicity, hepatic failure, and severe peripheral neuropathy.

Hydroxyurea Patient Counseling

- Hydroxyurea can lower your body's ability to fight infection and make you more prone to bleeding or becoming ill.

- Call your doctor immediately if you experience fever, chills, sores in the mouth, easy bruising/bleeding, purple or red point spots under the skin, pale skin, rash, shortness of breath, rapid heart rate, painful or difficulty urinating, and/or confusion.

- Wear disposable gloves when handling to reduce risk of exposure. Wash hands before and after handling. If you accidentally spill any of the contents, immediately wipe up with a damp cloth and throw cloth away in a sealed plastic bag.

Chelation to Reduce Iron Overload from Transfusions

Chronic RBC transfusions cause iron overload, which damages the liver, heart and other organs. Chelation therapy is used to remove excess iron stores in the body. Historically, deferoxamine, the antidote for iron toxicity, has been used but requires a pump for about 12 hours/day and has significant toxicities. Many patients will choose not to use it. Deferasirox (*Exjade*) is taken once daily by mouth, mixed with liquid. It is easier to take with less toxicity. Deferasirox is indicated for the treatment of chronically elevated levels of iron in the blood caused by repeated blood transfusions (transfusional hemosiderosis) in patients 2 years of age and older. It is also used for iron overload from chronic transfusions in patients with beta-thallassemia, a blood disorder causing decreased hemoglobin production.

DRUG	DOSING	SAFETY/SIDE EFFECTS/MONITORING
Deferoxamine (*Desferal*) Injection	Start at 20 mg/kg/day SC, max 2,000 mg/day At 1 month add: ascorbic acid 50-200 mg/d	**CONTRAINDICATIONS** Severe renal disease, heart failure **SIDE EFFECTS** Ototoxicity, visual impairment, arthralgia, headache, acute respiratory distress syndrome (dyspnea, cyanosis, and/or interstitial infiltrates), agranulocytosis, growth failure, hypersensitivity reactions (e.g., urticaria, angioedema), injection-site reactions (erythema, pruritus), hypotension **MONITORING** Serum iron, ferritin, total iron-binding capacity, CBC with differential, SCr, LFTs, chemistry panel, growth, and body weight, monitor at baseline and every 3 months, audiometry and ophthalmologic exams **NOTES** Pregnancy Category C

Chelation to Reduce Iron Overload from Transfusions Continued

DRUG	DOSING	SAFETY/SIDE EFFECTS/MONITORING
Deferasirox *(Exjade)*	Start a 20 mg/kg PO daily (round to nearest tablet), max 40 mg/kg/day Must be taken on an empty stomach at least 30 minutes before eating, mixed into orange juice, apple juice or water. Instruct patients using the Drop-Stir-Drink counseling method (refer to counseling section).	**BLACK BOX WARNINGS (3)** Gastrointestinal hemorrhage (including fatalities) may occur; monitor. Hepatic injury and failure (including fatalities) may occur. Acute renal failure (including fatalities and cases requiring dialysis) may occur; monitor carefully. **CONTRAINDICATIONS** CrCl < 40 mL/min or SCr > two-fold the age-appropriate upper limit of normal, platelet counts < 50,000/mm^3, advanced malignancies **SIDE EFFECTS** Headache, rash, abdominal pain, nausea, arthralgia, visual impairment, hepatic dysfunction, kidney impairment **MONITORING** LFTs, bilirubin, SCr and CrCl. **NOTES** Pregnancy Category C

Deferasirox Drug Interactions

- Deferasirox is a substrate of UGT1A1 as well as an inhibitor of CYP 1A2, CYP 2C8 and an inducer of CYP 3A4 and can be affected by many drugs; check prior to dispensing.

- Avoid concomitant use of aluminum hydroxide, bile acid sequestrants (e.g., cholestyramine), and potent UGT inducers (e.g., rifampin, phenobarbital, phenytoin) as they may reduce the efficacy of chelation therapy.

Deferasirox Patient Counseling

- Administer tablets by making an oral suspension in water, juice or in apple sauce on an empty stomach. Do not chew or swallow tablet whole, at least 30 minutes before eating. Use this method:

  - DROP the *Exjade* tablet(s) into a glass of orange juice, apple juice, or water. You can also use the *Exjade* mixer each day when taking your *Exjade*. Make sure that you use the amount of liquid directed by your doctor.

  - STIR the liquid and *Exjade* tablet(s) until you have an even mixture. The consistency of the mixture may be thick.

  - DRINK all of the *Exjade* mixture. Add more juice or water to mix anything that's left over. And then drink that.

- Avoid aluminum containing or milk products as they can bind the chelation therapy and reduce its effectiveness. Seek immediate medical attention if you experience any of these signs of an allergic reaction, including difficulty breathing, hives, and/or swelling of your face, lips, tongue, or throat.

INTRAVENOUS DRUGS, FLUIDS & ANTIDOTES

BACKGROUND

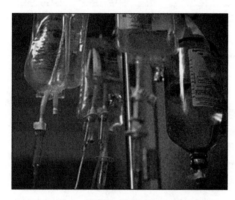

Intravenous therapy, or IV therapy, is the administration of liquid substances directly into a vein. The word intravenous simply means "within a vein". Medications can be administered through the IV route as intermittent bolus doses or by a continuous infusion, also known as a drip. Compared with other routes of administration, the intravenous route is the fastest way to deliver fluids and medications throughout the body. This may be needed given the patient's severity of illness (e.g., critically ill or cardiac arrest) or inability to take oral medications (nothing by mouth or NPO). Some medications may only be formulated for intravenous administration.

Many intravenous medications may be needed for a patient, particularly for critically ill patients. Several IV catheters (or lines) may be used at once and pharmacists are commonly asked about IV compatibilities of medications. Patients can also receive parenteral nutrition (PN) through the intravenous route. PN is discussed further in the Calculations chapter.

Intravenous Catheters

There are 2 main types of intravenous catheters, peripheral and central. A peripheral IV line consists of a short catheter (a few centimeters long) inserted through the skin into a peripheral vein, usually in the hand or arm. Central IV lines are placed in a large vein (e.g., subclavian, internal jugular, inferior vena cava) located in the chest, neck, or groin; or they can be inserted peripherally.

One commonly used central line is the peripherally inserted central catheter, or PICC line. PICC lines are used when access to the vein is required for a prolonged period of time or when the infused substance would damage a peripheral vein (e.g., patients that require long-term PN or long courses of IV antibiotics). The PICC line is inserted into a peripheral vein, typically in the upper arm, and advanced until the catheter tip terminates in a large vein in the chest near the heart.

A central IV line has several advantages over a peripheral line:

■ It can deliver fluids/medications that are overly irritating to peripheral veins (e.g., some chemotherapy drugs, PN, higher concentrations of potassium, vasopressor drugs, hypertonic solutions).

■ They can contain multiple parallel compartments (or lumens) within the catheter so multiple medications can be given at once even if they would not be chemically compatible within a single catheter. Larger volumes and rates of drugs and fluids may also be administered through these catheters, which may be required in hemodynamically unstable patients (fluctuations in blood pressure).

■ Some central lines can measure central venous pressure and other hemodynamics (cardiac output, etc.)

Central lines do have some disadvantages such as higher risks of bleeding, infection, and thromboembolism and they are more difficult to insert correctly (requires expertise and must be placed by a physician or other trained staff).

Infusion Pumps

Intravenous medications require the use of an infusion pump for administration. Infusion pumps can administer fluids in ways that would be impractical, expensive or unreliable if performed manually by nursing staff. For example, infusion pumps can administer as little as 0.1 mL per hour injections (too small for a drip), injections every minute, injections with repeated boluses, up to maximum number per hour (e.g., in patient-controlled analgesia or PCA), or provide fluids. They offer another "safety mechanism" to make sure the correct drug, correct dose and correct rate are given to the patient. See Medication Errors, Patient Safety, and the Joint Commission chapter for more information.

Intravenous Bags

Polyvinyl Chloride (PVC) Concern with IV Drugs

Polyvinyl chloride (PVC) is the 3rd most widely used plastic that can be made softer and more flexible by the addition of plasticizers. Virtually all medical devices made from PVC utilize one plasticizer, diethylhexyl phthalate, universally referred to as DEHP. There are 2 concerns with the use of PVC infusion bags, leaching and sorption.

Leaching Concern: Leaching means one substance is pulled from another; in this case, the primary concern is the leaching of diethylhexyl phthalate (DEHP) from PVC bags. In animal studies, DEHP has been shown to adversely affect the male reproductive system. There is little available study data in humans. Everyone is exposed to some degree of DEHP in everyday life and it is unknown what level may pose a risk in humans. Drugs with known leaching concerns should be put in non-PVC bags and use polyethylene-lined, non-DEHP administration tubing. The amount of DEHP that will leach out will also depend on the temperature of the solution, the lipid content and the duration of contact with the plastic. In addition to the drugs listed, there may be concern with leaching in neonates receiving lipids from PN in a PVC bag.

Drugs known to have leaching issues include <u>tacrolimus, temsirolimus, teniposide, cabazitaxel, docetaxel, ixabepilone and paclitaxel</u>. The rhyme "tic tac toe, craving delicious irresistible pho" may be useful (pho is Vietnamese soup.) Amiodarone, in the sorption group below, has some leaching potential. Practically speaking, it may be useful to know which drugs are best to avoid with PVC, rather than why, since the main point here is to avoid PVC bags with these drugs.

Sorption Concern: Sorption means that one substance pulls in another; in this case, the PVC bag pulls in some of the drug, which reduces the concentration of the drug in solution. Several drugs exhibit sorption to PVC containers and sets. With these drugs, pharmacists should use the newer polyolefin containers, which have reduced sorption and leaching potential. Occasionally, with some of these drugs, glass containers are used.

Drugs that have sorption issues are <u>amiodarone (for infusions greater than 2 hours), carmustine, lorazepam, sufentanil, thiopental, regular human insulin, and nitroglycerin</u>. The mnemonic <u>ACLS TIN</u> may be helpful.

Intravenous Fluids

When patients enter a hospital, they may be started on IV fluids to maintain their volume status. This is commonly done when there has been significant blood loss. Stopping the bleed and administering blood (a colloid) to replace what has been lost are first priority, followed by the administration of IV fluids. Fluids can also be used to treat the initial stages of hypoperfusion, or shock. There are 2 types of fluids: crystalloids and colloids.

- Colloids are large and do not readily cross the capillary membrane; therefore, they will primarily remain in the intravascular (inside blood vessels) space.

- Colloids may provide greater intravascular volume expansion than equal volumes of crystalloids; however, they are expensive and provide questionable clinical benefit over crystalloids.

- <u>Crystalloids are less costly and safer</u> (not as many adverse reactions associated with their use).

FLUID	COMMENTS

Colloids

FLUID	COMMENTS
Albumin 5%, 25% (Albuked, Flexbumin, others)	Natural colloid, pooled plasma protein More expensive than hydroxyethyl starch or crystalloids with no evidence of superiority May be considered in patients when clinically significant edema limits further administration of crystalloid; patients with albumin < 2.5 g/dL; use 25% albumin with diuretics for patients with clinically significant edema 5% albumin is isotonic (500 mL of 5% albumin = 500 mL of intravascular volume expansion); 25% albumin is hypertonic (100 mL of 25% albumin = 500 mL of intravascular volume expansion) Prepare 5% albumin by diluting 25% albumin with normal saline, not sterile water. Sterile water used as a diluent has been associated with hemolysis and renal damage due to hypotonicity
Dextran (Dextran 40, Dextran 70)	Semi-synthetic glucose polymer High risk for adverse reactions (urticaria, acute renal failure, increased bleeding time) Potential for allergic or anaphylactoid reactions Impairs hemostasis; sometimes used as anticoagulant 500 mL fluid volume = 500 mL intravascular volume expansion
Hydroxyethyl starch (Hespan, Hextend, Voluven)	Semi-synthetic colloid Larger molecular weight than albumin Potential for anaphylactoid reactions ↓ coagulation by decreasing concentration of hemoglobin and coagulation factors and impairing platelet function 500 mL fluid volume = 500 mL intravascular volume expansion

Crystalloids

FLUID	COMMENTS
Lactated Ringer's (LR)	Isotonic Lactate can be converted to bicarbonate which can help correct acidosis Considered equally effective as normal saline; historically preferred in surgical/trauma patients but no evidence of superiority 1,000 mL fluid volume = 250 mL intravascular expansion Risk for hyperkalemia; has 4 mEq/L potassium
Dextrose 5% (D5W)*	Equivalent to "free water"; metabolized to water and carbon dioxide and water can cross any membrane in the body; useful for patients with dehydration and adequate circulatory volume 1,000 mL fluid volume = 100 mL vascular expansion
NaCl 0.9% (NS, normal saline)*	Isotonic 1,000 mL fluid volume = 250 mL vascular expansion No evidence that hypertonic saline (e.g., 3%) is better than NS for fluid resuscitation Risk of hypernatremia and hyperchloremic metabolic acidosis

*There are various crystalloid combinations including: D5NS, D51/2NS, 1/2NS

CONDITIONS AND CONCERNS IN THE ICU

GUIDELINE

Dellinger RP, Levy MM, Rhodes A, et al. Surviving Sepsis Campaign: international guidelines for management of severe sepsis and septic shock: 2012. Crit Care Med 2013;41:580-637.

Shock Syndromes

Shock results from a lack of oxygen due to hypoperfusion. Hypotension, or low blood pressure (SBP < 90 mmHg), is a sign of shock. There are four main types of shock: 1) Hypovolemic (e.g., hemorrhagic), 2) Cardiogenic, 3) Distributive (e.g., septic), and 4) Obstructive (e.g., massive pulmonary embolism). Fluid resuscitation with crystalloids or colloids is generally recommended as first-line therapy in patients with hypovolemic shock. Blood products may also be administered in these patients. If the patient does not respond to this fluid challenge, then vasopressor therapy should be initiated. (It is important to note that vasopressors will not be effective without adequate fluid administration – at least 30 mL/kg). Patients with cardiogenic shock require the use of vasopressor and/or inotropic agents. Sepsis is the presence of an infection with Systemic Inflammatory Response Syndrome (SIRS). Septic shock is the development of hypotension in a patient with sepsis. The mortality rate of septic shock is 30-50%, so prompt interventions are necessary. Patients with septic shock should be administered crystalloids or colloids, vasopressors, and/or inotropic drugs. These patients also require antibiotic administration within an hour of presentation, and may be given corticosteroids.

Inotropes work by increasing contractility. Dobutamine is a beta-agonist and increases heart rate, which increases, cardiac output. Milrinone is a selective phosphodiesterase inhibitor in cardiac and vascular tissue. It causes vasodilation and inotropic effects, with little chronotropic effect.

Vasopressors work via vasoconstriction (think "pressing down on the vasculature") and therefore they increase systemic vascular resistance (SVR). Dopamine is an endogenous precursor of norepinephrine that stimulates different receptors depending on the dose. At low doses, D1 receptors are stimulated, leading to increased renal and mesenteric perfusion. At medium doses, β_1 receptors are stimulated, leading to increased stroke volume, and therefore, increased cardiac output. At high doses, α_1 receptors are stimulated, leading to vasoconstriction and increased SVR. Epinephrine is both an alpha and beta agonist. It increases cardiac output and SVR. Norepinephrine is both an alpha and beta agonist, with greater alpha effects. It increases contractility, heart rate and SVR. Phenylephrine is a pure alpha agonist, which means it increases SVR without increasing heart rate. Vasopressin is a V1 and V2 agonist. It causes vasoconstriction and increases SVR.

Inotropes and Vasopressors Used in Shock Syndromes

DRUG	DOSING	SAFETY/SIDE EFFECTS/MONITORING
DOBUTamine	2.5-20 mcg/kg/min	**SIDE EFFECTS** Dobutamine: hypotension, premature ventricular beats, tachycardia, angina Milrinone: ventricular arrhythmias, supraventricular arrhythmias, hypotension
Milrinone	0.1-0.75 mcg/kg/min; may consider a 50 mcg/kg loading dose	**MONITORING** Requires continuous BP monitoring, HR, ECG, CVP, MAP, urine output **NOTES** Amrinone (*Inocor*) is no longer used due to significant thrombocytopenia Milrinone: dose must be reduced for renal dysfunction Due to hypotension, only after adequate perfusion is achieved, dobutamine may be added for inotropic effect.
DOPamine	Low dose: 1-3 mcg/kg/min Medium dose: 5-10 mcg/kg/min High dose: 10-20 mcg/kg/min	**BLACK BOX WARNING** Dopamine, norepinephrine: vesicants, if extravasation occurs, treat with phentolamine **SIDE EFFECTS** Arrhythmias, tachycardia (especially with dopamine and epinephrine), bradycardia (with phenylephrine), tachyphylaxis, peripheral ischemia, necrosis (gangrene)
EPINEPHrine (*Adrenalin*)	0.1-0.5 mcg/kg/min	**MONITORING** Requires continuous BP monitoring, HR, MAP, urine output, infusion site for extravasation
Norepinephrine (*Levophed*)	2-12 mcg/min	**NOTES** *EpiPen, Adrenaclick, EpiPen Jr, Auvi-Q* – pre-filled auto injectors used for anaphylactic allergic reactions. Epinephrine used for IV route is 0.1 mg/mL or 1:10,000 ratio strength. Epinephrine used for the IM route is 1:1,000 ratio strength. Solutions should not be used if they are discolored or contain a precipitate. Dobutamine may turn slightly pink due to oxidation; however, potency is not lost.
Phenylephrine (*Neo-Synephrine*)	Initial: 100-180 mcg/min or 0.5 mcg/kg/min	Dopamine renal dosing is not considered beneficial for kidney protection.
Vasopressin (*Pitressin*)	0.01-0.03 units/min for septic shock; cardiac arrest: 40 units X 1	**SIDE EFFECTS** Arrhythmias, necrosis (gangrene). Doses > 0.04 units/min cause more cardiovascular side effects (asystole, MI) **MONITORING** BP, HR, CO, ECG, fluid balance **NOTES** Taper dose to avoid rebound hypertension

Treatment of Extravasation with Vasopressors

- Extravasation, or leakage of IV medication into surrounding tissue, of vasopressors/inotropes can cause tissue damage and necrosis. This is a medical emergency that requires immediate treatment.

- Treat with <u>phentolamine, an α-adrenergic blocker that antagonizes the effects of vasopressors</u>. Dilute 5-10 mg of phentolamine in 10 mL of NS and give SC to infiltrated area. Blanching should reverse immediately.

<table>
<tr><td>

GUIDELINE

Barr J, Fraser GL, Puntillo K, et al. Clinical parctice guidelines for the management of pain, agitation, and delirium in adult patients in the intensive care unit. Crit Care Med 2013;41:263-306.

</td></tr>
</table>

ICU Sedation, Analgesia and Delirium

Sedation (to reduce distress, delirium, pain and anxiety) and analgesia (to reduce pain) are commonly used for patients in the intensive care unit, particularly if the patient is receiving mechanical ventilation. It is often necessary to provide sedation/analgesia to limit the anxiety and agitation experienced by patients, to maintain synchronized breathing if on a ventilator (prevent "bucking" the ventilator), and keep patients free of pain and suffering in the harsh ICU environment. Patients in the ICU can quickly become disoriented, agitated, and delirious given the amount of interventions they experience, the constant noise of monitors and alarms, and the frequent interruptions from hospital personnel disrupting their normal sleep cycle. This, combined with fear and anxiety associated with their environment and current critical condition, can invoke an aggressive, agitated, disoriented and confused patient.

<u>Agents used for ICU sedation and analgesia can include a varied combination of opioids (morphine, hydromorphone, and fentanyl), benzodiazepines (midazolam, lorazepam), antipsychotics (haloperidol, quetiapine, risperidone) and/or hypnotics (propofol, dexmedetomidine). It is generally recommended to administer and optimize analgesia first.</u> Fentanyl is the preferred drug for achieving rapid analgesia. Benzodiazepines, propofol and dexmedetomidine are the recommended drugs for sedation. Midazolam is preferred for rapid achievement of sedation. Propofol is generally preferred for procedural sedation and when rapid awakening is desired. Benzodiazepines may be administered as either intermittent bolus doses or by continuous infusion. Propofol is administered by continuous infusion. <u>Care should be taken to limit the dose and duration of propofol due to the risk of propofol-related infusion syndrome, which can result in cardiac arrhythmias and death.</u> Dexmedetomidine produces a less sedating, more sleep-like state. It has been associated with fewer days of mechanical ventilation and less incidence of delirium, but it is significantly more expensive than benzodiazepines and propofol. A full discussion and review on opioids can be found in the Pain chapter, benzodiazepines are discussed in the Anxiety chapter, and antipsychotics can be found in the Schizophrenia chapter. Drugs such as ketamine may also be used, although there is a general lack of experience and evidence to support its routine use for ICU sedation. A brief review of several of these agents is found below.

<u>A tested and validated sedation scale should be used to frequently assess patient response to therapy and needs for continued therapy since requirements for treating agitation fluctuate over time.</u> Some commonly used sedation scales include the Richmond Agitation Seda-

tion Scale (RASS), the Ramsay Agitation Scale (RAS), and the Riker Sedation-Agitation Scale (SAS). Patients are monitored generally every 2-3 hours while receiving a sedation protocol to make sure patients are receiving the minimal amount of drug(s) to keep them calm and pain-free. Many ICUs have sedation protocols that are based on validated assessment tools. Daily interruptions of continuous infusions of sedative drugs have also been recommended to limit the duration of mechanical ventilation, doses of drugs administered, and length of ICU stay. Delirium may occur in critically ill patients and may be secondary to several factors, including drugs used for sedation and analgesia. Assessment for delirium is usually performed using the Confusion Assessment Method (or CAM-ICU). There is little evidence to support the use of haloperidol for ICU delirium, although this practice is commonplace. The ACCM guidelines recommend that patients with delirium be sedated with dexmedetomidine as opposed to benzodiazepines, as this may shorten the duration of the delirium.

Agents Used for ICU Sedation and Agitation

DRUG	DOSING	SAFETY/SIDE EFFECTS/MONITORING
LORazepam *(Ativan, LORazepam Intensol)*	LD: 0.02-0.04 mg/kg IV push (max 2 mg) MD: 0.02-0.06 mg/kg IV Q2-6H PRN or an infusion 0.01-0.1 mg/kg/hr (max 10 mg/hr)	**CONTRAINDICATIONS** Acute narrow angle glaucoma, sleep apnea **WARNINGS** Withdrawal symptoms may occur following abrupt discontinuation or large decreases in dose **SIDE EFFECTS** Respiratory depression, oversedation, hypotension, propylene glycol poisoning at high doses and prolonged infusions (look for metabolic acidosis and renal insufficiency) **MONITORING** BP, HR, sedation scale **NOTES** Mixed in D5W only Inexpensive, used for long-term sedation (> 48 hours), no active metabolite, longer t½ than midazolam Causes anterograde amnesia

Agents Used for ICU Sedation and Agitation Continued

DRUG	DOSING	SAFETY/SIDE EFFECTS/MONITORING
Midazolam	LD: 0.01- 0.05 mg/kg IV push MD: 0.02 – 0.1 mg/kg/hr	**BLACK BOX WARNINGS (3)** May cause severe respiratory depression, respiratory arrest, or apnea Start at lower end of dosing range in debilitated patients and geriatric population Do not administer by rapid IV infusion in neonates **CONTRAINDICATIONS** Intrathecal or epidural administration due to benzoyl alcohol in the formulation, acute narrow angle glaucoma, concurrent use of potent CYP3A4 inhibitors **WARNINGS** Withdrawal symptoms may occur following abrupt discontinuation or large decreases in dose **SIDE EFFECTS** Respiratory depression, apnea, oversedation, hypotension **MONITORING** BP, HR, sedation scale **NOTES** Many drug interactions (major 3A4 substrate), ↑ levels with 3A4 inhibitors; active metabolite accumulates in renal failure Used for short-term sedation (< 48 hours), shorter acting than lorazepam if patient has preserved organ function (no hepatic or renal impairment or CHF), drug is highly lipophilic and may accumulate in obese patients, has active metabolite that accumulates in renal dysfunction Causes anterograde amnesia
Propofol *(Diprivan)*	Initial: 5 mcg/kg/min over 5 min Maintenance: 5-50 mcg/kg/min	**CONTRAINDICATIONS** Hypersensitivity to egg, egg product, soy and soy product **SIDE EFFECTS** Hypotension, apnea, hypertriglyceridemia, green urine, propofol-related infusion syndrome (PRIS – rare but can be fatal) myoclonus, pancreatitis, pain on injection (particularly peripheral vein) **MONITORING** BP, respiration, triglycerides (if on longer than 2 days), signs and symptoms of pancreatitis, sedation scale **NOTES** Shake well before use. Use strict aseptic technique due to potential for bacterial growth. Discard vial and tubing within 12 hours of use. If transferred to a syringe prior to administration, must discard syringe within 6 hours. Do not use if there is separation of phases in the emulsion. Do not use filter of < 5 microns for administration Formulated in a lipid emulsion (provides 1.1 kcal/mL)

Agents Used for ICU Sedation and Agitation Continued

DRUG	DOSING	SAFETY/SIDE EFFECTS/MONITORING
Dexmedetomidine (Precedex) Alpha$_2$-adrenergic agonist	LD: 0.5-1 mcg/kg over 10 minutes (may be omitted) MD: 0.2-1.4 mcg/kg/hr for 24 hours	**WARNINGS** Use with caution in patients with hepatic impairment, diabetes, heart block, bradycardia, severe ventricular dysfunction, hypovolemia or chronic hypertension **SIDE EFFECTS** Transient hypertension during loading dose (may need to ↓ infusion rate), hypotension, bradycardia, dry mouth, nausea **MONITORING** BP, HR, sedation scale **NOTES** Mix with NS only Used for sedation in intubated and non-intubated patients. Duration of infusion should not exceed 24 hours per manufactuer labeling. Patients are arousable and alert when stimulated; causes less respiratory depression than other sedatives
Morphine	LD: 2-4 mg IV push MD: 2-30 mg/hr	**SIDE EFFECTS** Respiratory depression, hypotension, oversedation, bradycardia, pruritus, xerostomia, constipation **MONITORING** BP, HR, respiratory status, sedation/pain scale **NOTES** Has an active metabolite (morphine-6-glucuronide) which can accumulate in renal impairment; causes histamine release, preferred agent in patients who are hemodynamically stable
FentaNYL	LD: 25-50 mcg IV push MD: 0.7-10 mcg/kg/hr	**SIDE EFFECTS** Respiratory depression, bradycardia, oversedation, constipation, rigidity with high doses **MONITORING** BP, HR, respiratory status, sedation/pain scale **NOTES** Less hypotension than morphine due to no histamine release. Fast onset of action and short duration of action. 100 times more potent than morphine. Preferred agent in patients with unstable hemodynamics
HYDROmorphone (Dilaudid)	LD: 0.2-0.6 mg IV push MD: 0.5-3 mg/hr	**SIDE EFFECTS** Respiratory depression, oversedation **MONITORING** BR, HR, respiratory status, sedation/pain scale **NOTES** No active metabolites; not commonly used for ICU sedation

Agents Used for ICU Sedation and Agitation Continued

DRUG	DOSING	SAFETY/SIDE EFFECTS/MONITORING
Remifentanil *(Ultiva)*	LD: 1.5 mcg/kg over 1 min MD: 0.5-15 mcg/kg/hr	**CONTRAINDICATION** Intrathecal and epidural administration due to glycine in the formulation **SIDE EFFECTS** Nausea, vomiting, bradycardia, hypotension, respiratory depression, oversedation, pruritus **MONITORING** BR, HR, respiratory status, sedation/pain scale **NOTES** Metabolized by tissue esterases, no accumulation in renal/hepatic failure Use IBW if TBW > 130% of IBW
Haloperidol *(Haldol)*	0.5-10 mg IV push; may repeat Q15-30 minutes until calm, then administer 25% of last dose Q6H	**CONTRAINDICATIONS** Parkinson disease, severe CNS depression, coma **SIDE EFFECTS** Hypotension, QT prolongation, tachycardia, extrapyramidal symptoms (EPS), anticholinergic effects, neuroleptic malignant syndrome, esophageal dysmotility/aspiration, hyperprolactinemia, temperature regulation **MONITORING** QT interval and ECG, extrapyramidal symptoms (EPS), abnormal involuntary movements, vital signs **NOTES** Not to be given via continuous infusion Use for delirium in ICU patients is not recommended by recent guidelines due to lack of data

Acid-Base Homeostasis

An acid is a substance that can <u>donate</u> protons, or H^+ ions. A base is a substance that can <u>accept</u> protons. The degree of acidity is expressed as pH, or the negative logarithm (base 10) of the hydrogen ion concentration. Hence, the hydrogen ion concentration and pH are inversely related.

The normal pH of blood is 7.4 (range 7.35-7.45). The primary buffering system of the body is the bicarbonate/carbonic acid system. The kidneys help to maintain a neutral pH by controlling bicarbonate (HCO_3^-) resorption and elimination. The normal bicarbonate level is 24 mEq/L (range 22-26 mEq/L). The lungs help maintain a neutral pH by controlling carbonic acid (which is directly proportional to the partial pressure of carbon dioxide – pCO_2) retained or released from the body. The normal partial pressure of carbon dioxide is 40 mmHg (range 35-45 mmHg). Bicarbonate acts as a buffer and a base, whereas carbon dioxide acts as a buffer and an acid. Alterations from the normal values lead to acid-base disorders. Diet and cellular metabolism lead to a large production of H^+ ions that need to be excreted to maintain acid-base balance. The acid-base status of a patient can be determined by an arterial blood gas (ABG).

ABG: $pH/pCO_2/pO_2/HCO_3^-/O_2$ Sat

An acid-base disorder that leads to a pH < 7.35 is called an acidosis. If the disorder leads to a pH > 7.45 is called an alkalosis. These disorders are classified as either metabolic or respiratory in origin. For example, the primary disturbance in a metabolic acid-base disorder is the plasma HCO_3^- (bicarbonate) concentration. A metabolic acidosis is characterized primarily by a decrease in plasma HCO_3^- concentration whereas, in a metabolic alkalosis, the plasma HCO_3^- concentration is increased. Metabolic acidosis may be associated with an increase in the anion gap (difference in positive and negatively charged ions). The anion gap (AG) is calculated by $Na^+ - (Cl^- + HCO_3^-)$. An elevated anion gap metabolic acidosis is usually associated with an anion gap >12 (the anion gap calculation is in the Calculations chapter). In respiratory acidosis, the pCO_2 is primarily elevated and in respiratory alkalosis, the pCO_2 is decreased. Each disturbance has a compensatory (secondary) response that attempts to correct the imbalance toward normal and keep the pH neutral.

Some etiologies of acid/base disorders

- Metabolic acidosis

  ❑ Non-elevated anion gap – renal tubular acidosis, diarrhea, administration of acidic substances

  ❑ Elevated anion gap – cyanide, uremia, toluene, ethanol (alcoholic ketoacidosis), diabetic ketoacidosis, isoniazid, methanol, propylene glycol, lactic acidosis, ethylene glycol, salicylates (CUTE DIMPLES)

- Metabolic alkalosis – loop and thiazide diuretics, high dose penicillins, vomiting, cystic fibrosis

- Respiratory acidosis – opioids, sedatives, anesthetics, stroke, asthma/COPD

- Respiratory alkalosis – pain, fever, brain tumors, salicylates, catecholamines, theophylline

Treatment of acid-base disorders is always to stop the offending agent or cause (e.g., stop the drug or stop vomiting and assist respiration). In treating metabolic acidosis, sodium bicarbonate may be used to raise pH to ≥ 7.20, although there is no benefit in morbidity and mortality compared to general supportive care. Severe metabolic alkalosis may be treated using hydrochloric acid – this is rarely done.

ELECTROLYTE DISORDERS IN THE ICU

Sodium

Normal sodium concentrations in the blood range from 135-145 mEq/L. Sodium homeostasis is maintained with serum osmolality 275-290 mOsm/kg H_2O. Changes in serum sodium are usually from changes in water concentration.

Hyponatremia

Hyponatremia (Na < 135 mEq/L) may develop from many causes.

- Hypertonic – is a state in which serum osmolality is increased and is caused by hyperglycemia or use of hypertonic solutions that do not contain sodium.

- Isotonic – has normal osmolality and can be associated with hyperlipidemia.

- Hypotonic – may occur with changes in volume status:

  - Hypovolemic (diuretic use, salt-wasting syndromes, adrenal insufficiency, blood loss, vomiting/diarrhea). The treatment is typically to correct the underlying cause and to administer saline solutions. 3% NaCl may be necessary if Na <120 mEq/L or if severe symptoms are present. Refer to the Medication Safety chapter for ways to reduce the risk associated with the use of hypertonic saline.

  - Hypervolemic is caused by fluid overload, usually with cirrhosis, heart failure, or renal failure. Diuresis with fluid restriction is the preferred treatment.

  - Isovolemic (euvolemic) is usually caused by the syndrome of inappropriate antidiuretic hormone (SIADH). This results in the normal excretion of sodium with impaired free-water excretion by the kidney. Treatment for SIADH is usually directed to water restriction, and in some cases diuresis.

Conivaptan or tolvaptan may be used to treat SIADH. These drugs antagonize arginine vasopressin receptors (vasopressin V2-receptor antagonists), resulting in excretion of free water and maintenance of sodium. These drugs should be used with caution in patients with heart failure and should be avoided in patients with hypotension or hypovolemia.

DRUG	DOSE	SAFETY/SIDE EFFECTS/MONITORING
Conivaptan (*Vaprisol*)	LD: 20 mg IV over 30 minutes MD: 20 mg IV continuous infusion over 24 hours (0.83 mg/hr). Do not exceed 4 days.	**CONTRAINDICATIONS** Allergy to corn/corn products, hypovolemic hyponatremia, concurrent use with strong 3A4 inhibitors, anuria **SIDE EFFECTS** Orthostatic hypotension, fever, hypokalemia **MONITORING** Rate of serum Na$^+$ increase, BP, volume status, urine output **NOTES** Do not use if CrCl < 30 mL/min

Hyponatremia Continued

DRUG	DOSE	SAFETY/SIDE EFFECTS/MONITORING
Tolvaptan (*Samsca*)	15 mg PO daily; max 60 mg PO daily; for up to 30 days due to hepatotoxicity	**BLACK BOX WARNINGS (2)** Should be initiated and re-initiated in a hospital under close monitoring of serum Na$^+$ Too rapid correction of hyponatremia (> 12 mEq/L/24 hours) can be life-threatening **CONTRAINDICATIONS** Patients who are unable to sense or respond appropriately to thirst, hypovolemic hyponatremia, concurrent use with strong 3A4 inhibitors, anuria **SIDE EFFECTS** Thirst, nausea, dry mouth, asthenia, constipation, polyuria, hyperglycemia **MONITORING** Rate of serum Na$^+$ increase, BP, volume status, urine output; signs of drug-induced hepatotoxicity **NOTES** Not recommended if CrCl < 10 mL/min

Hypernatremia

Hypernatremia (Na > 145 mEq/L) is associated with a water deficit and hypertonicity.

- Hypovolemic is caused by dehydration, vomiting, diarrhea and is usually treated with dextrose to replace free water deficits and hypotonic solutions (0.45% NaCl).

- Hypervolemic is caused by administration of hypertonic solutions. Diuresis is usually the treatment of choice in these patients, with administration of 5% dextrose.

- Isovolemic (euvolemic) is frequently caused by diabetes insipidus (DI). DI can be central (impaired release of antidiuretic hormone) or nephrogenic (impaired response to antidiuretic hormone). Treatment of central DI includes use of desmopressin (either intranasally or subcutaneously). Nephrogenic DI may be treated by removing any causative medications and the use of hydrochlorothiazide or indomethacin.

Caution should be taken in treating patients with sodium disorders to prevent correcting too quickly. Corrections of sodium > 12 mEq/L over 24 hours have been associated with development of central pontine myelinosis, a devastating neurologic complication that can lead to quadriparesis, seizures, and death.

Potassium

Treatment of hyperkalemia is discussed in the Renal Disease and Dosing Considerations chapter. Hypokalemia (K < 3.5 mEq/L) is a common occurrence in the ICU. Management includes treating the underlying cause (e.g., metabolic alkalosis, overdiuresis) and administering oral or IV potassium. The oral route is preferred when available. IV potassium should be administered no faster than 10-20 mEq/hr with intermittent doses. Concentrations above 80 mEq/L should be administered through a central line.

Stress Ulcer Prophylaxis

Stress ulcers can result from the metabolic stress experienced by a patient in an intensive care unit (ICU). Patients with critical illness have reduced blood flow to the gut as blood flow is diverted to the major organs of the body. This results in a breakdown of gastric mucosal defense mechanisms including prostaglandin synthesis, bicarbonate production, and cell turnover.

Histamine H$_2$ receptor antagonists (H$_2$RAs) and proton pump inhibitors (PPIs) are the recommended agents to use for prevention of stress-related mucosal damage. H$_2$RAs can cause some adverse events such as thrombocytopenia, mental status changes (in the elderly or those with renal/hepatic impairment), and tachyphylaxis. PPIs have been associated with an increase risk of GI infections *(C. difficile)*, fractures and nosocomial pneumonia. These agents are fully discussed in the GERD and PUD chapters. Patients without risk factors for stress ulcers should not receive stress ulcer prophylaxis (see risk factors in the box above).

RISK FACTORS FOR THE DEVELOPMENT OF STRESS ULCERS
Mechanical ventilation
Coagulopathy
Sepsis
Traumatic brain injury
Burn patients
Acute renal failure
High dose corticosteroids

Venous Thromboembolism Prophylaxis

Venous thromboembolism (VTE) is a clinical manifestation of a deep vein thrombosis (DVT) and/or a pulmonary embolism (PE). DVTs can travel to the pulmonary arteries and cause a PE, which can be fatal. Many patients in the intensive care unit are at high risk of developing a DVT and/or PE.

The CHEST guidelines provide specific recommendations for the prevention of VTE depending on the level of risk and specific indication or type of surgery. Non-pharmacologic therapy consists of intermittent pneumatic compression (IPC) devices, graduated compression stockings (GCS), and/or the use of a venous foot pump (VFP). Drugs and their respective doses for VTE prophylaxis are below. A complete review of these agents can be found in the Anticoagulation chapter.

RISK FACTORS FOR THE DEVELOPMENT OF VENOUS THROMBOEMBOLISM	
Surgery	Erythropoietin-stimulating agents
Major trauma or lower extremity injury	Acute medical illness
Immobility	Inflammatory bowel disease
Cancer or chemotherapy	Nephrotic syndrome
Venous compression (tumor, hematoma arterial abnormaility)	Myeloproliferative disorders
Previous venous thromboembolism	Paroxysmal nocturnal hemoglobinuria
Increasing age	Obesity
Pregnancy and postpartum period	Central venous catheterization
Estrogen-containing medications or selective estrogen receptor modulators	Inherited or acquired thrombophilia

DRUG	DOSE
Low dose unfractionated heparin (LDUH)	5,000 units SC BID-TID
Low Molecular Weight Heparin (LMWH)	Enoxaparin 30 mg SC BID or 40 mg SC daily
	(If CrCl < 30 mL/min, give 30 mg SC daily)
	Dalteparin 2,500 – 5,000 units SC daily
Factor Xa inhibitor	Fondaparinux 2.5 mg SC daily (Do not use if CrCl < 30 mL/min or patient weighs < 50 kg)
	Rivaroxaban 10 mg PO daily (Do not use in patients with CrCl < 30 mL/min)

ADDITIONAL DRUGS USED IN THE ICU/OR

Anesthetics

Anesthetics are used for a variety of effects including numbing of an area (local anesthesia), to block pain (regional anesthesia), or to cause a reversible loss of consciousness and sleepiness during surgery (general anesthesia). Anesthetics can be given via several routes of administration: topical, inhaled, intravenously, epidural or spinal. More increasingly, anesthetics are being used concomitantly with opioids to reduce the amount of opiates a patient requires for pain control. They work by blocking the initiation and conduction of nerve impulses by decreasing the neuronal permeability to sodium ions. Patients receiving anesthetics must be continuously monitored to make sure the body is functioning properly (continuous vital sign monitoring, respiratory monitoring, and others).

The main side effects of anesthetics include hypotension, bradycardia, nausea and vomiting and a mild drop in body temperature that can cause shivering. Inhaled anesthetics can cause malignant hyperthemia (rare) and should be treated with dantrolene. Some patients may have allergic reactions to anesthesia. These drugs, if given too often or in too high of a dose, can cause respiratory depression and cardiac arrest. Below are some commonly used anesthetics.

- Topical, local – lidocaine *(Xylocaine)*, benzocaine

- Inhaled – desflurane *(Suprane)*, sevoflurane *(Ultane)*, isoflurane *(Forane)*, nitrous oxide, others

- Injectable – bupivacaine *(Marcaine, Sensorcaine)*, lidocaine *(Xylocaine)*, ropivacaine *(Naropin)*, others

Epidurals containing bupivacaine can quickly be fatal if given via the intravenous route. Do not give bupivacaine epidurals via IV infusion.

Neuromuscular Blocking Agents (NMBAs)

These agents cause skeletal muscle paralysis. Patients may require the use of a paralytic agent in certain scenarios such as to facilitate mechanical intubation, manage increased intracranial pressure, treat muscle spasms (tetany) and prevent shivering in patients undergoing therapeutic hypothermia after cardiac arrest. The use of NMBAs is typically recommended when other methods have been proven ineffective; they are not to be routinely used in critically ill patients. These agents do not provide sedation or analgesia. Therefore, patients should receive adequate sedation and analgesia prior to starting a NMBA. Patients must be mechanically ventilated as these agents paralyze the diaphragm. These are considered high risk medications by ISMP. All NMBAs should be labeled with bright red auxiliary labels stating "WARNING, PARALYZING AGENT".

There are 2 types of NMBAs – depolarizing and non-depolarizing. Succinylcholine is the only available depolarizing agent and is typically reserved for intubation. It is not used for continuous neuromuscular blockade. Succinylcholine has been rarely associated with causing malignant hyperthermia (particularly with the use of inhaled anesthetics). Resembling acetylcholine, succinylcholine binds to and activates the acetylcholine receptors and desensitizes them. The non-depolarizing NMBAs work by binding to the acetylcholine receptor and blocking the actions of endogenous acetylcholine.

DRUG	SAFETY/SIDE EFFECTS/MONITORING
Non-depolarizing NMBAs	**SIDE EFFECTS** Flushing, bradycardia, hypotension, tachyphylaxis, acute quadriplegic myopathy syndrome (AQMS) with long-term use **MONITORING** Peripheral nerve stimulator to assess depth of paralysis [also called train-of-four (TOF)], vital signs (BP, HR, RR)
Atracurium	Short t½; intermediate acting; metabolized by Hofmann elimination
Cisatracurium (Nimbex)	Short t½; intermediate acting; metabolized by Hofmann elimination
Pancuronium	Long-acting agent, can accumulate in renal or hepatic dysfunction, ↑ HR
Rocuronium (Zemuron)	Intermediate-acting agent
Vecuronium	Intermediate-acting agent; can accumulate in renal or hepatic dysfunction

Hemostatic Agents

With most surgeries there is minimal blood loss. In some cases, patients have hemostatic abnormalities, or may develop conditions in surgery that result in unexpected blood loss. In other cases, trauma produces acute blood loss, or emergency surgery is required in patients receiving drugs that increase bleeding risk.

The term "hemostasis" means causing bleeding to stop. A variety of hemostatic methods can be used, ranging from simple manual pressure with one finger to electrical tissue cauterization, or the systemic administration of blood products (transfusions) or "hemostatic" agents.

Previously, the primary treatment for intra-operative bleeding was transfusions. Transfusion with blood products is costly and has safety risks, including possible transmission of infectious diseases, allergic reactions and a high risk for drug-related errors. Partially due to interminable wars, the need developed for better agents to reduce blood loss. In warfare, the core is better protected than previously (in the gear of US soldiers); a soldier may lose a limb, but not die, and consequently require management to reduce the blood loss. Over the last decade, the number of effective hemostatic agents has increased dramatically.

The systemic hemostatic drugs work by inhibiting fibrinolysis or enhancing coagulation. Aminocaproic acid binds to plasminogen, blocking binding to fibrin. Tranexamic acid inhibits conversion of plasminogin to plasmin. Recombinant factor VIIa activates the extrinsic pathway of the coagulation cascade, increasing the conversion of prothrombin to thrombin.

Topical agents are now routinely carried by the military, law enforcement, and are used in inpatient and outpatient settings, including some formulations available in the community setting.

Systemic Hemostatic Agents

DRUG	SAFETY/SIDE EFFECTS/MONITORING
Aminocaproic acid (*Amicar*) Tablet, solution, injection	**CONTRAINDICATIONS** Disseminated intravascular coagulation (without heparin); evidence of an active intravascular clotting process **SIDE EFFECTS** Injection-site reactions, thrombosis **NOTES** FDA-approved for excessive bleeding associated with cardiac surgery, liver cirrhosis, and urinary fibrinolysis Do not use in patients with active clotting process
Tranexamic acid (*Cyklokapron*, injectable) (*Lysteda*, oral)	**CONTRAINDICATIONS** Acquired defective color vision, active intravascular clotting, subarachnoid hemorrhage, previous or current thromboembolic disease (oral) **SIDE EFFECTS** Injection: vascular occlusion, thrombosis Oral: retinal clotting **NOTES** FDA-approved for hemophilia-associated bleeding and cyclic heavy menstrual bleeding (menorrhagia)
Recombinant Factor VIIa (*NovoSeven RT*) Injection	**BLACK BOX WARNING** Risk of thrombotic events, particularly when used off-label **NOTES** FDA-approved for hemophilia and factor VII deficiency; has been used successfully for patients with hemorrhage from trauma and warfarin-related bleeding events

Topical Agents: There are many and most are used surgically. These include thrombin in bandages, liquids and spray forms, fibrin sealants, acrylates and a few others.

Intravenous Immunoglobulin (IVIG)

Intravenous immune globulin (IVIG or IGIV) contains pooled immunoglobulin (IgG), administered intravenously. The IgG is extracted from the plasma of a thousand or more blood donors (this is the FDA's minimum; typically the IVIG is derived from between 3,000-10,000 donors). IVIG is given as a plasma protein replacement therapy (IgG) for immune deficient patients who have decreased or abolished antibody production capabilities. Antibodies, which are produced by B cells, recognize a unique part of a foreign target called antigens – typically, on bacteria and viruses. Initially, IVIG was used only for immunodeficiency conditions. Currently, IVIG has

several FDA-approved indications, including primary humoral immunodeficiency, idiopathic thrombocytopenia purpura (ITP), chronic lymphocytic leukemia (CLL), Kawasaki syndrome, chronic inflammatory demyelinating polyneuropathy, and multifocal motor neuropathy. In addition, IVIG is used for a variety of off-label indications, with varying results. The majority of IVIG use today is as an antiinflammatory agent and has been tried in conditions such as SLE and rheumatoid arthritis. Recent reports cite efficacy for certain pain syndromes, possible benefit in Alzheimer's disease and many other conditions.

DRUG	DOSING	SAFETY/SIDE EFFECTS/MONITORING
Intravenous immunoglobulin (*Carimune NF, Bivigam, Flebogamma DIF, Gammagard, Gammagard S/D, Gammaked, Gammaplex, Gamunex C, Octagam, Privigen*)	400 mg/kg – 2,000 mg/kg per IV infusion; dose and interval depend on indication. Use IBW to calculate dose Use slower infusion rate in renal and cardiovascular disease	**BLACK BOX WARNINGS (2)** Acute renal dysfunction can rarely occur and has been associated with fatalities; usually within 7 days of use (more likely with products stabilized with sucrose). Use with caution in the elderly, patients with renal disease, diabetes mellitus, volume depletion, sepsis, paraproteinemia, and nephrotoxic medications due to risk of renal dysfunction. Thrombosis may occur with IVIG products even in the absence of risk factors. For patients at risk, administer at the minimum dose and infusion rate practicable. Ensure adequate hydration, monitor of signs and symptoms of thrombosis and assess blood viscosity in patients at risk for hyperviscosity. **CONTRAINDICATIONS** IgA deficiency (can use product with lowest amount of IgA) **WARNINGS** Use with caution in patients with cardiovascular disease (use isotonic products and low infusion rate) **SIDE EFFECTS** Fever, nausea, chills, hypotension, flushing, headache, myalgias, chest pain, tachycardia Renal failure, aseptic meningitis, hemolysis, neutropenia, thromboembolic disorders and anaphylaxis are rare but serious **MONITORING** Renal function, urine output, volume status, hgb **NOTES** Patients should be asked about past IVIG infusions, including product used and any reactions that occurred The pharmacy must keep track of IVIG lot numbers used for each patient

RESOURCES

Intravenous Compatibilities

Trissel's Handbook on Injectable Drugs and the *King Guide* to Parenteral Admixtures are commonly-used sources for IV drug compatibility.

Instability: occurs when a product/solution is modified because of storage conditions (e.g., time, temperature, light, absorption). A product is considered unstable when it loses more than 10% of its labeled potency from the time of preparation.

Incompatibility: occurs when one product is mixed or combined with another and changes occur that make the product unsuitable for patient use (e.g., degradation, precipitation, a change in pH).

There are 4 different types of tables listed in *Trissel's* – solution compatibility, additive compatibility, drugs in syringe compatibility, and y-site injection compatibility.

PHOTOSENSITIVE DRUGS

Some drugs are sensitive to light rays and may be broken down into inactive forms. These drugs require protection from light. Some light-sensitive drugs are available in packaging that is light-resistant. Drugs that do not come in such packaging may be protected by an amber or light-resistant bag. Below is a list of intravenous medications that require protection from light.

Amiodarone	Levothyroxine
Amphotericin	Linezolid
Ceftriaxone	Methylprednisolone
Cefepime	Metronidazole
Ciprofloxacin	Micafungin
Dopamine	Norepinephrine
Doxycycline	Ondansetron
Epinephrine	Pentamidine
Fentanyl	Phytonadione
Furosemide	Sulfamethoxazole/ Trimethoprim
Hydrocortisone	
Hydromorphone	Sodium nitroprusside
Levofloxacin	

Trissel's Handbook Example: Using Dopamine as an example

Look up dopamine (the drugs are listed in alphabetical order by generic name). There are pages of different charts for dopamine depending on how the drugs will be mixed (solution compatibility, additive compatibility, y-site compatibility, etc.). Find the correct chart to reference. Match the product information exactly to the product information listed in the reference. The last column will tell you if the drugs are compatible (listed as C) or incompatible (listed as I). The information is referenced so you can pull the trial information, if needed.

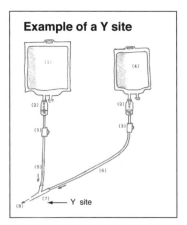

Example of a Y site

Y site

Additive Compatibility

DRUG*	MFR*	CON/L*	MFR	CONC/L	TEST SOLN	REMARKS	REF	C/I
Ciprofloxacin	MI	2 g		400 mg	NS	C for 24 hrs at 25°C	888	C

Y-Site Injection Compatibility (1:1 Mixture)

DRUG*	MFR*	CON/L*	MFR	CONC/L	REMARKS	REF	C/I
Cefepime	BMS	20 mg/mL	AST	3.2 mg/mL	Haze and precipitate form in 1 hr	1689	I
	BMS	120 mg/mL		0.4 mg/mL	Physically compatible with < 10% cefepime loss	2513	C
Heparin	ES	100 units/mL	AB	3.2 mg/mL	Visually compatible for 4 hr at 27°C	2062	C

*Info on the test drug (e.g., ciprofloxacin, cefepime, heparin)

Select IV Medications Requiring Filtration During Administration

DRUG	FILTER SIZE (MICRON)
Abatacept (Orencia)	0.22-1.2
Abciximab (ReoPro)	0.22
Albumin	15 – dispensed with filter tubing
Amiodarone (Cordarone)	0.22
Amphotericin B Liposomal (AmBisome)	≥ 1
Antithymocyte Globulin, (Thymoglobin, ATGAM)	0.22
Diazepam (Valium)	0.22 or 0.5
Digoxin Immune Fab (DigiFab)	0.22
Infliximab (Remicade)	≤ 1.2
Lipids	1.2 – dispensed with filter tubing
Lorazepam (Ativan)	0.22
Mannitol (Osmitrol)	0.22
Muromonab CD3 (Orthoclone OKT 3)	0.22
Phenytoin (Dilantin)	0.22
Parenteral Nutrition (without lipids)	0.22

Select Oncology Drugs

Asparaginase (Elspar)	5
Cetuximab (Erbitux)	0.22
Etoposide (VePesid, Toposar)	0.22
Gemtuzumab (Mylotarg)	1.2
Ibritumomab (Zevalin)	0.22

Select IV Medications Requiring Filtration During Administration Continued

DRUG	FILTER SIZE (MICRON)
Ixabepilone *(Ixempra)*	0.22-1.2 – non-PVC tubing
Paclitaxel *(Taxol)*	≤ 0.22 – non-PVC tubing
Panitumumab *(Vectibix)*	0.22
Temsirolimus *(Torisel)*	≤ 5 – non-PVC tubing

IV Agents that Should not be Refrigerated

Most IV medications, whether ready-to-use or prepared in the pharmacy, are refrigerated when sent to the patient care area. The drugs in the table to the right should not be refrigerated.

IV AGENTS THAT SHOULD NOT BE REFRIGERATED
metronidazole *(Flagyl)*
sulfamethoxazole/trimethoprim *(Bactrim)*
phenylephrine *(Neosynephrine)*
hydralazine, moxifloxacin *(Avelox)*
acetaminophen *(Ofirmev)*
esomeprazole *(Nexium)*

Poisoning and Antidotes

Antidotes reverse the toxicity of a poison, which could be a prescription drug or other substance. Ingestion of the toxic substance can be intentional, such as an acetaminophen overdose used in a suicide attempt, or be unintentional, such as farmworker exposure to organophosphate pesticides.

Childhood Poisoning

Children can have overdose from just one tablet of some common medications. The most toxic substances to a small child include iron, hypoglycemics (including sulfonylureas), cardiovascular drugs (including beta blockers and other drugs that lower heart rate), salicylates, anticonvulsants and illicit drugs. Or, the poisoning could be due to common household substances, such as toilet cleanser, furniture polish and antifreeze.

Iron poisoning can result in fatality in young children with as few as 5 iron tablets (depending on the size of the child and the iron salt). Fortunately, repackaged OTC iron formulations have brought down the rate of accidental poisoning. Acetaminophen poisoning is another high-alert OTC for accidental ingestion.

Poisoning Management

Symptoms at the time of presentation should not be considered to be conclusive; some compounds have a delayed reaction or the person could have taken a drug with delayed absorption. In general, treatment is given until blood levels are non-toxic.

Do not guess; <u>consult the poison control center for support</u>, and <u>refer the patient to the hospital emergency department</u> where they can receive rapid triage. Gastric decontamination, such as activated charcoal (which is sometimes used within 1 hour of ingestion) and gastric lavage are <u>no longer routinely recommended</u>. Syrup of ipecac (to induce vomiting) is <u>no longer routinely recommended</u>.

Insecticide Poisoning

Most household bug sprays contain chemicals called pyrethrins, which are not life-threatening. <u>Industrial insecticides are one of the most common causes of poisoning, particularly among farm workers</u>. These are <u>organophosphates, which inhibit acetylcholinesterase</u>, leading to the accumulation of acetylcholine.

The symptoms of organophosphate poisoning are <u>cholinergic</u> and can be remembered by the mnemonic MUDDLES: miosis (pinpoint pupils), urination, diarrhea, diaphoresis, lacrimation, excitation (anxiety) and salivation. The preferred antidote is the anticholinergic atropine, which is sometimes given with pralidoxime although the addition of pralidoxime is not thought to be beneficial. The table below lists common antidotes.

Antidotes for Select Toxicities

DRUG/TOXIC AGENT	ANTIDOTE
Acetaminophen	**N-acetylcysteine**
Anticholinesterase (industrial) insecticides/ organophosphates (nerve agents)	**Atropine**
Anticholinergic compounds	**Physostigmine (Antilirium)**
Arsenic, Lead	Succimer (Chemet)
Benzodiazepines	**Flumazenil (Romazicon)**
Beta Blockers	**Glucagon (GlucaGen)**
Botulism	Botulism antitoxin
Black Widow spider bites	Antivenin (Latrodectus mactans)
Calcium channel blockers	Calcium Chloride 10%, Glucagon
Carbon monoxide	Oxygen
Cyanide	Sodium nitrate, sodium thiosulfate, hydroxycobalamin (Cyanokit)
Digoxin	**Digoxin immune Fab (DigiFab)**
Ethylene glycol, methanol	**Ethanol or fomepizole (Antizol)**
Heavy metals	**Dimercaprol** or penicillamine or calcium disodium edetate
Heparin	**Protamine**
Iron	**Deferoxamine (Desferal)** Deferiprone (Ferriprox) – for iron overload from blood transfusions Deferasirox (Exjade)

Antidotes for Select Toxicities Continued

DRUG/TOXIC AGENT	ANTIDOTE
Isoniazid	**Pyridoxine (Vitamin B6)**
Methemoglobinemia	Methylene Blue
Opioids	**Naloxone (*Narcan*)**
Methotrexate	Glucarpidase, leucovorin, levoleucovorin
Salicylate	Sodium bicarbonate
Snake bites	**Crotalidae polyvalent *(Antivenin, Crofab)***
Scorpion stings	Centruroides immune FAB *(Anascorp)*
TCA's	Sodium bicarbonate
Warfarin, rat poison	**Phytonadione *(AquaMephyton, Mephyton)***
Vasopressors	Phentolamine

QUESTIONS

1. Which of the following statements about colloids is/are true? (Select **ALL** that apply.)

    a. An example is 0.9% sodium chloride
    b. Approximately 25% of the volume remains intravascularly after administration
    c. Significantly more expensive than crystalloids
    d. Have a higher risk of developing pulmonary edema compared to crystalloids.
    e. An example is 25% albumin

2. Which of the following vasopressors is considered first-line in treating patients with sepsis?

    a. Norepinephrine
    b. Vasopressin
    c. Epinephrine
    d. Phenylephrine
    e. Ephedrine

3. Which of the following is an antidote for morphine overdose?

    a. Naloxone
    b. Sodium thiosulfate
    c. Flumazenil
    d. Protamine
    e. Deferoxamine

4. Which of the following acid-base disorders is experienced in a patient with pH 7.25, pCO_2 39, HCO_3^- 18?

    a. Metabolic alkalosis
    b. Respiratory acidosis
    c. Metabolic acidosis
    d. Respiratory alkalosis
    e. None of the above

5. Which of the following is a cause of elevated anion gap metabolic acidosis?

    a. Renal tubular acidosis
    b. Vomiting
    c. Administration of HCl
    d. Diarrhea
    e. Diabetic ketoacidosis

6. Which of the following statements is true regarding neuromuscular blocking agents?

    a. Cisatracurium is a non-depolarizing agent
    b. Patients receiving these drugs do not require sedation/analgesia
    c. These drugs should be used routinely in critically ill patients
    d. NMBAs are not associated with significant adverse effects
    e. NMBAs are monitored using the Ramsay agitation scale

7. Which of the following statements is true regarding dexmedetomidine?

    a. It causes respiratory depression
    b. It induces deep levels of sedation
    c. It may cause urine to turn green
    d. It is associated with more delirium compared to benzodiazepines
    e. It may cause bradycardia

8. Which of the following electrolyte disorders is conivaptan recommended to be used to treat?

    a. Hypovolemic hypotonic hyponatremia
    b. Euvolemic hyponatremia
    c. Hypervolemic hypernatremia
    d. Diabetes insipidus
    e. Euvolemic hypernatremia

9. How much of a change in sodium should be _avoided_ in patients with sodium imbalances?

    a. > 4 mEq/L
    b. > 6 mEq/L
    c. > 10 mEq/L
    d. > 12 mEq/L
    e. > 20 mEq/L

Answers

1-c,e, 2-a, 3-a, 4-c, 5-e, 6-a, 7-e, 8-b, 9-d

48

DEPRESSION

We gratefully acknowledge the assistance of Jeannette Y. Wick, RPh, in preparing this chapter.

BACKGROUND

Major Depressive Disorder (MDD, or referred to here as "depression") is one of the most common health conditions in the world. The statistics are sobering. In any given year, approximately 15 million U.S. citizens will experience an episode of MDD. Although approximately half of these people seek help for this condition, only 20 percent – 10 percent of the total population with MDD – receive adequate treatment, and just 30 percent of those who receive adequate treatment reach the treatment goal of remission. People with depression suffer greatly with persistent feelings of hopelessness, dejection, constant worry, poor concentration, a lack of energy, an inability to sleep and, sometimes, suicidal tendencies.

Healthcare providers should remember that depression is usually a chronic illness that requires long-term treatment, much like diabetes or high blood pressure. Although some people experience only one episode, the majority have recurrent episodes. Recurrent disease generally requires long-term (often life-long) treatment. Effective diagnosis and treatment can reduce even severe depressive symptoms. And with effective treatment, many people with depression feel better, usually within weeks, and can return to the activities they previously enjoyed. A significant treatment problem is patients who discontinue their medication, or, continue medication despite an inadequate response. This is discussed under "Treatment-Resistant Depression." Due to high rates of

GUIDELINES

Institute for Clinical Systems Improvement (ICSI). Major depression in adults in primary care. Bloomington (MN): Institute for Clinical Systems Improvement (ICSI); September 2013.

National Collaborating Centre for Mental Health. Depression. The treatment and management of depression in adults. London (UK): National Institute for Health and Clinical Excellence (NICE); 2010 Aug. (Clinical guideline; no. 90).

Department of Veteran Affairs, Department of Defense. VA/DoD clinical practice guideline for management of major depressive disorder (MDD). Washington (DC): Department of Veteran Affairs, Department of Defense; 2009 May.

Diagnostic and Statistical Manual of Mental Disorders (DSM-5).

inadequate response, pharmacists should attempt to ensure adequate treatment trials: 6-8 weeks, at a therapeutic dose (the VA/DoD guideline recommends an 8-12 week trial).

CAUSES OF DEPRESSION

Depression's causes are poorly understood, but involve some combination of genetic, biologic and environmental factors. We are most concerned with biological factors, since these are treated with medications. Serotonin (5HT) may be the most important neurotransmitter (NT) involved with feelings of well being. Other NTs include acetylcholine (ACh) and catecholamines [including dopamine (DA), norepinephrine (NE), and epinephrine (EPI)]. Recent research has focused on complex or completely novel pathways that may be involved in depression. In patients with resistant symptoms, a recent trial with ketamine produced good results; ketamine interacts with glutamine receptors. The current medications used for treating depression affect the levels of (primarily)

DEPRESSION DIAGNOSIS
DSM-5 criteria includes presence of at least 5 of the following symptoms (even if they are in response to a significant loss like bereavement or financial ruin) during the same two week period (must include symptom 1 or 2):
1. Depressed mood
2. Marked diminished interest/pleasure
3. Significant weight loss or weight gain
4. Insomnia or hypersomnia
5. Psychomotor agitation or retardation
6. Fatigue or loss of energy
7. Feelings of worthlessness
8. Diminished ability to concentrate
9. Recurrent suicidal ideation

5HT, NE and DA. Since it is not possible at this time to measure brain chemical imbalances, treatment for mood disorders, including depression, depends on a competent assessment and trial. If a drug does not work, after a suitable trial of at least 6 – 8 weeks, a combination or different set of NTs can be targeted (see treatment resistance section). Patient history is critical in treating any mental illness; what worked in the past, or did not work, should help guide current and future therapy. Pharmacists should always counsel patients, family and caregivers that mood may worsen; this is essential, since the majority of antidepressants are prescribed by primary care providers, and patient follow-up (after the prescription has been written) rarely occurs. The patient needs instructions on how to respond to worsened mood. This is critical for adolescents and young adults in particular.

CONCURRENT BIPOLAR OR ANXIETY DISORDERS

It is necessary to rule-out bipolar disorder prior to initiating antidepressant therapy in order to treat the patient properly and avoid rapid-cycling (cycling rapidly from one phase to the other). This is why screening forms for MDD now include questions designed to identify mania symptoms such as "There are times when I get into moods where I feel very speeded up or irritable."

Benzodiazepines (BZDs) are often used adjunctively in depression with concurrent anxiety, although in many cases the BZD is the only "treatment" and the depression itself is left untreated. BZDs can cause and/or mask depression and put the patient at risk for physiological dependence and withdrawal symptoms when the dose is wearing off (tachycardia, anxiety, amongst others). Prescribers should also select BZDs carefully and monitor closely if patients have co-occurring substance use disorders.

MEDICATIONS THAT CAN CAUSE OR WORSEN DEPRESSION

Beta-blockers
(particularly propranolol)

Clonidine

Corticosteroids

Cyclosporine

Ethanol

Isotretinoin

Indomethacin

Interferons

Methadone, and possibly other chronic opioid use that can lower testosterone or estrogen levels

Oral contraceptives, anabolic steroids (medication-specific, patient specific)

Methyldopa

Methylphenidate/Other ADHD Stimulants/Atomoxetine: Monitor mood

Procainamide

Reserpine

Statins (patient specific, some cases)

Varenicline

And…antidepressants require monitoring for worsening mood, especially among younger people

---

In addition to the medications listed, medical conditions such as stroke, Parkinson disease, dementia, multiple sclerosis, thyroid disorders (particularly hypothyroidism), low vitamin D levels (possible link), metabolic conditions (e.g., hypercalcemia), malignancy, OAB and infectious diseases can be contributory.

LAG EFFECT AND SUICIDE PREVENTION

Patients should be told that the medicine must be used daily, and will take time to work. It is important to inform the patient that physical symptoms such as low energy improve within a few weeks but psychological symptoms, such as low mood, may take a month or longer. If the medicine does not help, the patient should not despair. If a patient reports suicidal ideation, refer to the ED or elsewhere for help. Do not take these statements lightly; this is a call for help. If someone has a plan to commit suicide, it is more likely that the threat is real.

PHARMACOTHERAPY

Treatment in the acute phase should be aimed at inducing remission of the depressive episode and returning the patient to his or her baseline level of functioning. Acute phase treatment may include pharmacotherapy; depression-focused psychotherapy; the combination of medications and psychotherapy; or other somatic therapies such as electroconvulsive therapy (ECT), vagal nerve stimulation (VNS) or light therapy.

The guidelines state that because the effectiveness of the different antidepressant classes is generally comparable, the initial choice of an agent should be based on the side effect profile, safety concerns and the patient-specific symptoms. For most patients an SSRI, SNRI or (with specific concurrent conditions or considerations) mirtazapine or bupropion is preferred.

Due to safety concerns (the risk of drug-drug and drug-food interactions) the use of the oral nonselective monoamine oxidase inhibitors (MAOIs – phenelzine, tranylcypromine and isocarboxazid) is restricted to patients unresponsive to other treatments. Serotonin syndrome can occur with administration of one or more serotonergic medications (and higher doses increase risk) but it is most severe when an MAOI is administered with another serotonergic medication.

All drug therapy trials should preferably be given with competent, concurrent psychotherapy, although this is not typically done. If a drug is being discontinued it should be tapered off over several weeks. In some instances a drug with a longer half-life (e.g., fluoxetine) can be used to minimize withdrawal symptoms. Withdrawal symptoms (anxiety, agitation, insomnia, dizziness, flu-like symptoms) can be quite distressing to the patient. Paroxetine and some other agents carry a high risk of withdrawal symptoms and must be tapered upon discontinuation.

Treatment-Resistant Depression

Prescribers should supervise a trial of 6-8 weeks at an adequate (therapeutic) dose before concluding that it is not working well. Only about half of patients respond to the prescribed antidepressant and just about one-third will reach remission (the elimination of depressive symptoms). The goal of therapy is remission. An incomplete response can necessitate any of the following:

- A dosage increase.

- A combination of antidepressants (which may or may not be appropriate).

- Augmentation with buspirone *(BuSpar)* or a low dose of an atypical antipsychotic. Agents approved as augmentation therapy with antidepressants are aripiprazole *(Abilify)*, olanzapine + fluoxetine *(Symbyax)* and quetiapine ext-rel *(Seroquel XR)*.

- Other guideline recommendations (as there are several, with various recommendations) include augmentation with lithium, thyroid hormone, and in some cases, electroconvulsive therapy (ECT).

- In 2012, good trial results were reported with the use of ketamine, which suggests alternative mechanisms may be targeted for improved treatment response.

Antidepressant Use in Pregnancy, Postpartum Depression

Untreated maternal depression, especially in the late second or early third trimesters, is associated with increased rates of adverse outcomes (e.g., premature birth, low birth weight, fetal growth restriction, postnatal complications). Depression in pregnant women often goes unrecognized and untreated in part because of safety concerns. All drugs carry risk, and the risk/benefit must be considered individually.

If a woman is on antidepressants and wishes to become pregnant, it may be possible to taper the drug if the depression is mild and she has been symptom-free for the previous six months. In more severe cases, medications may need to be continued, or started. The ACOG guidelines for mild depression in pregnancy recommend psychotherapy first, followed by drug treatment if-needed. SSRIs are often used initially and are pregnancy category C, except for paroxetine, which is D, due to potential cardiac effects. Paroxetine is the most difficult SSRI to discontinue, and requires a slow titration if stopped. The new formulation of paroxetine, *Brisdelle*, is pregnancy category X. Although SSRIs have historically been preferred, in December of 2011 the FDA issued a warning regarding SSRI use during pregnancy and the potential risk of persistent pulmonary hypertension of the newborn (PPHN). Tricyclics, also pregnancy category C, are the second group most commonly used.

Postpartum depression is common but often unrecognized and undertreated, with adverse outcomes for the mother, baby, and family. Breast-feeding is helpful for most women for physical and emotional symptoms, and is considered beneficial for the baby. Drug safety in breastfeeding, therefore, is essential. SSRIs or tricyclics are generally preferred (with the exception of doxepin, per the ACOG recommendations).

Post-Traumatic Stress Disorder (PTSD)

With the recent history of consecutive wars, the mental health of veterans has become a national focus. PTSD can be present after other traumatic events, and is common in a war torn country's civilian population. PTSD is defined by the VA as "the development of characteristic and persistent symptoms, along with difficulty functioning after exposure to a life-threatening experience or to an event that either involves a threat to life or serious injury." Symptoms are many and patient-specific. They include physical complaints (difficulty breathing, hypertension, fainting, fatigue, etc.), cognitive or mental symptoms (confusion, hypervigilance, nightmares, poor attention, etc.), emotional symptoms (agitation, anxiety, depression, fear, guilt, etc.) and behavioral symptoms such as increased drug and alcohol use, impaired sexual function, suspiciousness, social withdrawal, and others.

The FDA has approved the SSRIs sertraline and paroxetine for PTSD, although many others are used off-label. SNNIs are considered to have similar benefit to the SSRIs for PTSD, and there is some benefit with a variety of other classes. However, antipsychotics (as monotherapy or as adjunctive agents), trazodone, clonidine, benzodiazepines, topiramate and others have shown little benefit. The VA/DoD guidelines should be referenced when choosing an agent with possible benefit. As with other conditions, psychotherapy is essential. In cases involving military personnel, it is often preferable to involve others who have experienced similar conflict in the ongoing care/talk therapy of the patient. This is an area where clinicians have been slow to recognize disease severity, and therapy is evolving.

NATURAL PRODUCTS

St. John's wort or SAMe (S-adenosyl-L- methionine) may be helpful. Both are classified as "likely effective" for treating depression in the *Natural Medicines Database*, but there is less evidence of efficacy than with standard treatments. Both agents cannot be used with other serotonergic agents. St. John's wort is a broad-spectrum CYP 450 enzyme inducer and has many significant drug interactions. It is a photosensitizer and is serotonergic; use caution with other 5HT drugs. L-methylfolate *(Deplin)* is a medical food product being used for depression.

Suicide risk in Adolescents and Young Adults: Antidepressants Require a MedGuide that includes this Statement:

The FDA requires pharmacists to give a Medication Guide to all adolescents and young adults or their guardians. It indicates clearly that "antidepressant medicines may increase suicidal thoughts or actions in some children, teenagers, or young adults within the first few months of treatment or when the dose is changed. Prescribers must work closely with families to examine risks and benefits and monitor closely."

SSRIs: Selective Serotonin Reuptake Inhibitors

DRUG	DOSING	SAFETY/SIDE EFFECTS/MONITORING
FLUoxetine *(PROzac, Sarafem, PROzac Weekly)* + OLANZapine *(Symbyax)* – taken QHS, for resistant depression	10-60 mg/day (titrate to 60 mg/d for bulimia) 90 mg weekly 20 mg/5 mL liquid Premenstrual dysphoric disorder (PMDD): *Sarafem* daily, or weekly at 14 and 7 days prior to menses, through 1st full day of bleeding	**BLACK BOX WARNING** Antidepressants increase the risk of suicidal thinking and behavior in children, adolescents, and young adults (18-24 years of age) with major depressive disorder (MDD) and other psychiatric disorders; consider risk prior to prescribing. **CONTRAINDICATIONS** Potentially lethal DI: SSRIs and MAOIs: see wash-out information.
PARoxetine *(Paxil, Pexeva, Paxil CR, Brisdelle)* Preg Cat D *Briselle:* Preg Cat X	IR: 10–60 mg/day CR: 12.5–75 mg/day 10 mg/5mL Each 10 mg IR = 12.5 mg CR	Do not initiate in patients being treated with linezolid or methylene blue IV; concomitant use with pimozide or thioridazine (wait 5 weeks after fluoxetine before starting thioridazine); do not use in pregnancy *(Brisdelle* only). Do not stop suddenly – will get anxiety, insomnia, flu-like withdrawal symptoms. Fluoxetine can be stopped with less of a taper due to long half-life. **SIDE EFFECTS** Sexual side effects: include ↓ libido, ejaculation difficulties, anorgasmia
FluvoxaMINE *(Luvox, Luvox CR)*	100-300 mg/day IR form for OCD only, CR for OCD and SAD (social anxiety disorder) – fluvoxamine has more drug interactions	Somnolence, insomnia, nausea, xerostomia, diaphoresis (dose-related), weakness, tremor, dizziness, headache (but may help for migraines if taken continuously) Fluoxetine can cause activation; take dose in AM, others AM (usually) or PM, if sedating SIADH, hyponatremia (elderly at higher risk) Restless leg syndrome (see if this began when treatment was started)
Sertraline *(Zoloft)*	50-200 mg/day 20 mg/mL liquid Premenstrual dysphoric disorder (PMDD): *Zoloft* 150 mg/d continuously or 100 mg/d during the 2 weeks prior to menses	↑ bleeding risk with concurrent use of anticoagulants, antiplatelets, NSAIDs, gingko, thrombolytics ↑ fall risk; use extreme caution in frail patients, osteopenia/osteoporosis, use of CNS depressants **NOTES** All approved for depression and a variety of anxiety disorders except fluvoxamine.
Citalopram *(Celexa)*	20-40 mg/day 2011 FDA warning not to use > 40 mg/day due to QT risk; Max 20 mg/day with inhibitors	Note FDA warning regarding QT risk and citalopram at > 40 mg/day or > 20 mg/day if 60+ years, if liver disease, with 2C19 poor metabolizers or on 2C19 inhibitors. Similar, but lower risk for escitalopram at > 20 mg/day; do not exceed 10 mg/day in elderly. Bottom line: if cardiac risk better to avoid citalopram. Sertraline is often the top choice for an SSRI in cardiac patients. In 2011, the FDA issued a warning regarding SSRI use during pregnancy and the potential risk of persistent pulmonary hypertension of the newborn (PPHN). SSRIs are pregnancy category C, except paroxetine, which is considered more dangerous, and is D/X *(Briselle).* Citalopram/escitalopram not approved for use in children.
Escitalopram *(Lexapro –* S-enantiomer of citalopram)	10 mg/day (can ↑ 20 mg/d) 1 mg/mL liquid Do not exceed > 20 mg/day due to QT risk; Max 10 mg/day in CYP 2C19 poor metabolizers.	To switch to fluoxetine 90 mg/weekly from fluoxetine daily, start 7 days after last daily dose.

SSRI and Combined Mechanism

DRUG	DOSING	SAFETY/SIDE EFFECTS/MONITORING

SSRI and 5-HT$_{1A}$ Partial Agonist

Vilazodone (*Viibryd*) Dosing to the right is in the patient starter kit.	Titrate to 40 mg/d; start at: 10 mg x 7 days, then 20 mg x 7 days, then 40 mg all with food	**BLACK BOX WARNING** Antidepressants increase the risk of suicidal thinking and behavior in children, adolescents, and young adults (18-24 years of age) with major depressive disorder (MDD) and other psychiatric disorders; consider risk prior to prescribing. **CONTRAINDICATIONS** Potentially lethal drug interaction with MAOIs; see wash-out information. Do not initiate in patients being treated with linezolid or methylene blue IV. **SIDE EFFECTS** Diarrhea, nausea/vomiting, insomnia, ↓ libido (less sexual SEs compared to SSRIs and SNRIs) **NOTES** ↑ bleeding risk with concurrent use of anticoagulants, anti-platelets, NSAIDs, gingko, thrombolytics. Pregnancy Category C

SSRI, 5-HT$_3$, 5-HT$_{1D}$, 5-HT$_7$ Receptor Antagonist; 5-HT$_{1A}$ Agonist; and Partial 5-HT$_{1B}$ Agonist

Vortioxetine (*Brintellex*)	10 mg/d, can ↑ 20 mg/day, with or without food (5 mg/d if higher doses not tolerated)	**BLACK BOX WARNING** Antidepressants increase the risk of suicidal thinking and behavior in children, adolescents, and young adults (18-24 years of age) with major depressive disorder (MDD) and other psychiatric disorders; consider risk prior to prescribing. **CONTRAINDICATIONS** Potentially lethal drug interaction with MAOIs; see washout information. Do not initiate in patients being treated with linezolid or methylene blue IV. **SIDE EFFECTS** Nausea, constipation, vomiting ↑ bleeding risk with concurrent use of anticoagulants, antiplatelets, NSAIDs, gingko, thrombolytics **NOTES** Pregnancy Category C

SSRI Drug Interactions

- MAOIs and hypertensive crisis: allow 2 weeks either going to an MAOI or from an MAOI to an SSRI except fluoxetine which requires a 5 week wash-out period if going from fluoxetine to a MAOI (due to the long half-life of fluoxetine of at least 7 days).

- Fluoxetine: 2D6, 2C19 inhibitor. Fluvoxamine: 1A2, 2D6, 2C9, 2C19, 3A4 inhibitor. Paroxetine: 2D6 inhibitor. Note all three are 2D6 inhibitors and some other psych drugs are 2D6 substrates. Psych drugs are sometimes used in combination.

- Tamoxifen's effectiveness decreases with fluoxetine, paroxetine and sertraline (and duloxetine and bupropion).

- ↑ bleeding risk with concurrent use of anticoagulants, antiplatelets, NSAIDs, gingko, thrombolytics.

- Do not use with thioridazine or pimozide.

- Do not initiate in patients receiving linezolid or methylene blue IV.

- Caution with drugs that cause orthostasis or CNS depressants due to risk of falls.

- FDA warning regarding QT risk and citalopram at > 40 mg/day or > 20 mg if 60+ years, if liver disease, with 2C19 poor metabolizers and on 2C19 inhibitors. Similar, but lower risk for escitalopram at > 20 mg/day; do not exceed 10 mg/day in elderly. Bottom line: if cardiac risk, avoid citalopram. Sertraline is often the top choice for an SSRI in cardiac patients.

SSRI Counseling

- Dispense MedGuide & instruct patient to read it. Especially in adolescents and young adults: counsel on risk of suicide – particularly during therapy initiation.

- Fluoxetine is taken in the morning; the others morning or at bedtime.

- To reduce your risk of side effects, your doctor may direct you to start taking this drug at a low dose and gradually increase your dose.

- Take this medication exactly as prescribed. To help you remember, use it at the same time each day. Antidepressants do not work if they are taken as-needed.

- It is important to continue taking this medication even if you feel well. Do not stop taking this medication without consulting your doctor. Some conditions may become worse when the drug is suddenly stopped. Your dose may need to be gradually decreased.

- It may take 1 to 2 weeks to feel a benefit from this drug and 6-8 weeks to feel the full effect on your mood. Tell the doctor if your condition persists or worsens. You can try a medication in a different class. One will work or it may take different tries to find the right medicine that will help you feel better.

- Some patients, but not all, have sexual difficulties when using this medicine. If this happens, talk with the doctor. They can change you to a medicine that does not cause these problems.

- Sertraline oral concentrate must be diluted before use. Immediately before administration, use the dropper provided to measure the required amount of concentrate; mix with 4 ounces (1/2 cup) of water, ginger ale, lemon/lime soda, lemonade, or orange juice only. Do not use with disulfiram.

SNRIs – Serotonin and Norepinephrine Reuptake Inhibitors

DRUG	DOSING	SAFETY/SIDE EFFECTS/MONITORING
Venlafaxine *(Effexor, Effexor XR)* Depression, GAD	150-375 mg/day Can start low with 37.5 or 75 mg Different generics; check orange book	**BLACK BOX WARNING** Antidepressants increase the risk of suicidal thinking and behavior in children, adolescents, and young adults (18-24 years of age) with major depressive disorder (MDD) and other psychiatric disorders; consider risk prior to prescribing. **CONTRAINDICATIONS** Potentially lethal DI: SNRIs and MAOIs see wash out information. Do not initiate in a patient receiving linezolid or intravenous methylene blue. Duloxetine and levomilnacipran: do not use if uncontrolled narrow angle glaucoma.
DULoxetine *(Cymbalta)* Depression, Peripheral Neuropathy (Pain), Fibromyalgia, GAD, Chronic Low Back Pain, Chronic Osteoarthritis Pain	40-60 mg/day (daily, or 20-30 BID); max dose is 120 mg/day; doses > 60 mg/day not more effective Duloxetine is a good choice if the patient has both pain and depression	**SIDE EFFECTS** Similar to SSRIs (due to serotonin reuptake) and side effects due to ↑ NE uptake: ↑ pulse, dilated pupils, dry mouth, excessive sweating and constipation
Desvenlafaxine *(Pristiq)* Depression	50 mg/day, can ↑ 100 mg/day	SNRIs can affect urethral resistance. Caution is advised when using SNRIs in patients prone to obstructive urinary disorders. All have warning for ↑ BP, but risk is greatest with venlafaxine when dosed > 150 mg/day; yet all have risk especially at higher doses. (↑ BP may respond to dose reduction, use of antihypertensive or change in therapy) ↑ bleeding risk with concurrent use of anticoagulants, antiplatelets, NSAIDs, gingko, thrombolytics
Levomilnacipran *(Fetzima)* Depression	40-120 mg/day Start at 20 mg/day x 2 days Do not open, chew or crush capsules; take whole. Do not take with alcohol.	

SNRI Drug Interactions

- MAOIs and hypertensive crisis: 2 week wash-out if going to or from a MAOI.

- Duloxetine is a 2D6 inhibitor.

- Tamoxifen's effectiveness decreases with duloxetine.

- Do not initiate in patients receiving linezolid or methylene blue IV.

- ↑ bleeding risk with concurrent use of anticoagulants, antiplatelets, NSAIDs, gingko, thrombolytics.

- If on antihypertensive medications, use caution and monitor (can ↑ BP), especially at higher doses.

SNRI Counseling

- Dispense MedGuide and instruct patient to read it. Especially in adolescents and young adults: counsel on risk of suicide – particularly during therapy initiation.

- This medication may cause nausea and stomach upset (if venlafaxine IR can try change to XR).

- You may experience increased sweating; if so, discuss with your doctor. You should check your blood pressure regularly to make sure it stays in a safe range.

- Desvenlafaxine: When you take this medicine, you may see something in your stool that looks like a tablet. This is the empty shell from the tablet after the medicine has been absorbed by your body.

- Levomilnacipran: Take capsules whole. Do not open, chew or crush the capsules. Do not take with alcohol; this could cause the medicine to be released too quickly.

- To reduce your risk of side effects, your doctor may direct you to start taking this drug at a low dose and gradually increase your dose.

- Do not crush or chew extended-release formulations.

- Take this medication exactly as directed. To help you remember, use it at the same time each day. Antidepressants do not work if they are taken as-needed.

- It is important to continue taking this medication even if you feel well. Do not stop taking this medication without consulting your doctor. Some conditions may become worse when the drug is suddenly stopped. Your dose may need to be gradually decreased.

- It may take 1 to 2 weeks to feel a benefit from this drug and 6-8 weeks to feel the full effect on your mood. Tell the doctor if your condition persists or worsens. You can try a medication in a different class. One will work it may take different tries to find the right medicine that will help you feel better.

- Some patients, but not all, have sexual difficulties when using this medicine. If this happens, talk with the doctor. They can change you to a medicine that does not cause these problems.

TRICYCLICS

NE and 5HT reuptake inhibitors (primarily, and block ACh and histamine receptors which contributes to the SE profile).

DRUG	DOSING	SAFETY/SIDE EFFECTS/MONITORING
TERTIARY AMINES **Amitriptyline** *(Elavil* – brand N/A) **Doxepin** – *Zonalon* cream is for pruritus, *Silenor* is for insomnia ClomiPRAMINE *(Anafranil)* Imipramine *(Tofranil, Tofranil PM* – this is different salt, not interchangeable) Trimipramine *(Surmontil)* **SECONDARY AMINES** Amoxapine Desipramine *(Norpramine)* Maprotiline Nortriptyline *(Pamelor)* Protriptyline *(Vivactil)* (Secondary are relatively selective for NE – tertiary may be slightly more effective but have worse SE profile)	**AMITRIPTYLINE** Depression: 100-150 mg BID Neuropathic pain/migraine prophylaxis: 10-50 mg QHS **NORTRIPTYLINE** Depression: 25 mg TID-QID **DOXEPIN** Depression: 100-300 mg daily	**BLACK BOX WARNING** Antidepressants increase the risk of suicidal thinking and behavior in children, adolescents, and young adults (18-24 years of age) with major depressive disorder (MDD) and other psychiatric disorders; consider risk prior to prescribing. **CONTRAINDICATIONS** Potentially lethal drug interaction with MAOIs; see wash-out information. Do not use if urinary retention or narrow-angle glaucoma. **SIDE EFFECTS** **Cardiotoxicity** QT-prolongation with overdose – can be used for suicide-counsel carefully; get baseline ECG if cardiac risk factors or age > 50 years old Orthostasis, tachycardia **Anticholinergic** Dry mouth, blurred vision, urinary retention, constipation (taper off to avoid cholinergic rebound) Vivid dreams Weight gain (varies by agent and patient), sedation, sweating Myoclonus (muscle twitching-may be symptoms of drug toxicity) **NOTES** ↑ Fall risk – especially in elderly due to combination of orthostasis and sedation Tertiary more likely to cause sedation and weight gain

Tricyclic Drug Interactions

- MAOIs and hypertensive crisis: 2 week wash-out if going to or from a MAOI.

- Additive QT prolongation risk; see Drug Interaction chapter for other high-risk QT drugs to attempt to avoid additive risk.

- Metabolized by 2D6 (up to 10% of Caucasians are slow metabolizers); check for DIs

Tricyclic Counseling

- Dispense MedGuide and instruct patient to read it. Especially in adolescents and young adults: counsel on risk of suicide – particularly during therapy initiation. TCAs are dangerous if the patient wishes to kill themselves; a month's supply can be deadly. Counseling is critical.

- This drug can cause constipation. You may need to use a stool softener or laxative if this becomes a problem.

- This drug may cause dry/blurry vision. You may need to use an eye drop lubricant.

- This drug may make it more difficult to urinate.

- This drug may cause dry mouth. This can contribute to dental decay (cavities) and difficulty chewing food. It is important to use proper dental hygiene when taking any medication that causes dry mouth, including brushing and flossing. Sugar free lozenges may be helpful.

- This drug may cause changes in your blood pressure. Use caution when changing from lying down or sitting to a standing position. Hold onto the bed or rail until you are steady.

- If you experience anxiety, or insomnia (sometimes with vivid dreams), these usually go away. If they do not, contact your doctor.

- Take this medication exactly as prescribed. To help you remember, use it at the same time each day. Antidepressants do not work if they are taken as-needed.

- It is important to continue taking this medication even if you feel well. Do not stop taking this medication without consulting your doctor. Some conditions may become worse when the drug is suddenly stopped. Your dose may need to be gradually decreased.

- It may take 1 to 2 weeks to feel a benefit from this drug and 6-8 weeks to feel the full effect on your mood. Tell the doctor if your condition persists or worsens. You can try a medication in a different class. One will work it may take different tries to find the right medicine that will help you feel better.

MAOIs: Monoamine Oxidase Inhibitors

Inhibit the enzyme monoamine oxidase, which breaks down catecholamines, including 5-HT, NE, EPI, DA. If these NTs ↑ dramatically, hypertensive crisis, and death can result.

DRUG	DOSING	SAFETY/SIDE EFFECTS/MONITORING/
Isocarboxazid (Marplan)	20 mg/day, divided, max 40 mg/day	**BLACK BOX WARNING** Antidepressants increase the risk of suicidal thinking and behavior in children, adolescents, and young adults (18-24 years of age) with major depressive disorder (MDD) and other psychiatric disorders; consider risk prior to prescribing.
Phenelzine (Nardil)	15 mg TID, max 60-90 mg/day	**CONTRAINDICATIONS** Not commonly used but watch for drug-drug and drug-food interactions – if missed could be fatal. Hypertensive crisis (VERY high blood pressure) can occur when taken with TCAs, SSRIs, SNRIs, many other drugs and tyramine-rich foods (see interactions below).
Tranylcypromine (Parnate)	30 mg/day, divided, max 60 mg/day	**SIDE EFFECTS** Anticholinergic effects (taper upon discontinuation to avoid cholinergic rebound) Orthostasis Sedation (except tranylcypromine causes stimulation) Sexual dysfunction, weight gain, headache, insomnia
Selegiline transdermal patch (Emsam) MAOI B Selective Inhibitor Selegiline as Eldepryl and Zelapar (ODT) are oral drugs for Parkinson disease.	Start at 6 mg patch/day, can ↑ to 9 or 12 mg/day.	**CONTRAINDICATIONS** Avoid tyramine-rich foods and drinks while using 9 mg and 12 mg/d patches and for 2 weeks after stopping. Not approved for use in patients < 18 years of age. No dietary issues with 6 mg patch. **SIDE EFFECTS** Constipation, gas, dry mouth, loss of appetite, sexual problems

MAOI Drug Interactions

- MAOIs and hypertensive crisis: allow 2 week wash-out if going to or from a MAOI and an SSRI, SNRI or TCA antidepressant (exception: if going from fluoxetine back to MAOI need to wait 5 weeks).

- MAOIs CANNOT be used with many other drugs or the drugs will not be broken down and hypertensive crisis, serotonin syndrome or psychosis may result. The interaction could be fatal. These include any drugs with effects on the concentrations of epinephrine, norepinephrine, serotonin or dopamine. This includes bupropion, carbamazepine, oxcarbazepine, ephedrine and analogs (pseudoephedrine, etc), buspirone, levodopa, linezolid, lithium, meperidine, SSRIs, SNRIs, TCAs, tramadol, methadone, mirtazapine, dextromethorphan, cyclobenzaprine (and other skeletal muscle relaxants), OTC diet pills/ herbal weight loss products and St. John's wort.

- Patients taking MAOIs must avoid tyramine-rich foods, including aged cheese, pickled herring, yeast extract, air-dried meats, sauerkraut, soy sauce, fava beans and some red wines and beers (tap beer and any beer that has not been pasteurized – canned and bottled beers contain little or no tyramine). Foods can become high in tyramine when they have been aged, fermented, pickled or smoked.

MAOI Inhibitor Counseling

- Dispense MedGuide and instruct patient to read it. Especially in adolescents and young adults: counsel on risk of suicide – particularly during therapy initiation.

- Warn patients regarding the need to avoid interacting foods and drugs. See list in above drug interaction section. Stay away from tyramine-rich containing foods.

- Seek immediate medical care if you experience any of these symptoms: sudden severe headache, nausea, stiff neck, vomiting, a fast or slow heartbeat or a change in the way your heart beats (palpitations), tight chest pain, a lot of sweating, confusion, dilated pupils, and sensitivity to light.

- Use this medication regularly in order to get the most benefit from it. Take this medication exactly as prescribed. To help you remember, use it at the same time each day. Antidepressants do not work if they are taken as-needed.

- It is important to continue taking this medication even if you feel well. Do not stop taking this medication without consulting your doctor. Some conditions may become worse when the drug is suddenly stopped. Your dose may need to be gradually decreased.

- It may take 1 to 2 weeks to feel a benefit from this drug and 6-8 weeks to feel the full effect on your mood. Tell the doctor if your condition persists or worsens. You can try a medication in a different class. One will work – it may take different tries to find the right medicine that will help you feel better.

- *EMSAM* Patch Application: Change once daily. Pick a time of day you can remember. Apply to either upper chest or back (below the neck and above the waist), upper thigh, or to the outer surface of the upper arm. Rotate site and do not use same site 2 days in a row. Wash hands with soap after applying patch. Do not expose to heat. The wash-out period counseling above includes the patch.

Dopamine (DA) and Norepinephrine (NE) Reuptake Inhibitor

DRUG	DOSING	SAFETY/SIDE EFFECTS/MONITORING
BuPROPion *(Aplenzin, Budeprion SR, Budeprion XL, Wellbutrin SR, Wellbutrin XL, Wellbutrin, Forfivo XL)* *Buproban, Zyban* – for smoking cessation *Wellbutrin XL* is approved for Seasonal Affective Disorder (SAD) – start in early fall, titrate to 300 mg/day, if desired can discontinue in late spring by cutting to 150 mg daily x 2 weeks	Dopamine (DA) and norepinephrine (NE) reuptake Inhibitor 300-450 mg daily Wellbutrin IR is TID Wellbutrin SR is BID (to 200 mg BID) Wellbutrin XL is daily Hydrobromide salt *(Aplenzin):* Initial: 174 mg once daily in the morning; may increase as early as day 4 of dosing to 348 mg once daily (target dose); maximum dose: 522 mg daily. In patients receiving 348 mg once daily, taper dose down to 174 mg once daily prior to discontinuing. Alpha$_2$ antagonist effects, which ↑ NE & 5-HT. Blocks 5-HT2, 5-HT$_3$ and H1 receptors and (to a lesser degree) alpha$_1$ and muscarinic receptors.	**BLACK BOX WARNING** Antidepressants increase the risk of suicidal thinking and behavior in children, adolescents, and young adults (18-24 years of age) with major depressive disorder (MDD) and other psychiatric disorders; consider risk prior to prescribing. **CONTRAINDICATIONS** Do not use in seizure disorder Do not exceed 450 mg/d due to seizure risk Do not use if bipolar disorder Do not use if anorexic Do not use *Buproban* or *Zyban* and other form of bupropion together – same drug Do not use if discontinuing alcohol or sedatives, such as benzodiazepines Do not initiate in a patient receiving linezolid or intravenous methylene blue **SIDE EFFECTS** Dry mouth, insomnia, headache/migraine, nausea/vomiting, constipation, and tremors/seizures (dose-related), possible blood pressure changes (more hypertension than hypotension – monitor), weight loss No effects on 5HT and therefore no sexual dysfunction; may be used if issues with other antidepressants
Mirtazapine *(Remeron, Remeron SolTab)* Used commonly in oncology and skilled nursing since it helps with sleep at night (dosed QHS) & increases appetite (good for weight gain in frail elderly)	Inhibits 5-HT reuptake and is an α1-adrenergic blocker and a histamine blocker 15-45 mg QHS	**BLACK BOX WARNING** Antidepressants increase the risk of suicidal thinking and behavior in children, adolescents, and young adults (18-24 years of age) with major depressive disorder (MDD) and other psychiatric disorders; consider risk prior to prescribing. **SIDE EFFECTS** Sedation and ↑ appetite, weight gain Dry mouth, dizziness Agranulocytosis (rare)

Additional Agents Continued

DRUG	DOSING	SAFETY/SIDE EFFECTS/MONITORING
TraZODone Rarely used as an antidepressant due to <u>sedation</u>. Used primarily off-label for sleep (dosed 50-100 mg QHS)	100-150 mg BID TraZODone ER *(Oleptro)* – 150, 300 mg – may be less sedating and is dosed QHS	**BLACK BOX WARNING** Antidepressants increase the risk of suicidal thinking and behavior in children, adolescents, and young adults (18-24 years of age) with major depressive disorder (MDD) and other psychiatric disorders; consider risk prior to prescribing. **SIDE EFFECTS** <u>Sedation</u> Orthostasis (risk in elderly for falls) Sexual dysfunction and risk of <u>priapism</u> (medical emergency – requires immediate medical attention if painful erection longer than 4 hrs)
Nefazodone	Start at 200 mg, divided	**BLACK BOX WARNING** Antidepressants increase the risk of suicidal thinking and behavior in children, adolescents, and young adults (18-24 years of age) with major depressive disorder (MDD) and other psychiatric disorders; consider risk prior to prescribing. Similar to trazodone, but less sedating Rarely used due to <u>hepatotoxicity</u>: monitor LFTs, counsel on symptoms of liver damage Do not use concurrently with carbamazepine

Bupropion Drug Interactions

- Do not use with *Buproban* or *Zyban* for smoking cessation; same drug.

- Do not use in patients with seizure history; drug ↓ seizure threshold. Do not exceed 450 mg daily in anyone.

Key Counseling Points For Above Agents

- Dispense MedGuide and instruct patient to read it. Especially in adolescents and young adults: counsel on risk of suicide – particularly during therapy initiation.

- Counsel on lag time, need to take daily as with other agents.

- Bupropion: Include not to exceed 450 mg daily, or 150 mg at each dose if using immediate-release formulations due to seizure risk.

- Mirtazapine: Counsel to take at night, drug is sedating, and should increase appetite.

FOR TREATMENT RESISTANCE DEPRESSION ONLY

Rule-out bipolar disorder, check if antidepressant is at optimal dose, sometimes use combination standard antidepressants, or augment with various options. The antipsychotics below are approved for treatment-resistant depression.

All antipsychotics require MedGuides with this Warning:

Medicines like this one can raise the risk of death in elderly people who have lost touch with reality (psychosis) due to confusion and memory loss (dementia). This medicine is not approved for the treatment of patients with dementia-related psychosis.

And because it is being used to augment AD therapy:

Antidepressants have increased the risk of suicidal thoughts and actions in some children, teenagers, and young adults. See Schizophrenia/Psychosis chapter for more detail on the antipsychotics.

DRUG	DOSING	SAFETY/SIDE EFFECTS/MONITORING
ARIPiprazole *(Abilify, Abilify Discmelt)*	Start 2-5 mg/day (QAM), can ↑ to 15 mg	**BLACK BOX WARNING** Antidepressants increase the risk of suicidal thinking and behavior in children, adolescents, and young adults (18-24 years of age) with major depressive disorder (MDD) and other psychiatric disorders; consider risk prior to prescribing. **WARNINGS** Risk of Neuroleptic Malignant Syndrome Risk of Tardive Dyskinesia (TD) Risk of leukopenia, neutropenia, agranulocytosis
OLANZapine/fluoxetine *(Symbyax)*	Usually started at 6 mg/25 mg capsule QHS (fluoxetine is activating, but olanzapine is more sedating), can ↑ cautiously.	**CONTRAINDICATIONS** *Symbyax:* Do not use with pimozide, thioridazine, & caution with other QT prolongating drugs/conditions **SIDE EFFECTS** Each of these drugs can cause metabolic issues, including dyslipidemia, weight gain, diabetes (less with aripiprazole) All can cause orthostasis/dizziness **Abilify** Anxiety, insomnia, constipation
QUEtiapine extendedrelease *(SEROquel, SEROquel XR)*	Start 50 mg QHS, ↑ nightly to 150-300 mg QHS	**Olanzapine** Sedation Weight gain, ↑ lipids, ↑ glucose, EPS, QT prolongation (lower risk) **Quetiapine** Sedation, orthostasis Weight gain, ↑ lipids, ↑ glucose Little risk EPS

PRACTICE CASE

Steve is a thin, anxious-appearing 57 year-old male. He is married with two children. Steve's wife has brought him to the clinic due to his constant worry, anxiety, and feelings of worthlessness. When he was in college, Steve had several bouts of depression and was treated successfully with doxepin. He stopped using the medication when he graduated and moved to California. He felt the sunshine made him feel better. His wife reports, however, that this is the 3rd or 4th time in the past few years that Steve has felt so low that she became concerned he might harm himself. His wife reports that Steve is up all night, with constant worry. She does not think he has had a good night's sleep in months.

At the last clinic visit (2 months ago) the doctor started Steve on citalopram 40 mg once daily and lorazepam 1 mg 1-3 times daily, prn. Steve has been using the medication and states that it helps a little, but not much. He is taking the lorazepam 1 mg TID. His other medications include propranolol for hypertension/nerves and fosinopril for hypertension. He does not smoke and drinks occasional alcohol.

CATEGORY	
Medications	Fosinopril 20 mg daily
	Inderal LA 120 mg daily
	Citalopram 40 mg daily
	Lorazepam 1 mg 1-3 times daily, as-needed
Vitals	Height 5'10", weight 155 lbs, BP (in clinic today) 158/102

Questions

1. Steve has depression that has not responded to an adequate trial of fluoxetine or citalopram. Which of the following options represents the best alternative?

   a. Sertraline

   b. Venlafaxine

   c. Fluvoxamine

   d. Escitalopram

   e. Mirtazapine

2. If Steve was started on *Effexor XR* (he won't be), which of the following parameters should be carefully monitored in this patient? (Select **ALL** that apply.)

   a. Blood pressure

   b. Thyroid parameters

   c. White blood cell count

   d. Metabolic acidosis

   e. Symptoms of depression

3. A pharmacist counseling a patient on the use of any antidepressant should include the following counseling points:

   a. Your energy level may pick up before your mood starts to feels better.

   b. Your mood should improve; this usually takes about a month.

   c. If this medicine does not work, the doctor will try a different agent, which may work better.

   d. This medication needs to be taken every day; it does not work if it is taken occasionally.

   e. All of the above.

4. What is the mechanism of action of venla-faxine?

   a. Selective serotonin reuptake inhibitor
   b. Serotonin and dopamine reuptake inhibitor
   c. Serotonin and norepinephrine reuptake inhibitor
   d. Norepinephrine and dopamine reuptake inhibitor
   e. Norepinephrine and acetylcholine reuptake inhibitor

5. The doctor takes a thorough medication history and decides that it would be worthwhile to try doxepin, since the patient had a good history of use with this agent. Which of the following statements is correct?

   a. Doxepin is a monoamine oxidase inhibitor.
   b. Doxepin can cause excess salivation and has significant food interactions.
   c. He should be carefully evaluated for suicide risk.
   d. A and C only.
   e. All of the above.

Questions 6-10 do not apply to the case.

6. A patient has been started on bupropion for depression. His other medications include *Lopid, Pravachol and Zyban*. Which of the following statement is correct?

   a. Bupropion will raise his triglycerides.
   b. Bupropion will raise his HDL cholesterol.
   c. Bupropion will lower his HDL cholesterol.
   d. Bupropion should not be used in this patient.
   e. None of the above.

7. A patient has been started on bupropion 200 mg TID for depression. His medical conditions include partial seizures and obsessive compulsive disorder. His medications include fluvoxamine and phenytoin. Which of the following statements is correct?

   a. Bupropion will induce the metabolism of phenytoin.
   b. The bupropion dose is too high.
   c. Bupropion should not be used in this patient.
   d. B and C only.
   e. All of the above.

8. A patient has been using fluoxetine for depression for four months. He has suffered from sexual dysfunction and feels worse than when he started. Previously, he was well-controlled on tranylcypromine. The physician has decided to stop the fluoxetine and restart the tranylcypromine. Which of the following statements is correct?

   a. No wash-out period is required.
   b. A 2 week wash-out period is required.
   c. A 3 week wash-out period is required.
   d. A 5 week wash-out period is required.
   e. An 8 week wash-out period is required.

9. Which of the following statements concerning trazodone is correct? (Select **ALL** that apply.)

   a. Trazodone is activating and can cause insomnia; it should be taken Q AM.
   b. Trazodone can (rarely) cause a sustained erection.
   c. If priapism is present, the patient must go to the ER right away.
   d. A new form of trazodone called *Silenor* is less sedating and can be given in the morning.
   e. Trazodone does not require a MedGuide due to a lower risk of suicidal behavior in adolescents.

10. Which of the following statements concerning duloxetine is correct? (Select **ALL** that apply.)

   a. The brand name is *Pristiq*.
   b. Duloxetine can be useful for both neuropathic pain and depression.
   c. Duloxetine is a strong 3A4 Inducer.
   d. Bleeding risk will be elevated if a patient is taking duloxetine with an anticoagulant.
   e. Duloxetine is an SNRI and $5HT_{1A}$ antagonist.

Answers

1-e, 2-a,e, 3-e, 4-c, 5-c, 6-d, 7-d, 8-d, 9-b,c, 10-b,d

49

SCHIZOPHRENIA/ PSYCHOSIS

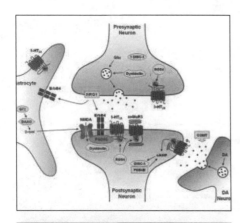

We gratefully acknowledge the assistance of Robin Wackernah, PharmD, BCPP, Regis University School of Pharmacy, Rueckert-Hartman College for Health Professions, in reviewing this chapter.

BACKGROUND

Schizophrenia is a debilitating thought disorder characterized by chronic, relapsing and remitting episodes that are a result of <u>excess dopamine</u>, and other changes in the brain. Recent research includes study of genetic variances in pathways that regulate neuronal development. Patients suffer from <u>hallucinations</u>, <u>delusions</u> (false beliefs), <u>disorganized thinking and behavior</u>. They may withdraw from the world around them and enter a world of psychosis, where they often struggle differentiating reality from altered perceptions. Schizophrenia ranges from relatively mild to severe. Some people may be able to function adequately in daily life, while others need specialized, intensive care. Treatment adherence is important and <u>often difficult to obtain</u>, primarily due to the patient's inability to recognize their illness. This is regrettable to the patient's family and to themselves since the patient with schizophrenia typically lives a life of torment where they may not be able to care for themselves. This condition has one of the highest suicide rates.

The onset of symptoms usually begins in young adulthood. A diagnosis is not based on lab tests, but on the patient's behavior, which should include <u>negative and positive signs and symptoms</u> (described on the following page). Schizophrenia occurs in ~1% in all societies regardless of class, color, religion, culture or national origin. The Diagnostic and Statistical

GUIDELINES

Diagnostic and Statistical Manual of Mental Disorders (DSM-5).

American Psychiatric Association. Practice guideline for the treatment of patients with schizophrenia. 2nd ed. Arlington (VA): American Psychiatric Association; 2009. http://www.psychiatryonline.com/pracGuide/pracGuideTopic_6.aspx (accessed 2013 Oct 14).

Manual of Mental Disorders, 5th Edition (DSM-5) is the current tool used to diagnose schizophrenia and other psychiatric disorders.

CAUSES OF SCHIZOPHRENIA

Schizophrenia is a thought disorder that manifests in the brain. Genetics, environment, stressors and some illicit drugs can be contributing factors. Abnormalities in the role of neurotransmitters is central. There is increased dopamine in the mesolimbic pathway. Antipsychotics primarily block dopamine receptors, although newer agents that block serotonin and additional receptors have benefit. The older "dopaminergic model" is being supplemented with a more recent understanding of the role of the glutamatergic N-methyl-D aspartate (NMDA) receptor and its role in the pathogenesis of schizophrenia.

Antipsychotics target the positive symptoms, but the lack of motivation, cognitive and functional impairment remain challenges for many patients and often take longer to respond to antipsychotic treatment, if at all. Researchers hope that a better understanding of glutamate receptors will improve functional levels. A problem with the current therapy is that the drugs that target dopamine hyperactivity also target dopamine involved in focus and the ability to pay attention; dopamine and glutamine modulate each other. Glutamine synaptic dysfunction is a large area of current research. It is hoped that as the pathways are better understood, along with drug development, a "fine tuning" of therapy will improve treatment.

DSM 5 DIAGNOSTIC CRITERIA FOR SCHIZOPHRENIA

Patients must have 2 or more of the following symptoms
(delusions, hallucinations or disorganized speech must be present)

Negative signs and symptoms	Positive signs and symptoms
Loss of interest in everyday activities	Hallucinations; hearing voices (auditory hallucinations are common), visual hallucinations
Lack of emotion	
Inability to plan or carry out activities	Delusions; beliefs the patient has, but are without a basis in reality
Poor hygiene	Disorganized thinking/behavior, incoherent speech, often on unrelated topics, purposeless behavior, or difficulty speaking and organizing thoughts, such as stopping in mid-sentence or jumbling together meaningless words
Social withdrawal	
Loss of motivation (avolition)	
Poverty (lack of) speech (alogia)	
	Difficulty paying attention

NATURAL PRODUCTS

Fish oils are being used for psychosis, as well as other psychiatric disorders including ADHD and depression. The evidence is preliminary, but promising. Do not recommend cod liver oil due to risk of vitamin A toxicity. Keep in mind that natural products have dose-response relationships; check the Natural Medicines Database for dosing recommendations that appear to have benefit from clinical trials.

PHARMACOTHERAPY

In general second generation antipsychotic agents (SGAs) are used first-line due to a lower risk of extrapyramidal side effects (EPS), however, they are not first-line in all patients and some respond better to a first generation antipsychotic agent (FGA).

In assessing treatment resistance or evaluating the best option for a partial response, it is important to evaluate whether the patient has had an adequate trial (at least 4-6 weeks) of an antipsychotic, including whether the dose is adequate and whether the patient has been taking the medication as prescribed. A previous positive or negative history with antipsychotics should be used to guide therapy.

Clozapine has superior efficacy, but has multiple black box warnings and is particularly known for agranulocytosis, seizures and myocarditis – in addition to having high metabolic risk. A clozapine trial should be considered for a patient who has had no or poor response to two trials of antipsychotic medication (at least one should be a SGA) or for a patient with significant ADRs.

MEDICATIONS THAT CAN CAUSE PSYCHOTIC SYMPTOMS
Amphetamines
Methamphetamine, ice, crack
Cannabis
Cocaine
Dextromethorphan (DM)
Phencyclidine (PCP), MDPV (bath salts)
Lysergic acid diethylamide (LSD) and other hallucinogenics
Anticholinergics (centrally-acting, high doses)
Dopamine or dopamine agonists used for Parkinson disease (Requip, Mirapex, Sinemet, etc.)
Interferons
Steroids (typically with lack of sleep – ICU psychosis)
Stimulants (especially if already at risk), including ADHD drugs, modafinil, etc.

High-potency FGAs such as haloperidol are associated with a high risk of EPS effects, a moderate risk of sedation and a lower risk of orthostatic hypotension, tachycardia, and anticholinergic effects compared to low-potency FGAs. In contrast, low-potency FGAs are associated with a lower risk of EPS, a high degree of sedation, a high risk of orthostatic hypotension, tachycardia, and a high risk of anticholinergic effects. Although other side effects also vary with the specific medication, in general, the first-generation antipsychotic medications are associated with a moderate risk of weight gain, a low risk of metabolic effects, and a risk of sexual side effects. With certain agents (thioridazine particularly), QT risk is significant.

Other possible side effects include seizures, temperature dysregulation, allergic reactions, and dermatological, hepatic, ophthalmological, and hematological effects.

With the commonly used SGAs, weight gain and lipid and glucose abnormalities (metabolic side effects) are common with clozapine, olanzapine, and quetiapine. Risperidone and paliperidone have a moderate risk of metabolic side effects. Aripiprazole, ziprasidone, lurasidone and asenapine have lower metabolic risk. The American Diabetes Association (ADA) screening and monitoring recommendations when initiating antipsychotics state that patients should first be screened for overweight and obesity, dyslipidemia and hyperglycemia, hypertension, and personal or family history of risk. While being treated, the patient should be monitored for treatment-emergent changes in weight, waist circumference, plasma lipid and glucose levels, and acute symptoms of diabetes (e.g., polyuria, polydipsia). QT prolongation with SGAs can be present and is highest risk with ziprasidone.

FORMULATIONS

Long-Acting Injections: Haloperidol is an older agent and comes in various formulations, including an IM injection for acute use, a long-acting decanoate, tablets and a solution. Long-acting injectables, including *Haldol* decanoate (every 4 weeks), *Risperdal Consta* (every 2 weeks), *Invega Sustenna* (every 4 weeks), *Abilify Maintena* (every 4 weeks), and a few others provide the benefit of increased adherence, or compliance, with the medication. They are also used in acute care settings prior to the release of patients to the street (such as with homelessness).

Orally Disintegrating Tablets (ODTs): These are used to help solve the problem of "cheeking" where the patient holds the medication in their cheek and then spits it in the toilet. With ODTs the medicine dissolves rapidly in the mouth, without the need for water. Several of the SGAs come as ODTs (clozapine, olanzapine, aripiprazole and asenapine).

Acute IM Injections: Intramuscular (IM) injections (short and fast acting injectables) work "stat" to help calm down an acutely agitated, psychotic patient for their own safety and the safety of others. They are often mixed with other drugs, such as benzodiazepines for anxiolytic and sedative effects and anticholinergics to reduce EPS risk. In contrast, oral absorption could take up to an hour to calm the patient down. The patient will be sedated and hopefully sleep through the acute symptoms. Olanzapine and benzodiazepines should not be given together (IM) due to orthostasis risk.

Choosing a SGA Based on the Side Effect Profile

Clinicians choose among the various SGAs based on the formulary availability and the following considerations:

- If a patient has cardiovascular risk do not choose an agent that has risk of QT prolongation/arrhythmia (ziprasidone-greatest risk, and although this is a review of SGA's, keep in mind that phenothiazines in general, and thioridazine in particular, are high-risk. The other SGA's are moderate or lower risk.

- If a patient is overweight, has little physical activity or has metabolic issues (elevated blood glucose and/or lipids) avoid agents that have significant metabolic risk (most notably olanzapine and quetiapine). Aripiprazole, ziprasidone, asenapine and lurasidone have the least risk of metabolic side effects and weight gain. Clozapine has high metabolic risk but is used in refractive cases and might be required. Olanzapine has the highest risk of metabolic issues (but does not have a high risk of QT prolongation).

- High prolactin levels causes galactorrhea, or milk production without pregnancy, sexual dysfunction, gynecomastia (painful, swollen breast tissue) and irregular or missed periods. After several years this can contribute to osteoporosis. This is a concern with risperidone and paliperidone, especially with higher doses.

- If the patient has a history of tardive dyskinesia (TD), or any type of movement disorder, avoid risperidone, paliperidone and lurasidone. Quetiapine has low risk of movement disorders and is the recommended agent for psychosis in a patient with Parkinson disease. Clozapine has very low risk but is not used lightly.

- Adherence Issues: see formulation section above. In addition an agent that comes as once-daily dosing (versus BID or TID) may be preferred.

Black Box Warning

Antipsychotics (APs) increase the risk of mortality in elderly patients with dementia-related psychosis, primarily due to an increased risk of stroke and infection. Note that APs are not particularly helpful to treat dementia-related anger/outbursts, but they are used and pharmacists are required to counsel on this risk. See the counseling section for wording suggestion.

Neuroleptic Malignant Syndrome (NMS)

NMS is rare but is highly lethal. It occurs most commonly with the FGAs and is due to D_2 blockade. NMS occurs less commonly with SGAs and with other dopamine blocking agents including metoclopramide (*Reglan*). The majority of cases occur within two weeks of starting therapy or immediately following high doses of injectables given alongside multiple oral doses. Occasionally, patients develop NMS even after years of antipsychotic use (antipsychotics used to be called neuroleptics; and thus, the name). NMS is a medical emergency as the intense muscle contractions can lead to acute renal injury (due to rhabdomyolysis from the destruction of muscle tissue) and death.

Signs Include

- Hyperthermia (high fever, with profuse sweating)

- Extreme muscle rigidity (called "lead pipe" rigidity)

- Mental status changes

- Other signs can include tachycardia and tachypnea and blood pressure changes

Laboratory results

- Elevated creatine phosphokinase (CPK)

- Elevated white blood cells

Treatment

STOP the antipsychotic.

- Provide supportive care: cardiorespiratory and hemodynamic support, body temperature modulation and control of electrolyte balance.

- Cool them down: cooling bed, antipyretics, cooled IV fluids.

- Muscle relaxation with benzodiazepines or dantrolene (a muscle relaxant, sometimes used) and some cases may require a dopamine antagonist such as bromocriptine.

First Generation Antipsychotics (FGAs) block D$_2$ and 5HT$_{2A}$ receptors.

DRUG	DOSING	SAFETY/SIDE EFFECTS/MONITORING
Low Potency		**BLACK BOX WARNING (ALL APs)** Elderly patients with dementia-related psychosis treated with antipsychotics are at an increased risk of death compared to placebo. Most deaths appeared to be either cardiovascular (e.g., heart failure, sudden death) or infectious in nature. This drug is not approved for the treatment of dementia-related psychosis.
ChlorproMAZINE	300-1,000 mg/d	
Thioridazine BLACK BOX: QT prolongation	300-800 mg/d	**SIDE EFFECTS** All are sedating and all cause EPS, however the lower-potency agents have ↑ sedation and ↓ incidence EPS (e.g., chlorpromazine), and the higher-potency agents have ↓ sedation (but still sedating!) with ↑ EPS (e.g., haloperidol).
Mid-potency		Dystonias, which are prolonged contraction of muscles (including painful muscle spasms) can occur during initiation. There is higher risk with younger males. Consider use of centrally-acting anticholinergic (diphenhydramine, benztropine) for prophylaxis during therapy initiation. May be life-threatening if airway is compromised.
Loxapine (*Adasuve* inhalation powder for acute agitation)	30-100 mg/d	
Perphenazine	16-64 mg/d	Akathisia, which is restlessness with anxiety and an inability to remain still. May be treated with anticholinergics, benzodiazepines or propranolol.
		Parkinsonism, which looks similar to Parkinson disease, with tremors, abnormal gait, bradykinesia, etc. May treat with anticholinergics or propranolol if tremor is the main symptom.
High Potency		Tardive dyskinesias (TD), which are abnormal facial movements, primarily in the tongue or mouth. The risk is higher in elderly females. If TD occurs the drug should be stopped as soon as possible. TD can be irreversible.
FluPHENAZine Available in **2-wk decanoate**	5-20 mg/d	Dyskinesias, which are abnormal movements, are possible however this is more of an issue with the Parkinson drugs.
Haloperidol (*Haldol*), see formulations to right Class: butyrophenone (and DA-blocker) Haloperidol is also used for tics and vocal outbursts due to Tourette syndrome	Oral (tablet, solution): start 0.5-2 mg BID-TID, up to 100 mg/d IV: usually 5-10 mg Decanoate (monthly): IM only, for conversion from PO, use 10-20x the oral dose	Cardiovascular Effects: orthostasis, tachycardia, QT prolongation; IV haloperidol has high risk Sexual dysfunction *Adasuve*: dysgeusia (bad, bitter, or metallic taste in mouth), sedation, bronchospasm risk, REMS drug
Trifluoperazine	15-50 mg/d	
Thiothixene (*Navane*)	15-50 mg/d	

Second Generation Antipsychotics (SGAs) block D$_2$ and 5HT$_{2A}$ receptors. Aripiprazole is unique; it acts as a D$_2$ and 5HT$_{1A}$ partial agonist and 5HT$_{2A}$ antagonist.

DRUG	DOSING	SAFETY/SIDE EFFECTS/MONITORING
Clozapine (*Clozaril*, *FazaClo ODT, Versacloz* suspension) Only if failed to respond to treatment with 2 standard AP treatments, or had significant ADRs	300-900 mg/d, divided (start at 12.5 mg and titrate, also titrate off since abrupt discontinuation can cause seizures) Clozapine has ↓ risk EPS/TD	**BLACK BOX WARNINGS (5)** All SGAs have same black box warning listed with FGAs on increased mortality in elderly patients. **Clozapine-Specific Black Box Warnings (4)** Significant risk of potentially life-threatening agranulocytosis. Tachycardia, orthostatic hypotension, syncope, and cardiac arrest; risk is highest during the initial titration period especially with rapid dose increases. Titrate slowly. Myocarditis and cardiomyopathy; discontinue if suspect. Seizures, dose-correlated; start at no higher than 12.5 mg, titrate slowly, using divided doses. Use with caution in patients at seizure risk; seizure history, head trauma, alcoholism, or concurrent therapy with medications which lower seizure threshold. **SIDE EFFECTS** Clozapine is thought to be the most effective, but use is limited due to the risk of agranulocytosis and seizures Myocarditis Orthostasis, with or without syncope Weight gain, ↑ lipids, ↑ glucose, prolongs QT Drowsiness, dizziness, insomnia, GI upset, sialorrhea (hypersalivation) **MONITORING** REMS: Patient must register with *Clozaril* Registry. Only pharmacies using Registry can fill this drug: To start: WBC must be ≥ 3,500/mm³ and ANC must be ≥ 2,000/mm³. Check WBC and ANC weekly x 6 months, then every 2 weeks x 6 months, then monthly. Monitor for metabolic effects; see counseling section.
OLANZapine (*ZyPREXA*, *Zydis ODT, Relprevv* injection)	10-20 mg QHS IM Injection (acute agitation) *Relprevv* inj suspension lasts 2-4 weeks, restricted use REMS drug	**Olanzapine-Specific Black Box Warning** Sedation (including coma) and delirium (including agitation, anxiety, confusion, disorientation) have been observed following use of *Zyprexa Relprevv*. (3-hr monitoring post-injection) **SIDE EFFECTS** Sedation Weight gain, ↑ lipids, ↑ glucose EPS, QT prolongation (lower risk) **MONITORING** For metabolic effects; see counseling section **NOTES** Smoking reduces drug levels.

Second Generation (SGA) Antipsychotics continued

DRUG	DOSING	SAFETY/SIDE EFFECTS/MONITORING
RisperiDONE (RisperDAL) and **RisperDAL M-Tabs ODT**, see injection to right Also approved for autism	4-16 mg/d, divided **Risperdal Consta**, 2 week injection, 25-50 mg	**SIDE EFFECTS** Sedation EPS, especially at higher doses ↑ Prolactin – sexual dysfunction, galactorrhea, irregular/missed periods Orthostasis Weight gain, ↑ lipids, ↑ glucose QT prolongation **MONITORING** For metabolic effects; see counseling section NOTES > 6 mg ↑ prolactin and ↑ EPS
QUEtiapine (SEROquel, SEROquel XR)	400-800 mg/d, divided BID or XR QHS XR is taken at night without food, or light meal (< 300 kcal)	**SIDE EFFECTS** Sedation, orthostasis Weight gain, ↑ lipids, ↑ glucose Little risk EPS – often used for psychosis in Parkinson disease, QT prolongation (lower risk) **MONITORING** For metabolic effects; see counseling section **NOTES** Take XR at night, without food or with a light meal (approximately 300 kcal). Smoking reduces drug levels.
Ziprasidone (Geodon), *Geodon* injection	40-160 mg/d, divided BID Acute injection: **Geodon IM**: 10-20 mg	**CONTRAINDICATIONS** Prolongs QT interval, contraindicated with QT risk **SIDE EFFECTS** Sedation, respiratory tract infection (some have insomnia) **NOTES** Take with food.
Aripiprazole (Abilify, Abilify Discmelt ODT, *Maintena* injection)	10-15 mg Q AM IM Injection, for acute agitation, *Abilify Maintena* is monthly injection	**SIDE EFFECTS** Anxiety, insomnia Constipation No/less weight gain, some degree QT prolongation
Paliperidone (Invega, *Invega Sustenna* is long-acting injection) Similar SEs to parent compound risperidone	3-12 mg/d (3 mg if CrCl < 50 mL/min) Active metabolite of risperidone; OROS delivery, enables once daily dosing *Invega Sustenna*, IM injection, give monthly	**SIDE EFFECTS** ↑ Prolactin – sexual dysfunction, galactorrhea, irregular/missed periods EPS, especially at higher doses Tachycardia, headache, sedation, anxiety Prolongs QT interval, avoid use with QT risk Weight gain, ↑ lipids, ↑ glucose **MONITORING** For metabolic effects; see counseling section

Second Generation (SGA) Antipsychotics continued

DRUG	DOSING	SAFETY/SIDE EFFECTS/MONITORING
Iloperidone (*Fanapt*)	12-24 mg/d	**SIDE EFFECTS** Dizziness, somnolence, orthostasis Prolongs QT interval, avoid use with QT risk Titrate slowly due to orthostasis/dizziness
Asenapine (*Saphris*)	10-20 mg/d <u>SL</u> No food/drink for 10 min after dose	**SIDE EFFECTS** Somnolence, <u>tongue/mouth numbness</u> EPS (5% more than placebo), prolongs QT interval, avoid use with QT risk
Lurasidone (*Latuda*)	40-80 mg/d	**SIDE EFFECTS** Sedation, EPS, dystonias, nausea, agitation, akathisia Nearly weight, lipid and blood glucose neutral **NOTES** Take with food ≥ 350 kcal.

Antipsychotic Drug Interactions

- Smoking can reduce plasma levels of olanzapine and clozapine, patients who smoke may require higher doses.

- All antipsychotics can prolong the QT interval – note that some are considered higher risk than others. The higher risk QT SGAs are noted. Thioridazine is a high risk FGA QT drug (black box warning).

- With clozapine: avoid concurrent drugs that lower the seizure threshhold. Some of the APs have CYP 450 drug interactions which could require dosing adjustments.

ALL ANTIPSYCHOTIC COUNSELING

- Dispense Med Guide and instruct patient to read it. In addition to individual warnings, several of the agents have anti-depressive properties and these include a warning for suicidality, particularly among adolescents.

- This medication can decrease hallucinations and improve your concentration. It helps you to think more clearly and feel positively about yourself, feel less nervous, and take a more active part in everyday life.

- There may be a slightly increased risk of serious, possibly fatal, side effects when this medication is used in older adults with dementia. This medication is not approved for the treatment of dementia-related behavior problems. Discuss the risks and benefits of this medication, as well as other effective and possibly safer treatments for dementia-related behavior problems, with the doctor. The pharmacist should review symptoms of stroke with family/caregivers.

- Contact your doctor right away if you experience uncontrollable movements of the mouth, tongue, cheeks, jaw, arms, or legs.

- Contact your doctor immediately and seek immediate medical attention if you experience fever, sweating, severe muscle stiffness (rigidity) and confusion.

- Use caution when driving, operating machinery, or performing other hazardous activities. This drug may cause dizziness or drowsiness.

- Dizziness may be more likely to occur when you rise from a sitting or lying position. Rise slowly to prevent dizziness and a possible fall.

- To reduce the dizziness and lightheadedness that may occur when you first start to take this drug, your doctor will direct you to start taking it at a low dose and gradually increase the dose. Your doctor may direct you to start by taking the immediate-release form of this drug, then switch you to the sustained-release form or an injectable form taken less often when you are regularly taking the same dose.

- Avoid consuming alcohol during treatment with this drug. Alcohol may increase drowsiness and dizziness.

- Tell your doctor if your condition persists or worsens.

Clozapine

- This medication can cause a serious immune system problem called agranulocytosis (low white blood cells). To make sure you have enough white blood cells, you will need to have a blood test before you begin taking clozapine and then have your blood tested regularly during your treatment.

- Clozapine can also cause seizures, especially with higher doses, or if it is increased too quickly when starting therapy. Let your doctor or pharmacist know if you have ever had seizures. While taking this medication, avoid activities during which a sudden loss of consciousness could be dangerous (e.g., driving, operating heavy machinery, swimming).

- This medication may rarely cause an inflammation of the heart muscle (myocarditis). Seek immediate medical attention if you have weakness, difficult/rapid breathing, chest pain, or swelling of the ankles/legs. The risk is highest during the first month of treatment.

Olanzapine, Clozapine, Risperidone, Paliperidone and Quetiapine

- This drug has a risk of weight gain, and elevated cholesterol, blood pressure and blood glucose (hyperglycemia). These must be monitored, and treated if they occur. Talk to your doctor if you experience any signs of hyperglycemia including excessive thirst, frequent urination, excessive hunger, or weakness.

- Your doctor will order blood tests during treatment to monitor progress and side effects.

Different Types of Oral Formulations

- *Asenapine*: Place the sublingual tablet under the tongue and allow it to dissolve completely. The tablet will dissolve in saliva within seconds. Do not eat or drink for 10 minutes. The tongue will feel numb afterwards.

- *FazaClo, Abilify Discmelt, Risperdal M-Tab, Zyprexa Zydis*: Immediately upon opening the foil blister, using dry hands, remove tablet and place in mouth. Do not push the tablet through the foil because it may crumble. Tablet disintegration occurs rapidly so it can be easily swallowed with or without liquid. Use liquid only if you need it.

- Most ODTs contain phenylalanine. Do not dispense ODTs to patients with PKU.

- *Risperdal* oral solution can be administered directly from the calibrated pipette, or mixed with water, coffee, orange juice, and low-fat milk; it is not compatible with cola or tea.

- *Latuda* is taken with food, at least 350 kcal meal. *Geodon* is taken with food.

- Quetiapine immediate-release tablet may be taken without regard to meals. The extended-release tablet *(Seroquel XR)* should be taken without food or with a light meal (approximately 300 kcal).

- Olanzapine is usually taken once daily at night (QHS), since it is long-acting and sedating.

PRACTICE CASE

Ruby is a 24 year-old college student. Her parents have attempted to help Ruby over the past year. Her academic performance deteriorated and she began to look unkempt. About a month ago, her Mom was sure she saw Ruby mumbling to herself. Ruby began to call her mother "evil" and told her mother that she was destroying her life. Later, Ruby accused her mother of trying to feed her poisoned food. Ruby has dropped her old high-school friendships, except for one girl who her mother feels is more troubled than Ruby. When the mother went to talk to one of Ruby's instructors, they found out that Ruby had accused the teacher of changing what Ruby had written on an exam, and that the teacher had seen Ruby mumbling to herself in class. The teacher also complained that Ruby lacks attention in class, and reported that her work is sloppy and disorganized. The teacher had assumed there was difficulty at home, since Ruby told her that her mother is dying from cancer. This report from Ruby was not truthful.

The crisis in the family came to a head recently when Ruby stole a bottle of vodka from the local convenience store and was caught. Fortunately, the store manager knew the family and declined to press charges. However, later that night Ruby took some unknown medication and attempted to drown herself in the bathtub. She was taken by ambulance to the hospital.

The psychiatric team, after a brief visit with Ruby and a history taken from her family, gave Ruby a tentative diagnosis of schizophrenia. She received an injection of haloperidol and lorazepam, and is sleeping soundly. The psychiatric resident has come to the family to discuss treatment options.

No current medications; no known medical history. Height 5'5", weight 125 lbs.

Questions

1. The physician gave the patient an injection of haloperidol. This medication comes in the following formulations. (Select **ALL** that apply.)

   a. Oral tablets

   b. IM injection

   c. Long-lasting (monthly) decanoate

   d. Oral solution

   e. Orally disintegrating tablet (ODT)

2. If Ruby is continued on haloperidol, she will be at risk for these side effects. (Select **ALL** that apply.)

   a. Painful dystonic reactions (including painful neck and back muscle contractions)

   b. Tardive dyskinesias, or abnormal facial movements

   c. Gynecomastia

   d. Agranulocytosis

   e. QT prolongation and possible arrhythmia risk

3. If Ruby were to experience neuroleptic malignant syndrome while receiving haloperidol, what therapies would likely be administered in this emergency situation? (Select **ALL** that apply.)

   a. Switch to fluphenazine

   b. Cooled IV fluids, ice beds

   c. Heating blankets

   d. Muscle relaxants

   e. Airway support

Questions 4-10 do not apply to the case.

4. Choose the potential adverse reaction/s from haloperidol which can be irreversible (and, if it occurs, the medicine should be stopped right away):

   a. Dystonic reaction

   b. Tardive dyskinesia

   c. Akathisia

   d. Dizziness

   e. Orthostatic hypotension

5. A patient is started on olanzapine for psychotic symptoms. This agent puts the patient at high risk for the following side effects. (Select **ALL** that apply.)

   a. Weight loss

   b. Elevated blood glucose

   c. Increased risk lymphoma or other malignancies

   d. Elevated cholesterol

   e. Elevated creatine phosphokinase

6. A patient has been prescribed *Risperdal Consta*. Choose the correct statement:

   a. The medication lasts four weeks.

   b. The medication is given by slow IV infusion.

   c. *Risperdal Consta* is an orally-dissolving formulation for use with dysphagia.

   d. There remains a risk of EPS with this formulation.

   e. The benefit with the Consta formulation is little or no risk of elevated prolactin levels.

7. A patient has schizophrenia, with constant auditory hallucinations which have instructed the patient to harm himself and others. He has failed olanzapine and chlorpromazine. His other medications include sertraline for anxiety. His WBC ranges from 2.3-3.4 cells/mm³. He also has a low platelet count of 120. Which of the following statements is correct?

   a. He should begin clozapine therapy.

   b. Clozapine therapy is contraindicated due to his WBC count.

   c. Clozapine therapy is contraindicated due to his platelet count.

   d. Clozapine therapy is not indicated since he has not tried haloperidol.

   e. None of the above.

8. A patient with psychotic symptoms takes the following medications for chronic conditions: metoprolol, warfarin, amiodarone, lisinopril and insulin. His physician wishes to begin an antipsychotic. Which of the following agents represents the best option for this patient?

   a. Thioridazine

   b. Haloperidol

   c. Ziprasidone

   d. Risperidone

   e. Aripiprazole

9. A patient is using olanzapine in the morning. He takes 10 mg daily. He is tired all the time, but has trouble sleeping at night. Which option is best?

   a. Add temazepam at bedtime.

   b. Add zolpidem at bedtime.

   c. Move the olanzapine to bedtime.

   d. Add modafinil in the morning.

   e. Add mirtazapine at bedtime.

10. A physician wrote a prescription for *Fanapt*. Which medication should be dispensed?

    a. Asenapine

    b. Olanzapine

    c. Aripiprazole

    d. Iloperidone

    e. Thioridazine

Answers

1-a,b,c,d, 2-a,b,e, 3-b,d,e, 4-b, 5-b,d, 6-d, 7-b, 8-e, 9-c, 10-d

BIPOLAR DISORDER

We gratefully acknowledge the assistance of Robin Wackernah, PharmD, BCPP, Regis University, School of Pharmacy, in preparing this chapter.

BACKGROUND

Bipolar disorder is a mood disorder where moods can fluctuate from depression to elevated moods referred to as "mania." Each mood episode represents a drastic change from a person's usual mood and behavior. Bipolar disorder is currently broken up into bipolar I and II disorder and a milder form called "cyclothymic disorder" where the criteria for depression or mania are not fully met. The Diagnostic and Statistical Manual of Mental Disorders, Fifth Edition (DSM-5) is the current tool used to diagnose bipolar disorder and other psychiatric disorders.

Bipolar I disorder is the most severe version of the disorder. The classic diagnostic symptom is mania, but patients may also experience bouts of depression with bipolar I disorder. Mania is characterized as an elevated mood where patients have a lot of energy, may feel euphoric, "on top of the world," and/or irritable. The symptoms of mania in bipolar I disorder can be so severe that they may require psychiatric hospitalization, impair social or occupational functioning or have features of psychosis such as hearing voices or delusions (false beliefs).

Bipolar II disorder has the same symptoms of bipolar I disorder, however the symptoms are described as "hypomania" because they are less severe than in pure mania.

GUIDELINES

Diagnostic and Statistical Manual of Mental Disorders (DSM-5).

WFSBP: Update 2012 on the long-term treatment of bipolar disorder. The World Journal of Biological Psychiatry, 2013; 14: 154–219.

APA, Treatment of Patients with Bipolar Disorder, 2nd Ed., 2005. Available at: http://www.psychiatryonline.com/prac-Guide/pracGuideTopic_8.aspx.

VA/DOD, Management of Bipolar Disorder in Adults, 2010. Available at: http://www.healthquality.va.gov/bipolar/bd_305_full.pdf

Hypomania by definition will not affect social or occupational functioning and patients with bipolar II disorder will not require hospitalization for hypomania, or have psychotic features.

The estimated prevalence of bipolar I disorder ranges from 0.4-1.6%. Bipolar II disorder is less common in the general population, however may be more common in women. Bipolar disorder can lead to problems with relationships, employment, disrupt lives, lead to suicide and/or a variety of risky behaviors.

Diagnostic Criteria

In addition to the elevated or irritable mood, the DSM-5 diagnostic criteria for mania include 3 or more of the below symptoms and note that 4 symptoms are required if the mood is only irritable.

- Inflated self-esteem or grandiosity (having an exaggerated belief in one's importance or talents)

- Decreased need for sleep

- More talkative than usual

- Flight of ideas (jumping from one topic to the next) or racing thoughts (the mind switches between thoughts very quickly)

- Distractibility

- Increase in goal-directed activity (either social, at work or at school)

- Excessive involvement in pleasurable activities that have a high potential for painful consequences (e.g., buying sprees, sexual indiscretions, gambling)

Pharmacotherapy

Mood stabilizers (lithium, valproate, lamotrigine), and the second-generation antipsychotics (SGAs) are first line for treating mania and for maintaining a stable mood and preventing the patient's mood from swinging into mania or depression. The definition of a mood stabilizer is a medication that can treat either mania or depression without inducing either. Hence, antidepressants are not considered mood stabilizers.

With the exception of clozapine, paliperidone, iloperidone and lurasidone all of the SGAs have indications for bipolar mania, lurasidone has an indication for bipolar depression. However, they all have the potential to be helpful for mania and maintenance either as monotherapy or as adjunctive therapy to mood stabilizers such as lithium and valproate. First generation antipsychotics (FGAs), such as haloperidol, have been used in the past for bipolar mania but have fallen out of favor due to the increased risk of extrapyramidal side effects (EPS). Patients with bipolar disorder are more susceptible to EPS and antipsychotic agents should be used with caution in this population, particularly the FGAs.

While some of the FGAs have been associated with causing depression, the SGAs do not induce depressive episodes, and some of them have antidepressant effects. The most current guidelines recommend either a mood stabilizer, SGA, or a combination of a mood stabilizer and SGA. Using one agent first enables clinicians to weigh individualized therapeutic benefits and to identify the cause of adverse reactions. However, severe cases may warrant initiation with combination therapy.

SGAs can be added to mood stabilizers or vice versa. If psychotic features are present it makes sense to begin with a SGA. In deciding which SGA to use, clinicians should consider the primary treatment goal: mania, depression or maintenance. In addition, comorbid health conditions and potential side effects may preclude using one agent over another. Aripiprazole and quetiapine ext-release have indications as adjunctive therapy in depression and can also be used for mania and maintenance.

Lamotrigine is used in bipolar depression and maintenance, however is not beneficial in mania due to the slow titration that is required to reach a target dose. Lithium is used in mania, depression and maintenance. Lithium is still commonly used today and is often paired with an SGA in severe cases. Valproate and carbamazepine (as *Equetro)* are both approved for bipolar mania.

Antidepressants are not recommended unless there is currently a mood stabilizer in the patient's medication regimen. When antidepressants are used as monotherapy in bipolar depression there is a risk of inducing mania and strict monitoring for mood stabilization is required if they are used in patients with bipolar disorder.

All antidepressants, anticonvulsants and antipsychotics require MedGuides.

MOOD STABILIZERS & PREGNANCY

Valproate, carbamazepine and lithium are pregnancy category D for treatment of bipolar and have known fetal risk. The benefit must outweigh the risk. Lamotrigine (pregnancy category C) is often considered the safer option, relative to the other agents. During pregnancy if the risk is not well quantified an attempt should be made to avoid unnecessary drugs during the first trimester when organogenesis takes place. The SGAs that are approved for bipolar disorder are pregnancy category C. Lurasidone is pregnancy category B.

- Lithium exposure in pregnancy is associated with an increase in congenital cardiac malformations.

- Valproate exposure in pregnancy is associated with increased risk of fetal anomalies, including neural tube defects, fetal valproate syndrome, and long term adverse cognitive effects. It should be avoided in pregnancy, if possible, especially during the first trimester.

- Carbamazepine exposure in pregnancy is associated with fetal carbamazepine syndrome. It should be avoided in pregnancy, if possible, especially during the first trimester. Carbamazepine is a third-line agent for treating bipolar but is occasionally used; see epilepsy chapter for a review of this agent.

- If an antidepressant is used, paroxetine should be avoided. It is rated as pregnancy category D due to the risk of cardiac defects, particularly in the 1ˢᵗ trimester. Other SSRIs and SNRIs should be considered to have some degree of risk as well.

Bipolar Mania or Illicit Drug Use?

A toxicology screen should be taken first (prior to start of treatment, and as-needed) to rule-out mania due to illicit drug use.

PRIMARY BIPOLAR AGENTS

Valproic Acid/Valproate

T-type calcium channel blocker and fast sodium channel blocker that increases γ-aminobutyric activity (GABA), an inhibitory neurotransmitter.

DRUG	DOSING	SAFETY/SIDE EFFECTS/MONITORING
Valproate/Valproic acid (Depakene, Stavzor, Depacon) *Depakene* – capsules, solution *Stavzor* – delayedrelease capsules **Divalproex (Depakote, Depakote ER, Depakote Sprinkle)** *Depakote* – delayed release tablet *Depakote ER* – extrelease tablet *Depakote Sprinkle* – capsules can be opened and sprinkled on food Also used for migraine prophylaxis	**Initial Mania** ER: 25 mg/kg once daily Delayed Release: 750 mg/day (divided doses) Max: 60 mg/kg/day **Adjust to serum levels** Serum levels: maintain between 50-125 mcg/mL Note the different serum levels with seizure disorders [Cannot substitute *Depakote ER* for the delayed release tabs *(Depakote)*; need to ↑ *Depakote ER* by 8-20%] If the albumin is low (< 3.5 g/dL) the true valproate level will be higher than it appears – adjust with the same phenytoin formula – see epilepsy chapter	**BLACK BOX WARNINGS (3)** **Hepatic Failure** Occurs rarely in adults (1:50,000) usually during first 6 months of therapy. Children (1:600) under the age of two years and patients with mitochondrial disorders are at higher risk. Monitor LFTs frequently during the first 6 months. **Teratogenicity** Including neural tube defects (e.g., spina bifida) and decreased IQ scores following in utero exposure. **Pancreatitis** Can be fatal in children and adults **CONTRAINDICATIONS** Significant hepatic disease, urea cycle disorders, prophylaxis of migraine in pregnancy, known mitochondrial disorders caused by mutations in mitochondrial DNA polymerase gamma (POLG) or children < 2 years of age suspected of having a POLG-related disorder **SIDE EFFECTS** GI upset (nausea/vomiting), abdominal pain, dizziness, asthenia, tremor, alopecia (treat with a multivitamin containing selenium and zinc), somnolence, weight gain, polycystic ovary syndrome (PCOS), vitamin D and calcium deficiency (bone loss), pancreatitis, lower IQ in children if exposed in-utero and hyperammonemia (treat with carnitine in symptomatic adults only). Dose-related: thrombocytopenia, diplopia, blurred vision **MONITORING** LFTs, CBC with differential, platelets, chemistry panel. For adults, monitor at baseline, 3 months, 6 months, and annually. For children, monitor LFTs every month for the first 6 months then annually. **NOTES** Pregnancy Category D/X (for migraine prophylaxis) Supplementation with calcium and vitamin D recommended Switching from valproic acid to delayed-release divalproex may reduce stomach upset

Valproic Acid/Divalproex Drug Interactions

- Valproate is an inhibitor of 2C9 (weak) and can ↑ levels of c arbamazepine, lamotrigine, phenobarbital, warfarin, and zidovudine.

- Use special caution with combination of valproate and lamotrigine, due to risk of serious rash (combo requires lower doses with slow titration and patient/parent counseling). The combination is synergistically beneficial where the effi cacy is greater when used in combination than either medication used alone.

- Salicylates may displace valproic acid from protein-binding site, leading to toxicity and valproate can displace phenytoin from albumin, resulting in phenytoin toxicity. Warfarin is highly protein-bound; valproate can displace warfarin and cause an increase in the INR.

- Carbapenems can ↓ valproate levels leading to seizures.

Valproic Acid Counseling

- Do not use if you have liver disease. In rare cases, this drug has caused liver failure. Notify your doctor if you develop severe fatigue, vomiting or loss of appetite. These could be early symptoms of liver damage.

- In rare cases, valproic acid has also caused severe, even fatal, cases of pancreatitis (inflammation of the pancreas). Some of the cases have progressed rapidly from initial symptoms to death. Cases have been reported soon after starting treatment with valproic acid, as well as after several years of use. Notify your doctor immediately if you develop nausea, vomiting, severe abdominal pain, or loss of appetite. These symptoms may be indications of pancreatitis.

- Do not stop taking the medication even if you feel better.

- Do not crush, chew, or break the capsules because they may hurt the mouth or throat. Swallow them whole. *Depakene* capsules contain liquid which will cause irritation to the mouth and throat. *Depakote* sprinkles can be taken whole or sprinkled on a teaspoon or very small amount of soft food. Do not chew even if sprinkled on food.

- Measure the liquid form of valproic acid with a special dose-measuring spoon or cup, not a regular eating spoon. If you do not have a dose-measuring device, ask your pharmacist for one.

- Valproic acid is FDA pregnancy category D. This means that it is known to be harmful to an unborn baby. Malformations of the face and head, heart, and nervous system have been reported. Do not take valproic acid without first talking to your doctor if you are pregnant or could become pregnant. This drug passes into breast milk. Tell your doctor if you are planning to breastfeed.

- Take each dose with a full glass of water. Take with food to help avoid stomach upset.

- You will need to have your blood checked occasionally during treatment. It is important for your doctor to know how much medication is in the blood and how well your liver is working.

Lamotrigine

Inhibits release of glutamate and aspartate (excitatory amino acids), fast sodium channel blocker and t-type calcium channel blocker stabilizing neuronal membranes

DRUG	DOSING	SAFETY/SIDE EFFECTS/MONITORING
LamoTRIgine [LaMICtal, LaMICtal ODT (orally dispersable), LaMICtal CD (chewable), LaMICtal XR]	**Bipolar Depression/ Maintenance** Wk 1 and 2: 25 mg/day Wk 3 and 4: 50 mg/day Wk 5: 100 mg/day Wk 6: 200 mg/day Target dose:200 mg/day Max: 400 mg/day This is adult dosing; children are dosed by body weight. Divide BID, unless using XR Adjust when taking valproic acid (reduce), carbamazepine, phenytoin or phenobarbital (increase)	**BLACK BOX WARNING** Serious skin reactions, including SJS (rate of rash is greater in pediatrics than adults) and TEN; ↑ risk with higher than recommended starting doses, rapid dose escalation, or co-administration of valproic acid which ↑ lamotrigine levels > 2-fold. To ↓ risk of rash, follow titration schedule – *Lamictal Starter Kit* and *Lamictal ODT Patient Titration Kits* provide the recommended titration schedule for the 1st 5 weeks. Titration schedule is based on whether patient is on valproate, inducer anticonvulsant, or no concomitant anticonvulsant. **WARNINGS** Risk of aseptic meningitis, blood dyscrasias **SIDE EFFECTS** Nausea, insomnia, drowsiness, fatigue, ataxia, impaired coordination, dizziness, diplopia, rhinitis, xerostomia, rash **NOTES** Pregnancy Category C Discontinue if any sign of hypersensitivity reaction or unspecified rash. Not used in mania

Lamotrigine Drug Interactions

- Strong inducers (including carbamazepine, phenytoin and phenobarbital) decrease lamotrigine. There are <u>higher</u> titration schedules when using these drugs concurrently. In this case, lamotrigine is generally started at 50 mg daily.

- Valproate/divalproex is an inhibitor and increases lamotrigine levels leading to a significant increase in the risk of a rash. There are <u>lower</u> titration schedules when using these drugs concurrently. In this case, lamotrigine is generally reduced to 25 mg every other day.

Lamotrigine Counseling

- This medication may cause a mild or severe (and potentially life-threatening) rash. There is no way to tell if a mild rash will develop into a more serious reaction. A serious rash is more likely to happen when you start this medicine or within the first 8 weeks of treatment. But, it can happen in people who have taken this for any period of time. Children 2-16 years old have a higher chance of getting this serious skin reaction. The risk of getting a rash is higher if you:

  - Use this medicine with valproate (valproic acid, or *Depakene, Stavzor or Depacon)* or divalproex (*Depakote*).

  - Use a higher starting dose than prescribed.

❏ Increase your dose faster than prescribed.

■ The dose must be increased <u>slowly</u>. It may take several weeks or months to reach the best dose for you and to get the full benefit from this medication.

■ Take this medication regularly in order to get the most benefit from it. To help you remember, take it at the same time/s each day.

■ A very small number of people may have worsened mental thoughts when using this medicine. Contact your doctor right away if you have recurrent thoughts of harming yourself or worsened mood or anxiety.

■ Do not stop this medicine suddenly; if it is stopped it will need to be slowly decreased by your doctor.

■ This medicine (rarely) can cause aseptic meningitis, which is a serious inflammation of the protective layer that covers the brain and spinal cord. You should get medical treatment immediately if you develop a severe headache, a very stiff neck, and possibly fever and nausea.

■ Less serious side effects can include dizziness, sleepiness, blurred vision, nausea, upset stomach or diarrhea, headache and feeling uncoordinated.

■ If you have difficulty sleeping (insomnia) or get unusual dreams, please let your doctor know.

Lithium

Lithium has various proposed mechanisms, including influencing the reuptake of serotonin and/or norepinephrine and inhibiting postsynaptic D2 receptor supersensitivity.

DRUG	DOSING	SAFETY/SIDE EFFECTS/MONITORING
Lithium *(Lithobid)*	Start at 150-900 mg/d, divided Then 900-2400 mg/d, divided Titrate to achieve therapeutic range **Therapeutic Range** 0.6-1.2 mEq/L (trough level) Acute mania may need up to 1.5 mEq initially Titrate slowly to help patient tolerate SEs Take with food (post-meal) if nausea, or try split dosing If tremor, thirst, confusion, or nocturia, try QHS dosing	Cannot use with renal impairment: lithium is 100% renally cleared – and if not eliminated, toxicity will result **SIDE EFFECTS** GI upset (take with food in the stomach, can change to ER forms) Cognitive effects, cogwheel rigidity, fine hand tremor, weight gain Polyuria/polydipsia, hypothyroidism – must monitor, serotonergic; avoid co-admin with other serotonergic agents Cardiac abnormalities (inverted T waves) Edema, worsening of psoriasis **TOXICITY** > 1.5 mEq/L (coarse hand tremor, vomiting, persistent diarrhea, confusion, ataxia) > 3 mEq/L (CNS depression, arrhythmia, seizures, irreversible brain damage, coma) **MONITORING** BMP (renal function), thyroid function (TSH, FT4), EKG in patients over 40 Pregnancy Category D

Lithium Drug Interactions

- These will ↑ lithium: ↓ salt intake, NSAIDs, ACE Is, ARBs, diuretics; aspirin and sulindac are safer NSAID options.

- These will ↓ lithium: ↑ salt intake, caffeine, and theophylline.

- These will ↑ risk 5HT-syndrome if given with lithium: SSRIs, SNRIs, triptans, linezolid and other serotonergic drugs.

- ↑ neurotoxicity risk (ataxia, tremors, nausea) with lithium in combination with these drugs: verapamil, diltiazem, phenytoin and carbamazepine.

Lithium Counseling

- Call your doctor if you experience severe nausea, vomiting, worsened diarrhea, slurred speech, extreme drowsiness, weakness, and noticeable (worsened) tremor. These symptoms may indicate that the lithium level is too high in your blood.

- Do not crush, chew, or break any extended-release forms of lithium (e.g., *Lithobid*). They are specially formulated to release slowly in the body.

- Lithium may cause dizziness or drowsiness. Use caution when driving or performing other hazardous activities until you know how you feel taking this medication. If you experience dizziness or drowsiness, avoid these activities.

- Lithium is FDA pregnancy category D. This means that lithium is known to be harmful to an unborn baby. Do not take lithium without first talking to your doctor if you are pregnant or are planning a pregnancy. Lithium can pass into breast milk. Discuss with your doctor if you are breastfeeding.

- Maintain adequate fluid intake by drinking 8 to 12 glasses of water or other fluids (do not count any caffeinated sodas, coffee or tea) every day while taking lithium. Vigorous exercise, prolonged exposure to heat or sun, excessive sweating, diarrhea, or vomiting may cause dehydration and side effects from lithium. Call your doctor if you lose a significant amount of body fluid as a result of sweating, diarrhea, or vomiting.

- Do not change the amount of salt you consume. Salt is high in many fast foods, luncheon meats, "TV dinners" and canned goods.

- You will need to have your blood checked occasionally during treatment.

- Do not stop taking this medication, even if you are feeling better.

SECOND-GENERATION ANTIPSYCHOTICS USED IN BIPOLAR DISORDER

The 2010 VA guidelines list other second generation antipsychotics as treatment options. These are the agents with FDA approval. For a more complete review of the SGAs, including mechanism, drug interactions and counseling, refer to the Schizophrenia and Psychosis chapter.

DRUG	DOSING	SAFETY/SIDE EFFECTS/MONITORING
Aripiprazole (Abilify, Abilify Discmelt) Approved for manic & mixed symptoms, maintenance, +/- lithium or valproate	15-30 mg QAM	These drugs can cause metabolic issues, including dyslipidemia, weight gain, diabetes Risk of Neuroleptic Malignant Syndrome Risk of Tardive Dyskinesia (TD) Risk of leukopenia, neutropenia, agranulocytosis All can cause orthostasis/dizziness
OLANZapine/FLUoxetine (Symbyax) Approved for bipolar depression, 2nd line option due to metabolic effects from olanzapine	Usually started at 6 mg/25 mg capsule QHS (fluoxetine is activating, but olanzapine is more sedating), can ↑ cautiously. CI with pimozide, thioridazine, & caution with other QT prolongating drugs/conditions	**COMMON SIDE EFFECTS** **Aripiprazole** Akathisia (esp in younger patients), restlessness, insomnia, constipation, fatigue, blurred vision
OLANZapine (ZyPREXA, Zydis ODT, Relprevv Inj.) Approved for manic or mixed episodes +/- lithium or valproate, or for monotherapy maintenance	5-20 mg/day, generally QHS	**Olanzapine** Cognitive dysfunction, dry mouth, fatigue, sedation, ↑ appetite/weight, peripheral edema, tremor, blurred vision. ↓ CVD risk than other listed APs
QUEtiapine extended release (SEROquel, SEROquel XR) Approved for mania/maintenance with lithium or divalproex, and for bipolar depression	Bipolar mania/maintenance: 400-800 mg QHS Bipolar depression: 300 mg QHS	**Quetiapine** QT risk, sedation, dry mouth, constipation, dizziness, ↑ appetite/weight **Risperidone** Sedation, ↑ appetite, fatigue, insomnia, parkinsonism, akathisia, nausea, some QT risk
RisperiDONE (RisperDAL) Approved alone or with lithium or valproate for acute mania or mixed episodes	Start at 2-3 mg/d, can ↑ to 6 mg In children start 0.5 mg/d Tablets, oral solution, M-tabs (ODT)	**Ziprasidone** QT risk (greatest), sedation, EPS, dizziness, akathisia, abnormal vision, asthenia, nausea
Ziprasidone (Geodon) Approved with lithium or valproate for maintenance, or alone for manic/mixed episodes	Start at 40 mg BID, can ↑ to 80 mg BID Take with food	**Asenapine** Numbs mouth, sedation, dizziness, weight gain (less than risperidone and olanzapine). Some QT risk.
Asenapine (Saphris) Approved for acute manic or mixed episodes, +/- lithium or valproate	5-20 mg Sublingual (SL) only: must dissolve under tongue, & no food/drink for 10 min after taking	**ADA Screening/Monitoring Recommendations** Patients being started on APs should first be screened for overweight and obesity, dyslipidemia and hyperglycemia, hypertension, and personal or family history of risk. While being treated, the patient should be monitored for treatment-emergent changes in weight, waist circumference, plasma lipid and glucose levels, and acute symptoms of diabetes (e.g., polyuria, polydipsia).
Lurasidone (Latuda) Approved for bipolar depression, +/- lithium or valproate	20-120 mg/day Dose titration NOT required Take with food	

PRACTICE CASE

Margie is a 65-year old female with a long history of bipolar I and hypertension. She has been reasonably controlled on lithium therapy for many years. Margie lives with her sister, who takes good care of her medical and social needs. Occasionally, her sister reports, Margie gets "back to her old thing" and becomes convinced that she is on a mission to "change the world." Margie is never quite sure what is involved with this mission.

Margie is brought to the clinic today by her sister. Her sister states that Margie has always had a fine hand tremor, but today her hand is visibly shaking. Margie is nauseous, and vomited the little she ate this morning. Her speech is slurred and confused. She appears to have difficulty walking into the examination room. She also has a bad cold with nasal congestion.

Her medications include *Lithobid* 450 mg BID, metoprolol IR 50 mg BID, calcium carbonate 500 mg BID with meals and a B-complex tablet.

Previous labs, taken on 11/15/2012: BUN/SCr 14/0.7, lithium level 0.9 mEq/L

Labs taken (today), 10/1/2013: BUN/SCr 28/1.7, lithium level 1.8 mEq/L

Questions

1. The following factors are likely contributing to the current symptoms of GI distress, coarse hand tremor, ataxia and confusion: (Select **ALL** that apply.)

   a. The use of a calcium supplement
   b. The patient's decline in renal function
   c. Lithium level of 1.8 mEq/L
   d. The use of a vitamin supplement (B-complex)
   e. The patient's ethnicity

2. Margie is using lithium. Describe lithium clearance:

   a. 100% renal clearance; no hepatic metabolism.
   b. 50% metabolized by 3A4, 50% excreted unchanged in the urine.
   c. 75% metabolized by 2D6, 25% excreted unchanged in the urine.
   d. 100% metabolized by 2C9, 100% metabolites cleared renally.
   e. Metabolized by 2C19, metabolites cleared renally.

Questions 3-10 are NOT based on the above case.

3. Which of the following statements are correct regarding blood pressure management in patients using lithium? (Select **ALL** that apply.)

   a. Lisinopril can increase lithium levels
   b. If a patient is using lithium and a diuretic is needed, furosemide may be a safer diuretic option
   c. Metoprolol dose should be decreased to avoid toxic lithium levels
   d. Margie's blood pressure should be kept under the maximum goal level of 120/70 mmHg
   e. In a patient using lithium the sodium content must be kept stable; increasing salt intake can cause the lithium level to become sub-therapeutic, and can increase the blood pressure.

4. A patient has a history of two myocardial infarctions. He has bipolar II which is moderately controlled with the use of lithium monotherapy. He has been using lithium for many years. His physician wishes to use an antipsychotic as augmentation therapy. Which of the following antipsychotics has either QT prolongation or other cardiac risk? (Select **ALL** that apply.)

   a. Quetiapine
   b. Risperidone
   c. Ziprasidone
   d. Thioridazine
   e. Haloperidol

5. Patient counseling for lithium should include the following points:

   a. You must keep the salt level in your diet around the same amount each day.
   b. You may notice that your hands develop a fine (light) tremor.
   c. If the tremor becomes worse and you feel nauseated, contact the doctor at once.
   d. A and B
   e. All of the above

6. A patient is using valproate therapy. Black box warnings for this medication include: (Select **ALL** that apply.)

   a. Neuroleptic Malignant Syndrome
   b. Severe Rash
   c. Hepatotoxicity
   d. Pancreatitis
   e. Teratogenicity

7. A patient has been diagnosed with bipolar II. Which of the following statement/s concerning bipolar II are correct?

   a. The mania symptoms are generally worse in bipolar II than in bipolar I.
   b. The depressive symptoms are generally worse in bipolar II than in bipolar I.
   c. Bipolar II is much less common than bipolar I.
   d. Bipolar II is much more common in men.
   e. In bipolar I, mania and psychosis can require hospitalization.

8. A patient received a prescription for asenapine. Choose the correct statement concerning asenapine. (Select **ALL** that apply.)

   a. Formulations of asenapine include an oral solution and tablets.
   b. Asenapine can make the mouth numb.
   c. Asenapine has little QT risk and can safely be used with cardiovascular conditions.
   d. The brand name is Saphire.
   e. Patients should be counseled to avoid driving when initiating or titrating therapy.

9. In the past few years, drugs typically used for schizophrenia have been approved for bipolar disorder. Which of the following antipsychotics have indications for bipolar disorder, according to the FDA-indications?

   a. Aripiprazole and Tiagabine
   b. Thioridazine and Topiramate
   c. Risperidone and Quetiapine extended-release
   d. Lamotrigine and Levetiracetam
   e. All of the above

10. A physician wishes to use an atypical antipsychotic for a patient with early Parkinson Disease. Her medications include ropinirole, metformin, glipizide, and a daily aspirin. He chooses to use quetiapine extended-release. Which of the following benefits would likely be experienced with the use of this agent?

   a. Little risk of movement disorders
   b. Little risk of metabolic issues, such as elevated blood sugar and lipids
   c. Little risk of sedation, orthostasis or dizziness
   d. No risk of stroke or worsened mental state
   e. No risk of increased appetite or weight gain

Answers

1-b,c, 2-a, 3-a,e, 4-a,b,c,d,e, 5-e, 6-c,d,e, 7-e, 8-b,e, 9-c, 10-a

PARKINSON DISEASE

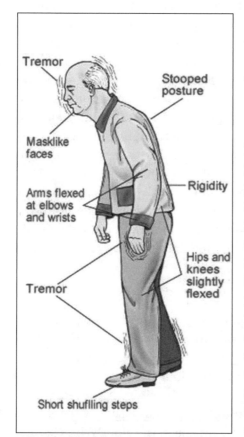

Tremor

Stooped posture

Masklike faces

Arms flexed at elbows and wrists

Rigidity

Hips and knees slightly flexed

Tremor

Short shuffling steps

GUIDELINE

Diagnosis and prognosis of new onset Parkinson disease (an evidence-based review): Report of the Quality Standards Subcommittee of the American Academy of Neurology. Neurology 2006 Apr 11;66(7):968-75.

We gratefully acknowledge the assistance of George De-Maagd, PharmD, BCPS, Associate Dean of Academic Administration, Professor of Pharmacy, Union University School of Pharmacy, in preparing this chapter.

BACKGROUND

Parkinson disease is a brain disorder. It occurs when neurons in a part of the brain called the substantia nigra die or become impaired. The cause of neuronal death is not well understood, but is multi-factorial. Normally, these cells produce dopamine. Dopamine allows smooth, coordinated function of the body's muscles and movement. When ~80% of the dopamine-producing cells are damaged, the motor symptoms of the disease appear. Non-motor symptoms can precede motor symptoms and may appear much earlier. These include loss of sense of smell (anosmia), constipation, sleep difficulties, low mood and orthostasis. While this disease usually develops after the age of 65, 15% of those diagnosed are under 50. Initially (in what is called Stage I) the disease appears as tremor on one-side (unilateral) and eventually spreads bilaterally. Bradykinesia (slow movement) refers to a reduction in spontaneous movement, which can give the appearance of abnormal stiffness and a decrease in facial expression. This causes difficulty with everyday functions, such as buttoning clothes and cutting food. Walking appears as shuffling steps. Speech is also affected. Rigidity causes stiffness and difficulty with movement. "Cogwheel rigidity" is a ratchet-like movement of arms. Postural instability, another cardinal feature of this condition, is a tendency

PRIMARY SIGNS/SYMPTOMS

TRAP:

Tremor – seen during resting, usually worsened by anxiety

Rigidity – arms, legs, trunk and face (mask-like face)

Akinesia/bradykinesia – lack of movement or slow initiation of movement

Postural instability – poor balance, which may lead to frequent falls

Other Signs of Parkinson Disease
Small, cramped handwriting (micrographia)

Shuffling walk

Stiff facial expression, reduced eye blinking

Muffled speech, drooling, dysphagia

Depression, anxiety (psychosis in advanced disease)

Constipation, incontinence

to be unstable when standing upright, and is due to a decline in reflexes. Some patients will sway backwards, which causes falls. Eventually, even with high doses of the two most effective classes of drugs (carbidopa/levodopa and the dopamine agonists), the "off" periods will increase – this is among the most frustrating and challenging of the complications. An off episode is a period of time with muscle stiffness, slow movements, and difficulty starting movements. Eventually, the patient will be unable to walk and have difficulty feeding themselves and swallowing foods. Amantadine can be useful to help with dyskinesias in later stage disease due to it's antagonism of the NMDA receptor. There is a newer drug (apomorphine) that treats later stage severe freezing episodes, but it is hard to take and provides increased movement for just about an hour. Patients with this condition have high incidence of depression. The agents with the highest efficacy for treatment in these patients are the tricyclic antidepressants, and the secondary amines (such as desipramine and notriptyline) are preferred due to less side effects than the tertiary amines. The majority of PD patients, however, use SSRIs since many clinicians are familiar with this class and think that they are better tolerated. Psychosis can present with advanced disease. Quetiapine is the preferred antipsychotic, due to a low risk of movement disorders, but will require monitoring due to metabolic complications, including increased blood glucose and cholesterol.

Drug-induced Parkinson Disease

Certain drugs can cause Parkinsonism due to their antagonism of dopamine receptors. These include phenothiazines (prochlorperazine, others), first generation antipsychotics (including haloperidol) the second-generation antipsychotics risperidone *(Risperdal)*, at higher doses, and the newer agent paliperidone *(Invega)*, and the dopamine-blocking agent metoclopramide *(Reglan)*. Metoclopramide is most likely to produce Parkinsonism when it is overdosed, which is not uncommon in the elderly since it must be reduced for renal dysfunction. CNS effects (sedation, dizziness) from this drug are another reason to avoid use in the elderly, if possible. Disorders with these drugs are always dose-dependent; higher doses (especially in elderly patients) are highest risk.

Therapy is directed at treating the symptoms. Medications can help improve movement, and may be used for related issues, such as psychosis and constipation.

Initial Therapy Selection

Levodopa, which is in the commonly used agent carbidopa-levodopa *(Sinemet)*, is the most effective agent and is sometimes better tolerated for initial treatment in the elderly than the dopamine agonists. Initial treatment of tremor in younger patients may be treated with an anticholinergic. The considerable side effects of the anticholinergics prohibit use in elderly patients. Amantadine is sometimes used for initial treatment of tremor, usually in younger patients. A monoamine oxidase inhibitor may also be used for a mild benefit as initial treatment.

As the disease progresses treatment will be directed at both reducing off periods and limiting dyskinesias.

Dopamine Replacement Agents & Agonists

DRUG	DOSING	SAFETY/SIDE EFFECTS/MONITORING

Carbidopa/Levodopa MOA: Levodopa is a precursor of dopamine. Carbidopa inhibits dopa decarboxylase, preventing peripheral metabolism of levodopa

Carbidopa/Levodopa (Sinemet, Sinemet CR) *Parcopa RapiTab* rapidly dissolves on the tongue without water. Levodopa and carbidopa are available separately. If switching from levodopa IR to levodopa-carbidopa CR, dosage should be substituted at an amount that provides ~10% more of levodopa/day.	Usual starting dose 25/100 TID IR: 10/100, 25/100, 25/250 mg tab SR: 25/100, 50/ 200 *Parcopa* comes in 10/100, 25/100 mg, 25/250 SR tab can be cut into half – do not crush or chew 70-100 mg of carbidopa is required to to inhibit the peripheral conversion (dopa decarboxylase) and to ↓ nausea	**CONTRAINDICATIONS** MAO inhibitors (non-selective) within prior 14 days, history of melanoma or undiagnosed skin lesions (melanoma risk higher with Parkinson's) **SIDE EFFECTS** Nausea, dizziness, orthostasis, vomiting, dry mouth, Dyskinesias (abnormal movements), dystonias (occasional, painful) ~1/3 of patients develop confusion, hallucinations, or psychosis (with disease progression; not initially) Can cause brown, black or dark urine, saliva or sweat, and discolor clothing **NOTES** Possibility of unusual sexual urges, priapism Response fluctuations after long-term use Separate from iron, possibly separate from protein (see counseling) May slightly increase uric acid

COMT-INHIBITOR: Used only with levodopa to ↑ levodopa duration of action. Inhibits the enzyme COMT to prevent peripheral and central conversion of levodopa

Entacapone *(Comtan)* Levodopa/carbidopa + entacapone *(Stalevo)* Tolcapone *(Tasmar)* – not used much due to hepatotoxicity	200 mg with each dose of carbidopa/levodopa (max 1,600 mg/day)	**SIDE EFFECTS** Similar to levodopa, due to extending levodopa duration of action: Nausea, dyskinesias Dizziness, orthostasis, hypotension Urine discoloration, diarrhea

Dopamine Replacement Agents & Agonists Continued

DRUG	DOSING	SAFETY/SIDE EFFECTS/MONITORING

DA-AGONISTS – Act Similar to dopamine at the dopamine receptor

Pramipexole *(Mirapex, Mirapex ER)* Both dopamine agonists approved in IR formulations (not long-acting) for restless leg syndrome (dosed QHS)	Start 0.125 mg TID, titrate weekly to 0.5–1.5 mg TID ER: Start 0.375 mg daily, can ~5-7 d to max dose of 4.5 mg/d A slow dose titration (no more than weekly) is required due to orthostasis, dizziness, sleepiness	**SIDE EFFECTS** Drowsiness, including sudden daytime sleep attacks Nausea, dizziness, orthostasis, vomiting, dry mouth, peripheral edema, constipation Hallucinations, dyskinesias, impulse control disorders **NOTES** Renal ↓ pramipexole dose if CrCl < 60 mL/min
Ropinirole *(Requip, Requip XL)* Restless leg syndrome, see above	Start 0.25 mg TID, titrate weekly to 1–4 mg TID XL: Start 2 mg daily, can ~1-2 weeks to max dose of 24 mg/d	Ropinirole: CYP 450 1A2 substrate; caution with 1A2 inhibitors due to increased drug levels. Bromocriptine *(Parlodel)* – no longer used for Parkinson's disease due to serious pulmonary complications; used as *Cycloset* for type 2 diabetes.
Rotigotine *(Neupro)* Patch formulation Like the other dopamine agonists, approved for both Parkinson disease and restless leg syndrome RLS: 1 mg/24 hours, can increase by 1 mg weekly	Patch: 1, 2, 3, 4, 6 or 8 mg/24 hours	**SIDE EFFECTS** Peripheral edema, drowsiness, headache, fatigue, orthostasis, sleep disturbance (trouble initiating/maintaining sleep), hallucinations, application site (skin) reactions, hyperhidrosis, nausea, dyskinesias, arthralgias. **NOTES** Apply once daily, same time each day Do not apply to same site for at least 14 days Do not apply heat source over patch Remove patch in MRI, avoid if sensitivity/allergy to sulfites

DA-agonist injection for advanced disease; a "rescue" movement agent; FOR "OFF" PERIODS

| Apomorphine *(Apokyn)*

 Lasts 45-90 minutes

 For hypomobility in advanced disease – SC injection restores temporary movement

 Used by patients for "off" periods; can be injected up to 5x/day. Taken in addition to other PD medications. | SC injection

 Start 0.2 mL (this is 2 mg, but do not write in mg) and can increase to a maximum recommended dose of 0.6 mL (6 mg) | **CONTRAINDICATIONS**
 With 5HT3-antagonists (ondansetron, others), due to severe hypotension and loss of consciousness

 SIDE EFFECTS
 Severe NAUSEA and vomiting, hypotension; monitor BP

 Supine and standing blood pressure should be checked pre-dose and at 20, 40, and 60 minutes post dose

 Trimethobenzamide *(Tigan)* 300 mg PO TID or a similar antiemetic should be started 3 days prior to the initial dose of apomorphine and continued at least during the first two months of therapy

 Yawning, dyskinesias, somnolence, dizziness, QT-prolongation |

CARBIDOPA/LEVODOPA *(Sinemet)* Drug Interactions

- Contraindicated with non-selective MAO-Inhibitors (2 week separation).

- Do not use with dopamine blockers – which will worsen disease symptoms (see front section) – this includes phenothiazines, metoclopramide, etc.

- Iron can ↓ absorption.

- Protein-rich foods can ↓ absorption.

CARBIDOPA/LEVODOPA *(Sinemet)* Counseling

- Do not stop taking this medicine suddenly. It may take several weeks before you feel the full effects of this medicine. Stopping suddenly could make your condition much worse.

- Do not crush or chew any controlled-release forms of carbidopa and levodopa *(Sinemet CR)*. They are specially formulated to release slowly into your system. If necessary, the tablets can be split in half where they are scored, then swallowed without crushing or chewing.

- Use caution when driving, operating machinery, or performing other hazardous activities. Carbidopa and levodopa may cause dizziness or drowsiness. If you experience dizziness or drowsiness, avoid these activities.

- Call your doctor right away if you have uncontrollable movements of the mouth, tongue, cheeks, jaw, arms, or legs. Contact your doctor if you experience fever or if your body feels very hot.

- Do not take carbidopa and levodopa if you are taking or have taken a monoamine oxidase inhibitor (MAOI) such as isocarboxazid *(Marplan)*, phenelzine *(Nardil)*, or tranylcypromine *(Parnate)* in the past 14 days.

- You may have unusual sexual urges – if this develops, discuss with your doctor.

- This drug may cause the urine to become darker, even dark brown, and can stain clothing.

- Iron can decrease the amount of medicine that gets into your body; if you take iron pills they should be taken at a different time.

- Foods high in protein may reduce the amount of drug that gets into your body (however, protein intake is important and usually not reduced).

- For males, in the very unlikely event you have a painful or prolonged erection (lasting more than 4 hours), stop using this drug and seek immediate medical attention or permanent problems could result.

- The *Parcopa RapiTab* disintegrating tablet contains phenylalanine. If you have phenylketonuria, you should not use this medicine.

Ropinirole & Pramipexole *(Requip & Mirapex)* Counseling

- This medicine can be taken with or without food. Taking it with food is helpful if the medicine causes nausea.

- Nausea and sleepiness are the most common side effects. If your ankles get swollen, let the doctor know.

- This medicine may cause you to fall asleep while you are doing daily activities such as driving, talking with other people, watching TV, or eating. If you experience increased drowsiness or dizziness, or episodes of falling asleep while performing daily activities, do not drive or participate in potentially dangerous activities and contact your doctor.

- This drug can cause dizziness, which may be more likely to occur when you rise from a sitting or lying position. Rise slowly and use caution to prevent a fall.

- Alcohol, sleeping pills, antihistamines, antidepressants, pain medicine and other medicines that cause drowsiness can make the drowsiness worse, which could be dangerous. Do not use alcohol.

- Hallucinations may occur, and may be more common in elderly patients. Please tell your doctor if you experience thoughts which seem like they are paranoid, or excessive worry, or hearing voices. There is medicine that may help, or the dose may need to be changed.

- It is likely that the doctor will increase the dose slowly, over time. This is normal, since the dose has to start low due to dizziness and sleepiness.

Rotigotine *(Neupro)* Patch Counseling

- Side effects from the patch can include ankle swelling, headache, fatigue, nausea, changes in blood pressure, difficulty getting a good night's sleep, and unusual thoughts. If any of these occur and are troublesome, discuss with your doctor.

- This medicine can cause you to become very sleepy. Do not drive a car or operate dangerous machinery until you are sure this can be done safely.

- If you have any unusual body movements, please contact your doctor.

- You may find that you sweat more than usual. It is important to drink enough fluids and avoid direct sunlight.

- The patch contains aluminum, which can burn your skin if you have certain medical procedures. The patch must be removed prior to magnetic resonance imaging (MRI) or "cardioversion."

- The patch can irritate the skin. It is important to rotate the patch site.

- Do not expose the patch to heat sources, such as heating pads.

- To apply the patch:

  ❑ Choose the time of day that works best for you so it is easiest to remember.

  ❑ Wear the patch for 24 hours. Remove before applying the next patch.

  ❑ Do not apply to hairy skin, or skin that has cuts. Do not use moisturizer before applying the patch or it will not stick well.

  ❑ After peeling off one side of the backing, apply to dry skin on the stomach, thigh, hip, side of the body, shoulder or upper arm. PRESS in place for 30 seconds.

  ❑ Do not cut the patch. If the patch falls off, you can reapply with bandage tape.

  ❑ The patch can irritate the skin. Report to the doctor if you get a rash, swelling or itching that persists. Rotate the place where you place the patch. Wait at least 14 days before applying in the same location.

Apomorphine *(Apokyn)* Counseling

- Do not take with any of these drugs: ondansetron, dolasetron, granisetron, palonosetron, and alosetron or any drug of the 5HT$_3$ antagonist class or group if using apomorphine.

- This drug causes severe nausea, and vomiting. A drug called trimethobenzamide *(Tigan)*, started before using this medicine and during treatment, will help reduce nausea.

- Other possible side effects include yawning, a runny nose, and swelling of your hands, arms, legs, and feet.

- Do not drink alcohol or any medicines that make you sleepy while you are using this medicine.

- Do not drive a car, operate machinery, or do anything that might put you or others at risk of getting hurt until you know how the medicine affects you.

- This medicine can cause dizziness or fainting. Do not change your body position too fast. Get up slowly from sitting or lying.

- Choose an injection site on your stomach area, upper arm, or upper leg. Change your injection site each time the medicine is used. This will lower your chances of having a skin reaction at the site where you inject.

- This medicine is given by subcutaneous (SC) injection. Never inject into a vein.

Additional Parkinson Disease Medications

DRUG	DOSING	SAFETY/SIDE EFFECTS/MONITORING
Amantadine: blocks dopamine reuptake into presynaptic neurons, increases dopamine release from presynaptic fibers; Used for mild disease, or for dyskinesias in advanced disease		
Amantadine *(Symmetrel)*	100 mg BID-TID ↓ dose in renal impairment	**SIDE EFFECTS** Dizziness (lightheadedness) and insomnia Toxic delirium (with renal impairment, ↓ dose) Cutaneous reaction called *livedo reticularis* (reddish skin mottling – requires drug discontinuation)

Additional Parkinson Disease Medications Continued

DRUG	DOSING	SAFETY/SIDE EFFECTS/MONITORING

Selective MAO-B Inhibitors: used with levodopa or *(Azilect)* with levodopa or as initial monotherapy

Selegiline *(Eldepryl)* *Zelapar*-ODT (rapidly dissolving oral formulation) Rasagiline *(Azilect)* Doses above max will become non-selective *Emsam* (selegiline patch) is indicated for depression May need to reduce levodopa dose when beginning therapy w/selective MAO-B Inhibitor--watch for side effects	Selegiline 5-10 mg daily *Zelapar* 1.25-5 mg daily Rasagiline 0.5-1 mg daily Selegiline can be activating; do not dose at bedtime. If dosed twice, take 2nd dose at mid-day. Selegiline only has benefit when used with levodopa Rasagiline can be used as initial monotherapy or adjunctive with levodopa.	**CONTRAINDICATIONS** Rasagaline: Concomitant use of cyclobenzaprine, dextromethorphan, methadone, propoxyphene, St John's wort, or tramadol; concomitant use of meperidine or an MAO inhibitor (including selective MAO-B inhibitors) within 14 days of rasagiline. **SIDE EFFECTS** Due to DA-excess, similar to levodopa Rasagiline, when taken as monotherapy, can cause headache, joint pain and indigestion. If taken with levodopa, any of the side effects from dopamine excess are possible. Drug Interactions: meperidine (can be fatal), tramadol, methadone, propoxyphene, dextromethorphan, St. John's wort, mirtazapine, cyclobenzaprine Tyramine Interactions: Low risk, but possible, of hypertensive crisis if used with tyramine rich foods – see MAO Is in depression chapter. (Rasagiline is more risky with both drugs and tyramine-foods, selegiline has had interactions with mostly drugs--this is dose dependent, keep doses at MAO-B selective levels or drugs become non-selective.)

Centrally-Acting Anticholinergics: used primarily for tremor in younger patients

Benztropine *(Cogentin)*	0.5-2 mg TID (start QHS)	Used primarily for tremor; avoid use in elderly **SIDE EFFECTS** Dry mouth, constipation, urinary retention, blurred vision
Trihexyphenidyl	1-2 mg TID (start QHS)	Drowsiness, confusion, tachycardia, high incidence peripheral and central anticholinergic side effects

PRACTICE CASE

Benjamin, a 70 year-old male, has been using carbidopa/levodopa for three years. His current dose is 25/250 TID. For the past month, he reports he has had trouble eating his breakfast and has difficulty with "off" moments, mostly in the late afternoon before the evening dose. While Benjamin is talking, he is having difficulty keeping his arms still and occasionally rolls his head in a circular motion. He had started ropinirole after the last doctor's visit but found it made him so dizzy and sleepy that he couldn't drive safely. His wife does not drive, and the excessive sleepiness caused the couple much distress. He self-discontinued the ropinirole. The initial ropinirole prescription was written for 1 mg TID. He is asking for advice on the worsening disease.

CATEGORY	
Medications	Carbidopa/Levodopa 25/250 mg TID
	Ropinirole 1 mg TID (not using, per patient)
	Ramipril 10 mg daily
	Amlodipine 10 mg daily
	Multivitamin daily

Questions

1. Choose the correct statement concerning the patient's Carbidopa/Levodopa therapy:

    a. The dose of carbidopa is too low.

    b. The dose of carbidopa is too high.

    c. The medication may make his urine turn brown.

    d. The medication will worsen his hypertension.

    e. The medication can cause severe rash.

2. When Benjamin started ropinirole, he found he could not tolerate the medicine due to excessive sleepiness. Choose the correct statement:

    a. The starting dose of ropinirole was too high.

    b. Pramipexole would be less sedating.

    c. The brand name of ropinirole is *Mirapex*.

    d. He should have been started on benztropine instead.

    e. He should have been counseled to increase his caffeine intake during therapy initiation.

3. Choose the correct titration schedule for ropinirole or pramipexole:

    a. Wait at least 2 days before increasing the dose.

    b. Wait about one week before increasing the dose.

    c. Wait at least two weeks before increasing the dose.

    d. Wait at least three weeks before increasing the dose.

    e. Wait at least four weeks before increasing the dose.

4. Benjamin is using levodopa therapy. He is taking carbidopa concurrently, in the combination medicine *Sinemet*. Choose the correct statement concerning carbidopa:

    a. Carbidopa inhibits decarboxylase and prevents the breakdown of levodopa outside the CNS.

    b. The dose of carbidopa should stay between 70-100 mg.

    c. Using carbidopa with levodopa will decrease nausea.

    d. A and B

    e. All of the above

5. Which of the following is a common side effect from ropinirole therapy?

 a. Brown urine
 b. Extreme hunger
 c. Somnolence
 d. Loss of consciousness
 e. Hyperglycemia

Questions 6-11 do not apply to the case.

6. A patient has been started on selegiline therapy. What is the mechanism of action of selegiline?

 a. Selective inhibitor of monoamine oxidase A
 b. Selective inhibitor of monoamine oxidase B
 c. Dopamine reuptake inhibitor
 d. Dopamine agonist
 e. Anticholinergic

7. Which of the following medications will require a dose reduction with renal impairment?

 a. Rasagiline
 b. Pramipexole
 c. Benztropine
 d. Levodopa
 e. None of the above

8. Choose the drug which can be safely administered to a patient receiving *Azilect* therapy:

 a. Tramadol
 b. Meperidine
 c. Dextromethorphan
 d. Methadone
 e. None of the above

9. Which of the following side effects can occur with the use of benzotropine, a centrally-acting anticholinergic medication?

 a. Dry mouth
 b. Urinary retention
 c. Confusion, drowsiness
 d. A and B only
 e. All of the above

10. A patient is having a difficult time swallowing pills. Which of the following medications would be the best option for this type of patient?

 a. *Comtan*
 b. *Cogentin*
 c. *Azilect*
 d. *Zelapar ODT*
 e. *Symmetrel*

11. Which of the following medications can worsen or cause Parkinson-like symptoms?

 a. Metoclopramide, especially in a patient with renal insufficiency
 b. Risperdal, especially when dosed high (> 6 mg daily)
 c. Haloperidol
 d. A and B only
 e. All of the above

Answers

1-c, 2-a, 3-b, 4-e, 5-c, 6-b, 7-b, 8-e, 9-e, 10-d, 11-e

ALZHEIMER'S DISEASE

We gratefully acknowledge the assistance of George DeMaagd, PharmD, BCPS, Associate Dean of Academic Administration, Professor of Pharmacy, Union University School of Pharmacy, in preparing this chapter.

BACKGROUND

Dementia is a group of symptoms affecting intellectual and social abilities severely enough to interfere with daily functioning. There are several types of dementia and Alzheimer's disease is the most common type and the type with well-defined treatment. Unfortunately, the treatments provide modest benefit.

Diagnosis

Exams include the Folstein Mini-Mental State Exam (MMSE – a score < 24 indicates impairment – and note that the MMSE is not a diagnostic tool for AD, rather it is a screening tool that indicates dementia or some type of memory disorder), DSM V criteria, National Institute of Neurological and Communicative Disorders and Stroke and the Alzheimer's Disease and Related Diseases Association (NINCDS-ARDA) criteria. The prescriber uses tests to diagnose dementia, which can be of variable types. A definitive diagnosis of the actual cause and type of the dementia cannot be made unless an autopsy is conducted post-mortem. If the diagnosis is a dementia that will progressively worsen over time, such as Alzheimer's disease, early diagnosis gives a person time to plan for the future while he or she can still participate in making decisions.

GUIDELINES

American Geriatrics Society. Guide to the management of psychotic disorders and neuropsychiatric symptoms of dementia in older adults. April 2011.

Qaseem A, Snow V, Cross T, et al. Current pharmacologic treatment of dementia: a clinical practice guideline from the American College of Physicians and the American Academy of Family Physicians. http://www.ncbi.nlm.nih.gov/entrez/query.fcgi?cmd=Retrieve&db=PubMed&list_uids=18316755&dopt=Abstract, Ann Intern Med. 2008; 148:370-8.

Memory loss

Difficulty communicating

Inability to learn or remember new information

Difficulty with planning and organizing

Poor coordination & motor functions

Personality changes

Inappropriate behavior

Paranoia, agitation, hallucinations

Pathophysiology
Neuritic plaques & tangles in brain tissue; neuron signaling is interrupted

Alteration of neurotransmitters (e.g., decreased acetylcholine)

DRUGS THAT CAN WORSEN DEMENTIA

Peripheral anticholinergics (including incontinence & IBS drugs)

Central anticholinergics (benztropine, etc.)

Antihistamines & antiemetics

Antipsychotics

Barbiturates

Benzodiazepines

Skeletal muscle relaxants

Other CNS depressants

Treatment

Acetylcholinesterase inhibitors, such as donepezil, are the mainstay of therapy. These are used alone, or with memantine for more advanced disease. At best, one in twelve patients has improvement with these medications. However, for a family, this may mean that the patient who responds can feed themselves for a little while longer, or use the bathroom independently for several more months. Many others do not have noticeable improvement and likely experience side effects (nausea, diarrhea, dizziness). A key clinical pearl with the acetylcholinesterase inhibitors is that although patients may not improve clinically, they may have a slower clinical progression versus if they were not on therapy.

A higher dose of donepezil *(Aricept)* was released in 2010 for advanced disease, however the benefit is very mild (2 point improvement on a 100-point cognition scale.) The motivation for the release of this product was the availability of generic donepezil. If a prescriber writes for the higher dose the patient will need to purchase the brand medication. With acetylcholinesterase inhibitors the patient should be monitored for both improvement and side effects; if no improvement or intolerable side effects the drug may be discontinued – this may also be advisable if the dementia has advanced to the point where it lacks clinical benefit. However, it may not be acceptable to the family and in some patients there will be noticeable deterioration when the medicine is discontinued. The timing of the dose should be considered: if nausea is present, evening administration can be helpful. Donepezil is administered QHS for this reason. If insomnia is a concern, the dose can be moved to the morning.

It has become more common to add memantine *(Namenda)* to an acetylcholinesterase inhibitor. It is approved for use alone or with donepezil.

Antidepressants (e.g., sertraline, citalopram, escitalopram) can be used to treat related depression and anxiety. Antipsychotics can be used to treat delusion/anger, but they increase the risk of death in elderly patients (mostly due to an increased risk of stroke) and provide little benefit.

NATURAL PRODUCTS USED FOR DEMENTIA

Vitamin E is sometimes tried for dementia, but doses (> 150 IU) carry risk. *Ginkgo biloba* is commonly used for memory; a well-designed, 8-year study completed in 2008 did not find benefit for prevention of dementia with the use of ginkgo, but many patients still use it, and in some earlier studies the use of ginkgo provided modest benefit – for both dementia and in slowing age-related memory decline. At this point, the benefit is not well-defined. Ginkgo can increase bleeding risk. But remember, there is not much available to treat this disease and the patient and family may want "something" to help. Huperzine A (derived from chinese club moss) is being used for dementia with promising efficacy. The adverse effects are similar to acetylcholinesterase inhibitors, and are mostly gastrointestinal, such as nausea. Other natural products such as A-phosphatidylserine and acetyl-L-carnitine may be helpful.

DRUG INTERACTION??

If adding an anti-muscarinic for overactive bladder, monitor for efficacy. These drugs are the opposite mechanism of the cholinesterase inhibitors, although the lipophilicity varies, and thus, the effect may be little. If there is no benefit with the incontinence drug (and these have little benefit), they should be discontinued in patients using a cholinesterase inhibitor as it may decrease the efficacy of the dementia drug. Incontinence causes significant stress for caregivers (families) and can cause nursing home placement; these factors should be considered. If possible, drugs with anticholinergic properties should be avoided in patients with dementia, or the lowest (useful) dose used.

DRUGS TO TREAT ALZHEIMER'S DISEASE

DRUG	DOSING	SAFETY/SIDE EFFECTS/MONITORING
Acetylcholinesterase Inhibitors – Inhibits centrally-active acetylcholinesterase, the enzyme responsible for hydrolysis (breakdown) of acetylcholine, which results in ↑ ACh		
Donepezil *(Aricept)* *Aricept ODT* 5 or 10 mg - disintegrating tablet Used alone or with memantine in more severe disease *Aricept 23 mg* used for advanced disease – minimal additional benefit	5-10 mg QHS for mild to moderate disease 23 mg QHS, for advanced disease, if stable on lower dose 1st x 3 mos Do not crush or chew	FOR MILD-MODERATE DISEASE (& IN COMBO FOR MODERATE-SEVERE AD) **SIDE EFFECTS** GI side effects (nausea, vomiting, loose stools) Donepezil given QHS to help with nausea Bradycardia, fainting, insomnia
Rivastigmine *(Exelon, Exelon Patch)*	1.5-6 mg BID 4.6, 9.5, 13.3 mg/24 hr patch 2 mg/mL liquid	**NOTES** Other oral formulations are BID or daily if long-acting Rivastigmine is with food – others without regards to meals (if GI issues can take with food) Recommend *Exelon* patch or *Aricept ODT* to decrease GI side effects – if the cost difference is acceptable
Galantamine *(Razadyne, Razadyne ER)*	4-12 mg BID 4mg/mL solution ER: start at 8 mg daily, then ↑ to 16-24 mg	*Exelon* patch: titrate Q 4 weeks, apply first patch the day after last oral dose *Razadyne* solution: can mix in 100 mL of non-alcohol liquid

Drugs to Treat Alzheimer's Disease Continued

DRUG	DOSING	SAFETY/SIDE EFFECTS/MONITORING

Memantine – blocks NMDA (N-methyl-D-aspartate), which inhibits glutamate from binding to NMDA receptors & ↓ abnormal activation

Memantine *(Namenda, Namenda XR)* Approved for use alone or in combination with donepezil *(Aricept)* for moderate to severe AD Take XR with food or drink, IR with or without food XR caps can be opened and sprinkled on applesauce	5-10 mg BID (titrate ~weekly) or 28 mg daily if XR (start at 7 mg daily and titrate not faster than weekly) Can switch 10 mg BID to 28 mg daily; start daily; begin XR the next day (not same day) Oral Solution 2 mg/mL (10 mg = 5 mL)	FOR MODERATE-SEVERE DISEASE **SIDE EFFECTS** Dizziness, constipation, headache Rare SEs: flu-like symptoms, arthralgia, UTIs, urinary retention, small risk seizures, hypertension **NOTES** Mostly excreted unchanged in urine; do not exceed 5 mg BID if CrCl < 30 mL/min

Acetylcholinesterase Drug Interactions

- Use caution with concurrent use of drugs that can lower heart rate (beta blockers, diltiazem, verapamil, digoxin, etc.) and with drugs that cause dizziness (antipsychotics, antihypertensives, alpha blockers, skeletal muscle relaxants, hypnotics, opioids, etc.) due to the risk of dizziness and falls.

- Drugs that have anticholinergic effects can reduce the efficacy (see previous table for drugs that can worsen symptoms). Monitor benefit with incontinence drugs; if no benefit, consider discontinuation.

Acetylcholinesterase Counseling

- These medicines can cause nausea and stomach upset. If this remains a problem, talk to your doctor about changing to the longer-acting formulations, or the *Exelon* patch, which has the least nausea. Taking the medicine with food should help.

- Tell patients that the drug dose may be increased, but is started low due to the risk of dizziness, falls, and nausea. Use caution when moving from a sitting to a standing position. Try not to use with other drugs that can lower your heart rate and make you feel dizzy. Try not to use alcohol when using this medicine.

- Please tell the pharmacist about all medicine you purchase over-the-counter since some of these can worsen memory problems.

- Please make sure the pharmacist knows about all prescription drugs you are using. Some of them can worsen memory problems.

- Donepezil is started at 5 mg, at bedtime. It is taken at night to help with nausea. If you experience sleep problems (insomnia), you can take it in the morning. If you have trouble swallowing the medicine, there is a formulation that dissolves in your mouth that can be used instead. Your doctor may increase the dose to 10 mg after about 4 weeks.

- Rivastigmine is started at 1.5 mg twice daily, with food. Taking this medicine with food should help reduce nausea. Your doctor may increase the dose after about 4 weeks.

- Galantamine is started at 4 mg twice daily, with or without food. Your doctor may increase the dose after about 4 weeks.

Exelon patch application instructions

- Apply to the upper or lower back, upper arm, or chest; rotate applications site. Do not use the same site within 14 days. Do not apply to an area of the skin that is hairy, oily, irritated, broken, scarred, or calloused.

- Do not apply to an area where cream, lotion, or powder has recently been applied. Do not place the patch under tight clothing.

- Do not remove the patch from the sealed pouch until you are ready to apply it.

- Remove the protective liner from one side of the patch.

- Place the sticky side of the patch on the application site, then remove the second side of the protective liner.

- Press the patch down firmly until the edges stick well.

- After 24 hours, remove the used patch.

- Do not touch the sticky side. Fold the patch in half with the sticky sides together.

Memantine Counseling (Caregivers)

- Take this medication by mouth, with or without food. When you first start taking this medication, you will usually take it once daily. Your dose will be gradually increased to lower the risk of side effects. Once your dose increases to more than 5 milligrams per day, take this medication twice daily (5 mg twice daily, and then it usually increases to 10 mg twice daily).

- If you are taking memantine oral liquid, read the instruction sheet that comes with the bottle. Follow the directions exactly. Use the oral syringe that comes with the product to measure out your dose. Swallow the medication directly from the syringe. Do not mix it with water or other liquids. Rinse the syringe with water after each use.

- You may experience dizziness; use caution when moving from a sitting to a standing position. Try not to use with other drugs that can make you feel dizzy. Try not to use alcohol when using this medicine.

- If you become constipated from this medicine, please ask your pharmacist, who can recommend a stool softener (if the stool is hard) or a different type of laxative that is taken at bedtime. These are available over-the-counter. The laxatives come in chewable or liquid formulations.

Memantine Extended Release *(Namenda XR)*

Same as above except:

- Take once daily with food or drink – if trouble swallowing can open capsule and sprinkle on applesauce (do not divide dose) but do not crush or chew the capsule.

- Start at 7 mg daily. Titrate weekly (as tolerated) to 28 mg daily.

ATTENTION DEFICIT HYPERACTIVITY DISORDER (ADHD) & STIMULANT AGENTS

BACKGROUND

The core symptoms of ADHD are <u>inattention, hyperactivity, and impulsivity</u>. People with ADHD often have difficulty focusing, are easily distracted, have trouble staying still, and frequently are unable to control impulsive behavior. Primary symptoms vary; some patients are more inattentive, and others are more impulsive.

The primary treatment for ADHD are <u>stimulant</u> medications, primarily methylphenidate formulations *(Concerta*, others) and lisdexamfetamine *(Vyvanse)*. The rationale behind using stimulants is to raise dopamine and norepinephrine levels. In ADHD it is thought that there is a lack of dopamine, or a lack of functioning dopamine receptors or some defect in the dopamine pathway, in the brains of persons with ADHD. Providing medications is challenging because this condition, more than many others, is marked by a wide variation in treatment response and in optimal dosing range. The range in treatment response and dosing has led research into the hypothesis that genetic factors may underlie such differences. Due to the positive response from using methylphenidate, the primary focus of research is on the catecholamine system (dopamine is catalyzed to the two other primary catecholamines, epinephrine and norepinephrine.)

Keep in mind that a focus on genetics alone is a mechanistic view; it is likely that <u>stressors</u> alter the brains pattern of catecholamine use in some patients, which leads to ADHD symptoms. In the popular book *Scattered* (Gabor Maté, MD), the author focuses on altering the environment to help control symptoms. Environment, as well as genetics, is a determinant in brain chemistry and alterations in the environment can change the chemistry. However, some require medications even with strong social support.

ADHD causes a good deal of emotional response from those who feel stimulant drugs are over-used and, on the other side, from parents who rely on the drugs to help their children do better in school, and from adults who use ADHD medications. As pharmacists, we should do our best to remain nonjudgmental and make sure that when medications are prescribed, they are used safely. Since <u>the stimulants are C II</u>, the prescriptions are for one month at a time, which makes it convenient to check blood pressure and heart rate (and weight and height, periodically, in children). Many prescribers issue three months of prescriptions at a time, which are post-dated. Stimulants are a common drug of abuse and have a high street value; these should be dispensed with caution, and counseling must include instructions <u>not to share with others and to store in a safe place</u>. Occasionally the "ADHD" stimulants are used for other conditions, including narcolepsy and shift work sleep disorder; these conditions are discussed at the end of this chapter.

About 10% of school-aged children are using ADHD medications, with boys outnumbering girls. The guidelines have age-specific treatment recommendations for children ages 4-18 years. ADHD should be considered a chronic illness; many children do not outgrow ADHD; up to 80% of children will continue to exhibit symptoms into adolescence and up to 65% of children will still exhibit symptoms into adulthood. Inattention and impulsivity often remain as the patient ages, and hyperactivity can be decreased.

DSM-5 DIAGNOSTIC CRITERIA

People with ADHD show a persistent pattern of inattention and/or hyperactivity-impulsivity that interferes with functioning or development. The DSM-5 requirements for an ADHD diagnosis:

<u>Inattention</u>: Six or more symptoms of inattention for children up to age 16, or five or more for ages 17 to adults; symptoms of inattention have been present for at least 6 months, and they are inappropriate for the developmental level:

- Fails to pay attention, has trouble holding attention, does not pay attention when someone is talking, does not follow through on instructions, fails to finish schoolwork, has difficulty organizing tasks, avoids or dislikes tasks which require mental effort, loses things, is easily distracted, and is forgetful.

<u>Hyperactivity and Impulsivity</u>: Six or more symptoms of hyperactivity-impulsivity for children up to age 16, or five or more for ages 17 to adults; symptoms of hyperactivity-impulsivity have been present for at least 6 months to an extent that is disruptive and inappropriate for the person's developmental level:

- Often fidgets or squirms, leaves seat unexpectedly, runs about when not appropriate, unable to play quietly, is "on the go" as if "driven by a motor", talks excessively, blurts out answers, has trouble waiting his/her turn, and interrupts or intrudes on others.

In addition, the following conditions must be met:

- Several inattentive or hyperactive-impulsive symptoms were present before age 12 years, symptoms must have been present in 2 or more settings (at home, school, at work, with friends or relatives), symptoms interfere with functioning, and symptoms are not caused by another psychiatric disorder.

PHARMACOLOGIC TREATMENT

First-line drug therapy for ADHD are stimulants. When stimulants do not work well enough (after trials of 2-3 agents), atomoxetine *(Strattera)*, a non-stimulant medication, can be tried next, or will be used first-line by prescribers who are concerned about the possibility of abuse by the patient or family.

The stimulant agent methylphenidate, which is available in various formulations, is tried first, or lisdexamfetamine (*Vyvanse*), the pro-drug of dextroamphetamine. Longer-acting formulations are preferred for children who would otherwise need dosing at school (which would require a nurse's office visit) and to help maintain more steady symptom control. Other stimulant classes can be tried.

Guanfacine (approved in the extended-release formulation *Intuniv*), clonidine (in the extended-release formulation *Kapvay*) are used most often as adjunctive treatments. For example, it is common to see *Concerta* with *Intuniv*, or *Vyvanse* with *Kapvay*, or vice versa. The guanfacine or clonidine formulation is being added-on to the stimulant after the stimulant was tried and provided some (but not enough) benefit. They are also used alone. Clonidine is also used in the immediate-release formulation to help patients on stimulants sleep at night. More commonly, diphenhydramine is used for this purpose.

Family therapy/psychotherapy may be required for an improved prognosis. The drugs described in this section are used off-label to help with some of the symptoms of autism.

NATURAL PRODUCTS

Fish oils are a natural product increasingly used for a variety of psychiatric conditions, including ADHD. Fish oil supplements (which provide omega 3 fatty acids) with or without evening primrose oil (which provides omega-6 fatty acids) may be helpful in some patients. Fish oils are rated as "possibly effective" to improve cognitive function and behavior in children with ADHD by the *Natural Medicines Database*. Check the dose prior to making a recommendation. The combo product used in the study that showed benefit used 6 capsules daily. Other products are occasionally used for ADHD, including SAMe, St. John's wort and ginkgo. If St. John's wort is used, check for drug interactions since this herbal induces CYP450 enzymes and will lower the concentration of the majority of other drugs. It is serotonergic, and has phototoxicity risk.

STIMULANTS FOR ADHD

CNS stimulants that block the reuptake of norepinephrine and dopamine.

DRUG	DOSING	SAFETY/SIDE EFFECTS/MONITORING

Methylphenidate

DRUG	DOSING	SAFETY/SIDE EFFECTS/MONITORING
Methylphenidate IR (*Ritalin, Methylin* chewable, oral susp) All of the stimulants (including modafinil and armodafinil) and atomoxetine require a MedGuide. Clonidine ext-release (*Kapvay*) and guanficine ext-release (*Intuniv*) do not.	2.5-20 mg tabs, and as oral solution and chewables BID-TID, 30 minutes before meals	**BLACK BOX WARNING** Potential for drug dependency; use caution if a history of ethanol or drug abuse. **CONTRAINDICATIONS** Marked anxiety, tension, and agitation, glaucoma, MAO I's use within the past 14 days, family history or diagnosis of Tourette's syndrome or tics. *Metadate CD* and *Metadate ER* only: Severe hypertension, heart failure, arrhythmia, hyperthyroidism, recent MI or angina; concomitant use of halogenated anesthetics. *Ritalin* and *Ritalin SR* only: Pheochromocytoma
Methylphenidate long-acting (*Ritalin LA*) ½ IR, ½ SR in one capsule	10-40 mg LA caps	**SIDE EFFECTS** Nausea, loss of appetite, insomnia, dizziness, headache, lightheadedness, irritability, blurry vision, difficulty with visual accomodation Stimulants ↑ BP ~2-4 mmHg, ↑ HR ~3-8 BPM, monitor, extreme caution with any cardiovascular disease; avoid use with known cardiac issues/defects
Methylphenidate sustained release (*Ritalin SR*)	20 mg SR tabs	Exacerbation of mixed/mania episodes if bipolar disorder, use caution with any pre-existing psychiatric condition; may exacerbate, including depression, aggressive behavior, hostility Withdrawal reactions (hyper); titrate both up and down Peripheral vasculopathy may worsen, including Raynaud's phenomenon
Methylphenidate ext-release (*Methylin ER, Metadate ER, Quillivant XR* – ext-release oral suspension)	10-20 mg ER tabs	Risk of seizures (use caution with seizure history) **MONITORING** Consider ECG prior to treatment, monitor BP and HR during treatment. Children: monitor height and weight.
Methylphenidate IR – ext-release (*Concerta*) OROS system Somewhat harder to abuse (harder to crush)	18, 27, 36, 54 mg ER tabs QAM, with or without food, swallow whole	Conduct cardiac evaluation if chest pain, unexplained syncope, or other cardiac symptom develops. Monitor CNS activity in all patients; signs of peripheral vasculopathy (e.g., digital changes), signs of misuse, abuse, or addiction.
Methylphenidate IR – ext-release (*Metadate CD*) Beads that dissolve at different rates	10-60 mg ER caps	**NOTES** *Focalin XR, Ritalin LA, Metadate CD* and *Adderal XR* can be taken whole or the capsules sprinkled on applesauce (if not warm and used right away, do not chew). *Concerta OROS* delivery The capsule's outer coat dissolves fast to give immediate action, and the rest is released slowly.
Methylphenidate transdermal patch (*Daytrana*)	1.1 mg/hr (10 mg/9 hr)-3.3 mg/hr (30 mg/9 hr)	*Concerta, Metadate CD* and *Ritalin LA* are all QAM (IRs and some others are divided), and *Daytrana* patch is QAM, applied to alternate hip 2 hours before desired effect (or as soon as the child awakens so it starts to deliver prior to school). Remove after 9 hours (at night, so the patient can sleep). C II; do not share, store in safe place.

Stimulants for ADHD Continued

DRUG	DOSING	SAFETY/SIDE EFFECTS/MONITORING
Dexmethylphenidate		
Dexmethylphenidate IR *(Focalin)*	2.5-10 mg tabs BID, 4+ hrs apart, with or without food	see Methylphenidate
Dexmethylphenidate ER *(Focalin XR)*	5-20 mg caps QAM	

DRUG	DOSING	SAFETY/SIDE EFFECTS/MONITORING
Dextroamphetamine and amphetamine		
Dextroamphetamine and amphetamine IR *(Adderall)*	5-30 mg scored tabs Given QAM or BID without regard to meals. First dose on awakening, additional dose 4-6 h later.	see Methylphenidate
Dextroamphetamine and amphetamine ER *(Adderall XR)*	5-30 mg ER caps QAM, with or without food	
Dextroamphetamine IR *(Dexedrine, Dextrostat)*	5-10 mg tabs QAM or BID, with or without food.	
SR and IR Dextroamphetamine *(Dexedrine Spansules, ProCentra)*	5, 10, 15 mg SR caps QAM, with or without food.	

DRUG	DOSING	SAFETY/SIDE EFFECTS/MONITORING
Lisdexamfetamine (prodrug of dextroamphetamine)		
Lisdexamfetamine *(Vyvanse)*	20, 30, 40, 50, 60, 70 mg caps Can mix capsule contents with water, drink stat. QAM, with or without food	see Methylphenidate **NOTES** Lisdexamfetamine is a prodrug composed of l-lysine (amino acid) bonded to dextroamphetamine (d-amphetamine). It is hydrolyzed in the blood to active d-amphetamine. If injected or snorted the fast effect would be muted. The design may ↓ abuse potential.

Stimulant Drug Interactions

- 14-Day wash out period after MAO I use.

Patient Counseling for Stimulants

- Dispense MedGuide and instruct parents/patient to read it. Stimulants should not be used in patients with heart problems or serious psychiatric conditions. Report at once if the child has chest pain, shortness of breath, or fainting. Report at once if the child is seeing or hearing things that are not real, believing things that are not real, or are suspicious.

- Your doctor should check your child carefully for heart problems before starting this medicine. Your doctor should check your child's blood pressure and heart rate regularly during treatment. Call your doctor right away if your child has signs of heart problems such as chest pain, shortness of breath, or fainting. The doctor will also periodically check the child's height and weight.

- This is a controlled medication (C II). It has a potential to be abused. Do not share this medicine with anyone else. Store the medicine where it cannot be taken by the wrong person or stolen.

- Most side effects are minor and disappear when dosage levels are lowered. Discuss with your doctor if the side effects remain bothersome. Your child may experience decreased appetite. Children seem to be less hungry during the middle of the day, but they are often hungry by dinnertime as the medication wears off. Some children get nausea or headache, which are most likely when the drug dose has been increased.

- Your child may have sleep problems. If a child cannot fall asleep, the doctor may prescribe a lower dose, or may move the dosing to earlier in the day, stop the evening dose or use a longer-acting formulation that can be dosed once-daily in the morning. Some children use diphenhydramine, or clonidine if needed for sleep.

- Less commonly, a few children develop sudden, repetitive movements or sounds called tics. These tics may or may not be noticeable. Changing the medication dosage may make tics go away. Some children also may appear to have a personality change, such as appearing "flat" or without emotion. Talk with your child's doctor if you see any of these side effects.

- If using a capsule formulation that can be mixed with applesauce *(Focalin XR, Ritalin LA, Metadate CD* and *Adderal XR)* and your child has difficulty swallowing the capsules, they can be sprinkled on a small amount of applesauce (if not warm and used right away). Do not chew the applesauce; just swallow. A small spoonful amount works well.

- If the child is using the medicine *Vyvanse*, the capsule contents can be mixed in water. It must be taken right after putting into the water.

Daytrana Patch Instructions

- The patch is applied to the <u>hip area in the morning</u> (avoid waistline on pants may cause it to rub off) and apply 2 hours before the desired effect.

- Use a new patch <u>each morning</u>.

- Alternate application site daily (left hip odd days, right hip even days).

- Hold patch on skin for 30 seconds and smooth down edges. It should stay on during swimming or bathing. Remove the patch after 9 hours so the child can sleep well at night.

- When peeling off to discard, fold in half, put down the toilet or lidded trash can.

NON-STIMULANTS FOR ADHD – 2ND LINE AGENTS – NOT CONTROLLED

DRUG	DOSING	SAFETY/SIDE EFFECTS/MONITORING
Atomoxetine (*Strattera*) Selective Norepinephrine Reuptake Inhibitor	40-100 mg/day, max 80 mg/day with CYP 2D6 inhibitors or if poor 2D6 metabolizer Take daily, or can divide BID	**CONTRAINDICATIONS** Glaucoma, pheochromocytoma, MAO I use within past 14 days. **WARNINGS** For risk of suicidal ideation in children Liver damage, severe (rare, most within 120 days of initiation). Risk of serious cardiovascular events including sudden death, stroke and MI (adults) in patients with pre-existing structural cardiac abnormalities or other serious heart problems; avoid use if known problems; conduct cardiac evaluation if needed. Use with caution if BP elevated. **SIDE EFFECTS** Headache, insomnia, somnolence, xerostomia, nausea, abdominal pain, ↓ appetite, nausea, hyperhidrosis, fatigue, dizziness, hot flashes, dysmenorrhea, ↓ libido, menstrual changes Orthostasis; use caution in patients at risk. Psychiatric effects, including hallucinations and mania, discontinue if symptoms. Urinary retention in patients with history or with outlet obstruction. Priapism (rare). **NOTES** Do not open capsule – irritant
GuanFACINE ext-release (*Intuniv*) For patients using stimulants for additional benefit, or alone *Tenex* – for hypertension Central alpha²ᴬ-adrenergic receptor agonist	1-4 mg, max 4 mg/day Start at 1 mg daily Do not take with high-fat meal (↑ absorption) With CYP 3A4 inducers, max dose 8 mg/day With CYP 3A4 inhibitors, max dose 2 mg/day	**SIDE EFFECTS** Somnolence, dizziness, headache, fatigue, xerostomia, constipation, abdominal pain, skin rash (rare, discontinue if occurs) **NOTES** All cardiovascular effects (bradycardia, hypotension, orthostasis, syncope) are dose-dependent; titrate carefully. Sedation and drowsiness can cause risk with physical and mental activities. Cases of skin rash with exfoliation; discontinue if rash develops. Do not interchange with other guanfacine formulations. Do not crush.
CloNIDine ext-release (*Kapvay*) For patients using stimulants for additional benefit, or alone Central alpha²-adrenergic receptor agonist	0.1-0.4 mg/day Start at 0.1 mg at bedtime, ↑ 0.1 mg/day Q 7 days until desired response Dose BID, if uneven give higher dose QHS Start 0.1 mg QHS, titrate weekly, using BID dosing	**SIDE EFFECTS** Headache, somnolence, abdominal pain, upper resp tract infections **NOTES** Rebound hypertension (with sweating/anxiety/tremors), if stopped abruptly – taper off by ↓ 0.1 mg Q 3-7 days Ext-release formulation has ↓ SEs Do not crush.

Atomoxetine Drug Interactions

■ Decrease dose if on strong CYP 2D6 inhibitors (e.g., paroxetine, fluoxetine, quinidine) or if 2D6 poor metabolizer, up to max 80 mg/day.

■ 14-Day wash out period after MAO I use.

Patient Counseling for Atomoxetine

- Dispense MedGuide and instruct parents/patient to read it. The MedGuide includes a warning for risk of suicidal ideation in children and risk of liver injury.

- Common side effects can include headache, insomnia, sleepiness, dry mouth, nausea, stomach pain, lessened appetite, nausea, sweating, dizziness and fatigue. Girls and women can get hot flashes, dysmenorrhea, ↓ sexual interest or menstrual changes.

- You may have suicidal thoughts or behavior while taking atomoxetine. Watch for symptoms of depression, unusual behavior, or thoughts of hurting yourself. Your doctor may need to check you at regular visits while you are taking this medication.

- The capsule cannot be opened. Do not use an open or broken capsule. If the medicine from inside the capsule gets into your eyes, rinse thoroughly with water and call the doctor.

- Atomoxetine can cause side effects that may impair your thinking or reactions. Be careful if you drive or do anything that requires you to be awake and alert.

- Monitor for symptoms of liver damage, such as weakness, abdominal pain, yellowed skin, light colored stool or darkened urine.

Clonidine and Guanfacine Drug Interactions

- Both clonidine and guanfacine are sedating; use caution with other CNS depressants.

- Both clonidine and guanfacine lower blood pressure; use caution with other anti-hypertensives.

- Both clonidine and guanfacine come as other formulations; do not use concurrently.

- Guanfacine is a CYP 3A4 substrate; see dosing in table for use with inducers or inhibitors.

STIMULANTS USED FOR VARIOUS SLEEP DISORDERS

Shift workers are at increased risk for a variety of chronic illnesses including cardiovascular and gastrointestinal disorders; the general health must be monitored. Some are able to accommodate with the use of melatonin to regulate sleep cycles, or by using a non-benzodiazepine such as zolpidem to fall asleep off-schedule, or with the use stimulants to stay alert during the work shift described below.

Stimulants used to improve wakefulness in adult patients with excessive sleepiness associated with narcolepsy, obstructive sleep apnea/hypopnea syndrome, and shift work sleep disorder.

DRUG	DOSING	SAFETY/SIDE EFFECTS/MONITORING
Modafinil *(Provigil)* C IV	200 mg daily	**SIDE EFFECTS** Headache, dizziness, anxiety, agitation, nausea, diarrhea, insomnia, dry mouth, risk of severe rash. **WARNINGS** Avoid use with pre-existing cardiac conditions. Use with caution with hepatic impairment, renal impairment, psychiatric disorders and Tourette's. **NOTES** Both of these agents require a MedGuide due to risk of severe rash, which can be life-threatening.
Armodafinil *(Nuvigil)* R-isomer of modafinil; similar drug C IV	150-250 mg daily	Similar side effects, similar drug to modafinil, including risk severe rash – give MedGuide

Note: Additional stimulants indicated for weight loss in weight loss/gain chapter, and the ADHD stimulants are sometimes used for these conditions.

Modafinil and Armodafinil Drug Interactions

May decrease efficacy of estrogen-containing birth control: The manufacturers recommend using nonhormonal contraceptives, in addition to or in place of hormonal contraceptives, during and for one month following treatment.

ANXIETY

BACKGROUND

Anxiety occurs for everyone occasionally, when faced with problems or challenges at work, home or school. These symptoms of normal anxiety dissipates when the problem is resolved. Fear and worry are the primary symptoms. Other symptoms include tachycardia, palpitations, shortness of breath, GI upset, pain (localized or generalized), chest pain, insomnia and fatigue.

Anxiety disorders are more serious than occasional anxiety and cause significant distress. Anxiety disorders interfere with the ability to lead a normal life. Common types of anxiety disorders include generalized anxiety disorder (GAD), panic disorder (PD), social anxiety disorder (SAD), obsessive compulsive disorder (OCD), post-traumatic stress disorder (PTSD) and specific phobias. PTSD involves a range of symptoms, and is described in the depression chapter.

In all cases, lifestyle changes can improve symptoms [increasing physical activity, talk therapy (with friends or a trained therapist), helping others, community involvement, and other methods] to broaden the patient's outlook and reduce stress. Currently, financial stress and uncertainty about the future is causing considerable stress and anxiety in many people.

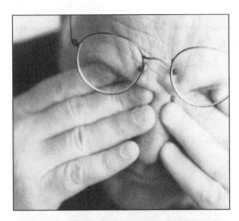

GUIDELINES

Diagnostic and Statistical Manual of Mental Disorders

Baldwin DS, Waldman S, Allgulander C. "Evidence-based pharmacological treatment of generalized anxiety disorder (DSM-IV-TR)." *Int J Neuropsychopharmacol.* 2011 Jun;14(5):697-710.

SSRIs and SNRIs are primarily used to treat anxiety disorders. Although only some of the antidepressants carry specific indications (see chart), often these agents are chosen based on the healthcare provider's familiary and/or the side effect profile. For example, although fluvoxamine was the first SSRI indicated for OCD, it is rarely used due to its drug interaction potential. Other SSRIs (prescribers tend to use the newer agents that have less drug interactions) are used instead. For example, dosing of SSRI and SNRI agents are initiated at

ANTIDEPRESSANTS WITH ANXIETY INDICATION

Bupropion – SAD

Citalopram – OCD, PD

Escitalopram – GAD

Fluoxetine – OCD, PD

Fluvoxamine – OCD, SAD

Paroxetine – GAD, OCD, SAD, PD, PTSD

Sertraline – OCD, PD, PTSD, SAD

Duloxetine – GAD

Venlafaxine – GAD, PD, SAD

Doxepin – Anxiety

Imipramine – PD

COMMON MEDICATIONS THAT CAN WORSEN ANXIETY

Theophylline

Levothyroxine

Acetazolamide

Albuterol (if used incorrectly-swallowed)

Aripiprazole, haloperidol

Caffeine, in high doses

Stimulants

Decongestants (pseudoephedrine and nasally inhaled agents)

Steroids

Bupropion

Fluoxetine, paroxetine

Illicit drugs, including cocaine, LSD, methamphetamine, others

half the initial dose used for depression and are slowly titrated to minimize stimulatory adverse events, such as anxiousness and jitteriness. Some clinicians often initiate these agents by overlapping them with BDZs by 2–4-weekto help alleviate some of the initial stimulatory effects and regulate sleep. Patients should be advised that immediate relief is not to be expected when initiating treatment with an SSRI. Noticeable improvement may be seen after 4 or more weeks of treatment. Specifics on the antidepressant drugs are located in the depression section.

Hydroxyzine *(Vistaril)* is FDA approved for anxiety but considered second-line and occasionally used for short-term anxiety rather than prescribing a potentially addicting medication such as a BDZ agent. This agent is a sedating antihistamine and works by sedating the patient, rather than treating any underlying cause. It should not be used long-term. Review hydroxyzine in the skin section; it is used more commonly for pruritus and is discussed in other chapters.

Pregabalin *(Lyrica)* is not FDA approved for anxiety and can be especially useful if a patient has neuropathic pain. Pregabalin has immediate anxiolytic effects similar to lorazepam, alprazolam, and venlafaxine. It is scheduled C-V since it is slightly euphoric – which can have a calming effect.

Propranolol *(Inderal,* others) is used to reduce symptoms of stage fright or performance anxiety (e.g., tremor, tachycardia). It is dosed at 10-40 mg 1 hour prior to an event such as a public speech. Use caution with this approach since CNS effects (e.g., confusion, dizziness) may be present. Non-selective beta blocker-avoid with asthma, COPD.

Buspirone is a second-line option for anxiety for patients who do not respond to antidepressants, at risk for benzodiazepines abuse, or added as adjunctive therapy. It is a commonly used agent.

GAD (FDA approved). There are inconsistent reports of efficacy with long-term use along with delayed onset of effect of 2 weeks or longer.

Quetiapine *(Seroquel)* is sometimes used for anxiety, but is not FDA approved for GAD. Quetiapine is costly and carries the same risks of extrapyramidal and neuroleptic malignant sydrome even a low doses and should be avoided.

NATURAL PRODUCTS USED FOR ANXIETY

Natural products used for anxiety include valerian, lemon balm, glutamine, passion flower and hops (both as teas), chamomile tea, theanine and skullcap. Kava is used as a relaxant but can damage the liver and should not be recommended. Valerian may rarely be hepatotoxic (or some valerian products may have been contaminated with liver toxins); this is unclear at present. Passionflower is rated as "possibly effective" by the Natural Medicines Database. For most of the other agents evidence of efficacy is scant or poor but individual patients may get benefit from the various agents.

BENZODIAZEPINE (BZD) TREATMENT FOR ANXIETY

BZDs are often used for anxiety symptoms. They provide fast relief for acute symptoms, usually within a few days, and tolerance to problematic adverse events generally occurs within the first 2 weeks of treatment. Situations in which BZDs are appropriate include short-term situations in which anxiety is acute and can cause extreme stress, prevent proper sleep, and disrupt life. These symptoms can be the result of a recent death of a loved one, an earthquake, a motor vehicle accident, or other stressful situations. In such cases, they are used less than 1-2 weeks and can be discontinued. Benzodiazepines can cover-up these symptoms, but do not treat the causes of anxiety, and, in most cases, should not be used long-term.

However, BDZs are often used chronically, including in the elderly, where they pose significant risk for confusion, dizziness and falls – the risk increases with concurrent use of other CNS depressants. BEERS Criteria for the use in elderly: May be potentially inappropriate for use in geriatric patients (Quality of evidence – high; Strength of recommendation – strong).

Benzodiazepines

Potentiate GABA, an inhibitory neurotransmitter, causing CNS depression.

DRUG	DOSING	SAFETY/SIDE EFFECTS/MONITORING
LORazepam *(Ativan)* Available: Tablet, solution (Intensol), injection LORazepam Intensol is solution (sol for solution) LORazepam injection--used commonly for agitation, sedation	1-3 mg PO BID-TID PRN	C IV Potential for abuse Physiological dependence and tolerance develop with chronic use Drowsiness, dizziness, weakness, ataxia, lightheadedness Anterograde amnesia (some of the events that occur after taking the benzodiazepine cannot be stored as memories – forgetting what happens)
ALPRAZolam *(Xanax, Xanax XR)* Available: Tablet	0.25-0.5 mg PO TID PRN	Withdrawal symptoms when discontinued: can include seizures, insomnia, mental/mood changes, increased reactions to noise/touch/light, N/V/diarrhea, loss of appetite, stomach pain, hallucinations, numbness/tingling of arms and legs, muscle pain, tachycardia, short-term memory loss, and very high fever
ChlordiazePOXIDE *(Librium)* Available: Capsule	5-25 mg TID-QID	**NOTES** L-O-T (lorazepam, oxazepam, and temazepam): these are considered less potentially harmful for elderly or with liver impairment since they are metabolized to inactive compounds (glucuronides)
ClonazePAM *(KlonoPIN)* Available: Tablet, wafer	0.25-0.5 mg PO BID-TID PRN	
Clorazepate *(Tranxene, Gen-Xene)* Available: Tablet	15-60 mg/day divided PO BID-TID	Chlordiazepoxide and diazepam also used for alcohol withdrawal and oxazepam has this indication. Diazepam is also used for muscle spasticity.
Diazepam *(Valium)* Available: Tablet, injection, solution (Intensol), rectal (Diastat)	2-10 mg PO TID-QID PRN	Clonazepam also used for seizures and clorazepate has this indication. Clonazepam patients who experience anxiety or panic attacks between doses due to its long duration of activity.
Oxazepam *(Serax)* Available: Capsule	10-30 mg PO TID-QID PRN	Pregnancy Category D; possible risk of cleft lip and/or palate if used during pregnancy. For lactation, if a benzodiazepine is required, use short-acting agents such as alprazolam or lorazepam are the safest with a peak effect about 60 minutes after administration.

Benzodiazepine Drug Interactions

- Additive effects with sedating drugs, including most pain medicines, muscle relaxants, antihistamines, antipsychotics, anticonvulsants, the antidepressant mirtazapine *(Remeron)*, trazodone, alcohol, among others.

- Some are contraindicated with strong inhibitors, such as grapefruit juice, azole antifungals (ketoconazole, etc.)

Benzodiazepine Counseling

- Only if used for insomnia: This medication should be taken before bedtime (for anxiety taken prn, if clinically feasible).

- Common side effects include drowsiness, dizziness, unsteadiness on your feet, slow reactions, lightheadedness and difficulty remembering what happened after you had taken the medicine. If any of these persist or worsen, contact your healthcare provider or pharmacist promptly.

- This medication may cause dependence, especially if it has been used regularly for an extended time (more than 1-4 weeks), if it has been used in high doses, or if you have a history of alcoholism, drug abuse, or personality disorder. In such cases, if you suddenly stop this drug, withdrawal reactions may occur. Such reactions can include seizures, trouble sleeping, mental/mood changes, increased reactions to noise/touch/light, nausea, vomiting, diarrhea, loss of appetite, stomach pain, hallucinations, numbness/tingling of arms and legs, muscle pain, fast heartbeat, short-term memory loss, and very high fever.

- Do not stop taking this medication abruptly or gradually reduce the dose unless directed. withdrawal symptoms can occur especially when taking extended regular treatment. Consult your healthcare provider or pharmacist for more details.

- This medication can also result in abnormal drug-seeking behavior (addiction/habit forming). Do not increase your dose, take it more frequently, or use it for a longer time than prescribed. Properly stop the medication when so directed.

- When used for an extended time, this medication may not work as well and may require different dosing. This is called "tolerance." Talk with your healthcare provider if this medication stops working well. Do not increase your dose without first talking to your healthcare provider.

- Do not take with other medicines that can make you sleepy, unless directed by your healthcare provider. Other sedating medications could cause a great deal of sedation and confusion if taken together with this medicine. Do not use alcohol with this medicine.

- After taking this medicine, you should not be driving a car or using any dangerous machinery.

- This medicine is a federally controlled substance (C-IV) because it can be abused or lead to dependence. Keep the bottle in a safe place to prevent misuse and abuse.

- If female: this drug may cause an increased risk of cleft lip and/or cleft palate if used during pregnancy.

- This medication is not recommended during breastfeeding.

BUSPIRONE

5-HT₁ partial agonist: <u>Not controlled, no abuse or physiological potential</u>.

DRUG	DOSING	SAFETY/SIDE EFFECTS/MONITORING
BusPIRone Available: Tablet	Start 7.5 mg PO BID Can increase by 5 mg/day Q 2-3 days until 30 mg/day, if needed. Max: 60 mg/day	2-4 weeks for optimal effect No potential for abuse, tolerance or physiological dependence <u>Nausea, dizziness, headache</u>, lightheadedness, excitement Avoid use if severe kidney or liver dysfunction When switching from a benzodiazepine to buspirone, the benzodiazepine should be tapered slowly **NOTES** Pregnancy category B

Buspirone Drug Interactions

- Do not use with MAO Inhibitors.

- ↓ dose with erythromycin, diltiazem, itraconazole, verapamil; consider dose reduction with any 3A4 inhibitor.

- 3A4 inducers, including rifampin, may require an increase in the buspirone dose.

- Avoid consuming large amounts of grapefruit juice.

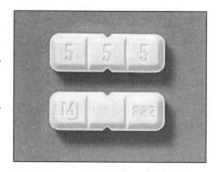

Buspirone Counseling

- Buspirone comes in a *Dividose* tablet designed to make dose adjustments easy. Each tablet is scored and can be broken accurately on the score lines into thirds. It snaps into pieces with finger pressure.

- Take this medication by mouth, usually 2 or 3 times a day or as directed by your healthcare provider. You may take this medication with or without food, but it is important to choose one way and always take it the same way so that the amount of drug absorbed will always be the same. This medication does not have immediate effects but takes 2 to 4 weeks to see its full benefit.

- Do not take with other medicines that can make you sleepy, unless directed by your healthcare provider. Other sedating medications can have additive effects when this medicine is taken together.

- Do not use alcohol with this medicine.

- Common side effects include dizziness, nausea, or headache. If any of these persist or worsen, contact your healthcare provider or pharmacist promptly.

- Grapefruit may increase the amount of buspirone in your bloodstream.

- Dosage is based on your medical condition and response to therapy. Use this medication regularly in order to get the most benefit from it. To help you remember, use it at the same times each day. When this medication is started, symptoms of anxiety (e.g., restlessness) may sometimes get worse before they improve. It may take up to a month or more to get the full effect of this medication.

- Avoid administering buspirone to nursing women.

INSOMNIA

DRUGS LIKELY TO CONTRIBUTE TO INSOMNIA

Bupropion

Stimulants (methylphenidate, etc.)

OTC appetite suppressants

Decongestants (pseudoephedrine, etc.)

MAO-B Inhibitors, if taken late in the day

Fluoxetine, if taken late in the day

Caffeine

Steroids

Alcohol (initially induces sleep, but prevents deeper stages of sleep and causes nocturia)

Any drug that causes urinary retention or nocturia, including antihistamines and diuretics taken later in the day.

BACKGROUND

Insomnia is having trouble falling or staying asleep. This is one of the most common medical complaints. A poor night's sleep reduces a person's ability to function well the following day, and can lead to depression and reduced quality of life. Most adults require seven to eight hours of sleep.

Poor "sleep hygiene" includes habits that contribute to insomnia and may be possible to reduce or stop, eliminating the need for drug therapy. For example, a retired, elderly person may have a daily routine that includes watching television and napping for much of the day. If the person can engage in a regular routine that reduces or eliminates daytime napping, they may not require a sleeping pill (a hypnotic). Changes to lifestyle are the preferred treatment for insomnia, not drugs, especially in light of recent concerns about increased mortality with the use of hypnotics--even with occasional use. The hypnotics are over-prescribed.

Heart failure or any condition that causes shortness of breath can worsen sleep. Anxiety and depression cause insomnia; if the condition can be corrected by therapy, a prescription agent, or both, a hypnotic may not be required. When sleep hygiene issues or medical conditions cannot be corrected, or when a problem causing the insomnia has not been identified, hypnotics may be used to help provide a good night's rest.

Natural Products used for Insomnia

If insomnia is due to depression, taking St. John's wort may be helpful but this will interact with many prescription drugs. St. John's wort induces CYP 450, is a photosensitizer and is serotonergic. Chamomile tea taken in the evening helps many people feel calmer. Melatonin is useful for some patients. Valerian can be useful. There have been isolated reports of valerian causing liver toxicity; this risk is unclear at present. Check the Natural Medicines Database for doses and the current safety profile.

DRUG	DOSING	SAFETY/SIDE EFFECTS/MONITORING

Non-benzodiazepines: Acts selectively at the benzodiazepine receptors to increase GABA

DRUG	DOSING	SAFETY/SIDE EFFECTS/MONITORING
Zolpidem *(Ambien, Ambien CR,* generic) C IV *Zolpimist*-spray *Edluar SL* tabs *Intermezzo SL* – for night-time awakening	5-10 mg PO QHS *Ambien CR*: 6.25-12.5 mg PO QHS *Zolpimist* 5 mg/spray (1-2 sprays) QHS *Edluar* 5-10 mg PO QHS *Intermezzo SL* 3.5 mg males, 1.75 mg females, and if using CNS depressants (decrease dose of these as well, if possible)	**WARNINGS** ↑ risk mortality (interferes with breathing at night, causes accidents/falls, confusion, and may ↑ risk infection and cancer) Potential for abuse and dependence **SIDE EFFECTS** Somnolence Dizziness, ataxia Lightheadedness "pins and needles" feeling on skin May cause parasomnias (unusual actions while sleeping – of which the patient may not be aware) Withdrawal symptoms if used longer than 2 weeks
Zaleplon *(Sonata,* generic) C IV	5-10 mg PO QHS	
Eszopiclone *(Lunesta)* C IV Not limited to short-term use (officially, although all 3 used long-term commonly)	1-3 mg PO QHS 1 mg if difficulty falling asleep, 2 mg if difficulty staying asleep, 3 mg if helpful for longer duration	**NOTES** *Intermezzo SL* Do not take unless planning to sleep 4+ more hours Lifestyle changes should be the primary method to improve sleep, not drugs. Preferred over benzodiazepines for 1st line treatment of insomnia due to ↓ abuse, dependence and tolerance Do not take with fatty food, a heavy meal or alcohol

Melatonin Receptor Agonist

DRUG	DOSING	SAFETY/SIDE EFFECTS/MONITORING
Ramelteon *(Rozerem)* Not controlled Not limited to short-term use	8 mg PO QHS	**SIDE EFFECTS** Somnolence, dizziness **NOTES** Do not take with fatty food

Tricyclic Antidepressant

DRUG	DOSING	SAFETY/SIDE EFFECTS/MONITORING
Doxepin extended-release *(Silenor)* Not controlled Generic doxepin, traZODone, mirtazapine used off-label for sleep Used for difficulty staying asleep (sleep maintenance)	6 mg PO QHS 3 mg if ≥ 65 years	**CONTRAINDICATIONS** Requires 2 week washout for MAO Is This is an antidepressant and requires MedGuide for unusual thoughts/suicide risk **SIDE EFFECTS** Somnolence, low incidence nausea and upper respiratory infections, possibility of anticholinergic SEs

Ambien, Sonata and *Lunesta* Drug Interactions

- Caution with the use of non-benzodiazepines with potent 3A4 inhibitors (e.g., ritonavir, indinavir, saquinavir, atazanavir, ketoconazole, itraconazole, erythromycin and clarithromycin).

- Additive effects with sedating drugs, including most pain medicines, muscle relaxants, antihistamines, the antidepressant mirtazapine *(Remeron)*, trazodone, alcohol and others.

Ambien, Sonata and *Lunesta* Counseling

- If using *Zolpimist*, spray directly into your mouth over your tongue (once for a 5 mg dose, twice for a 10 mg dose). Prime the bottle if 1ˢᵗ-time use. If using *Edluar* SL tablets, allow tablet to dissolve under tongue; do not swallow. For *Intermezzo*: this drug is not swallowed, it dissolves under the tongue. Do not take unless you are planning to sleep 4 or more hours.

- You should not eat a heavy/high-fat meal within 2 hours of taking this medication; this may prevent the medicine from working properly.

- Call your doctor if your insomnia worsens or is not better within 7 to 10 days. This may mean that there is another condition causing your sleep problem.

- Common side effects include sleepiness, lightheadedness, dizziness, "pins and needles" feeling on your skin and difficulty with coordination.

- You may still feel drowsy the next day after taking this medicine.

- This drug may (rarely) cause abnormal thoughts and behavior. Symptoms include more outgoing or aggressive behavior than normal, confusion, agitation, hallucinations, worsening of depression, and suicidal thoughts or actions. Some people have found that they get out of bed while not being fully awake and do an activity that they do not know they are doing.

- You may have withdrawal symptoms when you stop taking this medicine, if you have been taking it for more than a couple of weeks. Withdrawal symptoms include unpleasant feelings, stomach and muscle cramps, vomiting, sweating and shakiness. You may also have more trouble sleeping the first few nights after the medicine is stopped. The problem usually goes away on its own after 1 or 2 nights.

- Do not take with other medicines that can make you sleepy, unless directed by your doctor. Do not use alcohol with any sleep medicine.

SLEEP (INCLUDE WITH COUNSELING) HYGIENE METHODS TO IMPROVE SLEEP

Keep the bedroom dark, comfortable, and quiet

Regular sleep schedule

Avoid daytime naps even after a poor night of sleep – or limit to 30 minutes

Reserve bedroom for only sleep and sex

Turn the face of clock aside to minimize anxiety about falling asleep

If unable to sleep, get up and do something to take your mind off sleeping

Establish a pre-bedtime ritual to condition your body for sleep

Relax before bedtime with soft music, mild stretching, yoga, or pleasurable reading

Avoid exercising right before bedtime

Do not eat heavy meals before bedtime

Do not take any caffeine in the afternoon

- After taking this medicine, you should not be driving a car or using any dangerous machinery.

- This medicine is a federally controlled substance (C-IV) because it can be abused or lead to dependence. Keep the bottle in a safe place to prevent misuse and abuse.

BENZODIAZEPINES

Potentiate GABA, an inhibitory neurotransmitter, causing CNS depression. <u>BEERS Criteria</u> for use in elderly: <u>May be potentially inappropriate for use in geriatric patients</u>.

DRUG	DOSING	SAFETY/SIDE EFFECTS/MONITORING
LORazepam *(Ativan)* LORazepam Intensol is solution C IV	0.5-2 mg PO QHS	**WARNING** Potential for abuse and dependence **SIDE EFFECTS** <u>Drowsiness, dizziness, weakness, ataxia, lightheadedness</u> Chronic use can lead to tolerance and dependence. Anterograde amnesia (some of the events that occur after taking the BZD cannot be stored as memories – forgetting what happens)
Temazepam *(Restoril)* C IV	7.5-30 mg PO QHS	**NOTES** <u>Withdrawal symptoms when discontinued</u>: can include seizures, insomnia, mental/mood changes, increased reactions to noise/touch/light, N/V/diarrhea, loss of appetite, stomach pain, hallucinations, numbness/tingling of arms and legs, muscle pain, tachycardia, short-term memory loss, and very high fever <u>L-O-T</u> (lorazepam, oxazepam, and temazepam): these are considered less potentially harmful for elderly or those with liver impairment since they are metabolized to inactive compounds (glucuronides); <u>choose L-O-T if need BZD in elderly patient</u> Pregnancy Category D
Estazolam *(Prosom)* C IV		Cannot use with potent 3A4 inhibitors
Quazepam *(Doral)* C IV		Caution when use in elderly due to its long half-life: risk of falls, fractures
Flurazepam C IV		Caution when use in elderly due to its long half-life: risk of falls, fractures
Triazolam *(Halcion)* C IV		Associated with higher rebound insomnia and daytime anxiety; Tapering upon discontinuation. Contraindicated with efavirenz *(Sustiva)*, delavirdine *(Rescriptor)*, azole antifungals, and protease inhibitors & all 3A4 Inhibitors

Benzodiazepine Drug Interactions

- Additive effects with sedating drugs, including most pain medicines, muscle relaxants, antihistamines, the antidepressant mirtazapine *(Remeron)*, trazodone, alcohol and others.

Benzodiazepine Counseling

■ This medication may increase the risk of death, due to worsening trouble breathing at night (sleep apnea), and increasing the risk of falls, infection and possibly even cancer. It is preferable to use measures to improve sleep without drugs (such as avoiding daytime naps, and others.) Please ask the pharmacist for a hand-out on how to improve sleep without the use of drugs.

■ This medication should be taken before bedtime.Common side effects include drowsiness, dizziness, unsteadiness on your feet, slow reactions, lightheadedness and difficulty remembering what happened after you had taken the medicine.

■ This medication may cause dependence, especially if it has been used regularly for an extended time (more than 1-4 weeks), if it has been used in high doses, or if you have a history of alcoholism, drug abuse, or personality disorder. In such cases, if you suddenly stop this drug, withdrawal reactions may occur. Such reactions can include seizures, trouble sleeping, mental/mood changes, increased reactions to noise/touch/light, nausea, vomiting, diarrhea, loss of appetite, stomach pain, hallucinations, numbness/tingling of arms and legs, muscle pain, fast heartbeat, short-term memory loss, and very high fever. Report any such reactions to your doctor immediately.

■ When stopping extended, regular treatment with this drug, gradually reducing the dosage as directed will help prevent withdrawal reactions. Consult your doctor or pharmacist for more details.

■ Though it is unlikely to occur, this medication can also result in abnormal drug-seeking behavior (addiction/habit forming). Do not increase your dose, take it more frequently, or use it for a longer time than prescribed. Properly stop the medication when so directed. This will lessen the chances of becoming addicted.

■ When used for an extended time, this medication may not work as well and may require different dosing. This is called "tolerance." Talk with your doctor if this medication stops working well. Do not increase your dose without first talking to your doctor.

■ Do not take with other medicines that can make you sleepy, unless directed by your doctor. Do not use alcohol with any sleep medicine.

■ After taking this medicine, you should not be driving a car or using any dangerous machinery.

■ This medicine is a federally controlled substance (C-IV) because it can be abused or lead to dependence. Keep the bottle in a safe place to prevent misuse and abuse.

ANTIHISTAMINES

Compete with (block) histamine H1 receptors.

DRUG	DOSING	SAFETY/SIDE EFFECTS/MONITORING
Diphenhydramine *(Benadryl, Sominex, Unisom, others, store brands)*	25-50 mg PO QHS	**SIDE EFFECTS** Due to the side-effect profile, considered "DO NOT USE DRUGS IN ELDERLY" Possible anticholinergic side effects: Sedation; tolerance to sedative effects can develop after 10 days use. Confusion (can exaccerbate memory/cognition difficulty) Peripheral anticholinergic side effects: Dry mouth Urinary retention (will make it very difficult for males with BPH to urinate, can slow down/delay urination in females)
Doxylamine *(Aldex, Unisom Nighttime, store brands)*	25 mg PO QHS	Dry/blurry vision, risk increased IOP Constipation Best to avoid use in BPH (may worsen symptoms) and glaucoma (may elevate IOP)

Diphenhydramine *(Benadryl)* Counseling (for all indications – applies to other sedating antihistamines)

- Diphenhydramine is an antihistamine used to relieve symptoms of allergy, hay fever and the common cold. These symptoms include rash, itching, watery eyes, itchy eyes/nose/throat, cough, runny nose and sneezing. It is also used to prevent and treat nausea, vomiting and dizziness caused by motion sickness. Diphenhydramine can also be used to help you relax and fall asleep. It is occasionally used for involuntary movements and muscle stiffness from Parkinson's disease.

- When using this medicine, you will become sleepy. It can also make you feel confused and make it difficult to concentrate.

- Do not take with other medicines that can make you sleepy, unless directed by your doctor. Do not use alcohol with any sleep medicine.

- This medicine should not be used by patients with an enlarged prostate, or BPH, without getting their doctor's approval. It will temporarily make urination more difficult.

- If you have glaucoma, discuss use with your eye doctor. It may raise your the pressure in your eyes.

- If you have problems with constipation, this medicine will worsen the constipation.

- This medicine can cause your eyes to become dry and your vision to become blurry. It can also cause dry mouth.

- This medicine can make it difficult to urinate (it will take longer for the urine to come out).

- Although this drug is meant to be sedating, some children will experience excitability instead.

- After taking this medicine, you should not be driving a car or using any dangerous machinery.

- Take the tablet, capsule, or liquid form by mouth, with or without food. Diphenhydramine may be taken with food or milk if stomach upset occurs. If you are taking the suspension, shake the bottle well before each dose. Measure liquid forms of this medication with a dose-measuring spoon or device, not a regular teaspoon, to make sure you have the correct dose.

- The rapidly-dissolving tablet or strip should be allowed to dissolve on the tongue and then swallowed, with or without water. A second strip may be taken after the first strip has dissolved. The chewable tablets should be chewed thoroughly before being swallowed.

- To prevent motion sickness, take your dose 30 minutes before starting activity such as travel. To help you sleep, take your dose about 30 minutes before bedtime. If you continue to have difficulty sleeping for longer than 2 weeks, contact your doctor.

EPILEPSY/SEIZURES

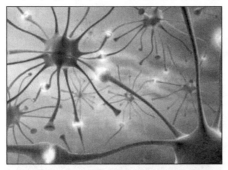

We gratefully acknowledge the assistance of Kimberly B. Tallian, PharmD, BCPP, FASHP, FCCP, FCSHP, Assistant Dean and Chair for Clinical and Administrative Sciences, Professor at Keck Graduate Institute, School of Pharmacy, Claremont Colleges, in preparing this chapter.

BACKGROUND

Epilepsy is a common neurological disorder, affecting up to 2.2 million Americans with approximately 150,000 new cases diagnosed in the United States each year. It is defined by unprovoked seizures or abnormal "electrical storms" in the brain. Unfortunately, many patients do not have complete seizure control, even with current medications. Seizures can damage and destroy neurons, which can cause cognitive deficits and be life-threatening.

Seizures are generally classified into two basic groups: partial and generalized seizures. Partial seizures start in one part of the brain where the patient is either conscious or unconscious. If there is no loss of consciousness, the seizure is called simple partial. If there is loss of consciousness, the seizure is termed complex partial. Partial seizures can spread to the other hemisphere of the brain, resulting in secondarily generalized tonic-clonic seizures. Generalized seizures, however, begin in both hemispheres of the brain where consciousness is impaired. Seizures that last longer than 5 minutes or 2 or more seizures between which the patient does not regain consciousness are known as status epilepticus, which is a medical emergency.

GUIDELINES

Drugs for Epilepsy Treatment Guidelines, Medical Letter 2013;11(126):9-18.

Efficacy and tolerability of the new antiepileptic drugs I: Treatment of new onset epilepsy: Report of the Therapeutics and Technology Assessment Subcommittee and Quality Standards Subcommittee of the American Academy of Neurology and the American Epilepsy Society. Neurology 2004;62:1252-1260.

Practice Parameter Update: Management Issues for Women with Epilepsy – Focus on Pregnancy (an Evidence-Based Review): Obstetrical Complications and Change in Seizure Frequency: Report of the Quality Standards Subcommittee and Therapeutics and Technology Assessment Subcommittee of the American Academy of Neurology and American Epilepsy Society. Neurology 2009;73:133-141.

INTERNATIONAL CLASSIFICATION OF SEIZURES

SEIZURE TYPE	SYMPTOMS

Partial Seizures

Simple Partial Seizures (consciousness not impaired)	Motor
	Autonomic
	Sensory (e.g., visual, auditory, olfactory, gustatory)
	Psychic (e.g., illusions, affective, cognitive, structured hallucinations, dysphagia)
Complex Partial Seizures (impaired consciousness)	Simple partial features
	Automatisms

Generalized Seizures

Absence Seizures	Formerly petit mal seizures
	Brief and abrupt staring spells lasting 10–30 seconds
Myoclonic Seizures	Brief, lightning-like jerk movements of entire body
Tonic-Clonic Seizures	Formerly grand mal seizures
	Characterized by five phases: flexion, extension, tremor, clonic, and loss of consciousness
Tonic Seizures	Flexion and/or extension only
Clonic Seizures	Rhythmic, repetitive, jerking muscle movements
Atonic Seizures	Loss of muscle tone and falls to the ground; known as "drop attacks"

RISKS ASSOCIATED WITH ANTIEPILEPTIC DRUGS

When anticonvulsants (or antiepileptic drugs, or AEDs) are used in women of reproductive age, it is important to consider teratogenicity and provide proper counseling. Carbamazepine, clonazepam, phenobarbital/primidone, phenytoin/fosphenytoin, topiramate and valproate are pregnancy category D – this means that there is known fetal risk, and the benefit must outweigh the risk. Health care providers should always consider that untreated or inadequately treated epilepsy during pregnancy increases the risk of complications in both the pregnant mother and her developing baby. Valproate also has been assigned pregnancy category X for migraine prophylaxis only. Valproate is thought to have the highest risk of fetal harm. All other AEDs are pregnancy category C. Metabolism of some of the AEDs increases during pregnancy (lamotrigine and others), resulting in breakthrough seizures. This can require a higher dose, which may increase risk to the baby. Managing epilepsy during pregnancy is complex.

CNS side effects such as dizziness, somnolence and cognitive dysfunction are common since these drugs have to penetrate the CNS to work. Side effects such as mental confusion and sedation can make it difficult for children to do well in school and for adults to perform well at work, and to drive safely. Recently, the FDA issued a warning that valproate is associated with decreased IQ scores in children following *in utero* exposure.

There are many drug interactions with most of the antiepileptic drugs. Several of the AEDs are strong inducers and can lower the concentration of other drugs, including other antiepileptic drugs the patient may be taking. AEDs that are strong inducers include carbamazepine, oxcarbazepine, fosphenytoin, phenytoin, phenobarbital, primidone, and topiramate ($\geq$ 200 mg/d). Drug selection depends on the seizure type, side effect profile, cost, and efficacy.

Individuals with epilepsy have increased fracture risk. Bone loss can occur as soon as two years after AED therapy. Modifiable factors that affect bone density should be addressed (see Osteoporosis chapter). The mechanism of AED-induced bone loss is not completely understood. Hepatic enzyme inducers lower vitamin D levels by increasing metabolism, which reduces calcium absorption. All patients on enzyme-inducing AEDs should supplement with vitamin D and calcium.

All AEDs require a MedGuide due to the risk of suicidality. The MedGuide warning states: "Like other antiepileptic drugs, this medication may cause suicidal thoughts or actions in a very small number of people, about 1 in 500."

Never discontinue seizure medications abruptly due to seizure risk but instead, taper the medication off slowly.

DRUGS/CONDITIONS THAT MAY LOWER THE SEIZURE THRESHOLD
Antipsychotics (e.g., clozapine, phenothiazines, butyrophenones)
Antivirals (e.g., amantadine, rimantadine, foscarnet, ganciclovir and acyclovir IV)
Bupropion
Carbapenems (in poor renal function – esp. imipenem)
Cephalosporins
Fluoroquinolones
Lindane
Lithium and theophylline (in toxicity)
Mefloquine
Meperidine (in poor renal function)
Metoclopramide
Natural products such as dendrobium, evening primrose oil, gingko, melatonin
Penicillins
Sleep deprivation, alcohol intoxication, menstruation, infection and fever (esp. in children) can worsen seizure.

FIRST AID FOR SEIZURES

First aid for seizures involves responding in ways that can keep the person safe until the seizure stops by itself. Protective measures include:

- Keep calm and reassure other people who may be nearby.

- Prevent injury by clearing the area around the person of anything hard or sharp.

- Ease the person to the floor and put something soft and flat, like a folded jacket, under the head. Turn the person gently onto one side. This will help keep the airway clear.

- Remove eyeglasses and loosen ties or anything around the neck that may make breathing difficult.

- Time the seizure with your watch. If the seizure continues for longer than five minutes without signs of slowing down or if a person has trouble breathing afterwards, appears to be injured, in pain, or recovery is unusual in some way, call 911.

- Do not hold people down or try to stop their movements.

- Contrary to popular belief, it is not true that people having a seizure can swallow their tongue. Do not put anything in the person's mouth. Efforts to hold the tongue down can injure the teeth or jaw.

- Don't attempt artificial respiration except in the unlikely event that a person does not start breathing again after the seizure has stopped.

- Stay with the person until the seizure ends naturally and the person is fully awake.

- Do not offer the person water or food until fully alert.

- Be friendly and reassuring as consciousness returns.

- Offer to call a taxi, friend or relative to help the person get home safely, particularly if the person seems confused or unable to get home without help.

STATUS EPILEPTICUS

Status epilepticus is generally defined as a continuous seizure lasting more than 5 minutes or 2 or more discrete seizures between which there is incomplete recovery of consciousness.

- It is a medical emergency.

- Treatment consists of using a rapid-acting benzodiazepine first (e.g., lorazepam), followed by AED therapy (loading dose followed by maintenance dose).

Status Epilepticus: First Line Treatment with Benzodiazepines

- Lorazepam *(Ativan)* is the benzodiazepine of choice for treating status epilepticus due to the longer duration of action in the CNS providing longer protection. Diazepam is highly lipophilic (quick onset) but rapidly redistributes into fat causing the CNS half-life to be shorter, hence a shorter duration of effect.

- Lorazepam: 4 mg given slow IV (adults); max rate 2 mg/min – may repeat in 5-10 minutes if no response.

- Diazepam: 5-10 mg given slow IV – may repeat every 5-10 min; max dose: 30 mg.

- Rectal diazepam *(Diastat Acudial)*: 5-20 mg PR (age and weight-based). May repeat once if necessary.

Status Epilepticus: Second Line Treatment

Start with one AED agent, and if it does not control seizure activity, move to another AED. Each institution usually has a treatment algorithm with the agents/doses to use.

ANTIEPILEPTIC PHARMACOTHERAPY

Treatment of Choice (Variable, Depends on Literature and Clinician Preference)

SEIZURE TYPE	1ST LINE TREATMENT
Partial, including secondarily generalized	Carbamazepine
	Lamotrigine
	Levetiracetam
	Oxcarbazepine
Primary Generalized Tonic-Clonic	Lamotrigine
	Levetiracetam
	Valproate
Absence	Ethosuximide
	Valproate
Atypical Absence, Myoclonic, Atonic	Ethosuximide
	Lamotrigine
	Levetiracetam
	Valproate

FIRST GENERATION ANTICONVULSANTS

Benzodiazepines (BZD)

BZDs enhance the activity of γ-aminobutyric acid (GABA), which is an inhibitory neurotransmitter, resulting in increased neuronal membrane permeability to Cl⁻ ions; this shift in Cl⁻ ions results in hyperpolarization (a less excitable state) and membrane stabilization.

DRUG	DOSING	SAFETY/SIDE EFFECTS/MONITORING
ClonazePAM (Klonopin) C IV Tablet, ODT	Initial: 0.5 mg BID-TID Maximum: 20 mg/day	**CONTRAINDICATIONS** Severe liver disease and acute narrow-angle glaucoma – for clonazepam only **SIDE EFFECTS** Drowsiness, ataxia, behavior disorder, dizziness, lethargy, cognitive impairment (limit other CNS depressants), depression, physiological dependence, tolerance, retrograde amnesia, pyrexia, constipation, drooling **NOTES** Pregnancy Category D (clonazepam)/C (clobazam)
CloBAZam (Onfi) C IV For adjunctive treatment of seizures associated with Lennox-Gastaut syndrome (LGS) in patients 2 years or older. Tablet, suspension	Initial: ≤ 30 kg: 5 mg/day; maximum: 10 mg BID > 30 kg: 5 mg BID; maximum: 20 mg BID	Do not discontinue abruptly as seizures can result (applies to all anticonvulsants); withdrawal symptoms will increase seizure risk; panic attacks can occur if dosing interval missed. Paradoxical reactions, including hyperactive or aggressive behavior, particularly in pediatric, adolescents or psychiatric patients, may occur.

Benzodiazepine Drug Interactions

- Clonazepam is a major 3A4 substrate; look for 3A4 inducers and inhibitors.

- Clobazam is a substrate of 2C19 (major), 3A4 (minor); inhibitor of 2D6 (moderate) and 2C9 (weak); inducer of 3A4 (weak). Use of an alternative, non-hormonal contraceptive is recommended.

- Caution for additive CNS effects, including dizziness, drowsiness, fatigue.

Carbamazepine

Fast sodium channel blocker; structurally similar to tricyclic antidepressants; stimulates release of antidiuretic hormone (ADH) promoting reabsorption of water.

DRUG	DOSING	SAFETY/SIDE EFFECTS/MONITORING
CarBAMazepine *(TEGretol, TEGretol XR, Carbatrol, Epitol)* *Equetro* – for bipolar Indicated for many seizure types and trigeminal neuralgia Capsule, tablet, suspension	Initial: 200 mg BID (XR is taken daily) Maximum: 1,600 mg/day (some patients may require more) **Therapeutic Range** 4-12 mcg/mL	**BLACK BOX WARNINGS (2)** Serious skin reactions, including SJS and TEN: If of Asian ancestry, MUST be tested for HLA-B*1502 allele prior to therapy; if positive, cannot be used (unless benefit clearly outweighs the risk). Fatal blood cell abnormalities (including aplastic anemia and agranulocytosis) **CONTRAINDICATIONS** Bone marrow suppression, hypersensitivity to TCAs, use of MAO inhibitors within past 14 days, concurrent use of nefazodone, concomitant use of delavirdine or other non-nucleoside reverse transcriptase inhibitors **WARNINGS** Risk of developing a hypersensitivity reaction may be increased in patients with the variant HLA-A*3101 allele. Serious skin reactions (onset usually 2 – 8 weeks after initiation) **SIDE EFFECTS** Nausea, vomiting, dizziness, drowsiness, headache, ataxia, fatigue, vitamin D and calcium deficiency (bone loss), SIADH/hyponatremia, hepatotoxicity; blurred vision and diplopia (esp. if toxic) **MONITORING** CBC with differential, platelets, LFTs, serum Na⁺ ophthalmic exam, thyroid function tests, electrolytes (esp. Na⁺), mental status, seizure frequency. Carbamazepine levels should be monitored within 3-5 days of initiation and again after 4 weeks due to autoinduction. **NOTES** Pregnancy Category D Potent CYP 450 inducer and autoinducer – ↓ level of many other drugs and of itself Supplementation with calcium and vitamin D recommended

Carbamazepine Drug Interactions

- Carbamazepine is a strong inducer of many enzymes (1A2, 2C19, 2C8/9, 3A4) and an auto-inducer. It will ↓ the levels of many drugs, including hormonal contraceptives, other seizure medications, levothyroxine, warfarin and others. Use of an alternative, nonhormonal contraceptive is recommended.

- Carbamazepine is a major 3A4 substrate. CYP 3A4 inhibitors will ↑ carbamazepine levels, and 3A4 inducers will ↓ carbamazepine levels.

- Avoid use of grapefruit products, nefazodone and non-nucleoside reverse transcriptase inhibitors.

- Caution for additive CNS effects, including dizziness, drowsiness, fatigue.

Ethosuximide

T-type calcium channel blocker that increases seizure threshold and suppresses paroxysmal spike-and-wave pattern in absence seizures.

DRUG	DOSING	SAFETY/SIDE EFFECTS/MONITORING
Ethosuximide *(Zarontin)* One of the drugs of choice for absence Capsule, solution	Initial: 500 mg daily Maximum: 1,500 mg/day Therapeutic range 40-100 mcg/mL	**SIDE EFFECTS** GI upset (weight loss, abdominal pain, nausea and vomiting), hiccups, dizziness, drowsiness, rash, including SJS and DRESS (drug rash with eosinophlia and systemic symptoms) **MONITORING** LFTs, CBC with differential, platelets, serum drug concentrations, seizure frequency.

Ethosuximide Drug Interactions

- Ethosuximide is a major 3A4 substrate; look for 3A4 inducers and inhibitors. Strong inducers including carbamazepine, fosphenytoin, phenytoin, phenobarbital, primidone and others may ↓ ethosuximide levels.

- Valproic acid can ↑ ethosuximide levels.

- Caution for additive CNS effects, including dizziness, drowsiness, fatigue.

Phenobarbital/Primidone

These agents enhance γ-aminobutyric acid (GABA)-mediated chloride influx; shift in Cl⁻ ions results in hyperpolarization (a less excitable state) and membrane stabilization.

DRUG	DOSING	SAFETY/SIDE EFFECTS/MONITORING
PHENobarbital *(Luminal)* C IV Barbiturate Tablet, solution, elixir, injection	Initial: 1 – 3 mg/kg/day Maximum: 300 mg/day t½:~100 hrs **Therapeutic Range** 20-40 mcg/mL in adults 15-30 mcg/mL in children	**SIDE EFFECTS** Drowsiness, cognitive impairment (limit other CNS depressants), dizziness/ataxia, physiological dependence, tolerance, hang-over effect, depression, vitamin D and calcium deficiency (bone loss), respiratory depression Rare: Serious skin reactions, including SJS and TEN, blood dyscrasias, hepatotoxicity **MONITORING** LFTs, CBC with differential, mental status, serum drug concentration, seizure frequency **NOTES** Do not discontinue abruptly as seizures can result (applies to all anticonvulsants); withdrawal symptoms will increase seizure risk
Primidone *(Mysoline)* Prodrug of phenobarbital and phenylethylmalonamide (PEMA) – both are active metabolites C IV Barbiturate Available: tablet		Paradoxical reactions, including hyperactive or aggressive behavior, particularly in pediatric and adolescent patients, may occur. Pregnancy Category D Supplementation with calcium and vitamin D recommended Strong CYP 450 enzyme inducers

Phenobarbital/Primidone Drug Interactions

- Phenobarbital (primidone is the prodrug) is a strong inducer of most CYP enzymes, including 1A2, 2C8/9, 3A4 and p-glycoprotein. These two drugs will lower the levels of the many drugs metabolized by these enzymes.

- Use of an alternative, non-hormonal contraceptive is recommended.

- Caution for additive CNS effects, including dizziness, drowsiness, fatigue.

Phenytoin/Fosphenytoin

Fast sodium channel blockers that stabilize neuronal membranes and reduce seizures by increasing efflux or decreasing influx of Na$^+$ ions.

DRUG	DOSING	SAFETY/SIDE EFFECTS/MONITORING
Phenytoin (Dilantin, Phenytek) Capsule, tablet, suspension, injection	**Oral** Initial: 100 mg PO TID **IV** Phenytoin max rate: 50 mg/min Fosphenytoin max rate: 150 mg PE/min Fosphenytoin is dosed in phenytoin equivalents (PE): 1 mg PE = 1 mg phenytoin Maximum: 600 mg/day Exhibits saturable, or Michaelis-Menten, kinetics; a small change in dose can cause a big change in serum level If the albumin is low (< 3.5 g/dL), the true phenytoin level will be higher than it appears – adjust with this formula: PHT correction = $\dfrac{\text{PHT measured}}{(0.2 \times \text{alb}) + 0.1}$ or can measure a free PHT level **Therapeutic Range** Total PHT: 10-20 mcg/mL Free PHT: 1-2.5 mcg/mL Phenytoin ER caps contain 8% less drug than chewable and suspension (dose adjust if changing formulations)	**BLACK BOX WARNINGS** Phenytoin IV administration should not exceed 50 mg/minute Fosphenytoin administration should not exceed 150 mg phenytoin equivalents (PE)/minute (if faster, can cause hypotension and cardiac arrhythmias) **WARNINGS** IV phenytoin is a vesicant; can cause venous irritation and "purple glove syndrome" (i.e., discoloration with edema and pain of distal limb); inject into a large vein slowly and follow with a saline flush. Serious skin reactions, including SJS and TEN HLA-B*1502 may be a risk factor in patients of Asian ancestry; DRESS **SIDE EFFECTS** With IV phenytoin (may need to lower rate): Hypotension, bradycardia, arrhythmias, cardiovascular collapse Dose-related (toxicity): Ataxia, dizziness, drowsiness, headache, nystagmus, slurred speech, behavior changes, lethargy, cognitive impairment, blurred vision and diplopia Chronic: Skin thickening (children), gingival hyperplasia, hirsutism, vitamin D and calcium deficiency (bone loss), connective tissue changes, coarsening of facial features, folate deficiency, hepatotoxicity **MONITORING** LFTs, CBC with differential, serum trough concentration, mental status, seizure frequency. For IV, continuous cardiac monitoring (rate, rhythm, BP). **NOTES** Pregnancy Category D Supplementation with folic acid, vitamin B12, calcium and vitamin D recommended Strong CYP 450 enzyme inducers Phenytoin IV is compatible with NS only, requires a filter and is stable for 4 hours; do not refrigerate as may cause precipitation (which may dissolve upon warming). Fosphenytoin can be mixed with NS or D5W and is refrigerated (good for 48 hrs at room temperature). IV to oral ratio is 1:1 Enteral feedings may ↓ phenytoin absorption; must separate
Fosphenytoin Prodrug of phenytoin (IV/IM) Injection		

Phenytoin/Fosphenytoin Drug Interactions

- Phenytoin and fosphenytoin are strong inducers of several CYP 450 enzymes, including 2C19, 2C8/9, 3A4 and p-glycoprotein. These 2 drugs will lower the concentration of many drugs including other anticonvulsants (carbamazepine, valproate, lamotrigine), contraceptives, warfarin, etc.

- Use of an alternative, non-hormonal contraceptive is recommended.

- Caution for additive CNS effects, including dizziness, drowsiness, fatigue.

- These agents have high protein binding [fosphenytoin (95-99%)/phenytoin (90-95%)]; they can displace other highly-protein bound drugs. Other drugs can displace fosphenytoin/phenytoin, causing an increase in levels and potential toxicity.

Valproic Acid/Valproate

T-type calcium channel blocker and fast sodium channel blocker that increases γ-aminobutyric activity (GABA), an inhibitory neurotransmitter.

DRUG	DOSING	SAFETY/SIDE EFFECTS/MONITORING
Valproate/Valproic acid (Depakene, Stavzor, Depacon) Depakene – capsule, solution, syrup Stavzor – delayed-release capsule Depacon – IV **Divalproex (Depakote, Depakote ER, Depakote Sprinkle)** Depakote – delayed release tablet Depakote ER – ext-release tablet Depakote Sprinkle – capsules can be opened and sprinkled on food Also used for migraine prophylaxis	Initial: 125-250 mg BID Maximum: 60 mg/kg/day **Therapeutic Range** 50-100 mcg/mL (some patients may need higher levels) Cannot substitute *Depakote ER* for the delayed release tablets *(Depakote)*; need to ↑ *Depakote ER* by 8-20% If the albumin is low (< 3.5 g/dL), the true valproate level will be higher than it appears – adjust with the same phenytoin formula.	**BLACK BOX WARNINGS (3)** **Hepatic Failure** Occurs rarely in adults (1:50,000) usually during first 6 months of therapy. Children (1:600) under the age of two years and patients with mitochondrial disorders are at higher risk. Monitor LFTs frequently during the first 6 months. **Teratogenicity** Including neural tube defects (e.g., spina bifida) and decreased IQ scores following in utero exposure. **Pancreatitis** Can be fatal in children and adults **CONTRAINDICATIONS** Significant hepatic disease, urea cycle disorders, prophylaxis of migraine in pregnancy, known mitochondrial disorders caused by mutations in mitochondrial DNA polymerase gamma (POLG) or children < 2 years of age suspected of having a POLG-related disorder **SIDE EFFECTS** GI upset (nausea/vomiting), abdominal pain, dizziness, asthenia, tremor, alopecia (treat with a multivitamin containing selenium and zinc), somnolence, weight gain, polycystic ovary syndrome (PCOS), vitamin D and calcium deficiency (bone loss), pancreatitis, lower IQ in children if exposed in-utero and hyperammonemia (treat with carnitine in symptomatic adults only). Dose-related: thrombocytopenia, diplopia, blurred vision **MONITORING** LFTs (at baseline and frequently during first 6 months), CBC with differential, platelets, serum drug concentrations, mental status changes, cognitive function, seizure frequency **NOTES** Pregnancy Category D/X (for migraine prophylaxis) Supplementation with calcium and vitamin D recommended Switching from valproic acid to delayed-release divalproex may reduce stomach upset

Valproic Acid/Valproate Drug Interactions

- Valproate is an inhibitor of 2C9 (weak) and can ↑ levels of lamotrigine, phenobarbital, warfarin, and zidovudine.

- Use special caution with combination of valproate and lamotrigine due to risk of serious rash (combination requires slow titration and patient counseling). The combination is synergistically beneficial where the efficacy is greater when used in combination than either medication used alone.

- Salicylates may displace valproic acid from protein-binding sites, leading to valproic acid toxicity.

- Carbapenems (imipenem, etc.) can ↓ the levels of valproic acid leading to seizures.

- Caution for additive CNS effects, including dizziness, drowsiness, fatigue.

SECOND GENERATION ANTICONVULSANTS

Lamotrigine

Lamotrigine inhibits release of glutamate and aspartate (excitatory amino acids), fast sodium channel blocker and t-type calcium channel blocker stabilizing neuronal membranes.

DRUG	DOSING	SAFETY/SIDE EFFECTS/MONITORING
LamoTRIgine (LaMICtal [tabs/ chewables], LaMICtal ODT [orally disintegrating tabs], LaMICtal XR) Adjunctive therapy for partial seizures, or conversion to primary therapy from older drugs Tablet, ODT	Initiate: Week 1 and 2: 25 mg/day Week 3 and 4: 50 mg/day Week 5 and on: can ↑ by 50 mg every 1-2 weeks. Dosing is different if on enzyme inducers such as carbamazepine, phenytoin, phenobarbital, or primidone. Also different dosing if on valproate (start with 25 mg every other day) Divide BID, unless using XR	**BLACK BOX WARNING** Serious skin reactions, including SJS (rate of rash is greater in pediatrics than adults) and TEN; ↑ risk with higher than recommended starting doses, rapid dose escalation, or co-administration of valproic acid which ↑ lamotrigine levels > 2-fold. To ↓ risk of rash, follow titration schedule– *Lamictal Starter Kit* and *Lamictal ODT Patient Titration Kits* provide the recommended titration schedule for the 1st 5 weeks. Titration schedule is based on whether patient is on valproate, inducer anticonvulsant, or no concomitant anticonvulsant. **WARNINGS** Risk of aseptic meningitis, blood dyscrasias **SIDE EFFECTS** Nausea, insomnia, drowsiness, fatigue, ataxia, impaired coordination, dizziness, diplopia, rhinitis, xerostomia, rash **NOTES** Pregnancy Category C Discontinue if any sign of hypersensitivity reaction or unspecified rash

Lamotrigine Drug Interactions

- Valproate increases lamotrigine concentrations more than 2-fold.

- Lamotrigine levels are decreased by strong enzyme inducers (e.g., carbamazepine, fosphenytoin, phenytoin, phenobarbital, primidone, rifampin, others) and oral estrogen-containing contraceptives. Dosage adjustments will be necessary in most patients who start or stop estrogen-containing oral contraceptives while taking lamotrigine.

- Caution for additive CNS effects, including dizziness, drowsiness, fatigue.

Levetiracetam

Unknown; may inhibit voltage-dependent N-type calcium channels and facilitate GABA-ergic inhibitory transmission through displacement of negative modulators; reduction of delayed rectifier potassium current; and/or binding to synaptic proteins which modulate neurotransmitter release.

DRUG	DOSING	SAFETY/SIDE EFFECTS/MONITORING
LevETIRAcetam *(Keppra, Keppra XR)* Adjunctive therapy for several seizure types Tablet, solution, injection	Initial: 500 mg BID Maximum: 3,000 mg/day ↓ dose if CrCl ≤ 80 mL/min	**SIDE EFFECTS** Somnolence, dizziness, behavior changes (aggression, irritability, etc.), asthenia **MONITORING** Mental status and seizure frequency **NOTES** Pregnancy Category C No significant drug interactions

Oxcarbazepine

Fast sodium channel blocker stabilizing hyperexcited neuronal membranes, inhibiting repetitive firing, and reducing the propagation of synaptic impulses.

DRUG	DOSING	SAFETY/SIDE EFFECTS/MONITORING
OXcarbazepine *(Trileptal, Oxtellar XR)* OXcarbazepine extended-release *(Oxtellar XR)* Partial seizures Tablet, suspension *(Trileptal)*, extended-release tablet *(Oxtellar XR)*	Initial: 300 mg BID *(Trileptal)*; 300 mg daily *(Oxtellar XR)* Maximum: 2,400 mg/day Reduce dose in renal impairment (CrCl < 30 mL/min); start 300 mg daily Carbamazepine to oxcarbazepine dose conversion: 1.2 – 1.5x carbamazepine dose	**WARNINGS** Serious skin reactions, including SJS/TEN (if rash with carbamazepine, 25-30% cross-sensitivity with oxcarbazepine) **SIDE EFFECTS** Somnolence, dizziness, headache, GI effects (nausea, vomiting, abdominal pain), diplopia, nystagmus, abnormal vision, ataxia, tremor, vitamin D and calcium deficiency (bone loss) Hyponatremia: monitor serum Na$^+$ levels especially during first 3 months (more common than with carbamazepine) **MONITORING** Electrolytes (esp Na$^+$), mental status, seizure frequency **NOTES** Pregnancy Category C Strong CYP 450 3A4 inducer Supplementation with calcium and vitamin D recommended

Oxcarbazepine Drug Interactions

■ Oxcarbazepine does not undergo autoinduction.

- Oxcarbazepine is an inhibitor of 2C19 (weak) and strong inducer of 3A4/5. Oxcarbazepine can increase fosphenytoin and phenytoin levels and decrease the level of hormonal contraceptives significantly. Use of an alternative, nonhormonal contraceptive is recommended.

- Caution for additive CNS effects, including dizziness, drowsiness, fatigue.

Pregabalin/Gabapentin

These agents bind to the α-2-delta subunit of voltage-dependent calcium channels within the CNS, inhibiting excitatory neurotransmitter release.

DRUG	DOSING	SAFETY/SIDE EFFECTS/MONITORING
Pregabalin *(Lyrica)* Diabetic neuropathic pain, postherpetic neuralgia, fibromyalgia, spinal cord damage, adjunctive therapy for adult patients with partial onset seizures C V Capsule, solution	Initial: 75 mg BID Maximum: 600 mg/day ↓ dose and extend the interval if CrCl < 60 mL/min	**SIDE EFFECTS** Dizziness, somnolence, peripheral edema, weight gain, ataxia, diplopia, blurred vision, xerostomia, mild euphoria **NOTES** Pregnancy Category C Often used for neuropathic pain treatment
Gabapentin *(Neurontin)* *Gralise* – indicated for postherpetic neuralgia *Horizant* – indicated for postherpetic neuralgia and restless leg syndrome Capsule, tablet, solution	Initial: 300 mg TID Maximum: 3,600 mg/day ↓ dose and extend the interval if CrCl < 60 mL/min	**SIDE EFFECTS** Dizziness, somnolence, ataxia, peripheral edema, weight gain, diplopia, blurred vision, xerostomia **NOTES** Pregnancy Category C Used more often for off-labeled uses such as fibromyalgia, pain, headache, peripheral neuropathy, drug abuse, alcohol withdrawal Take extended-release formulation with food

Pregabalin/Gabapentin Drug Interactions

- No significant drug-drug interactions; renally eliminated. Use caution with pregabalin and glitazones concurrently due to risk of additive edema.

- Caution for additive CNS effects, including dizziness, drowsiness, fatigue.

Topiramate

Fast sodium channel blocker, enhances γ-aminobutyric activity, antagonizes AMPA/kainate glutamate receptors, and weakly inhibits carbonic anhydrase.

DRUG	DOSING	SAFETY/SIDE EFFECTS/MONITORING
Topiramate *(Topamax, Topiragen, Topamax* Sprinkle caps) Topiramate extended-release *(Trokendi XR)* Adjunctive therapy for partial seizures, or conversion to primary therapy from older drugs Capsule, extended-release capsule, tablet Also used for migraine prophylaxis	Week 1: 25 mg BID or 50 mg daily Week 2: 50 mg BID or 100 mg daily Week 3: 75 mg BID or 150 mg daily Week 4: 100 mg BID or 200 mg daily Increase by 100 mg weekly until max dose or therapeutic effect Maximum: 400 mg/day ↓ dose if CrCl < 70 mL/min	**WARNINGS** May be associated with hyperchloremic nonanion gap metabolic acidosis due to inhibition of carbonic anhydrase and increased renal bicarbonate loss. Dose reduction or discontinuation (by tapering dose) should be considered in patients with persistent or severe metabolic acidosis Oligohydrosis (reduced perspiration)/hyperthermia (mostly in children) – try to limit sun and hydrate Nephrolithiasis (kidney stones) – keep hydrated Acute myopia and secondary angle closure glaucoma Hyperammonemia – alone and with co-administration of valproate **SIDE EFFECTS** Somnolence, dizziness, difficulty with memory, difficulty with concentration/attention, cognitive problems, psychomotor slowing, paresthesias, weight loss, anorexia, mood problems, ↓ sodium bicarbonate concentrations, taste perversions, vitamin D and calcium deficiency (bone loss) **MONITORING** Hydration status, electrolytes (esp. bicarbonate), SCr, BUN, mental status, seizure frequency **NOTES** Pregnancy Category D – use during pregnancy can cause cleft lip and/or palate in newborn *Topamax* Sprinkle Capsules: May be swallowed whole or opened to sprinkle the contents on a small amount (~1 teaspoon) of soft food (drug/food mixture should not be chewed; swallow immediately). Avoid alcohol use with topiramate ER within 6 hours prior to and 6 hours after administration Supplementation with calcium and vitamin D recommended

Topiramate Drug Interactions

- Topiramate is an inhibitor of 2C19 (weak) and inducer of 3A4 (weak/moderate). Phenytoin and carbamazepine ↓ topiramate levels.

- Topiramate may ↓ oral contraceptive effectiveness; ↑ risk with higher doses (≥ 200 mg/day). Use of an alternative, non-hormonal contraceptive is recommended.

- Caution for additive CNS effects, including dizziness, drowsiness, fatigue.

ZONISAMIDE

Fast sodium channel blocker, T-type calcium channel blocker and weak carbonic anhydrase inhibitor.

DRUG	DOSING	SAFETY/SIDE EFFECTS/MONITORING
Zonisamide *(Zonegran)* Capsule	Initial: 100 mg/day Maximum: 400 mg/day Do not use if CrCl < 50 mL/min	**CONTRAINDICATIONS** Hypersensitivity to sulfonamides **WARNINGS** Serious skin reactions including SJS/TEN; oligohydrosis (reduced perspiration)/hyperthermia (mostly children) – try to limit sun and hydrate; nephrolithiasis (kidney stones) – keep hydrated; metabolic acidosis **SIDE EFFECTS** Drowsiness, dizziness, anorexia, weight loss, vitamin D and calcium deficiency (bone loss) **MONITORING** Hydration status, electrolytes (esp. bicarbonate), SCr, BUN, mental status, seizure frequency **NOTES** Pregnancy Category C Supplementation with calcium and vitamin D recommended

Zonisamide Drug Interactions

- Major 3A4 substrate; look for 3A4 inducers and inhibitors.

- Caution for additive CNS effects, including dizziness, drowsiness, fatigue.

OTHER ANTICONVULSANTS

Eslicarbazepine Acetate

Eslicarbazepine is a fast sodium channel blocker and is a major active metabolite of oxcarbazepine.

DRUG	DOSING	SAFETY/SIDE EFFECTS/MONITORING
Eslicarbazepine (*Aptiom*) Adjunctive therapy for partial seizures Major active metabolite of oxcarbazepine Tablet	Initiate: Week 1: 400 mg PO daily Week 2: 800 mg PO daily Maximum: 12,000 mg PO daily CrCl < 50 mL/min: ↓ dose	**CONTRAINDICATIONS** Hypersensitivity to oxcarbazepine **SIDE EFFECTS** Dizziness, somnolence, nausea, headache, double vision, vomiting, feeling tired, problems with coordination, blurred vision, shakiness, hyponatremia **MONITORING** CBC with differential, platelets, LFTs, electrolytes (esp. Na$^+$), mental status, seizure frequency **NOTES** Pregnancy Category C Supplementation with calcium and vitamin D recommended

Eslicarbazepine Drug Interactions

■ Eslicarbazepine is an inducer of 3A4 (weak/moderate) and inhibitor of 2C19 (moderate)

Ezogabine

Potassium channel opener that enhances the M-current, regulating neuronal excitability.

DRUG	DOSING	SAFETY/SIDE EFFECTS/MONITORING
Ezogabine (*Potiga*) Refractory partial onset seizures C V Tablet	Initial: 100 mg TID Maximum: 1,200 mg/day ↓ dose if CrCl < 50 mL/min	**BLACK BOX WARNING** Retinal abnormalities that may progress to vision loss have been reported and were seen in about one-third of patients after approximately 4 years of treatment. **WARNINGS** Skin discoloration – typically blue in color (but may also be grey-blue or brown) and is mainly located on or around the lips, nail beds of the fingers or toes, face and legs, sclera, and conjunctiva. If detected, discontinue use. **SIDE EFFECTS** Dizziness, drowsiness, fatigue, confusional state, abnormal coordination, diplopia, disturbance in attention, memory impairment, asthenia, blurred vision, ataxia Rare: Urinary retention, QT prolongation, chromaturia **MONITORING** Eye exam at baseline and every 6 months, LFTs, bilirubin, electrolytes, QT interval, urinary retention, mental status, seizure frequency **NOTES** Pregnancy Category C Can cause urine to turn orangish/reddish/brown (chromaturia)

Ezogabine Drug Interactions

- Carbamazepine and phenytoin can reduce ezogabine levels.

- N-acetyl metabolite of ezogabine can inhibit renal clearance of digoxin; monitor digoxin levels.

- Avoid concurrent use with major QT prolonging agents.

- Caution for additive CNS effects, including dizziness, drowsiness, fatigue.

Felbamate

Felbamate increases γ-aminobutyric acid (GABA) activity, NMDA receptor blocker.

DRUG	DOSING	SAFETY/SIDE EFFECTS/MONITORING
Felbamate *(Felbatol)* Refractory seizures who have inadequately responded to alternative treatments where the benefits outweigh the risks. Tablet, suspension	Initiate: 1,200 mg/day divided TID-QID Maximum: 3,600 mg/day	**BLACK BOX WARNINGS (2)** Hepatic Failure and Aplastic Anemia **CONTRAINDICATIONS** History of blood dyscrasias or liver impairment **SIDE EFFECTS** Headache, drowsiness, nausea, anorexia, fatigue, insomnia, weight loss **MONITORING** LFTs, CBC with differential, mental status, seizure frequency **NOTES** Pregnancy Category C

Felbamate Drug Interactions

- If felbamate is being used in a case, there is likely a reason why it should not be used; look at LFTs, other concomitant drugs that are hepatotoxic, and the CBC. This is a drug used by neurologists only for refractive cases. Refer to the package insert for specific prescribing recommendations with inducing and inhibiting anticonvulsants.

Lacosamide

Slow sodium channel blocker, thereby stabilizing hyperexcitable neuronal membranes.

DRUG	DOSING	SAFETY/SIDE EFFECTS/MONITORING
Lacosamide *(Vimpat)* C V Tablet, solution, injection	Initial: 50 mg BID Maximum: 400 mg/day Max dose is 300 mg when CrCl ≤ 30 mL/min	**SIDE EFFECTS** Dizziness, headache, fatigue, ataxia, diplopia, nausea, tremor **NOTES** Pregnancy Category C Use with caution in patients with cardiac conduction problems and severe cardiac disease (MI, HF). Lacosamide prolongs PR interval and ↑ risk of arrhythmias. Obtain an ECG prior to use and after titrated to steady state.

Lacosamide Drug Interactions

- No clinically significant drug interactions.

Rufinamide

Fast sodium channel blocker, thereby limiting repetitive firing of Na⁺-dependent action potentials.

DRUG	DOSING	SAFETY/SIDE EFFECTS/MONITORING
Rufinamide *(Banzel)* Indicated for Lennox-Gastaut seizures only Tablet, suspension	Initial: 200 – 400 mg BID Maximum: 3,200 mg/day Must dispense oral suspension with provided adapter and dosing syringe	**CONTRAINDICATIONS** Patients with familial short QT syndrome **SIDE EFFECTS** QT shortening (dose related), dizziness, somnolence, nausea, vomiting, headache, fatigue **NOTES** Pregnancy Category C Take with food

Rufinamide Drug Interactions

- A weak inhibitor CYP 2E1 and weak inducer CYP 3A4. Monitor levels of other antiepileptics that are metabolized via CYP 3A4.

Tiagabine

Tiagabine blocks γ-aminobutyric acid (GABA) reuptake in the presynaptic neuron.

DRUG	DOSING	SAFETY/SIDE EFFECTS/MONITORING
TiaGABine *(Gabitril)* Adjunctive therapy for partial seizures Tablet	Initial: 4 mg daily Maximum: 56 mg/day	**WARNINGS** Worsening of seizures and new-onset of seizures when used off-label for other indications; serious skin reactions including SJS/TEN **SIDE EFFECTS** Somnolence, nausea, decreased concentration, dizziness, tremor **NOTES** Pregnancy Category C Take with food

Tiagabine Drug Interactions

- Major 3A4 substrate; look for 3A4 inducers and inhibitors.

Vigabatrin

Vigabatrin irreversibly inhibits γ-aminobutyric acid transaminase, increasing levels of GABA.

DRUG	DOSING	SAFETY/SIDE EFFECTS/MONITORING
Vigabatrin *(Sabril)* Refractory complex partial seizures and infantile spasms Tablet, solution	Initial: 500 mg BID Maximum: 3,000 mg/day Only available through SHARE distribution program (Support, Help And Resourses for Epilepsy)	**BLACK BOX WARNING** Causes permanent vision loss (25% in children, > 30% of adults) **SIDE EFFECTS** Fatigue, somnolence, nystagmus, tremor, blurred vision, vision impairment, weight gain, arthralgia, abnormal coordination, confusion **MONITORING** Ophthalmologic exam at baseline, every 3 months, and 3 – 6 months after discontinued; mental status and seizure frequency **NOTES** Pregnancy Category C MedGuide Required

Vigabatrin Drug Interactions

■ Vigabatrin is a weak CYP 2C9 inducer.

Perampanel

Selective, non-competitive AMPA glutamate receptor antagonist.

DRUG	DOSING	SAFETY/SIDE EFFECTS/MONITORING
Perampanel *(Fycompa)* Complex partial seizures in patients 12 years and older Tablet	Initial: 2 mg QHS (absence of enzyme inducing AEDs); 4 mg QHS (presence of enzyme inducing AEDs) Maximum: 12 mg/day	**BLACK BOX WARNING** Risk of serious neuropsychiatric events, including irritability, aggression, anger, anxiety, paranoia, euphoric mood, agitation, and mental status changes, mostly in the first 6 weeks of therapy **SIDE EFFECTS** Dizziness, somnolence, fatigue, headache, irritability **NOTES** Pregnancy Category C

Perampanel Drug Interactions

■ Major 3A4 substrate and weak/moderate 3A4 inducer; avoid concurrent use with other 3A4 inducers other than enzyme-inducing AEDs. If using with enzyme-inducing AEDs, start with higher initial dose (4 mg).

■ Use of an alternative, non-hormonal contraceptive is recommended.

Significant Toxicities

ADVERSE EFFECT	ASSOCIATED DRUGS	
Teratogenicity*	Carbamazepine	Phenytoin
	Clonazepam	Topiramate
	Phenobarbital	Valproic Acid
Hepatotoxicity	Carbamazepine	Phenytoin
	Felbamate	Valproic Acid
	Phenobarbital/Primidone	
Decrease effects of oral contraceptives	Carbamazepine	Phenobarbital
	Clobazam	Phenytoin
	Oxcarbazepine	Primidone
	Perampanel	Topiramate (≥ 200 mg/day)
Fatal pancreatitis	Valproic Acid	
Aplastic anemia	Carbamazepine (and agranulocytosis)	Felbamate
Skin rash (Stevens-Johnson syndrome)	Carbamazepine	Phenytoin/Fosphenytoin
	Lamotrigine	Tiagabine
	Oxcarbazepine	Zonisamide
	Phenobarbital	
Oligohydrosis – inability to sweat, risk of heat stroke – highest risk in children	Topiramate	Zonisamide
Nephrolithiasis (kidney stones)	Topiramate	Zonisamide
Weight gain	Valproic Acid	Pregabalin
	Gabapentin	
Weight loss	Felbamate	Topiramate
	Ethosuximide	Zonisamide
Hyponatremia	Carbamazepine	Oxcarbazepine (more common)

* Patients should be encouraged to enroll in the North American Antiepileptic Drug (NAAED) Pregnancy Registry if they become pregnant. This registry is collecting information about the safety of antiepileptic drugs during pregnancy (aed-pregnancyregistry.org).

Patient Counseling for All Anticonvulsants

■ All require counseling regarding the risk of suicidal behavior/ideation. Instruct patients/family to report any changes in psychological behavior. Dispense MedGuide and instruct patient/family to read it.

■ Do not stop taking this medication without consulting your doctor. Seizures may become worse when the drug is suddenly stopped. When stopping therapy, the dose needs to be gradually decreased.

- Seizure medications can impair judgment, thinking and coordination. You may experience dizziness and drowsiness, especially when starting therapy.

- Do not drive, operate heavy machinery, or do other dangerous activities until you know how this medication affects you.

- All have additive sedative/dizziness/confusion side effects with CNS depressants, including alcohol, hypnotics, benzodiazepines, skeletal muscle relaxants, etc. Avoid use of other CNS depressants drugs, if possible.

- Avoid use of drugs that can lower the seizure threshold (see chart at the beginning of the chapter). Avoid St. John's Wort with all anticonvulsants.

- Use caution with different generic substitutions; try to stick to the same manufacturer. Small dosage variations can result in loss of seizure control.

Carbamazepine

- If you have nausea, take with food or ask your doctor to change to a long-acting formulation.

- Carbamazepine can rarely cause very serious (possibly fatal) skin reactions. If you are of Asian descent, you must have a blood test prior to using this medicine to determine if you are at greater risk of developing a serious skin reaction. The serious skin reactions usually develop within the first few months of treatment. Seek immediate medical attention if you develop a serious skin rash or have blisters, peeling, itching or swelling.

- Carbamazepine can rarely cause a severe decline in bone marrow function leading to aplastic anemia or agranulocytosis. You will need to have your blood checked to make sure this is not occurring. Contact your doctor immediately if any of these rare but very serious side effects occur: signs of infection (e.g., fever, persistent sore throat, mouth sores), unusual weakness or fatigue, or easy bleeding or bruising on non-bony parts of the body.

- Carbamazepine is FDA pregnancy category D. This means that it is known to be harmful to an unborn baby. Do not take this drug without first talking to your doctor if you are pregnant or are planning a pregnancy.

- Avoid eating grapefruit or drinking grapefruit juice while being treated with carbamazepine.

- This medication can lower the amount of vitamin D and calcium in your body; it is recommended to supplement with calcium and vitamin D while taking this medication.

Gabapentin/Pregabalin

- This medication can cause weight gain and swelling of your hands, legs, and feet. Weight gain can be a serious problem for people with heart problems. Weight gain can adversely affect management of diabetes (if patient has diabetes).

- This medication can produce a slight "high" feeling (pregabalin only).

Lamotrigine

- Patients who experience headache, fever, chills, nausea, vomiting, stiff neck, rash, abnormal sensitivity to light, drowsiness, or confusion should contact their health care professional right away.

- This medication may cause a serious skin rash. These serious skin reactions are more likely to happen in the first 2 to 8 weeks of treatment (but it can happen in people who have taken the medication for any period of time). If you develop blistering of your mucous membranes around your eyes, nose, and/or mouth, seek medical attention immediately.

Levetiracetam

- Take levetiracetam with or without food.

- Swallow the tablets whole. Do not chew, break, or crush tablets. Ask your healthcare provider for levetiracetam oral solution if you cannot swallow tablets.

- If taking levetiracetam oral solution, be sure to use a medicine dropper or medicine cup to help you measure the correct amount of levetiracetam oral solution. Do not use a household teaspoon or tablespoon.

Oxcarbazepine

- This medication can cause low sodium concentrations in the blood. Symptoms of low blood sodium include apathy, confusion, frequent or more serious seizures, headache, nausea, and tiredness.

- Take oxcarbazepine with or without food.

- Before taking oxcarbazepine oral suspension, shake the bottle well and use the oral dosing syringe to measure the amount of medicine needed. Oxcarbazepine oral suspension can be mixed in a small glass of water, or swallowed directly from the syringe. Clean the syringe with warm water and let it dry after each use.

Phenobarbital

- Patients should be advised that barbiturates may produce psychological and physical dependency. Consult your healthcare provider before increasing your daily dose or abruptly decreasing or stopping the medication.

- This medication can lower the amount of vitamin D and calcium in your body; it is recommended to supplement with calcium and vitamin D while taking this medication.

Phenytoin

- Patients should supplement with folic acid (particular women of childbearing age), calcium, and vitamin D since this medicine can lower the amounts in the body.

- Contact your physician immediately if a skin rash develops, or you experience unusual weakness or fatigue, or easy bleeding or bruising on non-bony parts of the body.

- This medicine can cause inflammation of your gums. Brush and floss regularly; do not miss dental cleanings or appointments.

- Phenytoin is FDA pregnancy category D for treating seizures. This means that phenytoin is known to be harmful to an unborn baby. Do not take phenytoin without first talking to your doctor if you are pregnant or are planning a pregnancy. Phenytoin can pass into breast milk. Discuss with your doctor if you are breastfeeding.

- If using the suspension, shake the bottle well before each dose.

- Use this medication regularly in order to get the most benefit from it. It is important to take all doses on time to keep the amount of medicine in your body at a constant level.

Topiramate

- This medication may cause eye problems. Please contact your healthcare provider right away if you experience a sudden decrease in vision with or without eye pain and redness or a blockage of fluid in the eye causing increased pressure in the eye. These eye problems can lead to permanent loss of vision if not treated.

- Topiramate may cause decreased sweating and increased body temperature. Children in particular should be watched for signs of decreased sweating and fever especially in hot weather. Contact your healthcare provider as soon as possible if you have a high fever, a fever that does not go away, or decreased sweating.

- Topiramate can increase the level of acid in your blood (metabolic acidosis). Symptoms include rapid breathing, confusion, lethargy – contact your doctor immediately.

- Topiramate Sprinkle Capsules may be swallowed whole or may be opened and sprinkled on a teaspoon of soft food. Drink fluids right after eating the food and medicine mixture to make sure it is all swallowed. Do not store any medicine and food mixture for later use.

- Drink plenty of fluids during the day. This may help prevent kidney stones while taking this medication.

- This medication may affect how you think and cause confusion, problems with concentration, attention, memory, or speech. It may also cause depression or mood problems, tiredness, and sleepiness.

- Topiramate is FDA pregnancy category D. This means that it is known to be harmful to an unborn baby. An increased risk of oral clefts (cleft lip and/or palate) has been observed, particularly following first trimester exposure.

- This medication can lower the amount of vitamin D and calcium in your body; it is recommended to supplement with calcium and vitamin D while taking this medication.

Valproic Acid

- Do not use if you have liver disease. In rare cases, this drug has caused liver failure. Notify your doctor if you develop severe fatigue, vomiting, loss of appetite, or easy bruising/bleeding of non-bony parts of the body. These could be early symptoms of liver damage.

- In rare cases, valproic acid has also caused severe, even fatal, cases of pancreatitis (inflammation of the pancreas). Some of the cases have progressed rapidly from initial symptoms to death. Cases have been reported soon after starting treatment with valproic acid, as well as after several years of use. Notify your doctor immediately if you develop nausea, vomiting, abdominal pain, or loss of appetite. These symptoms may be early signs of pancreatitis.

- Do not crush, chew, or break the capsules because they may hurt the mouth or throat. Swallow them whole. *Depakene* capsules contain liquid which will cause irritation to the mouth and throat.

- Measure the liquid form of valproic acid with a special dose-measuring spoon or cup, not a regular table spoon. If you do not have a dose-measuring device, ask your pharmacist for one.

- Valproic acid is FDA pregnancy category D. This means that it is known to be harmful to an unborn baby. Malformations of the face and head, heart, and nervous system have been reported. In addition, children born to mothers taking valproate products while pregnant may have impaired mental development. Do not take valproic acid without first talking to your doctor if you are pregnant or could become pregnant. This drug passes into breast milk. Tell your doctor if you are planning to breastfeed.

- Take each dose with a full glass of water and take with food to help avoid stomach upset.

- You will need to have blood tests during treatment. It is important for your doctor to know how much medication is in the blood and how well your liver is working.

- This medication can cause weight gain and swelling of your hands, legs, and feet. Weight gain can be a serious problem for people with heart problems. Weight gain can adversely affect management of diabetes (if patient has diabetes).

- This medication can lower the amount of vitamin D and calcium in your body; it is recommended to supplement with calcium and vitamin D while taking this medication.

PRACTICE CASE

Lucinda is a 35 year-old female who was in a motor vehicle accident and suffered a head injury. She suffered one seizure in the emergency room. She had two broken ribs and has a concussion. During her hospital stay, she was treated with fosphenytoin initially, and continued on phenytoin. Her only other medication is *Loestrin*, for contraception. She does not smoke or drink alcohol.

Lucinda spent 2 weeks in the hospital recovering from the accident. She is being discharged on phenytoin 100 mg TID.

CATEGORY	
Laboratory Values	Phenytoin level at discharge 11.7 mcg/mL
	Albumin level 4.2 g/dL (normal albumin 3.5–5 g/dL)

Questions

1. Lucinda is receiving phenytoin for her seizure control. What is one of the brand names for phenytoin?

    a. *Trileptal*

    b. *Keppra*

    c. *Phenytek*

    d. *Stavzor*

    e. *Diastat*

2. The medical resident asks the pharmacist to explain when a phenytoin level needs to be adjusted for the albumin level. The pharmacist should give this response:

    a. The phenytoin level will appear artificially low if the albumin is low – and should be adjusted.

    b. The phenytoin level will appear artificially high if the albumin is low – and should be adjusted.

    c. The phenytoin level will appear artificially low if the albumin is high – and should be adjusted.

    d. The phenytoin level will appear artificially high if the albumin is high – and should be adjusted.

    e. Albumin levels have no effect on phenytoin levels.

3. Lucinda will be counseled to recognize symptoms of phenytoin toxicity. Which of the following should be included? (Select **ALL** that apply.)

    a. Shakiness/walking unsteady

    b. Severe rash

    c. Double vision

    d. Nystagmus

    e. Osteomalacia

4. There is a serious drug interaction between Lucinda's birth control pills and phenytoin. Choose the correct counseling statement(s):

    a. Phenytoin will lower the amount of contraceptive medicine in her body.

    b. She will need to use a different type of contraceptive method.

    c. Phenytoin will increase the amount of contraceptive medicine in her body.

    d. A and B

    e. B and C

5. If Lucinda continues phenytoin long-term, which of the following medical condition(s) could result if she does not use proper supplementation? (Select **ALL** that apply.)

    a. Osteoporosis

    b. Vision loss

    c. Alopecia

    d. Arrhythmias

    e. Anemia

Questions 6-13 do not apply to the case.

6. A patient is going to receive phenytoin via infusion. Which of the following statements are correct? (Select ALL that apply.)

    a. Phenytoin has saturable kinetics.
    b. The maximum infusion rate is 100 mg/minute.
    c. The therapeutic level of phenytoin is 10-20 mcg/mL.
    d. Phenytoin should be mixed in dextrose only.
    e. The brand name of phenytoin is *Felbatol*.

7. A child has been receiving divalproex for seizure control. Unfortunately, the seizures are not well-controlled. The physician has ordered lamotrigine as adjunctive therapy, with a careful dose-titration. What is the reason that a slow titration is required when initiating lamotrigine?

    a. Risk of multi-organ hypersensitivity reaction
    b. Risk of cardiac myopathy
    c. Risk of fluid retention and heart failure
    d. Risk of severe, and potentially fatal, rash
    e. Risk of fulminant hepatic failure

8. What is the mechanism of action of phenobarbital?

    a. Enhances dopamine
    b. Enhances GABA
    c. Suppresses dopamine
    d. Suppresses GABA
    e. Fast sodium channel blocker

9. Which of the following drugs decrease sweating and can cause heat stroke in children, and requires counseling to parents to help children avoid the sun and keep hydrated? (Select ALL that apply.)

    a. Rufinamide
    b. Zonisamide
    c. Felbamate
    d. Topiramate
    e. Oxcarbazepine

10. Which of the following drugs can cause kidney stones and require counseling for adequate fluid intake?

    a. Topiramate
    b. Tiagabine
    c. Pregabalin
    d. Valproic Acid
    e. Carbamazepine

11. Which of the following drugs is a preferred agent for treating typical absence seizures?

    a. Ethosuximide
    b. Lamotrigine
    c. Felbamate
    d. Topiramate
    e. Ezogabine

12. You find a patient actively seizing and call 911. What steps should you take to ensure the patient is safe? (Select **ALL** that apply.)

    a. Turn the patient on their side
    b. Remove sharp or hard objects away from the patient seizing and support their head
    c. Insert a stick into the seizing patient's mouth to prevent them from swallowing their tongue
    d. Loosen the patient's clothes
    e. Time the seizure

13. Which of the following statements are true regarding status epilepticus? (Select **ALL** that apply.)

    a. It is a medical emergency
    b. Lorazepam is preferred over other benzodiazepines since it has a longer duration of action in the CNS.
    c. Phenobarbital coma is preferred for patients still having seizure activity after the first-line agent is given.
    d. It is defined as sub-clinical seizure activity on an EEG
    e. Phenytoin is the drug that should be used first-line to break status epilepticus

Answers

1-c, 2-a, 3-a,c,d, 4-d, 5-a,e, 6-a,c, 7-d, 8-b, 9-b,d, 10-a, 11-a, 12-a,b,d,e, 13-a,b

STROKE

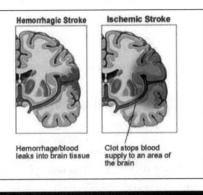

Hemorrhagic Stroke

Hemorrhage/blood leaks into brain tissue

Ischemic Stroke

Clot stops blood supply to an area of the brain

GUIDELINES

Guidelines for the Early Management of Patients with Acute Ischemic Stroke. AHA/ASA. Stroke 2013;44:870-947.

Guidelines for the Management of Aneurysmal Subarachnoid Hemorrhage. AHA/ASA. Stroke 2012;43:1711-1737.

Guidelines for the Prevention of Stroke in Patients with Stroke or Transient Ischemic Attack. AHA/ASA. Stroke 2011;42:227-276.

Guidelines for the Management of Spontaneous Intracerebral Hemorrhage. AHA/ASA. Stroke 2010;41:2108-2129.

BACKGROUND

A stroke, or cerebrovascular accident (CVA), occurs when blood flow to an area of the brain is interrupted by ischemia due to a clot (thrombus or emboli) or a ruptured blood vessel (hemorrhage). When a stroke occurs, it kills brain cells in the immediate area. When brain cells die, they release chemicals that set off a chain reaction that endangers brain cells in the larger, surrounding area of brain tissue (the penumbra). Without prompt medical treatment, this larger area of brain cells can also die. Acute ischemic stroke refers to a stroke caused by a thrombus or embolus and is more common than a hemorrhagic stroke. Intracerebral hemorrhage (ICH), subarachnoid hemorrhage (SAH) and subdural hematoma are all hemorrhagic strokes which indicate bleeding in the brain. Using agents that increase the risk of bleeding can be harmful (and fatal) in these cases.

When brain cells die, the abilities controlled by that area of the brain can be lost or impaired. Some people recover completely from less serious strokes, while others face chronic disability or loss of life. Stroke is the leading cause of disability and the 4th leading cause of death in the United States.

CLINICAL PRESENTATION & DIAGNOSIS

Signs and symptoms of a stroke can include:

- Sudden numbness or weakness of the face, arm or leg, especially on one side of the body (hemiplegia-paralysis on one side of the body, hemiparesis-weakness on one side of the body).

- Sudden confusion, trouble speaking or understanding

- Sudden trouble seeing in one or both eyes

- Sudden trouble walking, dizziness, loss of balance or co-ordination

- Sudden, severe headache with no known cause

Instruct the patient to call 9-1-1 immediately if any of these symptoms are present.

The evaluation of a stroke patient should be done expeditiously as time is brain. The clinical assessment (history, general exam, labs, and neurological exam) and stroke scales such as the National Institutes of Health Stroke Scale (NIHSS) assess severity of the stroke and provide prognostic information. Initial treatment includes supportive cardiac and respiratory care and quickly determining the nature of the lesion as ischemic or hemorrhagic via brain imaging. Brain imaging, either by computed tomography (CT) or, less commonly with magnetic resonance imaging (MRI), is essential to the diagnostic process and in selecting the appropriate treatment. Imaging should be interpreted within 45 minutes of the patient's arrival in the emergency department by a physician with expertise in reading these studies.

RISK FACTORS FOR STROKE
Hypertension – the most common cause (risk ↑ above 120/80 mmHg)
Atrial Fibrillation
Gender (males > females)
Ethnicity (African Americans highest risk, by ethnicity)
Age (55 and older)
Atherosclerosis
Diabetes
Transient Ischemic Attack (TIA)
Prior history of stroke
Smoking
Hypercholesterolemia/Hyperlipidemia
Patent Foramen Ovale (PFO)
Sickle Cell Disease

ACT F.A.S.T. (TEST TO LOOK FOR SIGNS/SYMPTOMS OF STROKE)	
Face	Ask the person to smile. Does one side of the face droop?
Arms	Ask the person to raise both arms. Does one arm drift downward?
Speech	Ask the person to repeat a simple sentence. Are the words slurred? Can he/she repeat the sentence correctly?
Time	If the person shows any of these symptoms, time is important. Call 911 or get to the hospital fast. Brain cells are dying.

HEMORRHAGIC STROKE

Hemorrhagic strokes include intracerebral hemorrhage (ICH), subarachnoid hemorrhage (SAH) and subdural hematoma. Patients with hemorrhagic stroke should use intermittent pneumatic compression for the prevention of venous thromboembolism in addition to elastic stockings since anticoagulants should not be used while the patient is bleeding. Overall, treatment of a hemorrhagic stroke is largely supportive.

Pharmacologic Management of Intracerebral Hemorrhage

ICH in intracranial pressure (ICP) has the highest mortality rate of all stroke subtypes. The progression of neurological deficits in many patients with an ICH is frequently due to ongoing bleeding and enlargement of the hematoma during the first few hours. As a result, an increase in ICP can result. Measures should be taken to lower the ICP such as elevating the head of the bed by 30 degrees and using mannitol. Patients with a severe coagulation factor deficiency or severe thrombocytopenia should receive appropriate factor replacement therapy or platelets, respectively.

Mannitol

Increases the osmotic pressure to reduce intracranial pressure (ICP) associated with cerebral edema.

DRUG	DOSING	SAFETY/SIDE EFFECTS/MONITORING
Mannitol *(Osmitrol)*	5%, 10%, 15%, 20%, 25% Mannitol 20% – 0.25-1 g/kg/dose IV every 6-8H: give over 20-30 minutes	**CONTRAINDICATIONS** Severe renal disease (anuria), severe dehydration, progressive heart failure, pulmonary congestion **SIDE EFFECTS** Fluid and electrolyte loss, dehydration, hyperosmolar-induced hyperkalemia, acidosis, ↑ osmolar gap **MONITORING** Renal function, daily fluid in's and out's, serum electrolytes, serum and urine osmolality, CPP, ICP, and BP **NOTES** Vesicant Maintain serum osmolality < 300-320 mOsm/kg Due to rebound phenomenon, use is recommended for ≤ 5 days

Pharmacologic Management of Acute Subarachnoid Hemorrhage

Subarachnoid hemorrhage (SAH) is bleeding in the space between the brain and the surrounding membrane (subarachnoid space). The bleeding usually results from the rupture of a cerebral aneurysm or arteriovenous malformation (AVM) or from traumatic brain injury. Surgical clipping, endovascular coiling or complete obliteration, when feasible, may be performed in patients with an aneurysm or AVM. SAH is associated with a high incidence of delayed cerebral ischemia 2 weeks following the stroke. Vasospasm is thought to be the cause of the delayed ischemia and can occur 4-21 days after the bleed. Oral nimodipine is used to prevent the vasospasm associated with delayed ischemia. The use of prophylactic anticonvulsants may be considered in the acute post hemorrhagic period to prevent seizures. The routine use of long-term anticonvulsants is not recommended, but may be considered for patients with known risk factors for delayed seizure disorder (e.g., prior seizure, intracerebral hematoma).

Nimodipine

Calcium channel blocker: lipophilic, favorable effect on cerebral arteries.

DRUG	DOSING	SAFETY/SIDE EFFECTS/MONITORING
NiMODipine *(Nymalize)*	60 mg PO Q4H for 21 days Start therapy within 96 hours of the onset of subarachnoid hemorrhage Administer on an empty stomach, at least 1 hour before or 2 hours after meals	**BLACK BOX WARNING** Nimodipine has inadvertently been administered IV when withdrawn from capsules into a syringe for subsequent nasogastric administration. Severe cardiovascular adverse events including death have occurred. **SIDE EFFECTS** Hypotension, headache, diarrhea **MONITORING** Cerebral perfusion pressure (CPP), ICP, BP, HR, neurological checks **NOTES** Label syringes "For oral use only". Have pharmacy draw up to reduce medication errors.

Nimodipine Drug Interactions

- Nimodipine is a major 3A4 substrate; strong 3A4 inhibitors can increase the levels of nimodipine and strong 3A4 inducers can decrease the levels of nimodipine.

- Avoid concurrent use of grapefruit juice.

Pharmacologic Management of Acute Ischemic Stroke

The goal of therapy is to maintain cerebral perfusion pressure (CPP) to the ischemic area, maintain normal ICP, control blood pressure and possibly remove the clot (e.g., *Merci Retrieval System* device, others) or dissolve the clot with rt-PA [alteplase *(Activase)*] if within the safe time frame.

Alteplase

Recombinant tissue plasminogen activator (rt-PA) causes fibrinolysis by binding to fibrin in a thrombus (clot) and converts entrapped plasminogen to plasmin.

DRUG	DOSING	SAFETY/SIDE EFFECTS/MONITORING
Alteplase (Activase, rt-PA) Must confirm clot on brain imaging (head CT scan) before use	Infuse 0.9 mg/kg (maximum dose 90 mg) IV over 60 minutes with 10% of the dose given as a bolus over 1 minute Dosing is different for MI and pulmonary embolism indications	**CONTRAINDICATIONS** Active bleed, PLT count < 100,000/mm³, ↑ INR (> 1.7), ↑ aPTT due to recent heparin use (within previous 48 hours), previous ICH, severe uncontrolled hypertension (> 185/110 mmHg), recent intracranial or intraspinal surgery, stroke or serious head injury (within past 3 months), intracranial neoplasm, and many others. **SIDE EFFECTS** Major bleeding (e.g., ICH), hypotension, angioedema **MONITORING** Neurological assessments every 15 minutes during infusion, then every 30 minutes for next 6 hours, then hourly until 24 hours after treatment. Check BP every 15 minutes for the first 2 hours, then every 30 minutes for 6 hours, then hourly until 24 hours after treatment. Obtain follow-up brain imaging (head CT) at 24 hrs before starting anticoagulants and antiplatelets **NOTES** Treatment must be initiated within 3 hours of symptom onset (guidelines state benefit in select patients up to 4.5 hours but this is not FDA approved). If severe headache, acute hypertension, nausea, or vomiting occurs, discontinue the infusion and obtain emergency CT scan. If patients are receiving fibrinolytic therapy, the drug should be given ≤ 60 minutes of the patient's arrival in the ED (door to needle time).

Alteplase Drug Interactions

- Most drug interactions are due to additive effects with other agents that can ↑ bleeding risk (e.g., anticoagulants, antiplatelet drugs, ginkgo and other natural products, dextran, NSAIDs, SSRIs, SNRIs and others). See Drug Interactions chapter for more information on drugs that can increase bleeding risk.

Additional Therapies in the Management of Acute Ischemic Stroke

Aspirin Therapy – for prevention of early recurrent stroke

- 325 mg PO initially

- Oral administration within 24-48 hours after stroke onset is recommended in most patients

- Not recommended within 24 hours of fibrinolytic therapy

Hypertension Management – qualify patients for rt-PA or ↓ BP

- If BP is not ≤ 185/110 mmHg, do not give rt-PA

- In patients with malignant hypertension (> 220/120) and not receiving rt-PA, ↓ BP by 15% during the first 24 hours after stroke onset

Hyperglycemia Management

- Maintain BG levels in the range of 140-180 mg/dL and closely monitor to prevent hypoglycemia

DVT Prevention

- Use of SC anticoagulants for DVT prophylaxis in immobilized patients is recommended

- Do not use anticoagulant therapy within 24 hours of receiving rt-PA therapy

Ischemic Stroke Prevention

Modifiable risk factors should be corrected.

- Hypertension – the use of ACE inhibitors and diuretics have shown a reduction in the risk of stroke in addition to lifestyle modifications. This recommendation also holds for patients without a history of hypertension as long as they can tolerate the BP reduction.

- Dyslipidemia – a target reduction of at least 50% in LDL or a target LDL level of 70 mg/dL for patients without known CHD. For patients with CHD or elevated cholesterol, treat per the NCEP ATP III guidelines.

- Use of existing guidelines for glycemic control and BP targets in patients with diabetes is recommended for patients who have had a stroke or TIA.

- Lifestyle changes including smoking cessation, increased physical exercise (at least 30 minutes most days of the week), weight reduction if necessary (maintain BMI 18.5-24.9 kg/m^2 and a waist circumference < 35 inches for women and < 40 inches for men) and limit alcohol intake (≤ 2 drinks/day for males, ≤ 1 drink/day for females).

- For patients who are screened and classified as having the metabolic syndrome, management should include counseling for lifestyle modification (diet, exercise, and weight loss) for vascular risk reduction

- Preventive care for patients with the metabolic syndrome should include appropriate treatment for individual components of the syndrome that are also stroke risk factors, particularly dyslipidemia and hypertension.

Primary Prevention

Primary prevention is only recommended for patients with atrial fibrillation. See Anticoagulation chapter for more detail.

Secondary Prevention

Patients with previous cardioembolic stroke should be placed on anticoagulant therapy for secondary stroke prevention. For patients with noncardioembolic ischemic stroke or TIA, the use of antiplatelet agents rather than oral anticoagulation is recommended to reduce the risk of recurrent stroke and other cardiovascular events (see table below). Aspirin, aspirin plus extended-release dipyridamole, or clopidogrel are all acceptable options for initial therapy. The addition of aspirin to clopidogrel increases the risk of hemorrhage and is not recommended for routine secondary prevention after ischemic stroke or TIA. For patients allergic to aspirin, clopidogrel is reasonable.

For patients who have an ischemic stroke while taking aspirin, there is no evidence that increasing the dose of aspirin provides additional benefit. Although alternative antiplatelet agents are often considered, no single agent or combination has been studied in patients who have had an event while receiving aspirin.

Antiplatelet Therapy

Aspirin binds irreversibly to cyclooxygenase-1 and 2 enzymes, resulting in decreased prostaglandin precursors and synthesis, and irreversibly inhibits thromboxane A2, a platelet-aggregating substance. Aspirin has anti-platelet, antipyretic, analgesic, and anti-inflammatory properties. Clopidogrel inhibits $P2Y_{12}$ ADP-mediated platelet activation and aggregation. Dipyridamole inhibits the uptake of adenosine into platelets and increases cAMP levels, which indirectly inhibits platelet aggregation.

DRUG	DOSING	SAFETY/SIDE EFFECTS/MONITORING
Aspirin *(Ascriptin, Bayer Aspirin, Bufferin, Bufferin Extra Strength, Ecotrin, St. Joseph Adult Aspirin, others)*	50-325 mg daily	**CONTRAINDICATIONS** NSAID or salicylate allergy; patients with the syndrome of asthma, rhinitis, and nasal polyps; children < 16 years old with viral infection (due to Reye's syndrome risk) **SIDE EFFECTS** Dyspepsia, heartburn, GI upset, GI bleed/ulceration, bleeding, renal impairment, ↑ BP, hypersensitivity, tinnitus (in toxicity) **MONITORING** Bleeding, bruising See Pain chapter for more information.
Clopidogrel *(Plavix)*	75 mg daily	**BLACK BOX WARNING** Effectiveness depends on the activation to an active metabolite mainly by CYP 2C19. Poor metabolizers exhibit higher cardiovascular events than patients with normal 2C19 function. Tests to check CYP 2C19 genotype can be used as an aid in determining a therapeutic strategy. Consider alternative treatment strategies in patients identified as 2C19 poor metabolizers. The CYP2C19*1 allele corresponds to fully functional metabolism while the CYP2C19*2 and *3 alleles are nonfunctional. **WARNINGS** Allergic cross-reactivity among thienopyridines has been reported **CONTRAINDICATIONS** Active pathological bleed (e.g., PUD, ICH) **SIDE EFFECTS** Bleeding, bruising, rash, TTP (rare) Thrombotic thrombocytopenic purpura (TTP): have patients report fever, weakness, extreme skin paleness, purple skin patches, yellowing of the skin or eyes, or neurological changes. **MONITORING** Signs of bleeding; Hgb/Hct as necessary

Antiplatelet Therapy Continued

DRUG	DOSING	SAFETY/SIDE EFFECTS/MONITORING
Dipyridamole ER/Aspirin (*Aggrenox*)	200 mg/25 mg BID	**CONTRAINDICATIONS** Allergy to NSAIDs; patients with the syndrome of asthma, rhinitis, and nasal polyps; children < 16 years of age with viral infections; pregnancy (third trimester; aspirin) **SIDE EFFECTS** Headache (> 10%), dyspepsia, abdominal pain, nausea, diarrhea, and bleeding **MONITORING** Signs of bleeding; Hgb/Hct as necessary **NOTES** Amount of aspirin provided is not adequate for cardiac indications (e.g., MI prophylaxis)

Drug Interactions

- Most drug interactions are due to additive effects with other agents that can ↑ bleeding risk (e.g., anticoagulants, other antiplatelet drugs, ginkgo and other natural products, dextran, NSAIDs, SSRIs, SNRIs, thrombolytics and others). See Drug Interactions chapter for more information on drugs that can increase bleeding risk.

- Clopidogrel is a prodrug metabolized mainly by CYP450 2C19. Avoid concomitant use with strong or moderate 2C19 inhibitors (cimetidine, fluconazole, ketoconazole, voriconazole, fluoxetine, fluvoxamine and others). Avoid concomitant use with omeprazole and esomeprazole as these agents may reduce the effectiveness of clopidogrel due to 2C19 inhibition.

GASTROESOPHAGEAL REFLUX DISEASE (GERD)

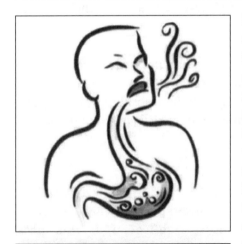

GUIDELINE

Guidelines for the Diagnosis and Management of Gastroesophageal Reflux Disease. Am J Gastroenterol 2013; 108:308-328.

BACKGROUND

Gastroesophageal reflux disease (GERD) is a condition in which the stomach contents leak backward into the esophagus. Normally, gastric contents are prevented from backflow into the esophagus by a ring of muscle fibers called the lower esophageal sphincter (LES). In GERD, the LES pressure or muscle tone is reduced (or transiently relaxes) and allows for backflow of the stomach contents. Typical symptoms of GERD include heartburn, hypersalivation, regurgitation, and/or an acid taste in the mouth. Less commonly, symptoms can include recurrent cough, sore throat, hoarseness, and chest pain, which may be difficult to distinguish from cardiac pain. GERD can lead to esophageal erosion, strictures, bleeding, Barrett's esophagus, which is a condition characterized by abnormal cell growth in the inferior portion of the esophagus, and esophageal cancer.

The stomach epithelial lining contains parietal cells that secrete hydrochloric acid and intrinsic factor, G cells that secrete gastrin, mucus-secreting cells, and chief cells that secrete pepsinogen. The parietal cells have receptors for histamine, acetylcholine, and gastrin, all of which stimulate HCl acid secretion. These substances activate the H^+/K^+ ATPase pump located in the parietal cell and represents the final common pathway for gastric acid secretion.

TREATMENT PRINCIPLES

Patient-reported symptoms are used in the initial diagnosis; invasive testing is not required in most cases. If there is a response to acid-suppressive therapy (generally proton-pump inhibitors or PPIs), a diagnosis can be established. Patients with alarm symptoms (e.g., chest pain, dysphagia) should be sent for further evaluation. Occasional and less bothersome symptoms may respond to antacids or histamine H_2 receptor antagonists (H_2RAs). Caution should be used with chronic acid suppression from H_2RAs and PPIs because of recent concerns of increased risk of GI infections (most commonly caused by *C. difficile*) and increased risk of nosocomial pneumonia in hospitalized patients. In addition, PPIs increase the risk of osteoporosis and fractures with long-term use. Caution with use of H_2RAs in the elderly, per the Beers Criteria: avoid cimetidine entirely (due to drug interactions, adverse reactions). Be aware of the risk of worsening dementia, delirium/confusion especially if overdosed. H_2RAs must be dose-adjusted for renal impairment.

Clinicians may follow "step-up" therapy – where over-the-counter products are used first, followed by prescription products only for patients with recurring symptoms. Another approach is "step-down" therapy – starting with more intensive therapy (PPIs), which is titrated downward and then discontinued as the symptoms decrease. In more serious conditions (where esophageal erosion is present), PPIs should be used first-line because they are the most effective agents at acid-suppression.

Misoprostol and sucralfate are difficult to use and hence, used infrequently. With these agents, there are a few important safety considerations to review. The American College of Gastroenterology (ACG) recommends against the use of metoclopramide as therapy for esophageal symptoms (risk outweighs benefit); unfortunately, it is still used commonly in the elderly, where it can pose significant risk of adverse events.

Recommended Non-Pharmacologic (Lifestyle) Treatment

- Avoid foods and substances that may reduce lower esophageal sphincter (LES) pressure or aggravate the condition. These include spicy foods, nicotine, coffee/caffeine/tea, alcohol, fatty foods, citrus, chocolate, and peppermint/spearmint. Carefully consider use of medications that may be irritating to the esophagus, such as as bisphosphonates.

- Decrease portion size and eat more frequently.

- Weight loss – best evidence in improvement, per AGA guidelines.

- Do not eat before sleeping (last meal should be 2-3 hours before bedtime).

- Elevate the head of the bed 6-8″ (not with pillows, but with a wedge, or by elevating the head-side of the bed under the mattress).

- Avoid tight-fitting clothing.

PHARMACOLOGIC THERAPY

Antacids

Antacids work by neutralizing gastric acid (producing salt and water) thus increasing gastric pH. This provides relief within minutes since antacids do not require systemic absorption. Antacids are good for mild or infrequent symptoms or if the patient is in need of fast relief.

DRUG	DOSING	SAFETY/SIDE EFFECTS/MONITORING
Calcium *(Tums, others)* Aluminum *(AlternaGel)* **Magnesium** *[Phillips Milk of Magnesia* **(MOM)**, *others]* **Magnesium + (Aluminum or Calcium)** **combo** *(Maalox, Mylanta, Rolaids, others)* **Mag-Al-Simethicone (anti-gas)** *(Maalox Max, Mylanta Max* **Strength**, *others)* Sodium bicarbonate + aspirin + citric acid *(Alka-Seltzer)* Sodium bicarbonate *(Neut)* – also used for metabolic acidosis with renal disease *Gaviscon* contains antacids in combination with alginic acid which theoretically forms a barrier to combat reflux (efficacy?) Calcium carbonate, magnesium hydroxide, famotidine *(Pepcid Complete)*	Many formulations including suspensions, chewable tablets, capsules 10-30 mL or 2-4 tablets 4-6x/day	**WARNINGS** Aluminum and magnesium can accumulate with severe renal dysfunction. Use is not recommended in patients with CrCl < 30 mL/min. **SIDE EFFECTS** Calcium may cause constipation or loose stools Aluminum may cause constipation Magnesium may cause loose stools (may use together to counter-balance, but still can get loose stools) **NOTES** Onset of relief within minutes; lasts 1-2 hours Antacids are the drugs of choice in pregnancy *Alka Seltzer* contains > 1 g Na$^+$ per serving

Antacid Drug Interactions

- Reduced absorption due to chelation is seen when administered with quinolone and tetracycline antibiotics. Doxycycline and minocycline are less likely to be of clinical concern. Separate extensively from these agents (2 hours before or 6 hours after ciprofloxacin; 2 hours before or 2 hours after levofloxacin; 4 hours before or 8 hours after moxifloxacin; 1-2 hours before or 4 hours after tetracycline).

- Refrain from administering less than 2 hours before or 4 hours after itraconazole, ketoconazole and iron, due to reduced absorption from increased pH.

Antacid Counseling

- Use all lifestyle counseling points (from above).

- This medicine provides immediate relief, but lasts about 1-2 hours. If you need longer relief, a medicine such as famotidine (the generic for *Pepcid)* will last longer (or PPI, but not used prn). If the symptoms remain bothersome, discuss with your doctor.

- If you are using this product more than 2 times per week, you may have a condition that requires stronger therapy. Discuss the symptoms with your doctor.

- Do not use aluminum or magnesium products if you have advanced kidney disease.

- If you experience constipation, discontinue use of aluminum-containing products.

- If you experience loose stools, you may wish to discontinue use of magnesium-containing products.

- Do not use antacids that contain sodium if you are on a sodium restricted diet, have heart disease, high blood pressure, heart failure or kidney disease.

- Do not use sugar-containing antacids if you have diabetes.

- See a doctor immediately if you have bloody stools or "coffee-ground" vomiting.

Histamine H$_2$ Receptor Antagonists (H$_2$RAs)

H$_2$RAs reversibly inhibit the H$_2$ receptors on the gastric parietal cells, thus reducing gastric acid secretion.

DRUG	DOSING	SAFETY/SIDE EFFECTS/MONITORING
	For all: Administered PRN for mild heartburn and twice daily for up to 12 weeks for documented GERD	**WARNINGS** Use with caution in the elderly, per the Beers Criteria: Risk of worsening dementia and confusion. Avoid cimetidine entirely (due to drug interactions, adverse reactions).
Famotidine **(Pepcid AC, Pepcid AC Max Strength)** **Pepcid Complete** – **calcium carbonate, magnesium hydroxide, famotidine** Famotidine 26.6 mg + ibuprofen 800 mg (Duexis)	Famotidine OTC Pepcid AC 10, 20 mg – Max Strength Famotidine Rx 20, 40 mg Powder for oral susp 40 mg/5 mL Injection 10 mg/mL	**SIDE EFFECTS** Agitation/vomiting in children < 1 year May increase risk of GI infections and may increase risk of pneumonia in hospitalized patients. Cimetidine: CNS effects (more common in elderly), gynecomastia, impotence **NOTES** Onset of relief: 30-45 minutes, effects last 4-10 hours. Longer duration of action than antacids, but shorter than PPIs.
Ranitidine (Zantac)	Ranitidine OTC 75, 150 mg Ranitidine Rx 300 mg tablet 150 mg EFFERdose tablets (contains Na$^+$ and phenylalanine) Syrup 15 mg/mL Injection 25 mg/mL	Generally no benefit to combining with a PPI. May occasionally be appropriate if used at bedtime for nocturnal reflux symptoms. H$_2$RAs must be dose-adjusted in patients with renal impairment. Use 50% of the dose when CrCl < 50 mL/min (famotidine, ranitidine, nizatidine); CrCl < 30 mL/min (cimetidine)
Nizatidine (Axid)	Nizatidine OTC 75 mg Nizatidine Rx 150, 300 mg Susp 15 mg/mL	
Cimetidine (Tagamet, Tagamet HB 200)	Cimetidine OTC 200 mg Cimetidine Rx 300, 400, 800 mg Susp 300 mg/5 mL Injection 150 mg/mL	

H₂RA Drug Interactions (All)

- CNS agents: Additive side effects, if elderly or reduced renal function; use lower doses. <u>Avoid cimetidine entirely in elderly</u>. Avoid use of any with patients on anticholinergics, if possible.

- Check package insert, other drugs may require dosing adjustments.

- Caution with concurrent use of itraconazole, ketoconazole, calcium carbonate and iron due to reduced absorption from increased pH.

H₂RA Drug Interactions (Cimetidine)

- Cimetidine is a CYP3A4 inhibitor and weak to moderate inhibitor of other isoenzymes. Avoid use with clopidogrel, dofetilide and warfarin. Use caution with many other drugs including amiodarone, phenytoin, carbamazepine, quinidine, theophylline, citalopram, and others.

H₂RA Counseling

- Use all lifestyle counseling points.

- This medicine provides fast relief (onset 30-45 minutes, lasts 4-10 hours). If you need longer relief, a medicine taken daily (such as omeprazole) may be more helpful. If the symptoms remain bothersome, discuss with your doctor.

- If you are using this product more than 2 times per week, you may have a condition that requires stronger therapy. Discuss the symptoms with your doctor.

- If elderly: caution for confusion, especially with higher doses – highest risk if renal impairment. This can cause memory problems, dizziness, risk of falls.

PROTON PUMP INHIBITORS (PPIs)

PPIs block gastric acid secretion by irreversibly binding to the gastric H⁺/K⁺-adenosine triphosphatase (ATPase) pump in parietal cells. They block the final step in acid production.

DRUG	DOSING	SAFETY/SIDE EFFECTS/MONITORING
	PPIs are taken daily, 30 minutes before breakfast. If this fails, BID (2ⁿᵈ dose before dinner) can be tried. For treating duodenal or gastric ulcers caused by *H. pylori*, dosing is usually BID.	**WARNINGS** May increase risk of *C. difficile*-associated diarrhea May increase osteoporosis-related fractures, especially when used long-term May increase risk of pneumonia in hospitalized patients
Omeprazole *(PriLOSEC OTC, PriLOSEC)*	20 mg (OTC), 10, 20, 40 mg (Rx) 2.5, 10 mg susp	
Omeprazole/Sodium Bicarbonate *(Zegerid, Zegerid OTC)*	20, 40 mg cap with 1.1 gram of Na⁺ bicarb 20, 40 mg powder for susp: both 1,680 mg Na⁺ bicarb (460 mg Na⁺)	**SIDE EFFECTS** Generally mild and infrequent (headache, diarrhea, nausea) Hypomagnesemia with long-term use; potential for vitamin B12 deficiency with long-term use
Pantoprazole *(Protonix)*	20, 40 mg tabs Granules for susp 40 mg/pk Injection *(Protonix* IV), 40 mg	**NOTES** PPIs are the most effective agents for severe disease/symptoms
Lansoprazole *(Prevacid, Prevacid SoluTab. Prevacid 24H-OTC)*	15 mg (OTC), 15, 30 mg (Rx) 15, 30 mg SoluTab (contains phenylalanine)	All available PPIs have similar efficacy, although an individual patient may respond better to one agent than another
Dexlansoprazole *(Dexilant)*	30, 60 mg	PPIs are not indicated for PRN use; they must be administered only as maintenance therapy for a duration to be determined by the physician or not to exceed 14 days if self-treating.
Esomeprazole *(NexIUM)*	20, 40 mg caps Granules for susp 10, 20, 40 mg/pk Injection 20, 40 mg/mL	Dexlansoprazole, lansoprazole, esomeprazole and omeprazole capsules can be opened (not crushed) and mixed in apple sauce or acidic juice if patient cannot swallow pill or for NG tube delivery
Esomeprazole + naproxen *(Vimovo)*	20 mg + 375 or 500 mg naproxen	Do not crush, cut, or chew tablets or capsules
RABEprazole *(AcipHex)*	20 mg	Pantoprazole and esomeprazole are the only PPIs available IV

PPI Drug Interactions

- Use caution when administering drugs that require an acidic pH for absorption including itraconazole, ketoconazole, calcium carbonate, iron, atazanavir, rilpivirine and others.

- PPIs inhibit CYP2C19: Do not use with delavirdine, erlotinib, nelfinavir, and posaconazole. PPIs may ↑ levels of methotrexate, phenytoin, raltegravir, saquinavir, tacrolimus, voriconazole and warfarin.

- PPIs may reduce the effectiveness of clopidogrel. If using these agents together, avoid omeprazole and esomeprazole. Dexlansoprazole, pantoprazole, and rabeprazole have specific wording in the product labeling indicating that they are safe to use with clopidogrel, although there are no data to support choosing one agent over another (except to avoid omeprazole and esomeprazole).

PPI Counseling

- Use all lifestyle counseling points.

- Take 30 minutes before breakfast. If twice daily, take before breakfast and dinner.

- If taking long-term, ensure that calcium and vitamin D intake is optimal. Recommend calcium citrate formulations (improved absorption in basic pH).

- If you are planning to stop this medicine, you should taper the dose to avoid acid rebound. Please discuss with your pharmacist (recommend decreased dose, then every other day over at least a couple of weeks.)

- Do not use for occasional mild stomach upset. This can be effectively treated with an antacid (such as calcium carbonate) or a stronger medication such as famotidine (the generic for *Pepcid*).

- Effervescent and orally dissolving formulations contain phenylalanine. Do not use in patients with phenylketonuria (PKU).

- If you are using for more than 14 days and heartburn persists, consult your doctor.

- Do not crush or chew any capsules.

- *Prevacid SoluTab*: Do not swallow whole. Place on tongue and allow to dissolve (with or without water), then swallow.

CYTOPROTECTIVE AGENTS

Misoprostol is a prostaglandin E_1 analog that replaces the gastro-protective prostaglandins removed by NSAIDs.

Sucralfate is a sucrose-sulfate-aluminum complex that interacts with albumin and fibrinogen to form a physical barrier over an open ulcer. This protects the ulcer from further insult by hydrochloric acid, pepsin, and bile and allows it to heal.

Cytoprotective Agents

DRUG	DOSING	SAFETY/SIDE EFFECTS/MONITORING
Misoprostol *(Cytotec)*	Start at 100 mcg right after dinner, increase (if tolerated) to 100 mcg QID or 200 mcg QID. Take right after meals and at bedtime.	**BLACK BOX WARNINGS** Abortifacient – warn patients not to give this drug to others Not to be used to reduce NSAID-induced ulcers in a woman of childbearing potential unless she is capable of complying with effective contraceptive measures **SIDE EFFECTS** Diarrhea, abdominal pain **NOTES** Pregnancy Category X
Sucralfate *(Carafate)*	1 g tablets QID before meals and at bedtime (usual), may be given 1 g Q4H (for treatment of active ulcer) Suspension 1 g/10 mL	**WARNINGS** Caution in renal impairment – sucralfate is an aluminum complex and can accumulate **SIDE EFFECTS** Constipation **NOTES** Used as an adjunct for GERD or peptic ulcer disease; not supported by the ACG GERD guidelines

Misoprostol Counseling

- Do not use in women of childbearing age unless strict compliance with contraceptive measures.

- Can start with 100 mcg right after dinner (with food in stomach), attempt to increase as-directed. Use of psyllium *(Metamucil)* may help decrease diarrhea.

Sucralfate Drug Interactions

- Avoid taking antacids 30 minutes before or 30 minutes after taking sucralfate.

- Avoid other drugs 2 hours before or 4 hours after administering sucralfate (difficult to use).

Sucralfate Counseling

- Major side effect is constipation; drink adequate fluids and use laxatives if directed.

- Discuss other drugs, including OTC products you are using, with the pharmacist. This drug can decrease the absorption of other medicines.

METOCLOPRAMIDE

Metoclopramide is a dopamine antagonist. At higher doses, it blocks serotonin-receptors in the chemoreceptor zone of the CNS. It also enhances the response to acetylcholine in the upper GI tract causing enhanced motility and accelerated gastric emptying (peristaltic speed) and increases lower esophageal sphincter (LES) tone.

DRUG	DOSING	SAFETY/SIDE EFFECTS/MONITORING
Metoclopramide (*Reglan, Metozolv ODT*)	5 mg, 10 mg tabs, ODT 5 mg/mL injection, 5 mg/5 mL solution 2.5-10 mg QID 30 min before meals and at bedtime.	**BLACK BOX WARNING** May cause tardive dyskinesia – increased risk in elderly and with high doses and long-term therapy **CONTRAINDICATIONS** GI obstruction, perforation, hemorrhage; history of seizures; pheochromocytoma; combination with other agents likely to increase EPS **SIDE EFFECTS** Primarily CNS – Extrapyramidal symptoms (EPS), including parkinson-like symptoms, acute dystonic reactions, drowsiness, confusion **NOTES** Must be dose-adjusted in patients with CrCl < 40 mL/min (use 50% of normal dose) CNS side effects are dose-related and more common in the elderly – use with caution and dose-adjust in renal impairment Avoid use in patients with Parkinson disease Metoclopramide has a short duration of action (must be present in gut when food is present)

Metoclopramide Drug Interactions

- Do not use in patients receiving medications for Parkinson disease (counter-effect).

- Caution for additive CNS effects, including dizziness, drowsiness and fatigue.

Metoclopramide Counseling

- Use caution when driving, operating machinery, or performing other hazardous activities. This drug may cause dizziness or drowsiness.

- Dizziness may be more likely to occur when you rise quickly from a sitting or lying position. Rise slowly to prevent dizziness and a possible fall.

- Avoid consuming alcohol during treatment with this drug. Alcohol may increase drowsiness and dizziness.

- Contact your doctor right away if you experience any unusual body movements, such as shakiness, stiffness, or uncontrollable movements of the mouth, tongue, cheeks, jaw, arms, or legs.

PRACTICE CASE

PATIENT PROFILE

Patient Name	Benjamin Specter				
Address	10 Pine Place				
Age	72	**Sex** Male	**Race** White	**Height** 5'6"	**Weight** 160lbs
Allergies	Aspirin (hives)				

DIAGNOSES

GERD	Seasonal allergies, occasional bronchodilator use
Prostate enlargement	Dyslipidemia, CHD, MI x 2 (last ~8 years ago)
Parkinson disease	

MEDICATIONS

Date	No.	Prescriber	Drug & Strength	Quantity	Sig	Refills
6/23/13	35421	Cooper	Clopidogrel 75 mg	#30	1 PO daily	6
6/23/13	35422	Cooper	Protonix 40 mg	#30	1 PO daily	6
6/23/13	35423	Cooper	Pravastatin 20 mg	#30	1 PO BID	6
6/23/13	35424	Cooper	Sinemet 25/250	#90	1 PO tid	6
			Albuterol inhaler	#1	Occasional use	4
			Loratadine 10 mg		1 tablet, as needed	
11/1/13	42877	Kreinfeldt	Metoclopramide 10 mg	#120	1 PO QID	

LAB/DIAGNOSTIC TESTS

Test	Normal Value	Results		
		Date 5/12/13	Date	Date
Protein, T	6.2-8.3 g/dL			
Albumin	3.6-5.1 g/dL			
Alk Phos	33-115 units/L			
AST	10-35 units/L			
ALT	6-40 units/L			
CH, T	125-200 g/dL			
TG	<150 g/dL			
HDL	g/dL			
LDL	g/dL			
GLU	65-99 mg/dL			
Na	135-146 mEq/L			
K	3.5-5.3 mEq/L			
Cl	98-110 mEq/L			
CO2	21-33 mmHg			
BUN	7-25 mg/dL	28		
Creatinine	0.6-1.2 mg/dL	1.9		
Calcium	8.6-10.2 mg/dL			
WBC	4-11 cells/mm^3			
RBC	3.8-5.1 mL/mm^3			
Hemoglobin	Male: 13.8- 17.2 g/dL Female: 12.1-15.1 g/dL			
Hematocrit	Male: 40.7-50.3% Female: 36.1- 44.3%			
MCHC	32-36 g/dL			
MCV	80-100 μm			
Platelet count	140-400 x 10^3/mm^3			
TSH	0.4-4.0 mIU/L			
FT4	4.5- 11.2 mcg/dL			
Hgb A1c	4-6%			

ADDITIONAL INFORMATION

Date	Notes
11/11/13	PCP (Cooper) on vacation. Reports bothersome heartburn. Reflux after eating dinner and during sleep. Eats dinner 8:30 pm, falls asleep 9:30-10 pm. Enjoys after dinner black tea with honey & pipe. Per discussion, symtpoms appear controlled.

Questions

1. The patient is using *Protonix* once daily. Which of the following is an appropriate substitution?

    a. Omeprazole

    b. Esomeprazole

    c. Pantoprazole

    d. Rabeprazole

    e. Lansoprazole

2. The patient is still experiencing symptoms despite his current therapy. The physician decided to add-on metoclopramide to control the reflux symptoms. Choose the correct statement:

    a. Inappropriate therapy; the physician should increase *Protonix* to 60 mg daily.

    b. Inappropriate therapy; the physician should either increase *Protonix* to BID dosing, or add ranitidine 75 mg at bedtime.

    c. Inappropriate therapy; the physician should add on magnesium citrate prn.

    d. Inappropriate therapy; the physician should start misoprostol 200 mcg QID.

    e. Metoclopramide is appropriate therapy; no change is required.

3. Benjamin can make several lifestyle changes that may help with his evening symptoms. Which of the following are correct counseling points the pharmacist can provide to the patient?

    a. Consider cessation of evening smoke

    b. Eat dinner at an earlier time

    c. Change his evening drink to a non-caffeinated, non-alcoholic option

    d. Elevate the head of his bead 6-8 inches

    e. All of the above

4. The substituting physician prescribed metoclopramide. Which of the following side effects may be present?

    a. Worsening of his Parkinson disease symptoms

    b. Worsening of his prostate disease symptoms

    c. Dizziness, sleepiness

    d. A and B only

    e. A and C only

5. If the metoclopramide was to be used in a different patient with this degree of renal function, what would be the correct dose?

    a. 10 mg four times daily

    b. 10 mg twice daily

    c. 10 mg daily

    d. 2.5-5 mg four times daily

    e. 5 mg once daily

Questions 6-11 are NOT based on the above case.

6. An elderly female presents at the pharmacy. She does not have health insurance coverage. Which of the following PPIs is available over-the-counter?

    a. *Zegerid*

    b. *Prevacid*

    c. *Prilosec*

    d. A and C

    e. All of the above

7. A patient has entered the pharmacy and asked the pharmacy technician to help her locate the store-brand version of *Pepcid*. Which of the following medications should the technician select?

    a. Famotidine

    b. Cimetidine

    c. Ranitidine

    d. Omeprazole

    e. Lansoprazole

8. A physician has written a prescription for *Prevacid*. Which of the following represents an acceptable therapeutic substitution?

    a. Omeprazole

    b. Esomeprazole

    c. Rabeprazole

    d. Pantoprazole

    e. Lansoprazole

9. Which of the following proton pump inhibitors is available in an IV formulation? (Select **ALL** that apply.)

    a. *Dexilant*

    b. *Nexium*

    c. *Protonix*

    d. *AcipHex*

    e. *Prilosec*

10. An elderly female patient has hypertension and heartburn. Her family states she has trouble swallowing large pills. She failed H$_2$-blocker therapy and has been well-controlled on a PPI. She is currently using *Nexium* 40 mg daily. Which of the following would be a better option?

    a. *Zantac EFFERdose*
    b. *Alka Seltzer*
    c. *Zegerid*
    d. *Prevacid SoluTab*
    e. *Maalox*

11. 11. Proton pump inhibitors can increase the risk of: (Select **ALL** that apply.)

    a. Bone fracture
    b. *C. difficile* infection
    c. Stroke
    d. Heart attacks
    e. Pneumonia in hospitalized patients

Answers

1-c, 2-b, 3-e, 4-e, 5-d, 6-e, 7-a, 8-e, 9-b,c, 10-d, 11-a,b,e

PEPTIC ULCER DISEASE (PUD)

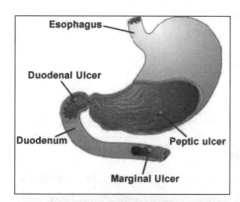

Esophagus

Duodenal Ulcer

Duodenum

Peptic ulcer

Marginal Ulcer

BACKGROUND

Peptic ulcer disease (PUD) occurs from mucosal erosion within the gastrointestinal tract. Unlike gastritis, the ulcers in PUD extend deeper into the mucosa. Most ulcers occur in the duodenum but a small percent also occur in the stomach. The three most common causes of PUD are *Helicobacter pylori (H. pylori)*-positive ulcers, nonsteroidal anti-inflammatory drug (NSAID)-induced ulcers and stress ulcers in the presence of critical illness and in mechanically-ventilated patients. *Helicobacter pylori (H. pylori)*, a spiral-shaped, pH sensitive, gram-negative bacterium that lives in the acidic environment of the stomach, is responsible for the majority of the peptic ulcers (~70-80%). Other, less common causes of PUD are hypersecretory states, such as Zollinger-Ellison syndrome (causes ↑ gastric acid), G-cell hyperplasia, mastocytosis, and basophilic leukemias.

Under normal conditions, a physiologic balance exists between gastric acid secretion and gastroduodenal mucosal defense. Mucosal defense and repair mechanisms include mucus and bicarbonate secretion, mucosal blood flow, prostaglandin synthesis, cellular regeneration, and epithelial cell renewal. These mechanisms protect the gastroduodenal mucosa from damage and irritation by noxious substances, such as NSAIDs (including aspirin), *H. pylori*, acid, pepsin, and other factors. Mucosal injury and, thus, peptic ulcer disease occur when the balance between the noxious mucosal irritants and the defensive mechanisms is disrupted.

SYMPTOMS

The primary symptom of PUD is gastric pain. This pain can be associated with a burning or gnawing sensation and may awaken a patient if it occurs at night. If the ulcer is duodenal (usually caused by *H. pylori)*, eating generally lessens the pain. With gastric ulcers (primarily from NSAIDs), eating generally worsens the pain. Other symptoms include heartburn, belching, bloating, nausea and anorexia.

H. PYLORI DIAGNOSTIC TESTS

H. pylori infection, if left untreated, can lead to cancer. If testing is positive for *H. pylori*, the infection should be treated. Common diagnostic tests for the presence of *H. pylori* include:

- Urea breath test (UBT): Breath test that identifies gas (CO_2) produced by the bacteria. False negatives can be secondary to the recent use of H_2RAs, PPIs, bismuth or antibiotics; discontinue H_2RAs and PPIs 1 to 2 weeks and bismuth and antibiotics 4 weeks prior to the test.

- Fecal antigen test: Detects *H. pylori* in the in stool. False negatives can be secondary to the recent use of H_2RAs, PPIs, bismuth, or antibiotics (to a lesser extent than the UBT); discontinue these drugs at least 2-4 weeks prior to test.

H. PYLORI TREATMENT

The American College of Gastroenterology guidelines recommend triple therapy with an anti-secretory agent (preferably a PPI) + 2 antibiotics (clarithromycin and amoxicillin) for 14 days. Metronidazole can be used in place of amoxicillin if the patient has an allergy. Several of the regimens (with various PPIs) are FDA-approved for a 10 day regimen. Due to recent failures with triple therapy, many patients are currently receiving quadruple therapy. This should be chosen if a patient has used a macrolide or metronidazole in the past, or if the local failure rates are known to be high. Quadruple therapy consists of a PPI, bismuth, metronidazole, and tetracycline for 10-14 days (can use *Helidac* or *Pylera*). Another option for resistant cases is "sequential therapy": a PPI and amoxicillin for 5 days, followed by a PPI, clarithromycin and tinidazole for 5 days. If the PPI is continued beyond 14 days, this is to help ulcer healing for a short period of time; it should not be continued indefinitely.

Do not make drug substitutions in *H. pylori* eradication regimens. H_2RAs should not be substituted for a PPI, unless the patient cannot tolerate a PPI. Likewise, other antibiotics in the same class should not be substituted in *H. pylori* eradication regimens (for example, do not use ampicillin instead of amoxicillin).

First-Line *H. pylori* Treatment Regimens

DRUG REGIMEN	NOTES

Triple Drug Therapy – Take for 14 days

PPI BID (or esomeprazole 40 mg daily) +	Penicillin or macrolide allergy: replace amoxicillin or clarithromycin with metronidazole 500 mg BID in this regimen
Amoxicillin 1,000 mg BID +	OR can use alternative therapy below
Clarithromycin 500 mg BID	See GERD chapter for PPI side effects and Infectious Disease chapter for more on the antibiotics

Quadruple Therapy – Take for 10-14 days

(Use if failed above therapy, cannot tolerate above agents, have taken a macrolide or metronidazole in the past, or if high local resistance rates to clarithomycin)

PPI BID (or esomeprazole daily) +	**Alcohol use** Do not use metronidazole
Bismuth subsalicylate 525 mg QID +	
Metronidazole 250 mg QID +	**Pregnancy** Do not use tetracycline
Tetracycline 500 mg QID	
	Salicylate allergy/children Do not use bismuth subsalicylate (or tetracycline in children 8 years or less)
	If patient cannot tolerate a PPI, substitute H$_2$RA (e.g., ranitidine 150 mg BID, famotidine 40 mg daily, nizatidine 300 mg/d)

Combination Products

Prevpac – BID x 14 days
Prevpac contains lansoprazole/amoxicillin/clarithromycin all on one blister card. One blister card is taken per day.
Pylera –QID x 10 days
Pylera contains bismuth subcitrate potassium/metronidazole/tetracycline in one capsule. Take 3 capsules QID. A PPI is obtained separately and given BID (or daily, if esomeprazole) for 10 days.
Helidac – QID x 14 days
Helidac contains bismuth subsalicylate/metronidazole/tetracycline all on one blister card. One blister card is taken per day. An H$_2$RA is obtained separately and given for 28 days.

Drug Interactions

- PPIs: Caution with concurrent use of drugs that require an acidic pH for absorption including itraconazole, ketoconazole, calcium carbonate, atazanavir, rilpivirine; PPIs inhibit 2C19: Do not use with delavirdine, erlotinib, nelfinavir, and posaconazole. PPIs may ↑ levels of methotrexate, phenytoin, raltegravir, saquinavir, tacrolimus, voriconazole and warfarin. PPIs may reduce the effectiveness of clopidogrel. If using these agents together, avoid omeprazole and esomeprazole. Dexlansoprazole, pantoprazole, and rabeprazole have specific wording in the product labeling indicating that they are safe to use with clopidogrel, although there are no data to support choosing one agent over another (except avoiding omeprazole and esomeprazole).

- Clarithromycin is a strong 3A4 inhibitor. See Drug Interactions chapter for more information.

- Tetracycline can chelate with aluminum, magnesium, calcium, iron and zinc leading to ↓ drug absorption. The administration time must be separated (1-2 hours before and 4 hours after). Monitor warfarin (may ↑ INR).

- Metronidazole: Avoid use of alcohol. Monitor warfarin (may ↑ INR).

- Bismuth subsalicylate can ↑ risk of salicylate toxicity with other salicylates, including aspirin.

H. Pylori Counseling

- It is important to take all medication as directed and finish the complete course of therapy. Drink a full glass of water with each dose. These medications may upset your stomach and should be taken with meals.

- Bismuth subsalicylate: The pink tablets are chewed while the other medications are swallowed. If taken with aspirin and ringing in the ears occurs, contact your doctor. If you are throwing up blood, have throw up that looks like coffee grounds or have bloody stools you need to be seen by your doctor right away. Bismuth subsalicylate may cause temporary and harmless darkening of the tongue and/or black stool.

- Tetracycline: Do not use if pregnant or in children ≤ 8 years old. Oral contraceptives may be less effective. Use a mechanical form of contraception, such as condoms, during antibiotic therapy. This medicine may make your skin more sensitive to the sun and you may burn more easily. Use sun protection such as clothing and UVA and UVB sunscreen (SPF 30 or higher). Refer to the Common Skin Conditions chapter for more details.

- Metronidazole: Alcoholic beverages should be avoided during therapy with metronidazole and for at least one day afterward.

- Clarithromycin may cause diarrhea, nausea and abnormal taste (each adverse effect occurs ~3%).

- If taking *Helidac* or *Pylera*, an additional PPI *(Pylera)* or H$_2$RA *(Helidac)* will be needed for entire course of therapy, as directed. The H$_2$RA is recommended for an additional 14 days after the end of *Helidac* therapy, to help the ulcer heal. Do not continue indefinitely.

- If diarrhea or loose stools develop during use, contact your doctor immediately.

NON-STEROIDAL ANTI-INFLAMMATORY DRUG (NSAID)-INDUCED ULCERS (PRIMARILY GASTRIC)

Background

The use of high dose non-steroidal anti-inflammatory drugs (NSAIDs) or chronic NSAID use greatly increases the risk for gastric (GI) ulcers. NSAIDs (including aspirin) can cause gastric mucosal damage by 2 mechanisms; direct irritation of the gastric epithelium and systemic inhibition of prostaglandin synthesis (by inhibiting COX-1).

Risk Factors for NSAID-induced ulcers:

- Age > 65 years

- Previous ulcer

- High-dose or chronic NSAID use

- Concomitant use of steroids, anticoagulants, SSRIs or SNRIs

Prevention and Treatment

Concomitant PPI therapy decreases ulcer risk. High-risk patients using a non-selective NSAID chronically can reduce bleeding risk by using concurrent PPI therapy. The clinician will need to consider long-term risks of acid-suppression therapy. Alternatively, a COX-2 selective agent (e.g., celecoxib) with or without a PPI can be used in high-risk patients if they do not have cardiovascular risk factors. Generic NSAID agents that approach the selectivity of celecoxib are meloxicam, nabumetone and etodolac. Some evidence suggests that naproxen may be preferable to other NSAIDs in patients with low-moderate GI risk and high CV risk.

If an ulcer develops, it would be best to discontinue the NSAID, if possible, and treat the ulcer with a PPI for about 8 weeks. Misoprostol is also an option, but diarrhea and cramping along with its four times per day dosing regimen contribute to poor patient compliance. If the NSAID therapy cannot be stopped, then reducing the NSAID dose, switching to acetaminophen or a nonacetylated salicylate or using a more selective COX-2 inhibitor should be considered.

Use caution with NSAIDs in any person with cardiovascular or renal disease since they can elevate blood pressure and decrease renal blood flow. If possible, avoid non-selective NSAIDs and celecoxib in patients with both high GI and CV risk and those at high risk of chronic kidney disease.

Patients who require antiplatelet therapy with a previous history of ulcers should be tested for *H. pylori* and treated, if positive.

Practice Case

PATIENT PROFILE

Patient Name	Edward Gilbert					
Address	560 Milton Drive					
Age	75	**Sex** Male	**Race** White	**Height** 5'10"	**Weight** 155 lbs	
Allergies	Penicillin (severe rash)					

DIAGNOSES

Shoulder/back pain, secondary to clavicle Fx 1/09	"Silent" MI, found on echo, no current Tx
Prostate CA	
Memory impairment	
Tremor	

MEDICATIONS

Date	No.	Prescriber	Drug & Strength	Quantity	Sig	Refills
8/11/13	77729	Sybell	Lupron 2 week-kit	#2	1 mg SC daily	
5/15/13	44825	Polonsky	Propranolol 20 mg	#90	1 TID	4
2/28/13	32187	Polonsky	Doxazosin	4 mg	1 PO QHS	7
5/15/13			Calcium carb+D 500-400	#120	1 PO BID	
6/15/13			Centrum MVI	#100	1 PO daily	

LAB/DIAGNOSTIC TESTS

Test	Normal Value	Results Date	Date	Date
Protein, T	6.2-8.3 g/dL			
Albumin	3.6-5.1 g/dL			
Alk Phos	33-115 units/L			
AST	10-35 units/L			
ALT	6-40 units/L			
CH, T	125-200 g/dL			
TG	<150 g/dL			
HDL	g/dL			
LDL	g/dL			
GLU	65-99 mg/dL			
Na	135-146 mEq/L			
K	3.5-5.3 mEq/L			
Cl	98-110 mEq/L			
C02	21-33 mmHg			
BUN	7-25 mg/dL			
Creatinine	0.6-1.2 mg/dL			
Calcium	8.6-10.2 mg/dL			
WBC	4-11 cells/mm^3			
RBC	3.8-5.1 mL/mm^3			
Hemoglobin	Male: 13.8- 17.2 g/dL Female: 12.1-15.1 g/dL			
Hematocrit	Male: 40.7-50.3% Female: 36.1- 44.3%			
MCHC	32-36 g/dL			
MCV	80-100 µm			
Platelet count	140-400 x 10^3/mm^3			

ADDITIONAL INFORMATION

Date	Notes
12/10/13	Patient's wife reports he is c/o severe epigastric pain for 2 weeks. Little relief with OTC antacids. Wife states she is giving spouse naproxen 250 mg #2 several times daily x 2-3 months for shoulder/back pain from his fall. Endoscopy report shows 1-cm gastric ulcer. A rapid urease test is negative. Evidence of anterior infarct reported during earlier hospital stay for cancer treatment. Family denies additional Rx or OTC medications.

Questions

1. Edward's wife is quite concerned about his severe gastric pain. Which changes should be initiated? (Select **ALL** that apply.)

   a. Discontinue naproxen

   b. Start PPI therapy

   c. Start antacid therapy

   d. Start *H. pylori* treatment

   e. Start ibuprofen therapy

2. Which of the following agents cause dizziness, syncope or fatigue and may have contributed to the fall that caused Edward to sustain a fracture? (Select **ALL** that apply.)

   a. *Lupron*

   b. Propranolol

   c. Doxazosin

   d. Calcium+D

   e. Multivitamin

3. Which of the following are risk factors present in Edward's case for the development of a gastric ulcer?

   a. Age

   b. High-dose, chronic use of non-selective NSAID

   c. Prostate cancer history

   d. A and B

   e. A, B and C

4. Eight weeks later, Edward has a follow-up endoscopy. The report states the ulcer has healed and the mucosa appears normal. PPI therapy is stopped. However, Edward is in pain, which he rates as a 4-5 on a pain scale. He states his back throbs when he sits or lies down. During this time, the oncologist has tried *Norco* and *Ultracet*, both of which did not offer much relief. Edward's wife asks if he can return to using naproxen, which was very helpful. Which is the most appropriate therapy at this time?

   a. Naproxen plus PPI therapy

   b. Celecoxib 400 mg once daily

   c. Piroxicam 20 mg twice daily

   d. Acetaminophen 325 mg, 1-2 tablets as needed

   e. Fentanyl patch

Questions 5-8 are NOT based on the above case.

5. A female patient presents to the pharmacy with a prescription for lansoprazole 30 mg BID, bismuth subsalicylate 525 mg QID, metronidazole 250 mg QID and tetracycline 500 mg QID for 14 days. The patient's other prescriptions include hydrochlorothiazide and the combination oral contraceptive product *Lybrel*. Choose the correct counseling statement:

   a. You will need to use back-up contraception, such as condoms and foam, for the 14 days you are using this antibiotic therapy.

   b. You will need to use back-up contraception, such as condoms and foam, for the 14 days you are using this antibiotic therapy and for 1 week afterwards.

   c. You will need to use back-up contraception, such as condoms and foam, for the 14 days you are using this antibiotic therapy and for 2 weeks afterwards.

   d. You will need to stop the *Lybrel* and use an alternative form of contraception for the 14 days you are using this antibiotic therapy.

   e. It is acceptable to use alcohol in moderation during use of this regimen.

6. A 16 year-old patient has the following allergies noted on her patient profile: ciprofloxacin, aspirin and erythromycin. The allergic reaction is not listed, and the patient is not available by phone. You wish to fill the prescription for *H. pylori* therapy, which includes rabeprazole, amoxicillin and clarithromycin. Choose the correct statement:

   a. It is safe to fill; most allergies to erythromycin are gastrointestinal.

   b. It is safe to fill; there is no cross-reaction with these agents.

   c. It is not safe to fill due to the use of amoxicillin in a patient with ciprofloxacin allergy.

   d. It is not safe to fill due to the patient's age.

   e. It is not safe to fill until the erythromycin "allergy" is clarified.

7. A 46 year-old man has received a prescription for lansoprazole 15 mg daily, amoxicillin 500 mg BID and clarithromycin 500 mg BID for *H. pylori* treatment. Choose the correct statement:

   a. Contact prescriber to correct dose of lansoprazole.

   b. Contact prescriber to correct doses of lansoprazole and amoxicillin.

   c. Contact prescriber to correct doses of clarithromycin and amoxicillin.

   d. Contact prescriber to correct doses of lansoprazole and clarithromycin.

   e. Fill as written.

8. A pharmacist is dispensing tetracycline. Which of the following are correct counseling points? (Select **ALL** that apply.)

   a. Take this medication 1-2 hours before or 4 hours after taking any products containing magnesium, aluminum, or calcium, iron, zinc including vitamins, supplements and dairy products.

   b. Do not use sunlamps while using this therapy.

   c. You should avoid getting pregnant while using this medicine.

   d. You may experience stomach upset, including loose stools and nausea.

   e. Do not take if you are allergic to penicillin.

Answers

1-a,b, 2-a,b,c, 3-d, 4-a, 5-a, 6-e, 7-b, 8-a,b,c,d

CONSTIPATION, DIARRHEA & BOWEL PREP

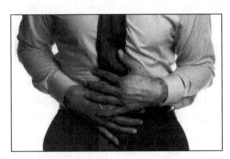

CONSTIPATION

Background

Constipation is defined as infrequent or hard stools, or difficulty passing stools. More specifically, constipation may involve pain during the passage of a bowel movement, the inability to pass a bowel movement after straining or pushing for more than 10 minutes, requiring digital evacuation, or no bowel movements after more than 3 days. The following are lifestyle modifications that may be helpful to reduce constipation:

- Look for offending drugs (see chart)

- Correct fluid intake (64 oz – caution with CVD)

- Limit caffeine and alcohol (to avoid dehydration)

- Replace refined foods with whole grain products, bran, fruits and vegetables, beans

- Increase physical activity

- Do not delay going to the bathroom when the urge to defecate is present; may need to schedule time (important for young children)

Treatment

In addition to the possible changes above, including the addition of fiber to the diet, if warranted, most patients self-treat constipation with OTC products. Per FDA-mandated labeling, use of all OTC laxatives should be limited to 7 days unless under medical supervision. Bulk-forming laxatives contain either psyllium, methylcellulose or polycarbophil and are usually recommended first-line. These come as powders, capsules and some (psyllium) in drinks and wafers. They require adequate fluid intake. The majority of patients use these safely. Any patient requiring longer use of a laxative should be referred to a physician. Another commonly used laxative is the stool softener docusate. It is especially helpful for iron-induced constipation since iron causes compact, hard stools which are difficult to pass.

CONSTIPATION NOTES

Medical conditions where constipation is common

Cerebrovascular events	Multiple sclerosis
Parkinson disease	Irritable Bowel Syndrome (constipation-predominant)
Spinal cord tumors	
Diabetes	Anal disorders (anal fissures, fistulae, rectal prolapse)
Hypothyroidism	

Medications that are constipating

Opioids	Aluminum antacids (magnesium often in combination with aluminum to counteract effect)
Anticholinergic drugs	
Antihistamines, phenothiazines, tricyclic antidepressants, antispasmodics, urge incontinence drugs, especially darifenacin (*Enablex*)	Aluminum complex in other drugs (sucralfate [*Carafate*])
	Tramadol, tapentadol
Non-DHP calcium channel blockers, especially verapamil	Colesevelam
	Milnacipran
Clonidine	Ranolazine
Bismuth	Varenicline
Iron (use docusate to avoid hard, compact stools)	5-HT3 receptor antagonists (e.g., ondansetron)
	Phentermine/topiramate
	Aripiprazole

Opioids and Constipation

Opioids are the worst drug offenders for causing constipation. A patient using "as-needed" opioids such as hydrocodone-acetaminophen may or may not require a laxative. The higher the dose the higher the risk of constipation occurring. The baseline is also important; some patients are more easily constipated than others. Once an opioid is scheduled, it is likely that a laxative is required. A stimulant laxative (usually senna) is given first, with or without a stool softener (docusate). If the patient has difficulty pushing the stool out, they require a laxative. If the stool is hard, a stool softener will help. Some patients on opioids get by with a stool softener alone. Certain opioids are more constipating than others; for example, morphine is more constipating than fentanyl, but both are constipating. A pharmacist dispensing opioids should always consider the risk of constipation by evaluating the dose, the frequency and the patient at baseline. It is preferable to recommend a laxative-even if you are unsure if they will need it. Store-brand senna and docusate are available everywhere and are not expensive. Senna is given at bedtime (usually two tablets QHS). It takes about 10 hours to work and the patient will be able to more easily defecate the following morning. Most patients defecate in the morning. Docusate is given twice daily (usually 100 mg BID) to make the stool softer while the food is being processed.

If the patient is constipated now and requires treatment, the options are different than those used for prevention. In this case, agents usually chosen include: lactulose, sorbitol, Milk of Magnesia (MOM), magnesium citrate or polyethylene glycol. If the patient is impacted an enema may be required. Digital evacuation (removing the drug with a gloved hand, sometimes by a physician or nurse) may be needed.

Laxative Agents Used for Bowel Prep

A screening colonoscopy is used to detect colorectal cancer, along with fecal occult blood tests. They are also used for other gastrointestinal conditions, such as Crohn's. A successful colonoscopy requires a complete and thorough bowel prep. Several of the agents below (the PEGs, and occasionally sodium phosphate) are used for both bowel prep and as laxatives. Sodium phosphate can cause fluid and electrolyte abnormalities, and is particularly risky in patients with renal or cardiac disease. Some of the PEG formulations are only used for bowel prep, such as *Golytely*. General counseling for bowel prep agents must include when to take the agent, what the patient can consume during the bowel cleansing process (i.e., after they have started using the bowel prep agent) and what must be avoided. Although usually safe and well-tolerated, in certain patients fluid and electrolyte loss could be critical. For this reason, some of the bowel prep agents require MedGuides. Use extra caution in patients with cardiovascular disease, renal insufficiency, if taking diuretics (loops, due to additional fluid loss) and NSAIDs.

OK to Consume

- "Clear liquid diet," which can include water, clear broth (beef or chicken), fat-free consommé, juices (apple, prune, grape, cranberry, and cider) without pulp, noncarbonated, sodas *(Sprite, 7-Up*, ginger ale, and seltzer), coffee or tea (without milk or cream), clear gelatin (without fruit pieces), popsicles (without fruit pieces or cream), fruit ices (no fruit pieces).

Do not Consume

- Anything with red or blue/purple food coloring (including gelatin and popsicles), milk, cream, tomato, orange or grapefruit juice, cream soups, any soup other than broth. No liquids that they cannot "see through."

- Alcoholic beverages

- No solid or semi-solid foods – liquid only until after the procedure is complete.

Laxatives for Chronic/Maintenance Therapy

Bulk-producing laxatives create a gel-like matrix in the stool, soaking up fluid in loose stool and adding bulk to hard stool. Emollients and lubricants (stool softeners) lubricate and soften fecal mass, making defecation easier. Lubiprostone works by activating chloride channels in the gut, leading to increased fluid in the gut and peristalsis. Linaclotide is an agonist of guanylate cyclase C, which increases chloride and bicarbonate secretion into the intestinal lumen, decreasing GI transit time.

Chronic/Maintenance Therapy

DRUG	DOSING	SAFETY/SIDE EFFECTS/MONITORING

Bulk-producing laxatives

DRUG	DOSING	SAFETY/SIDE EFFECTS/MONITORING
Psyllium (*Metamucil*, others)	2.5-30 g/day in divided doses	**SIDE EFFECTS** Increased gas, bloating, bowel obstruction if strictures present, choking if powder forms are not taken with enough liquid
Calcium polycarbophil (*FiberCon*, others)	1,250 mg 1-4 times/day	**NOTES** Onset of action – 12 to 24 hours Drugs of choice in pregnancy First-line treatment for constipation Increase bulk in diet slowly
Methylcellulose (*Citrucel*)	2 g 1-3 times/day	Adequate fluid intake required Take 2 hours before/after drugs (caution with other drugs that stick to fiber) Psyllium: tart-like flavor; sugar-free forms available

Emollients, lubricants (stool softeners)

DRUG	DOSING	SAFETY/SIDE EFFECTS/MONITORING
Docusate Sodium (*Colace*) Docusate Calcium Mineral Oil	Docusate – usually 100 mg BID (max of 500 mg/day)	**NOTES** Onset of action – 24 to 48 hours Bitter taste with liquid only Advise not to use more than 7 days without consulting physician (not that it's harmful, just to rule out more serious problem) Mineral oil – take a multivitamin at a different time due to risk of fat-soluble vitamin depletion (A, D, E & K)

Stimulants and irritants – Use caution when recommending agents by brand name as many brands can refer to multiple products

DRUG	DOSING	SAFETY/SIDE EFFECTS/MONITORING
Senna (*Ex-Lax*, others)	15 mg, usually 2 tabs QHS	**SIDE EFFECTS** Stomach upset, cramping, electrolyte imbalance with overdose (e.g., eating disorders)
Bisacodyl (*Dulcolax*, others)	Bisacodyl OTC: 5 mg, take 1-3 tablets once daily	**NOTES** Onset of action – 8-12 hours Do not crush or chew bisacodyl tablets (they are EC), do not take within 1 hr of milk or antacids – may require dose reduction with H_2RAs or PPIs.
Cascara (see Natural Products chapter)		Senna is well-tolerated at the usual dose. Side effects are increased when high doses are used. Caution, brand names can refer to multiple products.

Rx Agents

DRUG	DOSING	SAFETY/SIDE EFFECTS/MONITORING
Lubiprostone (*Amitiza*)	24 mcg capsule twice daily with food IBS dosing: 8 mcg PO once daily to twice daily Decrease dose with severe liver impairment	**SIDE EFFECTS** Nausea (30%) Abdominal pain & distention **NOTES** Take with food

Chronic/Maintenance Therapy Continued

DRUG	DOSING	SAFETY/SIDE EFFECTS/MONITORING
Linaclotide (*Linzess*)	Chronic idiopathic constipation – 145 mcg PO daily IBS with constipation – 290 mcg PO daily	**BLACK BOX WARNING** Do not use in patients less than 18 years of age **SIDE EFFECTS** Diarrhea **NOTES** Must be dispensed with a Medication Guide Take at least 30 minutes before breakfast

Acute (STAT) Treatments and Bowel Preps

Stimulants/irritants work by reducing water and electrolyte absorption by stimulating colonic neurons and irritating the mucosal lining of the colon. Osmotic laxatives cause fluid to be retained in the bowel lumen, with a net increase of fluid secretions in the small intestines. This distends the colon and increases peristalsis.

DRUG	DOSING	SAFETY/SIDE EFFECTS/MONITORING
Bisacodyl Rectal	10 mg PR	**SIDE EFFECTS** Rectal burning **NOTES** Onset of action – 10 minutes If too soft to insert, can cool in refrigerator or cold water first.
Osmotics **Magnesium salts (MOM)** Lactulose Sorbitol	 30-60 mL 15-30 mL 30-150 mL (as 70% solution)	**SIDE EFFECTS** Electrolyte imbalance, excessive gas, hypermagnesemia, hypocalcemia and hyperphosphatemia in patients with renal dysfunction, dehydration **NOTES** Onset of action – 2 to 48 hours Caution in patients with renal dysfunction (magnesium salts) Lactulose can also be used chronically – titrated to 2-3 soft stools/day
Sodium phosphates (*Fleets* enema, *OsmoPrep*)	1 enema PR PRN *OsmoPrep*: Evening before colonoscopy: 4 tablets with 8 oz clear liquids Q15 min for a total of 20 tablets Next morning: 4 tablets with 8 oz clear liquids Q15 min for a total of 12 tablets	**WARNINGS** Do not use sodium phosphates in CHF, renal disease, ↓ Ca^{2+} or ↑ PO$_4$ **SIDE EFFECTS** Electrolyte imbalance, excessive gas, hypocalcemia and hyperphosphatemia in patients with renal dysfunction, dehydration **NOTES** Onset of action – 1 to 5 minutes Ensure adequate hydration

Acute (STAT) Treatments and Bowel Preps Continued

DRUG	DOSING	SAFETY/SIDE EFFECTS/MONITORING
Nonabsorbable solutions; also used for bowel prep **Polyethylene glycol (Golytely, MiraLax, Carbowax)** *NuLytely, Trilyte* are sulfate free *HalfLytely, HalfLytely +* bisacodyl, *MoviPrep* are less volume (2 L)	PEG – 17 g in 8 oz water (for bowel prep, repeat every 10 minutes until 2 liters are consumed)	**SIDE EFFECTS** Nausea, abdominal fullness, bloating **NOTES** Onset of action – within 4 hours **To ensure adequate bowel prep** Clear liquid diet for one day prior, avoid red or blue/purple drinks If it will help, split the dose of the bowel prep, such as half the night before, and half 4-6 hours before procedure Use flavored agents, or add lemon juice or *Crystal Light* (no sugar-containing products)
Picosulfate, Magnesium Oxide, Andhydrous Citric Acid *(Prepopik)*	150 mL x 2 doses	**SIDE EFFECTS** Hypermagnesemia and reduced GFR Possible headache, hypokalemia, hypochloremia, hyponatremia, nausea, elevated serum creatinine **NOTES** Combination stimulant laxative and osmotic, enables lower fluid intake – used for bowel prep **Directions** If morning procedure, take dose the afternoon before and 6 hours later If later in the day, take first dose night before, 2nd 5 hours prior to procedure Drink 5 glasses of clear liquid after the 1st dose and 3 glasses after the 2nd dose
Glycerin suppository (adult size, peds size) *Babylax* is liquid in rectal applicator (squeeze out liquid around stuck stool into rectum)	Use 1 suppository, can repeat x 1	**SIDE EFFECTS** Anal irritation, stomach cramping **NOTES** Onset of action – 15-30 minutes Insert rectally towards side of rectal wall (at side of stool)

Opioid-Induced Constipation Treatments

Methylnaltrexone and alvimopan block opioid receptors in the gut to reduce the constipating effects of opioids.

DRUG	DOSING	SAFETY/SIDE EFFECTS/MONITORING
Methylnaltrexone *(Relistor)*	8 mg if weight 38-61 kg, 12 mg if 62-114 kg, and 0.15 mg/kg if > 114 kg. Given SC every other day	**CONTRAINDICATIONS** GI obstruction **SIDE EFFECTS** Abdominal pain, flatulence, nausea **NOTES** Decrease dose if CrCl < 30 mL/min Only for patients on opioids who have failed DSS + laxative (senna, bisacodyl). Do not use routinely; can often increase laxative until the patient can excavate
Alvimopan *(Entereg)*	12 mg PO, 30 min-5 hrs prior to surgery, and 12 mg BID for up to 7 days total (15 doses)	**BLACK BOX WARNING** REMS drug. Short-term hospital use only (max 7 days – no more than 15 doses) **CONTRAINDICATIONS** Patients who have taken therapeutic doses of opioids for more than 7 consecutive days prior to use **NOTES** Use is limited to post-surgical patients to decrease the risk of post-operative ileus

DIARRHEA NOTES

Medications that can cause diarrhea	
Antacids containing magnesium	Laxatives
Antibiotics, especially broad-spectrum antibiotics and clindamycin, erythromycin (due to prokinetic activity) – rule out *C. difficile* infection	Metoclopramide
	Misoprostol
	Quinidine
	Many drugs include diarrhea as a possible side effect
Colchicine	

DIARRHEA

Background

Diarrhea occurs when there is an increase in the number of bowel movements or bowel movements are more watery and loose than normal. When the intestines push stools through the bowel before the water in the stool can be reabsorbed, diarrhea occurs. Abdominal cramps, nausea, vomiting, or a fever may occur along with the diarrhea. Fluid and electrolyte replacement is essential; review counseling points at end of this section.

Treatment

- Most cases are viral. Diarrhea can be idiopathic, caused by diseases, or can be caused by stomach flu or food poisoning. Drinking untreated water, not washing fruits/vegetables properly, using untreated ice for drinks, or unpasteurized dairy products can cause viral, bacterial, or parasitic infections. *E. coli* is the most common bacterial cause. The treatment of diarrhea caused by a bacterial infection is discussed in the Infectious Disease chapter.

Antidiarrheals

Bismuth subsalicylate exhibits both antisecretory and antimicrobial effects when used as an antidiarrheal. Loperamide acts on intestinal muscles to inhibit peristalsis and to slow intestinal motility. Diphenoxylate works by inhibiting excessive GI motility and GI propulsion. A subtherapeutic amount of atropine is include in the formulation to discourage abuse.

DRUG	DOSING	SAFETY/SIDE EFFECTS/MONITORING
Bismuth subsalicylate (**Pepto-Bismol**, others)	524 mg (2 tbsp or 2 tablets) every 30-60 minutes as needed up to 8 doses/day; max 2 days	**CONTRAINDICATIONS** Children with viral infections (varicella, influenza) due to risk of Reye's syndrome, patients with a salicylate allergy, history of severe GI bleed or coagulopathy **SIDE EFFECTS** Black tongue/stool, hearing loss/tinnitus (toxicity) **NOTES** Bismuth subsalicylate should be used with caution in patients on aspirin therapy or anticoagulants or those who have renal insufficiency Salicylate toxicity can occur if used excessively
Loperamide (**Imodium, Anti-Diarrheal, Diamode,** others)	2 mg tab/cap; 1 mg liquid 4 mg PO after first loose stool initially; then 2 mg after each subsequent stool; not to exceed 16 mg/d	**CONTRAINDICATIONS** Abdominal pain without diarrhea, children < 2 years of age, acute dysentery (bloody diarrhea and high fever), acute ulcerative colitis, pseudomembranous colitis (C. difficile) **SIDE EFFECTS** Abdominal cramping, constipation, nausea **NOTES** Do not self-treat for > 2 days
Diphenoxylate 2.5 mg with atropine 0.025 mg (**Lomotil**) <u>C V</u>	5 mg up to QID (max 20 mg/day)	**CONTRAINDICATIONS** Children < 2 years of age, pseudomembranous colitis (C. difficile); obstructive jaundice **SIDE EFFECTS** Sedation, constipation, urinary retention, tachycardia, blurred vision, xerostomia, dizziness, depression

Counseling for All Diarrhea Cases

- Do not self-treat if high fever (> 101 degrees Fahrenheit) or blood in stool; see healthcare provider if no improvement in 2 days, if severe abdominal pain, infants (< 6 months), or if patient is pregnant.

- Diarrhea treatment should include fluid and electrolytes – this is important for all but especially so in children or adults with chronic medical illness.

- For moderate-severe fluid loss, replacement is best accomplished with oral rehydration solutions (ORS), which are available at stores and pharmacies (Pedialyte, Infalyte, etc) in developed countries. Gatorade or similar products are used as alternatives.

- Caution with *Imodium* and *Lomotil* if a decrease in intestinal motility may be due to infection from *Shigella, Salmonella*, and toxigenic strains of *E. coli* – toxic megacolon (usually due to *E. coli* or severe IBS) may occur. These products are also not recommended in *C. difficile* infections – the patient's body must be able to rid itself of the toxin.

- If fever/cold symptoms are present, aspirin rarely causes Reye's Syndrome in children and is avoided except under a healthcare provider's care (it may rarely be used in a child with a heart condition, where benefit may outweigh risk). For fever or mild pain, the parent can treat the child with acetaminophen or ibuprofen but should not exceed recommended daily amounts of acetaminophen or ibuprofen.

- Combination cough and cold products should not be used in children under 2 years old per the FDA (under 6 years old per the American Academy of Pediatrics). Any combination product may contain additional amounts of acetaminophen or ibuprofen – the patient must be counseled to count all sources.

- Rule out lactose intolerance as a cause of the diarrhea by stopping use of dairy products. Physicians can confirm lactose intolerance by tests.

Bismuth Subsalicylate Counseling

- Do not use if you have an allergy to bismuth, salicylates (including aspirin and NSAIDs, like ibuprofen), or any other part of this drug.

- Tell your healthcare provider prior to starting this medicine if you are also taking a salicylate like aspirin.

- Do not give to children and teenagers who have flu signs, chickenpox, or other viral infections due to the chance of Reye's syndrome.

- Some chewable products have phenylalanine. If you have PKU, do not use this product.

- This medicine may make your tongue and stool dark, this is normal. Contact your healthcare provider right away if you notice tarry or bloody stools or if you are throwing up blood or a substance that looks like coffee grounds.

- If you notice a ringing in the ears or a loss of hearing while taking this medicine, stop taking it and contact your healthcare provider.

- Do not take for longer than 7 days without the approval of your healthcare provider.

INFLAMMATORY BOWEL DISEASE (IBD)

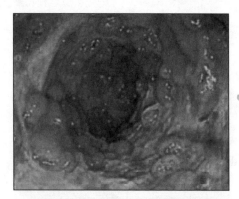

GUIDELINES

Management of Crohn's Disease
in Adults. Am J Gastroenterol
2009;104:465-483.

Ulcerative Colitis Practice Guidelines
in Adults. Am J Gastroenterol
2010;105:501-523.

BACKGROUND

Inflammatory Bowel Disease (IBD) is a group of inflammatory conditions of the colon and small intestine. The major types of IBD are ulcerative colitis (UC) and Crohn's disease. Symptoms include cramping, bloody diarrhea, fever and possible weight loss. Crohn's can cause malabsorption (vitamin deficiencies) and anal fissures. The treatment goal is to suppress inflammation to reduce symptoms. Acute symptom control (such as the use of antidiarrheals or antispasmodics) may be necessary. Symptoms can occur at any time but generally increase when the patient is under stress or eats foods that may be disease triggers. Food triggers, in some patients, include beans, alcohol, lactose-containing dairy products, cabbage and broccoli.

Ulcerative Colitis

Ulcerative Colitis (UC) is characterized by mucosal inflammation confined to the rectum and colon (often referred to as distal IBD) with superficial ulcerations (in contrast to Crohn's, where the ulcers can be deep). The larger the affected area, the worse the symptoms. When the disease flares, patients are usually running to the bathroom, often with pain, which can significantly decrease quality of life. Symptoms of UC include abdominal cramping, frequent bowel movements (often with blood in stool), weight loss, and fever and tachycardia in severe disease.

Crohn's

Crohn's disease (CD) is characterized by transmural (through the tissue) inflammation of the GI tract that can affect any part (from mouth to anus), although 2/3 of cases are in the ileum – the last part of the small intestine. Bowel wall injury is extensive and the intestinal lumen is often narrowed. The bowel wall first becomes thickened and edematous, then ulcerated and fibrotic. Fistula formation is common. Symptoms of CD include abdominal pain, frequent bowel movements, weight loss/malnutrition, and malaise. Bleeding in the stool can occur but is much less than with UC.

Treatment

Both UC and Crohn's, in mild cases, may only need antidiarrheal medicines, primarily loperamide (*Imodium*). Antispasmodics for UC may be useful. The most common antispasmodic is dicyclomine (*Bentyl*) which is an anticholinergic a high incidence of side effects (e.g., dizziness, xerostomia, nausea, blurred vision).

Short courses of oral or IV steroids are used to treat acute exacerbations of IBD. Aminosalicylates are used for maintenance therapy to control inflammation and reduce flare-ups. Mesalamine is the primary aminosalicylate used – it is well tolerated and can be taken once daily. The other aminosalicylates (sulfasalazine, basalazide, olsalazine) must be converted to mesalamine. Sulfasalazine is rarely used due to the many side effects associated with the sulfapyridine component of the drug. The efficacy of aminosalicylates has been proven in UC; however, it remains unclear in Crohn's. In moderate-severe cases, an immunosuppressive agent such as azathioprine, 6-mercaptopurine, or methotrexate may be used. Anti-TNF agents, such as infliximab, are used in patients with IBD that is refractory to aminosalicylates and immunosuppressants. These agents are extremely expensive and induce long-term remission in about 30% of patients. As a last resort, IV steroids or cyclosporine may be used.

Natural Products

Cascara and senna are "natural" stimulant laxatives since they are plant products and can be useful for patients with constipation. For diarrhea, psyllium (in *Metamucil* and other formulations) or other "bulk-forming" fiber products can be useful. These agents are relatively well-tolerated but the patient should consider the standard safety considerations (see Constipation/Diarrhea chapter).

Peppermint (oil, sometimes teas) can be useful as an antispasmodic. Some use chamomile tea. The probiotic *Lactobacillus* or *bifidobacterium infantis* may help reduce abdominal pain, bloating, urgency, constipation or diarrhea in some patients. Antibiotics and probiotics are not taken at the same time; separate the dosing by at least two hours. Fish oils (for the EPA and DHA, the omega fatty acid components) are being used, although the evidence for benefit is contradictory. Indian frankincense gum resin taken TID may be beneficial for UC, based on preliminary studies.

Watch for avoidable problems: Sorbitol is used as a sweetener in some diet foods and is present in various drugs. It can cause considerable GI distress in some patients with IBS. Sorbitol has laxative properties.

In addition, check if the IBS patient is lactose-intolerant. Lactose is not only in dairy products; it is also used in some oral drugs as an excipient. Both sorbitol and lactose are classified as excipients (or binders); they help hold tablets together.

Nicotine has been shown to worsen Crohn's but can be protective in UC. In fact, nicotine patches have been used as an adjunct therapy for UC; however, adverse effects (nausea, dizziness) limit their utility.

Agents Used For Mild Symptom Control: Diarrhea, Cramping/GI Spasms

DRUG	DOSING	SAFETY/SIDE EFFECTS/MONITORING

Antidiarrheals

DRUG	DOSING	SAFETY/SIDE EFFECTS/MONITORING
Loperamide (*Imodium*)	2 mg tab/cap; 1 mg liquid 4 mg PO after first loose stool initially; then 2 mg after each subsequent stool; not to exceed 16 mg/day	**CONTRAINDICATIONS** Abdominal pain without diarrhea, children < 2 years of age, acute dysentery (bloody diarrhea and high fever), acute ulcerative colitis, pseudomembranous colitis (*C. difficile*). **SIDE EFFECTS** Abdominal cramping, constipation, nausea **NOTES** Do not self-treat for > 2 days
Bismuth subsalicylate (*Pepto-Bismol,* others)	524 mg (2 tbsp or 2 tablets) every 30-60 minutes as needed, up to 8 doses/day; max 2 days	**CONTRAINDICATIONS** Children with viral infections (varicella, influenza) due to risk of Reye's syndrome, patients with a salicylate allergy, history of severe GI bleed or coagulopathy **SIDE EFFECTS** Black tongue/stool, hearing loss/tinnitus (toxicity) **NOTES** Bismuth subsalicylate should be used with caution in patients on aspirin therapy or anticoagulants or those who have renal insufficiency Salicylate toxicity can occur if used excessively
Diphenoxylate 2.5 mg with atropine 0.025 mg (*Lomotil*) C V	5 mg up to QID (max 20 mg/day)	**CONTRAINDICATIONS** Children < 2 years of age, pseudomembranous colitis (*C. Difficile*); obstructive jaundice **SIDE EFFECTS** Sedation, constipation, urinary retention, tachycardia, blurred vision, xerostomia, dizziness, depression

Antispasmodic

DRUG	DOSING	SAFETY/SIDE EFFECTS/MONITORING
Dicyclomine (*Bentyl*)	10-20 mg QID; max 160 mg/day Take 30-60 minutes before meals	**CONTRAINDICATIONS** GI obstruction, severe ulcerative colitis, reflux esophagitis, unstable cardiovascular status in acute hemorrhage, obstructive uropathy, breast feeding, narrow-angle glaucoma, myasthenia gravis, infants < 6 months of age **SIDE EFFECTS** Dizziness, xerostomia, nausea, blurred vision

Corticosteroids

DRUG	DOSING	SAFETY/SIDE EFFECTS/MONITORING

Oral Steroids

DRUG	DOSING	SAFETY/SIDE EFFECTS/MONITORING
PredniSONE	5-60 mg/day	**SIDE EFFECTS** Short-term: increased appetite/weight gain, fluid retention, emotional instability (euphoria, mood swings, irritability), insomnia, GI upset; higher doses can cause increase in BP and blood glucose Long-term: Adrenal suppression/Cushing's syndrome, impaired wound healing, hypertension, hyperglycemia, cataracts, osteoporosis, others. See Asthma chapter for complete list **NOTES** For acute flare management – steroids are not supposed to be used long-term – however, some patients use chronically due to severe condition. If used long-term, assess bone density (consider use of bisphosphonates, optimize calcium and vitamin D intake)
Budesonide (Entocort EC, Uceris – do not crush)	9 mg daily for up to 8 weeks; if changing from prednisone, taper prednisone while starting budesonide	Budesonide undergoes extensive first-pass metabolism so lower systemic exposure If used longer than 2 weeks, must taper (over 3-4 weeks) to avoid withdrawal symptoms. Budesonide is preferred if disease is in ileum or ascending colon May be using ADT (Alternate Day Therapy) to ↓ adrenal suppression Swallow whole – do not crush, chew or break

Topical Steroids

DRUG	DOSING	SAFETY/SIDE EFFECTS/MONITORING
Hydrocortisone (Cortifoam, Cortenema)	Cortenema: 1 enema (100 mg) QHS for 21 days, then taper Cortifoam: 1 applicatorful (80 mg) 1-2 times daily for 2-3 weeks, then taper	**CONTRAINDICATIONS** Obstruction, abscess, perforation, peritonitis, intestinal anastomoses, extensive fistulas **NOTES** Topical steroids have not been proven effective for maintenance of remission. Advantages of topical therapy include less systemic absorption and less frequent dosing schedule.

Budesonide Drug Interactions

- Budesonide is a 3A4 substrate; potent inhibitors (ketoconazole, itraconazole, ritonavir, etc.) may require a budesonide dose reduction.

- Avoid the use of grapefruit products when using this medication.

Maintenance Therapy

DRUG	DOSING	SAFETY/SIDE EFFECTS/MONITORING

Aminosalicylates

DRUG	DOSING	SAFETY/SIDE EFFECTS/MONITORING
Mesalamine *(Apriso,* **Asacol HD**, *Delzicol,* **Pentasa** and **Lialda** are all long-acting orals; **Canasa** – suppository; **Rowasa** – enema) 5-ASA (5-aminosalicyclic acid)	Suppository: 1 g rectally QHS Enema: 4 g QHS Oral: *Delzicol*: 800 mg TID or 400 mg QID *Pentasa*: 1 g QID *Lialda*: 2.4-4.8 g daily *Asacol HD*: 1.6 g TID	**CONTRAINDICATIONS** Hypersensitivity to salicylates or aminosalicylates or any component of the formulation **SIDE EFFECTS** Abdominal pain, nausea, headache, flatulence, eructation (belching), pharyngitis, acute intolerance syndrome (looks like symptoms of IBD exacerbation) **MONITORING** Renal function, CBC, symptoms of IBD **NOTES** Best to avoid concomitant use with antacids, H$_2$RAs, or PPIs (interfere with absorption). Patients with hypersensitivity to sulfasalazine may have a similar reaction to mesalamine; however, most patients do not Mesalamine is better tolerated than other aminosalicylates Topical mesalamine is more effective than oral mesalamine and steroids for distal disease/proctitis in UC; can use oral and topical together Topical agents should not be used in proximal disease Swallow caps/tabs whole; do not crush, chew, or break due to delayed-release coating
SulfaSALAzine *(Azulfidine, Azulfidine EN-tabs, Sulfazine, Sulfazine EC)* 5-aminosalicylic acid derivative	2-6 g/day	**CONTRAINDICATIONS** Patients with a sulfa or salicylate allergy GI or GU obstruction, porphyria **SIDE EFFECTS** Headache, rash, anorexia, dyspepsia, GI upset (N/V/D), oligospermia (reversible) (all > 10%); folate deficiency, arthalgias, crystalluria **MONITORING** CBC, LFTs, symptoms of IBD **NOTES** Can cause yellow-orange coloration of skin/urine Impairs folate absorption, may give 1 mg/day folate supplement Take with food and 8 oz of water to prevent cystalluria

Maintenance Therapy Continued

DRUG	DOSING	SAFETY/SIDE EFFECTS/MONITORING
Balsalazide *(Colazol, Giazo)*	*Colazol*: 2.25 g PO TID *Giazo*: 3.3 g PO BID	**CONTRAINDICATIONS** Salicylate allergy **SIDE EFFECTS** Headache, abdominal pain, diarrhea, vomiting (GI effects more common in children) **MONITORING** Renal function, LFTs, symptoms of IBD **NOTES** *Giazo* is only approved in males (it failed to show a benefit in females during trials)
Olsalazine *(Dipentum)*	500 mg PO BID	**CONTRAINDICATIONS** Salicylate allergy **SIDE EFFECTS** Diarrhea, abdominal pain **MONITORING** CBC, LFTs, renal function, symptoms of IBD

Immunosuppressive Agents – these agents can used if patient fails above therapy or they can be used in combination with above therapies

DRUG	DOSING	SAFETY/SIDE EFFECTS/MONITORING
AzaTHIOprine *(Azasan, Imuran)*	2-3 mg/kg/day given IV/PO	**BLACK BOX WARNINGS (2)** Chronic immunosuppression can ↑ risk of neoplasia (esp. lymphomas) Hematologic toxicities (leukopenia, thrombocytopenia) and mutagenic potential **SIDE EFFECTS** GI upset (N/V), rash, ↑ LFTs, hematologic toxicities (leukopenia, thrombocytopenia) **MONITORING** LFTs, CBC, renal function **NOTES** Pregnancy Category D Azathioprine is metabolized to mercaptopurine (avoid concurrent use due to myelosuppression) Patients with genetic deficiency of thiopurine methyltransferase (TPMT) will be more sensitive to myelosuppressive effects and may require a lower dose

Maintenance Therapy Continued

DRUG	DOSING	SAFETY/SIDE EFFECTS/MONITORING
6-Mercaptopurine (*Purinethol*)	1-1.5 mg/kg/day PO	Similar to azathioprine **NOTES** Take on an empty stomach
Methotrexate (*Rheumatrex, Trexall*)	15-25 mg/week PO	**BLACK BOX WARNINGS** Hepatitis, renal, pneumonitis, bone marrow suppression, mucositis/stomatitis, dermatologic reactions, others – renal and lung toxicity more likely when using oncology doses. **CONTRAINDICATIONS** Pregnancy and breastfeeding, alcoholism, chronic liver disease, blood dyscrasias, immunodeficiency syndrome **SIDE EFFECTS** Nausea, vomiting, ↑ LFTs, stomatitis, alopecia, photosensitivity **MONTIORING** LFTs, and SCr (baseline and every 2-4 weeks for first 3 months, then less frequently); chest X-ray, hepatitis B and C at baseline. Pulmonary function test if lung-related symptoms. **NOTES** Pregnancy Category X Folic acid can be given to decrease the side effects associated with methotrexate – commonly given 5 mg PO weekly on the day following methotrexate administration. May take up to 12 weeks to see full benefit Not proven effective in UC

If Failed Above Therapy: Monoclonal antibodies to TNF

Humira: Humanized monoclonal antibody (may have ↓ antibody development and ↓ resistance)

Remicade: Chimeric monoclonal antibody

Simponi: Humanized monoclonal antibody

Tysabri: Humanized monoclonal antibody that inhibits α4-integrin

Cimzia: PEG-linked humanized monoclonal antibody

Adalimumab (*Humira*)	160 mg SC, then 80 mg 2 weeks later (day 15), then 40 mg every other week (starting day 29). Some patients may need 40 mg weekly.	Similar black box warnings as infliximab **SIDE EFFECTS** Injection site reactions, increased CPK, upper resipiratory infection, headache, positive ANA titer, antibody development (reduced compared to infliximab) **NOTES** Approved for both Crohn's and UC Inject into abdomen or thigh Store in refrigerator until ready to use Injection technique is discussed in the Autoimmune chapter

Maintenance Therapy Continued

DRUG	DOSING	SAFETY/SIDE EFFECTS/MONITORING
InFLIXimab *(Remicade)*	5 mg/kg IV at 0, 2, 6 weeks, then every 8 weeks. Some patients may require 10 mg/kg to maintain response to therapy	**BLACK BOX WARNINGS (3)** Serious infections (some fatal) – discontinue treatment if patient develops a severe infection; lymphomas and other malignancies; perform test for latent TB prior to starting therapy **CONTRAINDICATIONS** Doses > 5 mg/kg in mod-severe heart failure (NYHA Class III/IV) **WARNINGS** TNF inhibitors can cause demyelinating disease, hepatitis B reactivation, heart failure, hepatotoxicity, lupus-like syndrome, and severe infections. They should not be used with other TNF inhibitors or immunosuppressive biologics, or live vaccines. **SIDE EFFECTS** Infusion reactions: hypotension, fever, chills, pruritus, (may pre-treat with acetaminophen, antihistamine, and/or steroids); infections, upper respiratory tract symptoms, headache, abdominal pain **MONITORING** Vitals (during infusion), TB test (prior to administration and annually), signs and symptoms of infection, CBC, LFTs, HBV (prior to initiation), HF, malignancies **NOTES** Alternative 1st line in mod-severe Crohn's or UC Should be infused within 3 hrs of reconstitution and dilution; 2 hour infusion Infusion requires a filter Antibody induction can occur, and will ↓ usefulness of drug Do not shake. Requires refrigeration (biologics will denature if hot). Do not freeze. Allow to reach room temperature before injecting (15-30 min)
Golimumab *(Simponi)*	200 mg SC initially, then 100 mg at week 2, then 100 mg every 4 weeks	Similar black box warnings as infliximab **SIDE EFFECTS** Infection, upper respiratory tract symptoms, injection site reactions **NOTES** Only approved for UC Injection technique is discussed in the Autoimmune chapter Vials refrigerated; good for 4 hours at room temp

Maintenance Therapy Continued

DRUG	DOSING	SAFETY/SIDE EFFECTS/MONITORING
Natalizumab *(Tysabri)*	300 mg IV over 1 hour every 4 weeks	**BLACK BOX WARNING** Risk for progressive multifocal leukoencephalopathy (PML) – monitor mental status changes. PML is associated with several factors including anti-JC virus antibodies, treatment duration and prior immunosuppressant use. **SIDE EFFECTS** Infusion reactions, headache, fatigue, nausea, respiratory infections, rash **NOTES** Only approved for Crohn's Discontinue if no response by week 12. REMS: Must be enrolled in manufacturer TOUCH prescribing program Cannot be used with other immunosuppressants
Certolizumab *(Cimzia)*	400 mg SC initially and at weeks 2 and 4, then 400 mg every 4 weeks	Similar black box warnings as infliximab **SIDE EFFECTS** Infection, upper respiratory symptoms, nausea, injection site reactions **NOTES** Only approved for Crohn's Inject into the abdomen or thigh Vials refrigerated; reconstituted vials are good for 24 hrs if in refrigerator or 2 hrs at room temp

Vedolizumab, another injectable biologic agent for CD and UC, is expected to be approved in early 2014

Mesalamine Counseling

- Do not crush or chew long-acting formulations. You may see a ghost tablet in the feces (*Asacol HD*).

- *Rowasa* enema: Remove bottle from pouch and shake well. Remove the protective sheath from the applicator tip. Hold the bottle at the neck so as not to cause any of the medicine to be discharged. Best results are obtained by lying on the left side with the left leg extended and the right leg flexed forward for balance. Gently insert the lubricated applicator tip into the rectum to prevent damage to the rectal wall, pointed slightly toward the navel. Grasp the bottle firmly, and then tilt slightly so that the nozzle is aimed toward the back, and squeeze slowly to instill the medication. Steady hand pressure will discharge most of the medicine. After administering, withdraw and discard the bottle. Remain in position for at least 30 minutes, or preferably all night for maximum benefit. *Rowasa* can cause staining of surfaces including, clothing, and other fabrics, flooring, painted surfaces, marble, granite, vinyl and enamel. Take care in choosing a suitable location for administration of this product.

- *Canasa* suppository: For best results, empty your rectum (have a bowel movement) just before using. This medication should be used at bedtime. Detach one suppository from the strip. Remove foil wrapper; avoid excessive handling. Insert the suppository with the pointed end first completely into your rectum, using gentle pressure. For best results, keep the suppository in your rectum for at least 1-3 hours. You may put a little bit of lubricating gel on the suppository. *Canasa* can cause staining of surfaces including, clothing, and other fabrics, flooring, painted surfaces, marble, granite, vinyl and enamel. Keep *Canasa* away from these surfaces to prevent staining.

Budesonide *(Entocort EC)* Counseling

- Take this medication with a full glass of water before a meal. <u>Do not crush, chew or break open the capsule</u>.

- Tell your doctor if you have changes in the shape or location of body fat (especially in your arms, legs, face, neck, breasts, and waist), high blood pressure, severe headache, fast or uneven heart rate, blurred vision, or a general ill feeling with headache, tiredness, nausea, and vomiting.

- You should have your blood pressure monitored on a regular basis. The blood pressure should remain in a healthy range.

- You should have your blood glucose ("blood sugar") monitored on a regular basis. The blood glucose should remain in a healthy range.

- Do not use grapefruit products with this medication. If you have been using grapefruit juice or fruit do not change the amount without discussing this with your doctor or pharmacist.

- Avoid being near people who are sick or have infections.

For counseling on the biologic agents, see Autoimmune chapter.

PRACTICE CASE

PATIENT PROFILE

Patient Name	Frank Clough
Address	1020 Darby

Age	75	**Sex**	Male	**Race**	White	**Height**	5'5"	**Weight**	148lbs

Allergies	Penicillin (severe rash)

DIAGNOSES

Ulcerative Colitis (distal disease Hypertension)

MEDICATIONS

Date	No.	Prescriber	Drug & Strength	Quantity	Sig	Refills
5/15/13	76740	Greer	Atenolol 100 mg	30	1 PO daily	3
5/15/13	76743	Greer	Mesalamine 1 g supp	30	1 PR QHS	3

LAB/DIAGNOSTIC TESTS

Test	Normal Value	Results
Protein, T	6.2-8.3 g/dL	
Albumin	3.6-5.1 g/dL	
Alk Phos	33-115 units/L	
AST	10-35 units/L	
ALT	6-40 units/L	
CH, T	125-200 g/dL	
TG	<150 g/dL	
HDL	>50 g/dL	
LDL	g/dL	
GLU	65-99 mg/dL	
Na	135-146 mEq/L	
K	3.5-5.3 mEq/L	
Cl	98-110 mEq/L	
HCO3	22-28 mEq/L	
BUN	7-25 mg/dL	
Creatinine	0.6-1.2 mg/dL	
Calcium	8.6-10.2 mg/dL	
WBC	4-11 cells/mm³	
RBC	3.8-5.1 mL/mm³	
Hemoglobin	Male: 13.8- 17.2 g/dL Female: 12.1-15.1 g/dL	
Hematocrit	Male: 40.7-50.3% Female: 36.1- 44.3%	
MCHC	32-36 g/dL	
MCV	80-100 μm	
Platelet count	140-400 x 10³/mm³	

ADDITIONAL INFORMATION

Date	Notes
12/10/13	Well-controlled on mesalamine supp x 5 months. Comes in today for acute flare; reporting 5-6 diarrhea episodes/day x 3d. Stool is bloody today only. Rx for prednisone 10 mg #28, 1 QID x 7 days, return to clinic in 1 week.

Questions

1. The patient was originally prescribed mesalamine suppositories for distal disease classified as mild-moderate. Which of the following statements are correct? (Select **ALL** that apply.)

   a. Oral therapy is preferred for initial treatment.

   b. Mesalamine is available in oral and rectal (suppositories, enema) formulations.

   c. Sulfasalazine is preferred over mesalamine for distal disease.

   d. Mesalamine cannot be used in a sulfa allergy.

   e. Mesalamine is considered 1st-line therapy for distal disease.

2. Mesalamine rectal suppository counseling should include the following points: (Select **ALL** that apply.)

   a. Peel open the plastic and remove suppository prior to use.

   b. Handle unwrapped suppository as little as possible.

   c. Should be kept in the rectum for at least 1-3 hours.

   d. Lubricating gel may be used to ease application.

   e. Insert suppository just prior to a bowel movement.

3. The physician prescribed prednisone therapy for the acute flare-up. Which of the following are short-term side effects that may occur and should be conveyed to the patient? (Select **ALL** that apply.)

   a. Elevated blood glucose

   b. Elevated blood pressure

   c. Osteoporsis

   d. Changes in mood

   e. Cataracts

4. ACG guidelines recommend against steroid treatment for long-term control of IBD symptoms; however, many patients use budesonide (or prednisone) daily. Which of the following are long-term side effects that may occur and should be conveyed to the patient? (Select **ALL** that apply.)

   a. Hepatotoxicity

   b. Poor wound healing

   c. Fat redistribution

   d. Adrenal suppression

   e. Peptic ulcers

Questions 5-12 are NOT based on the above case.

5. A female patient has failed her initial therapy for Crohn's disease, which included cyclosporine and methotrexate. Her symptoms are described as severe. She is prescribed infliximab. Which of the following statements is CORRECT?

   a. She can use *Enbrel* instead.

   b. She should have been prescribed *Tysabri* prior to use of infliximab.

   c. Infliximab suppositories are the preferred formulation.

   d. This medication comes in an IV formulation only.

   e. This medication can suppress TB activation.

6. A patient has been prescribed infliximab. Which of the following tests should be ordered prior to the start of therapy? (Select **ALL** that apply.)

   a. Pulmonary function

   b. TSH and FT4

   c. CBC

   d. TB

   e. HBV

7. Which of the following describes the mechanism of action of infliximab?

   a. Chimeric monoclonal antibody against integrin

   b. Chimeric monoclonal antibody against interleukin-1

   c. Chimeric monoclonal antibody against TNF

   d. Fully humanized monoclonal antibody against integrin

   e. Fully humanized monoclonal antibody against TNF

8. Which of the following can occur with the use of infliximab? (Select **ALL** that apply.)

   a. Infusion-related reactions

   b. Renal insufficiency

   c. Antibody induction

   d. Hepatotoxicity

   e. Reactivation of latent TB

9. A physician has ordered infliximab. The pharmacist calls the prescriber to ask if she wished to pre-medicate with acetaminophen, antihistamine and steroids. Which of the following statements is CORRECT?

   a. This regimen may be used for infusion-related reactions from infliximab therapy.

   b. This regimen may be used for infusion-related reactions from amphotericin therapy.

   c. This regimen may be used for infusion-related reactions from fluconazole therapy.

   d. A and B

   e. All of the above

10. A physician has written a prescription for *Entocort EC*. Choose the appropriate therapeutic interchange:

    a. Prednisone

    b. Budesonide

    c. Azathioprine

    d. Mesalamine suppository

    e. Sulfasalazine

11. A physician has written a prescription for *Pentasa*. *Pentasa* contains the following drug:

    a. Prednisone

    b. Budesonide

    c. Azathioprine

    d. Mesalamine

    e. Sulfasalazine

Answers

1-b,e, 2-a,b,c,d, 3-a,b,d, 4-b,c,d, e, 5-d, 6-c,d,e, 7-c, 8-a,c,d,e, 9-d, 10-b, 11-d

ERECTILE DYSFUNCTION

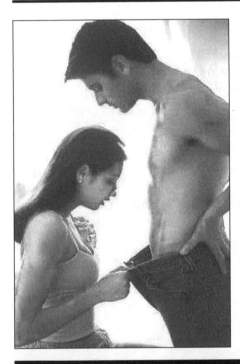

BACKGROUND

The most common direct cause of erectile dysfunction (ED) is reduced blood flow to the penis, which is commonly caused by diseases, including diabetes and metabolic syndrome, obesity, hypertension, heart disease, and nerve damage (commonly due to diabetes). ED is often the "canary in the coal mine" (an early warning) for cardiovascular disease. ED can appear first since the arteries supplying blood to the penis are smaller than those supplying blood to the heart; they can become restricted sooner than the larger vessels. Men with ED should be referred for cardiac evaluation. Hormone imbalances (such as <u>low testosterone</u>), psychological issues (including depression and <u>stress</u>) and <u>neurological</u> illness can also cause ED. Some men will need testosterone replacement therapy in order to sustain an erection. In these cases, they are likely to have other signs of low testosterone. See the Osteoporosis and Hormone

COMMON DRUGS THAT CAN CAUSE SEXUAL DYSFUNCTION

Blood pressure medications – especially beta blockers, clonidine, methyldopa

Antipsychotics – including haloperidol, chlorpromazine, fluphenazine and thioridazine

Antidepressants – particularly SSRIs and SNRIs

Atomoxetine

The BPH drugs finasteride, dutasteride (2013-warning of possible persistent sexual dysfunction after discontinuation with the these 2 agents), and silodosin

Chemotherapeutic agents that ↓ sex hormone levels, leuprolide (Lupron), etc.

Cimetidine – which blocks androgenic hormones

Opioids, chronic use, including methadone

Nicotine (smoking – the guy in the picture is a smoker)

Therapy chapter for more information on testosterone. Some men have more than one factor contributing to ED. Also, select drugs can cause ED.

PHARMACOLOGIC THERAPY

The phosphodiesterase 5 (PDE-5) inhibitors are the primary drugs used for ED in males. We are not discussing female sexual dysfunction since there is not, at present, drugs with an indication for this condition. If a patient cannot tolerate PDE-5 inhibitors (or has a contra-indication) there are a few other less effective options discussed at the end of this section. There may be surgical options, such as placement of a stent in a pelvic artery. Other patients use penile implants or penile pumps.

Note that the PDE-5 inhibitors are used under different names for pulmonary arterial hypertension (PAH) – do not use same drugs under different names concurrently (duplicate therapy). For PAH:

- Sildenafil *(Revatio)* is dosed at 20 mg three times a day (TID), (also available as 10 mg injection), taken approximately 4-6 hours apart, with or without food. Note the 20 mg dose; since this was the first PDE-5 inhibitor to become available as a generic, if used for ED more than one would be required. A common option to save costs is tablet-cutting. Vardenafil is available as a generic for ED.

- Tadalafil *(Adcirca)* is dosed at 40 mg once daily with or without food.

Note that the PDE-5 inhibitor tadalafil is used for Benign Prostatic Hypertrophy (BPH), with or without ED – do not use same drugs under different names concurrently (duplicate therapy). For BPH:

- Tadalafil *(Cialis)* is dosed at 2.5 mg once daily

Phosphodiesterase 5 (PDE-5) Inhibitors

Following sexual stimulation (which is required), PDE-5 inhibitors increase blood flow to the penis, causing an erection. They are used for problems with impotence. They do not increase desire.

DRUG	DOSING	SAFETY/SIDE EFFECTS/MONITORING
Sildenafil (*Viagra*)	25, 50, 100 mg Start at 50 mg, taken ~1 hour (0.5-4 hours) before intercourse In elderly patients (age > 65) start with 25 mg. Use this lower starting dose for patients with hepatic impairment, CrCl < 30 mL/min or if on strong CYP 3A4 inhibitors.	**CONTRAINDICATIONS** Concurrent use with nitrates **WARNINGS** Color discrimination impairment, dose-related, patients with retinitis pigmentosa may have higher risk. Hearing loss, can be sudden, with or without tinnitus/dizziness. Vision loss, rare but may be due to nonarteritic anterior ischemic optic neuropathy (NAION). Risk factors include low cup-to-disc ratio ("crowded disc"), CAD, diabetes, hypertension, hyperlipidemia, smoking, and > 50 years of age. Avoid use with known degenerative retinal disorders (e.g., retinitis pigmentosa).
Vardenafil (*Levitra, Staxyn ODT*)	2.5, 5, 10, 20 mg (*Staxyn* only 10 mg ODT, which is equiv to 10 mg *Levitra*) Start at 10 mg, taken ~1 hour before intercourse In elderly patients (age > 65) start with 5 mg. Use this lower starting dose for patients with hepatic impairment, CrCl < 30 mL/min or if on strong CYP 3A4 inhibitors.	Hypotension, due to vasodilation, higher risk if resting BP < 90/50 mmHg, fluid depletion, or autonomic dysfunction. Caution with other agents that cause hypotension, such as alpha blockers and BP drugs. Priapism, instruct to seek emergency medical care if erection > 4 hours. **SIDE EFFECTS** Headache, flushing, dyspepsia, color vision changes (blurred vision, increased sensitivity to light), epistaxis, erythemia, diarrhea, myalgia
Tadalafil (*Cialis*)	2.5, 5, 10, 20 mg Start at 10 mg, with or without food, taken ~ 1 hour before intercourse or 2.5-5 mg daily (for men who use *Cialis* > 2 times per week). ↓ dose to 5-10 mg with renal impairment or moderate liver impairment. Do not use if CrCl < 30 mL/min, or if severe liver impairment.	**NOTES** Sildenafil and Vardenafil: With all, use lower doses if concurrent strong CYP 3A4 Inhibitor; these drugs are 3A4 substrates, *Stendra* states not to use with strong CYP 3A4 inhibitors and use lower dose with moderate CYP 3A4 Inhibitors.
Avanafil (*Stendra*)	50, 100, 200 mg Start at 100 mg, with or without food, 30 minutes prior to intercourse Do not use with severe renal or liver impairment. Do not use with strong CYP 3A4 inhibitors and use lower dose with moderate CYP 3A4 inhibitors.	Best when taken on an empty stomach, avoid with fatty food (tadalafil is with or without food).

Drug Interactions

- PDE-5 inhibitors Are contraindicated with nitrates.

  ❏ Concurrent use of nitrate medications [any nitroglycerin-containing drug, including *Nitrostat*, *Nitrolingual*, isosorbide dinitrate-hydralazine *(BiDil)*, others] increases the potential for excessively low blood pressure. Taking nitrates is an absolute contraindication to the use of these medicines. These include the illicit drugs such as amyl nitrate and butyl nitrate ("poppers").

■ If a patient with ED has taken a PDE-5 inhibitor and then develops angina, nitroglycerin should not be used until after 12 h for avanafil, 24 h for sildenafil or vardenafil and after 48 h for tadalafil. Other anti-anginal and anti-ischemic therapies may be used – such as beta blockers, calcium channel blockers, aspirin, morphine, statins and percutaneous coronary intervention. (Sometimes nitrates are used in an acute emergency, despite this warning, with careful monitoring.)

Caution with PDE-5 Inhibitor and Concurrent Alpha Blocker Therapy

Wording from the PI, which is the same for selective and non-selective alpha-antagonists:

■ PDE-5 inhibitors may enhance the hypotensive effect of alpha$_1$-antagonist. Ensure patient is stable on one agent prior to initiating the other, and always initiate combination using the lowest possible dose of the drug being added. When tadalafil is used for treatment of BPH, concurrent alpha 1-blockers are not recommended. (Not in package insert: preferably, the selective alpha 1-blockers should be chosen, which do not cause as much hypotensive effect.)

If a person cannot or will not use PDE-5 inhibitors, there are several alternatives, however they have methods of delivery that limit the acceptance of these options.

Alternative Agents

DRUG	ROUTE	SAFETY/SIDE EFFECTS/MONITORING
Intracavernosal alprostadil *(Caverject)*	Injected via syringe into penis Causes erection 5-10 minutes after injection, lasts ~1 hr, max 3x/week and 1x/day	**BLACK BOX WARNING** Risk of apnea when used in neonates. **SIDE EFFECTS** Penile pain, headache, dizziness, hematoma, priapism **NOTES** Refrigerate vials, reconstitute prior to use. Syncope can occur within 1 hour of administration, most commonly with concurrent antihypertensives.
Transurethral alprostadil *(MUSE)* Refrigerate	Inserted into urethra (pellets)	**SIDE EFFECTS** Penile pain, headache, dizziness, priapism **NOTES** Alprostadil formulations are Pregnancy Category X/C *(Muse)*.
Tri-Mix gel (papaverine, phentolamine, and alprostadil) – compounded – not FDA approved	Gel inserted into urethra at a dose of 500 mcg	**SIDE EFFECTS** Penile pain

PRACTICE CASE

Jim is a 60 year-old African American male patient who has presented to his physician with complaints of impotence. He cannot sustain an erection. This has caused performance anxiety, which has worsened the situation. His medical conditions include hypertension, anxiety/low mood, obesity and prostate enlargement. The physician has written him a prescription for sildenafil 50 mg to be taken 1 hour prior to sexual activity.

CATEGORY	
Medications	Tamsulosin 0.4 mg daily
	Inderal LA 160 mg daily
	Fosinopril 10 mg BID
	Sertraline 100 mg daily
	Vitamin D 200 IU daily
	Aspirin 325 mg daily
	Acetaminophen 325 mg 1-2 tablets PRN headache
Vitals	Height 5'9", weight 210 lbs, blood pressure today 118/82 mmHg, HR 90 BPM.

Questions

1. Is sildenafil contraindicated in this patient? (Select **ALL** that apply.)

   a. Yes, the combination of tamsulosin and sildenafil is contraindicated.
   b. No, but he must be cautioned about dizziness, light headedness and fainting.
   c. No, but he has to begin sildenafil at 12.5 mg once daily.
   d. The tamsulosin should be changed to doxazosin; this is a safer combination.
   e. No, but he has to begin sildenafil at 25 mg once daily.

2. Which of the following medications could be contributing to Jim's problem with erectile dysfunction? (Select **ALL** that apply.)

   a. *Inderal LA*
   b. Sertraline
   c. Vitamin D
   d. Aspirin
   e. Acetaminophen

3. The pharmacist should call the physician and recommend possible medication changes that could reduce or eliminate the ED problem. Reasonable suggestions could include: (Select **ALL** that apply.)

   a. Change the sertraline to a medication that is not in the SSRI or SNRI class.
   b. Change the fosinopril to losartan.
   c. Change propranolol to a different class of medication, or try a trial with metoprolol.
   d. Change the fosinopril to amlodipine.
   e. Change the propranolol to furosemide.

4. If Jim begins sildenafil therapy, he should be counseled concerning the risk of priapism. Select the correct counseling statement:

   a. If you sustain an erection that lasts more than 4 hours, you should stop using the medicine. The erection will go away in about 24 hours.

   b. If you sustain an erection that lasts more than 4 hours, you should stop using the medicine and take 25 mg of over-the-counter diphenhydramine. The erection will go away in about 24 hours.

   c. If you sustain an erection that lasts more than 4 hours, you should stop using the medicine and rest in bed until the erection goes away, which takes about 4-6 hours.

   d. If you sustain an erection that lasts more than 2 hours, you will need to get medical help right away. Priapism must be treated as soon as possible or it can cause lasting damage to the penis.

   e. If you sustain an erection that lasts more than 4 hours, you will need to get medical help right away. Priapism must be treated as soon as possible or it can cause lasting damage to the penis.

Questions 5-10 do not apply to the above case.

5. A patient is using tadalafil three times weekly. He uses 10 mg, taken 1 hour before sexual intercourse. He has asked the physician to change him to the daily form of the medicine, since he uses it more than twice weekly. Choose the correct dosing range for daily tadalafil when used for ED:

   a. 0.125-2.5 mg daily
   b. 2.5-5 mg daily
   c. 5-10 mg daily
   d. 10-15 mg daily
   e. This medicine cannot be used daily

6. The PDE-5 inhibitors require lower doses, and in some cases avoidance, when a patient is using certain drugs, including saquinavir and clarithromycin. This is due to the following reason:

   a. These are strong CYP 3A4 inducers; they could cause the PDE-5 inhibitor level to decrease to a dangerous level.

   b. These are strong CYP 3A4 inhibitors; they could cause the PDE-5 inhibitor level to increase to a dangerous level.

   c. These are strong CYP 3A4 inducers; they could cause the PDE-5 inhibitor level to increase to a dangerous level.

   d. These are strong CYP 3A4 inhibitors; they could cause the PDE-5 inhibitor level to decrease to a dangerous level.

   e. There is no interaction between PDE-5 inhibitor's and these medications.

7. Jon is a 58 year-old male with dyslipidemia, type 2 diabetes, hypertension and coronary heart disease. His medications include insulin glargine 40 units QHS, metformin 1 g BID, lisinopril-HCT 20-12.5 mg daily, vardenafil 10 mg as-needed, clopidogrel 75 mg daily and aspirin 81 mg EC daily. He went to his doctor with several medical complaints, including a dry, intermittent cough. The physician discontinued the lisinopril-HCT and gave him prescriptions for valsartan-HCT, *Restasis* and nitroglycerin SL 0.4 mg. Which of the following action should the pharmacist take?

   a. Do not fill nitroglycerin SL
   b. Do not fill *Restasis*
   c. Do not fill valsartan-HCT
   d. Suggest to the physician that irbesartan-HCT would be a safer option than valsartan-HCT.
   e. Suggest to the physician that *BiDil* would be a safer option than nitroglycerin SL.

8. A young man is having difficulty sustaining an erection because he does not find his girlfriend to be sexually arousing but he does not wish to leave her because she has a lot of money. He has not had a problem with sexual dysfunction previously. Is sildenafil indicated in this case?

   a. Sildenafil is not indicated.
   b. Yes, the drug will work, but he should break up with this woman.
   c. Yes, the drug will work but at a higher dose.
   d. He would be better off using tadalafil, since it is a more effective agent.
   e. He would be better off using vardenafil, since it is a more effective agent.

9. A physician has written a prescription for *Levitra*. Which of the following represents an acceptable therapeutic substitution?

   a. Sildenafil
   b. Vardenafil
   c. Tadalafil
   d. Alprostadil
   e. Lansoprazole

10. A physician has written a prescription for *Cialis*. Which of the following represents an acceptable therapeutic substitution?

   a. Sildenafil
   b. Vardenafil
   c. Tadalafil
   d. Alprostadil
   e. Lansoprazole

Answers

1-b,e, 2-a,b, 3-a,c, 4-e, 5-b, 6-b, 7-a, 8-a, 9-b, 10-c

63

BENIGN PROSTATIC HYPERPLASIA (BPH)

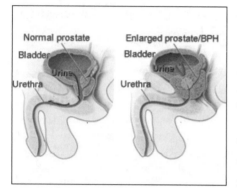

Normal prostate | Enlarged prostate/BPH
Bladder | Bladder
Urine | Urine
Urethra | Urethra

GUIDELINES

Update on AUA Guideline on the Management of Benign Prostatic Hyperplasia. The Journal of Urology 2011;185:1793-1803.

American Urological Association Practice Guidelines Committee. AUA guidelines on management of benign prostatic hyperplasia 2003. Chapter 1: Diagnosis and treatment recommendations. The Journal of Urology 2003;170:530-547.

BACKGROUND

The prostate is a walnut-sized gland that surrounds the urethra at the base of the bladder. As part of the male reproductive system, the main function of the prostate is to secrete slightly alkaline fluid that becomes part of the seminal fluid carrying sperm.

The prostate is dependent on androgens (mainly testosterone) for development and maintenance of size and function. Testosterone is metabolized to dihydrotestosterone (DHT) by 5 alpha-reductase. DHT is responsible for normal and hyperplastic growth (increase in the number of cells). Benign prostatic hyperplasia (BPH) results from overgrowth of the stromal and epithelial cells of the prostate gland. The enlarged gland contributes to lower urinary tract symptoms (LUTS) via direct bladder outlet obstruction (BOO) and increased smooth muscle tone and resistance. As the prostate enlarges, the layer of tissue surrounding it stops it from expanding, causing the gland to press against the urethra like a clamp on a garden hose. The bladder wall becomes thicker and irritated. The bladder begins to contract even when it contains small amounts of urine, causing more frequent urination. Eventually, the bladder weakens and loses the ability to empty itself. Interestingly, there is not a direct linear correlation between prostate size and symptoms; some men are more bothered even with a smaller prostate size, while others with a larger prostate are not as symptomatic. The enlargement does not usually cause problems until later in life with a peak incidence around 65 years of age. When the prostate becomes larger, prostate specific antigen (PSA) levels can increase; yet, BPH does not increase the risk of prostate cancer.

SYMPTOMS/COMPLICATIONS

The signs and symptoms of BPH are mainly LUTS which include difficulty holding urine (storage) and emptying the bladder (voiding). These disturbances significantly impact the quality of life for the patient. LUTS can include:

- Hesitancy, intermittency, straining or weak stream of urine

- Urinary urgency and leaking or dribbling

- Incomplete emptying of the bladder (bladder always feels full)

- Urinary frequency, especially nocturia (urination at night)

- Bladder outlet obstruction (BOO)

BPH rarely causes more severe symptoms – but if the blockage is severe, the urine could back up into the kidneys and result in acute renal failure. Urinary tract infections can also be present, but are uncommon in men.

DIAGNOSIS

Prostate cancer symptoms can be similar to the symptoms of BPH. Diagnosis requires a careful patient medical history including surgeries and trauma, current medications including herbal and OTC drugs, focused physical exam including a Digital Rectal Exam (DRE), and urinalysis and serum Prostate Specific Antigen (PSA) to rule out conditions other than BPH (e.g., prostate or bladder cancer, neurogenic bladder, others). Patient may be asked to complete a voiding diary as well to better tailor therapy. PSA, a protein produced by prostate cells, is frequently ↑ in prostate cancer, however, it can also be increased in other conditions including BPH. Note that the recommendations for routine prostate cancer screening have changed (they will be done less frequently than in the past); see Oncology chapter.

DRUGS THAT WORSEN BPH
Decongestants (e.g., pseudo-ephrine)
Anticholinergics (e.g., benztropine)
Antihistamines (e.g., diphenhydramine, chlorpheniramine)
TCAs, phenothiazines and other drugs with anticholinergic properties
Caffeine (can worsen symptoms)
Diuretics (increase urination–be sure to take early in the day to limit nocturia)
SNRIs (affect urethral resistance)
Testosterone products

TREATMENT

The patient's perception of the severity of BPH symptoms guides selection of the treatment modality in a patient. Validated questionnaires such as the AUA Symptom Score, are commonly used to quantify symptoms. The scoring system rates how bothersome the symptoms are to the patient, with higher scores indicating more severe or bothersome symptoms. Treatment options can include watchful waiting, pharmacologic therapy and surgical intervention. Choice of treatment is a shared decision-making process between the patient and the clinician. Mild disease is generally treated with watchful waiting, which entails having the patient return for reassessment yearly. Moderate/severe disease is generally treated with medications, a minimally invasive procedure, or surgery such as transurethral resection of the prostate (TURP). Medications include alpha blockers (selective and non-selective), alone or in combination with a 5 alpha-reductase inhibitor. The 5 alpha-reductase inhibitors should not be used in men with LUTS secondary to BPH without prostatic enlargement (as these medications work by decreasing prostate size). Peripheral-acting anticholinergic agents used for overactive bladder (such as tolterodine) are sometimes a reasonable option for men without an elevated post void residual (PRV) urine and when LUTS are predominately irritative. If anticholinergics are used, PVR should be < 250-300 mL (anticholinergics are discussed in the Overactive Bladder chapter). Another treatment option is using the phosphodiesterase-5 (PDE-5) inhibitor tadalifil. This can be used in men with BPH alone, and can be an attractive option for men with both BPH and erectile dysfunction (ED); the dose is sufficient for both indications. Tadalafil, in combination with an alpha blocker (especially a non-selective agent) would pose risk for additive hypotension and orthostasis in an elderly male.

Historically, alpha blockers have been considered the standard BPH drug treatment. They are used alone in mild symptoms, and often with a 5 alpha-reductase inhibitor with moderate symptoms. Recently, tamsulosin (the most popular alpha-blocker) has been associated with floppy iris syndrome, a condition that makes cataract surgery difficult to complete safely. Cataracts are common in elderly patients, and the use of alpha blockers increases the risk itself. The important thing is to let the ophthalmologist know if a patient has ever taken an alpha-blocker. This has been a "big news" item this past year and many men are asking pharmacists about the safety of their BPH medicines.

Natural Products

Saw palmetto is used for BPH, but it is rated as "possibly ineffective" by The Natural Medicines Database due to contradictory and inconsistent data. If men wish to try saw palmetto, they should be counseled to be seen first to rule out the possibility of prostate cancer. Pygeum is another natural product and it is rated as "possibly effective". Do not recommend a pygeum product unless it has been harvested ethically; ripping the bark off the trees to extract pygeum is not sustainable. Other natural products rated as "possibly effective" are beta-sitosterol (comes as supplements, in margarine substitutes, in African wild potato extract products, in pumpkin seed and in soy and red clover) and rye grass pollen. Lycopene is used for prostate cancer prevention, however, there is no good evidence for taking the supplement for this purpose. Pharmacists should not recommend natural products until the patient has seen a physician; it is not prudent to recommend a product that could be masking cancer symptoms. Although the symptoms will primarily be benign, the small risk of prostate cancer must be considered.

Alpha Blockers

These agents inhibit alpha-1 adrenergic receptors and relax the smooth muscle of the bladder neck reducing bladder outlet obstruction and improving urinary flow.

DRUG	DOSING	SAFETY/SIDE EFFECTS/MONITORING

Non-Selective Alpha-1 Blockers

DRUG	DOSING	SAFETY/SIDE EFFECTS/MONITORING
Terazosin *(Hytrin)*	Start at 1 mg at bedtime; titrate slowly to effect – generally 10 mg QHS (may ↑ to 20 mg QHS)	**WARNINGS** Orthostatic hypotension/syncope: typically with first dose, if therapy is interrupted for several days, dosage is increased too rapidly or another antihypertensive agent or PDE-5 inhibitor is started Floppy iris syndrome can occur during cataract surgery Priapism–seek medical attention if lasting > 4 hours **SIDE EFFECTS** Dizziness, fatigue, orthostatic hypotension, headache **MONITORING** BP, PSA, urinary symptoms **NOTES** The non-selective agents are often given QHS to help minimize the initial "first dose" effect of orthostasis/dizziness. This requires careful counseling (see below) as the man likely has nocturia, where getting up at night to use the bathroom with dizziness and orthostasis can be dangerous.
Doxazosin (*Cardura, Cardura XL*)	IR: start at 1 mg; titrate slowly up to 4-8 mg daily, usually given at bedtime XL: Start at 4 mg daily with breakfast; titrate to a max of 8 mg daily	There are 3 types of alpha receptors: 1A (prostate primarily has these receptors), 1B, and 1D; terazosin and doxazosin are non-selective and this results in more side effects (orthostasis, dizziness, fatigue, HA) than the selective agents. Alpha blockers start to work right away, but 4-6 weeks may be required to assess whether beneficial effects have been achieved; they do not shrink the prostate and do not change PSA levels. Take *Cardura XL* with breakfast.
Prazosin *(Minipress)* Off label	0.5 mg BID; titrate slowly to 2 mg BID	

Alpha Blockers Continued

DRUG	DOSING	SAFETY/SIDE EFFECTS/MONITORING
Selective Alpha$_{1A}$ Blockers		
Tamsulosin **(Flomax)** + dutasteride *(Jalyn)*	0.4 mg daily, 30 min after the same meal each day; max 0.8 mg daily	**CONTRAINDICATIONS** Concurrent use with strong 3A4 inhibitors, moderate to severe hepatic impairment (with alfuzosin and silodosin); severe renal impairment (CrCl < 30 mL/min with silodosin) **WARNINGS** Orthostatic hypotension/syncope: typically with first dose, if therapy is interrupted for several days, dosage is increased too rapidly or another antihypertensive agent or PDE-5 inhibitor is started Floppy iris syndrome can occur during cataract surgery Priapism–seek medical attention if lasting > 4 hours
Alfuzosin *(Uroxatral)*	10 mg daily, immediately after same meal each day CrCl < 30 mL/min: use with caution	**SIDE EFFECTS** Dizziness, fatigue, hypotension, headache Abnormal ejaculation (esp. with tamsulosin and silodosin). These agents are selective for alpha 1A receptors with ↓ incidence and severity of orthostatic hypotension and dizziness. **MONITORING** BP, PSA, urinary symptoms **NOTES** Do not use alfuzosin in patients at risk for QT prolongation – prolongs QT-interval
Silodosin *(Rapaflo)*	8 mg daily with a meal CrCl 30-50 mL/min: 4 mg daily CrCl < 30 mL/min: CI	Silodosin can cause retrograde ejaculation (stops with drug discontinuation) (28%) Alpha blockers – used for bladder outlet obstruction in women (off label)

Alpha Blocker Drug Interactions

■ Caution is advised when PDE-5 inhibitors *(Viagra/Revatio, Cialis/Adcirca, Levitra/Staxyn, Stendra)* are co-administered with alpha blockers. PDE-5 inhibitors and alpha blockers are both vasodilators with BP lowering effects. When they are used in combination, there will be an additive effect on BP. In some patients, concomitant use of these two drug classes can lower BP significantly leading to symptomatic hypotension (dizziness, light headedness, fainting). Patients should be stable on alpha-blocker therapy before PDE-5 inhibition is initiated and the lowest doses of the PDE-5 inhibitor should be used when initiating therapy. Conversely, if a patient is already taking an optimal dose of a PDE-5 inhibitor and an alpha blocker needs to be started, the alpha blocker should be started at the lowest dose, and the selective agents will be preferred (over the non-selective agents).

- Use caution with any hypotensive condition or with other drugs that lower BP.

- Tamsulosin, alfuzosin and silodosin are major CYP 3A4 substrates; avoid use with strong 3A4 inhibitors (ritonavir, itraconazole, ketoconazole, clarithromycin, others).

- Silodosin cannot be used with strong P-gp inhibitors, such as cyclosporine.

- Alfuzosin: can cause QT-prolongation; do not use with other QT-prolongating agents. Use with caution in patients with known QT prolongation (congenital or acquired).

5 Alpha-Reductase Inhibitors

These agents inhibit the 5 alpha-reductase enzyme which blocks the conversion of testosterone to dihydrotestosterone (DHT). This class of medications is indicated for the treatment of symptomatic BPH in men <u>with an enlarged prostate</u> to improve symptoms, decrease the risk of acute urinary retention, and decrease the risk of need for surgery including TURP or prostatectomy.

DRUG	DOSING	SAFETY/SIDE EFFECTS/MONITORING
Finasteride (Proscar) Affects 5α-receptors type 2 For hair loss (*Propecia* 1 mg daily)	5 mg daily	**CONTRAINDICATIONS** Women of child-bearing potential, pregnancy, children **WARNINGS** May increase the risk of high-grade prostate cancer. **SIDE EFFECTS** Impotence, ↓ libido, ejaculation disturbances, breast enlargement and tenderness, rash – sexual SEs ↓ with time and approach placebo levels at one year of use in some men; in others they persist **MONITORING** PSA, urinary symptoms
Dutasteride (Avodart) + tamsulosin (*Jalyn*) Affects both types of 5α-receptors (types 1 and 2), may have better efficacy; not proven.	0.5 mg daily	**NOTES** Pregnancy Category X Pregnant women should not handle nor take these meds: can be absorbed through skin, can be detrimental to fetus, semen of male taking this drug may present a danger 6 months (or longer) of treatment may be required for maximal efficacy Usually used in men with larger prostate size (40+ grams) or more severe symptoms; due to the slow-onset, often given with α-blocker 5 alpha-reductase inhibitors shrink the prostate and ↓ PSA levels

5 Alpha-Reductase Inhibitor Drug Interactions

- Finasteride and dutasteride are minor CYP 3A4 substrates; strong CYP 3A4 inhibitors may increase levels.

- Do not use finasteride in a patient using *Propecia* for hair loss; refer to prescriber.

Phosphodiesterase-5 (PDE-5) Inhibitor

PDE-5 mediated reduction in smooth muscle and endothelial cell proliferation, decreased nerve activity and increased smooth muscle relaxation and tissue perfusion of the prostate and bladder.

DRUG	DOSING	SAFETY/SIDE EFFECTS/MONITORING
Tadalafil *(Cialis)*	5 mg daily, same time each day CrCl 30-50 mL/min: 2.5 mg CrCl < 30 mL/min: do not use. Use 2.5 mg if using strong CYP 3A4 inhibitor.	**CONTRAINDICATIONS** Concurrent use of nitrates **WARNINGS** Rare: may cause color discrimination; sudden vision loss in one of both eyes – may be a sign of nonarteritic anterior ischemic optic neuropathy (NAION); decrease or a loss of hearing; priapism; concomitant use with alpha blockers is not recommended–discontinue alpha-blocker at least 1 day before initiating tadalafil. Please refer to Erectile Dysfunction chapter for a complete list **SIDE EFFECTS** Headache, flushing, dyspepsia, color vision changes, blurred vision, increased sensitivity to light, epistaxis, erythemia, diarrhea, myalgia **MONITORING** BP, PSA, urinary symptoms

For drug interactions/counseling for tadalafil, please refer to Erectile Dysfunction chapter.

Alpha Blocker Counseling

- Especially for non-selective agents, such as doxazosin: This medicine can cause a sudden drop in blood pressure. You may feel dizzy, faint or "light-headed," especially after you stand up from a lying or sitting position. This is more likely to occur after you have taken the first few doses or if you increase your dose, but can occur at any time while you are taking the drug. It can also occur if you stop taking the drug and then restart treatment. When you get up from a sitting or lying position, go slowly and hold onto the bed rail or chair until you are steady on your feet.

- Your blood pressure should be checked when you are sitting or lying down and standing.

- If you take the medicine at bedtime, but need to get up from bed to go to the bathroom, get up slowly and cautiously and hold onto the bed rail or chair until you are steady on your feet.

- You should not drive or do any hazardous tasks until you are used to the effects of the medicine. If you begin to feel dizzy, sit or lie down until you feel better.

- This medicine can cause side effects that may impair your thinking or reactions. Be careful if you drive or do anything that requires you to be awake and alert.

- Drinking alcohol can make the dizziness worse, and increase night-time urination if taken close to bedtime.

- Taking cold and allergy medications such as decongestants and antihistamines can make your symptoms worsen. Discuss what to use with your pharmacist if you need assistance.

- Tell your doctor (or ophthalmologist) about the use of this medication before cataract surgery. The doctor will want to know if you have ever taken this medication.

- Rarely, this medication can cause a painful erection which cannot be relieved by having sex. If this happens, get medical help right away. If it is not treated, you may not be able to get an erection in the future.

Tamsulosin
- The dose should be administered approximately half an hour following the same meal each day.

Alfuzosin
- Do not crush, chew, or break the alfuzosin tablets. Swallow them whole.
- Take the same time each day with food (food increases absorption).

Silodosin
- The most common side effect seen with this medication is an orgasm with reduced or no semen (dry orgasm). This side effect does not pose a safety concern and is reversible with discontinuation of the drug (lower risk with tamsulosin).
- Take the same time each day with food.

5 Alpha-Reductase Inhibitor Counseling
- This medicine can take several months or longer to help reduce the BPH symptoms. It is effective, it just takes awhile to work because it shrinks the prostate slowly. If your doctor has given you another medicine called an alpha-blocker, that medicine works faster.

- Women who are or may become pregnant should not handle the tablets. (These drugs can cause birth defects to a developing male fetus – Pregnancy Category X). The semen of males using the medicine may also be harmful.

- Your doctor may perform blood tests or other forms of monitoring during treatment with finasteride. One of the tests that may be performed is called PSA (prostate-specific antigen). This drug can reduce the amount of PSA in the blood.

- Tell your doctor if you experience any of these side effects: decreased sex drive, decreased volume of ejaculate, impotence, breast tenderness or enlargement.

- Taking cold and allergy medications such as decongestants and antihistamines can make your symptoms worsen. Discuss what to use with your pharmacist if you need assistance.

64

OVERACTIVE BLADDER

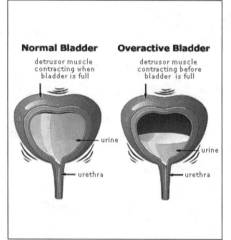

Normal Bladder

detrusor muscle
contracting when
bladder is full

urine

urethra

Overactive Bladder

detrusor muscle
contracting before
bladder is full

urine

urethra

GUIDELINE

Diagnosis and Treatment of OverActive Bladder (Non-neurogenic) In Adults: AUA/SUFU Guideline. J Urol. 2012 Dec;188(6 Suppl):2455-63. doi: 10.1016/j.juro.2012.09.079. (accessed 2013 Nov 17).

BACKGROUND

Overactive bladder (OAB) is a common, disabling urinary disorder that affects many people (1 in 6 people or over 33 million Americans). It is not a normal sign of aging. In overactive bladder, the detrusor muscle contracts frequently and before the bladder is full, leading to the classic symptoms of:

- urinary urgency (a sudden, compelling desire to pass urine which is difficult to defer), and

- urinary frequency (voiding ≥ 8 times in a 24 hour period), and

- nocturia (≥ 2 awakenings to void per night)

Overactive bladder can lead to urinary urge incontinence. About 1/3 of patients have incontinent episodes (OAB wet) and the other 2/3 of patients do not have incontinence (OAB dry).

IMPLICATIONS OF OVERACTIVE BLADDER

Many co-morbidities exist in patients with OAB including falls and fractures, skin breakdown and infections, UTIs, depression, and sexual dysfunction. Due to embarrassment of their condition, there are many social implications of OAB including low self-esteem, lack of sexual intimacy, social and physical isolation, sleep disturbances, limits on travel and dependence on caregivers; all leading to a reduced quality of life. Many patients become dehydrated because they limit their fluid intake. The cost of pads and adult diapers can be a huge financial burden.

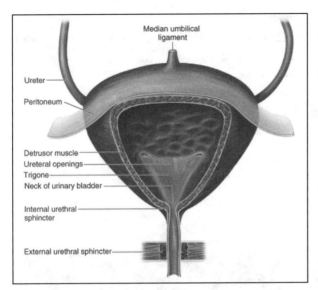

PATHOPHYSIOLOGY

The bladder is commonly referred to as a "balloon" with an outer muscular layer known as the detrusor muscle. The detrusor muscle and the bladder outlet functions are neurologically coordinated to store and expel urine. The detrusor muscle is innervated mainly by the parasympathetic nervous system while the bladder neck is innervated by the sympathetic nervous system. The internal sphincter is also innervated by the sympathetic nervous system and the external sphincter is innervated by the somatic nervous system. Both voluntary and involuntary contractions of the detrusor muscle are mediated by activation of muscarinic receptors via acetylcholine. Of the five known muscarinic receptor subtypes, the human bladder is comprised of M2 and M3 receptors (in a 3:1 ratio). It is the M3 receptor that is responsible for both emptying contractions as well as involuntary bladder contractions of incontinence. In overactive bladder, the detrusor muscle is hyperactive (overactive), causing the symptoms of frequent micturitions, urgency, nocturia, and/or incontinence.

Risk Factors for Overactive Bladder

- Age > 40 years

- Diabetes

- Restricted mobility

- Obesity

- Prior vaginal delivery

- Neurologic conditions (e.g., stroke, Parkinson's disease, dementia)

- Hysterectomy

- Drugs that can increase incontinence [e.g., ACE inhibitors (due to cough), alcohol, cholinesterase inhibitors, diuretics]

- Pelvic injury

FORMS OF URINARY INCONTINENCE

Functional
There is no abnormality in the bladder, but the patient may be cognitively, socially, or physically impaired thus hindering him or her from access to a toilet (e.g., patients in wheelchairs).

Overflow
Leakage that occurs when the quantity of urine stored in the bladder exceeds its capacity, often occurring without the urge to urinate (BPH is the most common cause).

Stress
Urine leaks out during any form of exertion (e.g., exercise, coughing, sneezing, laughing, etc.) as a result of pressure on the bladder.

Urge
Patient cannot hold in urine long enough to reach the toilet and is associated with neuropathy; often found in those who have diabetes, strokes, dementia, Parkinson disease, or multiple sclerosis (although people without co-morbidities are affected also).

Mixed
Combination of urge and stress incontinence

Approximately 1/3 of incontinence is stress, 1/3 is urge and 1/3 is mixed.

Diagnosis

Diagnosis requires a careful patient history including co-morbid conditions, duration of symptoms, baseline symptoms, fluid intake and type of fluids (with or without caffeine), a physical exam and urinalysis. Validated questionnaires such as the Urinary Distress Inventory (UDI) or the Overactive Bladder Questionnaire (OAB-q) are used to quantify symptoms. Patients may be required to complete a bladder diary to accurately measure intake and voiding information. A urine culture and post-void residual assessment may be performed to rule out other causes.

NON-PHARMACOLOGIC THERAPY

Behavioral Therapies

Behavioral treatments are considered first-line to improve OAB symptoms by changing patient behavior and/or their environment. Behavioral treatments include bladder training, delayed or scheduled voiding, pelvic floor muscle exercises (Kegel exercises), urge control techniques (distraction, self-assertions), fluid management, dietary changes (avoiding bladder irritants), weight loss and other lifestyle changes. Behavior therapies can be combined with other treatment modalities such as medications. Surgical intervention should be reserved for the rare non-neurogenic patient who has failed all other therapeutic options and whose symptoms are intolerable.

> **PELVIC FLOOR MUSCLE EXERCISES**
>
> **Pelvic Floor Muscle ("Kegel") Exercises**
> These exercises are done to strengthen the pelvic floor muscles and can diminish OAB symptoms.
>
> Proper technique is key and this means finding the correct muscles. Instruct the patient to imagine that they are trying to stop urination midstream. Squeeze the muscles they would use. If they sense a "pulling" feeling, those are the correct muscles for pelvic exercise.
>
> Pull in the pelvic muscles and hold for a count of 3. Then relax for a count of 3. Work up to 3 sets of 10 kegel exercises per day. Do these exercises 3 times a day to strengthen pelvic floor muscles and reduce wetting episodes.

PHARMACOLOGIC THERAPY

Behavioral and drug therapies are often used in combination in clinical practice to optimize patient symptom control and quality of life. Anticholinergic drugs are second-line therapy. These agents are antagonists of the muscarinic receptor and block acetylcholine, thus limiting contractions of the detrusor muscle. Patients with a post void residual (PVR) > 250-300 mL should not be started on an anticholinergic agent. Extended-release formulations are preferred over immediate-release formulations due to a lower rate of dry mouth. More selective (for the M3 receptor) anticholinergic agents (solifenacin, darifenacin, fesoterodine) have less CNS side effects over the nonselective, older agents such as oxybutynin. If a patient fails an antimuscarinic agent or develops an adverse effect, it is recommended to try at least one other anticholinergic agent or a dose adjustment before moving on to third-line recommendations, including onabotulinumtoxin A, nerve stimulation or surgical correction. Indwelling catheters are used only as a last resort in select patients. Additive antimuscarinic drugs should be avoided, if possible.

CHOLINERGIC & ANTICHOLINERGIC PHARMACOLOGY

Cholinergic drugs act like acetylcholine at the acetylcholine receptors and cause the "SLUD" symptoms: Salivation, Lacrimation (tearing), Urination and Diarrhea. The classic cholinergic drug bethanechol is used occasionally to treat urinary retention by increasing urination, which occurs with neurogenic bladder. Another cholinergic agent is pilocarpine, which is sometimes used for dry mouth (to increase salivation).*

Anticholinergics have the opposite effect: they block acetylcholine, which is present in the periphery (outside of the CNS) and centrally (inside the CNS) and will cause the anti-SLUD peripheral symptoms of dry mouth, dry/blurry vision, urinary retention and constipation and the central anticholinergic effects such as sedation and dizziness.

This is how diphenhydramine, which blocks acetylcholine in the CNS, works as a sedative. Diphenhydramine has to travel through the periphery (to get to the CNS) and will cause the peripheral side effects as well, including urinary retention. However, it is not an appropriate choice for an elderly patient because of the central effects, and the peripheral effects that are not desired.

When incontinence drugs were first developed the primary goal was to use agents that had low CNS penetration; therefore, exhibiting fewer of the central side effects. Oxybutynin is an older drug in this class and the prototype peripheral agent. Later on, drugs were designed to be specific for the M3 muscarinic receptor, the subtype present in high density on the bladder wall (the detrusor muscle). When this muscle contracts, there is a sudden urge to urinate; blocking the M_3 receptor can reduce the sudden urge to urinate. Darifenacin is an example of an M_3-specific drug. Unfortunately, the M_3 receptor is found in high density on the salivary glands, causing dry mouth when this receptor is blocked. The pharmacist must help the patient to manage dry mouth, which is quite uncomfortable and increases the degree of dental decay. It is possible to reduce this side effect with the use of longer-acting agents (over IR forms) and with drugs that bypass first-pass (patch and gel) since the drug metabolites contribute to the dry mouth. With the long-acting formulations, there are lower "peaks" and, thus, lower side effects. When the drug peaks there is more drug to hit the "right" receptors (producing the desired effect) and the "wrong" receptors (causing side effects).

* *Another way to increase acetylcholine is to block the enzyme that breaks it down: these are the acetylcholinesterase inhibitors, which are used for dementia and to reverse neuromuscular blockade.*

Anticholinergic Drugs Used in OAB

These agents are antimuscarinic receptor blockers that inhibit the binding of acetylcholine, thus limiting contractions of the detrusor muscle.

DRUG	DOSING	SAFETY/SIDE EFFECTS/MONITORING
Oxybutynin	5 mg PO BID-TID	**CONTRAINDICATIONS** Urinary retention, bladder outlet obstruction, gastric retention, decreased gastric motility and uncontrolled narrow angle glaucoma
Oxybutynin XL (Ditropan XL)	5-30 mg PO daily	
Oxybutynin patch (Oxytrol, Oxytrol for Women – OTC)	3.9 mg daily (Rx patch is dosed every 3-4 days; OTC patch is every 4 days)	**WARNINGS** Anticholinergics may cause agitation, confusion, drowsiness, dizziness, hallucinations, headache, and/or blurred vision, which may impair physical or mental abilities; patients must be cautioned about performing tasks which require mental alertness (e.g., operating machinery or driving).
Oxybutynin 10% topical (Gelnique)	Apply contents of 1 sachet to intact, dry skin (gel) daily	
Oxybutynin 3% topical (Gelnique 3%)	3 pumps daily	
Tolterodine (Detrol)	1-2 mg PO BID	**SIDE EFFECTS** Dizziness and drowsiness (greatest with oxybutynin and less with the newer, selective agents), xerostomia (dry mouth), constipation, dry eyes/blurred vision, urinary retention, application site reactions (with topicals and patch)
Tolterodine ER (Detrol LA)	2-4 mg PO daily	
Trospium (Sanctura, Sanctura XR)	20 mg BID or 60 mg XR daily and take on empty stomach	**NOTES** ↓ dose in renal impairment (CrCl < 30 mL/min) with fesoterodine, solifenacin, tolterodine, and trospium (do not use trospium XR formulation in these patients)
Solifenacin (VESIcare)	5-10 mg PO daily	Extended-release formulations have less incidence of dry mouth than their IR counterparts
		Oxybutynin patch and gel cause less dry mouth and constipation than oral forms.
		Darifenacin causes more constipation
Darifenacin (Enablex)	7.5-15 mg PO daily	Oxytrol patch is changed twice a week (every 3-4 days). Place patch on dry, intact skin on the abdomen, hips or buttocks. Avoid reapplication to the same site within 7 days. Available OTC for women ≥ 18 years.
Fesoterodine (Toviaz)	4-8 mg PO daily	Antimuscarinic agents should be used with caution in patients using other medications with anticholinergic properties.

Anticholinergic Drug Interactions

- All of the anticholinergics can have additive effects with other medications that have anticholinergic side effects. Use caution with acetycholinesterase inhibitors as the effect of these medications may be reduced by the anticholinergic.

- Tolterodine – do not exceed 2 mg/day when administered with strong 3A4 inhibitors.

- Solifenacin – do not exceed 5 mg/day when administered with strong 3A4 inhibitors.

- Darifenacin – do not exceed 7.5 mg/day when administered with strong 3A4 inhibitors.

- Fesoterodine – do not exceed 4 mg/day when administered with strong 3A4 inhibitors.

Beta$_3$ Agonist

Mirabegron relaxes the detrusor muscle during the storage phase of the fill-void cycle by activation of beta$_3$ receptors which increases bladder capacity.

DRUG	DOSING	SAFETY/SIDE EFFECTS/MONITORING
Mirabegron *(Myrbetriq)*	25-50 mg daily CrCl 15-29 mL/min: 25 mg CrCl < 15 mL/min: not recommended	**SIDE EFFECTS** Hypertension, nasopharyngitis, UTI, headache **MONITORING** BP, HR, urinary symptoms **NOTES** Efficacy seen within 8 weeks

Mirabegron Drug Interactions

- Mirabegron is a moderate CYP2D6 inhibitor. Use caution with co-administration of narrow therapeutic window drugs metabolized by 2D6. Levels of metoproplol and desipramine are increased when co-administered with mirabegron. Use caution when administered concurrently with digoxin (use lowest digoxin dose and monitor levels).

Botox for OAB

Botox is third-line treatment for patients who are refractory to first- and second-line treatment options. It affects the efferent pathways of detrusor activity by inhibiting the release of acetylcholine.

DRUG	DOSING	SAFETY/SIDE EFFECTS/MONITORING
Onabotulinumtoxin A *(Botox)*	100 units total dose, as 0.5 mL (5 units) injections, across 20 sites (given intradetrusor) – retreat no sooner than 12 weeks from previous administration In adults treated with *Botox* for more than one indication, do not exceed a total dose of 360 units in a 3 month interval.	**BLACK BOX WARNING** All botulinum toxin products may spread from the area of injection to produce symptoms consistent with botulinum toxin effects. Swallowing and breathing difficulties can be life-threatening. **CONTRAINDICATIONS** Urinary tract infection and urinary retention **SIDE EFFECTS** Urinary tract infection, urinary retention, dysuria **MONITORING** Post-void residual volume, symptoms of OAB **NOTES** Potency units of *Botox* are not interchangeable with other preparations of botulinum toxin products. Prophylactic antimicrobial therapy (excluding aminoglycosides) should be administered 1-3 days prior to, on the day of, and for 1-3 days following *Botox* administration.

Botox Drug Interactions

- AMG and agents affecting neuromuscular transmission can potentiate the effects of *Botox*.

Anticholinergic Patient Counseling

Ditropan XL

- This medication is used to treat symptoms of an over-functioning bladder.

- Certain medications can interact with this medication. Tell your healthcare provider or pharmacist of the medications you are currently taking including any over the counter products, vitamins and herbal supplements.

- The tablet must be swallowed whole with liquid; do not crush, divide, or chew; take at approximately the same time each day.

- This medication can be taken without regards to meals (unlike trospium which needs to be taken on an empty stomach).

- If you miss a dose, forget it. Just take your next scheduled dose. Do not take 2 doses within the same day.

- This medicine can cause dry mouth. Some formulations cause more dry mouth than others (the longer-lasting forms tend to cause less dry mouth). If dry mouth is bothersome, please discuss with your healthcare provider. Avoiding mouthwashes with alcohol, taking small sips of water, sucking on ice chips or sugar-free candy or chewing sugar-free gum can help with dry mouth symptoms. Take good care of your teeth since dry mouth contributes to tooth decay.

- Another possible side effect of this medicine is constipation. Some formulations cause more constipation than others [darifenacin *(Enablex)* causes the most]. Maintain adequate water and dietary fiber, including vegetables and whole-grains. A stool softener, such as docusate, may be helpful. If not, a laxative such as senna may be helpful. You may need to discuss this with your healthcare provider. If you have any type of serious constipation or constipation for ≥ 3 days, or "GI" problems currently, you should let your healthcare provider know.

- This medication can make you feel dizzy or drowsy. Using alcohol can make this worse. Heat can make this worse. Do not operate any dangerous machinery (such as driving a car) until you know how this medicine affects your concentration and coordination.

- Doing pelvic floor muscle (Kegel) exercises in combination with this medicine will work better than taking the medicine alone. You should get instructions on how to do this correctly, and do them for a few minutes three times daily, so you can slowly build up these muscles.

Oxytrol Patch

- The patch causes less dry mouth than oral formulations.

- Open one pouch and apply immediately. Do not use if pouch is torn or opened.

- Apply one patch to clean, dry, intact skin on the abdomen, hips, or buttocks.

- Apply to an area of skin that is under clothing and protected from sunlight. Avoid applying the patch on your waistline, since tight clothing may rub the patch off.

- The Rx patch is changed every 3 to 4 days; the OTC patch is changed every 4 days.

- Select a new site for each new patch (avoid reapplication to same site within 7 days).

- Do not apply the patch to areas of skin that are irritated, oily, or to where lotions or powders have been applied.

- The patch must be removed prior to having a MRI procedure.

- Contact with water (e.g., swimming, bathing) will not change the way the drug works. Avoid rubbing the patch area during these activities.

- <u>If the area around the patch becomes red, itchy, or irritated, try a new site. If irritation continues or becomes worse, notify your healthcare provider promptly.</u>

Oxybutynin topical *(Gelnique)*

- For topical use only.

- This formulation causes less dry mouth and less constipation than other formulations.

- For *Gelnique* 10%, each packet is for one use only. For *Gelnique* 3%, use 3 pumps (must prime the pump prior to first use with 4 pumps).

- Apply to clean, dry, intact skin on abdomen, upper arm/shoulders, or thighs. Rub into skin until dry. Use a different site each day (cannot use the same site two days in a row).

- Do not apply to recently shaved skin.

- Do not bath, swim or shower for 1 hour after application.

- Wash hands after use.

- Cover treated area with clothing after gel has dried to prevent transfer of medication to others.

- Oxybutynin gel is flammable. Avoid an open flame and do not smoke until the gel has completely dried on the skin.

65

GLAUCOMA, ALLERGIC CONJUNCTIVITIS, OTHER OPTHALMICS & OTICS

ABBREVIATION	MEANING	CAUTION
AD, AS, AU	Right Ear, Left Ear, Each Ear	These directions can be mistaken (interchanged) for each other & may mean other things: know how to interpret them but it is safer to write them out: use right eye, left eye, each eye, right ear, left ear, each ear.
OD, OS, OU	Right Eye, Left Eye, Each Eye	
Memory tip: A is from the Latin for ear (auris), O is from eye (oculus), D is from right (dextra) and S is from left (sinistra).		

- Eye drops and ear drops are either solutions or suspensions.

- Suspensions require shaking prior to use.

- Use Aux Labels: "For Use in the Eye" or "For Use in the Ear"

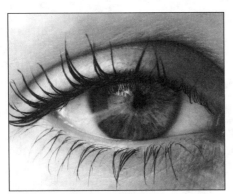

BACKGROUND

Glaucoma is an eye disease caused by an increase in intraocular pressure (IOP). If left untreated, glaucoma can result in damage to the optic nerve and gradual loss of vision. There may be no symptoms felt by the patient, although some may experience eye pain, headache, or decreased vision.

There are two main forms of glaucoma. Angle-closure, or closed-angle glaucoma is treated in the hospital and is a medical emergency. The more common type, open-angle glaucoma, is most commonly treated with eye drops.

RISK FACTORS

Include family history, increased age, African Americans and nearsightedness (myopia). A history of eye surgeries and diabetes can be contributory.

Drugs that May Increase IOP and/or Should be Avoided if Possible in Patients with Glaucoma

- Cough/cold/motion sickness medications (antihistamines)

- Anticholinergics (e.g., oxybutynin, tolterodine, benztropine, trihexyphenidyl, tricyclics)

- Chronic corticosteroids, especially eye drops such as prednisolone and others

- Topiramate *(Topamax)*

Pharmacologic Treatment

Either beta blockers or prostaglandin analogues (PAs) are used first-line. PAs lower IOP more than beta blockers and are approved for initial use, and beta blockers are inexpensive and can be used if only one eye needs treatment due to color discoloration from PAs. The other classes of agents do not lower the IOP as much as PAs and beta blockers, but can be helpful in patients who need additional decrease in the IOP.

The drugs can be absorbed systemically; improper administration technique can increase systemic effects. of the beta blockers used for glaucoma are non-selective agents and can be poorly tolerated in some patients. The other classes can have systemic effects. Pharmacists should make sure patients are inserting eye drops or gel appropriately in order to get the most benefit from the medication. If you ask, you will find that most patients do not hold the lacrimal duct down (closed) for an adequate time period (if at all) after inserting the medication.

Glaucoma Medication Therapy

DRUG	DOSING	SIDE EFFECTS/CLINICAL CONCERNS
Beta Blockers, Nonselective: reduce aqueous humor production		
Timolol 0.25% and 0.5% (Timoptic, Timoptic-XE, Istalol, Betimol) + brominidine *(Combigan)* + dorzolamide *(Cosopt, Cosopt PF)* Levobunolol *(Betagan)* Carteolol *(Ocupress)* Metipranolol *(OptiPranolol)* Betaxolol *(Betoptic, Betoptic S)*	*Timoptic* is QD or BID *Timoptic-XE* is a gel taken QD	**SIDE EFFECTS** Can cause burning, stinging or itching of the eyes or eyelids, changes in vision, increased sensitivity of the eyes to light, bradycardia, bronchospasm with non-selective agents **NOTES** These are non-selective beta blockers (except for betaxolol); although most medicine stays local, it is best to try and avoid in asthma, COPD, chronic bronchitis, emphysema, or advanced cardiac disease – some patients will have exacerbated symptoms – especially if used incorrectly Some contain sulfites, which can cause allergic reactions

Glaucoma Medication Therapy Continued

DRUG	DOSING	SIDE EFFECTS/CLINICAL CONCERNS

Prostaglandin Analogs: increase aqueous outflow

DRUG	DOSING	SIDE EFFECTS/CLINICAL CONCERNS
Travoprost *(Travatan Z)* **Bimatoprost** *(Lumigan)* **Latanoprost** *(Xalatan)* Unoprostone *(Rescula)* Tafluprost *(Zioptan)* Foil pouches of 10 single-use containers.	Once daily, at night except *Rescula* is BID Cannot be administered with contact lenses (preservative BAK will absorb into lenses) – remove and wait 15 min prior to re-insertion (most given QHS so this is not an issue but tell patient)	**SIDE EFFECTS** An increase in brown pigment in the iris and gradual changes in eye color may occur; eyelash growth and pigmentation may increase; skin on the eyelids and around the eyes may darken Eyelash changes: ↑ length, thickness, number (goes away when drug discontinued) Eye redness (ocular hyperemia), tearing, eye pain, or lid crusting **NOTES** Store unopened bottles of latanoprost in refrigerator. Bimatoprost *(Latisse)* is indicated for eyelash hypotrichosis (to↑ eyelash growth) – do not use concurrently with same class for glaucoma without MDs approval (using PAs more frequently ↓ effectiveness) *Travatan Z* does not contain benzalkonium chloride (BAK), instead has different preservative. This may be helpful to some with reaction to BAK or dry eye, but most people are fine with the much less expensive, generic latanoprost. *Zioptan:* After opening pouch use right away, throw it out after use (sterile, but no preservative – cannot keep). Keep refrigerated. Pouch contains 10 single-use containers; once pouch is opened it can be kept at room temp for 28 days.

Miotics: increase aqueous outflow

DRUG	DOSING	SIDE EFFECTS/CLINICAL CONCERNS
Carbachol *(Isopto Carbachol, Miostat)*	1-2 drops up to 3x daily	**SIDE EFFECTS** Corneal clouding, burning (transient), irritation, hypotension, bronchospasm, abdominal cramps/GI distress
Pilocarpine *(Isopto Carpine, Pilopine HS)*	Solution: 1-2 drops up to 6x/daily Gel: Instill 0.5" ribbon into lower conjunctival sac once daily, at bedtime	**NOTES** Use with caution with history of retinal detachment or corneal abrasion

Carbonic Anhydrase Inhibitors: reduce aqueous humor production

DRUG	DOSING	SIDE EFFECTS/CLINICAL CONCERNS
Acetazolamide *(Diamox)* Brinzolamide *(Azopt)* + brimonidine *(Simbrinza)* **Dorzolamide** *(Trusopt)* **Dorzolamide** **+timolol** *(Cosopt, Cosopt PF is single-dose)*	Acetazolamide 250 mg PO 1-4 x daily, or 500 mg ER PO BID *Azopt, Trusopt* are TID	**SIDE EFFECTS** Topical agents: allergic reactions, burning, bitter or metallic taste **NOTES** Acetazolamide (Diamox) comes in an oral formulation, which can cause many CNS effects (ataxia, confusion), photosensitivity/skin rash (including risk of SJS and TEN), anorexia, nausea and risk of hematological toxicities. It is used less frequently than the topical formulation.

Glaucoma Medication Therapy Continued

DRUG	DOSING	SIDE EFFECTS/CLINICAL CONCERNS

Adrenergic Alpha-2 Agonists: increase aqueous outflow, reduce production

Apraclonidine *(Iopidine)* **Brimonidine *(Alphagan P)*** +brinzolamide *(Simbrinza)* + timolol ***(Combigan)*** Dipivefrin *(Propine, Akpro)*	*Iopidine, Alphagan* are dosed TID	**SIDE EFFECTS** Blurred vision, macular edema, irritation/blepharitis

Patient Counseling (Eye Drops)

- Wash your hands.

- Before you open the bottle, shake it a few times.

- Bend your neck back a little so that you're looking up. Use one finger to pull down your lower eyelid. It is helpful, at least initially, to use a mirror.

- Without letting the tip of the bottle touch your eye or eyelid, squeeze one drop of the medicine into the space between your eye and your lower eyelid. If you squeeze in more than one drop, you are wasting medicine.

- After you squeeze the drop of medicine into your eye, close your eye. Then press a finger between your eye and the top of your nose. Press for at least one full minute (or longer if instructed by your doctor). This way, more of the medicine stays in your eye. You will be less likely to have side effects.

If you need to take more than one glaucoma medicine:

- Put a drop of the first medicine in your eye. Wait at least 10 minutes to put the second medicine in your eye. If you're taking three medicines, wait 10 more minutes before putting the third medicine in your eye. If you don't wait 10 minutes between medicines, some of the medicine may run out of your eye. If the medicine runs out of your eye, it does not help.

- If someone else puts your medicines in your eye for you, remind that person to wait 10 minutes between each medicine.

Prostaglandin Analog Counseling Specifics

- Remove contact lenses before using this medication because it contains a preservative that can be absorbed by the lenses, and cause them to become discolored. Wait at least 15 minutes after using this medication before putting your lenses back in.

- You may experience an increase in brown pigment in the iris and gradual changes in eye color (for this reason, they are not usually administered to patients with light eyes who have glaucoma in one eye only). Eyelash growth and pigmentation may increase (which is often pleasing to the patient). The skin on the eyelids and around the eyes may darken.

- This medicine is well-tolerated, but occasionally a patient can experience excessive tearing, eye pain, or lid crusting. If this occurs, please discuss with your doctor.

- <u>Latanoprost *(Xalatan)* unopened bottles should be stored in the refrigerator.</u>

- Tafluprost *(Zioptan)* is kept refrigerated. Once opened the pouch of 10 is good at room temperature for 28 days.

- Do not use this medicine if you are also using Bimatoprost *(Latisse)*, to increase eyelash growth, without your doctor's approval. *Latisse* may reduce the effectiveness of the glaucoma medicine.

Timolol *(Timoptic)* Counseling Specifics

- Common side effects from beta blockers include burning/stinging or itching of the eyes, and possible light sensitivity

- Timolol is a non-selective beta blocker, and although proper application should keep most of the medicine local, it is <u>best to avoid in patients with asthma, COPD, chronic bronchitis, emphysema, or advanced cardiac disease</u>. The medicine might exacerbate the disease symptoms. If you have any of these conditions, please discuss if this medicine is safe to use.

- <u>If dispensing the drops in the *Ocudose* dispenser</u>: To open the bottle, unscrew the cap by turning as indicated by the arrows on the top of the cap. Do not pull the cap directly up and away from the bottle. Pulling the cap directly up will prevent your dispenser from operating properly.

- Invert the bottle, and press lightly with the thumb or index finger over the "Finger Push Area" until a single drop is dispensed into the eye.

- If dispensing the gel *(Timoptic XE)*: Turn the container upside down once and shake the contents prior to use (the gel is a suspension and needs to be mixed). The gel is used once daily.

OTHER OCULAR CONDITIONS

Common agents known to cause vision changes/damage

- Alpha blockers (floppy iris syndrome-causes difficulty in cataract surgery)
- Amiodarone (corneal deposits, optic neuropathy)
- Bisphosphonates (ocular inflammation)
- Digoxin (yellow/green vision, blurriness, halos)

ALLERGIC CONJUNCTIVITIS TREATMENT

OVER THE COUNTER (OTC)
Antihistamine/Decongestant
Naphazoline/pheniramine *(Naphcon-A, Opcon-A, Visine-A)*
Antihistamine
Ketotifen *(Zaditor, Alaway)*

PRESCRIPTION
Antihistamine
Levocetirizine *(Xyzal)*
Emedastine *(Emadine)*
NSAID
Ketorolac *(Acular, Acular PF)*
Mast Cell Stabilizer
Cromolyn
Lodoxamine *(Alomide)*
Nedocromil *(Alocril)*
Pemirolast *(Alamast)*
Antihistamine/Mast Cell Stabilizer
Azelastine *(Optivar)*
Epinastine *(Elestat)*
Olopatadine *(Patanol)*
Steroids: Short term use, caution for ↑ IOP
Dexamethasone Na⁺
Loteprednol *(Alrex, Lotemax)*
Medrysone *(HMS Liquifilm)*
Prednisolone acetate 1%

- Ethambutol, linezolid *(Zyvox)* (optic neuropathy, especially with chronic use)

- Ezogabine *(Potiga)* (retinal changes, vision loss)

- Hydroxychloroquine *(Plaquenil)* (retinopathy)

- Isoniazid (optic neuritis)

- Isotretinoin (↓ night vision which may be permanent, dry eyes/irritation)

- Quinolones (retinal detachment)

- Sildenafil *(Viagra)* and other PDE5-Inhibitors used for ED and PAH (greenish tinge around objects, possible permanent vision loss in one or both eyes)

- Tamoxifen *(Nolvadex)* (corneal changes, decreased color perception)

- Telithromycin (blurry vision, diplopia)

- Voriconazole *(VFEND)* (abnormal vision, color vision change, photophobia)

Allergic Conjunctivitis

Background

A clear, thin membrane called the conjunctiva covers the eyeball and inside of the eyelids. If something irritates this covering, the eyes can become red, swollen and may itch. This is called conjunctivitis, or sometimes "pink eye." Common irritants include bacteria, viruses or allergens (animal skin or secretions, pollen, perfumes, air pollution, smoke).

Pharmacologic Treatment

Different classes of medicines are used. Two are OTC – naphazoline/pheniramine *(Visine* and others) and the antihistamine ketotifen *(Zaditor, Alaway)*.

Counsel patients to remove contact lenses prior to use (true for most eye drops) and wait 15 minutes afterwards before reinserting. Many eye drops cause a slight temporary burning or stinging when used.

If a corticosteroid is prescribed watch out for chronic use: these can cause glaucoma, or further raise intraocular pressure (IOP).

If any eye condition worsens after a few days or does not improve refer to the physician.

Antibiotic Eye Drops for Bacterial Conjunctivitis (Pink Eye) & Other Eye Infections

Common eye drops: pharmacists should know what is in them and be able to counsel for temporary stinging and reporting if situation worsens – and to limit contact lens use during an infection. Since these are antibiotics the patient should complete the duration of therapy. Some patients will have an allergic reaction to the eye drop and will need to return to the doctor if the condition worsens.

- <u>Azithromycin *(Azasite)* – stored in refrigerator, 14 days at room temp.</u>

- <u>Moxifloxacin *(Vigamox)*</u>

- <u>Besifloxacin *(Besivance)*</u>

- <u>Tobramycin/Dexamethasone (Antibiotic/Steroid)</u>

Other Common Antibiotic Eye Drops

- Ciprofloxacin *(Ciloxan)*, ofloxacin *(Ocuflox)*, gentamicin *(Garamycin)*, tobramycin *(Tobrex)*, erythromycin, sulfacetamide *(Bleph-10, Sulamyd)*, trimethoprim/polymyxin *(Polytrim)*, neomycin/bacitracin/polymyxin *(Neosporin)*.

Common Antibiotic Ointments Used For Blepharitis (Eyelid Inflammation)

- Note that treatment does not always warrant medication use – <u>warm compresses</u> such as a washcloth to the outer eyelids, gentle cleansing and gentle massage may be all that is required <u>and is considered first-line</u>. Occasionally, medications are used and in some patients blepharitis can be chronic and cause considerable distress.

- Bacitracin or erythromycin ointment, applied BID to QID.

OTICS

Background

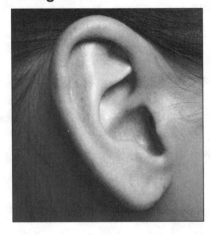

Common conditions treated in the ear include pain (such as from an otitis infection-which may be treated with topical antibiotics, although oral are much more common), inflammation from swimmer's ear (otitis externa) and ear wax (cerumen) impaction. Tinnitus (ringing or roaring or buzzing sounds) is caused by drug toxicity (primarily salicylates), noise exposure, or is idiopathic. There is no effective drug treatment for tinnitus. Eye drops may be used in the ear (as ear drops, for example to treat an infection), but never use ear drops in the eyes; the ear drops may not have an appropriate pH, may not be isotonic and may not be sterile.

Swimmer's ear, otitis media pain

- Antipyrine and benzocaine *(A/B Otic, Auralgan)*

- Benzocaine *(Americaine Otic)*

Ear drops with antibiotics may also be used for outer ear infections. A few common products:

- Ciprofloxacin and hydrocortisone *(Cipro HC)*

- Ciprofloxacin and dexamethasone *(Ciprodex)*

- Ciprofloxacin *(Floxin Otic, Floxin Otic Singles)*

- Neomycin and hydrocortisone (*Cortisporin-TC*)

Ear wax (cerumen) removal

- Carbamide peroxide (*Debrox*)

- Triethanolamine (*Cerumenex*)

- Antipyrine and benzocaine (*Auralgan*)

Otic Medication Application

- If cold hold the bottle for 1 or 2 minutes to warm the solution. Ear drops that are too cold will be uncomfortable and may cause dizziness.

- Lie down or tilt the head so that the affected ear faces up.

- Gently pull the earlobe up and back for adults (down and back for children) to straighten the ear canal.

- Administer the prescribed number of drops into the ear canal. Keep the ear facing up for about 5 minutes to allow the medicine to coat the ear canal.

- Do not touch the dropper tip to any surface. To clean wipe with a clean tissue.

Ear wax removal: flush ear with warm water after you have used the medicine for 2-3 days. (This may be done in doctor's office.)

66

MOTION SICKNESS

BACKGROUND

Motion sickness (kinetosis) is also called seasickness or airsickness. Symptoms are nausea, dizziness and fatigue. People can get motion sickness on a moving boat, train, airplane, car, or amusement park rides. This is a common condition.

NON-PHARMACOLOGIC TREATMENT

Some patients find benefit with a wrist band that presses on an acupuncture point located on the inside of the wrist, about the length of 2 fingernails up the arm from the center of the wrist crease. One popular brand is *Sea-Band* benefit. The best way to stop motion sickness, if possible, is to stop the motion.

Natural Products

Ginger, in teas or supplements, is used most commonly. Peppermint may be helpful.

PHARMACOLOGIC TREATMENT

Medications for motion sickness are anticholinergics and may cause drowsiness and may impair judgment. Pilots, ship crew members, or anyone operating heavy equipment or driving a car should not take them. The military uses combinations of products (such as oral scopolamine to reduce nausea, taken with a stimulant, such as dextroamphetamine, to counteract the drowsiness from the scopolamine) but these combinations have significant risk and should not be routinely recommended.

Scopolamine *(Transderm Scop)* is the most commonly prescribed medication for motion sickness. It is not more effective than generically-available OTC agents but is applied topically (behind the ear) and is taken less frequently (apply 4-6 hours prior to need, lasts three days, do not cut patch, alternate ears, wash hands afterwards).

Antihistamines used for motion sickness include cyclizine (*Marezine*), diphenhydramine (*Benadryl*), dimenhydrinate (*Dramamine*) or Meclizine (*Bonine*). Dimenhydrinate, meclizine and cyclizine are long-acting piperazine antihistamines and are a little less sedating than other antihistamines, but they are still sedating.

Promethazine is used and is prescription only. Do not use promethazine in children. All promethazine products carry a black box warning contraindicating use in children less than 2 years and strongly cautioning use in children age 2 and older. The FDA advises against the use of promethazine with codeine cough syrups in children less than 6 years of age, due to the risk of respiratory depression, cardiac arrest and neurological problems.

All of the antihistamines have anticholinergic effects similar to scopolamine. Make sure the oral agents are taken prior to travel (30-60 minutes prior) and ensure that the patient knows they will get tired. Instruct them not to consume alcohol or other CNS depressants.

DRUG	DOSING	SIDE EFFECTS/FORMULATIONS/CONTRAINDICATIONS
Scopolamine 3-day patch (*Transderm Scop*) Applied behind ear Q 72 hrs, rotate ears	1.5 mg, patch placed behind ear (hairless), 4-6 hours before needed (or evening before AM surgery – remove 24 hours after surgery) Primarily for motion sickness and occasionally used inpatient. Do not cut patch, wash hands after application.	**SIDE EFFECTS** Dry mouth, dizziness, stinging eyes (if touch eyes after handling patch), pupil dilation Confusion (can be significant in elderly, frail) **RARELY** Hallucinations, tachycardia Remove patch prior to MRI
Meclizine (*Antivert*)	12.5-25 mg 30-60 minutes before needed.	1st generation antihistamine: see diphenhydramine in allergies or insomnia chapters for complete discussion and counseling. Drug is highly sedating and causes anticholinergic side effects (dry mouth, urinary retention, constipation, dry/blurry vision, tachycardia) Will worsen BPH symptoms, can elevate IOP (glaucoma), and worsen cognition (elderly)
OTHER ANTIHISTAMINES USED Cyclizine DiphenhydrAMINE DimenhyDRINATE Promethazine [Rx-do not use in children due to (primarily) risk of respiratory depression.]		

Transderm Scop Counseling
- Wear only one patch at any time.
- No alcohol. Try to avoid other drugs that make you tired – this drug causes significant drowsiness. Do not use in children.
- The most common side effect is dryness of the mouth. Other common side effects are drowsiness, temporary blurring of vision and dilation (widening) of the pupils may occur, especially if the drug is on your hands and comes in contact with the eyes.

- Remover prior to an MRI procedure or the patch will burn your skin.

- Infrequently, some people get disoriented, and others can get confusion, hallucinations or heart palpitations. If any of these occur remove the patch and contact your doctor.

How to use

- Peel off the clear backing from the patch and apply <u>it to a clean, dry, hairless area of the skin behind the ear.</u> <u>Press firmly for at least 30 seconds</u> to make sure the patch sticks well, especially around the edges. The patch will slowly release the medication into your body over 3 days. Do not use the patch if it appears broken, cut, or damaged. <u>Apply at least 4 hours before activity that will cause motion sickness.</u>

- Be sure to <u>wash your hands thoroughly with soap and water immediately after handling the patch,</u> so that any drug that might get on your hands <u>will not come into contact with your eyes.</u>

- Also wash the area behind the ear where the patch was removed.

COMMON SKIN CONDITIONS

GUIDELINES

There are various conditions presented in this section and treatments for each are presented below. It can be difficult to determine the type of skin condition, which are often presented by the patient to the community pharmacist. *The Handbook of OTC Drugs* has pictures of common conditions, and many more are available at www.dermnet.com. If recommending OTC treatment it is important to tell the patient to be seen by a physician if the condition does not improve or worsens. You should be able to recognize a blemish that could be skin cancer; see the pictures and description in the oncology section.

Natural Products

Aloe is a natural product produced from the aloe vera plant that is used for many skin conditions, including sunburn and psoriasis. It has little proven efficacy but if used as a gel or lotion it may provide a soothing effect. Tea tree oil is used for a variety of skin conditions. It can be useful for treating acne. It may be helpful for onychomycosis symptoms (depending on the dose and application schedule), but is not useful in eradicating the infection in most patients. Tea tree oil may also be useful for athlete's foot symptoms if the 10% oil is used (not tea tree cream). Higher concentrations (25 or 50%) can cure the infection in up to half of patients, but are not as effective as the recommended antifungal agents. This efficacy data is from the Natural Medicines Database.

DRUGS THAT CAN DISCOLOR SKIN OR SECRETIONS		
Brownish Levodopa, Entacapone Methyldopa	**Blueish** Mitoxantrone Methylene blue	**Red-Orangeish** Phenazopyridine Rifapentine Rifampin
Purple/Orangeish/Reddish Chlorzoxazone	**Orange/Reddish/Brownish** Ezogabine	**Reddish** Anthracyclines
Orange/Yellowish Sulfasalazine	**Brown/Black/Greenish** Methocarbamol	
Brown/Yellowish Nitrofurantoin Riboflavin (B12)	**Yellow-Greenish** Propofol Flutamide	

Acne, Background & Treatment

- Most people develop acne, including infants, adults (and women, commonly, around the menstrual cycle) and, primarily, adolescents in puberty.

- Androgens (male sex hormones) are the primary determinant of acne (and is why boys often will have worse acne than girls) and the presence of the bacteria *P. acnes* and fatty acids present in oil glands. Where the oil glands are located is where acne occurs: the face, chest, shoulders and back.

- Lesions are classified as whiteheads, blackheads, small bumps, cysts and nodules.

- Treatment is determined by severity: mild (few, occasional pimples), moderate (inflammatory papules), or severe (nodules and cysts).

- Acne is treated with four primary groups of agents: OTC (benzoyl peroxide and salicylic acid), retinoids, systemic isotretinoin and antibiotics.

- Benzoyl peroxide (BPO) is the most effective OTC agent. It comes as Rx, including in combination with hydrocortisone, the retinoid adapalene or with the antibiotics erythromycin or clindamycin. Start with 2.5-5% BPO, which is generally adequate and less irritating than the higher strengths.

- Salicylic acid is a mildly useful OTC agent, and is primarily used in "medicated pads" for facial cleansing.

- Retinoids, primarily topical tretinoin and derivates are the usual Rx drug of choice. [They are also used to reduce fine wrinkles.]

  ❏ Retinoids are vitamin A derivatives. The mechanism is primarily to reduce adherence of the keratinocytes (outer skin cells) in the oil gland.

  ❏ They are well-tolerated when used topically, with mild skin irritation (redness, drying) and photosensitivity possible. Start at night (or every other night) with the correct (pea sized) amount. Use moisturizer each morning, followed by sunscreen.

  ❏ Retinoids take 4-12 weeks to work and acne may worsen initially. An antibiotic (often minocycline) taken concurrently can help.

❏ They are not used in pregnancy or breastfeeding; some are pregnancy category C, others are X. Tazarotene often works better than tretinoin; it is used with difficult cases and is pregnancy category X.

❏ Often a topical antibiotic is used concurrently – the retinoid allows the antibiotic to get into the pores to eradicate the bacteria.

❏ The oral retinoid isotretinoin has many safety considerations, including severe teratogenicity, and is reserved for severe nodular acne only. Cholesterol and pregnancy tests are required, among other monitoring.

■ Some women find benefit with birth control pills, especially if the acne is in combination with irregular periods or symptoms of androgenic excess.

■ Azelaic acid *(Azelex, Finacea)* is a topical dicarboxylic acid cream or gel available OTC and Rx for acne and rosacea. It is well tolerated and can cause mild topical burning or "tingling."

DRUGS	NOTES	SAFETY/COUNSELING
Retinoids 1st line agents Tretinoin cream *(Retin-A)* Slower-release, less skin irritation with: ■ Microsphere gel *(Retin-A Micro)* ■ Polymerized cream or gel *(Avita)* **Adapalene *(Differin)*** cream, solution Adapalene+BPO *(Epiduo)* Tazarotene (*Tazorac*, Avage-creams, Fabior-foam) stronger, more irritating Dapsone gel *(Aczone)* Tretinoin *(Retin-A Micro)* is a gel, and comes pre-formulated in a tube or pump dispenser and does not require refrigeration. Retinoids are popular and there are many other products, such as clindamycin + tretinoin gel *(Ziana),* others	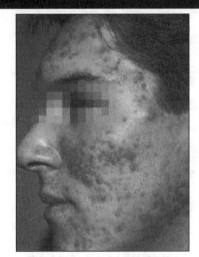 Severe nodular acne – this may be a suitable candidate for istotretinion (oral), but a retinoid with an antibiotic may be tried first.	Apply daily, usually at bedtime, about 20 minutes after washing face. If irritation use lower strength, or every other night. May need to reduce contact initially (wash off every a period of time.) A pea-sized amount is sufficient (for facial application); it should be divided into 4 equal parts and smoothed over the entire surface of the face – not just on acne. Avoid salicylic acid scrubs or astringents while starting a retinoid; this will worsen irritation. Wash only with mild soap twice daily. Takes 4-12 weeks to see response; may worsen acne initially. Limit sun exposure.

Acne Background & Treatment Continued

DRUGS	NOTES	SAFETY/COUNSELING
Benzoyl peroxide (most effective OTC agent), salicylic acid is weaker OTC agent OTC (many products) including *Benoxyl, Benzac, Clearasil*, If needed with retinoid. *Benzamycin* (BPO + 3% erythromycin) *BenzaClin* **(BPO + 1% clindamycin) (combo preferred)** **Clindamycin+BPO topical gel** *(Duac)* Azelaic acid *(Azelex, Finacea)*, OTC, Rx	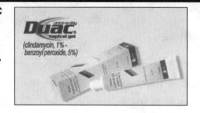 **Duac** Dispense with 60 day expiration. Apply QHS to affected areas. Can store at room temp, do not freeze. Limit sun exposure. **Clindamycin Topicals** **Cleocin T, ClindaMax** lotion/solution **Clindagel** gel, **Evoclin** foam Clean face, shake (if lotion), apply a thin layer once or twice daily. Avoid contact with eyes; if contact, rinse with cold water. Takes 2-6 weeks for effect and up to 12 weeks for full benefit.	BPO can bleach clothing, hair Limit sun exposure; skin will burn more easily. ***Benzamycin and BenzaClin*** Add indicated amount of purified water to the vial (70% ethyl alcohol for *Benzamycin*) and immediately shake to completely dissolve medication. If needed, add additional purified water to bring level up to the mark. Add the solution in the vial to the gel and stir until homogenous in appearance (1 to 1½ minutes). *Benzamycin* is kept refrigerated. *BenzaClin* is kept at room temp. Place a 3 month expiration date on the label following mixing.
Oral Isotretinoin *(Amnesteem, Claravis, Myorisan, Absorica)* Only for the treatment of severe recalcitrant nodular acne 0.5–1.0 mg/kg/day, divided BID with food (to absorption) for 15-20 weeks. Comes as 10, 20, and 40 mg capsules. Counseling about contraception and behaviors associated with risk of pregnancy must be repeated on a monthly basis. Two forms of birth control are required with taking this medication (not the mini-pill). DRYNESS! Carry bottled water, eye drops and lip balm.	Female patients must sign patient information/informed consent form about birth defects that contains warnings about the risk of potential birth defects if the fetus is exposed to isotretinoin. Must have had 2 negative pregnancy tests prior to starting treatment. Cannot get pregnant for one month before, while taking the drug, or for one month after the drug is stopped. Do not breast feed or donate blood until at least one month has passed after the drug is stopped. Do not use with vitamin A supplements, tetracyclines, steroids, progestin-only contraceptives, or St. John's wort. Must swallow capsule whole, or puncture and sprinkle on applesauce or icecream – this may irritate esophagus	Pregnancy Category X: severe birth defects or miscarriage. Can only be dispensed by a pharmacy registered and activated with the pregnancy risk management iPLEDGE program.1-month Rx at a time, fill within 7 days with yellow sticker attached. Teratogenicity, arthralgias, skeletal hyperostosis, osteoporosis, psychiatric issues (such as depression, psychosis, and risk of suicide), ↓ night vision (may be permanent), difficulty wearing contact lens (dry eyes/irritation), dry skin, chapped lips, elevated cholesterol and blood glucose, transient chest pain and hearing loss, and photosensitivity.
ORAL ANTIBIOTICS USED COMMONLY FOR ACNE **Minocycline ext-rel** *(Solodyn)* 12 years and older, dosed by weight Doxycycline and minocycline are more effective than tetracycline in eradicating *P. acnes* Trimethoprim-Sulfamethoxazole is also used. Erythromycin used to be commonly used but is not currently due to resistance.	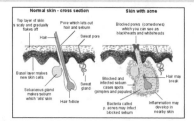	Photosensitivity, rash in susceptible patients, dizziness, diarrhea, somnolence Like other tetracyclines can cause fetal harm if administered during pregnancy. May cause permanent discoloration in teeth if used when teeth are forming (up to 8 years of age).

Dandruff, Background & Treatment

- Dandruff occurs when the scalp is itchy and/or scaling with white oily flakes (dead skin) in the hair and on the shoulders, back or clothing.

- Dandruff can be due to either eczema or fungal (yeast) overgrowth, and worsened by hormones, the weather or shampoo. Seborrheic dermatitis is a common form of eczema that causes flaking, itchy skin on the face, back, chest or head. If it is on the scalp it is commonly referred to as dandruff.

- Patients are not likely to know the cause of the dandruff. A store-brand, inexpensive dandruff shampoo can be tried first, and if this is ineffective, the pricier ketoconazole antifungal shampoo can be used.

DRUGS	NOTES	SAFETY/COUNSELING
Selenium sulfide ((*Dandrex, Selsun, Tersi)*, zinc pyrithone (*Head & Shoulders*), coal tar shampoos, *Suave* or store brands "dandruff" shampoos Ketoconazole shampoo *(Nizoral A-D)* Ketoconazole topical comes in many formulations for dandruff or seborrheic dermatitis (see notes above): cream, foam, gel & shampoo	 There are many different dandruff shampoos. Shown here is the antifungal shampoo *Nizoral A-D*. It is prudent to have the patient try less expensive formulations first, since these may work as well, including store brands or *Suave* dandruff shampoo.	Rub shampoo in well and leave in for 5 minutes, then rinse out. Shampoo daily. If the shampoo stops working, switch products. *Nizoral A-D* Apply twice weekly, for up to 8 weeks. Do not use if open sores on scalp. Can cause skin irritation.

Skin Fungal Infections, Background & Treatment

Tinea pedis, cruris, corporis, and topical candida infections (vaginal, onychomycosis, diaper rash see separate sections)

Athlete's foot (tinea pedis)

- A fungal infection of the foot caused by various fungi (commonly trichophyton rubrum)

- Symptoms are itching, peeling, redness, mild burning, and sometimes sores. This is a common infection, particularly among those using public pools, showers, and locker rooms. Diagnosis is usually by symptoms, but if unclear (psoriasis and other conditions can cause itchy skin), the skin can be scraped off and viewed under a microscope.

- It is treated topically with antifungals, except in severe cases.

Jock itch (tinea cruris)

- Affects the genitals, inner thighs and buttocks.

- The rash is red, itchy and can be ring-shaped.

- Jock itch is not very contagious, but can be spread person-to-person with close contact.

- Keep the skin dry (use a clean towel after showering) and treat with an antifungal topical. Creams work best.

- Change underwear at least daily.

Ringworm (tinea corporis)

- Not a worm, but a skin fungal infection.

- Ringworm can appear anywhere on the body and typically looks like circular, red, flat sores (one or more, may overlap), usually with dry, scaly skin. Occasionally the ring-like presentation is not present – just itchy red skin.

- The outer part of the sore can be raised while the skin in the middle appears normal. It can spread person-to-person or by contact with infected animals.

- Most cases are treated topically.

- Tinea capitis is "ringworm" on the scalp – this affects primarily young children, mostly in crowded, lower-income situations and requires systemic therapy, with the same drugs used for onychomycosis.

Cutaneous (skin) Candida infections

- Topical candida infections cause red, itchy rashes, most commonly in the groin, armpits or anywhere the skin folds.

- These are more likely in obese persons because they will have more skin with folds; the infection can be in unusual places, such as under the breasts, if the skin is moist. Diabetes is another risk factor.

- Occasionally fungal infections appear in the corner of nails (on the skin, not in the nailbed). If this is a suspected bacterial infection, OTC antibiotic topicals or mupirocin (*Bactroban* – excellent gram positive coverage) can be used.

- Candida can cause diaper rash in infants (discussed under diaper rash.)

DRUGS	NOTES	SAFETY/COUNSELING
Terbinafine and butenafine highly effective: Terbinafine (*Lamisil AT* cream and solution) Butenafine (*Lotrimin Ultra* cream) Clotrimazole (*Lotrimin* cream, lotion, solution, *Desenex*) Miconazole (*Monistat-Derm, Lotrimin* powder and spray) Miconazole+petrolatum (for moisture barrier, used in geriatrics) *(Baza)* *Monistat Derm* cream Tolnaftate (*Tinactin* powder, cream, spray) Undecylenic acid (*Cruex, Desenex*), others Rx Ketoconazole (cream), ketoconazole foam *(Extina)* Note the same name in OTC products can refer to different active ingredients – do not instruct patient by brand name alone or their could be a product mix-up. The FDA will be attempting to eliminate this confusion by restricting name allocations.	The top picture is tinea corporis (ringworm) – the rings can overlap, or be single) – note the redness. If pictures are not clear please refer to sources at the beginning of the chapter for online images.	Topical antifungals come in creams, ointments, gels, solutions Creams work best and are used in most cases. Solutions can be easier to apply in hairy areas. Powders do not work well for treatment but may be used for prevention, such as in shoes after a gym workout. Use cotton socks. Apply medicine 1-2 inches beyond the rash. Use for at least 2-4 weeks, even if it appears healed. Reduce moisture to the infected area If foot infection, do not walk barefoot (to avoid spreading it) Wear sandals in public showers (to avoid catching it)

Onychomycosis (Tinea Unguium – Toenail or Fingernail Fungal Infections), Background & Treatment

- Onychomycosis can cause pain, discomfort, and disfigurement and can lead to physical limitations, such as difficulty standing and walking. The discoloration and disfigurement can cause loss of self-esteem and psychological issues.

- Topical agents are limited to mild cases, patients who cannot tolerate systemic therapies, or are used concurrently with systemic treatment or as prophylaxis. They are not potent enough to cure most infections.

- Itraconazole and terbinafine are used most commonly and have FDA indications; fluconazole and posaconazole are used off-label. Griseofulvin is rarely used currently.

- It takes a long time for the nail bed to look better – sometimes up to a year in toenails. Toenails take longer to treat than fingernails, and are more commonly infected.

- Pulse therapy (intermittent) can be used to reduce costs and possibly toxicity, but may not be as effective.

- A 20% potassium hydroxide (KOH) smear is essential for diagnosis as other conditions can produce a similar presentation.

DRUGS	NOTES	SAFETY/COUNSELING
Itraconazole *(Sporanox)* Dose 200 mg Q daily x 12 weeks for 12 weeks, or "pulse-dosing" (fingernails only): 200 mg BID x 1 week, repeat 1-week course after 3 weeks off-time Terbinafine *(LamISIL, Terbinex)* – oral (topical is LamISIL AT, and is used for fungal skin infections) 250 mg PO daily for 6 weeks (fingernail) or 12 weeks (toenail) Ciclopirox *(Penlac, Loprox)* Apply evenly over entire nail plate QHS, or 8 hours before washing) to all affected nails with applicator brush	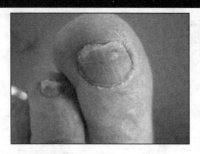 Ciclopirox (*Penlac, Loprox*) – used in combination with orals; poor efficacy when used alone. Occasionally used in patients who cannot tolerate systemic therapy, but generally cannot cure an infection when used alone. Occasionally used as prophylaxis.	For systemic azoles, see ID chapter. Primarily these drugs are hepatotoxic (monitor liver), are QT prolongers (Avoid in QT risk) and are 3A4 substrates & inhibitors (many drug interactions). Nausea and diarrhea are common. Itraconazole *(Sporanox)* Black box warning to avoid use in heart failure. Requires gastric acid for absorption; cannot use strong acid suppressing agents concurrently. Terbinafine *(Lamisil, Terbinex)* – oral Primarily headache, rash, nausea, risk of hepatotoxicity. Recurrence is common. Keep the nails dry. Practice proper foot care. Keep blood glucose controlled. Do not smoke. Monitor liver enzymes/symptoms liver toxicity in anyone on systemic antifungals.

Vaginal Fungal Candida ("Yeast") Infections

This is a common infection; about 75% women will have at least one episode, and half of these women will have recurrence. In a small percentage of women the recurrence is chronic.

- The infection is uncommon before a girl begins menstruating, and occurs most commonly during the week prior to menstruation – this makes treatment decisions around the period important. The woman can begin treatment during menses, or wait until the bleeding stops. Tampons should not be used when medication is applied.

- Vaginal fungal infections are also common during pregnancy. Pregnant patients are hopefully seeing a physician, and require longer (7-10 day treatment).

- Symptoms are primarily itching, with possible soreness and pain (burning) during urination or sex. Some women have a cottage-cheese like discharge (white, thick, clumpy).

- Diagnosis can be confirmed with either a vaginal culture to check for fungal growth or, via a pH test: a pH greater than 4.5 indicates the presence of either a candida or trichomoniasis infection. OTC test kits such as the *Vagisil Screening Kit* test for vaginal pH. Generally, testing is not necessary if the woman has been seen by the physician for the initial infection and is able to recognize the symptoms.

- If the woman has had the infection before and is able to recognize the symptoms, she can self-treat with OTC products. If there are more than four infections in a year, or if symptoms recur within 2 months, refer to the physician to rule-out an underlying condition that could be causative (most likely diabetes, HIV, receiving steroids or other immune-suppressing agents, pregnancy, or irritation from repeated douching or use of lubricants.) Women taking high-dose estrogen in birth control pills or in hormone replacement therapy are at elevated risk. Antibiotic use can be a risk factor; the antibiotic can wipe out the normal flora and lead to fungal overgrowth.

- Lactobacillus or yogurt with active cultures is thought to reduce infection occurrence; however, this is rated as "possibly ineffective" by the *Natural Medicines Database.*

- If self-treating, counsel that condoms and diaphragms may not provide adequate pregnancy protection; the oil in OTC antifungals weakens the latex.

- To avoid future infections, keep the vaginal area clean, wipe from the front to the back, use cotton underwear, avoid tight-fitting clothing, including pantyhose, change pads/tampons often, change out of wet swimsuits or clothing quickly, and recommend against use of vaginal douches, sprays and deodorant tampons; these can alter the vaginal pH and contribute to infection.

DRUGS	NOTES	SAFETY/COUNSELING
Mild-moderate, infrequent infection <u>1 or 3 day treatment</u>, with vaginal cream, ointment or vaginal suppository/tab **OTC, topical** Butoconazole (*Gynazole-1*, others) Clotrimazole (*Gyne-Lotrimin*, others) Miconazole (*Monistat 3*, others) Terconazole (*Terazol 3*, others) Tioconazole (*Vagistat-1*) **Rx, oral** Fluconazole (*Diflucan*) 150 mg PO x 1 <u>Complicated infections, Pregnancy</u> 7-10 days treatment, or send for referral	 The male sexual partner may be tested if the female's infections are recurrent; this is not commonly done. Always counsel on ways to avoid recurrence: avoid douching, wear cotton underwear, avoid tight-fitting pantyhose and pants, change out of wet swimsuits quickly. Some recommend avoiding hot tubs or very hot baths.	Counseling for OTC antifungals: Prior to using the product, wash the vagina with mild soap and water, and pat dry with a towel. Insert applicator, suppository, or vaginal tab at night before bed. Lying down immediately after insertion helps retain the medicine inside the vagina. It may be helpful to use a protective pad. The creams and suppositories are oil-based medications that can weaken latex condoms and diaphragms; avoid sexual intercourse. If you get your menstrual cycle during treatment, continue the treatment, otherwise a woman can wait until her menstrual cycle is over before starting treatment if she desires (this is not necessary.) Do not use tampons during treatment. Complete entire course of treatment. Medical care is warranted if symptoms persist/recur within 2 months after using an OTC product, or if > 4/year.

Eczema (Atopic Dermatitis), Background & Treatment

- Eczema is a general term for many types of skin inflammation, and is used interchangeably with the term atopic dermatitis (which is sometimes used to refer to other conditions – this makes the term "atopic dermatitis" confusing.)

- Eczema is most common in young children and infants, but can occur at any age.

- Eczema presents as skin rashes, which become crusty and scaly; blisters can develop. The rash is very itchy, red, dry and sore.

- Common locations are the insides of elbows, back of knees, face (often on the cheeks), behind the ears, buttocks, hands and feet.

- Outbreak "triggers" can be environmental irritants or allergens, including soaps, perfumes, pollution, stress or weather changes; patients should attempt to avoid triggers.

- Hydration is <u>essential</u> to reduce disease severity. Use <u>moisturizers</u>. Maintain humidity in the home.

- Treatment can include <u>topical corticosteroids</u> (and occasional oral courses, if-needed), antihistamines (for itching), or the <u>immune-suppresant calcineurin inhibitors, if topical steroids with hydration are not adequate</u>.

- In severe, refractive cases oral immune-suppressants (cyclosporine, methotrexate, monoclonal antibody-type drugs such as etanercept and others) can be used. These are described in other chapters.

DRUGS	NOTES	SAFETY/COUNSELING
Tx: topical or oral steroids, antibiotics, antihistamines, keep skin well hydrated (moisturized with petrolatum, lanolin, products such as *Aquaphor, Eucerin, Keri* or store brands) <u>Treat first with topical steroids, only use these agents if failed steroids:</u> **Tacrolimus *(Protopic)*** **Pimecrolimus *(Elidel)*** Do not use in children younger than 2 years of age.	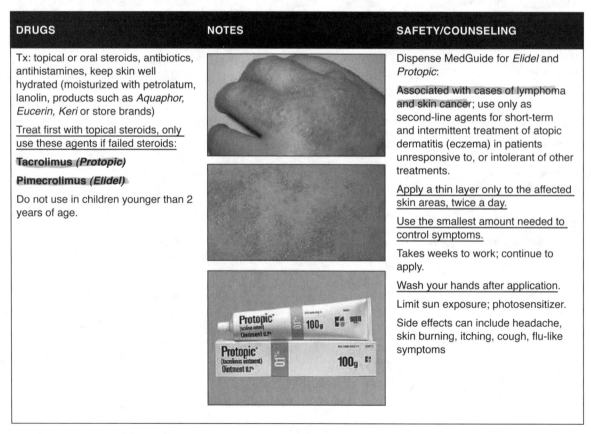	Dispense MedGuide for *Elidel* and *Protopic*: Associated with cases of lymphoma and skin cancer; use only as second-line agents for short-term and intermittent treatment of atopic dermatitis (eczema) in patients unresponsive to, or intolerant of other treatments. <u>Apply a thin layer only to the affected skin areas, twice a day.</u> <u>Use the smallest amount needed to control symptoms.</u> Takes weeks to work; continue to apply. <u>Wash your hands after application.</u> Limit sun exposure; photosensitizer. Side effects can include headache, skin burning, itching, cough, flu-like symptoms

Lice, Background & Treatment

NOTE this section discusses lice; SCABIES (mites) are treated with some of the same medications. Scabies are primarily spread through sexual contact. The primary treatment for scabies is permethrin in a cream formulation (*Elimite*) and the prescription drug ivermectin (*Stromectol*), two doses, taken one week apart. Ivermectin, when taken orally, can be difficult to tolerate due to lymph node enlargement, arthralgias, skin tenderness, pruritus and fever. Ivermectin was approved in 2012 in a topical formulation for lice called *Sklice*. Lindane (*Kwell*, others) used to be commonly used for scabies (and lice) but is not used commonly now due to neurotoxicity.

- Lice occurs most commonly in elementary school age children.

- Pyrethrins (permethrin) are the OTC drug of choice; can be used in infants as young as 2 months. Avoid with chrysanthemums or ragweed allergy.

- Malathion lotion 0.5% (*Ovide*) is an organophosphate. Only for use on persons 6 years of age and older. Can irritate the skin and is flammable; do not smoke or use electrical heat sources, including hair dryers, curlers, and curling or flat irons, when applying and while the hair is wet.

- Benzyl alcohol lotion (*Ulesfia* 5% lotion) kills live lice but not nits. Can irritate the skin and eyes; avoid eye contact.

- *Lindane* shampoo 1% is no longer recommended due to neurotoxicity and is reserved for refractive cases, and never in pregnancy, on irritated skin, or in infants, children, persons with small frames and the elderly.

- If the same medication has been used several times it may not be working.

- Repeating the procedure, and removing the nits from hair, bedding, and elsewhere is essential:

  - Wash clothes and bedding in hot water, followed by a hot dryer.

  - If something cannot be washed, seal it in an air-proof bag for 2 weeks or dry clean. Vacuum the carpet well. Soak combs and brushes in hot water for 10 minutes. Make sure to check other children in the household.

  - Do not use a combination shampoo/conditioner, or conditioner before using lice medicine. Do not re-wash the hair for 1-2 days after treatment.

  - After each treatment, check the hair and use a nit comb to remove nits and lice every 2-3 days. Continue to check for 2-3 weeks to be sure all lice and nits are gone.

  - Re-treatment is needed for OTC and prescription products (except *Sklice*) on days 7-10 (they vary; check the product) in order to kill any surviving hatched lice before they produce new eggs.

DRUGS	NOTES	SAFETY/COUNSELING
Permethrin, pyrethrins, OTC DOC for lice *(Nix, RID, Triple X)* 2 months+	Notice how the nit is cemented to the hair shaft.	In addition to OTC treatment, remove the live lice and nits by inspecting the hair in 1-inch segments and using a lice comb.
Spinosad *(Natroba)* –works well, expensive. 4+ yrs		Without removing live lice and nits, the OTC product will not work. Nits are "cemented" to the hair shaft and do not fall off after treatment. Nit removal requires multiple efforts, which should be continued for two weeks after treatment. See bulleted points above for additional counseling.
Malathion *(Ovide)* – flammable, do not use near heat source, organophosphate		
Benzyl Alcohol Lotion *(Ulesfia)* 6+ yrs		
Ivermectin (Sklice) 6+ yrs		
Lindane *(Kwell,* others) is no longer routinely recommended; high risk neurotoxicity/seizures, requires MedGuide – more commonly used for scabies (mites)		

Genital Warts, Background & Treatment

- Genital warts are caused by the human papillomavirus (HPV), a common sexually transmitted disease (STD), spread easily skin-to-skin. Consider recommending HPV vaccine, if series incomplete. *Gardasil* protects against the strains of HPV that cause most genital warts and reduces risk of cervical cancer. *Cervarix* protects against cervical cancer but not genital warts. Condoms reduce risk of STD transmission.

- Treatment may not be required if no symptoms, but if discomfort or emotional distress treatment can reduce or remove the warts.

- Imiquimod *(Aldara, Zyclara)* will reduce warts. Avoid sexual contact while the cream is on your skin; weakens condoms, diaphragms and can irritate the partner's skin.

In addition to the treatments below, the warts may be removed by lasers, cryotherapy (with liquid nitrogen to freeze the warts, after which they come off), freezing, electrocautery (electrical current burns off warts) or surgical excision.

DRUGS	NOTES	SAFETY/COUNSELING
Imiquimod cream *(Aldara, Zyclara)*	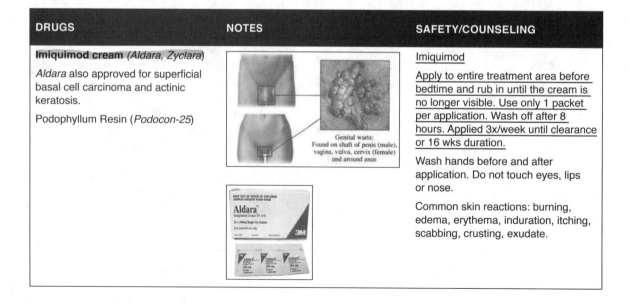 Genital warts: Found on shaft of penis (male), vagina, vulva, cervix (female) and around anus	Imiquimod
Aldara also approved for superficial basal cell carcinoma and actinic keratosis.		Apply to entire treatment area before bedtime and rub in until the cream is no longer visible. Use only 1 packet per application. Wash off after 8 hours. Applied 3x/week until clearance or 16 wks duration.
Podophyllum Resin *(Podocon-25)*		Wash hands before and after application. Do not touch eyes, lips or nose.
		Common skin reactions: burning, edema, erythema, induration, itching, scabbing, crusting, exudate.

Topical Inflammation (From Various Conditions, Rashes), Background & Treatment

- Primary treatment for skin irritation are topical steroids. Two strengths of hydrocortisone (HC) available OTC, 0.5% and 1%; all other topical steroids are prescription. A CHART OF RX TOPICAL STEROIDS is at the end of this chapter.

- The steroid vehicle influences the strength of the medication. Usual potency, from highest to weakest: ointment > creams > lotions > solutions > gels > sprays. Ointments have low water content; refer to compounding chapter for details.

- Parts of the body with thin skin, such as the face, eyelids and genitals, are highly susceptible to the side effects of topical steroids and low potency products should be used on these areas. Use low potency products on areas of the skin with folds, such as the armpits, groin, and under the breasts, as the absorption is higher.

- Local side effects (where the steroid is applied) are more likely but systemic steroid toxicity can occur if large amounts are used, and if over large areas.

- Local (skin) steroid side effects, if used long-term include skin thinning, pigment changes (lighter or darker), telangectasia (blood vessel) formation, rosacea, perioral dermatitis and acne, increased risk skin infections, delayed wound healing, irritation/burning/peeling, and possibly contact dermatitis from the steroid itself.

DRUGS	NOTES	SAFETY/COUNSELING
OTC steroids are low potency: Hydrocortisone 0.5% (infants) and 1% for mild conditions, thin skin (groin area, elderly) and for children. HC 1% lotion *(Aquanil)* See other steroids in chart at end of this section. Apply high potency Rx steroids once daily – Apply OTC/lower potency 1-2x daily. It is common to see a higher potency product, followed by a lower potency product, to treat acute inflammation. Severe rash likely to require oral steroids for 1-2 weeks.	Ointments often more potent than creams; use ointments for thick or dry skin. Ointments have low water content (reduced absorption) and form a skin barrier. Use lotions, gels and foams for hairy skin. No evidence for use of topical diphenhydramine – can use systemic but caution due to side effects. Skin should be lubricated (hydrated) with moisturizers for most conditions. The steroid vehicle can lubricate. Camphor, menthol, local anesthetics (often in combo creams with HC) can help relieve itching. COMMON STEROIDS, BY POTENCY, AT END OF THIS CHAPTER	 The "finger-tip" unit is used to estimate amount required: the amount that can be squeezed from the fingertip to the 1st joint covers one adult hand (about ½ g) Topical steroid over-use has risks; see top bullet points. Do not apply for longer than 2 weeks. Encourage patient not to use more than directed.
HydrOXYzine *(Vistaril)* 25 mg TID-QID	Used for general urticaria (hives) with severe itching	Anticholinergic; primarily sedation and dry mouth.

Diaper Rash, Background & Treatment

Diaper rash commonly occurs with nearly all babies. The skin is sensitive, and when exposed to the urine and stools, and a diaper moving back and forth, rash appears. Once the skin is damaged it is susceptible to bacteria and yeast overgrowth.

Prevention

- Change diapers frequently, do not cover diapers with plastic, use absorbent diapers.

- Wipe well with unscented wipes or plain water.

- Leave off the diaper, when possible, to let the skin air-dry. The baby can lie on a towel.

- Use a skin protectant:

  - Petrolatum ointment (*A & D* ointment, store brands) – this is a good preventative everyday ointment.

  - Petrolatum with zinc oxide, such as in *Desitin* – is thicker and contains a dessicant (zinc oxide) to dry out the skin; may be preferable for babies more prone to rash.

- "Butt paste" or "Triple paste" – are other alternatives.

- Clotrimazole, miconazole, others – for stubborn rashes, if yeast thought to be involved.

- Hydrocortisone 0.5-1% cream – can be used BID, but not for more than several days at a time.

- Combinations of the above are used.

DRUGS	NOTES	SAFETY/COUNSELING
Desitin (petrolatum + zinc oxide, a dessicant to decrease moisture) *A&D Ointment*, or plain petrolatum, or store-brands. Miconazole+zinc oxide+petrolatum (*Vusion*) Or other products mentioned above.		Review counseling tips above. Infants should be referred to the physician (especially if under 6 months) and older babies if condition appears serious or worsens. Topical antibiotics may be needed if bacterial involvement is suspected. Topical antifungals may be needed if fungal involvement is suspected. Topical steroids, low potency, may be used short-term. Diaper rashes can have more than one contributing organism.

Minor Cuts, Abrasions & Burns, Background & Treatment

- The basic types of minor wounds are lacerations, abrasions, cuts, bites and burns.

- Some can be effectively treated through simple first aid and others, depending on the severity, may need more medical attention than first aid can provide.

- Anything that involves puncture wounds should be referred out.

- Make sure tetanus vaccine is current (Q 10 years, after series has been completed.) If the wound is dirty a repeat tetanus vaccine may be required if it is >5 years since vaccination. The patient should be referred for medical care.

- If wound looks like abuse, contact authorities if able.

- Abrasions are minor injuries to the top layer of skin and are primarily treated with simple first aid.

- Abrasions such as a skinned knee can be cleaned thoroughly, antibiotic ointment applied and allowed to air heal.

- Lacerations are defined as irregular wounds with ragged edges, with the potential for deeper skin damage and bruising under the skin.

- If deep seek medical attention.

- A cut is different than a laceration because the edges will be more uniform or regular.

- After cleaning, if the bleeding does not stop, or it extends far below the surface layers of the skin, seek medical attention because it may require stitching to get the wound to close. If not, regular bandaging should get the edges of the wound to close over time.

- Antibiotic ointment can be applied prior to placing the bandage.

- Tissue adhesives *(Band-Aid Liquid Bandage, Nexcare Skin Crack Care*, others) create a polymer layer, which binds to the skin, keeping the wound clean and keeping moisture out. Some contain topical analgesics. *Seal-On* is a topical sponge (dressing) that can absorb blood and is used for nose-bleeds and other minor bleeds. There are other similar products.

- Bites (except minor insect bites) should never be treated with just simple first aid, because of the high risk of infection, especially with animal or human bites. Certain spider bites in the U.S. can be deadly: the brown recluse, the black widow and the hobo spiders. Spiders tend to stay hidden and are not aggressive. Bites can be generally be avoided by inspecting and shaking out clothing or equipment prior to use, and wearing protective clothing. If bitten, stay calm, identify the type of spider if possible, wash with soap and cold water, apply cold compress with ice, elevate extremity, and get emergency medical care.

- Minor, harmless insect bites can be treated with a topical steroid or systemic antihistamine (such as diphenhydramine) to reduce itching.

- Burns are characterized as first degree (red/painful, minor swelling), second degree (thicker, very painful, produce blisters) and third degree (damage to all layers of skin, skin appears white or charred.) Burns produced by chemical exposure, or in a person with underlying disease that reduces immunity should be referred for emergency medical care.

- If the burn is first or second degree OTC treatment is acceptable if the area is less than 2 inches in diameter and if the burn is not on the face, over a major joint or on the feet or genitals. In diabetes a burn on a foot, even mild, could lead to an amputation. Vigilance is required.

- Minor burns should be treated first by running the burn under cool running water or soaking in cool water for 5-20 minutes.

- Do not apply ice, which can further damage the injured skin. Bandages should be applied if the skin is broken, or if blisters pop. Burns heal best when kept moist (but not wet). Certain bandages designed for burns keep the environment moist, or ointments, such as antibiotic ointment, can be applied.

- Burned skin itches as it heals; the fingernails of children may need to be cut short and filed, or covered. The skin that has been burned will be more sensitive to the sun for up to a year.

- Ointments (80% oil/20% water, such as Aquaphor) should be used for skin protection over a minor burn to hold in moisture and reduce scarring risk.

- Silver sulfadiazene *(Silvadene; SSD; Thermazene)* may be used topically to reduce infection risk and promote healing, although it has not been shown to be very effective. If the skin is broken systemic toxicity could occur. Do not use if sulfa allergy or G6PD deficiency (due to hemolysis risk).

DRUGS	NOTES	SAFETY/COUNSELING
Triple antibiotic ointment (Neosporin, store brands) contains polymyxin, bacitracin & neomycin. If reaction to the neomycin component can use **Polysporin** (bacitracin and polymixin) or **Bacitracin** alone. Either of these is often sufficient. **Mupirocin (Bactroban) is an Rx antibiotic cream or ointment; very good staph and strep coverage, including MRSA; can be used for nasal MRSA colonization.** Tissue adhesives *(Band-Aid Liquid Bandage, Nexcare Skin Crack Care,* others) – "paint on" bandages to protect/keep moisture in skin via polymer layer. *Seal-On*, others (topical dressings for minor bleeds). sponge (dressing) that	The wound may be covered with a sterile bandage if it is in a place that could get dirty.  Leaving a wound uncovered helps it stay dry and helps it heal. If the wound is not in an area that will get dirty or be rubbed by clothing, it does not need to be covered.	To apply topical antibiotics: Clean the affected area and apply a small amount of medication (an amount equal to the surface area of the tip of a finger) to the affected area 1 to 3 times daily. If area can get dirty (such as a hand) or be irritated by clothing, cover with an adhesive strip (e.g., *Band-Aid*) or with sterile gauze and adhesive tape +/- antibiotic ointment. Change daily. Certain wounds, like large scrapes, should be kept moist and clean to help reduce scarring and speed healing. Bandages used for this purpose are called occlusive or semi-occlusive bandages. Burns require a moist (but not wet) environment by applying either ointment, or a bandage designed for burns.

Poison Ivy, Oak, Sumac, Background & Treatment

- Poison ivy, oak or sumac poisoning is an allergic reaction that results from touching the sap of these plants, which contain the toxin uroshiol.

- The sap may be on the plant, in the ashes of burned plants, on an animal, or on other objects that came in contact with the plant, such as clothing, garden tools, and sports equipment.

- Small amounts of uroshiol can remain under a person's fingernails for several days unless it is deliberately removed with good cleaning.

- Poison ivy grows around lakes and streams in the midwest and east. Leaves are green in the summer and red in the fall.

- Poison oak grows in the western (along the Pacific coast) and in the east from New Jersey to Texas. The leaves look like oak, usually in clusters of three leaves. The plant has clusters of yellow berries.

- Poison sumac grows in boggy areas, especially in the southeast and west. The leaves have 7-13 smooth-edged leaflets, with pale yellow or cream-colored berries.

DRUGS	NOTES	SAFETY/COUNSELING
Aluminum acetate solution (*Burrow's*) Colloidal oatmeal (*Aveeno*) Calamine lotion – *Caladryl, IvaRest* are calamine + topical analgesics *Zanfel* is supposed to bind urushiol (this is the toxin) – low evidence for efficacy	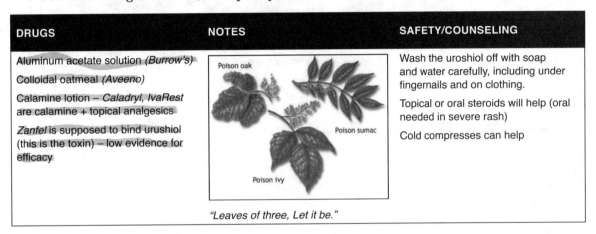 *"Leaves of three, Let it be."*	Wash the uroshiol off with soap and water carefully, including under fingernails and on clothing. Topical or oral steroids will help (oral needed in severe rash) Cold compresses can help

Psoriasis, Background & Treatment

- Psoriasis is a chronic, autoimmune disease that appears on the skin. There are several types of psoriasis. The most common is plaque psoriasis, which appears as raised, red patches covered with a silvery white buildup of dead skin cells, on any part of the body.

- Psoriasis treatments can be divided into three main types: topical treatments, light therapy and systemic medications.

- Topical treatments include steroids, vitamin D analogues (calcipotriene), anthralin, topical retinoids (some of the same drugs used for acne), calcineurin inhibitors (*Protopic*, *Elidel*), salicylic acid (primarily in medicated shampoo), coal tar and moisturizers.

- Ultraviolet (UV) light exposure causes activated T cells in the skin to die. This slows skin cell turnover and reduces scaling and inflammation. Brief, daily exposures to small amounts of sunlight can improve psoriasis, but intense sun exposure can worsen symptoms and cause skin damage.

- UVB phototherapy, in controlled doses from an artificial light source, can improve mild to moderate psoriasis symptoms. UVB phototherapy, also called broadband UVB, can be used to treat single patches, widespread psoriasis and psoriasis that resists topical treatments.

- There are other therapies, including combined treatments, photochemotherapy (ultraviolet A light with psoralen, a light-sensitizer), and laser light therapy.

- Medications for more severe symptoms may require immune suppressing agents, including methotrexate, cyclosporine, hydroxyurea and the immunomodulators, such as etanercept and infliximab. These are described in the rheumatoid arthritis and oncology chapters.

- This section focuses on the topical agents; most psoriasis is treated with topicals and UV light therapy. Soaking helps loosen and remove the plaques.

DRUGS	NOTES	SAFETY/COUNSELING
Most patients start with <u>topical steroids</u>, which is sufficient in some cases. Choose the type based on the location; see section on steroids at end of this chapter. High-potency steroid topicals are only used short-term due to risk of side effects. Other agents: Retinioids (see acne in above section) Coal tar, in many products, including *Neutrogena T, Denorex* Keratolytics (salicylic acid, sulfur), combo with cold tar *(Sebutone)* Anthralin *(Anthranol*, others) Calcipotriene *(Dovonex*, a vit D analog) **Calcipotriene and betamethasone ointment *(Taclonex, Taclonex scalp suspension)*** If topicals are not effective, can use: Oral steroids Psoralens+UV therapy Acitretin *(Soriatane)* (severe cases only)	White, scaly psoriasis plaque Psoriasis patients typically using products in combination.	*Taclonex* <u>If suspension shake well</u> Do not use > 4 weeks Do not use > 100 g ointment weekly <u>Tar products</u> are messy, time-consuming and can stain clothing and bedding. However, they are available OTC, including products applied to the skin and shampoo and bath products. Some patients get relief from these products at a reasonable cost.

Alopecia (Hair Loss), Background & Treatment

■ As people age, hair tends to gradually thin. Other causes of hair loss include hormonal factors, medical conditions and medications.

■ The most common cause of hair loss is a hereditary condition called male-pattern baldness, and less commonly, female-pattern baldness.

■ Hormonal changes in women that can result in hair loss are usually associated with pregnancy, childbirth or menopause.

■ Medical conditions that cause hair loss include hypothyroidism, alopecia areata (an autoimmune condition), scalp infections and some other conditions, including lupus.

■ Drugs that can contribute to alopecia include various chemotherapeutics (primarily because hair cells are rapidly dividing and therefore are targeted by the treatment) and infrequently with the following medications: clomiphene, heparin, hydroxychloroquine, interferons, lithium, some types of oral contraceptives, levonorgestrel, procainamide, valproate, spironolactone and warfarin.

■ Zinc and vitamin D deficiency is thought to contribute to hair loss.

■ Many people will seek surgical intervention for hair loss. The medications work modestly and are presented here. Bimatoprost in the *Latisse* formulation is for thinning eyelashes (hypotrichosis) and should not be used concurrently in patients using a prostaglandin analog for glaucoma (minimally, contact the optometrist or opthamologist to confirm because the IOP may increase if there is excessive use of prostaglandin analogs.)

DRUGS	NOTES	SAFETY/COUNSELING
Finasteride *(Propecia)* 5-alpha reductase type 2 inhibitor Do not dispense with someone on finasteride *(Proscar)* for BPH 1 mg daily, at least 3 months duration to begin to see effect Male pattern baldness "My Mom always said…god made a few good heads, and put hair on the rest of them."		Preg Categ X: females should not handle – can damage male fetus. Must be used indefinitely or condition reappears. **SIDE EFFECTS** Lower dose than *Proscar*; lower risk of sexual side effects; see overactive bladder chapter for further details
Minoxidil topical OTC 2% and 5% – 5% solution more effective, but more facial hair growth.	Rx tablets indicated for hypertension (very rarely used)	For men and women Must be used indefinitely or condition reappears.
Bimatoprost solution *(Latisse)* For thinning eyelashes (hypotrichosis)	Apply nightly to the skin at the base of the upper eyelashes only (do not apply to the lower lid). Use the applicator brush. Blot any excess. Repeat for other eye. Dispose of the applicator after one use.	May cause itchy eyes and/or eye redness. If discontinued, lashes eventually return to previous appearance. Eyelid skin darkening may occur, which may be reversible. Hair growth may occur in other skin areas that the solution frequently touches. Do not use concurrently with PG analogs used for glaucoma.

Sunscreens, Background & Treatment

- Applying sunscreen is important due to the risk of sun damage and skin cancer. Keep in mind that sunscreen blocks vitamin D production in the skin and many Americans are vitamin-D deficient. This is a difficulty in current practice.

- It is advisable to stay out of the sun when it is strongest (between 10AM-4PM). The sun damaging ultraviolet (UV) rays penetrate clouds; this applies to overcast days as well.

- Another method to avoid the sun is to wear protective clothing.

- Where skin is exposed sunscreen can be applied that provides both UVA (A for aging – causes damage below the skin surface) and UVB (B for burning) protection. Both UVA and UVB contribute to skin cancer. A "broad spectrum" sunscreen should be chosen; it protects against both UVA and UVB. SPF stands for sun protection factor, which is a measure of how well the sunscreen deflects UVB rays.

- Some dermatologists recommend SPF 15 and others recommend SPF 30. The key is to apply liberally and at least every two hours. The American Academy of Pediatrics says to keep all babies less than 6 months old out of the sun.

- HOW SPF WORKS: If someone would normally burn in 10 minutes, an SPF of 5 would extend the time they would burn to 50 minutes (5 x 10 = 50.) However, it is not accurate to calculate that if one normally would burn in one hour, then a sunscreen with an SPF of 10 would permit the person to stay in the sun for 10 hours (10 times longer) without burning, since the intensity of the sun varies during the day, and the sunscreen would not last more than a couple of hours.

- Sunscreen labeling is no longer permitted to use "waterproof" or "sweatproof" since they all wash off, at least partially, in the water. They can claim to be "water-resistant" but only for 40-80 minutes. Always reapply after swimming, or sweating.

- The American Academy of Dermatology (AAD) recommends sunscreens with any of the following ingredients: avobenzone, cinoxate, ecamsule, menthyl anthranilate, octyl methoxycinnamate, octyl salicylate, oxybenzone or sulisobenzone.

- Oxybenzone irritates some people's skin; this is not common.

DRUGS	NOTES	SAFETY/COUNSELING
Many products, choose one with UVA and UVB coverage, SPF 15+. UVA: Blocks aging (A for aging – wrinkles). Ingredients that block UVA: ecamsule, avobenzone, oxybenzone, sulisobenzone, titanium dioxide, zinc oxide (zinc and titanium are common barrier agents). UVB: Blocks burning (B for burning). SPF (sun exposure factor) – measures how long it takes to burn versus not using sunscreen (measures UVB only). An SPF of 15 takes 15 times longer for skin to redden than without the sunscreen.	 Apply liberally, at least every two hours, prior to sun exposure, and after getting the skin wet from swimming or sweating.	All sunscreens wash off; reapply after going in the water and at least every 2 hours. Avoid peak sun (10AM-4PM), even if overcast. Wear protective clothing. Consider vitamin D deficiency-if avoiding sun or little sun exposure may need supplementation. UVA and UVB exposure increases risk of skin cancer, including most common type (squamous cell). "Broad spectrum" covers both UVA and UVB. Water resistant – means resistant for 40-80 minutes.

Cold Sores (herpes simplex virus type 1 (HSV-1), Background & Treatment

- Herpes simplex I (HSV-1, oral herpes, or herpes simplex labialis) infection commonly causes cold sore or fever blisters.

- Herpes simplex virus 2, HSV-2, causes most cases of genital herpes. It is possible for either HSV-1 or HSV-2 to cause herpes sores on the face or genitals.

- There is no cure but antivirals reduce incidence.

- Complications rarely occur in healthy people with herpes simplex, but can be present in cancer, HIV and transplant patients, or those on immunosuppresants.

- Some patients may need an oral antiviral (e.g., valacyclovir, others).

- Other topicals include the OTC product docosanol (*Abreva*) and the combination acyclovir/hydrocortisone topical *Xerese*.

DRUGS	NOTES	SAFETY/COUNSELING
OTC Docosanol cream *(Abreva)* Rx Acyclovir/Hydrocortisone *(Xerese)* Acyclovir *(Zovirax)* cream, penciclovir *(Denavir)* cream, or oral antivirals		*Abreva*: apply 5 x/day until sore healed, max 10 days *Zovirax* cream, 5 x daily x 4 days *Denavir* cream, Q 2 hrs during day x 4 days Cold sores are not canker scores (these are inside mouth). Cold sores are on the lips. Sores brought on by triggers, primarily stress.

Potencies of Topical Steroid Products

TREATMENT	ACTIVE INGREDIENT

Very High Potency

TREATMENT	ACTIVE INGREDIENT
Clobex **Lotion/Spray/Shampoo, 0.05%**	**Clobetasol propionate**
Cormax Cream/Solution, 0.05%	Clobetasol propionate
Diprolene **Ointment, 0.05%**	**Betamethasone dipropionate**
Olux E Foam, 0.05%	Clobetasol propionate
Olux Foam, 0.05%	Clobetasol propionate
Temovate **Cream/Ointment/Solution, 0.05%**	**Clobetasol propionate**
Ultravate Cream/Ointment, 0.05%	Halobetasol propionate
Vanos Cream, 0.1%	**Fluocinonide**
Psorcon Ointment, 0.05%	Diflorasone diacetate
Psorcon E Ointment, 0.05%	Diflorasone diacetate

High Potency

TREATMENT	ACTIVE INGREDIENT
Diprolene **Cream AF, 0.05%**	**Betamethasone dipropionate**
Elocon **Ointment, 0.1%**	**Mometasone furoate**
Florone Ointment, 0.05%	Diflorasone diacetate
Halog Ointment/Cream, 0.1%	Halcinonide
Lidex **Cream/Gel/Ointment, 0.05%**	**Fluocinonide**
Psorcon Cream, 0.05%	Diflorasone diacetate
Topicort Cream/Ointment, 0.25%	Desoximetasone
Topicort Gel, 0.05%	Desoximetasone

Potencies of Topical Steroid Products Continued

TREATMENT	ACTIVE INGREDIENT

High-Medium Potency

TREATMENT	ACTIVE INGREDIENT
Cutivate Ointment, 0.005%	Fluticasone propionate
Lidex-E **Cream, 0.05%**	**Fluocinonide**
Luxiq Foam, 0.12%	Betamethasone valerate
Topicort LP Cream, 0.05%	Desoximetasone

Medium Potency

TREATMENT	ACTIVE INGREDIENT
Cordran Ointment, 0.05%	Flurandrenolide
Elocon **Cream, 0.1%**	**Mometasone furoate**
Kenalog **Cream/Spray, 0.1%**	**Triamcinolone acetonide**
Synalar Ointment, 0.03%	Fluocinolone acetonide
Westcort **Ointment, 0.2%**	**Hydrocortisone valerate**

Lower Potency

TREATMENT	ACTIVE INGREDIENT
Capex Shampoo, 0.01%	Fluocinolone acetonide
Cordran Cream/Lotion/Tape, 0.05%	Flurandrenolide
Cutivate Cream/Lotion, 0.05%	Fluticasone propionate
DermAtop Cream, 0.1%	Prednicarbate
DesOwen **Lotion, 0.05%**	**Desonide**
Locoid Cream/Lotion/Ointment/Solution, 0.1%	Hydrocortisone
Pandel Cream, 0.1%	Hydrocortisone
Synalar Cream, 0.03%/0.01%	Fluocinolone acetonide
Westcort **Cream, 0.2%**	**Hydrocortisone valerate**

Mild Potency

TREATMENT	ACTIVE INGREDIENT
Aclovate Cream/Ointment, 0.05%	Alclometasone dipropionate
Derma-**Smoothe/FS Oil, 0.01%**	**Fluocinolone acetonide**
Desonate Gel, 0.05%	Desonide
Synalar Cream/Solution, 0.01%	Fluocinolone acetonide
Verdeso Foam, 0.05%	Desonide

Lowest Potency

TREATMENT	ACTIVE INGREDIENT
Cetacort Lotion, 0.5%/1%	Hydrocortisone
Cortaid Cream/Spray/Ointment	**Hydrocortisone**
Hytone Cream/Lotion, 1%/2.5%	Hydrocortisone
Micort-HC Cream, 2%/2.5%	Hydrocortisone
Nutracort Lotion, 1%/2.5%	Hydrocortisone
Synacort Cream, 1%/2.5%	Hydrocortisone

WEIGHT LOSS

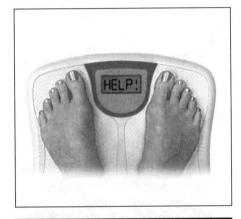

GUIDELINES

2013 AHA/ACC/TOS Guideline for
the Management of Overweight
and Obesity in Adults: A Report of
the American College of Cardiol-
ogy/American Heart Association
Task Force on Practice Guidelines
and The Obesity Society. Circulation. 2013;01. cir.0000437739.71477.
eepublished online before print
November 12 2013,doi:10.1161/01.
cir.0000437739.71477.ee (accessed
2013 Nov 18).

BACKGROUND

Overweight and obesity is a national health threat and a major public health challenge. Data from the CDC (2008) estimates obesity at 72.5 million adults in the U.S., with many more falling into the overweight category. Overweight puts patients at increased risk for coronary heart disease, hypertension, stroke, type 2 diabetes, certain types of cancer, and premature death. In addition to health risks, overweight reduces quality of life and causes social stigmatization and discrimination. This is sadly true for adults, and for children. Not too long ago it was uncommon to see an overweight child. Today, one-third of children are overweight or obese.

Weight loss is successful only when the patient (and usually the family) is able to make permanent changes in diet and exercise habits. Fad diets may cause an acute weight drop but do not contribute to long-term weight loss and can have harmful health consequences. Many people think they are just "born fat" or have low metabolism. Children become overweight (and grow into overweight adults) due to poor eating habits in the family and community. If low metabolism is an issue it will show up on lab tests (as hypothyroidism) and will be treated.

A healthy weight: value and achievement

In 2013 long-awaited obesity guidelines were released as a joint project between the American College of Cardiology, the American Heart Association and the Obesity Society. The guidelines support these actions:

Obesity needs to be confronted and addressed – which means it needs to be identified. BMI and waist circumference should be assessed at least annually. Overweight and obese patients should be warned of the health risks.

Counseling should emphasize that lifestyle changes that produce even modest, sustained weight loss of 3%-5% produce clinically meaningful health benefits (decreased triglycerides, A1C, and the risk of developing type 2 diabetes), and greater weight loss produces greater benefits.

Rather than emphasizing one particular type of diet, the guidelines state that "A variety of dietary approaches can produce weight loss in overweight and obese adults." Dietary strategies could consist of any 1 of the following methods:

- Reducing food and calorie intake: (1,200–1,500 kcal/day for women and 1,500–1,800 kcal/day for men or using a 500-750 kcal/day energy deficit; (a 500 kcal decrease per day equals 1 pound weight lost per week (3,500 kcal/pound), or

- Using "one of the diets" that restricts certain food types (such as restricting high-carbohydrate foods, low-fiber foods, or high-fat foods) in order to create an energy deficit by reduced food intake.

- In select patients and only under medical monitoring the use of a very low calorie diet (defined as < 800 kcal/day) can be provided.

To assist high-risk patients, high-intensity interventions led by a trained person is recommended. These could be live or delivered by phone or electronically. Some commercial-based programs that provide a comprehensive lifestyle intervention can be prescribed if there is "peer-reviewed published evidence of their safety and efficacy."

In all patients, weight loss support should include regular contact with a trained person, with body weight and diet monitoring and regular physical activity (i.e., 200-300 minutes/week).

The guidelines recommend bariatric surgery for adults with a BMI ≥ 40 or BMI ≥ 35 with an obesity-related comorbid condition. This will involve adjusting medications and nutrient support. Post-bariatric requirements are discussed in more detail later in this chapter.

Weight Loss Drugs: OTC and Rx

OTC

OTC weight loss drugs commonly contain stimulants, such as the ephedra alkaloid bitter orange or related compounds, along with excessive amounts of caffeine. Caffeine is packaged under different names – including as yerba mate, guarana or concentrated green tea powder. Tolerance develops quickly with the use of these agents, requiring higher doses. In patients with cardiovascular risk – which is often present in overweight patients – they carry significant risk. A newer OTC product called *Fastin* (the name is taken from the previous Rx drug phentermine) is being marketed as a "thermogenic intensifier." It contains stimulants, including synephrine and caffeine. For CVD-risk patients it should be viewed as a potential heart-attack-in-a-bottle. In February of 2012 Dr. Oz recommended raspberry ketones and sales took off. There is no evidence that this compound works for weight loss, and the structure is similar to synephrine. In 2013 "green coffee bean extract" became popular. OTC weight loss agents should not be recommended unless it is *Alli*, which contains a lower dose of the prescription agent orlistat (*Xenical*). This may be useful for patients who wish to provide a motivation to reduce fat intake, but use caution since *Alli* has tolerability problems, including flatulence, and is expensive. It would be better to help the patient adopt healthier eating for long-term benefit.

RX

Prescription agents are not appropriate for patients with small amounts of weight to lose. Prescription drugs should not be used in patients who are not obese or overweight with at least one weight-related co-morbidity (such as diabetes or hypertension). They are only used in addition to a dietary plan and increased physical activity, per the FDA. However, one may wish to consider what they are eating, as carbohydrates are a culprit to many in obtaining long-term weight loss.

Two new drugs were approved in 2012 for weight loss; both of these drugs were originally rejected by the FDA for psychiatric and cardiovascular effects (*Qysmia*) and for cancer and cardiovascular effects (*Belviq*). With these two agents, pharmacists should consider the "7 year rule" – which roughly translates to: do not recommend new agents until they have been out for awhile and used in millions--not including your patients, friends and family--in order to get a more complete understanding of the adverse effect profile than might have been evident in clinical trials.

DRUG	DOSING	SAFETY/SIDE EFFECTS/MONITORING

Phentermine: Sympathomimetic, with effects similar to amphetamines, causing increase in norepinephrine.

Topiramate: Effects due to decreased appetite and satiety, possibly by enhancing GABA, blocking glutamate receptors and/or weak inhibition of carbonic anhydrase.

| Phentermine and topiramate extended-release capsules (*Qsymia*)

C IV

REMS drug: only through certified pharmacy network; not all stores will carry. Psychiatric and cardiac monitoring required. | Start at 3.75-23 mg PO Q AM x 14 days, then titrate up based on weight loss. | **CONTRAINDICATIONS**
Hyperthyroidism, glaucoma, MAO I use within past 14 days, pregnancy, lactation

SIDE EFFECTS
Dizziness, headache, cognitive impairment, constipation, dry mouth, insomnia, paresthesias, ↓ serum bicarbonate, upper respiratory tract infection, pharyngitis

Decrease dose with moderate renal impairment

NOTES
CrCl < 50 mL/min max dose phentermine 7.5 mg/topiramate 46 mg daily

Pregnancy Category X |

Weight Loss Drugs Continued

DRUG	DOSING	SAFETY/SIDE EFFECTS/MONITORING

Serotonin 5-HT$_{2c}$ receptor agonist

| Lorcaserin *(Belviq)*

C IV | 10 mg PO BID

Discontinue if 5% weight loss not achieved by week 12 | **CONTRAINDICATIONS**
Pregnancy

SIDE EFFECTS
Headache, dizziness, fatigue, nausea, dry mouth, constipation, hypoglycemia (in diabetes patients, monitor, ↓ lymphocytes)

NOTES

Per FDA, company required to monitor cardiovascular outcomes after release

Pregnancy Category X

Serotonergic risk with additive agents |

Short term appetite suppressants – sympathomimetics, with effects similar to amphetamines, causing increase in norepinephrine

| Phentermine *(Adipex-P, Suprenza-ODT)*

C III | 15-37.5 mg PO, before or after breakfast, or in divided doses | **CONTRAINDICATIONS**
MAO Is within past 14 days

Avoid use with hypertension, PAH, hyperthyroidism, glaucoma, abuse potential |
| Diethylpropion *(Tenuate)*

C III | 25 mg PO IR, TID 1 hour before meals and mid-evening

75 mg PO SR, once in midmorning | **SIDE EFFECTS**
Dizziness, tremor, agitation, tachycardia, blood pressure elevations, insomnia, cardiovascular complications, dependence, psychotic symptoms possible

Used for 3-4 weeks to "jump-start" a diet. |

Long-term lipase inhibitor

| Orlistat Rx *(Xenical)* | 120 mg PO w/each meal containing fat

Both orlistat formulations must be used with a low-fat diet plan. | (Rare) cases liver damage

SIDE EFFECTS
GI (flatus with discharge, fecal urgency, fatty stool)

~13 lbs in 1 year

NOTES
Increased risk urinary oxalate stones

Reduces 1/3 dietary fat

Take multivitamin with A, D, E, K and beta carotene at bedtime or separated by 2+ hours from *Xenical*. Do not use with cyclosporine or separate by 3+ hours. Separate levothyroxine by 4 hours.

Must stick to dietary plan for both weight improvements and to help moderate side effects |

OTC

| Orlistat OTC *(Alli)* | 60 mg PO w/each meal containing fat | Same as *Xenical* (above) for counseling, vitamin and diet/fat intake, and drug interactions.

~5 pounds in 6 months

Reduces 1/4 dietary fat |

Post-Bariatric Surgery; Pharmacists Role

The guidelines recommend advising adults with a BMI ≥ 40 or BMI ≥ 35 with an obesity-related comorbid conditions who are motivated to lose weight and who have not responded to other options that bariatric surgery may be an appropriate option to improve health, and offer referral to an experienced bariatric surgeon for consultation and evaluation. This will correlate with easier payment for these procedures and therefore a higher number of patients receiving them. Bariatric surgery restricts food intake, which leads to weight loss. Patients who have bariatric surgery must commit to a lifetime of healthy eating and regular exercise. These are important to sustain the weight loss.

The procedure may use "open" approaches, which involve cutting the stomach in the standard manner, or by laparoscopy. Most bariatric surgery today is laparoscopic because it requires a smaller cut, creates less tissue damage, leads to earlier hospital discharges, and has fewer problems, especially less hernias occurring after surgery. Not all patients are suitable for laparoscopy. Patients who are extremely obese, who have had previous stomach surgery, or who have complex medical problems may require the open approach.

Weight loss surgery requires changes to the drug regimen, and adjustments in nutrients with decreased absorption, depending on the surgery type. This summary will not distinguish between the needs with various surgeries, but rather provide a short review of common problems.

Micronutrients

- One of the most common problems following bariatric surgery is calcium deficiency. Calcium is mostly absorbed in the duodenum, which may be bypassed. Calcium citrate is preferred as it has non-acid dependent absorption.

- Anemia may result from vitamin B12 and iron deficiency; both may require supplementation. Iron and calcium supplements should be separated.

- Some will require life-long supplementation of the fat-soluble vitamins A, D, E and K due to fat malabsorption.

Medications

- Medications may require dose-reduction, and may need to be crushed or in liquid or transdermal form for up to two-months post-surgery. Pharmacists will need to assess which drugs can be safely crushed.

- Due to the risk of gallstones with rapid weight loss, patients may need ursodiol *(Actigall, Urso 250, Urso Forte)*, which dissolves gallstones, unless the gallbladder has been removed. This drug is also used for primary biliary cirrhosis. It cannot be administered with aluminum-based antacids (if used, give 2 hours after ursodiol). *Urso Forte* can be split into halves for appropriate dosage, not chewed. *Urso* and *Urso Forte* should be taken with food. Ursodiol can be made into a sweetened suspension. The most common side effects are headache, dizziness, constipation or diarrhea (both about 26%) and nausea.

- Avoid drugs that are GI irritants – such as NSAIDs and bisphosphonates.

Dumping Syndrome

Dumping syndrome (rapid gastric emptying) occurs when undigested food moves rapidly into the small intestine, and may occur if the surgery bypasses or removes part or all of the stomach. Dumping syndrome can be separated into early and late forms, depending on the occurrence of symptoms in relation to the time elapsed after a meal. Common symptoms include <u>abdominal cramps, nausea and diarrhea.</u>

Methods to Avoid Dumping Syndrome

- Eat smaller meals, avoid fluids with meals (use only between meals).

- Reduce carbs, especially refined carbs, avoid sugar, including glucose, sucrose, fructose, dextrose, honey and corn syrup. Increase protein. Chew well.

- Increase fiber intake, including psyllium, guar gum and pectin. Avoid alcohol and acidic foods.

- Do not lie down after eating.

The prescription drugs Acarbose *(Precose)* and octreotide *(Sandostatin)* are used in some cases. Acarbose delays carbohydrate absorption (see diabetes section). Octreotide *(Somatostatin)* and the synthetic analogue *Sandostatin* is rarely used in severe cases. The usual initial dose of octreotide is 50 mcg administered subcutaneously bid/tid 30 minutes prior to each meal. Octreotide can cause bradycardia, chest pain, fatigue, dizziness, gastrointestinal and other adverse effects. It is sometimes (uncommonly) used for diarrhea.

APPENDIX

Top Sellers by Prescription Volume

This data is from 2012, the latest available.

RANK	DRUG
1	HC/Acetaminophen
2	Lisinopril
3	Simvastatin
4	Levothyroxine Sod
5	Omeprazole
6	Amlodipine Besy
7	Azithromycin
8	Amoxicillin
9	Alprazolam
10	Metformin HCL
11	Hydrochlorothiazide
12	Zolpidem Tart
13	Atorvastatin CA
14	Sertraline HCL
15	Tramadol HCL
16	Citalopram HBR
17	Ibuprofen (Rx)
18	Fluticasone Prop
19	Gabapentin
20	Furosemide

RANK	DRUG
21	Oxycodone/APAP
22	Prednisone
23	Metoprolol Succin
24	Metoprolol Tart
25	Atenolol
26	Clonazepam
27	Cyclobenzaprine
28	Pravastatin Sod
29	Proair HFA
30	Fluoxetine HCL
31	Lorazepam
32	Losartan Pot
33	Lisinopril/HCTZ
34	Ciprofloxacin HCL
35	Amox TR/POT Clavul
36	Warfarin Sod
37	Crestor
38	SMX/TMP
39	Cephalexin
40	Trazodone HCL

RANK	DRUG
41	Meloxicam
42	Nexium
43	Carvedilol
44	Pantoprazole Sod
45	Synthroid
46	Ventolin HFA
47	Cymbalta
48	Singulair
49	Fluconazole
50	Naproxen
51	Oxycodone HCL
52	Ranitidine HCL
53	Advair Diskus
54	Tamsulosin HCL
55	Diazepam
56	Doxycycline Hyclat
57	Potassium Cl
58	Escitalopram Oxal
59	Bupropion HCL Xl
60	Albuterol

RANK	DRUG
61	Allopurinol
62	Vit D
63	Venlafaxine HCL ER
64	Triamterene/HCTZ
65	Methylprednisolone
66	Triamcinolone ACTN
67	Acetaminophen/Cod
68	Amitriptyline HCL
69	Paroxetine HCL
70	Clopidogrel Bisulf
71	Clonidine HCL
72	Promethazine HCL
73	Diovan
74	Amphetamine Salts
75	Alendronate Sod
76	Losartan POT/HCTZ
77	Lovastatin
78	Valacyclovir HCL
79	Levofloxacin
80	Lamotrigine

Top Sellers by Prescription Volume Continued

RANK	DRUG	RANK	DRUG	RANK	DRUG	RANK	DRUG
81	Vyvanse	111	Mupirocin	141	Glyburide	171	Premarin
82	Montelukast Sod	112	Januvia	142	Estradiol	172	Diltiazem HCL
83	Carisoprodol	113	Sumatriptan Succin	143	Flovent HFA	173	Benicar
84	Spironolactone	114	Glipizide	144	Glipizide ER	174	Gemfibrozil
85	Metformin ER (G)	115	Cialis	145	Ondansetron ODT	175	Clotrim/Betameth D
86	Cefdinir	116	Hydroxyzine HCL	146	Tizanidine HCL	176	Doxazosin Mesy
87	Topiramate	117	Benazepril HCL	147	Buspirone HCL	177	Endocet
88	Metronidazole	118	Latanoprost	148	Famotidine	178	Ergocalciferol
89	Glimepiride	119	Fenofibrate	149	Oxycontin	179	Lovaza
90	Folic Acid	120	Isosorbide Mononit	150	Bystolic	180	Prednisolone Ace
91	Plavix	121	Diovan HCT	151	Ketoconazole	181	Klor-Con M20
92	Enalapril Mal	122	Penicillin VK	152	Levetiracetam	182	Tri-Sprintec-28
93	Risperidone	123	Diclofenac Sod	153	Verapamil SR	183	Niaspan
94	Nasonex	124	Lantus SoloStar	154	Clobetasol Prop	184	Medroxyprogesteron
95	Clindamycin HCL	125	Digoxin	155	Cheratussin AC	185	Prednisolone S Ph
96	Morphine Sulf	126	Ondansetron HCL	156	Methylphenidate	186	Ropinirole HCL
97	Methylphenidate ER	127	Quetiapine Fum	157	Methocarbamol	187	Hydralazine HCL
98	Lyrica	128	Ramipril	158	Methotrexate Sod	188	Hydroxychloroquine
99	Spiriva Handihaler	129	Nitrofurant Mono/M	159	Nuvaring	189	Actos
100	Celebrex	130	Phentermine HCL	160	Fentanyl	190	Namenda
101	Amlodip Bes/Benaz	131	Benzonatate	161	Finasteride	191	Dicyclomine HCL
102	Suboxone	132	Acyclovir	162	Lexapro	192	Methadone HCL
103	Viagra	133	Mirtazapine	163	Cd/Prometh	193	Minocycline HCL
104	Propranolol HCL	134	Lansoprazole	164	Dexilant	194	Proventil HFA
105	Lantus	135	Polyethylene Gly(R	165	Chlorhexidine Gluc	195	Nifedipine ER
106	Temazepam	136	Donepezil HCL	166	Symbicort	196	Clindamycin Phos
107	Lipitor	137	Zetia	167	Meclizine HCL (Rx)	197	Diltiazem 24Hr
108	Abilify	138	Butalb/Apap/Caf	168	Tricor	198	Zolpidem Tart ER
109	Amphetamin Salt ER	139	Loestrin 24 Fe	169	Baclofen	199	Hydrocortisone (Rx)
110	Bupropion HCL SR W	140	Nystatin	170	Trinessa-28	200	Phenazopyridine

We gratefully acknowledge the assistance of Bob Hunkler at IMS, in providing the top sellers list for inclusion in this text.

Common Laboratory Values
A few may change slightly depending on the laboratory that has issued the report.

ITEM	VALUE	
Albumin	3.5 - 5.0 g/dL	
Alkaline phosphatase	33 - 131 IU/L	
AST	8 - 48 IU/L	
ALT	7 - 55 IU/L	
Bilirubin, direct	0.1 - 0.3 mg/dL	
Bilirubin, total	0.1 - 1.2 mg/dL	
BUN	7 - 20 mg/dL	
Creatinine	0.5 - 1. 3 mg/dL	
	Male	Female
Hemoglobin (g/dL)	13.5 - 18	12 - 16
Hematocrit (%)	38 - 50	36 - 46
RBC's (x 106/mL)	4.5 - 5.5	4.0 - 4.9
MCV	80 - 100 micrometer^3	
MCH	26 - 34 pg/cell	
MCHC	31 - 37 g/dL	
Platelets	150,000 to 450,000/mm^3	
WBC	4,000 - 11,000/mm^3	

Electrolytes

Calcium	8.5 - 10.5 mg/dL
Calcium, ionized	4.5 - 5.6 mg/dL
Chloride	95 - 107 mEq/L
Magnesium	1.6 - 2.5 mEq/L
Phosphate	2.5 - 4.5 mg/dL
Potassium	3.5 - 5.0 mEq/L
Sodium	135 - 145 mEq/L

Diabetes

Estimated Average Glucose	< 154 mg/dL
Hemoglobin A1C	< 7%
Preprandial blood glucose	70-130 mg/dL
Postprandial blood glucose	< 180 mg/dL (ADA)

Common Laboratory Values Continued

ITEM	VALUE

Lipids

ITEM	VALUE
Cholesterol, total	< 200 mg/dL
HDL, low	< 40 mg/dL
HDL, optimal	≥ 60 mg/dL
LDL, optimal	< 100 mg/dL, or < 70 mg/dL
LDL, normal	100-129 mg/dL
Triglycerides	< 150 mg/dL

Thyroid Function

ITEM	VALUE
Free thyroxine (FT4)	0.8-1.7 mcg/dL
TSH	0.3 – 3.0μIU/mL

Iron

ITEM	VALUE
Iron	65 - 150 mcg/dL
Total iron binding capacity (TIBC)	250 - 420 mcg/dL
Transferrin	> 200 mg/dL

Uric Acid

ITEM	VALUE
Uric acid (male)	3.5 - 7.2 mg/dL
Uric acid (female)	2.0 - 6.5 mg/dL

Inflammation

ITEM	VALUE
C-Reactive Protein	Normal: < 0.8 mg/dL
	High risk: > 3.00 mg
Rheumatoid Factor, serum	< 40 IU/mL
Erythrocyte Sed Rate (ESR)	Male: ≤ 20 mm/hr
	Female: ≤ 30 mm/hr

SELECT NARROW THERPEUTIC INDEX DRUGS

DRUG	USUAL THERAPEUTIC RANGE
Amikacin (traditional dosing)	Peak: 20-30 mcg/mL Trough: < 5 mcg/mL
Carbamazepine	4-12 mcg/mL
Digoxin	0.8-2.0 ng/mL (Afibrillation) 0.5-0.9 ng/mL (HF)
Gentamicin (traditional dosing)	Peak: 5-10 mcg/mL Trough: < 2 mcg/mL
Lithium	0.6-1.2 mEq/L (can be as high as 1.5 mEq/L for acute symptoms)
Phenobarbital	20-40 mcg/mL (adults) 15-30 mcg/mL (children)
Phenytoin	10-20 mcg/mL
Procainamide	4-10 mcg/mL
NAPA	15-25 mcg/mL
Tacrolimus	4-20 mcg/mL (varies based on concomitant drugs and type of transplant)
Theophylline	5-15 mcg/mL
Tobramycin (traditional dosing)	Peak: 5-10 mcg/mL Trough: < 2 mcg/mL
Valproic acid	50-100 mcg/mL (can be as high as 150 mcg/mL in some patients)
Vancomycin	Trough: 10-20 mcg/mL
Warfarin	2-3 (INR) for most indications, use higher range (2.5-3.5) with mechanical mitral valves

Common Medical Abbreviations

Medical safety warning: Do not use any in the "DO NOT USE" abbreviation list in your institution; the meaning of abbreviations varies.

ABBREVIATION	MEANING
AAA	Abdominal Aortic Aneurysm
A&O	Alert & Oriented
ABG	Arterial Blood Gas
ACOG	American Congress of Obstetricians and Gynecologists
ACTH	Adrenocorticotropic Hormone
ADH	Anti-Diuretic Hormone
ADR	Adverse Drug Reaction
ADT	Alternate Day Therapy
AF	Atrial Fibrillation, or A.Fib
AIN	Acute Interstitial Nephritis
ALT	Alanine Aminotransferase
ANA	Antinuclear Antibody
ANS	Autonomic Nervous System
APTT	Activated Partial Thromboplastin Time
ARDS	Acute Respiratory Distress Syndrome
ARF	Acute Renal Failure
AST	Aspartate Aminotransferase
ATN	Acute Tubular Necrosis
BEE	Basal Energy Expenditure
BMP	Basic Metabolic Panel
BP	Blood Pressure
BPH	Benign Prostatic Hypertrophy
BPM	Beats Per Minute
BUN	Blood Urea Nitrogen

ABBREVIATION	MEANING
C I, C II, C III, C IV, C V	Refers to Controlled Drug Categories
C&S	Culture and Sensitivity
C/O	Complaining Of
CA	Cancer
CABG	Coronary Artery Bypass Graft
CAD	Coronary Artery Disease
CAPES	*Citrobacter, Acinetobacter, Providencia, Enterobacter, Serratia*
CBC	Complete Blood Count
CC	Chief Complaint
CCB	Calcium Channel Blocker
CF	Cystic Fibrosis
CH	Cholesterol
CHF	Congestive Heart Failure
CI	Cardiac Index
CMV	*Cytomegalovirus*
CNS	Central Nervous System
CO	Cardiac Output
COPD	Chronic Obstructive Pulmonary Disease
CP	Chest Pain or Cerebral Palsy
CPAP	Continuous Positive Airway Pressure
CPK	Creatine Phosphokinase
CPR	Cardiopulmonary Resuscitation
CrCL	Creatinine Clearance
CRF	Chronic Renal Failure

Common Medical Abbreviations Continued

ABBREVIATION	MEANING
CRP	C-reactive Protein
CSF	Cerebrospinal Fluid
CT	Computerized Tomography
CV	Cardiovascular
CVA	Cerebrovascular Accident
CVP	Central Venous Pressure
CXR	Chest X-Ray
D/C	Discontinue or Discharge
D5W	5% Dextrose in Water
DDIs	Drug-Drug Interactions
DJD	Degenerative Joint Disease (Osteoarthritis)
DKA	Diabetic Ketoacidosis
DM	Diabetes Mellitus
DOC	Drug of Choice
DOE	Dyspnea on Exertion
DRESS Syndrome	Drug Reaction with Eosinophilia and Systemic Symptoms
DVT	Deep Venous Thrombosis
Dx	Diagnosis
EC	Enteric Coated
ECG	Electrocardiogram
ESBL	Extended Spectrum Beta Lactamases
ESR	Erythrocyte Sedimentation Rate
ETOH	Ethanol
F/U	Follow-Up
FBS	Fasting Blood Sugar
FEV	Forced Expiratory Volume

ABBREVIATION	MEANING
FT4	Free Thyroxine (T4)
fxn	Function
GFR	Glomerular Filtration Rate
GI	Gastrointestinal
GNR	Gram Negative Rod
GTT	Glucose Tolerance Test
H/O	History Of
HA	Headache
HACEK	*Haemophilus, Actinobacillus, Cardiobacterium, Eikenella, Kingella*
HBV	Hepatitis B Virus
HCG	Human Chorionic Gonadotropin
HCT	Hematocrit
HCTZ, HCT	Hydrochlorothiazide
HCV	Hepatitis C Virus
HDL	High Density Lipoprotein
HF	Heart Failure
Hgb	Hemoglobin
HIV	Human Immunodeficiency Virus
HJR	Hepatojugular Reflex
HNPEK	Haemophilus influenzae, Neisseria spp, Proteus mirabilis, E. coli, Klebsiella pneumonia
HPI	History of Present Illness
HR	Heart Rate
HSV	Herpes Simplex Virus
HTN	Hypertension
HUS/TTP	Hemolytic-Uremic Syndrome and Thrombotic Thrombocytopenic Purpura
Hx	History

Common Medical Abbreviations Continued

ABBREVIATION	MEANING
I&O	Intake and Output
IBS	Irritable Bowel Syndrome
ICU	Intensive Care Unit
IE	Infective Endocarditis
IM	Intramuscular
INR	International Normalized Ratio
IV	Intravenous
IVP	Intravenous Push
LD	Loading Dose
LDH	Lactate Dehydrogenase
LDL	Low-Density Lipoprotein
LFTs	Liver Function Tests
LVH	Left Ventricular Hypertrophy
MAO	Monoamine Oxidase
MAO I	Monoamine Oxidase Inhibitor
MAP	Mean Arterial Pressure
MCH	Mean Cell Hemoglobin
MCHC	Mean Cell Hemoglobin Concentration
MCV	Mean Corpuscular Volume
MD	Maintenance Dose
MI	Myocardial Infarction
MRI	Magnetic Resonance Imaging
MRSA	Methicillin-Resistant Staph aureus
MS	Multiple Sclerosis or Morphine Sulfate (Don't use for Morphine – Dangerous)
MSSA	Methicillin-Sensitive Staph aureus
MVA	Motor Vehicle Accident

ABBREVIATION	MEANING
MVI	Multivitamin Injection
N/V	Nausea and Vomiting
N/V/D	Nausea, Vomiting, Diarrhea
NG	Nasogastric
NKA	No Known Allergies
NKDA	No Known Drug Allergies
NPO	Nothing By Mouth
NRT	Nicotine Replacement Therapy
NSAID	Nonsteroidal Anti-Inflammatory Drugs
NSR	Normal Sinus Rhythm
ODT	Orally Disintegrating Tablet
P-gp	P-glycoprotein
PAP	Pulmonary Artery Pressure
PCI	Percutaneous Coronary Intervention
PCN	Penicillin
PCOS	Polycystic Ovary Syndrome
PCWP	Pulmonary Capillary Wedge Pressure
PE	Pulmonary Embolus, or Physical Exam
PEK	*Proteus mirabilis, E. coli, Klebsiella pneumonia*
PKU	Phenylketonuria
PMH	Past Medical History
PO	Oral
PPD	Purified Protein Derivative
PRBC	Packed Red Blood Cells
PRN	As Needed
PT	Prothrombin Time, or Physical Therapy

Common Medical Abbreviations Continued

ABBREVIATION	MEANING
Pt	Patient
PTCA	Percutaneous Transluminal Coronary Angioplasty
PTH	Parathyroid Hormone
PUD	Peptic Ulcer Disease
PVC	Polyvinyl Chloride
Q	Every
R/O	Rule Out
RA	Rheumatoid Arthritis
RBC	Red Blood Cell
ROS	Review of Systems
RSV	Respiratory Syncytial Virus
Rx	Treatment, Prescription
rxn	Reaction
S/P	Status Post
SCr	Serum Creatinine
SIADH	Syndrome of Inappropriate Antidiuretic Hormone
sig	Write on Label
SLE	Systemic Lupus Erythematous
SOAP	Subjective, Objective, Assessment, Plan
SOB	Shortness of Breath
SC or SQ	Subcutaneous
STAT	Immediately
S/Sx	Signs and Symptoms
Sx	Symptoms
TB	Tuberculosis
TG	Triglycerides

ABBREVIATION	MEANING
TIA	Transient Ischemic Attack
TIBC	Total Iron Binding Capacity
TPN	Total Parenteral Nutrition
TSH	Thyroid Stimulating Hormone
TTP	Thrombotic Thrombocytopenic Purpura
Tx	Treatment
UA	Urinalysis
UFH	Unfractionated Heparin
ULN	Upper Limit of Normal
URTI	Upper Respiratory Tract Infection
UTI	Urinary Tract Infection
VF	Ventricular Fibrillation
VRE	Vancomycin-Resistant Enterococcus
VT	Ventricular Tachycardia
WBC	White Blood Cells
WNL	Within Normal Limits
WPW	Wolff-Parkinson-White Syndrome
y/o	Years Old
yr	Year

Auxiliary Labels

This list should not be considered exhaustive, but it does represent major categories for auxiliary labels.

LABEL	COMMENT
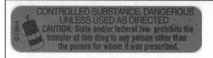	The federal warning label prohibiting transfer of ALL controlled substances must be on the bottle (see figure, or similar).
	Shake Well (all suspensions, most asthma aerosol inhalers and nasal steroid sprays, lidocaine viscous topical liquid).
	Refrigerate or Keep in Refrigerator: Do not Freeze (antibiotics): amoxicillin *(Amoxil* – refrigeration not required, but improves taste), amoxicillin/ clavulanate *(Augmentin)*, cefaclor *(Raniclor)*, cefadroxil *(Duricef)*, cefixime *(Suprax)*, cefpodoxime *(Vantin)*, cefprozil *(Cefzil)*, cefuroxime *(Ceftin)*, ceftibuten *(Cedax)*, cephalexin *(Keflex)*, erythromycin/benzoyl peroxide gel *(Benzamycin)*, erythromycin/sulfisoxazole, penicillin V. Others: adalimumab *(Humira)*, etanercept *(Enbrel)*, interferons (all), calcitonin NS *(Miacalcin)*, chlorambucil *(Leukeran)*, ESAs *(Epogen, Aranesp, Procrit)*, etoposide *(VePesid)*, filgrastim *(Neupogen)*, insulins (that patient is not using), nystatin pastilles *(Mycostatin)*, somatropin *(Genotropin, Humatrope)*, lopinavir/ritonavir solution *(Kaletra* – good at room temp for 60 days), alprostadil *(MUSE, Caverject)*, ritonavir softgels *(Norvir* - good at room temp for 30 days), sandostatin *(Octreotide)*, sirolimus suspension *(Rapamune)*, teriparatide *(Forteo)*, thyrolar *(Liotrix)*, mesalamine *(Canasa)* suppository, lactobacillus *(Lactinex)*, Nuvaring (if patient is not going to use right away), promethazine suppositories, typhoid oral capsules *(Vivotif Berna)*, formoterol *(Foradil* – prior to dispensing, patient can keep at room temp), dornase alfa *(Pulmozyne* – room temp only if < 24 hours). Eyedrops: latanoprost *(Xalatan)*, tafluprost *(Zioptan* – opened pouch good for 28 day room temp), trifluridine *(Viroptic)*.
	For External Use (topicals), may require: "For the Eye", "For the Ear", "For the Nose," "For Rectal Use Only," "For Vaginal Use Only," "Not to be taken by Mouth."

Auxiliary Labels Continued

LABEL	COMMENT
	Finish all this medication, unless otherwise directed by prescriber (antibiotics, antivirals, antifungals).
	May cause drowsiness. May impair the ability to drive or operate machinery. Includes analgesics with CNS effects, antipsychotics, some antidepressants including mirtazapine *(Remeron)* and trazodone *(Desyrel)*, dopamine agonists (ropinirole, etc.), antihistamines, antinauseants, anticonvulsants, skeletal muscle relaxants, antihypertensives with CNS effects, all C II, III, IV or V depressant or narcotic drugs, including hypnotics-controlled & not controlled.
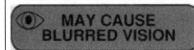	May affect vision. Includes amiodarone, anticholinergics, ethambutol, hydroxychloroquine, isoniazid, isotretinoin, PDE 5 Is (sildenafil, others), scopolamine patch, tamoxifen, telithromycin *(Ketek)*, voriconazole *(VFEND)*. Note: many drugs cause blurry or doubled vision (diplopia) if toxic, including alcohol and CNS depressants. Digoxin can cause yellow halos if toxic.
	Do not use alcohol while taking this medicine. Includes disulfiram, tinidazole, metronidazole (both of these avoid alcohol to 48 hrs after last dose), nitrates, opioids (all, but special warning for *Avinza, Opana*), tramadol, tapentadol *(Nucynta)*, benzodiazepines, barbiturates, non-benzodiazepine hypnotics (zolpidem, etc.), anticonvulsants, antipsychotics, some antidepressants, skeletal muscle relaxants, insulin, metformin, sulfonylureas.
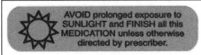	Avoid prolonged exposure to direct and/or artificial sunlight while using this medicine. Includes sulfa antibiotics, tetracyclines, topical retinoids (newer ones less risk), isotretinoin (oral), ritonavir & a few other HIV drugs, NSAIDs (piroxicam, diclofenac, some risk with ibuprofen and naproxen), metronidazole, isoniazid, diuretics.
	Take on an empty stomach. Includes ampicillin, efavirenz *(Sustiva/Atripla* – empty stomach, preferably at bedtime), bisphosphonates (at least half hour before breakfast or 60 minutes for *Boniva*), captopril (1 hour before meals), didanosine *(Videx)*, indinavir *(Crixivan)*, zalcitabine *(Hivid)*, iron (if tolerated), PPIs (variable times, but all before eating), tadalafil and sildenafil (light meal, avoid fatty food), levothyroxine (half hour before breakfast), *Opana*, mycophenolate *(CellCept)*, tacrolimus *(Prograf)*, sulfamethoxazole/trimethoprim *(Bactrim)*, voriconazole *(VFEND)*, zafirlukast.
	Take with food. Includes atazanavir *(Reyataz)*, carvedilol *(Coreg)*, itraconazole capsules, metformin (IR with breakfast and dinner, XR with dinner) *Mevacor* (with dinner), *Lofibra, Lipofen, Fenoglide*, niacins (with food, *Niaspan*—at bedtime with low-fat snack), *Lopid* (30 min before breakfast and dinner), phosphate binders (when eating), NSAIDs, opioids except *Opana*, steroids.

Auxiliary Labels Continued

LABEL	COMMENT
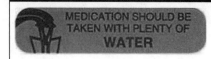	Take with full glass of water. Includes sulfamethoxazole/trimethoprim *(Bactrim)*, bisphosphonates, sulfasalazine *(Azulfidine* – take with water & food). Note: Drugs can get "stuck" going down, especially if dysphagia is present. It is preferable to take most with a full glass of water.
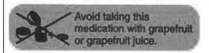	Do not eat grapefruit or drink grapefruit juice at any time while using this medicine. Includes lovastatin, simvastatin, atorvastatin, amiodarone, buspirone, carbamazepine, cyclosporine, tacrolimus, diazepam, triazolam, verapamil, nicardipine, felodipine, nisoldipine, nifedipine, telithromycin, voriconazole.
	Danger in pregnancy. If you are pregnant or considering becoming pregnant talk to your doctor before using this medicine. Includes ACE Inhibitors, Angiotensin Receptor Blockers, carbamazepine, isotretinoin, lithium, NSAIDs, phenytoin, phenobarbital, topiramate, valproic acid, ribavirin, misoprostol, methotrexate, leflunomide, statins, dutasteride, finasteride, warfarin, lenalidomide, thalidomide.
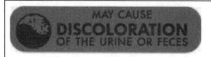	May cause discoloration of the urine, skin and sweat. May stain contact lenses and clothing. Includes entacapone, levodopa, metronidazole, nitrofurantoin, phenazopyridine.
	Check for peanut or soy allergy. Ipratropium/albuterol *(Combivent*, but not the *Combivent Respimat* formulation), progesterone (in *Prometrium*, not in other formulations).
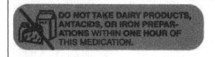	Separate from dairy products, calcium, magnesium or iron tablets, antacids. Includes tetracyclines, quinolones.
	Do not chew or crush. Swallow whole. Enteric coated formulations (bisacodyl, others), any drug that ends with XR, ER, LA, SR, CR, CRT, SA, TR, TD, or has 24 in the name, or the ending –cont (for controlled release, such as *MS Contin* or *OxyContin*), and timecaps and sprinkles. Note: Can cut metoprolol ext-release and levodopa-carbidopa SR at the score line (for half the dose), but cannot crush or chew.

INDEX